A DIN[illegible]
GOT MY BABY!

WORDS THAT DIVIDED A NATION

THE AUTOBIOGRAPHY OF

LINDY CHAMBERLAIN-CREIGHTON

A dingo's got my baby : words that divided a nation

National Library of Australia Cataloguing-in-Publication entry

Creator:	Chamberlain-Creighton, Lindy, 1948- author
Title:	A dingo's got my baby : words that divided a nation / Lindy Chamberlain-Creighton.
ISBN:	9780994280008 (paperback)
Subjects:	Chamberlain-Creighton, Lindy, 1948- Chamberlain-Creighton, Lindy, 1948---Trials, litigation, etc. Trials (Infanticide)--Northern Territory--Darwin. Criminal justice, Administration of--Northern Territory. Absence and presumption of death--Northern Territory. Judicial error--Northern Territory. Families--Psychological aspects.

Dewey Number: 345.942902523

Published by Lindy Chamberlain-Creighton with InHouse Publishing
www. inhousepublishing. com. au

IN HOUSE PUBLISHING

Cover Design: Dannielle Synot
Back cover photographs: Chamberlain family circa 1980 with Aidan (6) and Reagan (4) / Detail from *Forensic Analysis of Motherhood*, Felicity Marshall, 1987, pencil on paper

Lindy Chamberlain-Creighton can be contacted care of:
Harry M Miller Group
Fox Studios Australia
FSA#38, 38 Driver Avenue
Moore Park NSW 2021
www.harrymmiller.com.au

To broad shoulders,
the freedom of the outback,
a freedom kept at such high cost.

And to my Cricket.

INTRODUCTION

Judge ye not, lest ye be judged' ... so said Jesus Christ according to Matthew's gospel. Mark touched on it also. And It's a pretty sound concept really, even if you're not of the 'Christian' persuasion. Like, 'Do unto others...' It's a thoroughly decent, fair and balanced concept, uncomplicated and at the very least surely worth consideration. Unfortunately, generally speaking I think It's reasonable to suggest It's a notion not many of us subscribe to. Twenty-something years ago, a young mother of three and her (then) husband appeared on our television screens recounting a nightmarish incident concerning the disappearance of their youngest child. A beautiful nine week old baby girl named Azaria. We sat comfortably in our lounge rooms, glued to the evening news as the young woman, who' d been camping with her family at Ayers Rock (Uluru), described how she' d seen a dingo come out of the tent where Azaria had been sleeping in her bassinet alongside her older brother. With something in its mouth, it vanished into the pitch-black darkness of the desert night. At this point we sat forward in our armchairs, perhaps put our beers down for a second and tried to digest what we'd just heard. The nightly news journalist went on to report that she' d been barbecuing a short distance away with her eldest boy and her husband Michael, a Seventh-day Adventist Minister. Many of us then, I suspect returned to our beers, sat back in our comfy chairs and thought: 'That's a bit weird' .

And so it began. We all became authorities and experts on everything from canine behaviour to postnatal depression overnight. Pubs, homes, the workplace even schools became courtrooms. We seemingly arrived at our verdicts long before Coroner Dennis Barritt, who presided over the first inquest, arrived at his. And of course, most of us disagreed with his ruling. Debate, opinions, finger pointing and fist fights. Gestures of support and hate mail. Relentless hounding and sensational fabrications. A young family, torn apart.

I was fifteen when Azaria disappeared and at thirty-eight, I'm portraying Michael Chamberlain in the Liberty/Beyond produced mini-series *Through My Eyes*. I have to say It's been an extraordinary experience on so many levels. Certainly, meeting Lindy was a crucial ingredient in preparing thoroughly for this journey as an actor. I know

Miranda (Otto) who so brilliantly captures Lindy in our production would agree. But delightfully, something else was born out of our coming together something beyond answers to an actor's many questions. Friendship. Lindy, her husband Rick and I connected in a very open and comfortable way and if the planets aligned in such a fashion that I was destined to do this job just for that reason, I'm glad of it.

Strong and determined, that's Lindy. Loving and generous, absolutely. Armed with a razor-sharp mind and a knockout sense of humour, she's definitely wonderful company. But It's her enormous and enviable capacity to forgive that is so striking.

This is Lindy's story… judge ye not indeed.

Craig McLachlan (2004)

Actor and Musician

CONTENTS

PUBLISHER'S NOTE

All transcripts, taped conversations and personal correspondence appear verbatim in the text. Any inaccuracies, typographical errors, and grammatical and syntactical mistakes have been faithfully reproduced.

Uluru is referred to as Ayers Rock throughout this book. Uluru was frequently referred to as Ayers Rock in transcripts, conversations, personal correspondence and by the media at the time of the Chamberlain inquests and trial. As a result, the name Ayers Rock has been employed elsewhere in the text to achieve consistency and avoid confusion on the part of the reader.

This book has been written and published in different stages over the years. Throughout you will find references to "eight years", "twenty-four years", and "thirty-two years". These all refer to the number of years since Azaria died when I wrote the relevant sections of this book.

PART ONE

Why

This is the story of a little girl
who lived, and breathed, and loved, and was loved.
She was part of me.
She grew within my body and when she died,
part of me died,
and nothing will ever alter that fact.
This is her story, and mine.

I had been thinking for a long time that a book needed to be written to tell the personal side, the human side of the story—the side that people looking at the news tend to forget. People are often so anxious to look at someone's life as presented through the media, that they forget the people they are hearing about on the news are real flesh and blood, with real feelings.

Who is going to tell all those people the story of what can happen behind the scenes? Someone has to have the courage to tell what happens to innocent Australians who are being torn in shreds to feed the megalomanic media machine for our daily news. I felt that story should be told.

I still find it intriguing that when I consented to the magazine serialisation of my book I was asked, 'Will there be anything new in the book?' When I said that the majority of things in the book would be new, the reaction was astonishment. What could I possibly have to say that hadn't already been covered in magazines, newspapers, on radio, television, documentaries and even a Hollywood movie?

All this media coverage has tended to make the events of the last twenty-four years seem unreal, like a television soap opera. Things like this are talked about in hushed whispers, or in arguments, but one never knows the people personally. I suppose that is one of the things that's made the last twenty-four years so hard. It's never been real, the way the media reported it. It's never been true. I'd read the newspapers, and the reports would bear no resemblance to what actually happened.

People forget that my family has a private life. We have gone through a private hell as well as a private happiness in our battle to survive the last twenty-four years and most of our biggest battles have been fought in private.

This is my story of the way I saw those battles. It is not the story of my ex-husband Michael; he has a separate story to tell. What follows is the sort of thing that you normally read about in fiction, and it always happens to someone else. I'm just an ordinary person, yet the events of the last twenty-four years have been extraordinary: to live through the loss of my child, two inquests, accusations of murder, a trial, three years of prison, two appeals, a Royal Commission, then another Supreme Court, and another inquest, a Hollywood movie, an opera, and a TV mini-series of my life seems phenomenal.

As my story unfolds in front of you, all I ask is that you think of what I've said, and be slow to be dogmatic and judgmental. Evaluate carefully, be open to reason. Treat no person as you would not wish to be treated yourself.

I learned that you can coast along when things are fine and boast to yourself that you are tough, that you have faith and you are strong, but when everything you believe in and is dear to you, and everything that you know and own is crumbling around your ears, if you can be strong then, and if you can be tough then, if you can have faith then, *that* is when it is important.

It is only when your faith is tested that you know whether you have any or not. It is only when your temper is teased and provoked to the limit and you manage to control it, that you know you have succeeded. It is no use saying, 'I have got self-control' when there is nothing to provoke it.

Many years ago as a child in Warrnambool, Victoria, I sat on our front verandah steps and read stories of Marie Durand, a fifteen-year-old who was imprisoned in the Tower of Constance during the 1700s for her faith. For forty years she was held captive in the upper room of the tower where only a little light and air penetrated the narrow windows of the room. There she scratched deep into the stone wall one word: 'Resist'. As a child I could dream of what it really meant to her to resist under those odds. As an adult, when I looked back on the example she set me, I could mentally look at my wall and see 'Resist' written on it too, and I knew why she did it. I knew that resistance to temptation, resistance to all that was falsely offered was the only way to keep one's self-respect, one's allegiance to God and one's own character.

I was told so often, 'If only you will give up your fight for innocence and say you're guilty, you can go home.' I guess many a time Marie Durand was told if only she would say that God was not Lord of all, she could go home too. What a temptation. But that is the time that the tough get going.

Having 'looked at life from both sides now' I've gained a lot more tolerance. Having sat on a jury twice myself and then been on the other side, I can't help but see inadequacies in our British justice system. I know we pride ourselves on saying someone is 'innocent till proven guilty', but any person who has been through the system knows this means 'guilty till proven innocent' unless you have cash or influence. No wonder the innocent ex-criminal runs at the sight of the police rather than stopping to answer questions!

In my opinion there are astonishingly few 'straights' in the police, legal or justice systems who will not deal, accept payoffs, or use underhand methods. Nevertheless a few still exist. To win by cheating is worse than not to win at all. It would be so easy to do, but to live with yourself afterwards? I could not. God does not need to use cheats and liars to win. In the long run one person who will 'stand as true to duty as the needle is to the pole' is better than an army of corruption.

We must fight for the preservation of discerning laws in this country. One day I was just a happy housewife and mother, known only to my friends and acquaintances, next day a household word. I never dreamed it could possibly happen to me—how about you? If this continues will you be next?

How do you think we felt knowing most of you, our fellow Australians, were often maliciously discussing us over the morning coffee? It is amazing when one sets out to spread a rumour about another, just how quickly that rumour can take hold. Certainly the old adage that 'a lie goes round the world while truth puts its boots on', is a very accurate description of what happened in our case. But truth's boots can be big and crushing when they're on—and those boots just keep right on walking.

No matter how many years down the track it may be or how much they've proved to be untrue, it is still mind-boggling how some of these rumours started and were believed. How gullible people can be when lies are put over in a plausible way! We still hear these rumours coming back to us, although they have been discredited time and again.

Some people read the initial rumours and have *never* read the truth so continue to have misguided opinions, maintaining that they know the facts far better than any court or judge. It doesn't matter what anybody says—they *know*. I've learned, more than ever, not to show my true feelings. Whatever I did, in the early days, I was wrong. I didn't behave the way some people thought I should, so of course I *must* be guilty. That hurt. At least I have learned to ignore people staring at me, the whispers and, 'Look, there's Lindy Chamberlain.' Occasionally, I must admit, I can't resist turning to school kids, for instance, and giving them a big grin, or a wink. They either look terribly embarrassed, or else they grin back. Maybe it will teach them to be more open in the future and realise the people they discuss have ears too!

When we travelled to America in 1989 for a series of lectures and I could move around the shops freely without being recognised, I didn't even notice the difference until somebody said, 'It must be nice not to have people stare at you.' I was now so used, most of the time, to ignoring the attention I created that I didn't notice when it was missing any more.

It was a great relief to know that we didn't have to dodge photographers and reporters all the time, though. It is one thing to be photographed and quoted accurately with your consent but it's quite another to be deliberately bugged and find yourself in the papers with everything you've said misinterpreted or made up for the sake of a cheap story.

Most people, I guess, are like I was twenty-four years ago: average citizens thinking that in court all the facts are presented so that an intelligent assessment can be made by the jury as independent 'referees'. The law favoured those who told 'the truth, the whole truth, and nothing but the truth', and the police were to see that right and justice were followed. I still clung to that idea—despite evidence to the contrary—until the trial. Now I no longer believe a bar of it. 'Sadder but much wiser now . . .', yes indeed. I have come to the inevitable conclusion that the oath is interpreted, 'I promise to tell some of the truth, part only of the truth, and nothing but some of part of the truth.' That is how it works. It seems to me that the police often sort the evidence to suit their view only and manipulate witnesses to avoid mention of areas not supporting the prosecution case—after all if the defence doesn't know, it can't ask, can it? Before all this happened, Michael was happy. He was a progressive minister in the Seventh-day Adventist Church, ran his own Good Life radio program in both Innisfail and Mt Isa, and had a similar column in the local *Cairns Post* newspaper, with Mt Isa and Townsville syndication rights being discussed. He was an excellent semi-professional photographer. He took pride in his ability to counsel people and to discuss and interpret doctrine. He was the head of his family, with an assured position in the community; people looked up to him and he was doing a job he loved.

Then, because of his decision to take the photographs that a newsman requested on the day after our baby daughter died, because he thought it our duty to warn other parents about the danger of dingo attacks at Ayers Rock, people started to look at him differently. He was then thought publicity-hungry and a limelighter. As time went on, and he had to give evidence in court about the most devastating thing that had ever happened to him, he couldn't handle it; then people changed their perception of him and, with this change, he changed also.

On 15 September 1988 the Northern Territory Court of Criminal Appeal quashed all convictions against Michael and me. We had had to go through eight years of hell to be told officially what we always knew—that I did not murder our darling baby daughter, nor did Michael assist me.

I cannot begin to count the personal cost of the last twenty-four years. The total effects on the lives of my family and myself are permanent and far-reaching. No one who has been touched by our tragedy and the subsequent events can claim to have been unaffected.

The cost has been so great, and mere words just scratch the surface. They do not touch the deepest hurt, which *cannot be* expressed. In her poem 'Dreaming' my friend Joy Blackburn expressed it well.

There's a sadness
in this living,
There's a pain
that has no words.
There's a missing
and a longing,
And a sob
that can't be heard.
There's a grief
that can't be spoken,
There's a wound
that one can't see.
There's a dreaming
and a hoping,
When from pain
we can be free.

PART TWO

'Think Pink, Mum!'

A GIRL AT LAST

Early in 1980 our family (myself, Michael, Aidan and Reagan) moved to Mt Isa in north-western Queensland. I was pregnant and the first time I visited Dr Irene Milne, Michael decided to come with me to meet the new doctor and make sure I had decided on a good one.

When we got into the doctor's office and Dr Milne questioned me on my medical history, Michael gave the answers, much to my amusement. Although it seemed to throw the doctor a little, I was used to Michael doing that when we went out, so as long as he didn't give the wrong answers, I let it ride. After that visit I went alone and I could see that the doctor was quite relieved that I could actually talk and knew my own mind after all. (In years to come Michael's answering for me on that one visit still stuck in her mind as peculiar.)

The doctor asked me some questions about my first two births and said I was obviously one of those people who had a ten-month gestation period, not nine. 'I will not touch you until you have gone ten months,' she said, 'then, if we go *too* far over that, I will bring the baby on. We won't worry about it until then.' Sure enough, just a few days after the ten months, the baby started to make its presence felt. I felt a little uncomfortable the night before and wondered whether I was having contractions or whether, indeed, it was a false labour. It was my dad's birthday and I thought if I was going in, it would be lovely to have a baby then, especially if, as we hoped, the baby was a little girl.

Well, she wasn't to be born that day. At two the next morning, I got up and went to the toilet, then wandered around the house timing myself. When my contractions were five minutes apart, I knew it was time to go. My friend Jenny who was going to look after the boys couldn't come in the middle of the night, so another friend, Neroli Goss, was on standby if I had to go during the night. I woke Michael up and said, 'Honey, you'd better go and get Neroli in a hurry, I've got to go.' I expected him to be only a few minutes at the most, seeing she was half expecting him.

While he was away, I started to get anxious that he had been gone too long. That got my stomach in a knot and next thing I knew I was vomiting. That put my contractions out of order and from then on they came spasmodically. He arrived back nearly three-quarters of an hour later with Neroli and her husband Neville in tow—both looking sleepy but fully dressed. Michael asked how I was going, then said, 'We're pretty hungry. Do you think you could get breakfast before you leave?' Neroli's mouth dropped open and she was about to remonstrate with him, but I shook my head and said, 'Never mind, I'll get you breakfast. You've taken so long, I've done the washing ready to be hung out and I'm not going to go yet for a while after all, but we will have to get there fairly soon.' So they all had breakfast. Neroli had been watching me fairly closely and although she didn't have any children of her own at that stage, she said, 'It looks like it's time you went. Are you OK?'

I replied, 'Yes, but I do think it's time I went.'

She said, 'Right, I'll get him out the door.' So she shooed Michael out the door, and off we went. He then took close notice of the contractions I was having, decided it really was time to move and put his foot down. The more bumps we went over, the worse it was. When we got to the hospital, I was glad to get out and go in. We found the nurse was in a panic.

'I thought you were coming ages ago. We figured you must have had it on the way here or something had happened,' she said.

I assured her I was OK.

I was prepped and put into a room and Michael took off home. He had to be there before school, as Neville and Neroli were both teachers and would have to leave. He would get the boys up, send Aidan off to school and bring Reagan to see me for a while before taking him to Jenny's, then come back before the baby was born. I was having quite an easy labour compared to the boys. There was no pain in between the contractions and I was managing to deal with those.

Finally the nurse said, 'I think we will put you up in one of the rooms, there's a free one now. The baby's obviously getting closer; you're ten minutes apart now.' She would get a few things ready and was I OK?

'Fine,' I said.

As she went out, I said to her, 'I am starting to push.'

She said, 'Rubbish!'

'I am!' I said.

She said, 'I will wait for one contraction and see what happens.' Well, nothing happened. Not one thing.

'I don't care,' I said. 'The baby is very close. It is going to come in the next few minutes.'

She said, 'OK, do you want an injection?'

I said, 'Yes, please. Let's hope it will work before this happens.'

'It will work in about twenty minutes,' she said.

I thought boy! It better be before that, or this is going to hurt like hell. Although I was having an easier time, I knew what the final few minutes were like.

So she gave me an injection and said, 'I will just get all the other injections ready. I will wait for one more contraction, just in case you are right.' She turned around, picked up the syringe, and plunged it into the bottle ready to start drawing up the liquid, and I went into contraction. She took one look at me, said, 'Oh, gosh,' and pushed the emergency bell.

As a bell rang in the distance, we heard rushing foot steps down the hall. As Michael opened the door and walked in carrying Reagan, the nurse reached the foot of the bed, and the baby arrived in a whoosh. Michael stopped just inside the door and the charge nurse, who had been running behind him, almost went slap into his back.

'Well, that surprised everyone!' the charge nurse said. At the same time the nurse said, 'Well, it's a girl. Just what the doctor ordered.' I had seen as she was born that it was a girl and yet I thought—it can't be! I had been so disappointed when Reagan was another boy, and I thought, They're going to tell me in a minute that it is a boy and I have seen wrong. It can't be a girl. I wouldn't allow myself to get excited. I'd been too disappointed before, and yet I knew this time it was OK.

Well, Michael said it all for me. 'Are you sure?'

The nurse looked at him and said, 'Yes I am. Do you want to have a look for yourself? I'm sure it's quite plain.'

Michael, still standing there with his mouth open holding Reagan, looked at her and said, 'Oh . . . er . . . no thanks. I'm sure you're right.' He stood there for a few more seconds and then said, 'Do you hear that Reagan? You've got a baby sister . . . Did you hear that darling, we've got a *girl!*' And so we did. A beautiful little girl—3 kilograms (6 pounds 5 ounces)—with very dark violet eyes, so dark a purple they were nearly black. Black hair and olive skin. Apart from her eyes being darker, her hair just slightly bluer-black, and being smaller, she was the image of Aidan.

Michael rushed out to the car to grab his camera. When he came back he started taking photographs. He even talked Dr Milne into having her photograph taken with Azaria. She later said she thought he was a bit strange taking all those photographs but knew new fathers often did things she thought odd.

Reagan had seen his mum, and seen more than he bargained for. Michael took him out then and let him go and play while the doctor came to stitch me up.

When Michael came back later that afternoon I asked him what Reagan had said. He said, 'Nothing much, he just sat there quietly thinking about it and then later he commented, "Mummy had a lot of blood on her and so did bubby, didn't she, Daddy,"' and he never made any other comment than that.

Aidan, when he heard, was quite incensed that he had not been allowed to stay home from school. He said, 'I wanted to see bubby born too! How come Reagan was allowed?' We had to explain that it was purely accidental. Nevertheless, it was a bond that Reagan would never forget. He loved that little girl.

As Reagan had in effect been Aidan's 'baby' so Azaria was Reagan's. Aidan had guarded Reagan carefully. 'He is *my* baby, you stay away from him!' I worked in the camp store and when it came time for Aidan's meeting, Reagan had to go too. Aidan would push Reagan in the baby carriage across to the door while I watched, and the girls in charge would help him take the pram up the steps and park it. They were supposed to be officially babysitting for me while I was in the store, but no, they informed me, Aidan wouldn't let them near Reagan. He would sit at Reagan's side and if Reagan woke up, Aidan would roll him over and flop him forward on a chubby little fist, burp him and give him his bottle.

Reagan who, like Aidan, had pyloric stenosis (a restriction of the sphymeter muscle into the stomach, making feeding slow and bringing up wind without projectile vomiting impossible) was bottle fed not breastfed, so Aidan was able to enjoy feeding and taking care of his little brother to his heart's content. He was very possessive. If Reagan cried and he decided it was time to go for help, he would head towards the door and, on one occasion, he even told the girls that he could get down the steps with the pram by himself! Knowing that the handle of the pram was almost above his head and this wasn't true, they assisted him anyway. I heard him saying loudly, 'Don't touch my baby', looked out the door and saw him.

As they grew, Reagan and Aidan were great mates—and great enemies. Nobody fought together like those two but let anybody pick a fight with them, and that person would meet a solid wall of Chamberlain brothers who knew how to protect each other.

Reagan, of course, had been looking forward to his baby. For long enough he had said, 'How come Aidan had a baby and I didn't?' We had explained to him it was because he wasn't there at the time. Now he was getting his baby, and he was excited about it. When he saw her wheeled down from the nursery the first night and had his first hold, he was entranced at the tiny, weeny fingers and toes, and then the little black eyes opened and looked at him, and the smallest mouth he had ever seen in his life opened in a big 'O' and blew a bubble, the first of many. And so she got her nickname, 'Bubbles'.

Jenny was the only friend who visited me while I was in hospital, as I wanted a good rest (knowing I had two lively boys at home as well as the new baby), so the others all waited to see us when I came home five days after Azaria's birth. I had a private room and, although that is good for rest, sometimes it gets a bit lonely. Once when I wandered up to the nursery, I saw that the girl next door to me was on her own and starting to go into labour. She was obviously a little worried, her visitors had gone home and she was alone. I stuck my nose in to say hello. I was bored and so was she, so we sat and chatted.

It was her first baby and she asked me a few questions. She was a lot calmer when I went out. She said she was a local policeman's wife, and later that night I saw him arrive in his uniform. (I discovered that another woman I had met was also a policeman's wife, but I wasn't to find that out until quite a while later.) The other woman I befriended had obviously also delivered the day before. I asked her whether she had what she wanted and she said, 'Yes, a little girl,' quite delightedly, adding, 'I believe we had our babies fifteen minutes apart. I was in the other room yesterday when you had yours and heard all the commotion.' So we swapped news, as mothers do, of how our labours had gone, and later we compared little girls. They were very similar in size and we were thrilled with our daughters. I eventually went home and thought no more about it.

'Think Pink, Mum'

I decided that I would like to tell people myself that my daughter had been born. It always seems so unfair that the husband has the good bits—no pain, *and* the fun of announcing the news. I asked the nurses in the Mt Isa Hospital if I could use the phone. I was told I could make a couple of local calls, but I could not ring long distance. So, admitting defeat, I asked Michael to ring his parents and mine. He rang his parents but my parents were not on the phone so, rather than ring the neighbour like we usually did, he decided to send a telegram. It was very simple: 'Azaria born 9: 16, 11 June, 6 lb. 5 oz. Mother and baby both well.'

My parents had been waiting for some time to hear about the birth of their new grandchild. They had just gone for their daily walk when the telegram boy went past them. Mum said, 'I'll bet that telegram's for us,' and so they stood at the top of the hill and watched which house he went to. Sure enough, the boy stopped at their house. So they walked back to get the telegram, fully expecting it to be about the baby. They read the telegram.

'Azaria. Well, she's had another little boy,' said Mum. 'I wonder why they called him Azaria?' Dad commented that the spelling was odd—perhaps we had meant 'Azariah' and left the 'h' off. Maybe Michael had simply spelt it wrong, or we had chosen a different spelling. It really did not seem to fit with Aidan and Reagan. Mum thought I'd be disappointed because I dearly wanted a little girl; if the baby was a girl, they had planned to ring.

I thought this time they would be so excited, *surely* they would have rung now I was home. But we heard nothing from them until a tape arrived. Mum began very politely and cautiously, 'Well, congratulations, we've got a new little grandchild, a little boy. How lovely.' She went on telling Aidan and Reagan how much fun three little boys would have with cars and toys and playing cricket and football. I thought, she's really having me on. She must know I've had a girl and she's teasing me. But I knew this wasn't really Mum's style.

And then she went on, 'Now the name Azaria—have I said that right? It's not quite what we expected, and we would really like to know how to say it? Is it after the three Hebrew boys?'

Then I realised they *really* thought we had a little boy. I laughed so hard I nearly cried. I wondered how I was going to tell her. If I rang up and said that we didn't have a little boy, she might think that he had died and be very upset. I hadn't decided how to break the news without distressing them when Michael arrived home. His comment was, 'They can't be serious. Ring them up.' So I did.

I rang Lin and John's next door. Lin said, 'Hang on, they're here now.' Then Mum came on the phone, excited to hear from us as usual, and asked how we were going, and how the baby was, and I said, 'Fine.' By then my ideas of how to get the news across had flown out the window and I was madly trying to think of a way to tell them.

Mum said, 'Now, how do you say his name? Because we are not sure.' Suddenly I knew how to tell them, and I said, 'Well, Mum, you have to think *pink* first.'

She said, 'I beg your pardon.'

I said, 'You heard me. You have to think pink, not blue, before I tell you.'

A very puzzled voice came back, 'Think pink? Is that what you said? What do you mean? Oh, you don't mean it's a *girl*.'

'Yes, it's a girl!' I said.

I heard her say, 'Daddy, it's a girl, she's had a little girl,' and then I heard him say, 'Oh, how lovely,' and everyone else exclaiming in excitement too. For over two weeks they had thought it was a boy. It took a while for them to calm down again, then I was able to tell Mum all about Azaria and how to say it 'As-aah-rea', like in the aria you sing. It was great, she was really thrilled.

I tried again to persuade my parents to come out for a holiday to see Azaria while she was little, Mum had never seen any of our children when they were really small and I thought it would be nice. They had never been to Mt Isa, we could take them around, and they would really enjoy themselves. But Mum decided against it, they were busy and shouldn't really spend the extra money. So they didn't come.

Domestic Traumas

I tossed up whether to go on a mission appeal trip Michael and a volunteer were making to the Bourke region in the gulf country, or stay home. As we were going on holidays shortly, and Michael was only taking a small ute, things would be difficult and I decided against it. So Michael went without me, and the boys and I enjoyed the time on our own. We were in a routine and Azaria was easy to look after. Although she had a touch of projectile vomiting like the boys had had, it was mild and nothing that I couldn't cope with. She was troubled with wind because of that, but compared to sessions with Aidan and even Reagan, she was a joy to me. She would play quietly and soon had nice strong little rounded limbs.

She would stay on her bouncinette by my feet, keeping an eye on what I was doing as I worked around the kitchen, or lie beside Reagan watching him play with his toys on the lounge room floor. When she was tired, she went to sleep and when she woke up, we suddenly found somebody looking at us very quietly. She cried only when she had a pain or it was overtime for her feed.

She was quiet most of the time, but she talked to herself, her toys and her mat. I took one picture of her with a beautiful shawl my mother had knitted for her. I put it over the couch and lay her on it. She went cross eyed trying to look at the pattern of the knitting and talked about it to herself. I captured her talking, a picture that Michael never liked much, but then it didn't have the memories for him it had for me.

When Azaria was about five weeks old, Reagan stood on the side of the shopping trolley in the supermarket (one of those with the baby bed in the top) to get a better view of the fruit scales, and the full trolley tipped. Another shopper and I dived for the trolley and Azaria, but although I managed to stop the weight of the trolley, Azaria still fell out, trapped between the cement floor and the trolley. I immediately took her to the doctor as it had been a hard fall with a bang on the head. The receptionist got me in to the paediatrician as my doctor was busy and, noting no damage from the fall, he remarked on how strong she was for her age and how bright and well developed.

The next day, Aidan got chickenpox. He had two whole pox and apart from being a bit crabby and off colour, he was reasonably OK. He was hardly over it when Reagan succumbed. Reagan, like his mother, does a very thorough job of it if he gets ill, and he developed the worst chickenpox I have ever seen or heard of. He was covered head to foot in pox up to four centimetres (one and a half inches) across. At the height of it I would just get him off to a peaceful sleep, and then he would turn over. The weight of his little body would burst the pox and he would be stuck to the bedsheet. This would pull as he turned and he would wake screaming. I would have to sponge him very carefully off the sheet, he would turn over and go back to sleep, and shortly the process would be repeated. Michael was still away on his church trip at the time. On the third night, Reagan became delirious. I sponged him down, knowing that there wasn't anything more to be done. I'd read the medical book and knew that he wouldn't be any better off in hospital. At home he would get individual attention.

As he got worse and my attention to him was necessarily more, my time for Azaria was less. I was breastfeeding Azaria and carrying her around with one arm while talking and reading to Reagan and smoothing his hair with the other. The feeding was fine, although I was getting very tired. The problem was burping her. If he got delirious during the nightfeeds and woke up, I would prop her up and hope for the best.

By morning, not only did I have a very miserable little boy, whom I thought now needed additional medical attention, but also a baby screaming with wind. I'd lost the home number the doctor had given me so I rang his surgery. The receptionist there promptly told me he did not make house calls, so I asked to speak to him personally. She was extremely rude and refused even to put my phone call through. Furthermore, she said, no other doctors in Mt Isa made house calls either and I was a very negligent mother for not bringing Reagan down to the surgery where they would fit him in between other patients. I was desperately tired, I had a screaming baby and an extremely ill small boy. I couldn't drive them in that condition myself. I'd have to get the doctor's permission to call an ambulance—and how could I get that when no doctor, apparently, would come and see Reagan? The last thing I needed was somebody berating me for being a neglectful mother. I was angry now, as well as distressed, and I told her that I did not appreciate her attitude. I was not neglectful, but I would be if I brought him down in his condition. I then hung up and burst into tears.

Fortunately at that moment Michael walked in, having come home a day early. He found me sitting on the floor by the phone in tears. When I explained the situation he said, 'I'll have a piece of that woman.'

'Don't do that,' I said, 'she's a receptionist and I have to take Azaria there for a check-up shortly, it will only make things worse. It's not worth it.'

He said, 'Well, I think I'll have something to say about it. It's unethical. I happen to know that other doctors do house calls. We'll just find one.' And he did; a doctor was there within the hour.

He told me I was right—Reagan didn't need to go to hospital and I was looking after him perfectly well at home. There were a couple more things that I could do now, but he definitely shouldn't be taken outdoors in that condition.

He later said he rang the doctor in question and reported the misinformation I had been given. Michael went down and saw the doctor also. It wasn't so much that the receptionist had said no, but that she had told us no one did house calls, then tried to stop Michael reporting her to the doctor on top of it all. The doctor apologised profusely and Michael left. I never thought much more about it at the time.

For Azaria's six-week check-up, both of us were dressed in our matching black and red outfits. It was the first time I had ever taken her out publicly in a little black cotton dress I had made for Reagan and it caused quite a bit of comment. People either loved or hated it. Dr Irene Milne's nurse asked if she could show her off and walked around with her for a while. When she came back she said, 'Lindy, you have been here for ages. Who are you waiting to see?'

I said, 'Dr Milne. It's Azaria's six-week check-up.'

She said, 'I'm sure your card isn't out.'

I said, 'I wouldn't be surprised, I've been waiting at the counter for ages but the receptionist won't speak to me.'

She volunteered to check up for me, returning to say, 'No, it's not out.'

I saw the doctor within the next ten minutes. As with any other patient, the baby was stripped off ready for her check-up in the corridor and weighed by the nurse, so Dr Milne never did see the black dress.

Memories

It was still midwinter at that time and fairly cold at night. As I wanted to dry-clean Azaria's blankets, one of the easiest things to do was to put her in Michael's sleeping bag, so I popped it in her cradle, lay her on it and folded the top layer across. Because of her wind problem I had one end of the cradle propped up slightly to help her sleep. Like all my children she loved to sleep on her tummy, and when I put her down she would just put her head on one side and go straight to sleep.

As she moved in her sleep, she would wriggle down to the bottom of her bed, and she would be at the end of a warm tunnel with the top open. Of course, when she cried, the sleeping bag muffled the noise. I would hear a little scuffle, sense she was awake and go in and, sure enough, she would be worming around in the bottom. She sometimes used to make herself so hot with her wriggling that she would be red in the face. One time I went in, she had managed to make a little hole in Michael's sleeping bag and the super down was coming out. She had been playing with it and, because she was hot, it had stuck all over her and she looked like a brand new bird, just starting to grow down. Reagan thought it was a huge joke and called her his little bird for quite some time.

On one occasion, I went down the street to buy myself a new dress for church and a number of things that were coming up, such as a seminar Michael was running. I needed something decent and didn't have time to do any more sewing at that stage. I did not intend to take long, found parking close to the shop, and said to Reagan, 'Bubbles is asleep. I don't want to wake her up. Will you wait in the car out here with her? She will wake up for a feed soon and when she does, you call out and tell Mummy and I will come and get her and bring you both into the shop.'

I was trying on clothes when I heard a yell of 'Mum,' and a cry, and thought, hello, she's awake. I put my dress back on in a hurry and said to the saleswoman, 'I will be back in a moment. I will just go and get the baby.' As I walked to the door of the shop, Reagan stuck his little head out the car window and said, 'It's all right, Mum. I've just given her the bottle. You don't have to come and get us.'

I said, 'OK,' and went back to the woman and said, 'Mr Independence is feeding her.'

She laughed and said, 'That's all right.' I went on with my changing. A little while later, there was another yell, 'Mum! Mum!' I started to go out again. I got to the shop door and a clear little ringing voice came across to me, 'It's OK, Mum. She's just got some wind and I've burped her and she's done a *big* burp. But you'll have to change her pants because they're stuck.' This sounded interesting. The lady grinned at me and raised her eyebrows, and I grinned too.

I went over. Reagan had been trying to do everything for her, including changing her nappy. I have my own way of putting a nappy on. It doesn't come off in a hurry, it fits from newborn to two-year-old very tightly and manages to look like a nice little throwaway nappy without being bulky and floppy—often to my girlfriends' disgust, because they can't manage to put a nappy on anything like it. Reagan had got that nappy three quarters of the way off, then the pin had stuck and looked in danger of going in. She, of course, was not cooperating but happily and wildly kicking and cooing and playing.

He said to me in some disgust, 'I told her to lie still but she won't listen.'

I stifled a smile, 'Yes, babies tend to be a bit like that, you know. You were.'

'Oh,' he said and grinned delightedly.

When I changed her nappy and brought her into the shop the lady's face was comical when she saw the size of the child and the size of the baby. But when he perched beside Azaria to play with her and started telling the lady how wonderful she was, she soon realised I wasn't taking a chance, and had a real little pro on my hands.

It was no wonder Reagan was later hit so hard when she was taken from him and no wonder he initially rejected his new little sister, Kahlia, and took so long to accept her.

Michael was never good with nappies. When he did put them on, they seemed to come straight off again. They always seemed to be on upside down, inside out, or the wrong way round, they were thick where they should have been thin and vice versa. One day Azaria had had a lot of wind and I simply had to get down the street. As Michael walked in the door I said to him, 'Can you look after Azaria for a while? She's just been fed, bathed, changed, burped, and is asleep now, so she'll be right. She should be pretty tired and sleep solidly for at least three hours.'

He said, 'You better be right. Off you go and don't be long.' Promising to be not much more than an hour, I went.

I was quick as I could be because I knew she was unsettled, but still thought that she would be OK. Reagan went with me. As we came home, walking up the back stairs, we could hear her yelling. Reagan took off ahead of me and I heard him say, 'Where's bubby?' Michael looked at me and said, 'See if you can do something with her. I can't. I've tried everything. I even tried to feed her, she doesn't want a bottle.' There I saw the bottle I had given her about an hour and a half before, and left sitting on the bench ready to tip out. Michael had heated it up and reused it. It was only the comp bottle and she had had no more than two mouthfuls. The mixture can't have been too good sitting on the bench for that long but she wasn't interested anyway. I went round the corner and there she was propped up in the clean washing on the lounge, yelling.

I picked her up, gave her one pat on the back, at which she gave an almighty burp and immediately stopped crying. The exasperated look on Michael's face was probably indicative of all distracted fathers who try everything except what is needed. He uttered an explosive, 'Well, how was I to know she had wind? I never was any good at this sort of thing. I'm going down to my office.' And off he went.

Aidan, who was home from school, appeared round the corner and said, 'I told Dad she probably had wind, but he reckoned she couldn't have because she hadn't had anything to drink. Besides, he's put the nappies on all funny.' He had managed to take her nappy off but couldn't get the new one on. Thinking of boys, he had put three nappies on top and one underneath. Thank goodness she hadn't wet! I would have all my washing to do again and a wet couch as well. When Reagan and I had a look at the nappies, we had a good giggle and they both declared that when they grew up and had kids, they would know how to put nappies on because Daddy's Mummy couldn't have taught *him*.

Azaria was flesh and blood. She laughed and she cried and she talked, like you and me. It's no good saying she was only a few weeks old, she was just a baby and didn't have a personality. She knew and she understood. And when I sat with her in my arms at night feeding her, I talked to her and told her things. Sometimes we watched TV together, sometimes she stopped feeding and looked at it then looked at me and raised her eyebrows as if to say, 'Fair go. You don't expect me to believe that, *really*.' And then she'd laugh when I answered her. She knew. Maybe some babies are simply dull because their parents don't talk to them and don't give them the opportunity to respond. Some people said that Azaria smiled because she had wind, but when I took her to the doctor, we were talking and Azaria was listening then, she looked at the doctor and she smiled—a straight, knowing, direct smile. Dr Milne said, 'That's no wind, that one.' Dr Milne enjoyed babies. Azaria was small and dainty and pretty. She had little long legs and olive skin and big purple eyes, very expressive eyes, dark like her grandma's, very like Aidan but smaller and daintier, as a little girl should be.

I bought her a little white and turquoise frock. It was supposed to be for a one-year-old, but when I took in the little shoulder straps, instead of it being a bodice and short skirt, the bodice went to her waist and the skirt to her feet. It looked like a long frock and she looked like a little princess, with frills over her shoulders and around her toes. I bought her a little pink sunray pleated dress I was longing to put on her. I usually made all the things for myself and the boys, but I wanted something special, something pink I couldn't make. I hunted all over Mt Isa for that dress. It would have fitted her when we got back from the Rock. She had little shoes that were still too big for her, never worn. Now she wore the little dresses that Reagan had had.

She was small but strong. In my mind's eye I can still see her, at five weeks, bouncing in the Jolly Jumper I hung in the doorway. I used to put a magazine down the back of the harness to hold her head upright. She had the strength in her arms and legs but not quite yet in her neck to stay any length of time without support. She would jump and rest her head on the magazine, laugh and giggle and throw her arms around, strengthening her little legs and bouncing about on her toes. She loved it. It kept her occupied quite a bit while I got the dinner and talked to her.

In the evenings when the boys were asleep and Michael was still out, I would feed her. At first in hospital I had trouble, she didn't want to feed and I had cracked nipples and was extremely sore. As I hadn't fed the boys I was determined to feed her and I was feeling self-conscious—by your third child you should be an old hand but I wasn't. So instead of being uptight in hospital, I incurred the wrath of one of the sisters by telling her that I was going to put Azaria on a bottle because of the way she was vomiting. I held out for that and I did it, despite the fact that she told me I was an unnatural mother because of it. I went home, let my nipples heal, and then decided to try again and see whether I could feed her. I knew you could breastfeed a baby if you wanted to, even it if was adopted, so I decided to try and see if it worked.

I started in the bath and, instead of giving her a dummy, I gave her the breast. Gradually she started to suck and got used to the change of shape. As she sucked, my milk came in, as it does to a new mother. I discovered my milk was not as plentiful as I would have wished and found out how to resolve that too.

When Azaria was five and a half weeks old, Michael had to give an all-day seminar for which I was doing the catering. About seventy people were enrolled. I took Azaria with me and put her down in the kitchen; as people came down they said, 'Where's Azaria?'

I would say, 'Over there.'

'Goodness, she's quiet!' and there she would be playing in the basket on one of the benches.

The day went well all except for a minor mishap. I went to change her nappy and noticed that she had managed to hit her umbilical cord and it was three-quarters off, dried and bleeding. I wasn't quite sure what to do, it was swinging free and, like a broken toenail, was going to pull and really hurt if not cut off. So I went down to the car, got a tiny pair of scissors and used them to chop her cord a lot closer down. Then I pressed the cord back into shape and put her nappy on without any further trouble. I wiped the scissors clean and put them back in the glove box. As far as I knew I hadn't got blood on anything.

At her six-week check-up Azaria was fit, well, and healthy, and Dr Irene Milne was impressed and proud of her progress. She was interested that I had managed to start breastfeeding again, even though I had initially stopped. Things like that were interesting to her because that was her field; so many people had said it couldn't be done. By the time we got to the Rock, Azaria was fully breastfed, and I was carrying only emergency comp feed bottles.

In the evenings I would sometimes sit watching television while she went to sleep in my arms. I kept telling myself to put her down before she got big enough to realise she was being held so much and was being spoilt. And yet always it seemed as if tomorrow was soon enough. I felt that I needed to hold her; she was so beautiful that it seemed as if it wasn't true I'd had her in the first place, and she would disappear if I blinked. So I continued to hold her although my instincts said I shouldn't.

Sometimes for hours at a time I would sit up at night just holding her in my arms and cuddling her. How glad I am that I did. I have got that special time to look back on, and I know that I spent much more than her fair share of time with her. She knew she was loved, she knew she was wanted, she loved her family, she responded to them all very happily and, despite her tender age, it was obvious that she knew she was loved.

THE HOLIDAY OF A LIFETIME

Michael loved photography and enjoyed finding different and unusual things to photograph. For years I had been wanting to take him through the Centre as I knew how much he would enjoy taking pictures of its unusual landscape. We had previously lived in Tasmania and coastal areas and tried to take our holidays in different places close to where we were living, as Michael's job meant that we stayed in each area only for a few years. In this way we saw different parts of Australia as cheaply as possible.

In Mt Isa we were close to Darwin, Alice Springs and Ayers Rock. Michael was keen on barramundi fishing and was thinking just of going to Darwin. I suggested we extend our holiday plans and go to Alice Springs and Ayers Rock first, then back via Palm Valley and some of the other tourist spots making a circle to Alice Springs, then up 'the Track' to Darwin, finishing our holiday with the beach, tropics and barramundi. Michael agreed, so we completed our plans.

With everything packed we were all in the car ready to go except for Azaria's blankets, which were still at the drycleaners, so we called there to pick them up. Everybody was excited and looking forward to the holiday. The boys were in their seats up the back, and Azaria was wide awake on my knee, so Michael went in to collect them. Michael knew the woman fairly well as he often took his clothes in to her, but I only knew her slightly as I had avoided moving around in the Mt Isa heat as far as possible while I was pregnant. As the woman had known I was pregnant but hadn't seen the baby yet, she came out to the car to have a look at Azaria and we talked a little, then she wished us well before we left. We had no idea then how important that woman would be in our lives.

The road wound in and out of creek beds the first part of our trip as we drove to Camooweal on the Northern Territory border. We had heard a lot about it and it turned out to be a typical small outback town with wide streets, a few dogs, cafes, service stations and the usual local pub. We had a look around, bought some drinks, and continued on our way. I had made sure the drinks were in little plastic bottles with resealable lids. Each of us had picked a bottle with a different coloured lid, which I would later refill from the large insulated drink containers at my feet as we travelled along. This saved us hours over the trip, as we only needed quick pit stops for going to the toilet.

Now the road was flat and brown and fairly boring in a long straight stretch to Three Ways, where the road from Mt Isa met 'the Track' from Alice Springs to Darwin. We stopped to refuel, get something to eat and have a look at their souvenir shop, then travelled further south to Tennant Creek.

Tennant Creek had been a very small settlement with unpaved dusty roads and an open-air picture theatre when I went through it with my parents in 1964. Now it was a thriving metropolis, the fourth biggest settlement in the Northern Territory. In fact, the whole highway from the South Australian border to Darwin was now tarred. On my last trip only very small narrow sections had been tarred.

We enjoyed looking around through the local shops, then continued south to the Devil's Marbles. We pulled up just on sunset and decided to camp, as there is no twilight in the tropics. We found a position amongst the rocks, put a tarp down on the ground and laid our sleeping bags out under the stars. Michael and I thought of putting Azaria's basket between us but were worried that a snake or even ants could crawl into the basket and bite her while we were asleep, so we decided to leave her in the car (which was parked beside us) with the windows down fractionally for air so we could hear every move, but nothing else could get in.

The boys thought it was wonderful to sleep without a tent, they had never done it before. In coastal areas there is often a deluge of rain during the night when you are least expecting it which gives you a nasty surprise and ruins your sleep, so we always pitched a tent in those areas.

In the morning, we woke to discover we were very close to a picnic area with large 'No Camping' signs. We had breakfast and a good look around then continued to Alice Springs. The roads are long, straight and flat, so although fairly boring the miles pass quickly between tourist spots, and the boys were well occupied with little books and their toy cars.

The trip was great. Because of Michael's work in Mt Isa, and me so busy as a minister's wife, Aidan at school and somebody always studying or doing homework, we didn't get much time together just as a family. At Central Mt Stuart we had one of our happiest times relaxing as a family, we were all conscious of being on holidays.

We stopped for lunch to coincide with Azaria's feed. The boys were running around and playing, racing up to their sister. I was changing her on the ground in the picnic area, and she was wide awake and happy after her feed, and laughing and playing, doing her best to kick furiously while I tried to clean her. This wasn't the easiest task—she was a wriggling, squirming little worm, doing her best to get her feet into it! I was trying to keep the persistent bush flies off her bottom and out of her eyes. Then the boys would run back, Reagan playfully holding his nose and keeping the flies out of Azaria's eyes, while I tried to get her other end in order and keep away some of the flies myself. Aidan fetched the nappy and was playing some sort of chasing or kicking game with Michael. Then we packed up and the kids were all laughing, and so were Michael and I.

That seemed to be one of the last times we had totally alone together, relaxed, away from people and shops and away from camping areas. So often I picture those waving little arms and legs and that happy, laughing, little face talking, blowing bubbles, animated and excited, playing with the rest of the family, joining in, enjoying it. That was very much our little princess.

When I was last there, Alice Springs had consisted of a paved main street with a few shops carrying essentials, a news stand with week-old papers, and a two-story art gallery and souvenir shop. The main part of town, or should I say all of it, seemed to be contained in four streets that ran around a central open paddock known as the Park. Most of the shops were on one side and that seemed to be it. The Todd River was a windy stretch of sand that meandered along near the front of the shops and water had obviously flowed along it at some stage. The railway terminal from the south was within easy walking distance and seemed to be half the whole town area. At the edge of town, also within easy walking distance, was the one bump on the landscape—a lookout with a cenotaph atop a small rise.

When we hit the outskirts of a modern city the sign said 'Alice Springs', but nothing bore a resemblance to any of my memories. After several kilometres we entered the centre of town—a large thriving business and commercial area which now dwarfed the end of the rail link. The lookout was now in the centre of the city and you could look on houses spreading in every direction into the distance, stretching almost to the Gap in the MacDonnell Ranges leading south and beyond.

When looking around the shops, I actually recognised the old souvenir and art shop which was still there. We bought a few souvenirs and enquired where the camping grounds were, then left town for the Gap caravan park which had been recommended.

We were able to secure a campsite, pitched our tent and decided that one really had enough room for all of us after all. Pitchi Ritchi (William Ricketts gallery in Alice Springs) was across the road and, having seen his work in the Dandenong Ranges in Victoria and loved it, we went across to have a look at his outback works and spent what was left of the afternoon there.

When we went back to the caravan park, we discovered that the entrance area and round the small park shop was crowded with Aborigines settling down for the night. Michael and the children were fascinated as they had never seen them camping out before, or realised that a lot of them spent most of their lives sleeping in river beds or wherever they happened to be. The sadness of this is the introduction of cheap alcohol which means a lot of drunken disorder and litter.

We drove back to our campsite, prepared tea, had showers and started to settle for the evening. We had noticed a number of new campers but things seemed fairly quiet. Just as the children were going to bed, loudspeakers crackled and we discovered we were very close to the rodeo grounds and it was the weekend of the big Alice Springs rodeo. People had come from miles around for it, including most of our new neighbours. Between eleven and midnight, the rodeo revellers returned in hotted-up cars ready for an almost all-night party; sleeping was rather difficult. It was Friday night.

When we rose on Saturday morning, our neighbours were all soundly sleeping in tents, cars and where they sat from the night before. We had a few choices: to stay round a noisy campsite and go to church for part of the day, as it was our Sabbath; or we could raise camp and travel slowly to Ayers Rock, our next destination, and enjoy the scenery along the way. If we had gone for a local drive we would still have to come back to the same racket that night. If we went to church, Michael as a visiting minister would have been asked to speak; a visitor was always too good to miss and the locals would be disappointed if he did not. The only way for a minister to actually have a holiday is to avoid going to church. We opted to travel on slowly. Seeing one tent was big enough for a short stay, and we were not staying in one place for any length of time, we left one tent pitched at the Gap caravan park, along with our extra gear and Aidan's cricket set, which one of the permanent campers had agreed to store for us.

Our first stop was at the Finke River, which was nearly a mile wide at that point and didn't even have puddles at that time of year, although there were water-holes further along. A huge scrub bull was standing in the river bed, and Michael got some good photographs of it. The rest of us kept our distance from those wicked-looking horns. We stopped at various points of interest along the way and then realised the light was fading fast, so Michael put his foot down. The road was still unpaved and had deep corrugations for miles. The car performed well, apart from us deciding that in one more mile we would all shake to pieces. We arrived just too late to get the sunset colours on the Rock that Michael wanted, as we had to register at the park office first, which took too long. We were simply told where the amenities and the camping area was, and we could find our own site within the designated area. It was 16 August 1980.

Lots of families had decided to visit one of Australia's great tourist attractions during the school holidays and we could tell, even in the darkness, that the camping area was fairly full. Later we learned there were around 2,000 there. Because Azaria was so little, we looked for a camping spot that was quiet and far enough away from most of the other campers so they wouldn't be disturbed if she cried. We drove around the camping area and finally found a site at the back next to Sunrise Hill, the local name for the sand dune that campers climbed to view the sunrise.

Michael and I loved camping. We'd been to a lot of places together in New Zealand and in Australia. This wasn't my first visit to the Rock. When I was a teenager, my parents and I had gone through the outback from Adelaide through Coober Pedy in South Australia to the Rock, Alice Springs, Katherine and Darwin itself. I remembered that at the time the camping area at the Rock had consisted of one ranger's house and a small joint ablution block, with two showers, and a couple of toilets each end. You put two shillings in the slot and if you hadn't finished washing your hair before the money ran out, you had to dash outside and put another two bob in. Water was very scarce then because there was only one bore and a tank.

A long time afterwards my father reminded me that, even then, he had been a little concerned that the dingoes at the Rock came rather too close to human beings. The ranger had warned him to be careful where we put our food because the dingoes would be after it during the night. No one warned us on this night.

I later learned the West family—Bill, Judy and their twelve-year-old daughter, Catherine—were camped next to us. Not long before we arrived, Catherine had an encounter that gained great significance because of what happened afterwards.

In the words of Judy West:

> Catherine was near the tent, and noticed a sleek, healthy dingo standing about a meter from her. She said, 'Look at that!' and sounded pretty upset.

> She told me the animal had come up while she was writing, had taken her elbow in its teeth and shaken it. She was wearing a fairly thick cotton fleecy windcheater: it wasn't cut or marked, and the skin on her elbow was unbroken. This was the first dingo we'd seen in the area. We had never left food out to feed the animals because notices posted in the toilet block advised against it.
>
> After dinner that night, I approached a clothes line knotted at an angle between the low fence and the roof of the caravan [next to their tent]. As I approached, a dingo was systematically ripping the clothing off the line. It ran off when it saw me, but I knew it wasn't the same dingo as the one we'd seen earlier. When I spoke about this to Mrs Daniell [the owner of the clothes] she told me that none of the clothing had rips, teeth marks or tears in it.
>
> Later that evening, after tea, I heard a baby crying, quite a loud cry, coming from the Chamberlain tent.

By the time we had pitched the tent it was fully dark and, as usual in the desert, the temperature dropped dramatically after the sun went down. I finished feeding Azaria but she had decided not to settle and I thought that perhaps she wanted a little more, so while Michael was cooking tea in the gas barbecue enclosure near the tent, I plugged her comp bottle warmer into the car's cigarette lighter. Normally when we were travelling it was very quick, but with the car stationary and the night extremely cold it took some time to warm, and Azaria started to cry. Before it was warm she actually went to sleep and I didn't need it after all. I put her to bed in her carry basket in the car and left her there with the windows only slightly open as usual while I set up the tent, attended to the boys, and had my meal. Finally when we were all ready to settle for the night I lifted her basket into the tent and placed her beside me next to Reagan's feet for the night.

I had bought a special torch that worked like a lantern with a high spreading beam good for general light in the tent, but it was useless to use walking about as it shone in your face instead of on your feet. It also had a subsidiary bulb which gave a very dim light, just sufficient to see what I was doing for night feeds but not enough to disturb everyone else. I had an icecream container and sterilisation tablets, which I used overnight for sterilising the juice and comp bottles and refilled every morning for the day's supply. As I was using throwaway nappies, camping was a cinch.

Azaria always woke just before sunrise so we did not need an alarm to wake Michael for the photographs he desired of the beautiful colour changes on the Rock as the first rays of the sun hit it.

The kids and I stayed in bed playing until a more reasonable hour when the sun warmed the landscape up a little. We dressed and were just beginning to get breakfast when Michael returned. We decided to cook our meal to eat about ten o'clock and then spend the rest of the day looking around the Rock. I met one of the other campers, with her daughter, at the barbecue area and she introduced herself as Judy West.

While I was cooking I had Azaria's carry basket resting on the bench beside me. The boys were happily playing nearby with some little friends they had discovered. At one stage Aidan came back very excited that he had found a little mouse that hopped like a kangaroo. Months later we discovered that Ayers Rock actually has a species of wildlife called a kangaroo mouse and this was apparently what he had seen.

Judy West remembers:

> On Sunday morning, we met the Chamberlains in the barbecue shelter. I was admiring the baby in the carrycot and Lindy told me she was their long-awaited girl after two boys. They had called her Azaria because it meant Blessed of God.
>
> Lindy was wearing a mid [grey] parka almost literally covered in travel badges. I commented on the badges and Lindy explained that her family went camping wherever her husband's profession sent him. The badges were an indication of their travels; she collected them for herself and the two boys. She said she had even collected two already for Azaria, ready to sew on a parka for her as she got older, although she was only nine weeks old.

I finished my preparations and Michael returned from his local wanderings so we all got in the car for our day's sight-seeing We headed west around the Rock, having a look at the local airstrip and the sections of rock called the Brain and the Kangaroo Tail, then stopped at the Climb. Azaria was now asleep. We wanted to take some photographs on the Rock because most of the photographs my father had taken years before were overexposed and I wanted some replacements.

When my parents, a friend and I had previously been to the Rock there was no chain to cling to up the steep part of the climb. We just asked where the Rock was climbed and clambered up. The book that was kept on the cairn at the top in those days was changed once every couple of years and, at the very least, you could go back and look at names scattered months apart.

I was later informed by a ranger that the book we had signed was probably about the second or third ever placed at the Rock. Now (1989), in holiday seasons it is often changed every couple of days, as so many people visit the area. Back then it was still and beautiful, despite the fact that we went there right near the end of the big ten-year drought. I can remember sitting on the top and looking at the scene below me and counting the spinifex bushes through binoculars, they were so sparse. That trip stands out as one of the happier memories of my childhood.

The boys were excited but had no desire to climb all the way to the top. Knowing Michael would be tired when he returned from his intended climb I wanted to take the photos beforehand, so I organised the boys while Michael got ready.

There was a nice-looking woman sitting in the vehicle next to us so I asked her if she would mind listening for when the baby woke up, as she was due for her feed shortly, and we agreed that she would wave if Azaria woke. We climbed up to Chicken Rock, the nickname given to an outcrop of rocks near the base of Ayers Rock. These look low, but many people find they lose their nerve when they no longer have them to hold on to and have to walk straight up the Rock from there on, so they chicken out, hence the name. The chain which goes up the two steepest sections of the Rock for people to hold on to starts a little distance above Chicken Rock. This discourages fainthearted climbers from proceeding beyond their limits before they realise their predicament.

It was in this area just before the main climb that we had all our photographs taken. Michael used a fluorescent filter on his camera which would give the Rock a slightly redder hue than the midday sun gave it naturally. I took some shots of Michael and the boys and he took some of us. The lady below waved, and I saw her go around to the car to pick Azaria up. Michael waited with the boys while I went down to fetch Azaria and bring her up for her photograph. When I got down the lady said she was surprised the baby was so little, but commented on how well set up the car was. I thanked her for her help and went back up the Rock to where Michael was waiting.

I had hoped to climb the Rock with Azaria in a backpack but realised my legs were still too weak and not recovered from her recent birth, so gave up the idea. This short climb only helped convince me I had made the right decision. We took photographs of Azaria, one of which is now famous; it shows me holding Azaria upright on the Rock. Then Michael left to climb the Rock with his camera bag (which weighed over 8 kilograms) over his shoulder.

The boys and I stayed near the car and they played while I fed Azaria, after which I got them some food. Michael had still not returned and the boys were tiring of their game, so we went across the road to the seats placed at the bottom of the climb where we could watch the various people come and go. Watching really is quite a sport. A number of bus tours came by, dropping off or picking up their loads of climbers, so it was not at all boring. I had sat down next to an elderly lady whose husband was climbing the Rock. They were from an earlier bus tour and because he had a heart condition, he was taking it very slowly and the bus captain had taken the rest of the people to another location and was coming back later to collect him.

The lady and I had quite a conversation, and she explained how her husband was climbing slowly so he would not upset his heart. We also discussed Azaria and, of course, her age, size and name. The boys were playing around by our feet but at one stage they took off over the road. As I got up to go and fetch them, the elderly lady offered to hold Azaria for me while I ran to catch them as a number of large buses were approaching. I got the boys settled and we were watching as her husband came into view. He waved and sat down on the flat part of the top of the major climb for another rest before he descended.

I was fascinated to see the progress of a guy who had gone up in ordinary street shoes with steel caps on his heels and toes. At that stage I would have been inclined to go barefoot if I'd been him but he had left his shoes on and lost his nerve. He was crouched helplessly on the Rock holding on to the chain for dear life, three quarters of the way up the steep part. I could remember from my initial climb that somewhere about there you could stand upright and by holding your arm out directly in front of you, both your feet and hands would touch the Rock, as the gradient was so steep in that spot. Eventually the coach captain had to climb up to the man and walk him down.

While we were watching, another family of four also sat down on the bench and the subject of conversation was, as usual, mainly the climb. The man had a pair of binoculars through which he was watching the climbers. Way up on the top of the Rock a man appeared running. That is one thing that you do not do unless you are extremely surefooted because one slip and you roll to the bottom, usually to your death. We were commenting on the chance he was taking and as he came into full view, his clothing looked familiar. I borrowed the binoculars and, sure enough, Michael was galloping down the Rock, knees locked and well in control, but I was glad it wasn't me and it made me feel rather nervous. When the others started commenting, I informed them it was my husband before they said something which would embarrass them later when Michael came across to us and they realised who he was. Shortly afterwards the family left.

By now Aidan had decided that he wanted to climb the Rock too. As Michael was feeling fairly fresh, he decided that he would take Aidan back up after he had removed his socks and cut his toenails, which were annoying him. Then he was annoyed to discover that I didn't have any scissors with me in the car. All I had was a pair of nail clippers, which he hated. After some fuss and grumbling he finally used the nail clippers, left his socks off and went to collect the boys, who had both just started off. Reagan was not going to be outdone by his big brother and had every intention of going too. Michael had to wait for Reagan's little legs of course—but not Aidan. He scampered up ahead like a little mountain goat. Unable to be in two places at once, Michael called for Aidan to wait but Aidan had tacked himself on to the back of a group from a bus tour and either didn't hear or decided it was wisest to play deaf, and kept going.

When they got to the steep part at the top of the chain, Reagan took one look down, announced that was far enough and he was going hack. As Aidan was well out of sight and Michael could neither catch him with Reagan on his back nor leave Reagan sitting there alone while he fetched Aidan, he decided to bring Reagan down and then go back up a third time to get Aidan before he got back to that steep section. I saw them turn around and Michael descended slowly while Reagan held on to the chain and slid down on the seat of his brand new nylon pants. I figured when he got to the bottom they would be smoking hot and have holes, but they didn't seem to be any the worse for wear and nor did he. Michael left him with me, then returned for his third onslaught. Reagan told me that he thought 'big rocks like that are too high for little boys and they should stay on the ground.'

I was amused, but knew Michael wouldn't think it was funny as Aidan appeared at the top of the chain just as Michael got there. They turned round to come back together and Aidan once again galloped off well ahead of Michael who was left to come down alone anyway. When he got to the bottom Michael said he was getting so stiff he would not be able to move later and wanted to go straight home as he was now very tired. I told him I had promised the boys they could have a look at Maggie

Springs as they had found it difficult to believe that there was water anywhere between where we were and the ocean!

As it was on the way home and Michael was also interested that a pool of water existed, it was agreed that we would go after all. The family of four that I had been talking to were walking back to the campsite, looking at the various features on the way. We passed them and waved, then they passed us as we stopped for Michael to get photographs of the lichen on the Rock. To use the right lens he had to walk away from the Rock in order to get the view he wanted. We waited in the car as usual. Michael took over one hundred shots of the Rock and its environs that day and was having a delightful time (apart from aching calf muscles) as it was a photographer's paradise. He was really excited that I had finally talked him into coming.

We continued on around the ring road and stopped at a place where my memory told me there were rock paintings, although there were no tourist signs there. We all got out of the car and sure enough, some paintings were there, although the site did not seem to be quite what I remembered. The boys had fun and found a natural rock slide which kept them occupied for a while. We all wandered out the back entrance to the cave while Michael continued to take pictures.

The family of four caught up to us again. I was standing talking to them when I sensed something watching me. I looked up and saw a dingo steadily gazing at me. It made me feel a bit creepy to see it standing there so quietly like that, so I made light of the situation and said to the people jokingly, 'That your dog?' nodding my head towards the dingo. The man answered me very seriously that it was a dingo which was a native wild dog to this area. It didn't seem right after that to enlighten him that I was only joking and knew all that perfectly well, so I just kept quiet. In later years I came to wish I had risked hurting his feelings.

We called Michael, but he just missed out on a photograph as, although the other man got a quick photo and the boys playing about didn't seem to disturb it, Michael's arrival did. Normally a dingo seems to keep its eye on all activity in the area but what struck me as peculiar with this one was that it seemed to have its gaze fixed on Azaria and me; she was awake and sitting over my shoulder. It was not the least bit interested in Reagan's activities though, and he was playing in a crack along the base of the boulder on which the dingo was actually standing. From where I was standing looking from below it, the dingo had looked fit, healthy, and reasonably young.

We left after that and continued round to the Fertility Cave and Maggie Springs. This cave was the one I had remembered the rock paintings in from years ago and behind it was Bullari (translated into English as 'Cut Throat') loosely called Echo Cave by tourists because of its ability to cast a great echo. It was the spot where a number of Dreamtime men had been caught and murdered for stealing a maiden from another tribe, and the gap in the Rock was where they had tried to scream for help after having their throats cut. The boys and I clambered up to the echo spot and I sat nursing Azaria while they played about. A Koala bus pulled up with a load of school children aboard. They came and climbed around the area as well. I sat and talked to a number of the children and noticed that one of them had his arm in a sling and another one had a bandage around his head which, I was told, came from a recent injury. They all left and we left shortly afterwards.

We didn't get to see Maggie Springs after all because it was another two or three hundred meters (two or three hundred yards) further on and Michael had really had it by then, so we went straight home, promising to return the following day on our way to the Olgas.

When we returned we discovered that the disposable nappies I had placed in a bag and pushed right up inside the low camp fireplace had all been pulled out. The inner wet patches on the nappies had been scooped out and shredded. Michael cleaned them up and told me he had actually seen dingoes doing this earlier on, and that I had better be more careful where I left things in future. So much for trying to protect them from marauding dingoes.

Judy West's story continues:

> I was cooking on the southern barbecue when Lindy came down with the baby. We sat on the bench and talked. She was holding Azaria, sitting up in the crook of her arm. Azaria was wearing a little bright pink cotton dress—I noticed this particularly because when my own children were babies the only acceptable colour had been white or very pale pastels and colour was a new innovation. Azaria seemed to me to be tiny, quiet and good as I'd only heard her cry once, when the family had arrived the previous evening.

I started to prepare tea and get things ready for our return from Sunset Strip, then decided to bath Azaria early while it was still her playtime. I took the little square washing up dish I was using as a baby bath across to the ladies' toilets, put it in the washtubs and gave her a bath. Later, when I returned to the barbecue area, I dressed and changed her out of the strawberry pink Angel suit she had been wearing all day and put on a clean nappy, singlet, white stretch jumpsuit and matinee jacket. The knitted matinee jacket had a pretty pale lemon scalloped edging. I had put her bootees on underneath her jumpsuit because I got sick of taking the bootees on and off every time I had to change a nappy during the night. They were nice little ones that my mother had knitted for Aidan, with special hand-twisted ties in them, instead of ribbon. I wrapped Azaria up well and, as Michael had returned, I asked him if he would get her a juice bottle while I bathed the boys before we left for Sunset Strip, which he did.

I left Michael talking to Judy West and, much to the boys' disgust, I took them across to the ladies' toilets and insisted they have a bath in the small square concreted bath area just inside the door. Aidan was in and out in a hurry before anyone came and I took him back to Michael. Reagan, on the other hand, did not wish to be bathed where someone might come in the door. No way. We had quite a discussion and then he had his bath anyway. Fortunately no one came in. By now we were running close to sunset time and Michael was anxious to leave. I put Reagan straight into the car and hurriedly grabbed the rest of the bath gear and threw it into the tent, then we drove off.

We had a fast trip to the sunset area and Michael decided to stop much closer to the Rock than most, as he had a special lens which allowed him to do that. We could avoid other cars' dust and noise this way. There was one other young couple there and I thought they were probably honeymooners because she was the photographer and he was very patiently waiting for her, which I couldn't imagine him doing unless he was still starry eyed. I fed Azaria in the car and when I turned round to put her in the basket, I discovered Reagan was sound asleep. I got out and talked to the others for a little while, then climbed back in the car as it was already starting to get quite cool. The light went and we returned to the campsite. Michael went ahead to start getting tea and was cooking baked beans and mushrooms while I organised the boys and the tent.

As Azaria had woken up on the way home and was grizzly with wind, I gave her to Aidan to hold in the car while I settled the sleeping Reagan in the tent in his sleeping bag for the night, and organised clean clothes for the morning. I was in the habit of setting out clean clothes at the foot of the children's beds so they could get up whenever they chose, whether I was there or not. I also gathered the dirty clothes and damp towels, which I had flung into the tent at the last minute and placed them in the plastic laundry bag in the back of the car.

With us at the barbecue were Greg and Sally Lowe and their daughter Chantelle. Greg Lowe later recalled:

> We started to prepare and eat our evening meal, and noticed a stranger walking towards us.
>
> The stranger was soon joined by a lad of about six or seven and shortly afterwards, a woman approached along the worn track that linked the barbecue shelter with the sites on the eastern edge of the camping ground.
>
> As she neared the shelter we saw that she was holding a young baby against her shoulder. She sat next to me on the railing. In any company a small baby is a sufficient reason to enter into conversation with complete strangers. We asked the usual question: 'Boy or girl?' The lady, who introduced herself as Lindy, proudly announced that the babe was a girl named Azaria and the little boy was Aidan. We all introduced ourselves and engaged in an informal conversation. We learned that Mike, her husband, had spent time in Tasmania some years before; that formed a bond because we came from Tasmania. Lindy said she had been born in Whakatane, on the North Island of New Zealand. We had friends in the same town, whom we hoped to visit the following year. Mike was a university graduate; I was into the third year of a part-time university course. We shared an interest in sport. Lindy and Mike and I all jogged, and I had been making haphazard runs around the home block in an effort to get fit for pennant squash.

Someone noticed a dingo fossicking fairly close to the barbecue shelter. We continued to talk and Greg was trying to guess Michael's occupation. As people usually did, he guessed Michael might be a schoolteacher or a bank employee.

Greg Lowe:

> A few minutes later, the dingo reappeared on the northern side of the shelter. It was fossicking around the base of some bushes directly behind the rails upon which Lindy and I were sitting. I drew the dingo's presence to the attention of our toddler, Chantelle, who was standing at my feet. She pointed excitedly, and said, 'Oggie, oggie.' I was about to stand her outside the barbecue railing to pat the 'oggie' when the words of my brother-in-law, Bruce, echoed in my mind. On seeing a dingo in the wild, on a previous day trip out of Alice, he had remarked, 'Where's my gun? I'll shoot the bastard.' If an Alice Springs resident of many years' experience didn't like dingoes, who was I to argue? So I prevented Chantelle from touching the dingo, and removed her to a more secure position inside the barbecue shelter. Not an unwise decision, in the light of what later happened. The dingo was apparently hot on the trail of a mouse that had earlier fled through the grounds of the barbecue site.

I remonstrated with Michael for trying to throw the dingo some food and reminded him that there were signs in the toilet requesting people not to feed the dingoes. The sign said it helped to break down their natural reticence towards man and that the dingoes were wild animals and anyone attempting to pat them may be bitten. The faded typing indicated the main reason for not feeding them was that they were considered sacred by the Aborigines and it would be a pity if tourists changed the dingoes' habits so much that they became pests and had to be shot because they were a nuisance to the public.

Azaria was still squirming and wriggling with wind. I walked her around for a while patting her back while she was leaning over my shoulder, then sat down on the railing beside Greg Lowe.

Suddenly from the dark, we saw the little mouse again. It was one of Aidan's hopping variety which he had previously seen and was searching for. Greg called Aidan to bring his torch quickly as it was sitting at the base of the post between where Greg and I were sitting on the fence. Before Aidan could arrive, the dingo, which had previously disappeared, pounced out of the darkness scaring us, and the mouse became no more.

Azaria was sleeping intermittently and still squirming all the while, obviously uncomfortable. I had lain her across my knees on her tummy and was patting her bottom gently, which helped her in her troubled sleep. She wriggled so much that she squirmed out the bottom end of her blankets and her little legs could be seen kicking.

Sally Lowe was later to describe it this way:

> Lindy was holding the baby here like—she was actually resting on a pole, so was quite comfortably holding . . . definitely kicking towards her hand. You know, just like a little kick towards her hand.

I stopped to rewrap her and Aidan asked if bubby was still awake. I pulled the blankets down a little for him to see that she had actually settled now and Greg Lowe asked if he could have a look too. He did, then commented, 'Geez, that's a little one. Come and have a look, Sally, and bring Chantelle.' Sally did. Azaria wriggled in her sleep and pulled a face, as babies do when they sense they are being disturbed or checked. It is a movement that is difficult to describe but which all mothers recognise.

Greg loves kids and has told me since that he was about to ask to nurse Azaria. I don't know how I would have reacted to that; he had a tinny in his hand! I would probably have said no because she was asleep. If she was awake, I might have handed her over but I never used to hand my children around to be nursed a lot unless I knew the person really well. They end up crying if they're handed from one person to the other, and then it's a mess.

Greg Lowe remembered the incident this way:

> Mike was about to put a billycan of water on the barbecue plate he was using. Sally and I had finished our meal and had no purpose for the boiled water still simmering on the adjacent plate, so we offered him our water to use for herbal tea.
>
> Lindy was still having problems getting the baby to settle. Azaria had kicked the blankets loose so Lindy rested the baby on her knee and began wrapping her up again. The source of her problem was obvious. The child was squirming against Lindy by kicking its feet. As soon as Azaria was rewrapped in the cocoon of blankets, I moved a step nearer to closely examine the little one. Azaria's eyes were closed, so I, a near total stranger, dare not undo the good work done by her mother, and refrained from tickling her cheek. Sally remembers Azaria wincing when I poked my face next to hers.
>
> Lindy finally won the struggle to settle Azaria, and was relieved enough to comment, 'At last it's worked.' She got up from the railing alongside me and moved closer to where Mike was busily engaged at the other barbecue plate. I was tempted to ask if I could hold the baby, but desisted because not every new mum likes a stranger to have control of her infant.
>
> Once again (ignorant of his profession) I offered Mike a can of beer; once again he declined. Lindy added that a drinker ought to be concerned not only with his own future health, but also the future welfare of his wife and children. I dismissed her statements with the words, 'I'm a bit of a fatalist anyway,' but she was quite right in her attitude.

Michael was pressing me to eat so he could clean up and finish for the night. Aidan announced he was tired and as Azaria was now sleeping soundly, I suggested that Aidan come with me to go to bed while I put Azaria down for the night.

Greg continues here:

> Lindy began to retrace her steps along the worn path that led from the barbecue to their tent with the obvious intention of putting the sleeping Azaria to bed. Aidan went with her. I watched her, with natural curiosity to find out what tent belonged to our new acquaintances. Even though the scrub between the barbecue shelter and the tent partly obscured the view, it was obvious that Lindy had to kneel to enter their tent.

Aidan unzipped the tent and we crawled inside. Aidan tenderly kissed his baby sister good-night and watched while I put her down on her stomach in the carry basket. She stirred slightly and turned her face towards the back of the tent as I tucked her in securely. By now she had been sleeping soundly for about half an hour. It was getting really cold already so I made sure the blankets came up within one and a half centimetres (half an inch) of the crown of her head and she had a warm tunnel to sleep in. She actually had six layers of blankets over her, with a soft bunny rug nearest to her body. When I had made sure she was asleep, I turned my attention to Aidan, who had taken off his parka and thrown it by the door with Reagan's parka and was now sitting up in his sleeping bag. Then Aidan said, 'Is that all the tea I'm getting?'

I said to him, 'Why, are you still hungry?' It seemed to me that he had had a great deal to eat that night but after climbing the Rock I supposed he had developed hollow legs. He said, 'Yes,' he was hungry.

I told him he could have some more tea and asked what he would like. He wasn't sure so I suggested some more plain baked beans. He said yes. I went to talk to him as he had already crawled out of bed again and was standing in front of the tent. I stood with my arm around his shoulders while we discussed whether or not he would eat in the tent or come back to the barbecue again. He wanted to eat in the tent but as I remembered he still spilled things frequently I suggested he had better come back to the barbecue to eat. I told him to get his parka but now he decided he was hot and didn't need it, so I went to the car.

The car was parked so close to the tent that if the door had been opened carelessly the corner of it would have ripped the tent. I walked to the back hatch and opened it, then realised I was looking in the wrong food box and moved around to the driver's door. Aidan started talking to me again and I realised he was still standing at the front of the tent without his parka. I took the two steps to the driver's door while he watched and got the tin of baked beans out from behind Michael's seat, gave up on the parka and said, 'You'd better come back and tell me which plate was yours anyway and I will get the same plate—save me washing it twice.' I didn't zip up the tent again as I was planning to come back fairly quickly and go straight to bed, having decided by then I was far too tired to eat after all.

Can in my hand, Aidan and I had a race to the barbecue, he going one way round the bushes and I another. Nearly back to the barbecue, I saw Sally Lowe start to look up and slowed to a walking pace immediately. I was still very conscious of being overweight and I hate seeing floppy women running so I had no desire to get caught.

Greg remembers it this way:

> Aidan had followed Lindy and waited patiently for his mother alongside the tent. The sounds of the voices at the barbecue site must have attracted his attention because he was looking in our direction. Lindy came out of the tent, joined Aidan and moved towards the car that was parked on the southern side of the Chamberlains' tent.

We climbed the low railing and I walked round the gas bottles to the barbecue stove we were using. I put the can of beans down and picked up the can opener.

The front of the tent was visible from where we were. If the children got up or stirred, I could see and hear them if they got restless. Sounds carried further at night, so movement in the tent next door could also be heard. It is not surprising that the Wests, who were sitting quietly in their tent, heard a dingo growl, though not very loudly. The distinct sound came from behind their tent and towards ours. They interpreted it as an unusual noise for that area, one that Bill West later described as a warning growl to let another dog know he was encroaching on private territory and to keep off his property. We discovered later that we may have camped in the territory of a particular dingo.

Greg remembers:

> Lindy must have questioned how much Aidan had to eat because she asked him, 'Is that all you've had?' Mike and I again took up our lapsed conversation. I was pondering a reply to his questions about my work when Aidan interrupted, 'Was that bubby crying?'
>
> Sally agreed, 'Yes, it was.' Mike had also heard the cry and asked Lindy, who was bending over the barbecue plate, if Azaria had been settled when she was put in the tent. Lindy replied positively, so Mike said, 'I think you had better go and check.'

From my position behind the barbecue gas bottles, working with the can opener, it was not surprising that I missed hearing Azaria cry out. The others, standing quietly talking and in a direct line, *had* heard.

I was sure that Azaria was well settled and was not convinced that she had started to waken, but Michael looked determined that something should be done, so rather than argue I thought the quickest thing would be to go back and check before I got on with preparations for Aidan. I immediately put the can opener down and started to walk back towards the tent. I was halfway between the fence and the barbecue railing, when I saw the head and shoulders of a dingo emerging through the tent flap.

It had its head down, shaking vigorously, and I thought, it's got Michael's shoes, which were at the front of the tent. It seemed a pretty golden colour; the light from the barbecue shining through its coat made it look shiny and in beautiful condition. It wasn't one of the mangy ones we had seen before and the way it had its head down made the hairs of its neck stand out in the light like a ruff. The light shining through the hairs on the outer edge of the ears made them look fluffy (I was later to have my description of the dingo criticised because of that mention of its ears). Its nose was in the shadow cast by the bushes and railing in front of the tent but the way it was swinging its head around made me think it had the shoe by the shoelace and couldn't get it through the tent flap properly. The dingo appeared to be having difficulty in getting whatever it had free and through the door. It was these observations that gave me the impression it was probably a young dog.

I mumbled, 'Go on, get out!' and then turned to tell the others. I briefly noticed Aidan trailing a few feet behind me. As I was about to speak I suddenly thought there was no food in the tent and the realisation that Michael had said Azaria had cried hit me. It flashed through my mind that the dingoes were wild. When first asleep she slept heavily and it would have had to actually touch her to disturb her and it could have bitten her. The only thing visible was her head. She might need first aid. I was now one step closer past the bush and I could see into that dreadful ravaged tent. I started to scream to the others as I burst into headlong flight—'The dingo's got my baby!'

A few weeks later I wrote down my devastated feelings in an effort to get the horror out of my system and start dealing with life again.

'THE DINGO'S GOT MY BABY'

Bubby, no God, oh no, not my baby. It's not true. She is there. Something else, God, not her. She must be dead or she'd cry. Not a sound and those empty scattered blankets. My feet feel like lead as I clear the fence and dive into the tent headlong. I scream to Michael as I run that the dingo has the baby, with one hand on Reagan to feel his heartbeat and check he is alive and the other lifting those awful scattered blankets. The basket rolls as I bump my hand on the edge. It wouldn't do that if she was in it. I think I'm going to be sick. I touch the carry basket. It's really empty. It's no bad dream—and it's still warm, even her dummy is still warm. She's so little. So little and so precious. Reagan has his sleeping bag hood up and his face buried in the pillow. He never sleeps like that. Not ever. Boot him hard. He wriggles at last. He's alive. Thank you God for his life—it could be both of them. Azaria, oh Azaria, what's happened to you, what is happening to you? Your bed's still warm and it's so cold out there. 'Oh God, oh God help me,' I cry in my heart. I turn and dive out of the tent again the direction the dingo went. It is like standing outside myself and watching someone else moving in slow motion. So many things done so quickly, so little time gone. Three seconds, five seconds, from that first terrifying glimpse of an empty bed, and my scream to Michael. He seems to turn slowly as if someone has made a slow motion movie. Why hasn't he run too. 'What?' God, he thinks I'm joking. Please God let him realise I'm serious and help me quickly. He's had time to get to me, to chase that dingo, to get to here and help. He hasn't moved and I've checked the tent and am out already. I scream again, 'The dingo's got my baby!' I run to the right where the dingo headed and, and . . .

I reached the front of the car. There was a dingo, standing motionless slightly behind the rear of our yellow Torana in the shadow. It had its back to me and its head was turned slightly towards me, as if it was listening. As it saw me, it ran swiftly and silently across the road on an angle, to my right, into the scrub towards the sandhills. I ran madly and reached the edge of the scrub. Suddenly all light ended and the night was dark, impenetrable. I listened for movement but it was so silent that it was as if the animal had vanished completely. Michael and Greg Lowe madly raced towards me.

'Which way?' yelled Michael. I pointed and they ran straight into the scrub.

'It's no good, you can't see, you'll need a torch!' I knew that our own torch, a powerful Big Jim, wouldn't work; the batteries were flat.

'Has anybody got a torch?' I screamed as loudly as I could, 'The dingo's got the baby, has anybody got a torch?' *Dear God, don't let them think I'm drunk or joking.*

Two men appeared immediately to my left. It seemed to me almost as if they must have had the torches in their hands and been on their way out the door when they had heard my call.

‘Which way?’ they called. I pointed and called the answer back. They called to each other, ‘Spread out!’ and ran into the scrub after Michael and Greg.

A third man ran from the right, calling, ‘Which way did the dingo go and how big is the baby?’ I ran towards him as I answered and we met briefly in the middle of the road as I pointed my instructions and told him Azaria’s size and that she was wearing white. (For years that meeting was a source of confusion and irritation.) I did not know then that that man (Haby) had photographed a dingo right in the doorway of his campervan only minutes before, and the animal had headed in our direction.

Sally later said, ‘My husband Greg yelled at me to get the torch as Michael was still a bit stunned.’

Judy West continues:

> I went back into the tent and said to Bill and Catherine, ‘I think something terrible has happened. I think a dingo’s got the baby.’
>
> Bill put his sandals on and Catherine her sneakers and we went outside to see what was happening, but no one was around. We went to the back of the Chamberlains’ tent where Aidan was standing by himself. I asked him if it was true that a dingo had taken the baby. He said, ‘Yes,’ and started to cry. I felt quite devastated because it had been an unthinking thing to do to a child and he had realised the situation and it had hit him with full force.

When I had first half turned to tell the others about the dingo in the tent, I had seen Aidan there but had no idea what he had done after that. He hadn’t gone to the tent while I was there although I later learned he must have looked into the tent himself. Being small, behind me, and behind the bush, I knew he would have been prevented from seeing that dingo, thank God.

Aidan came running from around the car. He sort of screamed at me, ‘Mummy, don’t let that dingo eat our baby.’ He put into words what my mind wouldn’t accept. There could be no doubt that he was quite aware of what had happened and what was going on. I held out my arms and he ran into them. I cuddled him and said, ‘Darling, we’re trying to find her. Jesus will look after her but she’s very little.’

I didn’t know whether to stay with him, or go and look for her, or what. He wanted to come out searching with me but I explained that I wanted him to stay back because if Reagan woke up he wouldn’t know what had happened and would be frightened on his own.

It was not until a long time later that Reagan told me he had woken to feel the dingo walking over him and had been terrified to move or look (thank God). He could remember me poking him and, terrified, had played possum at first, then, on hearing my voice, that had calmed him and being so tired he had immediately gone straight back to sleep, once again sleeping deeply. The West Australian woman (Judy West: I couldn’t remember any of their names after what had just happened, but learned them all again later) approached me. She had been following at a distance behind Aidan and, hearing the conversation, said to me, ‘Don’t worry about him, I’ll look after him if you want to go out with your husband and look, you can.’

Greg Lowe had gone back for his own torch, and Judy West thrust her fluorescent-lamp torch into Michael's hands.

He seemed to be in shock as he wouldn't take it and kept saying 'Where's my keys?' (He later said that fluorescent lights weren't good for looking under bushes.)

I couldn't understand why Michael was looking for the keys. The car was open and he had access to the torches and things although I knew the battery was flat because we had accidentally packed something against the switch and it had been on the whole time we had been travelling. It didn't seem to be important to me. I doubt in the trauma of the moment whether I would have remembered that I had dropped the keys under my pillow even if Michael had told me then that he wanted to use the spotlight in the glove box. (I was also unaware that the car had to be turned on for the light to work.)

Somebody produced a torch for Michael initially but the batteries were well worn and he couldn't see very well so he came back to exchange it for something better. It was only then I realised he had Aidan's small green rubber-coated torch. I presumed Michael had found it somewhere and grabbed it but later learned that Aidan, hearing me call for torches, had rushed and got his from where he had been using it in the barbecue to look for the mouse. Seeing Michael looking desperately for a torch, he had handed his over, and Michael in his agitation had not even been aware that his own son had handed it to him.

Finally Bill West provided Michael with a powerful torch, and he went back out again with Greg Lowe into the bush, sand and spinifex.

Greg later indicated he wanted to go searching with Michael regardless of what was found, because Michael was in a state of shock and Greg didn't want him to find her alone. He said he knew, no matter what they discovered out there, there would be no joy for us.

In a piece called '*A Night We'll Never Forget*', Sally Lowe wrote:

> Yes, I grabbed Chantelle all right. The fear of what had happened, and could happen to our daughter, made me hold her so tight against my body all night, it was as if we melted into one. Greg yelled at me to get the torch. I raced back to our vehicle and frantically grabbed it to give him. I felt helpless as I stood behind the Chamberlain tent with Lindy and watched Michael and Greg rush off into the darkness with the only available torch. Greg yelled at me to get the police; I realised I could not drive our borrowed four-wheel-drive vehicle.
>
> By this time the people from the tent next door to the Chamberlains' had appeared and I asked the man to get the police. He nodded, but said he didn't know where to find them. His daughter said she did and off they sped.
>
> Aidan was crying nearby and said, 'That dog's got my bubby in its tummy.' Sobs were nearly shaking his body apart. I thought that the best thing I could do was to put Aidan to bed in the tent.
>
> When I first looked into the tent, I saw the empty little carry basket towards the right hand rear corner and a crumpled blanket that appeared

> to be torn. I quickly looked away and asked Aidan to tell me where he slept. This quietened him down a little. While he was telling me where he slept, and where his mummy and daddy slept, a pool of blood in front of me had caught my eye. It was still wet and gave the impression that it had soaked into something padded. I realised it was a lot of blood for a small baby to lose. At that moment in my mind I recalled the baby's cry I had heard earlier. The awful realisation dawned on me that the babe had died then and there in the tent. I just wanted to get myself, Chantelle and Aidan out of there as quickly as possible. To quote words Mike himself later used, 'The tent was like a morgue.'
>
> The blood was a little to my right and Aidan was on my left so I tried to shield him from the sight of it. He must have already followed my gaze, because at that point his little body started shaking again with hysterical sobs. He managed to blurt out something like, 'Reagan's dead, the dog's killed him too.' I had not even noticed the other child, although I had *seen* some drops of blood earlier on what must have been his sleeping bag. As I turned towards the other boy who was asleep, I saw more drops of blood on what appeared to be clothing and sleeping bags on the floor of the tent. I quickly shook Reagan as Aidan's distress was increasing and finally I managed to make him stir. This helped me convince Aidan that his brother was unharmed. We left the tent and Lindy, myself and another woman comforted Aidan.

I told Aidan, 'I want you to go and get into bed,' and explained what was happening. I said, 'There's nothing we can do,' and told him the policeman's coming soon . . . [and to go] to bed because if Reagan woke up he would be frightened 'cos Reagan slept through the lot. And I said, 'I want you to be there, so that he's all right, because he knows you and those other people . . . will be right here.' And Aidan said he didn't want me to go away . . . The other lady that he knew . . . 'she's going to stay right there on the fence where you can see [her].' People were still coming from all directions with torches and Michael reappeared with a short, motherly woman and spoke my name. The woman then walked straight up to me and put her arms around me saying, 'God is good.' It seemed an unusual thing to say but I realised immediately that she was a Christian and I knew what she meant, so I replied, 'I know, and the Bible says that children will be returned to their mother's arms.' She understood. It was much later that I learned she was a fully qualified sister and social worker, presently specialising in grief and trauma counselling and she had decided that the best thing she could do was to stay near us in case she was needed.

The woman (Amy Whittaker) stayed there and shortly her daughter arrived. We were looking for a light to place near the car so that the police and searchers and those assisting knew immediately where to go. Amy asked her daughter to get their gas light which sat on a 1.8 metre (six foot) stand. It was initially placed by the front of the tent, but in order to let the children stay sleeping I asked for it to be transferred around the southern side of the car and it was put a few feet from my passenger door (in later years that light was something that the police wished had been forgotten).

Greg Lowe:

> On the immediate feverish search Mike and I raised our torches above our heads to illuminate as wide an area as possible. I was looking for the colour of the child's clothing or for drops of blood that would indicate the dog's movements. An inspection of the sandy ground showed that nobody except an experienced tracker could possibly identify the many indentations in the sand as dog prints. I thought our pursuit might cover dog prints but logically, unless Azaria was found quickly, the best tracker in the world would be too late to help.

Judy West later commented:

> The situation was so appalling that no one could say very much at all, just wait and pray that someone would find the baby. At this stage everyone felt quite hopeful that the baby would be found, that the dingo would have dropped her and any minute one of the searchers would find her. But it took half an hour before the police arrived and it was a strained and terrible time.

Bill and Catherine West had found it hard to raise the police who believed at first it was a hoax.

I was later told by the nurse on duty that the first radio call to the hospital at the Alice was to prepare Emergency, because an Aboriginal baby had been taken by a dingo.

Greg continues:

> Mike and I were still busily looking for Azaria on the sandhill. The initial fruitless search caused us to widen the search area. After all, a dingo could have disappeared into the scrub for a few metres and then changed direction.
>
> We started combing the sandhill in a grid pattern. I was amazed that both Mike and myself could think so logically, given the nature of the situation. Although the search was carried out with a haste that could only be described as mad panic, we were cool-headed enough to realise that the scrub on the sandhill east of the tent would have to be searched methodically.
>
> I have had the experience of identifying the body of a close relative, so I thought that Mike ought to be prepared for what we may find and suggested to him that if we found the child there wasn't going to be any joy. Mike quietly agreed.

For Michael's peace of mind we both checked the tent again for any sign of Azaria. This time we changed the angle of the torch beam so that light fell on one of the sleeping bags, and there we saw large blood spots. We later showed these to the ranger who immediately felt concern, knowing that Azaria had been hurt. We knew that because she had a slight cold, because it was freezing and because she had been taken out of her warm rugs, received a shock, and was bodily injured, that if she was not found within the first twenty minutes to half hour, there would be no hope of saving her life. If she had not already been killed, the shock and the cold alone were enough to cause an infant of that age to die.

As the night dragged on we realised there was no longer hope of finding her alive. I wanted to see her, regardless of how she was found. Michael initially did, but probably felt differently as the hours passed.

I was worried, too, because I didn't know what her blood group was, I had wanted her tested at birth but the hospital had said it was not important right then, so I waited—too long. Now I didn't even know whether anyone else in the family had a blood group compatible with hers so we could give her some blood if she was found alive. I realised even by immediate emergency flight to Alice Springs it was still a couple of hours away.

We personally did not see or know of any other blood in the tent that night except what we saw on the sleeping bag near the door—where I had seen the dingo so vigorously shaking what I had mistakenly thought to be a shoe.

In the middle of the semi-organised confusion a four-wheel-drive vehicle arrived, following Bill West.

The driver appeared to be in uniform and he introduced himself. I presumed he was the policeman. He spoke to us briefly and asked to see the tent which he inspected thoroughly by torchlight. He questioned me closely about the dingo that I had seen behind the car and assured us that because Azaria was injured and the night was cold, she would indeed need to be found very quickly, and that he could not promise anything. It appeared that dingoes might sometimes drop their prey and run, but not always, and he assured us that if the attack was the worst, and had been fatal, that it would have been quick. He then went to organise the search, instructing us it would be best not to disturb the tent until the police had seen it for evidence. It was then I realised the man was a ranger, and I later learned he was the senior ranger Derek Roff.

(Mr Roff later said that he expressed some of those opinions in order to gently reassure us as much as possible without giving us false hope, although at the time he was still hopeful of finding our baby alive.)

Greg Lowe commented that from where he was searching he 'could see that two Land Rover-type vehicles had arrived, parked so their headlights lit up the search area. Presumably the police had finally arrived. Their powerful lights failed to penetrate the scrub well enough for a ground search to be carried out, but at least the lights provided a focus for the searchers.' (In later years, Michael and I were heavily criticised for not turning the car around, but it was so low set all it would have done was shine into the railing and create more shadows for the searchers to penetrate.)

Another four-wheel-drive arrived and the driver swung out of the vehicle, leaving his door open and heading towards us at a run. It was Frank Morris, the head local policeman. He asked briefly what had happened and how I knew. I told him of course about the dingo in the tent and the dingo I had chased from behind the car and where I had lost sight of it. I explained how I had thought the dingo had a shoe, and how I had then seen the tent and known it was my baby. He asked if I had seen the baby in the dingo's mouth, and I told him no.

That was one thing that privately worried me. In one way I had got a good look at that dingo behind the car and yet I could not remember seeing whether it had anything in its mouth or not. Even while I was chasing it I tried to puzzle that out, but my mind would not register what my eyes were seeing. I briefly thought it might be the wrong one, but it was there and the animal surely couldn't have gone far. I had to do something, so I chased it. Not for many months was I to discover that I had chased the wrong dingo.

The description was brief and hurried. Constable Morris kept rushing off to organise someone, then coming back to continue the conversation. Several times he questioned me as to whether I had seen something. He seemed confused over me saying I had *seen* nothing in the dingo's mouth, and his mental impression that I had said that there *was* nothing in its mouth.

The policeman left again, then returned to ask the age and the size of the child he was looking for. To most men, a baby is any age up to two years old. He was surprised when I told him that she was only nine and a half weeks old and about 4.5 kilograms (10 pounds) when dressed. I told him quickly that she was dressed in white, a jumpsuit and matinee jacket. He left at a run, as I was still calling out and I was not the least bit sure that he had heard all I said. I guessed it didn't really matter as long as he knew she was wearing white. Both the jumpsuit and the matinee jacket had long sleeves, and in the dark it wouldn't make much difference what the article was, I supposed. (How wrong I was to be! I had no inkling of the future trouble over that hurried conversation that night as everybody pulled together to find a precious little baby.)

Michael walked away and I became aware that he was calling for the attention of the searchers, who were regrouping for instructions. He stood in the road near our tent, and said, 'I want to thank you all for what you're doing . . . I'm a minister of religion and I know that nothing happens in the world unless God allows it.' I had gone over to the edge of the group to see what Michael was doing and noticed that some of the searchers were looking embarrassed, some astounded, some pitying or thankful. I was later told most of them couldn't believe that Michael was praying for them. Michael was led away and I couldn't really help him. I felt too dead inside and helpless myself.

As I sat on the fence I could not believe I was going through this. One moment I had my baby in my arms, the next minute she wasn't there. It was not possible to believe—how could one even dream such a thing could happen? It was beyond all my knowledge and understanding—so far away from anything I had ever known. Part of me wanted to sob uncontrollably and part of me couldn't cry at all. I felt a numb sense of unreality, alive and dead all at once. I sat staring into the dark, my stomach churning and rolling over, wanting to vomit, yet feeling there was nothing there. I was no longer tired, or hungry—that ceased to be important. I was simply there.

Sally Lowe was later to comment,

> 'Words couldn't express the sense of bereavement that prevailed.' zzzzGreg

> Lowe remembers:
>
> As the night dragged on there was no question in my mind that we could expect to receive news of any sort that could bring us hope.

People were around me. They occasionally talked, but none of it mattered. It was unimportant. I wanted to rush here and there screaming, I wanted to close my eyes and pretend it wasn't happening. I wanted to go and be searching and doing and yet I wanted to be waiting the moment news came through, as I was sure it would.

Judy West:

> At about nine, everyone had gone searching—police and rangers. There seemed very little to do once the search had been organised and I thought maybe a hot drink would help to ease the situation so I went with Catherine down to the barbecue area to heat water for Milo. Before I'd put it on, Greg Lowe came down and told me that he thought it inadvisable to be in the barbecue area as I could be destroying evidence of dingo tracks. I thought this wasn't necessarily so, and went ahead. While we waited for the water to boil, Catherine and I looked for dingo tracks and found fresh ones overlaying all the other footprints; a dog or dingo had been there since the baby was taken. After this we stayed close to the gas stove so that we didn't interfere with them, as they ran between the two entrances of the north and south side.
>
> When the water was hot I asked whether anyone would like a cup of Milo. Michael Chamberlain, who was on the path between the tent and the barbecue, refused politely, saying he'd had a drink with his meal. When I asked Lindy, who was near the car, she simply replied, 'No, I couldn't. I'd just bring it straight up again.'

Greg Lowe:

> Within the hour, the number of searchers grew considerably as news of the baby's disappearance quickly spread. On one of my periodic returns to the tent site, a young man appeared with a dog like an Irish Red Setter and it was quickly agreed the dog should sniff the baby's clothing so that it could follow the trail.

Greg brought the dog over to the car where I collected Azaria's singlet and the pink outfit that she had worn earlier that day. I stood in the passenger side doorway and let the animal smell the clothes. It had a good sniff and then the owner of the animal took it out into the sand dune area to hopefully do some good.

Later another dog was brought over, and because the clothes were still out, I simply sat in the front seat, leaned over the back and got them. I placed them in my lap and the animal smelt them there. Neither dog was distracted by any other scents the car might hold, and willingly went off with their respective owners to continue in the general searching. My actions on those occasions and the actions of those dogs was something that others were to wish in the future could be forgotten, as it created an embarrassing problem for them.

Sally Lowe:

Lindy and I went back and forth desperately looking under and around the bushes between the tent and the barbecue area. We didn't have torches so could not join the others searching the scrub areas. For a short while we held on to the hope that the dog had perhaps circled back somehow with the baby. I was a bit wary as I'd seen the blood and knew the sight would not be pleasant. But the thought that Azaria might have been close by and in need of help spurred us on. When I made my way back to the barbecue area there was a track of large paw prints clearly defined across the sandy floor of the barbecue area where we had been standing earlier. I now know what they mean when they say in the movies that 'a cold shiver ran up my spine.' It shook me so much that I made sure I did not wander far from the other women who were on the rail in front of the car until Greg had returned.

Greg Lowe:

I rejoined Mike near the tent. The temperature had dropped considerably and nearly all hope of finding Azaria alive had vanished. Mike and I both sat on the timber rails. I gave him a gentle backhanded pat to his midriff and stated, 'I'm a drinking man, mate, and I need a drink. I'm going to the nearest pub.'

I assured him that I would return at first light the next morning to continue the search. Little did any of us realise that this was to be the final personal contact between the two families until the . . . inquest.

After an hour or so of searching we packed up our tent and tucker box and gave the distressed parents a few words of reassurance. Words were all we could offer. It was probably our light chatter that allowed Lindy to lower her guard. Some time during the course of the night she told us how she had been so careful the previous night.

Sally Lowe:

We drove to one of the nearby motels and Greg ordered a drink. We just sat there like zombies. Through the fuzz in my brain I heard a few of the staff talking about joining the search. A chap sat near me and was saying something about how a dingo wouldn't harm the baby. We mumbled, 'She's dead, it's too late!' Their discussion continued and then we shakily told what we knew. The lass behind the bar mentioned other occasions when children had been attacked, including that of an Aboriginal baby who had been taken by a wild dog. I then remembered that the woman from the tent next door to the Chamberlains' had said that a dingo had grabbed her daughter's arm while she was in their tent writing in her diary. I know the dingo is a hunter, and I've seen one tear at a rabbit. I don't believe campers were warned sufficiently, and I believe a high fence should be erected around the camping area.

Greg Lowe:

Needless to say, Sally, Chantelle and I transferred to the nearest motel. That night we hardly slept. As soon as our eyes closed, we saw dingoes. We

> became paranoid about any slight noise outside our room and eventually slept huddled together in a single bed, Chantelle tightly snuggled between us.

The rest of us sat forlornly on the fence. All the searchers had moved further afield now and the immediate area was deserted. There wasn't much anyone could say. Time wore on and then the lights appeared, a whole long stream lighting the top of Sunrise Hill, the whole crest lit up as the string of searchers swept over the top and down towards us around in a big sweeping arc. It had seemed as if there was nobody there who cared, and then the whole hillside lit up and I knew they were all looking. It was a wonderful, comforting feeling.

I had been worried that the search seemed to be well out over the hill and no one was in the immediate sand dune area. Eventually Amy Whittaker persuaded Michael to take me out in that area searching so I would be convinced in my own mind that Azaria had not been dropped close by and was simply dying through neglect. Amy promised to keep an eye on our torch so that she could immediately locate us if the police came back with news.

Judy West remembers it this way:

> Michael was still searching. Amy Whittaker was comforting Lindy but at one stage Lindy became very upset and she and Michael went away alone. When they came back Michael suggested we say a prayer together. I hesitated because I wasn't certain whether Michael, with his firm Christian belief, had felt affronted by my talk of Guru Maharaj Ji, and Lindy must have sensed this diffidence because she said to me, 'Yes, let's pray together. After all, we all worship the same God.' It was a sensitive and reassuring gesture from someone young enough to be my daughter and under terrible stress, and I was extremely grateful.
>
> Michael began his prayer by saying, 'We must remember that this is not the time for bitterness or anger . . .' The prayer gave everyone strength and we went back to waiting for news of the search.

There seemed little to say as we sat on the fence silently going over our own thoughts. Eventually one of the police vehicles returned, but there was no more news and it turned out to be just the younger constable bringing the local bush nurse around to see how we were.

Judy West:

> Constable Noble drove up with the bush nurse, Bobbie Downs. He introduced us to her and she talked to Lindy to find out how she was coping. Bobbie told us about her job, but no one felt like talking except to relieve the tension. By now we had realised that, even if the baby was found, there was very little chance of her being alive due to the intense cold. We'd always had a spark of hope, but it had begun to wane and we grew really depressed.

> While the Chamberlains were talking to Bobbie Downs, Reagan started to cry, so I crawled into the tent to hush him back to sleep. I didn't have to crawl in very far as he was sleeping on the south side with his head towards the opening. I noticed three or four cot blankets strewn on the floor from the carrycot, which was on the eastern end of the tent. I patted him off to sleep. He was cold, I think, so I pulled the sleeping bag higher up around him and looked around at Aidan who was sleeping quite peacefully on the other side of the tent.

Judy might have thought Aidan was sleeping, but I know better. He'd fooled me too for a while, but when I bent closer he said, 'Mummy I'm praying that Jesus will shut the dingo's mouth just like he did for Daniel in the lions' den.' There was nothing I could say.

As I hadn't realised he was awake when he first spoke it nearly scared the wits out of me. It was only then that I realised he was lying still too frightened to move and trying hard to be good as I had asked him not to call out while we searched and waited. He was able to see those who were on the fence from where he lay, so he knew he wasn't alone. From then on each time I checked he always answered me if I spoke, so I know he was awake a lot. He later told me he had not slept at all in the tent that night.

The nurse wanted to take us to a motel, but I didn't want to go. I wanted to stay there. I was OK. Michael looked at the tent and said he would never sleep there again, it reminded him of a morgue. To me that tent was my only remaining link with her. I knew that even now if they found her it might be too late. We had seen some of the blood in the tent, we knew she was bleeding. The cry Michael had heard indicated that either she was dead or unconscious. Either way, there wasn't much hope. She was just so little.

We were cold, we had sleeping bags around us. I had gone and put my tracksuit pants on again under my dress and put on an extra jacket. Michael had put his trousers on over his shorts. I knew I was cold and yet I felt numb enough almost not to feel it. I knew I would never feel the same again. All my life I had wanted a little girl, and I had had her for so fleeting a time. I knew that I had been blessed of God and she had been well named because of the short but wonderful weeks I had had with her.

Judy continues:

> Michael and Lindy were wrapped in the Whittakers' blankets. At about ten o'clock Michael said, 'This will be headlines tomorrow.' Both he and Lindy became worried that Lindy's parents would hear of Azaria's disappearance through the media and they badly wanted to tell them themselves. We discussed the availability of a phone or radio contact but no one knew very much.

Because of Michael's media involvement (he had his own newspaper column and radio program, plus having his regular rostered turn on the local weekly religious radio broadcast), he had had a fair bit to do with small town media and basically knew what sorts of things drew comment as news items. Michael said that we probably wouldn't need to let a lot of our friends know what had happened because it was something so unusual, so horrific and different that they would find out. We had no idea that it would become *such* a news item for years to come.

When I Left My Heart Behind

We couldn't afford a motel and said so, but after a lot of discussion and the assurance that it would not cost too much, it was finally agreed that if the police were told, we would go to a motel for the night. And so Amy Whittaker (we discovered her name later) and Bobbie Downs went away to see if they could find us a room in one of the hotels or motels.

They came back ages later and Bobbie said that she had found a place for us to go. She had told Constable Frank Morris and he was sending over the other policeman, Constable Noble, to help us move. When he arrived, I crawled into the tent and handed the gear out to the waiting hands. Blankets, sleeping bags and mattresses were piled willy-nilly into the back of the open four-wheel-drive police Toyota and things were thrown into our car as well. Judy West, Constable Noble, the nurse and Amy Whittaker all helped us move. It seemed odd to me though, as the ranger had told us not to move anything until the police had been able to have a good look—and the senior policeman hadn't even been back, but this one had been sent The worst thing I had to do was to pick up Azaria's bottle container from the picnic table nearby, as it was all ready for the following morning with sterilising solution in it. As I walked across to the railing during the packing and transfer of our gear and tipped that solution out, I realised I was saying goodbye to my little girl. If she was found at all, she wouldn't need a bottle. The least she would need would be a life support drip, and that was taking the most optimistic view of things at this time of night.

It was suggested that I travel in the front of the police Toyota with Constable Noble and the boys. Aidan was lifted in his sleeping bag and Reagan was carried across and put on my lap, still sleeping. Michael offered to take Nurse Bobbie Downs with him in our car.

We went round to the motel. I carried Reagan in and Constable Noble carried Aidan. We put them down on their beds, then started carrying things in from the back of the police vehicle. I saw the empty carry basket and my baby daughter's rugs and our sleeping bags and I couldn't bear the sight of them. I knew I would have to tidy up in the morning, but that was soon enough. Michael asked me what else I needed and I looked at him slightly dumbfounded noticing they were starting to carry things in from our car now, and said, 'Oh, nothing. We've got beds here, we don't need anything.' So the rest was left in the car. It was wide open with doors open, internal lights on and hatch up. People were milling around.

I looked around the motel as if it was a foreign country. It didn't seem like home, as the tent had. Something was missing, missing out of that little carrycot now sitting piled with the sleeping bags in the corner. The rest of the dishes at the barbecue we had left, the Wests or the Whittakers or somebody promising to pack them up and bring them to us the next day. Constable Noble saw we were settled and that there was nothing else we needed. We were introduced to some of the motel staff and a young man called Mike, who brought down a tray of sandwiches and some hot Milo for us. At least they said it was hot Milo, but it had coffee in it. I am sure they thought they were doing it for the best and didn't realise they were giving us something that would keep us awake when we least needed it, as our bodies weren't used to coffee. I asked Bobbie Downs before she left for some tablets to help dry my milk and she promised to send them along. As we were settling the children down and generally tidying up a bit in preparation for going to bed, she returned with the tablets and then went off again. Michael was exhausted and prepared for bed.

I said to him, 'We had better make arrangements to tell our parents and also ring Pastor Harker (Michael's conference president) too, if we don't want them to hear in the newspaper, we had better be up pretty early.'

I went outside to check everything was OK. The car was still lit up and wide open. I poked things back in as much as possible in order to close the hatch, and left it, messy and untidy as it was, even though it was against my normal nature to leave it in such a state. I locked the front doors and walked off with the keys.

I went up to the bar. Mike had said if we wanted anything just to come in the back door and ask for him, so I did. I could hear a lot of people in the bar. I didn't want to walk in there and meet anyone. I didn't know whether they knew who I was or not, but I didn't want anybody looking at me and I didn't want to hear, 'That's the mother, that's her there.' I couldn't stand the thought of it.

I stood for a moment in the back section, wondering whether to poke my head into the kitchen, or whether I should go through, when a young lady came through some swinging doors. She seemed a little surprised at seeing me there, but asked if she could help, and I said I was looking for Mike.

She said, 'Oh yes, the barman. Just a moment, I'll get him.' It seemed that my asking for him had given her a clue who I was. She went off and very quickly returned with him. I explained how we wished to make some calls and he suggested that the best time would be about seven in the morning. They only had radio phones, a two-way system used for the flying doctors and the School of the Air. Anyone could listen in on the open airways, and before the general sessions it was a little quieter. So it was agreed that I would meet him in the office in the morning. I went back, shut the door and got ready for bed.

The air conditioner in the room was on. It was quite warm, but I was still bone-chillingly cold. It seemed that I would never be warm again. I was doing everything on automatic pilot, as if I would wake up soon, but I knew I wouldn't. I wandered around a little, checking the children, picking up things and putting them down in a rather aimless manner. The lights were off and I could see just a little by the outdoor lights of the motel. I drew the curtain across the window for privacy and Michael said to come to bed. I picked up my sleeping bag to bring it with me and he said, 'You're not going to use that thing in bed, I hope, it's got blood on it.' We argued and I told him that it didn't. It was his that had blood on it, not mine. I put my sleeping bag down on the bed then climbed in, in my clothes, the blankets on top of the lot. We tossed and turned. I slept a little. Michael appeared to be having a better rest than I was, because I could hear him snoring on and off.

I woke again at about four, and got up and looked out the window. I could see the dark outline of the Rock against the night sky. I got back into bed and lay there blankly; finally I saw the faint lighting of dawn and got up.

I took my dress off and put another one on that was clean but had permanent stains down the front. It was one I usually used for cleaning the house. I woke Michael and told him it was time to get ready to make the phone calls before the boys woke up. He got up and was in the middle of shaving while I stood looking out the window, just gazing absently towards the Rock, when I saw the policeman, Frank Morris, drive up. I knew who he was because I had met him briefly the night before. He came walking towards the room and I opened the door as he reached it. Before I could say anything he shook his head and said, 'I'm sorry, Mrs Chamberlain, there's no news.' That was that. We didn't have to ask, we'd been told.

He asked how we were and whether we had everything we needed, and I explained we were shortly going to make some phone calls. He agreed that was a good idea and said, 'I guess the news will be on to it pretty soon. You can't keep things like this quiet for long. I will be back later in the morning, if it is all right with you, to get you to sign a form of release for the coroner's court. There will have to be a short inquest.' He couldn't have told us more plainly that they had given up hope, and she was dead. We agreed to see Frank Morris later, and if we weren't in our room we would be at the office ringing up. He left.

Aidan had already woken and I wondered how he would be. He looked like I felt—depressed and quiet. We explained we were going to ring up and just as we went to walk out the door I heard a little voice say, 'Mummy, where's bubby?' Reagan was awake. He was disorientated, having gone to sleep in the camping area and woken up in a motel. I thought that he had slept through the terrible tragedy the night before, not knowing he had woken and perhaps thought he was waking up after a nightmare. I was dreading having to explain what had happened to his precious baby sister.

I looked at Reagan. What could I say? How do you tell a little boy that his baby sister has died and been carried away by a wild animal and that he will never see her again? She was his pride and joy. He was so proud of her and loved her so much. He had been Aidan's baby; Azaria was his. He had wheeled her in her pram, helped burp and change her, given her bottle of juice. He loved doing that so much that sometimes he begged me to let her have juice instead of a feed, and I had quite a job to convince him that Azaria was really hungry, not thirsty, and she had to get the feed from Mummy. He could not understand why I could not put my milk in a bottle, so he could feed and hold her instead.

Now I had to tell my four-year-old son what had happened to *his* baby.

I sat down on his bed and explained as best I could that while he had been asleep last night, a naughty dingo, who didn't know any better, had come into the tent and taken his little baby sister away. He interrupted and said, 'But he can't carry her. Bubby's too heavy,' no doubt thinking of his own struggle to carry her now. I tried again and explained that despite that, the dingo had taken her and that she was dead. Jesus would look after her and one day if we were all good, we would see her again when Jesus came back to take us all home to live with Him. He looked at me with his wide unblinking eyes fixed on me. He was quiet for a while and then asked, 'Mummy, did the dingo take our bubby to the shoppin'?' That floored me. Shopping was his favourite occupation at the time. It was a real treat and he loved it, and he thought the dingo was somebody giving Azaria a treat. I said no, and Aidan told him not to be stupid.

I said to Aidan, 'Don't worry, sweetheart, he doesn't understand right now. Leave it be and he will understand later. Just be kind to him.'

I explained that we were going to ring Gran and Grandad, and Nanna and Pa, and we wouldn't be very long if they'd be good boys. We went up to the office and met one of the motel girls who was on her way down to see whether there was anything we needed or if she could get us breakfast. She thought perhaps we would rather avoid the dining room. We asked if she would mind taking breakfast down to the boys—just cereal, milk and toast—and look after them until we got back.

In the meantime Bill and Judy West called, and seeing we were busy, talked to Lizzie, the lass from the motel staff. Judy later said: 'When I asked how the boys were coping she replied that they were taking it more calmly than she had ever imagined. I knew this was because Lindy would have explained the situation to them to hurt them as little as possible . . .'

Neither Michael nor I was hungry, though the motel staff brought us some toast and hot Milo in the office anyway. We both nibbled, but that was about all. We made our necessary phone calls and Lizzie came to the office door. She told us Bobbie Downs had arrived and was now looking after the boys so she was returning to work. We thanked her and she left.

Alan Barber, the assistant manager in charge of the motel, came into the office to tell us that Frank Morris was back again and looking for us. We finished our call, went out and spoke to him.

It was still early and we went back to the room with Frank Morris. He needed to collect a few things for evidence, and he had not had time to check the night before. The most important thing then had been to try and find Azaria. Because things had just been dumped in the corner Michael, for something to do, had started to pick them up, shake them and fold them, but had soon lost heart and left the rest there. Every time I looked at the stack it made me shudder and think of things I had no wish to remember so I had also been avoiding it.

Now we had no choice. As we inspected the gear from the tent, item by item, we discovered that Michael's sleeping bag had large spots of blood across the bottom. It was decided that he would take that with him for evidence as we were obviously not going to continue our camping trip to Darwin but had every intention of returning straight home from the Rock. All the carry basket items were inspected and we discovered that Azaria' thick 'Penthouse' blankets had some spots of blood on them and were also torn; one tear in particular was a 'W' shape and went straight through the blanket. It must have been caused by something very sharp because I had bought a large blanket and cut it down to make the smaller cot and cradle and carry basket blankets and I knew just how difficult it had been to cut with sharp dressmaking scissors. This cut was three-cornered and a drop of blood was not far from the jagged cut. Morris decided to take the sleeping bag and the two cot blankets. He thought there was enough blood on those items to get a grouping to identify any clothes found at the Rock.

Aidan came to me very quietly, while Sergeant Morris was still looking at the blankets, and said, 'Mummy, there's blood on my sleeve.' I looked down at the parka he had put on. Around the right cuff was nearly a 6 millimetre (quarter inch) ring of blood, almost as if the sleeve had been dipped in it. I was initially sceptical and looked closely to make sure. As I squeezed it between my fingers, they came away red; it was unmistakably blood. The parka was dry on the outside but the inner side of the cuff was obviously still wet. I took Aidan across and showed Morris the cuff, saying 'What do you think about this? It is his only parka.' He looked at it and looked at Aidan and said, 'I think we have enough evidence without taking that.' Although the days were hot, the nights were cold and Aidan needed the extra warmth. In fact, Reagan had kept his jacket on all day because for us, coming from Mt Isa, it was cool, although anyone coming from Melbourne or Sydney would actually find it hot. Later I attracted some heavy criticism because I hadn't shaded Azaria's head in the hot sun, and I couldn't help thinking that the temperature of a place is simply relative. To us, used to temperatures in the upper thirty degree range (88°F), the weather was not hot.

So we kept the parka. I washed the cuff under the tap, squeezed it well and let it dry. Aidan wore the parka the rest of the way home. Later I used salt and cold water and any remaining blood came out easily. During his evidence Morris couldn't remember being shown Aidan's cuff, only the conversation.

We finished going through the things and then walked across to the police vehicle while Morris collected the notification form for the coroner. We leaned on the bonnet of his truck and filled out the information on the death form.

Morris told us the Aborigines were following some tracks which they didn't really think were the right ones, but they were doing their best.

Meanwhile Greg Lowe had risen after a fitful night and returned to the tent site, prepared for the day's searching. He later wrote:

> I approached an obviously empty tent, but things seemed totally different in broad daylight. It was difficult to imagine that this had been the scene of so much activity the night before.

He left as the police had called the rest of the search off, feeling that it would be much better just to let the Aborigines and a few of the locals work without too much hindrance.

Morris didn't tell us that the rangers, Inspector Gilroy and Sergeant Lincoln, had found paw prints and a wet substance they took to be saliva down the outside of the back right hand corner of the tent, near where Azaria's carry basket had been located. When they lifted the bottom edge of the tent a little, they found a damp patch which they took to be the 'saliva' which had run down the tent. It had stayed protected overnight because the tent had slackened, sagged and billowed out over the area. They also saw sprays on the side of the tent that they thought could well be arterial blood sprays. They took samples of the 'saliva' patch, and sent that and the tent to Darwin for testing. (It was tested for blood instead of saliva and, of course, got a negative result, so was shoved in a cupboard along with the tent and nothing further was done.)

We were still asking Frank Morris about details of procedures in an inquest when Alan Barber came out to tell us that there were press on the phone and they were wanting to talk to Mr or Mrs Chamberlain. Michael turned to Frank Morris and said, 'What will we do? Do you think we should take the call, what would you advise?'

Frank suggested that we take it, saying, 'They will hound you if you don't, they will be on your doorstep when you get home with cameras rolling. You may as well talk to them here and get it over and done with by the time you get home.' So Michael went back to the office to take the call.

I stayed and talked with Frank Morris a little longer. He was urging us to pack up and go home because there was nothing more, he felt, that we could do there at that time. We, on the other hand, were hoping that some sort of news might be found, even if it was only her clothes—*something*. But he told us that it would be better to go and that he didn't expect there would be any more news, until a tourist found the clothes somewhere around the Rock. I thought it was a little odd that he thought a tourist would find the clothes instead of one of the trackers, but I gave his comment no more thought until later.

I went back into the office to hear Michael on the radio phone telling them that his wife had seen a big *yellow dog* at the door of the tent.

I said to him, 'Michael, it was a *dingo*, not a dog,' but he said, 'It's not important. It doesn't matter.'

I said, 'It does,' but he was talking again. I don't know why getting details wrong like that irritates me, but it always has. I have always tried to be careful in getting things correct—and that was incorrect. I had the feeling that it would have more far-reaching consequences, though I didn't know why. (I found out as time went on and the Crown tried to maintain I had changed my story, saying a dingo had taken her instead of a dog when I became aware dingoes were dangerous. It was no such thing.)

I went back across to our room then, and sat down on the step talking to Bobbie as she looked after the boys. She had pencils and paper for drawing and the boys were squabbling, out of sorts and niggly. It was to be expected. I looked down at my dress and in the light I realised that it really looked too stained to be worn, even if it was clean, so changed back into the dress I had had on the night before.

Michael came back from the office and said that Trevor Scadden of the Adelaide *News* wanted him to take some photos of the tent and the surrounding area and to send through by air a picture of Azaria if we had one. We had the photographs we had been about to send to my parents, intending to write on the trip. They were already in the envelope with a letter half-written, waiting to go. He looked at me and said, 'We don't have to send the pictures, but I think it might be a good thing. At least we can warn other people this way.' I agreed and went to the car to get out the photograph. Looking at those photos again, the morning after it happened, I couldn't bear it. I started to cry. Bobbie Downs either saw or heard me and came out to the car too.

She said, 'Look, you don't have to do this if you don't want to.'

I pulled myself together and said, 'I know.' And yet sending the photos to be published in the paper seemed to be the only way to warn everybody. She was a beautiful child, why *not* show them how beautiful she was? So I selected a photograph that had been taken of her the moment she came home from hospital, sound asleep and relaxed, at five days old. (I didn't realise what a fuss there would be about that photograph, because she was so tiny and her little hand and wrist were just relaxed. Later on it was represented as a current photograph of a nine-and-a-half-week-old baby and people said that because of the formation of the hands, she must have had a physical disability, or be a cretin, or spastic.)

Michael intended to go to the tent site to take the photographs in our car, then realised that it had stuff thrown everywhere. I wanted him to take the boys with him. I wanted to cry and needed some privacy; tears were welling up inside me. Bobbie Downs volunteered to go with Michael to look after the boys and they arranged to go in the motel bus which the owners had kindly placed at our disposal. I emptied Azaria's milk bottles down the sink and brushed them out for the last time. But even then I couldn't cry. Tears were churning inside me, but they couldn't get out. I gave up and wandered outside and saw the others still there, so told Michael I would go too. Bobbie then said she would go back to the clinic if I was going with the boys and would be all right, so we agreed to see her later on.

Everywhere we went that day Reagan kept reminding me I didn't have the carry basket, and would need it when we picked bubby up. I tried to explain she wouldn't use it any more several times, but he really wasn't taking it in.

We all hopped in the bus. First we went round to the Red Sands Motel where the pilot of the plane that was organised was, so he would know not to take off before we brought the film to him, then we went to the shop. Lyttle, the bus driver, and Michael got out and went and told the shopkeeper in the Ininti store that they wanted a black and white film; the newspaper didn't want colour. Then they got back in the bus and went to the campsite. Bill and Judy West were packing up the last of their things and their friends were just pulling out as we drove in. Michael and the boys hopped out of the bus. The tent was standing there, all forlorn, on its own. The camping area that had been so full the night before was nearly empty. Momentarily I wondered whether the police had moved people away, or whether they had simply gone home. I stayed in the bus and Lyttle stayed too. Nobody talked. The boys walked around a little near the tent while Michael set up his camera and took a few shots. One of them had the boys standing beside the tent. He then took a shot out into the sand dune area where I chased the dingo and we searched, and another shot back towards the Rock. The Wests came across and spoke to him and then Judy came to the bus and leaned in to say goodbye and wish me well, if such a thing could be possible. None of us knew what to say. Then Bill came over and thrust his hand out and roughly shook hands. His gruffness more than anything else said how he was feeling, words weren't really needed.

Judy West described our parting this way:

> About midday the motel bus drove up. Michael got out and was photographing the tent. He came over to say goodbye and thank us—he

> gave us a blessing but although we tried to talk, the whole situation was so terrible that we couldn't speak. He stayed with Bill while I climbed into the bus to say goodbye to Lindy, but once again it was impossible to talk. Lindy was wearing dark glasses—she looked completely drained and as though she was on a fine edge.
>
> At about eleven o'clock, Catherine went to the shop and when she came back she said she had heard someone say, 'She only wanted to get rid of the baby,' which we found incredibly depressing.

It was obvious that public disbelief that the dingo killed Azaria had begun very early in the piece.

I felt too dead to care much, just like a lump of stone, and I was walking around in a dream. Surely all this was happening to somebody else. If somebody had walked up right then and told me they were going to shoot me, I would have said to go ahead. It would have been a blessed release.

We drove back to the Red Sands Motel and delivered the film to the pilot of the plane, and told him who would collect it and that they were expecting it, and then went back to our motel. We just sat around in the shade in front of the motel unit. Early in the day while we were in the office ringing up I had seen a number of Japanese coming out of the dining room and noticed two of their little girls with beautiful white fake fur coats, just as I had been planning to make for Azaria when she grew a little bit bigger.

My mind flew to all the clothes I had designed to make her when she was a few years older. I thought of the little girl I had been going to dress up, make things for, do things with—the little girl I would never have again. There were the cooking lessons I had been going to give her, the embroidery and sewing lessons, and art—all the things my mother and I had enjoyed doing when I was a child, and I was going to be denied that. Boys were fun, and I dearly loved my boys, but they weren't the same as a little girl. Girls liked different things.

We sat around the pool and a couple of other people walked in, one of them a man with very bloodshot eyes. I guessed he had just had a hard night on the town. We quietly said a few commonplaces, then we realised he was tired. Something was said to that effect and we then realised he'd been up all night searching for our little girl. We told him who we were and he said how much he wished that his friend Harry Butler, the Australian naturalist, had been there, because he had been at the Rock the day before. He was sure Harry Butler would have known about dingoes' habits and where to look and if only he had been there he might have found her sooner. But it was not to be. He told us a little of what he knew about the habits of dingoes and it confirmed the little we knew of how they killed sheep.

Lizzie came and told us that Michael's president had rung and the local Seventh -day Adventist minister from Alice Springs, Pastor Bert Cozens and his wife Norma, were on their way up to be with us and would arrive some time later that day. She figured they must already be on their way because apparently they had been trying for some time to get through and it was now already after lunch.

We were on our way back from the office when we saw a television crew walking down the path. We couldn't help realising why they were there and Michael wondered what to do. 'Well, I'm not waiting for them. They can come and find me if they want me,' I said and took off for our unit. Michael followed me.

It wasn't long before we heard voices and a knock on our door. Sure enough it was the media men. Still following Constable Morris's advice of getting the press coverage all over and done with, and still having a burning desire to warn other Australians of the potential danger of dingoes, we agreed to do an interview.

The television reporter introduced himself as Geoffrey de Luca, his cameraman was Erwin Chlanda, a local Alice newspaper reporter and freelance television stringer (we were to get to know him much better later on), and they had another southern newspaper reporter with them also. We went briefly over the basic facts, gave our warning, and the interview was over. It was very brief. Michael was used to interview situations from his own programs so it was not difficult for us to do, only personally traumatic. I was upset as I went over the details again, but I had made sure I was wearing my dark glasses so it wasn't quite so obvious that I had been sniffling off and on all day. Tears were never far away, yet for most of the time not *quite* there. I did cry a little during the interview though, much to my disgust as I don't like crying in public.

We didn't know, till long afterwards, that de Luca told Inspector Gilroy later that night that he was suspicious of us because he thought it had been too easy to interview us. This might have been the first time in history that people cooperating with police and journalists under extremely difficult circumstances were judged and condemned because of it.

Ignorant of the suspicion we had aroused, we went back to sit under the trees where it was slightly cooler. Lizzie was off duty then so she came and talked to us for a while.

In fact, we were still sitting talking to her on some benches under the trees when a couple walked down the path. The man was tall, with silvery hair, and he was accompanied by a woman no taller than I: they were dressed casually, like the other locals. We looked up and they said, 'Hello, are you the Chamberlains?' We realised at the same time who they were. We nodded, and they said, 'We're the Cozens.' We just nodded again, there didn't seem to be much to say. Norma sat down beside me and said, 'We thought you must be. The description fitted and there is something about Adventist ministers and their wives. You can kind of pick them.' I didn't tell her that I wouldn't have picked *them*. She was short and plump and motherly. She just put her arm around my shoulder and said, 'We came as quick as we could.'

I mumbled something about it being miles and she said, 'Oh pooh. What's that? We often do long distances. Besides, you needed us.' That was typical of the Cozens; they went miles wherever they were needed. They were well loved in Alice Springs and they were a real blessing to us. We sat and talked, and as we talked she said to me, 'You know, we spent a lot of our early years in the islands in the mission field and I have got a little one to bring up in heaven too. It's not easy, lovey. You never quite forget, but at least we know we will see them again.' We spent some time just getting to know each other. The Cozens planned to sleep in their campervan so they left to look for a campsite, and arranged to eat with us later.

Someone from the motel came to see if we would like a meal sent to our room that night. We decided we had to face everyone again sometime: if we didn't do it then it would be so much harder. I knew how easy it would be for me to shut myself away in the motel room and never come out again and once I shut myself away, I would be in trouble. So I forced myself to face people and we decided that we would try, for the sake of the boys, to get back to normality as soon as possible. We decided to have dinner in the dining room that night, when the Cozens could join us.

It wasn't long before the Cozens rejoined us and we prepared to go to the dining room for dinner. Just before the boys and I left the room there was a knock on the door. I opened the door to find Inspector Gilroy and Sergeant Lincoln had arrived to take our statement. The Cozens volunteered to look after the boys for me and to inform Michael the police had arrived.

Inspector Michael Shamus Gilroy was a softly-spoken, well-mannered Irishman that one would describe as a gentleman. Lincoln was a typical Aussie. Inspector Gilroy questioned me, using a small hand-held tape recorder to record the interview. Michael arrived and contributed to the conversation when we were part way through. It was routine, although we certainly didn't enjoy it, but realised that this kind of questioning was normal in a situation where you are a witness.

We went right through the whole thing, from our arrival at the campsite to the end of the evening. I had to go over what Azaria had been wearing again, in detail, including the brand names of the clothing.

I said, 'The throw-away nappy she had on was a new Johnson's panty nappy that have only been out a few weeks, a little Bonds ribbed singlet, her jacket was a Marquise jacket, the bootees, they don't carry brands in them, but they were little sox bootee types, they were ribbed up the leg with moss stitch at the top of the toe, and instead of having ribbons in them, they had twisted, a twisted little tie on them and her um, the little stretch suit, I'm not sure whether that was a Bonds or whether it was another brand, but it was one of the more expensive ones, with the little pieces that flip over their hands at night when it's cold and I had that folded over her hands and she was all rugged up to the neck.'

Michael interjected '. . . The animal that attacked her, did have probably, very sharp long teeth and again I think that this is another reason why probably the death of the child was very quick.'

I added, 'We feel it was an instant death. If she'd been alive at all, we would have heard some sort of whimper or cry from her, and there was nothing.'

Michael later said something that was on both our minds. 'I'd like to pay tribute to the people who went out quickly and so voluntarily, and anyone who was able to go out appeared to be on the way out and it was very heartening to see it, very grateful.'

Inspector Gilroy asked, 'Is there anything else you would like to make a comment about to finish off our conversation?' (And it was a conversation; Gilroy was such a nice, friendly person that we never felt at any stage that we were being 'grilled by the police.')

Michael said, 'Yes, this is an observation, um, I have listened very carefully to a lot of people about their comments regarding this incident, I wouldn't be so unkind as to say that some would try and defend the dingo and look at you and consider that you are a bit daft suggesting it, the dingo, but I have noticed that some of the more authoritative people have been the ones to try to knock the idea, not openly, er, through enuendo's, well not enuendo's *[sic]* but questioning, whereas when you talk to those who have lived here and know the dingoe *[sic]*, none of them have been at all surprised . . . I've got nothing against dingoes, the other thing is my suggestion would be, would be rather expensive, that perhaps that one of the alternatives to keep these dogs away, would be a dingoe-proof *[sic]* fence around the camping area.' (Spelling as per police typist.)

They left and Michael and I made our way to the motel dining room to rejoin the boys and Pastor and Mrs Cozens. The hotel staff had been surprised and pleased that we had decided to mix again so soon, so they had prepared a nice vegetarian meal for us and from somewhere or other they dug up a couple of bottles of non-alcoholic wine for us to drink as well. They had gone to a lot of trouble and it was nice of them. They wouldn't take anything for our stay at the motel and they bent over backwards to try and accommodate all our needs.

The following morning we decided to pull out from the Rock as Frank Morris had urged us to. It was Tuesday. I had to tell Bobbie Downs the breast pump she had lent me had been broken. The boys had been fighting over it and the glass had smashed. At the time it had seemed like the last straw. I was so sore, and it seemed that my very last link with Azaria had gone, but the stress and trauma had dried my milk up as effectively as those tablets Bobbie Downs had given me, and I ended up not needing the tablets very much anyway. They had a tendency sometimes to cause lumps in the breast and I wasn't keen on that. As Bobbie Downs didn't have another pump, Mrs Cozens said she would be able to borrow another for me from the Nursing Mothers' Association in Alice Springs because she knew a couple of girls who were members and they would be happy to help.

It was arranged that we should meet about eleven that morning at the turnoff and the Cozens parked so they could see whichever way we came from around the Rock and not miss us. It was the only way out from the Rock. (How fortunate that was; later the Crown tried to suggest that we could have dropped Azaria's clothes off somewhere but the Cozens were sitting guarding either direction so we couldn't have without being seen.) It seemed as if every moment of every day we had been under observation somewhere. Even at the motel the bar closed at two in the morning and the kitchen opened at four and there had been people around most of the time in between on that particular night as some of them had never gone to bed.

We drove back around to the tent site. It was bare sand now. Michael had initially wanted to burn the tent because it gave him the horrors now, but Pastor Cozens had convinced him that he ought to keep it and sell it if we didn't want to use it again. Michael suggested that maybe Pastor Cozens would like to do it because he couldn't bear to. When the Cozens went around to pick it up, they found the police in the process of taking it down for evidence. Michael had asked for the tent pegs, as we had another tent and only one good set of pegs. So the police handed them over. (What a fuss that was to cause later!)

Now the camping area was empty, except for one tent being pitched very close to where ours had been. Little did the new campers know what had happened near that spot not so many hours before. I hopped out and got a little bagful of sand. It was my way of saying goodbye to Azaria. Besides, I had a sand collection and it wouldn't be out of place, it would just go with everything else. I was never going to have any ashes from a cremation, or a grave that I could go and visit. So I took that little bit of sand from the tent site underneath where her carrycot would have been, and then we called into the ranger's station to see if there was any more news and see about erecting a memorial plaque in memory of our little girl. The workman on duty had told us that we'd find the senior ranger, Derek Roff, at the Aboriginal camp and so we pulled in there.

Just as we pulled in, we saw that both policemen were there as well as Derek Roff, talking to a group of Aborigines. When we pulled up, Mr Roff came across and said, 'Just the people I wanted to see. You are on your way, are you?'

We said, 'Yes,' and told him what we wanted to know. He explained to us that we would have to put our request in writing and send it through to Canberra and gave us the name of the person to contact.

Mr Roff then asked if I would mind inspecting the Aboriginal camp dogs to see if there was any amongst them that I might recognise as the animal that I had seen on the night. Although he had questioned me closely about the animal (even asking me whether I had seen its foot size or knew whether it was a male or female), and was convinced from my description that I did know what a dingo was, there was always a slim chance that a crossbreed from the Aboriginal camp might have fooled me. As both police were already there with their guns waiting to shoot, my identification might save some heartache for the Aborigines. I inspected all the dogs with the senior ranger, but none were remotely like the animal I had seen. Most of them were hound-like creatures with big bones, floppy ears and slobbery jowls, small terrier or cattle-dog type beasts, all a good range of bitsers. I guess there would have been some relieved dog owners in the camp that day.

Derek Roff introduced us to the Aborigines who had been tracking and had just arrived back in camp. They spoke to us in broken English and their own lingo which Derek Roff translated for us, also our replies back to them. Michael asked if he could take a photograph of the trackers with Mr Roff in memory of our daughter and the service they had rendered her, and they shyly agreed. He then persuaded the two policemen also to have their photograph taken leaning against their truck. He also asked if he could photograph the mouth of one of the dingoes they had shot, lying in the back of their vehicle. I thought it was a rather gruesome request and was rather glad when they refused permission. In later years that request reverberated on Michael badly.

We left and headed towards the Ininti store which was owned and run by the local tribe. I had promised my nieces and nephews to bring them something special home from Ayers Rock and I had no intention, because of my own grief, of disappointing little children or of breaking my promise, so I picked out four picture tumblers and got one each for our own boys as well.

The store, I noticed, had a visitors' book which I idly leafed through while waiting for the boys to look around. I noticed that most other people who entered the shop also leafed through it, so it occurred to me to be an ideal way to warn people of the local danger of dingoes, seeing there were no warning signs around, and so I signed the book. When I went to write my comments I could think of nothing direct enough to say which was adequate warning, so I simply put, 'The dingo took my baby.' Michael came in and told me Frank Morris was looking for me so I left.

Constable Morris had changed his mind and decided it would be a good idea to look at the clothing after all, as I had previously told him I had some identical to what Azaria had been wearing. I showed him a similar-sized and coloured jumpsuit and a matinee jacket. I also gave him a new nappy out of the same packet that Azaria had been wearing.

I stressed that the identifying feature of the clothes was that the bootees were inside the jumpsuit and that they were hand knitted with self-twisted ties. Frank got himself confused with the lemon edging on the matinee jacket and thought the bootees had lemon ribbons. I told him several times that it was the jacket that had lemon edging and the bootees had twist ties, but when he left I was still not sure that he wasn't totally confused.

I arranged with him to ring the Alice Springs police on our way through to let them know our local address and that we were all right. They would also let us know if there was any further news. I went back into the store to let Michael know I was ready to leave. We decided to take something home that would remind us of the local Aborigines and the assistance they had given tracking our daughter, and so we purchased a locally made goanna decorated in the traditional Pitjantjatjara wood-burning style.

We pulled out and headed towards the nurses' residence to return what remained of the breast pump Bobbie Downs had lent me. We had a good talk, said goodbye, then Michael asked whether he could take Bobbie's picture too. Although she was a bit shy, when Michael assured her he had no intention of giving it to the press or of publishing it, but that it was just a last link to those who had helped us so much on the night our lovely daughter had been taken, she understood our reason for wanting the picture and happily complied, realising our need for some sort of record and reminder of the little girl we had lost in the events whose dreadful reality we were still finding so difficult to grasp.

Just down the road at the intersection, we met the Cozens waiting for us to travel back to Alice Springs. Michael soon decided the Cozens were travelling too slowly, put his foot down, and they were left in a cloud of dust.

All the way back to Alice Springs we seemed to be playing leapfrog with a police paddywagon full of Aborigines. When we stopped for the boys' pit stops they would pass us, and later we would pass them stopped beside the road. For some reason, to take his mind off what was happening perhaps, Michael decided to do a fuel economy test on the way back to Alice Springs. Just as the Gap and Alice Springs came into sight, our car coasted to a stop. We pulled up on the side of the road and refuelled, but because of the excessive outback heat and the fact that we had totally drained the tank, we had to sit and wait till the engine cooled down enough for the petrol to stop vapourising so it would flow through the carburettor again. We were stopped with the bonnet up and had refilled all our drink bottles, had the usual pit stop and were about to try the engine again when a car pulled up beside us and asked if we were OK. We told them we were fine now, thank you, and they left. Michael tried the engine again and the car started immediately, so he shut the bonnet and we passed the people not far down the road.

We went straight to the Gap camping area which we had previously telephoned and they had our tent already pulled down and waiting for us to collect. (We forgot Aidan's cricket set but the man was nice enough to post it to us later.) Then we proceeded straight to the address Pastor Cozens had given us and pulled up just in front of them.

During the whole trip back to the Alice, Reagan kept asking me to take bubby's carry basket, because she would need to sleep in it when we got her back; I kept trying to explain. When we packed up to leave he watched me packing things into the carry basket. (I couldn't bear to see it sitting empty in the back seat, so I packed it full of her things, and tied it down.) He asked why—again; and I told him that we didn't need it this time—again.

We stayed overnight in Alice Springs with the Cozens. The newspapers were waiting. This was the first time we had seen any publicity; the story was splashed in headlines all over the papers. We hadn't been expecting that. As we drove down the main street of Alice Springs, Aidan, who was very proud of his reading ability, read: 'Baby taken by dingo from tent at Ayers Rock' from the bulletin board outside a newsagent's. Reagan started to take notice.

After we had arrived at the Cozens's, Aidan started reading some of the newspapers to Reagan. I came back into the kitchen to see the two little boys with their heads together at the table with Aidan reading aloud. I sat down beside them and saw the expression on Reagan's face change as Aidan read. Finally Reagan turned to me and said, 'Mummy, our bubby isn't coming home, is she? We're not going to get her back any more, are we?' I said to him, 'No, darling.'

He said, 'Is that why you and Daddy have been crying so much?' All I could do was nod. He broke down in my arms and sobbed, and I knew I didn't have to explain any more. Aidan also sobbed then, for the first time since that night. I had two little boys breaking their hearts in my arms and there was nothing, *nothing* I could do about it but hold them and tell them I loved them, and sob too.

How can you understand that hurt unless you have been there too and it has happened to you? You can't. Nothing prepares you for that or for the hurt in your child. It is *much* harder than taking that hurt yourself.

Because we were emotionally drained, we felt physically drained as well. We ate, then everyone settled fairly early for the night's rest. We had barely showered and got into bed when Pastor Cozens came in and said that Constable Buzzard from the Alice Springs police would like to come around and have a talk to us. He had been having Bible studies with Pastor Cozens and he really wanted to meet us and emphasised that it was *not* an official visit. Because he was a friend of Pastor Cozens (who vouched for him) we agreed to get up again and meet him. He was a slim, intense young man who seemed fairly disgruntled with the job he was doing and with his associates at the police station. A number of the statements he made about his fellow workers I thought were rather unwise in view of the fact that he was talking to complete strangers but supposed he felt he was getting it out of his system among friends, Michael being another clergyman.

Then we got on to the subject of our recent tragedy and he launched into a full description of how he, as the coroner's assistant, would be preparing the case for the coroner's court. He then proceeded to enlighten us with his knowledge of dingoes and dingo attacks. The information he gave us became so specific on the way a dingo would eat a child that I was feeling physically ill and wondering just how Michael was coping. Normally a discussion like this would turn his stomach very quickly and the fact that he was still sitting there indicated to me that he was not assimilating the details and that shock was still controlling his actions. I figured if the conversation didn't stop shortly I would have to leave the room as Constable Buzzard blithely babbled on with his gruesome details.

Mrs Cozens looked at him and at my face several times and finally went and spoke to her husband. Bert waited for a break in the conversation and then politely and gently told him it was time he left. Afterwards Norma said to me, 'Well I don't know about you and how you stood it, but any more of that and I was ready to give him a piece of my mind. I don't understand how he could be so insensitive.' First thing in the morning we called the police station, identified ourselves and asked for news. There was still nothing. We told them we were planning to travel home and were wondering whether they had had time to type our statement up yet as we were to sign it. They asked us to wait a while. It was thought that perhaps we needed to have blood tests for the whole family in order for them to work out what Azaria's blood group was for the purpose of identification when or if her clothing was found.

Eventually we rang back and they had decided that it wasn't necessary for us to have blood tests because of the blood on the baby's blankets and sleeping bag which could be used instead. The interview tape had not yet arrived from Ayers Rock and they advised us that they would send it through to Mt Isa some time later and we could sign it there. In view of the late hour, we were now only going to travel to Tennant Creek to stay the night before proceeding on the long final stretch home. We arranged to check at the Tennant Creek police station on our way through.

The Cozens had given us the key to a church member's house in Tennant Creek where we could stay for the night. They always stayed there on their regular fortnightly visits and had a key because the owners were away down south on holidays. They knew the owners would welcome our staying there if they knew.

We pulled in at the address we had been given, the key fitted so we went inside and made ourselves at home in Ros and Steve Peers' place. Steve was an ambulance officer and an hour or so after we arrived another ambulance man walked in the door. We were surprised to see each other as neither party knew the other was staying there. It turned out to be Steve's temporary replacement. We had an interesting conversation with the man and he gave us some details about dingoes that we were unaware of.

We had always understood that dingoes were shy creatures and thought that it was only in camping areas like Ayers Rock where they had become accustomed to man that they would approach so close. He told us that when the ambulance had to travel to outback stations where patients were unable to be airlifted out, sometimes the length of trip meant they had to camp out overnight. In this case a tarpaulin was put on the ground, sleeping bags thrown on it and the other half of the tarpaulin was thrown back on top of them. They slept well down the tarpaulin leaving a tunnel through to their faces for air and, in the morning, they would gently bang the tarp and emerge slowly because they often found dingoes checking them out and any sudden move would cause them to attack. This happened in areas where humans were rarely seen.

The next morning we once again checked with the police as promised and continued on our way home to Mt Isa.

As we drove home, between Tennant Creek and Mt Isa, we were quieter than we had yet been on the trip. As the day wore on, I was thinking that travelling on these long, lonely stretches was fine while the sun was up, but there was a horrible foreboding about the gathering darkness. I was not at all anxious to travel several hundred kilometres in the dark. Previously I had enjoyed travelling in the evening, around dusk and after dark. I had no wish for that to happen that night.

Around lunchtime, we saw a little wayside service station with a cafe and pulled in to get some petrol and something to eat, because the next stop might be hundreds of kilometres away.

While we were getting petrol, a carload of Aborigines came in. When I say a carload, I mean it. Out they piled, one after the other, until our eyes boggled and we wondered just how many exactly could fit in that car. We watched them with some amusement. One man hopped out and seemed to be giving directions to the driver. The latter pulled up, and the fellow would say, 'Nooo, too far. You go again.' He had another go at positioning the car right in front of the bowser. Finally our boys went across to talk to them. Aidan said, 'That car's a bomb, you know. It's not like my daddy's.' I thought: Oh dear, this is *not* the sort of thing to say to a strange Aborigine. It's rather rude and they can take exception fairly quickly. The man looked down at Aidan and said to him, 'Which is your car?' Aidan promptly and proudly pointed out our yellow hatchback Torana, and they started talking. Everything appeared to be OK. We were keeping a fairly steady eye on Aidan and Reagan, but decided to wander across to collect the boys before they became nuisances.

The Aborigine who appeared to be in charge asked, 'These your kids, are they?' We said, 'Yes.' He said, 'This one's very proud of Daddy's car. Thinks this one's an old bomb. We've got no brakes, you see, and we have to keep going round until we stop in the right place for petrol, because if we stop too far away we've got to push it.' They were standing around in various places—some still in the car, some in the shop, one getting petrol. Then he looked at us and said, 'You're the people with the little baby that's lost at Ayers Rock, aren't you?'

We said, 'Yes, how do you know?'

He said, 'My people, they tell me.'

'Oh, you read the papers?'

'No,' he said, 'not yet. We've just come in from the mission now.'

We said, 'Well, how do you know?'

He said, 'My people, they tell me. In my head they tell me. We know.'

Michael asked, 'And you recognised us from that?'

He said, 'Yes, the little boys, the car, you, I know. And Jesus, He will look after your little girl. You be all right. You don't worry. My people, they keep looking till they find something. Maybe next year, maybe the year after, maybe nothing, but if they can, they find.'

We said, 'Thank you.'

He said, 'Jesus loves you. He look after you, after your little boys. He be with you, you travel tonight. You be fine and you not worry about your little girl, you see her in heaven.'

Thank you Lord, I thought. That angel had a black face.

His friend came back from the shop with a pile of newspapers under his arm, and we were introduced. Michael said, 'I see you've got the papers.'

He said, 'Yes, I only come in every couple of weeks to pick them up.' This was quite obviously true. We knew they hadn't read about Azaria. We thanked them and went over to the shop, and they left to go home.

When we got in the shop we asked whether any of the Aborigines had been in for the week. The man said, 'Oh, no, they only come in once every so often. It's pension day today; they're in to get their supplies and they'll be off partying tonight. No, they haven't been in.'

So we asked him about this talking in their heads, and he said, 'Yes, if he said his people told them in their heads, that's how they'd find out, because that's what they do.' We thanked him and drove off, marvelling at the way God had sent us help from such an unexpected source. We travelled home without any further mishap.

Expecting us earlier, our friend Jenny Richards rang up a mate in the police force and said, 'Look, these people who lost their baby at Ayers Rock, Mike and Lindy, they were due back early today and they're not back yet. I'm getting a bit worried. I don't know what to say to them, but I do want to know that they're home safe. Have you heard any news? There haven't been any accidents or anything have there?' She was well known in town so they promised to let her know when we arrived.

'WELCOME HOME, LOVE JEN'

On Thursday, 21 August we drove across the edge of town through the back way to where we lived. Just a few hundred yards from our house we saw a police car going down a different road. We didn't think any more about it till later. As we walked up the front steps, there on the front verandah was a huge basket of groceries, with a note saying, 'Welcome home, love Jen.' It was from Jenny Richards. We just stood and looked at it; we knew why it was there and what wasn't written on that little note.

I said to Michael, 'You know, she's worried. I'm going to ring her. I don't think she's coming over.' I got on the phone and rang Jenny, who was absolutely speechless. After a moment, she said, 'You know, if you hadn't rung me, I wouldn't have rung you. I didn't know what to say. I didn't know how you were taking this. I wanted to be there but I just couldn't. I couldn't face you.' We talked for nearly two hours. She said, 'I knew you were home.' I asked her how, and she said, 'The police rang and told me. They were keeping an eye out for you and they saw you drive into your yard.' And then I remembered the police car that we'd seen.

Several weeks earlier I had told another friend about the New Zealand inter-island ferry, the *Walvine*, which sank in Wellington harbour. A young mother on board, fearing she couldn't throw her baby from the deck to the lifeboat, had given her precious baby to one of the sailors, thinking he would be stronger. He had thrown the baby but not far enough and the mother had had to stand and watch her child drop between the ferry and the lifeboat, into that boiling sea and out of sight. I had cried as I told my friend, Neroli, that story; we were both looking at Azaria, who was then about the same age as the baby had been and contentedly feeding at my breast at the time.

Neroli had told Jenny the story after Azaria died. 'I don't know what Lindy's going to do,' Neroli had said, 'I saw her reaction when she talked about that other baby. Whatever are we going to do when she comes home?' Jenny had been wanting to see me, yet avoided ringing me, because of the pain in her own heart.

But I was too numb for tears. I'd tried to cry, but I couldn't; I wanted to be on my own and cry. The crying came later at various times. As the years go by, it gets easier. But then I felt as if I were dead, as if somebody had killed my whole reason for being. I had to remind myself I still had two dear little boys and that they were the reason for going on. I had to pull myself together for the sake of my family who still lived. I told myself that life must go on, even though I felt dead inside. Azaria died, but it might as well have been me. A part of me will never live again. It doesn't matter how many years you go on; you look at a child, you see the turn of a head, the flick of an eyelash, the shrug of a shoulder, and it brings back a memory, you remember the age *she* would have been, see a resemblance and wonder what she would have been like. And it hurts.

Jenny said to me that night, 'Don't you blame God for this? Don't you think, "How can this be?"' I said to her, 'It's not God's fault. He doesn't want anyone to hurt. For His part, He made it quick so that she didn't feel any pain.'

'It's no good tormenting ourselves about what happened afterwards, the details after her death, the way she might have been handled by that animal. That's the sort of thing the devil wants us to do. He wants us to torment ourselves, tear ourselves to pieces and think what might have been. God would not choose this. God didn't choose sin in this world, that's not His way. He loves us and He wants us to be with Him and have no more pain.' Who knows? I thought, there might have been something later that precluded Azaria from going to heaven, or some awful tragedy, or rape, or something that would have been far more painful than her death had been. Who knows what her future would have been? I don't. I do know that her death was quick, because if she had been alive at all, I would have heard her cry. But her cry was cut off, so at the very least, when she was taken from that tent she was unconscious, which meant she felt no more pain. The cry that Michael had heard was so very short that I had not even heard it. I had been in the wrong place at the wrong time.

If only we had known and been warned that there was danger, she would have slept in the car that night, and so would the boys, with the windows only slightly open for air. But there were *no* warnings about dingoes for the families with young children. We went about our chores suspecting no danger. We were in a public camping area; not like a few nights before at the Devil's Marbles, when we had slept on the ground under the stars, with Azaria in the car because we were afraid of ants. We hadn't even thought of bigger animals such as dingoes.

As I spoke to Jenny, I thought of Job, who suffered horribly without knowing why, only remaining faithful to God, his Lord and Master. God rewarded him in the end, but still he did not know why. Maybe we will never find out in this world either.

I'm sure Job has many questions to ask God when he sees Him. I have a few to ask Him, too. Maybe we can queue up together. But suffering is not God's will. He will help us to bear what we must, and to hang on until the end, but it's not something He delights in.

Jenny said, 'Lindy, you have got such a strong faith that you've encouraged me. Why don't you talk to the newspapers about this?'

I said, 'You know there's already been something in the newspaper. It's there, that's fine, that's it. It's not for me to go to talk to the newspaper. I really think, if there's been an article, it's over.'

She said, 'No, I want to ring them up.'

I said, 'Leave it, Jen. If one person's been helped by what's happened, then that's fair enough for me. Maybe that makes it worthwhile, and one day I'll find out the reasons.'

The day after Azaria died, the only thing that kept me sane was having to do things for my remaining children. That continued to make me fight to retain normality. They needed to be fed, have their clothes unpacked and washed and ironed. I was forced to keep going. Although in one way I felt very together, in another way, looking back on it, I was not terribly aware of what was going on. I would start preparing a meal and then an hour or two later would realise that I'd gone off to do something else and hadn't advanced any further. My friends were dropping in and saying, 'She's disappeared again. I think we'll finish peeling the potatoes and put them on,' and they would do it. Half the time I realised I wasn't sure whether I had finished doing something or someone had finished it for me. The phone rang non-stop. I was answering the phone and answering the door, and trying to do things in between.

Jenny and June, another woman from the church, turned up to help. I was floundering around, still confident that I could manage on my own, as I always had. I had always been very independent. I was proud of my neat house, the way I looked after my children and coped with the church work and my husband's typing, and the other things a minister's wife does. And yet I was beginning to realise that my grip had slipped. I was trying to keep things normal, and yet they weren't normal; they weren't staying in the pigeonholes I had designed for them. Things kept getting out of hand; the routine was upside down. I couldn't work the way I normally did. My mind was playing games with me, and still I felt dead inside. We had only been home one night and half a day and things were already in chaos. Jenny and June were doing some tidying up, helping answer the door and phone, getting food for the boys.

The women sorted the washing as it came out of the back of the car; others helped Michael unload while I put things away upstairs. As I was working, Jenny called me down to the laundry underneath the high-block house to ask me various things: 'Is this washing? Is there any dry-cleaning here? What do I do with this?' My tracksuit was there and I asked Jenny to get it dry-cleaned. 'Point out to them that it's got some marks on it, would you please,' I said, 'because it's wool, it's new, and I don't want to wash it.' However hard you try, it seems, if you wash some wool things by hand, they can sometimes change their shape. I was not in the mood to do any washing myself. I had bought the tracksuit on sale at the local sports shop and was proud of owning my first good one. I had been travelling in it all the way to Ayers Rock, pouring drinks and spilling them down myself, feeding Azaria, having her jump up and down on my knees, and that tracksuit was well and truly dirty. I had put those tracksuit pants on the night she disappeared hauled up under my dress for extra warmth as the temperature dropped below zero, and climbed in and out of the tent several times later. After that I hadn't worn them the rest of the way home. We were going to warmer areas and they weren't needed; they just sat in the washing pile. I hadn't given them another thought until Jenny mentioned them. I also sent a couple of Reagan's little woollen jackets to the dry-cleaners.

There were several other things that I had pointed out to Jenny, including Aidan's parka with blood on the sleeve. She was horrified and wondered what to do with it. I said, 'We'd better leave that for a bit. We'll just keep it out of Michael's way until we know what is happening with these things. Blood upsets Michael. If you find anything like that, put it to one side.' So she did.

As I opened the cupboard door in the kitchen, I saw all the cans of baby formula—one more grim reminder. After a shaky start, I had been totally breastfeeding Azaria during our holiday with a comp bottle for emergencies only. Not only were my breasts sore now, but I had a cupboard full of food for a little girl who no longer needed it. Our budget was too tight to simply throw it in the bin, and I couldn't face the thought of going back to the shop to return it, seeing the chemist's eyes on me with sympathy I couldn't stand. I asked Jenny, who went to the same chemist, if she would take it back. She put it in the boot of her car with the dry-cleaning and promptly forgot it, unknown to us, for nearly a week. That slip of memory was to plague her in the witness box for years to come. Was it *deliberate* hiding of evidence for a friend?

Woman's Day had rung us at Ayers Rock and talked us into giving an interview on Friday 22 August. They said this was one way we could tell people about the dangers at Ayers Rock so that no more babies were taken. There seemed to be no records of dingoes attacking anyone before. We didn't want to see this happen again, and so we agreed. They were due to arrive at any time.

The reporter and photographer from *Woman's Day* duly arrived. The plane carrying my parents, my brother and sister-in-law and their two oldest children was due to land about twenty minutes later. Jenny offered to help pick up the family while I dealt with the press.

By the time she had collected them and returned, we were not very far into the interview; I had had to answer the phone and the door, and I wasn't finding it easy to concentrate.

I heard a car pull in, went downstairs; there was my family. I gave Dad a hug and he held me tight. Then I hugged Mum. I could see the way she was feeling by looking at her face. There was not much anyone could say. I had tried so hard to convince them to visit us when Azaria was born, and for some reason, that time especially, I had particularly wanted them; I didn't know many people in Mt Isa and was feeling it would be good to have some family around me. But it was a long way and it cost money.

I know that is something they will regret for the rest of their lives, and so will I. They came over when we needed them most, but not in time to see their dear little granddaughter. They hadn't even seen a photograph of her until one was published in the newspaper after her death.

There was no point in saying this, but we knew it was going through everybody's mind; they had come now, come for a little girl who was no longer there for them to see. It was all there in Mum's eyes. I didn't have to ask her what she was thinking; she would always wonder what Azaria was like, always wish she had been able to hold her. And so would I. My brother, Alex, his wife and boys were there too.

Eventually we decided to ask the reporters to stay for lunch with the family; at that stage we considered journalists to be people doing a job, trying to be helpful. We had no reason to believe otherwise, and they were treated as ordinary guests in our house. (This attitude did not remain the same.)

To Reach Out and Touch

When you have not been part of a pregnancy, not been part of a life and not been part of a death, it is very difficult to accept the existence of another family member you did not know. I don't think the reality of Azaria's birth, life and death struck home to my parents until they were able to see and handle some of her clothes that had been at Ayers Rock. When we were unpacking and sorting the washing I had put her baby clothes out to wash by hand, which I always did instead of through the washing machine, and Mum asked me if she could do the washing. It brought her close to the little granddaughter she had never known, whom she dearly wished she had seen while she was still alive. In one way, I wanted to wash her clothes myself but I knew I had been able to wash her bottles out and clean up her things afterwards, and I felt I could allow Mum to do Azaria's washing because that was her way of saying goodbye.

I happened to walk downstairs while she was washing the clothes. She turned her head away, not fast enough, because I realised that, although she hadn't cried in front of me, she was crying as she washed those clothes for the last time. I forgot why I was downstairs, put my arms around her from behind, hugged her and we both cried.

Today Tonight, the Brisbane TV show, had also asked for an interview similar to the *Woman's Day* article. They had heard about our faith in dealing with Azaria's death and asked whether we would give some hope and comfort to other parents who might have lost a child. We thought about this and, because ours was a minister's home, we felt we should give what assistance we could, so we agreed. The following day was our first Sabbath home, and the camera team came to church, filmed part of the service, did an additional small interview and then went away.

We thought no more about this until a crew from another program rang. We had had trouble with them already, they had given us the tired old story that they *had* to have an interview because we had given one to their opposition. We had given the only interviews we were going to, and this group had bad manners and a reputation to match, so we politely and firmly refused. Next thing we knew, we had a phone call saying that their reporters were on their way up on the aeroplane. Although we *still* refused to give them an interview, they arrived on our doorstep with cameras rolling; they were going to talk to us whether we wanted it or not. Rather than have them say we refused to talk and so we must be hiding something, we agreed to a five-minute interview.

The first few minutes of the interview went fine, and then we were asked whether we realised that Azaria's clothes had been found folded and people were saying she had not been killed by a dingo. This was the first we had heard of any such rumours and we found them devastating. Michael immediately started asking where they had heard these stories, but they wouldn't tell us. Michael told them we didn't appreciate their mischief-making, that they were there under false pretences and we wanted them to leave. Easier said than done; they wouldn't go. I had the phone number of the decent crew from *Today Tonight* who had been there the day before, so I rang and asked them what we should do with these people, who were coming out with such horrible rumours. The *Today Tonight* people said they had heard the rumours too, but had ignored them. They advised us to say we'd had legal advice and our lawyers would contact them.

We said this to the hostile camera team and with bad grace they left. We did not have a lawyer then, but we got one fast and served them with an injunction on that part of the program. Years later, it was claimed that we were annoyed over this incident because we were guilty. The thought that innocent parents might be upset because of lies did not seem to be taken into account!

Meanwhile Azaria's clothes—her disposable nappy, singlet and jumpsuit—were found by Wally Goodwin, a tourist, on Sunday 24 August, a week after her death.

When we finally met Wally Goodwin much later he told us that they had gone into the area where the clothing was found because it had poured heavily the night before. So heavily, in fact, that some of the bus tours started packing up to leave at about 4 a.m. in case they got trapped by flash flooding. As Wally was a keen bird photographer, he and his family were investigating any areas on the Rock apart from the main tourist area of Maggie Springs that looked as if they may have water catchment areas that would attract bird life.

As there was an obvious area where water cascaded down the Rock near the rockface with the lichen, they had parked on the road and the family was walking in to see what they could find. Although there was an animal track near the area, they had to make their own path across from the road and as they got closer were clambering over small boulders. Wally's daughter was a little ahead of him and suddenly stopped and screamed.

As he looked at what was frightening her, he could see what he immediately recognised as a baby's small jumpsuit.

His wife Margo stopped the children from going any further, and took them back to the car while he went to investigate. He said what had frightened his daughter was the fact that the jumpsuit was sitting on its back, slightly concertinaed with the feet rounded and pointing upwards as if the lower part of the baby's legs were still inside.

(Azaria's nappy I learned later had received similar treatment to those we had seen shredded near our tent that day.)

They had heard so much news that he knew immediately he had found the missing baby clothes that the police were looking for. Because he was so conscious of warnings to the public never to touch evidence, although he had his camera around his neck he knelt down and carefully bent over the clothes having a close look at them but took no photographs and did not disturb them in any way before he went to call the police.

He saw no human footprints of any sort other than his own in the area but did note that the surrounding area looked as if the vegetation had been rolled on. He left his wife standing guard while he went to notify the police. Frank Morris was on the radio telling Alice Springs there was no further news. When the conversation finished Wally told Frank Morris that he had just found the missing baby clothes and was asked how he knew!

Frank Morris travelled back with him and he once again left his wife and children on the road while he took Morris to the clothes. When they got there he was amazed to see Constable Morris put his bare hand down and pick up the clothes. Morris must have realised Wally was looking shocked because he told him not to worry, he was just checking to see if they were the right ones because if they were, there should be bootees inside the legs of the jumpsuit. Constable Morris, having large hands, had to undo a number of the press studs which were still done up in order to get his hand in. Wally was interested to note that Morris's hands shook badly and he came to the conclusion that it must be the first time Morris had investigated a dead body and was fearful of what he might find, which was making him extremely nervous. When Morris had satisfied himself he had the right article, he asked Wally Goodwin to go and fetch assistance and stayed alone with the clothes while Wally did so.

Wally had difficulty in contacting anyone and finally saw a ranger driving towards him, whom he stopped and notified. The ranger was then able to use his two-way radio to contact the others, so Wally left.

One of the church members heard the news on the radio and rang us. We rang the police in Alice Springs, who confirmed the information. They had only just been informed from the Rock themselves and the media wanted permission to film the clothes, so they had to contact us. We, of course, wanted to see the clothes, but as they were at the Rock and we were in Mt Isa, we thought this was one way for us to see them. So it was arranged and the police gave the television company permission to photograph the clothes.

I saw the telecast of my baby's clothes, and a very odd experience it was. Even being mentioned on television was strange, it happened to movie stars, politicians and other famous people—not us.

It was difficult enough to believe that Azaria was dead, and here I was looking at clothes that were said to be hers. They were certainly the same design and shape and I knew they were hers. But they weren't white, and they weren't clean and fresh and beautiful. And they weren't on *her*. She had never been dirty like that.

Besides, her clothes were supposed to be going to an inquest. They were supposed to be dealt with by scientists and by the court; here was a policeman on television, handling them with his bare hands. When I thought about it, I knew this was contrary to every cop show and every bit of reading I'd ever done about police procedure. They always said, 'Don't handle the evidence.' They would pick it up carefully with penknives or with a biro, or tweezers, or with gloves on, and painstakingly put it into specimen bags and send it to the lab to be tested.

This can't be right, I thought. I must be imagining it; they must have done tests on her clothing already, finished them, and it doesn't matter any more.

It was many years before I learned that Azaria's clothing had been handled like that—carelessly, sloppily—all the time.

Something else about that initial TV film disturbed me, too. I noticed that the reporters were saying that the clothes had been found folded, and inferring that maybe the dingo hadn't put the things where they were found about 4 kilometres (2.5 miles) from the campsite. There was some implication that people might have been involved. This annoyed me, because I knew it couldn't be true, but nothing in what we first heard was to warn us that we were being considered possible murderers. It was, of course, something that did not even enter my head.

Michael tried to get back into his work as soon as possible, while I tried to pick up the pieces and answer the phone at home. By this time Michael's mother had also arrived from New Zealand. We were very crowded: my parents and Michael's mother were staying in the house, and my brother Alex, sister-in-law Felicity, and their two boys were in a caravan in the yard.

We arranged to have a memorial service for Azaria as soon as possible after Michael's mother arrived. Because so many people in Mt Isa wanted to come, it was difficult to find a big enough venue and it was suggested we hire the town hall. Eventually we settled on the local Adventist church which could be extended if necessary. We were asked by the local ministers' fraternal to have the service on a weekday after work so as many people as possible could come.

The women were eager to decorate the church beautifully, perhaps with white flowers all across the front, as well as a floral arch: all for a little girl they loved. I didn't think I could handle that, Michael and I wanted something simple; after all, this wasn't a wedding, or even a funeral—we had no coffin.

Jenny said, 'All right, if that's what you want, tell me exactly and I'll organise the ladies.'

We decided to have one vase of flowers on each side of the church. Below the pulpit on a small table was to be a white, heart-shaped cushion with a spray of pale pink flowers and maidenhair fern; something I could keep as a memory of her, something frilly, beautiful, sweet and dainty. We set the little phial of earth I had collected from the tent site (to me it was almost like having a phial of ashes), and her dedication certificate, one each side of the cushion on the table. That was all.

The day came and, as usual, everything happened at the last minute. Jenny came in upset—the florist hadn't followed instructions about the cushion and it looked awful, so I had to redo it myself. Getting dressed one of my shoes got lost, Reagan managed to get dirty twice, the kids had scuffed their shoes and they needed cleaning again, and our parents and relatives were trying to use the bathroom at the same time as we were. Michael had to go across early to see to one or two things as Pastor Harker and Pastor Kennaway had arrived from Townsville for the service—we had asked for them specially. Pastor Kennaway had dedicated Azaria a few weeks before; now he was to take the memorial service.

Pastor Harker, the president, had been very good to us and it was decided that he should have some part in the service too. We had originally wanted just Pastor Kennaway up the front; one man for the dedication and the same man for the memorial service. However, Pastor Harker very much wanted to be part of the proceedings for Azaria's sake, as well as feeling that the local church should have representatives there too. So, in the end, several men stood on the rostrum. It was less simple than what we would have liked to represent the life of a little girl.

Somehow or other the media, for once, had overlooked the fact that the memorial service was being held, and they stayed away, which left us in peace without the unreality of cameras spoiling the solemnity of it all. The church was filled to overflowing with our friends and acquaintances from throughout Mt Isa. As Michael and I stood at the door afterwards to accept sympathy and condolences, we saw many people we barely knew, as well as close friends. The owner of the local store had hired a temporary replacement and came across. The local policeman's wife, whose baby had been born on the same afternoon as Azaria, came too.

During the service I managed to stay fairly calm, at least inwardly, by refusing to think about what was happening. The moment I saw her face as she was coming through the door towards me, all those memories hit me and I broke down, because we had shared the happy time when our two little girls were born. We cried in one another's arms. She had not known whether to come or not, or whether she could handle it. I am so glad she did. Then I was able to collect myself and the rest of the people went past.

A Nightmare Relived Daily

I went to hang a couple of Aidan's little shirts in the wardrobe. It was morning and the sun was shining directly into the wardrobe as I opened the door and there, hanging up in front of me were the boys' parkas. I saw two splashes of blood—one large one and one slightly smaller on the sleeve of Reagan's parka near the shoulder.

I hadn't realised because I had put it away at night without seeing any blood. The parkas were an army green, with darker lining, and didn't show marks easily, so how much more could there be? I now realised Azaria had initially bled a lot more than we knew. I pulled it out and looked at it, and pulled Aidan's out as well. Apart from the cuff, it had splashes of blood right across the lining on the inside, which had not been visible in normal lighting. Reagan's parka had splashes on the outside across the back as well as on the sleeve.

Both the boys' parkas were splattered with it; the parkas had been on top of the sleeping bags near the tent door where the dingo had come through and I had seen it shaking its head.

I knew I had put Reagan's parka on the pillow when I tucked him into bed, thinking he might wake up and need to put it on if he had to go outside the tent. Aidan had taken his parka off himself when he climbed into the tent, and I could tell from looking at it that he'd just put it down as he'd taken it off, upside down. I called to Mum and when she came in I said, 'Look, I don't want to upset you, but you said you wanted to see anything else I found.' I knew she was still trying to come to grips with the fact that this was all real. Mum needed something tangible other than little dresses in the wardrobe to convince herself it *was* all real and that she wasn't in some horrible nightmare. We didn't even have any photos of Azaria at home with us at that stage; those we had developed already we'd sent across to Michael's mother, and we had given our other copy (which had been for my parents) to the newspaper.

I told Mum about the parkas, showing her what I'd found on them. She took them in her hands and cried. I held her in my arms, and my eyes watered, but I couldn't cry. The tears just wouldn't come. That hurt, angry, dead feeling was blocking them.

At Ayers Rock, Inspector Gilroy had asked us if we thought of anything significant, or wanted to know anything, to feel free to contact him direct, and he would chat to us at any time. We had contacted him several times and always found him very gentlemanly, courteous and kind.

The blood on the parkas seemed important evidence so I immediately rang to let the police know what I'd found. They thought perhaps they'd better pick Reagan's parka up and sent someone round to collect it. They still weren't interested in Aidan's, and said I could wash it. So, I washed it and put it away in the cupboard again. Within the next couple of weeks, we realised just how much more blood there was in the tent than we had initially seen.

Then I found my jogging shoes. I had always been a jogger, and I started jogging again in Mt Isa very soon after Azaria was born with a group of women who were also keen to get fit together. One of the women could only do a short distance so she would jog up and down past the car, keeping an eye on Azaria in her carry basket and her own little girl, while the rest of us did longer distances. We gradually built up to 4 or 5 kilometres (two or three miles). I had to be careful because my milk was still coming in and excess physical exercise affected its flow. I discovered that yeast tablets doubled the quantity of milk, so then I was able to jog normally every day. I was beginning to get fitter and do longer distances when we went to Ayers Rock.

Now I threw myself wholeheartedly into my running. I always noticed that when I had been jogging I could cope better, and I was trying to get back to a normal routine as fast as possible for the sake of the boys and Michael. The other girls turned up to go jogging and I went to put my shoes on. It was the first time I had worn them since that awful night at the Rock. When I picked them up I noticed that besides the fruit juice stains there were blood stains on them. I burst into tears.

It was just too much. Mum heard me and came in. I asked her to wash them while I was away as it was too much of a reminder for me. The police didn't seem to be interested in any more evidence at that stage, so I didn't even bother to ask them about the smeared blood on my shoes; I must have got it when I crawled in and out of the tent so many times that night. I put on another pair of shoes and Mum removed the offending ones. I wiped my eyes, washed my face and went out to the other girls. My shoes were washed and hanging out on the clothes line by the time I got home.

It was good to be running again. On the other hand I needed another kind of outlet, something different to do, and Jenny di Silva asked me whether Reagan and I would like to learn to roller skate with her and her daughter. Michael said I was too old and, if I broke anything, not to expect any sympathy from him.

When we arrived at the rink I stuck my nose very dubiously in the door. It seemed a lot of people were getting to know me these days, and making a fool of yourself seems to be worse when you're well known; at least I thought it was then. There weren't many people there so I quite enjoyed it and managed not to fall over too much. After a few sessions I got cocky, turned quickly and slipped over, landing hard on my right wrist. It felt like it was broken and I was unable to use my right hand, but an x-ray said it was only a bad sprain. I had to have it in a sling for a while, so Michael was pleased not to have me skating. I have only been skating a couple of times since. At least the boys enjoyed me going with them and I didn't quite disgrace myself by falling over, but I haven't improved any further.

Finding Crucial Evidence and Meeting a Phantom Cop

The interview we'd done for *Today Tonight* was to be on soon. On the evening of the telecast we decided to get the kids' baths over early and have them all in their pyjamas. Alex's boys brought their sleeping bags to lie in, so Reagan and Aidan decided it would be a great idea to have their sleeping bags also. We'd been finding bits and pieces here and there with sprinkles of blood or marks on them, but I realised I hadn't examined everything yet, so as I got the sleeping bags out, Felicity and I checked them. The boys' were fine but we found that my sleeping bag had blood on it after all, so we also checked the space blanket that had covered Reagan on the night.

I started to open it up and immediately saw some little puckers on its surface, which was annoying because the blanket had been new. Mum was also getting tea, so was Felicity, my sister-in-law. Felicity said, 'Oh, there seems to be some more.' So Mum held one end of the blanket and Felicity held the other end for me so I could have a good look. I noticed a diagonal line of rip marks across the blanket. Mum said, 'Hey, what's this? They're paw prints.' Felicity and I looked, and there on the space blanket near where Mum was holding it were two unmistakable canine prints, one very clear, the other one looked as if the animal had stopped very quickly with a propping action, and skidded slightly.

I touched the tip of my fingernail on a print. They would not rub or scrape off, but they weren't dusty, nor were they thick like mud. The impression was that the animal had walked on damp earth and then walked on the blanket, leaving a caked-on pattern that was thin yet very distinctive. I would have needed to get a damp cloth to actually *rub* it off if I had wanted to remove it. The prints were dry but although they looked sort of dusty wouldn't blow away. When the question of the space blanket came up in court later, those who had seen it gave descriptions ranging from 'dusty' to caked'; the prints were actually very difficult to describe, and much was made of this.

Michael was called in to have a look, he walked through the door, said 'Oh, no!' and disappeared, refusing to look again. The thought of it was obviously too much. From then on, he was unable to remember whether he had actually seen the blanket or somebody had told him about it; he had not been able to handle further evidence at that stage.

Once again I telephoned the Alice Springs police immediately, and they said that they would send someone around to collect it. Several days passed and no one arrived. Then one day I came home from shopping and Michael said, 'Do you know where that space blanket is? The police have been here to pick it up, and you'd better know where it is, because I couldn't give it to them.'

I said, 'Well, that's fine. It's in the lounge ready for them.'

'OK,' said Michael, 'I didn't know that. The police'll be back shortly. I have an appointment and I've got to go.' So he took the car and went.

Shortly afterwards a police car pulled up outside and I heard a knock on the door. Mum opened it to find a blond policeman in uniform. He didn't look any older than about twenty-four. Someone else was waiting in the car. Dad was fixing the back screen door where he could hear through to the front door and I went to the door also.

I gave the young policeman the space blanket, and said 'Now, do you know what you're taking in?'

He said, 'Just a blanket I was told to collect.'

I told him, 'You'd better know what is significant about it, so you can point it out to your superiors when you get back. This is the blanket that was over Reagan on the night Azaria was taken. We think the dingo actually walked over him to get to where she was in the carry basket at his feet, because there are rip marks right across the blanket and footprints on one end.' I opened out the space blanket and showed him the rip marks and the footprints. He looked at them intently as I spoke, and when his eyes lit on the footprints, he said, 'Oh, yes, there's no dou . . . Yes, thank you very much, Mrs Chamberlain, I'll hand that in.'

The formal manner was so apparent after his involuntary exclamation that I knew he had been talking to us as an ordinary person and then suddenly realised he was a policeman, picking up evidence, and he wasn't supposed to comment.

I asked him, 'What about my sleeping bag? Do you want that too, or can I get it dry-cleaned? The police were going to let me know.'

He said, 'Oh no, that's fine, they don't want it. You can get it dry-cleaned.' I said goodbye to him after he'd collected the space blanket and Reagan's parka and thought no more about it.

When Michael took my sleeping bag in to the dry-cleaners he told them that there were blood spots across the hood; it was Azaria's blood and he wanted it taken out. When he went to pick it up, he checked to see whether the blood had come out, and he could still see the telltale marks of blood, which had now been set. They evidently hadn't used the blood spotter properly. He told them they would have to try again, as he would not accept it in that condition. The dry-cleaning lady apologised and he left the sleeping bag there to be put aside to have another go.

Another customer in the drycleaner's at the time looked at them both but said nothing.

When Michael went to pick the sleeping bag up again, a very embarrassed drycleaner told him that the police had turned up with a warrant and collected the bag. Michael, annoyed, went down to the police station and asked why this had happened, asking why they hadn't asked for it as we'd have given it to them. They didn't need to get a warrant for it. They mumbled a bit and gave him no particular reasons.

Not until much later, in fact in court, did we discover that the other customer who had been in the drycleaner's that day had thought that Michael had been trying to get rid of some evidence. She had rung the police who had turned up in a hurry. They had forgotten having given us permission to get it dry cleaned.

Now they decided they had better have Aidan's parka after all so Michael dropped it off to the Mt Isa police station on Friday 29 August 1980 for them to send on to Alice Springs. Days later the Alice Springs police rang me looking for it. They tried to say we still had it. I told them they had it, but they assured me they couldn't find it. I thought that, instead of taking it to the police, Michael *might* have taken it to the drycleaners absentmindedly (because that's the one that was washed) although he said he hadn't. We checked in case. But no, it wasn't there either. Then I got a phone call from the Alice Springs police saying they had it there after all; they had just forgotten about it.

In years to come, the reason why Aidan's parka had been washed became very significant. Had we tried to destroy evidence? Why were we looking for it so hard? When we reminded the police that they had *asked* us to look for it, and we were trying to assist them in their enquires, they said they hadn't known about that and were very sorry, and apologised. But by that stage the damage had been done, and as far as the public was concerned we were hiding evidence.

The Sympathy of a Nation and Lessons on Dingoes

Sympathy cards and letters were pouring in from all over Australia. A number of people who had lived in the outback and northern Queensland in early settlement days wrote to us about their experiences with dingoes. When out mustering cattle and camping overnight, one mentioned waking up and finding a dingo by the large wooden cot that their two-year-old slept in. They remembered being afraid and thankful that he wasn't on the ground, and how extra precautions had to be taken.

Some children had to be escorted home from school, with guns, because packs of dingoes were tailing them daily. They had been coming closer and closer each successive night and the parents had feared for their children's lives, as winter was coming on and food for the dingoes was growing scarcer.

In one case a four-year-old boy had wandered away from his home. After a frantic search by family, friends, and neighbours from the district, his partially eaten body was found with dingo tracks all around it.

When we tried to document some of these incidents for court, we were told they were too early to be listed in court records, considered irrelevant, or misleading (since they were usually listed as death by 'misadventure'), or just reported in local newspapers of the day.

Rangers, Aborigines and old trackers all said that a hungry dingo could consume its whole prey within two or three minutes. The dingo was a very tidy eater that would not necessarily leave evidence of where it had eaten. It could then pick up the clothes (in this case) and take them to some other location.

As for the skin (or clothes in this case) dingoes like to roll in something that has the smell of blood about it, or they may simply bury it. Sometimes they bury what is left of the carcass and come back to eat it later. After the kill, when a dingo gets to a location where it feels at ease to stop and consume its meal, it will bite the head off its prey, put its feet on the carcass, and use its teeth to peel back the whole skin in one piece, so it is very neatly turned inside out. Often if something was wrapped or parcelled they would just place their feet on it and gently extricate the contents without tearing the packaging. We had evidence that dingoes are capable of cutting through a seatbelt as if it has been sliced through neatly with a knife or scissors. They are also capable of biting through the standard No. 8 fencing wire used by farmers.

The jumpsuit, which was a little loose on Azaria at the time of her death, would also have caused no problems. With only the two top press studs undone, a dingo could easily extricate a body from a jumpsuit without further damage, as tests done at the Adelaide Zoo were to show. On Azaria's jumpsuit there was a small amount of damage near the top press stud and a little on the collar, which the dingo experts felt was quite consistent with the dingo damage around the throat and also on one arm. Other than that there was nothing visible on the jumpsuit except extensive staining caused by blood running down from her head and neck area. Experts said this was all consistent with the type of damage to be expected from a dingo attack.

We also learned from the old doggers (dingo trappers) that human urine was most effective in causing dingoes to come to traps. They seemed to be in no doubt that if Azaria had a wet nappy, it would have attracted dingoes faster than anything else.

Dingoes hunt either alone or in packs; they have been known to kill up to one hundred sheep in one night simply for fun. The animals are almost undamaged, they just have bite marks around the neck, and the bodies are left where they fall. There was evidence of dingoes having carried large wallabies for long distances, with the dingo's head held erect and the body of the wallaby well off the ground, or with just its tail dragging. They can move at quite a fast trot without the prey's weight being an apparent problem. The experts considered that the near 4.5 kilogram (10 pound) weight of Azaria would have been no impediment whatsoever.

Les Harris from the Dingo Foundation of Australia later gave several instances of cats and even female dingoes being tossed into the air by other dingoes with the greatest of ease.

Trying to Handle an Avalanche of Press

The press invasion began in earnest. A lot of reporters were ringing, and I didn't seem to be getting much done except trying to avoid answering questions.

But reporters always had information faster than anyone else—certainly faster than we did. So we thought we might as well question them to find out the latest news about developments, seeing we couldn't avoid answering the phone.

The phone rang hot. The calls often began at five or six in the morning and would keep going till sometimes one o'clock the following morning. We had to keep our line open; it was the only one available to police as well as church members, family, and friends. But it seemed the phone just *never* stopped.

I had a slight cold at the time and, with the shock of Azaria's death and the aftermath, I developed laryngitis. As Michael was always out, the phone answering fell to me and the continual talking made my throat worse and worse. I actually strained my voice and it will never fully recover. When I listen to myself talk now on television or on a tape recorder, I hear a scratchiness that was never there before. Not only did I lose my voice, but the battery in our phone also went flat. I gathered from Telecom that a phone battery relies on being able to recharge itself when the receiver is down and as ours was in use for hours on end, it actually had to be replaced. Even Telecom's phones in the exchange didn't have that problem.

We got an increasing number of crank calls, and in desperation we asked the local exchange to monitor our phone. We found this a great relief, because we could then choose which members of the press we wanted to talk to as well. Some names kept coming up over and over again; one in particular was Malcolm Brown from the *Sydney Morning Herald*. I very quickly discovered that if he reported something, all the newspapers would ring up and say, 'Malcolm Brown, from the *Sydney Morning Herald*, reported . . .' He seemed to be regarded as the reporters' reporter. We also learned that his information in those days was accurate, for which we were very grateful.

Not all reporters were as careful as Malcolm Brown, though, even though they quoted him. Newspapers are supposed to tell the truth and give us facts, aren't they? Or is that a figment of the imagination? Is this something we have convinced ourselves is correct, even though we *know* it is not.

CB or not CB

Michael had a week of ministers' meetings in Townsville and took his mother with him in the plane so she could see some of the countryside and he would have company on the twelve-hour trip. Within hours of their departure, Jenny Richards rang.

She said, 'I don't like doing this, but there is some pretty devastating stuff going around. You're going to hear it from somebody and it may as well be from me first, so that you will know what to do.' She told me that a friend of hers had a CB radio in his work truck and had picked up a conversation between two policemen who were swapping stories about Azaria. She had been mistreated; her father had murdered her and would shortly be picked up for murder; she was dressed in black and she was a Mongoloid, deformed or at least a cretin, they said. Soon I had another phone call, this time from Bundaberg in Queensland; a friend of ours had picked up the same information from the CB. Another call later that day came from friends in Western Australia and they had also heard the information on their CB radio. Were these CB conversations accidental? I have since wondered. Or, were they part of a well-thought-out plan?

I knew the *Today Tonight* crew were still in town as they had not been able to pick up their plane, and they had mentioned they had heard the rumours too. So, after these phone calls, I decided to see whether this material was what they were referring to. It was, plus a lot more they had picked up around town that day. The day before they had been unable to get anything much from the pubs, now they were buzzing. The crew said, 'Can we do another piece with you? We'll answer some of these rumours, and we'll put a stop to them in an authoritative way, this is totally intolerable.'

By this time we had had thousands of letters, plenty of which contained information from outback people and from old doggers, telling us the way dingoes behaved. We were getting to know quite well what the expected activities of these animals were. You also only needed to put your common- sense together with the information that was available, to get a fairly clear picture of what had happened.

The Lowes too heard and saw the news reported incorrectly and wrote to us, saying:

> It is with regret that we peruse newspaper reports that indicate callous rumours are circulating in your home town in connection with Azaria's disappearance.
>
> We offer our deepest sympathy and trust that you are able to ignore these slanderous statements. We are at a loss to understand why some people would deliberately cast a slur on the integrity of your family and its faith.

The Whittakers also were distressed to hear the flood of gossip spreading over the countryside. They wrote on 8 September 1980:

> As we were having tea last night, Max's brother rang to tell us of the interview on the Mike Willesee show [as we never did an interview for Mike Willesee we presumed this was the *Today Tonight* program part two Willesee used]—we turned it on just as the interview began. You and your boys have been very much in our thoughts and prayers as we have journeyed homeward, and occasionally we have met with people who seemed puzzled by what they had heard or read about Azaria's disappearance. We have been glad of the opportunity to set them straight—but had been disturbed by such distortions. However, it was not until we reached Melbourne at the weekend that we heard of newspaper reports and finally hearing what you were saying tonight, that we realised the extent, and horror, of the rumoured innuendos.
>
> Our hearts go out in love to you both—we are saddened and distressed, and angry also that this further anguish and heart-break should be added to the pain and sorrow of separation that you already know and feel.

In the trauma of the events of that awful night at the Rock, people's names had slipped our minds, and funnily enough we either didn't know a lot of their names or couldn't remember what they were. We did not realise these letters were actually from eyewitnesses until after the inquest when they told us they had written, so we went home and looked for them amongst the piles of mail we had opened.

I was really hurt at the rumours, and angry that the police should be so stupid and careless.

I decided I'd had enough. Previously, Michael was mainly the one who talked in the interviews. I told Mum and Dad I was sick of having all these things said about us, and I was going to fight them myself.

In my anger at the rumours and the ignorant misconceptions, with the deadness of my spirit making emotion very difficult to show to those who did not know me well, I agreed to do another interview for the *Today Tonight* crew.

The second interview, quite short and pithy, was done totally about the rumours. I was asked about the clothes not being found inside out, and information I had been given on dingo habits. I described how dingoes could have removed the clothes. My face was swollen and blotched from crying. I had makeup on, after all. I was too angry and dead to cry any more, and already I was learning to cover my emotions well. Besides, it seemed academic to me, whatever happened later was not part of my little girl alive and happy. It was not relevant in my mind.

Watching the video years later, I found it obvious that I had red eyes and a face swollen from crying. But I guess most viewers only saw what they wanted to see—a hard-faced, murdering bitch.

Between the starting of those rumours and the going to air of the program, we suffered dingo howls, whistles, toots and calls past our house at all hours of the day and night.

As Michael was still away, I had to ring him in Townsville to let him know that the latest rumour was that he would shortly be arrested because *he* had murdered Azaria. I didn't feel that Michael would handle that very well over the phone, so I rang Pastor Harker, his president, and explained to him what was happening. I asked him to take Michael aside and tell him gently. Things were under control, but we wanted him to hear before somebody walked up to him on the street, or something. So Pastor Harker told him gently.

At the time the response was terrific. The *Today Tonight* program allayed many of the local rumours which almost stopped dead. Peace reigned and life was more tolerable again for a while.

But the interview, plus the rumours, started to affect our relationship with people around Mt Isa. One of these was Dr Irene Milne, who had delivered Azaria. By the time Azaria's disappearance had become headline news, I was due to go back for my final check-up. The appointment had been made before our holidays but when I rang up to confirm, I was told that Dr Irene had cancelled it and I could see one of the other doctors. There was no explanation and we never did have a word of sympathy from her. I found that quite strange; perhaps all the publicity had made her uncomfortable. Then I met her in a shoe shop while I was buying shoes for Reagan. She stood next to me at the counter and I knew she realised I was there, so I stayed facing her, waiting for her to turn around. She glanced towards me quickly, I was looking straight at her and said, 'Hello, Dr Milne. How are you?' She looked embarrassed and said, 'Oh, hello. I am well, thank you,' grabbed her receipt and walked straight out of the shop. She was obviously avoiding me. We didn't speak again, and I only saw her in the witness box, but she was never a hostile witness.

She had been quoted as saying that I was not a normal mother, but she denied that and I believe her. One of the sisters in the Mt Isa hospital had argued with me about demand feeding Azaria (the hospital was in the process of changing over so that mothers could demand feed if they wanted to and this sister was against that), but other mothers demand feed also. Dr Milne thought that the rumours had probably come from that dispute. Although her attitude to us personally was unsympathetic, she did stick professionally to her field of expertise and did not evade the hostile reports attributed to her. She was also a very competent doctor.

Another doctor in Mt Isa called the police with the helpful information that I was a strange mother and the name Azaria meant 'sacrifice in the wilderness.'

This message was passed on to Inspector Gilroy in Alice Springs who checked it out, found it to be false, that it was the meaning of Azazeal which was the name underneath Azaria in the baby names book, so he took the matter no further. But the rumour did not rest there, it grew. The rumour that at six weeks of age Azaria had been taken to the hospital bashed and battered and dressed in black, spread like wildfire throughout the town.

One day Jenny asked me if I would mind picking up her young daughter from preschool. I agreed, so Jenny rang the preschool and notified them that a friend would be collecting her daughter. I went along and stood outside, waiting for the children to come out. The few mothers who were standing around when I got there seemed to know one another. The children were a bit late that day, so I walked around the corner into the sun, not really wanting to talk to anyone. I didn't want to explain who I was or answer questions about my own children just then.

Very soon I realised the six or seven mothers waiting there were talking about Azaria's death, and there were two points of view. One view was that I had done away with the kid because I didn't like it, the other was that it was definitely a dingo, or at the very most an accident. Maybe I just didn't get on with children and didn't like them.

The group went on to talk about the TV interview and one woman said,

'Well, I reckon she is hard. She didn't talk like a normal mother.' Another stood up for me quite forcibly and said she thought I was very brave—going on TV and fighting back at the rumours that were going around. After much to-ing and fro-ing of conversation, the same woman added that she probably would have done the same thing to try and protect her family from the things others were saying.

I was shaking and felt as if I was going to explode, and after hearing a little more I decided I had had enough. I walked around the corner and confronted them, saying, 'Excuse me, but that is my baby you are talking about,' then I walked away.

There was dead silence. When I got back around the corner, one of them said, 'Shit. Where did she come from? I didn't know there was anyone there.' There was an immediate 'ssh' and then in a quieter voice I heard someone say, 'She came early, she's just been leaning around the corner in the sun. She's been there all the time.' The voices dropped right down, then stopped. For the next five minutes while we waited for the children to arrive there was little or no conversation. It was rather obvious that they were all having their own thoughts and felt very badly about the way they had been discussing me.

When Jenny's little girl came bouncing out the door, I walked across to collect her and realised all the ladies were watching to see who I collected. I met her just as she reached the group of women and she said, 'Oh, Auntie Lindy! Goodie! Am I going home with you?' When I said 'Yes,' she said,

'Oh, good. I *like* coming with you,' and happily reached for my hand. I couldn't help thinking, out of the mouths of babes. There couldn't have been a better way of informing the group that I liked children and that they enjoyed being with me. No one could have done it better.

There was no mistaking that Azaria's disappearance was the topic of conversation right throughout the town. We were still not aware, however, of how much publicity it was creating down south. We had a lot of phone calls from the press but we didn't know, as 1980 drew to its end, that the case was making front-page news almost daily. In Mt Isa I could walk into a shop knowing the people there had seen only the initial TV news, the *Today Tonight* programs, and nothing about it since.

I could still stand next to people who were discussing us and hear everything they said, knowing they didn't recognise me. Most of the time I managed to hold my tongue, but occasionally the shopkeeper knew me and did his best to make the customer be quiet. Quite often he would say loudly,

'Can I help you, Mrs Chamberlain?' The conversation would then come to a dead stop. At other times people had no idea who I was and the conversation would just ebb and flow around me. That had been yet another good reason why I went on air and did that interview for *Today Tonight*.

A local retired chief inspector of police knew the local undercurrents better than we did though and told Michael that we really ought to be represented at the inquest. We didn't have any money for that and really we couldn't see why. Lawyers were only to represent you if you were guilty of something and this was simply to find out the method of our daughter's death, which we knew anyway. The inquest was just a rubber stamp. Constable Morris had said it would probably only take a couple of hours, maybe a day at the most, and it would be all over. We may have to stay in Alice Springs overnight, nothing more.

A Phone Call, 'Clark Kent' and a Goat

One day as we were working in our yard a woman rode in on a bicycle. She jumped off and stood glaring at Michael and I, then asked, 'Are you the parents of that kid that got taken by the dingo?'

It was rather a blunt introduction but we tried to hold our tongues and merely said, 'Yes.'

Then she started on a tale of woe about her daughter's disappearance, saying that she knew what we felt like because she had been through it all. Her thirteen year old had run away from home, been traced and returned. The woman was distraught and bitter. She couldn't understand how we could forgive people and why we weren't going insane. It became apparent that she was quite drunk.

She said, 'You didn't really have a kid, did you? That's just media talk.' We said, 'Yes, we had one.'

She said, 'Well, didn't you want her? I heard you dressed her in black, is that true?'

We said, 'We wanted her, and yes, that was true.'

She was looking very unsure and I asked, 'Would you like to see it? It's not sinister like they make it sound. It's a very ordinary little dress.'

She followed me up to the house and had a look at some of the baby's things hanging in the wardrobe, including the black dress, complete with red ribbon trimming, then she sat on Aidan's bed and cried.

'I can see now that you did like the kid after all,' she said, 'and I am really sorry that you lost 'er and all that. But I still can't see 'ow you can be so calm about it, 'cos you haven't got her any more. It can't be just 'cos of your religion.' I explained that God had given us the strength to go through with it and she could have that too, if only she would ask for it.

She looked wistfully at me. 'Oh, I don't think 'e comes to the likes of me. It's only ones like you 'e takes any notice of. I've gotta go.' She got up quickly and left as abruptly as she came. She left me feeling very sorry for her. She had no hope and nothing to cling to and was being eaten up by bitterness. It made me realise just how lucky we were.

Life went on, then one Sabbath I came home from church early to start preparing lunch, and heard the phone ringing as I walked up the stairs. It was *the* Malcolm Brown I'd had quoted to me so much. He asked me if I would like to make a comment on the 'zoo tests with the baby goat'? I answered, 'What zoo tests with what baby goat?' He thought that we, as parents, would have had to have been informed on things like that, and all the tests they were doing for the inquest. I told Malcolm that most of our information came from reporters rather than the police; otherwise we had no idea what was happening. I also told him his name kept coming up as the reporters' 'bible.' He seemed surprised at that.

Malcolm told me that Ken Brown, a forensic dentist, had conducted an experiment at the Adelaide Zoo, by dressing a decapitated goat kid in a jumpsuit and putting it in the dingo enclosure after they had been starved for several days. They wanted to see whether the dingo could extricate the kid without damaging the jumpsuit. The dingo apparently managed to take the body out without undoing more than two studs at the top of the suit; and had then buried the garment. Michael walked in halfway through Malcolm's account of this, and was able to pick up the connecting phone in the study, so we could both hear the facts. We then rang the police and asked for details. They confirmed what Malcolm had said, assuring us that the test was 'just routine'. They couldn't tell us when the inquest would take place, but said it was coming up shortly' and they would let us know when.

I had a good chat to Malcolm over the phone and I liked what I heard of him. The mental picture was a very businesslike, very together sort of gentleman. He said he'd keep us informed after that, and he did. Much to our amusement, when we later met him we found him to be very much the Clark Kent of the newspaper world, down to the glasses and the brown suit which he wore, and sometimes was known to sleep in! The brain was just as sharp as the Superman alter ego was, though.

ROI: RECORD OF INTERVIEW OR RECORD OF INTERROGATION?

The inquest was expected to take place within three or four weeks at the most, and somebody had to look after the boys. Aidan's life needed as little disruption as possible as he was in grade two at school and it did not seem fair to take him and Reagan back to Alice Springs. After the memorial service my parents agreed to stay with us (as Dad was retired), until we returned from Alice Springs after the inquest.

Things appeared static for a few weeks, then, after months of hearing nothing about his previous application, Michael received the news that he was to be sponsored for the new MA program at Avondale College, Cooranbong, which is near Newcastle, and was to be transferred from the North Queensland Conference (in charge of all Seventh-day Adventist churches in that region) to the Northern New South Wales Conference. We got in contact with their president. He told us that Michael was to have a church part time while he was studying and at the end of the twelve months when he graduated with his Master's degree he would then be placed full time in a church somewhere else in that conference. They gave us an approximate moving date, but they hadn't reckoned with the wet season in the north. If Funnell Creek flooded north of Rockhampton, we would be stuck for weeks. It was imperative that both us and our furniture left Mt Isa before the wet season started if we were to arrive in time for Michael's early December registration date. We gave them the latest date we dared to leave because of the wet, and they assured us that they would have a house ready for us by then.

Our move wasn't the only one to take place. For some reason, the preparation for the inquest was taken out of Inspector Gilroy's hands and given to Sergeant Graeme Charlwood. We later discovered that this had been done without Inspector Gilroy's knowledge or consent; he simply came back to his office one day to discover Detective Sergeant Charlwood at *his* desk looking through *his* papers. I still think it's most unusual for a subordinate to tell his superior that he is taking over. But that's the way it went.

A policeman who was there at the time told us that Gilroy was pushed out because he believed we were innocent. Inspector Gilroy was right, of course. He checked up the leads, found then incorrect, so let them die.

We were not told that Gilroy had been replaced until on 29 September there was a knock at our door. When I opened it there were two gentlemen who introduced and identified themselves as police. I invited them in saying, 'I haven't seen much of the Alice Springs cops; it's about time somebody did something useful.'

One of them said, 'Actually, I'm from Alice Springs.'

'Oops,' I laughed. 'Foot in mouth disease.'

He said they had come across to take our statements, and that he was now actually in charge of the case. I thought we had already given our statement to Inspector Gilroy who had said they would just type it up and we could sign it.

I told him I was surprised they wanted further statements as we had waited an extra half day in Alice Springs especially for them to get our statements and blood groupings done. He said they needed a few more details and apologised; they had had financial problems and had to wait for the OK and the money to come over.

I told him they were welcome to take the statement at our place but he wanted a typewriter. I offered our electric one but he said he wasn't a typist, and it was 'about one hundred words a minute faster than me'. He suggested it might be more private if we went down to the police station, as they had typists there, so I agreed. He also wanted to talk to both the boys and Michael. After several abortive attempts to talk to Reagan (who just looked at him and wouldn't even say his name or age) they gave up.

I heard Michael drive in shortly afterwards and suggested we should go down to Michael's office which was underneath the house.

By this time we were starting to pack up to go to Cooranbong. Michael's visual aids were mostly packed but one was sitting on the garage floor, where we had to step over it to get into Michael's office. It was a 1.4 metre (4 feet, 6 inches) wooden pauper's coffin.

Charlwood asked, 'What on earth's that?' I explained it was just a coffin Michael used for his anti-smoking five-day plan campaigns. He got people to throw their cigarettes, cigars and pipes into it before they ended up there themselves. It worked quite well. Charlwood said 'Oh,' and laughed and the coffin was not mentioned again at that stage.

I introduced both policemen to Michael and we discussed who would make their statement at the police station first. I was busy the next day and I also had the beginnings of migraine, so I hoped Michael would go first so I could re-organise my program and recover. They seemed quite insistent that they wanted me first, though, and I thought, oh well, if that's the way they want it, get it over and done with. We arranged for them to pick me up about one o'clock. They would ring Michael when they were ready for him, and Aidan could go after school so his routine wasn't altered.

Michael was surprised they wanted evidence from a six-year-old.

'Children are very observant,' explained Charlwood. 'They see things which, you know, we may miss out on. They're at an age where—particularly six—where they're taking in a fair bit of the world, even though they may not talk about it. Certainly we're not going to put him through any trauma.'

How you can put anyone through questions of a traumatic event they have just been through and not upset them, I don't know!

I offered to show them quite a few things before they left, including the mattress we had had in the tent and Azaria's carry basket, and I went through all the information I'd already given Inspector Gilroy.

After a discussion on the contents of Azaria's carry basket, Charlwood said, 'Mmmm, all right. We'll take this [the carry basket] and have a look at it, um, this afternoon. We might get you to bring some of the . . . the blankets, the equivalent of what you had, perhaps to reconstruct how the baby was and we can perhaps get a couple of photographs of just a reconstructed arrangement.'

They left after completing those arrangements, and Charlwood accidentally taped himself in a most enlightening conversation he had with the other policeman in the car (after they had just met us) where he referred to Michael as a 'fucking little weed'. Interestingly enough, Charlwood was a similar build to Michael. Years later when these tapes were subpoenaed I nearly got the stitch laughing.

That afternoon, at one, the police picked me up as arranged and I was taken down to the local Mt Isa police station.

When we arrived I was taken to a fairly bare grey room. It had an old desk, a battered manual typewriter, two chairs behind the desk, and a couple of kitchen-type chairs, one of which I sat on. The room was otherwise bare, with a small high window for light. A local man, Detective Sergeant Morris, was to do the typing, and young Detective Constable Scott was there as a witness.

Charlwood asked me to tell him everything once so he could familiarise himself with the details and then we would do it again and type it up as we went. I went right through the story of that terrible night in excessive detail; I even drew diagrams and explained just where everybody was in the tent. But, although he had said that the more detail I put in the statement the better, I couldn't really understand why I had to list all the children's clothes, right down to descriptions of their bathers, and where we had been from the time we left Mt Isa until the night of the 17th. It really didn't seem to be relevant to me, but if that's what the man wanted, I guessed I could handle it.

Charlwood was on the other side of the desk and fiddling around. I noticed him open a drawer but thought nothing of it, just continued to answer his questions. Sometimes he took notes, sometimes not.

It wasn't until nearly twelve months later that I learned he had been secretly taping me, hoping to use the tape to contradict my record of interview. There was no reason why he could not have taped the whole thing and told me so.

Finally Charlwood decided it was time to start typing, and he said again that the more detail I put in that statement, the more it would help them, so into detail we went—over the various places we had been and what we did.

I started off again explaining when we arrived at the Rock, where I'd seen the dingo at the Fertility Cave, Michael and the boys climbing the rock, viewing the sunset, the whole thing. Charlwood was very particular about times, for some reason. He didn't seem to be using the information from his familiarisation session to base any of his questions on, and he asked some very obvious questions.

'What then was the baby wearing when it was taken from the tent?'

'Um, I already explained to you before,' I said. 'The . . . the bootees, the stretch jumpsuit, the singlet, the throw-away nappy and the matinee jacket.'

'The matinee jacket,' he repeated thoughtfully.

‘They’ve got them all back except that matinee jacket,’ I said, ‘and that, um, it wasn’t a tight one, it had elastic around the wrists and the buttons were loosish. In fact, I know that if she wriggled a bit in bed they would undo themselves. So there is as much chance of it being off on a bush on the way from the Rock somewhere as there would be of it being down a den, and left away from the other clothes, I should think.’

When I later heard the tape played back in the courtroom I noticed certain controversial segments of conversation were not on it. One occurred halfway through the record of interview. While he was fiddling around with the drawer Charlwood asked me what I thought of hypnotism. The other police present had gone out for a break; I told him I didn’t believe in hypnotism because it meant giving your mind over to someone else and it was possible to tell you, while in that state, to say or do anything they want you to whether you believed it or not. I asked him whether he was aware of the story of Saul when he went for advice to the witch and the familiar spirits, and how the Bible said it was displeasing to God to give your life or mind into the control of others.

We ran out of time and it was decided to break the interview overnight and I would return the next day. I told them that because of some information they had given me, and because Michael had not yet been interviewed, I would not discuss it with him overnight.

When I arrived home Mum had the boys fed, bathed and organised and I was in time to kiss them goodnight and no more.

It had been arranged that Aidan would be picked up from school the next day by Michael and they would come in for simultaneous interviews. The police wanted to check our car, so they could have a look at it while they were there also; this was ‘just a formality’.

Once again the police came to pick me up on my second day, I October. Before we left they once again attempted to interview Reagan. (They seemed reluctant to mention that episode in court later.)

Reagan was talkative, and proceeded to tell them his name and age. He went over the trip a little for them, his most vivid memory being made to bath in a square bath in the ladies’ toilets—that would be what he chose to remember! When Charlwood asked him details of the sleeping arrangements in the tent he quit answering questions for a stranger. Asked what colour his sleeping bag was he said correctly ‘red’—and then proceeded to say ‘red’ as the answer to every question from then on. Smart child! He was right though in a way; the Rock and the blood were all red. Charlwood gave up. We left and went down to the police station to begin again.

Right near the end of my interview some questions were thrown in about forensic reports that had come through. Charlwood went on to tell me some of the test results. He showed me only summaries of the scientific reports, which he said were all he had at that stage. There were results of saliva and hair tests and some confusing details on blood.

I was asked whether any of the family had sustained any cuts, scratches or injuries while we were at the Rock. None of us had. I was told that blood and small pieces of bone had been found near the Fertility Cave at Maggie Springs, an area we had visited on the afternoon of 17 August. I was told that the blood not only was the same group as mine, but they inferred it *was* mine; I found that fantastic. I was told this was where the clothes were found and where I had seen the dingo earlier. Was I going crazy? They were all looking at me as if I was lying and I knew I was not. I *knew* I had seen that dingo. All of us at the tent site that night knew that there was no way that any person could have gone into that tent. The police attitude seemed really strange to me.

Charlwood stopped the interview and talked to me for a while. 'You realise that these tests mean it is not a dingo at all, but it was murder?'

Detective Sergeant Morris joined in. Without saying it outright, they almost seemed to be hinting that *I* might have done it. I thought, this is just not realistic. The only thing that came into my mind was that somebody had tried to set us up. But this wasn't feasible; this didn't happen except in novels, not in real life! But here it was, happening to me. I dismissed that idea as preposterous and thought no more along those lines as I felt I *must* have misunderstood them.

Now, I knew it was *not* murder, and I knew it *was* a dingo. I really couldn't see how they could be stupid enough to consider murder as a possibility, but I presumed they probably had to cover all possibilities. They seemed to think that maybe somebody had found the clothes later, or even found Azaria that night and removed the clothes and put them somewhere else. What could possibly be a motive for that was a puzzle to me, but it was a thought.

I commented in question 141 of my official record of interview,

'Obviously the space blanket with all the cuts down the end are going to be very interesting when it's done. The pad marks on the blanket were very distinctive and a number of people saw them before it was given to the police.'

Charlwood asked, 'Who were the people that saw the pad marks?'

'I think we all examined it initially before the police got it,' I answered. 'But the ones were my mother, who drew my attention to it, my sister-in- law and myself. My husband, father and brother all saw it, also my mother- in-law.' (I was really keen to see the results from that blanket which Charlwood told me was still in Adelaide being tested. I didn't find out until much later that it was actually still in the Mt Isa police station while I was there doing my interview.)

The subject was dropped and they left me to read through my record of interview and then they came back. Off the record they had asked me if there was anyone I could possibly think of who might have been able to get to our tent that night without being seen. I knew from personal experience that sound in the desert can travel at least 8 kilometres (5 miles) on a clear night. On 17 August, despite the fact that the camping area was crowded, sound still carried. It was impossible for anyone to walk around in that area without being heard. We were all relaxed and there was nothing much to do; in those circumstances, you tend to take notice more than ever of where people go and what they are doing. The Wests' tent was only half a dozen yards away from ours, they could not have gone to our tent without being either seen or heard, yet they were the only people who could possibly have got across, but *that* thought was ridiculous. Yet I remembered him (Bill West) coming quite a bit later from who knows where saying. 'What happened?' and 'Is it really true?' Maybe their tent *was* close enough to use the fence line as cover and crawl along to ours, so to include all possibilities, I mentioned it, but told them it was not a logical conclusion and I did not believe those people were involved. (I discovered twelve months later when we went out to Ayers Rock again that the police had dug up a large area looking for a body and the whole of the Wests' tent site had been dug up as well as ours. The road, the barbecue site, the hillside nearby and the place we had stopped to refuel on our return to the Alice had all been dug up to see if there was any possible way to fit their theory that the baby had been murdered.)

They also asked whether I knew anyone who might hold a grudge against us for any reason.

Michael and Aidan arrived about 3. 30, parked the car around the back at the police station and came inside. They had to wait for a while because I was still reading my lengthy statement, which had to be signed and a few formalities completed, until all that happened there were no police available to deal with them. While they were waiting, Senior Constable Graham was supposedly searching the car for evidence. We were informed later that he used a Big Jim torch to provide extra clarity. He was looking for blood, and if I'd known that, I would probably have been more puzzled than I already was. I didn't know at that time that a police theory was that I had murdered Azaria in the car and put the folded clothes nearly 4 kilometres (2.5 miles) away from our campsite.

It was almost sunset by the time Michael and Aidan started. When I added all the segments of my interviews up later, I had been with the police for a total of thirteen hours. Michael went away with two of the police while the younger Detective Constable Scott and I went to another room with Aidan to give his statement. Another policeman was in the room when we got there trying to look as unobtrusive as possible, probably so Aidan would not be so shy and would talk freely. Well, he did and was quite chatty. Scott started the interview by telling him what he wanted to know and Aidan complied. The only time he stopped was when he couldn't remember whether Reagan had gone to sleep before or after his tea. He asked me what I thought, and then made up his own mind without waiting for an answer, and continued to chat.

At every stage of where we had gone that day Detective Scott would stop him and query, 'And who was in the car then?' Aidan would say, 'There was Mummy and Daddy and Reagan and bubby and me.' Each time this process was repeated, you could see Aidan getting more and more puzzled and impatient as he went through the cast of characters again. Finally he said to Detective Constable Scott, 'Can't you remember? I have already told you lots of times. You better listen this time. There was Mummy and Daddy and Reagan and bubby and me!' Whereupon Scott looked at me with a grin and said, 'Guess I'd better not ask him that any more.'

After a few more questions Aidan announced, 'I can't talk any more, my throat's dry and besides, I've got to go to the toilet.' Whereupon he hopped up, went out the door and up the hall. Scott looked surprised, then laughed and said, 'Mmm. I've got one like that at home too, only it's female. Does he know where the toilet is?'

I said to him, 'Well, I don't know. He was waiting out there with his father for a while, but I shouldn't think so.'

He said, 'Mmm,' again, then grinned. 'I guess I better go and tell him where it is.' He followed Aidan and pointed out where the toilet was and made sure Aidan knew his way back. He also promised Aidan a drink that he could choose himself, then he returned. His whole attitude was relaxed and friendly, contrasting with Charlwood's non-committal professional style.

When Aidan came back Scott asked him if he would like a Coke.

'Don't drink Coke.' It was no good offering him tea or coffee either; what about orange juice? He finally settled for a Fanta but informed Scott he couldn't possibly talk any more until his drink came. Fanta seemed to be the only thing they were out of, so Senior Constable Graham went across the street to the shop for it. Aidan wandered around the room and had a look at various things until it arrived. He had his drink then said, 'All right. I can talk now.' So they continued.

Sergeant Graham looked as if he didn't think he was needed any more as we were nearly finished, I asked whether we could go home in our car; I was to take Aidan home and the police would bring Michael when he was finished. Dusk had settled into night already. Aidan was getting tired and hungry and Reagan would be wondering where we were. Scott turned to Senior Constable Graham and asked if he knew what was happening about the car. He answered that it was fine, finished with and ready for me to take. But he just had to check with the others.

A compilation of what Aidan said had been typed up by Detective Scott. I had checked it over to make sure he hadn't put words into Aidan's mouth, and then this statement was given to Aidan to sign.

Aidan was very good in his interview (although he was described on one of the tapes as being 'weird' too). This is his summary of what happened:

> Daddy went to the barbecue and got some tea. There was a man, a lady and a little girl there too. Me and Reagan were watching. Daddy cooking tea and Mummy was there holding bubby in her arms. I think Reagan had some tea and then he went to bed in the tent. I think Mummy took him to bed. After I finished my tea I said that I wanted to go to bed and Mummy said she would take me and bubby up to bed. I went up to the tent with Mummy and bubby and I said to Mummy is that all the tea that I get? Mummy said I could have some more tea. While we were in the tent Mummy put bubby down in the cot and then I went to the car with Mummy and she got some baked beans and I followed her down to the barbecue area. When we got to the barbecue area Mummy opened the tin of baked beans and Daddy said is that bubby crying and Mummy said I don't think so. Mummy went back to the tent and said the dingo has got my baby.
>
> Mummy shouted has anybody got a torch. And Daddy went around and asked if anybody has got a torch. When Mummy saw the dingo come out of the tent I was behind her but I didn't see the dingo come out of the tent. I went back to the barbecue and got Daddy's torch and I gave it to

Mummy or Daddy. After I gave them the torch I stayed with a lady and then I went to bed.

Before I went to bed there was *[sic]* lots of people there searching. I went to bed at the motel. I went to the motel in a police car with Mummy, Reagan, me and a policeman. Reagan was asleep on Mummy's lap. When we got to the motel Reagan woke up and then he went to sleep.

When I was standing with the lady near the tent Reagan was asleep all the time.

While I was at the tent I was in my bed but I didn't go to sleep. Bubby's blankets were spreaded *[sic]* over the tent and I saw some blood on them. I saw some blood on a sleeping bag, I think it was on Mummy's. I saw that the tent post at the front of the tent was knocked over away from the thing that it sits in, Mummy told me not to touch it. I saw some blood on Reagan's parka on the sleeve. There was some blood on the wrist band of my parka. There was no blood on my parka before that night.

What has stuck in Aidan's mind to this day is the angle of the tent pole. It was very tightly fitted into a little cup on the floor of the tent and had been knocked nearly 15 centimetres (6 inches) right out of that cup. Later when forensic tests were done, a blood splash was discovered on one of those poles. Aidan had tried to straighten the pole alone but, at nearly seven, it was so tight that his strength alone had been inadequate so he asked for assistance. It must have taken a really hard whack to push it out like that. I had told him he must leave it like that until the police had a look, and he had. I hadn't thought of it again until his interview.

Charlwood was right about the surprising things kids would remember. It was a shock to realise he'd seen blood on Reagan's parka that night. He hadn't mentioned it, and we hadn't shown it to him when we found it at home.

Well, almost seven Aidan may have been, but he insisted on reading every last word of his statement himself, to check it was right. Senior Constable Graham was away no more than five minutes when he returned, saying the car was fine and ready to go when I was. Aidan was happy with his statement, so he signed and we were ready to leave. We followed another policeman through the police station and out the back to a very well lit area that had a big indoor parking bay with large fluorescent lights. The cells were along one side of the parking bay, and our car was parked near them. We hopped aboard and drove home. When we asked about the car later, Charlwood told us it was clean. Not until much later was I to realise the significance of what I had witnessed, as all mention of the car being checked was quietly put into the background for many years.

On 3 October 1980, I complained to Sergeant Charlwood that the press were releasing information that had been read to me during my interview the day before. Unknown to me at that stage, our conversation was being taped by the police and went as follows:

I said, 'I had an Adelaide radio call me up. They said it was on one of the radio stations and also in one of the Adelaide papers that the evidence on the clothes and—

er—the piece, he didn't read it all to me but the piece about there being no saliva and the rip being caused by something else other than a dingo, was almost word for word from that report.'

'Yeah,' said Charlwood.

'So it's out,' I said.

'Yeah. And—urn—did you or your husband give that information to the media?'

'No. No way,' I said. 'We didn't speak to them at all, but they were on to us and told us what was in it, well there had been several on to us and on to Michael while I was talking to you . . .'

'Yeah,' Charlwood broke in. 'I'm certainly as perplexed as you are. I, as I said, I haven't heard the TV or radio, but have heard rumours as to what is in the southern and eastern papers and what has been in radio and television. And, you know, I'm as perplexed as to where it came from. It's just . . .'

'Well, I know where it came from,' I broke in. 'I'm not sure—one . . .' I was thinking aloud, then continued. 'I definitely know the name of a policeman in Brisbane that it came from. I know that his source was a forensic mate in Adelaide.'

'Do you know the name of this chap down there?' asked Charlwood.

'Oh what, the one in Adelaide?'

'Hmm.'

'Or the one in Brisbane?'

'Well, both,' he asked.

I know the name of the one in Brisbane, but I promised that I would not reveal his name even under oath,' I said.

'Hmm.'

I continued, 'It was a reporter that told me and oh, you are well aware that there is corruption here and there in the police force and the particular gentleman, um, I was told by two different sources who it was and he is high up in the Brisbane police force. He is a constant source of information to the press. He is well respected—ah—he is usually correct and obviously they don't want to close the doors on their information and of course if one of them lets it out, even if he does want to, the rest of the reporters will turn on him.'

'Yeah,' he agreed.

(The policeman I meant was later named in the Fitzgerald Inquiry, a Queensland-based commission of inquiry into police corruption.)

'The other thing is a number of newspapers carried . . . that the clothing was found neatly folded. Inspector Gilroy seemed to indicate that it had been in a . . . a . . . well like I mentioned it to you, he said it had rained the night before at the Rock. It was muddy and in a heap and he had told them to pick it up with a stick and put it in a plastic bag, now you said there was no rain so I was just wondering was it folded or was it in a heap?' I queried.

'Yeah, I wasn't there when it was found, um,' Charlwood said.

'You probably heard how it was found though or something,' I asked hopefully.

'Well, everyone's got an idea of, and my idea of neatly folded probably certainly not the way a woman's is. Um, I wouldn't describe it as neatly folded.' *[sic]*

The discussion continued with me asking how information could be so correct from those summarised reports, supposedly secret, and yet be known by the press, and their sources. With wider experience later, we were to watch how some people were able to get others to do things for them and still appear in the clear, and how people could tell only part of the truth, such as, 'I wasn't there at the time.'

We began to wonder if the local police inspector had known more than he'd told us. We were leaving to go back to Innisfail for the Johnson Jog (a 13 kilometre [8 mile] road race that Michael and I had run in before). I was not fit enough to run that far yet but Michael was and he was taking some of the Mt Isa Good Life team members to run with the Innisfail Good Life team. My Mum and Dad would come too. The visit with all our old friends would do us good, and after living there for three years, it still felt more like home than Mt Isa did.

We finally decided to take legal advice, because we thought the police seemed to be acting strangely. We were fairly new in Mt Isa and with nasty rumours and bad feeling now spreading, we thought we should find somebody outside Mt Isa who we knew we could trust. So we booked an appointment with a lawyer in Innisfail whom Michael knew fairly well.

The day of the jog we were up early to drop Michael at the start line. I waited halfway down the course to see Michael pass, then went to the finishing line at the local racecourse in time to see the winner arrive. The spectator stands were crowded, with many people (mainly runners' wives and families) standing near the finish as well. I joined them.

If you were in the stands you could see the runners for their last full 1. 6 kilometres (1 mile) as they ran around the track. The local radio commentator was broadcasting live and it was going over the loudspeaker as well. The first place runner was given a cheer and a clap as he arrived.

A number of other runners arrived and then the announcer gave the number of the next runner, went to look it up, then exclaimed excitedly that it was Michael Chamberlain. He explained that Michael was a previous winner who had come back with a full team from Mt Isa to run.

Michael had been a well-known local and the announcer expressed the town's support. Michael was well up the front of the field and when he arrived near the finishing line he received more applause than the winner. I felt thrilled for him and then I realised the spectator stands were giving him a standing ovation, which really gave me a lump in my throat.

We later learned that the announcer was one with whom Michael had worked on radio in Scottsdale, Tasmania, years before.

We really enjoyed our time. It gave us a good break from the press and harassing publicity in Mt Isa and we enjoyed the company of close friends and acquaintances.

Later we went to our legal appointment and explained the situation we were in and what the retired policeman had told us about legal representation at the inquest. The lawyer advised us to simply answer any questions the Crown had and a separate lawyer would not be necessary. He said if we went into the inquest with legal representation, it could look as if we had something to hide. If we went alone, like lambs led to the slaughter in the way that normal country folk do, we would be fine. So we relaxed again.

We were still looking for actual evidence of dingo attacks because we had been told our experience was unique. The lawyer told us that a client of his had just sued a touring circus because her small daughter had been attacked by a dingo in Babinda, far north Queensland. The animal was a female with pups, and was chained up in an area where people could go and view the animals. The small child had wandered too close and the dingo had managed (by stretching to the end of her chain) to bite the girl on the bottom and hold on. There had been a tug-of war between the aunt who was with the little girl and the dingo who was determined to pull the girl closer and not let her go.

The child's clothes had been ripped in straight lines due to the tugging as if they had been cut with a knife. They had very little blood on them. The child's body, on the other hand, had deep puncture wounds. The parents received quite a reasonable out of-court settlement from the circus and they offered her clothes for police research because it was different from domestic dog damage.

We interviewed the woman, and took some photographs of the child's injuries. When we returned home to Mt Isa we rang the Alice Springs police, telling them this material was available and where to get it. They thanked us, but said they had enough material, and told us it would not be needed, so we supposed they had found material from elsewhere. Little did we know at that stage that they had none.

The Misconception Grows and We Hear Our First Evidence

The Wests had no idea about any of the aftermath publicity. They were farmers in Western Australia, and saw the papers about once a week—mainly local papers at that. When the police called to take a statement about the night at Ayers Rock, Judy West was puzzled; why on earth did they want to know how Azaria was treated and what she had been wearing? For some obscure reason this seemed important to the police.

It troubled Judy so much she tried to phone us but couldn't get through as we were still in Innisfail, so wrote instead. When we returned from Innisfail the letter was waiting so we rang the phone number they had given.

This was the first direct contact we had had with any witnesses. When Judy questioned us, we told her about the newspaper reports and rumours. Bill and Judy were aghast; they had known nothing about that. After the phone call, they went into town to look at the newspapers and discovered the headlines. Judy was absolutely devastated. As a result, she called in to the local police station and said she wished to add to her statement. She had suddenly realised why they asked her such apparently stupid questions; it was because they thought Azaria had been neglected and mistreated.

Judy West wrote to us again on 31 October 1980:

> We had never spoken to anyone [the police or the media] about the night of Azaria's death since it had always seemed so totally and irrevocably

true that she was taken by a dingo and the possibility that it could be questioned—however remotely—simply didn't arise. Anything we could have contributed would have been unnecessary. However, after hearing the latest news and reading the *Woman's Day*, I realised how appalling gossip and innuendo can be, so I am writing to say that if there is anything we can do or say to help we will do so with all our heart.

And perhaps telling you why we were so utterly convinced that the dingo had taken the baby will help. Being camped within feet of your tent and with the night so still and clear meant that Bill, Catherine and I were aware of what was happening maybe more than most people around.

First I must say that both Bill and I heard the dingo growl. We've had a Labrador dog at home who gives the same kind of growl and we both heard it (and noted it for the same reason) without commenting at the time. I don't remember hearing the baby crying—I guess because it would be a sort of ordinary sound that I wouldn't bother to register.

The next thing I was aware of was you, Lindy, crying something like, 'O God, the dingo's got my baby.' And I simply couldn't believe my ears—in fact the whole idea seemed so completely incredible that we were stunned. Almost literally. And then everyone started moving with torches. Bill moved the car to shine the lights into the sandhills, and then he and Catherine drove down to tell the police.

Never for a second, at the time, or since, had it crossed the minds of Bill, Catherine or myself that there was any question that the baby had not been taken by a dingo.

The night before all this happened Catherine (who is twelve) was sitting outside the tent writing up her diary, about 6 o'clock when a dingo came up, and after sniffing around took her elbow in its teeth and started to worry it. She was quite scared when I came out and shooed it away. I was pretty diffident about shooing it off as I knew they were wild. . . . but the dingoes at Ayers Rock were a most peculiar acting dog and people who have never seen them in action would find it hard to believe that they could be accustomed to humans and still retain all their savage instincts.

Dear Lindy and Michael, Azaria was truly named 'Blessed of God'. She was blessed in having you for parents.

Saying Goodbye to the Old and Hello to the New

Not long before we were due to leave for Avondale College for Michael's ma, my hospital acquaintance, whose baby had been born just after Azaria, came to say goodbye. She had offered to get a babysitter and come alone, but I said, 'No, bring your baby too; I have to get used to seeing other mothers with their babies. It won't get any better as time goes on, and it's better for me to face that now.' So she brought her little girl with her; she was about five months old at the time. She was really taking notice of things, smiling and playing and kicking about. She was the same build as Azaria had been, and seeing her brought everything back again. I finally managed the courage to pick her up and hold her. My heart bled silently as we talked and I played with that sweet little girl.

We continued packing slowly, and the week before we were to move to Cooranbong, the North New South Wales Conference president said they were having difficulty finding a house and it would be better if we could find our own. The inquest was due to take place just after we arrived at college and we had to have somewhere to leave Aidan, Reagan and my parents, who would care for them while we were away. Also, of course, we needed somewhere to at least store our furniture. If they couldn't find us a house when they were locals, how were we going to?

We knew Dr Eric Magnusson, then president of Avondale College, and I decided to ring him up. I phoned and explained the problem. He said to me, 'Look, Lindy, what is the latest that I can get some information to you before you have to start down?' Our trip down would take us nearly a week pulling the trailer and following the van through, so I named a day. He said he would get some sort of information to us regarding housing before we left and not to worry. That was one man I knew would do exactly what he said, so I said, 'Lord, help him to find a house,' and promptly stopped worrying. We kept packing and finalised everything. The truck was actually being loaded when the phone call from Dr Magnusson came through. He said they had found a house for us but it was not yet vacant. They could store the furniture at college and give us one or two college married students' units to move into until our house was vacant. If anything better became available, he would let us know when we arrived.

When you move around continually the only home you have is what you create around you. You have to put up with the colour scheme, the size and shape of the house and yard, so your 'home' is your furniture, your ornaments and pot plants. I took about eighty potted plants with me in the trailer, covered with plastic (I still have one I brought over from Tasmania with me). Michael mumbled about what would happen at the border but when I declared them they simply squirted them with something, gave us a sticker for the next checkpoint and sent us on our way.

I didn't expect people to recognise us. Admittedly our pictures had been in the paper, but it had been a few months ago and we thought things had died down. Still, we were taking some precautions like not using the children's names where we could be heard because they were so unusual it would be a dead giveaway.

We stopped at a roadside stall to buy some fruit. The others were on their way back to the car with our purchases, when the gentleman, handing me back my change, said, 'There you are, Mrs Chamberlain. Have a good trip, and all the best to you.' I managed to say, 'Thank you,' dumbfounded that he had known my name. He hadn't *asked* me, he just *said* it matter-of-factly, as if there was absolutely no question. That was something I was to get used to over the next few years.

When we arrived at Avondale College we saw our furniture truck had just beaten us and was starting to unload at a house in College Drive. We thought we ought to call at the office first anyway, as we had been instructed. Dr Magnusson welcomed us and told us that the young man who was going to be moving into that house was still living in the married students' quarters. He was happy to stay where he was for a while so we could use the house until ours became available. The house internally was much bigger than it looked, and when the young guy saw we had a family *and* carpets, he suggested we swap houses. As the house we were to rent was carpeted, semi-furnished and too small we agreed. They had no furniture and their family was still on the way so they were delighted, and we heaved a sigh of relief to be settled. We were very happy there.

When talking to Dr Magnusson, he enquired if we had been in contact with our lawyers yet.

We said no, as we weren't going to get a lawyer. We had checked our legal advice with the Division (our Australian church headquarters), who'd asked Victorian lawyer Lloyd McMahon's advice. Everyone thought it wasn't necessary, but we weren't *really* happy about it all the same. Dr Magnusson looked at us strangely, and said, 'I beg your pardon, did you say that their advice was that it was all right to go without a lawyer?' We nodded. 'Well,' he said, 'I hate to argue with them, but Lloyd McMahon happens to be a close friend of mine and when I asked him the same question that is *not* what he told me. Do you mind me ringing him and asking in your presence what his advice to the Division was?' We readily agreed. He rang and explained we were with him and that we were still without a lawyer. Was that really his advice? Lloyd McMahon was aghast. He told the Division that we *did* need a lawyer. It wasn't his field, though. This was a few days before the inquest was to start! Dr Magnusson then rang someone in the Division and said, 'Look, I am very concerned. I have the Chamberlains sitting here. They indicate to me that you have told them they don't need a lawyer. I have just talked to Lloyd McMahon . . . he tells me there are crossed wires somewhere . . . This matter is larger than the Chamberlains. The church is involved, and I think that we ought to get a lawyer and help them with the financial aspects . . .' Whoever it was obviously did a double take.

Dr Magnusson said, 'Lloyd's there now. This is his number. Ring him . . . I'm in my office, I'll be waiting for your call.' He received a call back not five minutes later.

Dr Magnusson was right, and now they didn't know what to do. He took matters in his own hands and said, 'Thank you very much. I knew you would think that way, and I know the church can arrange it and have a lawyer there for them when they go on Sunday.' Meanwhile, we had gone to the trouble of having a lawyer put on standby, just in case we needed one. We had simply asked Pastor Cozens to find us the most honest lawyer in Alice Springs, and after making enquires, he gave us the name of Peter Dean.

So the Division rang Peter Dean and formally engaged him. We met him for the first time just after we arrived in Alice Springs on the Sunday afternoon before we went into court on Monday morning. Irene Heron knew us both well from our stay in Bowen and volunteered to go to Alice Springs to act as a mum and friend during the time we were at the inquest. Having no children of her own, she had 'adopted' both of us as if we were hers: because Michael's parents were in New Zealand and mine were looking after the boys, Irene thought that the moral support might be appreciated. We were happy to accept her offer, so she came.

Irene was coming from Maryborough and it took her all day to get to the Alice and we were glad to see her when she arrived. She was able to stay with Pastor and Mrs Cozens so she had no excess costs and a ride to court every day with them as well.

Irene regularly carried an umbrella with her for the sun. Because of this and her lovely manners, she gained the reputation of being a *real* lady.

AN INQUEST FOR THE HISTORY BOOKS

When the inquest finally began on 15 December at the Alice Springs courthouse, we thought we were as well prepared as we could reasonably be. We had a lawyer; we knew what had happened; we had gathered a reasonable amount of information about the habits of dingoes. We knew nothing to suggest that the inquest would be anything other than a rubber stamp.

When we arrived at court we were met and told they had saved us a couple of seats near the front as the courtroom was packed out. I was initially to wait up the back until called because I would be the first witness. I sat down at the back near the door and was amazed to note that the jury box was full of media representatives. It seemed extremely appropriate in view of the fact that we were already being tried and found wanting by a curious and unrelenting press.

The coroner was an earnest gentleman named Dennis Barritt, a local magistrate; the counsel assisting the coroner was Ashley Macknay, and Michael O' Loughlan was the solicitor assisting him. We had Peter Dean.

And the press, of course. We were besieged by television reporters and print journalists all through the inquest and—as it wasn't over nearly as quickly as we had anticipated, continuing through the Christmas recess and not finishing until February—we had ample opportunity to get to know them.

Peter Dean did make a comment about the appropriateness of using the jury box for the media which caused a laugh, but was duly noted as our objection. Because of the lack of seating, however, those seating arrangements continued to be allowed, the coroner stressing that no relevance should be attached to the placement of the press.

Ashley Macknay proceeded with the initial summary of this case. As we sat in court, we were amazed at the amount of evidence that had been acquired about what seemed to us to be a perfectly straightforward, though horrific incident. Mr Macknay said that scientific evidence suggested that Azaria had lost at least twenty per cent of her normal blood volume. Well, she was very small—but seeing that the police hadn't wanted all the evidence of blood we had, how could they be so sure of the percentage? There was also a lot of material in reports about hairs, blood, and about various kinds of stains. All this was the forensic case:

> Firstly, the deceased was removed from her clothing by a person rather than by a dog or a dingo. Secondly, the damage to the clothing was more consistent with having been caused by a person rather than a dingo. Thirdly, the state of the clothes suggests that the clothes were put in the

> place in which they were found by a person, rather than being dragged there by a dog or dingo.

Barritt wanted to make clear that he had jurisdiction to hear the case. What he said was: 'I agree that because of the nature of the damage to the clothing and the manner in which the clothing was found, it would indicate that there has, at some stage, been human intervention in the disposal of the body, and that the body cannot now be found. I find that the body is in a place from which it presently cannot be recovered. On those grounds I find that I have jurisdiction.'

Person or persons unknown? A human agency? Rubbish! Those remarks of Barritt's, however, caused no end of trouble because, though no evidence had been given by anyone, they implied that he believed somebody had taken Azaria and possibly killed her.

After that day's proceedings, the coroner mentioned that the press had inferred a suggestion that Azaria had been murdered in the tent, or taken from the tent by human hands. 'This is not my understanding of what was said yesterday,' said Mr Barritt, and Mr Macknay agreed; he said it had not been supported by any evidence. Although the court complained about the misreporting, I think everyone listening thought the same thing initially.

I was the first witness called and, for the fourth time at least, I officially went through the events of the night on which Azaria had disappeared. It wasn't any easier. Every time I spoke about it, I could see the scene again, reliving that ghastly moment when Azaria was supposed to be in the tent and wasn't. Sometimes I found it difficult to speak as sobs just kept closing my throat.

Bill Barnes was the court orderly, a dapper little gentleman close to retiring age. He was responsible for swearing in the witnesses, and looking after all the exhibits. He wrote to me later:

> One of your rare breaks—and everyone signalling for me to get you a glass of water. God—I thought—why does everyone think a mouthful of water cures heartbreak and distress. I got it, and gave it to you but I wanted to touch you—to help you—to say something—but that microphone was right there in front—and after my many years behind one I shied off. Gee, I felt frustrated—and sad.
>
> I remember Ashley Macknay calling for exhibits which I couldn't find—my embarrassment for I was proud of the way I could put my hands on whatever was required. Ashley smirked 'as the orderly was having trouble finding his exhibits'—he'd move to something else. I thought long and hard and asked Lesley, a staff member, to bring me the Exhibits Book. There it showed the exhibits in question had been signed out to Crown Prosecution, signed by—A Macknay. The exhibits were, in fact, in Adelaide for tests!! Dinny [Dennis Barritt] amused—I relieved.

Once the exhibits required had been located, the court continued. We started discussing the baby blankets that Constable Morris had picked up from the motel room the morning after Azaria was attacked. They were the ones we had seen rips and spots of blood on.

Macknay asked, 'See if you can find the rips for me?'

I obliged, '"That's one, and that's another one, there's another one there. One of these two was in it previously. I think from memory that it may have been this one; I am not sure. There was also a rather large three- cornered tear in it. I don't know whether that has been cut out of this hole.'

'That hole was not in it at the time when you gave it to the police?' he questioned.

'No,' I answered. 'I presume that the forensic department has done that.' He asked further, '. . . in respect of those marks, are you able to say with certainty that those marks were not on the blanket beforehand?'

'There was one very small mark that I just indicated that had been made by moths. The larger of the two blankets had only been dry-cleaned once. It had never been washed. It was relatively new and there were no other marks on it. Actually they look a little to me as if they have been washed and shrunk since I gave them to the police,' I answered.

That was the first of many items I was shown in the box to identify and received a shock over their condition.

I had been in the box some time when Mr Macknay said, 'If I can refer you to a report which I have already mentioned to you, I think, by a forensic dentist. If you were told that the forensic dentist had examined the jumpsuit and the singlet and had found, firstly, that none of the damage to that clothing was consistent with having been caused by a dog or dingo, what would you say about that?'

I answered, 'If you are referring to the shapes of the rips and the absence of saliva, he is an expert and I am not but I note that at the time these tests were done they were looked at from the angle of what would be expected to be found by a domestic dog. I have not been specifically told but my observation seems to be that any tests done on dingoes have been ones in zoos, or semi-domesticated and no tests have actually been done on wild dingoes from what I can gather. In talking to old doggers, as I mentioned, I have discovered that they all agree that dingoes have a very dry mouth with very little saliva and that marks left by them are completely different to those left by domestic or domesticated animals. I have also seen clothing of a little girl who was attacked by a semi-domesticated dingo—had her clothes ripped—and there is no doubt in my mind that ripping by dingoes, even semi-domesticated ones, is distinctive compared—I was going to say ordinary dogs—with domestic dogs. It raises questions in my mind as to just perhaps how much we know about dingoes, rather than the evidence found, because it is something which has not necessarily been dealt with or investigated before. To comment on that at this stage without reading any of the reports on a lot of these other tests that they have done, I would not like to do so.'

'Let us just hypothesise for a moment,' said Mr Macknay, 'that the forensic dentist in examining the clothing was able to determine the difference between a cut and a tooth mark. We hypothesise that and we also hypothesise that some of the damage on the clothing—for instance, the collar and the sleeve of the jumpsuit—was consistent with having been cut rather than being torn by a dingo or dog. Do you understand what I am suggesting to you?'

'Yes,' I answered.

He continued, 'If we also hypothesise that the forensic dentist who examined the blankets which you have identified determined that the damage to the blankets was a cut rather than damage caused by teeth, what have you got to say about that?'

'I have simply got to say that we are hypothesising and that's all,' I stated.

'So if the forensic dentist says that the damage to the blankets, which were in your custody up until the time that you gave them to the police and which were undamaged on your evidence prior to your seeing the dingo, had in fact been caused by cutting you would not have any explanation for that at all?' Mr Macknay queried.

'No, I would wonder if he determined that—I would like to know what he determined did it,' I said.

Mr Macknay continued his questions. 'Apart from being unable to explain those cuts, if they were cuts in the blanket, you are also unable to explain the cuts, if they were cuts, in the jumpsuit?'

'That is correct,' I said. 'I gathered from the tests that nobody else is able to explain them either.'

Mr Macknay changed the subject then. 'There is some other material I would like to put to you in relation to the examination of the singlet and the jumpsuit. If it was put to you that there was a hole in the back of the jumpsuit in about the middle, a corresponding hole in the singlet these holes being roughly three millimetres in size, and that there was a hole in the right hand collar region of the singlet which appeared to be caused by an object going from inside out—?'

'Did you say "the collar of the singlet"?' I asked.

'Yes, around the top right hand front of the singlet?' he replied.

'You mean the shoulder strap?' I queried.

'Below the neck on the right hand side, and that that last hole was from the inside out, assuming that the singlet was on the child in the same way as when it was examined—that is, inside out?' Mr Macknay finished.

'I beg your pardon?' I asked surprised.

'Inside out?' He repeated.

'Did you say that the singlet was inside out?' I asked, stunned.

'Yes, assuming that,' he replied.

I wasn't paying attention to what he wanted to know, only thinking of the singlet evidently being inside out according to them. That was totally wrong.

'Well, it wasn't,' I said aloud.

It was his turn to be surprised.

'You are absolutely certain about that, are you?'

'Yes,' I said positively, 'I am absolutely certain about that. I never put my children's clothes on inside out.'

A little later Mr Macknay returned to the puzzling question of the singlet.

'If I suggested to you that this singlet was found inside out amongst the clothing when it was located, what would you say about that? That the dingo had turned it inside out?'

'I would only be surmising what happened to it,' I answered.

'What is your supposition about it?' he queried.

'I don't know that I have got one at the moment and it would only be a supposition,' I said. 'I prefer to deal in facts.'

'If I suggested to you that an examination of the clothing which you have identified today compared with clothing that was used in the experiment in Adelaide which I think you are aware of, are you not? He paused.

I told him, 'A reporter did tell me a few details of it. The police have not told us anything about that.'

Macknay returned to the zoo tests. 'Now, if it were the case that the clothing that was located at Ayers Rock did not have any consistent features with those taken from the zoo, would you then accept that the damage to the clothing at Ayers Rock was not caused by a dog or dingo?'

The information seemed pretty scanty and incomplete.

'I would like to question what differences there are between domesticated dingoes and wild dingoes,' I stated.

Macknay continued. 'If the forensic dentist told you that there were no significant differences between wild dingoes, tame dingoes and dogs insofar as the present purposes are concerned?'

It wasn't enough to *just suppose*. 'Have tests been done on wild dingoes?' I wasn't going to accept that inference.

He didn't answer but continued. 'If we hypothesise that the forensic dentist knows what he is talking about . . .'

I interrupted. 'You are still hypothesising. I was just asking "Have there been any tests done on wild dingoes?"'

Well, no one had told me I was supposed to act dumb and go along with pretended scenarios.

Mr Macknay seemed determined to try and blind me with experts. 'The position is, Mrs Chamberlain, is it not, that insofar as the experts have concluded from their observations that the damage etcetera was inconsistent with having been caused by a dingo, you do not accept that?' I certainly *didn't* accept having my words twisted, so I tried to explain.

'What I am saying is that in the three different reports that I have read there have been considerable personal opinions and comments . . .'

'Do you accept them or not?' he interrupted.

I patiently tried again, 'I am answering the question and if I am allowed to . . .'

'My question is: Do you accept them or not?' he interrupted again. This was getting nowhere. 'Your Honour, may I finish what I was going to say?' I asked.

The coroner answered, 'No, I am sorry, you are not in a position where you are permitted to ask questions, only answer them.'

This was weird. Did the courts want the truth or only bits of it? Maybe they didn't want to know what I thought at all. I had begun to wonder, when I had sat on juries in Innisfail, whether our jury and court system, and the adversary system, was all that we thought it to be, too. Was there a problem that we were unable to put our finger on there as well? Was something withheld from the normal person that we weren't quite sure of? It was not enough to complain about, just a gut feeling that something was wrong, somebody knew and we weren't being told.

I answered the coroner, 'That is what I was trying to do. I find that I cannot answer that question with a straight "yes" or "no".'

'Well, it does not matter,' said the coroner. 'If you cannot answer it with a "yes" or "no" answer you can answer it and qualify your answer in any way that you feel you ought to.'

'Then if you don't mind I'll qualify the answer,' I said. Mr Macknay was resigned. 'Well, what is the answer?'

'The answer is that in reading those statements I have found a lot of personal interpretations in them and from reading them myself I find that they give no hard evidence one way or the other; it is interpretive depending on who is reading it.' That seemed to throw him.

'Did the fact that the forensic dentist concludes that the damage to the blanket, that you had up until the time you gave it to the police, was caused by cutting have anything to do with your assessment of his report and his conclusion?' Macknay questioned.

'I beg your pardon?' I asked, stunned. Macknay repeated his question.

'No,' I answered, puzzled. 'There is no reason why it should have anything to do with the way I accept the report, is there?'

'It does not cause you any concern at all that the forensic dentist has concluded that the damage which had not been there before you went back to the tent was caused by cutting?' he queried.

'I have not read anywhere that it is specifically proved that it was caused by cuts. I have only read that it seems inconsistent with dog marks, and I feel that that is perhaps being a little interpretive,' I explained.

Mr Macknay said, 'Perhaps I could just read something out and see if you are prepared to accept the accuracy of what I read in relation to those blankets: "There were several small cuts in the blankets but there was no evidence of tooth marks".' That seemed really odd.

'Well, teeth cut, don't they? Teeth cut, knives cut, scissors cut—several things cut,' I said. Surely they could see that!

'The fact that the forensic dentist has concluded that there was no evidence at all of tooth marks on that blanket does not cause you any concern at all?' he asked.

'It does cause me concern in the fact that they cannot tell what it was done by, and if they can be so accurate in one thing why can they not be so accurate in stating what it is?' I asked.

Later Mr Macknay continued, 'So your answer to that is "Well, you are not prepared to accept his expertise in saying that there were no tooth marks"?'

'I am not saying that at all. I am saying that I would like a full answer not just a partial answer to this. I would like to know more, perhaps, than anyone else what happened to my daughter, and I would like the tests to be done as fully and as accurately as possible, and if they have gone so far I would like a full and accurate conclusion as to exactly what it was, otherwise it is pure supposition,' I explained.

So that is your assessment of what I have told you about the forensic evidence?' he asked.

'My assessment is that the gentleman who did it has gone as far as he is able, and he has also put some of his own opinions as well, as no doubt you are doing at the moment,' I answered.

He continued later, 'In any event, you are not satisfied with what you have read and what has been put to you?'

'All I have read at the moment is a précis, if I may call it that, of what was indicated to me at the time to be quite a lengthy paper.

I asked some questions at the time on it and was told that they had only seen the short one, that there was a longer one. I have heard you quote certain pieces out of the longer paper, but I have not read it myself in context at all and I am not prepared to make full comments on it without doing so,' I stated. This was all a bit useless, only a fool would jump to conclusions on incomplete information.

When I read my evidence years later it sounded as if I was being tried, rather than attending an inquest into the death of my daughter, but I was so engrossed in assisting them to find out the truth that I missed the whole inference of the questions, which was unlike me. If I had not been so numb from Azaria's death and so intent on helping the police, we may even then have been able to stop a lot of the future heartache, but we could not see into the future.

It was obvious that Ken Brown the dentist had made some observations based on the singlet being put on inside out. Apart from my memory, even the dirt staining indicated that I was right in how she had been wearing it, regardless of how it had ended up later. Whatever these observations would turn out to be, it seemed whether or not I was careful in the way I put the children's clothes on was very important for some reason.

'In that regard, what was your practice as far as singlets and the clothing were concerned? Did you have any particular set practice after you got them off the clothes line?' Mr Barritt, the coroner, asked.

I explained, 'When I fold the clothes, I always turn them in the right way before I put them away. I am one of these people who, when they hang clothes on the line, put matching pegs on each garment and that sort of thing. I suppose I am fussy but it is one of those things; it is a habit and upon occasion when I have put something away by mistake or somebody else has put it away for me inside out, I have always made sure that it is the right way on; even when the kiddies dress themselves and put their pants on back to front, I take them off and turn them around before they go outside the door.'

'On the way to Ayers Rock, had you had to do any washing of singlets for Azaria?' the coroner continued.

'I hadn't done any washing for her at all,' I answered.

'So any singlets that you were using at Ayers Rock would have been singlets that you had previously folded at your home?' he queried.

'That's correct,' I answered.

The coroner had realised the difference between routine jobs at home, and holidays. Washing at home, of course, meant that I was not distracted by any awkwardness caused by camping.

During my evidence I went to show the footprints on the space blanket to the coroner and discovered they had gone. They could only have come off if rubbed by a damp cloth. They would not brush off simply by wear and tear, particularly in the short time between handing it over and the inquest. The tears and puckers were still there, of course, but *no* police seemed to know *anything* about these footprints. Charlwood said yes, I had mentioned it but no, he didn't see them, and no tests had been done as they didn't realise it was important.

I didn't accept that because of the conversations I had had during my record of interview and over the phone with him later when he had actually told me it was being tested.

It was stated that I had refused an official request to be hypnotised for no reason. When cross-examined, Charlwood actually admitted that I had refused because hypnotism was against my principles and said hypnotising me had just been an idea which he had subsequently rejected, that he had not actually told me it was an official request. It had just been an off-the- cuff remark he had made while all the other policemen were out of the room. Funnily enough, none of our conversation about this came through on the tape recorder. Mr Barritt said that my refusal to be hypnotised should not be held against me as he would have refused a similar request also.

We went through the physical evidence, and then at the end of Mr Macknay's examination, he brought up the question of the meaning of Azaria's name. I told him that 'Azaria' was Hebrew for 'blessed of God'; 'Chantel' was the name gypsies use for their lead singer, and 'Loren' is Teutonic in origin and means a branch of laurel leaves.

Macknay then proposed what he called the 'alternative explanation' for Azaria's disappearance.

He said the other explanation was 'that a dingo did in fact remove your child from the tent but that somebody else disposed of her remains and placed the clothing where it was found.'

Not knowing as much about the habits of dingoes then as I do now, I agreed that that could be an explanation, but added that the police would have to round up and interview all the people who had helped search the area that night.

After that, Mr Macknay called on Michael, a lot of whose evidence was substantially the same as mine.

Bill Barnes remembers:

> An early day (the second, I think) when Mike was continually referred to as 'Mr'. On adjournment I asked Mike how he preferred to be addressed. He simply answered he was a minister of religion. I pointed out to Dinny he was being incorrectly addressed. And at the first opportunity on a query—Dinny called him Pastor. Mike broke—whether for this reason or not, I, of course, don't know—but at the Bowling Club that night Dinny

blamed me!! You caused the Pastor to break! A compassionate man, he really felt it had been the reason for Mike's brief loss of control.

Not until the inquest did a number of the people involved in the case get together. They were sitting outside the courtroom, waiting to give evidence, and they struck up conversation to pass the time.

The Wests and Lowes knew each other by sight from that awful night, but there were others waiting there too. No one was discussing evidence, so reasons for being there were obviously something to talk about. It was soon discovered that they were all there for the same reason—the Chamberlain inquest. Well, the eyewitnesses knew one another, but who were these others? They turned out to be Wally Goodwin, who had found the clothes, and Mrs Mona Wilkin, who had held Azaria for me while I rounded up the boys at the climb.

After all of them but Wally Goodwin had been in the witness box, they were sent for lunch to a bistro at the Telford Territory, the hotel where we were staying and lunching also. They came across to us, able to talk freely now because we had all given our evidence but nobody knew much about court etiquette. Then a stocky man with jet-black hair and intense very dark brown eyes, whom we had never seen but who seemed to know everyone else, asked 'Can I join you?' 'Sure,' the others answered. He sat down and everyone continued talking about their time in the box to us, and he listened intently, chipping in here and there. Greg Lowe suddenly realised we had blank looks on our faces, laughed and introduced him as Wally Goodwin, the man who had found our baby's clothes. As we had been inside the court and he was still waiting to give evidence after lunch, he didn't know what we looked like. I don't know who was more surprised, him or us! It was almost like a family reunion.

The inquest was obviously going to be much longer than we had initially been told. The evidence continued with detailed descriptions of search patterns from the police and rangers.

For the first time we discovered there was a large discrepancy in the way Frank Morris said the clothes were found and the way Wally Goodwin described them. No one knew until Wally actually saw the photographs in the witness box that those tendered in court were merely of a reconstruction that Morris had attempted after handling the clothes. Until that time everyone, including the rangers, had been unaware that they were not looking at the original positioning of the clothes. No wonder the rangers said there was no way a dingo would leave the clothes in that position.

After court one day I tried reconstructing them from the photograph for our lawyers and discovered in order to put them in the position shown in his photograph you had to actually tie them in knots. Not only that, but bootees which were inside the jumpsuit mysteriously appeared separately on the reconstruction.

Although no common ground was found in court over the way the clothes were originally found, to my mind the fact that Wally's small daughter had screamed was the telling piece of missing information. If they had been found as Frank Morris claimed, nothing about a pile of dirty old 'rags' would scare a child. On the other hand, it seemed quite feasible to me that she would have screamed when it appeared that a part of a dead body was still there in the way Wally Goodwin described.

Bill Barnes remembers the early days of the inquest this way:

> My earliest memories of those first days are of an attractive, intelligent, meticulous young lady perusing exhibits after the day's enquiry—recording with Peter Dean, putting *me* at ease—I remember thinking—what a beaudy—an intelligent lass with a sense of humour! And the immediate future didn't then seem too bad.

Bill was very careful when he had to walk across in front of us to the witness box with exhibits and did his best to keep them as much as possible out of our line of vision. Several times he came and apologised that he had to put us through the trauma of having these things brought in front of us time and time again while they were being discussed. We assured him that it wasn't his fault. It was something necessary and please not to worry about it. He hung around very solicitously with drinks and things when necessary, realising from the beginning that we were not guilty of any of the rumours that he had heard. Although *we* weren't aware of the internal police rumours at the time, *he* had certainly been in a position to hear them.

Bill Barnes became more and more concerned about the treatment we were having as the court progressed. He looked as if he had been through it all and knew it all. He smoked little brown cigarillos fairly heavily (they smell like cigars and when you are confined in a room with them for some hours you think they must be among the deadliest missiles around). Over time, Bill became a very good friend. He was also a close friend of Barritt's.

One day while we were sitting in court, we watched a note being handed up to the Crown. Ashley Macknay looked concerned and handed it across to Peter Dean. Peter read it quickly and then immediately stood up and asked for a recess. The Crown supported the motion. A buzz ran through the courtroom. The coroner, realising that something serious had happened immediately granted it, and the courtroom was cleared. Peter came across to us and said, 'Look, um, I don't want to alarm you but there have been death threats made on your life by phone and it appears that it is someone in the courtroom. Because of the nature of the phone calls it has become apparent that the person must be in here as the threats are made during court breaks and information given at the last session was mentioned in the latest call. No news media has reported these things yet, so the person must be in here.'

That really shook me, but Mrs Cozens talked quietly to me and I settled down again before court was resumed.

I was immediately assigned a bodyguard and the court reconvened. Frank Gibson was a jovial Englishman; ex-Scotland Yard, he had dropped rank when he migrated to Australia and had to go through the system all over again. He was now public relations officer for the Alice Springs police and well liked in the Alice. Frank came with us everywhere. He ate with us; he *almost* slept with us (he was in the room next door), although it caused many jokes as the news media said that Frank Gibson was sleeping with the Chamberlains. Barely twenty-four hours after he had been assigned, Frank told us that apart from being a bodyguard, the police had asked him to report back any information he could glean. He said, 'Look, I am telling you this because it is quite obvious to me that you have nothing to hide and I am going to tell them that.'

He did and from that time on, the police gave him a very hard time. He lost friends; people he had known for years now cut him off. One night, when things were quiet, and he was off duty, he went to a barbecue with his wife. When I asked him how it had gone the next morning, he pulled a face. I said to him, 'You didn't have trouble over us, did you?' And he said, 'Well, put it this way, Lindy. Friends like that I can do without.' And sure enough, his wife later said there had been an argument. Although his colleagues knew him well, and knew he was guarding us, they preferred to listen to the lies rather than listen to him. He felt that if his friends had so little trust in his judgment, they were ones he didn't need any more.

We were lent a motorbike one weekend and planned to go trail riding. Frank also rode trailbikes and, as our bodyguard, had to go too. So he went to his friends to borrow a bike. The first one he tried said he could have the bike, but then refused, saying that if he was going riding with the Chamberlains he couldn't have it. That was one more friend down the drain. However, he found another friend who would lend him a bike quite happily.

So we went and enjoyed a Sunday riding all around the hills on the outskirts of Alice Springs and ended overlooking the city. We met no one and enjoyed the freedom of it all. I, of course, was just on the back of Michael's bike, not being able to ride myself then. But it was the next best thing, and lots of fun.

When the inquest recessed for Christmas, we knew enough to realise that it had become far too complicated for Peter Dean to do all the work on his own, and he needed some assistance. I was doing the best I could, but he needed another legal mind: it really did look odd, having me tell him what questions to ask and trying to point out the relevance of certain things but I didn't understand all the intricacies of the law so there was only so much I could do. After all, Peter had been given the case just the day before the inquest started; he had had no material or time to prepare and was trying to discover the significance of things on the run. As the Crown had two lawyers and were working well with that number it was decided we should find another lawyer to assist Peter.

Peter was a nice guy, but not the most organised one that you had ever seen. His girls had already knocked off and we needed copies of the affidavits. So I said to Peter, 'Never mind the girls, we'll go down and photocopy them off and staple them ourselves.' Instead of the couple of hours he thought it would take, we were there for nearly five hours, working steadily, and were almost at the end. I was stapling and sorting the last few stacks. Peter was packing them and Michael had momentarily run out of steam and was sidetracked reading instead of sorting. We had been discussing various aspects of the case and suddenly Michael became very excited. 'Look, look at this! Why hasn't this been mentioned? He was reading Scott's evidence, and had come across in Dr Scott's list of results the mention of a large splash of blood which had tested and grouped foetal positive, identified as Azaria's blood on one of the floral mattresses that had been under Reagan.

Dr Scott had given his evidence in court, but had not been asked about this at all so it remained unmentioned. The only reference to this blood had come from Sally Lowe who had seen a large patch in the tent that night. Here we were now with a reference to a large-sized patch on a mattress. Seen in the dark it could well fit the description of the blood that Sally Lowe had described.

One thing that had puzzled the novices at first was the unexpected lack of large amounts of blood in the tent, but we were told that it was not unusual for a dingo attack to cause very little bleeding. When the teeth are clamped shut and pressure is applied, less than the normal amount of blood flows from the wound. However, there was the pool of blood on the mattress that Sally Lowe had seen right next to the two rugs that had covered Azaria at the time of her death.

Michael then showed his find to Peter Dean, who became just as excited as Michael and me, and later we were able to use that evidence in court. Because of the extremely cold temperatures that night, there could well have been blood that had frozen and actually shaken off elsewhere in the trip between the motel and the campsite; who knew? Judy West even voiced the same opinion.

When I had gone into the tent that night and found Azaria missing, I had touched her carry basket to make sure I was not seeing things and that it *was* empty, and it had rocked towards me. Because of the way it was situated and because it was empty, it tipped very easily. I thought it would not have been difficult for a dingo to roll Azaria out of the carry basket; and the blankets would have landed about where they actually were in the tent. The initial point of attack would have been near where Sally Lowe had seen that pool of blood.

The other thing that had indelibly ground itself into my mind was the quick cut-off cry that Michael had heard. There was no doubt in my mind that Azaria had been roughly rolled out of that carry basket, which had given her a fright and caused her to wake with a cry, but that her cry had been cut off very quickly at the moment of attack.

A Fundamental Problem

The Division headquarters told us they would see what they could do about another lawyer but, at such short notice, men they would normally suggest would already be engaged. As soon as we came home, I was told of a Mr St John (once again by Dr Eric Magnusson) who had been interested in the case and said he would be glad to help any time if it was necessary. Initially, of course, it was felt that a QC wasn't needed. Now the matter was obviously far more involved than we expected. Dr Magnusson got on to Mr St John who was amazed that we did not have a QC. As he had not heard from us and had been very busy with another case, he had presumed that the Chamberlains were all right. He was unable to take the case himself, because he had just accepted another brief, but he undertook to find us another lawyer and shortly rang back to say Phil Rice QC would take the case and that he was a good man, familiar with the Territory and was excellent in an inquest situation. The church, which had undertaken to guarantee our legal fees, would engage him for us.

Meanwhile Mum, in Cooranbong, had unpacked what she could for me while I was away, so now I could move ahead and arrange my cupboards as I wanted them, and finish the rest of the unpacking. Michael and I had some soft-brimmed ex-army giggle hats that we had taken to the Rock with us; we actually didn't wear them because the sun hadn't got hot enough in the end. They had been in the tent on the night of 17 August. I had packed them up, unused, and put them straight into the cupboard with the rest of the camping gear when we got back to Mt Isa. I hadn't thought of them again until I found them in a packing box after Christmas; then I discovered what appeared to be blood on them.

I showed the hats to Dr Magnusson who, as well as being the college president, was a scientist whose specialty field was blood, and he agreed they looked blood-spotted and suggested we could run tests.

'I'd certainly tell the police,' he said, 'though they probably won't need them at this stage.' I eventually mentioned the find to our lawyers as soon as I could contact them. They thought, as I now did, that the inquest had enough blood splattered items. So I put them away again.

For some reason we were being stopped from finding out where to contact Mr Rice.

Eric Magnusson had transferred now, and we were supposed to be going through Sandy in the Australian Division headquarters of our church. I wanted to see what progress had been made and whether they had officially engaged Phil Rice QC. Yes, the man had been engaged, things were going nicely.

I asked, 'Could you tell me a contact number for the new lawyer, please? I need to get in touch with him.' Peter Dean at this stage was away on his Christmas holidays.

No, no, it is fine, we have things in hand.' I hung up feeling a little frustrated.

Time passed and we still had no communication from either the Division or Mr Rice. The time was growing shorter. The brief needed to be sent to the new lawyer and instructions given. There were a number of things that Peter had set us to look up and check, and we were endeavouring to do that. Now in his absence, we should be passing that information on. Peter had gone away secure in the knowledge that we would hand on the information to our new QC when we had engaged one, so when he came back they were ready for a conference and he could pick things up from there. It was obvious that we couldn't go into court cold turkey with our new man knowing absolutely nothing, as we had with Peter Dean.

I tried ringing again. A couple of times Sandy was 'not in'. The third time I rang he took the call. He once again told me everything was under control, calm down, it was fine, they were organising things nicely.

I said, 'Look. I appreciate this, but I need to talk to him myself.'

'There is no need for you to talk to him,' he said.

'Excuse me, but you seem to misunderstand,' I said. 'This is *my* case. Not yours. It is not the church's case either. I appreciate what the church has done in guarantoring the lawyers for us, but we need to contact them ourselves.' He said no. I exploded, 'It is all very well for you in your fancy office sitting up there protected from the world saying everything is in hand. It is my family we are talking about and I want to speak to that lawyer. Now, would you kindly, simply, give me his telephone number.' He told me what he thought of me in no uncertain terms and hung up. (I didn't find out for over twelve months how true my words were about his office.)

I came away from that call very upset. I started to cry and I couldn't stop. I wanted to go to the toilet and I couldn't. My body had shut down and gone into semi-shock. My parents, with their first aid experience, realised that I was in trouble. I was determined that I would not give in to it. I *must* stay in control of myself or I'd go crazy. Dad had worked in the same conference as Sandy, so my parents decided to see what they could do. They didn't tell me what they were going to do at the time, just afterwards. That phone call was unsatisfactory as well, and they also came away upset. It is extremely difficult to make my father angry, but after that phone call he was obviously very disappointed. They had pointed out what the effect of his phone call to me had been, and said they did not appreciate what he had done. They knew their daughter and it was very difficult to upset her this way. Despite the pressures upon her, they said, she had been coping well—until she spoke to him. His phone call had brought on more stress and distress than anything else during the whole time, and they told Sandy of my physical response. Sandy went quiet; out of all of them he *knew* the significance of that because he had a medical background.

Unknown to any of us, there was another circumstance at work which, on top of the two phone calls, had made a profound impact on Sandy.

A little over a week before, we had called in on our way through Sydney to see our friends Breece and Rosalie Rickards, whom we hadn't seen for a while. They had asked how we were going and I mentioned that I was having great difficulty getting past Sandy to contact our new lawyer. The very morning he was supposed to ring back, Sandy's only daughter, a girl I knew as a child and who I haven't seen since, had dropped in to see my friend Rosalie. Knowing them to be mutual friends, she asked how I was going. Rosalie (realising it was this girl's father I was having trouble with) explained and said she hoped Sandy had given me the information I wanted as I was having difficulties with him.

The girl was absolutely incensed. (I was older than she was and she used to tag around after the bigger girls, who thought she was a nuisance. Frequently I let her tag along with me, promising to be responsible for her when she was lonely; I could do my thing later, and she would be happy. Although I had forgotten her, she had not forgotten me.) I was told she said that somebody who had been so kind to her deserved all the help they could get, and he'd better do something about it. My phone call, then my parents' call had rocked him a little, and now his daughter was confronting him as well. Meanwhile Michael and Dad went to see the new College President, Dr James Cox, and got him out of bed near midnight. He came to our home with clothes hastily pulled on over his pyjamas. Near 3 a.m. he walked home, facts in hand. What he did after that I don't know but very shortly I had the number I so desperately needed.

That was not the only run-in we had with certain of the Division hierarchy. Over and over again a similar process was repeated. The Division seemed very concerned that we represent the church aright: we must be careful, the church was involved. It didn't seem to matter how often you told them that it was our case and yes, we were Adventists, but it really was not the church's case. They were taking it a little too personally.

We took a trip to Adelaide to meet our new lawyer and for him to interview us about the case. Phil Rice had steel-grey hair, and was about 178 centimetres (5 feet 10 inches) tall with a tendency to portliness. He was very professionally dressed in a dark suit with immaculately polished black shoes and white shirt, half glasses perched on the end of his nose—very much a gentleman of the old school.

So Phil Rice was there for the second half of the first inquest.

Imagine our surprise when we saw him get off the plane in Alice Springs carrying an old battered suitcase tied up with string, and wearing an old blue short-sleeved shirt and moleskin trousers held up by an old leather belt. Phil wore those clothes for most of the inquest. We learned later he had worked in the Territory and knew what sort of image would give him the most advantage in that area. On top of this, he knew a number of people involved. So when the case resumed there he was with Peter Dean assisting him.

We soon discovered that he was a specialist in his field and realised God had led us to the right man for the job, which he did brilliantly.

Muscles and the Media

One night Michael and I were sitting in our hotel room, reading the evening papers and wondering more or less what to do with ourselves when we realised that a commotion was going on outside. Looking out the upstairs window, I saw a lot of people milling about on the road; it seemed that a crowd was gathering for something. I was feeling restless, wishing I could go down and be part of it, but knowing that if I stuck my nose out at that time of night I would probably end up with a drunken reporter trying to get information about something that he wouldn't remember in the morning, or at best would get totally scrambled anyway.

It is no wonder they call some afternoon papers 'screamers'. When I saw reporters reeling to the phone to put their story through, so drunk that they couldn't quite make it through the doorway, and then have them blissfully stutter to me what a good story they had written, I just felt disgusted, yet sorry for them. Under pressure, produce or you're out—living on the move, chain smoking and drinking to get themselves through. It wasn't much of a life.

I realised it would be better to stay in the room. We had had a number of death threats. It seemed we ran the gamut—everything, Frank said, except a bomb. This became the standard joke. If you joked about things like that, you see, they didn't hurt so much, and so we kept saying, 'Who's got the bomb now?' Then that evening I heard knocking on what seemed to be every door along the corridor in the hotel coming closer and closer.

I said to Michael, 'I bet there's a bomb. They are going along warning everybody to get out of the hotel. What else explains what is going on?'

He said, 'Don't be stupid.' But when the knock came on our door, I opened it and there was a policeman.

I said to him, 'So there's a bomb, is there?'

He said, 'I see you've been told, Mrs Chamberlain.' I didn't enlighten him that I hadn't. I looked at Michael and raised my eyebrows (well, it's not ladylike to say, 'I told you so').

The policeman told us that we would need to evacuate. The whole hotel had been emptied except for us, and we could either go out the front, into the street with everyone else or down the back way to the swimming pool. It was far enough away from anywhere they thought might be dangerous and everyone else had been put out in the street.

They considered that the bomb was intended for us according to the information they had received. Had any packages been recently delivered? Did we recognise all our luggage? Was there anything strange in it? Was there anything under the bed, in the cupboards, in the bathroom? I hadn't noticed anything different.

Another quick glance through the side of the curtains showed us that the road was now full of people and a number of cameras were down there as well. The pool it would be.

I was sure it was just a hoax, and I was even more convinced when I knew that the smart photographers had managed to grab their cameras before evacuating their rooms. They were hoping to get shots of the Chamberlains being rushed out of their bomb threatened hotel in their pyjamas. Those who had forgotten their cameras or were in the bars and unable to get theirs were grumbling about it now.

The policeman informed us that they were hoping to get a pyjama shot as we came out the doors. Well, we weren't in our pyjamas, we were fully clothed. I grabbed my shoes and bag and Michael picked up his briefcase and we followed the policeman down the lift and across to the swimming pool.

We met a poor unsuspecting man who had been left in his room with his family, with no idea what was happening in the rest of the hotel. He thought the pool was a bit quiet that night, and we looked too dressed up for swimming. When we told him about the bomb threat, he grew alarmed, wondering which important people in the hotel had caused that. We realised he had no idea who we were, which suited us fine. We assured him that the management had sent us down to the pool because it was safe and he had no need to fear or to go anywhere else. So he calmed down and relaxed, and we had a good chat.

After a while we were told that it was safe to go, and he saw nothing unusual in that; until he read the newspaper the following day, he wouldn't realise who his companions had been.

Within a couple of days, the same thing happened. We could hear the hotel being emptied again. By this time I was bored at the thought of being kicked out of my room. The police said, 'We're pretty sure it's another hoax, but is there anything abnormal in the room again?'

We said, 'No.'

They said, 'Well, look, you can stay here if you want to, or you can go down to the pool again.' We opted to stay in the room, being sure by this stage that the bomb scare was simply a hoax. We wondered whether the media were trying to get different pictures. They had got together before and decided that if they didn't report the scares, nuts would not be encouraged to do this sort of thing. It seemed unlikely that anyone would have deliberately created a scare again because the media policy didn't appear to have changed. That left us wondering just what had happened and then outside the room we heard a voice we recognised. Kevin Hitchcock of Channel 10 was discussing with his crew whether one of the other newsmen had set it up for a story or whether someone else had, perhaps even the Chamberlains, for publicity.

Maybe the police had set it up, he said. I was interested to hear that. Nobody knew.

They were arguing whether we were in the hotel or not and finally Kevin, despite the arguments of his men, decided to knock on our door and see whether we really were there or not.

He knocked on the door, and I simply said, 'Hello. Yes we are here, Mr Hitchcock, what would you like?'

He was taken aback and said, 'How did you know it was us?'

I said, 'Because I can hear you talking and recognised your voice.' They wanted to get some pictures, and I said, 'No.'

Michael said Kevin could come in by himself for a chat off the record if he wanted to, but if they planned to come in with the camera, we wouldn't open the door. So he told his crew they could go.

We talked about Kevin's background, his wife and children, and his philosophy of life. He was surprised to see us in our room when the rest of the hotel was empty. When we asked him why he was there too, he said that he and his crew had actually hidden in the wardrobe until the police had checked that the room was empty and gone on past. When the coast was clear they had come out with their cameras to wander around the hotel and see what they could find.

Not for a number of years did Kevin express the thought that it was most unusual that the Northern Territory police, who were so anxious to protect everyone, had moved all but the people for whom the bomb was intended out of the hotel. They had been quite happy to leave us in what was supposed to be the priority danger spot. This was something that I hadn't considered before, either; they weren't willing to take the risk of a bomb with anyone else, but it was quite OK for the Chamberlains. Who knows?

That was our first close encounter with Kevin Hitchcock. He didn't seem to have any particular opinion about the case. His reporting was straight, maybe slightly swinging towards the Crown, but fairly impartial. He had decent manners and integrity.

I teased him about his scuffle over the cable bearer to Sydney. Apparently Channels 10 and 9 had been the last to get cable bearers, and as there was one short, they had to make an arrangement to share and evidently took turns to use it—so that one day, one got the news to the air first, and the next day the other did. On this particular day, one crew had thought to steal a march on the other and had got there early out of turn, and were in the process of using it when the other crew arrived. There had been a show of strength between Kevin Hitchcock and Mike

Lester, the reporters (on behalf of their crews) which everyone had watched with interest in the foyer of the courthouse. Both men were very much the same bulk, although Mike was slightly taller and Kevin was slightly more solid. They had their fists clenched tightly by their sides while fronting up to one another, chest to chest, reminding me of two stags in the mating season. There was quite a deal of angry, red-faced discussion, and shoving with their chests although they never actually came to blows. The confrontation ended but apparently was resumed at the bearer's location where both crews also joined in.

The outcome in the end was amicable but it did leave a nasty flavour for a while in the press ranks.

We had had slight dealings with both these men, and were to become good friends with both of them in the future.

Mike Lester was known by everybody at the court as the 'clean gentlemanly one'. Despite the fact that Alice Springs was very hot and most of the reporters turned up in sports shirts, both Kevin Hitchcock and Mike Lester usually wore white shirts and always looked very clean and fresh. (It was a real contrast to Geoff de Luca's deep green sports shirt with the red strawberries over it! Whatever he spent his money on, it certainly wasn't shirts.)

Because Mike Lester was an ethical reporter, he was generally trusted by those in the courthouse and others, and he always kept his word. He seemed to be the only general reporter there; the others were mainly court reporters.

The threats made Michael nervous but made me get the giggles, much to his disgust.

Then the Telford Territory motel said they had had enough, the threats were giving them a bad name. We would have to move. Finding somewhere else to take us after that was not easy, but eventually the Midland Motel, where our bodyguard Frank's wife Cath worked, gave us rooms. Only Cath cleaned our rooms, so we could be sure of security.

Bill Barnes remembers:

> That day, although you tried to be your usual bright self in court, I voiced my concerns—that of your well-being—to Frank. You didn't look well to me. Frank told me you'd had a sleepless night (you were then at the Midland Motel). Then had to put up with comments that you were 'sulky' or you didn't care or whatever. Very hard for me to say nothing, and, as Mary [Bill's superior] exhorted, 'Keep out of things—don't get involved.'

As the evidence continued, we heard from Ken Brown the forensic dentist. He had hung a singlet, spring loaded with a scale of 4.5 kilograms (10 pounds) across the tooth of a dingo skull (from the museum), and left it hanging there overnight to see what amount of pressure it would need to penetrate the cloth. I was thoroughly disgusted. Muscles and tendons are on *live* creatures that go chomp, not on museum skulls. This never seemed to have entered the calculations, though. It is as bad as hanging a slice of bread on your false teeth overnight and expecting them to bite it. It seemed ridiculous to me. The whole court broke into laughter, much to Mr Brown's indignation.

The evidence moved on and we discovered the clothes had not only been picked up and checked out *before* any photographs were taken, but they had been handled quite extensively with bare hands and transported in a box (whether transferred again at Alice Springs or not, we do not know). When they got to the Northern Territory, Moira Fogarty, the young policewoman who was asked to do the initial forensic work, admitted in court to having taken everything out of the box and shaken it all. Anything that had dropped off (such as dirt, plant material, or hairs) had simply been swept off the bench or floor on which it was dumped. What was in the transportation boxes and the boxes themselves, as well as any plant and whatever other fragments there were, she had simply tipped out. Then she had put the clothes on the bench and vacuumed them. The material she had got off the clothes in the vacuuming she had put in containers and shoved under the bench in the back of the cupboard somewhere.

Miss Fogarty didn't see anything she thought was hair, and when asked how she distinguished what a hair was—she said she'd pulled one out of her own head and compared that, because she didn't know what sort of hairs she was looking for! When asked whether there had been *any* animal or natural material in the vacuumings at all, she had said, 'No.'

Her evidence brought out confusion over the saliva test on the dirt from the tent site having been done as a blood test, and the complete neglect of any tests at all on the tent. All that material had been placed in the back of the cupboard also. When found it was sent down to Dr Andrew Scott in Adelaide for testing. By this time it had been in an uncontrolled situation for so long that any saliva tests were useless. As for the 'arterial spray' Sergeant Lincoln and Inspector Gilroy had seen on the tent, Scott could only say that it was blood of some sort. He could not determine whether it was human or animal blood due to denaturisation, and was unable to take it any further.

Coroner Dennis Barritt considered the blood to be very important and that a major forensic mistake had been made in not testing it originally, particularly as the whole Chamberlain family at that stage were total vegetarians and were not likely to have blood of any sort in or near the tent from cooking, shooting or fishing.

Dr Harding, the specialist on hair, was asked whether he knew of the evidence Miss Fogarty had given as a background to his tests. The information was obviously a surprise. As another witness had to catch a plane, Dr Harding stood down overnight to resume his evidence the next morning. He asked for the transcript of Moira Fogarty's evidence to read overnight. When he resumed his evidence he stated that he wished to change his testimony, in light of the fresh material he had read, because he discovered the clothes had been vacuumed *before* he saw them. Seeing this evidence now appeared vital, the Crown located the containers of vacuumings which were fortunately still under the bench, and had them flown down for him to see.

When they arrived in court it turned out there were bird feathers, quite a number of animal hairs, and quite a few of what I would identify as Michael's blond hairs off his sleeping bag. All the vacuumings were in together.

Dr Harding was critical of the fact that the clothes had been vacuumed, as this had damaged the hairs. He said it was standard procedure when hair was to be removed that a small piece of sticky tape was used and the hair was lifted off carefully in order not to damage the shank of the hair or make it appear more worn than it actually was. Under the microscope, a fresh hair that has come into superficial contact with a garment looks very different from one that is old and embedded, or one that has been embedded in the clothes and rubbed. It was his opinion that the garments should not have been handled at all until they had been sent to the hair and botany departments where scientists could look at the surface of the garment together and decide what material would be on the surface of the garment, before handing it on to be subjected to vacuuming and odontological (forensic dental) examination. In actual fact the garment hadn't gone to the hair or plant men until much further down the track. (In the years to come, with the addition of further evidence and better forensic testing methods, Dr Hans Brunner, a world expert, was able to prove conclusively that there had been dog or dingo hairs from the vacuumings of the garment. How much material had simply dropped off those clothes we will never know.)

An English/Irish Jokester and Ties and Jogs and Things

Because tensions were high and the atmosphere morbid, Frank Gibson did his best to lighten the occasion for us. It certainly worked with me, even though it sometimes frustrated Michael. Frank kept telling us the most awful Irish jokes (and others) that he could find. The hard part was to try and keep a straight face in front of other people. It didn't do to be found smiling too much. I soon learned that when the press came up and said, 'Come on, don't look so solemn. Give us a smile!' and finally their antics would make me smile, they would snap a photograph and next thing I was presented as unfeeling at the inquest into the death of my daughter. So I quickly learned to school my face into blankness.

Pastor Wal Taylor had been sent by the Division to report back to the church on the progress of our case, seeing they were our guarantors, as well as having the local man there. One day when driving to court he was with us. Frank was driving the car. He had been telling me jokes all through breakfast, including some crazy ones about policemen. As we went to court, he started telling me (seriously) that he had often escorted royal parties, including the Queen, around the area and to the Rock, as it was a favourite visiting place. I grabbed his hat and put it on my head and started waving to the non-existent crowds with a royal wave. I informed Wal that I intended to wear the hat right into court. He immediately grew very concerned.

Frank just looked at me in the mirror and grinned. He knew very well that I would not cause him trouble by taking his hat from him in a public place, let alone be seen wearing it. Nor, of course, would I have had the power to stop him taking the hat from me anyway. After several minutes, Wal suddenly realised I was teasing, and he broke into a reluctant grin, saying, 'Oh, you naughty girl, you are teasing me again.' He took the bait so well it was just too tempting *not* to tease him.

One day fairly tedious forensic evidence had been presented all morning and lunch had been a welcome break. I was settling myself in, trying to convince myself that I shouldn't wriggle and must sit still early after lunch. As the tedium continued I noticed Dennis Barritt start to squirm. Then I realised he was feeling his throat. He patted it, looked down and realised he had come in without his tie. He tried to look unconcerned, then wrote a note he handed to the court reporter, who promptly sent it out. It was obvious to me what he was doing, yet nobody else seemed to have noticed. Shortly Bill Barnes the court orderly came in with the missing tie in his hand. He was doing his best to keep it invisible and as he walked past me, he saw I was watching him with a grin, well aware of what was happening. There was nothing much he could do, so he gave me a bit of a sheepish grin back and kept going.

I looked up at Mr Barritt, who could also see I knew what was happening. He tried to bluff it out for a minute then broke into a huge smile as he realised Bill Barnes was having great difficulty trying to figure out how to get the tie, which he held bunched up tightly in his hand, up to him. Realising there was no way he was going to get that tie on without being seen, Barritt sheepishly said that he was afraid he forgot and came in without his tie. Would we all excuse him while he got dressed for court. That sent a ripple of light-hearted laughter through the court and helped us all settle in for the afternoon session. He promptly put his clip-on tie on, and then announced he was ready to go again.

Pastor Cozens, because he lived in Alice Springs and was continually coming up against people who took their information from the local gossip trail, asked to tape the proceedings of the inquest, and was given permission to do this for his own private use. Halfway through the session one day, a tape was completed, and he turned it over quickly, pushing the button. Just as the coroner paused for breath, the Hallelujah Chorus rang out, then was abruptly stopped. There was a startled silence, then Pastor Cozens, not the least bit embarrassed, looked up and said, 'Sorry.' Everyone smiled and court continued. It had been a fairly tense moment and helped lighten the atmosphere considerably. A number of the reporters were expecting to see action taken on the 'illegal' taping until they discovered Pastor Cozens had permission. He was the only person allowed to tape the whole inquest apart from the court itself.

Over one weekend of the inquest the local Alice Springs fun run was held. Although still jogging while in Alice Springs, we didn't enter during the inquest because of the press interest, but Peter Dean and a couple of our friends did. They came back highly amused to report they had seen Malcolm Brown in street dress shorts and normal street shoes. His only concession to the event or to the heat was a T-shirt. He was puffing along with his reporter's pad and pencil in his back pocket.

Malcolm reported the race at the start, he ran in it, and covered it again at the end. Everybody else, of course, was in running gear and shoes, but that was no problem to Malcolm. Despite his ungainly style of running, he could move over the ground quite fast and didn't seem to tire, nor did incorrect footwear seem to affect his knees, ankles or feet. He was a source of amusement to many of the locals with his perspiring red face, glasses and southern pallor as he ran along, splay-footed. You could hear him coming, clap, clap, clap, from away down the road, but he finished well up in the field, putting many of the locals to shame.

A Rocky Trip and an Outback Court

It was announced that the court would move to Ayers Rock. Irene Heron dearly wanted to come with us but the extra fare was beyond her means. There were no regular flights to Ayers Rock then, so you had to hire your own plane or go by car. We were going by legal plane with Peter Dean and others so as there was no room Irene was to stay behind in Alice Springs.

When one of the reporters heard this, they offered her a free seat in the plane they had hired. Irene accepted happily. One of the other reporters sharing the plane, knowing they had spare seats, agreed to take some other reporters including a local female reporter, so the plane was extremely well loaded. Irene was sitting at the back of the plane and the reporters were merrily downing tinnies. In a small plane on a two-hour flight, heavy fluid intake has predictable results.

One of the reporters who had been drinking a little more freely than some of the others decided he simply couldn't wait and had to go. Having no facilities on board the plane, he asked for his mates' empty tinnies. As he was sitting next to the female reporter and three people were sharing two seats, quarters were cramped. As he filled the empty tinnies, he jettisoned them out the plane window over the desert. (The female reporter was absolutely disgusted and broke the reporters' unwritten rule by writing about the incident when she returned to Alice Springs and it was published in the local paper.)

During this process, Irene pretended to get very interested in something out the window on the ground. She enthusiastically drew the attention of the reporter next to her to her supposed 'find' and those with her on the plane supposed that she was totally unaware of what had happened.

We had all not long arrived at the Rock when Kevin Hitchcock walked into his room at the Red Sands Motel to find a large venomous tiger snake under the bed. He had his crew film him with the snake and put it on the news the next evening. *That* was an exclusive the other crews missed out on!

On the same evening I walked across to the ladies' toilets and just as I went to open the door and step inside, something slithered across my foot. I smartly kicked it off. As the lights in the ladies' had blown and not been fixed (they weren't fixed the whole time we were there) I could not see what it was. I ran back to our unit and grabbed a torch. When I shone the beam on the slithery thing I discovered it was a 30 centimetre (1 foot) desert sidewinder. It was now down a crack in the side of the building. As sidewinders are one of Australia's deadlier snakes, I was very thankful it had not bitten me as I walked in.

The coroner, learning of both incidents, was not impressed with the care taken for the personal safety of tourists and was later to be misunderstood when he commented upon it.

When the court moved out to Ayers Rock it was the first time a coroner's court had ever been held there and was therefore history in the making. It had been previously agreed that there would be some technical evidence and all the Aboriginal evidence would be heard on the spot, particularly from the women. The court started indoors with some of the technical evidence.

Bill Barnes recalls:

> The first day at the Rock in the makeshift court—tables and chairs—papers everywhere.

> After swearing in . . . Phil Rice pointed out to Dinny that the witness had not been correctly sworn. I hadn't used the Bible!!! It was under a heap of papers.

When we moved outdoors, evidence was taken fairly briefly from Constable Frank Morris who took the court around the various locations of significance. I was at a loss to know why the Aborigines hadn't been asked to point out the important locations instead of Frank Morris. After all, they had done the tracking and that was what he was mainly pointing out.

Only then did I discover that the clothes had not been found near Maggie Springs behind the Fertility Cave where the blood was, but nearly half a kilometre (a third of a mile) away. The place I had seen the dingo was halfway between the two, and was called not the Fertility Cave but the Maternity Cave. This confusion was righted while at the Rock, but it wasn't particularly significant until nearly a year later.

There had been a lot of discussion over the lighting at the campsite on the night, so the court was to see it for themselves.

When we arrived everyone gathered around the coroner. He opened his mouth and immediately every television camera switched on. Only then did they realise they were in a complete circle around the 'Lone Ranger' in the middle, and their bright night lights (like airport landing lights) were shining directly into each other's lenses. None of them could film anything. Poor Mr Barritt exclaimed, 'I was only going to ask where the court recorder was!' Everyone laughed and decided on a rearrangement before the court started.

To all the campers who had been there since dusk and whose eyes had slowly grown accustomed to the density of the night, it had been quite light although there were no stars. The night had been cool, clear and still, certainly light enough to see without having a light on, apart from the large light on the barbecue shelter. When I testified that I was able to see in the tent quite well enough without a torch and you could actually read if you wished, most people didn't believe me. To Frank Morris and some of the rangers who had come from lit houses, it looked very dark, because their eyes had not grown accustomed to the light difference, so it appeared I could have been lying.

It became such a point of contention that it was decided to try whether or not it was possible to read from the one light there during the night view. Because the television lights were blinding everyone and it could not be assessed this way, the coroner asked for all lights to be turned off for about twenty minutes to half an hour so that people's eyes could become accustomed to the light from the barbecue only. Before long one could see quite clearly the area that had appeared dark before. When our QC, Phil Rice, drew the attention of the coroner to the fact that it *was* light enough to read because all the reporters were walking around taking notes, Mr Barritt asked one of those reporters to read back to the court from a randomly chosen page what he had written. This was done. Mr Barritt agreed that anyone with reasonable eyesight could indeed read a book by that light if they wished.

Frank Gibson, our bodyguard, was a big man and was always complaining that I could duck under people's shoulders while he had to go around them. While at the campsite, where it was dark he couldn't see who was milling around. Anyone could be there, and would I *please* not dodge about so much when he was supposed to protect me? It seemed pretty safe out there to me, so I didn't take much notice. Finally Irene said that Frank really was worried; I had better go easy on him and stick a little closer. So I agreed to be good and stay near him.

Frank had been continually cracking funnies and telling me jokes in order to try and relieve some of the tension the night view had engendered. Trying to repress a mixture of tension and laughter had got to me.

Sick of standing around, I sat down at the picnic table situated next to where our tent had been located. Nearby was the double low open fireplace with barbecue plates across the top into which I had stuffed Azaria's used nappies that day in August. The moment I sat down the newspaper photographers rushed round the other side of the table to get a new 'angle'. In the resulting melee one of the photographers overbalanced, flung his arms out and almost landed on top of the barbecue, bumping the camera of the photographer next to him and making its flashgun go off. Pastor Cozens, an ex-missionary from New Guinea, commented, 'Nearly had long pig.' Having been brought up with mission stories, I knew 'long pig' was what the cannibals called the white man when cooked, but the comment obviously passed over the heads of everyone else except Irene.

It had been bad enough trying to repress my laughter before, but Bert's quip was just *too* much and I burst into laughter. As soon as I did, I realised a camera was being raised so I quickly covered my face with my hands just before the flash went off. (A photograph of me laughing at the campsite would have immediately created headlines to the effect that 'mother laughs at daughter's death site'—which was the last thing I was doing.) I hoped the photograph would be a dud. However, when we returned from the Rock, there was a full front page photograph of me, hands over my face, with the large headline reading, 'Mother's Agony'. They had got the 'angle' they wanted after all.

While the court heard other technical evidence given by Kuchel the botanist we were told that a relative of Barbara Tjikadu, one of the trackers, had just died. She would be leaving shortly for the funeral at Docker River, so it was important to get her on the stand quickly. For some reason technical evidence continued to be heard indoors at the makeshift courtroom in the Information Centre, and Barbara left.

Eventually none of the Aboriginal evidence was heard in *situ* at the Rock. There were apologies but it was decided that the Aborigines should be called back at Alice Springs after all, as the time allotted for the court at Ayers Rock had run out.

Back at Alice Springs the technical evidence continued, then Nipper Winmatti was called. He was the tribal elder and the first of the Aborigines called to give evidence. After waiting for the day and still not being called into the box, he was paid his day's witness wages and told to come back the next day. Unfortunately, like most Aborigines in town, he enjoyed himself that night and the next day came back to court and went to sleep on one of the benches in the court foyer. Having been out with his friends the night before, he did not have a clean shirt, was embarrassed at his state of dress and did not want to get into the witness box until it improved. Finally the coroner's assistant stated that he had been bought a new shirt and would be in the box as soon as he had changed.

There were problems with Nipper's evidence that did not appear on the surface. Nipper seemed to be uncomfortable but I was at a loss to know why. I found his evidence fairly easy to follow, but the lawyers did not. Mr Macknay continually swapped from Nipper's English to the interpreter and back again, ending up by wondering just how much help the evidence had been.

Mr Macknay asked Nipper general questions to begin with.

'How long have you been tracking dingoes?'

'Many years,' said Nipper.

Then Mr Macknay continued asking him about Azaria's disappearance: 'Did you do some tracking for the police at that time?'

'Yes, I have been tracking for them for four days up until night-time,' Nipper answered.

'. . . Whereabouts did you see those dingo tracks?' asked Mr Macknay.

'In the sandhills near the tent,' Nipper replied.

'How close to the tent, just a little bit or a big bit?' continued Mr Macknay.

'On the corner of the tent,' Nipper stated.

Mr Macknay then asked Nipper: 'Could you look at those two photographs and tell me whether you can see in those photographs where the dingo marks were?' Nipper looked at the photograph. 'Yes, on the corner of this side here,' he said.

'Photograph AJ1, the front right hand corner,' Mr Macknay identified it for the court transcript, and asked, 'Did you see just one paw mark or did you see a track?'

'Several tracks, four tracks,'replied Nipper. The interpreter interjected: 'They only count up to five in Aboriginal.'

Mr Macknay queried: 'Could you see where those tracks led?'

Nipper answered, 'From the corner of the tent and leading up towards the hill and near the bushes.'

Macknay identified, 'Photograph AJ3, indicating the front right hand corner of the tent as one looks at the photograph, heading towards the background or the Rock.'

Then he asked Nipper, 'Could you see whether they were fresh tracks or old tracks?'

'Old tracks,' said Nipper.

That was a surprise to Macknay. 'Not fresh?'

'Like they came at night-time on Sunday,' said Nipper.

I was interested in that. Nipper obviously knew what he was talking about.

'When did you see the tracks?' asked Macknay.

'In the morning time,' said Nipper.

'Which day?' queried Macknay. Nipper replied, 'Monday.'

'Did you see any other dingo tracks around the tent?' Macknay wanted to know.

'One big track. A big one,' said Nipper.

'Which way did that go?' asked Macknay.

Nipper explained, 'It was going up the sandhills. There were two tracks and one cut short and the other went further into the bush.'

'Perhaps if you hold the photograph up, could you point out for me which way those tracks went?' Macknay requested.

Nipper explained and indicated on the photograph with his finger:

'Came around the corner and go that way, like that. Goes around that hill, Ayers Rock.'

'Did it go around the front of the tent or did it keep going?' queried Macknay.

'It came around, up and that way,' answered Nipper.

Mr Macknay continued later: 'You know the Sunrise Hill behind the tent?'

'Yes.'

'Did you see any tracks up there?'

'I have seen tracks,' said Nipper.

'You saw those tracks?' questioned Macknay.

'Yes.'

'Whereabouts were those tracks?'

'Climbed up the hill, the sun hill, and came on the road,' explained Nipper.

Macknay started, 'Climbed up the hill . . . ?'

'Yes.'

'And what did it do then?'

'All the people in the night-time go round that little road and are frightened to come on the road that way—don't like it—take it round there, that way, that little corner.' Nipper answered.

Later Mr Macknay was having difficulty and decided to use the interpreter for a while to see if it was any better. He continued 'Which direction were those tracks heading?'

'West. He found them on the east and they came back on the west,' the interpreter translated.

Mr Macknay asked, 'Which direction were the tracks heading?'

'West. Maggie Springs way,'replied the interpreter.

'Did you see tracks on that big dune?' Macknay asked Nipper through the interpreter.

'Yes, on the east side,' she answered.

'Which direction were those tracks that you saw on that sandhill?' Mr Macknay wanted to know.

'On the sand dune, on the east and they went to the west,' the interpreter answered again.

Later in Nipper's evidence, Mr Macknay asked, 'When you saw the tracks on the sandhill, did you see any other marks apart from the paw marks?'

'I saw one track. I saw one dingo,' the answer was translated.

'Was that dingo you saw on the hill carrying anything?' Macknay asked.

'Yes,' came the answer. 'I tracked it halfway and I saw it [the dingo] put it [the baby] down and left it and then after that carry it again but after that I cannot find it [the dingo]. Too many [people] have been there at night- time. There has been no track because the marking is gone.'

Mr Macknay was having difficulties in understanding: 'It seems that there are some difficulties whichever way we approach the matter. Perhaps if I can just try speaking to Nipper again in English and you listen to me, Nipper, and then tell me what you think. That dingo was carrying something was it?'

'Yes,'replied Nipper. 'It was carrying something. I track it and see it put it down.'

I didn't find Nipper difficult to follow. Having gone to schools with large migrant enrolments, I was used to following broken English but it seemed the lawyers were not.

Macknay continued with evidence on some other tracks which turned out to be those of a second dingo, apparently the one that I had mistakenly chased on the night.

He then continued: 'Did you find that other dingo again, the one you had seen on the sandhill?'

Nipper agreed, 'I find the dingo again when he came for water, the same like it, the paw'

'It came around to the water?' queried Macknay.

'Yes,' said Nipper.

'Which water?' Mr Macknay wanted to know.

'Maggie Springs,' stated Nipper.

'Was that paw a big or a little paw?' asked Macknay.

'Big one, big track. He is hungry,' stated Nipper.

I had always been told dingoes go for water before or after food and Maggie Springs, where the culprit dingo had stopped, was on the way to the place the clothes were found near the dingo lair.

'Did you track a dingo that went to the water tower, water tank?' asked Macknay.

'Yes, wrong one,' said Nipper.

'That was the wrong one, was it?' queried Macknay.

'Yes,' said Nipper.

'So the right one went down to Maggie Springs, did it?' asked Macknay.

'No, the wrong one,' answered Nipper, misunderstanding and still thinking of the irrelevant dingo. 'I track the wrong one. The right one, he go west.'

'He went west?' asked Mr Macknay.

'Maggie Springs,' stated Nipper again.

'Did you track him after Maggie Springs?'

'No,' said Nipper.

'Did you track him past that tent?'

'Yes,' said Nipper. 'I track him going from tent.'

Macknay wanted to be perfectly clear: 'When the dingo that went west left the tent, did it head straight across to the west?'

'It go the east side and he come back along the road, the motor car road,' patiently explained Nipper again.

'Did you track him along the motor car road?'

'No,' Nipper answered again, after all he'd already told them too many people had wiped out the tracks.

‘Do you know how far out east he went before he went west?’ Macknay queried.

‘How far?’ Nipper repeated. ‘It might be two hundred yards.’

‘Two hundred yards?’

‘Yes.’

‘Past the sandhill or not?’

‘On the sandhill.’

Macknay queried, ‘Which way did he go then from the sandhill?’

‘West.’

‘Back to the tent?’

‘No, he go on that way, west, the Maggie Springs way.’

Then Peter Dean had some questions: ‘Nipper, have you ever known dingoes to take babies from Aboriginal camps?’

‘No,’ said Nipper.

‘You have never heard of that?’ Peter wanted to know.

‘No, I have never known about the baby,’ Nipper replied uncomfortably.

‘What about camp dogs?’ Peter pursued.

Nipper made the statement ‘Camp dogs cannot take away. They cannot take them, camp dogs.’ This was a taboo subject; we learned later that he could not discuss it.

The court had supplied a female interpreter for Nipper and had two male interpreters standing by for the four Aboriginal women. Sensing some sort of hidden inhibition in Nipper, I went to quite a deal of trouble to make inquiries as to what the problem might be. I learned that what the court did not realise was that a woman interpreting for a tribal elder was not the done thing. It was actually an insult.

I also learned that Nipper, as head elder, was entitled to use the word ‘I’ when he spoke of himself, another member of the tribe, or of the tribe as a whole. This had created quite a deal of confusion over whether or not he had tracked on the night of Azaria’s disappearance. He said he had, yet others remembered a different Aborigine (Nui Minyantiri). When the ranger Derek Roff and his associates were asked whether Nipper had been tracking that night, of course they said no. A lot of Nipper’s evidence was therefore discounted as hearsay or confusion when Nipper was actually using his right to speak on behalf of a tribal member in the first person.

Much later I discovered that the women were unable to speak freely away from their tribal ground either, and not through a male interpreter without the permission of the tribal council. Even with the permission to speak to white men away from their tribal grounds, there were some things that they would still be unable to say. I had to gain the confidence of the Aborigines before I was even able to find out that much, and am still unclear about some of the implications.

The coroner asked Nipper questions about Aboriginal babies and dingoes and from a white man’s point of view he seemed to be claiming to have no knowledge of this. Once again there was a confusion in the white man’s understanding of the Aboriginal code of ethics. It was later obvious that when Nipper said he had no knowledge, he meant he was constrained by tribal laws to admit no knowledge of forbidden subjects, even though it was in his memory.

Some subjects are considered taboo and may only be spoken between initiated elders and no one else (including other tribal members). It is also forbidden to speak of the dead and anyone named after a person who dies must immediately change his or her name; and the former name must never be mentioned as a mark of respect to the dead (this often frustrates the police when looking for fugitives from the law).

Nipper's evidence was actually quite clear when you understood a few of these factors. He had told them each time they questioned him about the wrong dog, but had still suffered their confusion and answered their questions, continually adding after erroneous questions, 'But that wrong dog, right dog go down motor car road.' One of these tracks was going east, however, the correct track—according to Nipper—was going west.

Ian Cawood, one of the rangers, gave evidence of a previous dingo attack in June 1980. Another child had been dragged by the throat from her parents' car and the culprit dingo, a semi-pet known as 'Ding', was shot. The victim was a four-year-old girl, but Mr Cawood was unable to remember the name of the people. We were anxious to interview the parents but could not without their name or address. We asked permission to advertise but the coroner felt we would be opening the floodgates to a lot of nut cases. However, he agreed to make a general appeal for anybody knowing anything about dingo attacks to contact the court.

A survey had been sent out to all park entrants, with questions about us and dingo attacks. The Cranwells (as we much later discovered their name to be) had filled in theirs with details of the attack on their daughter, Amanda, and returned it to the police. None of us were aware that the police already knew who they were from the park files and surveys, and that they were withholding the information. As the Cranwells had reported to the rangers at the time and filled our the police survey they had been sent, they thought their evidence would have automatically been included and handed on to us, so they didn't reply. Besides, because of the feeling against us at that stage, they wanted to keep their case as quiet as possible. They were hoping their daughter would get over the attack without any mental scars, so were trying to make things as easy for her as possible.

The evidence continued, and Bill Barnes remembers:

> Jim Muirhead's assistant [a judge whom we were to get to know well in the future] asked me if I could find a seat in court for Mrs Muirhead! I gave her my seat by my table and sat on the other side of the court. [That must have been prophetic!]

Finally the last witness was dismissed from the stand. It was time for the summations.

'That Such Innuendoes, Suspicions and Gossip May Cease'

Ashley Macknay, for the Crown, stood and commenced his summary. He said, in part:

> Pastor Chamberlain at page 111 says his wife called out 'Michael, that dog's got my baby'. At page 188, Mr Lowe says, 'Mrs Chamberlain cried out that the dog had her baby'. Mrs West at page 134 says she heard 'My God, my God, the dingo's got my baby'. Mr West says at page 149, 'A dog

has taken my baby'. Of course, there was Aidan's account, which is also consistent.

Bearing in mind the remarks I made earlier about the question of publicity and the like, there was a lot of evidence to suggest that Mrs Chamberlain did call out words to that effect and that she called it out either immediately before or immediately after she checked the tent. [Of course there was a lot of evidence seeing I had done both, and Judy West had even heard me when I was mumbling to myself!] There is not perhaps much significance as to whether it was before or after. Apart from the fact that words to that effect were used, I think one can also be satisfied from the witnesses who heard her say them and observed her immediately after she said them that there was a certain amount of urgency about it and there was a certain amount of distress that followed, which perhaps is significant in terms of whether the fact of the words or the fact—I am not expressing that very well—whether she meant what she said or not.

On the evidence as it appears to me, one could be satisfied (a) that she said the words and (b) that she meant them. If one is satisfied as to that, one can perhaps move onto the following point and that is what the foundation was for Mrs Chamberlain coming to that belief. Now, that question to be answered properly has a number of considerations contained in it, not the least of which is the type of witness that Mrs Chamberlain impressed one as—whether as an accurate witness or a witness who was inclined to embellish things or dramatise things or perhaps leave things out.

There are also other elements contained in that question. For instance there is the question of paw marks outside the tent, in particular. Now, the thing that most impressed me about Mrs Chamberlain as a witness was her meticulous attention to detail which one could really say was quite extraordinary.

I think that one does not often see a person who is so meticulous about detail and one who is so often found to be accurate as to that detail, which is obviously the most important factor.

There are those matters which Your Worship raised yesterday in relation to Constable Fogarty and without in any way detracting from what Your Worship said yesterday I think it is perhaps unfortunate that the wrong person was in the witness box, in some ways. The person who bears and has to bear ultimate responsibility is the supervisor of Constable Fogarty who gave a box of items from Alice Springs to her with those bald instructions, 'Look for hair, look for blood'—the most junior person in the forensic science division who had had no training and three months on the job experience.

For that sort of thing to happen, it really shows almost derogation of responsibility on the part of the supervisor . . . The only way of preventing those mistakes from becoming as serious as they did in this case is for the supervisor to supervise properly. That obviously did not occur here.

> In my submission it would be quite proper for Your Worship in this case to recommend to the Commissioner of Police that people not be permitted to handle potential exhibits until they have had at least basic training in the identification of things that are going to be important; the people who are receiving on the job training not be permitted to work unsupervised particularly with the more serious matters involving deaths or serious injury to people; that only experienced people handle them in any event and really there needs to be a long hard look at that section.
>
> I have spent the last fourteen months or so in Alice Springs and just about every case in which I have been involved and Your Worship has been involved, Your Worship has made valid constructive criticism of the forensic science section in Darwin. There have been some improvements but there are still some major areas of difficulty . . . It would be my submission that Your Worship should recommend to the persons involved at the highest level—I presume the responsible minister or head of department that the question of the dingoes at Ayers Rock be examined immediately by somebody with expertise in the area and that his advice be followed. That does not necessarily mean that one is going out and kill all the dingoes at Ayers Rock—perhaps there are other things that can be done with them.
>
> Given what I have concluded, it is open to Your Worship to find on the facts that a dingo did take this child and one cannot permit the present circumstances to continue any longer. That point is perhaps reinforced by the fact that the suggestion that was made by the expert some years ago was not based on any tragedy having occurred but was simply based on his knowledge of the animal both in the wild and in captivity. The fact that a tragedy has apparently occurred at the hands of a dingo reinforces his advice of some years ago.
>
> As I said, there is no point in recriminations now. In my submission the thing to be done is to simply ensure that it will not and cannot happen again.

After that there was not a lot we needed to say, and Phil Rice's summary was short, then the court adjourned to wait for the coroner's finding.

Dennis Barritt made a controversial decision. Because there had been so many rumours about us, and because it seemed all Australia was talking about it, he decided to televise the delivery of his verdict in the hope that, as he said, 'by direct and accurate communication, such innuendos, suspicion and gossip may cease'. No private cameras were to be allowed.

Bill Barnes remembers the events overnight:

> That morning at seven, media blokes knocked on my door for the 'finding'. They really wanted a copy from Dinny, but weren't game to go to his house. We went up to Dinny's, collected him and went to the courthouse where Lena [Barritt's secretary] was waiting to photostat thirty odd copies

> for the media (with an embargo, of course). Reading that first copy was like having a refreshing drink. It was wonderful and I agreed with it about ninety percent. That, of course, is where it should have all finished.

As we walked into court on 20 February 1981 to hear Barritt's verdict, a reporter quickly drew one of our lawyers aside and told him that the finding was favourable and we would be happy with it. The reporters had only just discovered that we didn't know. We seemed to be the only people who didn't know. What Phil Rice and Peter Dean said about not giving the defence counsel the same courtesy as the press was unprintable.

The court was crowded, with people even standing in the aisles and around the walls. The door was left open to allow those in the foyer to see, as it was crowded also. One camera crew had their camera with them, supposedly not operating. As the court officials couldn't see the running light from where they sat, the crew got away with it. It was upsetting to have the finding filmed illegally like that.

Barritt, looking nervous and official, gave a long summing up. He said:

> In the Territory, whose economy is substantially centred on tourism, it is surprising that nobody sought to represent at this inquisition of which department of whatever government is finally responsible and possibly liable for the overall conservation policy at Uluru national park.
>
> In an area where advance planning is in hand to provide for the overnight needs of upwards of 6,000 tourists, a policy of conservation appears to have been activated that has its ultimate aim the intermingling of tourists with an ever increasing number of dingoes, death adders, desert brown and king brown snakes. The dingo is a dangerous animal and is known to be dangerous.
>
> Prior to 17 August 1980, the conservation authorities had received reports of several instances of dingoes attacking children. The significance of a dingo's range and a dingo's territory was known and understood by the rangers.
>
> In fact, Dr Newsome, a zoologist, had said that the growl the Wests heard was probably a warning signal to another dingo; Derek Roff the senior ranger agreed that there were probably two dingoes at the tent and that one was warning the other off his territory.
>
> The existence and whereabouts of a number of their lairs were known and known to be in areas where children might be expected to wander whilst exploring the many areas of interest around the base of the Rock.
>
> The conduct of dingoes around campsites, together with their propensity to enter tents, was known or ought to have been known. The propensity of a dingo reared by homosapiens and treated as a pet in a domestic environment to violently attack children was known; yet in the face of this knowledge dingoes have been retained and indeed allowed to virtually infest the area as a tourist attraction.

> I would hope that as a moral responsibility to protect children visiting national parks would appear to have been avoided in the past, the legal consequences of such conduct in the future ought lead to the elimination of any species dangerous to man from such parks or at least from those areas frequented by tourists. Every person in our community is under an obligation to conserve human life and those charged with the added task of conserving wild life ought remember and apply this primary tenet of our law. If those charged with the protection of wild life within national parks would rely on laws forbidding the destruction of such creatures then they ought to be made to publicise the inherent dangers that exist and are permitted to exist in such parks, and also what medical care would be available in an emergency in such remote regions.
>
> Such publicity should be included in any tourist promotion to fulfil the requirements governing fair advertising. This case clearly emphasises that a choice has to be made between dingoes and deadly snakes on one hand and tourism on the other. The two ought not be expected to co-exist creating hidden traps for decent people where formerly our forebears set hidden traps for deadly creatures. Dingoes are not and never have been an endangered species. Despite constant effort by man they have held their position as the most dangerous carnivore of the canine species on the Australian continent.
>
> Tourists in national parks should be able to observe native fauna in its natural state but I maintain only from a safe distance. To be able to observe a deadly snake under one's motel bed, as apparently was the fate of one of the media personnel on the court's recent visit to Ayers Rock, appears to be taking the cause of conservation too seriously. Lessons ought to be learnt from this inquest and applied. The death of this babe in an area where previous attacks causing bodily injury or potential bodily injury is too high a price and a totally unnecessary price to pay in the cause of conservation.
>
> I recommend that all animals dangerous to man be either safely enclosed or else eliminated from areas of national parks likely to be frequented by man . . .

As we later found out, this criticism of the conservation authorities did not exactly please them. Nor—as we discovered to our cost—did Barritt's following words endear him (or by extension, us) to the Northern Territory police force.

> Once again during this inquisition I have had occasion to criticise the work performed by the Northern Territory Police Force Forensic Science Section. Police forces must realise, or be made to realise, that courts will not tolerate any standard less than complete objectivity from anyone claiming to make scientific observations . . . any standard less than the highest attainable, where the rights and interest of suspect and prosecutor

alike are protected, negates the credit of such a section, and renders the probative value of its conclusions useless.

The forensic scientists certainly did everything possible to prove their diligence later.

He ended his summing up with great compassion:

To you, Pastor and Mrs Chamberlain, and through you to Aidan and Reagan, may I extend my deepest sympathy. You have not only suffered the loss of your beloved child in the most tragic circumstances, but you have all been subjected to months of innuendos, suspicion and probably the most malicious gossip ever witnessed in this country.

> I doth find that Azaria Chantel Loren Chamberlain, a child then of nine weeks of age and formerly of Mount Isa, Queensland, met her death when attacked by a wild dingo whilst asleep in the family's tent at the top camping area, Ayers Rock, shortly after 8 p.m. on 17 August 1980.
>
> I further find that in attempting to remove this babe from the tent, the dingo would have caused severe crushing to the base of the skull and neck and lacerations to the throat and neck. Such injuries would have resulted in swift death.
>
> I further find that neither the parents of the child, nor either of their remaining children, were in any degree whatsoever responsible for this death.
>
> I find that the name Azaria does not mean and never has meant 'sacrifice in the wilderness'.
>
> I find that after her death the body of Azaria was taken from the possession of the dingo and disposed of by an unknown method, by a person or persons unknown.
>
> This part of Barritt's comments was both publicly and privately quoted many times in the future.

I find it impossible to describe the depth of relief and vindication that Michael and I felt as we left the courthouse that day.

As we stood on the steps with the press surrounding us, Michael said a few words of relief and thanks to the court and Australia. We unrolled a poster print of myself holding Azaria so that the press and public could see once and for all the central reason for the inquest—and why we were so concerned that our experience should never happen to anyone else in Australia. We had been proud of our baby daughter and loved her very much. We wanted the world to see her and understand why we had fought so hard for the correct verdict.

But we weren't the only ones to give an interview on the court steps after the verdict—so did Mr Brown. He was upset his evidence had been discounted and said so, we learned later. When we went to apply to get out belongings back we were told they had to be officially held for one month. During that time anyone could apply to see them or do further tests. They would all come back; it was only a formality, but the jumpsuit and singlet may be a little longer as Mr Brown had applied for access.

Nothing could bring back our darling baby girl, of course; that was a loss that will make my heart ache for the rest of my life, but we had been publicly cleared; the rumours had been put to rest at last and now we could get on with our lives.

We also discovered later that the girls on the switchboard of a large well- known hospital in Brisbane, desperately wanted to watch the telecast of Barritt's summary so they took a portable television into work, just in case they could catch the inference of a few words during phone calls. One of the girls told me later that normally the only time the switchboard was quiet in the whole year was during the running of the Melbourne Cup. Much to their surprise, as soon as the coroner started his actual telecast, the switchboard went silent and not one phone call came through until the end of his summation. (This was about twenty minutes.) The girls couldn't believe their luck as they were all able to watch the complete program.

During the inquest, Erwin Chlanda, the chief reporter for the local *Centralian Advocate* and a freelance TV documentary maker, had approached us, asking us to consider doing a TV documentary on the case. We thought this sounded a good idea to clear up lingering doubts. One television program on our own terms would save a lot of hassling as well as giving us full control over what was being said (and oh, the bliss of not being misquoted yet again). Erwin seemed a reasonably nice guy and fairly genuine, so we agreed to a split of profits, if any.

As soon as the inquest was over, we headed out to Ayers Rock in a private plane. This was the first time we had been low over the area by small plane, and it helped to emphasise the vast loneliness. We flew across kilometre after kilometre of orange sand, here and there broken by small patches of white or yellow sand, scattered clumps of desert oak and spinifex. Occasionally we saw rolling ranges and deeply cut waddies where the water raced through in the wet season. It was spectacular.

Michael took all the photographs he wanted and Erwin asked him whether he would like to have a go at flying. He wasn't interested, but I was, so we swapped places and Erwin let me take the controls, after explaining what was what. I thoroughly enjoyed it. After a while Erwin said, 'You're doing well, but it's a bit bumpy. Keep your eye on one spot on the horizon and steer for that rather than just worrying about keeping the plane straight, because it feels as if you are flying by instruments.'

I said, 'Well, I am, because I can't see out of the front window. I was just flying by this little thing here you said to keep straight and by the compass.'

He looked stunned, slid down to my level and said, 'Shit! You can't see, either. Here, we'll have to do something about that.' He promptly made me sit on his briefcase, which raised me several centimetres so that I could look through the window and see where I was going. Things immediately improved. I flew for another half hour and as we got near the Rock and I started bringing the plane down, Erwin radioed that he was coming in. A real bush strip it was then, without a control tower—it just had a local two- way radio. When we were only thirty metres or so off the ground, he took over the controls. I was allowed to keep my feet lightly on the pedals to feel what happened as we came in to land.

In preparation for filming the documentary, Erwin's wife and a mate had gone out to the Rock by truck carrying a small motorbike. When we arrived, they had put up a tent similar to ours, on the spot where ours had been on 17 August, according to maps and plans we had drawn for them. They wanted to look as if they were tourists accidentally camped there. They were to officially register, while we would mainly stay clear of the national park, landing on the brand new airstrip at Yulara.

We checked locations and went out to the camping ground, making sure we stayed well out of sight to avoid any speculation or gossip. That night we all sat around and talked under the stars, feeling very relaxed. We pulled out beds and put them on the ground on the end of the airstrip. Erwin, his wife and their friend slept there; Michael was still very nervous about sleeping outdoors again so soon, particularly at the Rock, so we folded the seats down in the plane and slept there. The plane made a cosy bed and rocked a little when we moved, as a caravan does.

The following morning we were up early, ready to go around the Rock and film the various important locations. We filmed the area where Azaria's clothes had been found, as well as the animal track that ran directly between the clothing site and the dingo lair. During the inquest and later, when asked where the dingo lair was, the court was always taken to it through the scrub and boulders. This was supposed to illustrate that if the dingo had gone through between those sites, Azaria's clothing would have been a lot more damaged than it was, and other vegetation would be evident on it. The court was never shown that there was a clear dingo track through to the lair.

The lair was obviously still occupied; the scent around it was strong, and fresh paw prints were visible around the opening. You can tell a dingo track because the vegetation is worn away like a regular walking track and the rocks are often worn shiny in the small openings because they have been rubbed. At the site where Azaria's clothes had been found, you could see a crack in the rock with the typical greasy surface from the dingoes' coats polishing it, as well as paw prints. A side entrance to the lair opened directly onto this track which led straight to the clothing site with little or no hindrance. The front entrance of the cave was relatively difficult to approach due to thick scrub and boulders. Nevertheless, we saw one of the so-called 'rare' plants that we had been told didn't grow around that area, as well as small ferns and milk thistles that had been found on the clothing.

We filmed the area on a video camera, then checked the lair and the front entrance. We thought that perhaps Azaria's matinee jacket had been buried in the lair, but we couldn't get down there, although we could see by torchlight into the centre.

Because I was the smallest of the group, I could with some difficulty wriggle part way into the hole, balance the camera and take some time- exposure photographs of the centre of that lair. We discovered later that, by using a remote control arm (a special instrument to hold cameras in odd places) we could have dug in the area to see whether the matinee jacket had indeed been buried there.

Just inside the front entrance was a cavity in the rock, obviously used by the puppies as their toilet area. They had almost completely filled it with droppings, and we discovered the small bones and skulls of local animals the dingoes had been eating. We had been told by an expert that if anything was left of Azaria at all, the only evidence would be teeth. Even at her age, the teeth are hard and formed within the gums, whereas the bones are still very soft. The bones would have been consumed by the dingo without difficulty and its digestive system would dispose of them, whereas the teeth would go straight through the body as a waste product. This was a point that later caused great consternation. I always wished we were able to analyse the dingo faeces we found that day. Nevertheless, we felt the pictures we had taken clinched the matter. The case was now closed, and there didn't seem any point in wasting more money.

We finished filming the dingo lair with its side entrance track to the clothes site and the lush vegetation, then went to the Maternity Cave and filmed there. We then went to check out the Fertility Cave, where the blood, represented as being mine, had been found, and to see the area where I had initially been told the clothing was found. This was almost a kilometre away from the actual site. We did some filming there, then went straight to the tent site, endeavouring to get as much as possible done before we were recognised. We stayed out of sight while Erwin set up his camera, then filmed the actual barbecue site where we had all been standing on that fateful night. I followed my movements back to the tent; where I was when I saw the dingo and which direction I thought it had gone. What I saw in the tent, how I had called out, and where I had seen the other dingo, given chase and finally lost sight of it, all followed in sequence, then it was Michael's turn. He explained where he had been standing when he heard Azaria cry and where he searched that night. We quickly finished filming and hopped in the car to go back around the Rock before anyone knew we were there.

At one stage we had to wait for Erwin and I decided to start walking to the next location. It seemed fairly safe: there didn't seem to be anyone around and no one would recognise me anyway. Nobody was looking for us; it didn't occur to them that people they had seen on TV dressed up in court might be at the Rock, walking around in jeans. Michael was still very self-conscious and he decided to stay, lecturing me on the danger of blowing our cover. I set off anyway and walked quite a distance. Then, coming towards me, I saw a ranger's vehicle. As luck would have it, the ranger was Derek Roff, the very man who did know me. I thought this would be a good test whether I was recognised or not. Derek Roff has two different ways of waving to people: his 'I am the ranger, how are you going?' wave, and his 'Hello, nice to see you, I recognise you and know you' wave. I couldn't duck away—it would look most peculiar if I suddenly took off into the bush, so I decided to keep sauntering along. As Roff got close enough I just casually waved an Australian salute and kept walking. Roff acknowledged me with his brief polite ranger wave and kept going. It was obvious that he hadn't recognised me, so I jauntily went on my way.

Just after that, Michael and Erwin arrived. Michael was sitting in the passenger seat with a newspaper held up in front of his face. He said, 'You realise the ranger's vehicle just went past? He could have seen you. Now, get in quickly.' I grinned, 'Well he did see me,' I said, 'it was Derek Roff, and I waved to him and he didn't even know me.'

Erwin burst out laughing. 'I don't *believe* you two,' he said. 'One of you sticks a newspaper over his head to avoid being noticed and couldn't be more conspicuous if he was naked, and the other wanders around and waves to the very people you are trying to avoid and they don't even *know you*. Geez, what a story this would make if I was writing about it.' Michael and I always approached life differently. I was the practical one.

We finished our filming and left, arriving back in Alice Springs without any trouble. I flew almost the whole two hours back because Erwin started going to sleep at the controls (he claimed my flying soon woke him up) and I thoroughly enjoyed it.

The next day in Alice Springs we heard a news item saying that we had been to Ayers Rock but had been evicted. We weren't the only ones who heard that news item; so did the rangers, who were extremely upset. They assured us that the news item had not come from them and that they were annoyed about the adverse publicity. We informed them that we actually had been at the Rock but hadn't been evicted, and discovered they had not known about our presence at the Rock at all, confirming our belief that we had not been recognised by anyone. The local newspaper published a small retraction later, but the damage had been done. The rumour stayed for weeks. As a result of this, however, I was able to have a good phone conversation with ranger Ian Cawood, who told me the location of all the dingo lairs in the area around where the clothes had been found.

Peace at Last?

We came home to Cooranbong with a sense of utter relief. Once again, it was a totally new environment so we didn't know many people. A number of the young married couples and singles from Mt Isa had also enrolled at Avondale College in 1981 so we had a few friends apart from Michael's MA mates. Now that the legal proceedings were over, the whole business of our daughter's disappearance could be laid to rest, and we could get on with our lives. We knew, of course, that people with sick minds wouldn't be convinced by what Dennis Barritt had said, but we couldn't worry about them. Michael had study to do, I had a home to run and two little boys to look after. And our friends were all around us. We could begin the process of healing. I was going to start a Bachelor of Education (secondary) degree with a triple major, something I'd always wanted to do, and now I had the chance it would also help take my mind off the past.

But in my heart there was an ache that nothing could touch. My baby daughter had been such a delight, such a source of joy . . . and she had gone. We didn't even have a grave for her. We didn't know where she was. I felt we had been denied even mourning her properly.

Soon after our return, we were asked to do a number of radio, television and newspaper interviews and articles. Not about the inquest itself: the findings had been accepted (or so we thought). People wanted us to talk or write about dealing with our stress and grief, coping with a family in crisis—and what Seventh-day Adventists actually believed. But the church authorities didn't want us to speak out. They felt the inquest had harmed their image, and asked us to remain quiet, keep a low profile, let the issue disappear as quickly as possible. Michael and I agreed.

I always felt uneasy about this. I have never pushed my religion or my philosophy of life at other people, but if they asked about my beliefs I had always been perfectly willing to tell them. Now, here we were, being given the opportunity to speak and being told to remain silent. Perhaps this was why the media turned ugly later: because we had not spoken, they tended to print all sorts of things about us—rumours, fantasies, stories masquerading as fact. But this was still to come.

Peter, one of the young Mt Isa guys, was doing the farm maintenance course. When he realised I went jogging on my own, he offered to come straight after work (still in his work clothes and big work boots as a handicap) to jog with me.

Quite often he arrived with his deep pockets filled with two or three potatoes, a carrot, a parsnip, once even a small cabbage; things that had been turned up when ploughing or digging, and normally would have been left to rot. He knew we were having a rather hard time, and this helped stretch our budget.

It was his practical way of saying 'I'm sorry and I care'. He and his mate Brian had worked at the mines and had often come over to have Bible studies with Michael. They had delighted in playing with Azaria while waiting for Michael. They were among the few who really knew her and loved her.

On a trip Peter took to Ayers Rock, he made it his business to chat to a number of the rangers without letting on he knew the Chamberlain family and the baby that had been taken just weeks earlier. He asked about the dingoes. One of the rangers told him that over sixty dingoes had been shot after a small baby had been taken, but that they were only admitting to half a dozen or so officially. We chased that information because we kept coming up with similar reports from people travelling through, and having locals tell them there had been many more dingoes shot in the area than had been admitted to. But we could not at any stage prove that. Peter always wished afterwards that he had taken his tape recorder with him and also asked the ranger's name.

Les Smith, an acquaintance of ours, was a scientist working for the Plant Development Division of the Sanitarium Health Food Company. He had always been interested in the fact that spurts of blood had been found along the side of the tent, and although they had been rediscovered too late (due to the tent material and denaturation) for any definitive human or animal tests to be done, other than the fact that it was blood, he thought the blood spurts presented a range of possibilities. Les asked me whether I could tell him whereabouts on the tent and how far apart those blood spurts were. I was able to gather that information for him and hand it over. When I asked him why he wanted it, he said, 'I've just been wondering about something. If I feel there is any light in it I will let you know, just as a matter for your own curiosity.' He knew the average heart rate of a baby and then calculated the speed with which a dingo, from a standing start, might travel alongside the tent. He concluded that the blood spurts were spaced at about the right distance apart to tally with a dingo that was gathering speed and carrying an unconscious baby whose heart was still beating for a few seconds before she died. The fact that the first two spurts were closer together than the last ones had initially started his thinking.

In actual fact, the dingo would have been a long way away before I came out of the tent to chase it. This had been worrying me because I now realised that there had been two dingoes and it was very possible that I *had* chased the wrong one. Les had done this exercise to relieve my mind; to let me know, even if I had chased the right dingo, there would have been no way I could have caught it.

Life started to settle into routine again. The media had now lost interest: the nine-day wonder was over and we could be normal people again. I landscaped my front garden and finished setting up our new residence. Reagan started school and I began a Bachelor of Education course at Avondale College. Michael resumed his MA and we got to know our neighbours.

Helen from next door had to go to the dentist so she asked me as usual to look after her baby, Murray, who was about four months old. She took longer than usual, and Reagan enjoyed his time with Murray. Helen collected him on her return and I thought that was that. For days afterwards Reagan seemed to be looking for something. I asked him occasionally what it was but he always said, 'Oh nothing.' Finally I realised he was really worried, and said to him, 'Darling, what *is* it you are looking for? Can Mummy help you look for it?' As he still wasn't forthcoming I said, 'If Mummy knows what you are looking for maybe I can help find it.' He thought for a moment, then looked straight up at me and said, 'Mummy, has the dingo come and got our new baby too?'

My heart lurched as I suddenly realised he was looking for Murray.

'No, darling,' I replied, 'You know Murray. That was Murray from next door. He has gone back home to his own mummy and daddy.'

I could tell from the look on his face that he wanted to believe me but he wasn't convinced so I went on. 'Darling, would you like to see Murray?' and he said, 'Yes.' So next door we went, knocked, and when Helen answered the door I said to her, 'Auntie Helen, we've come to see Murray.' She said, 'Oh, he's asleep at the moment,' obviously thinking Reagan had come to play.

I looked at her and said, 'That's all right; we just need to see him right now.'

I pointed at Reagan over his head and raised my eyebrows. She cottoned on very quickly and said, 'All right. You'll have to be very quiet though, because he's asleep.'

We went in and saw him sleeping in his own cot, in his own room, with his own toys around him. Reagan was happy then as he had seen that Murray really was there and was all right. He never said any more about it. When we got home I explained to Reagan that Azaria had been mummy's baby born in a hospital as he had seen.

'Well, let's go and get one, then,' he said immediately. I explained that it wasn't *quite* that easy. A baby had to grow in Mummy's tummy first, just as Azaria had. When it was ready to be born you went to the hospital and it was your own special baby they gave you back, not just any baby. When our next baby came, I said, he could come to hospital like he did with Azaria, and it would come home with us all together.

All the exhibits were returned—except the baby clothes; they would come when Mr Brown was finished with them.

Things may have looked normal on the surface, but the hurt was still barely covered for all of us, and I felt as if there was unfinished business while Azaria's clothes had no final resting place.

Then, for us, the final word came in a letter we later received from Derek Roff, the senior park ranger at Ayers Rock; it had been written five days after Barritt's verdict had been brought down.

> Dear Pastor and Mrs Chamberlain,
>
> I am writing to pass on to you and your children the best wishes of the staff of Uluru National Park.
>
> Both I and my ranger staff are sorry that your visit to this park in August 1980 resulted in such a tragedy as the loss of your daughter which also led to the long period of suspicion and gossip that you were all subjected to by ill-informed people. I am glad that the inquest hearing exonerated you and I hope and trust that you will be permitted to live in happiness and peace and that your traumatic experience is over although I realise that the events of 17 August will remain with you all forever.
>
> May I and my wife Roberta and our children extend our sympathy and the hope for a happy future to you all.
>
> Yours sincerely, Derek Roff,
>
> Senior Park Ranger, Ayers Rock

PART THREE

Raided and Invaded

HOWLING IN THE NIGHT

At Easter we went camping with friends in the Wattagans, not far from home. The weather was cold and clear and after a walk, we camped around the fire. It was fairly cold by this time so we had stoked the fire up well. After we had all gone to bed in our separate tents, Michael and I sat looking at one another. We had borrowed a large family tent with the floor enclosed, which felt reasonably safe, yet we knew the Wattagans had dingoes. This was our first camping trip since August and we were feeling restless and unsure of ourselves. We left the lantern burning low at the front of the tent all night and put both boys in the middle of the tent with Michael on one side of them and me on the other.

At one or two o'clock in the morning, the howling started. It woke me with a shiver and before long I realised that Michael was also awake. We just lay there, looked at the boys, looked at the edge of the tent and decided to turn our lantern up. As I stuck my head out of the tent, thinking that it wouldn't be a bad idea to build the campfire up as well, I noticed that our friend Neville McKenzie was doing just that.

In the morning, one of the women said she had also heard the dingoes. She said, 'It has never worried me before, but having you with us and knowing the associations dingoes have for you, the howling really sent shivers up my spine. I got up and checked on my kids to see that they were all right.' Neville said he had built the fire up because he had heard that it would keep them back a little; he was also hoping if anything came near the tents it would serve as a light for him. Fortunately, most of the smaller children had slept right through it, so they weren't frightened. The adults had all had trouble returning to sleep, though. The next night we made sure we had plenty of firewood on hand and we kept the fire stoked.

Not long after our Easter trip, we heard from Erwin Chlanda again. He hadn't quite finished the work he wanted to do on the documentary, and came down to Cooranbong to see us, and stay for a couple of days so he could do the final taping.

I had arranged to pick him up at the airport in Sydney. On the way I was late and managed to collect a ticket for speeding. It was a Friday and I knew I wouldn't get my shopping done before Sabbath if I left it until I got home, so when I had picked up Erwin I told him he would have to come shopping with me on the way home. When we got to Wyong, I went into the supermarket. Erwin thought it would be interesting to observe people's reactions and as I walked around, he pushed the trolley and followed at a distance. He certainly got some response. People gaped and reacted as if their heads were connected on swivels. I no longer took a great deal of notice of them.

At one stage, Erwin came over and whispered, 'Look at those old ducks down there having a real argument, deciding whether it is you or not! They've worked out you are with me, and I don't fit the description of Michael. One says it is definitely you with someone else, and the other one says no way. We have got enough groceries for parcel pickup, so we'll tell them my name at the checkout, OK?' The two elderly ladies stood in the queue behind us and we could see them craning their necks to see the name on the pickup docket. When they saw it was Chlanda, one said to the other, 'See! I told you it wasn't her.' Erwin went off chuckling and he laughed to himself for most of the half hour journey home.

We eventually sold the short documentary to the ABC's 'Four Corners'; we made just enough to cover the production costs. What I found interesting was Erwin's difficulty in selling it. Whereas everybody in the media had been clamouring to talk to us on their terms, suddenly when we told our story, they decided there was no more to be said. What's more, people have thought at various stages through the last ten years that they knew the whole story—they had heard it all before. Yet they always asked the same questions, over and over again.

Later Erwin told us the police had asked to see his rough footage of the film. Having seen Erwin being friendly to the police on several occasions, we felt we could not trust him to the same extent that we had before so did not disclose why we wanted it given to our lawyers first. I'm sure he thought I was anxious because there was some hidden clue of guilt. We did not want them to realise the significance of the puppy litter in the lair for fear it disappeared. We were told later that the police had not subpoenaed the footage but that Erwin had actually offered it to them. When we were next able to visit Ayers Rock, our fears were confirmed. The area of puppy litter, where infant teeth might have been found, had been totally cleaned. Clean as a whistle. And it could not have happened on its own. The dingoes no longer used that area; they had been shot, moved off, moved camp. The rock formation was like a very deep baby's bath and it would actually have had to be scooped or sucked out with something like a vacuum cleaner. No mention was ever made of that area being searched, cleaned or tested. It simply ceased to be.

Quite a lot of other things were happening that we didn't know about. The forensic dentist Kenneth Brown was so incensed about Barritt's findings he had applied to the Northern Territory government for Azaria's clothes, saying he wanted to take them to London to be examined by an 'internationally renowned' forensic pathologist named Professor James Cameron. Permission was granted, and he went in June. He didn't tell Professor Cameron that the clothes had already been examined at an inquest, nor did he inform him that a method of death had been established by the coroner, Dennis Barritt. Kenneth Brown was a Seventh-day Adventist: proof, if any were needed, that not all Adventists were on our side.

Cameron found that the neck of Azaria's jumpsuit had been stained with blood while it was fully done up. He said that Azaria's neck hadn't been cut by dingo teeth, but by a cutting instrument—scissors or a knife. The jumpsuit, he said, had been buried with her body still in it. He even found what he said were impressions of an adult female hand (later simply a 'small adult' hand—though how you tell the difference between small adult and large child I've yet to find out) on the back and shoulder of the jumpsuit, caused by somebody (me, presumably) holding the baby upright with bloodstained hands. His conclusion was that it was reasonable to assume that Azaria met her death by unnatural causes; basically, I cut her throat while holding her upright.

It was this finding that opened the second inquest, and led to the whole subsequent chain of events.

When the Northern Territory heard about all this, they really got going. According to the police tapes tendered at a later court, Paul Everingham, the Chief Minister, personally convened and directed a police conference and the cops formed teams, one for each state of Australia, to interview the witnesses. Simultaneously (so we couldn't all compare notes) the police called on the Lowes, the Whittakers, the Goodwins, the Wests and the Elstons—all people with whom we had had no contact since the end of the first inquest. When the police called on Greg and Sally Lowe, they told them to grab their coats and get down to the police station. At the station they were interviewed; Sally, who was three weeks away from having her second baby, was left sitting on an upright kitchen chair for five hours without being offered food, water, or the use of the toilet. She was later to give evidence that she felt they treated her as if she was a criminal, and that she was badgered to change her evidence. Had she heard Azaria cry? How did she know it had been a baby's cry and not a wild animal's? In later evidence it was clear the Lowes and other witnesses were told to forget the dingo. No one wanted to know. In later years they compared notes and found they had all been told the same thing—'Forget the dingo'. The police also arranged to record every conversation (without telling anyone they were doing so). They called this Operation Ochre.

Raided and Invaded

On Saturday 19 September 1981 a team of police, led by our old 'friend' Detective Sergeant Graeme Charlwood, arrived at our home. It was Sabbath morning—Saturday—a day for God, church, and friends, not work: and I regard answering questions from police, armed with a warrant to collect about sixty items, as work. They weren't mucking around, either; before we knew it, it seemed, police were swarming all over the house. They could have waited another day . . .

Did they start at the back and work through, collecting their items? No way. They were deliberately searching everywhere—behind the water heater and up unlikely ledges. I began to wish a redback spider would bite in some of the places one of the policemen put his hands. He was so sour I couldn't help mentioning to his colleague that he must have had razor blades for breakfast. Interestingly enough, when the transcription of the hidden taping was produced later, that was one of the segments marked 'inaudible'. So was the section where I asked them to tidy up.

The questions were puzzling. Where were the tent pegs we'd used during our Ayers Rock holiday? We couldn't find them and couldn't work out why on earth they were needed anyway. (We later found that one of the cops—Metcalfe—had found our family Bible supposedly underlined at the Old Testament story of Jael, who murdered an enemy general, Sisera, by hammering a tent peg through his forehead while he slept in her tent. In reality the 'underlining' was the marking caused by the old-fashioned woodcut picture rubbing ink on the opposite page.) They seemed particularly interested, for some reason, in knives and scissors, and went right through all my kitchen drawers, asking questions about the cutlery and cutting implements we had taken on our holiday, and taking a number that hadn't even gone with us to Ayers Rock. Other items that appeared to rivet their attention were camera bags. Now, Michael is an inveterate photographer, and he always drove with a camera bag wedged under his legs in the driver's seat. We couldn't see why this was so important. They picked up a brown one, and Michael had to fetch the correct one for them—eventually they took away three of his bags just to be sure.

Then they asked to look at our car. (We didn't know then, but the theory was that I had cut Azaria's throat in the car with the scissors and that her body had been stowed in Michael's camera bag to be buried later.) We had no objection to their examining the car, though yet again we couldn't see the reason for it; after all, Constable Graham searched before the first inquest, supposedly thoroughly. It was being repaired after a road accident and was still in pieces over the floor of a private garage not far away. But Michael said, 'Sure, you can examine it if you want to.'

We gave them what they wanted, including some items that they hadn't had before. These included the giggle hats I had found during the first inquest. I got them out and explained when I had found them, and began to hand them over to Charlwood: I let one go, thinking he had hold of it, and it dropped to the floor between us. We laughed and apologised, both tried unsuccessfully to pick it up at once, and then I stood up and left Charlwood to pick up the hat, which he did.

I thought no more of the incident until we got to court and one of the policemen stated I had angrily thrown the hats. Of course I hadn't at all. When Charlwood came into the witness box, he was asked for his version of the incident, and agreed that it was as I said and the earlier statement had been a mistake. It was just one example of the police attempting to misrepresent my actions.

The police finished in the house and started loading the boots of their cars. I could hear them grumbling that we couldn't possibly have fitted all the stuff they took in one car. Well we hadn't, of course, as they had taken extra gear, but they *didn't* take a few items that *did* surprise me, especially knowing what I do now.

We have a large Esky; metal with plastic lining, that has numerous miscoloured stains in it. We had had it at the Rock. They looked at it carefully then rejected it as of no use. Would it have ruined their camera bag theory, I wonder? A leakproof, sealed container with ample space would seem more likely than a much-too-small and awkward camera bag. Then there were the two large polystyrene foam drink containers I had kept on the floor of the car at my feet. They were also left behind. Their presence made it impossible to kill anything in the space under the dashboard—but that would also mean I had liquid readily available to clean up with, *if* I had killed Azaria, as they said.

When we moved outside, Charlwood inspected the doona we had used for Aidan's mattress, but as it was old and the boys used it for cubby houses under the tree outside, it was rejected. (Later the Crown tried to maintain that one of the two floral mattresses under Reagan had been used on the other side of the tent for Aidan, so it couldn't fit Sally Lowe's description, of course.)

They had a further hunt for the tent pegs and were surprised to find them where they should have been—wrapped with the tent. But then we didn't know Metcalfe had found his tent peg murder incident underlined in our Bible, did we!

They all eagerly looked in the pauper's coffin they had stepped over in Mt Isa which Michael used in his anti-smoking program, and found it full of program aids. An inspection of the garage revealed a cane knife, which they promptly took. Seeing this, Aidan volunteered that there was another one on the garage roof, and promptly climbed up to fetch it. Their eyes sparkled and one of the police climbed on the garage door so he could see onto the roof. He jumped down again with a shrug.

The police wanted statements and we needed to show them where the car was or they would never find it. It was lunchtime and the boys were hungry and upset. I arranged to go down to church (at college) to get a babysitter and had every intention of seeking legal advice while I was away if I could, as we were not on the phone at home.

Most people had left as I ran down the path to the church. Suzanne Silvasti from Mt Isa, the very person I was looking for, was walking towards me with her husband, Harry, and behind them walked the new college president, Dr Jim Cox, and his wife Alice. They obviously realised from my dress and demeanour that all was not well.

I blurted out, 'Suzanne, can you look after the kids for me?' She nodded yes, and her smile turned to dismay as Dr Cox said, 'What's wrong?' I broke down when I said, 'They've reopened it all over again!' I quickly regained control and asked to try and ring for advice. While Suzanne and Harry hurried off to Michael and the boys, Alice hugged me then went home to pray for us while Jim took me to his office so I could use the phone.

Peter Dean wasn't at home, nor was Phil Rice, so I didn't know what to do. Jim suggested a local Adventist solicitor he had met, Stuart Tipple. After several phone calls we finally got his home number, but he was obviously out to Sabbath lunch. Where next to turn? Then I remembered Mr St. John, QC. He was at home mowing his lawn and happy to help. He questioned me closely and told me if they were taking more things from us and hadn't let us read their warrant, they were up to no good. 'As they have very full statements already I would strongly advise you not to talk to them without your lawyer present,' he said. I thanked him and hung up, just as Dr Cox told me Suzanne was back.

I met Suzanne in the corridor and was astonished to see Charlwood with her. Before he could say anything to me, she whispered, 'The press have arrived, and there are helicopters, photographers and journalists everywhere.'

'Where's Michael?' I asked. Charlwood then came up and told me Michael had bundled the kids into the police vehicle and gone off to the police station in nearby Toronto. The cops had managed to convince him that they would be safe from the press there. This was the very last thing I wanted; I had been hoping to keep Reagan and Aidan home and settled. The descent of the press on the house (almost literally, as the helicopters landed over the road) had caused Michael's precipitate departure for Toronto—anything to get away.

Charlwood told me that Michael had been quite happy to go with the police and that, because we had agreed to give a statement anyway, they had gone on ahead. I told him, 'The lawyers have told us not to give any interviews without them being present and as Michael doesn't know, I'll have to tell him and pick him up from the police station with the boys.'

Charlwood asked—quite humbly for him—whether I'd be good enough to give him a lift down to the police station, saying that his mates had left him. Because the press were everywhere, we decided that Charlwood would drive the Honda Civic we'd borrowed while our own car was being repaired. The press wouldn't be expecting to see me in that, and we could probably leave without being spotted.

As we passed our gate I remarked on the press there. 'Oh, they're not press. They're our boys,' Charlwood said. So he hadn't been left behind at all. I was starting to really simmer now, silently.

Charlwood began our conversation by saying, 'You haven't asked me why we're here yet, Mrs Chamberlain.'

'No, I haven't, have I?' I said in an offhand tone.

'Aren't you going to?'

'I think it's pretty obvious,' I said. 'You took all the scissors and knives. It's back to us again, isn't it?'

'Er, yes. You could say that,' Charlwood replied. 'Aren't you going to ask?'

'OK,' I agreed. 'What are you here for?'

'If I tell you,' he said, 'I want you to understand that I will deny that this conversation ever took place, and that I was ever here with you in this car. This is entirely off the record.' What a laugh.

'In that case, I might do it also!' I said. 'Anyway, I won't be quoting you, except to Michael and the lawyers.'

'One of the questions you would have been asked is: Did you kill your baby?'

I was disgusted. 'If I answer that,' I told him, 'I'll be giving you an interview.'

'No, you won't.'

'Why not?'

'You have my word,' he said.

'Once before I was caught, about hypnotism,' I said. 'That was off the record also, and it was brought up as an official enquiry.' It had been a nasty surprise during the first inquest.

'I didn't write that in my notes,' Charlwood said. 'I kept my word.'

'Then how did they know?'

'Someone must have found out about it and I was asked in the box.'

'I wonder how!' I said sarcastically. There was no reply.

'Well,' he said a moment later, 'you haven't answered my question.'

'No,' I agreed, 'I haven't, have I?'

'Well, did you kill your baby?'

'No, I did not,' I said. 'But I think you know that deep down anyway, don't you?'

'Do you want an honest answer?' he said.

'Of course,' I said.

'I don't know,' said Charlwood.

He didn't know! I took a deep breath and said, 'Do you think I could look you straight in the face and lie?'

He told me he'd had to deal with people he could have sworn were innocent but they turned out to be guilty of the most horrible things, and people who seemed guilty who were in fact innocent.

'I now try to remain entirely impartial and not make a judgment,' he told me. 'Some people are excellent liars.'

'Fair enough,' I said. 'Let me state that I am not a good liar. I could never look you in the face. I know that, if you don't. Well, what are you here for, then?'

'We have a report from a Mr Cameron in England who has been doing some further testing on the clothes, and he has found hand-prints on the baby's suit in the underarm region belonging to a female.'

When I commented that I didn't know there were any dingo experts in London, Charlwood gave me a dirty look.

'So we're back to that, are we?' I said.

'Something like that.'

'You're crediting me with a few extra brains than I've got, aren't you ?'

'You're being facetious, Mrs Chamberlain,' he said.

'Are you making fun of me?' I asked.

'No, I'm not,' he said, 'Don't sell yourself short.'

'Oh, come on. If I had done it, why come up with such an unbelievable story? There would be something more logical than that, surely!' I was coldly angry, but underneath I felt an amused detachment that seemed completely unreal.

'Don't sell yourself short,' he repeated.

'You are crediting me with the brains and ability to commit the perfect murder!'

'Don't sell yourself short,' he said again.

'What else is in the report?' I asked.

'Cameron indicates the baby was decapitated.'

Now I knew the reason for their interest in knives and scissors. 'I guess that puts me in the hot seat,' I said.

'Mmm,' he replied.

'What else?' I asked.

'That's about it,' he said. 'Except there is no animal involvement, never was.'

'Well, how do you explain the dingo then?' I demanded.

'I thought you might have some ideas on that.'

'You've heard my ideas, in court. I didn't make them up,' I told him.

He then told me that there would be a new inquest, with an opposing verdict.

'Well,' I said, 'I know it can be reopened with disposal of the body—' I meant that I knew further evidence could be given about what had happened to Azaria, in view of Barritt's finding that human intervention had been involved.

But Charlwood said that Barritt wouldn't be working on the case. 'It will all be annulled at the Supreme Court,' he added, 'It won't be a dingo verdict this time.'

In fact, the police had applied to the Northern Territory Supreme Court for an order quashing the findings of the first inquest so that the matter could be reopened.

We hadn't been told about that until Charlwood mentioned it to me. All the proceedings would take place in camera. I couldn't believe all the fuss and trouble, or that the police hadn't told us a thing.

'You've got yourself a headache and more questions than answers,' I said sarcastically. 'I'm glad it's you and not me. How did the press know—again?'

'I don't know,' said Charlwood. 'You know I don't talk to the press. The statement must have come out earlier than expected. I thought it wouldn't be until Monday possibly.'

There was nothing more I could say. Unknown to me, while the police were raiding us, Paul Everingham, NT Chief Minister, was holding a press conference. That announcement had allowed the press to reach our house before the raid was over. We had a general conversation until we arrived at the Toronto police station.

'You know, sometimes good people do something accidentally and it is much easier for them in the long run if they own up as soon as possible,' Charlwood said as he pulled up.

I knew what he was hinting at, but I wasn't about to confess to something I hadn't done. 'Yes, I agree with you,' I said, 'I have always held that view, and it is the sort of thing I would do if faced with that situation, but I'm not.' I added, 'Anyway, how am I supposed to have done it and washed my hands, cleaned up, etcetera, and got back to the barbecue in that short time? There aren't even any taps out that way.'

'You're presupposing it was done then,' said Charlwood.

'Oh, well! Yes, I hadn't thought of that,' I said. 'That's a whole new ball game. Boggles the mind.' And as we got out of the car and walked into the station, I added, 'You have more coincidences than I care to think of. I don't envy you your job.'

We went in. I realised the police were stalling for time and wondered whether Michael's interview had already started. I knew that Michael would be talking to the police quite openly, as we had before, not realising what they were up to. If they had some theory, not just mischief in mind, they could have simply asked for the items they wanted to be handed over and known that we would have complied. The fact they had a warrant (even though they hadn't let us read it) and had appeared on our doorstep so abruptly indicated that the police had another motive, but the conversation with Charlwood had now told me what their purpose was.

Some Records of Interview

I expected to be led straight to Michael, but was put into a room on my own. Charlwood said he'd get Michael and went out, closing the door behind him. I was immediately wary and got up to watch him through the other open connecting door. He was simply talking to a colleague. Unaware I had a continual view of him, he was not writing up his notes, as he later claimed, or calling Michael. I heard a door open and shut, with Michael's and the boys' voices coming from that direction. It was obvious that Michael was not being told I was there and then I heard one of the kids say, I want a drink, Daddy.' I walked back out into the main corridor area where Charlwood was making a phone call and said, 'Where is my husband? What's the hold-up?'

He said, 'Oh, they have just gone to get him.' The children, hearing my voice, came running out calling, 'Daddy, Mummy's here!' Michael came then and said, 'Hello, I didn't realise you were here already.' Later we discovered that he was being taped without his knowledge on what was actually an informal interview. Although I had scanned Charlwood for a tape recorder, he had actually had one strapped to his leg when we talked in the car, and he later claimed it had malfunctioned. Well, if it hadn't, his version wouldn't have coincided with the tape he had! The police later subtly tried to make out I'd asked for a deal when I'd asked what my position would be in answering questions, in view of the fact I'd refused to give an interview.

When this was taken in context it held a totally different meaning, but context didn't seem to matter to the police. They weren't interested in truth, just in their own theories it seemed to me. It was the closest Charlwood came to verballing me.

I explained to Michael that we had had legal advice not to give an interview to the police again, but that some extra forensic tests had been done. Charlwood explained about the baby being decapitated and hand- prints in human foetal blood being on the clothing. This was obviously as much of a shock to Michael as it had been to me. Charlwood said they would like to have my hand-prints too. I told him that was fine if my lawyers agreed.

The police gave up on the interview and hand-print idea after we had tried several more times to get through to Peter Dean without success.

Then they wanted the car. We had to hang around for quite some time until a low loader and a crane could be found, as the car was without its engine and it had to be lifted everywhere. As the car's location was difficult to find, even with directions, we had to take the police there. They had almost finished loading the car when the mechanic came tearing down the road, demanding to know what they were doing; he thought that the car was being stolen. He too was a Seventh-day Adventist and did not appreciate a visit from the police on Sabbath. But there was nothing we could do about it. My impression was that the police had deliberately chosen Sabbath.

Michael signed the police notebook as a sort of receipt that they had taken the car, and we came home. I immediately made full notes of the conversation that I had had with Charlwood in the car.

On the police tapes handed in as evidence years later, there was a discussion about the seizing of the car. It was one thing not listed on the warrant and the police had had no right to take it. They were worried that it would not be able to be used in evidence, until they remembered that it was a 'bloody good piece of luck' that Charlwood had got Michael to sign his notebook, because that meant he gave his consent and the Chamberlains couldn't do anything. At the time, Charlwood assured us that we would be compensated for any damage done to our car and other things. We both raised our eyebrows and I bluntly stated we hadn't received any the last time. He disclaimed knowledge of that and assured us it would be different this time. Our goods would only be gone a few weeks. Seven years later the equivalent of $19,000 of damaged goods and what was left of our car and most of our goods were returned. Compensation took even longer.

During the raid Noel Bainbridge, one of the policemen, was taped in a phone conversation with Superintendent Neil Plumb. These tapes were later used in evidence and these are all precise extracts. No one could believe they had taped themselves, as the tapes were so self-incriminating. The general comment was, 'It was a wonder they didn't lose *them* when they got subpoenaed.'

'What's doing?' asked Bainbridge.

'Not doing too well. Just stand by, mate. We've got no admissions [by the Chamberlains] or anything as yet, mate,' said Neil Plumb.

'Well, we've finished interviewing the Lowes,' Bainbridge stated. 'We've had them for about four and a half hours. They don't advance any more than what they've already said, really. The only thing that Mrs Lowe came up with was that Mrs Chamberlain had no sooner got to the barbecue area than the sound of the cry came and she turned around and went back. She put it down to about thirty seconds. So there's no way that a bloody dingo could get in there and get the baby out from the time she took to walk from the tent to the barbecue and back again.'

Plumb questioned urgently, 'What—the sound of the cry, did she hear the sound of a cry?'

Bainbridge replied, 'She's pretty sure that it was a baby's cry, it was loud—not a shout—like it wasn't a shout, a shout—I will just find the part. In relation to seeing the baby, she remembers seeing the face but she can't recall the actual image. She only saw about a third of the face. She saw the feet and the legs where the blanket came adrift down the legs. The baby didn't cry at all; she didn't hold the baby over her shoulder as if it had wind. I asked her if she had a definite recollection of the baby squirming. She said, no, it was more or less assumed.

'Question: "Can you recall if Mrs Chamberlain had her hand near the baby's feet when the baby kicked?"

'Answer: "It was in that area. In the court they tried to indicate that Mrs Chamberlain moved the feet but I recall the definite kick from the baby."

'Question: "Just to clarify that, would you say that it was possible that the kicking was simulated by Mrs Chamberlain or that the feet kicked of the baby's own volition?"

'Answer: "From what I could see, the baby kicked on its own behalf."No mention of the baby having wind.'

'Yes,' mused Plumb.

'Mrs Chamberlain and Aidan didn't run back to the barbecue after putting the baby down, they walked back,' Bainbridge said.

Plumb said, 'Now if she walked back to the barbecue . . .'

'Yes,' Bainbridge said.

Plumb continued, 'After she put the baby in the tent?' Bainbridge agreed, 'Yes.'

Plumb expanded, 'Yes, and then it was within ten seconds of her getting there—'

Bainbridge interrupted, 'No, the time lapse from when she would have left the tent or—yes, thirty seconds from her getting there to the cry going up was virtually almost simultaneously that she got back there.'

Plumb asked, 'Did she see the face of the baby? She didn't.'

Bainbridge said, 'She reckons that she [saw] a third of it, looking down at an angle through the blankets but she can't recall the image.'

Plumb questioned, 'Was it dark at this time?'

'No, there was a fair amount of light from the—light near the barbecue there. I said, "During the time Mrs Chamberlain was at the barbecue, did you see any part of the baby at all?"

'Answer: "I can remember seeing the face but I don't recall the actual image."

'"How much of the face would you have seen?"

'"She was quite tightly wrapped up but I remember seeing the feet kicking. I suppose I would have seen about a third of the feet, just looking down on the baby at an angle."

'I don't know whether they just kind of think that or what, mate,' Plumb sighed.

'I think she's assuming a lot, to be quite honest,' Bainbridge said.

'What about the hypnotism part?' Plumb queried.

Bainbridge said, 'Well, we went into that. Unfortunately we couldn't get anyone in here—there was a couple quite prepared to do it but they were going away for the weekend.'

Bainbridge wasn't happy though. 'The only problem is that Dr Burroughs says that people can lie under hypnosis and that unless you can corroborate what they say in some way—'

'Yes,' agreed Plumb.

'—then you're putting yourself out on a limb,' worried Bainbridge. Bainbridge went on later, 'We sort of tried to tie the Lowes down as much as possible but it's just time and sort of in the memory.'

'Yes,' Plumb agreed.

Bainbridge continued, 'And there's very little difference to what they said originally.'

'Yes,' Plumb said.

Bainbridge, 'Certainly nothing worthwhile,' he said. 'I don't think they honestly remember, you know, about—'

Plumb agreed, 'Yes.'

'Things sort of got blotted out because of the circumstances,' Bainbridge said.

'Yes,' said Plumb.

Bainbridge started, 'But . . .'

Plumb said, 'I think it will be all or nothing, mate. I think we might have to get that bloody hypnosis done.'

'Yes, all right. As I said, the only problem is that if we do get something, will it be—would we be able to get it into court?' wondered Bainbridge.

Elsewhere on the tapes, Superintendent Neil Plumb and Detective Sergeant Graeme Charlwood were comparing notes on the key eyewitnesses after Operation Ochre. Plumb said, 'We can't shake it that the baby was at the barbecue early—you know, at least twenty past seven.'

Charlwood agreed and said they had worked out that I had raised the alarm at about five minutes to eight that night. He continued, 'We can't break the Lowes down. Are we putting them under hypnosis, or have they declined that?'

'Well, no. I don't know whether that is going to do us any good because of those people in Esperance [the Wests] who have got them at twenty past seven,' Plumb answered.

Plumb added, 'What we've got to be prepared for, mate, is quite a long, lengthy investigation.'

'Yes,' agreed Charlwood.

'You know, it's just one of those things, and we're not going to do it in five minutes. We'd hoped that something might happen, but it hadn't. That's all it amounts to,' Plumb complained.

Plumb and Charlwood also demonstrated their biblical knowledge.

'They did find an open page in an old Bible in the house, which mentions Deborah and—Christ, someone else—Deborah and Barek, or something, and the child is spiked in the head and then the throat is cut, and they found some bloodstained giggle hats that we never knew about before. But a lot of it is going to depend on forensic. They [the Chamberlains] had the bloody press descend upon them and buggered everything up,' said Plumb. (Well, whose fault was that? Paul Everingham had held a press conference.)

Charlwood and Neil Plumb continued discussing the Bible story. Charlwood said, 'You know, the significance of it wasn't that great. But had it have been underlined, you know, to show that they were in fact really particular[ly] interested in that section of the page—'

Plumb interrupted, 'Yes, but it's just one little thread, that's all. But it's still a little thread.'

That statement describes the case against us in general—a lot of little unrelated threads joined together. And not often correct; the Bible episode proved embarrassing to them later during the Royal Commission, when the Bible was actually produced.

Charlwood told Plumb that they had a photograph of the baby's coffin.

'They use it in—he does a five-day stop smoking campaign,' he said.

'I get you,' said Plumb.

Charlwood added, 'And he uses it as a prop in that.'

Plumb questioned, 'That's just a prop—the relevance of that?' Charlwood said, 'Yes.'

'Oh, Jesus!' the superintendent exclaimed.

We kept trying to ring Peter Dean, and Dr Cox kept trying Stuart Tipple. He reached Stuart Tipple first and we engaged him. When we finally got through to Peter Dean he agreed we should have a local lawyer as his assistant.

Finding Stuart was a great piece of good fortune. He was local, for a start, living not too far from the college and Cooranbong. He was an Adventist, and a New Zealander as well. He had known Michael's family when he was growing up. Peter Dean arranged a meeting with him and us at Cooranbong. This was the first time I met Stuart. When he drove into our driveway I wondered at first if he was another reporter, but Michael assured me it *was* Stuart. I was surprised he was so young, but very quickly realised that he had his head screwed on all right. We were pretty sure we could trust him.

We didn't realise then what a goldmine we had struck. I am sure God picked him for us, if we had looked around all the lawyers in Australia, we couldn't have chosen a better one. Stuart's tireless, unshirking work became apparent during the preparation for the second inquest.

Dr Harry Harding heard of a new test that could definitely distinguish between cat and dog hairs, so speculation would end about the hairs found on the jumpsuit. He rang the police, and was taped giving them some information. 'The Chamberlain thing—they've got now a computerised program for trying to discriminate between cat and dog hairs and they've offered to process the information if we can get that across to them . . . specialists get a hold of a couple of the hairs and make microscopic measurements on them and telex them across to the UK. That's what I was trying to chase up.'

The police didn't want to know anything about hairs, wild animals and particularly dingo involvement and the 'fanciful lie' that Mrs Chamberlain had claimed as an alibi.

Noel Bainbridge and Jim Metcalfe were also recorded on the telephone.

'Just a thought on my part, mate—it might be worth checking with Aidan's schoolteacher to see what sort of little—sort of bloke he is, you know?' said Bainbridge.

Metcalfe agreed, 'Yes.'

Bainbridge continued, 'Whether he's got any strange behaviour . . .' Metcalfe agreed again, 'Yes.'

'One of the fellows here reckons he's got very weird eyes,' said Bainbridge.

'Everyone reckons that she's got killer eyes,' Metcalfe added. Graeme Charlwood and Jim Metcalfe also discussed evidence.

'I went to the Mitchell Library on Friday,' said Metcalfe. 'I went through dozens and dozens of name books and I could not find one of them which had . . .'

'Azaria,' Charlwood broke in.

Metcalfe continued, 'Azaria, Chantel, Loren in it.'

Charlwood stated, 'Actually, if you go out to the—as far as Azaria—if you go out and see the Sheila that teaches the Hebrew studies—I think it's the University of New South Wales . . .'

'Yes,' Metcalfe broke in.

Charlwood continued, 'She's the one that phoned Barritt and told him the definition.'

Metcalfe asked, 'What about this doctor at Mt Isa who looked up the Oxford . . .'

Charlwood broke in, 'Milne, yes, but he got it wrong. He got it with the name—the letter "H" on the end of it.'

They *knew* Dr Irene Milne had not rung; her brother *had*, and had given his name. They also knew the rumours about Azaria's name were wrong.

Metcalfe continued, 'I looked up the same book and it mentions nothing about sacrifice and all of those things.'

'No, it's a load of shit, mate,' agreed Charlwood.

'Yes, that's for sure,'reiterated Metcalfe.

Charlwood mused, 'I don't think it's of significance, you know, really.'

'No,' said Metcalfe.

'It's not going to—in the long term it's not going to worry us,' stated Charlwood.

'No, that's right,' agreed Metcalfe.

It wouldn't, would it. The rumour that the name 'Azaria' meant 'sacrifice in the wilderness' did far more damage for them in the public's mind than any facts.

We worked on various things steadily with Stuart, and Stuart liaised with Peter. They agreed we had given the police very full statements and there was little more we could add. They also said, in view of the fact that the police were not telling us what particular information they had, they were just trying to cross-examine us out of court, so we would trip ourselves up to their advantage. We should ask them to submit a written list of questions. The things that we had taken to Ayers Rock and since given away I *was* trying to get back, as the police had asked. I had collected all but one, and was waiting for them to be picked up, but the police never collected them.

Mark Plumb was talking to the superintendent again. 'I'd say that once we get the gear out of here, all we can do then basically is wait for the result, right? Particularly on items we could interview on. We have interviewed Peter Dean in the office here this morning.'

Neil Plumb remembered, 'Yes, that's what I was trying to get back to you about, too—about Dean. What was the outcome of Dean's interview?'

'We taped him,' Plumb asserted.

The superintendent added assent, 'Yes.'

Mark Plumb stated, 'He produced a letter—I don't know if you're aware of it.'

'No,' said the super.

Mark Plumb enumerated, 'He produced a letter stating that we were not to approach the mob [Chamberlains]; they will not answer any questions—right?'

'Yes,' answered Neil Plumb.

Plumb continued, 'And if we wanted questions asked, we would have to list them and put them through to the solicitors for their approval or denial.'

So they taped Peter, eh? Taping a lawyer was against all ethics. That would really set the cat amongst the pigeons if the legal profession found out.

Phil Rice was re-engaged and immediately concurred with what our two solicitors had told us. They got their heads together and planned a campaign. Phil suggested that we use Andrew Kirkham, a junior barrister he had worked with before and thought was good. Using four lawyers seemed absolutely overwhelming to me, but we were learning fast about the way the legal system worked, so we agreed. Extracts from the police tapes (tendered at court later), clearly indicated their hopes and thoughts during the days following the raid.

This time Superintendent Neil Plumb was Charlwood's superior in charge of the case.

'Neil Plumb again, Graham. The blood in the car—can you just go through it again? Where exactly was it?'

'Driver's side,' replied Charlwood.

'On the driver's side, yes,' Plumb repeated. Charlwood added, 'Front floor well area.' Superintendent Plumb parroted, 'Front floor well area.'

Charlwood said, 'Right up against the base of the front of the seat.' Plumb parroted again, 'Right up against the base of the front of the seat.'

He must have had trouble letting this sink in.

He added, 'If you're sitting in the car, directly under your crotch, right at the very base of the seat.'

Plumb said, 'Yes. Now, mate, do you recall [Bobbie] Downs saying that the sister. . .'
Charlwood interrupted, 'That's where the camera bag was . . .'
Plumb continued, 'That the camera case—he wouldn't shift it from that place.'
Charlwood agreed, 'That's right.'
Plumb said, 'So there may be nothing in the camera case.'
Charlwood replied, 'No, got a positive on blood inside the camera case.' Plumb exclaimed, 'You got a positive blood inside it?'
Charlwood answered, 'Yes.'
'What about underneath?' questioned Plumb.
Charlwood misunderstood. 'Well, that's where it was—yes, in the carpet, underneath where the camera . . .'
Superintendent Plumb interrupted, 'No, no, no. What I mean—on the camera—the bottom of the camera case?'
'No, they got nothing . . .' started Charlwood.
Plumb exclaimed, 'They got nothing there at all, eh?'
Charlwood continued, 'But, you know, it's only a haemostix positive. They're still looking at it to get a presumptive positive on it.'
Plumb said, 'Yes. That was inside the camera case?'
Charlwood stated, 'Inside, yes. Jim just went round—wiped round the inside. They used six inside the case. [One at a time] Jim just wiped it round and one came up positive. Haemostix aren't a real good indicator. They do react to other things apart from blood. They're, I understand, a protein indicator rather than blood indicator—indicates protein.'
So it took *six* sticks till they found something and only *one* was positive. They were obviously persistent! This tape proved they knew all along the tests only indicated protein, not blood, as newspaper leaks indicated.
The superintendent then spoke to Jim Metcalfe, whom I discovered was the man I'd called Grumpy during the house search. He had been with me when they picked up the car. I had pointed out a small pair of scissors in the console, and went to pick them up. 'Don't touch them!' he had exclaimed sharply, so I left them there. *He* rummaged around and handled them, though, then found the old fishing knife, torch and the towel we used to dry the car with; all in the wheel well. They were wrapped together so they wouldn't rattle when we were travelling. Obviously he thought they had a find.
Superintendent Plumb asked, 'Now, you're taking the knife across, I take it?'
Big Jim Metcalfe questioned, 'The knife out of the vehicle?'
'Yes,' said Plumb.
Metcalfe answered, 'That's still with the biologist here, but I can get it. She [Joy Kuhl] tells me that there is a trace of blood on the knife.'
'There is a trace of blood on the knife, eh?' Plumb mused. Now maybe they were getting some results.
They talked again about the towel.
Metcalfe said, 'Yes. Now, that towel is the most promising thing we have. She's [Joy Kuhl] working on it now, of course, and the stains on it are visible to the eye and she's hoping to get the best results off that . . .'

‘How much blood’s on it?’ Plumb questioned.

Metcalfe replied, ‘There’s a spraying of area about 2 inches by 3 inches [5 centimetres by 7.5 centimetres] on a bottom corner, and then there’s a smear about 10 inches by 2 inches [25 centimetres by 5 centimetres] halfway up the towel; another smaller smear about a third of the way up the towel, all on one side. That towel was found in the boot wrapped around a torch.’

‘It was wrapped around . . . ?’ queried Plumb.

‘A torch—and it was in the wheel well area. As far as the mats are concerned, she’s still working on that—definitely blood, but there may not be enough there to say whether it’s foetal blood or not,’ Metcalfe stated.

Funny they already knew the results; scientists are usually very particular about *not* releasing *any* information until *all* results are completed.

Mark Plumb rang Superintendent Neil Plumb. ‘We’re working on the car. By the way, that blood on the towel isn’t foetal blood after all.’

‘It’s what?’ exploded the superintendent.

‘It’s not foetal blood,’ Mark Plumb said.

‘We were told that it was,’ Neil exclaimed.

‘We were told that it was, too,’ agreed Mark Plumb.

‘Apparently further tests have been done and it hasn’t come up foetal so anything coming from here now, we won’t be saying nothing about it until we’ve got it absolutely confirmed.’

‘Jesus,’ exclaimed the superintendent disgustedly.

Mark said, ‘I thought that would set you on your heels. I don’t know what happened there. We were told straight—and I know that for a fact—that it was foetal blood but I’ve just been told this morning that it isn’t foetal blood so I don’t know what the score is but it’s no good like that, of course.’

Well, that was that.

‘Yes,’ Neil Plumb continued. ‘What’s happened about the scissors?’

‘The scissors, a definite trace of blood but they don’t think they can group and the towel is the same way—It’s blood but not foetal. Whether or not they can group it at this stage, I don’t know. I don’t think they can. It doesn’t leave you with anything,’ Mark Plumb replied.

Mark Plumb and Bainbridge also talked about the towel. Plumb said,

‘Apparently on this towel business, there was a test done that come up as foetal [blood] and then a further test was done later which come up as negative.’

Bainbridge queried, ‘Have they done more tests on it?’

‘Yes. Apparently the further test is sort of more a confirmation test and it doesn’t come up that way. We got told in between times, “You beauty, it’s foetal blood,” so I’m a bit nervous about making statements at the moment,’ Plumb said.

‘Yes,’ Bainbridge agreed.

‘Neil didn’t sound too happy on the phone either,’ commented Mark Plumb.

Bainbridge mused, ‘No. Well, the boss’s arse hit the ground yesterday, I think, when he found out.’

Plumb said later, 'We don't have the camera case.' Bainbridge queried, 'That's in Adelaide, is it?' Plumb affirmed, 'That's in South Australia.'

Bainbridge said, 'Sorry, yes. What about the scissors? Did they go to

Adelaide too, or have you got them?' Plumb asked, 'What's that? The scissors?'

'Yes,' said Bainbridge.

'The scissors are in Adelaide,' agreed Plumb.

'They're in Adelaide, too. Yes,' mused Bainbridge.

Mark Plumb interrupted, 'Now hang on. Yes, the scissors—no, the scissors are here, mate, sorry. They were recovered out of the car.'

This sounded like the saga over the boys' parkas before the first inquest when they finally found they had the parkas themselves. They never could quite get their act together.

They continued. 'On the hinge, but that got traced. It's blood but that's it. They can't group it or say whether it's foetal or anything like that,' stated Plumb.

Bainbridge thoughtfully asked, 'They can't?'

'What have we got—just between you and I—we have got blood in the car,' Plumb said.

'I see,' said Bainbridge.

'I'll go one step further back: we have got positive indications—and I mean, you know, positive indications—and you can view a certain amount of blood as well so I think—put it this way: if we could come up with a grouping on it, it would be a very good step,' Plumb stated sounding hopeful.

Mark Plumb continued, 'But what we have got is, I was up till lunchtime or after lunch yesterday with them and we located blood under the seat at the rear—I told Neil about that yesterday and I told him I wouldn't tell him anything on it until we had it in writing but while I was up here, they found more and I know that Joy [Kuhl] said this is what she's been looking for and she's stopped on the car now and is going through the gear she's got.'

Bainbridge and Mark Plumb again.

'No, no. I won't tell anyone, mate,' said Bainbridge.

Plumb continued, 'You might mention to Neil [the superintendent] on the quiet, if you like, that . . .'

'No,' exclaimed Bainbridge, 'I'd rather not at the moment.'

'Right. He sounds pretty down,' agreed Plumb.

Bainbridge agreed, 'Yes, they're both pretty down, I think. I'd rather not build them up. I'd rather let it come. No, I'll keep it to ourselves, mate.'

After Plumb's disappointment when they had to break the news they had given him wrong information before, they weren't going to do it again.

Joy Kuhl, according to the conversation, was working on the car.

Mark Plumb said on tape, 'I'll just give you the facts as they are now. We have, as I said, foetal blood on the coin under the mat, under the floor, against the metal. Where the coin was, we have foetal blood on the floor, right. On the area around the thread stud into the floor on the right hand stud, the right hand rear bracket, we have foetal blood there. Now, that metal bracket I told you that is bolted on by three bolts on the side of the seat against the seat plastic—vinyl, right?—we removed that this morning and we have quite a large amount of blood in behind it.

Now, it hasn't been tested yet for foetal [blood], right. And I think we're going to have big problems coming up with grouping but we have got foetal in the area and there is a lot of blood and we have been told by the biologist—and we also had the top pathologist there have a look—he didn't commit himself but he said it is consistent with blood flow.'

Plumb continued, 'Now, she's [Joy Kuhl] terribly excited. She's quite happy and what we appear to have is either the child was killed across the area of the console or was put there immediately after.'

According to the tapes, Joy Kuhl actually travelled to Cooranbong to see where we lived during the time she worked on the car.

Mark Plumb discussed the case with Boag, another policeman. 'I'd like to sit down with the brains trust again and start going back over other theories,' he said.

'Yes. Now, as far as the pathologist—you've got his name and everything else. Is there any chance of getting a statement off him?' Boag asked.

'We'll ask him for one,' said Plumb. 'He seemed a little bit hesitant in a way: not the fact that it was blood flow but he sort of backed off when he asked what the case was [i.e., what case he was being asked to comment on]. I don't know, but Joy [Kuhl]—who is a biologist—says she gets asked that question in court and she's quite capable of giving that answer. Now, as you know, you can get a smear—you can't get a smear in behind there of blood.'

Boag questioned, 'What about the grouping?'

'The groupings? We haven't got anything as yet,' said Plumb, then he explained that Joy Kuhl would try and establish the group on the blood they had found, to determine whether it was Azaria's or one of the boys'.

'Well, she'll go for the test for the foetal first and I dare say she'll be trying to establish the groupings—hang on. I just remembered she said something about she couldn't get a haemoglobin on the coin. She couldn't get the haemoglobin test on the coin—she can't break the blood down. Now, she expects it this way; she expects it from the age of the blood to be able to get the grouping but the fact that the child—it would possibly be the same blood group as the other children. Right?' Plumb stated.

Later Joy Kuhl claimed she got her most positive reaction to foetal blood on that coin.

They came back to the role of the supporting pathologist.

'About the pathologist. You want another view if you can get . . .' began Plumb.

Boag interrupted, 'Well, if he will say that that [the appearance of the blood] is consistent with blood flow, we'd like it on paper.'

'Yes, all right,' agreed Mark Plumb.

Boag said, 'He is supposed to be a top pathologist.' Plumb agreed, 'Yes, yes. As I said, I just had a funny feeling about him but we'll see how he goes. We may have to bring our own down.'

This, of course, was important. They had to have someone who would corroborate what Joy Kuhl said.

To make the murder theory really stick, they would have to find blood on my clothes. I'd told them before some was on my shoes but Mum had got that off so well they couldn't even find traces of it—nor could they on the cuff of Aidan's parka. It just showed what I could have done if I had been guilty of a crime as they claimed.

It was feasible that I could have transferred blood to my slacks when I crawled in and out of the tent door, because the other items there had blood on them; my dress too could have had some on it. But according to their conversations, they were not doing well. That dress over the top of the slacks was a real nuisance to the Crown, as it protected them. If they could find some blood on my clothes they could maintain it was evidence of murder. My statement that I had crawled over blood in the tent would be scoffed at as another 'fanciful lie' that I merely told as a cover-up.

Sergeant Bainbridge, asked Charlwood, 'And no luck with the track pants? Tracksuit pants?'

'No,' Charlwood said, 'We tried everything that they know down here.'

Bainbridge asked, 'They can't even bring up the outlines as to whether they were . . .'

'No,' Charlwood said baldly.

Bainbridge was disappointed. 'Gee. What about her dress?'

'No, nothing on that either,' Charlwood replied.

'Nothing on that?' questioned Bainbridge.

'No,' Charlwood stated. 'They've got a thing called Luminol down here that we've been using. It's extremely good. It brings up stuff that you can't even see. If there's anything there, it will bring it up.'

Bainbridge said, 'Yes. Gee, it's a bloody shame, isn't it?'

'That's right, yes,' Charlwood agreed.

They just couldn't win, it seemed, with the carpet on the floor of the car either.

'Well, the carpet is out as far as I'm aware. They just can't do anything with it. They are going right over it again. Hopefully, they might come up with something somewhere else,' Charlwood said.

'Gee, you couldn't credit it, could you?' said Bainbridge dishearteddly.

'Yes,' agreed Charlwood.

'Nothing is going for us.'

Later, Bainbridge said, 'Listen, did they seize anything from the car that might have been at the panel beater or the wrecking yard? Like seat covers? [Mark] Plumb was chasing after seat covers this morning. We can't get anyone who actually pinpoints the car as having seat covers.'

Easy to see what they were thinking—maybe we had thrown them out to get rid of telltale evidence.

'I'll tell you who could—Barry Graham down at the . . . We took Barry with us to Mt Isa when we went over it. He had a look at the car there. He would probably be able to tell you whether it had seat covers or not,' Charlwood answered.

How interesting. *They* obviously hadn't forgotten the car had been gone over thoroughly in Mt Isa. If we had realised we would have subpoenaed Graham to testify on our behalf at the trial, as he had looked at the car before the first inquest and said there was no blood in it. Rather an embarrassment, that. I wouldn't have liked to have been accused of a shoddy job if I was Sergeant Graham either.

But they spent a long time going over the car—yet again.

Everything had to be eliminated in the car's history. There were to be no last-minute loopholes. Mark Plumb was on the phone again.

'Yes. You're going to have to get a full medical on it and you're going to have to get a full test . . . of the car. We also want the car checked back—its whole history—through the RACQ and all that sort of thing. Insurance companies to find out whether they've had a claim on an accident or anything before at all. We're too early to jump but I think we've got it without a doubt in my mind. Even the foetal is hard to come up with because she'd get the foetal under the floor because it's not exposed to anything but the other areas, it's too hard to break down because foetal is not an easy test.'

Plumb said to Charlwood, 'You know, that car is very important, mate.' Charlwood agreed, 'Well, that's generally the only card we have to play.' The superintendent wanted an update.

'Right, now what's happened this morning? They were taking the seats out of the car, right?'

'Yeah,' reported Mark Plumb. 'The seats are being taken out of the car. The wheels are being taken off.'

Bainbridge and Mark Plumb later discussed the same subject. Bainbridge said, 'Yes. Good.'

Plumb continued, 'She's had it once before where the seat's been cleaned but it hadn't passed through the rubber backing.'

Bainbridge agreed, 'Yes, plus you've got the seams and that, you know; the stitching and things like that. That's very good, mate.'

'As I said, mate, the last thing I want to do is get them excited about finding something and then be dashed,' Mark Plumb reiterated.

A DE-PRESSING SITUATION

We were in a dreadful situation. We had gained the impression from our conversations with the police and from press reports that started appearing that the Northern Territory had gathered a lot of scientific evidence that seemed to raise a strong case against us. But what was it? We couldn't find out any details, except in the daily papers.

Although information was readily 'leaked' to the press, no indication of the Crown's plans were given to our lawyers. Day by day we'd read the newspapers to find out what the latest information was. There was enough information in the newspapers to keep the public at a fever pitch of accusation.

I could see what effect all this was having on my family. My parents called in just after the raid and I noticed the hair at Dad's temples was now white; a few weeks before it had been very dark.

As the pressure increased, so did the tension within our family and traumatised Aidan and Reagan even more. The restlessness and aggression they had shown during the lead up to the first inquest had slowly abated as the months wore on and we returned to a normal, peaceful existence. It took about five months to get them back to a secure state. But with the reopening of the case when our house was raided, they took only two weeks to go back to that state of trauma and thereafter their behaviour became both wild and aggressive. If someone knocked on our door, they would deliberately fight to get my attention back to them, but if we were alone they were fine. I found it frustrating. They took to screaming and kicking one another. The neighbours noticed the difference in their behaviour immediately. Fortunately they understood and all helped the boys to cope, even turning a blind eye when necessary.

One night, most of the neighbours weren't home, it was getting dark, we were hungry and getting cold. We were still hopping back fences to get into our home undetected. The press were parked in a different position and we were able to get to our back door without being seen if we were careful. As we were hopping over one of the back fences, Michael ripped his good trousers. This seemed the last straw: he swore. That was the first time I had ever heard Michael swear, he was so frustrated. No matter how expertly I could mend the three cornered rip it would always show. I felt like asking the press for a new pair of trousers.

The only way to make it look as if there was no one home was to leave the lights off, so I was trying to get dinner by the light of one small candle. In the gloom I reached for the electric frypan cord to plug it in, and grabbed the control pin. I usually left it plugged in and turned off, but this time someone had pulled it out of the frypan and left it switched on at the wall. I got a real kick out of that discovery!

The shock made my whole arm, shoulder and neck stiff for days; I was lucky I wasn't killed.

I wondered whether the house was bugged by the police too, and have since been told the press had special microphones that pick up what you are saying from metres away, so nothing was private anyway.

At the end of the first inquest, Russ McPhedran, a photographer from the *Sun* newspaper, had sent me a large bunch of flowers, and Steve Brien, the reporter from the same paper, asked if they could simply have a couple of photographs. Because they were the only press who had managed to find us, we couldn't see the harm in a decent out-of-court photo so we agreed.

Some weeks later, the *Sun* approached us for an interview. As things had settled down, we agreed. They also wanted pictures, and took a couple of shots in the backyard, including one of me collecting eggs from our half dozen chooks. We gave them lunch and later they sent us the article. It wasn't too bad, although I was disgusted to see that the picture in the chook house was 'Lindy on the college farm', which didn't even have chooks. I supposed it was some editor somewhere who had got things wrong.

Steve Brien sent us occasional notes, representing himself as a friend. Not until the case reopened did he start showing his true colours. He stayed outside our house for weeks at a time, waiting to get a glimpse of us, and put notes under the front door, although we had gone elsewhere. The boys were staying away from home so they could go to school freely. Most of the time we were at college, but occasionally we came back to the neighbours' and hopped over the back fences until we got to the back door of our house unseen, got what we needed and left again by the same way. We would stay at one of the neighbour's houses or at college and only return home after the press left at night, about five o'clock. Usually they didn't arrive until about eight-thirty in the morning, but the last few days they had been arriving at six and staying until eight, nine or ten, which was a real pain. We couldn't do *anything* freely.

We did not have the telephone on, so we put an intercom from next door where our friend Gavin, the assistant college accountant, lived. He had a phone, so if anything happened or news broke, he could call us on the intercom and let us know what was happening. If somebody came looking for us at the college office, Gavin, working there, was able to ring up his wife to warn us that there were press on the campus and to lie low. We had just got another message and were grabbing our gear to get out of the house before we got blocked in, when Phyllis, our neighbour from over the road, came across to say my Mum had rung and was calling back in five minutes. She took most of the calls from our parents and one or two others (such as Bill Barnes, who was keeping in contact now he was retiring from being head court orderly in Alice Springs).

I opened the door for Phyllis just as Steve Brien pulled up, and dragged her in quickly. We walked straight through the house and left by the back door, hopping over three or four sets of fences until we were behind the car and then crossed the road and went through the cow paddocks, down the back lane and over Phyllis's back fence. By this time her neighbours were out, standing at the back fence laughing at what we were doing and watching the press. She told them to go away somewhere else or they'd give away our position. They apologised then and went back inside.

We got inside just as Mum phoned. When I put the phone down again, I went to see if I could get home. By this time Steve was out walking around and it was obvious that I was not going to be able to get home for some time. I was able to get a message through Faye's husband, another neighbour, to Michael in class at college and let him know the house was well and truly staked out again. He was on his motorbike, wearing full gear and helmet so could move reasonably freely as the bike seemed to be one detail they'd missed. Hours later we decided to ring Faye and see if she knew where Michael had gone. Michael had ridden his bike to Faye's and the boys had been collected by car, but as it was not our house, no one bothered to check who it was coming and going. By going to the window we could see one another and wave.

A mutual friend staying with Phyllis at the time observed a number of times during the day that Steve Brien had got out of the car and put notes under our front door. As he was still there we decided to find out what he was doing. She had a reversible coat, so she put that on and went across and let herself in with my key, collected all the notes, waited a little while inside and then came out again. As she came back past the car he stopped her and wanted to know why the Chamberlains weren't answering the door. She said that the Chamberlains weren't home, and that she was just collecting any mail from under the door and see to things inside on her way home and did not know when we would be back. This was quite true; it depended quite simply on when *they* left. She returned with his notes. Why wouldn't we come to the door? He would give us an extra half hour; this was very rude—he had been supportive and was a good friend and why wouldn't we talk to him now? The notes grew more irate. Not the sort of note to inspire anyone to actually go out and talk to him!

By now it was getting on to dinner time. I could eat with Phyllis and go home much later or try and get across the road to rejoin the rest of the family, so my friend's reversible coat became very useful. I reversed it and she went coatless. The coat was big on me. I turned the collar up and put my head down, holding her arm as if I were a little old lady being helped across the road. We were only fifty yards from the reporters and they watched with disinterest as I shuffled slowly across.

We got to Faye's door, I took the coat off, reversed it to its original side, then she returned to Phyllis's once again wearing her own coat, and they never knew the difference.

That night we watched the Royal wedding on Faye's TV while the frustrated Steve Brien and friend still waited outside our house.

Eventually Michael couldn't bear being on his own when I wasn't there. If he had free time and I didn't, the house would be totally empty, no children, no noise, and he would either remain in the library or go and find somebody to stay with until I came home, knocking on the neighbours' doors for company to keep him away from that hollow empty house; he asked my parents to come back to stay. They hadn't been gone more than a few weeks but readily agreed to come back for company and to answer the door, take messages, and transport the children when we had to keep out of sight. And *all* Dad's hair had gone white in just those three weeks since we had last seen them.

The police claimed they would only have our vehicle for a few weeks at most, and gave us a written authorisation (which did not specify any time limitation) to hire a replacement vehicle. After several months the hire firm asked us to pay for the car as it was now a month overdue. On enquiry we discovered the police had written to the firm and stated they would no longer pay as from one month before. They had not informed either us or the hire company so that we could return the vehicle. We returned the car immediately. Now the company wanted to sue us for the money. After some legal hassles we reached consensus with the company as co- respondents in action to be taken against the Northern Territory government.

One morning Dad decided to walk to college with me. We didn't have any car then, and I was early enough to walk to class. We set off briskly down the drive, feeling great because there were no press around that morning, when a press car drove past us. The nearest building was the cowshed, several hundred metres away. There we were, sitting ducks for any photographer. We had been praying steadily for weeks that if it was God's will, we be protected from reporters and, believe it or not, that car went past us without the occupants even glancing in our direction. We heaved a sigh of relief. When Dad and I were only about 9 metres (10 yards) from the car, they pulled up by the roadway that went down to the cowshed, backed in and turned around. We had to stop and wait for them to finish their turn. They looked right at us and through us as if we weren't there; we could hear them talking about sitting in front of the Chamberlain home to see whether or not they could catch us.

I felt just like Daniel in the lions' den, when the lions didn't harm him, and as Jesus must have felt on the clifftop when he passed through the mob and away, when they were angry and looking to stone him. Dad and I were silent for some time, then remarked together that God must have shut those reporters' eyes so they didn't see us. Sure enough, when Dad had walked me to college and returned to the house, the reporters hopped out of the car and ran across to him, recognising him and asking when Michael or I would be home. A number of times similar things happened.

Often I would be returning to the house, only to find a press car parked out the front. But it always seemed to be facing in the opposite direction, so I could hop the neighbours' fences and come in the back door without being seen.

I didn't know at the time, but as soon as you answer the phone and a reporter recognises your voice, he or she can say that you have given them an interview, simply because they have said hello to you.

We actually watched this in action one day. Mum and Dad were working in our front bedroom and saw the Sydney *Sun's* Steve Brien walk to the front door. While waiting for him to knock, they noticed that he seemed to be bending over instead. Then there was a shuffling noise and he walked away again. He hadn't knocked so Dad went to see what he'd done and found a note under the door saying, 'Dear Michael, sorry I was unable to contact you.' Michael was home.

The following day, under the headline, 'Long Interview With Michael Chamberlain', Steve Brien wrote a totally fabricated 'personal interview' that he claimed he'd had with Michael the previous day!

Steve Brien, who said we were some of the nicest people he had ever met—and claimed he was our best friend, later authored one of the most scurrilous books ever written about our case with incorrect evidence and rumours put in as fact. Because we were convicted at that stage he had no reason to fear we would sue as anything could be said libel free. Later when we should have been able to obtain retribution, the statute of limitations had run out. What the police couldn't say publicly about 'white babies' coffins' and 'underlined Bible texts', Steve did—and the myths grew.

Press were still walking through the college corridors looking for me and so far I had successfully avoided them. One day I went to the college bank. I swapped the latest college news with Daph, who ran the enquiry counter, switchboard and post office, then left. Along the corridor, nearly to the door, I looked up and there only a few feet away was a reporter whom I knew quite well. I'm really a goner this time, I thought to myself.

It was class changeover time and there were a lot of students in the corridor. Fortunately he hadn't seen me. I dropped my head, patted my pockets as if I had forgotten something, and turning on my heel, sauntered back with the other students. I was in my art clothes, all covered in clay because I had been down in the pottery studio, and had just run up in between classes. I reached the stairs, ran up and stood around the corner, while I watched the reporter walk straight to enquires and ask Daph whether she knew what class I had at that time.

Daph panicked when she saw me coming back and realised that there was a reporter behind me. I was sure her face would give her away, but I disappeared safely and she presumed that I was well away so told him with a clear conscience that she had no idea where I was at that moment. Just as she said this, she looked up and saw me above her. I saw her start but fortunately the reporter was looking in the opposite direction and she was able to recover. He thanked her and went to see whether I was in the library.

I came bouncing down the stairs again. Daph looked at me and said, 'I'd like to throttle you, you little minx! Quick, get out of here, you make me nervous.' I gave her a cheerful wave and took off.

Several times, I nearly walked into the media. As long as I kept slightly behind or beside someone when they walked, I could go almost anywhere without arousing any suspicion. If I moved quickly, ran or tried to hide, they would look to see what had caused the commotion and I would be sprung. I could see why anyone who worked in the Resistance movement during the war needed nerves of steel.

For weeks the press wandered freely around the college. They became quite cheeky and actually walked into classes looking for us. They even parked in the college faculty car park near where the main body of the college students walked to and from the Education block and the main lecture theatres. Most of Michael's classes overlooked where they were, so he could note their locations, and wait quite happily until it was safe to leave without being seen.

The college became absolutely fed up with the journalists. They had become such a pest that the college asked them, very politely, to refrain from coming onto the grounds. The college was private property and the Chamberlains did not wish to see them; they would now have to stay outside the gates, otherwise the college would get a court injunction against them. So for weeks they camped by day at the gate, and stopped anyone coming and going to ask them information about the Chamberlains. The locals had had enough, they gave no information and were very protective. The reporters must have had a very boring time. It was hot, there was no beer to be bought locally and even cigarettes were quickly sold out at the one local takeaway shop that stocked them, because the local supermarket does not have them at all.

Although Aidan and Reagan were only seven and five years old, they were able to pick out the press cars almost as well as we could. This wasn't hard. Although the journalists tried to dress like students, they never seemed to realise that the college is full of non-smokers. Any smoker could be picked instantly because of the smell on his or her clothes, and it was not a time of year when parents visited, so strangers were usually reporters.

Another giveaway was the fact that reporters had nice modern cars, often with hire car stickers. The students knew the cars belonging to all the faculty members, as well as the Sanitarium factory workers and the locals. The students themselves had old bombs, of course. One of the reporters was smart enough to realise this, so he got himself a bomb and travelled around in that. However, he didn't realise that not all that many students had cars, and those who possessed them didn't tear around the campus as he did, but had their own distinct parking spots. The students thought it was hilarious to see the reporters trying to blend in with the locals.

OH, DEM EYES AND A PACK OF LIES

Michael, Stuart and I travelled to Adelaide for a meeting with Phil and Andrew Kirkham. Stuart had said, 'Well, this will be interesting. This Kirkham character sounds to be pretty good on the phone. He seems to have his head screwed on and be pretty quick. Other than that I don't know much about him.'

When we arrived, we discovered that information Stuart had passed on had not reached either Kirkham or Rice. This made it rather embarrassing. There was a slip up in the system somewhere and it became very apparent that we would need to get something in motion in a hurry.

This small awkwardness was soon overcome as Phil Rice introduced us to Andrew Kirkham. Andy, as we later came to call him, was about Michael's height, a fine wiry build, with aquiline features, piercing eyes and a surprisingly deep voice when he chose. The one thing I noticed about him was that he gave me a very intense look of interest mixed with curiosity in his summing-up glance. I suppose I was doing the same thing to him. It was almost as if, after a mutual quick evaluation, we both realised we could work on similar wavelengths and that was it. We went to business.

It frustrated and amused me to see that Phil followed strictly correct legal procedure. Messages could *not* be relayed directly, but passed from person to person in order. Although he was in the room, he did not talk to us directly very often, but basically had his questions relayed to the junior barrister, then to the solicitor, and on to us. By the time we had been through this several times I felt like screaming, because so often the differences in interpretation ended up like the children's game of whispers. A couple of times when frustrated I spoke to him directly and was told that we must follow correct procedure.

Bill Barnes, the court orderly from the first inquest, was intending to retire, but when he heard that the inquest finding had been quashed and the case reopened, he decided to wait until after the second inquest was completed. Interestingly enough, both he and Frank Gibson, our ex- bodyguard, were told that although they knew us, they were not to come anywhere near us. They were not to be seen. Dennis Barritt was apparently told the same thing, though when we got to Alice Springs everybody was working in the same building. They had to be very careful to keep out of the way while we were there. All this we learned later.

For the first part of the second inquest, we stayed in a unit in a local motel. We had been told we had an empty room next to us, yet we continually heard the phone being picked up and realised it was connected to ours. We could hear movement in there and the beds being made up every morning, yet the motel steadfastly maintained that the room was unoccupied. We were on the second floor and across from us in another section, also on the second floor was Charlwood, who spent most of his time while we were there sitting on his balcony talking to various women while he kept an eye on the back door of our unit. Across from us were a couple of policemen. Of course, these men were all supposed to have come from Darwin, and this was the motel that the law was paying for.

Well, maybe that was so, but some of them certainly were never in court, and it struck me that they must have been locals simply sent there to keep an eye on us. What did they think we were going to do? Bolt, or something? How stupid can you get? If we had been going to do that because we were guilty, there would have certainly been better chances than letting ourselves get right to court in the middle of Australia with very few exits and lots of police, not to mention media. Every time we went to eat, the dining room was full of police and reporters. Our every movement was observed. It was not a relaxing situation. Even our lawyers were uneasy about their rooms and the thinness of the walls. Whenever possible, we had conferences outdoors, anywhere away from prying ears.

At the first inquest when I had just been myself, I got so much criticism. I laughed when I shouldn't laugh, I cried when I shouldn't cry, I smiled, I scowled—it didn't matter what I did, it was wrong. How does one react to that? My dressing was wrong, the way I walked, the way I talked, everything was wrong.

By the time the second inquest came up, my lawyers said, 'Well look, it doesn't matter what you do, it will be wrong. So try and keep as neutral an expression as possible.'

I did, and I was *still* wrong, and I started to be known as a hardfaced bitch, unfeeling and uncaring.

Michael's parents and relatives were absolutely aghast at what was happening and because the New Zealand news media was so spasmodic, they were frustrated in finding out what was happening. It was decided that a family representative should come across and be able to report to them direct, so Michael's brother Peter was sent across. Peter came to court with us the first half day and then wandered off. He was driving us crazy. He seemed to be wandering out and mixing with the press while the court was on and then mixing with us in between. We knew he wasn't used to the press and felt that they would be watching his actions and quoting him. Michael's mother had spent the money for him to come across to court, and here he was outside instead of in. His association with the press was frustrating, and we asked him not to do it, but he still did.

It wasn't until some years later that he admitted that once he had been in the court the first day, he simply couldn't bear it. He *couldn't* sit there and hear what they were saying about his brother. Although he put up a brave front to us and said nothing to Stuart, with whom he was rooming, when he returned home after the inquest Lois, his wife, told us that he had gone to bed and cried for hours. His seemingly uncaring bravado had just been to hide his own deep hurt and was his way of trying not to add any further to our upset. He tried to spend as much time as possible with Michael out of court, which helped, because at this stage all Michael and I were doing was getting on one another's nerves.

All police information is supposed to be confidential. We, like gullible fools, believed this. We discovered how the process worked, though you could never pin it down to claim it in court. Somebody 'told' somebody else loudly, particularly if they knew they would be overheard. Then, of course, it wasn't *their* fault; they hadn't *told*. Sometimes they had a drink with a friendly reporter, and if they happened to be indiscreet, well, that friendly reporter knew exactly what to print and what not to—if you get my meaning. And they always got *their* meaning. Fortunately not all police are like this.

'Tame' police reporters managed to get an incredible amount of 'leaks', as they're called. When we actually got to court we found that the papers had somehow known accurately what line certain scientists were going to take.

On 14 December 1981, in an atmosphere of total frustration for us, the second inquest began. This time Brisbane barrister Des Sturgess was the Crown's man working with Mick O' Loughlan.

The press had already dubbed it 'the inquest by ambush', and being ambushed we certainly were. Right at the start we were being forced to give evidence and be cross-examined with no prior knowledge of what was coming or any way of combating it.

Michael was called first to give evidence. Andrew Kirkham objected, referring to a witness's privilege against self-incrimination and adding, 'Inasmuch as they have the choice, it can only be a real choice if it is known what evidence is going to be called. We don't know the nature or extent of the fresh evidence to be put before you, and neither of the parties we represent is in a position to effectively exercise their rights without knowing the nature of the evidence to be called. The fairer course would be to call the evidence, then call the Chamberlains and allow them to make an election [a choice], or to make submissions as to their rights, on the basis of what has gone before.'

But this had no effect on Sturgess. 'I am subject to Your Worship's direction,' he said to chief magistrate Gerry Galvin, who was presiding, 'but apart from that, I control who shall be called, and when they shall be called, and the order in which the evidence is presented, not the witnesses themselves.'

So we got nowhere. All our lawyers—Stuart Tipple, Peter Dean, Andrew Kirkham, Phil Rice—were furious. The whole thing was subject to such misinterpretation. A radio station had already announced that Michael had refused to give evidence to avoid incriminating himself.

If we gave evidence there would be just that much more to cross- examine on if we came to trial. Our evidence was comprehensive as it was and we were only going to be asked about blood, which we knew nothing about. Yet if we refused we had to make a statement saying we wouldn't on the grounds that we might incriminate ourselves, that in itself was damning. That choice was no choice, as the Crown knew! The best we could do was try to appear *after* all the other Crown witnesses, so we could hear all their accusations first. Andy had sent for copies of a legal precedent, but it got held up on the way from Melbourne (they were sent promptly) and we eventually ran out of time and had to give in and go into the box early. (I wonder what happened to the material on the way?) When it finally arrived too late—Andy *was* right. We *were* entitled to be called last.

Michael handled the question of blood badly. He is good at accidents and first aid, as long as they don't affect his own family. If they do, or simply if blood is discussed, he goes to pieces. When Sturgess asked Michael about blood, Michael answered as if he was talking in his sleep. What he said made no sense and the more they tried to push him, the less he knew. It was quite obvious that he was so stressed that he had absolutely no knowledge of what he was saying. And yet the Crown pushed and pushed. Michael had enough sense to say that he was under stress, but *still* they pushed. I listened, horrified. It was patently obvious that Michael had gone to pieces and still Sturgess pushed. Even the reporters behind Stuart and me were embarrassed and saying, 'Give him a break!' quite loudly.

I would have liked to get up and kick Sturgess. It was so obvious that he was trying to denigrate Michael. In actual fact, all it did was make the reporters say, 'If they wanted to make him look like an accomplice, all they've done is make it look as if he couldn't possibly be an accomplice to anything . . . it's made him look like he hasn't got the brains . . . it's pretty obvious he would never have the stomach to carry through a charade like that . . . Any jury watching that performance would drop the bloody charges straight away.'

When court recessed for tea break, Stuart grabbed me by the arm and moved me to the door in a hurry, before Michael left the courtroom. As soon as we got into the little side room we used, he said, 'Listen, young lady, just you get your face straight in a hurry, before Michael comes in. Don't you *dare* let Michael see you like that. He has to go back in that box with confidence, and if he sees your face now, he will know exactly how bad a job he has done. We can't afford him to see that right now. He needs all the help he can get.' I did my best to pull myself together and a few moments later Michael came in. He said, 'Well, how do you think I went?'

All I could think of to say was, 'You had Sturgess really working hard, sweetheart.' It was true, he did. Sturgess hadn't a clue what Michael was going to say next and was having great difficulty in getting any sense out of him. I didn't lie, but neither did I say what I really thought. Stuart knew Michael's difficulties in discussing blood and said that, under the circumstances, he was doing well. Michael seemed to relax until Andy Kirkham walked in. We hadn't bargained on him saying anything, forgetting that he didn't know Michael's weakness. He breezed in the door and straight to the point said to Michael, 'Geez, mate, you're a bloody bad witness.' Michael looked aghast. We hadn't even been able to kick Andy to shut him up, the damage had been done. We were able to rectify things slightly, bolstering Michael up by assuring him that he had gone to pieces on the blood but everybody could see that, and he would probably be questioned on something else when he went back in, and would be fine. Andy quickly got the message, recovered and, with difficulty, kept his mouth shut until we got Michael out of the room again.

When Michael went back into the box, he was totally different. He was accurate and to the point about people and number plates. I suppose if you had been looking on without knowing Michael, you could have thought he was play acting deliberately, but he wasn't.

Then it was my turn.

Sturgess had asked Michael about cutting his toenails, but he simply couldn't remember anything about it at all except that he had cut them.

So Sturgess tried again with me as I was the one who had mentioned it originally. He said, 'I would now like you to look at a pair of scissors, exhibit147. You were in court this morning when I asked your husband questions about those scissors, is that so?'

'Yes,' I answered.

'Don't take them out of the packet,' Sturgess snapped. 'I don't think it is necessary. You understand I am not suggesting they were in that condition, but do you remember those scissors?'

'We have a number of little pairs of scissors. I would think this is one of them,' I explained.

'You had scissors in the car on 17 August 1980, is that correct?' queried Sturgess.

'I would think we did. There should have been a pair of scissors in the first aid kit and there is usually a pair of scissors in the console box of the car although the children quite frequently take them out and it is not always the same pair,' I said. 'Do you remember this morning I quoted a passage that came from your evidence?'

'Yes,' I agreed.

'And spoke of your husband coming down the climb and then cutting his toenails or someone cutting his toenails for him?'

'That is correct,' I stated. I could see where he was leading now.

'That was your evidence I was quoting?' Sturgess said.

'That is correct.'

Sturgess said snappily, 'Well, there is no doubt about it, is there, the scissors would have been in the car at some time that day at least?' He really was walking head on into unknown territory.

'I would not be sure whether the scissors were in the car or not,' I answered.

'Well, where else would you have got them from?' he asked, exasperated.

'What for?' I questioned innocently.

Sturgess exploded, 'What *for?* Do you recall evidence given by you in which you spoke of your husband coming down from the climb?' (He meant the Ayers Rock climb, of course.)

'Yes,' I said, trying hard not to look at Andy grinning and Phil fiddling with a pencil.

'I will quote it exactly,' said Sturgess. 'I will read it again. Your counsel will check me if I misreport you, "Michael said he was feeling fairly fresh and Aidan wanted to climb the Rock and he said he would climb it again. He would take [Aidan] back up, so we removed [Michael's] socks because they had been annoying him, cut his toenails and then went back up with the children. "?'

'That is correct,' I agreed again.

Sturgess really was annoyed with his 'thick' witness.

'Well, is there any doubt about it—there were scissors in the car that day at that time?'

'I don't know whether there were scissors in the car or not. I don't see the connection between scissors and that statement,' I explained.

'You don't! Well, you have spoken here of the use of scissors?' Sturgess exclaimed.

'Excuse me, I didn't,' I stated.

Phil Rice jumped to his feet. It was time to reel Sturgess in. 'There is no reference to use of scissors in that statement, Your Worship.'

'It just simply says he cut his toenails,' I added helpfully.

'Well, not with scissors?' Sturgess was beginning to see a trap.

'No, not with scissors,' I replied.

'With what?' he asked impatiently.

'A nail clipper.' There, I had said it.

'Oh, a *nail* clipper. I see. Very well, Mrs Chamberlain. You remember that, do you?' he asked sarcastically.

'Yes,' I said.

'They were nail clippers and not scissors?' he reiterated.

'Yes,' I agreed.

'Do you remember that positively?' Again he was sarcastic.

'Quite distinctly, because my husband makes a fuss every time he has to use nail clippers. He does not like them so it is quite a job to get him . . . to persuade . . . that that is the only thing that is available,' I finished.

He abruptly changed the subject. 'Have a look at this towel, please.'

Part way through Sturgess's cross-examination, Andy came out during the break, looked at me and said, 'Geez, Lindy, I'm glad you are our witness and not theirs. I'd hate to have to cross-examine you in the box.'

'Why?' I asked.

'Because I never know what you are bloody going to say next! We have asked you every question we can think of and think we know you inside out, and you *still* surprise us. Even when we know what you are going to say, you still say it in a way we don't expect!' I grinned.

Sturgess questioned me over the conversation I had with Charlwood in the car and tried to twist it. I was thoroughly disgusted by now, but the more annoyed with him I grew, the clearer my brain became.

Sturgess asked, 'Did Mr Charlwood say, "Mrs Chamberlain, did you kill your child?"?'

'Yes.'

'And did you say, "You have asked me that before"?'

'No.'

'Did you say this, or something to this effect, to him,"Well, what are the implications if I tell you?"?'

'That's correct.'

'Why did you ask him that question?'

I had had just about enough of this. 'Because I had told him that our legal advice was not to give an interview, and although I've learned very fast how far to trust the police, I was still expecting them to honour their word. And I was not sure what he considered an interview and what he didn't; as I had no legal advice there, I was asking him the question. Unfortunately, I was given the wrong advice.' I managed to add Charlwood's comment that he'd deny the conversation if it ever came up. That threw him a bit and caused a stir.

'Did you say this, or something to this effect?' Sturgess asked. '"I am prepared to let you have my hand-prints, but I would like to talk to my solicitor first"?'

'That's correct,' I said.

'And he said, "Yes, that's all right." Is that correct?'

I said it was. 'And he promised to contact us the following day,' I added. 'We haven't heard from him since.'

That surprised him. 'Steady on,' he said. Then he asked, 'Mrs Chamberlain, would you be prepared to give your palm prints to the police?'

Phil Rice jumped to his feet, objecting that it was unfair to put me on the spot without giving me the chance to take legal advice, and we adjourned. Andy Kirkham said to me, 'Look, it's a no-win situation. If your hand-print on the jumpsuit's too small, they can say it's only part of the hand. If it's too big, they can say the jumpsuit was bunched. We still say no.' I shrugged. Phil grinned, and told me the adjournment was really to give me a break and let them know what I was going to say next. How did I know?

When I went back into the witness box I said, 'I told Sergeant Charlwood, and I say the same thing again, I would have been quite happy to provide my palm prints to them provided my lawyers agree. They do not agree that I give my palm prints at this stage. They know I am quite happy to give my palm prints.'

Sturgess just looked at me and raised his eyebrows. 'You are not prepared to give to the authorities your palm prints so they can be compared with . . .' he said, then he gave up and sat down—having done his level best to make me seem a totally uncooperative witness. He seemed to have lost his steam all of a sudden like a tired old man.

The Continuing Ambush

Stuart had tried to get copies of various scientific reports before the inquest, but his requests were refused. This was astonishing, because the lawyers who assist coroners at inquests are, I believe, normally cooperative. But Stuart got no help from Des Sturgess and Gerry Galvin said he had no power to intervene on our behalf to help us find out what scientific evidence the Crown had.

Whatever we could glean we did, and our experts tried to work on it. We realised we were fighting a setup, one that couldn't exactly be proved in court but was very obvious anyway.

I had always thought that if you were innocent, you had nothing to worry about in law. I supposed that all this scientific stuff was interesting, but in the end it didn't matter too much because the truth would be revealed. I was about to find out how wrong I was.

A tip-off we had had about Galvin's non-co-operation and verdict proved correct, and his reactions were anything but favourable to us. We watched him in court. He didn't seem at all interested in whatever was going on; he yawned, he looked around the room, he even went to sleep occasionally at the bench. As you don't have a jury during an inquest, and the inquest continued without a pause, Heaven help the fate of information put in front of him during those times.

When Sally Lowe arrived in Alice Springs for the second inquest, two interviewing officers came to see her on behalf of the Crown the night before she was due to give evidence. They harangued her for two hours, trying to get her to change her story, but they could not. She gained the clear impression they were inferring Azaria was already dead when I brought her to the barbecue area before settling her down for the night, and I was deliberately moving her legs to make it appear she was still alive. Sally said, 'I knew this wasn't true because I had been seated alongside Lindy when Azaria's blanket had parted and had seen her little legs kick.' They also suggested that the cry from the tent that Sally had heard could have been tape recorded!

Sally was so upset she wanted to complain about her treatment to the newspapers. She rang Greg and he told her it might upset her evidence if she did, so she tried to see us. Not only was the Crown treating her very badly, but they had made no provision for her welfare while she was in Alice Springs. She had been obliged to bring her very new baby with her, because she was only a few weeks old and was being breastfed. No provisions had been made for babysitters, or indeed for a travel allowance for the baby. Sally had to arrange her own babysitters in a town she did not know for the whole time she was required to be in court.

From Stuart's room we saw Sally heading to our room. Fortunately Stuart was able to talk to her and calm her down. He told her if she saw us before she had been in the box it could jeopardise her evidence, so she restrained herself. He also advised her not to go to the press as the matter was *sub judice*. She was so upset at the Crown's badgering that she thought she needed her own legal representation. Stuart told her this was not possible, but if she got into any real problems, our lawyers would help her as much as they could and, if she felt she was being badgered on the witness stand, she was entitled to tell the magistrate.

We discovered that Sally was not the only witness who was being harassed. Mrs Hansell, the drycleaner in Mt Isa, had been interviewed before she went in the box and put through such a mill about blood on parkas, sleeping bags and tracksuit pants that she emerged from the Crown interview room in tears. When she met our friend Jenny Richards (who had become Mrs Ransom and moved away from Mt Isa) she said,

'Whatever you do, don't go in there without your husband. They are absolutely *awful*.' She formed the impression that the interviewer was extremely rude, not wanting to hear all the information she could give about the blood on my tracksuit pants (for instance, the fact that the reagent substance she used to remove blood also got rid of other substances, such as chocolate sauce, milk, some fruit stains and household products). She was terribly upset that she was not able to tell the whole truth as the oath stated.

So Jenny took her advice and her husband Jim went in with her. She said her own interview wasn't very pleasant, but nothing like as bad as Mrs Hansell's must have been. Nevertheless, she was extremely concerned that they dug up a phone tape they had made of her, wanting to use it in the inquest as evidence against me. She had not been told they were taping her at the time and, because she had been vague about some things and not confident about what she had been saying, the inference was that she was changing her story about the blood that had been discovered on my tracksuit pants.

Proving the presence of blood on my clothing was, of course, important to the Crown case. They were trying to get Jenny to say that her impression that I meant 'blood' when I said 'stains' on my trousers was not an impression she had, but a clear statement of guilt from me—an admission of known blood, and therefore guilt, by me, and a cover up by her. When they tried that in the box—both at that inquest and later—the sparks really flew.

Things were going very badly. It was obvious what the police were trying to do. I just couldn't believe the way we were being steamrolled. Stuart looked at me, knowing my strong faith and his own stand, and said quietly,

'Well, Lindy. I guess they did worse to Jesus. Look at it like this. Even if you went to the electric chair, you would know you had a clear conscience.' It was the first time anyone had voiced to me what I was thinking. My fear that the Crown could persuade the whole of Australia to believe that I was guilty and that I would end up in prison with a murder sentence on my head, simply because they told lies.

Hearing this actually voiced really threw me. I had to excuse myself from the room as soon as possible. If anyone else but Stuart had said that, I probably could have laughed it off, but I knew he was serious and genuine, and not trying to hurt me—which made his words all the more devastating. From that time onwards I knew Stuart would always tell me the truth. Albeit information I sometimes dreaded.

Colin Lees, a running mate of Michael's who had given evidence about the way Michael normally kept his camera bag beneath his legs as he drove, followed me out of Stuart's room where we all were. He had seen my face when Stuart was talking to me and although he didn't know what had been said, he simply thought he could help. I was on my way back to our room, hoping I wouldn't meet any press on the stairs and doing my best not to cry until I was indoors.

Col said he guessed we'd had words, as Michael had commented about my reactions to things and he had tried to explain to Michael why I was as I was. He said he told Michael at one point, 'Look, mate, you know you get your strength from her and if she goes down, you go down. It is the very fact that she *is* strong that is holding *you* together, and she knows that. Don't blame her for laughing if that's her way of coping. It doesn't mean she doesn't feel.' Colin had seen me cry one minute and laugh the next often enough to know that I felt just as strongly as anyone else. I simply didn't like people to see how I felt. I didn't even tell Col what had actually upset me, but I felt much better after I had talked to him. At one stage when Michael and I had a particularly bad fight over our different reactions to things in court and Michael's out-of-court activities, Colin and Peter were able to take Michael out for a while.

That evening I released some of my frustration by writing of the last few days' events:

> *Every snippet of whatever they can invent is being hurled at us. It seems so incredible that Azaria is gone and all this too. My beautiful daughter, and they are making up so many incredible accusations that my mind cannot take it in anymore. It seems as if my mind is numb to the actual reality. Oh, I know exactly what is happening, but each dastardly new piece of evidence setup seems to leave me cold, without emotion. I have prepared for it—the word we had leaked to us warned us.*
>
> *There is no way we can prove a set-up—It's so obvious, but then we know the facts and it's so subtly done that no one would really believe you if you told them. When the set-up first became obvious to me I sat down and started to deal with the horrifying reality of being accused when innocent.*
>
> *I have often wondered how Joseph felt when Potiphar's wife unjustly accused him. Now I am beginning to understand just a little of how he felt. God help me to be as faithful as he was. I know your answer is 'not yet' and I won't give in. I know you need me as I am. What is it you wish me to do, Lord? Help me to know, and above all help me to cope day by day, moment by moment as each new thing arises . . . I know they are out to try and prove that the female hand-print is mine. Lord, we both know it is not mine, so help me keep my face straight at all times and keep my feelings to myself so I don't upset the others. I have howled all afternoon. My eyes feel sore and swollen, my nose puffed up too, and my head swimming. I am so tired, but my brain is awake. It's an awful feeling, and when you eventually do get to sleep, morning comes too soon. Hold my hand, God; I'm not going to take any tablets. They only muddle my brains. We can manage together, God. I must be strong for Michael.*

The court adjourned to Ayers Rock. All the Crown lawyers, the court orderly, the court reporters, the coroner and some of our lawyers went to the Rock in the one plane. That caused a lot of jokes; all those high- powered legal people would go down in one hit if something happened to the plane. If there was any complaint about the inquest, all you had to do was put a bomb on the plane and it would all be history! Fortunately, nothing like that happened. Along with Stuart Tipple, we engaged a local hire car to drive the four hours to the Rock, arriving early enough to eat our breakfast in peace at one of the deserted tour bus picnic tables. Just as we were packing up, we spied a press car approaching in the distance. We hurriedly finished packing and drove off, congratulating ourselves on avoiding them. Later we learned the press *had* seen us and created headlines reading 'Picnic at Death Rock'.

The questions Sturgess asked the witnesses on the stand were concerned with blood—on objects found in the tent and elsewhere. The Crown kept insisting that there wasn't very much blood in the tent at all. Sally Lowe, for one, knew that this simply was not the case; certainly, if the tent itself had been examined, little blood would have been found. The floor of the tent had been covered not only by mattresses and sleeping bags, but by articles of clothing, and blood had been scattered over all of these. She said so. Phil Rice objected to the way she was being questioned. 'Mr Sturgess,' he said, 'for reasons best known to the authorities who instruct him, is proposing simply to call witnesses without giving a summary, even to Your Worship at this stage, of the nature, extent or their purpose in being called.' It was a vain attempt to force Sturgess into handing over the witnesses' statements that he was basing his information on, or even a witness list for the day.

Sturgess said he would see what he could do about that, but offered no further explanation. Coroner Galvin overruled Phil Rice's objection.

The court then adjourned to the police compound to look at our yellow Torana hatchback. 'Big Jim' Metcalfe, the senior constable from Operation Ochre day, and the forensic pathologist, Mrs Joy Kuhl from the New South Wales Health Commission, were sworn in together. Then we had to endure a tediously long and boring account of forensic evidence, interspersed with fluttering eyelashes. Joy Kuhl referred to Sergeant Metcalfe throughout her evidence at the car.

The car was pulled apart and the inside wrecked. The dash was cut in two with a hacksaw, where simply undoing two screws could have removed the lot. The vinyl upholstery had been slit next to the stitching instead of the stitching itself being undone. The carpet had holes cut in it, the seat hinges had been broken off. To add to it all, Metcalfe removed the loose car seat to better show the court where blood was supposed to have been found. He took it out and plonked it hard on the roof of the car; bare metal on newly resprayed duco. At times like these I needed a superhuman effort to keep my mouth shut, and face straight. I didn't dare look at Michael—I'd already heard him gasp and Stuart quickly speak to him.

Metcalfe showed where he'd found a pattern of sticky droplets in a spray formation and other areas which, he said, had been tested by Joy Kuhl.

From this point onwards, the so-called experts took over. We listened with a growing feeling of unreality.

Joy Kuhl said she had done screening tests for blood in the car, and the chemical she had used got positive reactions from the door handles in the car, the console, the seats and the carpet. There was an impressive battery of scientific terminology and equipment; test tubes, swabs, slides, photographs, diagrams, the lot. All this, she said, went to demonstrate that there was blood on the hinge of the passenger seat, underneath the seat and on a number of things taken from the car, particularly on a 10 cent coin under my passenger seat, stuck there by 'foetal blood'—her most positive finding. She said she had tested two droplets removed from the steel plate cut from the under- dash area of the car and, though they reacted negatively to the chemical test she had run on them, when she dug into the material removed she could show that it contained 'foetal haemoglobin which could only have come from a child under three months'.

While Kuhl and other experts were giving their evidence, I was trying to assimilate it all. All this discussion about foetal haemoglobin and haeptoglobin and the composition of blood, and chemicals, and the rest of it! I was glad I had just done one unit of physical science and one of biology at college. I was able to understand a little of molecular weight and structures and DNA chains, and was thankful not to be too stupid in that respect, so I had no trouble understanding with only a couple of minor questions here and there.

Still, *none* of it had anything to do with my baby daughter and what had happened to her that night. One thing that really shook me was all the fuss about the blood that had supposedly been found in the car. The way the press had made it sound, there were gallons. Yet when all the evidence was in, the quantity was five millilitres. *One teaspoon.* By comparison with that, the tent had been awash with blood, and the Crown had refused to accept that. One teaspoon of blood. In the car, where I hadn't been. If the newspapers had said one teaspoonful, people would have looked at it and said, 'You have to be kidding!'

True, the kids had had nosebleeds at various times, and we had picked up an accident victim, some time before, and he had bled fairly lavishly over my knees and maybe down between the front seats onto the console. But that had been a couple of years before—ancient history.

All Joy Kuhl's evidence was reported in great and sensational detail as the inquest progressed, and we were faced with the alarming possibility that this barrage of scientific tests and terminology would influence the public. I mean, science can't be wrong . . . can it?

We continued to face the media circus daily as we walked in and out of the court. The ABC camera crew just did not have their act together. We called them the Push and Pull Gang. Normally, a cameraman can film running flat out backwards if necessary (and some can go almost as fast backwards as forwards), being guided by the soundman who puts his hand in the cameraman's belt, steering him by pushing or pulling to the left or right, so even steps present no problems. This particular crew who had obviously not been together very long were never attached to each other when required. In a crowd the soundman would go one way, the cameraman another, and when they came to the end of their 1. 8 metres (6 foot) length of cord, it either pulled out or they came to a dead halt until they got their act together again. They continually managed to tangle people up in their flex and even got it wrapped around themselves sometimes.

Joy Kuhl was followed by other scientific experts. A South Australian policeman, Sergeant Cocks, cut a jumpsuit with a pair of curved scissors, demonstrating that, when you cut terry towelling, small tufts of material fall out. He said he discovered similar tufts in the material vacuumed from our car, and three in the material vacuumed from the camera bag. This was supposed to show that I had cut Azaria's head off with the scissors, while she was wearing her jumpsuit, and put the body in the camera bag, apparently. He had a small problem, however: at least some areas of Azaria's jumpsuit had been heavily bloodstained, but he couldn't detect any blood on the tufts of the jumpsuit material removed from the car or the camera bag. When the boys grew out of their old jumpsuits, I had cut the legs off to make them last longer. The pieces were used for rags, so what was so odd about jumpsuit tufts in the car anyway?

Then came the star Crown witness: Professor James Cameron, the London forensic scientist who, the newspapers and court informed us had done tests on the famous Turin Shroud. (Well, that was no great claim to fame because its authenticity is still hotly disputed.) He said Azaria's death had been caused by a cutting instrument, possibly a pair of scissors, making an incisive wound to the neck. He produced a coloured video which he said showed the hand print on the back of a jumpsuit and how it was made. It didn't look anything like it to me, and other people had trouble seeing it as a hand print also. No mention was made of the hand being female now, either. Phil Rice summed it up quite neatly when he said: 'Like beauty, it has to be in the eye of the beholder.'

Cameron's conclusions were supported by an odontologist named Sims, also from London, who had examined Azaria's clothes and found none of the characteristics he would have expected to see if they had been damaged by dog's teeth. He had examined only one dingo skull to see how the teeth were positioned, and hadn't actually seen a wild dingo in his life—nor, of course had Professor Cameron. (Sims had once been bitten on the ankle by a terrier, though.)

Malcolm Chaikin, one of Australia's top textile experts and a professor at the University of New South Wales, was next. He gave evidence that the teeth of dogs could tear fabric, but not cut it, like scissors. He'd looked at the damaged areas of the jumpsuit both with the naked eye and with an electron microscope, and said that the severed fibres had been cut, not torn, and that the damage had been caused by scissors or another cutting instrument, not by the teeth of a dog or other canid, as only scissor cuts could produce tufts. That statement was refuted with dramatic style in later years.

Charlwood was called, and gave evidence of interviews he'd had with us. He admitted he had attempted to record conversations without telling us that this was his intention. We asked him to list them all; that way we would be protected from any surprises he might later produce.

Still neither reports nor the daily witness lists were given to the defence team beforehand, so our lawyers could not study them and know what questions to ask. This put them at a disadvantage because it meant they had to think on their feet. Quite often they would be reading the report the person in the box had given while trying to cross-examine them at the same time.

One or two reporters were friendly enough to get the day's witness lists for us, as they *were* given to the press, sometimes even the day before (thank God for the *Sydney Morning Herald's* Malcolm Brown). Sometimes the press were even given the reports, and getting those was very helpful. Time and time again, Phil or Andy got to his feet and protested that he had been unable to have the evidence given to him, and could it please be handed across. Sometimes some was given; at other times the Crown would maintain that it wasn't ready yet. Our objections fell on deaf ears, but at least they were on the record.

A Cool Load of Incompletes

Court recessed for the Christmas break, and we returned home. We got back into routine as soon as possible. We had had 'incomplete' on our studies again because of being away and because he was now behind on his thesis, it was certain that Michael would not be able to graduate with the rest of his mates that year. He got straight back into that with a will and I endeavoured to catch up on my studies and sit for some belated exams I had missed.

Apart from this, I had a lot of my art to catch up. I was hoping to have it all finished by the start of the college year, realising of course that I had the last half of the second inquest to come, with the ensuing disruption to our lives. The press had seen so much of us during the first half of the inquest, they fully realised we weren't going to talk to them, so most of the time they gave up pestering us over Christmas. I spent many hours in the pottery shed way down the back of the college, soothing my troubled spirits by watching the clay on the wheel go round and change shape. No wonder pottery is often recommended for therapy.

I caught up on some dressmaking, too; I had always made my own clothes. I had done a four-year certificate course in dressmaking, tailoring and drafting, at technical college, and managed to top that course both years (I did the four years in two). When I left I was offered a teaching job with the college but Michael had a transfer to north Queensland and I was unable to accept. It would have been something that I loved doing. Along with the teaching job went free extra education in other subjects I was looking forward to studying. I designed my own clothes as well. Occasionally I bought a dress when I was pressed for time in my program of caring for children, church work and looking after Michael, plus doing all the typing for the local radio programs he did. But I made most of the family clothes, including some suits for Michael. People often commented on the way I dressed my children. I made trousers for Michael, Aidan and Reagan all alike, and shirts for the boys to match their father's. They all had several sets of similar clothing.

When the first inquest came there was no problem; I had my own clothes. When the second inquest was held, I had the same clothes, but because time was short I went down to the local swap shop to see if I could pick up some more clothes suitable for wearing in court. It was cool inside the court, but extremely hot outside. Court dressing in the north is far different from what it is down south. It is quite acceptable to wear shorts and long socks as business dress up north, and short-sleeved shirts minus coats. Not so in the south. The fact that it was still cold in the south when it was hot in the north meant the southerners thought we were under- dressed, and the northerners, used to the normal mode of very casual dress, thought we were over-dressed. It didn't matter where we were, we couldn't please everyone.

One woman had complained bitterly to my mother about a certain dress of mine she had seen pictured in the newspaper. I was walking down College Drive with Mum one day and met the lady walking up. She stopped and, part way through the conversation, looking at my dress, she said, 'Now, *that's* a beautiful dress. Why didn't you wear that one at the inquest?' Mum, quick as a flash, said, 'Oh, she did. That's the dress that you were remarking about.'

I discovered there had been a lot of flack over my dressing, particularly by some Adventists who thought that it was very indecorous to have bare shoulders. Well, if they had been up north, they would have been very lucky not to be in bikini tops and shorts. Indeed Dr Geoffrey Edelsten's wife Leanne got her first modelling break because of it. At least somebody got something useful out of the second inquest.

It was obviously very important indeed for us to find our own expert witnesses. Stuart Tipple tried to find some forensic pathologists who could duplicate the tests that Joy Kuhl had described at the second inquest. It was very difficult, not to say impossible: she had used up all the 'blood' found in her tests.

The testing procedure had not been photographed, so there was no way of getting a second opinion on her tests. (This was 'standard procedure', she claimed at any forensic laboratory.) The plates she had used for the immunological tests had not been stained or preserved either.

What could we do? We couldn't check anything and the Crown was still being unhelpful. Not only that, but we'd voluntarily given the police whatever they'd asked for—including our car—and they had carried out tests without our knowledge or consent. Then, when no material was left to test and we thought we couldn't counter what they said, they had presented us with a whole lot of evidence.

While the inquest was in recess over Christmas and in January 1982, Stuart wrote to Joy Kuhl asking for information about the antiserum she had used in her immunological testing. She didn't reply. When she gave her second lot of evidence at the beginning of February, we asked her again to provide the material we'd asked for. She agreed, but nothing happened. Stuart contacted her again in early March, and yet again at the end of April, and he phoned her as well. Finally she told him (in her letter dated 25 May 1982) what he wanted to know.

Stephen Garrett, a friend of ours who was head of the Avondale College laboratory with an honours degree in science, was doing further study at the University of Newcastle under Professor Barry Boettcher. Professor Boettcher was head of the Department of Biological Sciences and one of the world's IVF pioneers, with some world firsts to his credit. Stephen asked if he could read the evidence on blood, as it was his field. We agreed and later he asked for permission to show it to his teacher in Newcastle who was 'OK in this stuff'. 'Sure, why not?' we said.

Professor Boettcher came up with some very interesting results. In the first place, Joy Kuhl had said with great authority that the blood tested had fifty per cent foetal haemoglobin in it. Boettcher knew that this was incorrect for Azaria's age; with the help of Dr Andrew Scott, who had tested Azaria's clothes, he learned that Azaria's blood contained about twenty-five per cent foetal haemoglobin. Therefore it seemed unlikely, to say the least, that the blood Joy Kuhl had tested had been Azaria's.

Second, he found it peculiar that her tests had suggested that the antiserum had reacted more strongly with the blood samples taken from the car than with the control sample she had used, which had about seventy per cent foetal haemoglobin (or nearly three times the concentration to be found in Azaria's blood). Besides, she had carried out tests on blood taken from the hinge of the passenger seat, and found that they contained *only* foetal haemoglobin.

There was a great deal about crossover electrophoresis testing, haeptoglobins, haemoglobin, and a lot of other complicated stuff, but basically Professor Boettcher came to the conclusion that either the bloodstains Joy Kuhl had tested had not come from Azaria, or that there was something radically wrong with her testing procedure.

He started some testing for his own curiosity's sake.

He came to the conclusion that her methodology was severely at fault. In fact, Professor Nairn was later to testify, 'It's not just only of immunological techniques, I think her basic knowledge of immunology was deficient' and that 'her level of understanding doesn't seem to move to being able to appreciate the significance of double banding'. The more Professor Boettcher investigated her work notes, the worse they became. Controls were missing, steps left out, and incorrect conclusions reached. We were told that Barry Boettcher's scientific honour was aroused. We contacted Stuart and he rang Professor Boettcher and asked him officially to work on our behalf with a view to actually appearing in court. He agreed.

This was all very well, but how were we going to get it across at the inquest? I now knew it certainly wasn't enough to say that the evidence was all on our side and truth must win. It seemed that people have much more of a chance if they say, 'I'm wrong; I can scheme; I can lie; I can cheat and, whatever I do, because I am telling lies, I will get more attention and probably win my case, and it will be much better for me than if I tell the truth.'

Barry was very keen to uphold the impartiality and the correct scientific methods of all scientists. He wrote to various places in the world for information on forensic testing to make sure that he was completely accurate. He went to the highest recognised authorities in each field and each time the answers were the same. He did a number of his own tests and had these checked and each time, as predicted, he was proved right, so we were able to go back to the inquest with that material.

Michael knew that Webber Roberts had a Torana hatchback of the same vintage as ours, so he asked whether he could see where the plate came from. He examined the underdash area and found a spray similar to the one that had been presented in court. Webber let him cut the plate out so we could test it and see what the droplet spray pattern might be.

We knew that it wasn't blood, as Joy Kuhl had said, but couldn't find out exactly what it was. We approached General Motors, the manufacturers, to no avail. Try as we might, before the trial, we could find no further information about it. Les Smith had broken it down into ingredients but we could not identify the product, as many things could contain those substances—and what if the real one had some of Reagan's blood on it from when he'd bitten his lip under there? Surely it would have denatured by now, but who knew? We didn't have any access to the original, only some small samples, which didn't react as blood. So we were at an impasse.

Stuart regularly called for information. Often various scientists requested additional information not indicated in the transcript, or they wanted the history of various items for tests in any forensic field that we could provide. We decided to simply ask Joy Kuhl as many useful questions as we could when the inquest resumed so our men could work, and save our forensic rebuttals for the trial. We were unable to gain access to any of the exhibits before the inquest and soon decided presenting the little evidence we did have would only give the Crown more time to come up with more scenarios. The best thing was to wait and leave it for the trial which we now realised would be unavoidable, the way the evidence was being presented. If they would not cooperate with us, we would not give them *any* information ahead of time that we did not obviously *have* to, either.

Blocked Communications

It was time to return to Alice Springs. As the plane came in to land we saw a huge crowd of reporters waiting. We hoped that Peter Dean was there with the car for us to leave in a hurry. He had excelled himself. His mate Paul Brann (manager of Ansett Industries) had organised a car to drive out onto the tarmac. The airport security van was to clear a path for us. Our vehicle was not easy to see into. It pulled up beside the plane and we climbed in without too many photographs.

To avoid the press, it was decided to go straight up the runway so we could leave by the light aero club gates. The press, seeing this, raced to their cars, blocking the exit. We turned around to see if we could beat them back to the normal gates. Although we sped along that runway (we didn't manage to take off like the planes did), the media once again beat us, so we used the two-way radio to obtain permission to use the restricted air force gates where the press could not go, and so back to our motel.

As we drove along observing the speed limit we soon had ten press cars following us. At one stage we thought we'd lost some but when we rounded the motel corner, we discovered that they had gone a different way and beaten us there. There they were, all standing around the reception area where we had to get our keys and walk up the outside stairs to our room.

Paul had said on the way back, 'Why don't we give them the slip? Come and stay at our place instead.' I was still shy with strangers then, so we had declined, but as we recoiled at the sight of the press again, he reiterated, 'Just come around for a while until things die down. You can check the place out. We've got a nice room at the back of the garage. It's like a little motel unit, all self-contained. If you want to stay there you can, otherwise we can bring you back tonight when things have died down a bit.' We quickly agreed, and took off again. The reporters followed.

Peter looked at Paul and said, 'How about we give these guys the slip?' Stuart, cautious legally and not anxious for us to have any more bad press, said we should take things carefully and just leave well alone. We dropped Stuart off at the Alice Springs Casino where our other two lawyers were already staying, then we were to continue on to Paul's. Peter looked at Paul again, and then at us and said, 'Well? What about it? Shall we lose them?' I grinned, 'Why not!'

There was a short discussion and it was agreed that we would go down the back lane to Peter's office and see what we could arrange. It was obvious he and Paul had something in mind, but we were not sure what. As we drove down the back lane, sure enough, all ten cars followed. The guys grinned and said, 'It will work!' We stopped; the reporters stopped. Peter jumped out and went through the back gate to his office and we took off again, slowly. We drove around several streets. As far as anyone else was concerned, we were simply driving around to avoid photographs while we waited to go and collect Peter again.

Actually, we were simply waiting for Peter to arrange a trap. He made two phone calls and both parties were home. One call was to Barbara, Paul's wife, and the other one was to the deputy headmaster of the Alice Springs high school. A few blocks later Paul said, 'Ah, he's done it. I recognise that vehicle.' As we looked down the street we saw a big four-wheel-drive vehicle edged up on the nature strip, out of sight of the opening to the back lane. 'In that case,' Paul said, 'Barbara should be around shortly.' We went around two more blocks, and saw Barbara's vehicle. 'Now, let's do it, guys,' he said.

Around the block and down the lane we went again, pulled up, opened the door and made as if to get out. The press jumped out of their cars, cameras in hand, and started rushing forwards, all except the red car behind us, whose occupants stayed, simply watching warily. When the rest of the press were all out, we slammed the door again, and took off in a cloud of dust. You could see the reporters swearing. All except the red car, which took off after us. The driver had stuck like a stamp all the way, just *too* smart, and we couldn't shake him.

We got to the end of the lane. The four-wheel-drive started coming across, but that red car was so close on our bumper that it had to be let through as well. Then that big four-wheel-drive went straight across the lane, and stayed there. The driver, Peter's friend the deputy headmaster, climbed out of the car and removed the keys. The rest of the reporters had got back into their cars and raced after us—too late. Now they were blocked. They got out and abused him. He was a fairly stocky man, fit, and had a black belt in karate with two dan to boot. As they swore at our unknown friend, he bowed politely, grinning hugely, and said, 'Thank you, thank you very much. Thank you. A lovely day to you, too.' When they could not disturb his equanimity with more swearing, they got in their cars and backed to the other end of the lane, and, lo and behold, there was one very small van parked across that end too—locked with no driver in it.

Peter Dean, meanwhile, had hopped on his little step-through motor scooter and came around to see if all was OK and create some diversion if necessary. He was opposite the four-wheel-drive as we came through. Seeing the red car, he called, 'Follow me!' and went in front, guiding us to the Todd River bed. The Todd River is dry sand for all but a few days of the year. The roadway through it was narrow and sandy. Midway across he pulled to one edge and let us go through and then drifted in between us and the red car—and I mean drifted, from one side of the road to the other. Paul put down his foot and took off while Peter slowed down deliberately, knowing the red car couldn't pass him there. As we got out of sight, we sped the wrong way down a one-way street to Paul's place and out of sight in his backyard before anyone was able to catch us and see where we had gone. Peter led the red car a merry dance and then simply went back to his office, where he rang us in great glee.

We took one look at the room behind the garage and saw how comfortable, quiet and peaceful it was beside the pool. Home. No press, no police next door, across the corridor or balcony keeping an eye on us.

Then Barbara came in laughing. She was my size with a cheerful happy face and cute, turned-up nose. She had a lovely disposition and was intelligent too, we were to discover. Realising her van was light and she was no match for angry men,

Barbara had simply parked and locked it, ran two or three houses away and hidden in someone's front garden to see what would happen!

Well, they walked around and around that van swearing, and demanding it to be opened and moved! Finally four of them picked it up bodily and moved it out of the way. As the last car drove through, Barbara stood up to go back to her vehicle. One reporter, seeing her, waved his fist threateningly. She grinned and waved her fingers back in a cheeky hello. Years later we discovered that Kevin Hitchcock was that reporter. By then he was a friend (they finally met and reminisced in 1988).

If the incident had been scripted in a Hollywood movie, I am sure they couldn't have done it in one take, but we did it unrehearsed and unplanned and nine cars were blocked down that lane.

Fred Schepisi, when planning the final stages of the movie *Evil Angels (A Cry in the Dark)*, complained that he couldn't put the chase in because, if he did, everyone would think it was Hollywood hype instead of reality, therefore detracting from the accuracy of the rest of the film. With one of his huge grins, he said, 'Wish I'd seen it happen, though.'

Well, we had met both halves of the family now and Barbara was as adamant and kind in her invitation to stay indefinitely as Paul had been, so we did. Despite the fact that they ate meat and we didn't, and Paul liked his tinnies and we liked our juice, we became firm friends and stayed there for the rest of our time.

A CROWNING INDIGNITY

When the inquest resumed on 1 February 1982, Joy Kuhl came back into the witness box and said there was blood in various places in the camera bag, and identified the presence of 'foetal blood' on the zipper clasp and part of the buckle, and Andy Kirkham cross-examined in as much detail as possible for our scientists. She later testified this annoyed her. All the evidence had now been given.

The Crown summation had been given to our lawyers the day before. The Crown was asking for my indictment for first degree murder, with Michael as accessory after the fact—the murder of our beautiful baby girl!

I was devastated and angry but had realised for some time they were after this. It was awful, printed in black and white, like that. So many lies. I ground my teeth and slept fitfully that night. Justice was being made a mockery. I prayed and chatted a long while with God that night and was calm and ready for the new day by morning.

I was surprised that Michael seemed only a bit annoyed, but not upset as I thought he would be. Maybe it hadn't sunk in yet.

I waited for Sturgess to sum up the Crown allegations. As he spoke I sat there impassively, numb. He said the Crown case was that I had taken my daughter to the car and cut her throat. I had then put her body in the camera bag, or concealed it some other way, until later in the evening when I had had the chance to take the body away from the camping area and bury it. I must have told Michael what I had done, and he had cooperated in concealing the crime. The body was later dug up and the clothing removed before it was buried again. The jumpsuit had been cut by scissors in such a way to look as if a dingo had caused the damage. Then Michael or I—or both of us—had supposedly jogged nearly 4 kilometres (2.5 miles) out to the little gully below Bularo on the Rock and left the clothing there to be found, giving the impression that a dingo had discarded it.

We were committed for trial as the Crown had requested.

When Michael heard the summation actually being read in court, it hit him like a ton of bricks. He was distraught, in a really bad way, and I wasn't sure what he was going to do.

When we arrived back from court that day, Paul Brann met us at the back gate. He was dressed in an orangey-red, flowery laplap, a comical straw hat with feathers in it, had bare feet and a tinny in one hand. He had heard the news and was worried about Michael, but didn't let on. He took one look at him and obviously said the first thing that came into his head.

'I heard you haven't been having a good day. I've been listening to the wireless. *I've* had a bloody bad day too. The ducks upset the garbage and then wouldn't get out of the swimming pool so I could have my swim!'

Well, that was the end. It was so ludicrous in comparison that Michael cracked up and laughed. It seemed the earth was falling apart around his ears, and this helped put things in perspective. I walked off, so grateful to Paul for his shrewdness and understanding, and left to go into the house for a cool drink. Later the guys swam and relaxed.

Paul later admitted that when he took one look at Michael's face, he realised that if he sympathised with him, he would probably break down altogether, and decided that maybe a joke, although perhaps in bad taste, was probably the best thing he could do. He just kept his fingers crossed that it worked. Thank God that it did. I guess Paul never thought he looked much like an angel that day, but I sure did.

All the way through, from the nightmare of Azaria's disappearance until the raid, I had done my best. I had cooperated with the police, answered questions I couldn't see the point of, spoken to the press, and to television and radio journalists. I had thought the truth must come out. During the first inquest, I had tried to be myself, to keep the family going, to support Michael . . . and people still condemned me. Nothing I did was right. If I smiled, I was heartless; if I cried, I was just acting.

This time, I had sat and listened while a lot of people with university degrees and expensive equipment did their level best to show—scientifically—that I had murdered my baby girl. And because I didn't show the cold, dead anger I was feeling, because I just listened to all this evidence, I was wrong again. I'd had to listen to so many words about what other people said had happened to Azaria that the whole thing didn't seem to have any relevance to me because I knew it was not murder. It was just an expensive farce put on for the benefit of a privileged few forensic, legal and political identities. A lot of words: all addressed to somebody else.

And all people saw when they looked at me was what they wanted to see—a hard-faced, murdering bitch.

Thinking About Pink and Other Things

When we planned another baby, we were very careful lest it appear that we were going after public sympathy. At the end of the first inquest, we had been planning a second daughter, and had been about to start when they reopened the second inquest, so we put off my pregnancy because of that.

Now with the devastating result of the second inquest, Michael wondered if we should postpone it still further.

I desperately wanted to have another daughter, so I said to Michael, 'Look, if they have their way, I'm going to prison. That will be the end of it; there will be no way we can have another baby. By the time I come out of prison I'll be too old, and if they don't get their way, we're all right anyway.'

At the end of the second inquest the date of the trial was announced for June. I told Michael I was going to ask Stuart's advice, so I waylaid him on the way home from court and asked, 'What if I get pregnant now? I won't be showing at the trial, and nobody will be any the wiser. Then when it's all over, and the baby comes, there'll be no problems. If anything does go wrong, they still can't stop me having this baby. I'll be pregnant, and I'll have the baby afterwards in jail. They can't do anything about that. What do you think? I don't think they should be allowed to ruin our plans any longer.'

He smiled and said, 'Sounds OK to me.'

I raced gleefully back to Michael and told him Stu had given the OK. He grinned and I could see he was pleased. In the movie *Evil Angels (A Cry in the Dark)* the bed scene in our Cooranbong home looks horribly calculating, with me trying to force a reluctant Michael to get me pregnant. It was a far cry from the mutual agreement and the great holiday we had at the beach where our second daughter was conceived.

Although I had had amniocentesis and we knew I was expecting a girl, we hadn't told the boys—just one or two of our closest friends whom we could trust. We were afraid that the boys might accidentally tell, or the press would get hold of the information somehow, and would use it as a publicity gimmick before the trial.

We had to decide on a name for the baby, but were very conscious that it would be blown up as media headlines if the press were given half the chance. Azaria's name had been taken out of context and created such a furore that we were particularly anxious not to have anything like this happen again.

Whenever we looked for names for our children, we had always been particularly careful of their meaning. Now we couldn't find anything we really liked. We were looking for something unusual. We wanted to give her three names, as Azaria had had, and even rhyming with them if possible. But there seemed to be nothing we could agree on.

In a book one day, I noticed a name that had the basis of something I liked. I sat and fiddled with the spelling and when Michael came home I said to him, 'I think I've found a name I like. It has the same type of ending as Azaria, and we have Aidan and Reagan both ending in "-an", so what about the girls ending in "-ia"? What do you think of Azaria and Kahlia?' Michael said the name over to himself several times and said, 'Yes, I like it.' I smiled as I watched him. I had to have a subtle approach or he'd disagree without thinking. 'What does it mean?' I replied that it really didn't have a meaning, I had made it up. Nevertheless, it was derived from Charles, which means 'the strong one', and this little girl would need to be strong to handle the insinuations she might have to endure.

We decided on Nikari as a third name, after the daughter of a friend of ours. We had almost used it as a first name, but didn't want her to be called Niki: something that couldn't be shortened was much nicer for a first name, we thought. But the middle name remained a problem.

After the second inquest and before the trial, we obtained photographs of some exhibits, and test samples were supplied to us from the under-dash spray. Our biggest difficulty was the rest of the so-called blood in the car. Kuhl had used all of it in her testing, so we only had access to her worknotes and the court notes of Andy's close cross-examination.

Certainly Professor Boettcher had agreed to appear for us, but there was also further evidence the Crown had come up with. We were faced with the strength of public opinion against us, and this grew stronger as the trial approached, the 'accidental' forensic leaks to the press continually drumming up the public to fever pitch. Sometimes it seemed that all the copy journalists wrote for weeks had the words 'blood' or 'trial' in it. You didn't have to be a genius to work out what people thought about us. It was everywhere.

We could see that people thought if we hadn't been guilty, we wouldn't have been charged and bound over for trial, would we? The law can't make a mistake like that (can it?). Then, because I hadn't apparently acted 'appropriately' and fitted some people's idea of 'the norm', lamenting, screaming, yelling, abusing, or bursting into tears all over the place, I was unfeeling and therefore a murderess. I'm neither a watering pot nor of Latin temperament. That's not my way.

Then there was the belief that 'dingoes just don't do that sort of thing'. People who lived in the cities, who had never seen a wild dingo in their lives, suddenly became experts on their behaviour. Despite the fact that there were dozens of letters from Australians living in the bush and who knew about dingoes, giving many examples of what they were capable of doing to human beings, they couldn't be right.

For the time being, we had to contend with prejudice against our religion, too. Anybody who knows anything about religion is aware that Seventh-day Adventism is very much in the mainstream of the Protestant faiths: we believe in the Trinity—one God: Father, Son and Holy Spirit. We take the Ten Commandments literally, which is why we have Saturday Sabbath instead of Sunday services. We believe the dead are asleep until Jesus returns again, at which time they are resurrected, as II Thessalonians 4: 16,17 teaches. We hold communion, and baptise by immersion, as Jesus was baptised, but not until people are of an age when they can choose. We dedicate our babies so we may set a good example as parents and give them a Christian upbringing.

Australia isn't what you'd call a deeply religious country on the whole, and these small deviations from the so-called 'norm' caused people to think we were weird. I don't believe in ramming my religion down another's throat . . . but I know that I wouldn't have survived without knowing that God was looking after me. His guidance was always made plain to me when I needed it most.

We needed a new set of lawyers for the trial. Each lawyer has his own specialty field and though Phil Rice was excellent in an inquest, we now needed a trial specialist. Andy Kirkham would definitely be on the team. We were on the same wavelength and had often held discussions where, much to Michael's bewilderment, Stuart, Andy or I began a sentence and the others finished it.

As we were all strong-minded, this was interesting, too! We decided if Andy could recommend a good QC we would be happy to accept that and Stuart agreed, so on the way out of court I asked Andy whom he would suggest.

'Now, young lady,' he said with his piercing look, 'that's an unethical question. Your solicitor must advise you.'

'Well, who would you get if it was you?' I asked with a grin.

'John Phillips,' he answered immediately with his head on one side and a twinkle in his eye once more. 'Geez, Lindy, now get lost before you get me into trouble!'

Stuart agreed we engage John Phillips so, as soon as we all got home from the Alice after the inquest, John was asked and agreed. He was sharp- witted, honest, clean living, and wouldn't stoop to deceit. He later became the Victorian Director of Public Prosecutions and then a Supreme Court judge. Like Andy Kirkham, he came from Melbourne, which was handy, because they could work together closely before the trial. Because we had applied for legal aid, we were bound to have a legal aid solicitor from Darwin, which we were all wary about. Eventually Greg Cavanagh was appointed and he proved to be very nice.

We were told by the Law Department that we would be staying in the Travelodge motel. But it was decided that we should look for private accommodation where we would have more protection from the press and more room to move. Stuart found us a comfortable flat with two bedrooms, which he rented. Irene Heron's local church knew how much she worried about and appreciated us, so her local church members clubbed together, as she was now a pensioner, and paid her fare and accommodation so she could be with us. My parents would once again look after the children. Irene would cook our meals and generally look after the house, spending her spare time at court. She would answer the phone and the door. The arrangements seemed ideal and it was much cheaper than the motel. So it was arranged.

A Dressing Down

When it came to the trial, everybody was *still* telling me how to dress. I shouldn't look too well dressed. I must be careful to project the image of an ordinary mother; I shouldn't look too well off or too well groomed because the jury wouldn't like it. I was supposed to look motherly. I was very pregnant and said, 'What in the hell do you think I can look except motherly? I'm looking like Porky the Pig!' You can't look too fashionable when you are pregnant. You have to wear low-heeled shoes, and there is not much choice in your style of dress.

I had had winter maternity clothes when Aidan was born, which were far too hot for the trial; Reagan had been born in summer but I only had a couple of dresses left that were suitable for court wear. The day-to-day and cooler dresses that I had had for both Reagan and Azaria had long since worn out or been handed on, and here I was going from winter to very hot weather. All my girlfriends around college rallied round to lend me maternity frocks. Mum and I spent a couple of weeks before I left taking up the hems of some, and letting down others. I went to the swap shop and looked for old-fashioned dresses that were the same style as modern maternity clothes. I removed grease, scrubbed off stains, washed and mended them, added lace to some and, lo and behold, I had a new wardrobe. I was ready to go. Shortly before we were due to leave, Stuart got a phone call from Blu Border, saying that it would be much more convenient if we stayed in the accommodation in their backyard. It would be cheaper and it would be easier to keep an eye on us there, and keep the press away. Blu had done this for our benefit, he said. Stuart rang us and said, 'There's a change of plans. Did you ask for your accommodation to be changed?'

We said, 'No.'

He replied, 'Well, Blu is giving us other accommodation'.

'You're kidding!' I said. 'I'm not accepting that. I know where he's talking about. It's an old tin shed! We can't stay there.'

'Are you sure?' Stuart asked.

'Of course I'm sure. I've seen it. It's dreadful,' I said.

'Well, I'll check up,' he replied.

He rang back to tell Blu that we wanted it left as it was but Blu informed him that he had already cancelled our flat and it was too late to do anything about it. I was extremely annoyed.

Michael said, 'Maybe it is not as bad as we think. I can't remember what it's like.' I could.

In *Evil Angels (A Cry in the Dark)*, our 'suite' is shown as being quite pleasant—freshly painted and carpeted. The truth was very different. The new carpet was old seagrass matting, the beds in the front room were simply old, metal framed, single bedsteads. Certainly they had foam mattresses on them, but no covers of any sort, and the pillows were without pillowcases. These we used as a lounge. The room also held a small Laminex table and three chairs. We also had an overhead fan, which only served to move the hot air under the corrugated iron roof down onto us. The front room had a 15 centimetre (6 inch) gap underneath the adjoining wall, through which cockroaches periodically crawled. We had an Esky type drink container. We were given an electric frypan, but the power plug was somewhere next door and we were told they really didn't think it was a good idea to use the electricity.

There was a window with tin louvres and wire screen. Outside tangled trees and vines blocked what would have otherwise been a direct view for the press.

There was a very narrow middle section, without a door. I jammed a broom handle across between two walls and hung clothes on it, creating a makeshift wardrobe. A local church member, horrified at the spartan conditions, had supplied an ancient dressing table with four drawers. (These same people also supplied the Laminex table.) Beyond that was our bedroom. The room had an ancient, threadbare carpet square. I used a packing case to put my things on, and there was one kitchen chair out the back also. We couldn't use the huge, built-in cupboard because of the cockroaches.

Fortunately the previous tenant hadn't yet removed his air conditioner and we were able to persuade him to leave it for us. The tin louvres were kept permanently shut with the air conditioner going full blast all day so that it would be cool enough for us to sleep at night. That meant it was pitch black all day with no view. The room had two more ancient single beds; for these we were supplied two sheets and one blanket.

I whispered to Michael, 'I'm not staying here. It's awful.'

'No, I don't think we'll stay either,' he replied. Turning to Blu he said,

'Look, thanks for the offer, but I think that we would be better situated at the flat, and we will see if we can get that back again.'

Blu said, 'You can't. It's been re-let. You won't find any accommodation in town. It's full.'

I said, 'Yes, thanks to us. They've all come up for the trial.' He just laughed. We were stuck there.

This was the 'suite' from which we had to conduct the preparations for our trial. It certainly wouldn't make our job any easier.

It was time for Irene's plane to arrive, and Blu returned to the airport to pick her up. Later we heard the car pull up and Irene came and gave us a big hug. As she was to stay with us I had mentioned to Blu how good it was that there were plenty of beds and two rooms—Irene could sleep out the front and we would have the back. He never said a word. When she came in I started telling her which was her bed. He picked up her case and said, 'Irene will be staying upstairs with us.'

She said, 'No, it's fine, I'll stay here.'

'You will be upstairs with us,' Blu repeated. Taking the case, he walked upstairs and inside. She looked at me and raised her eyebrows; I shrugged.

'Maybe I'd better for a while, anyway. I'll see what's happening,' Irene said. She went upstairs, was given a nice room, unpacked, met them all and then came down to see how we were going.

TRIAL OF THE CENTURY

The trial began at Darwin courthouse on 13 September 1982 before Mr Justice James Muirhead. The prosecution team consisted of Ian Barker QC, who had been the Solicitor-General of the Northern Territory; Des Sturgess, QC, who had led the team at the second inquest; Darwin barrister, Tom Pauling, and Alice Springs solicitor, Michael O' Loughlan who had been the solicitor at both inquests.

John Phillips, our QC, was a very gentlemanly person. John, along with Andy and Stuart, always wore really clean shirts, either white or pale blue. Both Andy and John sent their clothes to the cleaners and their shoes were always highly polished (unlike the Crown lawyers, who quite often looked as if they had slept in their clothes). None involved themselves in the gutter tactics sometimes used by other lawyers. All were proud of their straight reputation and had every intention of remaining that way. The locals sometimes laughingly referred to our lawyers as 'the choir boys'—not inappropriate for John, who sings opera.

I was seven months pregnant—the trial had been postponed far past the original June date we had been given—and I found it almost unendurable to sit in that room hour after hour. We were being watched by prison officers on duty and were told that their job was to keep the public away and give us privacy. (I now realise that they were really there so we wouldn't get away, since we were out on bail on our own recognisance.)

This was where I first met Mrs Barham, the head of the female section of Darwin Prison. She was slim, had jet-black hair, and was near retiring age. I thought she was tough as old boots; she was strictly official and didn't seem at all sympathetic to me. I discovered how wrong I was on the first day (and continued to find out in the years to come). We had to sit in the accused's box, which only had a narrow, hard, built-in bench. I came back after the midmorning break on the first day to find a comfortable office chair provided for me behind our lawyers and Michael was allowed to sit there as well. I later discovered that this was Mrs Barham's doing. She had gone to the officers of the court and said that a very pregnant lady could not continue to sit on a hard bench without any support for her back. She said nothing about it to me, and I didn't find out who had helped me for a few days. At one stage, I thought I caught her blinking very hard, as if she was trying not to cry, and I thought I'd imagined it. Knowing her better later, I am sure she was trying to blink back tears on that first day.

Mrs Barham also helped in another very practical way. Initially when I wanted to go to the toilet I had to use a lavatory outside the courtroom, this meant walking past what seemed like hundreds of people. I had had enough of that, I was so hot that I thought I was going to explode because I was so pregnant, and it was generally very uncomfortable. Mrs Barham arranged for me to use the toilet downstairs, away from the public. The cells were about three metres square and could take about a dozen people if necessary; there was a hard bench along one wall and a lidless toilet bowl in the corner. The female holding cell was right next to the officers' section, and the male officers could watch me go to the toilet. I used it once with her standing guard (she even sent the men outside and locked the main door), and she decided this was ridiculous and that I should have better treatment. Because she had seniority, she ordered that I was to be allowed to use the officers' toilet.

It wasn't for some time that I realised that Michael and I could have been kept in those holding cells all day, every day, separately, without any means of communication with each other or our lawyers and been sent to prison at night. We wouldn't have had the power to object; I am very thankful that this did not happen.

We knew that the picking of a jury was able to be rigged. Although it is not supposed to happen, it is quite possible to pick people who are known to favour one point of view so the whole list, regardless of who is rejected, turns out to be favourable to the Crown. In a small town this is easy and I was feeling nervous. We could have only eighteen rejections (twelve for me, six for Michael). After that whoever was left that the Crown didn't object to could go on the jury. The Crown has an unlimited power of rejection.

There were 150 potential jurors, and choosing the twelve for our case was very difficult indeed. I can see the worth of the jury system—the need to find unbiased people from a whole group of assorted citizens—but finding twelve people who hadn't been influenced in Darwin, the chief city of the Northern Territory, where a dingo had taken our baby, was incredibly difficult.

There were local issues to consider. For instance, one potential juror turned out to be the wife of a policeman, and asked to be excused. There was much laughing and joking about this, but why had she not been excluded in the first place? How could she be expected to be impartial about a case that involved her husband's work? Even if he was not directly concerned with the investigation, some of his colleagues and friends would be. Similarly, how can a local government worker be impartial in this case, when his or her job is on the line if they go against the boss?

One cartoon aptly depicted the problem. An old desert tramp was shown with two police bending over him. As he said, 'Lindy who?' one policeman remarked, 'Only eleven to go.'

The judge was very conscious of the particular problems our jury faced. Before the evidence started, he said to them,

> 'If you were on trial for a serious offence, how would you feel if you found that jurors had been influenced by matters not mentioned in the court, by matters heard outside the court, under circumstances where neither you nor your counsel could explain it or challenge it? That, ladies and gentlemen, is why it is so vital that you keep your eyes entirely on the evidence. Your job in this case is to administer justice according to law, not according to rumour, not according to preconceived notions. You will hear much of this, ladies and gentlemen, for the simple reason that possibly the publicity concerning this matter has been without precedent in our lifetime.'

Two video cameras recorded everything that happened throughout the whole course of the trial. Judge Muirhead said to the jury,

> 'I do not want you to feel as you sit here that you are more or less being directly telecast to Australia or that there is any direct broadcast of these proceedings. That is not so. They were put in for the convenience of the press to avoid overcrowding, to enable the press to observe these proceedings in another place close by if they wished to do so. So do not get the idea that you are erupting to stardom or something, because you are not.'

The jurors—nine men and three women—nodded.

Ian Barker, QC, a shortish man with stooped shoulders, grey curls ringing a bald pate, and an insecure furtive way of hanging his head and peeping up at you from under his lashes, set out the Crown case. He didn't take long.

He said,

> 'A baby was killed at Ayers Rock on 17 August 1980 during the evening between eight and nine o'clock. It was a Sunday. The child was just under ten weeks old, having been born on 11 June. She was called Azaria Chamberlain, and was the daughter of the accused Michael Leigh Chamberlain and Alice Lynne Chamberlain. The body of the child was never found but, having heard the evidence concerning the baby's disappearance, you will have no difficulty determining that she is dead, and that she died on the night she disappeared. As to the manner and the cause of death, one cannot be precise because the body was never found. However, what will be proved, largely upon scientific evidence of the baby's clothes, is that the child lost a great deal of blood, in all probability from injury to the major vessels of her neck. She died very quickly because somebody had cut her throat.'

He dealt with the weaknesses to the Crown case—why on earth I would do such a thing—very quickly.

> 'The Crown does not venture to suggest any reason or motive for the killing. It is not part of our case that Mrs Chamberlain had previously shown any ill-will towards the child. Nor do we assert that the child was other than a normal, healthy baby. The Crown does not, therefore, attempt to prove motive, nor does it invite speculation as to motive. We simply say to you that the evidence to be put before you will prove beyond reasonable doubt that, for whatever reason, the baby was murdered by her mother. Shortly after the event the mother asserted, and thereafter continued to assert, that the dead child had been taken from the tent by a dingo. The Crown says that the dingo story was a fanciful lie, calculated to conceal the truth, which is that the child Azaria died by her mother's hand.'

The trump card in all this was the scientific evidence, particularly that of Joy Kuhl. Barker said,

> 'The discovery of foetal blood in the car is a critical part of the Crown case. It would be preposterous to suggest that the dingo took the child from the tent and into the car, and we will submit that the discovery of Azaria's blood in the car destroys the dingo attack explanation given by Mrs Chamberlain, whatever else there may be to support such explanation, and the Crown says there is almost nothing.
>
> 'So, ladies and gentlemen, this is a case of simple alternatives. *Either a dingo killed Azaria, or it was homicide*, because the child could hardly have inflicted injuries upon herself. *If she was killed in the car, one can at once forget the dingo.*' (Italics mine.)

When we adjourned on the first day, it was quite clear that the case Barker was presenting was quite different from the one put forward by Sturgess at the second inquest. There I had been accused of premeditated murder; now apparently I was supposed to have killed Azaria for some unknown reason, in the car, at about eight in the evening. The reasons for this were not to be given, but it was apparently unpremeditated.

Communication Breakdown

The ABC push and pull gang turned up again for the trial in Darwin. Once, when the press of people was intense and we were trying to walk through it with all the cameras following us, the Gang moved with their usual lack of precision; one man went one way, one the other. Michael and I were caught in their flex, the cameraman, feeling the flex tug, turned round and his camera whacked me hard on the head. We just had to learn to live through things like that. That wasn't the only time I was cracked on the head by a camera, and I just had to keep smiling as if I had never noticed the difference.

We tried to watch the news on television to see how the case was being reported. The Borders' TV was in their bedroom. They would bring it out from their room to watch the news when asked, but we always seemed to manage to miss the headlines. Sometimes we would miss the reports of the day's proceedings altogether, or have to wait until the later news, which wasn't so comprehensive. When one of the members, John Parry heard we intended to hire our own television, he loaned us their spare set for the rest of our stay.

It was obvious from the second day of the trial that we wouldn't have time to go back to Borders for a midday meal. There were so many people to get past, we had to run the press gauntlet twice more if we left for lunch, and we only had an hour. Rather than go back to where we were staying, it was much more convenient to send out for sandwiches. So every lunchtime Irene would slip out of court and, while we had our conference about what had happened that morning, she would be down at the shop waiting in line.

One shop attendant kept her waiting deliberately and served everyone else until there was no one left in the shop. Even though our lunch had been ordered in the morning it still wasn't ready. She never went there again. We would eat our sandwiches with Irene in the lawyers' rooms during the break; it was cool, we could sit down, and we were away from the press. During lunchtime and recesses, I spent my spare time crocheting a round tablecloth of locally spun silk.

I quickly realised we would be eating fewer meals at the Borders. Even some evening meals would be awkward. I said to Michael, 'I'm not going to pay for food we are not getting. I think that we ought to negotiate a fee per meal and pay only for what we eat.'

'Well, I'm not going to upset things by saying that,' he replied. 'I would rather leave it as it is.'

'Well, I'm not. We can't afford to pay extra money. I'm going to say something,' I said. So I spoke to Mrs Border. 'I don't want you to be put out by preparing meals we cannot attend—we can't always let you know in advance. Unless we order the night before and tell you that we are going to arrive, please don't prepare food for us. We will just pay you a set amount per meal. We will have breakfast, but we won't worry about other meals.' It was agreed; in some ways I could see she didn't like it, in others she was relieved.

Our breakfast was meagre and Irene gained the impression that her food was very expensive, although she was paying full board and lodging. Because of this, Irene bought her own supply of hot drink material, milk and sugar. But she could never have a hot drink without asking if others would also like one, so ended up supplying them all with hot drinks for breakfast. That drink was all she had; she would then buy her breakfast on the way to court because she felt so uncomfortable.

As Irene conducted open house for people as they passed through, and nothing was too much trouble for her she found it difficult to understand. She would even give up her own bed for you. She often picked up a hitchhiker on the road, the needy or the homeless, took them home and fed them, and gave them extra food and sent them on. That was Irene's mission in life, to love and help people. She said God had allowed her to do that by giving her the talents of love and hospitality.

Later Irene observed we were having no juice sent down for breakfast, and knowing how much Michael liked it, she went to the local supermarket and purchased quite a large supply, which she gave to Mrs Border, informing her it was for Michael and Lindy's breakfast. Several days later she asked me whether we had received any juice. We hadn't.

The first witness was Sally Lowe. She was called by Barker's junior, Tom Pauling (who had accepted a brief by Peter Dean for us, but was now appearing for the Crown. We'd have objected if we'd known but, as Peter Dean had transferred overseas, we hadn't any idea.) Sally gave substantially the evidence she had supplied before, and she did it with reason and conviction. She rejected all suggestions that she hadn't heard Azaria cry, and explained in a very down-to-earth fashion why she, a young mother, couldn't possibly have been mistaken. She added that until she and Greg moved to the motel at about ten o'clock that night, Michael and I were never out of sight of somebody. 'They were quite visible because you could see them crying,' she said. She never saw us trying to clean the car or taking any object at all out into the scrub. (As we hadn't, that was quite understandable.)

She was followed by her husband, Greg, who repeated much of his evidence on the search from the first inquest.

Greg Lowe was later to write a submission to the Australian Law Reform Committee called 'Conduct intended or likely to prejudice fair trial'. With Sally's treatment at the second inquest, and similar incidents in mind, he wrote, 'Our experience with the Chamberlain case makes us aware that extra judicial influence can be exerted on witnesses.

'Lay witnesses assume that law officials are obliged to act in a certain unbiased manner in an attempt to assist the courts of law. This is not always the case.

'To whom does one turn when an attempt is made to influence the evidence to be given by a witness?

'Many of my friends, relatives and work colleagues in Tasmania were so influenced by the media coverage of the second Chamberlain inquest, as to openly comment to both my wife and I that the woman must be guilty. The mere fact that the Chamberlains were committed for trial seemed sufficient information for our acquaintances to assume guilt of the couple. This ought not to be the case.'

Judy West came next, and said she heard Azaria cry too, 'fairly quickly after the growl of the dog'. She said that Michael and I had left the area of the car twice for about ten minutes each time. On neither occasion were we carrying the body of a child or a digging implement.

Amy Whittaker agreed, and said on one of the occasions she had actually told Michael to take me out searching so I would be satisfied Azaria hadn't been missed somewhere close by.

Murray Haby was called next. He turned out to be the man who had been in the nearby blue campervan. He gave most of his evidence slumped in his seat, head bowed, uncomfortable. When Pauling asked Haby what he had done next, he screwed around in his seat to stare at me in the box. Decision made, Haby's hunched back straightened, then he took a deep breath and spoke quickly before he could be stopped. 'I went back to my vehicle and got a torch and then proceeded up the sand dune. There were two other torch lights flashing around on the dunes at that stage. I looked around in the low part, and we exchanged calls a couple of times to check if we had found anything. The answers were no. Then I thought, well, if there was a dog carrying something, it would have to cross the ridge of the sand dunes, so I thought well, I'll go up to the sand dune and I went to the top of the sand dune and then walked along the sand dune until I came across some tracks—there were a lot of tracks down lower but this track stood out because it was a bit bigger than the other ones and quite easy to follow and came along to an area where obviously it had put something down—this dog or dingo—and had left an impression in the sand which to me looked like a knitted or woven fabric and then it obviously picked it up because it dragged a bit of sand away from the front and kept moving, and I followed it around past the Anzac memorial to where a car park comes off that road to the south of the sand dune, and lost it in on that sand dune there—not the sand dune, the car park.'

Haby let out a long sigh and relaxed. There! He'd got it out at last. He felt much better now. He also mentioned what he thought were blood spots. We later learned from Haby's evidence they hadn't wanted him to mention the last bit about the dingo and the jacket. In the corridor during the break I heard Barker say to Pauling, 'If I wanted the defence on my team I would have invited them. Thanks a lot.'

I wondered why we hadn't heard from Haby at the first inquest.

The other eyewitnesses were called; those immediately involved on the night. Frank Morris, the policeman who had carried out the initial search; Senior Ranger Derek Roff, Inspector Michael Gilroy and Sergeant Lincoln. They told the story of what they had done and what they had seen.

Each one supported what I had said. None of the witnesses could be shaken in what they said, because it was all true.

Once again, Jenny Ransome was called over the 'blood' on my tracksuit pants and her taped conversation. The jury had to be sent out while she argued with the Crown—forcibly telling the judge what she thought of the Crown's methods. She won her point and the Crown had to retreat.

But the Crown had all the eyewitnesses and favourable evidence in and out in a matter of days. Nipper, the tracker, was not called. When we suggested that *we* would call him, the Crown indicated they would have something to say about his English and his eyesight. We refused to have him humiliated by calling him under those conditions.

So far we were doing well; we had evidence from unbiased witnesses about what had happened on the night. But, as Andy and Stuart pointed out, the Crown strategy was becoming clear. They had called all the eyewitnesses first, the people sympathetic to us. But the Crown case depended heavily on scientific evidence and, by the time the 'experts' had given their evidence, there was a fair chance the jurors would be confused by its weight. They would then forget their original sympathy for us (supported by the eyewitnesses) and be heavily influenced by the scientists. Then we began weeks of scientific evidence the Crown had found.

It was incredible. I thought they must be crazy. *Surely* the jury would not believe that line of bulldust. In *ten minutes* I was supposed to have taken Azaria back to the tent; put her down; put on my tracksuit pants; taken her to the car; cut her throat; and cut her head off—with the nail scissors, mind you—in the front passenger seat of the car. Blood had supposedly sprayed the dashboard, run down the console and dripped on to my tracksuit and running shoes. I had then stuffed her into the camera bag (which was too small, by the way); hurried to clean up the blood; got a can of baked beans, because Aidan, who was there all the time, presumably watching, was still hungry; taken him back to the tent; taken off my tracksuit pants; and sprinkled my own baby's blood around the tent and on Reagan. Sometime about then, I suppose, I made dingo tracks around the side of the tent, then Aidan and I had a happy race most of the way back to the barbecue as though nothing had happened. Later I buried Azaria's body; dug it up again (I liked this bit!) and removed the clothes she had been wearing, used the scissors again to simulate dingo damage to the clothes, then went for a jog and deposited them in a small gully 4 kilometres (2.5 miles) away from the campsite. Maybe Michael helped me.

It was ridiculous, preposterous, whichever way you looked at it, but that was essentially the Crown case. It was obvious that two completely different sets of evidence were being presented for the trial.

I couldn't believe the way evidence was presented. Where it was a fair and orderly succession at the first inquest, now the Crown simply tendered slabs of evidence from the first or second inquest haphazardly, and picked and chose what evidence they wished for open court. Sure the tendered evidence was available to the jury, but I'll bet they didn't get time to read it all. I've since learned that at least one juror thought they *weren't supposed* to read it!

The two sets of evidence were irreconcilable. What the jury in the trial would have to decide was whether they would believe a whole series of statements from reliable witnesses, or the conclusions drawn from scientific testing. Ian Barker, for the Crown, was adamant that it was simply a choice—*Mrs Chamberlain or a dingo. No other.*

Stuart Tipple was trying to work behind the scenes composing a 'dingo file' with evidence about the behaviour of dingoes when confronted by humans.

John Phillips applied for permission to advertise in the papers for people who knew of dingo attacks (as Peter Dean had during the first inquest), but once again we were not granted permission. We still didn't know where to contact the parents of Amanda Cranwell, who had been attacked at the Rock not long before Azaria and the Cranwells still thought we knew about them.

Mr Justice Muirhead dismissed the application, saying, 'There is an abundance of evidence as to dingoes, their capacity to get very friendly, and to get very vicious, to go into rooms, and to go into tents and upset rubbish bins and behave like pests. It seems that the jury will have to approach this case knowing that.'

Roe Bowhey (the uncle of Ken Brown, the dentist who initially took the clothes to London which reopened the case) and his wife, Jackie, had been convinced that the Chamberlains *must* be guilty, because they believed what Ken had said. Besides, there was so much information around the place about what was *supposed* to have happened, and so many rumours in Darwin, they decided they must hear first hand what was happening. So they came to court daily.

Irene used to sit in the back row and she made friends with this lady who knitted. Irene preferred to crochet, because knitting would make a clack of needles in the quietness, and that could have been objected to.

Jackie, watching Irene, and also keen on handcrafts, started chatting to her in the corridor during court intermissions and they realised they were very much on the same wavelength (they were also both retiring age). Jackie used to import all sorts of handcrafts from her American homeland. She and her husband Roe invited us all to their home one Sunday.

We got on so well that on the following weekend Roe and Jackie invited Irene to stay with them. From then on she often stayed for weekends.

CROSS OVER PLATES AND SCIENCE AND THINGS

One day a stranger was called to the witness box. I leaned over and asked Stuart who it was. He laughed and said, 'You ought to remember *this* one, Lindy. It's Detective Sergeant Brown from Mt Isa CIB, who picked up the space blanket from Michael.'

I blinked. 'He's not the one! They got it from me and mum too, *not* Michael.' I said. Now it was his turn to be surprised. Brown's record of interview claimed that he had picked up the space blanket from Michael.

Stuart said, 'Look, the fact that it is here and in evidence is actually the main thing. We could chase it up, but if we ask for the records and they have the wrong cop here, he'll be here for a reason and by the time we alert them to it, all files will have disappeared or changed and there will be nothing you can do about it. The main thing is that the space blanket is here, and I think we'd better just let it go at that.' So I agreed.

That night my mother rang up, after seeing the news, and said, 'That's not the man who collected the blanket.' Then she described him: her description tallied with my memory—young, blond, uniformed, mid to early twenties.

The only others home when the blanket had been collected were Reagan, who was making himself a great mud puddle out in the backyard, and my father, mending the back screen door, in direct line with the front door where he could see the policeman quite clearly. He also said it was the wrong man.

My mother wrote to the Queensland Premier, Joh Bjelke-Petersen, asking him to investigate the identity of the young policeman and whether he could find out why another man had been substituted at the trial. He did talk to Brown about it, but went no further. Though we were never able to take the inquiries any further, we did place a submission about it before the Fitzgerald Royal Commission of Inquiry about five years later.

What was wrong with the correct young policeman? Why was a substitute in his place? Was this even the second policeman driving the car, or someone else again?

The Crown's array of 'expert' witnesses gave evidence intended to prove their theory. First of all, they called forensic textile experts to demonstrate their assertion that the fibres had been damaged by cutting with an instrument like scissors.

Sergeant Cocks (whose evidence was backed up by Professor Chaikin from the University of N. S. W.), impressed the jury with his scissor-cut demonstration and their resulting tufts, which they said *only* scissors could make. His results didn't bear any resemblance to the dingo damage on Azaria's jumpsuit to my way of thinking, but Blu was impressed. I figured as soon as Blu got to know us better he would realise what a load of rubbish the Crown case was, and would also hear evidence apart from the Crown material presented. Well, he did warm during the time we were there.

We then saw what seemed hours of Chaikin's slides, and heard discussions about the nature of fibres when cut and when torn. I couldn't believe that anyone could seriously make such a big deal out of literally nothing. They made forensic science sound like God. What effect was it having on the jury?

The basic wrong assumption, of course, was that a dingo's teeth will not cut, but only tear. Not only that, but at least one expert witness admitted to never having seen a live dingo bite anything, and had not examined the clothes of anyone bitten by a dingo.

Joy Kuhl came to the witness stand again. She had a very convincing and authoritative manner when she was giving evidence, and it stood her in good stead. John Phillips cross-examined her this time, and she was most uncomfortable. I fixed my eyes on her most of the time she was in the box. Maybe if she felt uncomfortable enough she would tell everything that happened, not parts of it. As Proverbs 18: 17 in the *Living Bible* says, 'Any story sounds true until someone tells the other side and sets the record straight.' Despite close questioning from John Phillips, who forced her to admit she had not used proper controls here, none there, or not enough time elsewhere, the court didn't really pay attention until we asked her to produce the plates from her tests. She didn't have them. Where were they?

'They have been destroyed,' she said. A gasp shook the courtroom. She added defiantly that this was standard practice. Standard practice to put someone's freedom in the bin? My blood boiled but I had to just sit there. She had apparently been disconcerted by Andy's cobra stare and sweet choirboy smile at the second inquest and, complaining she had been disbelieved, she had done many more tests to prove her point. (She tried to imply she had run the tests earlier, but her notes proved she hadn't.) She complained that Mr Rice had been rude to her during the second inquest and when it was pointed out that Mr Kirkham was the cross-examiner, she had nothing to say. In our room later Stuart remarked, 'Got to her, Andy boy,' and Andy replied with a self-satisfied air of innocence, 'Now I thought I did that most politely.'

'Yes, like a crocodile,' Stuart joked.

'I'd love to have been doing the cross-examining when she said that—my bloody oath, I'd be polite now!' Andy said and grinned wickedly. Michael and John walked in and we subsided. We were slowly becoming more optimistic, though.

Despite the fact that Joy Kuhl admitted destroying all the test plates, and hadn't taken any photographs (though she had managed to present slides in court for demonstration purposes), she *wouldn't* change her story that she found Azaria's blood in the car and elsewhere. She said, quite firmly, that she had tested the substance found on the plate underneath the dashboard of our car and discovered that two of the droplets that formed the famous spray pattern contained foetal blood. Yes, the antiserum she had used for testing *was* specific to foetal haemoglobin. She wouldn't be shaken. Another Darwin pathologist, Dr Anthony Jones, made the helpful contribution that the spray droplets indicated pressure from 'a small orifice such as a small artery'.

Andy Kirkham asked Dr Jones to look at the other steel plate we had with a similar spray pattern. (The one Michael had found in Webber Roberts' car and cut out.) The pathologist agreed that it looked very much the same. We still couldn't prove what the spray droplets were, though we had tried, and couldn't take it any further just then. Even on the face of it, it seemed most unlikely that Webber would have cut the throat of a baby under his dashboard too!

The media were relentless. We were staying next to church property, which had a park attached, and the photographers staked us out, waiting for us to leave for court in the morning and return at night. Someone seemed to have a wretched telephoto lens trained on us most of the time. Our bathroom was underneath the house where we were staying, and the press waited around when they knew we were there. If I wanted to go to the toilet, Irene went with me and I used her as a decoy or a shield, or waited until the photographers were distracted by something else and made a dash for it. Fortunately, they knocked off at about six at night (contrary to the movie which shows me rushing out to the toilet after dark to avoid the press). As I couldn't leave the small, dark tin shed in which we stayed, I was bored stiff in the evenings. Most of the time I stayed in the front room of our shed, Irene would come down and we would sit and crochet, talking or watching our borrowed TV.

Even Michael had to go for his jog about 4 a.m., in order to be back before sunrise, so he wouldn't be followed and photographed. He could slip out more easily than I could; he was mobile enough to avoid the media if necessary. Just as well he could get out, give them the slip, and go down the street, because when he was in the rooms he reminded me of a caged tiger, pacing backwards and forwards and making anybody who happened to be there utterly exhausted and uptight by his continual pacing.

I could barely get out of my own way. Although pregnant, I had been jogging 3 kilometres (2 miles) a day regularly until I left for Darwin, when I suddenly had to cease all exercise. Not only could I not jog because of the press ('rubber ball come bouncing back . . .' horrors!) but any form of exercise in that heat made me want to faint. I now looked like Humpty Dumpty and probably would have rolled better than I walked. I always had low blood pressure during pregnancy and the dramatic change of climate put paid to even mild indoor exercise. I was entering my heaviest months of pregnancy, and the lack of exercise, the dearth of fresh fruit and vegetables and sedentary days in court meant I gained excessive weight rapidly. In fact, my normal pregnancy weight was 59 kilos (130 pounds) but this time I went to 76 kilos (167 pounds).

It was very frustrating. Michael's abhorrence of fat people is well known, and as he was under enormous stress as well, he continually harped at me about my size. It reached the point that he couldn't bear to look at me, and said I should go on a diet. As I was barely getting enough to eat, and was pregnant as well, this added pressure did nothing to help my peace of mind. I couldn't exercise, I couldn't get the right food, and Michael was adding to my stress.

The baby also gained weight; she was almost a kilogram (2 pounds) heavier than any of my other babies at birth. She soon lost her weight, but I have a continual fight to keep weight off. I find it easy to put on nearly 3 kilograms (6 pounds) over a weekend out, but not as easy to lose it again. To make matters worse, I always hold weight under stress. Once I got a bad dose of the flu. I vomited for ten days, and lived only on water. My friends all seemed to lose between 2 to 7 kilograms (4 pounds to a stone) under the same circumstances, but I *gained* a kilogram!

Because there was so much strain and we were unable to invite friends to the house, we took to getting takeaway food in our room at night as well, whenever we wanted friends across. Because they had the transport, we would decide what food we wanted, order it, and they would pick it up on their way over. We would then eat in the front room of our shed. One night when there was a group of us there, something was said about the standard of the accommodation. I passed the comment that the motel would have been better accommodation at the same price. One of them said, 'What do you mean the same price? You're not *paying* for this!'

I said, 'Oh? Didn't you realise we were paying for this?' They tried to pass it off in a hurry but the comment and look between them had been a dead giveaway. Later we discovered that although we paid for our food separately we *were* supposed to have been given free accommodation by the property owners the Borders rented from.

The word soon spread among the rest of the church members about our situation then each weekend we were invited out to different homes for meals so that we could get some sort of balanced diet with fruit, salad and vegetables. We had freedom to walk about and were treated normally. We really enjoyed that.

In the evenings, seeing the Borders watched television in their bedroom, Irene spent more and more time with us. One night, when she returned to the house at about 9 p.m., she discovered she was locked out! She had a great deal of difficulty alerting the Borders, but finally they opened the door. They told her that they always locked the doors at 8 p.m., even though she was only in the backyard. Not only were the upstairs doors locked then, but so were those downstairs, so we were locked out of our bathroom and toilet! We had to ask for a key and agree to lock up at all times from a certain time onwards. To unlock it to let ourselves in and lock it up again afterwards in the dark was a nuisance, as the back light was also off. Irene was given a key with strict instructions to lock up after herself. She came in giggling after receiving the key, saying she felt like a naughty, escaped teenager.

Phoning was also difficult. The Borders had said we could use the phone whenever we liked, as long as we paid for the calls. Well, that was to be expected. After we rang the children a couple of times, I became aware calls were being monitored. I didn't make any more phone calls and waited until Mum rang again and then I said to her, 'Look, I'm sorry. I can't talk now, we have discovered our phone calls are being listened to by unscrupulous people. I will ring you when I can,' and hung up. As far as possible we tried never to use the phone again.

From then on, we went to Greg Cavanagh's office at Legal Aid, as we were allowed one free phone call to our family per week, and we knew the lawyers' phones were the safest we could find. Only then was I able to explain to Mum exactly what was happening. (Hence the little scene in the film where, when the children want to phone us, Grandma says, 'I don't think we can ring just now.')

As Irene sat inconspicuously at the back of the courtroom, she watched people's reactions and listened closely to their comments. In this way she could get a good gauge of the courtroom feeling. By sitting near the jury room door she could study the jurors coming and going and try to work out what they were thinking. (She said this helped give her peace of mind.) When the jury was making a racket, the noise came through the door. During breaks Irene sat near the door when the court wasn't cleared, and occasionally heard things that were said.

Blu Border began sitting at the back also, next to a gentleman who had something to do with the court or police force. The two men would talk very loudly during breaks; Blu's voice definitely carried. Soon everybody knew about various cases that had been set up and things that happened behind the scenes in the police force.

Irene was absolutely horrified and thought that it was in extremely bad taste. She asked him and his companion several times to lower their voices, knowing full well they would be heard clearly in the jury room.

When they started talking, Irene would, if possible, begin a loud conversation on knitting, handcrafts, anything with whomever was closest to her, so that listeners to Blu's conversations would be confused at least.

After the first couple of weekends, we again met Liz and John Parry. John invited us to their place for the weekend, and to stay whenever we liked. They had a pool in the backyard and a self-contained flat downstairs. We could have moved there permanently and it would have been a good arrangement, except for the fact that it was too far out for easy access to the lawyers and court every day, and we did not have transport available for that.

As I was feeling fairly shy and extremely tired, Michael visited the Parrys on the Friday afternoon alone, with the arrangement that I would come out on the Saturday night, stay, and spend the Sunday with them. I went to bed on Friday night and slept right through until about 3 p.m. Saturday afternoon.

John Parry and Michael picked me up and I went out and met the rest of the family. I fell in love with them and the place straight away. So began a friendship between Liz and I that grew ever closer. From then on John would pick us up on Friday afternoon and bring us back late Sunday afternoon or even early Monday morning before court.

We could relax and be ourselves there, away from the pressure of the media and hostile influences. Irene sometimes came too, or visited other friends. Stuart was also welcome on these weekend trips; it was a welcome break for him, away from the Travelodge.

On Sabbath morning Stuart would come to church, then go with us to lunch. He had to be back late in the afternoon ready to start work again after sunset on Saturday night.

It wasn't until I was watching the Commonwealth Games at the Parrys' one weekend during the trial that I found the second name for Kahlia. I saw a black girl, whom I think came from England, winning the long jump. Her name was Shonel. I immediately fell in love with it and told Michael. We had had Azaria Chantel Loren—how about Kahlia Shonell Nikari? Michael liked it. We could hyphenate her name and call her Kahlia-Shonelle. Michael said, 'No way! You can have double "l" at the end but you can't have "lle"! That's putting it on a bit thick. And no hyphen.' In the end we agreed; Kahlia Shonell Nikari it was to be. 'Nikari' means 'blithe spirit' or 'happy person', and she is indeed a strong, happy person. The meaning of 'Shonell' I have never been able to discover, but it's French, we think.

Being away weekends we gradually became more comfortable domestically, and this was important, during the boring part of the trial—the difficult forensic evidence, was coming thick and fast.

Bernard Sims, an odontologist (i.e. a dentist—why they couldn't say so I don't know) from London, produced a dingo skull and a doll dressed up as a baby about three months old, and demonstrated that the jaws wouldn't admit the doll's head. Wouldn't fit within the jaws, he said. A dingo couldn't possibly have picked up a head that size. Andy Kirkham showed him the photograph of a live dingo with the head of a doll, very similar to the one Sims had used for his demonstration, in its mouth. Sims's jaw dropped nearly as far as the dingo's and he had to admit he was wrong, if the dingo's jaw wasn't being forced; it didn't appear to be. A crack from the Crown bench about disarticulated jaws and the dingo being sorer than the doll made the jury laugh.

Then came the famous Professor Cameron. He said that the dingo couldn't have grasped Azaria's head from above, because the blood wouldn't have collected around the collar of the jumpsuit. With a head injury, he said, rivulets of blood drain down and miss the collar. He said that the blood pattern on the jumpsuit could only have been described by 'a cut-throat type of injury'.

When Barker showed him the plate cut from under the dashboard, he said that the pattern looked like an arterial blood spray spurting upwards. (I must have been a contortionist in that confined space as well!) The water bottles and gear stowed at my feet were never mentioned. The styrofoam covers on the water bottles should have been blood spattered to fit this theory, and they weren't—how inconvenient!

John Phillips got Cameron to admit that he had made mistakes in forensic evidence in the Confait case in England. This had resulted in two boys spending three years in prison; they were subsequently declared innocent and awarded compensation after further inquiries were held.

He finished by taking up Cameron's assertion about the hand print on the back of Azaria's jumpsuit. 'Would you not agree that blood from an injury, purely by accident, can take up apparent shapes of objects?' he asked.

'They must have a contact point,' agreed Professor Cameron. 'By or against an object.'

'It can occur purely by accident, an apparent pattern of an object?'

'Yes.'

After all, that was one of his mistakes in the Confait case—a wrong conclusion about the pattern of a blood flow in the wrinkles of the victim's neck, which he claimed to be a word written in blood.

Surely, I thought, looking at the faces of the jurors, *surely* they must see that these so-called experts are absolutely *wrong*. I knew they were; I've always known they were. But the jurors were influenced by other things too: the press reports, even walking to the courthouse every day through crowds with some demonstrators wearing T-shirts that said THE DINGO IS INNOCENT. After all, they couldn't pre-empt the court and say Lindy was guilty, could they?

John Phillips must have had some of the same thoughts in mind when he opened for the defence on 13 October.

John said to the jury: 'I want to begin by mentioning some legal matters of fundamental importance to the trial. Very shortly you are going to see and hear witnesses for the defence, and it is of critical importance that, when you are listening to and looking at witnesses for the defence, you never once allow yourself to slip into an attitude of mind where you say, in effect, to the witness for the defence: "Come on, you convince me that the Chamberlains are innocent. "You see, as His Honour will tell you later on, persons accused of crimes like these under our law never ever have to prove their innocence.'

He outlined our case to the jury by summarising the points that were in dispute. Firstly, the presence of foetal blood in the car and camera bag; Cameron's conclusions that Azaria's throat had been cut by a sharp instrument and that there were hand prints on the jumpsuit; and the suggestion that a dingo hadn't been involved at all—that Azaria's clothes had been damaged by a sharp instrument.

This was the second time we'd heard all the forensic stuff in court—some of it was for the third time. For the most part, except when something startling was disclosed (such as Joy Kuhl's admission about throwing away the evidence), it no longer had any power to shock. We were more bored than horrified—and I was explosively hot and uncomfortable. Try as I might, I couldn't see this as anything but academic—irrelevant to the case. To the jury, hearing it for the first time, the evidence must have seemed overwhelming and my reaction to it mostly hard and uncaring. By now I'd had a lot of practice at hiding my feelings pretty well from the press and had no intention of giving away any more than I could possibly help.

You can never wear a dress for more than one day in that climate. You get absolutely wet through, your clothes are sticky, sweaty, and smell of perspiration at the end of the day. The fact that this happens to everybody didn't seem important. Sure the media changed their shirts every day, but that was different, they were mostly men, and many of their shirts looked similar anyway. But I was a woman; what they expected me to do I don't know, but they recorded how I changed dresses every day. Big deal! I washed at the end of the week and I had enough dresses for two weeks—ten dresses. I would wash and by the time they got ironed it was time for the next week. I rotated my dresses and as I grew out of the smaller ones I grew into the bigger ones. Everybody knows as you get bigger you have to change your clothes, and so did I. But that created quite a hassle and media attention.

The night before I went into the witness box, Michael and I had a roaring fight. I felt hot, sick, and the size of an elephant. Most of my clothes were too tight to wear now without discomfort; some pulled so tight when I was sitting down that I could see Kahlia had the hiccups and my stomach was jerking. (Once when I'd looked over at the jury unexpectedly, I noticed one of the men interestedly staring at the movement of my stomach as the baby kicked within. He blushed slightly when he saw me looking and quickly looked away.) I didn't want that distraction while I was in the box.

Michael once again suggested I ought to lose weight. This added pressure did nothing for my peace of mind. I'd been eating little enough as it was, hampered by inactivity, restless as I watched him come and go as he wished (he'd just spent a weekend away fishing with the guys), while I grew bigger and bigger. His continual comments about my weight gain were just *too* much. For once he noticed I looked upset and said, 'Now, what's upset you?' How like a man! The straw pile was getting *much* closer to the last one.

I let him have it. 'I'm so fat, you hate fat, don't you Michael? You can't stand me being fat. You'd like me to be skinny again, wouldn't you? Well, if Mr Barker has his way, the decision may be taken right out of your hands.' He looked shocked then, but I was too hurt to feel sorry and told him to get lost, which he did, smartly, then I burst into tears.

That night Michael wanted to turn the air conditioner off! I suggested he put his sheet and blanket on if he was cold, but no, that was too restrictive.

'Well, go out in the other room then where there is no air conditioner. You forget I've got a furnace attached to me. Don't be selfish!' I said.

'I will,' he replied, grabbed his sheet and pillow, and went.

The next morning we barely spoke, and he wouldn't hold my hand on the way into court as he usually did. I felt really alone. Even the lawyers noticed something wrong and told us to at least show a united front in public even if we didn't get on in private. They too had noticed Michael shy away from holding my hand that morning. So things basically returned to normal, but Michael chose to sleep in the front room for the rest of the trial.

I was the first defence witness. I could have read a statement, but why should I? I had nothing to hide and no fear of cross-examination. I had a migraine, I was nervous, and prayed silently. Once again, like the first Inquest, my head cleared and my mind became clear and sharp. Why did I always have migraines or the flu when I had to go into the box?

John, Andy and Stuart reiterated that I was not to appear too bright when Barker cross-examined me. Even if I did realise what he was going to say next, I should let him finish. I must not be cross or too quick, as that would not go over well with the jury, who would think I was trying to be smart, they said. If I showed my intelligence too much, Barker would only use it as evidence that I was smart enough to do exactly what they had accused me of. (I should hope that if I had done anything like the Crown said, I'd have done a better job than the botch up they claimed!) No wonder they didn't verbal me. If they had, they would have had to stick to it, and then they'd have been in a mess. They had to keep shifting as their so-called evidence was proved false.

And so I went into the box.

John Phillips went through the preliminaries, and I explained exactly how blood could have been found in our car: Reagan and Aidan had had nosebleeds while we were travelling, Reagan had cut his lip, Keyth Lenehan, the accident victim, had bled so badly that he had left two blood- soaked T-shirts on the roadway.

Then John showed me the clothes Azaria had been wearing. I looked at the jumpsuit, the nappy, the singlet and it was all academic. I identified them and the cot blankets and then, there in front of me, was the blue bunny rug. I wasn't prepared for the wave of feeling that hit me in the gut as I held the rug in my hands. *Then* it was no longer academic. It was clean and fresh- smelling, untainted by scientific tests, dirt and blood. It was part of *her*, alive and smiling and kicking: the blue bunny rug that was wrapped closest around my darling baby daughter on the night she died.

I heard a voice and found it hard to draw my attention back.

'Are you all right, Mrs Chamberlain?' asked the judge.

'Yes,' I said.

'All right. You let me know if you are not.'

John Phillips could see how distraught I was, so he said, 'Without opening any of those articles, do you confirm that they were the clothing your child was wearing, apart from a matter I will ask you about in a minute?'

'Yes,' I said in a small voice. It wouldn't go any louder, try as I might.

'Please state what other article Azaria was wearing,' John Phillips asked. I couldn't do it straight away. It took several tries. 'She had . . . a white knitted Marquis matinee jacket with a pale lemon edging.' And then I had to stop. I could see her wearing it.

I heard the judge say to John Phillips, 'Some of the jury are upset now.'

'I am sorry, Your Honour,' apologised John. 'It was my fault . . .'

'It's all right,' said Judge Muirhead. 'Mr Foreman, how are you getting on?' The foreman of the jury said nothing; his face *told* everything.

'Right,' said the judge, 'we'll take a break for a quarter of an hour.' When I came back, I felt better. At the end of his questions, John made me put my hand on the photograph of the ultraviolet fluorescence that Professor Cameron had said was the impression of a handprint on the jumpsuit.

My finger extended beyond the black mark by about 1 centimetre (1/2 an inch). When I held it up, everybody could see that it had the normal number of joints and bones—that is, two joints, three bones. The print or 'impression' on the back of the jumpsuit, if it *was* a hand, showed another joint and bone in the middle 'finger'.

Barker then cross-examined me and got onto the question of blood immediately. He asked me about the 'blood' on the tracksuit pants (I had supposedly been wearing as I sat in the car and cut Azaria's throat).

'Do you accept there was blood on the pants?'

'No.'

'Do you *deny* there was blood on the pants?'

Here it was again. Try to get me to accept there was blood, then later say I had said there was. Barker was brilliant at taking statements out of context afterwards and making them mean the opposite, so one condemned oneself with it.

'I have never seen any blood on the pants at all.'

'When do you say the blood got on the pants, if it was blood?'

'Well, I would think it would be at the same time as it got on the parkas, because they were all together.'

'Where do you think it came from?'

'My personal opinion is that it came from Azaria.'

'How?'

'The attitude of the dingo coming out of the . . . head shaking indicate to me that blood from Azaria [was] going on the garments, and the description that is given is very similar to my impression of the marks on the parka and the sleeping bag.'

The scientists so far had conveyed the impression there was little blood in the tent. I couldn't help noticing that if I said there was blood on something, the Crown didn't hesitate to express doubt and was keen to contradict me, but if I said there was none, I was a liar, and there was a large amount (which I had attempted to clean up, of course!). The use of a little logic and commonsense would have gone a long way.

For example, they had said when examining one of the other parkas, that there was only a 'minimal amount' on it. Because of the direction of the blood spray, they said, the wearer—presumably Reagan—would have had to be carrying the injured baby.

What nonsense! When the dingo was shaking the baby at the tent flap, blood would obviously be flung on to that garment because of its position in the tent—by the entrance. Because the night was cold and the parka was made of nylon material, blood would not dry quickly; any blood spots on it would simply continue to run when it was picked up. I still fail to see why such a simple fact was made to appear so difficult and complicated. I guess the truth was too easy.

Further blood was found on the baby blankets, on the sleeping bags, and also on the floral mattress—Sally Lowe's pool of blood—which tested by Dr Andrew Scott to be made by a minimum of 7 millilitres of blood. The Crown always described this as 'minimal'! On the other hand, they said, 'oceans' of blood was found in the car. The actual amount was five millilitres—*one teaspoonful*—and less than on the mattress without the rest of the articles.

'And you say that the dog shook its head at the entrance?' Barker asked.

'That's right.'

'And that, therefore, blood must have been dropped at the entrance to the tent?'

'Yes.'

'Splashed around, is that what you're saying?'

'Yes.'

He asked me about the dingo leaving the tent, and I said that it went south for a couple of feet but I hadn't watched it after that.

'Did you see it again at all?'

'I saw a dingo which I have been led to believe was a different dingo.'

'Did you see the dingo standing by the side of the car on the southern side?'

'I saw a dingo standing by the car on the southern side. The trackers told me that it was a different animal. It was the one I chased, though.'

'There were two dingoes, were there?'

'According to the trackers, there were two.'

But the trackers hadn't been called to give evidence at the trial at all—and when Derek Roff had been questioned, he wasn't asked about the likelihood of a second dingo.

I thought Barker would never get off the subject. If the jury *wasn't* aware we were arguing back and forth over whether the dingo's nose was 7 centimetres (3 inches) inside or outside the tent flap when I saw it, I was. He spent over ninety minutes on just that. Finally I told him, barely patiently, that the dingo was moving, not a still photo; the judge told him he didn't think he could elicit much more from this line of questioning.

We moved on at last to the bloodstains in the car. How would they have got there?

'Children crawling around the car, or people moving. Or from people Michael had fixed up with injuries,' I said. 'I don't know.'

Judy West had thoughts of her own. 'The nights were so cold—below freezing—that friends of ours had photographed a wet tea towel which had frozen into a right angle after being left outside on a table overnight. So it seemed possible that the blood Sally Lowe described as seeing ("a pool as big as a dinner plate or bread and butter plate") could have frozen on something lying on the tent floor, been packed into the car in the space between the front and back seats, and unwittingly spread on the floor of the car next morning when the clothes were moved and the blood had thawed!'

Maybe if there really *was* blood on the console, Judy was right.

Barker went through the items that Joy Kuhl had got positive reactions from—the window handle, underdash spray, scissors, camera bag, underneath the dashboard of our car. It just didn't make any kind of sense at all, of course.

Barker then asked me whether the dingo had been carrying 'a bleeding baby'. I was pretty disgusted by this time.

'That's my opinion,' I said.

'Well, is there any doubt about it?' asked Barker.

'Not in my mind.'

'Is it merely "your opinion" or is it something you know as a fact?'

'It is something my heart tells me is a fact,' I said. 'Other people don't think so.' That seemed to put the situation in a nutshell.

Barker couldn't leave it alone, though. Later, he said, 'Mrs Chamberlain, you say this child was in the mouth of a dingo which was vigorously shaking its head at the entrance to the tent. That is what you firmly believe, is that right?'

'That's right.'

'The dog having taken Azaria from the carrycot?'

I said, 'Yes,' unsteadily. Judge Muirhead, who was sympathetic all through the trial, said, 'Take it steady, Mrs Chamberlain.'

'You saw blood on the parka?'

'Yes.' I had spoken clearly, but Judge Muirhead could see I was physically and emotionally distressed.

'Would you like a spell, Mrs Chamberlain?' he asked.

I was definite about that. 'No, I'd rather get it over with, Your Honour.' This didn't quite satisfy him, though. 'I do not want you to have to answer questions when you are feeling distressed. Would you like me to give you a ten minute break?'

'No,' I told him, 'I'd prefer to go on. This has been going on for two years. I want to get it over with.'

Barker picked up the point again. 'You say the blood on the parka must have come from the baby.'

'Yes.'

'When it was in the dog's mouth?'

'Somewhere around that time.'

'What other time could it have come from the baby?' I was getting really angry by this time. I didn't like Barker, I didn't like his nitpicking, his needling attitude. And I was sick of having every statement I made questioned. 'Look, Mr Barker, I wasn't there. I can only go on the evidence of my own eyes. We're talking about *my baby daughter*, not some object.' I broke down.

The judge intervened, 'I'll give you a break, Mrs Chamberlain. For ten minutes.' Some of the jury members were crying again, too.

Barker annoyed me by calling Azaria, 'Ass-area', not 'As-*aah*-rea'. (Similarly he called Boettcher, 'Botchup' or 'Bootcher'.) His mispronunciation of 'Azaria' reminded me of cinerarias, and I never could stand those flowers. One of my guys told me to calm down and hold my tongue. If I was angry while being questioned, it looked bad in front of the jury.

Barker put the Crown case to me, point by point. Thank heavens we had had that recess, I could look at him with reasonable calm and deny everything without getting angry or my dislike of him showing too much. Suddenly, he gave up and sat down.

A Scientific Defence

We called Barry Boettcher, who refuted a lot of what Joy Kuhl had said. But what he had to say was so complicated and took so long that I could tell we had lost the jury. Not only that, but Barry, though a terrific bloke, wasn't as effective as Joy Kuhl in the witness stand. He had a serious academic manner that contrasted unfavourably with Kuhl's conviction and impression of conspiratorial understanding with the jury. He claimed that the anti-serum used by Joy Kuhl in testing was 'defective', but nobody understood why; it was too difficult. Barker attacked on the grounds that the other scientists, who had agreed with Kuhl's conclusions, were *forensic* scientists, not academic purists like Barry Boettcher.

The judge made a few comments of his own: 'You say you did find fault with her methodology, do you not?'

'I am critical of the conclusions derived from those results, Your Honour,' Barry Boettcher said.

'You are critical of the interpretation of what she saw?'

'Yes.'

'And her scientific examination? Am I right in saying you believe she was misled by believing that the antiserum was specific, where you say it was non-specific?' Because, of course, part of our case was that the testing substance used by Joy Kuhl could have given positive results for both foetal and adult blood, as proved by her own tests.

'Yes.'

Barker said, 'You don't know whether it was specific or non specific, do you? Apart from what she can tell you, and what Dr Baxter can tell you?'

'Unless one of the two batches I used was the same batch as Mrs Kuhl used,' said Boettcher.

This, of course, was the weakness in his argument. Stuart Tipple was still trying to get details of the antiserum (specifically the batch number) from Joy Kuhl, who wasn't telling him. So we couldn't ignore the possibility that Joy Kuhl had used another batch of antiserum that didn't show the same deficiencies as the one in Barry's tests.

Barker followed up on this by reiterating that Boettcher wasn't a forensic scientist anyway, so he didn't have the same day-to-day experience as Joy Kuhl and the other forensic biologists.

Les Harris was called to give evidence about the habits and abilities of dingoes, and he did it very well. He told the jury of his dingoes biting through seat belts which looked as if they had been cut by scissors. They were also capable of biting straight through number 8 fencing wire as cleanly as wire cutters would. One of his dingoes could even open the latch door on his fridge to fetch her food! He also gave evidence of the strength of their neck muscles, the weights they could easily carry, and the fact that a dingo can disarticulate its jaw—which a dog cannot. We already knew most of what he was saying (from his letter to Coroner Dennis Barritt at the first inquest) but a lot of what he said, I could tell, was news to the jury. And to the southern press, of course.

Andy Kirkham asked him: 'With your knowledge of dingo behaviour and capacity, are you able to offer an opinion as to whether a dingo would be capable of grasping and carrying the child?'

'Yes, it would,' said Les Harris. 'There is enough (of the baby) showing (in the demonstration photo of a doll in the carry basket) that the dingo would make the assessment that it was a mammal and therefore viable prey. I would envisage that a dingo would, immediately after the instant of identification, make seizure, which would be of the entire head, and it would close its jaws sufficiently to render that mammal immobile. As a continuous operation, it would then continue by immediately making off with the acquired prey. It would have made the seizure by the head, and it would be unlikely that it would change its grip in any way. That would have been adequate to immobilise the prey.'

When he cross-examined Harris, Barker asked a lot of questions about the dingo's strength. He later said that a dingo could easily have held the baby well clear of the ground, so it need not have continued to keep its head down as I had initially seen it and described, and so the body or the clothing wouldn't necessarily have dragged on the ground. As somebody pointed out later, this was a very interesting twist. The Crown had originally said that a dingo wouldn't have been capable of carrying a child of Azaria's size and weight. Now, Barker was saying that I shouldn't be believed because a dingo *would* have been able to carry it, not drag it.

The accident victim Keyth Lenehan (we had learned his name), whom we had rescued from the roadside near Cairns, described how we had loaded him, bleeding, into the back of our Torana hatchback with his head protruding forward towards the aperture between the front seats, therefore accounting for any blood found in the car.

The Crown then made jokes about a 'six-foot' baby bleeding in the car, which made the jury laugh.

Our witnesses were all starting to drop in to check how soon they'd be on and whether they could go sightseeing if they weren't on until the next day, or if the lawyers needed to interview them. One day a young man came in barefooted wearing jeans and a singlet top. Several of our forensic men were waiting around to go in the box, and I supposed this new person was driving them around or something, as he looked at home with everyone. Nobody had asked him to leave so he couldn't be a member of the public who had strayed in past the security guard.

Stuart came out of the office so I asked, 'Is that your new messenger boy?'

'Shush!' he said, grinning. 'That's your doctor, the smart one on electrophoresis, and he's *your* age, not a kid!'

Dan Cornell *was* a surprise packet—and he looked very much the science whiz next day dressed for court.

Dr Cornell had introduced the screening technique known as crossover electrophoresis to Australia and used it regularly. He stated boldly that Joy Kuhl didn't know what she was doing with it. Her boss, Simon Baxter, wriggled uncomfortably; it had been claimed *he* introduced this test to Australia, but he was only the first person to use it for forensic purposes.

Other witnesses came and went, each an expert in a particular field. Barker attacked expert after expert of ours on the grounds that they weren't forensic scientists, but only university professors of science. (Well, who developed the new methods, anyway?)

I was looking forward to seeing Dr Vernon Pleuckhahn in court. Stuart said he was a colleague of James 'Taffy' Cameron's and equally good. He regularly worked in forensic and wouldn't be cowed by accusations of being an academic professor. He knew his own standing, was confident and an excellent scientist. Stuart, who was waiting for John and Andy, sat next to me to chat.

'Where's this guy with the swollen head?' I asked cheekily. I received a whack in the ribs. Stuart pointed to the quiet man beside him and whispered, 'He'll think I said that! That's him there. What made you say that?'

'Well you did say he was a very confident man!'

'That's different,' said Stuart. Trust me! Pleuckhahn must have heard, but didn't turn a hair.

Professor Vernon Pleuckhahn, Director of Pathology at the Geelong Hospital and senior examiner in forensic medicine at Melbourne University, was the last forensic witness. He was almost scathing about Professor Cameron's conclusions that the pattern of bleeding on the jumpsuit could only have been produced by a cut throat, saying he had seen people brought into hospitals with severe head injuries that had produced patterns of bleeding similar to those on the jumpsuit. He also said there wouldn't have been a lot of bleeding. 'Depending on the vessels punctured at the time; if it's a vein punctured as such, a tooth could well form a plug. It depends on how tight he gripped,' he said.

Barker questioned, 'You don't agree with Professor Cameron that there is evidence of the impression of a human hand?'

'As I've said before,' said Plueckhahn, 'with due respect to his eminence—I'm sorry, that's the wrong word—to his prominence, with due respect to that, his opinion, I cannot postulate, even with proper—with full examination, having viewed it also under ultra violet light without his photographs, and all that sort of thing, and seen it, I cannot in the wildest imagination from this, see the imprint of a hand. And as I've said, I've tried to convince myself there could be.'

The judge asked, 'With imprints, you include impression, do you ?'

'Impressions, yes,' said Dr Plueckhahn. 'There is nothing in this, looking at it, which would even remotely suggest to me that it is any part of the human hand.'

He added that he could find no evidence of a handprint on the highly contrasted ultraviolet fluorescent photograph, either. 'If I really want to I could say it was an emu's foot, or something or rather like that, which is more like it, but I wouldn't conceive that—that doesn't conceive anything to me.'

Pleuckhahn was great, but he was used to big-city juries. In Darwin they thought he was a pompous snob talking down to them. He didn't go down well at all.

Who's Confused?

Others came and went, and then it was Michael's turn to be examined. John Phillips led him through his evidence; there had been no confession that I had murdered Azaria, no cover-up, no burial, no cutting up the clothing, no midnight jogs to plant the jumpsuit and other things.

The next day Barker asked, 'Have you discussed this with your wife overnight?'

'Not overnight,' said Michael.

'Discussed the evidence you've given—just a moment?' queried Barker.

'We have talked about it, yes,'remembered Michael.

'Last night?' asked Barker.

'We talked about it briefly this morning,' said Michael.

Barker asked, 'You discussed with her the question whether Morris visited you at the motel room did you not?'

'This morning?' queried Michael.

'Yes?' Barker queried.

'I think so, yes,' agreed Michael.

'She said: "Don't you remember that Morris came to the motel room with the form?"?'

'No, she didn't say that,' disagreed Michael.

'You didn't tell us yesterday he came to the motel room, did you?' accused Barker.

'No, but I've known for a time that he came to the vicinity of where our room was.'

Barker asked, 'What did she say to you this morning?'

'Well, she said a lot of things to me this morning.'

'About your evidence?' queried Barker.

The judge intervened. 'Just about this motel room, if anything?'

'She may have asked me about Morris at the motel room,' Michael replied.

'What time was this?' asked Barker.

'Pardon?'

'What time was this, that she may have asked?' repeated Barker.

'What, this morning?' asked the judge, confused.

'Yes,' said Barker.

Michael said, 'It would've been some time probably before eight-thirty.'

'Eight-thirty this morning?'

'Yes.'

'Tell us what she asked you, please?'

'She mentioned something about the motel room, and Morris.'

'What did she say?'

'I don't remember exactly what she said,' Michael shook his head.

'It's not very long ago, is it?' Barker said exasperated.

'No, it isn't, I've had a lot of . . .'

'You finish that, "I've got a lot . . . ",' the judge said.

'I've had a considerable number of things on my mind this morning, as you can imagine,' said Michael, all at sea.

'Could you tell us again what she said to you?' Barker said patiently.

'Just do the best you can.' The judge interposed kindly.

'Yes,' agreed Michael.

'Just about this motel room?' continued Barker.

'She mentioned about Constable Morris and the office, and I think made the comment that that wasn't the only time that he saw us that morning,' said Michael.

'What did you say?'

'Well, I remember that I had been waiting—lying awake in the morning waiting for him to knock on our door—and that I believe that he had called on us to say that there was nothing as yet been found.'

'You said that to your wife this morning, did you?' added Barker.

'No, that's what I thought, I didn't say that to her,' said Michael, surprised at the question.

Barker tried again, 'Do you know why she raised the matter with you this morning?'

Michael answered, 'Well, she was concerned because Morris had seen us on at least two occasions on that morning, probably three.'

'Did she say anything else to you about your evidence?' Barker was getting exasperated.

'Not anything in particular,' said Michael.

'Can you remember anything in general?' asked Barker as a last resort.

'Yes, stay calm,' said Michael, following something he was clear on. At last Barker was getting somewhere. 'What else did she say?'

'Listen carefully, I think,' said Michael.

Barker continued. 'Did you discuss any subject matters about which you've given evidence?'

'Yes,' Michael answered.

Barker really had to work for answers. 'What?'

‘I think we talked about the Olgas,’ mused Michael.

‘What about the Olgas?’ sighed Barker.

‘About whether we could go there or should go there,’ stated Michael.

‘What did she say about the Olgas this morning?’ asked Barker.

‘Well, the question was raised who mentioned or who suggested that we go to the Olgas, and I said that I thought it was the Cozens,’ Michael replied.

‘Did you? What did she say?’ patiently continued Barker.

‘Well, the transcript said that she had suggested it,’ Michael replied.

‘Transcript of the first inquest?’ questioned Barker.

‘I don’t know which inquest. One transcript,’ Michael supplied helpfully. Barker continued, ‘Who drew your attention to the transcript?’

‘Well, I remembered that from last night,’ Michael said. Barker asked, ‘Did you read the transcript last night?’ Michael replied, ‘No, I didn’t read it last night.’

This was really confusing Barker. ‘Who raised the question of the Olgas this morning?’

‘Well, it might’ve been me, I don’t know. It was either Lindy or myself. We talked about it briefly,’ Michael was muddled again.

Barker queried, ‘What time was it?’

‘Sometime probably before eight-thirty,’ Michael thought.

‘You’re not sure which one of you it was?’ Barker asked.

‘I can’t remember who it was that brought it up,’ Michael said perplexed. Barker tried again, ‘What did you say about it?’

‘Well, I wanted to be sure what I’d said,’replied Michael.

‘Said where?’ asked Barker.

‘In the transcript,’repeated Michael.

‘What transcript?’ asked Barker, confused.

‘This is the inquest transcript?’ asked the judge, also confused.

‘Yes, the inquest transcript,’ answered Michael.

‘Have you got a copy of the transcript?’ Barker then asked Michael.

‘No.’

‘Has she got a copy?’ Barker pursued.

‘Not now, no,’ Michael said.

Barker tried another tack. ‘Did you—who first raised the question of Morris and the motel room, you or your wife?’

‘I think she may have, I don’t know—yes, she could’ve,’ Michael thought aloud.

‘She could’ve?’ queried Barker.

‘Yes,’ agreed Michael.

‘You’re not sure?’ said Barker.

‘No,’ said Michael.

‘This was this morning?’ Barker asked.

‘Yes,’ agreed Michael.

They were getting somewhere.

‘Who raised the question of Mt Olga, you or your wife?’ Barker wanted to know.

‘Well, that question wasn’t raised this morning, it was talked about last night,’ Michael answered.

Barker didn't want to know when just then, he wanted to know by whom. He tried again. 'Who raised it, you or your wife?'

'Well, I didn't talk to my wife about it last night,' Michael was still on another wavelength.

'What do you mean, the question was raised last night?' Barker asked confused.

'Well, I wanted to know who it was that suggested that we go to the Olgas.'

So did Barker! That was the question.

'Who did you raise the matter with last night?' he asked.

'One of my lawyers,' said Michael.

'Did you? Were you told what was in the transcript?' queried Barker.

'Yes,' said Michael.

Barker tried again. 'Did you discuss the matter with your wife?'

'Not last night,' said Michael.

'Last night?' queried the judge, confused.

'Not last night,' Michael said again.

If Michael was going to talk of the lawyers, Barker would follow that up.

'You discussed the evidence with one of your lawyers, did you?'

'Yes. I went over there,' explained Michael.

Maybe that was the answer. 'For that purpose?' Barker asked.

'Not for that purpose particularly,' Michael answered.

'Discuss any of the other evidence with him?' Barker asked exasperated. Michael replied, 'Just in a general sense. How things were going.'

'Discussed the cross-examination with him, did you?'

'Not particularly, no,' Michael was doing strictly as he had been told, answering only the question as briefly as possible. This could go on forever.

Barker was stung. 'At all?'

'There were several basic things said, but not much more,' said Michael.

'What sort of basic things?' Barker asked.

'Just to concentrate; to listen carefully,' said Michael. I thought Barker was going to have apoplexy.

'You had a discussion about Mt Olga?'

'Yes. It was a brief discussion; just to know what was in the transcript.'

'Mt Olga's an embarrassment for you, isn't it?'

'No, it isn't.'

I wasn't sure whether to laugh or cry. Either way Barker was just as confused and frustrated as Sturgess had been. It was typical of a discussion with Michael though—they just weren't used to it.

The End of an Episode

When the evidence had all been presented, somebody tallied up the elements in the case; 73 witnesses, 145 exhibits and a transcript running to more than 2,800 pages. And what was going on in my head was equally bewildering: there were so many words, there had been so much talk about what had happened over the past seven weeks.

And now we had to listen to the summing-up. John Phillips, who spoke first, ridiculed Barker's failure to prove any motive for my cutting Azaria's throat. He said:

> 'There was one allegation, the most important allegation in this trial, that was never put, and it's the allegation which would have started with the words, "Mrs Chamberlain, I put it to you that the reason you cut your child's throat was . . ." It was never put, because Mr Barker, one of the best men in the business, just cannot think of any reason why she would do it. The prosecution has had two years and three months to think of a reason, any reason, good, bad or indifferent, but they can't. They can't supply you with a reason why this mother would kill her baby, the prosecution are bereft . . . But we're not bankrupt in this area of the case. We have been able to obtain from witness after witness after witness, ninety per cent of them independent of the Chamberlains, proof after proof after proof of this mother's love and affection for her baby.'

He ran through the evidence very logically and forcefully, reminding the jury about the spate of dingo attacks around Ayers Rock at the time, reminding them that we had had no chance to bury Azaria and clean up the car. He finished by saying;

> 'Now you don't want a lecture from me about beyond reasonable doubt, do you? We've all got that perfectly clear. We all understand the fundamental importance of it. You can't go wrong, in our respectful submission, if you keep that centrally in your thoughts while you're considering the case. By all means give Mr Barker the same fair hearing you've given me. But remember, he has got to prove his case beyond reasonable doubt. The defence does not have to prove anything.'

When he sat down, we all felt that the case was as good as over; John had presented the defence evidence so persuasively that Barker would have an impossible job to sway the jury his way.

But we had reckoned without Barker's rhetorical skills, and his oratory. He said:

> 'This is a classic textbook case of circumstantial evidence. We don't have eyewitnesses in the sense that anyone saw the child killed, so the whole case must be, in substance, a drawing of inferences from established facts. If these inferences point to the guilt of the accused, and if there was no room for alternative reasonable inferences, well then, your duty is to convict . . .
>
> 'What is this dingo supposed to have done? It managed, if her story is true, to kill the child in the bassinette, drag her from the basket, divest her of two blankets and a rug and shake her body vigorously at the entrance to the tent, and carry her off into the night in such a way that it left virtually no clues in the tent in the way of blood or hairs or anything else . . .
>
> 'At the shortest it walked 4 or 5 kilometres (2.5 to 3 miles), if the story is true, to the base of Ayers Rock, and if during part of that distance it walked through the bush, it managed to do so without tearing or pulling

the fabric of the jumpsuit, collecting almost nothing in the nature of seeds or sticks or other vegetation along the way. So, all in all, ladies and gentlemen, it was not only a dexterous dingo, it was a very tidy dingo . . .

'It managed to cut the collar and the sleeve with a pair of scissors. An unlikely circumstance, you may think, even if we're dealing with the most intelligent and perceptive of animals.

'But supposing the dingo were on trial here. How could you possibly convict it on this evidence? Where is the evidence? Where is there one substantial clue, apart from the account given by this child's mother, pointing to the killing of this child by a dingo? There isn't one. The case against the dingo would be laughed out of court because it's a transparent lie.

But don't be confused by all that. The way the defence is presented, we are here dealing with a man-eating dingo who raided the tent like a tiger in an Indian village . . .

'Now I don't contend, ladies and gentlemen, that dingoes are gentle creatures, nor do I contend that they are never dangerous, but what we do know as Australians, and you don't need experts to tell you, is that they are not notorious man-eaters. In the same way that you know as Australians, particularly as Northern Territorians, you don't need experts to tell you that crocodiles are notorious man-eaters. Now, no doubt the ordinary crocodile would go out of his way to eat this baby. The experience of Australians suggests that the dingo does not bear such a reputation and in saying this I am conscious of Mr Roff 's evidence about the peculiar conduct of dingoes at Ayers Rock, and that is something you will take into account, but if this case was set at Cahills Crossing on the East Alligator and not at Ayers Rock, and if this were a crocodile case and not a dingo case, well, you might have much less difficulty with it and questions of inherent improbability might not arise. But you are entitled to take account of your general knowledge and commonsense in a case like this, and if your general knowledge tells you that dingoes are not known as a species for killing and eating human beings, then you can take all that into account, in deciding the likelihood of the truth of the dingo theory.'

Of course, Ian Barker was a local identity, a well-known person in Darwin. He managed to get across to the jury that John Phillips was a smart southern lawyer and that only people who lived in the Territory could understand what dingoes were or were not likely to do.

Then he discussed the scientific evidence, starting with Professor Cameron:

'I am sorry, ladies and gentlemen, I can do no more than give you the world's leading forensic biologist . . . The fact is you've heard from a man who commands international respect in the field of forensic biology, who you will remember was neither assertive nor dogmatic nor disdainful of the opinions of others . . .

'Mrs Kuhl says it is foetal blood, and I suggest to you that she ought to know, and Dr Baxter ought to know what it is he is dealing with because you know really, if the suggestions made about their work in this court have any substance, people in New South Wales are in constant danger of being wrongly convicted whenever there is some blood involved.'

(In the later commission into Rendell's murder conviction Kuhl was again accused of incorrect forensic evidence which helped lead to a wrongful conviction; fortunately the conviction was thrown out and the accused pardoned as a result. When the ombudsman investigated the NSW forensic laboratory, Joy Kuhl left just before the report was released for a new job—in the Northern Territory forensic laboratory.)

'And it's really, I suggest, rather too ridiculous to contemplate that she would come into this, in the course of her daily work, as a professional forensic biologist, and muck it all up, not knowing whether she was dealing with adult blood or the blood of a child under three months of age. What we ask you to do is to respect her opinion. She didn't come here for her greater glory; she came here because she got into the case as an employee of the New South Wales Health Commission.

'Well, as with some other issues in this case, the defence side found experts to disagree and Professor Boettcher came along and criticised Mrs Kuhl and criticised the quality of the antiserum without ever asking her if he could test the actual antiserum which she used.' (This, of course, was completely untrue.) 'Professor Boettcher, whose academic university life was preceded by life as a schoolteacher, and who has never been actively engaged in the day to day routine work of testing bloodstains . . . who teaches and engages in pleasant research and writes for learned journals, has never been confronted with the difficulties which the poor old practical, hardworking forensic biologist is confronted with . . . a biologist whom, we say, does an honest and competent day's work and goes to court to offer her honest opinion and finds herself confronted with the criticisms of academics who have probably never in their lives entered a forensic science laboratory.'

I couldn't believe the jury would swallow this. Joy Kuhl's evidence had been discredited and, though Barry Boettcher hadn't been as forceful as he might have been, the jury must have picked up that Joy Kuhl's notes and methods were, at the very least, suspect.

Barker dealt with the question of the spray on the underdash of Webber Roberts's car by saying that it was irrelevant, and that nobody knew how the spray got under there anyway.

'We were not favoured with an explanation of how the spray got there,' he said. 'We were not favoured with an explanation of how long it's been there. We were not favoured with an explanation of what it is . . .'

He finished by saying,

> 'The blood in the car came from Azaria. The blood in the camera bag came from Azaria. All these things we put to you, you are entitled to find as facts. If there was no dingo, the child was murdered. The question who did it is brutally answered. You can leave out Michael Chamberlain, and you can leave out the two boys, and no one else was there. It is not consistent with reason to suggest that it was anyone but the accused, Alice Lynne Chamberlain.
>
> 'You are entitled to find that she invented the dingo lie. She had blood on her pants and her shoes. She had the opportunity. She's lied about the animal, its appearance, what it did, where it went, what she did. We submit to you, with respect, you are entitled to find that she's lied constantly and persistently and so has her husband . . .
>
> 'There's only one conclusion, we say, there's only one verdict open to you, and that is that each accused should be found guilty.'

On 28 October, Mr Justice Muirhead summed up for the jury. He absolutely bent over backwards to be fair and sympathetic to us. He pointed out:

> 'It was not only Mr Chamberlain who heard the baby's cry . . . Mrs Lowe, the first witness in the case, told you on oath she heard a baby's cry which definitely came from the tent. She says she is positive of that and she was there, and she is an apparently independent person.
>
> 'You are here to determine whether you are satisfied beyond reasonable doubt that Alice Chamberlain murdered Azaria, and whether her husband is proved to the same degree of proof to have been an accessory after the fact to that murder. If upon that evidence you are so satisfied beyond reasonable doubt, your duty of course is to convict. If you are not so satisfied your duty is to acquits simply because by law they are entitled to the benefit of any reasonable doubt that the evidence may leave in your mind.'

He finished his summing up (which seemed to take a long, long time) at twenty past two on the afternoon of 29 October.

And then the jury went out to consider its verdict.

NEWS OF A LIFETIME

Everybody was feeling that we had won by this time. We knew that Judge Muirhead had done everything he could to make the jury acquit us. We thought there was probably one juror who was holding out against it being unanimous; ironically, ours was the last case in the Northern Territory to require a unanimous verdict.

As the hours dragged on towards evening and the jury was still out, one of our lawyers returned from a walk saying, 'Well, obviously they think they have lost. Barker has just approached us asking how much compensation we will be suing for!'

This was encouraging, of course, but something told me it was better to wait for the jury before getting too excited about things. As the lawyers came and went it was comforting to have Irene stay there with us.

It grew dark. We couldn't continue sitting in our lawyers' rooms near the courtroom; as soon as the lights were switched on everybody could see us (though the windows were one-way glass, quite private during daylight hours, it was like watching television when the lights came on). We would look as if we were on a big TV screen, visible to hundreds of other people outside the courthouse, also waiting for the jury to come back. We'd also be on display for the media who were reporting every move we made. At this time, particularly, we felt we could do without that, and someone suggested we might like to go downstairs near the cells to the prison officers' area and wait there. At least we would have some privacy. Outside huge crowds had gathered. It was a big event.

Downstairs we went. It was a Friday evening, coming on Sabbath. Irene was with us and Blu Border was very much in evidence at this time, supposedly to whisk us away afterwards, although we had never needed his help before then. The police wardens were maintaining they were bored. Blu was in high spirits talking to them and, although the last thing I wanted at that time was the television, he actually offered to go home and get his own very precious set and bring it down for the prison wardens to watch. This was against the rules; prison officers aren't allowed to watch television while on escort duty, but the prison wardens accepted anyway, and they seemed to enjoy it. It was a comedy program, and the female prison warden's coarse laughter echoed around the quarters, and her mannish guffaws were not what I wanted to hear right then.

I felt that the jury was taking a long time to make up its mind. We were actually in custody at that time, but because Muirhead had summed up heavily in favour of our acquittal, we were not being treated as prisoners, but allowed to stay free. So Irene was allowed to stay with us downstairs. She didn't appreciate the TV either.

At one stage Michael wanted to get something from upstairs, but because the doors were locked up there, one of the prison wardens had to go with him. He discovered that he had taken the wrong key to get Michael out the way they wanted to go, so decided to go via the courtroom. They had obviously forgotten Muirhead had said that everybody was to stay out; the jury was to have full access to the whole of the courtroom, especially the exhibits, while they were making up their minds. Michael and the prison warden returned quickly, both looking shocked. The jury was in high spirits, clowning. Michael seemed beyond speech. They got the keys and went the way they were supposed to go in the first place.

Well, I thought, that means that the jury have come to a decision and are happy with it. I remembered being on a jury myself, and we had been told that we could have a meal after reaching our verdict because then we would be entitled to another half day's pay and get our dinner for nothing. We had decided there was doubt about the guilt of the lad we were trying, but thought it wouldn't hurt him to sweat for a while; we'd deliver our decision after we'd eaten. I thought as the jury was now relaxing a verdict would be given very soon.

About half an hour later we hadn't heard anything and I felt that something was wrong. I went into the toilet—it was the only place I could get away from the prison wardens, the TV and from Blu bounding in and out where he wasn't supposed to be—and I prayed about it. Finally I said,

'Well, Lord, if You have got a reason for me going to prison, I am prepared to go, provided you leave Michael out because the children need someone and I don't think Michael could handle this.' It was something I had often done, I suppose, bargaining with God, and yet I felt it wasn't an unreasonable bargain.

When I had finished praying, I felt peace and calm come over me. I heard footsteps down the hall and the prison warden called out, 'Lindy, the jury is ready to come back in—we have to go as soon as you are finished.' I felt God had allowed me that extra time to come to terms with what was happening. I felt within almost as if I knew I was going to prison, and when I went upstairs I had an inner calm that could not be explained in any human way. Blu helped the prison wardens rush Irene out the back way. Now the jury was back she mustn't be seen leaving from where she shouldn't officially have been. We said hasty goodbyes on her way out and she said, 'I'll see you soon.'

We took our normal places. Stuart came in and told us we would once more have to sit in the dock for the verdict. He was quiet and serious. He said they hadn't a clue about the outcome but I could see the length of time the jury had been out had made them all uneasy. He said, 'Look guys, I'm going to wish you all the best and even if it sounds inappropriate, I'm going to tell you now that if this goes wrong I'm going to fight and keep on fighting for you until it's clear. I want you to know that so you know it is not just an afterthought.'

Michael said, 'Oh, mate,' and I just took his hand, squeezed it and said,

'Thanks.' The prison wardens came to escort us to the dock then, and we left with them, making our way and sitting quietly.

At 8.33 p.m. the court rose while Mr Justice Muirhead came in and took his seat, directing the Sheriff's officer to bring in the jury.

The foreman stood and was asked whether the jury had reached a unanimous verdict.

'We have, Your Honour,' he said.

'Do you find the accused, Alice Lynne Chamberlain, guilty or not guilty of the charge of murder?'

'Guilty,' he said.

There was not a sound in the courtroom. The foreman repeated, 'Guilty,' a little more loudly. Later he repeated the word for Michael.

It was like a nightmare, a bad dream when you can see and hear everything, but know you are about to wake up and it will be OK. I went numb. Thank God He had prepared me a little, so the verdict did not have quite the impact it could have had otherwise. I was determined not to let them see what they'd done to me. I sat hardly breathing, waiting for the foreman to say he'd made a mistake, played a joke, something. He didn't. He looked embarrassed. Two of the women jurors and one of the men were crying; obviously they weren't happy about the verdict. My eyes turned to Muirhead. Under his wig his face was an ashen white. The whole courtroom seemed to be suspended. The lawyers all sat like statues. No one moved.

Mr Justice Muirhead said, 'Alice Lynne Chamberlain, you have been found guilty of murder by this jury. There is only one sentence open to me under the law. You will be imprisoned for life with hard labour.'

Michael's sentence was deferred and he was to be released on licence again in the custody of our lawyers.

The 'court dismissed' call broke the spell. Malcolm Brown jumped up, shook his fist and shouted, 'Bastards!' Bedlam broke out in the gallery. Some people cheered or were smirking delightedly, others sat stunned, while still others were crying or dumbly shaking their heads in disbelief. Barker was very red in the face and hunched, head down, looking furtively around under his lashes, as if he thought he was going to be attacked. The female prison warden said, 'Let's get out of here.'

As I turned to go downstairs to the cell block, this time for real, John and Andy were motionless, staring at the now vacated bench. John looked an old man of seventy at that moment, white-faced and drawn. Even Andy was pale under his tan and he looked stunned. My eyes travelled on as I turned to leave and the movement must have caught Stuart's eye because he looked up and our eyes met. *His* eyes looked like those of a wounded deer. One split second said everything. Those eyes will haunt me for the rest of my life when I think of that verdict. No words were needed. The pain and compassion mirrored spoke volumes. I never want to see that look again in anyone's eyes for the rest of my life.

I followed Gardner, the prison warden, through the door to go downstairs to the cell block. As I turned at the head of the stairs and looked behind me I noticed that Michael's legs were not steady; they looked as if they had turned to rubber and he was about to fall. I turned to the prison warden and said in a dead voice, 'You better hold him up or he's going to fall down the stairs.' It didn't occur to me to do anything myself, I simply saw something that needed doing but was nothing to do with me. I was in another world. Gardner heard me and repeated my words loudly and quickly to the male prison warden beside Michael, who took one look and grabbed him, then assisted him downstairs. They sat him on one of the chairs at the lunch table, and I sat in the other one. The prison wardens stood around, nobody knowing much what to do. I heard Gardner ask whether a car had been called for, and someone said yes. I was in immediate custody; Michael, still on his own recognisance, was to go home alone and I was to go straight to prison.

Everything seemed useless. I knew Michael wouldn't cope on his own and I thought he should be free. So in a low voice I said to him, 'Love, I want a divorce.' He broke down at that and said, 'No. I don't want a divorce. I want you.' There was no point in saying anything more then, he was too upset. Maybe this would be the catalyst for change. He was begging me not to go and I had no choice. I had to go. It wasn't *my* wish to go to prison. He was so upset he got through my apathy and upset me; I started to cry too.

I had gathered, from my reading, that there were a number of things you couldn't have in prison. I had talked a little to Stuart about it because Michael didn't even want me to mention the thought that I might go to prison. I discovered that you couldn't have watches or wedding rings. There was no way I wanted my ring left sitting for who knows how many years in a property bag somewhere, especially in Darwin where things get mildew and are ruined. It could also get lost or disappear, so I took off my ring and watch. I guess that seemed so final to Michael. I put them in my handbag and gave it to him. That started him sobbing afresh. I tried to comfort him as best I could, but there was nothing I could do.

John and Andy came down with Stuart, very briefly, to say goodbye. There wasn't much they could say. I knew they had tried every last possible thing. They had left no stone unturned. We had all agreed on everything. There was no blame to attach to anyone, we had all done our best. No one knew exactly what had gone wrong at that stage, we were all too stunned for words. John and Andy were still white. I don't remember Andy saying much at all except shrugging and grasping my shoulders. Then he turned on his heel and went out the door and up the stairs. John just stood there white-faced and dumb; his face told us how much he was hurting too, but his words were few. Stuart told us later that their wives had said neither of them had slept much for a week after the verdict and that Andy had slammed things and sworn a great deal, whereas John had not eaten much and been extremely quiet. One or both of them had got very drunk at some stage. I heard that Barker was so stunned I guess it didn't register for a while that he had actually won.

Much later, an Auckland judge having dinner with Jim Muirhead asked him about the case. Muirhead said, 'Shit,' then stated he 'wrote on the file "not guilty"' very early 'and went about my jobs'. When he was asked what went wrong, he stated that he had underestimated the power of the press. (He was later to sign 'once a judge!' for me when I asked for his signature in my book when it came out in 1990. This book was later stolen.)

Stuart stayed just a few moments longer, waiting for Michael to go with him. He looked at me and said quietly, 'Well, you *know* what I'll be doing,' and I knew what he meant; I didn't have to worry, I wasn't forgotten. *He* wasn't going to go to pieces. He might feel as upset as I was, but he was going to fight in whatever way he could, and I knew eventually we'd get there because, although now wasn't the time, we had God on our side and we *would* win.

The prison wardens said the car was there, and Michael would have to go. Stuart went to help him up. He said, 'Come on, mate.' Michael didn't move. As I came round the table, he grabbed my arm and wouldn't let me go. I had to drag my arm away from him and told him he *had* to be strong, too. He had to look after my two little boys. He couldn't forget them. He had to be strong, too. Stuart had his arm around him and I know he knew how hard it was for me to walk away. He looked at me and tried his best to make me crack a smile, by saying, 'And to think I had to cough up for that case of champagne for this.' Well, I did crack as much of a grin as I could at that. It was standard procedure to chip in for the typists, win or lose, and they had asked for champagne. I don't think even the typists would have felt much like celebrating after that, either. They had already told us what they thought and wished us well, so they weren't going to be too happy.

INNOCENCE INCARCERATED

I walked through the door. It shut behind me and I was in a big double garage. There was a car waiting there instead of the paddy wagon. I was told later that they thought I would be more comfortable in that. I'm sure they didn't think at all. A paddy wagon couldn't be seen into, but the car sure could. We were informed that there were crowds lining the driveway out of the back entrance to the court. Gardner suggested I crouch down in the back seat and that she would sit on me. I was pregnant! I looked at her with contempt. I wasn't guilty, I had nothing to hide, I never had, why should I act as if I was guilty now? I didn't appreciate the thought of her sitting on me in a space that was far too small anyway. I refused her offer and sat bolt upright in the back of the car.

Now I was away from Michael, my tears had dried. I felt as if I was dead on the outside and crying on the inside. My face was blotched from crying and I didn't care. It was about 9.30 p.m. The roll-a-door went up and there was a roar from the outside. Then as the car moved forward, it became strangely quiet. One woman jumped forward and banged on the side of the car and said, 'Good on yer, love. We're with you.' It took me some moments to realise that she wasn't being nasty, but had actually had the guts in front of that crowd to say she believed in me. The noise didn't start up again until we were well away down the road. It seemed as if even those who were against us were momentarily ashamed as they saw me come through that door on the first stage of my trip to prison.

Darwin Prison is at Berrimah, about 15 kilometres (9 miles) east of Darwin (and not to be confused with Berrima Gaol in New South Wales). I had been down the first part of the road many times before, and now as I looked around I kept saying to myself, 'This is the last time for years you will be going here. You won't see this any more. Take a last look.' And yet I wasn't even really interested enough to look. All I could remember later was that it was dark and the street lights went past in blurs. I kept telling myself this was temporary. They had made a mistake. We would appeal shortly, and they would realise that it had all been a mistake. It wasn't permanent. I would only be here for a few weeks and then I would go home again. Dear God, it was only yesterday I was on the phone to my little boys and telling them everything was fine and that Mummy would be home soon. I had been so certain that at last all was well.

We drove into a compound. I thought I must be at some halfway station and was to be transferred. But no, they said this was the female section, and I walked into a fairly well lit area that could have been any country motel in the outback, except for the locks on the outside of the doors and the bars on the outside windows. It was clean and spartan, and looked OK. Gardner handed me over and went home.

I was taken down to a room and showered. To add insult to indignity, the prison warden, Mrs Wallace, stood and watched me. No largely pregnant woman wishes to be observed naked, and I certainly didn't. She stood there with a half-sneering smile on her face, taking notes. She had to observe whether I had any scars, she said. I later noticed that they did this to some prisoners to intimidate them, but not all, but I wasn't to know that then. The other woman on duty was much nicer. She was matter of fact and careful of the rules, but she had a soul, and was well liked by the girls. She left shortly after, unfortunately.

I was changed and given a uniform. They actually gave me some new knickers. They thought the second-hand ones they normally handed out wouldn't be very good for a pregnant woman, just in case I caught some sort of disease. How kind of them! At least it was more than they did for most of the girls who came in. I was allowed to keep my own knickers too because they thought they would be more comfortable. (I think what they really meant was that they didn't have any more that were big enough for me at that particular time.) I was taken up to the day room, introduced very briefly to the girls. There didn't seem to be many of them and I presumed the rest were in other rooms, but no, I later learned there were no others. They were watching TV, happily enjoying the programs.

Although they didn't say, I supposed they must have all been watching what happened to me on television that night. It was on all the stations, breaking into the regular programs with updates of what the jury was doing. I didn't realise then how much they knew, but I later discovered just how much the papers were watched. They knew when the trials were going on, what they were all about, and even what the prison wardens thought about the girl being charged before she came near the prison. They knew whether she was likely to be charged and fined or sentenced, and they would have known all that about me too. The Aboriginal girls were quiet but polite. I didn't feel like mixing so they put me on early lockup, probably because they didn't know what I would do. I had been quiet, but quiet ones sometimes throw tantrums at the most unexpected times. Until the prison wardens get used to that person, they treat them with caution. My bed had been made up by one of the other girls. I didn't realise this was unusual. I just went in and lay down to rest. They asked me if there was anything else they could do for me.

I said, 'No, except that I would like a drink.' They brought me down a plastic cup. I had a little drink and then put it on the floor, thinking to use it throughout the night, as I normally did, but no, a plastic cup was dangerous and had to be taken out of the cell. They were sorry. They locked me up and said that if there was anything I needed, just call, or press the button. There wasn't anything I needed that I could think of—well, nothing that they could give me anyway. Just my freedom, and they weren't at liberty to do that.

I lay there too spent to cry any more. I talked to God. I said, 'Well, Lord. I made a bargain and here I am. It is your turn to keep Michael out of prison tomorrow. I have kept my promise, you keep yours. Right now, Lord, I need some sleep. I've had it. Please help me to be calm and give me rest so I can face whatever the morning brings.'

Although others might have slept badly that night, I had the sleep of an exhausted innocent. I woke early in the morning. I wasn't sure what had woken me, but the sun was just up and I looked out the window. There, in the early light of dawn, I saw a dingo in the distance facing towards me. It was free, anyway.

Also Sentenced

Back at Cooranbong, Aidan had gone to bed with the jury still out. Like my parents, he had been absolutely confident that Michael and I would be exonerated, that the truth would be known at last. And then Mum had to tell him that the jury had said that his mummy and daddy were guilty of killing his little baby sister.

She described what had happened much later and her words nearly broke my heart:

> The verdict was given—we lay in bed in absolute stunned silence, but not for long. The doorbell rang and in minutes folk began to arrive, before long filling the room to overflowing. Some were crying; all felt stunned as we did that such a decision could be arrived at in the light of evidence so clearly indicative of innocence.
>
> Aidan stirred and needed to go to the bathroom. My heart missed a beat—would he hear the conversations and discover the truth? I quickly breathed a prayer, 'Oh Lord, please don't let him find out this way.'
>
> He questioned, 'Grandma, why are all the people here?' I replied that they had come to talk with Grandma and Grandad.
>
> 'Oh,' was his only response. It was with gratitude I saw him drowsily snuggle down as I tucked him in and soon he was once again fast asleep.
>
> Around 11 p.m. the last person reluctantly left after being assured we would be all right. God was our help and comfort.
>
> As we closed our eyes in a vain attempt to sleep, our hearts torn and bleeding, I knew that when dawn broke I would have to face two little boys and tell them their precious Mummy would not be coming home to them. In agony I prayed for strength and courage for the right words to carry out a task I felt so unequal to, for words to say that would soften the awful blow.
>
> Hour after hour I lay in the darkness, praying for our own precious daughter and pleading for strength and help I so much needed to face her boys. I clung to and repeated over and over again one of my favourite texts: 'Fear thou not for I am with thee, be not dismayed for I am thy God: I will strengthen thee; yea, I will help thee; yea, I will uphold thee with the right hand of my righteousness' (Isaiah 41: 10). What a comfort it was.
>
> Dawn came at last and with it Aidan awoke. I sat beside him on the edge of his bed, took his hands in mine and explained that the naughty people still thought Mummy had hurt little bubby and that they had put her in prison so she would not be able to come home, but I said, 'You know Mummy didn't hurt bubby because you were with her all the time.'
>
> 'Yes,' he whispered.

His face went pale, he dropped his head back against the bedhead and broke into deep dreadful groaning noises with dry eyes. And my mother, feeling devastated herself, knew there was little she could do for him. Her letter continues:

> I would not wish such agony on my direst enemy—if I had one. It was only by God's grace I was able to remain outwardly calm and comfort him with the assurance that Jesus knew too that Mummy loved wee Azaria so very much and would not, and did not, hurt her and that He loved Mummy and would look after her and not let the naughty people hurt her. He would send lots of beautiful shining angels to be with and protect her all the time.
>
> Soft footfalls on the carpet heralded Reagan's arrival. Soon he was perched on the bed beside us. The dreaded message was repeated. Poor little man, he sat there poker stiff, just looking at me with big wild frightened eyes. Oh, the agony as I did my best to comfort those little fellows. If only the false accusers could have looked in on that scene, they would never have been the same again. I changed the subject and asked the boys if they would like to spend some time that day at the home of a friend who had kindly offered to look after them for the day. We all knew what the day would be like, both at church and at home . . .
>
> Sunday morning I woke to what I thought was someone crying. I listened—yes—soft sobbing was coming from Aidan's room. I jumped out of bed and went to him. I suggested he come and get into bed with Grandad and Grandma. He didn't need a second invitation. We both put our arms around him and snuggled him up between us. Again we assured him that Jesus and the angels were with Mummy and she would be all right. Saturday evening someone from Melbourne had rung and told us of an article in the paper that day describing the women's section of Darwin prison, so we were able to tell Aidan that Mummy had her own little room with a shower and toilet, a bed, wardrobe and little table. This seemed to give him quite a deal of comfort. No one knows what ideas he might have had in his head.

And so began the lonely days and nights for two small boys who were left motherless so unnecessarily for what stretched into years. God alone knows the hurt, the agony, the heartache that can never be erased from our minds.

Who can imagine Michael's hurt, knowing he had to go home alone? He was leaving his wife miles away and going home to face his children to tell them their mother wasn't coming home for years. The sight of him on his own, although excited and grateful to see him, would bring home to them all the more that their Mummy wasn't there, and that that was Australian justice.

The rest of the prison woke with a jangling siren that I learned to dread. That siren gave us just a half an hour to get out of bed, shower, tidy our room and turn up for breakfast. Much as I hated it, I had to face everyone in the daylight. I looked at my face in the polished piece of metal that served as a mirror and in that wavering surface I could see my face was swollen and blotched and I had no makeup to cover up the ravages of the night, nothing but a toothbrush, toothpaste and comb. I dressed and when it was time to leave the room, one of the officers came down to tell me what to do with my washing (your towel and uniform had to be washed daily), and to take me up to the kitchen. She introduced me to one of the girls who was then on kitchen duty and told me where to sit. The other girls were fairly quiet and subdued, recognising that morning is not always best for some people and respecting the privacy of those who wished to be quiet.

After breakfast, we sat and talked a little. One of the girls told me the program for the day—the girls certainly updated you a lot more on what happened than the prison wardens did. They told me I would probably be put on washing, because a girl who had been there before with a baby had been put on laundry. That way you did your own baby's nappies without causing any one else work. Women with babies were mainly given indoor work. Well, I thought, at least it wouldn't be impossible for me to keep Kahlia.

After breakfast I was called across to the office and informed that my lawyer would shortly be coming to see me and possibly even my husband. I was taken across to see the sister to be weighed and poked and prodded and signed in—just a routine matter. Then I had to have my photo taken—mug shots—left side, right side, front, with a number underneath. I must say I looked extremely unglamorous with my face like that and the uniform they gave me was a horrible lime green colour. Besides, in order to be large enough to fit around my stomach it was far too long and far too wide for me at the shoulders. But that was not the point. Maternity dresses of any sort were not provided in prison. You wore whatever was there, and this was a size 20.

By lunchtime I was back with the other girls and they told me a little more of what happened in prison. They were obviously curious but didn't ask too many questions at that stage. I learned it was an unwritten law that you don't pry into another's business unless given the opening to do so.

When Stuart arrived he told me that Michael had received a suspended sentence, as we had expected—a twelve months' suspended sentence on his own recognisance and a three-year good behaviour bond. I was pleased for the boys' sake at least.

He also told me a little of what had happened to Irene. When the verdict was handed down, Irene had been so shocked and upset she almost collapsed. She flatly refused to go back to the Borders' and wanted to go to a hotel. She was so distraught that Jackie and Roe Bowhey offered to take her home with them. She accepted gratefully. She wouldn't even go near the house to pack up her gear, so Jackie went.

Jackie packed Irene's gear and took it with her, only explaining to the Borders that Irene was going to stay with them for a few days, nothing more. Irene never saw them again. She went through a physical collapse after that and couldn't even use a pen for nearly two months. When I eventually heard from Irene months later, her writing was so shaky I could barely read it. Irene never holds a grudge, but even now she can't talk about our stay in Darwin with any comfort, as she gets so upset at the treatment we all received.

I knew our lawyers would appeal against the verdict to the Federal Court. I was convinced the verdict couldn't be permitted to stand; justice in Australia in the 1980s *couldn't* go so wrong. 'We can't tell how successful we'll be until we go through the transcript of the trial,' Stuart told me. 'It's a very technical area. The judge could easily have made a slip in summing up which we could use as grounds for an appeal.' The trouble was that the summary had been so fair that we couldn't easily find those grounds. I knew the jury was completely wrong, of course, but the problem was in getting a separate court to see how the evidence presented to them was inconsistent with a guilty verdict. This Stuart explained to me, urging me, as he was bound to, not to get my hopes up, but at the same time I knew he'd move heaven and earth and find that gap.

When his legal visit ended he said that Michael was waiting outside. Stuart had asked if my things could be brought in and, as Michael and I had already packed our suitcases for a quick getaway after the 'innocent' verdict, his clothes and mine were mixed together. A lot of the things I had in my suitcases I certainly didn't want left behind, so they were all brought in. The prison wardens stood by anxiously while I quickly went through them and pulled out some of my things for Michael to leave behind. The rest Michael took out with him. The process seemed to cause problems for them, but little enough in comparison with the problem they had caused me.

Both Stuart and Michael were aghast at my appearance. The lime green did nothing to enhance my complexion and I guess it brought it home to them with a real shock the situation I was in. Michael was still distraught, but a little more together now he knew that at least he was going home to the boys. Even though he was going home alone.

That night as I got up to get a drink at the water fountain, I heard Michael's sentence on the TV news.

His suspended sentence was in 'the interests of the motherless boys'. One of the Aboriginal girls on the other side of the room commented, 'That's all very well, but they forget that kids need their mums too and they don't care about that, do they?' The Aboriginal girls were very sensitive about family. Too often they had seen mothers pulled away from children and thrown into jail for things they knew little about.

At first I was kept in the inner compound almost continually, away from the prying eyes of the journalists who camped around the gate hoping to catch a glimpse of me. It was only after they'd packed up and gone home in the late afternoon that I was allowed outside. Then I had to shift the hoses. I wasn't allowed to do any heavy work (I might damage the baby), but pulling those long, heavy, industrial hoses was more likely to damage the baby than anything else, the way they strained and hurt my stomach. But the hoses were outside, it was cooler, and a chance to go for a walk around, looking at the grass and trees directly instead of through the bars.

I later wrote of my feelings in one of my circular letters:

> I cannot pretend to know exactly why things are as they are, except that God in His great plan knows every step of the way, and why should I fret and worry when He had my hand in His, leading all the way. I know He

will reveal His plan when He is ready. Maybe we need to wait until we meet face to face at His feet in Heaven, but this I know—that Jesus loves Me, He died for Me, and I willingly follow the path He has for me. I cannot doubt His love for me. He holds my hand and does not let go. Jesus is my real and personal friend and we talk together. He has promised to be by my side and not leave me and I know He keeps his promises. Sometimes He says, 'Wait a while yet', sometimes He even says 'No', but always He loves me. I can do no less than love Him back. He has been so good to me and has answered so many prayers in my behalf and for my family. The fact that Michael is home right now with Aidan and Reagan is only a small example of this.

An Unborn Dilemma

For the next three weeks I was subjected to one of the worst possible forms of unkindness; that of being given hope and then having it dashed over and over. I was told I would be able to keep Kahlia, then told I could not. Then I was told that I could have her in hospital for as long as I was there, then I was told I could not. Then I was told it would depend on my doctor how long I could have her at birth, then I was told by my doctor that he had been instructed that I was not to have her at all.

Finally it was settled that I was allowed to have my baby daughter for one hour after birth, and that was all. It would have been much kinder to tell me first off that I was allowed to see her just for a little while than to let me live in hope until then. All the time I was told I could, but Paul said no; 'We want to let you, but Paul says no.' 'I would be happy to let you, but Paul says no.' Always it came back to Paul Everingham. Why the Chief Minister, rather than the courts, police or prison, had so much say was not clear.

Tapioca, a prison official, was continually coming across to call me up before him and give me the latest news. I got so that when I saw Tapioca standing at the gate, or indeed even heard the bell ring and thought that it might be him, I felt sick in the stomach and wanted to vomit. Morning after morning I would wake up with a funny feeling, wondering what was about to happen, then I would realise there was sure to be another session. Not only did he literally make you stand on the mat, but he was always cracking bad jokes about babies, particularly when I was told I wasn't able to have Kahlia with me.

Mrs Barham happened to be in the room when a particularly nasty joke was told. When the interview came to an end, she called me in and apologised. Girls may be there for punishment, but that is bad enough without having salt rubbed into their wounds and people being nasty to them.

To say I was miserable would be an understatement, but I have always tried not to let my misery rub off on those around me and to see the best side of things if I possibly could. Because I was pregnant I was not allowed to work (apart from those awful hoses, of course) except for occasionally sewing on buttons, but they left that very much up to me. Sometimes I did it, sometimes I didn't.

I was told to answer as much of my mail as possible so they could put it away in the storeroom. One day I got more than 250 letters in one mail and it continued much the same, day after day. I tried to open and read them all. I realised it was pretty hopeless, but I listed them carefully, thinking in future I would write an open letter and have it printed and sent to everybody. That way nobody could complain they had been missed out. The other girls thought it was a great diversion and helped me list all the names and addresses too. That helped a lot.

But my very mail was a source of irritation. One of the other girls who was used to getting half a dozen or so letters a week and thought of it as part of her status in the prison became very jealous. Her remarks were thinly veiled with civility, which I realised very quickly. I was not the only one; the other girls remarked on her jealous attitude.

She didn't like the fact I was white, or that I was about to have a baby. (She badly wanted children.) I often saw her watching me from the other side of the room and knew that she was planning and scheming to throw any sort of a rub in my way she could.

The mail helped the time pass quickly and there were some lovely surprises in it. One letter I got, despite my misery, made me grin. It was from someone called Jim who said he had known me years ago and how he wished it was the days of the knights of old where you could come riding up on a white charger and spirit the damsel in distress away from the forbidden castle, but he presumed his old white Valiant Charger was not the sort that would leap any fence with grace. It would probably stall on the way. What a pity the days of chivalry no longer existed. I couldn't help smiling. In subsequent letters I realised just who he was, and that I had indeed known him as one of the older guys around the place when I was a first-year high school student.

Then one day a tape arrived. I was informed I wasn't allowed to have tapes. As I didn't have a tape recorder and as it had a letter attached I could take it to my room with the rest of my mail and return it when read and it would be put into my property. By then I was getting to know Smiley fairly well. She was one of the Aboriginal girls and she had her own tape recorder. I arranged to borrow it, longing to know what was on the tape. The accompanying letter simply said it had been prepared especially for me and so, after work that night, we managed to sneak the tape recorder from Smiley's cell to mine. I plugged it in and put it under the bed with my tape in and turned it on.

Lying on the floor, because it was hot, I put my head near to the bed and listened to the tape recorder just the other side of the draped bed quilt. With it on very low I could hear clearly the beautiful music, and the words:

It's not over now, though the world says it is,
Many will forget, but we never will.
Can you believe That many think about you?
They fall asleep at night
Praying silent prayers
To the Lord, who doesn't forget.
So try and understand, it's not over now,
Though the world says it is.

Lindy, they know that you're up there
Not alone in your room.
Seems the world don't care for you any more,
But part of it, part of it still does.

Lindy, they know that you're up there
Not alone in your room.
Seems the world don't care for you any more,
But part of it, part of it still does.

Lindy, Lindy, Lindy . . .

Lyndon Bidmead, one of my art classmates, had written the words and had given them to Steven Martin to compose the music. Steve I knew from the Outdoor Club, and he had been one of the best music students at college. We had often stopped and talked, although we had no classes together. Lyndon and Steve had managed to get Shirley Lewry, the assistant girls' dean, to sing the song for them. At 1 a.m., while the college was quiet, they had sat in the music studio with a little hand-held tape recorder, taping it for me so I would get their message as soon as possible.

When I heard the song I lay on the floor and cried, listening to it over and over again, till we were called for tea. I had to sneak the tape recorder back in a hurry, wash my face and pretend nothing had happened. But I was thrilled they had thought of me and I knew they weren't the only people who hadn't forgotten, and that they would fight until this thing was cleared, as hundreds and thousands of other Australians had started to fight for me and for truth and justice at that time.

Years later when the movie *Evil Angels (A Cry in the Dark)* was made that piece of music should have been its theme song. The producers, however, were too afraid to use it, realising it was so poignant and such a catchy tune that if that music was put across it might have detracted from the story of the movie and they wanted it to stand on its own without the music. I have no doubt that had it been used, it would have become a popular tune.

One day I was told to get ready for a visit, my brother Alex was there. I waited and waited, then I was told the visit was off. The press had paid his fare and he was to interview me, so he was a media representative and would not be admitted. I had to watch my beloved brother walk past my window and out. He looked tired and old. I tried to whistle and couldn't utter a sound. Something was fishy. Alex knew I wasn't giving interviews so that wasn't the whole story. I felt frustrated and angry.

A Contractual Fight and a Depressing Celebration

On 16 November Dr Fred Smith came to do a series of psychological evaluation tests for use in the appeal to the Federal Court and also for my bail application. All the time I was doing those tests, I was having contractions. I knew they were a fair distance apart and I was able to time them on the office clock from where I sat. I told Mrs Barham that I had started but didn't expect to be in labour properly before morning. She arranged for an extra female to be called in on the male side in case I needed an escort before then, and added to the next day's roster for hospital duty, before she went off duty. We told no one else.

Miss Tonks was on night shift when I was woken by stronger and more regular contractions. It must have been about two in the morning. I lay awake for a long time before I decided they were getting fairly close and needed timing. I pushed my buzzer; Miss Tonks came to my window and I asked her whether she'd mind timing my contractions. She went into a panic and wanted to ring the tower immediately. Just what I needed—several large, burly men hanging round timing my contractions and flapping about. If *they* came across, the whole section would wake up.

'No!' I said forcibly. 'I'm nowhere near going to the hospital. I just need to time them at this stage so I know what is happening. It's my fourth birth and I know how soon to go. Don't worry, I'll give you plenty of notice. You'll only look like a fool if you ring up now and don't know anything about it. We'll time a few and then we'll see what happens.' We were not allowed to have watches, of course. She grabbed a chair and sat outside the cell window and when I started a contraction, I told her and she timed it. She didn't need to time the duration of the contraction, however. I explained this to her, and the second time she timed how far *apart* they were and we got it right. She very conscientiously recorded everything in the day book, which was supposed to be a complete record of everything that happened during the day, such as 'Chamberlain first notified of contractions . . . Chamberlain's first contraction was timed at . . . Next contraction timed at . . .' I thought, Goodness, you can't even have a baby in peace without them writing it up. They couldn't just make the entry

'Prisoner Chamberlain had a baby at such-and-such a time' could they? No, all the details had to go in.

When the contractions were getting a bit closer, we decided it was time to notify the tower. They decided to move me to hospital just before dawn, as that was the most likely time to avoid the press, who were now parking outside the prison gates from early morning until late at night. There were also journalists camping outside the hospital waiting for me to arrive. The sun was just rising, spreading the darkness with brilliant apricot and orange as we travelled to the hospital in the bumpy prison paddy wagon.

Madam, the officer who accompanied me, did everything correctly. She had been given a sealed envelope with the instructions for Chamberlain's confinement. She had a new day book, specially for me, in which she was supposed to write down every contraction and movement I or the nursing staff made. She drove the hospital sister mad, following her around; every time the sister turned, Madam almost banged into her. Finally, the sister said to her, 'Perhaps if you sit down somewhere, you could take your notes from there and see what's going on. We are just going to do the prep.' Most mothers know what that means, but either Madam had no children or she was so nervous she had forgotten.

The sister said to me, 'I'm just going to give you an enema and shave you, then we'll go into the other room and you can stay there.'

I said, 'Fine' but still Madam either didn't understand or wasn't listening. She found a seat and promptly sat down at the foot of the bed. The sister and I looked at each other, and the sister asked the prison officer, 'Are you sure you are comfortable there? You might be better elsewhere.'

Madam said, 'Well, what are you going to do?'

Having already explained, the sister simply gave up. She shrugged and said, 'I'm going to shave her bum and give her an enema, right?' Madam turned scarlet and said, 'Oh, oh, I am sorry,' and jumped up and sat in the only other available chair in the room, which was further from the bed.

When I rose to go to the toilet, she went to follow me. The sister said,

'Look, I think she'd be better on her own. It's only the enema working. She can't get out of there, but if you want to check before she goes, OK.' Madam duly inspected the toilet to see there was no exit apart from the door, where she parked herself while I was inside. Every few minutes she called out, 'Are you all right, Lindy?' When you are having contractions before a birth, it is most unlikely you would attempt a prison break. I was too miserable to want to go anywhere. Finally the sister convinced her I was fine.

I came out and we went into the other room. The sister leaned over and whispered to me, 'Is she *always* like this? What a pain! Do they always follow you around like that?' I just had time to nod assent before Madam came over again to see what we were talking about. It was, of course, strictly against the rules to talk to a prisoner like that—you may be passing confidential jail information or planning a break!

I went into the main delivery room, where Madam once again took a perch right next to the bed-head. Every time I had a contraction she asked me whether I was all right, whether it hurt, if she could get me a drink of water or do something for me. If she had sat there quietly, it wouldn't have been too bad. But having the birth of your baby spoiled by a prison officer sitting right under your nose was bad enough without her asking if she could make me more comfortable. I know she was trying to be helpful but she was really getting on my goat.

Madam went out for a few moments and in came Mrs Yardley, another officer. Was I glad to see her! Good old Mrs Barham had called her in an hour early. Mrs Yardley had had her last baby only three months earlier and it was fresh in her mind. No more pestering; she just stayed unobtrusively in the background. Besides, she was not afraid of the superintendent. Madam came in to say goodbye and wish me well.

When the doctor finally came, he looked at the time and said, 'Mmm. Shift change coming up. I think we will bring this baby on.'

'I don't want this baby brought on. I want to have it naturally,' I said. 'It's being fairly quick. I would like to leave it alone.'

He replied, 'No. I think for your sake and ours, the fewer people who know the better. If we can use one shift instead of two, we have only one set of nurses to worry about. We know who's on this shift, the hospital is secure and we can keep the news away from the press as much as possible.'

I said, 'OK, if you put it that way, I guess it is the best thing.'

He decided to break the water and let me progress from there, which I did fairly quickly. (Much to their disgust they discovered later that, despite their careful vetting of staff, one of the delivery staff was the wife of a reporter!)

I had the oddest feeling. Apart from being so emotionally drained, I didn't feel I could stand the pain as I normally did and fought every contraction I had. Instead of trying to cooperate and relax and let the baby come in its own time, I was fighting to hold her inside me. I knew I had to give her up, but while she was inside me she was still mine and mine alone; I had her and nobody could take her from me. As soon as Kahlia was born, I would have her for only one hour. She would then be taken away and I wouldn't see her again for twelve months. Because I was 'dangerous', and supposed to have murdered Azaria, I wouldn't even be permitted to see Kahlia on family visits, under the supervision of prison wardens and family until she was a year old. Apparently they considered that she would then be out of danger from me.

Losing one baby was bad enough, but this one was being taken from me by a jury who couldn't see past the lies they were being told by the Crown and the police. Lies were separating my baby from me. I fought the contractions and consequently they hurt twice as much. The sister said, 'You are having strong contractions but you are not opening very much.' She said she would try to open the cervix a bit, but I said, 'I don't want to.'

She said, 'Look, you are in pain and you might as well get it over as quick as you can. I understand you feel you want it naturally, but you might be in trouble and tear. I'll do it. We'll ring the doctor and he will be here pretty soon.' I agreed; no use in fighting the inevitable. I knew Kahlia was going to be born anyway.

The sister said, 'When you have the next contraction, I'll see if I can open the cervix slightly. It will hurt, but you will be OK.' Hurt it did, and then she exclaimed, 'Oh, my goodness!' I knew exactly what was happening because, once that cervix was open, my babies came in a rush. When Azaria was born, the nurse didn't even have time to get from the head to the foot of the bed, and this baby was obviously going to be the same. I said to her,

'You've done it, haven't you?'

She replied, 'Yep. The doctor's going to be cross.'

The assistant asked, 'Do you want me to get the doctor?'

'Forget it,' the sister replied, 'It's too late. Just help me here.' She sat with her hand still in the cervix pushing against me. It felt odd and very uncomfortable.

When I commented on this she said, 'Yes, I know. One woman nearly kicked me off the end of the bed when I did this to her, but it will make it easier and stop you tearing. I'm holding the baby in. You were right, but you would have torn badly otherwise.'

Michael came rushing into the room while the sister was still holding the baby inside me, only just in time to see Kahlia born. The timing had echo's of Azaria's birth. He'd been held up at the lift and if the doctor hadn't come along he wouldn't have been there at all. No wonder Dr Mouncie wasn't there: he was still squaring it with the officer and the superintendent!

When Kahlia was born Mrs Yardley was as excited as Michael and the sister. Asked by the sister to hold the phial to collect some cord blood, she could hardly keep it still. While the nurse was attending to the baby, Michael picked Mrs Yardley up and swung her around, right off her feet, which was quite uncharacteristic of him. Later on he couldn't even remember having done it. Mrs Yardley was delighted that Michael had included her in our celebration, despite the fact that she was a prison warden. Trying to be as unobtrusive as possible, she then wandered out of the room for a while; she was only writing essentials in the book and being as natural as possible under the circumstances.

I didn't feel any joy—only sadness. I was longing to hold Kahlia, yet I didn't want to touch her because I knew if I held her in my arms she would be more mine than ever, and it would be even harder to give her up. It would be much easier if they took her away immediately and I didn't touch her. The nurse must have sensed that, because she didn't give me any choice. She just plonked that little wet, squiggling, squirming bundle straight onto my stomach. The automatic reaction when something lands on your tummy is to grab it. So there was my little daughter in my arms, whether I wanted to have her or not. The blood from her birth was all over me and my gown and I didn't care a bit.

She was so fat, I couldn't believe it. She had a little double chin and a round belly. My biggest baby: 3.8 kilograms (8-1/2 pounds)! She had got fat—just like me; not the best possible start in life. She didn't look like any of the others at that moment.

Mrs Yardley was pretty understanding. She came back, looked at the baby and retired into the corner saying she had to write her book up. After being so excited and passing all sorts of comments, she settled down and left Michael and me to talk on our own. Then Dr Mouncie arrived. The superintendent had obviously not told the officer on the lift that Michael had permission to be there. It was an old trick. Too late to make amends, they would always apologise profusely and claim a slip up in the system; the orders 'hadn't got through'. Dr Mouncie had to pull rank pretty firmly—*he* was in charge at the hospital and he *knew* Michael had the superintendent's permission. This time they were caught out.

Dr Mouncie administered a few stitches and saw that everything was fine. And, Kahlia had indeed been born before the first shift change.

The first time Reagan saw his little sister was when Michael took the boys down to the nursery and there, in one of the little cribs, they saw their baby sister. Reagan was quiet. Mummy had said his baby would be with her and you didn't collect them from hospital nurseries. He wasn't going to be tricked. That baby had nothing to do with him. Aidan, though, was ecstatic. Here was his new sister at last. Of course it was a girl. He had asked Jesus for one, hadn't he? Nobody could persuade him otherwise.

My parents were in Darwin with Michael, waiting to take his brand-new baby daughter home and care for her. The boys had also come, so they could see their mother and their new sister. It was the first time they would see me since before the trial started, so we had been apart almost three months.

TENTATIVE JOY AT LAST

The bail application came due the day after Kahlia was born and it was held up overnight for a decision, so I had to wait. I didn't know whether to hope or not and after the trial, could I ever dare to hope again that a court might be reasonable? I slept badly, between hope and despair.

In the morning my day guards came on. I still had Mrs Yardley, thank goodness, as the female on duty, and Mr Schubert, a decent male officer. Hospital security was also there—three guards and I was several floors up! The reason there were so many there, however, was to keep others away from me rather than on my account. Prison wardens were usually enough, but the hospital was genuinely worried about my security. There was so much publicity, good and bad.

I was trying hard to pretend it was just another ordinary day when Mrs Yardley came in to say good morning.

'This is the big day, eh! Are you excited, eh, eh?' I just smiled. 'You will be. I am,' she said. I didn't tell her how my stomach was churning and my hands shaking. I had the hospital radio on very low to catch the first news—the press would have it to me sooner than Stuart, who would have to break red tape. I was trying to appear unconcerned by doing crochet, but my hands shook so much I had to put it down and hide them whenever anyone came close or they'd have noticed. I was only pretending to work—I couldn't even get the hook through the loops. There was no news—just because I had access to a radio my case wasn't mentioned, I'm sure!

The phone rang, as it often did. Mrs Yardley came in. 'You got it.'

'Got what?' I said, momentarily puzzled.

'Bail. You got bail.' She did a little whirl. 'Still not excited? It'll take a while for the papers to come through from Sydney, but as soon as they do, you can have your baby back, and Michael can come in. Oh, you'll be excited as soon as it sinks in.' And off she rushed to talk to the guys at the door. She was in a real buzz. I turned to the radio. If it was on there, it must be true. It was at last. I let my breath go in a long sigh. I must have been holding it for ages, surely. 'Thank you, God,' I whispered.

Then I had to wait. Michael turned up unannounced but I wasn't officially free yet, so he couldn't visit. Mrs Yardley told him to talk to her.

Grinning, she said, 'Talk loudly, I'm deaf! Lindy, it's a bit dark in there, I'll pull your screen back in case you need to talk to me.' She continued to smile broadly. At that stage she was far more excited than I was.

We then had a three-way conversation. I asked her all sorts of questions and Michael gave her all sorts of information. She had a ball, and the rules were strictly adhered to. There were flowers and messages for me all over the foyer, too. The afternoon shift arrived at four o'clock with the same story. The bail papers were due at any time. They were taking ages and I was free, yet not free. Mrs Barham rang to check she had packed all my gear—Mrs Yardley handed the phone to me, which was not normally done. Mrs Barham wished me well.

Afterwards, Mrs Yardley said, 'I saw that baby taken off you, eh. I'm going to see her given back. Who cares about overtime pay!' She dismissed the afternoon shift who left reluctantly after a trip with Michael to the nursery. Mr Schubert also wanted to stay. He was shy, but nice. He came and spoke to me for the first time then, as male officers weren't supposed to talk to the female prisoners. He quietly wished me well and I knew he meant it.

The court officers duly arrived. I listened to the bail conditions and then signed. From $5,000 bail and $5,000 security between the second inquest and trial and, once Kahlia was born, no access in prison for a year after the trial. Now I had Kahlia with me and $300 bail. Someone got their sums wrong.

It was over. I was free again, but no one wanted to move. Michael was allowed in and then Mrs Yardley informed me they *all* wanted to see me get my baby back—court officers as well. Heavens! I couldn't get out of it gracefully so off I went down the corridor with a retinue following. Other new mothers gazed as we passed on the way to the nursery. Kahlia was around the corner out of sight in the special care section, where she couldn't be seen during normal visits.

The nurse handed her over, whispering that she had given her extra cuddles while her Mummy couldn't—all her special nurses had. She wished me luck. The others took a peek at my daughter and wished me well, then melted away, leaving hospital security to see us safely back to my room and avoid the press. I thought to myself later how fitting it was that Kahlia had had an Aboriginal nurse as her main attendant.

As soon as I was officially released, Picceen the owner of the Golden Wattle flower shop arrived. She had been a little smarter than the rest of the florists in town, waiting until she knew I was able to have flowers and would receive them, before putting her orders together. If she hadn't been able to deliver she was ready to send me a cheque and a note with everybody's names and their wishes and bouquet instructions. I thought it was a very sensible thing to do.

When she discovered she could finally get flowers through, she tracked down my mother and asked what I would prefer and what my colour schemes were at home. All the flowers came through in those tones except the fresh ones. She had chosen some long-lasting fresh flowers so that I would have some there on the spot, for example tropical orchids, that would travel home with me. Apart from that she had stuffed toys, artificial and dried flowers, chocolates, lollipops and other mixed lollies that she thought would travel well and the whole family could enjoy.

I still hadn't seen the boys because the prison authorities would not let them in while I was in hospital. They had let Michael in a couple of times, but the others would have to wait until I was back in prison. Now with the bail application won, and Kahlia in my room like a normal newborn, Michael brought Mum and Dad and the boys in. There she was, the new, little baby sister with me. I had taken Kahlia out of the hospital gown and put her own clothes on. Aidan was absolutely delighted. He looked at her little fingers and toes and commented on the length and size of them.

Reagan, who was normally more interested in babies than Aidan was, just stood back and looked. I said to him, 'Do you want to feel her little feet?'

'No thank you, Mummy.'

'*Uh oh*,' I thought. I said to him, 'Darling, this is your little sister. Remember Mummy said that she would be with her. Well, here she is with Mummy. Do you understand that?'

'Yes, Mummy.'

'Wouldn't you like to hold her?'

'No, thank you, Mummy.'

I let him be, knowing that he would come round in time. He hurt so much; everything he had been promised had fallen through. He had no confidence any more that people kept their promises. It was easier to stay detached.

When I got out of hospital and took her home, I thought things might be different.

Now I was released on bail, my brother Alex (knowing that he was there on a contract arranged by Shane McGuire of the Murdoch-owned *Daily Telegraph* and *Mirror* to provide information to the press) didn't come in with Mum and Dad on their first visit. He knew before the baby was born that it was impossible to answer most of the press questions about the day and hour of the baby's birth and such things. (I knew the prison authorities were paranoid about anything to do with the press but rejecting a pre-birth visit because of the list of questions Alex had submitted was going overboard especially when he needn't have been honest and told them in the first place.) He would have fulfilled his contract by simply saying that Lindy wouldn't answer this one, she doesn't know that, etc. Now it was different: he knew that we didn't want any publicity about the baby at least until we got out of the state and, hopefully, interest in her would die down (apart from her name and that she was doing well). So he asked my permission to come in. I gave him permission, but said he couldn't see the baby, and I wouldn't tell him her name or anything about her.

The press were not happy with that and, in order to keep his word to me and to them, he could not see me at all before I left because he was honour bound. He would not see me, then lie to them and say he hadn't, so he didn't come in. McGuire threatened to 'throw the book at him' if he caught the plane without giving them the information they required. Alex told McGuire in that case he would miss the plane, check out of the hotel and stay in Darwin. So he did. After the plane had gone he rang McGuire again. This time McGuire said he wouldn't take action provided Alex stayed up there for a while. So Alex remained, knowing I was home and that he lived only a block away from me in Cooranbong. Alex had only agreed to the contract as he couldn't afford to get to Darwin to see me any other way.

As the *Mirror* was one of the papers I didn't respect because of its sensationalist content, I was not surprised by all this. I only felt sorry that it was a week before I was able to see my big brother again.

I think most journalists don't know how to react when they are confronted with a person who gives and keeps their word. It seems to throw them into total confusion. To find a reporter with the same integrity is also uncommon. My dad always told us that 'what the world needs most is men who will be as true to duty as the needle to the pole'. And certainly in this day and age, that is what we need. So many people are spineless, gutless, miserable shadows who no longer realise that a person's word is his or her bond or recognise the worth of a good name.

It was announced in church on Sabbath morning that I was now allowed visitors. Visiting hours that afternoon would be their only chance to see me as we were leaving Darwin the next day. Shifts were arranged in the corridor of about ten at a time, so they all had a chance to talk to me individually, see Kahlia and wish us well for the trip home. It was a wonderful day, but very exhausting. Everyone left at about 3.30 p.m., and the hospital let Michael, the children, and my parents stay on their own for a while. When they left, I gave Kahlia her afternoon feed.

Later Michael returned with Picceen. We had arranged that she would pick up the flowers, fruit, toys and lolly baskets that she had brought and repack them for the trip home. (Somehow the flowers that everybody had told me were in the hospital foyer never arrived. They were supposed to have been checked for bombs and then sent up to me. I didn't even see the cards, so I never knew who sent them and was unable to acknowledge them. Apparently there were also stuffed toys. I imagine they were distributed among other wings of the hospital.)

It took a while to do, and Michael helped Picceen carry it all to her van. By the time they had finished, it was evening visiting time again, so Michael stayed until it was feed time and then left, taking most of the extra gifts with him. The feed was over by 11 p.m. and it took me a little while to pack the rest of the gifts I had received that day into the last suitcase. I had gone into hospital with nothing but my toothbrush, comb, Bible, nightie and brunch coat, and here I was coming out with boxes and suitcases full of stuff. I had my shower and climbed into bed, exhausted, half an hour after midnight.

At 2 a.m. Kahlia woke for her next feed, so I got up, fed, changed, and dressed her, and popped her into her carry basket ready to go. Just as I was about to climb into bed again, the hospital security man stuck his head round the door to wake me earlier than planned. Our contact, whom I will call Footsie, had rung to say he would come early, as there was a photographer down there. It would take us about twenty-five minutes to get down to the exit, so I dressed and we left.

Getting Kahlia and me out of the hospital took on the smoothness of a military operation. They produced a wheelchair for me and I sat in that with a small suitcase on my knee, and Kahlia in the carry basket across the arms of the chair. Away we went, one security man leading the way, the other pushing me. We went down back lifts and came out somewhere in the bowels of the hospital, through boiler rooms and down long corridors where the air was stale. Finally we came out to a loading bay. By then the security men's walkie-talkies had told them that it was raining outside. We were grateful for this because the press photographer who had been waiting all night for a picture had gone back to the corner. Even if he had realised that an escape car was pulling up, he wouldn't have got a very good picture in the rain. Footsie timed it perfectly, pulling up as we arrived. One security man opened the car door, we were loaded straight in and took off past the photographer in the rain. He obviously didn't expect me to emerge from the loading bay and was gazing steadfastly in the opposite direction.

We drove to the house of our friends Liz and John Parry without any hitch at all. As we came around the corner John was waiting to open the gates and let us through. Nobody could see into his yard and the press did not seem to be aware that Michael and the children were staying there. I walked into the downstairs flat where Michael and the children were sound asleep. There I was again, in the room where I had stayed for many weekends during the trial. It was the weirdest feeling. I was in a familiar room, but in unfamiliar company; instead of Michael and I on our own, the boys were there. It was the first time they had been to Darwin. I had a new baby at my feet and family luggage was strewn from one end of the room to the other.

The dawn light was streaking the sky as we arrived. I walked over, kissed Michael and he woke up. He was going to wake the boys, but I told him I had only had about two hours' sleep, and wanted some rest while the baby was still sleeping. They would wake soon enough; we had to go home that day.

I managed about half an hour's sleep at the most, then everybody started to stir. The boys realised I was there, the baby woke up and so did the rest of the household. Everybody was excited because we had not seen each other in a natural situation for so long and, of course, we were travelling home on the plane with a new baby. I set about repacking the cases, and just as well I did; there was so much stuff I had to sit on the cases to close them. What with people dropping in to say hello and packing the cases, I finished just in time to load them into the van for the plane.

Mum, Dad and the boys went to the airport in the car and we took the van. We couldn't be seen with the gear in the back and we were fairly low down. Footsie had arranged for us to arrive early and drive directly to the plane steps, so we were able to park with the doors of the van facing the plane. The van gave some protection against the media who were lined up at the departure area waiting to take photographs of Lindy with her new baby. I managed to arrange the little quilt cover of the carry basket over Kahlia's head so there was only a tiny bit of black hair showing.

We walked straight up the stairs into the plane and sat down. There was little opportunity for photographs at all. We had arranged for Greg Cavanagh, our Legal Aid lawyer, to travel back with us to fend off the press. Kahlia and I took up the very back three seats of the plane next to the toilet. I sat next to the aisle and she was strapped on the two seats beside me. Greg was in the seat in front of me and the boys, Michael and my parents took up the rest of that row and the next. This kept us as far away from prying eyes as possible. The only people who would walk past us here were those who were going to the toilet. We recognised all the members of the press, and as soon as one of them got up to walk to the toilet, Greg, who is about 190 centimetres (6 feet 3 inches) tall, would get up and lean right over me, ostensibly talking, so that those with cameras didn't have a chance to take a photograph. All they would get was the seat and Greg's back.

Kahlia slept right through, except when she woke for her feed during takeoff. I fed her, feeling quite safe because everyone was safely buckled in their seats. She fed hungrily and quickly. Because I had not fed her for the first few days, my milk had

had plenty of time to come in and I was hard and sore. She was starting to feed quite well but as she got bigger she was getting stronger and hungrier and she latched on hard. I noticed when she finished feeding that she had blood around her mouth and checked to see whether my nipples had cracked. I couldn't see anything and decided that she must have bitten the inside of her mouth in the turbulence of takeoff. Having had a good feed, she soon fell asleep.

Michael turned around casually and said over the back of his seat, 'Oh, by the way, we are moving tomorrow.'

I said, 'Oh yes, where are we going?'

He replied, 'Down by the college.'

I said, 'What do you mean "down by the college"? Do you mean moving house?'

He said, 'Yes.'

I said, 'No way. I'm not. I refuse to move.'

'It's a condition of bail,' he told me. 'You have to go down beyond the security gates. You are, and that's all there is to it.'

I fumed silently the rest of the way home. Hadn't they done enough already to our lives without this disruption? It seemed I'd only just got things straight from our last move. Oh well, move number thirty-four coming up!

The rest of the trip was uneventful; Kahlia was invisible inside her basket as we walked through the Sydney airport buildings and out to the car.

Hardly had we got into the car than Kahlia woke up again. We had arranged for two cars: Michael, Kahlia and I were in Ron Craig's car with Greg Cavanagh; the boys, Mum and Dad in another. We were hoping to avoid the press, who were waiting for us.

When I began to feed Kahlia I realised where the blood was coming from; she had sucked so hard she had cracked both my nipples and I was bleeding badly on both sides. We decided that Mum, Dad and the boys should go on ahead while we stopped off at the Sydney Adventist Hospital for medical attention and hopefully time on a breast pump to help my milk start flowing and reduce some of the inflammation and engorging due to Kahlia's absence during those first few days. It turned out to be a lot more difficult than they thought. Although my milk supply was good, it never expressed easily. They had to put the electric pump up on a high setting in order for me to get relief. As the sister in charge was concerned that my breasts were still so engorged with milk after the use of the pump, it was decided that I should take one of the spare ones home. I was given dressings and spare bottles of milk as well.

Kahlia was, after all, a hungry five-day-old baby and the quality and quantity of breast milk changes with the baby's age. I had to put my expressed milk into bottles, leaving the cracked nipples to heal quickly, and then wean her back onto me. (The process was time-consuming, but it worked.)

On the way home, we stopped at Stuart Tipple's house in Gosford and had dinner. Here we parted company with Greg, who was to stay with Stuart and return to Darwin in the morning.

While we were there Stuart rang up to see how things were at college and was told the place was still staked out by the press. We were advised to go to our house via one of the neighbour's driveways. I said to Michael,

'There is no way I'm going to climb over back fences with stitches from a new baby. We'll drive up to the front door, hop out and walk in quickly.' This was going to be the last night in that home, and we had been happy there.

Shortly after Kahlia was born, we had a letter from Bill and Judy West. They wrote:

> It came over the news yesterday that your new babe has arrived and I do so much want you to know that our thoughts of love and a boundless joy are with you and Michael and the boys to have a new baby girl to share your life. I know how truly you are a beautiful and loving mother and how truly lucky the new one is to be born into your care. Michael and the boys must be so proud.
>
> My heart is aching for the inhumanity of men. And as abyss after abyss has opened in front of you, I pray in my heart that your courage and faith and trust are as unwavering as ever . . .
>
> Catherine loved seeing you again for the brief ten minutes [on her way out of court after testifying at the trial—she was only about fourteen then]. She said it was beautiful to feel your warmth and aliveness again. It was just so beautiful to see you and Michael. Nothing changes the inner truth that is really you.

That letter meant a lot to me. Here were three people who had been through so much with us, who had been present on the night Azaria disappeared, reaffirming their faith in our courage. It helped to offset some of the dreadful T-shirts I had heard of, worn of course by Territorians: *Watch out, Kahlia, Mummy's coming home.*

Home But Not At Home

We arrived at the college at one in the morning. Stuart had seen my point about climbing fences with stitches. After discussion it was decided that we should stay in one of the college guest rooms overnight. Mum and Dad had gone ahead with the boys and had already put them to sleep in one of the rooms and had a room ready for us. Dr Jim Cox, Mum and Dad had persuaded an excited 'welcoming committee' at the college that I was absolutely exhausted. It would be a couple of hours yet before we arrived, so they should go to bed. They left messages and went. I was so glad when I was told as I was ready to drop.

We walked in and put our things down. I washed my face and started to prepare for bed when Kahlia woke for her feed. Michael went to sleep and I sat up feeding Kahlia. Of course, when finished I had to use the breast pump. This meant that each feed took about an hour and a half because it was like double feeding. At 3 a.m. I climbed into bed; by 5 a.m. Kahlia was awake for her next feed. I gave her the next feed and used the pump again. By this time I felt as if my head was floating away from my body because I was so tired. I was just about to climb into bed again when Michael's alarm went. He woke up and said it was time to start moving; the students would start to bring our furniture down to the new house at 7 a.m. I just had time to walk down to the house and decide which room was which when the first lot of furniture arrived.

That was that. For the rest of the day, I was kept busy telling people where to put boxes, furniture and arm-loads of things. Several volunteer crews were working. Mum went to supervise at the old house and I didn't even get back to check up.

Unpacking was quite a task. Volunteers were plentiful but somebody had to tell them where to put things, so there was only a certain amount that they could do. Some boxes would be unpacked and put on the floor, which really was more inconvenient than having things left in the boxes. We had to find things and eat as well. Michael's mother arrived from New Zealand and took over the cooking, and my Mum tried filling cupboards in a way that would be as near to my own method as possible—she was the most familiar with my style of housekeeping. Even then I had to shift some things around afterwards. And I had a baby to feed.

The next fortnight was absolute bedlam. People from everywhere were arriving for graduation. The new house had three fewer rooms than our previous place and we had one extra child. Because of the second inquest and trial, we had accumulated many papers and manuscripts and hundreds of letters from supporters, all of which needed filing. Where to put them in that small house was a problem, to say the least. My parents stayed in the college dormitory guest rooms, while Michael's mother shared Aidan's room.

I met Ann Deegan during this time. We found we had similar ideas and she was a big help around the house and in organising everyone and leaving me free. There came a stage, however, when it was impossible for anyone to do anything without me around if I was to find things later. I was also trying to do other things in between.

I was still very independent and found it frustrating to have strangers helping me. I would open a cupboard to put something in and find some well-meaning person had shoved things in there out of sight, so it would look better. It meant I couldn't put anything in that cupboard until whatever it was came out. I would have it all out, when somebody would come to the door. While I was at the door, someone else would reload the cupboard with whatever they could find. I would rush back to continue my job, only to find that I was back where I started!

After about a week of this, I was just about at screaming point. I didn't want any more visitors, well meaning or not, just family or people who knew me and who could help intelligently, like Ann and her mum, Lois. The last straw came one day when I was feeding Kahlia and Ann came in saying that some students were at the door to help. I said, 'No, thank you.' Ann returned and said they insisted Michael had sent them, so inwardly groaning, I said they could take out all the dead flowers and rearrange the live ones, but they must *not* throw out my orchids. Ann dutifully carried the message.

Later Ann came in and said, 'One girl has now gone, but you are not going to be happy with what the other one is doing and she won't listen to me—she's started throwing your orchids out.'

I stopped feeding, emerged and said, 'Look, please could you leave the live flowers. Take the rest out and make up one or two vases with the live ones. I want the containers saved. Don't put them in the rubbish bin, and please don't throw out those orchids.' She agreed and said she was very happy to help.

Not long afterwards, Ann came in and said, 'You'd better get back out there', indicating the lounge. I came out. Not one live flower was to be seen, just a vase of very dead roses! I had almost $100 worth of tropical orchids that Picceen had packed in Darwin, which would have lasted for at least another month. That student had thrown out the lot! When she walked in the door, I tore strips off her, telling her to get back down to the rubbish heap, find my orchids and bring them back in. The rubbish heap was visible from the kitchen window and I could see the orchids lying on the top. It looked as if she had just thrown them away out of spite; what her motive was I have no idea. She said she would go and get them and I went back to finish feeding Kahlia. When I went to wash my hands in the bathroom, I could see the girl standing by the compost heap doing nothing. After about twenty minutes, she came back in saying she could only find one orchid, which she put in the vase with the dead roses. I had had enough. I told her in no uncertain terms to get out and not to come back inside my door unless she apologised.

Michael returned soon afterwards and I let him have it as well for loading me with useless people. He was left with his mouth open as I stormed off to the bedroom. Later, when I cooled down, I went to see if I could rescue my orchids but they had been scattered across the top of the heap in the blazing summer sun.

It became obvious after a while that some people were genuine in their offers of help, while others had no intention of doing anything, just thought it was the right thing to offer anyway. People like that needed teaching a lesson. The next time a group of ladies from a local do-gooder society arrived offering flowery speeches such as, 'If there is anything we can do, tell us. We are praying for you, dear. You are a very strong lady and you will cope.'

'Why thank you!' I said.

Then they sat there smiling and waited to be entertained. I could tell they didn't mean a word of it, so I thought, Right!

'Yes, there is, as a matter of fact,' I said. 'I haven't been able to do the dishes and the fridge needs cleaning out. If you could do that I would appreciate it very, very much, thank you. Now, if you will excuse me, I am in the middle of feeding the baby.' I left them standing there with their mouths open and walked off. There was nothing for it but to oblige! When the fridge had been moved, the food inside had spilled and set hard when it was turned on again. Nearly an hour later they emerged, saying they had done as much as they could and hoped they had been of service. I thanked them. They didn't offer further help, but left as quickly as they could. I hope it taught them not to offer help unless they meant it after that.

After that, if I sensed people were not genuine in offering help, I made sure I found work for them on the spot, even if it was only sweeping the patio, and left them to do it or squirm in embarrassment. There is nothing worse than falseness. People like that very quickly withdrew and we ceased to see them.

Other women would walk in, apron in hand, sleeves rolled up, and say, 'I've come to help, I have an hour to spare, if there is anything I can do. If I'm a nuisance, tell me and I'll stay out of your road. I just want you to know I am here if you can use me.' That help really *was* appreciated. If I was feeding Kahlia, some started of their own volition washing dishes, making beds or doing the obvious jobs that didn't need my supervision.

Being very independent I had quite a battle convincing myself that allowing people to help me was not a confession that I couldn't cope, because the situation was so abnormal. I was coping with ten times my normal workload and still expecting to do it on my own. That was unrealistic of me. I had to come to terms with the fact that people I had helped before now wanted to do the same for me. I had to learn to take as well as give, and to do it graciously without feeling I had to embarrass people by paying them or giving them something in return. That was a difficult lesson for me. For a while I felt guilty about babysitters and sharing the housework. Even now, when things blow up again, journalists ring, visitors call and the family wants attention, I have to tell myself it is all right to ask for assistance.

Many people called round with large quantities of food during this time: hot meals ready to eat, or meals to heat up or freeze as was necessary. It was a marvellous help and one of the reasons I would be able to start my next year at college on time and still handle the work at home.

Mum said she had someone she would like me to meet. Not more people! I sighed.

'Yes, I know what you are thinking but you will like this one and she has been so lovely to us. She said you haven't met.'

A couple of days later Mum came down the hall and said, 'I have someone special here to meet you.' Jenny's smiling face came around the corner.

'Hello, I'm Jenny.' She appealed to me straightaway. She often popped in briefly but never stayed long enough to be in the way.

The second time I saw her she casually asked what I was wearing for Michael's graduation. When I said one of my maternity dresses I supposed (I hadn't lost any weight yet), she snorted and went. Friday night before graduation, Mum brought a shopping bag into the room where I was feeding Kahlia. Jenny had dropped it off and left. It contained two dresses on approval, one of which I was to choose for the graduation. One was a perfect fit and colour (she didn't even know what colours or styles I liked and had just guessed). I proudly wore it on graduation weekend.

I have since wished that I kept a register of visitors by the door; I kept a rough daily tally though and I saw more than 2,000 visitors in the first fortnight, an average of 143 per day. I know more called during Kahlia's feed times but were unable to wait, so I didn't see or count them.

Peter Stojanovic rang the college so regularly to locate us that finally they told us, 'Look, we've got the Yugoslav Adventist pastor from Melbourne on the phone. He is really persistent. He sounds very nice. He has been doing petitions and all sorts of things for you and they are coming through for the weekend, and they want permission to drop in and give you something they have from the Yugoslav churches in Melbourne.' We had had a number of messages from the Yugoslav churches and always found them to be very supportive.

Although we had had countless people through and were trying *not* to book ourselves up, we agreed that Peter could have our phone number. He sounded fine on the phone and told us that he was going to bring us, among other things, one of their special national cakes.

I didn't think much more about this until one day a tall guy knocked on the front door. He was large by any standards, not fat then, but tall and broad, the type you wouldn't want to pick a fight with. He had a cheerful manner and happy nature. Then we realised he was *the* Peter. He explained that his brother and both their wives were in the car and asked whether they could come in.

Danny and his wife, Dusanka, were more voluble than Peter, but Pete's wife Mary sat fairly quietly, contributing a little more as time passed. They handed us various gifts from people: small, handmade items for Kahlia; some envelopes containing money to buy things for Kahlia, Christmas presents for the boys or us. They were gifts from Pete's churches to tell us that they loved us and thought of us.

Then came the *piece de resistance*—the cake. It was about thirty-eight centimetres (fifteen inches) round and about ten centimetres (four inches) tall—a special walnut cake that did not keep out of the fridge. They told us they had spent two nights travelling up from Melbourne to Cooranbong and had had to choose their motel rooms according to the size of the fridge to accommodate the cake! It was wonderful: rich and delicious. After we spent a couple of happy hours with them they left, giving us hugs all round.

From then on we got frequent calls and occasional letters from Pete to see how we were going and to let us know they were still thinking of us. It wasn't, however, until much later that we really got to know them.

My feeding problems with Kahlia still took up ten to twelve hours per day. I soon learned not to be shy because people I knew really well just walked in while I was feeding anyway, but I kept strangers at bay. The nervous tension was enough without that added strain during feed times. I had to use the breast pump for nearly a month before my breasts had healed and I could send it back to the hospital.

Reagan, meanwhile, would still have absolutely nothing to do with Kahlia. He would get me a nappy or bottle when I asked, but would refuse to have any physical contact with her, although she shared his room.

One morning after a particularly heavy night with Kahlia I was really tired. The first thing I knew was that one of the boys was standing at the bed saying, 'Mum, bubby's hungry. You'd better feed her.'

Normally I gave her a 5 a.m. feed and would then go back to sleep. Aidan would wake for school and get up. Being an early bird in those days, he would get Kahlia up and play with her. When she was getting hungry, he'd cart her in to me and unceremoniously dump her beside me to feed, which I would; then we would finish getting ready for school, and off he'd go. This particular morning, something was different. I fed Kahlia, changed and settled her and went straight back to sleep; it was a weekend and I didn't have to get up for school. At about 8. 30 a.m., I woke and thought,

'I'm sure it wasn't Aidan who brought her in this morning.' So I asked Aidan, 'Did you bring bubby in?'

He said, 'No. Reagan did.'

That's what I had thought. So I said to Reagan, 'Did you bring bubby in this morning? That was good.'

He said, 'Well, she was making a racket, Mum, and I was trying to sleep, so I thought I'd take her in to you.'

I left it at that, but grinned to myself. He had had physical contact with his sister for the first time. After that, he would pick up her toys and put a bottle in her mouth when there was no one around to 'cut the racket' she was making. Slowly but surely he came to accept Kahlia, to play with her and enjoy her company. The relationship between Reagan and his new little sister was starting to blossom at last, as it once had with Azaria.

By now things were beginning to be fairly normal. We had settled in properly although after the other house, it was like living in a shoebox. Things were stacked on top of one another; it was what one would describe as 'over-cosy'.

When we were free of visitors, I spent the Christmas holidays trying to finish the college work I had missed because of the trial and I had almost completed it when the new college year started. By the time college started I still had a number of things to do, but I knew that I basically had things under control.

I took Kahlia along to lectures with me in her pram. When she got hungry, I sat at the back of the class where I fed her, using the tape recorder to tape my lectures. She was very good, sleeping when she was tired and just making a few noises when she was ready for her food. She popped her head up, looked around and watched the lectures with great interest, drinking it all in, following the different people as they spoke in the discussion groups and obviously enjoying everything. She still loves people and is very outgoing and outspoken.

When I was granted bail, the Northern Territory government made it quite clear that this had happened only so I could make arrangements for Kahlia, but that I would soon be back in prison. All the time I had in the back of my mind the knowledge that all their threats had been carried out so far, despite the fact that I had been through a number of courts at different levels. It almost seemed that they had some way of regulating those courts.

We now had greater access to exhibits, but they were in Canberra in the custody of the High Court. This meant we had to arrange trips specially so our program coincided with the availability of a court official to supervise them. Our men worked feverishly and I fully expected to win our Federal Court appeal, nevertheless I knew I had to consider the alternative. I was careful to ensure that Kahlia was used to a variety of people so that, if the impossible happened and we lost the appeal and I went back to prison, she would not be so traumatised. When she was awake, I let her be handed around in class and cuddled by various people. It helped her to be a very outgoing baby and stopped her from being shy and clinging. As she was quiet and a delight to be with, the other girls at college enjoyed this, and visitors came through wanting a cuddle also. I did not allow her to be disturbed if she was hungry or tired, however, so her routine was not interrupted despite this.

One of the things we probably enjoyed most was the pottery studio. She was fascinated by watching the clay grow to various sizes, being pushed up, pulled down and changing shape on the wheel as I worked. Occasionally she managed to grab some clay. Then followed an interesting spectacle of me with clay-covered hands trying to rescue the clay from her and stop her eating it or getting it all over the place.

I enjoyed the freedom of mind that the task gave me. Immersing myself in an enjoyable activity, I could blank out everything else and didn't have to think about the traumas I had gone through and those that might be coming. During the time before the second inquest the studio was perfect; although I was not deliberately hiding, the press never discovered I was a fine and applied arts student, so did not look in those departments for me. The art area was away from the other classrooms and people unfamiliar with the college were unaware of its existence.

The food lab was also out of the general way, so both of my majors were in rooms that were in basements and virtually invisible from the road.

Because of the stir over my parole, the district officer, John Duffield, assigned himself as my probation and parole officer. Instead of having me call into the parole office, where other parolees and staff members would be curious, and which the press could stake out, he visited us at home. He used to pop in at irregular times, spend an hour or so with us and then go on his way, which saved me leaving the college grounds. He had a timetable and could call in when I was not in classes, or at least know where I was. My bail had stated that I had to stay in my own home every night, which meant I couldn't go away on a holiday. I could, however, go on day trips.

John had been warned by the Crown to beware—they said I was an extremely good actress and that he should be very careful because I would pull the wool over his eyes. This was the initial reason he had decided to come to the house, having used the excuse that my appearance would cause disruption if I went to the parole office. He admitted later that he really wanted to see me at home, in my own home, with the baby there, because I didn't necessarily need to report with her. But if he hung around at home he would see the interaction between me and the baby. Because of the circumstances I would be under more stress with her than I had been with Azaria, so if there were any problems, they would show up. Certainly that was true!

John and I got on very well. We discovered that his birthday was very close to Michael's and mine, and that we are all two years apart in age, Michael being the oldest, then John, then me, with our birthdays all three days apart.

One evening we had visitors for dinner: our friends Gordon and Sally, and another friend, Ted, from Tasmania. After Sally and I had chatted for a while, she asked to see Kahlia. 'Sure,' I said, happily going off to get Kahlia. I discovered that her carrycot was empty. I didn't worry much at first, because I thought one of the children had taken her outside. But Aidan and Reagan hadn't seen her either.

I flew from room to room, my heart pounding in my throat. It was only a small house, with five rooms and a hall, and yet I couldn't find her anywhere. I searched thoroughly, then told Michael I couldn't find Kahlia. He said, 'Oh, she's around somewhere' and went on talking to our friends. Like Azaria's, the carrycot was empty! I wanted to vomit.

That absolutely finished me. My legs almost buckled, I fled to the bedroom, shut myself in and collapsed on the bed, shaking and crying. Michael came in, took one look at me, and said, 'Oh, you're *really upset*. I'll have a look.' And he hurried out, very concerned.

I stayed there, unable to move. About five minutes later he returned, carrying Kahlia. He explained that Ted had picked her up and had been sitting outside nursing her while he talked to the other children who were playing. In the stress of the moment, I had forgotten Ted; I thought he and his kids had gone home. It was all right.

But I knew, straightaway, that if anything happened to Kahlia or the boys—whatever it was—I'd be blamed for it. Nobody would believe it was an accident. So, from then on, I was very anxious about where Kahlia was and I had to know at all times. When I had to leave the house, for whatever reason, I worried constantly until I got back and saw her. And the same with Reagan and Aidan. I simply couldn't face the thought of what the media and the public would do or say to me if the slightest thing went wrong.

Now, all the time I was home on bail, I had to fight the feeling that something dreadful was about to happen to Kahlia, and I would lose another daughter.

Michael's birthday drew near so I gave him a surprise birthday party a little early, which he enjoyed. He wanted to make it a double birthday party, but I just didn't feel in the mood. For my birthday a few days later Michael decided to surprise me. He asked me whether I wanted a birthday party. I replied, 'No, I have had enough of people at the moment. I would prefer a quiet family day.'

When the day came nothing went right. Michael was flurrying here and there and obviously keeping secrets; I was trying to get things done to no avail. Ann had invited us over for dinner that night and, although I really didn't want to go out, I agreed to go provided *nobody* else was there, because I felt I couldn't face any more people. I just wanted to be quiet and alone. She promised, but I was a bit suspicious, saying, 'Are you *sure* nobody else is coming? It will just be us?'

'Yes, yes, that's fine,' she said.

'OK,' I said, 'but if anybody else does turn up, I'm going home and I want you to understand that. I can't handle people at the moment.'

'Fine, that's all right,' Ann and Michael assured me.

I worked flat out all day and was looking forward to a relaxed evening. But no, it wasn't to be. Kahlia was difficult and the boys weren't cooperating. When Michael came home late, I was in the bath. I said,

'Hurry up, we've got to go. We've got fifteen minutes.'

'Well, I have to go out for a minute. I've got a couple of things to do,' he said.

That was almost the last straw. We were going to be late for something again and I'd be blamed. I said, 'It's my birthday and you promised to be here early for once. What's holding you up?'

'Oh, I can't tell you.'

I had had enough of his secretive attitude, as it usually did not mean a happy ending. This was looking the same.

By this time I was so wrought up I burst into tears. I said, 'I'm not going. You can go on your own tonight.' Then Michael snapped at me, which only made me more upset. All I wanted to do was crawl into a corner and sleep, but there was too much to do. He said, 'All right, I'm not telling Ann. You will have to tell her yourself.'

And then he finally dropped the bombshell. About fifty people were waiting for me at Ann's. That made me see red. They both *knew* what I wanted. Both had deliberately misled me and done exactly the opposite to what I asked. I rang up Ann and told her I was not coming. She wanted to know what to tell the rest of my friends who were there excitedly waiting for me. I said, 'Tell them the truth. I'm tired. I had asked for no people. It has been done deliberately to annoy me, and I'm not coming. I told you if anyone was there I wouldn't come, and I am not coming.' I slammed the phone down, went into my bedroom and continued crying.

Michael said he thought I would be pleased. I was sobbing uncontrollably by this time. Everything seemed to go at once. I had been working both ends of the clock and knew I had been very close to the edge. Once I let myself go, I couldn't stop. Now Michael was alarmed and didn't know what to do with me. He disappeared for a while and came back with a couple of my close friends. They came into the room and tried to calm me down, which only made me worse. I started hyperventilating and nearly blacked out. That frightened me and I started fighting for control. I knew if I continued, not only would I black out, but I would break completely. The only thing that stopped me from having a total breakdown was sheer will-power and prayer. They were the only things I felt I had left to hold on to.

As my friend Pauline talked softly and prayed with me, I doggedly held on and slowly but surely managed to calm myself down with God's help. Finally, I was sitting quietly. Kahlia's next feed was almost due and there was no way that I could feed her in that state. I knew she would get extremely bad wind, which was unfair to her, and would only add to my burden when I needed sleep. Pauline rang SOS to Jenny who, because she was also breast- feeding, was able to feed Kahlia for me.

By that time quite a few people had dropped in; about eight of them were with me. A number of my girlfriends (one was a doctor) sat on the bed talking to me, half of them quite upset; a couple of the guys kept Michael company in another room.

We had a scrap tea. My beautiful birthday cake was sent back to our house. That started me crying again because it was chocolate. Michael knew I liked chocolate, but had completely forgotten that while I was breast- feeding I was unable to eat it.

By the next morning I felt much better. I had cried a lot out of my system and relieved much of the tension. I knew I couldn't go back to that state so pulled myself together. That certainly was a party to remember to forget.

Finally all the visitors died down and I tried, slowly but surely, to do those things that can only be done by the mistress of the home. I wanted to have the house totally arranged and spotless, just in case the Federal Court appeal failed and I went back to prison again, as the Northern Territory government had threatened. Stuart had always maintained that if things went wrong I would go to prison and Michael would be remanded on a good behaviour bond because it was extremely rare for both parents to be sent to prison where children were involved. As it had turned out that way, we knew if the Federal Court went wrong once again, I would be in custody and Michael would be out, so I did my best to leave the place so he could run it with as little trouble as possible.

Kahlia—To Love and Cherish

If things did go wrong, we needed someone to care for Kahlia. We knew Michael would be unable to care for her. We discussed a number of alternatives but both agreed our new friends, Jenny and Wayne Miller, would be ideal.

For us to agree was one thing, but we had to ask them, and they already had four children of their own. How do you say, 'Look, I may need someone to look after my baby. If I go to prison how would you like to do it on a semi-permanent basis until I get out again?'

I prayed about it and waited for some opening. One day they called in. Jenny ran in quickly while Wayne and the children waited in the car. Jenny delivered her message, then said, 'You know lady, if anything did go wrong—and I am sure it won't—but if it *did* and you needed someone to care for this lovely pot of jam, we'd have her.'

I was speechless. Here was the answer to my prayer. Jenny continued, 'I just wanted you to know.' I had recovered by then and didn't want to appear too eager.

'What would Wayne say?' I questioned.

'He's in the car. Ask him yourself,' she replied brightly, as we walked out the door.

'Ask me what?' Wayne asked, leaning his head out of the car as he caught his name.

'Jen is just volunteering to adopt another kid,' I joked as lightly as I could. I saw his eyes meet Jenny's and the slight nod in reply. He knew the subject.

'Yep,' he grinned, then said seriously, 'Lindy, what's five when you have four and would like six?' So that was it. Later, when making tentative arrangements, we found they had also prayed about it and hadn't been sure how to offer either.

Meanwhile, college started and I got back into my classes. In April 1983, when I had been home for about five months, there was one day when John Duffield, my probation officer, failed to turn up. I thought he had been delayed and tried to ring him at work and at home to report in, but couldn't get through. The following day, I still hadn't heard from him. I had just completed taking a fourth-year art tutorial class when the lecturer's phone rang. I had moved on to the darkroom for my photography class when the lecturer, Marty Willis, came to get me. He had a very serious look on his face and said, 'Lindy, Michael is trying to contact you urgently. He has some news. You can ring from my office.' I rang Michael back on the internal phone at home (a blessing because we could ring from anywhere in college and find out, for instance, whether it was safe to go home or whether the press was considering another ambush). Michael said Stuart had just rung him to say that the Federal Court appeal finding would take place in two days' time.

I was devastated: here we were again. I told Marty and the look on his face told me he felt the same—bad enough to forget to mark the tutorial I had just given I discovered later, and he'd been pleased with it too. John Duffield had still not called and I was suspicious now. This time, however, I managed to get through and tell him our news. He said that he had been notified himself that the appeal was coming up, and had been told not to come out and see me in case he gave away some information.

I asked him whether he had any indication of the result, and he said he wasn't at liberty to say. I said, 'Well, that sounds as if you know. It's not too good, seeing they told you to stay away, is it? The police are up to their old tricks again, letting us be the last to know anything.'

All he said was, 'Well, let's just put it this way. I would take some precautions.'

'Are you telling me I should pack my case?' I asked.

'I can't tell you that,' he replied. 'But it's better to be sure than sorry.'

I then phoned Stuart and asked him if he had heard any rumours. No, he said, just the date of the finding. I told him what I had gleaned from John and he replied, 'It won't hurt, packing up. It might be a pain, but it'll be great fun unpacking later, and that would be better than going unprepared, wouldn't it?'

So I set about packing my cases. I put in every conceivable craft item I could think of, and a number of items I wasn't allowed, like nail files, but would be able to use occasionally with permission if I brought them in. I also packed a separate case for Kahlia, because I hoped she would be able to come with me.

I let Jenny Miller and Ann Deegan know that they should get ready to come too.

The Law is an Ass—Again

On 30 April we went to Sydney for the Federal Court appeal. We were allowed to park in the car park underneath the court building to avoid the press as much as possible. This was quite convenient, although I learned later they wanted to ensure I did not skip and they could keep their eye on us. We were ushered to a room upstairs and were only there a few minutes when Stuart arrived and told us that it was time to go. Jenny and Ann stayed in the room with Kahlia.

In the lift on the way down we met our new appeal QC, Michael McHugh, who had been acting for us, and our junior, Glen Miller. (John and Andy withdrew so we could criticise them in the appeal if we chose.) Michael and I walked into the courtroom and sat down; the judges entered and we stood and bowed with the usual rigmarole. Chief Justice Sir Nigel Bowen was in charge with Judges Forster and Jenkinson assisting. Sir Nigel Bowen said the appeal had been denied. I was to go back to the custody of the Northern Territory's Darwin Prison. I was to be held for transportation and my bail was revoked. The court burst into uproar and we were whisked out the door.

In just three minutes my life had been rearranged by those same old lies. I was still having that waking nightmare. I walked back upstairs with the police escort, just beginning to feel the shock of what had happened. Ann and Jenny looked at us when we came in. Ann said, 'What, you're back already? Is it over?'

'Yes,' I said baldly.

'How did it go?' Ann asked. Jenny just looked at me and I shook my head, incapable of saying anything at that stage. She immediately knew what I meant and her eyes filled with tears. She started to weep quietly. In the back of the room Ann looked at me dumbfounded and said, 'But they *can't*. It *can't* be over that fast. It's not true.'

By then I had recovered my voice and confirmed it was true and that I had to go back to Darwin again. Ann was beside herself and didn't know what to think or do. Stuart Tipple, who had come up with us, said he would see the other lawyers and would be back in touch as soon as possible. Michael and I were left alone with Jenny, Ann and now two Federal policewomen. Ann was allowed to say goodbye but was told that, as I was now in custody, she would have to leave and I could make arrangements to see her at some other stage. She was so upset she disappeared for several days. Because Jenny was to take care of Kahlia, she was allowed to stay a little longer for the changeover with the baby.

We waited while arrangements were made to get me out to Mulawa, the women's prison in New South Wales, where I was to be held for transfer and extradition to the Northern Territory. The police officer in charge was very matter-of-fact, but tried to be as unobtrusive as possible. A woman doctor was summoned to examine me. She said it was just a precaution because I was recently pregnant, asked if I had had a recent examination to which I said yes, and she went to leave. She had a minor altercation with the officer at the door—obviously she was unwilling to do some thing. She then returned. Apologising, she told me as I had recently been pregnant she really should give me a standard vaginal check. She was very unwilling to carry it out. I later learned that this is a standard examination for all high- security and drug prisoners. Some minor offenders are not searched like that. (They can also, of course, use a mirror and make you touch your toes in case you are anal drug smuggling as well. I think they decided there was no point doing that with me!)

I was told it was time to go. I was not willing to hand Kahlia over, because we wanted permission for her to go with me. So we waited. Michael and I had both agreed, but I knew whatever the decision, one of us would be without our daughter that night.

Finally the news came through that I was not allowed to take her to Mulawa because if I was allowed to have her in New South Wales, that would pressurise the Northern Territory into doing the same thing. New South Wales did not want to encourage a political furore. But if Michael was able to stay close by with Kahlia, Mulawa would allow her in for feeds until we got word for certain. He looked at Jenny, Kahlia's standby foster mum; she nodded. As soon as they said that I could feed Kahlia, Jen rang her husband, Wayne. Their own baby was only thirteen months older than Kahlia and they had three other children as well. Wayne didn't murmur, but immediately took over the role of Mr Mum until she could come home.

Michael said he couldn't handle any more, said goodbye and went for a walk. Then I had to hand Kahlia over to Jenny and walk out of the room without her. It broke my heart and hers too.

It wasn't easy for Reagan either. When we lost the Federal Court appeal, once again those that he loved were precipitously taken from him. I went back to jail and Jenny and Wayne Miller took Kahlia. Even though the Millers lived only a few kilometres away, Kahlia was not with him in his home. He withdrew once more. It wasn't until nearly three years later that people observed that Reagan was once again starting to accept and play with his little sister, so great was his hurt and fear of loss.

The policewomen escorted me to the downstairs car park again and into a police car with three other police. I was driven past the press at the back entrance of the courthouse, but fortunately I was shielded somewhat by police on either side of me. They were packing pieces (guns), I discovered, and seriously worried about trouble. Feelings about the case were running high and no one was neutral. Once again I felt numbness and cold anger, because the lies that the Darwin jury had believed were still there. We had had new evidence about the underdash spray, but couldn't use it because of the way the stupid system worked. If it wasn't in at the trial, we were told, we couldn't use it now. Well, if we'd had it then, we wouldn't have been trying to use it now!

Some media reported that the three judges had found us guilty. They had *not*. They said they had been unable to demonstrate that the jury had made an error. This time it was all based on legal technicalities, not on evidence. An appeal is usually trying to do something when it is already too late, or as Barker aptly put it, 'Trying to kick goals in the moonlight.'

All I could do was say, 'Lord, I know you have a reason for this. I don't know what, but just give me the strength to go through with this until you tell me.'

Here We Go Again

We drove through the western suburbs of Sydney until we reached Mulawa. The police had radioed ahead, the gates opened and we went through. The way into the female prison was then via the men's prison, and you actually travelled through a section of the male prison at Silverwater before reaching the gates of Mulawa. They had already heard I was coming in; the prison grapevine is most efficient. As we drove through, a lot of the guys were out on exercise or work parties. They lined the driveway. They were all supportive. A good many of them were waving, and some called out, 'Good on yer, Lindy! Keep fighting!' or 'Sock it to them, girl!' I found that encouraging. At least the criminals of Australia knew I was innocent. A crim knows a crim—and they knew I wasn't one, and they'd stand up for anyone who would stand up to a crooked system.

The gates of the female section opened. I walked into Admissions, and was handed over to the prison authorities. I was signed for, fingerprinted—for the *first* time in my life—then issued clothes and showered, with none of the standover tactics of Darwin.

The girl on clothing distribution was a friendly lifer whom I was later told was working there because she had killed an infant while under the influence of drugs. Offenders were ostracised for committing crimes against children, and this job kept her apart from the other prisoners. But she seemed a nice girl. (I was told later that it was standard practice for incoming prisoners to jump the counter and 'punch her one in the mouth' for her crime. I was asked whether I had done so. How barbaric!)

I was put in a bleak, square cell, with a handbasin, toilet, cupboard and bed. One window was high up on the wall; the door was thick and solid, with a viewing pane set in it. I was locked in and left alone until the dinner tray arrived. I wandered around slowly. There were magazines here to read at least, a Gideon's Bible and an old *Readers' Digest*. I had been allowed to keep my own Bible and makeup bag also. Toiletries, including deodorant, were supplied, I noticed.

There didn't seem to be much activity around. I looked through the door window. No one was down my end, so I climbed on the bed to look through the other window. As I wasn't tall enough, I climbed up on the old iron bed end and could just see out on tiptoes. Old buildings, some grass, paths and prison fences were all I could see. Voices were coming from two of the buildings (remand and the kitchen, I later learned), but no one was in sight. I climbed down and idly leafed through some of the magazines. I was emotionally exhausted and, after dinner, fell asleep early.

I couldn't believe the clothes I got at Mulawa: two pairs of jeans, two shifts, a long winter dressing gown, a short summer brunch coat, slippers, gym shoes, sandals, four pairs of socks, three T-shirts, a jacket, a choice of nightie or pyjamas, all brand new. Brand new clothes! Brand new shoes! Brand new socks! At Mulawa, you could earn a minimum wage of $4.50 a week and a maximum of $40 if you did piece work in the tailor's shop and were fast. You could do a hairdressing course or a tech course; even an arts course. There were also facilities for day release in New South Wales!

I could not believe my eyes when my food came over. I was served a beautiful vegetarian meal and given a bagful of vegetables as well in case I didn't like the meal and wanted to cook my own as an alternative. All the vegetarians got that; very different from the 'eat it or leave it' junk I had received in the Northern Territory. I was informed that the officer usually in charge of kitchens had broken her arm and that the meals were coming across from the men's side. They apologised for the fact that they were so awful and told me that the meals would improve once they started cooking their own again. There was no need to apologise; if they set eyes on the slop Darwin served, they would realise why I appreciated the meals so much.

It was a relief to me to be able to stagger Kahlia's feeding from Jen to me, so Kahlia had no ill effects and I was able to dry my milk more slowly. An instant cut-off once was enough, and this made twice.

Jenny was absolutely marvellous. Kahlia had been demand fed, and now we had to set feeding times for the prison, so if Kahlia's bedtimes were irregular or she woke up during the night, Jenny would feed her on demand; otherwise she would hold her off until she could come in to me. Jenny did the late-night feed, and if Kahlia woke too early in the morning, she would give her a little feed before she came in, and the officers would give me a message not to expect a full feed. When Jenny returned home she breastfed both the babies until she weaned her daughter, Tiana. No wonder the little girls are now so close. It takes a very special lady to do what Jen did. Not everyone could do it. But Jenny did, and Wayne supported her. Thank God for the dedication of two Christian parents who were willing to do this for me.

One morning at Mulawa I was roused at about 5. 30 a.m. and told to shower across in the office block. Something was happening in the reception area that day, and obviously they wanted me out of the way for the time being. Grabbing my clothes, towel and makeup, I stumbled out of bed three-quarters asleep. When we arrived (I was escorted by a male and a female prison officer) there was not a soul in sight, the door was unlocked and I was told to go in alone. The female officer looked amazed at her male counter part, but was assured it was OK, so didn't say any more. I had no watch, of course, so I didn't know the time but I know I spent a long time under the shower, washing and blow-drying my hair, and putting my makeup on. Still nobody appeared. I thought I'd have some breakfast, so I cooked eggs and tomatoes on toast from the officers' fridge, having been told to help myself and eat anything that was in there.

A male prison warden finally appeared on boundary duty outside. Every time he came past, he got closer. Then he came right over to the window to look in. I turned my back to him; I had had enough of being stared at. I kept my back to him whenever he got close. He was getting frustrated because he obviously wanted to see my face. Finally, as I was sitting at the table, head down, almost asleep, the assistant superintendent arrived.

The male officer came right up to the window to have a look through then. She saw him and said, 'What's he doing there?'

I said, 'Oh, he's just perving. I feel like pulling the blind down.'

She said, 'Well, I am going to pull it down' and she did, right in his face, which must have annoyed him. Later she told him off.

She took one look at me then and said, 'Do you want to go and lie down upstairs? You might as well sleep as stare at walls.' (Girls often have that sleep reaction after court.) I said, 'Thank you.' So I went upstairs to what turned out to be the disused mother and child section of the prison.

It was like an ordinary house. I wandered around and saw the empty cots and beds where former prisoner mothers and their babies had been allowed to cohabit. That was another slap in the face. It was kind of them to send me upstairs, but I wished I really hadn't seen it because it only brought home to me what I did not have. I then slept for hours, waking only for lunch before sleeping again.

I had tried everything, and so had Mulawa, to get permission for me to take Kahlia to Darwin with me. It *had* been done before, I knew. There were facilities up there, if necessary, and right or wrong, I wanted Kahlia with me. So often when we think we know what's best, God lets us struggle on our own until we decide to let Him do things His way. Once again I found this to be true. I'd struggled and prayed so hard and I had been notified that sometime that day the answer would be coming through. Once again Kahlia was brought in for me to feed. Michael brought her to the gate and the officers brought her over to me. I wouldn't see Michael again until the night feed. Just before I got her, the superintendent, Mrs Storrier, said to me, 'Well, there's still no news.'

I had the feeling that this might be the last time I saw Kahlia and certainly the last time I saw her alone. I knew I was due to be sent to Darwin the following day. I had two more feeds, that was all. And so I prepared to enjoy the time I had with Kahlia as much as possible. They called me to tell me she was there. I went downstairs and got her, and took her upstairs. I was grateful then to have the top, empty part of that old house. No one disturbed us; there was none of the Northern Territory suspicion, and the constant surveillance here. I sat alone with my baby and fed her.

I had wanted to have Kahlia dedicated, but Michael didn't want that until after our names had been cleared and the press lost interest. He had been quite confident that the Federal Court would do this. I had learned to be much more sceptical where the Northern Territory government and legal system were involved. I wanted Kahlia dedicated like the others while she was still little and we had the chance. I was quite happy to have a private ceremony, but Michael wanted to celebrate. Well, there wasn't going to be any 'later'. Either he dedicated her without me or we waited an indefinite period of time; I didn't want to do that.

I decided there and then that, although there was no church, or minister, I would dedicate my daughter myself. As I held her in my arms and prayed to God, promising her life to Him and asking that He would look after her as He saw fit, peace came over me. No longer was I asking that He make the way clear for me to take her north, but simply that He did what was best for her. I knew He would. I knew I was prepared to accept now whatever answer came because it would be right for her. My heart was at peace because I knew I had promised to leave her life in God's care and He had promised me that He would look after her, do what was best for her and keep her safe.

I had just finished my prayer when I heard the phone ring. It came to me that that was the answer. Now I had committed Kahlia to God and was ready for whatever happened, the answer came through. The prison officers called up to tell me that feeding time was over; I finished changing Kahlia and went downstairs. I asked if there was any news. Mrs Storrier looked at me and said, 'Not yet.'

It was time to go back to my cell and for the first time I was allowed to carry Kahlia back to the gatehouse myself. On the way back past the kitchen block the girls saw us coming and all lined up to wave and call out their best wishes.

Every meal so far, I'd had smiling faces, and one- or two-word messages to cheer me up. They would have got solitary in Darwin for that. The kitchen officer, as she brought my night meal, told me that they had been thrilled to see me with the baby. They had watched Kahlia's progress to and from feeds every day, and that was the first time they'd seen us together. They were very happy about it, and they hoped everything would be OK for me. I found none of the animosity I had been told to expect.

I had my meal and then Mrs Storrier came in. She said, 'Well, the news has come through. They've said no, love.'

I said, 'That was the phone call I heard, wasn't it?'

She looked at me and said, 'Yes, it was the phone call.' I knew God had let me come to the decision to accept His will before He let me know.

Many times, later, in Darwin when I discovered more fully the rules they had for children, I realised what Kahlia had been spared. Although they had the facilities for a fairly normal life in that section, they were so paranoid that Kahlia would have been locked in the cell most of the time. We would not have been allowed outside in the grounds at all. She would have been kept virtually a prisoner inside. She would have been allowed a minimal amount of nappies, toys and clothes. Certainly she would have gone through the regulation quantity of nappies in about ten hours, judging by her standards at home, unless she was left wet, which I didn't like the thought of.

I was more and more thankful that God in His foreknowledge had not allowed me to have my own way. I also realise she was very much an anchor for Michael and a tie to me through her. She helped keep him sane.

When I was told about Kahlia, I managed to keep a brave front. Mrs Storrier asked me gently if I was all right and when I nodded, she said, 'Tonight will be the last feed. You will be going to Darwin early in the morning, and that will be your last visit. We've told your friend Jenny and your husband that they can have a special last visit tonight. We'll give you a short time to visit, then you can feed the baby, and later you can have some more time with your husband.'

That last feed I gave Kahlia was a very difficult one, to say the least. I had to contend with my own feelings about having her separated from me again, knowing that I would miss all those milestones mothers love: her first words, steps, teeth, etc. And what about the boys? Would they be all right? How would they cope with Michael bringing them up on his own? He wasn't used to babies, doing housework, and being with the children a lot. That was my job.

I might not see any of them until the children were almost grown up, at least until Kahlia was a teenager. I felt helpless. That ache will never go. No one, nothing, can replace that. For quite some time I blamed the jury.

Jenny, Kahlia and Michael came in together. I was determined to be calm and brave. We had a quiet visit. Michael played with Kahlia, while Jenny and I swapped last-minute details, then they left while I fed Kahlia. During the final feed I was concerned that the tension and pent-up emotion might affect my milk flow, giving Kahlia bad wind. If there was one thing I didn't want to do, it was to upset Kahlia.

I was glad of that last time on my own. I stayed as long as I could. Kahlia rolled over on her tummy and raised herself up on her hands and knees, rocking, trying for that first crawling step, and nosediving as she failed. I picked her up and wandered to the door where the others were waiting. Michael came back and the three of us shared our last visit. It was short and painful as I tried to hide my hurt. Time had well and truly run out.

Although it was out of hours, Mrs Storrier came across from her home specially for the visit; she had been waiting in the other room. Jen was with her. I handed Kahlia over to Jenny and we just looked at each other. I bravely watched them out of sight, my baby's face over Jenny's shoulder . . .

I went back to my cell, broke down and cried. Mrs Storrier locked up outside, then came to my cell. She took one look at me, walked across, put her arms around me and held me. I could never be quite sure afterwards whether she cried too, or whether I imagined it, but she said to me at the time, 'Look, girl, we have had many people come through here, and we get to sense whether they're guilty or not. I know you're where you shouldn't be. We wish we could keep you here and we'd treat you well, but we can't. We have to transfer you back. When you get back there, girl, give them hell; they deserve it.'

She told me not to do anything they could put their finger on, but just to keep my opposition at nuisance level, creating subtle hell and staying under their noses till they let me out. If I wanted to transfer back to Mulawa they'd look after me, but I shouldn't say anything while I could be a pain to them because 'If you're under their noses, it's going to be more of a pain to them than if you're down here with us, although it will be hard on you,' she said. Her words proved prophetic.

When you go through severe stress the body finally says it's had enough. Sleep takes over regardless. I was very grateful for that because while I was sleeping I didn't have to think. That night I prayed and asked God to be with me, and once again fell into an untroubled sleep.

I was woken early the next morning to change and get ready before leaving to catch the plane to Darwin under escort. The same Federal policewoman who had taken me to Mulawa from the court once again escorted me north. She appeared brash and mannish with an abrupt manner. I thought the trip would probably be an unpleasant one.

Michael, as he'd left the night before, told me he'd have a surprise for me as I left. Hearing there were some cars around, the police took a disused back gate out. As we whizzed past the corner where the two roads met, the press cameras went off. The police were jubilant they had escaped 'all those sticky noses'. I looked down the road to the main gate. It was Michael with my darling boys and my friend, Ann, who had finally been located. My escorts thought they were so smart. I quietly said as we went past the last lot of press, 'That was my husband and children, with a friend, not the press or a demonstration.' They quietened suddenly and quickly, embarrassed, and remained quiet the rest of the way to the airport, where the press again caught them unawares. It seemed ironic that I'd been whipped away from my husband and children straight into the arms of the press.

When we got onto the plane, I said to the woman police officer, 'Look, I'm sorry you got this job. I know you've got no choice, nor do I, and although I know I shouldn't be here, I am, so let's make the best of this, and try to make the journey tolerable.' She looked at me and didn't say much but obviously agreed. I did my best to make it as easy as possible for all of us. It was obvious that she and the others appreciated that. The police did their best to shield me from the press on the plane. Because they were Federal police and we were on a Federal airline, they could confiscate cameras or film if necessary to protect me. For this I was grateful. The plane trip was reasonably uneventful and quiet; Mrs Storrier had, without my knowledge, organised vegetarian meals for me too.

When we got to Darwin, we transferred to a car and drove on roads I'd often travelled before. I wondered when I'd next travel them free. It seemed so unrealistic that this was to be my permanent home. I hadn't *done* anything, yet here I was. I wondered how others who had also been set up had felt. It was so unreal, it was laughable, yet who was laughing? Not me.

Instead of going to the female section as I had last time, we were directed straight to the main gates. Darwin prison is a harsh-looking place of concrete and brick: high, solid concrete front walls, a great iron door, cyclone mesh fences with razor wire along the top elsewhere. A warder controls the observation tower. During the wet season the humidity is almost unbearable, and the stench from the abattoir across the road adds insult to injury. It was no longer the frightening unknown. I'd seen it all before. This time I was ready for them.

PART FOUR

Prisoner Chamberlain Number 2958

TO LIFE ON THE INSIDE

The huge gate of Darwin Prison groaned upward and we drove into the sallyport. (This was the loading area for all escorts and where any new arrivals were dropped off. The reception and administration blocks opened onto here, and it was out-of-bounds to prisoners at all times except those on work details or passing through under escort. Heavy steel side doors and the huge automatic gates blocked each end of it, and only one end was permitted to be opened at a time.) We got out and were all ushered in to wait in the male reception area.

The male prison wardens, or screws as we called all the wardens, were cocky and rude; they did not like southerners, and the southerners reciprocated. They weren't even offered something to quench their thirst, and when they asked, the screw on the gate said, 'You won't be here long enough, you don't need a drink,' and refused to get them one!

When the superintendent came in, he did not bother to say hello to the Federal police. I had some money and although this had been sealed and signed by Mulawa Prison, he ordered the Fed who was transferring it to break the seal and count it, otherwise he would not accept it.

The Feds soon left and I was taken across to the female section. My old mug shot was still on file, and it would do. I was amused that one of the male screws was ordered to carry the heavy case across for me! Usually you had to carry your own.

The difference between Mulawa and Darwin was very obvious. In the former, I had been issued with new clothes and plenty of them, and good bags to put property in. Up here things were in your own case, a cardboard box, or shoved in anything they could scrounge to go into the storeroom.

My cases had everything imaginable in them: writing, craft, art and study materials including scissors, glue, paints and turps. I had nothing that would deteriorate in that climate, but if things continued to move slowly I didn't intend to be bored. Everything had to be listed individually. The prison officers moaned at the quantity of stuff I had brought, thought of their small storeroom and had the horrors. My subtle nuisance campaign had begun. I grinned because I knew eventually I would get permission to use most, if not all, of it (and I did).

This time round I went through the normal entry: write things in the admission book; go and change; have a shower if you want one (unless you had to use the delousing gunk!); you'll be right—you know the routine. I was left alone, nobody stood over me, and it was a much more pleasant entry than before.

Darwin Prison, because it is located in the suburb of Berrimah, is often called the Berrimah Jail. Berrima Jail (without the 'h'), is in New South Wales and Tapioca, one of the prison officials, got upset if you put

'Berrimah Jail' on your letters. It caused quite a bit of confusion in mail, and sometimes my mail used to go to Berrima and then have to be transferred north. I was told unless I corrected it and corrected the people writing to me, my mail would cease to be sent out. Eventually I complied and put an explanation in one of my circular letters. It didn't make a lot of difference but at least no one could blame me any more. Tapioca did call me in on parade when I got a letter addressed to Her Majesty's Free Guest House! It was a comical card from some apple pickers and it gave me a grin. As there was no signature, no one could be blamed.

When I initially entered prison and the girls realised I had taken my wedding ring off and given it to Michael, they informed me that I could have filled in forms and got permission to wear it after a few weeks. (I noticed one of the others wore her ring.) Forms were something I learned very quickly had to be completed in triplicate for just about anything you could think of. Whether by us or the officers, every detail of life had to be recorded in paperwork. The screws had a day book in which they made running reports around the clock. Routine things like head counts and their rounds were recorded between such things as girls not sleeping at night, or even talking in their sleep!

During my first stay in prison Hypo had been very helpful in explaining the routines and telling me what requests I could make and how to use them. She had explained that we were paid 30 cents per day on ordinary jobs and 35 cents for kitchen or administration cleaning over the other side of the prison. This money was credited on worksheets and at the end of each fortnight, if we were not on punishment with loss of privilege, the sheets were brought in with our daily work tallies and the fortnightly total.

There was a master sheet which listed specified products and their prices from which we could choose to buy. This included pads, pens, envelopes, stamps, shampoo, conditioner, soap, deodorant, baby oil, hand cream, coffee, biscuits, lollies, cordial, cigarettes, Milo and canned drinks. Each item was either one brand or a maximum selection of four specified brands. Four or five days later, the packages would arrive. This engendered great excitement as buys were checked and signed for, one by one, in the presence of an officer.

If anyone had private money, which they had either brought in or had sent by family and friends, they could have a monthly private buy. This was done on a request form in triplicate, which was also used for anything else that you wanted to ask for, or do. Once again, the specified buy sheet had to be used, but this time you were allowed a larger quantity. You could also try requesting items not specified, which *occasionally* you were granted permission to get.

Some craft work was also allowed to be bought from one selected shop, providing it wasn't anything too complicated as the buyer was usually a man. Fortunately, a number of the female screws also did a lot of craft and dealt at the same shop. The ladies in the shop sent out colour sample boards for tapestry, macramé and wool so selections could be made by specific order numbers. Occasionally they also sent tapestry and embroidery catalogues for us. Special occasion cards, some underclothes, makeup and, on rare occasions, plain earrings could be requested also.

Special buys had to be handed in to the office by a certain date each month. The block senior wrote a behaviour report, then forwarded it to the administration chief (one was specifically rostered for requests) and he wrote his report and granted or denied our requests. Then it went upstairs to the deputy superintendent and finally the superintendent who wrote more reports and 'rubber stamped' the approval. Finally the forms were sent to one of the secretaries who had to go and do the buying. Special buys were eagerly awaited and came anything up to three weeks later, depending on how busy the person doing the buying was.

Not until the buys arrived would you know if they were fully or partly approved. If we were knocked back on something, we would wait until a different chief was on duty over the other side and try again. Frequently we were successful the second or third time around, even if we unluckily struck the same chief.

With all this information in mind, when I returned to jail I wore my wedding ring and took cash to buy the toiletries and craft I needed to keep me fully occupied. Almost as soon as I arrived, I asked for a heap of request forms. When you do this, you must state the reason for wanting them and that is also written down. A separate form is required for each type of request. I filled one form out asking for permission to jog; another for a special buy to get shampoo, conditioner and deodorant as soon as possible; a third requesting makeup and writing materials out of my property specifying a little more than the limited amount of makeup we were allowed to wear. You always tried for more than you wanted. The fourth form requested permission to do craft work and had to specify what type and where I got it from. In this case I asked to complete some I had with me. This was quicker than requesting to start some from scratch as they were able to inspect your ability and assess the fact that it was not just an excuse with an ulterior motive. Once you had had permission for craft work, it was then easier to get permission again, as each time you changed crafts or wanted something new out of your property you had to repeat the whole process. Next I requested permission to wear my wedding ring. Amazingly, all my requests were granted fairly quickly, some forms returning the following day.

That evening I wrote:

> My darling family, Michael, Aidan, Reagan and Kahlia:
>
> I finally have my property through so my very first letter is to my darlings. It is hot up here but not too bad—no blankets and a fan till early morning for me. I finished my first full week of work roster and bought myself a small can of Milo with the money (it cost $1. 71 and I received $1. 90) so now I don't have to drink only water—now it's water and Milo! You get barley sugar instead of smokes now but I've only had about five and given the rest away, so I've plenty to spare. I am doing my exercises every night—seem to be losing inches but not weight (yet!).
>
> I wish I could give you all a big hug, but I'm trying to be cheerful. I hope you are all helping each other to be happy too. How's the housework? Beds made for Daddy and room tidy, kids? I hope so. Look after one another won't you. I love you all very, very much, you know. One day we'll all be back together again—Azaria too in heaven. Try to all be good, strong, true

men for Jesus. Give our Princess a big hug and a kiss from Mummy and tell her I love her lots. And one for each of you too.

Love, Mummy

When I asked for my ring, you would have thought I had asked to rob the mint. I was given a lecture on the value of gold, the dishonesty of prisoners, and the availability of a 50 cent ring from K-Mart—we came to an understanding that I was requesting my wedding ring, not a piece of kid's jewellery. I pointed out that as it was to be put on my finger and left there, it would be very difficult to steal without taking me with it. Tapioca wanted to know where this precious piece of metal was. Mrs Barham, our senior, fetched it from her safe and he held it up to the light to inspect it, reading the inscription and commenting that, he supposed that that would identify it as mine. Then he weighed it in the palm of his hand and compared its weight to that of his own ring, which he took off and put in the palm of his other hand. Finally, he estimated its value. I agreed, although he was way off what it was worth. I wasn't going to enlighten him mine was worth over double the value as he probably would have refused permission on the grounds that it was too valuable.

Finally permission to let me wear it was granted. I didn't let on that my hands were still too fat and I would have to put it on my little finger. Ironically, when I finally lost weight, I had to deny the ring was loose. They were worried that if I lost it I might accuse someone of stealing it and they would never be able to disprove that, so I had to sign a release form relieving the prison from all responsibility.

The amount of mail I received when I first went to prison was enormous. A lady called Cath wrote official 'cheer-me-up letters' just to give me a laugh. They were all sorts of funny little 'Pam Ayres with an Australian flavour' poems, anecdotes and stories. In one of her first letters she said that she was overweight and going on a diet, but she had a problem; every time she went to the fridge the Smarties attacked her and she had to defend herself with her teeth!

I shared most of her letters with the whole section and the girls thoroughly enjoyed them. Other people, like a lady called Kyla, virtually wrote diaries, telling me of normal daily things. People who wrote only about my legal situation were all right in small doses, but I wanted to know what was happening in the real world; everyday things, especially if they knew or accidentally ran into my own family and told me what they were doing and saying.

Some letters were sad, telling stories of sorrow and hardship in families where there was controversy, loss or sickness. My heart went out to those people. Some I communicated with, others I was not able to. Always the worst letters to get were those from other prisoners who thought I might be able to help them in their desperate struggle against the law. Usually I was not able to do anything except give occasional encouragement to keep fighting. I'd have to write circular letters again.

Once again I made lists which I sent to my brother Alex who had volunteered to catalogue them. He listed how many times a particular person had written to me and wrote a little relevant information about each. Any stamps sent in I sent out to Alex also. When I wrote a letter, he organised printing, addressing, stamping and posting. He sent out up to 5,000 at a time. Even with a gang of people helping it was a mammoth task, but Alex managed it with minimum fuss and great efficiency. Just one of the many things my big brother did for me while I was in prison.

He even wrote me regular letters—something, like me, he normally loathes. Whenever any photocopying, filing, or stamping was needed for court, I could always count on Alex. He spent many, many hours behind the scenes working alone. Fortunately the press didn't discover that he lived close to us in Cooranbong, so was able to move about freely without being pestered as my parents and Michael were.

In one of the early public circular letters my brother sent out for me I wrote of the parting from my children.

> 30 June 1983: . . . I miss my little family very much. I know they are in good hands though, as Jesus is babysitting for me. Now He's just got four of them instead of one, and their Daddy and friends are assisting Him instead of me. He has other things for me to do right now.

I missed my little family in more ways than one. Kahlia's abrupt removal from my breast had created physical problems. With no daily feeds my breasts had become so engorged that even dressing myself hurt. I asked to see the doctor, but the sister kept saying he was too busy and I could wait. At the end of a painful week Granny, a trained nurse, came back on evening shift and commented on my appearance. She checked me lightly and I flinched. She recommended I see sister and get a breast pump. I told her I had one but wasn't allowed to use it without sister's permission and couldn't see her till at least Monday. She snorted, and, when she realised I had the pump in my property, gave me immediate access to it. I expressed

330 millilitres (11 ounces) of milk and felt much better. In the morning I used it again and almost felt normal. Overall I had lost 35 centimetres (14 inches) from my bust. One of the girls commented I looked as if a steamroller had just run over me. I felt much more comfortable but the large red angry streaks which had been developing took several more days to subside. Later the sister commented she 'knew [I'd] be all right'!

The abattoirs were across the road from the female section and some days the smell was phenomenal. It was particularly bad in the mornings after they had killed pigs all night. We knew the nights they slaughtered, and nobody looked forward to them. We could hear the stun-gun going off at regular intervals all night and if we lay awake, we could count the number of animals being slaughtered, but the nights they butchered the pigs were the worst. The pigs cried when being killed, and the younger pigs sounded like human babies. Even the toughest girls used to jam their fingers in their ears.

The smell was awful. If the wind blew from the wrong direction, not only did we get the smell of the slaughter, but also from the offal pits. When it got *really* disgusting, the officers would complain from their air- conditioned comfort. We girls had no air-conditioning and the smell used to waft in regardless. We had to bury our faces in our pillows to filter it out. Once in, smells would hang around, because the placement of the walls meant wind couldn't readily blow through.

I remember one morning going across to cleaning duty with Froggie. We had been walking around with cloth over our noses and mouths in the section trying to block the smell and, not being able to take these cleaning, we had to use our hands. Froggie started dry retching at the smell. It was at its very worst on long weekends when the health inspector was off duty. If they killed on a Friday night, the smell would linger till Sunday, and was usually gone by sometime on Monday before the inspector started work on Tuesday. Eventually the abattoirs, their offal pits conveniently full, bulldozed them and put new pits much further away, so we only got the smell when the wind was in the wrong direction which fortunately was not often. What a relief that was.

The wet season created a muddy area around the animal holding yards and at one stage a lot of ibis decided that was exactly the place to feed and roost. There were two or three big dead trees that a couple of hundred of them roosted in. Although they looked beautiful perched in the trees, the smell they created was not. The stirred up mud smelt like a combination piggery and chook farm. Eventually a deterrent was used to get rid of the birds.

On one of Stuart Tipple's early visits we discussed an advance plan of action for my case which took in as many possibilities as we could think of. This way Stuart knew what he was to do without the delay of having to continually check with me and communication through the prison where the phone calls were monitored was minimal. Our security was kept as tight as possible, even if it did cause Stuart to be unfairly talked about. I knew Stuart would follow my instructions to the letter, regardless of the personal cost of keeping my instructions and additional information confidential.

Quite often, when he gave an immediate answer, it was taken the wrong way and people got irate, supposing he hadn't communicated with me and that he was making the decision off his own bat.

Also, sometimes the prison authorities wouldn't let Stuart contact me when he needed to, even though local lawyers were allowed at any time of the day (sometimes I saw them call up to ten o'clock at night). Stuart was not allowed to contact me without prior appointments, even when he was in Darwin. The prison authorities seemed to be absolutely paranoid about my southern lawyers so if Stuart wanted to send me any messages for immediate answer without going through the system, we could use Greg Cavanagh, our tall Legal Aid lawyer at the trial.

If Greg was seeing a client and had a few minutes to spare, he often popped in to say 'hello' on the pretext of legal business. He would chat about anything, including the screws and Tapioca. He also kissed me hello and goodbye just to see the disapproving looks on the screws' faces. They didn't approve of prisoners being on normal friendly terms with people classed as professionals, so they tried to maintain his was a personal visit and remove him. He pushed them as far as he could without totally antagonising them. When leaving for further study in England, he came out especially to say goodbye. He said, 'They are standing there like big leeches. Just watch their faces.' Without warning, he picked me right up off the ground, gave me a big hug and kiss, said, 'See you, kid,' and walked off laughing. He always called me 'kid'.

When Stuart was in Darwin staying with Greg and his wife they had some friends to dinner. After a number of drinks, one of the guests, who had an important position in the Northern Territory, became talkative. He said something and added, 'Boy, wouldn't those Chamberlain lawyers like to get their hands on that!' There was dead silence, then Greg said, 'Stuart here *is* one of the Chamberlains' lawyers.' The poor man didn't know what to say.

Stuart laughed as he told me, but he did keep the poor man's confidence. He wasn't one to take advantage of a drunken indiscretion.

Reaping What Was Sewn

Hypo, who considered herself 'head' girl in jail because of her length of sentence and knowledge of the prison system, had her nose thoroughly out of joint now I had returned. One of the other girls warned me that, neatly veiled under a polite exterior, she was as mad as a hornet.

She was a little younger than I, and it rankled having someone claiming innocence in there and saying, 'Well, I don't care what the others do, you may do whatever you like, but *despite* what you think, I'm *not* guilty and I'm *not* going to be treated as if I am, so you will just simply have to put up with it.'

I made it quite clear I would do what I was told by the screws, but I would not be dictated to by another prisoner. It seemed important to Hypo that she be considered the best in everything, and until I came, she was the one to whom everybody (including some officers) turned for assistance—whether in the use of correct English for writing letters, spelling a word, doing some sewing, or any other project.

Now, not only was I continuing to get more mail than her, but far from her being able to teach me to sew, and tell me what to do, I was trained to teach dressmaking and tailoring, and could sew anything I set my mind to. I had just come from tertiary education studies, was halfway through a secondary teaching degree, I could spell and I didn't need assistance with my English. The girls quickly realised somebody else could do things as well as, or better than, Hypo. Most of the girls had already accepted me fully, despite my short time there.

The male officer in charge of sewing machine maintenance 'showed' me how to use Hypo's machine and told me to 'practise'. There was nothing complicated about her machine. We'd had them at tech years ago, breaking down, and this was no exception—she just didn't know how to use it properly. The officer (a tailor) was pleased to find that I knew what I was doing, and was able to fix the machine most times, so he would not be called across constantly. This did not go down well with Hypo.

She managed to get a ruling through that she was the only one who could use that particular machine without special permission, as it was 'complicated'. Others could use the other older machine which they couldn't 'break'. She waited until I started to use 'her' machine as 'practice' after work on some sewing for Kahlia and reported me for using it without permission. The screw blew me up for using it and for doing my own sewing. Of course, being new, I stated that I had permission and when asked who'd given me permission, I told her.

Then she tore strips off me because I had spoken to a male officer, even though I'd had a female officer with me! That officer was now off duty; by the time the two were rostered on together again and she could back me up, the whole issue would have blown over, so I had to sit there and take it. I was told to remove myself immediately and I would be on report in the morning.

I was summoned before the senior next day, in front of Hypo, who denied that the male officer had spoken to me in her presence, so she was told she could go. Then the senior explained quite nicely that male officers had no right to give any of the female prisoners directions to do anything—and he should have at least notified them. (I thought of the absent female screw who hadn't written the instruction down. Was that deliberate too?) I was told until further notice not to touch Hypo's machine, because she was touchy about it. In the past others had broken it, and her work had been disrupted. They would see the male officer next time he came across and maybe get me my own machine also. As far as my own sewing was concerned, although I had permission to do it, and had the ability to use a machine and could use it for prison mending during the day, I had to fill in another request form for permission to use the machine for my own sewing out of hours. (No prizes for guessing who had told me the previous exact wording needed to request permission to sew—omitting the use of the machine!)

It wasn't long before Hypo's machine broke down again (just a little dust in the wrong place). The male officer came to repair it, and was called straight in to the office on arrival. He managed to tell me afterwards that he'd 'been ticked off' for giving me instructions about the machine, thought this was ridiculous, and would see I got my own sewing machine. He said he would send me his own industrial one, and specify it was to be used 'exclusively' by me. He would arrange it via head office as he realised what was going on, but I 'officially' didn't know that.

Half a day later the machine arrived and, because it was so big, it was to be permanently positioned. I was to choose where to put it in the day room sewing corner. There was only one available place where the new machine and the large sewing table would fit. It had good light and, best of all, I had my back safely to the wall. Coincidentally, this spot had the best view of the room, the gate, the office and staff room. As her machine was portable, Hypo was told to move and she now didn't have a good view. The thunderous look on her face told me what she thought about the move and my industrial machine. Her plan had backfired. Most of the girls were delighted and thought she was getting her just desserts.

The commercial machine was a blessing and a curse. It would go at two or three times the speed of any of the other machines. As a result, boy, did I ever have to work! I got through two or three times as much mending in the same time as the others.

I hadn't been there very long at that stage. Many a day I spent inside sewing while the others were outside working on the lawns and gardens, because there were still photographers or journalists somewhere. I had to stay well out of sight, sometimes for a week at a time.

I could well have done with a break out in the sun, but it wasn't to be. I soon became expert at putting zips in the men's trousers. Oh, how I hated putting in those zips—hundreds of them! The germicidal, caustic soda type washing powder worked on the cotton, rotting the seams almost as soon as the zips went in, it seemed.

Mending sheets was another matter. Nobody liked that job. They were huge and bulky in the machine, besides which, when sheets did come across to be mended, they were rotten. I couldn't believe they kept and *used* things that were really even too old for rags! (Seeing they occasionally issued second-hand toothbrushes I shouldn't have been surprised, I suppose.)

No one bothered to tell me for quite some time the criteria by which we recognised whether something could be mended or not. Consequently, a number of the nasty screws took advantage of this and I was given some atrocious mending. Later I realised that it had come out of the 'too hard to be mended' box, and had already been ripped for rags, which was why it was in such a bad state. I was expected to stitch it back together again and turn it into a workable pair of shorts or sheet, or whatever.

After I had been there for over two years and become quite expert at their mending, I decided to time mending one particularly bad pair of shorts. It took me an hour and a quarter. As a point of interest, we had just been pulling a whole lot of brand new Yakka shorts to pieces, because there had been a factory special and we were cutting them down to make smaller sizes for the guys. A pair of those shorts that had been pulled apart and re-cut to make up only took fifteen minutes if you went flat stick, without a zip, and half an hour for those that had zips *and* pockets!

Our uniforms were pale blue, turquoise, or a bilious limey green. When the supplies got impossibly low, the senior ordered some more. Finally they arrived. I walked up to the office and found her mumbling frustratedly. When she looked up to see what I wanted, I said to her, 'You don't look happy.'

She exploded, 'Navy blue!'

'Well, why did you order it?' I asked.

'I didn't. That stupid man got me navy blue. It looks dreadful on my black girls. He should have had more sense.' Then realising I was looking blankly she explained the prison bought end of factory lines, seconds, and samples in whatever colour was available as these were much cheaper. I liked navy—but most of the girls hated it, and it did look awful on the Aboriginal girls. We also thought the style with tight sleeves was unsuitable for the tropics.

Unlike the guys, we all had to wash, iron and mend our own uniforms, and kept the same two until they were paper thin, which took about twelve months. After that we ripped the sleeves out of them, patched them where we could, and used them for gardening uniforms until they disintegrated totally.

Masking Feelings and Fences

With continual media exposure over the preceding years, I had learned to keep my feelings to myself more and more. By the time I got to prison I thought I was doing very well, but in my first three weeks I had learned a lot more about how to control my face. It was necessary: the moment you showed emotion you were vulnerable—to the screws and to the other girls. Weakness or fear shown when relating to another prisoner will be used to their advantage, and if you want to be your own person you cannot afford to let them know anything you are thinking. If you look afraid they will stand over you; if you are despondent, they will kick you in the dirt; if you are elated, they will try to bring you down or use it as an excuse to put you on report. Some screws were the same.

Eventually, people had to know me extremely well before they could tell whether I was really happy or upset about something. Even Michael said he didn't know what I was thinking any more, and when he did try and guess he was usually wrong.

In jail you have to learn at all times to keep a straight face and be like the three wise monkeys: see no evil, hear no evil, speak no evil. Yet you must remain extremely alert, *notice* everything that is going down, and make it your business to *know* in order to *survive*. If somebody intends to report you falsely, you must be able to turn the heat onto them. More than one screw in that jail would ask us to do sewing and later, in a fit of pique, want to report us for some minor thing. All one had to do was drop a word at the right time or place, or just say loudly that the topic under discussion reminded you of a certain occasion, and they would change their minds quite quickly. It was a form of emotional blackmail used right throughout the system and one had to at least know how to use it in return.

A fair cop for something you have done should be taken on the chin, but a setup is something you should fight. I always stood up for a principle when one was involved, even to the point of occasionally getting myself disliked and the officers knew this. If there was anything that was *not* a principle and somebody wanted to break it, that was their business.

After the first few months in prison, setting me up was rarely attempted. When anyone did try they learned very quickly that I fought back with facts opposing their fiction, and *they* would end up in strife as I didn't jump to conclusions or invent things. When I did end up in front of Tapioca, the problem usually worked itself out fast.

Although I was no longer pregnant, the conditions for the first few weeks remained the same as my first stay in prison—inside work and no work on the male side or gardening until things settled down and the press lost interest in me. Every time some new piece of evidence appeared in the paper, one or two journalists would arrive and hang around near the gate. As the interest lessened I was allowed out more, but if I was on a work party and the press were seen, I was under instruction to go inside immediately.

As my story and location became widely known, tourists started stopping off at the prison to take pictures. They would photograph anything and anyone in sight. The prison authorities soon erected a huge sign saying no photographs were allowed to be taken within the prison precincts (as the press already knew). Then tourists stopped their cars near the gate or down the road further, and walked along with cameras in their hands, stopping to take a quick picture then keep going, much to the annoyance of all the girls in the section.

It was like having somebody stand outside the front of your home, take a picture, and then quickly drive on. I always wondered why they wanted to do that and what they would do with the photographs. The Aboriginal girls in particular got upset. Some of them were doing twelve-year stretches, and this was home to them. It was also home to me and the other long-term girls. There was no point in thinking of home somewhere else; that was where we lived, that was our turf, our private area.

The longer I spent in prison, the more I resented outside intrusions of this kind, and the more I understood how the other permanent girls felt. Initially, it was something different, adding an extra dimension to the boredom of life and something to pass the time of day. But the longer I stayed, the more I realised it was simply an intrusion.

One of the screws decided that she had an absolutely foolproof plan for stopping the press and public from seeing me. A piece of shade cloth about ten metres (11 yards) long was stretched along one section of the fence! It stopped us seeing the road from our cells but that was all. We could see through it a bit, but not clearly, and it just made us feel hemmed in even more.

What possessed them to believe that photographers would only stand in that section, I don't know. We heard on the grapevine that it was Rambo's brainwave, so every time she was on duty, the girls made audible comments about the stupidity of the officer responsible for the idea. She would get a peculiar look on her face, but kept silent. After a couple of weeks, Froggie and I had her for office cleaning one afternoon, and decided that it was time to speak.

The prison could apparently be held liable for subjecting me to press coverage, so they were paranoid about it. We knew this time the local press were on the gate because there were negotiations with the prison officers and their union, so it was fairly safe.

As Rambo still hadn't seen the photographers, I said, 'Golly, look at that, press on the gate, and the cloth's in the wrong place. They can see straight down here!'

She didn't stop to think, just looked up, saw the press, rushed to open the gate in a hurry and fumbled it badly. We grinned at one another, then Froggie turned and, very innocently said, 'Do you know who was responsible for that harebrained idea up there? I can't figure out why they thought that would be any protection, because all you have to do is move a few feet to one side.'

'Oh,' Rambo said. 'Well, it was an idea that it would be some protection, but it doesn't seem to have worked and it will have to go.' The guys came over and took it down first thing the next morning!

A Real Head Trip and a Body in the Bed

We had heard of a drug-related murder, but not much more than the fact that a young white woman was involved. One day the woman, Janus, arrived in jail. By the time she had gone through reception, we were all eating dinner. We discovered her table manners were unusual (to say the least) and she seemed to be extremely proud of what she had done. It was then we discovered she had actually shot a guy in the back because she had asked for some grass and he had refused. She told us he had tormented and insulted her by blowing the smoke of his joint in her face, so she had gone and applied for a firearms licence, got it, bought a rifle and ammunition, and asked for instructions on how to use it. She then went home, called the guy's name through the window, and shot him in the back as he started to turn. On numerous occasions when she got annoyed with us or had one of her turns, she would say, 'Well, you're not brave enough to shoot a man in the back,' which invariably left us speechless. (Janus was a certified mental deficient that is lowered mental responsibility not mentally retarded in several states at this time, but not yet in the Northern Territory. They were still waiting on classification for that.)

Janus was extremely artistic and intelligent, a brilliant and informative conversationalist on a large range of current and historically accurate subjects, but she tended to get over-excited and flip easily. Because of this, she was on constant sedation and was awaiting the Governor's pleasure (that is, found guilty but not given the normal sentence due to diminished responsibility). The girls were told that if she got upset when talking to us, we would be transferred to Alice Springs, which we all dreaded, as it had a shocking reputation and was maximum security. Some of the girls had already been there too. Consequently, *any* conversation with her at all was avoided and with the cold war she only got worse.

The girls continually got on her back when they were out of the officers' earshot, digging at her about her murder until they sent her off on a rampage and she would be put on lockup.

Mostly new prisoners were brought in around four o'clock after court finished. One afternoon another new girl arrived, and after reception was brought down and introduced to the rest of the girls. We were all standing around talking while waiting for dinner, and the talk turned to prison escapes, rules, and security. The new girl, Shelion, seemed fairly quiet, but nice. Our section was fairly full at the time and everyone was watching television when Shelion came up to the day room after dinner to have a drink from the water cooler and say an early goodnight to everyone.

This wasn't unusual as new girls had often had a hard time in court or on police lockup. A short while later I was walking out of the day room and Smiley (one of the Aboriginal girls) was returning from her shower when she announced excitedly that a man was climbing in. She was worried that whoever it was might be coming in to hurt us! That thought amused me, but Smiley was quite serious. I checked where she said on the fence and, sure enough, there was something flung over the razor wire that had not been there before. When I convinced her that no one would be stupid enough to climb *into* a prison, she calmed down.

'Maybe it is the new girl's husband come to break her out,' she decided.

'Maybe,' I agreed to calm her. We told the screws that Smiley was serious and there *was* a blanket there. Nearly everyone came to look then, except the screws. Firstly they rang the tower to see if they had noticed any unusual activity, then came and had a look themselves. They went back and told the tower there was definitely something there.

It was obvious to me the only person missing was Shelion, the new girl. She must have done a bunk. Before they decided to keep us in one area, I decided to go down to my cell, which was next door to Shelion's, and check if she had really gone. As Janus was also walking to her cell on the other side, I casually walked with her. As we came to Shelion's door it was obvious she had shaped the bedding to look like a body in the bed. I grinned to myself; this would set the cat among the pigeons. I said goodbye to Janus and turned to backtrack to my cell. As I did she turned to face me and saw into Shelion's cell also.

Suddenly she also realised it wasn't Shelion in the bed and went tearing up to the office, calling out excitedly that the new girl had escaped. I went into my cell, where I would have a good vantage point. Anything to break the monotony. The screws came back with Janus and checked out the cell. Then they finally called all the girls and took a head count. One missing, of course. After that, the tower gave instructions to put us on lockup while the escape was investigated. Being next door, of course, I could hear all the comments as they checked Shelion's cell. The police came later, photographed, measured, checked everything and had a long conversation outside my window before they went to the office to interview some of the girls.

Janus, meanwhile, was excitedly telling her story repeatedly to the police who by now realised that she had worked herself into such a hyped up state she was no longer giving reliable information. At one stage she started telling the police that as I was the last one who had been talking to Shelion before dinner and escaping had been under discussion, that I must have assisted her in leaving. Then she started on what was wrong with the girls' treatment of herself. The screws removed her promptly from the office and we could hear them telling her she would be put in her room on lockup if she didn't stop talking nonsense, and she was not to discuss any of the other girls either.

I thought it was extremely funny as I had heard the police trying to work out how Shelion had managed to scale the sheer brick wall and decide she must have had help from either the drainpipe or a chair. Janus had obviously heard the conversation also, so had solved the problem in her own mind by suggesting I helped. Shelion later revealed she had simply vaulted it. What was even funnier, I thought later, was that she had the nickname, 'the jumper', in another state because she had once vaulted a 1. 8 metre (6 foot) corrugated fence when being escorted to court between two policemen—only to find she had actually jumped into the police compound where all the police were training! That one didn't get her very far!

When the police discovered from Janus that I had actually been with her when she saw the 'body', I was called in for an interview to learn what I knew, which was negligible. But I was able to inform them that Smiley had actually seen her escape, not Janus. They were grateful for the information. (From Smiley they learned Shelion looked like a man, and so she must have been in her own jeans, not a prison nightgown and sandals after all; so they checked her property and found all her clothes missing.)

Later Shelion told me she had not handed her clothes in after registration as instructed. As no one had questioned her, she had thrown them over the inner wall. Later she jumped the wall and sat there waiting for someone to discover she was missing and take her back inside. When no alarm was raised, she dressed, then wandered to the outer fence and waited for the tower to see her and raise the alarm. *Still* nothing happened, so she climbed the cyclone wire fence, threw the blanket over the razor wire at the top, and went over (which was when Smiley had seen her and thought she was a man). There was still no alarm, so she casually sauntered to the main road and hitched a ride to town! She had checked out her friends' places and warned them she was out before the cops arrived, then she went bush. As she was part Aboriginal, or a 'chocky drop', as she liked to refer to herself ('milk chocolate' at that) she had learned all the tribal ways of existing in the bush from her Aboriginal heritage.

Janus, now in her cell on lockup like everyone else, continued to get worked up over the escape and periodically for the rest of the evening called the officers over to demand they call the police back so she could deliver some smidgin of information that she had remembered and needed to pass on. They, of course, refused. By morning she was really playing up and had to be sedated and left on lockup when we were released.

That day we saw an extremely bad mug shot of our escapee, claiming her to be dangerous, part-Aboriginal, and having a blotchy complexion, which certainly appeared so from the mug shot. None of us could even recognise her from it. She certainly did not have a blotchy complexion at that stage without a tan, nor did she look to have Aboriginal blood in her, unless it was pointed out.

Meanwhile we suffered the removal of our two rotary clothes lines from inside to outside the section in case we used them as a jumping off point to go over the wall. (Even Tarzan would have had trouble trying that!) We also had all the beautiful trees in the yard cut down (the screw in the tower said that was the reason he hadn't seen the escape) and gained razor wire around the inner roof of the section above our cell verandahs and along the brick wall that Shelion had scaled. This meant some of the guys came over on a work party and, of course, livened up the dull routine of the section some more. Some of Hypo's friends were amongst them, so we got extra news as well. One of the guys was extremely confident and talked to us whether the screws were around or not. He seemed to be classed as harmlessly incorrigible, so they left him alone. Eventually only Blondie was left. He was nearing the end of his sentence, married and probably about thirty, so could be trusted to work around the female section without too much supervision. He and the work officer were to complete the rest of the work on the installation of razor wire around the edges of the inner verandah and end wall on their own. We promptly dubbed it 'Christmas decorations'.

Whenever Janus got off lockup for exercise, she would go and stand near his ladder and stare at him. It got to him so much at one stage he nearly fell off! Eventually the screws told her if she didn't leave him alone, she would stay on permanent lockup.

Eventually Shelion returned, and was taken straight to solitary. Later she told us she had stayed in the bush and gone to a phone box to ring the police up and make a deal. Not till they finally agreed to keep her in Darwin for twelve months instead of immediately extraditing her interstate did she come out of the bush at an agreed place and walked up to the police car. Although the cop was looking for her to 'capture' her, he hadn't seen her arrival. She tapped on the window and gave him a fright. They found it hard to believe she had lived in the bush for days and still looked as fresh as if she had just gone down the street from home.

That afternoon when Janus woke up from her daily drug-induced sleep, she discovered our escapee had returned and started to play up in earnest again. As soon as the TV finished and we were all on lockup for the night she had a real captive audience. All her grievances about being on lockup now centred on Shelion as the cause of it, since she had been on lockup since Shelion disappeared. Janus got progressively worse in her accusations until she worked up a tirade against all the girls in turn. It was such a mixture of truth and nonsense that muffled snorts of outrage and laughter alternated from the cells as the girls endeavoured to hide their reactions to the 'floor show'. It sure helped pass the night away. We were used to it but Shelion must have wondered if the jail was a madhouse and she was in the wrong place!

Eventually Janus was classified and transferred to a mental institution in another state, where she is very happy and decently treated.

Introducing Lena the Lock Lady

When Helena first came to prison she was very unpredictable. Not long after her arrival while Smiley and I were in admin cleaning, she made her presence felt. Two of the Aboriginal girls were having an inter-tribal argument, which was quite minor until Helena decided to involve herself on behalf of one, her friend. This, of course, is not done. You can say, 'Hey, you two, you're not fighting, surely? Let's be happy together,' and they will accept that; but you cannot tell one off without the other one, particularly if you are new in the section and don't know anyone very well. But Helena decided to teach the other girl (who was very small and barely old enough to be in prison in the first place) a lesson.

We all had to dust, mop and clean our cells out daily after breakfast. Anyone whose cell hadn't been done by the specified time was in trouble, unless they were on kitchen duty, which had to be completed first. Remand girls were also allowed to take longer. Occasionally the officer inspecting the cells would deliberately wear white gloves to check for dust on things like the lintel across the top of the door or the top of the fan. Helena was not finished with her argument. She waited until the girl was alone in her cell cleaning the bathroom and walked in, shutting the louvres.

The Aboriginal girl's cell was opposite mine and I was still cleaning, too. Soon I heard angry muffled voices and scuffling. I didn't take much notice until there was a big bang and both girls landed on the cell floor near the doorway in a fighting heap. The Aboriginal girl went to scramble up but Helena grabbed her, threw her down hard, sat on her, and started punching her about the face. Meanwhile she appeared to be saying, 'Are you going to say yes? Are you going to say yes?' What it was all about I had no idea, but as Helena was twice the weight of the other girl, I realised that quite some damage could be done. I hadn't decided what to do; if it ended soon, it was best left alone because neither girl would be charged, and they would have sorted their own problems out. On the other hand, if one looked like being badly hurt, somebody needed to intervene.

However, Hypo, who walked past and saw what was happening, didn't wait. She went flying up to the office and told them. By then the fight was quite audible all over the section and why the screws hadn't heard it I don't know. Hypo later asked me,

'Didn't you see what they were doing? Why didn't you report them?' I told her it was no business of mine to dog (dob in a fellow prisoner). She gave me a dirty look and walked off.

The screws broke up the fight. By then the Aboriginal girl had a bleeding nose, a split lip and her front teeth knocked out—and Helena spent a month on solitary in midsummer. Lockup was very hot, with water at tap temperature only, all food lukewarm, nothing to read and nothing to do. The incident earned her the ire of the other girls in the section, particularly as she was very new and they resented her brashness. They never spoke to her in solitary, and she was left totally alone. Hypo decided that when she was allowed out she was to be blacklisted by everyone, and decreed no one was to speak to her until she learned to conform and who ruled on the inside.

Being locked up was not to Helena's taste either, and she played up. The screws decided to put the cuffs with the restraining belt on her. This belt was about 10 centimetres (4 inches) wide and made of very thick leather, with a D-loop centre front for the handcuffs to pass through. The cuffs gave just enough movement for the wearer to go to the toilet—at least it did for males, and, with difficulty, for slim females, but it was *almost* impossible for fat ones! The belt was buckled at the back so it could not be undone (they hoped), especially by somebody who was broad.

This action was like a red rag to a bull. Helena stood with both arms held out like a scarecrow. I could hardly believe my eyes when I saw the screws using all their weight one on each arm trying to force her arms down to put the cuffs on her. Speedy (who was probably about 85 kilograms (190 pounds)) was using all her force nearly swinging on Helena's arm to try and lower it. She was not actively resisting, but simply standing there. They had not said what they wished her to do, or said please, so she just stood—with a screw suspended from the end of each arm. Tapioca arrived and went to assist them.

Between them someone finally asked her to 'put your bloody arms down'. She immediately did. As soon as she did Speedy grabbed her arm and twisted it up her back. I heard her say, 'My arm! My arm! You're hurting me.' At this Speedy gave an extra shove upwards and I heard an ominous crack. (Helena later told us she thought a bone in her shoulder somewhere had broken and she still has trouble with that shoulder to this day. She received no medical attention.) She was then thrown to the floor, although no longer resisting since she had lowered her arms, and Tapioca put his knee in her back and knelt on her while the restraining belt was put on. Every time they opened the door for regulation security checks she had the belt undone. As it could be used as a weapon they gave up and took it away, just leaving her handcuffed. Now each time they checked her she would hand them the locked cuffs, which she had removed, despite the fact that they were put on progressively tighter each time. Eventually they gave up and removed them as well. The next time they opened the door she handed them the basin taps. She was not hurting herself, or doing actual damage, just slowly dismantling things with her bare hands to show them what she could have done to *them* if she had chosen. It was a successful way of making them look complete fools. She had proved her point and caused them no further trouble when the next shift came on.

On the other hand, when Del first came in I thought she wouldn't be much trouble as she looked sweet, demure, shy and much younger than she turned out to be. As she lost a little of her shyness the first night, starting to chat more freely with the other girls, it was obvious that, despite her looks, she could have quite a coarse manner.

As she spoke openly about herself it became obvious that she had lost her temper, had a fight, and been put in prison as a result. She took this philosophically, saying that she could have been caught for other things many times, and was paying her dues to society for all the times she'd done something and got away with it. Win some, lose some.

Her victim, Angel, who was alleged to have been mass raped, had a rather chequered history herself, it seemed. Del told us she and Angel had had words when drinking in the pub then had later gone outside where Del had 'bashed Angel up' and left her. Some of the guys with Del had gone out, found Angel still there and raped her, then returned and told Del, who went out to see if Angel was OK. She was still there. The rest of the group had now appeared and apparently, after an argument with the guys, Del left.

Angel had then gone to the beach with the guys, who all enjoyed themselves—some more than once—after which they all slept the night together on the beach. Waking first in the morning, Angel then apparently decided to report them all for rape. Del had always claimed that she wasn't present during the initial rape and didn't know anything about it until after. It was claimed in court that she was there and actually held Angel down while her mates raped her. So many stories go around one finds it difficult to know, without being there, what the actual truth is.

Del went through many court and committal appearances. When all the guys involved were taken in for their identification lineups, they eventually realised the ventilation grille had been removed from the door base and Angel was sitting behind it. The police were stopping the suspects for their final instructions right by the grille. In the lineup Angel then only had to look for the feet of the guys the police had spoken to and she knew that she was picking the right person. When the group realised this they were able to tell the last guy to stop so that his feet were not in view of this gap—Angel was unable to identify him.

For Del's lineup the other four females were all older tall blondes, while she was a young brunette, short and slight. Angel was told within Del's hearing to remember to look for a short, brown-haired girl. There could be no mistake; there was only one short, brown-haired girl in the whole lineup. Del came back spitting.

Del was willing to plead guilty to assault and bashing, but not guilty to first-degree rape or any other kind. Three of the four guys were pleading guilty, while the last one also wanted to plead not guilty to a couple of his charges (such as stealing a cigarette which he maintained she offered him!). Del said she and the other young guy were eventually told openly that if they didn't change their pleas the cops would spin the case out so they spent their time on remand anyway and all their mates' cases would be held up also.

She had so many court dates and postponements, mentions, and deferments that it was like living on the edge of an active volcano—never quite sure if today would be the day or not. Once she told us they read her charges for the record and the Crown forgot some—she couldn't believe it when her solicitor reminded them that they had left some out! Often she complained at the slackness of her appointed Legal Aid solicitor—and he rarely came to see her. She even tried to have him changed, but didn't succeed.

At the end of her fourteen months—apparently the longest time any female had spent on remand in the Territory at that time—Del decided to do a deal and plead guilty if they would backdate her sentence, as the guys were still being held up waiting for her to plead also. It was done. Sentence was duly passed and backdated, and she ended up being halfway through her bottom sentence already! Sentences are passed ('on the top') then a minimum non-parole period is given ('on the bottom'), but good behaviour in some states can reduce this again, so a seven-year sentence may end up only two and a half years or so. As crims know this, but most of the general public don't, the legal system can keep most people happy. Del was really pleased—and so were we. The long-running saga was over and we could all relax as she planned her sentence.

Frequently the girls would come back from court and say their lawyer had said, 'I've done a deal. You plead guilty, you get so many months. That's it. We've got it all worked out.'

It was their life on the line, but who cared? Certainly not most of those lawyers. They had a heavy workload and they really weren't interested. Girls often said they were advised, 'Plead guilty. It'll only be a little time. Do your time sweet and you'll be out. I don't want to know if you're going to plead not guilty. That's work for nothing—just do a deal.'

During Shelion's extradition hearings, she had told her lawyer she was pleading not guilty. She had been in and out of courts long enough to know the procedure, so when he stood and entered a guilty plea (for pending Queensland charges), she stood up and told the judge she was pleading not guilty and had instructed her lawyer so, notice. She accused him of doing deals with the Crown, and said she wished to conduct her own defence instead. I hope he learned a lesson.

Where can a homeless street kid complain about treatment like this? These kids have no public weight and no one wants to know. Their brief is given to a busy Legal Aid solicitor who has so many, it's often just one more passing face. Such is our justice system in Australia at this time.

We think things happen to someone else or to those who deserve it—until it happens to someone we know. Unless we stick up for the underdog, one day it will come back and reverberate on us. The big criminals rarely go to jail. They are far too smart for that. It is the petty criminals who take the rap except where someone higher wants to dump someone else as a payback, and then you find the occasional criminal we really *should* be frightened of.

Lawyers, although they may alleviate some discomfort, can also cause it. Some get so puffed up with their own importance they tend to forget they are dealing with fellow human beings, not mere puppets. They're not God. No matter how much they can look like vengeful demons coming towards you with their floating robes and pompous expressions, they are simply human. It's time we learned to shun those lawyers who are willing to do anything for a price, and accept only those who are honest, true and just. Then we would shortly find that in order to make a living most would either behave themselves and toe the line, or leave the profession, thus ridding it of unfair, unjust, barely legal practices that eat like a cancer into our society.

WHAT'S YOUR CLASSIFICATION?

When the doors clang shut behind you, locking you in, and you have nothing to rely on except your own strength of body and mind, it can be terrifying if you let it. At a time like this, if you thought God was a figment of your imagination, He now either becomes a very real and personal friend, or is totally disregarded as a mirage only relevant to a distant Biblical past.

Like others before me, I came to that knowledge while in prison. There is no way that one can put this into words, it is simply something that slowly but surely happens. Time and again when there was no one else to turn to, nowhere else to go, I could turn to God and say, 'Lord, you've got to help me here. I can't manage on my own. What do I do? How do I do it? Teach me Lord, lead me step by step. I'm tired. I don't know what to do, you're going to have to tell me.' Often I would stick my finger into the middle of my Bible and let it fall open. Time after time a verse would just leap out at me from the page encouraging me to relax, trust God, leave it to Him and stop struggling.

I don't believe we should expect God to do everything when we say, 'Your will be done,' any more than your food flies through the air to your mouth once you've asked God to bless it. As you must pick up your fork and eat, so you must assist God in His plans for you. I believe if you attempt the wrong thing after asking for God's guidance, He will stop you and lead you in another direction; but we must not get discouraged and mad with God when He says, 'Don't!' God's way is the right one, and, had you access to all the alternatives, that would have been your ultimate choice also.

I often used to go to my shower recess when I became really frustrated. It was the only place where I could be unobserved, even the toilet could be seen from the door. In the shower recess I could spend just a few minutes alone. I would lie on my back on the floor with my feet up the wall, both to cool my back and head and to give my feet a rest before I went out again. In the dimness I could relax and talk to God. I'd argue with Him and He would answer: sometimes immediately, although at other times I'd have to wait. But there was always an answer, and I'd go away calmer, more refreshed, no longer as uptight and distressed. I could go back out to the others, or to the prison officers, and I could hold my tongue. I would appear calm even though I was often inwardly shaking or seething with unspoken words and thoughts. Once again I could look as if nothing had happened. But that was not my doing, it was His.

I went through several months of what was, for me, serious depression after I had heard the officers discussing what sort of treatment they were going to give me. I had been at the clothes line and was walking back. Apparently they did not realise that I was on washing duty and thought I was still inside; I don't think they ever realised how much their voices carried. From ten or twelve feet away I could clearly hear the discussion of how they were going to 'break Lindy': how they would get me to fit into what *they* wanted me to be. They'd fix that high-and-mighty goody-two- shoes who said she was innocent. They were going to keep on my back continually. I could have named those officers, but I never let on I had heard.

To be forewarned is to be forearmed. I was given the dirtiest jobs they could find and continually kept working. When I was working, if there was something else to do, I was called away to do that and then abused because my original job wasn't finished. One officer would tell me to do one thing and another tell me to do something else, and as I had to obey both, I got into trouble with both because neither was ever satisfied. It reminded me of Paul Newman's classic movie *Cool Hand Luke*, when he had to continually dig and refill a hole. I was told I had to work on my own, not with the others, because I wasn't classified yet but I knew that had nothing to do with it.

The screws would always say, 'Don't let the other girls get you into trouble. Mind your own business. Keep your nose clean and you'll be fine.' The screws were really afraid that if the prisoners all got together to do something, they would lose control, so they tried to keep each person isolated and wary of the others.

One or two of the girls held the officers' view but they were the type that I wouldn't trust any further than I could throw anyway. As I recognised that, it was not something that worried me. A number of girls rallied around, to the obvious annoyance of those officers. After work, they would want to be with me, even though they'd been told I wasn't a very nice person and shouldn't be mixed with. Because most of them had suffered the same type of treatment at some stage or other, they recognised the mind games the officers tried to play.

One of the dark girls said, 'They get on your back. We sorry, we can't help. We're not allowed, true, but you be our friend.' So, night after night, I was asked to play pool with the Aboriginal girls and had fun with them teaching me how to play.

I borrowed a book from the library and set about learning something that looked scientific about angles and directions, where to place the balls and how. I began to enjoy the game. I was having quite a bit of fun and eventually winning more than I was losing. Well, at least it was an occupation nearly everyone liked.

During this time the dark girls started referring to me as 'Gulla', or 'Lindy Gulla'. I asked them what it meant, but they would only giggle, especially when I told them they might be swearing at me in their own language for all I knew. It seemed to be a friendly name though, so I wasn't really worried if they wanted to call me that.

(I was not to find out what it meant for over a year, until we had a lot of new girls in. One of the girls asked me at lunch why they called me Gulla and what it meant. I replied that I had no idea because Shy and Smiley wouldn't tell me. One of their relatives who was friendly and outspoken chided them to tell me, and they finally gave her permission to tell me. She said it meant a good fellow, or good one as near as she could translate it into English. I realised this helped explain why I never had the trouble with difficult new Aboriginal girls that a few of the other white girls did. Hearing me called 'Gulla' was an automatic acceptance signal.)

We seemed to spend hours in the yard 'gardening' for exercise. It seemed a useless occupation mainly designed to fill in time, and we hated most of it. Cutting edges with scissors, usually blunt paper scissors, was one of the most loathed jobs. We actually owned a whipper-snipper but that was too fast, so always seemed conveniently 'out of order'. Scissors, of course, kept more of us working longer hours. We got blisters on blisters and hot tempers to match. The perimeter we clipped was on both sides of the fence surrounding a block of approximately two acres. We also clipped all our garden bed edges this way—one reason why the permanents hated new girls inventing new garden beds.

Another thing we hated was weeding the lawn by hand. Short-term girls merely pulled the tops off the weeds and we had to do the job all over again when they regrew. One of the screws even sowed weeds in an area we were trying to re-grass in order for it to look green till the grass grew. When I asked her why she planted weeds she stated that the girls needed something to do anyway! This also gave us blisters on our thumbs, particularly in the dry season when the ground was rock hard, and that was the season when we did most of our gardening.

It was on one of these abortive lawn weeding days that I was told to come inside and shower quickly for my classification. I had not been looking forward to this and felt some trepidation: then I discovered I had Mr Dewsnip! I hurried as much as possible, feeling nervous of the unknown. Dewsnip had a reputation for being stern and tough. Because of his height, bulk, and the terror in which he was regarded, I held him in some awe. I made up my mind under the shower that I would bluff it out.

When I entered the room he looked up quite politely. This didn't seem the ogre I had been led to expect. The first question he asked me, apart from my name and enquiries about my family and children, was my previous occupation before I became a student. I told him I was a homeologist and clergical assistant. He looked up and said, 'A what?' I repeated it and he asked me if I meant clerical. I said no and explained. Then he asked if I worked at home. When I agreed, he said, 'You mean a housewife?' I told him that mine was the work of no ordinary housewife and I refused to be called one. He openly grinned and said, 'OK, spell it.' So I did. Then we came to where I was born, and I had to spell 'Whakatane' for him. His eyes merrily glinted through all the rest of the session although his face remained straight and impassive. It was enough of a clue for me to realise that an entirely different person resided behind that stiff exterior and reputation, and that he was not the monster I had been led to believe. From then on we got on quite well. Although most of the guys seemed to be petrified of Mr Dewsnip, they really should have counted him as a friend; he was fair and would listen to what you had to say, so you knew where you stood with him. I discovered his straight no-nonsense approach, and the fact that he would not stand for any underhanded methods or practices upset the nasty screws and some of the prisoners.

Can I Have a Little More, Sir?

There were between twenty and thirty vegetarians in the prison altogether, so we got special vegetarian meals. Most were on drug-related sentences and just simply chose not to eat meat, but some did not eat meat for religious reasons. There were two in this latter category in our section: Hypo, who said she was a Muslim, and me. Hypo had previously tried a hunger strike for several days. She was told that she was causing a hassle and if she didn't behave herself she'd lose her vegetarian food privileges. Chagrined, she was unable to think of any payback that wouldn't directly land on her own head, or cause the removal of a privilege *she* wanted. So, when a number of new vegetarian girls came in, six out of the eleven in our section were vegetarians, she saw her chance and got their support to go on another hunger strike.

It wasn't hard. The food was always a shock to newcomers. We were supposed to have the same food, including fruit, as the male prisoners. We saw very good food go past on its way from market to the kitchens, but by the time it got to the table, it had been so mutilated one sometimes thought it was done on purpose. The main supervisor was a five-star French chef—the only one in captivity, as the superintendent was fond of telling us. He didn't seem to bother checking whether the prisoners under him washed or cooked the food at all, though.

We knew cases of fruit came in on the truck, but that fruit never came across to our side, and we discovered the guys weren't getting that fruit either. Those in the kitchen claimed it went out in the officers' bags. Wherever it went it certainly didn't reach the prisoners. The officers' meals were supposed to be the same as ours, though they had dessert every meal, whereas we were only allowed it every second night. Although officers weren't supposed to, if they were friends of the kitchen officer, they often ordered special meals, and the guys were ordered to prepare it, like it or not.

It was easy to tell when there were visitors in the prison because we would get a very nice, palatable meal. Even if we didn't have visitors, we knew somebody was in one of the other blocks around lunchtime, or inspecting the kitchen, because the food was so drastically different. The grapevine would later tell us who, where and when. If there were any complaints about the food and someone came out from head office to check, they never saw what we complained about.

It got so bad at one stage that the girls were given stew for at least one meal, if not two meals a day for three months. I got an identical salad every day, which I would have happily thrown at the nearest wall. This might have been temporarily gratifying, except that I would have gone hungry and probably got a dose of solitary as well.

For Darwin Prison food it wasn't too bad just then. The vegetarians still got better food than those on meat. Hypo told of the benefits the strike would have; how head office always listened; how they could go to Mr Barrier and he would do something—and the food would be improved. She was unaware that after she had been on her previous strike Mr Barrier, who was second in charge at head office in town, had called me in on another matter. He finished what he had wanted to see me about, and then asked what my opinion was.

I had approached him before on behalf of some of the Aboriginal girls as well as myself, asking whether he could do something. The lettuce was gritty; the pumpkin was unwashed and partially cooked with the dirt mixed in; frequently vegetables (often the potatoes) were cooked until they were covered with a sort of slimy scum; the rotten parts of the potatoes were still left in, and the pork had hairy skin still on the outside. I know very little about pork, but the hairy skin visibly poking through the stew certainly didn't look too good to me, and it obviously made the meat-eating girls feel ill. Complaints the screws had made on our behalf to the kitchen went totally unheeded, and they were even abused sometimes for passing our complaints on.

We heard later that almost every block complained one particular day. The rice was hard, and practically broke our teeth fillings in half. It literally bounced just as raw rice does so we had to get special permission to finish cooking it ourselves. After adding boiling water from the urn and turning it on high, the rice was barely soft twenty minutes later.

On a number of occasions when things deteriorated we let Mr Barrier know and he had a chat to the kitchen staff. Things would then improve considerably for a number of weeks, or indeed months.

Now I told Mr Barrier my opinion hadn't changed since we last spoke about the way they handled the food, but at least it was palatable just then.

The food wastage was phenomenal. Quite often, with only three or four girls in, we would get enough potatoes for twenty. We counted 132 slices of cucumber one day which were sent over for nine girls, and two-thirds of one of the big containers full of beetroot (that would be about equivalent to six or seven large tins-full). Things that did not need to be cut up in the first place, or would keep until the next day, were sent across anyway. We used to send our food back at one stage so they would see how much there was left over. Then the kitchen complained because they would have to clean the bain-marie. Often we had to throw away two or three times as much food as was eaten, and the prison complained about the cost of food and how expensive the running costs were! The prison also had some new rule that they were not allowed to give the slops to the pigs at the prison farm. Officers, at one stage, could take home the leftover stew or vegetables to use for their animals, but even that wasn't permitted any more. It had to go in the rubbish bin and to the tip. I could never see the point of the waste.

When Hypo and the others started making trouble, Mr Barrier was interested again. I told him there wasn't any variety in our meals, but the quality was probably as good as the prison seemed to be able to manage. He said, 'If Hypo continues to whine about her meals, she will lose the privilege of vegetarian meals altogether.' In fact, he added, they were having so much trouble with these 'grass-eating hippies', as they called them, that they were thinking of removing the privilege of vegetarian meals from all those except the prisoners who had genuine religious beliefs.

'I can tell you now, they will all lose it except you,' he said.

I said to him, 'Well, thanks very much, you know what *that* will do.'

'Yes, I know,' he said, 'and if you can help to calm them down, we'd appreciate it.' It was a gentle form of blackmail—if they continued to complain and lost their meals and I did not, they would be furious and take it out on me. I got his meaning.

He said, 'I *hate* telling you, but no one else will and I know you would rather know what is happening. They have every intention of using you, so if there is anything you can do, we'd appreciate it. I'm sure you'd find it easier yourself, too.'

The strike was imminent. One of the girls asked me if I was going to strike too, as I had been non-committal so far and hadn't entered in the discussions that had been going on for days.

I said, 'No,' and told her, 'Hypo was warned when she did this a few weeks ago. I've gone to Barrier about the food and I'm happy to do that again, but I will not strike.'

She gave me a piece of her mind and walked off. At the next meal the whole group faced me and I told them the same thing. The meat-eaters thought I was sensible and very brave, the others told me in no uncertain terms I was an idiot.

The strike started. Meals at full tables with only three of the people eating was an interesting experience. The strikers made constant comments about the food, particularly about the revolting meat stew being eaten. The meat girls had a rather nasty time trying to eat in peace with this going on, besides being glared at for not going out in sympathy as one of their number had, and thus making it a total strike (apart from Helena on lockup who therefore didn't count), which the vego girls thought would have been more effective.

Of the three meat-eaters who were eating, Del thought it was ridiculous and a great joke so she argued with them throughout each meal. Smiley was angry at their stupidity and the way they commented about her food, so sat in sullen silence (which was probably more effective than Del's arguments), and the third (a young Aboriginal girl) was scared stiff, embarrassed and uncomfortable.

The first few days of the strike, I had a migraine and was so ill I couldn't eat. Although I made it plain, the girls apparently thought I had capitulated due to their pressure, and was using my headache as a blind. I had made it quite clear to the officers (who knew I had been having medication for days), that I was not striking, simply ill, and would eat again as soon as I was able, so they had not put me on report for going without food. Deliberately refusing food was written up in the day book. Continuation put you on report for a dressing down by Tapioca or a chief, a visit to the doctor, and probably punishment.

My migraine went and I started eating normally again—then of course the trouble started. Tempers flared. It was like sitting on stage with a packed audience watching you through binoculars—they watched everything I did, every mouthful, the way I chewed, what I ate. I did my utmost to look as if I was unconcerned and ignore the comments but I must say it decreased my appetite considerably. (Previous practice in ignoring being stared at in public helped greatly!) I ate just enough to take away the hunger pangs and got out of there as quickly as possible, without looking hurried (I hoped).

After the first few days of their strike, as Barrier had indicated, the girls were called on report and informed they were on probation and if they didn't get back to normal, their vegetarian meals would be taken away altogether. They came away looking quite devastated, but with Hypo's leadership and their own confidence, they still thought they would win. They decided it was scare tactics and continued to strike for several more days. Then, without warning, they were all given that day's particularly vile meat stew for lunch, except me. I still had my regular vegetarian meal.

They were absolutely furious and asked to go on parade. Before their request even had time to be put in, the superintendent and Mr Barrier arrived and they were summoned on parade again. They were told their tactics were not appreciated: the prison did not accept strikes and because of their complaints, the whole prison had lost their vegetarian food privileges, except those who couldn't eat meat on religious grounds. Hypo herself as a Muslim was to have the meat meals, except when there were pork, ham or bacon dishes of any sort, then she would receive the vegetarian meal.

This made her even more furious. Not only did it single her out, but at breakfast we cooked in our own section and the girl on duty had to prepare special meals for me anyway, so there was no reason why there should be any problems at that meal for anyone.

I was summoned separately and informed, because I had not gone on strike and had genuine religious reasons for not eating meat, I was the only one in the whole prison whose vegetarian meals would continue. The prison would require a statement from my church as to why I did not eat meat. Pastor Bob Donaldson duly did that for me. I was later informed that some of the other girls *would* have been allowed to keep their vegetarian meals *if* they had been totally consistent in refusing to eat meat, but the officers had observed some of them tasting a mouthful or two occasionally, including Hypo, who occasionally ate fish.

With no officers sitting in the dining room at that stage, this should have gone unnoticed. If I had ever been seen doing the same, I would also have lost my vegetarian privileges. This just showed how much we were under a microscope. It also taught me how much others take notice of our actions, even when we were unaware of it, observing things which in the future would either help or hinder us.

The girls were almost in shock. Not only had they had a resounding loss, but they'd succeeded in removing the guys' meals too—and facing them wasn't going to be pleasant. After all, there was a husband and a boyfriend over there who'd just lost their meals, thanks to the girls.

While all this was going on, work was scarce, except for sewing. A number of the girls volunteered to build some rock-edged, tiered gardens just outside the main female gate. It was very hot and I was not displeased to have a lot of sewing to do. It meant I could get my work done without being hassled while they were employed elsewhere.

(Once on his way to visit me Michael saw some of the girls voluntarily breaking open the soft, cracked sandstone rocks to reduce their size for the border. He was shocked. No amount of persuasion would convince him he had not seen hard labour!)

The Aboriginal girls weren't pleased as they would have had time off, but eventually had to 'volunteer' also. They justly grumbled about girls who made work, then went home and left those who were 'permanent residents' to care for it for years to come. It simply made our workload heavier.

Officially the female section, and presumably the male section in Darwin, had no set rules at all, and it just depended on the whim of the particular officer concerned. Rules were passed along by word of mouth. I was fortunate enough to get a copy of the one sheet of old rules (from the turn of the century) which were in existence, and they later disappeared entirely, leaving none. Apparently to have an official set of rules and let the prisoners know what they were lessened the fun and authority of the screws.

Tension at mealtimes continued to remain extreme. The girls did manage, because our section was so small, to arrange internally for their meat and vegetables to be dished up separately so at least their food was unpolluted and they could throw the meat out. Nearly three weeks later, the girls came in to find that one of the nastier officers had forced a fairly new Aboriginal girl on kitchen duty to dish the meal out together. All the vegetables were ruined because they were covered in stewy-looking meat juice.

The girls had been working hard on their new garden and after their strike they were still trying to catch up. To come in hungry and face that was a blow. Shelion had absolutely had enough. She was starved, and had a fairly short fuse anyway. She took one look at the meal, picked it up, threw it in the bin and ran out of the room in angry tears. There was no lunch for her or any of the other vego girls that day—except the regulation two slices of bread and two small pats of butter.

On days like this, when I had my meal and they had none, life was not at all pleasant. The kitchen used to send me across a huge meal—enough to serve three or four people. This was done on purpose because I had got a message to the kitchen guys to send me a good-sized serving, to share with the other girls. I offered, but the others simply would not have it. It was obvious a number of them would dearly have liked to share but resolutely said no. If one had broken they all would have and forgotten their stupid pride—but no one was strong enough to stand alone. They would rather have the extra food thrown out and give me a hard time.

Show and Don't Tell Time

The Darwin Show was an annual event on the prison calendar, and the girls were expected to 'volunteer' to enter exhibits, at least in the floral art section. In my first year, I was asked by the male officer in charge of the greenhouse and gardens (who knew I was good with my hands and had worked in clay) if I could do a special project for him and make a stockyard. I said I thought this was hardly a dried floral arrangement, but he maintained it was all natural material. If I could use twigs to look like a bush stockyard and make animals, he'd make the metal tray and sand would do for the ground. Easy. So I used my imagination. I fashioned some range-cattle, a bony stock horse, drover and dog (complete with tongue lolling) from floral clay. With lashed sticks for the stockyard, trees and 'campfire', and a few rocks, I turned out what he wanted. It was not what I thought the judges meant, but they were apparently so impressed they put it in the miscellaneous section and it got a first prize. The officer was rapt. Hypo, who had put herself basically in charge, had also begrudgingly told me she supposed I had 'better arrange a couple of vases' of flowers.

I did, then helped Smiley to make a floral saucer. When the displays were judged, I received first prizes for both my efforts, and Smiley got a prize too. This upped the prison record quite considerably, although I'd encroached on Hypo's turf again.

The following year, with much glee, the garden officer announced that because of what we'd done the previous year, the judges had added to the Show categories a new section called 'A Rural Scene'. There were two sections and specific sizes for the trays—one was a living tray, the other a natural dried arrangement.

The living tray didn't appeal to me particularly, but Froggie and I both entered anyway. I let moss and tiny little ferns grow wild in mine. At the last minute I added a swagman, contrived from the clay, a fire, a watery billabong, and some twigs. It gave the effect of trees, bush and fallen logs—I had created a jolly swagman camped by a billabong, with a crocodile making the swagman look in some danger, and a few rabbits and a dingo behind the tree as well.

I was also asked by the screws to take a greater part in the floral work, so I asked whether we could get the flowers the night before. If they were put in the fridge overnight, the majority of them could be done out of work hours. With more time and a lot less pressure, we'd probably get more prizes. This was done, and we did win a lot more.

Froggie was a keen gardener, but not artistic, and was having a problem with her entry on Show morning. As I had finished my work, I assisted her and helped her contrive an English lady sitting in her manicured garden in no time at all. A sundial and 'flowering tree' overhead made it a very pretty tray.

For the dried rural setting, I had decided to make part of a sheep station. I called it Drogheda, as the idea came from the novel *The Thorn Birds* by Colleen McCullough.

Helena's Aboriginal mates had now left and she would be with us for the next year. The girls were right—she did need changing—but I felt blacklisting and ignoring her existence wasn't going to help in this case. Eventually Helena was allowed short exercise breaks outside lockup once a day. This was the first we had seen her for weeks, apart from occasional glimpses when the screws opened her door for meals or something. She refused to walk around in the courtyard but chose to sit on her cell door step (under guard), was hostile to all the girls and avoided eye contact. Towards the end of her time in solitary I was on kitchen duty. The weather was stifling hot with little breeze. When one of the decent officers came on I asked if Helena could have iced water instead of tap water for a change. Even a dog deserved that. She agreed so I crammed as many ice cubes in the plastic cup as I could so it would last for a while—at least one refill—or have some to rub on herself if she wished.

Apparently they told her I was responsible and later I caught her studying me several times when she thought I wasn't looking.

How was I to know she had set her heart on murdering me because I had supposedly killed my baby daughter, and this had completely thrown her off balance? Why would a murderer like me be kind? She later said she decided to investigate and get to know me before she did anything further. I decided, as I saw her attitude begin to soften, that I would try and make things a bit easier around the section by making an effort to understand her.

When she finally got off lockup, she was moody and unpredictable. The white girls avoided her and the Aboriginal girls were frightened of her. She could stay in a bad temper night after night. The daytime wasn't so bad because she had to work, but at night when she was in a bad mood she wanted to be entertained. I didn't have any time for myself; she would follow and badger me: 'Help me do this', 'Help me do that', 'You aren't any fun. Why can't you think of something to do?' I could, but, whatever I suggested was never what she felt like doing. Meanwhile, everybody else was trying to relax and do their own thing.

She was at a loose end, not yet able to get any buys through because of her misbehaviour. Her range of activities had been reduced to reading magazines and games—not exactly congenial to a restless personality.

I was well on the way to completing the shearing shed, sheep and shearers, when Helena got off lockup. She kept pestering me to allow her to help. There is nothing worse when you're working on a project than somebody else trying to assist, unless you know each other well and plan it together. (The year before, Janus had continually wandered in and out, changing our work around until we'd had to get her removed. It was frustrating to have our work undone after it was just finished.)

This year I was working alone. Someone I knew nothing about, who might have been all thumbs for all I knew, was not in my plans. Helena pestered me so much to let her make a stone wall that I finally said, 'Well, go for it, make the wall!' under the strict conditions she did what I said, otherwise she couldn't help at all. She argued, but finally agreed and made some nice stone fences. Helena turned out to be quite artistic, and when the project was finished we were very proud of it.

We kept right out of what the other girls were doing because the food strikes were not long over and there was still a lot of tension around. Talking to Helena, whom the older vegetarian girls had persuaded the section to blacklist because of her fighting and cockiness, didn't go down well at all. That got me more in the black books than ever, except with the Aboriginal girls, who had refused to blacklist me as well just because I was talking to Helena and didn't strike.

I did enter personal handcrafts I felt would not compete with those of the other girls, competition would only have made them angrier.

One of the screws returned from the Show telling the girls we'd won the Grand Champion Floral Art prize but couldn't remember which entry. Everybody was curious to find out which exhibit had won. Then the male senior in charge of the Show entries came back. Our senior called Helena and me in and told us we'd won the Grand Champion Floral Art Cup for our sheep station, but because there'd been so much jealousy in the section, they were not letting the other girls know, just telling them it was won by our section. No cup had ever been won before.

We told Smiley but added that it was a secret. She was thrilled; we thought it was great, too. When it was announced the girls crowed and decided they must have won it for the aggregate number of entries. Helena got mad and went to tell everybody that my big project had been the winner, but Smiley and I cut her off fairly quickly and convinced her to let it be. Later the certificates were hung on the wall, and the category number was there on the front. Someone would drop to it one day, we knew, but by then the fuss would probably have blown over.

Helena now had permission to do high school work and would start that but her interest span was very short, then she would begin throwing whatever she could get her hands on—starting with her books—until I stopped what I was doing. Sometimes I could handle that, but at other times I simply had to give up until I settled her down like a spoilt two-year-old.

She admitted nearly a year later that she used to pester me and ask what I was doing, partly to work out my personality and partly because she was bored. Like many of the younger women in prison, she had virtually brought herself up. Girls like that often have temper tantrums when they can't get their own way, and quite frequently this appeared to be the root of why they were in prison. If they can't have what they want, they steal it. If someone refuses to do their bidding, they will bash that person up. Brute strength and 'what I want' counts for them. So Helena tried, in various ways, to make me bend to her will. Fortunately Helena didn't stay like that.

When she couldn't command me, she became more and more curious. She also became quieter and started to listen to what I had to say to her, and I tried gently to settle her down and advise her. She was young enough to be my daughter; there was the same age relationship between us as there was between her mother and elder brother. She had problems and desperately needed the guidance of her mother but, although she loved her, they had very little in common, and seemed always to be warring. She started looking to me as an additional mother-figure, coming to me with her problems. As she changed and matured, she started to become a nice person, although still very volatile. You still had to watch her temper and mood changes, but she was settling down and you could see the real personality that existed underneath all the street bravado.

She started drawing, first of all, because she was bored on one of her many stints of lockup. I discovered that although self-taught she was naturally very talented artistically. She also wrote some very interesting poems. Obviously there was more to this girl than met the eye. Her education might have been lacking, but with higher education and a lot more self-control and confidence, there was obviously a long way she could go. I encouraged her to do more high school work and to get into crafts and something useful, instead of just being frustrated at her time spent in jail. Slowly but surely she opened up like a flower. Over the eight to ten weeks that most of the other girls did not speak to her, she grew and changed quite considerably.

The other girls started to realise that Helena wasn't so bad after all. She had a good sense of humour and could be the life of the party, making them all laugh. Shelion had a similar sense of humour, and little by little she and the others started to accept Helena as part of the normal prison family—then the fun started.

When everyone had long faces, Lena, as we often called her, started looking for 'Mum'. She would look in the bookshelves, knock on cupboard doors then search inside them. She would even knock on walls and the water cooler calling out 'Mum? Mum? Are you there, Mum?' Then putting on a forlorn face she would say, 'No, Mum's not there. Why won't she answer me?' Then she would giggle when she went back to work and say, 'They [indicating the older girls] think I'm nuts. I'll have them convinced soon.'

The Aboriginal girls didn't know if she was serious or not, but decided she couldn't be, as her mother couldn't fit in some of the places she looked. When Shelion heard that said quite seriously she cracked up and started laughing so much she nearly cried. Then all the dark girls joined in thinking they had made a huge joke. When Shelion told the others later what had been said, Hypo turned up her nose—it was beneath her—but the others appreciated it for what it was. From then on Lena calling for Mum became a real game, with everyone in the section suggesting places to look and Lena looking. The screws shook their heads in disbelief when she knocked on the back of a nasty one calling for Mum, then mournfully announced there was 'nobody in there'.

We all knew she wanted us to take the double meaning, which we did, but the screw couldn't say anything because of the way it had been done. *She* didn't think it was funny at all!

Some weeks later one of the male chiefs was doing his inspection and, on seeing Helena and me in the day room with everyone else, said, 'Oh, by the way, girls, congratulations on getting the Grand Champion prize for your big model.'

One of the other girls immediately said, 'That was the section prize, because of the number of entries.'

He said, 'Oh, rubbish! That was Lindy's project.' Now the fox was in the henhouse! No one had thought to warn him, as he was usually an officer who didn't talk to any of the prisoners.

One of the girls started to hit the roof as soon as he walked out. Helena would not be still this time, and spat, 'Go and have a look at the board. They have numbers on them.' Smiley surprised everyone by backing Helena up. Wanting to prove a point and not believing she could have had it hanging in front of her that long without realising, Hypo looked, then asked for the Show book to check the category; there it was in black and white. The group looked shocked. Shelion quietly said, 'Congratulations' and the others silently dispersed. I felt uncomfortable and wished it had stayed quiet.

Later Hypo announced she wouldn't be working on anything for the Show the following year. Most were amazed at such a blatant display of pique, nevertheless we let it go.

Because of the ill feeling, I informed the senior before I started work on Drogheda or entered any private sections that year, that I had decided not to enter any private entries the following year, as I would be competing with other girls within the section. If I won again there would be more ill feeling, and as I had already won in those categories before, I knew the standards required for success. I would only consent to do the large rural scene, as the other girls found this difficult. Later when I also discovered that Mr Mercer was boasting to visitors who came through the section about how smart his girls were and what prizes they took off, I was glad I had made that decision. Nevertheless, I have forty-odd prizes to my credit from the Darwin Show. Mr Mercer would not even permit Lena and me to have the trophy we won (a small cup) in our section, let alone let us keep it, as we did our certificates. I'm sure he somehow felt he had earned it himself!

We were never allowed to enter in our own names, because credit had to be given to the prison, not to an individual. One year my friend Liz Parry entered a pair of crocheted size two baby shoes for me, after seeing them in a parcel she was holding for Michael to pick up on his next trip. The head office guys, wandering around just before the exhibits were opened to the public, saw my name on the First Prize card and removed them from the Show. When Liz went to inquire about them, she was told that they'd been confiscated, and she went to a lot of trouble trying to find out where they were.

It was during this process she discovered the little shoes had won, and when they had been removed the Show judges had had to reallocate the prizes. The hierarchy considered a little pair of child's shoes entered by me would be considered inflammatory to the public! They wouldn't even enter them in the prison's name because the public would guess they were done by me, I was told! Both Liz and I received a lecture from the superintendent. I even had a visit from Mr Donnelly of head office 'to explain the situation'!

One of the things we always did for the Show was arrange a fruit basket. Kiwifruit, five-star apples, strawberries, grapes, paw-paws and pineapples were bought—things that we were never served—as well as common oranges, apples and bananas. Bananas and pears we saw occasionally, apples frequently, and oranges, of course, regularly. The rest we only saw once a year at Show time. Because the fruit was so scarce, the girls worked quite democratically. When the fruit came back from the Show we were allowed to make and eat a fruit salad, so the girls would check out who did *not* like certain fruit and share up the special fruit between those who did (unless a nasty screw was on and forced us to pool the lot, which ruined it for some). For instance, when five-star apples came in one year, it was discovered that only three girls liked them, and so whole fruits were handed out to those girls who had a rare treat. Pineapples were liked by everyone, so they went into the fruit salad. By this stage the fruit had been handled by many of the patrons going through the Show; some of the strawberries had started to brown and go off, but because of their rarity they were still eagerly consumed by the girls.

One occasion I remember, the officers had paw-paws in their fridge that had gone clear and overripe. They threw them out in our rubbish. Several of the girls who saw them realised although the officers would not wish to eat them in that state, they were not beyond eating. They were certainly not rotten, just overripe. For us they were like nectar from the gods. We rescued and washed the paw-paws and divided them among those who liked them, and had quite a feast. But not for the world would we admit taking food out of the rubbish and eating it. We even happily put up with the stomach aches we got due to the unaccustomed diet change.

I saw that the Frank Moorhouse docudrama about our case was advertised to come on local television. As I had already heard about it, I was hoping to watch it. I didn't really expect to be able to see it as it was still too soon after the food strike. As the date drew nearer, Duckie asked if I was looking forward to seeing the feature. I told her I hadn't asked to see it as I didn't want to create a scene.

'Rubbish!' she said. 'I'll just put it in the book and make sure you see it. Something special like this—you *ought* to have precedence no matter *who* you are.' I said thank you and left. When it finally came to the evening and the duty screw came over to change the television channel, a lot of the girls made the predicted fuss. I felt bad but had no intention of backing down now it was in the book, but I didn't have to say anything. The screw told them they were selfish and if they didn't like it, to lump it; they could leave the room. Most promptly did. Del and I remained on our own, and Smiley, who hadn't been in the room initially, joined us later.

It was quite inaccurate, and having to watch sets that didn't even remotely look like our home, and people purporting to be us yet wearing clothes that looked as if they had come from the local op shop was embarrassing. Watching Elaine Hudson's attire and interpretation of me gave me the shudders. Seeing the whole thing was a weird experience. This piece of journalistic licence is being marketed overseas as a feature movie available from video stores and it still ends at my conviction *without* a postscript.

There were huge fights over the type of TV programs watched—soapies or news. When one group won, they would all walk in with smirks on their faces and exit with scowls when it was changed back for the other group. Programs invariably changed in the middle of something *someone* was watching, and tempers constantly flared. It got bad enough for the whole section to be called up for a lecture from one of the big chiefs. After they said the TV would be removed if it didn't stop, *I* ended up with the unenviable task of having to negotiate between the two groups.

The strike girls by now grudgingly accepted me as an equal and the Aboriginal and younger girls as a sort of spokesperson and mother figure rolled into one. Lovely! It didn't help much but we were able to negotiate a strained compromise, which basically worked.

Helena could do a monkey act that was very realistic, and she was totally uninhibited. She would jump from chairs to table and up the side of the cupboards, scratching and hooting and making monkey noises, which set the section on its ear. The Aboriginal girls, in particular, developed a great liking for the monkey act. Often when we had a visitors' tour through (or 'zoo' visit as we called them), Lena would go into her act when they were being let in the gate, and noise carried. All the girls would be laughing, and then, as the visitors walked past the window and came to the section door, we would suddenly all become very demure doing our sewing with straight saintly faces, eyes lowered. The visitors would come in with puzzled looks on their faces, and walk around the section, most were not game or too embarrassed to meet our eyes. The moment they walked out the door, we would start again. They must have wondered what on earth we did in there. The senior would come back and berate us, with a big grin on her face:

'Helena, do you know what it's like trying to keep a straight face down there with all those people looking at me and trying to pretend I'm stone deaf, and there's nothing happening? You'll be the death of me yet, you girls. I don't know.' And off she would walk with a big smile. We had to be careful Lena didn't do her monkey routine when Tapioca was with the visitors, because he would recognise only too well who it was and what we were doing, and we would all be in trouble.

One day a reporter and a photographer came in to do an article on Australian prisons. Before we realised what they were doing, they came into the kitchen during the end of smoko. I was on kitchen duty and I didn't have time to get away. I managed to casually stand between the two fridges (it was the regular walkway around the bench but provided cover from where they were standing) while the photographer took some shots. I stayed well out of range until his camera was put down. When he had finished he too leaned against the fridge, and so I was trapped there. The other girls all knew I was standing there but he obviously didn't see me until he backed straight into me. Surprised, he turned around and immediately apologised. I was no longer easy to recognise as I had lost nearly 32 kilograms (70 pounds) in five months due to my jogging and exercise routine. The reporter realised then that there were three girls in the room, instead of two. I had to answer a couple of questions generally but said nothing of significance. She finished her interview and left, expressing her disappointment to the screw, as visitors invariably did, that she hadn't seen Lindy Chamberlain in there. The Imp said to her, 'Oh, but you did. She was one of the girls you were talking to in the kitchen.' She said, startled, 'Was she? Which one?' The Imp just looked at her and said, 'Well, if you don't know, I'm not telling you.' She delightedly watched the reporter walk away with an extremely puzzled look on her face.

When prisoners answer questions in monosyllables, it's not because they resent being talked to, simply that they do not like their private lives being investigated. If you were to talk to them as if they were ordinary people on the street about news, sports, or current opinions, you would find no problems. Questions on your own life are none of their business, and reporters don't tell prisoners their surnames or where they live (except for personal visitors, no visitor is allowed to for security reasons in case of a 'hit' by a prisoner later), so the conversation is one way and therefore resented. Also, if an officer is standing there when you talk to a reporter, you have to be very careful what you say, because you may be charged for it later.

On one occasion Sister X, a local nursing sister acquaintance of mine, came to take blood samples from all the prisoners because of a nasty infection that was running rampant through the male section. After the first little while the screws allowed her some freedom. Sister X wanted to make some impersonal observations of what actually went on in prison. As she was with the prison sister and medical personnel the screws didn't stand on ceremony but continued as normal.

Sister X must have been really waterlogged because she kept maintaining she was thirsty, in order to visit our day room to get a drink from the water cooler to observe our work and treatment. She was never quite able to get close enough to talk to me, as we had been told to keep out of their way except when called, and my sewing machine was not on her path to and from the water cooler.

Sister X later commented that although a few of us were working quite hard, the rest were all just sitting around watching, and the screws made those working do everything and ignored the others as if they didn't exist.

This was a favourite trick. Willing workers were loaded with all the extra jobs that could readily have been passed over to someone not particularly skilled—like running messages, sweeping, emptying a rubbish bin, or pulling a hose. Often we would be removed from sewing detail or whatever, to do these jobs in preference to somebody merely reading.

On a number of occasions, when the screws were on my back, the whole section was left sitting while I did every job they could think of, until the afternoon shift came on, and then often had to do the bins and/or the hoses at night as well. Girls who were willing to work and had to sit (which was boring) became upset when they saw this happening to their mates. It happened to everyone at different times as the screws got a set on someone, and this caused unrest through the whole section.

Although the guys could mix freely in each other's cells, which we were forbidden (we'd be on a charge if we did), we had the advantage of more readily getting permission for handcrafts. At times selected girls could even get permission to have scissors in their cell during lockup if they were doing tapestry or similar crafts (as suicide or vandalism was a possibility, this was normally forbidden). Each cell block had to have a minimum number of staff, regardless of the number of prisoners it contained, so it was obvious the smaller the number the easier it was to keep track of what they were doing. On the other hand the guys could get away with certain scams because of their higher numbers, where we couldn't as we were under the spotlight all the time.

Our leatherwork classes, for instance, continued for months after the men's were discontinued due to lack of supervisors. We could jog nightly for the same reason; the men couldn't—the guards in the towers might mistake them for escapees and shoot them! But then of course they had good, regulation basketball courts, and enough men to play occasionally.

Poles Apart

The question of exercise was always in a state of flux. We were supposed to be able to have recreation time. The men had weights (the weights were kept locked in a small room off the stage in the assembly hall) and they could go across every night to use them—provided there was an officer free to supervise. The prison was quite proud of this service, and used to tell visitors about it. They made sure it wasn't *seen* though, as the reality never matched the mental picture. It also wasn't mentioned that if an officer didn't think exercise was important or was scared to be alone in the 'weights room', excuses would be found for not opening up, so the guys would be lucky to sustain any sort of regular muscle-building program, and often got stiff muscles from alternate disuse and overwork.

We had similar problems. The prison made a big deal about their intention to give us a basketball and volleyball court; plans were drawn up, and we were all excited. For some reason no one stopped to think that we never had any more than sixteen girls in at the one time, and even if all those girls were fit, we still didn't have enough to play a decent game. That is, of course, provided everybody knew the game and wanted to play. Quite a few of the girls were far too lazy, and a number had never held a basketball in their lives, didn't have a clue how to play, and weren't about to make fools of themselves now.

The area was ploughed up for the basketball court (about three quarters of an acre, in all) and we had to rake it, get the rocks out, flatten it out, carefully level it, then sow it with lawn. This seemed a bit odd—it had been good, flat weed-free lawn—and we had only just got it in that condition before they ploughed it! But we did it anyway—day after hot, dry, dusty day, with tempers flaring and the screws pushing. It was extremely dirty, tiring work with plenty of blistered hands, and it took several weeks.

Later when Mrs Barham, our chief, returned from leave she was extremely annoyed at what we had been made to do. Only a small problem section of grass near the fence was supposed to have been ploughed and re- sown! All those blisters because of someone's mistake! Mrs Barham didn't let the male officer responsible for that mistake near our section for some months after that.

Finally the goalpost went in at one end and we waited for the other one. We knew by now the court would only be grass. Then we were told that we were only having one goalpost! The two poles went in for the volleyball net, but it seemed nobody had ever bothered with measurements. The distance was at least twice what it was supposed to be and the net wouldn't reach. When they got a long piece of rope to extend the net ties, it sagged in the middle and really wasn't very satisfactory. Our dreams of having a good court like the guys were blown completely.

Anyway, the girls enthusiastically tried to play a few games. One girl, who was quite good at basketball, managed to get one of the officers to go out with her a few nights to play one-on-one, but we soon realised we had the same problem as the guys did. The screws complained that there were too few on duty to let one go outside; they would be busy, or there would be a girl on lockup. We'd get all ready, and an officer would say, 'Oh sorry, it's too late, you've got to stay in, tea's here early,' or 'The sun set too quickly, I'm sorry I didn't realise the time,' or 'The girls were late from cleaning tonight'. So the pole sat in the yard, unused.

Tapioca came across and said, 'See, I told you you wouldn't need two poles, you don't even use the one you've got. That proves my point.' Nobody bothered to argue with him. We'd had our say, and who was going to tell him that it wasn't our fault we couldn't play? It really wasn't worth the effort.

Inside was a little different. When I arrived in prison, Froggie was jogging daily. As I badly needed to get fit again and needed something to work out my frustration, I started jogging again also. I loved jogging, but hadn't done any since before the trial and was well out of condition. We only had our daily uniform and sandals to wear; the uniforms were hot, tight, and ended up wet and smelly with perspiration. A few weeks before Tapioca had refused us permission to jog and caused a furore over our sporting activities.

Froggie and I wrote to head office and managed to have the decision reversed. Having won that round against Tapioca, Froggie and I decided to ask for running shoes and clothes—she optimistically asked for shorts. I wasn't so hopeful and asked for a sports skirt instead—so we filled out our request forms. At worst they could only say no again, but at least we had a slim chance they'd say yes to at least part.

Froggie was called in on parade one day to say that her request had been denied, but she *would* be able to have a pair of prison sand-shoes for jogging, as well as those supplied for gardening. Then she was given a lecture about the type of company she kept and how she shouldn't let other people influence her. She pretended to be very dumb about that, and told them she was very careful about her company, and was quite capable of choosing her friends without anybody influencing her. She was allowed to go.

Then I was called in. Froggie had reported briefly as she came out that she had got most of what she wanted, so I was quite encouraged. Well, I was in for a shock. Three people were there—Tapioca, Duckie and another good but fairly new chief, who had previously been the senior in charge at our trial for the first five to six weeks. Tapioca told me to stand to attention at a very specific distance from the table on a mat (I hadn't realised until then that the term 'on the mat' was literal) and pay attention.

I could see that he had several of my letters, sent across before Mrs Barham went on holidays. Both she and I knew certain others were only too happy to check on my business and report it far and wide. She had come over specially with the last of my inward mail before she left, telling me she had arranged for only one person to do it while she was away, and also that she had asked Duckie to take my outward mail over to the post rack, as she had completed censoring, signed and sealed that as well. A few minutes later, through my window, I had witnessed it being handed over, and she left.

Seeing my letters there in Tapioca's hand, I knew that there was only one way he could have got them, as a senior's work was not rechecked. Duckie had not done as she had been told. I glanced at her, and saw a very embarrassed and mutinous look on her face. Tapioca told me I did not have permission to write things about the prison, and these letters would not be sent. They would be rewritten, the offending pieces taken out of them, and then they would be sent back across for his censorship. Everything I wrote in future would be censored in the same way. I said to Tapioca, 'Could you please tell me specifically what's wrong with my letters?'

He was only too happy. I had made comments about the prison food. Would I please like to tell him why? Didn't I *like* my food? Wasn't it *good* enough? I was being cared for at great expenditure of public money. I privately thought this was their own fault; if they wanted to keep me in prison, innocent as I was, it could cost them triple for all I cared. It certainly didn't cost as much at home as the amount he quoted. I could have kept my whole family for months on the amount it cost them to feed me for the year, so I wasn't impressed.

I was puzzled where I had mentioned prison food, though, and as Tapioca read the quote from my letter, I realised he had fallen into a beautiful trap. I had been discussing the college cafeteria food, in reply to something that was said to me by a young college student. Tapioca didn't like me pointing out his misconception. I was amused at his discomfort and had difficulty keeping a straight face.

Then he said I wasn't to write about the work I did in the prison. I knew very well I hadn't said anything about that either and asked him, 'What work is that?' He had to be specific; it was about my own craft work. I said, 'That is not prison work, it has nothing to do with the prison.' He looked to the other officers for help—the chief looked out the window, Duckie grudgingly told him that the girls were allowed to talk about their own craft work. So he put that letter down.

The next letter mentioned that my husband was not coming to live in Darwin. I was not to put *that* sort of information in my letters either, Tapioca said. By this time, my blood was boiling. I was having a job to control my face and refrain from telling him to go jump in the lake, probably less politely than that. Finally, I said to him, 'Excuse me, we're told that in our letters we are only able to talk about personal subjects. I consider it is personal for me to state whether or not my husband and family are coming to live in Darwin. It has nothing whatsoever to do with the prison or the state, and therefore cannot be censored.' He mumbled and said my remarks were really inflammatory and that I shouldn't be making that sort of comment, but he would take the letter back and review it, and he would let me know.

The fourth letter was written to one of my lecturers at Avondale College, explaining that any letters about my study courses in prison should go to the teacher, Mr Kerry Gardner, care of the Darwin Prison (and I gave him the address). Kerry would pass on the relevant parts to me. I was told I was naming an officer and that was against the rules. I said I was very sorry, but Mr Gardner (who was not a regular officer at all but a part-time teacher) had asked me to do that so I had thought that was all right. Well, Mr Gardner had no excuse for telling me to do that, said Tapioca. I said I'd ask Mr Gardner to write to my teacher. *That* would be all right, wouldn't it?

But Tapioca hadn't finished yet. He said, 'We are not pleased with your seditious influence in here.' I said, 'Oh?' That was all. By this time I was fuming and standing looking out the window past his ear. I was sick to death of having him sitting there in silence with his eyeballs rolled up at the ceiling, staring at me with only the whites of his eyes showing. If he was going to subject me to that, I wouldn't bother to take notice. He got sick of doing it, then kept talking. I had no right to come into the prison and think I could have everything. Asking for a jogging skirt was absolutely ridiculous and that would be denied.

I said, 'That's fine. Would it be all right if I jogged in my gardening uniform? I can't wear my other one; it gets too sweaty and the officers complain afterwards.' He was just about gnashing his teeth but said he would take that into consideration and let me know.

'Thank you very much,' I said. He then informed me that I could not have shoes sent in, but that I would be given a pair of prison-issue sand-shoes (K-Mart's cheapest) when they became available, and that was all. Again I thanked him. Did I have a pair of gardening shoes? he wanted to know. I said, 'No, I've never been issued with them.' I knew I was supposed to be, like everyone else, but I had not been. That was passed over, and I was told to stop stirring up trouble and making the bullets for other girls to fire. Whereupon I assured him that if I had any bullets to fire, I would do so myself. I also informed him, 'As you know, if I have something to say to you, I say it myself.' He mumbled and passed that over—'Well, what do you intend to do about your behaviour? You realise, of course, that with continued behaviour of this kind, any privileges will be lost?'

I said I did.

'Good, we understand one another,' he said. I looked him straight in the eye and said, 'I believe we do.' I then asked if he could explain what behaviour of mine he found unacceptable. No, he would not. I said, 'Well, I'm sorry but if you can't tell me what it is that I'm doing wrong, I'm afraid I can't do anything about it.'

'You know very well what it is you're doing.' I said, 'No, Mr Tapioca, I don't.'

'Do you mean to tell me you don't know?' I said, 'Yes, Mr Tapioca. I *don't* know.'

He said, 'Well, I'm not going to explain it. You just think about it.'

Once again I said, 'I'm sorry, but if you can't tell me what it is, I'm afraid I can't do anything about it.' We then stared at one another for what seemed like five minutes, but was probably no more than thirty seconds. I was determined I wasn't going to blink, and if he was going to roll his eyes up and stare at me, I was going to face him back. His eyes eventually dropped before mine and he curtly stated, 'You can go.'

I walked out, coldly furious. I had maintained a calm exterior and had mainly held my tongue simply by looking out the window past his ear and ignoring him. I knew our senior officer was quite happy about my behaviour and the way I was settling in. She, too, knew I would be in for a rough time with her gone and had said to try to keep my chin up until she returned from her holidays. This time I had to bear it for a while, but I wasn't fazed by Tapioca any more.

We weren't working, just hanging around, so I stewed in the corner until shift change. I told some of the other girls what had happened. He had no right to keep my letters.

'Don't worry about him,' they said, 'he can't do a thing. He just likes to threaten you. He'll get over it and it'll blow over.' Well, that was okay for them. Froggie finally got near enough to let me know she got the 'firing bullets' bit of the lecture also, so that was explained, but I never did work out what my 'seditious influence' was. Perhaps it was constantly maintaining my innocence. So they really *were* going to try and break me. Well, they could try, but they *weren't* going to win.

A couple of days later I received a visit from head office. I wondered what I had done now. I was in for another surprise. This time *they apologised* for the inconvenience I had been having over my mail. I was informed all my letters would be mailed and it would not happen again. When I asked who told them, I was told they 'had their ways' of finding out. As I hadn't said anything I could only surmise that the chief on duty with Tapioca had said something, as I knew by the look on his face that day that he had been embarrassed.

I still had the problem of footwear to consider, though. The gardening sand-shoes were supposed to protect our feet more than sandals but I had still not been given a pair because my feet were 'too small'. The day after Tapioca's 'interview', Duckie called me in and asked what size I took, so I tried another girl's shoes on, which were too big. Depending on which brand it was, I took different sizes, so I worked out the size in both brands. The money came specially out of petty cash, they said. The storeman went to town and brought back a size smaller than I had asked for and, of course, they wouldn't fit. Smiley was delighted—her feet were smaller than mine and so she was given them for gardening shoes. I was told I would have to wait for the petty cash to mount up again.

Time went by and another pair of sand-shoes were sent over. I had asked for one size larger in the same brand, but no, they bought two sizes up to just make sure. Of course, they were too big. They went to another girl, and I had to wait *again*. Then

I received a pair of *another* brand; a completely different fit again. This process was repeated several times, after which I was told that they had tried their best to please me and I would just have to wait until the next lot of shoes came in.

Mrs Barham returned and Duckie was demoted to the normal ranks again. Time passed, and then a lot of shoes came in. Everyone else had at least gardening shoes by this time, but I still only had one pair of sandals. I wore them all day and after gardening and working in the mud I would come in, wash them out under the shower and put them straight on again. Being leather they cracked and shrank, drying lumpy. My sandals had been second-hand in the first place and this only made them worse. Every bump was in the wrong place and they hurt my feet; I had no choice but to wear them anyway.

A friendly male screw informed us that the female section owned a trampoline, and it stood unused against the wall of the remand section on the male side. They could not use anything of ours without permission. This information was then confirmed by our officers, so we decided to request permission to have the trampoline brought across to use. The officers had always known it was there, apparently, but a number of them didn't want it across because that meant giving us something we would enjoy. The girls asked me to talk to either Mr Donnelly or Mr Barrier from head office in town about it, knowing that I got on reasonably well with them and that Tapioca would refuse.

Because of the jogging furore some weeks before Tapioca had been forced to give in, but it was consent grudgingly given and he had given us a half-hour time limit. If we were called to do any work, such as moving hoses, or bins, during that time (which nasty screws delighted in making us do, our turn or not), we were not allowed to make up lost time. I wanted the right to do our jogging at any given time we were free in the evening, so I wrote to town again.

When Mr Barrier came out we discussed it and permission was granted. Then we started talking about other facilities and I requested the trampoline. Barrier grinned and said, 'Oh, the girls are flying a bit high there. We'll put in your request, but trampolines are expensive.' I pointed out we already had a trampoline and all we needed was direction from head office for it to be brought across and permission to use it. He laughed and said, 'I might have known you'd worked it all out. OK, you can have your trampoline.' It was obviously a good day! I tackled the question of running shoes again. My sandals were nearly impossible to run in and bare feet were forbidden. I had had enough games so I asked Barrier's permission to run barefoot until shoes arrived. He looked aghast that my shoes hadn't arrived yet, and immediately granted my request. It would be duly written up in the day book so no one could stop me or charge me.

Prison was a constant battle of mental one-upmanship without being obvious or, in prison language, 'head trips'. Initially I nearly skinned the soles of my feet on the rough concrete, but after my feet toughened up I enjoyed the freedom.

The trampoline soon arrived, carried over from the male side by a number of the guys, and was set up in the middle of our courtyard—and it had another beneficial effect. Now—wonder of wonders—we were allowed to have shorts; we were not permitted on the trampoline without them, it would be immodest and unladylike. I was called to the office and told to design shorts for the girls, provided they had elastic waists, no zips or pockets and were at least mid-thigh length! (Boxer shorts, of course.) They were individually made to measure, and inelegant or not we were delighted as we also received T-shirts to wear with them. Froggie was particularly delighted, because now she had her shorts for jogging.

Eventually one of the other girls noticed the state of my sandals and asked, 'Why don't you ask for some more?' Well, I had, and had been told the same thing as with the sand-shoes; they had to buy me special shoes because of my small feet, and there weren't any in stock (there never seemed to be any problem with Smiley, and her feet were smaller than mine). They would get some as soon as possible. I knew on a number of occasions Mrs Barham had gone over with it on her list, and come back without any, having been told to wait again.

I noticed the whole front sole of my sandal was now flapping, and I had almost worn it through in one place. Having found it was pointless to keep reminding them, I had just kept quiet about it for a number of weeks.

I was chatting to our chief one day when one of the male chiefs came over. He stood talking with the officers and girls who had finished their jobs. When I went to brace my foot on a pot plant, I hit the front loose flap of the shoe, lost balance and nearly tripped myself up. One of the other girls quickly quipped to the chief that they would be paying insurance for broken legs if they didn't buy Lindy some decent shoes soon. Whereupon all eyes focused on my shoes and the male chief said, 'They are a bit worn, aren't they?'

I thought, now's my opportunity, so I flipped my foot up. His eyebrows almost went past his hairline, and he looked questioningly at Mrs Barham. She said she'd had sandals on the request forms continually for months but the store didn't hold any size smaller than a four in stock, which were too big for Lindy and Smiley. The Foreman would have to get smaller for the female section. He said, 'Well, what's the problem? You can get them in any time.' She looked at him, raised her eyebrows and said, 'There isn't enough petty cash?' He said, 'Oh. Petty cash. Oh yes, Mrs Barham.' Then he changed the subject and everybody pretended they hadn't heard the exchange.

That afternoon across came a new pair of sandals for me and within the week I had my jogging shoes as well. (Then I had to contend with blisters while running them in.) Nevertheless, the whole time I was in there I was never issued with a pair of gardening shoes. Those sandals were the only new pair I ever got. Eventually I was told I could use three pairs of Indian- type sandals (sent in by St Vincent de Paul) in the storeroom, as they were for a narrow foot. Once I had managed to wear them to shape, they were more comfortable than the regular shoes, so I was grateful for that. The whole shoe episode showed yet again that clothes had to be practically threadbare before the prison replaced them. It was just another form of harassment.

How to Foster Local Discontent

The radio was simply switched on from the tower and came through the intercom system into the cells. You could switch it on or off in your own cell, but not choose the volume or the station, except in the office.

As the section was built around a hollow courtyard the noise reverberated like a sound shell, and I grew to hate the nerve-jangling racket. It was hard to even think straight at times. My cell, near the middle of the section, gave me a four way reception at night. The cell radios were the loudest (playing 'She's A Maniac' and 'Innocent Man' often), then I could hear the private tape recorder in the cell next door playing Richard Clayderman's piano pieces, the tranquillity of which I enjoyed when heard alone. Usually Smiley played her own tapes of Aboriginal music, and finally there was the television in the day room trying to drown out everything else so the commentary could be heard. It was particularly lousy when I had a migraine. Sometimes I thought my head would burst and I'd go crazy, but I never quite did.

Silence was supposed to reign at eleven o'clock for the television and eleven-thirty for the cell and private radios, but sometimes the tower left the radios on until midnight or later and as a lot of the girls slept like logs, they left theirs switched on permanently, driving the lighter sleepers crazy. The addition of snoring didn't help either.

When I first went to prison we always had the radio on at lunchtime. The talkback session was sometimes interesting. We had an hour for lunch when I first arrived and were allowed to leave the table as soon as we wished to return to our cells, sleep, do craft or stay in the day room as we wished until work resumed.

Once I was in my cell resting and the cell radio opposite was going. I heard my name mentioned so pricked up my ears and discovered that the prison was being discussed. A listener rang in to say she was the wife of one of the officers who worked at the prison and she thought it was disgusting the way Lindy Chamberlain was being given special treatment. She happened to *know* that I had just put in a request for a trampoline, so they had bought one specially for me, and what was taxpayers' money for? Of course, it wasn't new, or for me! Whoever she was, that screw's wife was just causing mischief.

The local papers had continually complained I received special treatment. Certainly I did—but not the way they meant. I was not allowed 'outside' at times in case I was seen. Stuart had to have permission, time limits and restrictions for my legal visits, sometimes even those visits were *monitored*, which *never* happened in the case of other prisoners. A lot of my visits were conducted in a different way and different areas to those of the other prisoners. It all showed a degree of paranoia on the behalf of the Northern Territory authorities that was not there with other prisoners' visits.

I often heard 'facts' about myself discussed on that program by people who always 'knew' but when a number of people tried to ring in to correct these mistaken views, they weren't allowed on air. Darwin didn't want to hear the truth, it seemed.

The radio wasn't all bad, though. One day when I was feeling particularly low, I heard an interesting quote on the wireless from Abraham Lincoln. It went something like this: 'It is not as important to have to do the things that you like to do as it is to learn to like the things that you have to do.' That was very appropriate for me just then because I was having to do a lot of things I did not like, such as scrubbing toilet walls. I found I could, indeed, learn to like and appreciate jobs that I formerly hated because there was a sense of satisfaction in overcoming something and in a job well done. To be able to truthfully say, I have mastered this situation, it has not mastered me, is important.

Despite the unwelcome or unexpected interruptions, I used these times as learning experiences rather than letting them grind me into a state of hate and despondency. Over and over again I was to find that if I gave up and let a situation master me, I became discouraged, and found myself falling into a sense of despondency very difficult to extricate myself from. I knew if I gave way to that feeling and let go, I would end up having a physical breakdown as well. There is no doubt in my mind that if it hadn't been for God's help and strength, plus grit and determination, I would have landed up in a mental asylum. At times I felt myself so low I knew I was losing my grip, not only on life but on reality. I knew I had to find it again in a hurry; only God could give me the strength and courage I needed for that and calm me down. Time and time again I asked Him to give me healing sleep, peaceful oblivion in order for my body to heal and wake with renewed strength in the morning, and He always did.

At times when I could not form the words to pray I would just say, 'Lord, take over!' and He would. In the morning I could get up and say, 'I will master this moment,' and I would ask God for the strength, moment by moment, to go through that day, not a day or hour at a time, but minute by minute. I often had to develop 'diarrhoea' in order to be alone and pray for strength for the next few moments and to keep myself calm and together so that nobody knew what I was feeling internally when things looked bleakest and blackest; and God always saw me through.

Part way through my sentence our lunchtime break was reduced to half an hour and the radio was not switched on. Lockup was also moved from 11 p.m. to 10.30 p.m., but the radio still stayed on till 11. 30 and later. We missed the end of *all* movies and TV mini-series then, as we usually had to leave the day room by 10. 25. The programs and movies always finished five to fifteen minutes later. It was a constant source of frustration, as we always missed the punch line. A decent screw would watch the ending for us and come around and tell us what happened often, but that was never quite the same. The television was the only thing that took your mind away from the reality of your situation and stopped you from dwelling on where you were. It was an agreeable form of escapism.

How to Clean a Pigsty and Other Useful Hints

Some male screws certainly earned their name of 'pigs'. We had to cope with unflushed toilets and excreta up the walls. These men were often no lovers of hygiene. They threw lunch wrappers around, and some left a terrible mess. We knew which officers were tidy and which were emphatically not. Some cleaned the fridge or the stove in their kitchen (this was not part of our job and relied on a volunteer), some even cleaned the toilets, while others spilt fat all over the ovens and left it there. Dirty frypans would even be hidden in cupboards until they were mouldy. They spilt coffee, soup and other food all over the floor, knowing of course that the female prisoners would come across each morning and clean it up. Some of these men would mess up the place on purpose right in front of us. I hated to think about their personal habits in private life.

On one occasion, we had been getting a run of absolutely filthy toilets day after day. Some of the decent male screws told us it was because some of the men came on duty for night shift the worse for drink, left it too long to go to the toilet, and couldn't be bothered cleaning up after themselves. We had complained a number of times over the weeks, and finally Mr Keo agreed to check out what we were saying. He did not normally use those toilets and was aghast to see what we were cleaning up. He said we were to stop cleaning them immediately and would organise the cleaning himself. The instruction was not passed on to us 'officially' until I had done one more shift on the toilet section. I did the normal cleaning job when Rambo told me I was to scrub down all the walls and showers (which were almost as bad as the toilets). I hadn't been in very long at that stage and the officers were still on my back. Rambo delighted in it. My partner Smiley finished, then seeing me scrubbing said, 'You don't do that. We not supposed to scrub here any more. Why you do that?'

Well, that was my understanding of the talk with the chief the day before also. Maybe it was still lost in the paperwork somewhere. 'She said I had to,' I said, indicating with a thumb in Rambo's direction.

'Is not right,' Smiley said, but realising that I was deliberately being told to do extra work, she started to help me. Rambo saw and stopped her, saying it was my job and if I was slow, that was my fault; Smiley could not help. Smiley was obviously furious. She had to just sit and wait, when she could have been back in the section for smoko with her mates, so she was annoyed on her own behalf as well as mine, knowing we weren't supposed to do what I was doing at all, even if we did still have to clean the toilets. She felt so strongly she even spoke up to Rambo and told her we 'shouldn't do it' . Smiley was usually quiet, but if you got her going she could be very stubborn. She said 'This wrong, Miss Rambo. I tell Miz Barham.' The screw looked uncomfortable and told Smiley to mind her business and be quiet or she'd be charged.

For quite some time Rambo stood over me while I scrubbed and Smiley glowered. I had no gloves and only a toothbrush to do the job. All very well for getting into cracks, but not very efficient for scrubbing a floor! Later Smiley got the regular scrubbing brush and swapped it over when Rambo was easily distracted by one of the male screws. I finished scrubbing quickly then.

Smiley, still irate, did 'tell'. The next day one of the good officers was on, and on our way across to cleaning she told us the directive *had* arrived before we had gone cleaning the day before (as we had suspected).

Nevertheless, while I was cleaning, I had managed to get my own revenge on those filthy screws. I had used the same cloth and brush to clean all the hand basins, after I cleaned the showers and toilet bowls. I knew some of them drank with their mouths over the hand basin taps, and often others had obviously been peeing in the hand basins and left their urine there for us to clean. I figured it was only fair for them to get a few other things in their hand basins as well. I wasn't the only one who 'cleaned' the bathroom like that when we knew the nasty screws were on. We thought if they got stomach upsets, all the better; maybe that would teach them to be a bit cleaner. There was no way of seeing what we did, but it was possible to leave enough film of the dirty toilet water on their hand basins (without getting it on ourselves) to make them quite ill, yet still appear clean.

If a visitor or one of the male screws asked us a direct question, we were permitted to answer but were not supposed to initiate conversation. Whistling, singing and laughing were all against the prison rules, and we could be had up on a charge for doing any of those (fortunately the laughing part wasn't adhered to). Some of the male screws, also forbidden to talk to female prisoners, totally ignored this, and they managed to get away with it, too. In fact, if we had a nasty officer on and got a good male screw, it was not unusual for him to pull faces behind her back or make some pretty rude signs just to make us feel better.

On the way back from cleaning the medical centre a few days after the shower scrubbing episode, my partner and I were waiting to be let back through the security gate into the sallyport. We had the Chameleon with us and could be seen by half of B block, male maximum security, as we leaned on the wall patiently waiting for the gate at the other end to close so our gate could be opened.

Suddenly we heard a loud bellow, 'G'day Lindy! Good on yer, Lindy!' The whole male prison must have heard it, and I saw somebody's arm madly waving through the concrete reinforcing walls (the holey type that let the air through). I have no idea who was in there, but every day I went cleaning that week, he called out something like, 'Good on yer, Lindy! Keep lettin' them have it. Don't lose courage girl!' That cheered me immensely, as it was a lousy week. The Chameleon couldn't blast me for it as long as I didn't answer because I hadn't initiated it (I did wave an acknowledgment behind my back as we went through the gate, but she didn't see that)—and he couldn't get lockup for calling out as he was already on it!

Treat of the Week

The only regular visitors we had the whole time I was in prison were Sister Mary Louise Serafini and a lady from St Vincent de Paul (different each week from a pre-approved list). Sister was available for a few moments during that time if anybody wanted counselling, but mostly they simply talked generally. They would keep in contact with girls who had left, and let you know what they were doing. This visit gave the girls a lot of fun, and a respite from work as well.

If any of the girls were leaving and didn't have clothes, they could ask Sister for some. Lots of girls put on or lost a lot of weight in jail, and occasionally girls needed clothes for court or other reasons. One girl was picked up for an unpaid fine without warning. It was hot and as she was still doing her morning housework, all she had on were knickers and one of her husband's long shirts. She thought the police were joking when they told her to pack for prison, and laughed at them, so they grabbed her and hustled her out. They didn't even let her lock the house, let alone ring her child's preschool to tell them she wouldn't be picking up her son that day; she had to get special permission to make a phone call from prison to arrange that and tell them where she was. She had no money and wasn't in prison long enough for work permission to earn any so, consequently, when she was released four days later, she was barefoot, semi-dressed with no money for even a phone call. She had to walk several kilometres into town or hitchhike. When situations like that occurred, if they were in over a week, or girls had to go into court, they could ask for clothes and St Vincent's would supply them or get them from their homes.

Other church or welfare groups tried to join St Vincent's or come in on their own with other projects. One group offered to give cooking or craft classes, but after a Salvation Army lady teaching china painting transferred no replacements were allowed to fill the gap. It seemed the prison wanted no outside influences.

We were fortunate the St Vincent's ladies were still allowed to come in. Often the St Vincent de Paul visits were the one bright spot of the week, especially if we had a particularly bad-tempered screw on duty who was on everybody's back. Then the visit was usually the one hour when we were left alone. Sister knew immediately when the girls were having trouble with the staff. The St Vincent's ladies said when they were let in the gates they could feel the tension and when they walked in the door, Sister would say, 'Who's on today, girls? Everything OK?' We would shake our heads imperceptibly and nod towards the screw.

On those days, the ladies would watch themselves very carefully so they didn't infringe the rules, and so did we. For instance, one girl might have had a photograph from home, which she wanted to show Sister just as if she was part of the family. But if a screw was in a bad mood, Sister would get into trouble and the photo would be confiscated; the girl could be forbidden a future visit, too. Sister would be very sure to keep off any topics that could be interpreted as discussing prison policy. She would be careful not to ask too many questions about our Christmas sewing, because that might be considered asking how much prison work we had to do and how much spare time we had for sewing, which was against the rules, of course.

I'd been there for several months when Sister Mary Louise announced that Mary Ehn was coming in the following week. There was such a buzz of general enthusiasm and approval that I was interested to see who this was. The next week in walked an English redhead, cheerful and relaxed. She was a driving instructor, who also taught the disabled how to drive. She treated all the girls the same, regardless of what she thought privately, and many kept in contact with her when they left.

Mary would tell you funny little things that happened to her and the experiences she had had during the week. She had the ability to make the daily and commonplace come alive (like the new Australian man who insisted on letting out his crutch, as opposed to his clutch). She was great fun and we enjoyed her visits. Mary never missed the birthday of any long-term girl. And since I have left, there has not been one birthday she has ever missed.

We were all thrilled when she won a Churchill Fellowship to go to England and get her ticket to become a driving instructor's educator on how to teach the disabled.

Over the years I got to know Mary well. She joined my Darwin support group and was a great encouragement. She was cheerful even when she was feeling down, and if you guessed and mentioned it to her, she'd say, 'Oh, yeah, a bit down today,' but toss it off lightly in passing, and say, 'Just a little prayer for me and I'll be right.'

(This was one 'Pom' who never whinged!) If one of the girls was having problems, Mary would manage to talk to her. She would go round every girl individually for a private chat and say,

'Saying a little prayer for you at church. Keep your courage up.' The girls were very grateful to her for her constant cheerfulness and helpfulness.

By now Speedy was one of the few screws still determined to break me. Her main method was to try and overload me with what she considered to be the worst jobs available. I discovered she hated you to like your work and ask for more, so I determinedly adopted a permanent smile, rushed through my jobs and continually begged for more. She had me clean everything she could think of, sew everything she was able to lay hands on (she even rang the laundry specially to get them to search for anything still lying around over there!), and now she was really getting desperate to keep it up.

Then Speedy suddenly had another brainwave. The pair who had been rostered for tower cleaning were always anxious to get back quickly for Sister's visits. Froggie and I were equally looking forward to it today as Mary Ehn was coming in and Speedy had already found extra places to clean, keeping us late. On our way back the visitors caught up to us. At the gate Speedy let the visitors in and told us to wait. Froggie whispered, 'She's at it again.' Sure enough she turned and asked us to pick up papers in the officers' car park—and it was a really windy day. Froggie exclaimed 'Oh, detention!' I cracked up and Speedy exploded. Then Froggie and I hastily explained that we had only been referring to old memories of schooldays. Speedy bought it, after some convincing, and calmed down again.

We energetically rushed around, going further and further afield in opposite directions. Soon Speedy was getting desperate to keep an eye on us both at once, and tried to call us back. We both enthusiastically called that we only had one or two more, so she said 'OK', not realising they were a further 50 metres (55 yards) away from both of us! After that she decided it was time to finish as we'd 'done a good job and that should be enough for the day'. We went, and as soon as we got inside we told the other girls what had happened, and all of us collapsed in helpless giggles. (They had all watched us out the windows.)

Apart from Tapioca and several of the nasty screws in our section, I didn't have any problems with the rest of the officers. They knew I didn't deliberately go out of my way to cause any trouble, and if I said no to something, it was because it was against my principles, and there was a legitimate reason. If any nasty jobs needed doing across the other side, they usually asked me knowing I would go willingly enough, even though I might not like it.

To Penalise a Child

My stomach had been churning for days and I had a feeling something was wrong, and I was waiting for the phone to ring to give me bad news. Then it happened. On a Monday Speedy came over and said, 'Lindy, you're wanted on the phone. It's your husband.' I did not immediately understand the significance of this, then it registered—I could request to ring Michael reverse charges, but he couldn't ring me, and the prison was letting the call through!

My stomach was churning again by the time I got to the phone, and sure enough, the news was bad. Reagan had had an eye accident on the Saturday evening. Michael had sent him across to call Aidan for dinner and he had lingered to look at a neighbour's bonfire of leaves in the yard. The neighbour's son, a classmate of Reagan's, had earlier thrown a bottle with its lid on into the fire and the bottle exploded. The flying glass sliced the side of Reagan's face, went through the cornea and the lens of his right eye and the bridge of his nose. None of the others were injured. *They* were hiding.

Michael rushed him into hospital and he was operated on immediately. Our friend, Darryl Kent, sat with Michael through those awful waiting hours and helped organise things for him. At this stage they were pleased with his progress but said he had lost the sight of his right eye and that there was a fair chance of his left eye going blind in sympathy, but they would not know for certain for a few more days.

Reagan had been asking for his Mummy ever since the accident, but, although he had tried, Michael had been unable to get a message through to me. I knew that no attempt had been made to put him through.

Speedy had been on my back off and on for months but had almost stopped by this time. When the phone call about Reagan came through, I noticed an immediate change. I didn't tell her any details, but she could tell from my end of the phone conversation, that one of the children had had a bad accident. It was as if she now no longer desired to try and test me, and was genuinely sympathetic. She asked, 'What would you like to do? Do you want to go outside and work for a while, go to your room, or what?' I asked for a bit of peace. If I worked on my dried arrangement for the Show, perhaps I could get myself together before everybody came inside. I was pretty upset. She agreed. I went out to the greenhouse to get what I needed. Froggie was working out there, she took one look at my face and asked, 'What's wrong?' I told her Reagan had had a bad accident and was blind in one eye . . . maybe both . . . then the full impact hit me and I started to cry.

Not being fully aware of the animosity towards me, Speedy went over to the main office for the daily report on the section.

The Panther was relatively new at that stage and was still on probation. She was on yard duty and when she saw us talking she blew us both up. I turned away, dropping my head so my face was hidden, not trusting myself to speak, knowing if I did I would let her have all the pent-up anger I had been feeling for weeks over her treatment of me.

Froggie, trying to cool the situation, glibly said she was just getting some advice about the plants from me (which she often did, as I prepared the plants for the Show for her) and apologised.

I had got what I needed, so started to go back inside. By that time I was sort of under control again, but the Panther had not finished with me. She told me I had to go and do some weeding. Weeding the lawn! We all hated it—such a useless task.

I stated, 'I have permission to work on my project. I was just collecting these things then going back inside.'

She said, 'You do as you are told!' and bitingly told me 'go and get a bucket'. She was aware I was pretty upset but did not know why. I was doing my best to hold my tongue, so started to walk off to do some weeding on my own. She again came after me and told me, aloof and cold, that I was to 'work with the black girls'. For weeks while the 'get-on-Lindy's-back' pact was on, I had to work solo. Now when I wished to be alone, I was being forced to work in a group. I went across and sat down with the Aboriginal girls. Smiley, Blackie and Shy were also lifers and knew me really well; the Bird was fairly new but also a Christian. They had been having a happy time, talking and laughing together in their own language, but they were very sensitive to people and, when they took one look at my face, they fell silent. I knew that I owed them some sort of explanation. I told them not to worry, but I was very unhappy because I had just been told my little boy was going to be blind in one eye and was very sick. He wanted me, but they wouldn't let me go and see him.

Smiley had two children herself, and the Bird was also a mother. They were very quiet and I noticed their hand signals to each other and the other two girls to give me silent support. I said to them, 'I don't want to make you unhappy too. You were laughing and happy before I came, I just want you to be as you were and help me take my mind off it. You keep talking and don't mind me.' After a little while and some persuasion, they told me they were very sorry, and they started talking again.

We were all talking about it, and as usual the Aboriginal girls stopped working to do so. The Panther approached telling us to get on with our work. I quickly told the girls not to let her know what had happened or that I was upset. She'd be on my back more than ever if she knew. The Bird was a big, fat, happy girl and she suddenly called out an invitation for her to come and sing with us—and promptly started singing even though we weren't supposed to; that was enough to drive the Panther off in a hurry and, in spite of feeling miserable, I had to laugh. The girls were all Christians from mission stations and loved singing, which took their minds off their own troubles, as well as mine. It was a lot better than all crying in sympathy with each other, which we had been in danger of doing.

The Panther left us out there until the bain-marie was coming across, instead of letting us shower beforehand as normal, which meant she could later growl at us all for being late for lunch. I picked up a number of buckets and tools to bring in and called Froggie, knowing she had not been called and the Panther would use it as an excuse to go crook at her later.

We came in last, a little behind the Aboriginal girls, and the Panther prepared to have another go at me. I was all ready to have a go at *her* this time. Prison officers are not supposed to goad prisoners under stress. I could plead being upset and that she was hassling me, and I would get away with telling her what I thought without being charged or punished. I opened my mouth to speak but Froggie, seeing me about to do it, stepped in quickly to avoid trouble, and the moment passed.

Unbeknown to us, Speedy was quietly observing from around the corner, and saw the Panther's behaviour was overstepping the mark. After lunch we had to go outside again so I asked her whether I could stay inside this time. Surprised, she said, 'Yes, if you want to. You know I said you could do whatever you like.'

I said, 'I asked to stay inside before and was told I had to go out.' She looked at me and asked what I meant. I told her and she replied that she would have come and got me if she'd realised. She thought I had decided I *wanted* to go out.

She told me not to say anything, just leave it to her, so after muster I went to go about my business and the Panther started again. Speedy was waiting for it and just said, 'No, no. Lindy's staying inside. I have work for her. You take the other girls, I'll look after her.' She said it with quite an airy note as if to say, 'I'm in charge and don't argue,' and the Panther just had to swallow it.

I went to bed early to pray for the strength I needed. I was so angry at the prison authorities, knowing I could and should have been told about what happened on the Saturday night, but they hadn't even tried. They didn't care. Some of the screws did and showed their support where they could, but there was nothing they could do to let me see Reagan while those in authority said no.

As I wept on my bed that night, I pleaded with God to look after my little boy. I said, 'Lord, if he needs to be blind in that eye, then You know what's best. You're the only one that can look after him, but Lord, please don't let this hurt him emotionally, don't let him be bitter, and don't let me be bitter. Help him, Lord, I left him in Your care. I'm doing my part and doing my best here. When I came, You promised me You would look after my kids, and I'm holding You to that promise. Don't You let my son be emotionally scarred by this. He's only a little boy. Do what You want to with me, Lord, but make the Devil leave him alone. Help him through this, and keep him safe. May Your will be done about his eye, but please don't let it hurt him emotionally.' I knew that God heard me and that Reagan's other eye would be all right, but I had no confirmation of that yet. I was able to face those next few days calmly, at least with an outward serenity, which I was desperately trying to maintain on the inside. I knew God wouldn't let me down.

The next evening after work on 20 July 1983, I was able to write to Reagan in a calm way that I hoped would help settle a frightened little boy, although I still felt shattered.

> Dearest Reagan,
>
> How's Mummy's little pirate? Daddy tells me you had a bad accident to your eye and now you have a big bandage or patch over it. I'm very sad your eye is hurt and you hurt too. I'd love to be with you and give you a big cuddle. You'll have to have an extra one from Daddy for me.
>
> Did you know Mummy had her left eye hurt in an accident once, and I couldn't see for a long, long time. I had to use just one eye too. It's kind of funny at first 'cause things look flat, like the gutter and the road, and stairs look flat too but I made a game and soon got used to it. You will have to play a game too, eh? Maybe the doctor will give you a pirate patch! I bet you've been winking at the nurses too! Daddy said you have been a very good boy in hospital, darling. That's my brave boy. Mummy is very proud of you, my darling. Jesus will be with you, sweetheart. Cruel men hurt Him once and He knows what it's like to be hurt. One day He'll fix your eye up, if not soon, then He'll give you a brand new one in heaven when

> we see our baby Azaria and get her back again too. Won't that be lovely? Try and be a brave happy boy for Mummy and Jesus, my darling. I love you very much.
>
> Yours lovingly always,
> Mummy

A number of the other screws told me how sorry they were to hear Reagan had had an accident, and they asked about his progress. Although the Panther later learned what had happened, she never said anything to me.

A few days after I got the news of Reagan's accident I got a letter from Michael that had been held up in the post. In it were some photographs, one was a portrait shot of Reagan, taken before the accident. It was a long time before I could look at those two bright little eyes and feel no anger welling up in me against the Northern Territory. I knew if I had been home, if it hadn't been for the Northern Territory, we wouldn't even have been living in that house with those neighbours. We would have been nearly a kilometre away and Michael would have been able to call the children instead of having to send Reagan while he prepared the meal and looked after Kahlia on the weekend. It is, of course, no good even thinking about the 'what ifs' and 'might have beens'.

The Panther continued to watch me and would manage to stand in such a way that she could always see me from wherever she was. Several days later I was working on the big floor polisher resurfacing the floors. I went to the office to ask to be let out of the section and into the kitchen from the back door to continue polishing. The Panther heard and went to leave what she was doing to take me, but the chief, who seemed to be busy, jumped up to take me herself, telling the Panther to keep an eye on the girls. I wondered whether she was aware of what was happening.

When we got to the kitchen door the Panther was standing where she could see me through two sets of windows. I commented to the chief, 'You realise we are both being spied upon? We are naughty girls and are going to get into trouble!' Then the chief told me she had realised that the Panther had taken a set against me for weeks, so had deliberately brought me out herself.

I said to her, 'Thanks very much. I had noticed but I didn't realise anyone else had.'

She replied, 'Oh my word, and she'll be getting another edge of my tongue shortly.' Whether she got another edge of the chief's tongue or not I don't know, but I did notice that was the last day there was any more deliberate hovering around me.

At last the break-Lindy campaign was at an end and I could finally relax most of the time and settle down without living permanently on my guard. Michael rang again, telling me that they thought Reagan's left eye would be saved, but Reagan was still asking for me. They were doing all in their power to get me down to see him; he was in the Sydney Eye Hospital having further tests and operations and not in a position to come visiting me. Apart from anything else, the pressure of taking off and landing in a plane could damage his eye further, and they were now hoping to save some sight in it.

Friends had offered to pay the fares for me *and* my escort (all prisoners have to be escorted) to Sydney, so I could stay in Mulawa. I could go from Mulawa to the hospital on day leave or escort during the day, and be taken back at night for a week or two until Reagan's condition stabilised and then be sent back to Darwin. The New South Wales authorities, however, needed to have the Northern Territory's agreement. This was refused. Once again I was told Paul Everingham said no. Always Everingham said no. I would get the official reason and would then ask point blank whether Paul had a hand in this, and it was always, 'Yes, Paul says no.' No to my keeping Kahlia, no to my comforting Reagan. I wondered why—I'd never even met the man. In the *Living Bible* Matthew said, 'Don't be afraid of those who threaten you . . . the time is coming when the truth will be revealed: their secret plots will become public information.' I hoped this was true. The Territory authorities said we had to get a psychiatrist's report saying that Reagan would suffer irreparable psychological damage if he did not see his mother before they would agree to me going down.

I knew when he was sick, his mummy was the only one he really wanted because he knew she understood. One thing I knew about Reagan; he would not ask for me unless he was absolutely desperate, and like me, he would not show his feelings to a stranger. Only seeing us together would they know how much he missed me. When he was little, if I went away for a day or so on business, and left him with friends he would not mention me at all, but when I got back, he would cling to me like a limpet for days afterwards. He knew where I was and that I *would* come back but he would not let on how he felt to those people. It was the same with prison. He asked his father whether his mummy could come, and he asked friends; he even sat with head in hands at school one day and asked his teacher, 'Why can't I have my mummy like other kids can?' But when confronted with strangers (psychologists or not), he would not discuss it. So, of course, he seemed 'to be coping fairly well'.

Friends, knowing what they would like done for their own children if they were unable to be there, helped. Ann Deegan, although she had children younger than Reagan, arranged babysitters and went to the eye hospital to stay with Reagan hour after hour, as I would have done if I could have been there. Her only breaks were when Michael could get down to sit with him, or when others, like Denise, an old friend from Tasmanian days, now married and living in Sydney, relieved her. Denise wrote telling me all the news of the operations and details of how he was coping and how his teddy bears were bandaged up with sore eyes, arms and legs to match. I was very grateful to her for that, as Ann was too. I also received a photograph of him in hospital which showed a listless, lonely little boy. It spoke volumes to a mother who was also lonely.

That was my lowest time in prison. I knew the damage that emotionally could be done in my absence, and yet I was powerless to do anything about it. Once again it seemed to me that jury had a lot to answer for. Not only had I lost one little girl tragically, they had then been responsible for taking my next little girl away from me twice, and had also punished two little boys who had done nothing in their lives to deserve the punishment of parting them from their mother. I felt like asking them how *they* would like to be parted from *their* children under similar circumstances.

My little boy was hurting so much and I could have been there, done something, and they were stopping me. So was all their red tape. I felt angry and desperate, the closest I came to losing control in all my time in prison.

The next time the family were able to visit after the accident, I had to look at Reagan walk in the gate with an eye patch on, scars across his nose and at the corner of that eye. It brought home to me again the cruelty of other human beings against their own kind, something that God never intended or ordained should be. Once again I knew a parent's helpless wish that I had been hurt instead of my child. I saw a very withdrawn and lonely little boy, desperately needing to be loved and not getting the love that he wanted.

Reagan's disposition is fairly similar to mine; every time he came to visit me I noticed he had grown more remote and inward. Aidan would come in with arms outstretched and run to me, his huge smile first wobbling, then dissolving into tears as he finally hugged me. Reagan came seriously and shyly, taking his time before giving me a cuddle. When he finally did, however, he perched himself on my lap and refused to move. By the time the end of the visit came, he didn't want to go home.

On one occasion, I was disappointed because I thought he had already gone while I was still saying goodbye to the others, and it was the last visit before they flew home. When we counted heads, he was missing and couldn't be found anywhere. Suddenly a thought occurred to me; he had asked if he could stay with me. We looked in the section, my cell, the toilets, outside—nothing.

It occurred to me then to move the interview room door, and there crouched down, hiding behind the door, was Reagan. He figured if he hid behind the door they wouldn't notice he was missing and he could stay behind with his mummy. I had to tell him he couldn't. He couldn't understand why; he wouldn't be any trouble. He hadn't realised the others had also seen where he was, and begged me to let him stay hidden. He could hide under my bed all day and see me at night when it was dark.

Reagan didn't know we had to sleep with the lights on and the screws would see him. He hadn't thought of how much little boys wriggle, how hungry they get, how hot it was under the bed and that he would get found anyway. He *desperately* wanted to be with his mummy. My last sight on that visit was of him crying his eyes out on Michael's shoulder. As they got to the gate he just looked back. He was no longer crying. He didn't wave, although he knew I was standing watching in the window as I always did. He just looked. It took me days to settle back into the prison routine after that.

From Slag to a Breath of Fresh Air

When Janus left, her cell was in a disgusting condition. She had regularly spat on the walls and this had dried on. Somebody had to clean it and I got the job. I had no gloves, as usual, and when using the water, slimy patches of thick yellow secretion reconstituted themselves. I went through quite a lot of toilet paper endeavouring to remove the globules without getting it on me. When I started, the smell and look of the cell left much to be desired, so I finished that job in record time. Walls, ceiling and floors had to be scrubbed and not before time.

At one time we had a new superintendent, Mr Sutton from head office. That was a totally new era and a much happier one for most. The whole prison was far better run with minimal hassles. I first met him regarding some medication that was not on the free list and which I needed. It was simply a cream for mosquito bites (which I was allergic to) and could be bought over the counter in the Northern Territory, but it created a problem. They were complaining and finally said I could only have this cream, provided I paid for it myself. I said, 'That's fine, as long as I get it.' Next thing I had a visit from Mr Sutton, telling me when medicines were not on the free list but a prisoner needed them, and the doctor had given a prescription, they were allowed and paid for. Mine came into this category. He apologised that I had been told I had to pay myself. He would personally rip up the papers I had signed. The prison had been given orders from head office not to hassle me, and my medicine would arrive shortly. It did.

Not only did Mr Sutton remember me again, but he addressed me as 'Mrs Chamberlain'. It surprised me because staff tended not to remember one prisoner from another. Even though I was well known, I had lost a lot of weight, so I didn't look like the same person he had seen before.

Although I was supposed to be referred to as 'Prisoner Chamberlain' (numbers weren't used except on your buy sheets), in the smaller female section everyone was called by Christian names, which we appreciated. It was much nicer to be called 'Lindy' than 'Prisoner Chamberlain' or simply 'Chamberlain'. I noticed certain chiefs who came across started addressing me as 'Mrs Chamberlain', then later 'Lindy'. Usually they didn't use our names at all. Slowly but surely, a number of the male screws also started calling me 'Lindy', as if they were talking to an acquaintance, and I appreciated that. It was quite rare to be given the title 'Mrs', and usually caused raised eyebrows and comment from those around.

Mr Sutton asked if Lindy and another girl who could be trusted would come across to scrub his office out. I had seen the state it had been left in. Sure enough, the two of us spent several hours. The furniture was filthy, caked on dirt shiny with wear. Hand and boot marks (up to a metre in height), were smeared all over the safe. As the room smelt stale, we opened everything we could to let the place air as much as possible. The cupboards were turned out and cleaned, the bookcases cleaned and scrubbed, the carpet vacuumed . . . Still we didn't finish. The toilet was enough to make you sick—it stank. It was so stained I had to get some rubber gloves and get down on my hands and knees and scrub it off with Jex because the toilet cleaner would not lift if off!

The following day I went along to do the fridge and finish off. It took hours. The fridge was a mini-bar, with only a small area left in the middle that had not frozen solid with ice—in the whole fridge compartment, not just the freezer. I eventually unearthed cans of Coke, frozen for months amid the ice. It took hours with hot water and knives to chip the ice out. I was able to scrub the desk back, oil and polish it. The whole place smelt much better and it looked quite a decent room.

Mr Sutton wanted to keep his room tidy and requested the girls on cleaning do his office too. Frequently we would go in and clean it while he was there. He would always stop to talk to us as if we were humans; even when he was obviously extremely busy he would not ignore us but address us politely though briefly, before immersing himself again.

Within a couple of weeks he knew a number of the prisoners by name. He spoke kindly and he didn't treat us as if we were some piece of unseen dirt, or worse; he commented on our work and how much he appreciated the way we kept the section. The males were treated with similar respect. Where once you would walk through the sallyport where the Aboriginal boys swept and see screws deliberately walk in their dirt and spread it all around again; now we would see Mr Sutton nod and smile at them, stand back for them to move out of the way or detour around them. He would say good morning or good afternoon and smile at them and the men with him would follow suit.

When we asked to go on parade before Mr Sutton, we could guarantee he would come at least within two days, if not the same day. We could talk to him alone, or with one of his men, without having one of the screws standing over us. If we hadn't made our requests plain and he had any questions, he would ask us clearly and intelligently, and then, most of the time, he would give us an immediate yes or no. If the answer was 'no', we could put a case before him stating why we thought he should alter his opinion. If the reasons were good, he would say, 'I will give it some thought and let you know,' and it was not beyond the realms of hope. In fact, quite frequently, he would come back across and say, 'I have given your reasons some thought and decided that you may have permission.'

Anyone on parade for a misdemeanour was encouraged to speak out, instead of being told what the crime and the punishment would be. The rule 'an officer is always right, and a prisoner is always wrong', did not work with him. He asked you to explain, and listened before he told you what *he* knew; only then would he act. Sometimes he even called officers across to his office and remonstrated with them instead. A bad officer could often get another officer's backing so that it was the word of two officers against you. Because of this, if he was told another officer had been there at the time, that officer was called across to be questioned as soon as they came on shift before that could happen.

During Mr Sutton's term, interstate visitors were allowed one hour twice daily visits, and we were still permitted our local half-hour visit if booked, as well as a one-hour religious visit, if our clergyman called. This was great; normally religious visits were cancelled if we had interstate visitors (and they were limited to a maximum of five visits). On one of my family's visits during Mr Sutton's time, Michael brought me a photo album, which he showed Mr Sutton and asked permission to leave. Not only was this granted, but he was told he could actually *hand* it to me, and I could keep it in my cell. I thought Michael had made a mistake and it must be for my property as we were only allowed six photographs in our cells at a time.

So I thanked him, but told him he better take it home as it would get mouldy stored in my property. He said he had permission and could give it to me, but I was still doubtful and thought he should check. So he asked Mr Sutton again the next day and he said Mr Sutton seemed indignant that Michael didn't believe him when he gave his word.

I was very excited about actually getting a photo album, and one or two of the other girls also got permission while Mr Sutton was there. Once permission was granted it was not revoked, unless a prisoner was badly behaved. Then everything was taken away and you had to ask for your possessions to be reinstated one by one, as you regained a good behaviour record.

Mr Sutton also gave me permission to do a number of different crafts and the other girls likewise found him accommodating. His belief was (as it should be) that the punishment of being away from your friends and loved ones was enough without further harassment and that we did not need to be stood over, which caused us to be upset and play up. Hence he was not liked much by some of the nasty screws. But the others got on better. We had better meals during Mr Sutton's regime than we had in the rest of the time put together. Food was cooked and cleaned properly and it became quite palatable, with variety as well as taste. Much-needed supplies arrived and badly needed new clothing was bought for the guys. Rules were tightened or relaxed where necessary and became much more even handed and sensible.

After he left, once again the office wasn't cleaned, and before long the smell was wafting out the door again. The only times we got in there to clean were after they had a party for something or the ashtrays were overflowing. We would dash in, grab the ashtrays, and dash out again. The old regime had returned. The place reassumed the appearance of a pigsty with a pig in residence.

Azaria aged nine weeks four days standing on Ayers Rock with me.
(Michael Chamberlain courtesy Reagan)

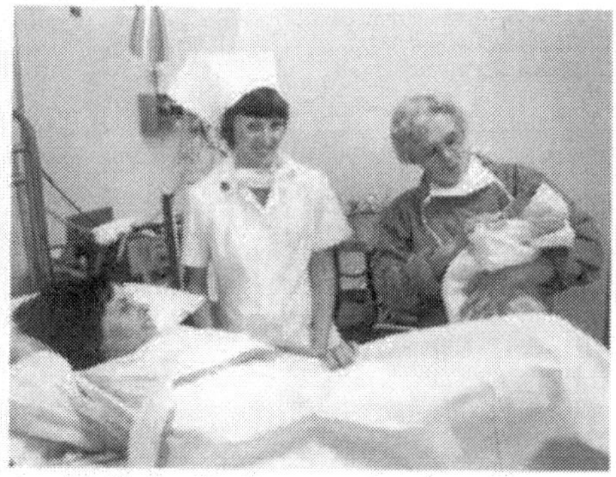

Azaria's birth with the maternity sister who delivered her and Dr Irene Milne.
(Michael Chamberlain – court exhibit)

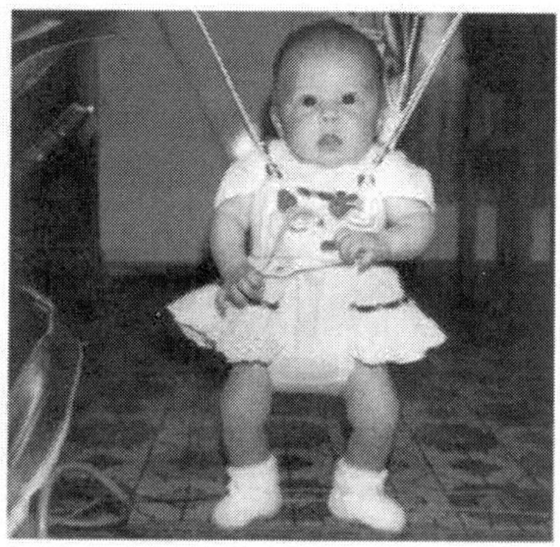

Azaria aged five weeks and three days enjoying her jolly jumper. *(Lindy Chamberlain)*

Reagan feeding Azaria her comp bottle.
(Lindy Chamberlain)

Azaria 'talking' to the shawl my mother knitted. *(Lindy Chamberlain)*

A carefree Aidan aged six and Reagan aged four on the way to Alice Springs. *(Lindy Chamberlain)*

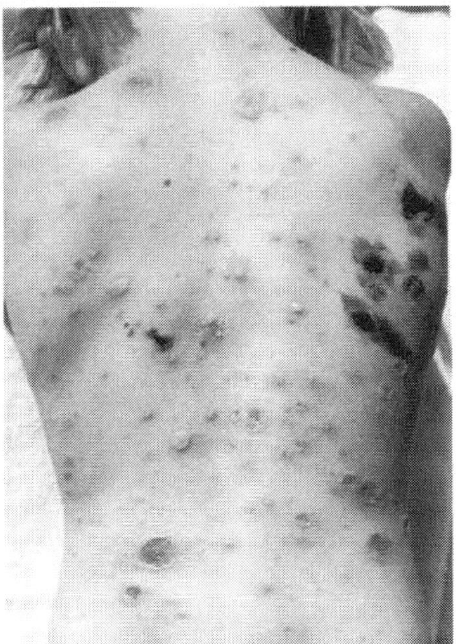

Reagan's chicken pox (four days later when he had recovered quite a bit) that caused ill feeling and started rumours. *(Lindy Chamberlain)*

Aidan and Reagan before we left our overnight campsite at the Devil's Marbles. *(Michael Chamberlain courtesy Reagan)*

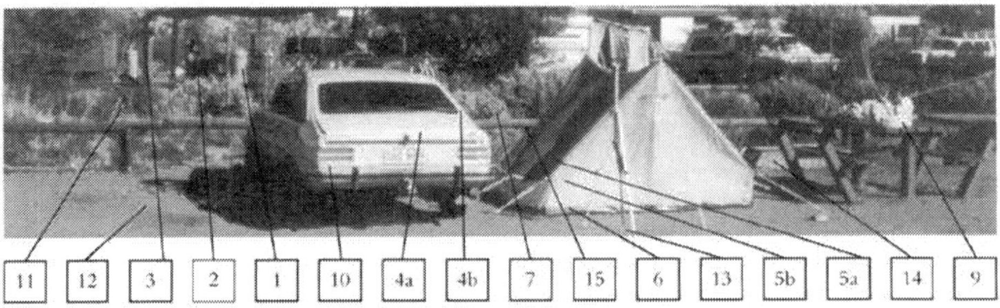

Our campsite at Ayers Rock. The gas bottles (1) blocking the view from the stove (2) to the tent, with Reagan (5a), and Azaria's carrybasket (5b). The car hatch (4a) and door 4(b) where I collected the baked beans. Azaria's bottles and sterilization solution (9) which the Crown maintained I had in the tent. The wet salivery substance and dingo footprints (6) found by Inspector Gilroy and the trackers. The bush (7) that blocked my view of the dingo, and the spot (10) where I saw the second dingo behind the car and the direction it ran (12). The culprit dingo's track (13) discovered by the trackers later. The 'long pig' barbeque (14) and the light on the barbeque shelter (3). Whittaker's gas light (11) moved from outside the tent (15) to beside my passenger side car door (11).
(*Michael Chamberlain – court exhibit*)

Greg, Sally and Chantelle Lowe with whom we shared the barbeque shelter. (*Courtesy Greg Lowe*)

From right to left: Senior Ranger Derek Roff, with Nipper Winmatti, his wife Barbara Tjikadu (the key tracker), Daisy Walkabout and another woman tracker. (Other key trackers Nui Minyintiri and No. 1 were absent.)
(*Michael Chamberlain – court exhibit*)

Wild dingo. (*Michael Flowerdale*)

The family gathered after the memorial service. *Back row left to right:* my brother Alex, Dad (Pr Cliff Murchison), Michael. *Middle row:* sister-in-law Felicity, Mum (Avis Murchison – grandma), me, Mother (Greta Chamberlain – Nanna). *Front row:* nephews Malcome and Alex jnr, Reagan and Aidan. (*Courtesy Lindy Chamberlain*)

The first day of the first inquest. *At the bar table left to right:* Council assisting the Coroner Ashley Macknay (1) and his solicitor Michael O'Loughlan (2) our solicitor Peter Dean (3). *In the press seats left to right:* Geoff de Luca (4), Michael (5), Shane McGuire (6), Kim Tilbrook (7), unknown (8), Bill Hutchings (9) and Malcolm Brown (10) behind the TV cameraman. Mike Lester is standing (11). I'm at the *back* near the door (in dark glasses) (12). Bill (13) and Judy West (14) are in the *second back row*. (*Barry O'Brien*)

Taking botanist Rex Kuchel's (kneeling) evidence at the spot where the jumpsuit, singlet, nappy and booties were found (undergrowth present when initially discovered is dead at the season this photograph was taken). I'm in the white hat. (*Russell McPhedran*)

Ashley Macknay, Crown forensic pathologist Dr Andrew Scott, solicitor Michael O'Loughlan and forensic dentist for the crown Mr Ken Brown, who requested the clothes for an opinion in London, which re-opened the second inquest. (*Russell McPhedran*)

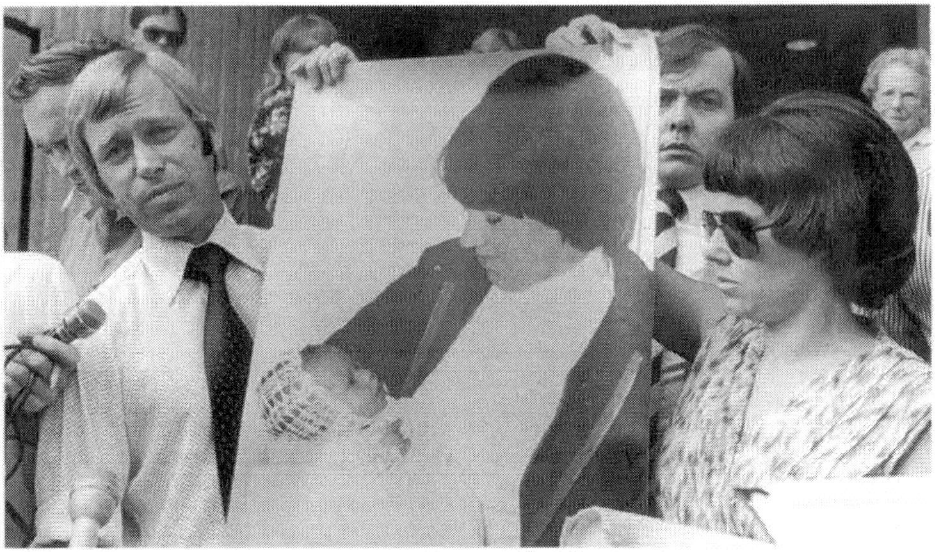

On the steps of Alice Springs court house. With the inquest over, Michael and I hold up a poster of the reason for it all – our beautiful baby Azaria. (*Barry O'Brien*)

Coroner Gerry Galvin (left), and Des Sturgess barrister for the Crown, discuss one of Michael's photographs of the Rock. (*Russell McPhedran*)

At last they post some signs at the rock. (*Russell McPhedran*)

Our team for the trial *left to right:* Legal Aid solicitor Greg Cavanagh, solicitor Stuart Tipple, Junior Counsel Andrew (Andy) Kirkham, Queen's Counsel John Phillips. (*Barry O'Brien*)

Crown Queen's Counsel Ian Barker. (*Barry O'Brien*)

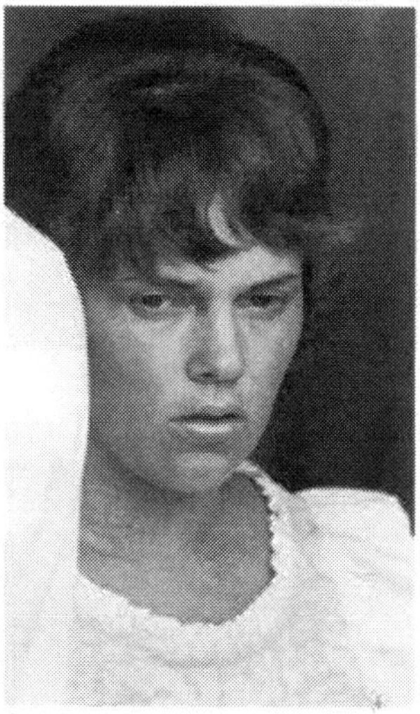

At the end of a day in the box. (*Barry O'Brien*)

Detective Sergeant Graeme Charlwood. (*Barry O'Brien*)

Leaving the courthouse en route to prison after being sentenced. (*Barry O'Brien*)

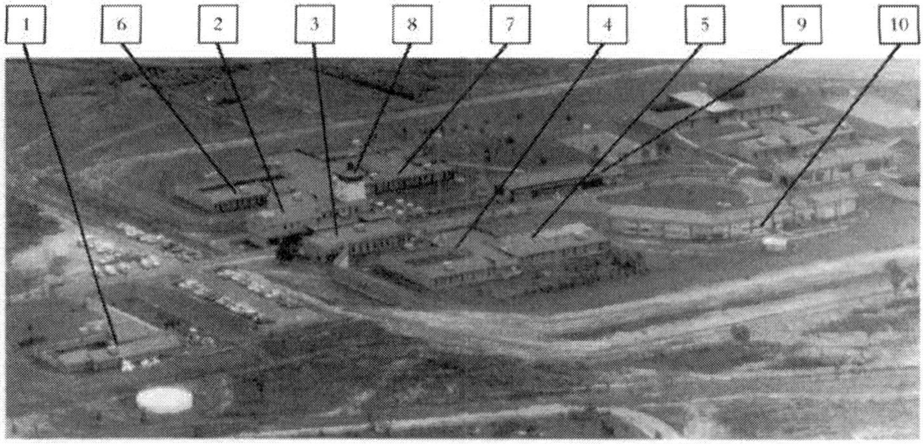

Darwin prison: (1) The Female Section (2) Administration (3) Southport (4) Medical Centre (5) B-Block (6) Remand (7) Library (8) Observation Tower (9) Assembly Hall (and weight room) (10) Kitchen, Laundry and Workshops. (*Russell McPhedran*)

My brother Alex, distressed after being refused a visit with me. My cell is in the building immediately behind his right shoulder. (*Russell McPhedran*)

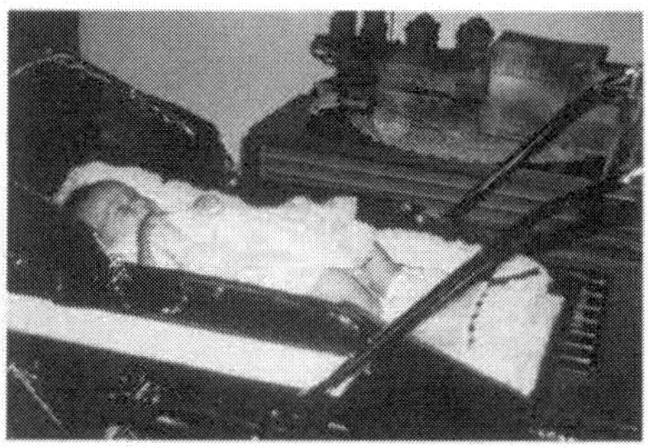

Kahlia ready to go to class with me. A few weeks later she was taken from me for the second time when I was returned to prison after the Federal Court. (*Lindy Chamberlain*)

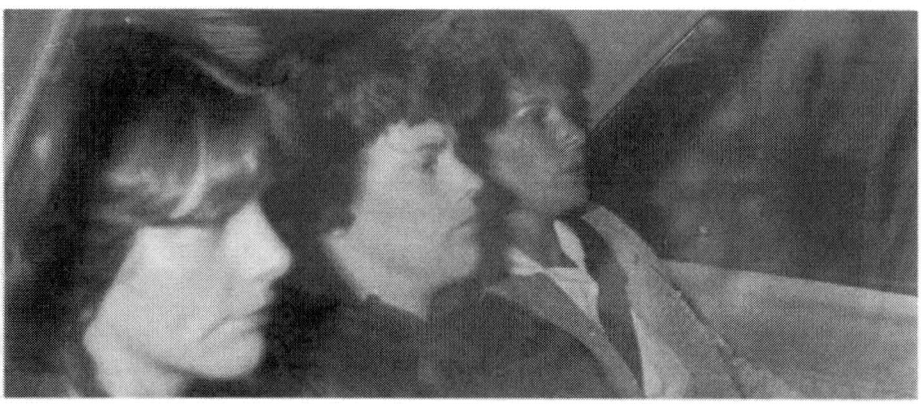

Being taken from the Federal Court to Mulawa Prison for transfer back to Darwin. (*Russell McPhedran*)

Michael and Reagan bring Kahlia for a prison visit. (Aidan caught measles and had to stay in bed.) (*Russell McPhedran*)

Kahlia (*right*) and her foster mummy Jenny Miller and foster sister Tiana (TJ), the greatest of pals. TJ was weaned so Kahlia could continue to be fed. (*Wayne Miller*)

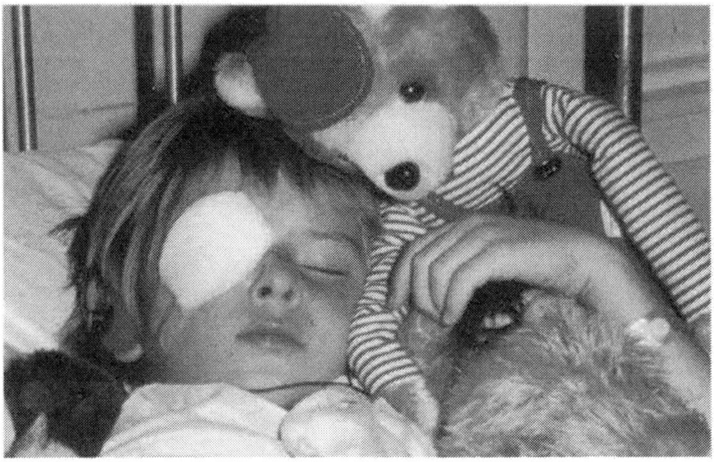

A lonely Reagan in hospital after his eye accident. (*Michael Chamberlain courtesy Reagan*)

Kahlia with her first foster family, the Millers, after Wayne's graduation. (*Lynley Potts*)

Kahlia happily working with her second foster family Jan and Owen Hughes with three of her foster brothers and Aidan and Reagan. (*Michael Chamberlain courtesy Kahlia*)

The Innocence Committee at the media conference with Gordon Elliot presenting the 'Blue Book'. *Top left to right:* Guy Boyd, Dr Weston Allen, Senator Malcolm Colston, Mr Justice Francis Gallagher, Gordon Elliot, Sir Reginald Sholl, chairman. *Bottom, left to right:* Stuart Tipple, Pro Hart, Betty Hocking, Dr Frederick Smith, Arlyn Tombleson, Senator Colin Mason. Absent: Dr Anthony Noonan. (*Bruce Miller, courtesy Fairfax*)

Mum and Dad with some of the petitions during the presentation at Parliament House. (*Betty Hocking*)

Mike Lester (*left*) and Peter Stojanovic. (*Michael Chamberlain*)

Liz and Tony Noonan with the flowers I took him weeks before he died. (*Michael Chamberlain courtesy Liz Noonan*)

Yvonne Cain, the juror with a backbone. (*Bernie Ollevou*)

Me with friends Simon, Chip, John and Liz Parry only hours after my release. (*Stuart Tipple*)

Stuart Tipple with Kahlia and his son James at my home-coming party. (*Lynley Potts*)

With Mum and Dad at my home-coming party. (*Lynley Potts*)

Me, Pat Stanley TNT Security (ex Mulawa screw), Mike Lester and Michael on Kerry Packer's shooting wagon, 'hiding out' at the Barrington tops. (*Michael Chamberlain*)

Michael with Helena (Lena) after her release from prison. (*Lynley Potts*)

Michael and me leaving the Royal Commission with friends George Rollo (*right*) and Ron Craig in the background. (*Bruce Miller, courtesy Fairfax*)

Aidan leaving the Royal Commission after his evidence. (*Paul Matthews, courtesy Fairfax*)

Stuart Tipple and me arriving at the press conference about compensation in 1989. (*Craig Golding, courtesy Fairfax*)

Justice Morling the Royal Commissioner. (*Robert Pearce, courtesy Fairfax*)

Our guys line up for a final photo wearing their 'presents' *Left to right:* David Re assistant solicitor, John (Jack) Winneke QC, Joan Simmons secretary, Brind Zichy-Woinarski Junior Counsel, Stuart Tipple, Ken Crispin Junior Counsel
(*Michael Chamberlain courtesy Brind Zichy-Woinarski*)

Constable Francis (Frank) Morris. (*Barry O'Brien*)

Mrs Joy Kuhl, Crown forensic pathologist. (*Barry O'Brien*)

Professor Barry Boettcher, defence pathologist. (*Ken Chapman*)

Professor Gustafson, defence odontologist. (*Courtesy Liz Noonan*)

Professor Ouchterlony, defence forensic expert. (*Courtesy Liz Noonan*)

Mr Les Smith, defence scientist (*Courtesy Liz Noonan*)

Dr Ken Chapman, defence scientist. (*Lynley Potts*)

Dr Anthony (Tony) Raymond, Commission forensic expert. (*Courtesy Tony Raymond*)

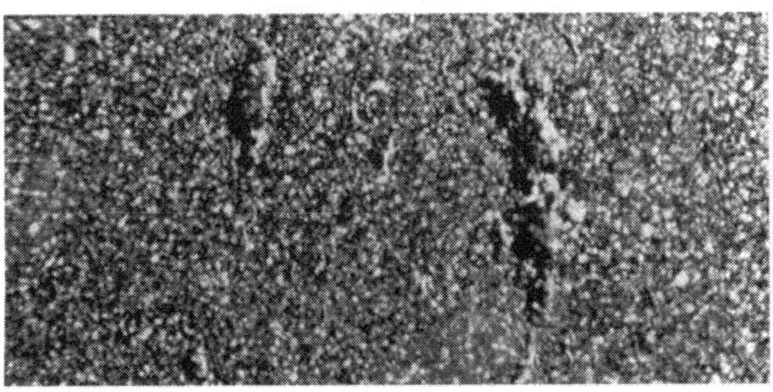

The underdash spray from our car, enlarged about ten times. The paint overspray is clearly visible, yet the Crown (using a microscope magnified to forty times) was unable to distinguish this and claimed it was a foetal blood spray. (*Les Smith*)

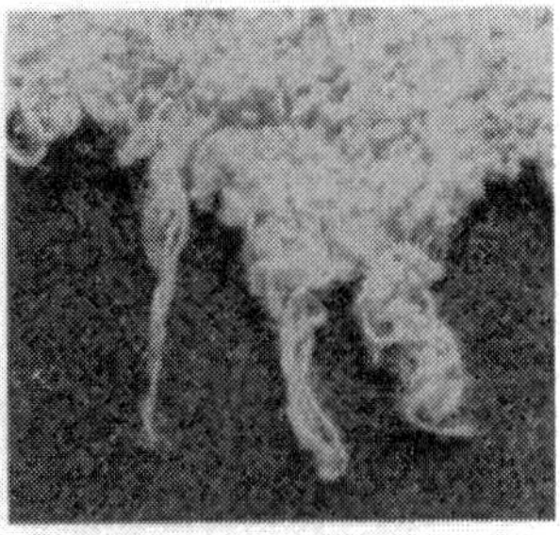

Azaria's jumpsuit damage.
(*Les Smith*)

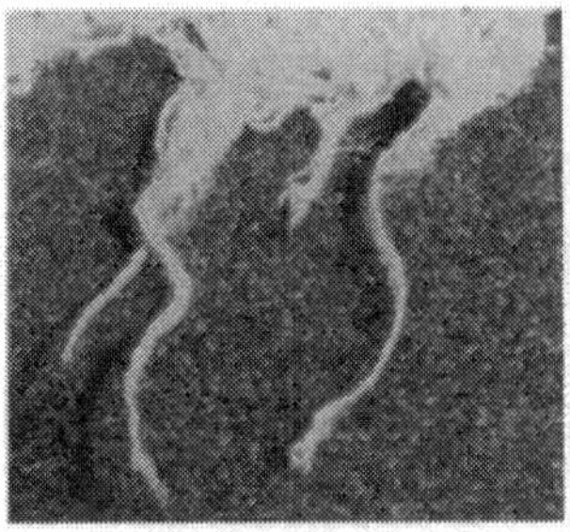

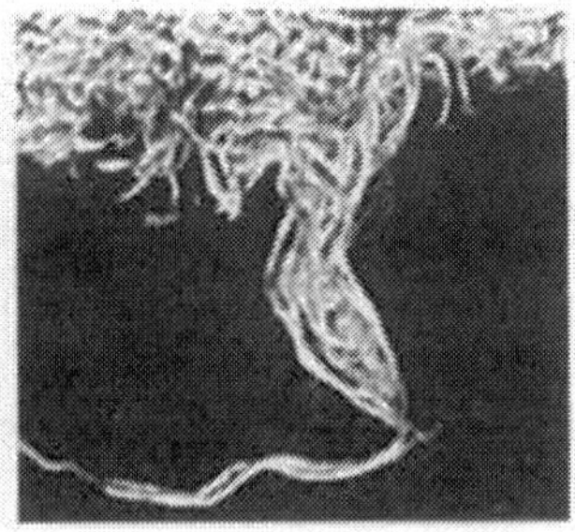

Test sample dingo damage showing typical 'tassels'.
(*Ken Chapman*)

Left: Azaria's jumpsuit collar damage showing five nylon threads in 'planar array' and an uncut nylon thread, impossible to explain with a scissor cut but easily recognized as a thread left between the cuts of two adjoining teeth. (*Les Smith*)
Right: Damage to Azaria's jumpsuit showing more 'tasseling'. (*Les Smith*)

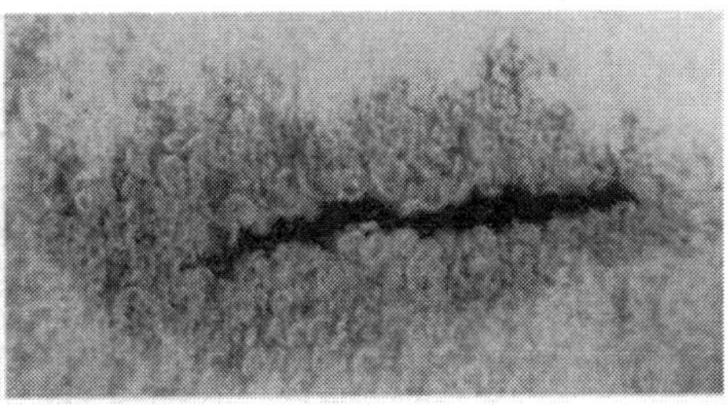

Left: Test dingo cut damage showing the famous 'planar array' over a 15 mm cut which is similar to that in Azaria's jumpsuit collar damage. (*Ken Chapman*)
Right: A dingo cut by 'Suzie' showing just how straight an animal can cut. (*Ken Chapman*)

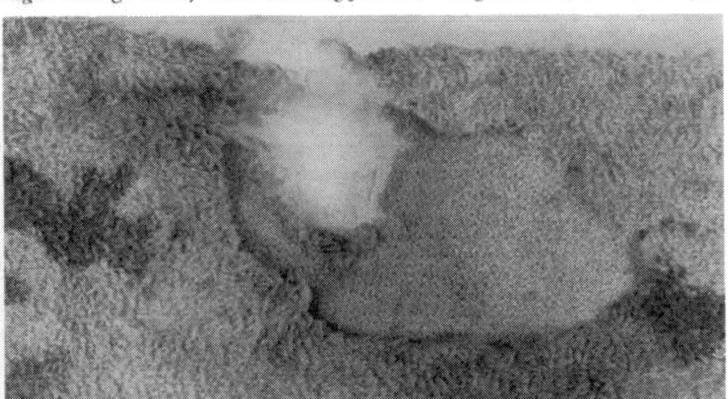

The sleeve damage to Azaria's jumpsuit is made up of cuts 5 to 15 mm long with tassels and discontinuations interweaving between them. The Crown claimed this was faked scissor damage. Dingo cut experts and world authority discredited this. (*Michael Chamberlain – court exhibit*)

Working with Robert Caswell on the movie script. (*Michael Chamberlain*)

Final script consultations with Robert Caswell (*centre*) and Fred Schepsi in Melbourne. (*Michael Chamberlain*)

Working on the script with Sam Neill and Meryl Streep the first time I met her. (*Michael Chamberlain*)

Pausing for a photo after our first consultation. *Left to right:* Craig McLachlan, me and Miranda Otto. (*Rick Creighton*)

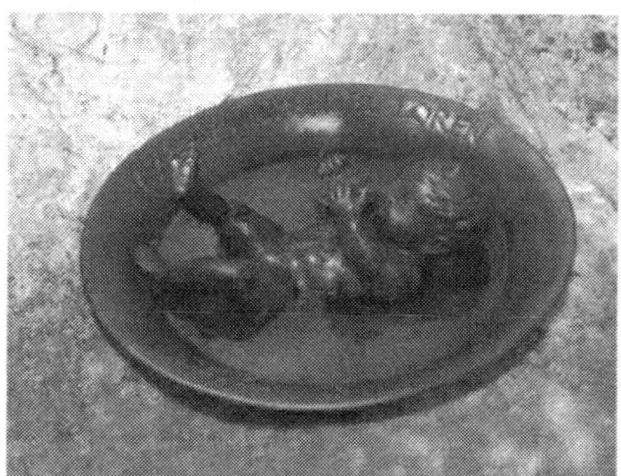

My celebration of Azaria's life. Her fountain. (*Barry O'Brien*)

Rick, Kahlia and me with my favourite 'human Alsatian' Harry M (Miller) back on holiday from the USA. (*David Hahn*)

Barbara Brann who helped block the press down the lane. (*Margo Goodwin*)

The victory party, *left to right:* Margo Goodwin, Greg and Sally Lowe, Michael, me, Wally Goodwin (who found the clothes), Liz Noonan – Darwin Support Group Leader. (*Courtesy Barbara Brann*)

Me hiking in New Zealand. (*Darryl Kent*)

Still keen on the outdoors – morning ablutions for the family when camping out in 1990. *Left to right:* Reagan, Kahlia, Aidan and Michael (*Lindy Chamberlain*)

My most precious possessions: Aidan 16, Kahlia 7 and Reagan 14. As they were in 1989 trying to lead a normal life and put the last 10 years behind them. (*Kevin Brown courtesy Women's Day*)

Going home to America at last (1993). On our way to the plane. *Left to right:* Reagan, me, Kahlia and Rick. (*David Hahn*)

All of my most precious possessions. The day Rick married 'us' in 1992. *From left to right:* Reagan, Aidan, me, Kahlia and my lovely man Rick. (*www.tombrewsterphotography.com*)

Greg Lowe, with Lindy, Stuart Tipple, and Michael Chamberlain, after Fourth Inquest Submissions
(photo: Rick Creighton)

Our conference room view of the waiting media, at the end of Fourth Inquest Submissions
(photo: Rick Creighton)

Lindy does one of many interviews for overseas *(photo: Rick Creighton)*

Final Victory pose: Cherie Tipple, Michael, Stuart, Lindy, and Aidan *(photo: Rick Creighton)*

Addressing the media at the end of our 32-year saga. Triumph at last: June 2012 *(photo: R. Creighton)*

Reagan Chamberlain
(photo: Kahlia Chamberlain)

Our whole family at Aidan & Amber's wedding *(photo: H. Mantz)*

Kahlia at her wedding
(photo: Lindy)

Left: Lindy & Rick today

30th Year Witness reunion. Top: Greg, Sally, Murray, Lindy, Diana, Catherine, Judy, Phyllis, Amy, Max. Bottom: Chantelle, Aidan, Reagan, Margot, Wally. Sadly missing: Max Cranwell, tragically killed in PNG Kokoda Track plane crash just months before. *(photo: David Hahn)*

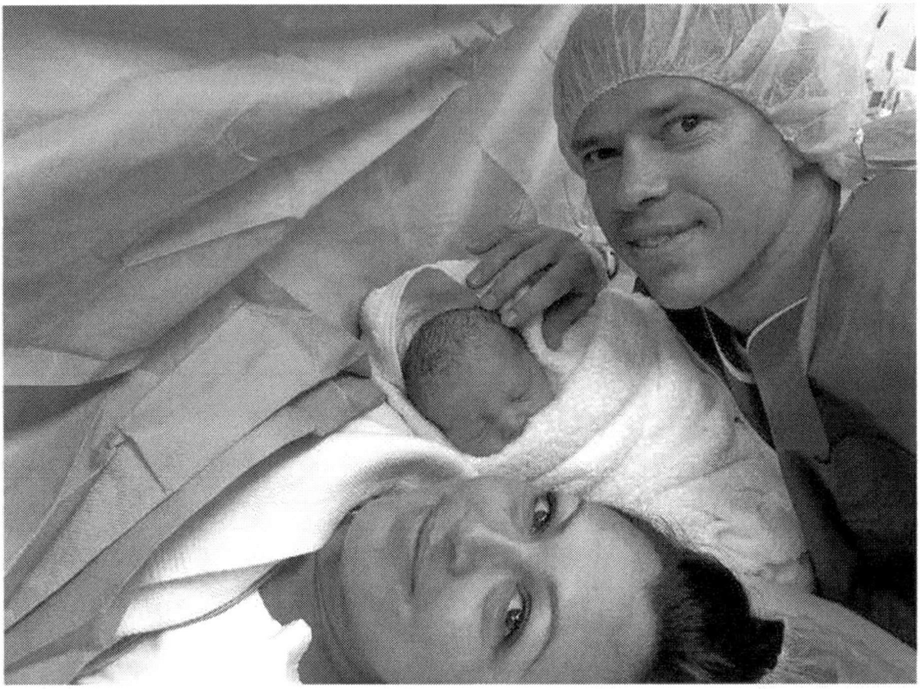

Aidan & Amber, with our very first grandchild, Amelia 'Milly' Loren Chamberlain

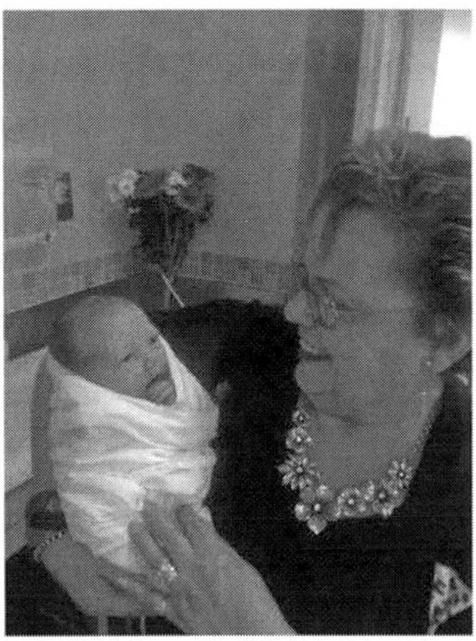

'Milly', meeting Grammy, for the first time
(photo: Aidan Chamberlain)

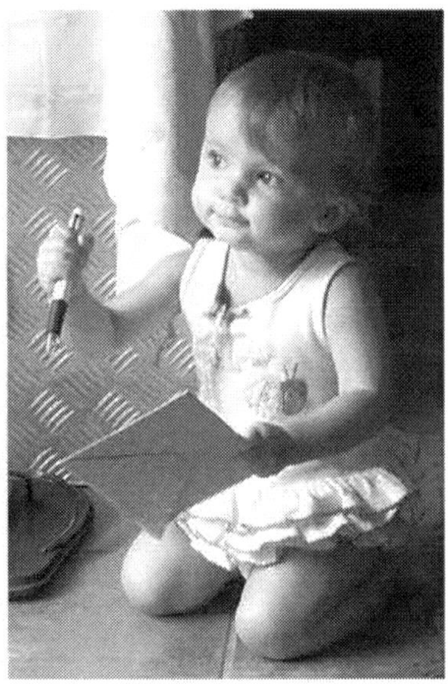

Amelia Loren Chamberlain, 1 year old
(photo: Lindy Chamberlain-Creighton)

Northern Territory Of Australia
Births, Deaths and Marriages Registration Act

CERTIFIED COPY OF DETAILS IN DEATH CERTIFICATE

DECEASED Name Sex Date of Death Place of Death Age and Date of Birth Place of Birth Occupation Usual Residence Period of Australian Residence Marital Status	 Azaria Chantel Loren CHAMBERLAIN Female 17 August 1980 Ayers Rock N.T. 9 Weeks 11 June 1980 Mount Isa, QLD Infant 3 Abel Smith Parade Sunset Mount Isa QLD Life Single
MARRIAGE DETAILS To whom married Age of deceased at marriage Date and place of marriage	
CHILDREN OF DECEASED Names (Sex, Age/Date of Birth)	
PARENTS Father Mother (Maiden Name)	 Michael Leigh Chamberlain (Pastor) Alice Lynne Murchison
CAUSE OF DEATH Coroner When deceased was last seen	INQUEST HELD 12 JUNE 2012 ELIZABETH MORRIS - NT CORONER The cause of her death was as the result of being attacked and taken by a dingo.
BURIAL Date Place Funeral Director or Arranger Witnesses	 Body Not Recovered
REGISTRATION Informant Name, Occupation Registration Number Registering Officer Date and Place	 Peter J. Buzzard, Police Constable 20098813 D. Van Aalst (Daniel Van Aalst), Deputy District Registrar Of Births, Deaths And Marriages 2 March 1981 Alice Springs

I certify that the above are particulars contained in an entry in the Register of Deaths.
Dated this 12th day of June, 2012

Northern Territory Government

217347

Peter Howell Shoyer
Registrar of Births, Deaths & Marriages

The final death certificate (left)

Below: Azaria's place in art and history (artist: Andy Collis)

THE ENDLESSNESS OF NOTHING

One of the guys got a book sent in called *The Long Huey* by a New Zealander, Greg Newbold, who did time for drugs. It was smuggled over to us and I enjoyed reading it also. There were a lot of similarities in his work release prison and where we were—I could relate to a lot of the screws' attitudes he described, and even identify with certain characters and compare them to certain of our screws.

He described the petty tyranny—being directed to do a job and being stopped just as you felt you were accomplishing something, then being told to do something else. This meant you never actually *finished* anything. If you were doing a good job and enjoying it, they would deliberately ask somebody incompetent to finish it, so your good work was negated at the last moment. Then again, they may ask someone who had a grudge against you to finish off and that person would claim credit for your work, so it looked as if you had done nothing all day.

The pettiness of some people was amazing. Rambo delighted in walking about briskly and deliberately rattling her keys, looking at you with a smirk as they rattled. The Panther and one or two of the others did the same. (Their personal insecurity showed in the way they liked to rub in their authority: 'I hold the keys and you're the prisoner. You are locked in here.') Officers mainly brought their food from home and ate wherever they chose, although they were supposed to use their own staff room. Rambo, if on with another nasty screw, liked to take her food to our day room. Normally her food wasn't much—she thought the prison food was great as she couldn't cook for nuts. If she knew we had been enduring particularly lousy food, she would wait a couple of hours after our meal when she knew we would all be in the day room and hungry, then come in with her food and give us a running commentary about how *nice* her food was. She would also bring in exotic fruits such as grapes, peaches, apricots and plums which she ate in front of us, slurping to make us well aware of it; if we couldn't bear to watch, we had to listen. This was accompanied by a running commentary: 'Do you like . . . ? Pity they don't give them to you in here, isn't it?' When she finished eating she would smirk at everybody and go back to the officers' staff room, where she should have been all along. This annoyed us all, as she knew, but it also disgusted both us and the decent screws.

The next time Michael came to visit I told him about Rambo eating her fruit (even though officially we weren't allowed to discuss the other girls, the screws, or any of the prison routine). The stupidity and futility of it all so overwhelmed me that tears came into my eyes, my throat closed over and I couldn't speak. I saw the devastated look on Michael's face but knew he hadn't understood. I knew he would get a mental picture of me being hard done by and not getting the fruit I loved, but that wasn't what I meant.

The point was that I was somewhere I shouldn't have been, having rules forced on me that were unnecessarily stupid in their pettiness. I knew one day I would walk out of there with a clean record, yet other girls would stay there for years to come, serving no purpose, no more prepared for life on the outside than they had been when they came in. They would emerge from prison totally out of touch with the outside world. They would have no friends except those they had made in prison, and in most cases, although they hated being in prison, they would be so unfit for ordinary life now that they had little choice except a life of crime; or they would do something to get themselves back inside where they now felt safe.

One girl had spent a considerable part of her life in prison; she was younger than I was, and still had several years to go after I left. Her educational standard was extremely low, and she was obviously not used to ordering her own life. She had been in institutions so long that she was like a child being looked after by its parents; when she was told to do something she immediately hurried to do it. Prison was home. She joined in the talking, grumbling about the food, the screws and the general prison policy with all the other girls, and yet if all that had been taken from her, she would be at sea, desperately longing to get back.

There is no sense in a system like that. Criminals are not retrained and prepared to re-enter society with a purpose. They are just held in limbo and then put out at the level they were before, or lower. If a person of twenty- five spends fifteen years on a life sentence, then at forty he or she picks up where they left off as a twenty-five-year-old, they can't cope. People expect more of them because of their age, yet their emotional maturity has been retarded. This is difficult for people to understand as they expect that people develop more maturity with the years.

Prisoners are told *not* to think for themselves, *not* to do *anything* on their own initiative. They are told where to go, when to rise, shower, eat, drink, clean their teeth, sleep, and sometimes even when they can go to the toilet, what sort of hobbies they can have, what to read, whom they can write to and whom they can't. It is like kindergarten. If they throw tantrums, they can get their own way. If they are good girls (or boys), they 'get a buy' as a reward. If they are naughty, they don't. They don't earn subsistence money so they come out of prison broke. (I only had a few dollars when I got out myself, and I'd used my private money to buy things like shampoo and deodorant. It wasn't enough for a taxi to town.)

It is no wonder the system doesn't work. Sometimes I think it is there, more as a security blanket for the public than anything else. The majority of people in prisons are there for minor crimes; things that could be corrected in other ways with far less public expense. But then, of course, there wouldn't be so many jobs for government employees.

Those who bash people up would be far better used as compulsory sparring partners for boxers in a gym or work in hospital casualty wards. A work order in a hospital casualty would be far more effective than prison for reckless or drink driving offenders because they could see the results of their stupidity. Vandals would think twice about it if they were forced to clean walls, repaint or rebuild. They do not like work, their intention is to destroy and let others repair, and if they were forced, even under guard, to do it themselves, it would act as a very effective deterrent. If drug users did time assisting in mental institutions and morgues, only hardened and amoral criminals would come away wishing to continue pushing and/or using. These are the sentences *they* fear and consider deterrents.

Over and over again, girls said prison was easy, especially when they had been in once and got used to it. It was a cinch, you could do your time standing on your head. They learned how to use the system very quickly. Once learned, it is easy to fall back into the routine quickly each time they returned. (I agreed—after only a few weeks the first time, my return to prison was simple in comparison, now I knew a lot of the ropes.) Prisoners could still work their 'outside' rackets from the 'inside'. Beside this you could create a tremendous nuisance to the system and cost the taxpayers quite a bit of money per day.

Prison had enormous advantages: you got free room and board (which was certainly a lot better than sleeping on the street and scrounging for food); you could get all your dental work done free; your medical problems attended to; gain weight, get fit and healthy, ready to go out and have another stint of no food, and no bed. Your health wouldn't suffer too badly for another year then you could repeat the process and go to the free government 'health farm' for homeless cons—prison. You also had a fantastic alibi for any scams you ran from the inside.

Some of the Aborigines quite clearly came in near holidays and long weekends, because they knew they would have a good feed and they didn't like to be on their own then. One bloke knew exactly what would put him in over Easter and Christmas, so to be with his mates inside, he regularly put a brick through a window. The judge knew him and if he fined him, the man would tell him he wasn't going to pay and they may as well give him the time. Close to a public holiday, it was less trouble for the courts to do it. Eventually everyone expected him to be brought in for some minor offence just before the holidays, which would give him his two or three days with bed and board.

Once a prisoner walked through the gate, sentences were forgotten and everyone basically became equal. You did not ask anyone why they were in prison. If they wanted to tell you about their case, you could ask questions; if they did not volunteer the information, it was a case of live and let live, and leave them alone; but you *did not ask*.

The young woman who spent a week in prison for having no tail-light on her bike was, for that week, as guilty as anyone doing life for murder. Although that is hard to understand for some short-term prisoners, and also some drug offenders, who tend to think their crime is in a completely different category from others, these prisoners quickly realise they are just criminals and putting on airs and graces is not going to get them anywhere inside.

In my letter dated 7 February 1985, I wrote:

> Prison life is like leaving a sponge above the high tide mark. It withers and dies slowly, drained of anything useful till it's just a skeleton for scratching backs—a mere shadow of its former self.

If you want respect or position, you have to earn it, although, funnily enough, length of sentence does have a bearing on this. The longer you're there, the more respect you gain within the system, even if you don't deliberately set out to do this. As you live within the prison and learn the rules, the system and how it works, you learn how to use that system as much as possible to your own advantage. Only through time do you learn how far you can go. It also depends on how many of the screws know you and your capabilities, and whether you will abuse the trust placed in you or not. If you are keeping your nose clean and doing your time sweet, they will let you do things that perhaps you would not be permitted to do otherwise, because they know that privilege will not be abused.

You learn how to write letters to headquarters; to deal with the screws and their personalities; to play off one screw against another, and the little idiosyncrasies of the different officers. In a prison like Darwin where there are no set rules, you have to know the rules of each officer because what one considers a misdemeanour, another will readily allow. The new girls learned the system from the longer-term prisoners, to ask how to fill in forms, what phone calls and visits they're allowed, the rules about buying things and how to get money sent in. They also learn all prisons invariably have a network of communication, which even now I would not describe as it is often the lifeline to a person inside. No doubt many of the same methods used while I was there are still used now.

It was no secret that certain officers brought drugs into the prison for certain prisoners and those drugs were transported between the male and female sections. I knew when others in the section were taking drugs and I was even offered some.

Some days it was more difficult to get a message to the outside than others, but it generally took no more than three days to set up communication. Even on solitary, you could get a message out. Over and over, the screws wondered how we knew things, and where we got our information. All we needed, apart from some intricate channels, were good eyes and ears.

If we were observant when we went to clean the offices and medical centre, we knew exactly what was happening, often ahead of the officers. Everyone knew, when certain coloured papers were on desks, someone was on report and you'd soon find out who plus the details. It was easy to pick up information from the male screws and from the guys themselves through our cleaning detail, the library, or from the cells with coded whistles and hand signals. The Aborigines had no problem at all; they simply talked in their own language. It didn't matter what room searches or strip searches were done, sending a message was easy enough, and the messages slipped through frequently.

One girl wanted to send out some photographs of herself and the prison to her family, and the Cat owned a camera and film. The Cat had her property out, going through it, when someone came to the gate. She saw her chance and took it, smuggling her camera out before the screw came to lock the property away after the visitor had been attended to.

As soon as the section door shut, the Cat moved like lightning, getting her camera and taking pictures of every facet of the female section; office, storerooms, cells, kitchen, day room, and some of the girls. She then raced back, put her camera away, closed the door, and stood, leaning nonchalantly against the workbench in the day room, talking to the other girls, while waiting for the officer to let her back into the property room as if nothing had happened when they returned!

They never fully realised the agility and ability of the Cat who was quite an accomplished burglar, and it was no trouble for her to do whatever she wanted.

We had to get special permission for a tape recorder; even when we did, the recording part was removed. The Cat had a big stereo in her property but they wouldn't give her permission to have it. A stereo is not something that can be easily hidden, but that didn't worry the Cat. She managed to get it out one day when the property room was open for cleaning and hide it in different places until she got it to her cell. She kept the stereo up on top of the cupboard that backed into her shower cubicle most of the time, and at night brought it down, enjoying the music as she played her tapes and those she borrowed from others.

We had been expecting a cell search for some time, and knew Mr Dewsnip was on duty. Mr Dewsnip was so tall he had to take his hat off and duck his head to get through the kitchen doorway. Because of this he could see things that we had to stand on chairs to dust. He was forever putting his finger on something we couldn't reach and finding dust then looking at us with a grin as we groaned. A couple of girls had things hidden on top of their fan blades, stuck there with sticky tape. If ever he was around, they would pull them off in a hurry because he was sure to find them. If he found the Cat's stereo she would be put on lockup with all her personal belongings confiscated again. We'd get a lecture on dishonest girls who would have known what she was doing and should have reported her. Nobody wanted her to be caught as she was pretty popular.

Because of what Helena and some of the others had done to the security cell, it was changed to wall-to-wall concrete. The authorities made a concrete bed—a 15 centimetre (6 inch) high platform in one corner—concreted the toilet in and removed the fan to an air vent set into the ceiling, as were the lights, controlled from outside. The bars were replaced with heavy mesh and bar, and a double glass viewing window ('unbreakable', of course, but which Lily managed to break on one of her visits!) was put in the door. Prior to that it had just been a cell that was a little more heavily barred than ours.

The officer plus the four guys remodelling the security cell were having their morning tea-break. The Cat's cell was almost opposite. Mr Dewsnip was already through the gate and walking the 60 metres (65 yards) up to our section door when she found out he was there. She moved like the wind—down to her cell, climbed on top of the shower, took her stereo down, ran back with it past the guys to the day room and hid it in one of the cupboards among the sewing, where they would never look. She was casually standing in the day room once again, talking to us all, when Mr Dewsnip and the other officers entered the room.

One of the guys later asked what the excitement was about! The Cat had been so fast they had totally missed her actions, even though she had been in full view most of the time!

We discovered the administrators and secretaries kept sandwich spreads and cheese in their fridge, and certain girls would grab grease-proof paper or Glad Wrap, take a big scoop of peanut butter or Vegemite and bring it back to share at mealtime. This was risky; we had to get back to our section, with a body search as we went through the main prison gates if they suspected anything was wrong.

The girls wrapped the spread up well and down it would go into their bra or knickers. One night I could smell my partner's peanut butter all the way back to the section and was amazed that the screw did not.

On another occasion the Cat had just returned from cleaning when the phone rang. She was on kitchen and guessing the phone call would be the gate saying to go and get the food cart, she stuck her head into the interview room, where I was, and said, 'Here catch, before they come and get me.' I caught without thinking and found myself holding a big fistful of Vegemite, which had already started to seep through the paper in which it was wrapped.

I had barely caught it when both screws came back together, one taking the Cat with her, the other coming into the room to see what I was making and to have a chat. I had automatically shoved the Vegemite hand in my pocket as I heard them approach. There I was, sitting with a pocketful of Vegemite, hoping to goodness she couldn't smell it, not knowing what to do with it and wondering, if I had to take my hand out of my pocket, whether it was covered with the telltale brown spread. I was also hot and the additional heat was making it perspire through the paper and smell strongly.

Prison forcibly demonstrated how good the human nose is. We were allowed no scent or aftershave, as you could make a brew and get drunk on it. The soap was a specified type and everything was fairly basic. My sense of smell developed to the point where I could identify each screw by their particular scent. It was easy to understand how in bush warfare, the native guerrillas could smell strangers coming (quite apart from cigarettes, which a non-smoker can smell a mile off).

It was amazing how much more acute our sense of smell was than any of the screws'; this helped with the smuggling, of course. To my relief the screw didn't smell my pocketful of Vegemite, as the one caught red-handed cops it sweet. You don't dog; if you were caught you'd be charged with at least loss of privileges and maybe solitary if the offence was really bad.

The girls brought all sort of things across from the officers' section—pens, pencils, rulers, rubbers, paper clips (they were difficult to conceal in the section, as the screws knew where they came from). Sometimes the girls brought across paper and envelopes and certainly food—usually cheese and biscuits.

Nothing ever seemed to be missed, or if it was, they never searched us and, of course, none of the screws would admit that the girls were stealing from right under their noses because it reflected on their ability as officers.

No one ever played up on a decent officer, because if you were caught they also got into trouble. Because of this, any misbehaviour was deliberately done on a bad screw's shift. Because they claimed they were such perfect officers (they were really afraid of their own reputations), if they didn't catch us personally they would go to any length to disclaim any stealing had been done while we were in their care, so we knew we were quite safe.

Vegemite was at such a premium that when the girls had some special birthday or send-off party, if a nice officer asked us if we would like a special treat, we usually asked for Vegemite to make sandwiches. On one occasion, a screw brought in some hundreds and thousands and the girls made fairy bread. Only a couple of the girls ate the fairy bread and the rest dived into the Vegemite. We had it so rarely and we needed it to boost our vitamin B.

With several accomplished burglars and other enterprising girls, nothing was impossible. On a regular basis a number of the girls had the ability to open the locked office door and the filing cabinets and search for anything they wished to find. There was no problem in setting a lookout and going through the day book, request forms, drawers or cabinets for any information wanted, and being back again at their work by the time the officers returned. I watched this procedure on many occasions. Officers' home addresses and confiscated property were among the most popular items.

One night I was rostered with Helena on office cleaning over the other side. She was on the office end and I was on the kitchen and toilet end. If the superintendent's office had to be cleaned, we usually did that together so the screw could keep an eye on both of us at once. For some reason we were split up and I was sent on to do my work alone. I hadn't been more than five or ten minutes when Helena darted down excitedly saying,

'Quick Lindy, where can I hide these? I've got his keys!'

'What! All of them! However did you get those and where's the Chameleon?'

'Oh she got called away and the silly fool left me there, so I went through all his drawers and they were just sitting in the top drawer. It's the big master set he uses!' After a bit of persuasion she put them back. Seeing we were the only two there, we would both get the blame, and I finally convinced her that she should do it another time. I wasn't keen to take that rap! The problem of where to hide them gave me the creeps.

On the way back that night she told me she was *only* going to put the keys in the rubbish and throw them away, as they would never look there and it would create a real replacement problem for them. The Chameleon would be left to explain why Lena was there on her own, and the superintendent would have to explain to head office why his keys were in such an accessible place! Now, knowing the whole plan, it really was a great idea and I'm sorry I talked her out of it.

I believe the only thing ever taught by prisons is the perfecting of old and learning of new criminal skills.

An Answer to Depression

One thing I learned was to appear busy doing nothing, and make any job last six times longer than it should. It took me months to learn not to do my jobs at the same speed I did them at home. When the screws weren't watching, we often sped up if we knew we could get free time when finished because a good screw was coming on. We worked particularly slowly when nasty screws were on because they invented extra work—often weeding lawns—and we hated most of the things they invented. I had to dig holes once for a screw; another then decided that they weren't necessary after all, and I had to fill them in again. If there was no work we still had to look busy, and it was amazing how effective it was to pick things up, put them down in the same place and wander around touching things, or bending over and looking studious. Quite an art.

One lass had been doing this all day, as well as pulling our work from under our noses. We were quite busy that day, and were trying to finish fast. She was taking our cotton or scissors, spilling the buttons on the floor, and really creating a nuisance, frustrating everybody. When work was over I was glad to get out of the place and decided to do some leather-work. I got all the leather-work out in the interview room and was thoroughly relaxed. Not for long. When the girl returned from cleaning, she decided to wet my leather where I didn't want it wet, try and use tools on it and bang things around. It is very difficult to work when you are having shoes thrown at you and your work jerked out of your hands, especially when you are doing delicate work with a cutting blade. To stop it being totally ruined, I decided to pack up in a hurry.

I went back to my room for a while. She followed me, and I thought, No way! Next thing I'll go on report because she is in my room. She knew we were charged if we went into each other's room, but she came in anyway. Maybe the best thing to do was go to the day room after all. I had really had enough and wanted some space, so I went to watch TV and took my tapestry with me. She followed and hassled and annoyed me. One of the officers told her to get out because she was noisy and irritating everybody. We had a lot of girls in at the time, too. She went and things quietened down. I thought that she might go to sleep early or *something*, to give us all a break.

Next thing I heard her screeching my name at the top of her voice. I ignored that as well. After a while, Sunshine went down to see why the girl was creating such a racket and tell her to settle down. She came back and said, 'She's all right, just playing up a bit as usual. You know what she's like. But she's demanding to see you. Maybe you can give us all some peace if you just go down and tell her to shut up and you don't appreciate it.'

I thought, OK, I'll get this over and done with in a hurry and went down to her cell and stood leaning on the doorframe. She was sitting quietly on the bed, obviously really depressed and her eyes now had a dangerous quality about them. She was cross-legged on the bed with her arms in her lap, her hair a bit wet, and she said she had just come from the shower. I could accept that, but there was something odd.

Glancing down I noticed a big splash of bright red blood on the floor. I knew that it was not time for her period because I had seen her using the sanitary burner about ten days before. I looked again at the towel and noticed how it was being held—she wasn't actually holding it in her hands; it was mainly over her wrists with her fingers poking out the end and I thought, uh oh, slit wrists. I asked 'Why do you want to be such an idiot and cut your wrists?'

Her mouth fell open and she asked, 'How did you know?'

I said, 'Look, if you are going to do that in here, you could at least be serious about it. You are just after sympathy.'

She looked as if she would fly at me but then calmed down again and said, 'What made you say that?'

I said, 'Let's face it. If you were serious you would wait until lockup when it's dark and you couldn't see the blood, which you now have splashed on the floor for anyone to see.' She looked down, saw it, realised she was caught and showed me her wrists. She had started cutting them, not deeply yet, but enough to cause quite a bit of blood, which the towel was absorbing. She had used a razor blade from her shaver.

I said, 'Give me the razor.'

She said, 'No. You try and take this razor off me, and I will do a good job of myself and they won't be able to get to me in time.'

I said to her, 'Oh, yeah? What are you intending to do? You haven't even cut the right way.' She looked at me again. She had cut crosswise, and anyone who wants to do a job doesn't do that.

I leant over to pick up the razor, but she immediately grabbed it and held it to the carotid artery in her neck. That was a different proposition. If I grabbed for it, she definitely could, and would, cut deep in her neck. In a few minutes she'd bleed to death. It would take longer than a few minutes to get help. We only had one officer on at that stage; the other was taking the kitchen girl back with the food cart.

I decided to try and talk her around. We began discussing some of her favourite projects, which she wanted to do when she got out, and she began to relax. Then I got her talking about her latest project, and she wanted to show it to me. It was on the bench and she told me to get it. I said, 'No, I'm not going in to your cell. You can go and get it yourself. You're not helpless.' After some grumbling, she got up to fetch it, leaving the razor blade on the bed.

As soon as she was at the other end of the room, I dived for the blade, grabbed it and ran. I knew she was fast and if she got near me while I still had the blade, her superior weight and strength would overcome me and that would be that. Besides, a sharp razor blade is not something you really like to grab tightly in your fist. I made a beeline for the day room with her after me and Sunshine looked up to see why we were running. We weren't allowed to run anywhere, certainly not through the day room, and it looked as if we were playing chase As I came through the door, I said to Sunshine, 'Quick! Open your hand.' She immediately did so, I placed the blade in her hand, shut it and said, 'Don't give it back to her.' Then I walked across to the water fountain to get a drink as if nothing had happened.

The lass rushed into the day room hot on my heels and Sunshine immediately turned round and said to her, 'Why are you running? You know that's something you shouldn't be doing.'

She said, 'Lindy's got something of mine.' She looked at me, and I opened my hands. She glanced toward Sunshine and then back to me and exclaimed, 'You didn't!' I said, 'I did. Now go and behave yourself.' I could see Sunshine moving her hand in her pocket, working out what I had given her. Her quick glance had also taken in the fact that the lass was holding a towel in her hand. The lass backed out in a hurry then, not wanting Sunshine to notice what she had done. Sunshine called me aside and said, 'OK, spill it.' I told her, adding, 'I think she's OK now, but you may need to do something.'

Sunshine went down and spoke to her, straight and to the point. She told her she was being 'a silly girl', and not to 'create hassles like this', or 'make problems for Lindy'. If she settled down and promised to behave herself, it would go no further. But any more problems and she would put a report in, and 'you know what's going to happen then'.

The lass promised, so her cell wasn't searched or her property confiscated. Some of the officers and the other girls were trying to find out what happened but I said, 'She was just mucking about and playing up and got told off a bit. Nothing to worry about.' I discovered the next day that no report had been put in, and, although Sunshine personally kept a close watch on the girl for three or four days (fortunately that was her last evening before a stretch of day shift), she left it at that. The girl was able to calm down and settle in, realising that she had been doing something on the spur of the moment, simply for attention. She never tried that in prison again.

If any prisoner was considered a suicide risk the officers removed pencils, pens, shavers, paper, cigarette papers, matches—anything they could hurt themselves with from their cell. They did with Froggie. She started to cut her wrists with the big vegetable knife when on kitchen duty just before lunch, then changed her mind and went to the office to ask for a dressing! They also took away her eyeliner pencils for weeks, which she hated.

I couldn't figure out why they took pens and pencils until I discovered one of the guys had picked open nearly 5 centimetres (2 inches) of his wrist vein with a pen! Where there's a will, there's a way, and some prisoners would use anything. Being a long-term prisoner is so boring that even a trip to hospital, with great pain, is worth it to alleviate the boredom.

It used to amuse me when I first went inside to discover the safe in the administration section was not full of money and keys, but paper clips, pens, rulers and rubber bands. One day, when Mr Keo, a good chief, was on duty I asked why. He told me prisoners made themselves very ill by stealing a paper clip, straightening it out, putting a rubber band round it to hold it like a circle and then swallowing it. The stomach juices broke down the rubber band, letting the paper clip spring to full length, which then dug into the stomach, causing tremendous pain. Usually the clip will not pass through the bowel and must be removed surgically. A stay in hospital can mean a welcome break from routine, but it is an agonising way of committing suicide, if not discovered in time. So paper clips had to be kept in the safe.

Razor blades can be made using roll-your-own cigarette papers. By wetting them, letting them stick together, and rubbing the fingers along one edge, gradually building up the thickness, a very sharp blade with a fine cutting edge can be made. Although it is more fragile than a normal razor blade, it can be used for the same purpose. I understand it has been known in some prisons in the USA for prisoners to ritually murder fellow inmates using these blades. Certainly they are effective for slashing wrists.

One morning when we went across for cleaning we heard talk about a suicide in remand. A guy who had been due to appear in court the following day had become so distraught he had hanged himself from the ceiling fan in his cell. Immediately, our screw's face lit up. She pumped the male screw on duty for all the information she could get out of him, and questioned anyone else who might possibly know. The incident created a great stir, and the screws were laughing and talking excitedly about it. It seemed to be their greatest piece of news for the week.

Later in the week when we went to the library, we were able to find out more information for ourselves. It appeared the guy had shown definite signs of harming himself or others. He had been deliberately left where he had all the means available to do something to himself if he wanted to—and he had. What upset us the most was that the screws on duty had thought it was funny. The guys who were there at the time said that, when they found him hanged in his cell, the screws had laughed. The word was passed around and screws from other blocks came over to view his hanging body before it was taken down. Of course, as soon as the chiefs found out what had happened, that was stopped and the police were called, but those who got in first enjoyed the free show. We had seen similar reactions from some of the screws on our side, and the disappointment of those who had missed out.

This peculiar attitude seemed to be common to all the nasty screws, although a suicide unsettled all the prisoners. The decent screws would not discuss it. It often appeared to me that the nasty screws felt some need for their authority to be recognised and we had no choice but to bow to their every wish. It was apparent that this work pandered to their egos immensely.

Yarns for the Deaf and Dumb

I was sent a book on macramé, which I had always wanted to do, and I thought I'd have a go at it. When I applied for permission, the request was sent all the way to head office! Finally Tapioca consented but imposed restrictions. I had to be locked in my cell while I was doing it—one of the other prisoners might suicide with the macramé cord. We knew in our section this was absolutely ridiculous, and how the men might get it we weren't sure. The girls were kept in the day room while I cut the correct lengths. My shower was the only hanging place I could find and as I couldn't be seen there, most of the screws soon relaxed on the cell idea, so I was allowed out in the day room provided the work disappeared when Tapioca or some of the chiefs came over. When I did a 3 metre (9 feet 9 inches) hanging table, I was finally given open permission to hang it permanently from the day room ceiling until it was completed. However, I was still only allowed to cut my long lengths of cord when certain girls were not present.

Similar restrictions applied to gaining permission for other types of craft requiring paint, knives, scissors or needles.

I was told (I never did time in solitary) if you were on lockup the most boring thing was not knowing what was going on. You didn't hear the gossip to keep up with the news; you weren't even told the new rules. What else was there to do? There was no TV, just the wireless at night turned on from the tower. A system was devised so girls on lockup could keep abreast.

Shelion was the first one to give us the idea. When she escaped she was brought back and put straight in solitary. We'd had one evening with her, but nothing more. She settled down immediately, not hassling the guards or girls, but whenever anyone walked past she would talk to them. It was against the rules to talk when on solitary—that was part of the punishment. But when you are already on solitary, what's the point? If someone went past and you wanted to talk, well, they can't take anything else away from you.

Most wouldn't answer anyone on lockup, not only because it was against the rules, and we'd get lockup too, but often the person had fought someone in the section and played up, so the girls showed their disapproval this way. Of course if it was a fight, verbal or otherwise, with a nasty screw, that was different.

Whenever I went jogging, Shelion would hold a conversation with me as I went past. I held out on answering for a while, watching the screws and her. I realised she had an indomitable spirit and was a fairly happy person, so cautiously started communicating. Eventually answers were refined to a system of hand or body movements, which all the regulars knew.

My cell was opposite solitary, and at one stage when the Cat was in, if we turned both lights on so we were silhouetted against it, we could talk slowly, in two-handed deaf and dumb language, as long as we stood back in our cells out of sight and kept an ear out for the screws or 'unsafe' prisoners.

The Chameleon must have realised that something was going on once but couldn't quite decide what. Some girls, when jogging at night, used to hold conversations with those on lockup as they ran around. One night in particular, there were several of us jogging, and we all held a conversation for over half an hour with the girl on solitary. The Chameleon stood there with her arms crossed, watching us like a hawk. We had been going in one direction, as we always did half our jog one way, then reversed for the remaining half the other way, so we didn't develop muscles in one leg more than the other, when running in such small circles.

As we were facing the Chameleon with our lips moving, we did an early turn so we had our backs to her. Then one girl had to sprint to a half-circle in front so at all times someone was facing the screws, while the others had their backs to them, talking or listening on the way past the lockup. At any problem, a hand signal from the 'guard' would warn that the officers were creeping up, then everyone would simply be jogging and the girl on lockup sleeping or at the other end of the cell. The Chameleon watched for about twenty minutes before she gave up, frustrated that she couldn't catch us.

Interior Decorating, Darwin Style

Lily, a plump Aboriginal girl, regularly came back, for a couple of days or several weeks. We got to know her reasonably well. She rarely went off the deep end in public, but when she did, she spent a longer spell in prison. Sometimes she just wanted somewhere permanent to live, so she would throw a brick through a window or something to get her back to the Darwin Prison to watch television again. She was known to have put the full length of dressmaker's pins into the top of every finger so that all you saw was the heads of the pins sticking out; she also did other masochistic things. She didn't seem to feel pain when she was about to 'go off'. Things like these made the officers very wary of Lily.

Lily arrived back in again, under escort from Alice Springs on a Friday. This was about the third time I'd seen her now and she seemed quite happy to be back. As the day wore on she maintained that because she had been in the prison before, she did not have to be classified again or get early lockup like other new arrivals. She wanted to watch television that night. Duckie said to her, 'I'll see what I can do, Lily, but I won't promise.'

The whole reason Lily had asked the judge in Alice Springs to serve her sentence in Darwin was because there was one more TV station than at Alice Springs! As long as Lily was happy, drawing pictures or something, she did not go off the deep end, but if something upset her, the reason she had been certified as a mentally deficient became obvious; she became most cantankerous, agitated and violent, to say the least.

As the shift change approached, Lily became more and more agitated. Her eyes were starting to glass over. I thought if I sat and talked to her for a little while, she may settle in, accept early lockup and be OK. Normally if she got upset she would ask to go to her room, but this time she didn't.

I said, 'Lily, if you are a good girl, you just have one early night and have a big sleep because you have had a big trip today. Tomorrow morning they get the videos in and you can watch them then and TV all afternoon.'

She said, 'No, no, I am going to do something soon. I am going to get upset and I am going to hurt somebody.'

'You don't want to do that because you will go in lockup for a long time and then you won't see television,' I pointed out.

'No, I'm going to make them let me watch television. They have to let me watch television.'

I tried to calm her down, and she looked as if she was responding. The afternoon shift arrived and I noticed Duckie leave. One screw had gone across on administration cleaning, and the Panther was sitting in the office reading the afternoon paper, as usual. I went to my room to get my tapestry. I had barely opened my wardrobe to get it out, when one of the other girls came flying to my door.

'She's done a split,' she said excitedly. 'Lily's run for it.'

'What do you mean?' I asked.

'She's outside. The door was open and she's gone, and they don't even know. The Panther's still sitting in the office.'

I thought I had better do something, so walked up, knocked on the office door and asked, 'Do you realise Lily has gone outside?'

She gave me a peculiar look and said, 'Mmm, you're sure she is out there? I'll take a look.' She did so and said, 'Yeah, she's gone all right. I thought I saw her.'

I thought it was a funny attitude, but as it was no business of mine, I walked back to my room. Then I realised Lily was sitting under a tree near my window. The Panther, who was outside some distance away, called,

'Come on, Lily, you've got to come back inside.'

Lily said, 'No way. I'm stayin' here,' in no uncertain terms. She was going to 'camp under the tree'; she 'wasn't going to get no lockup'. So the Panther calmly walked back inside and rang the tower. Across came the outdoor work supervisor, a Fijian who was a boxing coach still in training. The screw with him was about 180 centimetres (6 feet) tall and well built though fairly quiet. They talked quietly to Lily, telling her to go back inside. She started to yell.

The Fijian took a step towards her and she started to scream and back away. He told her, still quietly, to walk inside on her own or they would have to force her. She stayed put, so they put their hands on her arms to get her up. She suddenly jumped up, pulled away from them and started to swear. When Lily swore, she became anything but the meek and mild young lady she normally was and developed one of the foulest mouths possible. She swore in two or three Aboriginal dialects, I think, plus English, and the combination of the words made even the men shudder. At last, she walked in ahead of them and they took her straight to solitary. She went in and suddenly realised the door was being shut.

Lily started to scream in earnest then, to rant and rave, and then the filth really poured out of her mouth. As he walked off, the Fijian said, 'Where did she learn to swear like that? Even the guys don't swear like *that*. I haven't even *heard* some of those words before.' She got worse. The men headed back to the male blocks agreeing to come over later with the seniors to feed and prepare her for the night.

When the cleaning party returned, they were updated about Lily. Because Lily started swearing at anybody within her range of vision through the window, the officers decided it was time to act again. The rest of us were put on lockup and the men were summoned again.

When something like this happened and the inmate was known from past experiences, the big boys always came. If they were not extremely tall, they had the weight to compensate. My cell was directly opposite solitary, so I had a good view of what happened.

I had seen a lot but I had never seen anyone manhandled like this before. Darwin Prison normally seemed to prefer psychological to physical warfare. This time it was different. Lily had worked herself into such a state that she started screaming again the minute they came in sight. The sight of the restraining belt was the final straw. She went off the deep end, and as one of the officers leaned over to put it on her, she grabbed his hair and tried to punch him. He was quicker than she was, and as soon as he felt her hand in his hair, he punched straight into her stomach, while his other arm warded off the blow to his face. He caught her blow on the side of the head, rather than full under the jaw. I thought a fist in the stomach would settle her down, as she really had asked for it by flying for him first, but no.

As the others grabbed her hands when she doubled up, one of the screws started kicking her viciously with his steel-capped boots, not once but several times. Of course she screamed and struggled violently, then did her best to kick back, grab or head-butt. Whatever she tried was ineffectual because she was so heavily outnumbered. It still took three or four screws to hold her down and eventually they got the belt on. She was then told to be quiet and settle down.

When Lily let fly she had the strength of six demons and a tongue to match—and she could stay like that for weeks. She was pleading and screaming, 'Don' hit me, don' hit me, you're rotten. Ooh, don' hurt me, don' hit me.' Then, with her next breath, she would swear and have another go at them. She couldn't control her own actions, and the screws knew that. But the sight of her being deliberately kicked, when the first punch would have been enough, turned my stomach. I sat on the bed in my cell shaking and feeling sick for ages after Lily had been subdued. This wasn't the last time I was to see things like this, but like anything else, the first time makes the biggest impression. It's never quite the same again.

Lily continued alternately to rant and rave, beg, plead and scream for hours. At lockup, she was still going strong. We knew we were in for a bad night, and we had to rise at 6.30 a.m. the following day regardless, ready to start work. We were right—nobody got much rest. If we slept through the siren, the screws came around and checked to see if you were awake. If you weren't, they woke you by banging hard on your window and calling your name. If we went back to sleep we were charged and got early lockup. We staggered around, three-quarters asleep; cold water on our faces and showers made little difference. Breakfast was bad. The cook was so sleepy that she'd lost the fight with the toaster, which was troublesome at any time. The toast was somewhat overdone and the food underdone, so we blamed Lily instead of the cook. Nobody had much of an appetite anyway and we were all short tempered from lack of sleep.

When Duckie came back on duty again, I spoke to her about the door being open and asked her why.

She looked at me and said, 'Well, Lindy, we could tell she was going to go off. It was done on purpose, because when Lily goes off, it is not the cause of her problem she attacks, but the person nearest her. It was much better for her to go off outside, away from the other girls than near the cells where anything could happen.' They had left her talking to me though!

Only Smiley had seen Lily like this before and knew her full potential, and Smiley wasn't around. Lily had a violent history and more than one of the officers had come out on the wrong end of her outbursts. One officer in particular had been bringing Lily back from the doctor one day when Lily had grabbed her by the hair and forced her down to her knees, banging the officer's head up and down on the concrete, while the officer screamed for assistance. Lily had also apparently stabbed that same officer in the stomach with a kitchen knife while she was pregnant. Incidents like that made the officers wary, and forced them to change their rules in regard to the handling of violent or potentially violent prisoners. Everything that happens in jail usually has a history.

They dosed Lily, so while we tried to do our jobs during the day, she mostly slept, with a few small outbursts. The screws woke her up for meals, which she sometimes ate and they sometimes wore. In the evening, refreshed after her sound sleep, she went off again, she continued this way for night after night. When it was time for the TV to go on after the dinner dishes were finished, Lily would start to scream. She continued through our free time and often until about 3 a.m. She yelled a peculiar mixture of Bible verses, hymns, praise, and some of the foulest pub songs, ditties and language imaginable—often put to tunes like 'The Old Rugged Cross' and other well-known hymns. It showed the two sides of Lily's personality—her violent tendencies versus the charm when she was stable. This continued for weeks.

The situation became intolerable through lack of sleep and harassment, and everyone was bad tempered, including the officers. They were not there to babysit mental patients; they were there to look after prisoners. The Northern Territory, however, had no facilities for mental patients, so whenever somebody in that category misbehaved, he or she was sent to the prison. The screws got extra money for looking after them, but nobody liked it. As two officers had to be on call at all times like this, all outside work had to be postponed also.

Petitions from girls and officers alike flew to head office, asking for Lily to be moved elsewhere, but to no avail. The situation in our section grew steadily worse. Finally, Lily was to be transferred to maximum security on the men's side where a couple of similar male prisoners were kept, as only the men could handle her.

Lily refused to use the toilet in her cell, preferring the mattress, floor, walls, or whatever was handy, and wearing clothes was no deterrent, so her physical state was disgusting. Whenever the door of the cell was opened, urine cascaded out the doorway. She had ripped up the toilet paper (not choosing to use it) into tiny pieces and thrown it all over the floor, squirting water from the hand basin around to add to the mixture of urine and faeces. From outside, the odour of the room pervaded everything.

When four large men came across to transfer Lily to the other side, we were put on lockup. When they finally opened solitary we saw her properly for the first time in weeks. Her eyes were wild, her hair was matted with excreta, muck and dirt, her clothes were dripping wet with water and urine. She had unzipped her uniform right down the front and managed to half-strip her bra off so her huge breasts were swinging loose, and she would not let anyone do her dress up to make her decent before the men came across, or even while they were there.

When they told Lily she was being transferred, she started screaming again, although she had been given a tranquilliser. As she fought to stay where she was, it looked, for quite a few moments, as if a number of the officers would end up on their backs in the filth. She eventually came out and dropped to her knees, so they dragged her along; she screamed, 'No, you're hurting me.'

'Well, Lily,' they said, 'get up or we'll drag you all the way.' She got up but still struggled and screamed. Three male officers surrounded her, one on each side and a third a short distance behind; a fourth, the biggest one of the lot, had her by the back of the belt and dress collar, keeping her upright because she kept trying to stop and kneel down.

The officer was obviously having a struggle, though Lily was less than 150 centimetres (5 feet) tall; however, she weighed about 90 kilograms (198 pounds) and was angry. Through my window I watched her struggling, pulling and kicking her way across to the other gates. We later learned on the prison grapevine that the officer holding her upright had deposited her in her new cell, then rushed out to be violently sick because he couldn't stand the stench of handling her in such close proximity. He was also given the following day off.

Lily was put in a cell where they could watch her activities and she could at least be given a shower from a distance with a hose for hygiene's sake.

As soon as Lily had gone, our officers said, 'Well, girls, that's it. Back to routine.' They started cleaning out her cell with hoses. It was a dreadful job. They used as much pressure as possible and hosed whatever they could. The mattress was hosed for a long time but the urine still poured out of it. When the water running off it looked clean, they left it upright to drain; there was no way it could be moved in its present state. It was left for several days to dry in the hot sun and the cell was left open to air. The next day the cell was given another cleaning, and a good scrub out with disinfectant, but the smell lingered. Thank goodness the screws did that job.

Eventually the mattress was dry, but it could not be used again. It stank. It had been one of the better mattresses, and as some of us were sleeping on very bad ones, we didn't appreciate the ruin.

Mrs Wallace started to drag the mattress out. I offered her a hand.

'I wouldn't ask you to do this. This is a filthy job, it stinks.' I helped anyway. We picked the mattress up and off we went. We must have bent the mattress sufficiently to encourage a trickle of dark yellow urine with the most vile smell. I was carrying the back end and occasionally the urine dripped on my feet. I was not amused. We carried it out our gate, putting it in the huge industrial rubbish bin near there.

Mrs Wallace told me to go straight to the shower after that and she would bring me down some special soap. She also gave me disinfectant for my shoes, and some temporary ones to put on until the others had dried out. Unusual! So I got some ill-fitting but dry shoes to wear and had a really good scrub in the shower after rinsing my feet under the outside taps first. It took nearly three weeks for the remnants of the toilet paper that Lily had ripped up to come off the footpath and the smell to subside.

Behaviour like this in the past had prompted the screws to negotiate through the union for alternative housing for mental deficients.

We weren't sorry about this because having to make sure we watched our backs whenever one walked behind us with knives and forks at the table was not restful, especially with Janus' and Lily's history!

While the Cat's Away . . .

My jaw was aching continually because my lower left wisdom tooth had decided to grow, not upright, but sideways. It started to pressure my other teeth out of alignment. The dentist decided to put me into hospital and have the tooth removed under a general anaesthetic as it had to be cut out in pieces. It was duly arranged, and I went to hospital. That was quite an outing. I enjoyed it, except for one thing. Here was a chance of getting some real food. I know that sounds odd because hospital food doesn't have a gourmet reputation, but it looked absolutely delicious after prison food—a meal fit for royalty. But with my post-operative swollen jaw I couldn't eat any of it! Jelly and ice-cream were all I could have, and then I was sent back to the prison.

The stitch removal date was arranged—no problems there. The healing progressed well, but I could only have soft food. The prison, however, didn't have any provision for special situations like that. First they sent across something called soup that looked like a mixture of Vegemite in dishwater with meat. One could hardly call it food. Great for a vegetarian! The screws returned it asking for vegetarian soup—tinned tomato would do—but nothing arrived, so I had to make do. Soft boiled eggs would have been fine (if they had been on the breakfast menu, which they weren't), but almost anything else I couldn't eat, so warm cordial became my staple diet.

A week later, by the time my stitches were due to come out, I was really hungry and looking forward to eating again. The day arrived and it was obvious there was some unrest. The unions had been having discussions about whether mentally retarded and mentally ill inmates should be hospitalised or whether one wing of the prison should be converted to a mental institution, cared for by the prison officers. The officers were frequently called across for stop-work meetings and discussions. Every time they went we would be put on general lockup, and all rooms switched through to the tower control. One of the chiefs would look after the tower, and everybody else would leave. They invariably came back, but when they came back this time they collected their hats and left us there without a word; it was obvious they were going home. Soon we watched their cars leave, and it became very quiet.

I was due to leave for the hospital to get my stitches out when they picked up their hats and left. For some reason stitches tighten more than normally with me and usually have to be removed early. Already my jaw was being pulled so tightly shut I could only just manage to get a pencil between my teeth. The time passed, and my appointment time came and went while we were still on lockup.

About three-quarters of an hour passed before there was any movement or activity. We were simply left, wondering what was happening. They didn't even bother to say from the tower, 'Girls, the officers are out on strike. Somebody will be across later; in the meantime, you're there on your own.' They don't believe in telling you what's going on.

Across came Mr Donnelly and Mr Barrier (from head office) and one of the chiefs. They called out, 'Hello, girls, we'll be with you in a minute,' then went into the office. They were obviously reading the day book to see what we were all supposed to be doing; they then came around to unlock our doors.

'Right, girls,' Mr Barrier said. 'There's a general strike on. If you behave yourselves you can be unlocked. You know what to do. We think you're OK on your own. You'll be having me over here with one of the other head office guys relieving, and the guys' blocks are being manned by the superintendent and the chiefs. It will take us a while to sort ourselves out. Food will probably be late tonight, but if you're patient, things will be fine.'

Free time was great. As I was unlocked, Mr Donnelly said to me, 'Hello, Mrs Chamberlain, how are you going? You're right, aren't you? You've had your stitches out and everything is fine with you? You'll be OK to eat?'

I said to him, 'No, I haven't had my stitches out. I was due to go when they walked off. Now what happens?'

He swore. They looked at each other in consternation, then at their watches. It was too late to get me there that day, so they promised to do their best for first thing the next morning.

They made another appointment but the first one available was two days away. They apologised, said they hoped everything would be back to normal by then, and if not, one of them would take me themselves. In the meantime they gave me a fistful of pain killers, said they thought I was old enough to know what I needed and ask for more when necessary. Two aspirin, or the equivalent, every four hours (strictly written down and timed) was sheer hell for girls who had just had major operations and should still have been on pain-killer injections. Migraines were also deadly for this reason. Now it was nice to be treated as an adult for a change.

By the time my appointment came, my teeth were jammed shut as if my jaw had been wired together. In the meantime, because we were not under the normal prison rule, I was able to get some food I could eat; Mr Barrier got me some tinned spaghetti, which I could mash and suck through my teeth. I also made some really soft scrambled eggs, using food from the officers' fridge, which we had been given permission to raid. Because dinner was late the first night, Mr Barrier had said, 'Well, girls, are you hungry? Use whatever you like in the fridges and get something to eat.' So we got our food out of the officers' store fridge and whipped up scrambled eggs and toast. The girls had a great feed; all they wanted for once. A couple of hours later, dinner came across from the kitchen. It was better than normal because the guys had done what they wanted to and everyone pigged out. Who knew when we'd eat like that again—and I had to just watch!

At night, Mr Barrier asked, 'Will you girls be OK if I just put you in contact with the tower?' We agreed. If anything was desperately needed, if Del had an asthma attack for instance, a push of the button and they would come across, otherwise they would leave us alone. Because they were short- staffed, he said to us, 'We need to get the guys up first because they get fairly restless, and get them fed. Do you mind if we're late?' We cheekily asked if we could sleep in, in that case, instead of the normal 6. 30 a.m. Mr Barrier grinned and told us to stay in bed. 'You can get up when I come cross. You will get your own breakfast, so that's fine.'

We thoroughly enjoyed ignoring the rising bell, rolling over and going back to sleep. They didn't come until about eight o'clock. Bed till then was absolute luxury.

We had also asked if we could have the lights out and sleep in the dark for once. When you're used to sleeping in an area that is as well lit as the main street of a town at night, you really look forward to sleeping in the dark. Mr Barrier agreed, and turned the lights in the section out for us that night, leaving only the perimeter security lights on. Mr Mercer happened to be on night patrol, and when he came over between midnight and two o'clock to do his first rounds, he switched the lights on again. Several nights later, Mr Mercer was not on night shift, and his replacement turned the lights off. Using a little torch he whipped round making sure the right number of bodies were in the cells. Mr Mercer, on the other hand, loudly rattled every door on his way round, waking us. We found out later they regularly did that in the guys' section on the hour every hour—I guess you would learn to be rather like a cuckoo clock and sleep in between your hourly rattle.

Mr Barrier opened all the storerooms for us and said, 'Right, girls, get whatever you need. You know where things are.' Because he trusted us, not one girl overstepped the mark and took anything she should not have. One of the younger ones suggested pilfering, but the others soon put her straight and said, 'No, we're on trust. Don't you ruin it.' We were able to go right through the uniforms, swapping them for the best ones we could find. Some also got better sandals instead of their awful old ones. When the screws came back on duty they were still wrapped up in their own affairs, and the shoes were so well worn in they didn't notice the difference. We didn't take brand new things, of course, because that would have been too obvious.

Mr Barrier told us if we had any request forms to put in, to do it, as he had the power to deal with them then and there, so girls who had craft or special buy requests, or anything that normally went to head office were approved on the spot, if appropriate. He also ordered new sneakers for jogging and decent mattresses and pillows from supply on the other side, which normally we wouldn't have got. He rang the store-man and said, 'The stuff the girls have got here is disgusting. Get me some decent stuff. I'll collect it next time I'm over there and bring it back myself.' And, apart from the mattresses, which unfortunately they didn't have in stock, that's what happened. He was interested to see from the inside that money allocated for replacement supplies was obviously not being used for that purpose, at least not in our section, and we took the opportunity to show him the mending we got and tell him how badly off the guys were.

During the strike everyone was supplied with a packet of cigarettes and a can of Coke. Those who didn't smoke were issued sweets; chocolate- centred ones, not the same old barley sugar rations we normally got. We shared them with the other girls.

We automatically did our jobs in the morning, because if we left them, they would only be extremely dirty and hard to do by the time the strike finished, so we did the minimum—a basic clean-up instead of the extra scrub usually dictated. There were no jobs over the other side, so those girls pitched in with the girl on kitchen duty and lessened her job. After that we did what we liked. We had the TV on during the day, did hand-crafts, played pool and other games, and generally enjoyed ourselves.

When a union meeting was held, we held our breath until Mr Barrier came back and told us talks had broken down again. We heaved a sigh of relief and cheered. He was amused at our reaction.

It was obvious that one of the men would have to take me to hospital to get my stitches out after all. I was told Mr Donnelly (secretary to the minister) would take me. I wondered how he would like driving one of the paddy vans, if he would wear his uniform, whether I would be handcuffed, and what he would say if seen out on an escort during a strike.

I didn't have long to wonder. Donnelly arrived in his usual civilian clothes and I was called to the office. When I walked through the door, before he said hello he exclaimed, 'Haven't you got any other clothes?' I explained that we weren't allowed to have our own clothes (I thought he would have known that) except for court or release. He was sure he could make an exception if I wanted them. I didn't really have anything to fit now I had lost weight and would have to iron it anyway, so as time was short, it was mutually decided my uniform would do. When I enquired about the striking screws' reaction to an escort, they just replied 'Too bad, it's their fault.' We left in Mr Donnelly's private car, without handcuffs.

As we drove to the hospital I pointed out that as my uniform was similar to many office uniforms (the girls' section didn't have one set colour, only the same style, so it wasn't immediately recognised as the male uniforms were), people wouldn't realise he had a prisoner with him as we weren't in the paddy wagon and he wasn't wearing his uniform either. He blushed and immediately denied that was the reason he had exclaimed over my uniform. He had just thought it would be a nice change for me. I personally thought it would have had repercussions if I had accepted.

My stitches had tightened so much that the dentist could only remove the stitches from the outer side of my gums. I would have to return the following week to get the inner stitch out after my jaw relaxed enough to allow the dentist access to it. On the way back we seemed to be going down unfamiliar streets. When I commented on this Mr Donnelly said he thought I would like the change in scenery, so he was taking a longer route. That was rather nice of him, I thought.

Very few of the guys were allowed out for normal work. The cooks were, obviously, as were the laundry, repair and maintenance guys. Apart from them, no one stirred much. We discovered that the guys, because there were thirty or forty in each cell block, were only being allowed out on a rostered basis for an hour or two at a time, and in B block (maximum security) only some were let out for meals. The men were naturally becoming discontented.

As a matter of interest, I asked Mr Barrier just how many of the prison inmates would be considered dangerous and *should* be on lockup at a time like that, and prohibited from wandering. (We even had our inner section doors open so we could wander into the yard if we chose; only the perimeter gates were closed.) Of the 1150 odd prisoners at the time, my personal estimate was three or four only. He quickly agreed with me, saying five at the most. Of those, two were mentally retarded and one was a psychopathic killer. As I had no actual contact with maximum security, I was not aware of who was in there and never met the other one or two he classified as dangerous.

Most of the guys were averaging twenty-one hours of lockup out of twenty-four. Fortunately it wasn't the hottest part of the year, as the guys didn't have showers in their cells as we did, so their towels were outside also. They only had hand basins and toilets, so if they exercised in the evenings or on lockup they could wash, but they had to use one of their bed sheets to get dry on. Whereas we were issued two uniforms on arrival to alternate (they were washed together but we had to iron our own), the guys got a clean towel, shirt, and shorts issued to them on the way to the shower daily. All dirty washing was dumped in the bins and sent to the laundry. The detergent used to kill the bacteria was so strong it rotted the clothes fast. As the guys weren't issued jocks (we did get knickers—although usually second-hand), they tried to get shorts that were tight around the legs. If they put on weight inside or had a pot belly, it wasn't an uncommon practice to slit the waistband of the shorts to make them fit better (when caught they were charged)—and we continually had to mend them.

Very few of the guys had permission for hand-crafts or studies, so all most of them had were a few books, if they were lucky, and four walls to stare at, even playing cards was still banned at this stage. Normally, they were allowed to play pool in the daytime or watch television, but as that was in the day room they didn't even have those diversions. No wonder they were bored and unhappy.

I was able to catch up on some sewing for the family, and was sitting pinning a dress for Kahlia while some of the girls were having a leisurely extended smoko. Suddenly Smiley called excitedly, 'Lindy Gulla, come quick! Michael come with Kahlia! You come quick. True.'

Smiley didn't get excited over nothing, so I did—quickly! The pins on my knee scattered over the floor as I jumped up. Everyone else went to the kitchen windows too. Michael was walking slowly in front of the car on his way back from the main gate to the road, holding Kahlia in his arms. She was waving what looked like a red flag. I tried to whistle to let them know I was watching, but a lump rose in my throat and I couldn't.

Helena had been released several weeks before, and she was the section whistler. (She was only out for a few months, then was returned for a second, longer stretch.) Everyone tried unsuccessfully to whistle for me, then Smiley remembered one of the new, shy, dark girls could whistle, and persuaded her to do so. Michael was almost to the end of the road when he heard the whistle. He knew it wasn't me, but turned to look, just in case. One of the girls had grabbed a tea-towel for me to wave, as something white was just visible from the road. He saw it and waved Kahlia's arm, then we realised she must be holding a single red rose.

It was Mother's Day and we'd all forgotten about it. Special days have no real meaning in prison, as the days are all alike. Only the television programs changed. (Michael later told me he had tried to persuade the gate box official to give me the rose, seeing they wouldn't let them visit—no visiting was supposed to be allowed over the strike due to lack of staff.)

Sadly for the female section, the strike eventually came to an end, although I *was* glad to see my family before they had to leave. Mr Barrier brought us each a large family block of chocolate—diabetic specially for Smiley—to say thank you for our good behaviour (and for washing and ironing Mr Donnelly's shirts as his wife was away, but they didn't know that and we weren't talking). He also, much to the obvious disgust of the presiding screws now back on duty, gave us a blow-by-blow account of the final strike negotiations before he left to go back to his 'lonely old head office'.

It was the one relaxing time I had during the whole period I was in prison. In fact, I really looked forward to another strike, but unfortunately, although it was brewing, it never quite came to that.

With routine into full swing again, things once again deteriorated drastically. At one point, a couple of the nasty screws said we had been stealing food. We knew this was untrue. At every meal we were issued two slices of bread and two small packets of butter. If, at the end of each meal, we hadn't eaten our share, we couldn't save it—it was taken back by the staff and reissued for the next meal. Some officers delighted in deliberately leaving the rations in our kitchen fridge so they could accuse us of stealing them. We often returned them ourselves to save being accused. This time it was forgotten, and after days of trying to avoid a scene we copped a lecture on stealing and our bad morals. Certain of the screws took a great delight in delivering such lectures.

Tips on Exam Techniques and Expediting Education

My application for study approval to continue my BA by correspondence finally came through and I was allowed to have my first books and assignments. Permission for art and some other subjects took longer, or were rejected altogether.

Then there were the books I needed. I had to apply for a library card; then a town library card, and one from the Darwin College of Advanced Education in order to get all the textbooks needed. Everything took time. Sometimes it took six to eight weeks before a required book would finally be procured.

Invariably when I sat down to study, I would be called away. I was told, the other girls were watching their TV program. They knew I wouldn't mind, 'so just do this, will you?' It got so bad in the end that I had to do most of my study between midnight and one in the morning, when I was supposed to be asleep, ducking when the screws came by on their rounds and pretending to be asleep, then once again sitting up and trying to read and write by the security light outside my cell. Not the best for the eyes, let me assure you, but it was the only way I could get some consecutive time without hindrance.

Assignments had to be typed, and although there were two typewriters, I couldn't even use the teacher's one that came across especially for students. One girl wanted to learn typing, and that was fine, but the typewriter wasn't for those who could type, because they might break it! It was for practice only, and so I went through more rigmarole.

I could never get over the amount of futile work that was found to be done when we could have been quite gainfully employed. The Aboriginal girls had primary school once a week, and a number of the girls wanted to do high school courses. I wanted to finish my Bachelor of Education course. Those who were doing high school work eventually got permission to study in their cells or work on their assignments in the day room when there was no other work to be done.

Coming straight from Avondale College as a fourth-year student used to the language spoken around tertiary institutions, I quickly realised the majority of inmates did not understand most long words, so I quickly simplified my speech. I knew they would often ask the meaning of a slightly longer word and I would explain it, but it wasn't until several months later when one of the girls said to me, 'Shit, you use big words! I can never understand what you're saying. What does "vertical" mean?' that I realised the *extreme* limitation of their grasp of what I thought of as simple, everyday language. I asked, 'When you read the paper, do you understand it?' Most said they didn't, unless they sat with a dictionary beside them. I could not believe the girls (most of whom had gone to at least grade six and quite often grade eight or ten) were not grasping the language written in the daily newspapers. I learned if a word was above two syllables, and at most an easy three, most did not know what it meant. English had to be extremely basic. So I adapted accordingly. Dropping g's and h's with a little street slang added, also helped.

I could only surmise that much of what these prisoners heard in court about themselves was totally beyond their comprehension, particularly when normal language was interspersed with legalese. Although extremely streetwise, using what to most people would be a totally foreign language, the language used by the average person did not convey a great deal of meaning to them at all.

As girls came in, most decided that the way to increase their education and standing in the community was to be able to carry on a conversation that included big words. To do this, they frequently sat and read the dictionary or thesaurus, picked out words that sounded good and practised using them in sentences to anybody who would listen. They also did crosswords (even fighting over who got a new one first), using the thesaurus or dictionary to assist in understanding the clues. This helped them feel more ready to face the 'straight' community upon release.

I noted nearly two-thirds of the screws in our section resorted to the use of the dictionary when writing special letters or reports to head office so they didn't sound ill-educated. A number were quite open in their use of the dictionary, but others tried to hide it when anyone else was around.

It was OK to read a book or magazine, if you had no work. Staring into space or talking was fine, but we couldn't do anything useful. When the wet season came, if we had caught up on all our work (scrubbing the walls, ceilings and windows; stripping and polishing the floors; cleaning the storerooms; mending; and 'voluntary' Christmas sewing), if it was pouring rain so we couldn't weed the lawn, mow or dig, *then* we were given permission to do our own craft work or play games. But during the whole time I was there, I was never granted permission to study during the day when there was no other work on. The only 'study' time I had in work hours was for tutorials and exams when the education officer set the time during *his* working hours.

Taking an exam in jail was a memorable experience. One of my lecturers at college had stated that if I could get someone to give me extra tutoring in the figure drawing I had been doing when I was sent back to prison, I could complete this subject. Kerry Gardner, the education officer, was in favour of tertiary students and assisted them wherever possible, so he managed to get the head of the art department at the College of Advanced Education in Darwin to give me private tutorials. The problem was, I had to have live models to draw. I was not allowed to draw any of the other girls or the screws. Nor was I to draw myself, and the course called for me to do a self-portrait (I didn't have a mirror) plus three more studies, one of them a group study.

Kerry Gardner volunteered himself as a model for the two-hour session at least once a week for several weeks. The art tutor was a terrific teacher and I learned more from him in half an hour than I had done in a whole college semester. Now my talent began to accommodate my dreams instead of my vision being limited by my skill.

When it came to the practical exam, a friend of the tutor volunteered to sit. Because I had the sitter, the education officer and my teacher with me, the interview room was too small for the four of us. Strangers (particularly men) were not allowed in the section where the cells were, so we had to go outside underneath the carport near the section door. The model was set up by my tutor. I was given the time by Mr Gardner and told to begin. Within five minutes, the door opened and one of the girls came out in her gardening uniform. To walk out, she had to pass between me and my subject. Others followed in dribs and drabs until finally everyone was out. Then they returned for tools and came out again; then mowers and yet again for wheelbarrows. Every time I looked up there seemed to be a body between me and my subject. The wind was flapping the paper and doing its best to rip it from the board entirely, despite being securely pinned down. Drawing on what felt like a cushion of air instead of solid board was a peculiar experience.

I battled for half an hour, and my frustration increased. The conditions put me off, I was stiff and everything went wrong. I asked the tutor, 'Do I have to hand this in? Is there anything stopping me from starting again?' He said, 'No, as long as you finish within the allotted two hours.' I grabbed new paper, got a break in the interruptions and went for it. This time the drawing came on nicely, and I'm sure the prayer I said in desperation had everything to do with that.

After an hour I had to make a decision—whether to try and finish the drawing another stage or not. It would take half to three-quarters of an hour. If I finished it, I would get another mark or two, but if still incomplete, I would lose marks. It was perfectly satisfactory at the stage I had reached, so I decided to stop rather than chance failing to complete. Within fifteen minutes the girls would start packing up again, they would all return at once, with a lot of noise, and the wind had increased.

I couldn't help thinking wistfully of the exam conditions at college; a quiet two hours with extra time for a break for the model—and us. My poor model had to sit still for two hours straight! The model was very nice and pleased with the finished product. He asked whether he could have it if ever I no longer wanted it. I was not allowed to know his name or address; as he was not a visitor of mine, his anonymity had to be preserved according to the rules.

Some months later I received a letter that mentioned my exam, and I realised it was written by my mystery sitter. He coached the Northern Territory team for the Disabled Olympics.

The marking of my exam proved to be a long-running saga. My tutor was to give me a mark comparable to his own art class in Darwin (doing the same level art I was), taking into consideration the conditions under which I sat the exam, and my college work (I had some marked college work with me.) An exam is compared with what you are capable of, as well as marks averaged out with the rest of the class. The tutor marked my exam and wrote an accompanying note to my lecturer, Mr Painter, while I watched, and it was sent away along with a number of other fourth-year drawings.

I awaited my results with eager anticipation. I knew (so I thought) what my practical mark was, and as I had done my theory exam and sent in some of my term work as well, I was waiting for quite a number of marks. My teacher finally communicated the marks I had received for my theory exam, and that he had re-marked my practical exam.

Mr Painter had decided it shouldn't really be marked in the way he had formerly told them. He should mark it along with the rest of my college class. So he calculated the class average and adjusted my marks accordingly without any background facts. Because there had been a prior agreed procedure, I didn't think that was particularly fair, but I wasn't going to do anything about it.

The only thing that really did concern me was the list of other marks he had sent me. It struck me with fascinated horror that, despite going to a great deal of trouble to name and describe the paintings I had sent down for marking so there could be no mistake, I got quite a different list back with first, second, and third-year art, and unfinished works mixed with *some* of the ones I'd sent. For my fourth-year art, I got the marks I was expecting. Some of my first-year art got better marks than it had when originally marked! Unfinished paintings got dreadful marks—and comments about being better if they'd been finished off. I knew that! I wrote and told him of the mix-up, asking for my marks to be left in abeyance, until I could be released and straighten everything out in person. Receiving no reply, I assumed he had agreed.

I was also working on my major fourth-year art written assignment and it took major battles to make any headway. Eventually I finished it. I was very proud of that effort; I knew it was a good essay. I went through quite a rigmarole to get photocopying done through the jail for my illustrations, not to mention the battle royal (which finally meant having to go to head office) for permission to study in the first place.

I got limited permission only for use of the typewriter and, as I had a deadline to meet, I got special permission to hand the assignment to a southern visitor to take it with instructions for a friend to type it then hand it in. Finally, I hadn't had marks for so long, I wrote to my lecturer and asked what had happened. No assignment had been handed in.

After much to-ing and fro-ing of letters with Michael, he wrote back and said he was sorry, but somewhere along the line the assignment had been mislaid and no one seemed to know who had it. He had some more bad news. My photography portfolio had also been lost. The portfolio of notes, photography and the assignment was the entire work for that subject and made up the total mark. I had finished the portfolio in Darwin and sent it home with Michael by hand.

Both Michael and my lecturer agreed they had both looked at my work together but neither knew which one had kept it. All they *could* agree on was that, between them, they had lost it. They were both very sorry. As my lecturer couldn't remember the work now, he was afraid he couldn't mark it, and I would have to repeat the whole subject again. This would be for the *third* time. I had already been over halfway through the subject when I had to leave for the trial. After getting bail, the following year I had started again. This time I had got about a third of the way through, finishing off a number of things I hadn't been able to do the semester before, then was returned to prison again where I had finally finished it. I certainly had my lecture hours up, so was only lacking practical work in two small areas. My lecturer knew what my regular work and standards were. I knew Michael's work had been marked by the same teacher, sight unseen, and he had received an A. My work *had* been seen and he had simply forgotten it, so he was telling me to repeat it a third time.

I had had the same problem with this assignment as with all the others: lack of books; lack of research material; lack of time to do it; not being able to get the glue to stick in the pictures. I had to wait and get request forms for everything. The thought of all I had gone through to complete this work and then being told I would have to repeat it when I was finally released, because of their carelessness, was just *too* much. I was determined to fight this.

After I had been inside for quite a while it was announced that there would be a pottery school coming for one week. We would all be allowed to join free and those participating would be relieved of work duty. That was a good reason to join, even for those who hated pottery. I was pleased because I hoped to do some extra work towards a fourth-year assessment I was working on, and hopefully I would be able to experiment with some different methods.

When the potters arrived, the screws would not let us do our own thing but insisted on everyone keeping at the same level. The first day was fun but very basic. At the end of the day, I was able to talk to one of the potters, who asked how far I had progressed. From then on he assigned me various other things to do and got me to help teach the other girls, so I wasn't bored. This way I did get some additional experience.

The following year the same guy was with the pottery crew and knowing I was still inside, he had managed to get permission for the pottery wheel (the prison owned one which was stored) to be brought over and used. He made sure I had enough time to get the feel of it again, a skill easy to lose through neglect. The school was two weeks long this time and I was able to do quite a number of hand-built pieces which he had agreed to fire properly for me. When firing time arrived they came in on a Saturday morning without notice. As it was Sabbath I was in my room and not told. Later I discovered the screws had decided there was not enough room in the kiln and some works would have to wait. Seeing I had done it before, they were sure I wouldn't mind mine left on the shelf. It was typical of what happened when they knew I wanted work specifically for my educational program.

The pottery crew called in especially on their return trip to collect and fire my work. The potters didn't realise all those left were delicate pieces that had taken me hours and would not transport. The screws had already moved some of them in the storeroom and broken pieces. The potters did their best, but on the way to the university kiln, the fine filigree work either dropped off or cracked and made the pieces useless. When the work was returned, not one piece was intact out of a dozen pieces and I had to destroy them all. I think the crew were as upset as I was.

It was OK to do primary or high school study—but if you were studying for a higher level it seemed that was a threat to most.

To Test a Theory and End Speculation

Meanwhile, Kevin 'Muscles' Hitchcock, the journalist we met during the first inquest bomb threat, figuring I must be guilty from what he'd understood at the trial, decided to go to Ayers Rock and investigate for himself. (If you really want to find out what has happened accurately and quickly, ask a good investigative reporter. They'll be quicker than most police any day. Whether they will let you know what they've found out is another matter, of course.) Kevin thought it would be easy to quell the Chamberlain supporters once and for all with hard facts.

First he decided to test the Aborigines' tracking ability. Because they aren't used to speaking in public, on the witness stand, or to journalists, he'd come to the conclusion that Nipper and the others weren't quite sure what had happened. When he spoke to them, he discovered they had *very* definite ideas. They were in absolutely *no* doubt, in fact. True, Nipper wore glasses with lenses like milk bottles, but it was quite obvious that, whether or not he had been wearing them while tracking in August 1980, he could still see somebody coming at a distance, identify them, knew what they were doing and where they were going when he was *not* wearing his glasses.

Kevin asked Nipper and his colleagues to track for him. They did, and Kevin had to admit that the Aborigines knew precisely what they were doing. So now he listened, carefully, to how they *knew* a dingo had been involved, and what it had done. Kevin came home with changed views. He was upset that the information leaked to the media by the police outside the court proceedings had been rumour, hearsay, and in some cases total fabrication. He then had the guts to contact Michael and apologise to him, telling him he had originally thought I was guilty. Realising the influence of the press, he said he was ashamed of what he, as a newsman, had helped to do and now intended to take whatever steps he could to make people realise the miscarriage of justice that had taken place. And he did. He produced a very useful documentary called *Azaria: A Question of Evidence* that helped people realise what had really happened, despite their own scepticism.

To test the Aborigines' tracking ability once again, another Victorian journalist and one of his mates laid a trail, making it as difficult as they could. They wore each other's shoes, walked, ran, walked backwards. One left someone else's shirt stuffed in the crevice of a rock as he walked through. The two men even met at one point and carefully exchanged shoes. They leaned over and broke twigs off in different places to cause confusion also.

The Aborigines went through the track at a walking pace, pointing out everything the journalist and his colleague had done, as well as their reasons for doing it: where they had swapped shoes, how heavy they were, when they walked backwards, which man was wearing which shoes. The reporters thought they would miss the shirt in the crevice, at least, but as they went past, one Aborigine just reached in, pulled it out and handed it to its owner! The journalists were even more impressed than Kevin Hitchcock had been. It was obvious these Aborigines were no amateur trackers. Those journalists were also now convinced that something really odd had happened in our court case.

Funnily enough, even though the Northern Territory Crown claimed Nipper was too blind to be any good any more, they happily used him to track Crabb, the truck driver who drove his truck into the crowded bar of the Inland Motel in a fit of anger. Crabb was tracked and captured to stand trial for murder and served time in Darwin—although we never met. That was over two years after Azaria's death!

Dash It All!

Les Smith, who worked in the Plant Development Division of the Sanitarium Health Food Company, had done work on the under-dash spray before the trial, but that wasn't enough. Stuart came to Les after the trial and said, 'Is there anything you can do to help?'

'What would you like me to do?' asked Les.

Les had already proved, by means of scientific tests and infrared spectroscopic analysis (similar to a chemical fingerprint), that the spray was sound-deadening material. On the drawing board at work Les had calculated by means of drawings and measurement the angle the spray had come from when it was applied. Then he went and had a look at a similar Torana car.

Right where he had calculated, he saw a small drain hole under the front wheel arch that allowed the sound deadener (sprayed into the arches to cut down the sound of stones being thrown up by the tyres) to penetrate at exactly the right angle. It was called the plenum drain. It was through that little hole that the sound deadener and body paint had been sprayed on to the under-dash plate. He tested the sound deadener and, sure enough, it was the same thing he had been working on. You could actually see quite clearly the yellow paint over the top of our so-called blood spray under an ordinary magnifying glass.

By this time Wally Goodwin had heard about our inability to fully identify the under-dash spray, and, realising that his brother-in-law was in charge of the spraying department at General Motors Holden, got the cooperation we needed. That mystery was now over. We knew that it was *not* blood on the plate, but sound deadener, before the High Court appeal came up.

Les gave us his final report on 24 November 1983, four days before the High Court was scheduled to begin. But this new vital evidence that wasn't given at the trial couldn't be used in an appeal to the Federal Court (Les later said he never did quite understand that facet of the law), nor could evidence not used at the Federal Court be used at the High Court! If material is new and cogent, it can reopen the case, but this was *not* considered new and cogent because the under-dash spray had *been* there during the trial. We just had a new way of looking at it, and therefore this couldn't be accepted; the evidence of the fatal flaw in the Crown case could not be demonstrated. The High Court's job was to evaluate the evidence that had been presented and decide whether it was sufficient to continue to pronounce me guilty. It was frustration upon frustration. Like banging your head against a brick wall.

The dingo damage was a field that did not have any precedents, and we were not making much headway. Given a mind like Les's, with plenty of unplumbed depths, who knew what he was capable of? He was original, analytical and thorough, so Stuart asked him to have a go at this untouched field of the dingo evidence. He was more than willing.

Les read the court transcripts, then started working on dog bites and the resulting fabric damage with his dog, Suzie, to see if what the Crown had said was true. Suzie, now deceased, made a great contribution towards the Chamberlain case. Les found a very interesting range of damage, and discovered the Crown evidence about tufts and loops was totally wrong. He started talking to Ken Chapman, then chief analyst of the Australasian Food Research Laboratory, and between them the two men seriously started thinking about research. Eventually Ken ended up doing more of their travelling research than Les, because Les was involved on more fronts than one.

It was the combination of the work on the blood and the dingo damage that 'broke the back' of the Crown's so-called forensic science in my case, and without Les's keen brain and involvement, I don't think that would ever have come about. We'd had so many look, but just not realise the implications of what they were actually beholding.

The High Court appeal was heard before five judges: Lionel Murphy, Chief Justice Sir Harry Gibbs, Sir Anthony Mason, Sir William Dean and Sir Gerald Brennan.

When the decision was about to be handed down, I was torn between hope and despondency. The local rumours had not been good, so I was not expecting much. The local news always seemed to have foreknowledge of what was happening. Then I received a phone call from Stuart saying, 'I don't want to get your hopes up, but I feel you should know it is a swinging vote, two and two, and the verdict will depend on the fifth man. We are in with a chance.' Try as I might, I could not keep that seed of hope from growing.

The day of the result dawned. The night before I had cleaned a lot of things out of my cell so I could pack up and go very quickly if my release came. I had prayed about it: 'Lord, if it is the right thing, send me home. You know what is happening and I don't know what the reasons behind this are. You know how desperately I want to go home, but maybe your reason for me being here has not ended yet. I don't know.'

I was on kitchen duty. I had cleaned everything that I could possibly scrub, and was three-quarters of the way through scrubbing the floor when I was called across to the office and told Mr Tipple was trying to get through, and would ring back within the next half hour. I could see the press at the gate but still didn't know what the news was. Hypo looked at me strangely as I went back to the kitchen and I could tell that she knew something she wasn't telling. She had a private radio in her room and I was sure something about the appeal result had been broadcast but she wasn't telling. I was too proud to ask, because I knew she would rub it in.

If it had been good news, there would have been some indication. The press were slowly leaving—there was no news here today, if there was, they'd stay. I felt sick as I realised the answer must be no, and my heart sank. As I scrubbed that floor on my hands and knees, I prayed to God to give me the strength to hide what I felt from the other girls.

This was officially my last chance in law; I was in prison for life, and that, according to Northern Territory law, meant I would be in prison until the day I died. It appeared I was already the longest-serving prisoner in Australia for the type of crime I was supposed to have committed. Mrs Barham, our section chief, had done some research of her own and had told me that no woman in prison for the murder of a child under two years of age had been there for longer than a few months, as far as she had been able to find out. My sentence already ran into years.

Stuart eventually phoned again and told me we had lost by three votes to two. I could tell by his voice that he was extremely upset, especially as we had come so close. He said the strongest voice in our favour had been Lionel Murphy's, who, I discovered later, had said:

> The error is that the jury's view of the exculpatory evidence may well have been taken in the light of their acceptance of the scientific evidence as reliable, an acceptance contributed to by the trial judge's summing up. Likewise with other adverse conclusions, and the finding of guilt itself. If in accordance with the directions, the jury accepted the evidence that the blood was foetal, it was irresistible that they should then disbelieve Mrs Chamberlain and other evidence pointing to her innocence . . . Once it was accepted that it was unsafe to conclude that there was foetal blood in the car, then the conviction of Mrs Chamberlain was unsafe . . . Not only for that reason, but because I am of the firm view that the rational hypothesis advanced by the defence was not excluded beyond reasonable doubt and that the presumption of innocence was not displaced, Mrs Chamberlain is entitled to a judgment of acquittal.

He said, further, that if I was acquitted, the judgment against Michael could not stand, but in any case 'the presumption of his innocence was not displaced. He should have been acquitted'.

What a pity Lionel Murphy died before he had the advantage of hearing the additional evidence and the Report of the Royal Commission. During the Commission Michael and I took time off and went to his memorial service in the Sydney Town Hall, along with hundreds of other mourners, as a last mark of respect for a great man. He was a man who wasn't afraid to get up and speak against the majority when he knew they were wrong. In a sense, he paid for that in the end.

The other judgment in our favour came from Sir William Dean, who said:

> I have finally come to a firm view that notwithstanding the jury's verdict of guilty, the evidence did not establish beyond a reasonable doubt that Mrs Chamberlain killed Azaria. That being so, the verdict that she was guilty of murdering her child is unsafe and unsatisfactory and constituted a miscarriage of justice. It necessarily follows that the evidence failed to establish beyond reasonable doubt that Mr Chamberlain was guilty of the crime of which he was convicted.

Four out of the five judges found that the jury should have 'entertained reasonable doubt' about whether Joy Kuhl's tests had shown that there was foetal haemoglobin in the car. They also clarified the law that governed cases that, like ours, depended on circumstantial evidence, saying that every primary fact that forms a basis for guilt to be inferred must be proven beyond reasonable doubt. Yet three out of the five had upheld the court's finding that we were guilty as charged.

I found out all these details later. When I put the phone down after talking to Stuart, I was shaking. The cold, dead feeling I'd lived with for so long surged up inside me again.

I stayed inside the office for a time to collect myself and then walked straight back to the kitchen. When I passed her, Hypo looked at me and raised her eyebrows. The other girls all looked expectant also.

I simply said, 'I've lost my appeal' then continued to the kitchen to finish scrubbing the floor. That at least enabled me to work some of the anger and hurt out of my system and be on my own. The other girls could not come in to the kitchen except at mealtimes. As long as I kept my back turned I was able to cry silently without them knowing. As I scrubbed, I prayed to God to give me strength.

Psalms 82: 1, 2 in the *Living Bible* seemed terribly appropriate. 'God stands up to open heaven's court. He pronounces judgment on the judges.' How long will you judges refuse to listen to the evidence?

By lunchtime I had calmed down and was able to go to my cell, clean up and come back as if nothing had happened. By the time I needed to go over to get the food cart for lunch, all the press had left and I had a free walk across.

Many was the time, if the press had waited a few minutes more or been there a few minutes earlier, they would have seen me. It seemed they weren't meant to get photographs. I was so slim by this time that no one recognised me anyway. I was still doing an hour and a half to two hours' exercise every night.

At lunch Hypo admitted she had known some three-quarters of an hour before I did because she had been listening to her radio.

I said to her, 'Why didn't you tell me?'

She shrugged, 'I didn't know how you would react. You might have gone crazy or told the screws or something and so I thought you'd better learn through official channels.' She really *had* to know everything first.

Losing was a real blow and I felt really down over the next few weeks. Living with God's silence is perhaps the hardest part. I knew He knew all about it and would help me cope, but He also knew I was innocent. Why was He *still* making me wait? God's silence on things is probably the biggest religious issue of our times. After Auschwitz and the death camps, many thousands of Jews could no longer believe. With unchecked violence, sexual perversions, AIDS, greed, and death, many non-Jews cannot believe that God cares or intervenes in human affairs any longer either.

I *knew* He cared, but I wished I *also* knew His plan for me. I had to trust a little more each day and my faith was stretched to its limit daily. It was like swinging on a slim cord over a deep mountain chasm. The signs said someone held the other end, but in the mist you couldn't see them. You had to trust and just swing across. Not until you did could you *know* you were securely held. So it was with me and God over the next few weeks—and *He held me up*. I clung to the Bible text: 'It is time Lord for thee to work: for they have made void thy law.' (Psalms 119: 126, King James Version.) In His own time I knew He would work.

In my next circular letter about six weeks later, I couldn't show my fight with initial depression. I didn't want the Northern Territory to know just then how I really felt, so I said:

> The High Court finding was a bitter disappointment—so near and yet so far. Each time it happens, you tend to die a little inside, which means to an

> onlooker that you appear to handle it better each time. You don't really—you just learn to cope better with the pain. I just keep looking at a motto I have on the wall:
>
> 'Tough times don't last, but tough people do!' and I keep telling myself 'this too shall pass' and with God's help I will bounce back on top again. My favourite book states in Isaiah 59: 14-15: 'Justice is turned back and righteousness stands afar off; for truth has fallen in the public squares, and uprightness cannot enter. Truth is lacking, and he who departs from evil makes himself a prey.'
>
> In the meantime we are working on our next legal step, yes, despite the news saying there was none. The fight is far from over and it is not the end of the case. I'm not meek and mild and never was. Rather too outspoken for comfort if you ask Michael and my friends, but that's me. Just yet it is too soon—and I do have a fair share of patience. Jail develops that too.
>
> We must fight for the preservation of discerning laws in this country. One day I was just a happy housewife and mother, known only to my friends and associates, next day a household word. I never dreamt it could possibly happen to me—how about you? If this continues, will you be next?

I also wrote:

> Total freedom is in the mind, not the body. One needs the former to enjoy the latter. The High Court decision had not changed my innocence. Their action was the finishing touch, the ultimate act in framing an unworthy picture of justice.
>
> People can blacken my reputation, but they can never change my character. I am not afraid of presenting myself before the Judge of the universe for His ultimate decision.

As well as keeping me fit, jogging kept me sane and helped expend pent- up frustrations. Jogging was always best just before sunset. When I stopped I would often stand looking through the bars on the doors, watching the beautiful wild cyclamen pinks, purples and mauves with a tinge of orange thrown in; seeing them change quickly as night took over and the stars came out. The sunsets are deep, vivid and very tropical, with none of the lingering afterglow you see further south. In my mind's eye I could blot out the bars and the cyclone wire fence around the prison, with its razor wire

'Christmas decorations'. In the mornings I could watch the sunrise outside my cell window as I rose and dressed. It was different, but beautiful also, bathing the flat, brown, arid landscape, so typical of Australian outback, in a pinky, purple glow, or wild orange colours. Sometimes there were even greens.

Eventually the curiosity over my appeal failure and how I was taking it faded, and the whispering ceased. Life returned to its normal humdrum boredom again, but my mind continued to tick over.

We had massive legal costs, and the press for years had been making themselves fat and rich over our story. We had received nothing and we were the ones with the bills to pay. Because the press had not seen me for years and I had changed so much, the history-making aspects of the case so far and the continued public interest, made it obvious it would be possible to make a deal and sell an interview. I wasn't sure how one went about it, but I was going to find out. I was sick of being the 'bunny' that was used all the time, so I devised a plan whereby I could 'escape' without being seen as I was sure one day they'd simply walk in and say, 'Come on, you're going home.'

I had been tossing ideas over for some months. Finally I got Liz Parry to bring her husband, John, in to outline the plan. Now, John and Footsie were our specialist 'escape' artists. Footsie normally did the planning and John filled in where necessary. This time I did most of the planning as I knew the prison. John normally came in about once every six months, so he took the time off work and came in just as if it were another normal visit, instead of a clandestine committee meeting, and I outlined the plan.

That may have seemed foolhardy at a time after the High Court failure when there seemed no chance of my release but the case was unknown from day to day, so we all thought it best to be ready. John thought my plan sounded great, and went off to tell Footsie. They would arrange the details between them. We'd have to work on who could be a decoy, though.

A couple of weeks later, Sue Priory came in on a visit. We always had a fun visit when she accompanied Liz. Something was said about us being alike and all of a sudden Liz and I looked at one another and said, 'Hey, that's it!' Suzie was sitting there saying, 'What? What? Tell me! What?' Sue was about 2.5 centimetres (one inch) taller than me, of similar build, and we both had short dark hair, although she had a darker complexion than me. I knew that we could look even more alike if our makeup and clothes were the same. Sue got excited when I explained and agreed instantly. A phone call would make Sue drop all her office work, and run.

Liz assured me some weeks later again that the conference had taken place with Footsie, and everything was set to go when needed. The others they'd rely on for help would only be told on a need-to-know basis, but could be relied on.

To Help a Stranger and Find a New Friend

While life settled down on the inside again, it really started to bubble and boil over on the outside. Too many people were aware of the injustice I had suffered to let things lie. So many were working to help me and in *Cry for Justice: An Untold Story*, Lenore Stevenson, the eldest daughter of well- known Australian sculptor Guy Boyd, told the story of setting up and running a support group, and why she had become involved. This is a personal note she thought might be useful, and it is reprinted here with her kind permission:

> It was a cold, bleak day in October 1982. The afternoon was proceeding on its customary course at our house. That evening the fracas was at last subdued as babies and children were finally tucked into bed for the night. Stuart [her husband] was tired after coming home late from work and had already gone to sleep. I curled up alone on the couch in front of the TV to

see the end of *The Sound of Music*, savouring the solitude which seems so rare to mothers of young children.

Suddenly the program was interrupted. It was another news- flash about the Chamberlain trial which had dominated the headlines for so long. I felt disgruntled and annoyed about having my reverie disturbed. I wished that the media would leave the Chamberlains alone and cut out the sensationalism which always seemed to surround the case. These thoughts fled through my mind in the second before I grasped the meaning of the news-flash.

'The verdict was handed down tonight in the Darwin court. Mrs Alice Lynne Chamberlain has been found guilty of the murder of her nine-week-old daughter, Azaria, at Ayers Rock camping ground on 17 August 1980. A unanimous jury has found that Mrs Chamberlain removed the baby from the family tent to the car, where she cut her daughter's throat. She and her husband, Michael Chamberlain, later disposed of the body by means unknown. Mrs Chamberlain has been sentenced to the mandatory 99 years imprisonment with hard labour. Michael Chamberlain will be sentenced tomorrow for his role as accessory after the fact. The Chamberlains' claim that a dingo took their baby from their tent is now discredited.'

Ninety-nine years in jail! Hard labour! The television screen was filled with the image of Lindy's swollen, tear streaked face glimpsed through a police car window as it drove away from the court. Lindy's face was branded on my consciousness. I caught my breath as if a bucket of ice water had been thrown over me. *The Sound of Music* came back on the screen, but the characters seemed faceless, colourless and dim. All I could see was that suffering face, the head bent forward, the eyes hooded with grief.

Mechanically, I switched off the set and went to bed. All night I tossed wakefully, the grieving image before me and sympathetic tears eking their way hotly into my pillow. I tried to wake Stuart to tell him what had happened, but he groaned, turned over and remained obstinately asleep.

No matter what had happened in the Chamberlain case, I felt it could not justify such a harsh sentence. Lindy was a mother, like me. Aidan, Reagan, Azaria were of similar ages to my children. Lindy had been a consistently loving and devoted mother. The murder allegation was totally out of character and now her whole family was being penalised. This much I had gathered from the media. The rest evoked an illusion of the French guillotine . . . people gossiping and knitting as heads rolled.

The next day I broached the subject with Stuart [her husband].

'It's nothing to do with us,' he said, 'What can we do about it? It's the law.'

I didn't see it that way. I would do something about it. I would write to politicians and newspapers. It seemed such a glaring injustice, so there must be a public outcry.

Michael Chamberlain was given a good behaviour bond. During a phone conversation with my father, we discussed the case. My parents [Guy and Phyllis Boyd] had been overseas during much of the publicity storm surrounding the disappearance of Azaria, and Dad was unfamiliar with many of the details, but still he was amazed at the severity of the sentence for infanticide. Homicidal psychopaths had been given much lighter sentences for much more violent crimes. There was also a mysterious lack of evidence to convict Lindy. Dad's constant concern for justice prompted him to see about starting a petition for mercy in Melbourne. He promised to look further into it.

So Guy Boyd and his daughter Lenore spearheaded the biggest support movement and petitions this country has ever seen:

Dad was deeply grieved by the fact that Lindy was still in gaol [after the High Court appeal failed]. 'I can't sleep while that woman remains locked up,' he said. My mother was more philosophical. It would take years to see a result for our efforts. She went on working quietly behind the scenes, ever the mainstay to Dad.

'We'll turn this into a political football by the end of the year,' said Dad. 'We'll approach people individually. We'll get the information out about what really happened in this case and no government will be able to turn a blind eye to it.'

I collected signatures in the Geelong City Square.

Two tall, dark men in jeans and checked shirts stopped to read the literature that I had displayed on a bench. 'We are from the Territory,' claimed the taller of the two. Apparently he felt that this gave him authority about the subject at hand.

'The press in the Territory don't make a big deal of the Chamberlain case the way your southern ones do. You just don't read about it up there.'

His friend was rocking from foot to foot, looking at the literature, but listening to our conversation.

'There was a lot of confusion about the story in the press,' I said, not sure where the conversation was leading.

'People down here have got no business mucking around in affairs that don't concern them,' he said firmly, clearly disgusted by our ignorant southern ways. 'You should keep your nose out of it. She's guilty. Lindy's guilty.'

His message delivered, he strode up the street, indicating with a jerk of his head to his friend to follow. The friend began to walk away from me but turned back, hesitant and anxious. He looked at me with a clouded brow, obviously struggling with an inner argument of his own which would have made my comments superfluous, so I said nothing.

'Give it here. I think I should sign it,' he said at last, indicating the petition.

He hurriedly signed his name and headed towards his outraged mate, who had been waiting indignantly, halfway up the street. As they disappeared into the distance, I could hear their voices raised in heated argument.

The two ladies who had helped me for a while had gone home. I stood there alone. The sound of someone spitting on the pavement behind me caused me to turn quickly around, but I couldn't see anyone.

A middle-aged couple approached me. I was trying to guess who would be 'for' and who would be 'against'. This couple appeared very flustered, so I guessed that they were 'against'. I braced myself.

'I heard you on the radio, and what you said convinced us that we should sign the petition,' said the woman. 'We've driven five miles from our home to come and sign.'

This was the highlight of my day. So much for trying to guess by appearances what people would think. I was beginning to learn that it was impossible to do this. People's reactions were highly individual and unpredictable and I could never judge correctly.

'They should have hung her before the trial!' shouted a young man angrily as I packed up to get home in time to pick up the children.

A sad countenanced, shy little man approached me. He looked around nervously before thrusting a stack of signed petitions into my hand.

'Charlie Gentle,' he introduced himself. 'Give those to your father. It's taken me six months to collect them. This case is making life quite unbearable for us Adventists, do you find?' he continued with a conspiratorial air. I told him that I wasn't a Seventh-day Adventist, like the Chamberlains, as he (and many others) assumed.

'Oh!' he exclaimed in startled surprise at this unexpected revelation.

Although the Boyds and a number of others became involved immediately after the trial, the work was fairly slow while there were still legal steps open to us. As soon as the High Court appeal failed, all stops were pulled out and the support group movement blossomed rapidly.

Before I knew him, Pete (Pastor Peter Stojanovic) had been petitioning in pubs, on street corners and the City Square in Melbourne. Once when he walked into a pub he saw two gentlemen wearing dingo shirts, which he found very offensive. When you have a towering, broad, solidly muscled gentleman confronting you and telling you to 'Take that off, it offends me!' you tend to do what you are told. One of them, after an initial attempt at saying no, hastily took his T-shirt off and he and his mate headed for the door. This was sensible because Pete was a former boxer. On one occasion when a gentleman annoyed him because of what he had said about me, Pete knocked him out cold.

Despite his ill health, my father slowly but surely knocked on doors throughout whole sections of Nowra with the petition, collecting signatures to try and get an inquiry. He didn't identify himself because he wanted people to sign of their own volition, not because they felt sorry for the father of the lady concerned. Occasionally he told them his name, but many was the time he bit his tongue and remained silent while they abused his beloved daughter. During this time he suffered what was thought to be a heart attack and was rushed to hospital. When given all the tests they discovered it was not his heart. The doctor asked him if there was any particular reason he might have been under severe stress. Dad looked at him and said, 'Well, Lindy Chamberlain is my daughter.' The doctor said, 'Oh, I see.' And that was the end of that conversation.

My parents hand wrote nearly a thousand letters each (all members of state and Federal Parliaments at least three times) even though my mother has arthritis in her hands. On two different occasions my brother Alex also wrote handwritten letters to the same Parliamentarians.

Mervyn Whittaker, a Victorian man, decided to go to the Dandenong markets and set up a stall with the petitions to see if he could get names. At the end of the day he went home with two hundred signatures. He said those signatures had cost him up to five minutes arguing and persuading for every one. Not one person voluntarily signed when first asked. He went home totally exhausted, emotionally and physically.

South Australia was headed by Arlyn Tombleson, a chiropractor.

In the far north of Queensland, an old friend, Mavis Butler (of necessity a warrior war dog from way back), took one look and said, 'Something's wrong.' She started a support group on her own and eventually spearheaded the far northern groups. She was afraid of absolutely nothing and a lot of her unique methods were adopted elsewhere. Mavis is a small, wiry woman. But it is not the size of the dog in the fight that counts, it is the size of the fight in the dog, and this dog had no lack of fight. She found a lot of opposition was coming through university students. Her sons were mixing in this group and she realised these were the people who talked, so she took matters into her own hands. Mavis waltzed into the university and asked to put a notice on the notice board. She issued a challenge to the debating society, or any other interested university member or group, to meet her at a certain place and time to debate the Chamberlain case. They accepted and she turned up to find a lot of students waiting, fascinated to see who was brave enough to stick her nose into a university on such a topic. She brought the video, *A Question of Evidence* by Kevin Hitchcock (which showed a lot of the new evidence, as well as the trackers' evidence), plus a number of leaflets and booklets. She had learned the case inside out.

At the meeting Mavis insisted the students watch the tape and then she'd answer any questions they threw at her. Grinning, they complied, and later every objection they raised she answered. The meeting went longer than it was supposed to but nobody minded. She was then asked to run a second meeting. The change in attitude was marked and the influence spread.

She took the petition and knocked on doors. She entered shops, school gates or wherever she thought she would find people. She stood on soapboxes, speaking and arguing and got results.

Many people were not game to stand up and say what they believed. There was no sitting on the fence in our case, and people who had the guts to stand up and make a public stand for the Chamberlains' innocence certainly needed the guts to live with the flak that came afterwards.

Many of the groups had their mail tampered with. They had to put up with graffiti and signs on their properties, hate-mail, anonymous phone calls and being accosted in the street; but *all* of them realised that what had happened to us could happen to them, and if they weren't prepared to stand up and fight for us, heaven help them if the time should come in the future, that they ended up in a situation like ours. There was a principle involved, so they fought very hard.

Many people thought the support groups were run by Adventists. Sure, many Adventists belonged to support groups, but they were often support groups initiated and run by others.

There were factions of supporters, however, probably because there was initially no central coordinating committee but spontaneous and independent efforts made by thousands throughout the country. Stuart Tipple didn't support the line of some who were convinced there was a vast conspiracy organised by the Northern Territory to conceal the identity of what they considered the culprit dingo, and there was some controversy over that.

In fact, some support groups banded together and tried to convince the Chamberlain Innocence Committee to transfer allegiance to a legal team nominated by them, instead of Stuart Tipple. On the surface these groups looked very supportive but were actually very disruptive and caused me a great deal of stress.

They had tried to force me to use their lawyers and had been very scathing in their attacks on Stuart, saying that he would never manage to get a Commission for us and was taking our money under false pretences. I called them the counter-support groups. We knew their lawyers had less information than ours did, nor were they as good as our past lawyers had been. We could not guarantee information given to those support groups and lawyers would not end up in the media, so I had ceased instructing them. Any leaks gave the Northern Territory the chance to disparage correct evidence, making it seem irrelevant.

I'd had to leave a lot of people with the impression they had gained from the newspapers without trying to correct it, simply because we wanted to keep our information strictly confidential until ready to use it ourselves. The supportive public would just have to wonder and agonise; just taking our word that things were being done, even if they might not know what.

Because Stuart Tipple wouldn't give any information to the do-gooders, these people were given a very high profile in the media and in the counter-support groups. They had done their best to discourage Stuart, as well as disparage him, complaining about his competence as a lawyer. He had managed to weather all that, although it had been difficult. At one stage, when Stuart was working full time for us, he estimated he was spending almost a third of every work day in phone calls from irate people telling him how to do his business. In order to take the pressure off Maurice Neil, our QC, who was silently working, and off me, Stuart had taken the brunt. Often when he came to visit me in jail I would say to him, 'How are the shoulders?' He would grin and say, 'Still pretty broad.' But I knew what sort of a battering he and his family had taken over the malicious stories and rumours that were around about him.

A lot of the hassling was caused by professional jealousy, I am sure. Stuart lost a number of his regular clients because he was involved in the Chamberlain case but he gained others. He also became a partner in his firm during that time.

The Bushfires of Justice Spread

Occasionally someone told me some member of the jury had moved or took long detours because they normally had to pass the jail every day and they could no longer stand it. I thought, Good! It serves them right, they brought it on themselves. And yet I knew deep down they hadn't; they had been set up, too.

Some people in Darwin, though, were very supportive. Tony Noonan was the consultant surgeon at the Royal Darwin Hospital, and his wife Liz (a trained nurse) looked after their small children at home. I was told about them, but didn't give them a great deal of thought, then Liz Parry kept saying Liz Noonan would like to see me.

I was fairly careful whom I allowed to visit me because I knew I couldn't talk freely to many people; whatever I said tended to be misquoted and misunderstood then blown out of proportion. I trusted Liz Parry and I kept the list of people who came to visit with her restricted to friends and people I *knew* could keep their mouths tightly shut. People had enough information about me; they didn't need private details.

When I eventually agreed, Liz Noonan came in with Liz Parry and we just chatted generally. She was fairly well on in her pregnancy with Josh, her last child, and we enjoyed talking. That night I heard repeated on the evening news some of the things I had said that afternoon, so I mentally crossed her off the visiting list and told Liz Parry not to bring her again.

Some months later, a number of rumours got back to me. By this time I was well aware that Liz and Tony Noonan were being very supportive, and headed the Darwin Support Group, but I also knew they had been influenced quite strongly by the counter-support groups. I had heard that Liz and Tony were being fed wrong information by these groups, a lot of which they believed.

Now the rumour was that I would not have anything to do with other lawyers was because I had fallen in love with Stuart started. It was said he had me totally hoodwinked and was dictating to me—I had no mind of my own. Those who knew me and saw me every day knew this was utter rubbish. Longstanding friends know that I have a mind of my own, and of course so did Stuart. I know he told a friend of mine that if the counter- support group lawyers wanted me to do something badly enough and thought I would refuse, they ought to tell me it was exactly the thing I *wasn't* to do, then I might do it! I must say that amused me, even if it has been known to work on occasions! Because I am never one to lie down and say die before the last possible facet has been investigated, it is amazing how many impossible things you *can* do if you try *before* somebody tells you they're impossible.

Misconceptions had got to Dr Noonan, who repeated the latest rumour to Pastor Bob Donaldson. On his clergy visit, Bob let me know and I decided to set this Tony Noonan straight. It was arranged for him to come in with Liz Parry, even though he wasn't on the approved list.

I said to Mrs Barham, 'Don't worry if we have an argument because I think we have differing views, but don't butt in, I will be perfectly all right and I know what I'm doing.'

Mrs Barham said to me, 'I have been waiting for this. I've been watching the situation.' (She censored my mail.) It was not the easiest thing to get strangers past Tapioca, but with Mrs Barham's approval we did, so Tony arrived.

That was a memorable meeting. We all said hello, and Liz sat down with a grin; she knew what to expect. I said, 'Well, we all know what we're here for. Let's go for it. We've only got half an hour.' I told Tony Noonan, 'I know you've got questions. You go first.'

I let him talk for about five minutes and immediately saw that his problems were based on some scurrilous rumours that were totally groundless. I stopped him in midstream and said, 'Hang on a moment. Let's get some points straight. Do you realise I've been instructing their lawyers for six months?'

His mouth dropped open. He said, 'What did you say?'

I repeated my words and added, 'You weren't told that, were you?'

'No,' he said, amazed. I told him to check up and ring his source and ask, because they knew this was correct. He agreed to check wondering aloud why they had omitted to tell him.

I continued, 'What's more, I have given them some very simple affidavits to do to see how they work. So far I have not had one word back, and even the slowest lawyer would have had time to finish what I have given them.'

He said, 'Oh!'

'I am continuing to instruct these non-support-group lawyers, but I have sent them a letter saying that if they don't produce work in the time allowed, they have an extension of one month. After that I am going to discontinue their services because they are wasting money, and I will not be responsible for what they are doing. They are hoodwinking good people who are pouring money into their cause and they are doing absolutely nothing in return for that money.' I said I had read all their material, had asked questions, and asked them back again, but they still had not produced any different material. It was still incorrect, and they hadn't even read my record of interview yet. This indeed was a grave oversight for anyone supposed to be working on any case.

Once again he said, 'Oh!'

Then I gently told him about some of the rumours *I'd* heard. Such rumours as I didn't know my own mind and was in love with Stuart. I laughed as I said that so he wouldn't suspect I knew *he'd* repeated that one. I continued, 'They don't know me too well.'

He swallowed and said, 'Oh, er, I had heard that.'

The half hour went quickly and I ended up giving him a thumbnail sketch of what was being done by us.

At the end, Tony commented that the visit had been far different from what he'd expected. He had a lot to think about and would make some enquiries and get back to me.

I thanked him.

When leaving, he said that his wife Liz would love to see me again. I said, 'Look, I am sorry but after her last visit she went to the newspapers, and I cannot allow that.' He was totally aghast. I said, 'I'm sorry, I like Liz, but can't afford these security slips and that's the reason Liz hasn't been in again.'

He said, 'Right, well, I will tell her. Thank you for letting me know.' Within a few days I heard back that Tony had done a complete reversal in his thinking and that Liz was devastated. She said she hadn't spoken to the media, she hadn't realised that information from her visit had been on the news and she was racking her brains to work out how this had happened. She had only spoken to four people—her main officers in the support group. I sent the message back to her that one of them was leaking information and her committee was not secure (she located her leak there). All of a sudden she realised just how careful we were trying to be and how the leak had occurred.

After that, there were no further worries about leaks from the Darwin Support Group. It learned the hard way, as most of the other groups did, who you could speak to and who you couldn't.

And so the inner groups were screened, not just by availability of time and talent, but also by their ability to keep security. Liz Noonan came in more often after that.

During this time I wrote in one of my circular letters:

> Thank you for all those letters, photos, cards and telegrams. The trust and support shown me in the last nearly four years has been gracious. It shows me the real mateship of Australia is not dead. I do not believe it is just for me that you are fighting, but Australia's basic community is at stake. Honesty remains a very precious virtue.

Then I continued on the subject causing all the furore—lawyers:

> On the legal front various lawyers have been working for me for quite some time, some alongside Stuart Tipple, some freelance, and one group paid for by my support groups. You have heard most about the group led by Mr Lloyd-Jones due to some of the support groups publicising it, but others are working equally as hard, but quietly, in other areas. Shortly I expect all areas to be completed. When this is so I will be choosing my team for the next legal move and not before.
>
> There have been a lot of legal men involved and a lot of pressure lately to use this or that lawyer—whomever I use, someone will be disappointed. It is impossible to please everyone, so I will simply be choosing the best men for the work, based on their qualifications, grasp of the case, and work input. It will not be a hasty decision, nor one that is made lightly. All your contributions in this field have been much appreciated, so I hope none of you feel disappointed when the final team is named. There is a lot I would like to say about what is coming, but think it best not to just yet. In the next few weeks hopefully we will be able to see some positive moves made. In the meantime don't be too misled by the well-meaning but erroneous press releases some are putting out.

Things settled down a little after that, but it still took a lot of Stuart's precious time.

Pastor George Rollo was a man I had known more as a friend of my parents and grandparents than as a friend of my own. When I was sent to jail, George started to write to me. His letters were up-to-date, interesting and informative. I could guarantee to find a letter from George, my parents and one or two others weekly. Michael's parents' letters took a little longer to come across the Tasman but they were regular as well. This helped keep me informed. Then I learned George had compiled a small booklet, with questions and answers about our innocence, called 'A Reason to Kill'. He distributed this far and wide. Despite his seventy-odd years, he was an avid writer and researcher with seemingly endless energy. He also had the ability to talk to anyone and his contacts were phenomenal, from all walks of life. He was the major solo influence in keeping our case before the public.

George at the very least was extremely astute. He could sift information and pick out fact from theory quickly. He rapidly summed up a situation recognising how it could be used. This quality was extremely useful. He stayed apart from the support groups so he could act as a liaison point between the two warring factions of support groups. This he did with great effect; so effectively in fact, that he became the link, not only between the support groups, but between the groups and politicians. He could handle the media and lawyers, asking and answering difficult questions.

Anne Campbell (a nursing sister and my gynaecologist's wife) ran the Sydney group and also had the unenviable task of trying to mediate between the support and 'anti' support groups (those trying to run *our* case *their* way—a desire accompanied by threats and flying tempers). She and Mavis Butler were two of the few Adventists who did lead support groups.

Guy Boyd (who neglected his own work for the sake of our cause), headed Bob Sutcliffe and Mervyn Whittaker, with the Victorian groups. They ran packed meetings in the Melbourne Town Hall. During one meeting, which included talks by key eyewitnesses and engendered a lot of emotion, an elderly woman stated that she would be happy to swap places with me and serve the rest of my sentence for me. When one of the organisers heard about this, the woman was asked if she would go up the front and tell the congregation. She did and said that because she was eighty, she had already lived a lot of her life, and wouldn't mind spending the rest of it in jail, whereas I was a mother with young children who needed me, and she thought that she could change places. Unfortunately, the law does not work that way, but the thought was wonderful and at the end of her little talk to the people, she walked across to the piano, sat down and played and sang 'Rock of Ages'.

At the same meeting a woman approached one of the organisers and gave him a ring that she said was worth a considerable amount of money. She wished it to be used for my cause. The committee was not used to being given jewellery and was unsure how and where to sell this ring. After several attempts to sell it (they didn't want it to be sold under its value), I was released from jail, so they decided to let me deal with it. More than three years later I received it, but by then no one knew the name of the donor. (This ring was to become very significant later.)

Some of the most prolific letter writers were Helen Brown of Ipswich, who worked tirelessly and cooperated with Dr Weston Allen's groups; Mary Knipe of

Queensland and her grandchildren who not only wrote letters but lobbied and collected signatures for hours; and Birdie Swift, a fearless octogenarian with a keen brain and a sense of justice. Mary Milton, another elderly Brisbane lady, regularly collected newspaper cuttings, which she used her pension to photocopy. She sent them to me in jail, as well as to Michael, both our parents, George Rollo, Stuart, the Chamberlain Information Centre, and others who were vitally engaged in other areas of the fight and didn't have the same time to scour the papers.

Danny Stojanovic videoed everything he could on TV and the Victorian Yugoslav church members saved all the Victorian news clippings for us. Often a vital piece of information was gleaned this way.

Miss Veronica Flanagan, a retired lady from New South Wales, wrote a pamphlet that she published and lobbied with far and wide on the reasons, facts and myths of the case. She called it 'The Azaria Evidence: Fact or Fiction'. It was used effectively in the support groups.

Some women combined in groups to organise massive mailings to politicians. One lady regularly made pumpkin scones and other goodies in aid of their local support group efforts on my behalf. Some simply contributed money to assist those who had more time, but all worked together.

The numbers were phenomenal; so many people were involved that it's impossible to name them all. Ordinary people committed themselves—they lobbied politicians, their fellow Australians, the media, all with the message: 'Free Lindy'. Large numbers of the vocal ones were women (which contradicted the view that women were more hostile than men).

Supporters calculated that Liberal members in Western Australia alone got about 17,000 letters, and chief minister of the Northern Territory Ian Tuxworth (a successor of Everingham), said he got about 1,400 letters a month about our case. Mr Barrier of the Corrective Services head office regularly told me they were nearly driven mad with mail about me and wished I would ask people to stop. I would just smile and say they knew a really easy way to make it stop if they wanted to! He would just sigh.

People didn't just write letters to Parliamentarians, either. They organised letter-boxing, bumper stickers, distribution of leaflets, rallies—and even T-shirts, though they were much less provocative than those used by people who were against me. Betty Hocking's was typical: 'LINDY'S GUILT MAKES NO SENSE . . . NO MOTIVE, NO WEAPON, NO BODY, NO DEPRESSION, [i.e. I wasn't suffering postnatal depression] NO CONFESSION, NO SENSE'.

The support groups, although consolidating, were still working separately. It was obvious there needed to be some central control for accurately swapping information. Our phone was driving Michael crazy. It was felt some sort of coordination was necessary to give a push for a Royal Commission. So *The Azaria Newsletter* and the Chamberlain Information Service were set up. This existed to give our supporters the latest news about the case, and keep them in touch with each other. Three Cooranbong young women volunteered and they did a marvellous job. Marie Alford opened mail till it came out of her ears, wrote regularly, answered queries, and also did the bookkeeping. Nonie Hodgson made it her job to gather the information and edit it, with Michael's assistance when he was available; Linda Driscoll typed for hours on end, getting it ready for printing; then crews of ladies, not known by me, would fold it, and get it ready for mailing to the various support groups and interested people around the country.

The newsletter gave politicians' addresses, summarised vital documents, and kept people informed of various news items. Later newsletters included comprehensive summaries of new evidence presented years later. The newsletter initially carried a subscription rate in order to cover printing and postage. It continued until September 1989—we were still fighting for compensation, although now it was no longer self-supporting and had to be subsidised.

The girls also ran a dial-for-information prerecorded service, which really ran hot when major lobbying was done, and distributed books and tapes that were coming out about the case.

With the establishment of the Information Centre the groups got in contact with one another. Guy Boyd's support group was now joined by others.

A number of people had set up bigger groups and were capable of coordinating some sort of action within their states. Betty Hocking, an Australian Capital Territory House of Assembly member who was already running the Plea for Justice Committee in Canberra, eventually co-spearheaded the campaign nationally. She and her committee were prepared to give information through their established newsletter, which already had a wide circulation. She worked closely with Guy Boyd and Lenore supporting the spread of their petitions nationally. Bob Sutcliffe and his family ably acted as Guy's secretaries and coordinators. In Queensland Dr Weston Allen formed the Brisbane Justice Committee. He was very influential in the Brisbane support area, and a number of outlying Queensland groups, on hearing he had started a support group, joined with his, forming one large consolidated committee.

In March 1984 a delegation including the Lowes, the Wests, Barry Boettcher and Les Harris had met with the senior staff of several prominent Parliamentarians, Federal Attorney-General Gareth Evans, Senator Peter Durack (the shadow Attorney-General) and Ian Sinclair (deputy leader of the Opposition) to ask for a judicial review of my case. But Senator Evans said that the authority to hold such a review rested solely with the Northern Territory government, and later added in Parliament that there was nothing to suggest 'that the criminal process has been other than followed in a normal and entirely satisfactory manner through all the successive stages of appeal'.

They collected no fewer than 131,000 signatures, Australia wide, from people demanding a judicial review of our case. This was presented to the Governor-General, Sir Ninian Stephen, in May 1984. Twelve days later in a letter to the Adelaide *Advertiser*, Betty Hocking wrote that 7,000 of those signatures 'came from countries as far afield as Britain, Germany, the USA, Malaysia, Mauritius, New Zealand and Hong Kong'. She added, 'Although the petitions were presented on May 3, another 1,000 signatures were on hand by May 4 and they are still coming in.' Eventually it totalled 150,000 signatures.

When the petitions were presented to the Governor General, Federal Parliamentarians could hardly still deny that thousands of dedicated persons had organised to express their dissatisfaction with the course of Australian justice.

Senator Colin Mason, the deputy leader of the Australian Democrats, announced in June that he intended to introduce a private member's bill into the Senate to set up a Commission of Inquiry. He did this after consulting with Stuart. Stuart, a number of our supporters, and some scientists went to Canberra. The bill called upon the Federal Parliament to appoint 'a Commission of Inquiry, with all the relevant powers of a Royal Commission' into our case. In his second reading speech, Senator Mason reminded the senators that justice may be wrongly dispensed and expressed his concern at 'the way in which circumstantial evidence is increasingly being used to convict persons of major crimes'.

Labor Senator Gareth Evans released a press statement restating that the government's view 'remains that the matter is one to be resolved by the Northern Territory government'.

Senator Mason wanted to come and visit me and after a lot of fuss, I managed to gain permission for a visit from him. (The Northern Territory didn't like this at all: the day after Colin Mason's announcement, the *Northern Territory News* quoted the Northern Territory Attorney-General, Jim Robertson, as saying that his proposal was extremely dangerous, and urged all senators to reject it.)

While in jail I was constantly kept abreast of what was happening outside in all facets on government, public, community, Michael, family, and support groups' activities. In fact, I often think I was better informed while I was in there than I am now. I knew a number of politicians had decided to join our cause and both Senator Colin Mason and Senator Harry Edwards requested a visit. At first I was a bit scared at the thought of meeting politicians.

When Colin Mason and his wife arrived, it was the first time I had ever met a politician and I wasn't sure what I should say. I'd always thought of politicians as people you never meet at close quarters. I eventually decided he was probably an ordinary bloke doing a very public job.

We are all nervous of meeting others because in our minds we give people a presence, an authority, that they don't actually have. I knew people were occasionally intimidated by meeting me too. I remembered advice on how to avert nervousness when meeting someone important: think of that person in his or her underwear and the pomp and dignity surrounding them will rapidly disappear; so I did. I found Senator Mason an extremely pleasant man, friendly, sympathetic and down to earth. The same applied to his wife. I was able to meet both senators naturally. Senator Edwards and I discovered a Christian bond that I found heartwarming and we prayed together before he left. That was the last time I felt really nervous when meeting new people. It made me realise we all have our secret fears about being accepted. If we treat people in a normal friendly manner, they will respond; there is no barrier except that of our making. I have since met people with much bigger reputations, such as Meryl Streep. One quickly learns that anybody can be just like the friend next door, if only we are prepared to treat them that way.

Eventually Hypo's sentence finished, things calmed down quite a bit, and mealtimes got back to normal. The girls stopped grumbling and made the best of what they had. Without Hypo's leadership, they began to get to know me and soon treated me normally. Before long Shelion was the only one of the vegetarian girls left from the group, and had no one else to communicate with except the Aboriginal girls, Helena, Del and myself.

Now all the others had left, Shelion came in and said, 'Look, I am not really into TV. I'd like one news program a week, but other than that, you have what you like.' And that was that—all the arguing ended. There were few problems to disturb the peace now. I was glad as the whole section had been extremely tense.

Del soon told Shelion there was nothing wrong with me. She kept to herself for quite some time, watching us all, then she got stuck with a leather-work project and asked one of the intelligent officers for help. She was promptly told to ask me about it.

I had been watching her for a couple of weeks and knew what her problem was. We were working in the same room one evening and I watched her continue to struggle to fix it by herself. After watching her give up hopelessly swearing, I finally said to her, 'Do you want me to tell you what's wrong with it?' She told me in no uncertain terms what she thought of me and that she did *not* want to know. She tried twice more, getting more and more furious, then said, 'If you sit there quietly any more, I'm going to *throw* it at you. For goodness sake, say what you've got on your mind.'

I said, 'Well, turn it around the other way. If you don't do it upside down, it will work.' Her mouth dropped open, and she looked at me, looked at it, started to swear, looked at it again and turned it round. Then she laughed so hard she nearly cried.

She fixed the problem very quickly and when she had finished, she told me, 'If you dare say *one* word, I will throw it at you still! Fancy sitting there all that time and not telling me it was upside down!'

I said, 'I thought you would eventually realise what was wrong, and besides you told me I wasn't to say anything!' She stalked off to her room furious, cranky and embarrassed because I hadn't let her have the rough edge of my tongue, as most of her striker friends, or indeed she herself, would probably have done in the same circumstances.

She ate her meal in silence that night and went back to her room. At lunchtime she came up to me and said, 'Right, that's it. I give in. I apologise. I was rude and I'm sorry. I really deserved that, and I don't know how you've held your temper. I can't believe it, but thank you. And now I don't know how to do the next piece, so will you please tell me before I get frustrated again?'

I responded, 'Sure.' Once she had swallowed her pride and was ready to accept help, I showed her in about five minutes the rest of what she had been struggling with for weeks. New respect dawned in her face. When she had a problem, she would come up to me and say, 'All right, Miss Smarty Pants Know-It-All, how do I do this?' And I would tell her.

Finally Shelion asked, 'How come you can do all these things?' I told her I had studied tailoring and had always done hand-crafts. I found reading instructions easy, so if she wanted to know anything, I didn't mind helping her. She was extremely puzzled, and for weeks I would catch her looking at me with a frown on her face, but she soon came round and joined in with the rest of the girls. The other younger girls were pleased. After that we became quite good friends.

We soon discovered that we all had a lot in common, and we used to have some hilarious times together for the rest of her stay.

One or two of the officers could cut hair, but weren't allowed to cut ours, so we had to wait until a prisoner appeared who said she was reasonably proficient with the scissors. One church group offered a fully qualified hairdresser to come in on a regular basis free for the whole prison but the offer was rejected. The girls soon discovered that I could cut hair, and when the girl who formerly did it left, I took over. Then another girl came in who could cut hair, and that was a relief. Although I didn't mind doing it, it meant I had less free time for craft, so I was quite happy for someone else to do it. She was good but only had a short stay, then Shelion took over and she too, for a non-professional, was good with the scissors. By now I had a fairly reasonable ponytail; it might not have been the most glamorous thing, but there wasn't much choice. I didn't want my hair hacked—the thought of a sudden release and looking like a scarecrow put me off that. At least I could tie my hair up out of my face instead of it hanging around with no hair spray or proper hair care, but it still had to be washed every day because of working in the garden, and as it is thick it took ages to dry.

When I had watched Shelion do a few good haircuts, I got her to cut mine, and got it cut very short, about an inch long at the top and tapered down at the back and the sides and around my ears almost like a boy. The first time Michael saw me with that style he nearly fell over. So did the screws when they came on the next day, but it was easy to care for and I enjoyed finally being able to have regular haircuts.

One day when I was having a haircut, the Imp walked past and stood watching for a while. When the other girl was called away for a few moments, she leaned over and asked would I please save my hair clippings for her. When I asked in surprise, 'What for?' she replied, 'I take them home for my little birds to make their nests out of.'

As she was extremely superstitious (she would make us all walk one side of a pole to avoid splitting friendships), I supposed it was just another of her idiosyncrasies and agreed, saying, 'Well, I'll save all the clippings for you, if you like.'

'No. I only save the really nice girls' hair,' she replied.

'Oh,' I laughed, 'all right.'

She took hair on a number of other occasions as well. Sometime later she giggled a little bit and said, 'Guess what? I was making my son's bed the other day [he was over twenty-one and in a certain state cricket team] and I found a lock of your hair under his pillow. He must have nicked some from the birds. I didn't know he had it.'

I said, 'If I'd known he wanted some, I'd have autographed it for him.' I bet he never knew his mum told me.

The Imp was one of the officers who was into tapestry, as were a number of the girls. Occasionally when we ran out of wool and needed a little bit extra she, Sunshine or Speedy would have leftovers that they gave us so we did not have to wait a month until our next buy.

The Imp was such a tiny little thing she made *me* feel huge, even though I was only 44 kilograms (98 pounds). She was near retiring age and the other screws, for some time, had been trying to get her to retire. As she loved the job, she was resisting. Finally, after her long service leave, she announced her retirement. The girls were upset to see her go as she was an extremely good officer and treated us all fairly. When she actually left, Lena picked her up and whirled her around in her arms and then put her down again. The Imp was horrified.

'Maybe they were right. You know, I didn't realise you girls could do that so easily,' she gasped.

That was one thing that had caused concern with the other officers, but they needn't have worried because any *good* officer who was attacked by a rampaging prisoner would have been protected immediately by the other prisoners. This was *not* something that was done for screws in general.

Alternatives to an Inadequate Diet

Depending on the cultural or socioeconomic background of the inmates, they either thought the food was wonderful or disgusting. Some, who arrived half starved found the food too rich, while the average white prisoner found it low in nutrition. After an extended time in prison, the long-term white girls became run down due to the inadequate diet. As we were not given gloves to wear when cleaning, we developed infections from slight cuts, which quickly became septic (dirty swabs containing mucus, pus and blood were left around on the floor for us to pick up with our bare hands). On one occasion I was put off cleaning for a week because of a small surface cut I received when cleaning the medical centre; my whole finger became swollen and poisoned within hours.

When an AIDS sufferer came to prison, head office finally issued an order that we were not to clean without gloves and could refuse to do so without being charged if they were not supplied. The risk of infection to cuts was minimised, and our health safeguarded.

Shelion got ill as time wore on and blood tests revealed she was extremely low in vitamin B12, so she was put on injections.

I had been feeling weird for ages. I had heaps of sleep, but still felt tired and light headed. Working in the daytime I often felt faint, unusual for me except when I had low blood pressure during pregnancy. When I lay down to rest though, I found I was wide awake and all desire to sleep had left me. Finally I saw the doctor. He decided I had lethargy anaemia, and might be low in B12 like Shelion, so ordered blood tests for me too. Sure enough I was way down in iron (I dropped four points on the scale in four months on their diet and needed to be on iron tablets); now I, too, was very deficient in B12. After a course of injections I began to improve, at least I didn't feel like fainting any more, and could enjoy physical activities again. But I still had to continue the injections for almost four years before my levels began to stabilise once more. (Although a lacto-ovo-vegetarian, I had never been low in iron or vitamins prior to my prison sentence. In fact, a lot of my levels were higher than normal.)

We kept daily lists of both the meat and vegetarian diets, with assessments on the cleanliness and cooking so they could see what we got when they were absent. I smuggled copies out to a nutritionist working on a submission on prisons who was aghast at the food we were served in Darwin.

At times I got six eggs a day in my diet and thought I would cackle if I had any more. When I saw the doctor about it (he was responsible for ordering special diets), he agreed it was unbalanced (too high in protein) and substituted some eggs with cheese! The authorities had rejected an offer from local Adventist ladies to supply meat substitute dishes (or tinned substitutes if this was unacceptable) for all the vegetarians free of cost.

Things improved once again for a while on the general food scene, but I still had personal diet problems. Because I was allergic to powdered milk, I couldn't have any milk for three years, except when it was smuggled in for me twice. While the prison supplied tea, I and others who preferred it could buy Milo or coffee to drink instead. I quite enjoyed it, but Milo without milk is rather an odd drink. I discovered the best way to drink it was half a teaspoon in a cup of hot water and I could nearly get used to it. More than that and it tasted more like dirt in water than chocolate. In the long run, I settled for cordial in hot water in winter. I wouldn't recommend it as a regular hot drink, but it is amazing what you can get used to when you have to. I even got used to having no salt in the food.

It had been many months since our china painting classes had been discontinued. Our leather-work classes had also recently been discontinued as that teacher had transferred also.

Although the Aboriginal girls enjoyed hand-crafts they did not have friends on the outside who could send them money so they could participate, as we had to pay for our own materials. Head office, realising this, arranged for Saturday afternoon pool games to be played socially with some girls from town. It was primarily for the Aboriginal girls but everyone could watch. As the girls arrived, there was great interest.

As time passed, we realised one of the girls had managed to get one of the pool players to act as a courier for messages and for smuggling various small items. If it was a private visit and anyone was caught, she was the only one to suffer, so the other girls didn't care. The girls *were* upset this time because, if it was discovered the whole pool afternoon would be cancelled. After a conference, with the offender carefully excluded, it was decided to voluntarily discontinue the games on a pretext rather than have the whole situation blow up. Even Sister Mary Louise and her ladies could be banned if this type of visit was exploited.

Often if something special had been smuggled in for the girls and they wanted to keep and use it over a period of time, there were only a couple of places where it could be kept. One was in the officers' own storeroom to which only they had the key, and access to it was very difficult. One of the girls regularly hid things in the greenhouse while she was overseer of that area, and she used to almost go berserk when somebody else was occasionally allowed in there. She ran the risk of a new girl or someone who didn't like her digging it up and saying, 'Look what I've found!' The same applied to a lot of other areas, so you had to know the right spots.

Swapping drugs on inter-prison weekly visits was easy. The guys simply hid a trip in their mouths, and transferred it during a kiss to their wife, lady or girlfriend, who then swallowed it. The evidence was gone. At least it gave the girls one weekly shot of their favourite drug. Sometimes this was done on an external visit also, but it was more risky then.

Drugs could also be brought across in the supplies for work repair parties, by hiding them in the tools earlier. Access to storerooms was easy if you knew how; when the tools were picked up in an officer's presence, they weren't searched—after all, they had just come out of the storeroom, and the guy collecting them had already been searched when he left the blocks.

All that had to be done then was to drop the goods on the way in or out in a prearranged spot in the garden, where the girls collected them. Sometimes they could even be handed over directly if the opportunity arose. Or it could be done without the maintenance guy even knowing he was a courier as others could plant it, and the girls had plenty of opportunity to remove it from the tool box themselves if necessary.

Several of the girls hid things in the fan connection that actually attached to the roof. No screw wished to put a hand in and grab a live wire, so it was never searched. I wonder if they are aware that there is a little space in there. Provided you weren't scared of grabbing live wires, you could have quite a little stash put away safely.

Once one of my visitors brought me something and left it behind in full view of the watching screws. It was a large can of art fixative (about 15 to 20 centimetres [6 to 8 inches] tall) which I later put with the rest of my art gear and used. No one even noticed its addition.

Froggie lost one of her earrings, so her sister bought her a diamond stud and passed it over the table on a visit. Only the girls noticed. Weeks later a screw commented, so Froggie told her it was a cubic zircon she'd had in her property, and they happily accepted that. I decided you could smuggle in an elephant if you wanted to, and they wouldn't notice.

Lulu Chucks a Doughnut

When I first went into prison I couldn't make out why the girls spent so many hours looking at old magazines pointing out the advertisements for food and reading recipes. When I asked about it later they told me they imagined what those foods tasted like, so they wouldn't forget. When they were doing long stretches, this was a very valid point of view.

One of the new male prisoners was a fully qualified sweets chef, so they put him in the kitchen. He was good, but prison authorities don't like to see you doing what you can do well if they can possibly help it, so they put him on vegetable preparation, and the guy on sweets couldn't cook for nuts. When the permanent kitchen overseer went on holidays or had days off, we always got better meals, and on these occasions they would let the sweets chef cook dessert so we got something really nice; a special type of cake or a pie. Occasionally we even got doughnuts. One of the screws was very partial to them, and because he was friendly with the officers in the kitchen, he would request this particular prisoner be allowed to make them, so we *all* got two each.

The Aboriginal girls were very fussy about what desserts they ate. Where normally they would eat anything sweet, they wouldn't even try a dessert they hadn't seen before, and would give it to one of the other girls.

Most of the good officers ignored this trading, preferring to see food used rather than wasted, and we made sure the nasties didn't catch us. Some days a roaring trade was done, almost like an auction and the girls had a lot of fun as well. One day doughnuts arrived for dessert for the first time. The rest of the meal had been terrible and the white girls were rapt that there was a good dessert at least. (The Aborigines had a much higher tolerance for stew than the white girls.)

A number of the Aboriginal girls had already given their doughnuts away and most of the white girls had had a fair feed of them. One of the new Aboriginal girls didn't like her doughnuts either so tipped them in the rubbish, as she was fully entitled to do. A number of the white girls got upset and one of them said to her, 'Why didn't you offer it to somebody else if you didn't want it yourself? You could have offered it around. We don't get them very often. It's all right for you, you have only been in for a few days, and are going home soon. Some of these girls don't get stuff like this for years at a time.' Well, the Aboriginal girl looked daggers, and went out. That should have been the end of the matter.

Then Froggie kept on nagging, saying how disgusting it was these black girls threw out their food and how they should have more consideration for others. Another Aboriginal girl, Lulu, sat and listened to this, getting crosser and crosser. One thing Aboriginal girls do *not* like is being called 'black girls'. They are Aborigines.

Froggie kept on and on about the doughnuts. Lulu had stopped eating quite some time before and was staring at her plate. Her face was getting more and more stormy. Finally she got up very deliberately and tipped her uneaten doughnuts into the rubbish, poking them under the other slops, where they couldn't be rescued.

Froggie, who had got up to take her plates to the sink saw what Lulu was doing and gave her a mouthful of abuse. Lulu said, 'Don't you tell me what to do, you.' Froggie turned her back and continued getting her coffee ready, all the time mumbling about girls who had been told what to do and deliberately went and did the opposite.

Froggie seemed to be feeling quite pleased with the way she was getting at Lulu. If she hadn't turned her back, she would have realised that Lulu had something in mind; she was standing by the door, with arms held rigidly by her sides, fists clenched, staring at Froggie. I could see Froggie was in for big trouble. Smiley, knowing Lulu well, caught my eye and rolled her eyes in Lulu's direction. I just shook my head slightly; nothing could be done, and we had to wait for something to happen. Smiley hopped up to take her dishes to the sink and surreptitiously looked to see where the screws on duty were. They weren't far away, and we figured if anything blew up too much, we could grab Lulu in a hurry. Froggie continued to mumble and complain.

Lulu waited just long enough for Froggie to fill her coffee cup with boiling water at the urn, walk back to the table and sit down. Then she went for Smiley's empty chair opposite me. Smiley was still around the other side of the bench at the sink. Del had her back to Lulu, totally unaware. To say anything would have put the rest of us in danger because she would have gone for all of us then. As she picked up the chair I started to move. The chair came flying across the table around Del just as Froggie started to look up. I managed to catch it by the legs, stopping most of its force by my arm but the top flicked around, hitting Froggie's cup, and dumped scalding coffee into her lap. Del jumped up in a hurry, spluttering, wondering what the hell had happened.

Lulu was glaring at me now, as well as Froggie, who was now swearing at her. Everybody thought Froggie was lucky she'd only got boiling coffee on her clothes, the way she had been carrying on. The screws heard the commotion and came across. Lulu was obviously about to explode again. The chair was in the middle of the table, with me trying to take it off without spilling anything else. The screws sized up the situation, looked at me with the chair, and Lulu's face. They told her, 'Get out of here, down to your room immediately!' When Lulu started to protest, they marched her out in a hurry and everybody else was told to stay put.

When the screws came back they said, 'Right girls, what's going on?' We all explained what had happened. They nodded, then said, 'Right, settle down and get yourselves out of the kitchen as quick as you can. Your mealtime is over now, anyway.'

As I went jogging that night, Lulu stood in her doorway staring at me. I realised I would be unwise to keep my back to her because she was still in an angry, sullen mood and I had foiled her plan of revenge. Some of the Aboriginal girls had a really short fuse and Lulu had a history of flying off the handle. I made sure I ran where I was facing her most of the time; her cell on the corner gave me a chance to keep an eye on what she was doing, giving minimum time with my back turned.

One of the screws came out on her rounds and realised she was standing at the door just staring. She said, 'Lulu, go in your cell. You go in your cell this instant when you are told, or I am locking you up.'

Lulu went into her cell and slammed the door; a difficult thing to do because cell doors open outwards (not inwards) and when the doors were unlocked in the mornings the bolts were deliberately locked, protruding outwards to stop the door from fully closing. This meant if you were in a bad mood and decided to shut yourself in, you couldn't put your weight against it to stop the screws getting in; but had to pull, giving them the advantage. Because Lulu was Aboriginal (it was sometimes very difficult to know how to discipline them) she was not locked in, but told she could not come back to the day room to watch TV that night.

By the next day, the problem was over. Lulu was just told off by the section chief, and that was all. A white girl who had done the same thing would have been put on report and immediately locked up, with a fair chance of spending time in solitary later, but then missing TV was not a big deal to them, as it was to most of the dark girls who were generally much more childlike in their responses.

For several days, I had a lump the size of an egg on my lower arm where I had stopped the leg of the chair. I was glad it was no worse; if I hadn't been aware of what was going on, I would have copped the chair as well as Froggie, instead of being able to catch it.

Eventually, one of the girls who was mentally retarded, started causing real problems at mealtimes, complaining that she got less to eat than the rest of us (all meals were identical) and generally being disruptive. Two of the nasty screws got their heads together and decided this was a good excuse to have our mealtimes monitored, so we were subjected to having a screw sit by the table to oversee every meal. This effectively dampened conversation; mealtimes *had* been one of the few times we could relax and chat together without the screws listening and hanging on every word of the conversation.

The nasty screws would sit and stare at us. It was like trying to eat a meal with someone you'd just had an almighty row with who wasn't speaking to you—you could feel the hostile vibes. The nicest screws used to simply bring a crossword puzzle or magazine, and sit just outside the door where they could hear any unusual activities, but otherwise appear to totally ignore us and let us relax. We found that much better, both for the community spirit and the digestion.

To Weed a Snake, Cut a Sham, and Train a Rookie

Being hassled perpetually, you couldn't get into a routine. Invariably we went through cell-searches to see what 'mischief' new girls were up to. Meal routines were altered and new rules added. Not only was it the new girls that caused this, particularly those on drugs and doing from three- to nine-month sentences, but new officers caused similar problems—every so often, we would get a batch of new recruits or 'rookies' who needed to learn how things were 'done' in prison.

The rookies were a humbug. They were always so eager and anxious to get good marks that they often tended to be officious. They usually went exactly by the book, and beyond. We would have to fight for our rights all over again, so the girls had various ways of working out what officers they liked, and what officers they would like to get rid of, and worked to that end.

If we could work it right, an unwanted screw could be got rid of during training. They would come in on 'zoo' tours first to see the prison and the way it worked. At that time some suddenly lost their great desire to assist mankind and humanity, working for the poor unfortunates in the prison, despite the good pay.

When the rookies finally arrived at the end of their theory period for their practical sessions (or rookie weeks), there were 'set-ups' —deliberate misbehaviour, mock disobedience and fights—sometimes even including the officers. It would give the rookies a taste of what it was like when someone really did play up. Usually we found it scared the hell out of them. One very quick set-up reduced the school by two females after their introductory 'zoo' tour before they even got to 'rookie' week, but this was unusual.

The new batch of rookies contained some awful ones. As some would go to Alice Springs and we would end up with the rest, the thought of thinning the ranks a little was appealing. We had a fortnight's grace before being permanently stuck with a bad one.

Helena decided she did not like one of the new rookies in particular, who was already showing bad signs on her first day. Even most of the officers weren't really rapt. One of them complained she had been reported for swearing *at* one of the girls. This rookie decided it didn't suit her idea of what should happen in a prison. Instead of going to the female officer and asking whether or not this was permitted, she took it to the training officer, and the complaint went full circle back to the officer concerned. It turned out to be a jovial conversation between the officer and prisoner. Swearing *to* and not *at* each other made all the difference. The report was highly resented. We did *not* need somebody else like the Chameleon, officious and always on your back.

We were told often enough by the nice screws that their rules said only that they must see we did our work and were not to stand over and harass us. They were simply there as a form of 'babysitter', to see that those 'naughty children' in jail did what they were told, and as long as we did it, they weren't to interfere in how we did it. (Pity all of them didn't remember that one.)

Helena hoped scare tactics might work on some of the rookies and decided to set up a tantrum with me and the sewing machine. Duckie was the only regular officer on, and as she knew I could handle Lena's tantrums, she wouldn't rush to put her on lockup.

So, in the quiet workroom, Lena started to yell at me and swear at the machine. Then she belted her machine and banged her fist on the table. The rookies, blissfully enjoying their smoke, dropped everything and ran in, but they didn't know what to do. Lena was ranting and raving and the rest of us were either simply looking at her or ignoring her. She threw a book at me, which I didn't even bother to dodge; I merely picked it up slowly and said, 'What did you do that for? You've broken the back of your book.' I then put it down again as if nothing had happened and continued sewing.

The rookies were huddled around the door, peering in, whispering to each other, trying to decide what to do with her. Realising something was going on, Duckie came across and said, 'What's going on here? Oh, it's you, Helena.' Then returned to the office. The expressions on the rookies' faces were comical; they backed out the door and slunk away. From where I was sitting I could see them discussing the incident in the staff room.

Duckie could hear a lot of what they said from her office and when they had gone, she came over to us and said they were all wondering what Lena was like, and discussing her when Grannie came on shift. She told them Lena had a terrible temper and spent more time on lockup than any of the other girls, so they were totally scared of her now. And off she walked with a grin. Lena, for the next two days, continued to throw many tantrums with good effect. It kept the rookies on their toes and obviously nervous, but we only lost one, and not the one we wanted to. (Lena's outbursts, however, weren't always so premeditated. In a real fit of temper one day over a recalcitrant zip she had punched her machine so hard it rolled completely over and off the other side of the table—she was so astounded at the force of her fist and the results that she said, 'Oh shit!' and burst out laughing. The outburst was over and the machine, miraculously, still operated afterwards!) When a lot of rookie officers were on, jobs that were only done occasionally could be tackled because there were enough officers to take all the girls outside the perimeter fence (where it was easy just to walk on to the road and off, with only a few strands of no. 8 fencing wire between us and freedom).

A favourite activity was cutting the grass where it was too close to mow against the concrete edgings of the outside boundary fence. This was done in one of two ways; by hand with a pair of scissors, or by banging the spade head against the concrete and cutting it off, jarring your bones and ruining the spade in the process. (We could have done it differently but weren't allowed.) Scissors, of course, were more favoured (they gave us the most blisters and took the longest). As some of the grass roots we were expected to cut were as thick as my little finger and much harder, it was a thankless occupation. Once we had cut the grass, we were supposed to weed along that area also. During the wet season, the concrete footing that the cyclone fence was embedded in acted as an embankment to stop the water flowing freely. This meant pools of water up to 20 centimetres (8 inches) deep continually lay around this area. Before this I had not realised it was possible to mow grass under water!

On one of these futile and frustrating weeding trips, we were being stood over by almost as many rookie screws as there were girls. While weeding in a very incompetent manner as instructed by a young rookie (*our* methods were not good enough for *her*, although tried and true), I 'weeded' a small snake approximately 30 centimetres (12 inches) in length. I dropped that 'weed' with great speed and it landed somewhere in the water we were paddling in.

Smiley, not believing her eyes, said, 'What that? That snake?'

'Yes,' I said, 'and I don't know where it's gone.'

'Aargh!' said Smiley, and immediately climbed on the concrete edging. I had great difficulty in persuading myself not to do likewise. Smiley was then asked, 'What's the matter?' by the screws. 'Lindy picked up snake! True!' she explained, then all the Aboriginal girls followed her example! I didn't think they'd be scared of snakes, as they kill and eat them. They were all told not to be stupid and go back to work. I pointed out I had thrown the snake somewhere in the direction that screw was now standing. She moved elsewhere like greased lightning. The girls then said *they* had no intention of going back to work as *she* wouldn't even stay there either! After a screw conference, our work that day was relocated and that area was avoided until the water went down and we could see what creepy crawlies were beneath our feet.

During rookie week, the mind games between the officers and girls were often heightened. On one occasion, Froggie decided it was a good chance to train the new officers into giving us matching sheets. Most of the officers did, but we had some who didn't care, and one or two who deliberately gave us mixed sheets. They maintained that this was to stop fights over the floral sheets! The girls actually found it more frustrating to get one of each than they did to get a pair of plain white ones.

Froggie who was rostered on washing, deliberately mixed the sheets up. On sheet night Blackie, the rookie, distributed the sheets, just as they came. She reached Froggie's room last, leaving a mixed set. Froggie let her walk out, then called her and said, 'Oh, excuse me, but you've given me the wrong sheets. We have to have the sheets matching, otherwise you will get into trouble.'

The rookie then went into a flap promising to fix them all. Froggie came in with a grin from ear to ear and told us what she'd done. 'For goodness sake back me up,' she added. We watched with some amusement as the rookie tried to pair all the sheets and pillowcases in sets without the senior noticing—and there *weren't* enough to match.

Finally Blackie returned explaining worriedly that some didn't match. We all managed to keep our faces straight, assuring her some were in the mending.

'You did very well,' we assured her.

Blackie heaved a sigh of relief. When she came to say good-night, the senior screw was grinning from ear to ear—she knew what had gone on. She always gave us matching sheets if available herself, so she didn't enlighten the rookie either. Sunshine, when she found out, still fairly new herself, but a good officer and well accepted already, proclaimed us little wretches and told us, 'The poor thing is in a real panic.'

That rookie turned out to be a good one (even if a little vague), and was permanently assigned to Darwin. Every time she was on sheets, we got matching ones.

One night when she was running around again matching up the sheets, the Chameleon noticed.

'What are you doing that for? Just hand them out. Doesn't matter what order they're in,' she snapped. Blackie's mouth was observed to drop open, then close.

Blackie finished putting the sheets and pillowcases out, still trying to match them without the Chameleon noticing, then she came in to Froggie and me, looked at us with the biggest grin on her face and said quietly, 'You girls have been hoodwinking me for months.' Much to our delight, she wasn't cross. She just gave a big grin and we smiled back and said, 'Really?' She grinned as she walked off. Later she said, 'I can understand why you did it, though. I hate sheets that don't match too.'

We all knew by the look on the Chameleon's face when she rang the gate bell on sheet night whether or not she would give us mixed sheets. We often surreptitiously swapped, taking the risk of being charged for doing so. Our rooms were small and bare, so if we had a chance of making them better, even by obtaining matching patched quilts, this became very important to us.

How to Catch a Dangerous Mouse

One night I noticed the number of screws turning up for the midnight shift seemed to have doubled or trebled and I realised there must have been a jail break. I watched awhile, and early in the morning, after fitful sleep, I saw the screws and police out with dogs and some of the Aboriginal guys, obviously tracking.

It was no big deal; all we wanted to know was who had skipped. It happened occasionally; it was a part of life. Someone ran; usually they were caught. If they weren't caught after a week or two we would all cheer, unless of course we thought the escapee was dangerous. That was very rare, although the police would always advertise the escaped prisoner as 'dangerous' or 'armed and dangerous'. Often we knew the 'dangerous' ones wouldn't hurt a fly. In fact, if a fly said 'Boo!', they would run away. Most of them wouldn't think of hurting anyone unless frightened out of their wits and then, only if cornered and desperate, they might lash out. It you treated them normally they would not touch you.

On this occasion, just before breakfast, we were abruptly told to shut all the windows down the road side. The girls on the far side had apparently slept through it all and wanted to know why.

'Orders from the chief,' the screws said.

We asked about the escapee and they snapped, 'Who told you that?' We pointed out that it was obvious, with all the activity we had seen.

'Who was it?' we asked. 'Did one of the kids get out of remand again?' The screw walked out.

Later that morning, we heard Smiley's relatives had been the trackers so we knew we'd get details soon. The new shift came on and some of them had been involved. The escapee had actually climbed the fence, cutting himself so badly on the razor wire on the way over that he felt sick. He was so frightened in the dark he'd only gone just beyond the prison boundaries, across the road into the abattoirs and had huddled down in the grass, too frightened to move. He had watched them looking for him most of the night, but was afraid they would shoot if he moved. As soon as the trackers came they went straight to him, following the trail of blood easily. They said, 'Come on, mate, let's go,' and that was about it. On the radio news bulletin it was stated that the special squad had been called out and they had found this man with the aid of police trackers (not prisoners!). A 'dangerous' escapee was caught and the public could relax. Phew!

Another time, one of the guys escaped by mistake. He was at the hospital under escort, went to the toilet and, not realising there were two doors, walked out the wrong one. He couldn't find his escort and thought he had been forgotten and left there. He wandered hospital corridors for some time, looking for them, without knowing about the furore he was causing as a so-called runaway. He then walked all the way back to the prison, about 9 kilometres (approximately 5.5 miles), arriving considerably later. He knocked on the main gate of the prison and asked to be let in. They asked him to identify himself! It was considered quite a joke for a prisoner to knock on the door and ask to be let back in, but he had nowhere else to go. Though it was later joked about among the screws he, too, had been listed as a 'dangerous' escapee.

It wasn't always that way, though. Once some of the boys down at the low security prison farm had got some smuggled grass and were high as kites. They had apparently made an illegal brew and were rolling drunk and fighting. Normally the guys on the farm didn't see a screw from one week to the next, as long as they worked and reported in when required. On this particular night things became so rowdy the screws had to go down. It was decided they should be taken back to town, over an hour by vehicle, the road untarred and corrugated, giving a bone-shaking ride.

The guys were furious at not having been given a chance at least, and *all* of them, heavily involved or not, were told they were coming back. If the screws had waited until morning the prisoners would have accepted it and copped it sweet, but here they were still drunk, and they were losing everything. The actions of the screws only exacerbated the problem. The meals that they had out there would be exchanged for our lousy food, their more decent clothes for our thin and worn ones, their virtual freedom for total restraint in the maximum security section (until reclassified out to the other blocks again). All the men sent out to the farm were low-security prisoners, most with little time left to do. Now everything was gone at once, with perhaps a sentence extension to add to it all too. They had nothing more to lose.

Two Aboriginal boys were asked back immediately. On the way back, the jolting was such that they were apparently able to use their hands (they were either very strong, desperate, or both!) to pull out the window of the paddy wagon. Once they got that out, they then had to pull out the back window of the ute cab (don't ask me how the screws didn't notice the wind difference in the vehicle, at least). The heads and upper bodies of both prisoners simultaneously came through the window and grabbed the screws around the neck in throttle holds. The truck came to a standstill, as the officers tried to fight off the prisoners. The driver jumped out and ran into the bush, leaving the keys; the passenger fought a little more to gain control, but was whacked by an iron bar on his right hand, mangling the last two fingers badly. Then he too cut and ran into the scrub. The boys took off in the paddy wagon. Some weeks later they were found in Katherine.

The injured screw had nerve and tendon damage, and it was feared he might not use that hand again. With physiotherapy it improved, but it will never be completely right again, I gather.

When we heard about it the next day, everybody cheered. He happened to live next door to a friend of mine, who commented one day how sad it was that such a nice young chap had been injured. I thought she was joking and told her of his behaviour at work.

My friend could hardly believe that the nice young man she knew treated the prisoners differently. I later realised screws were often two faced. It helped me understand why some people in Hitler's regime were seen as kind to their families, yet authorised the terrible atrocities we now know occurred.

Neither of the boys in that escape attempt had a record of violence. If they had been left to settle down overnight without being hassled, they would have taken their punishment decently. There is no accounting for the way some officers act.

After three months off because of his hand, the screw returned to work on lighter duties. For some time he was the officer in the medical centre, and we saw him when cleaning in the morning. It was not unusual to hear him answering the phone with, 'Medical. You stab 'em, we slab 'em. What can I do to help you today?' The attitude was typical of him. Prisoners were not regarded as people; he would walk past us or bump into us and keep going as if we didn't exist, and was not the least bit helpful. He'd deliberately stand in the dirt pile we were sweeping or drop mess on the floor. Other officers would jump up voluntarily, even when we *didn't* want to sweep underneath them. Some would be very polite, even when they were extremely busy or even offer us a seat if we had to stand for long periods waiting somewhere.

All Stitched Up

Shelion used to make it her business to try and brighten up the section. One day she'd been assigned to clean out the garden storeroom (which had laundry supplies, sport and art equipment and old uniforms as well as the tools). She came across Lily's bras. When she saw the size of those cups, it was just too much. After a bit, she emerged. She'd put on a gardening uniform, belted it with twine, and hoisted it up to make a mini-skirt, and had put 'those' bras on over the top and stuffed them with volleyballs (yes, volleyballs)! She had arranged a piece of old, bright-coloured rag around her leg, in a very creditable garter, and she'd cut a piece of cardboard box into the shape of a tennis racquet and drawn the strings and a striped handle with a felt tip pen. A white rag headband completed her outfit. Out she minced in her tennis outfit, asking, 'Anyone for a game of tennis, girls?' The girls went into hysterics, then she cracked up too. There was so much noise, the screws came round the corner to see what was going on. Even one of the nasty screws, trying to tell her off, ended up with a grin on her face and simply gave up. We redid the episode for Sunshine that evening. The guy in the tower saw too, and it created a topic of conversation and hilarity for days, lightening the gloom of the section considerably, as Shelion had intended.

Although Shelion was fairly clear thinking and able to analyse her own feelings and actions, she continually claimed to be muddleheaded. Because she was not afraid of authority in prison and knew herself very well, she was not cowed, as a lot of the other prisoners were. When Mercer came across to tell her off (as he often did, because she pushed them to the limit nicely and like me, kept putting in unorthodox requests), she was not in the least perturbed, and would give as good as she got. No matter what they did to her, it didn't faze her. She was normally cheerful and easy to get along with, so if she flew off the handle they knew there was usually a specific reason for it. As they knew exactly what she was capable of from her long record, they kept a respectful distance then.

I understand Shelion was the first woman ever to make the Queensland top ten wanted list, and since then some of her friends have also been on it. To know her in the ordinary course of daily life in prison, she was just another fun 'girl next door'. We knew she was capable of setting the police on their ears, though, and carrying it through (as she'd proved by her escape). But if she gave her word and you had her confidence, you knew that she would stick by it.

Tapioca was decidedly a figure of fun for her, and she took the mickey out of him time and time again. If he came over to complain about something, she would laugh in his face. On one occasion he came across complaining about the whole female section, and she said, 'Hang on, hang on, I can't handle this. Just a minute, Mr Tapioca.' Not being used to this treatment (it was in the middle of an official lineup, screws and all), his mouth literally dropped open. The rest of us tried to keep straight faces.

She grabbed a nearby chair, sat down and, pretending to play an imaginary violin, humming to herself, she said, 'Right, now I've got my violin, you can keep going . . .

hummmm.' His grumpily delivered homily to us was ruined. He knew he had lost our attention (although he told her off, she continued to laugh) and while we tried to look as if we were listening, he knew we were taking absolutely no notice. Nor, incidentally, were the screws. We were all just managing to keep straight faces for his benefit. He threw up his hands in disgust, rolled his eyes and stomped off back to the other side.

Time and again she managed to do this to him. There was nothing he could do. He would tell her to go, and she'd say, 'Keep your shirt on, keep your shirt on. I'm going. Don't you like me saying hello? Where's my flowers? Didn't you bring me any flowers today? Oh, I'm disgusted. Oh well. I'll have to go if you haven't come to be nice to me.' She would totally ignore the fact that he was trying to put her on report, interrupt her or get a word in edgewise.

One day she said, 'How's your mother's ducks?'

Stunned he forgot himself and replied, 'What ducks?'

'Doesn't she have ducks? Well, chickens then? Goats?' Shelion asked as he gaped at her. Then she walked off laughing, while he was left still trying to recover. No amount of threat or punishment altered her, so she got away with it. Sometimes one of our officers would tell her she had been naughty and she'd say, laughing, 'I know.' You couldn't be cross with her.

When some of the chiefs or officers who weren't acquainted with Shelion saw her in action, they would look at her in absolute amazement, as she gave Tapioca a hard time. The guys had heard of her reputation but thought it was exaggerated until they actually saw her in action. They would inevitably draw their finger across their throats, eyes boggling and mutter to whoever was with her, 'How do you girls get away with it? We'd be for the high jump.' High jump or not, she'd still laugh and give it to him, so there was no point. People like that survive any system.

One day Shelion and I were on evening office cleaning together (usually we were on different rosters). We were halfway through mopping the stairs when Tapioca came up with an entourage. He never bothered to wipe his boots or wait for the floor to dry like the others, but plopped all over our clean wet floor. I had the mop and bucket, she had the broom and dustpan. We squeezed into the corners on the landing because there wasn't room for all of us at the same time—most of them were big blokes.

As Tapioca came by, Shelion gave him a cheerful greeting and received a grunt. Seeing Mr Dewsnip next, and not being the least bit afraid of him, she pulled a face at Tapioca's retreating back.

Although he was loyal, he obviously had no great love for rudeness and he apologised for walking on our floor as he went past. The others had no choice but to follow Tapioca. The twinkle in Mr Dewsnip's eyes as he caught that grimace caused me to stand to attention with the mop and salute, very seriously. He cleared his throat and nodded imperceptibly, indicating he'd seen, but not enough for those behind him to know. Shelion followed suit with the broom, and we stood there like two guards of honour until they had all gone past.

The visitors openly grinned (we knew most of them from head office) and we kept straight faces. We gave them a military at-ease after they left, and Dewsnip glanced back. The unholy glint in his eyes and the slight lift at the corners of his mouth were not lost on us. Dewsnip would stop bad behaviour immediately but appeared to believe harmless high jinks never hurt any one.

One of the screws was very short, so all his trousers had to be specially taken up. That was my job. When I was told the length of the trousers and looked at the size, I knew they could only belong to one man—an unpopular screw. I had almost finished them and was racing against the clock, hoping to return them that night. Shelion, also realising who they belonged to, asked, 'Can I help you with them?' The look on her face made me say, 'What are you going to do with them?' She replied, 'Never mind, just leave it to me.'

I said to Shelion, 'Whatever you do to them, I don't want it coming back on me because I am supposed to be the one who has done these pants.'

'That's all right,' she said, and yelled out, 'Lindy's running late, so can I help with the pants? I'm just going to do a bit of snipping on them for her.' They agreed. 'Snipping' was right. She got those trousers and cut every second or third stitch in the back seam, from top to crutch, on each of his three pairs of trousers. They would have held quite nicely while he put them on, but all of a sudden without warning, either in the first or the second day of wear, they would split wide open, and we all hoped he would be in a most embarrassing position when this occurred. We never heard another word, so presumably he had them mended himself, realising what we had done but not being game to say. A man like that would not admit that he'd had a nasty practical joke played on him.

Another screw, the Panther fell in the same category. She would never lift a finger to help any of the girls in any way, no matter how difficult their job was. When the food cart came across with a cooked meal, it was often so heavy that a lot of the lighter girls had great difficulty in pushing it up the ramp to the kitchen door. Usually the escorting officer would assist in pushing or pulling it up after the door had been unlocked.

One evening I was on kitchen duty with the Panther as escort. Instead of letting me wait at the bottom of the ramp as normal, she insisted I push the food cart part way up and hold it there while she unlocked. While I was waiting, the heavy machine started slipping back on top of me. I couldn't jump out of the way and let it slide, so had to try and hold it.

As the machine far outweighed me, I lost the battle, my feet slid from under me, and I landed hard on my knees with the food cart still sliding down on top of me. I asked the Panther to grab it quickly to stop it. Not her. She merely stared over the top of the machine at me, still sliding down the concrete on my knees and said, 'Having trouble? I'll call one of the girls to help you.' Fortunately they had been watching from inside and got there quickly, but both my knees were already raw. If the other girls had been any further away it wouldn't have been just my knees.

'Bitch,' commented Shy with unusual venom when she saw my knees. The Panther had walked off with her nose in the air.

When the Panther was in a bad mood, she would stand over us while we worked; not behind us, but *just* in front of us all the time. If we were sweeping, she would insist we sweep the way *she* told us to, then would deliberately stand right in our way. We swept up one way, leaving a dirt pile, then back again. When we turned, she would be standing right in the middle of our dirt pile spreading it around. We would say, 'Excuse me, I need to sweep there now,' and the Panther would only move about 30 centimetres (12 inches).

We soon learned how to get her to move. When we mopped if we went backwards we could keep an eye on where the Panther was by looking under our arms as we went. If we mopped other areas at a fairly fast rate, then when we got near her, we made a beeline flat out backwards towards her (particularly if she was looking away), and mop straight into her. Because you were going backwards, of course, you could turn around, feigning surprise, and say, 'Oh, sorry! I didn't realise you were standing where I was mopping.' The Panther would look daggers then and go elsewhere. There was nothing she could say, as she shouldn't have been there in the first place, and, after all, *she* was supposed to be watching *you*.

On a good day (when she was in a bad mood), you could manage that at least once or twice. When you were sweeping, if you did something similar with your head well down 'concentrating on what you were doing', you could manage to sweep dirt over her feet which delighted the girls. After she got her shoes dusty and full of grit several times, she would walk right away to the other end of the room and you could return to normal.

Everybody had their favourite routine on medical and administration. Let's face it, we had cleaned the same things for months, and in some cases, years. We had our system, then we would get a new screw who insisted we did things *her* way. She would have us walking from one side of the room to the other and then back again. You would still have the same time limit and you wouldn't get your job done. When we went overtime, we would miss smoko with the other girls, the senior would complain about us being back too late, or the screw would say, 'I know you girls can work faster. Now I want you to do your best, otherwise we will have to have some words about this.' Either way we were in trouble, so the more they kept out of our way, the more we could get our heads down and go for it.

When we finished our morning job, particularly if it was over the other side, we could sit down until morning tea-break on most days, unless everybody was finished early. Then they sometimes had the horrible notion that they could take us weeding the lawn early, and that *wasn't* a pleasant thought.

When all the new evidence was unable to be presented at the High Court, the problem arose of how to bring it before the public. It was decided a special inner committee would be formed of prominent people and legal minds to decide what to do. These people were drawn from support groups all around Australia and those who had been outspoken on their own behalf. Sir Reginald Sholl, Justice Michael Kirby, Guy Boyd, Pro Hart and Betty Hocking made up the inner committee. As time wore on we were still aiming for a Royal Commission but not getting anywhere;

we had the evidence but were unable to use it. After looking at and discussing the evidence available, the Innocence Committee, as they called themselves, decided to produce this material in booklet form, hold a major press conference and distribute it. We would try again to use a public push to get this information into some sort of a court situation where we could use it.

We finally produced the *Blue Book* (so called because of its blue cover), containing only two strains of the new evidence, in comparative photographs and information. One was on the under-dash, sound deadener spray, while the other set was on dingo damage set out so even a child could evaluate it.

At times our scientists used black and white photos so you couldn't tell by the colour of the garment which was the real one, scrambled them and asked scientists who had not been working on the case to pick which was the Chamberlain one, and they could not. The only ones they *could* pick were those with the obvious scissor cuts made by Cox. They could not distinguish between the original jumpsuit, the Adelaide Zoo test jumpsuit and the other dingo test jumpsuits.

A request for an inquiry was forwarded to Brian Martin, the Northern Territory Attorney-General, together with the *Blue Book* and a more detailed report by the Innocence Committee. A nationwide press conference was held to coincide with this. No reply from the Northern Territory was received for months. This material, along with the petitions, started a national push for an inquiry and my release.

Meanwhile, people kept fighting, urging the Northern Territory to grant the request. Australian Democrat Senator Mason said in an adjournment speech to the Senate in September that 'Mrs Chamberlain's continued imprisonment is an affront to all reasonable opinion and an affront to any rational view of what ought to constitute justice' and said another mass campaign to free me could easily be mounted (our supporters were waiting to see what the Northern Territory decided). He was supported by Bob Collins, the leader of the Opposition and shadow Attorney-General in the Northern Territory, who wrote to Chief Minister Ian Tuxworth, asking him to consider the request as 'a matter of urgency'. Like so many others, he was fed up with the Territory's delay in making a decision.

As well as Les Smith's findings on the under-dash spray, there were other factors. Stuart was busily gathering further scientific evidence. On 18 September, Hans Brunner, one of the world's leading experts on hairs, wrote to him saying that he'd examined hairs removed from Azaria's clothing and held by the High Court. He found that several were definitely the guard hairs of a dog. During his summing up at my trial, Barker had said that if a dog had been involved in Azaria's disappearance, hairs would have been found on the jumpsuit. Well, they thought they hadn't found any then—but now, here they were.

Just before Christmas, Professor Randall R Bresee, a textile expert from Kansas State University, also wrote to Stuart. He too had examined Azaria's clothing. He said:

> 'I agree that the damage of [the] jumpsuit was caused by cutting, but very strongly disagree that the most likely method used to produce the cutting of the jumpsuit has been shown to be the rather complex scissor mechanism proposed by the prosecution.

> 'Great effort was expended in reproducing damage to the Azaria Chamberlain jumpsuit using scissors and a complex combination of operations was proposed in surprising detail to reproduce the jumpsuit damage. On the other hand, no experiments were performed to investigate cutting in a way that is remarkably similar to cutting with a sharp object such as a knife.'

Les Smith's report of the experiments done in conjunction with Ken Chapman (about feeding meat wrapped in cloth to dingoes in pens), included a series of photographs (reproduced in the *Blue Book* of new evidence compiled by the Chamberlain Innocence Committee) showing that features of the cloth damaged by dingoes could be compared with the damage done to Azaria's jumpsuit. Professor Bresee was impressed by this, and wrote:

> 'The evidence presented in this report clearly demonstrates that canines are capable of producing the type of cutting damage seen in the Azaria Chamberlain jumpsuit. It is important to note that all the damage by the results of this study. Further, the results of this study are consistent with what is known about canine cutting of animal skin . . . Explaining the damage by cutting with scissors on the other hand requires a complex set of operations and there is no evidence available to conclude that the scissor mechanism is "the most likely that was used" to produce the damage to the Azaria Chamberlain jumpsuit.'

It was obvious that the evidence already collected flew in the face of the so- called 'facts' on which the High Court decision had been made.

The men working on the scientific evidence in my case became so involved with the battle for truth and justice that even their sleeping hours were taken up with dreams of blood cells, cuts, sprays, Ouchterlony plates, haptoglobin, crossover electrophoresis and precipitin tests, cuts, tufts, loops, teeth and dingo damage until I am sure their wives felt like screaming. But their wives put up with it, too. Like Cherie Tipple, they were grass widows for many, many months while their husbands fought on solidly for an absentee lady.

Bob Collins, Leader of the Opposition in the Northern Territory, came to visit me in prison on 27 September (he had been to see me once before too) and told me he intended taking the request for an inquiry to Canberra. He was going to discuss it with Bob Hawke PM at an ALP executive meeting.

When this was reported, it brought the whole question squarely into the Federal sphere, and it meant the Northern Territory also couldn't ignore one of its own Parliamentarians any longer. Tuxworth asked the Labor Party in the Northern Territory to bring their Leader into line and also telexed Bob Hawke asking him to 'discourage the Territory Leader of the Opposition from continuing to conduct a public campaign—a campaign which has the potential to discredit both the political and judicial systems of this country.' The support groups also lobbied both houses of Parliament, State and Federal. A number of Parliamentarians eventually did a lot of work behind the scenes. Michael and friends went to Canberra and visited politicians; some listened attentively to what he had to say while others brushed him off as quickly as they could or refused to see him. A number favoured a review of the case but nobody would openly demand one. There was no doubt that I was a political hot potato—Guy Boyd's prediction had been correct.

On 18 October 1985, Lionel Bowen, who was acting Prime Minister, replied to Tuxworth's telex to Bob Hawke by reiterating that 'the question of an inquiry into the Chamberlain case is entirely a matter for the Northern Territory'—the position that the government had always maintained.

Then, on 12 November, the Northern Territory Attorney-General Marshal Perron tabled the report of the Solicitor-General, Brian Martin in the Northern Territory Legislative Assembly, rejecting the fresh evidence out of hand and recommending that the application for a review be declined. He produced, in answer to it, a paper entitled the Martin Report, in which he said, 'No one has suddenly come forward to give evidence which could not have been given at the trial by that person or someone else, nor are they putting forward any recent scientific advance.' Bob, who had obviously not been worried by the censure of the Northern Territory ALP, noted that part of the Martin Report had been compiled from material supplied by none other than our old friend Ian Barker QC, the chief Crown lawyer at our trial. Collins pointed out that Barker was perfectly entitled to be consulted, but the government should have realised the 'substantial body of scientific evidence now available' demanded an objective, impartial assessment from somebody who hadn't been the leader of the legal team that prosecuted me.

Nothing was altered. This was utter nonsense, of course, but the Cabinet accepted the recommendations, and once again, our hopes were dashed.

It seemed Psalm 58: 1, 2 in the *Living Bible* was right without a doubt when David said, 'Justice? You high and mighty politicians don't know the meaning even of the word! Fairness! Which of you has any left? Not one! All your dealings are crooked: you give "justice" in exchange for bribes.'

Habakkuk also knew what he was talking about when he said so long ago, '*The law is not enforced and there is no justice given in the courts, for the wicked far outnumber the righteous, and bribes and trickery prevail.*' (Habakkuk 1: 4, *Living Bible*.)

The day after the Martin Report was tabled, Senator Colin Mason raised the whole question formally in Parliament, accusing the Northern Territory government of having conducted 'a secret inquiry into the new evidence presented to it by the Chamberlain Innocence Committee'. He told his fellow senators that because the Northern Territory had refused to initiate an inquiry into our convictions, a whole new set of circumstances had been created, and it was time the Commonwealth did something. He asked for a suspension of standing orders so all senators could vote on his bill, but got nowhere.

Betty Hocking wrote the following pamphlet, which sums up the situation. It was headed 'The Need for a Federal Review of the Chamberlain Case'.

> The Chamberlains came to the end of the legal road in Canberra in 1983 when the High Court dismissed appeals to have their conviction set aside.

The only possibility of obtaining an inquiry now lies with the Federal Government; the Northern Territory has rejected a request to hold an inquiry.

The Federal Caucus of the ALP will consider its attitude towards an inquiry at its first meeting in 1986.

Many calls for a review of the Chamberlain case have been made . . . Since the trial new evidence has emerged on the case, including:

1. A statement by the manufacturers of a blood testing reagent stating that their product was unsuitable, by itself, for the identification of foetal or infant blood.
2. A demonstration that material, which the Crown identified as a spray of blood containing foetal haemoglobin, was, in fact, a bituminous/sand compound sprayed into the car by GMH during the assembly process.
3. Cuts in the jumpsuit of the missing baby, which the Crown claimed were scissor cuts made by the Chamberlains to fabricate dingo damage, were cuts made by the teeth of a dingo.
4. Dog or dingo hairs were found on the jumpsuit and singlet of the missing baby.

Other aspects of the trial, although dealt with at that time, have caused concern. These include: the Crown's inability to produce a motive, murder weapon, body or confession, and the impeccable character of the Chamberlains.

While the preceding arguments for an inquiry may be compelling, the real reason for instituting a Federal inquiry is alluded to in the *Sydney Morning Herald* editorial, documented in Bryson's book, *Evil Angels*, and demonstrated in the Solicitor General's reply to the Chamberlain Innocence Committee's call for an inquiry. There is a clear antipathy on the part of the Territory authorities against the Chamberlains.

A single example will suffice to illustrate how any information that does not suit the viewpoint of the NT authorities is misinterpreted by them. Namely, Behringwerke AG, the German manufacturer of the reagent used in the blood tests, provided a report that stated in part: 'The antiserum against haemoglobin F of Behringwerke, therefore, is not suitable on its own for the identification of foetal/infant blood and adult blood'.

The Solicitor General of the NT, who received the above information, wrote: 'The identification of HBF in blood stains . . . is enhanced by everything learnt since the trial, emanating from the manufacturers of the antiserum' (report of Solicitor General to Attorney General, p. 25).

Further examples comparable with that above could be cited.

To help obtain an inquiry, contact your local Federal MP—either by a letter of your own wording or in a well thought out personal interview—and request his support for an inquiry into the Chamberlain convictions. Representation should be made to members of all parties, both in the

> House or the Senate. The telephone number and address of MPs can be found under the heading 'Commonwealth Government—Federal Members' in the front of the phone directory.
>
> Once a decision has been taken by Caucus either for or against an inquiry the issue will be decided. It is therefore important that action in support of an inquiry be taken now. Support the maintenance of justice—request support for a review of the Chamberlain case from your Federal MP now.

Early in December, Sir Reginald Sholl, who was the chairman of the Innocence Committee, wrote a letter to all Federal Parliamentarians. It was a biting attack on 'the system'. He said:

> The reasons for the decisions [i.e., not to reopen the case] were apparently: (1) to intervene could be interpreted as an invasion of the 'State rights' of the Territory under its recent self-government legislation; and (2) as the Chamberlains had exhausted their legal remedies up to the High Court, it would constitute a threat to the judicial system, and to public confidence in it, to allow a further inquiry . . .
>
> With great respect, both reasons make nonsense. As to (1) the Northern Territory is still a Territory of the Commonwealth, and it is acknowledged that by all parties that the Commonwealth still has the right to intervene by legislation in its affairs . . .
>
> As for (2), if it is based on the naive belief that courts can never be wrong, it is time that Members of Parliament woke up to the serious defects in our legal system . . . It should surely be obvious to any intelligent Australian that Parliament must retain the right to remedy cases of miscarriage of justice . . .
>
> Finally, if one assumes that there is even a possibility, let alone a practical certainty (as four million Australians according to a recent poll believe) that an innocent young mother is rotting away in a Darwin jail for a crime she did not commit, may we ask how any decent, fair minded Australian politicians can bring themselves with a clear conscience to say to her: 'Well, we know we have the power to intervene and, at any rate, to investigate the case again, but—sorry, young lady—we are afraid of offending the Northern Territory government in its new found grandeur; we know there is quite a lot of new evidence which, if accepted, would most likely completely exonerate you, but . . . we, like Pontius Pilate, wash our hands . . .'

Things seemed particularly bleak, but God's leading was obvious. I knew all was under control, though I couldn't see why things weren't moving quicker at the time, or why He was working the way He was. All I knew was that He *was* working. I wrote of my feelings in a newsletter to all those corresponding with me:

> Don't despair the way things are. God is still on His throne and He is still in my heart. He never leaves me and ever upholds and strengthens me. I

will need your prayers particularly now. God and I will manage OK. He is a wonderful friend to have, and no one can take away, lock out, influence or apportion visiting hours to Him. He's totally available all the time, and He's mine—but I don't mind sharing Him and introducing you, if you like.

What is the time on the clock of the universe? God has eternity to set the record straight and He can see every anguished tear and pain. He will not ask what we cannot give.

To Shield or Not to Shield

On 3 January 1984, I was really upset. The Chameleon had given me an unwarranted tirade and put me on report. I was upset because I had been following directions and it wasn't a fair cop. I turned to my Bible and opened it at random to seek some message there.

I found a passage in Ezekiel 35 on a prophecy against the perpetual enmity of Mt Seir to the Israelites during a calamity which had befallen them. It strengthened my resolve and I thought, No, I'm not going to sit and take her perpetual enmity either. I don't mind being reported for something I've done wrong, but not for something I haven't. And so I wrote my own counter report.

The anger I felt when facing a setup is indescribable. Frustration, anger, powerlessness and deep hurt are only part of those feelings. Nobody bothers to accept the truth at face value any more, no matter how impartial they think they might be. Even now I sit and analyse whether or not I'm being told the truth, because I have been hurt so many times by some I trusted most I no longer just accept things as they are. Once or twice you might be able to forgive and forget, but as it continues over and over again, the hurt and the disillusionment become deeper and deeper.

It was interesting to note the reactions people had while I was in prison. The most frustrating thing is that people decide they should shield you from what is happening outside because they don't want to cause you more stress than necessary.

Those who *pretended* to be friends told me what they *thought I* would like to hear, particularly if it concerned things they didn't wish me to hear. I would get very pleasant information, assured that I was thought of, prayed for, and cared for above all else; yet, I knew their activities belied this. I often thought of the line in *Hamlet*, 'Methinks the lady doth protest too much.'

My *real* friends told me the score exactly as it was, straight from the shoulder and kept me abreast with events concerning my case in the outside world, and with anything that happened to my family (their life certainly was not private and everything they did was relayed by many) without embellishing facts.

I thought things personally couldn't get any worse, then discovered they could. Later, everyone had assured me it had improved (I was sure it hadn't, but I wanted to believe otherwise.) To have those who call themselves your friends lie to your face is perhaps worse than anything else. Sometimes I already knew outright, at other times you can sense they are lying and something is wrong, even though you may not be sure of the reason why just then, and then you worry until you find out what it is. You invariably find out sooner or later and the frustration of not having been told at the time is worse than knowing. It is much better to be told straight on the chin at the time, than have all your disillusions come at once when you get out. I had few illusions when I got out, but didn't expect personal betrayals by some of the friends I thought to be closest to me.

Even when not sure of the facts, I learned very quickly that when certain people were anxious and overly careful they were usually trying to cover up the truth. It simply made me more curious till I eventually found out the full story.

When I did, of course, it made that person go down considerably in my estimation. From then on, I would never accept them at face value. I might still have loved them as a friend, but knew that no longer could I accept what they said as a fact. Their main aim was usually self-preservation.

The desire to shield out of kindness can often harm more than help, and can backlash badly. One of my old teenage mates became very ill and was given only a limited time to live. His mother wrote and told me that he was sick, but didn't say how sick. Reading between the lines I felt that he was perhaps more ill than she had indicated, but it was still not quite enough to alarm me into writing immediately. We hadn't been in contact for quite some time and I thought perhaps it would give him a bit of a shock if I wrote straight off, so I waited until the newsletter went out and put a note on for his mother to give him my love and to find out what was wrong. Several weeks later she wrote telling me she was sorry, she hadn't wanted to worry me, but Perry had died only a little more than a week before my newsletter arrived. He had been very supportive and worried about me, and his last words, she said, were of me—only she didn't tell me what they were (how I wish I knew). It broke my heart. If only I had known I could have written personally and he would have known I was thinking of him in his illness after all those years. Friends are irreplaceable.

Receiving a 'Dear John' letter may be traumatic, but it is better to know where you stand so you can start building a new life for yourself, than to find out when you are released that all the castles you have built in the air of happy times and plans suddenly crash in dust around your feet—and you are left with less than nothing. There is no such thing as 'breaking it gently' in this situation.

When I first went to prison, the days flew by as long as I looked on it as a new challenge and did not think about home. Each day was different. Although physically restricted and mentally invaded, being summoned on parade and pressured for various reasons all the time, the activities were different and in some way novel. But as time went on, three, four months, I felt I'd settled in and begun to be accepted. In six months, I thought I knew the system fairly well; then in twelve months, all there was to know. In eighteen months, I realised I'd learnt a lot more and didn't know as much as I thought I did. In two years I realised how little I knew at twelve months, and how much more I knew now. In two and a half years, I knew I had really settled in, knew the system and what was going down, and felt very much at ease. From then on it was a breeze.

New girls coming and going through the prison no longer provided a diversion, someone different to talk to; they were simply a nuisance. They were there; they disrupted your pattern of life; they came with what they thought were new ideas but which had all been tried before; they agitated to get new things, not realising as soon as they got those, they would lose something else. They failed to realise if they worked quietly, they would get what they needed and have a reasonable lifestyle under the circumstances.

All Zipped Up

Whatever mending was still on my stack on Friday would be mine to finish on Sunday, my next work day. I would do my normal job, the rest of the mending, if any, and the remainder of the day was mine to watch TV, do hobbies—whatever I liked. If anything came up, such as hoses or errands on the other side, I was the one who was sent because I officially worked that day, whereas the others did their job on Saturday morning, followed by a video, then pool or hobbies in the afternoon. Usually the work content of the day was very light. They had their day off on Sunday instead.

Initially I swapped just with the one girl who did my rostered Saturday job, and I did hers on Sunday so we both had a totally free day each. The senior was rostered off every second weekend and that was when things went wrong. I was often made to do all the work. The girls knew I could handle it, but didn't think it was fair. It had been going on for some time. The other girls had been having an easy day Saturday, and I'd been kept working all day Sunday. This time I was still working when the afternoon shift came on, and we were supposed to be packed up by then.

Grannie asked why I was still working when she came on shift, and one of the girls told her I was being made to sew all day while they were watching TV (my commercial machine was really noisy). Grannie was basically decent and after early hassles, I now got on reasonably well with her. She had suspected I was doing too much work for weeks, so she used this as an excuse to complain to the senior about the amount of work I was given, saying it was disrupting others. The senior then came to see me about it, and finally wrote a rule in the book saying exactly what my Sunday routine was to be, giving me agreed set work after which I could relax. If anybody gave me more than that to do, I was to tell them to look in the book and let her know. I finally ended up doing every morning rostered job in the section, with only occasional sewing and extras, so everyone else had a peaceful full day off. From then on things became much easier. Normally our *one* morning job was spun out till nearly smoko. Sunday was the one day I worked full speed and could usually finish *all* the work by smoko or soon afterwards, then have most of the day free. At least I did until Del played up.

She took a vehement dislike to putting zips into trousers; she hated sewing and refused to do them. That was at a time when I was getting most of the sewing, and some screws had decided to have another go at me. (Some always did when there was a court case coming up, or a visit from the family 'down south' . They would make sure they made it as hard as possible, because those were the times they were *most* likely to get someone on report, and some of them thoroughly enjoyed doing that. This applied to all the girls, not just me. Other officers, like the Imp, prided themselves on their record of *not* provoking anyone.)

Del quite openly told us she was not going to do any more zips. When asked what she would do if the screws made her, she replied she would throw a tantrum and that would be the last zip she would see. She knew how to play the system! When there were only three of us in the section—Del, Smiley and me—we divided the mending equally in piles, and went for it. Because of my dressmaking experience, the worst mending was picked out for me and the others evenly shared what was left, zips included, so we finished about the same time. Usually if I'd finished early, I'd help the one with the most left and then we'd all basically finish around the same time. Smiley dutifully did her zips, even if it took her a full half hour to put one in; but Del refused. She continually threw them on my pile and occasionally on Smiley's.

Finally I bucked and told her to do her own. She still refused. I had noticed that if there were a dozen things left to be mended on Friday, there would be perhaps twenty on Sunday, my next work day. I watched this happen for two or three weeks, then I realised that Del was putting her Saturday mending on my pile. I spoke to Duckie and told her I was not going to do any more of Del's zips.

She said, 'Oh, look, Lindy, you can do them, you don't mind. You know there are not many.'

I said, 'Duckie, it's the principle of the thing. I hate doing zips too—everybody does. I may be able to do them faster, and usually without complaining, but I *hate* it. I don't even mind doing more than my share but she should do *some*—Smiley does hers. She is skiting deliberately that she'll throw a tantrum and won't be made to do it, and she is. I'm not going to pander to that. It's not good for her or anyone else. I'm sick of it. Any more of hers on my stack and I won't do them. You can charge me if you like.'

Duckie asked thoughtfully, 'How do you know she puts more in your stack?'

I told her and offered to leave my stack in a prearranged order on Friday afternoon. She could watch on Saturday morning and see what happened. The next day Del was told to do her zips and Duckie supervised—or thought she did.

I was sceptical, but hopeful. I went to the cupboard and got out my pile of mending—and had extra again. I went straight back to the office and said to Duckie, 'You might have kept an eye on her, but you weren't smart enough.'

She asked, 'What do you mean? Has she added to them?' I said, 'Come and have a look.'

Duckie checked the special stack that I had left on Friday, and sure enough I was right. Not only had Del loaded my sewing up but now she had disobeyed a direct order as well.

Duckie called Del over and told her precisely what she could do with her zips! Del looked daggers at me, but that was too bad. Once she got something into her head, Duckie was fair and stuck to it. Occasionally she went off, but usually she was reasonable, and since she and I had come to an understanding that she wasn't going to put anything over me, and I was straight with her, we got along famously. In fact, we'd got to be quite good friends and happy to tease one another without any fear of retribution.

Del grumbled at me all Sunday and hoped Duckie would have forgotten by the following day. Duckie was in her office, and over came the Chameleon to the day room and told Del all her zips would be inspected on completion. This was the height of indignity. Del grumbled all that week but no amount of sulking moved Duckie this time.

Del was about the same age as Helena and they both looked on me as a friend, and in some ways a substitute parent, I suppose, as Del's mother had died when she was a child, and Helena did not have a lot of contact with her mother.

There was a lot of rivalry between them. At times they both wanted to have most of my attention and wouldn't join in when the other one was there, so instead of enjoying one another's company, they often got on each other's nerves. They were very similar in a lot of ways but vehemently denied it.

When it came to polishing floors, we often had a lot of fun. The floor was sloppy, wet and slippery. We were allowed to wear our old gardening clothes. If it was done the right way, we could fall and skid halfway across the room. On one particular day, Del and Lena decided to play an odd sort of tag. They had pulled each other round and round on rags on the floor in order to scrub it (what scrubbing it did, I don't know!), they tired of that, then each was trying to grab the other one's legs and trip her as she went past. This started off in fun, but became more serious because, although they were laughing, each trip got harder and harder. Lena didn't seem to worry because she knew how to fall and seemed to bounce; she had more fat on her, too. Del crashed down hard on several occasions, till finally they decided it was time to call it quits. The next day, Del had an enormous black bruise on her hip. It was at least 15 centimetres (6 inches) round, red, yellow and purple. That game, needless to say, wasn't played again for some time.

The permanent girls used to look after one another whenever possible, just as family members would. When doing our cells, we would sneak back and put extra coats of polish on—a number of thin ones polished in between, if we could. This made a surface that would last long enough to match the other rooms, which were only in partial use as girls passed through, so didn't scuff and scratch as much. Certain screws used this as an excuse for aggravation against us and for a grievance saying we were careless and not keeping our rooms tidy enough.

Oh, Dem Shirts and Pants and Things

Mr Dagg was a pretty good sort, one of the most recent class of rookies who was obviously going to become a decent officer. Males on regular shifts in the female section were just being introduced at this time, and volunteers were being used as pioneers, as some of the male screws had hangups and were reluctant to come. He was confident in his own ability like Sunshine, and could handle being teased about being 'Mrs' Dagg, or when he would be 'applying for the issue of a dress', so he volunteered. The first time he came across to the female side on duty after his training course, we asked his name; he told us and quickly quipped, 'It's not Fred, either.' From then on, we called him Fred, but he didn't really seem to mind. When his uniforms came (they were issued five), we told him that he could get his badges done by us, as all the other screws did, instead of racing around to do them himself.

Like the rest of the rookies, Mr Dagg hadn't been tipped off about the service. His shirts duly arrived and I put his insignia on all five. Then I ironed them beautifully—

tacked the short sleeves shut so he couldn't put his arms in them, and sent them back. The following day, we went across to the garden garbage heap underneath where the tower was situated. Out of the corner of our eyes we could see wildly gesticulating arms in the tower. We looked up and there was Mr Dagg on duty, hanging half out the window, waving his arms about and pointing at us. Next thing he had his shirt half off and was graphically demonstrating how he had tried to get his arm into the sleeve of his shirt and it wouldn't go. When the nasty screw who was with us, realised that we were looking at something, she turned around to look too. Quick as a flash, he turned his back to the window looking as if he was wearing his shirt, and we instantly became engrossed in something else. When she looked away he hung out the window again, whistling and waving his arms.

We managed (with difficulty) to keep our faces straight when our screw was looking at us, and carried on a conversation totally unrelated to his antics, and he managed to be doing absolutely nothing every time she glanced at the tower. She could hear the whistling (which wasn't forbidden) and was sure we were talking to the officer in the tower, but she couldn't prove a thing. When she looked to see what he was whistling at, he appeared to be communicating with a male officer by means of hand signals. If she'd had better eyesight, she would have realised that the screw on yard duty with whom he was supposedly communicating had his back to the tower, and had no idea that he was the subject of a false conversation!

A couple of days later when Mr Dagg was rostered on our section again, we teased him about nearly getting us into trouble and trying to commit suicide by falling out of the tower windows. He was totally unrepentant and said, 'Sorry about old Sourface, but she didn't count anyway. A bitch like her deserves all she gets.' He was sure we could stand up for ourselves anyway, which of course we could. He also told us that he thought it was one of the best jokes he'd had played on him for years, and his wife also enjoyed the joke.

When Alex Stiff, one of the male seniors was promoted to chief, he sent all his shirts across to have their new insignias put on. His name lent itself to all sorts of jokes, so I decided to have some fun. I stitched them up very nicely, ironed and folded them neatly, but inside each I labelled them with indelible marking pen on his name tags; a different pun on his name for each of the five shirts. As he was now a chief, he had also personally requested me to shorten his trousers and 'stitch them up'.

I said to him, 'Are you *sure* you want me to stitch them up?'

He said, 'Yes.' So I did. I hemmed them, then stitched all the cuffs of his trousers together and sent the whole lot back, packaged in a big box neatly ironed and folded. The screws commented on how nicely they were done and how pleased he would be. I got the message back the next day that he was extremely pleased with the job I had done on his clothes, particularly the stitching that I had done on his trousers!

The other officers had no idea I had stitched his pants up in the first place, and the way he had worded his message did not allow them to know, but told me what he thought of it. The next time I saw him, I said with a very straight face, 'I'm really pleased you liked the way I stitched your pants up.' With just the tiniest quirk at the corner of his mouth and the slightest twinkle in his eye, he replied quite gravely that I had done 'an excellent job'. After our chief retired and I had left, Mr Stiff became the regular chief of the female section.

The very tall officers had to have their trousers either let down to the limit or extra length added; Mr Natt was one of these. He had obviously noticed the sewing, and when it was my roster for administration office cleaning one afternoon, I was summoned to go to his room. The Chameleon was on duty and tried to follow me. He sent her back to look after my partner who was cleaning elsewhere. He was quite capable of taking charge of a prisoner.

I was not sure what was coming, whether there had been a message from home he wanted to give me without her knowledge (unorthodox though it might be, that sometimes occurred), or whether I was in trouble and he would tell me and my senior but not the Chameleon.

He simply pointed out he had ripped his new office chair and asked whether I thought it could be mended. *That* was something new. I had a look, decided I could mend it reasonably easily and asked whether it could be sent across to our side. He said he really needed it and asked how long it would take me to mend it on the spot. I estimated that a decent job would take half an hour to an hour, and suggested that perhaps I could come across the following evening, if he put the request through to my section. I would fix it for him while the other girls were doing their cleaning. He agreed. I warned him if he did not ask our senior direct someone else may be sent. He said he wanted me to do it, and would see that it was done.

He then let me out of the office and didn't inform the Chameleon what had occurred. I didn't either and she could not question me about my conversation with a chief. She avoided me for the rest of the evening, and I heard no more about it.

The next night when the cleaning girls were due to leave, the Chameleon came into the day room and said, 'You're to come as well and bring your needle and thread.' So I did. I selected the right colours and the senior, who had a grin on her face said, 'You won't be annoyed. I know you know what the cotton's for. I've instructed the Chameleon you are to do the chair while the other girls do the cleaning. If there are any problems, she can contact me!'

I got over there and the Chameleon told me to wait. Mr Natt saw me and beckoned me in. Once again the Chameleon tried to follow, but he told her she wasn't needed, 'I'm here, thank you' and shut the door abruptly. I saw the look on her face and my sense of the ridiculous came to the fore and I started to grin. I dived down behind his chair in a hurry before she saw me (the office was glassed in for maximum view).

I said to Mr Natt, 'She's going to *kill* me when I go out. You know that don't you? Last night she was furious.'

He replied with a bit of a grin, 'Leave her to me.'

Much to her obvious annoyance, he not only stayed in the room, but remained in his chair and continued working while I mended it. I could not mend it at the normal angle, as there wasn't enough room for me to get behind it, so he had to sit with the chair awkwardly sideways while I worked. The papers he was working on contained reports about other prisoners, and requests—all confidential. They were all over his desk and very visible. He knew I would not try to read them (you only do that to nasty screws) and made absolutely no attempt to hide what he was doing.

The other girls finished (his office hadn't been done that night because he was too busy), so they sat and waited for me outside the partition. The Chameleon paced up and down like a caged lion. He finally had a look at how my work was going, got up, went out and told the Chameleon she could take a seat and I would not be very long. He obviously intended to give the impression that her pacing was annoying him and he was going to have the job finished regardless. He was one of the true gentlemen there.

I could see the other girls thought it was very funny. Mr Natt came back inside, shut the door and told me to take my time, so I did. I did a decent job, then told him I'd finished. He said, 'Thank you,' and I went. He sent an official thank you message across the following day.

I had to lengthen Mr Dewsnip's trousers also, and having never seen such large trousers in my life, I decided, when I had finished, to have some fun with them. I put them on, rolled up the legs (about a foot) and stuffed the waist with pillows. I also had a dress shirt with all the braid, feathers, ribbons, and fancy buttons I had just been putting on for Mr Donnelly from head office in town, so I put that on as well and belted the trousers with some fancy cord from our Christmas sewing. Del came in, saw what I was doing and raced across to the male chief, who was one of our favourite officers and relieving for the day. He was known to us all as Gentleman Jim because it was so rare to see a real gentleman in the prison system who treated the guys on the other side, and us, humanely. He was there alone as all his other officers were on escorts. As he was bored he made himself useful doing some repairs around the section; he was in the courtyard with a hammer and nails mending something. Del asked whether she could borrow his hat, and promptly took it. Normally we would be told off for having the cheek to ask, let alone taking an officer's hat. He knew we wouldn't do anything bad to it and just grinned, not even asking what she wanted it for. She handed it to me and I put that on as well. I grabbed a duster stick, put it under my arm for a baton (like Tapioca) and trotted out.

Gentleman Jim had his head down working when I reached him, so I banged the stick on the table and said in a deep voice, 'Here, here, you know this is against the rules. I will *not* have my officers doing repairs. This belongs to the prisoners' work section.' He looked up startled (officers *weren't* supposed to do useful things—might upset the union), saw trousers belonging to a man, straightened up, and suddenly it registered that Tweedledum had come to town. He just cracked up. He laughed so hard he held his stomach. By then the other girls, who had been in different parts of the section, came to see what was funny and roared too. I marched out and was taking off the trousers, when Del decided that minus the pillows there must be room for two, so we tried it out. I stayed in the back and she hopped in the front (we were both about the same size). We had to hold the edge of the pool table to balance at first, but eventually, by cooperating and with much giggling, we managed to walk. I said, 'Hup, two, three, four!' and off we went, keeping our feet in the right place and not standing on each other.

That was really the end for Gentleman Jim. He gave up his repair job and had to sit down, helpless, until he stopped laughing and cooled off. We'd had our fun for the day, so we put the trousers back. I ironed them, and replaced them on the return stack in the office.

That afternoon at shift changeover, Gentleman Jim sent the other screw cleaning, then came over to us and said, 'Please—will you put those trousers on again? I want you to do it for Sunshine.' So we did, and headed for the office. She was sitting facing the other way. He kept her in conversation until we got nearly across then couldn't keep his face straight any longer. She turned around to see what was happening and doubled up with laughter. As she and Duckie were on in the morning, she said, 'I won't send the trousers across tonight, girls, just one more night. We'll keep them to show Duckie.' The following morning we repeated it for the third time and Duckie was also duly appreciative. Then the trousers went back to Mr Dewsnip.

There was much hilarity about the girls wearing Mr Dewsnip's trousers. Sunshine without realising what she was saying once said, 'Did you see these girls in Mr Dewsnip's pants?' That cracked up the whole section. Everybody said, 'Goodness, you can't tell him *that*.' We learned later somebody *had* let him know, but he said nothing. Next time he came across he thanked me for doing his trousers. He said he'd found them very satisfactory, and added, with a very straight face and a twinkle in his eyes, 'I understand you had quite a time with them.' That was all, and *I* was not going to expand on the conversation either!

We tended to do crazy things like that during the 'suicide' season (the lead up to the Wet). Everybody was bored; it was getting towards Christmas again. We were still there, our sentences were interminable, and if anybody could think of something hilarious, funny or different to do, they would. This would take our minds off where we were, what we were doing, the length of our sentences and, of course, the fact that we weren't going to see our families and friends *again* for Christmas.

Officers and visitors commented that the girls in the female section seemed always to be laughing and cheerful. But they didn't see behind the masks. Tears were never far away. We all knew this, and encouraged each other to laugh at ourselves, trying to keep each other's spirits up. The real feelings were pushed deep. At night, on lockup, you would often hear girls quietly sobbing or swearing to themselves. The letters would come out from home, or you'd see them sitting on their beds looking at pictures and listening to some tapes over and over again, and you would know that their thoughts were of home.

Most of us tried to spend as little time as possible in our cells in order to minimise the length of time for thought, because that's when it hurt the most. In the middle of the night, if you were still awake, you often heard an officer on her rounds bend close to a window and ask a girl whether she was OK, and you would know that someone had been caught sobbing into her pillow.

Del had been having one of her remorseful periods for quite some time. Her father was ill; things weren't right at home. Despite the hard life Del had led, she thought a lot of her family, and was really upset that she would be in prison over Christmas again.

No wonder it's called the suicide season—it gets so hot and sticky. There is no relief day after day. If only it would rain, you think. You're waiting for the Wet to come, and the build-up gets oppressive and difficult. You develop headaches because of the high temperatures and humidity. Everybody, without exception, gets listless and crabby, but particularly the prisoners because, unlike the officers, we couldn't go home to air-conditioning or into air-conditioned offices to cool down. The ceiling fans did nothing except stir the hot air around. As the build-up grew, the humidity was regularly over ninety-five per cent.

The girls had been bickering and warring for days. One particularly bad day, without stopping to think, I said to Del, 'Oh, grow up and stop bitching. You're always grumbling. Just lay off and give everybody a break.' Well, that was the end of her temper. She swore at me; called me every name she could think of and told me I thought I was smart—I was no Christian to say things like that to her. It was all a setup, for show she added. I was no smart little saint, just a goody-two-shoes. Her fists came up and she wanted to fight. She did everything she could think of to provoke me to hit her. (The one who hit first would be charged, the other person could claim self-defence.)

I just stood there and said, 'Well, if it's going to make you feel better by hitting me, hit me!' She came very close to doing it. She was as enraged and hostile as a caged tiger. Her fists were clenched so tight, her knuckles were turning white. I just stood looking Del straight in the eye, and the longer and more calmly I looked at her, the more you could see the fight dying out of her. Finally, she said loudly, 'You're nothing but a religious sham!' turned on her heel and ran off. The thing was over, but the other girls thought that I had got the best of her and they were pleased.

I said, 'Look, she's just upset. I shouldn't have said that. Everybody gets that way occasionally. It doesn't matter. Leave it; she'll be right later.' Sure enough, within a couple of hours, she came back and apologised. Her words had been hurtful because she, of all people, knew that they weren't true. When she apologised, this time very quietly on the side, I said to her,

'Del, you are also a Christian and do you think that it was very nice of you saying what you said?'

She looked very shamefaced and said, 'No, I lost my temper. I'm sorry.'

I said, 'Well, Del, you did it in front of all the girls in the rec. room, and I think if you're going to apologise, seeing you did it so publicly, you ought to apologise publicly as well.' She flushed at that and admitted she should, but said, 'They hate me enough as it is. I can't.' (They didn't really—just her present mood.) She said she didn't have the courage to do that, and wanted me to forgive her then, so I did. (I wasn't the only one who'd had enough of her grumbling though. Later, as she was sleeping soundly one lunch hour, one of the girls sprinkled sugar all over her. The heat and humidity quickly made it a sticky mess and attracted the ants. She woke furious and turned the air blue swearing. None of us knew who'd 'done it' either, of course, which made her madder still.)

Her outburst cleared the air somewhat and everyone calmed down a little after those two incidents.

Christmas is Coming but We Won't be Getting Fat

One of the more difficult times I spent in jail was before one Christmas when I knew Michael was going home to New Zealand with the children. We had always gone hiking in New Zealand, something we both loved. Now Michael was not only going to his parents without me but he was planning to go hiking with his cousin and some others at Copeland Crossing near Mt Cook, which I had always wanted to do. He wrote and told me he would keep a diary and tell me all about it later, which he faithfully did. I found it difficult reading about the planning. When he returned home he sent me all the leaflets, booklets, and his pictures with the story of his trip. I sat there and read the leaflets, then tried to read his essay. I simply couldn't do it. I could not face the reasons I had missed out on that holiday and the implications behind it. It is only recently that I have been able to cope with reading about that trip.

Despite our private joys and sorrows, Christmas in prison was something that we all got excited about no matter how hard we resisted the memories it evoked. The girls who were going home for Christmas were excited, and talking about being back with their families. Occasionally there were visits. Most who didn't have contact with their families for the rest of the year at least got some sort of a Christmas card, or hoped they would, and they talked a lot of past Christmases at home. Whether you wanted to or not, you got caught up in the spirit of things because we had to decorate our section. Often the decorations would drop down because they were not always put in practical positions and when you were on day room cleaning, they were a real curse. But it made a change and gave us something to do. We usually managed to talk the screws into getting a fairly big tree in for us, either a living tree, an old plastic one or a large branch. It stood in one corner of the day room. The female section prided itself on having the best tree in the jail and over the years they had accumulated decorations for it. Some screws had donated unwanted baubles, and occasionally we were given new ones by good officers. We had lights, and over the years various girls had made ornaments for the tree, which made them special for sentimental reasons.

One week we were doing some Christmas sewing, and the Aboriginal girls were putting patches down on the floor for the patchwork quilt they were making. Smiley had wanted my opinion whether it looked alright. She had worked all year crocheting the squares, and some of her mates had contributed a few to help as well.

The Aboriginal girls were all sitting around on the floor, stitching, and I was going backwards and forwards helping them. We always seemed to get a lot of extra girls in the weeks just before Christmas and the majority of them were Aborigines. Some of them had done very little or no sewing before, and their work had to be watched fairly carefully, otherwise it fell apart later. Often the joining colours they used were wrong as well. Del kept coming past and deliberately moving the squares and getting them messed up. Our dark girls worked slowly and methodically through their task with care, and they were getting more and more upset at her interference, as the changing expressions on their faces indicated.

The girls asked me to intervene. I decided to sit down with them before there was a big blowup, because we all knew what would happen if Smiley and Del had a row. They would both fly; they'd both be in trouble. Smiley would go on lockup because she was the senior of the two and should know better, while Del might have one night on lockup for being a pest. (Although Aboriginal, Smiley, being a permanent, had been conditioned to prison rules and could go out on lockup just like the rest of us. She was also older and therefore the automatic tribal senior for most of the dark girls who came in.) Then they wouldn't speak to one another for a week. It would be awkward for everyone, and tempers would be short. One being white and the other black didn't help either, as the new dark girls wouldn't understand the 'family' squabble of those two, and would think it was racial and it could get nasty. They would automatically protect Smiley, she being their elder.

As I sat down with the others, I made sure I sat on some of the squares that Del kept moving. Then she kept coming after the scissors (which she had decided cut better than her own), waiting until someone was just ready to use them, then removing them. She would use them and then just leave them sitting in her lap for several minutes before giving them back. She was being deliberately annoying. About the fifth time she went to grab the scissors without asking, I was waiting for it and put my hand out first and picked them up. She knew the girls were objecting to her and was just waiting for a fight. As she went to punch me, I saw her fist coming and grabbed her round the wrist and held tight so she couldn't move it. She twisted her hand enough to grab my wrist too so that I couldn't move it, but she hadn't been able to connect with the punch.

I asked her to, 'Let my arm go, Del.' She wouldn't, so I just squeezed her wrist tighter, and repeated myself. As I did so, she tried to twist my arm around but couldn't, and I just held on. As my hand got tighter and tighter, my nails apparently dug into her wrist. In the end, it was hurting so much she wanted me to let go.

She said, 'You let go and I'll let go.'

'No,' I said, 'loosen your hand and you can go, otherwise you'll stay put. You can go into the other room away from the girls and leave them alone, because they've had enough.' She let go so I released her wrist. She jumped up and flew out of the room, disappearing for about an hour. The officers must have sensed something had gone on because they came in and said, 'What's happened?' One of the Aboriginal girls said, 'Nothing. Del be a pain and Lindy stop her. She gone now. No more trouble. Is all right now.' They looked at me and said, 'Is everything all right?' I said, 'Yes' and off they went.

Later that evening Del said, 'Do you realise you hurt, you little beggar?' I said, 'Well, I'm sorry, but you don't annoy like that and get away with it. It's time you also learned you can't just hit people because you lose your temper.'

She looked at me and walked off. Some time later she came back and said to everyone, 'I'm sorry about what happened this afternoon. I don't know what got into me. It won't happen again.'

This was one of the things about Del you could really like. She would go away and think about what she did. If she lost her temper, she would come and apologise. If she had done something to you publicly, she would usually apologise publicly at meal time, which takes a lot of guts.

We worked very hard on finishing batches of the craft work and Christmas sewing for St Vincent de Paul. The girls on sewing would sew nearly all year until we ran out of materials, storing it to finish until the wet season, when it was too wet to garden. Everyone else could stuff them, or sew on buttons just before Christmas. We always hoped we would run out early, as then we would be allowed to do our own thing for a little while over the wet season. We made children's and women's clothing, pillowcases, mats, rugs, cot sheets, coat-hangers, cushions, stuffed animals, rag dolls and other items. One year we made padded picture frames. St Vincent's put them in their Christmas packages or sold some of the toys to raise money for food. We also made dresses for some of the retarded children in the area who had trouble getting special clothes. We made them two or three new dresses each year to order. St Vincent's or the children's home sent in the material needed. I'm sure there are many little girls in Darwin who have something that came from the girls in prison. Although it was called voluntary work, it really was compulsory, but the girls didn't really mind doing something different.

Sometimes the workmanship on some of these things was not of the highest standard, but everything was done with love and care by those assigned to it. We gathered that the knee rugs were very much appreciated by the elderly. We also made many stuffed toys. This put a lot of pressure on the girls who could sew, and they would work steadily throughout the year.

On Christmas Day we actually got a holiday. One whole day to ourselves. (The only other day we got off was Easter Day.) All we had to do was give our section jobs a lick and a promise in the morning, then we were allowed to open our presents. If long-term prisoners wanted to make something for each other, we could put our gifts underneath the Christmas tree too. Generally we agreed we wouldn't bother doing that. There was nothing much we were allowed to have and could make for each other that we didn't have already (like mats or coat-hangers), and we couldn't buy anything. The long-term prisoners bought extra stuff on their fortnightly buy for birthdays to have a 'pig out' on the designated evening with their mates. That was about all the celebrating we did (except occasionally when a long-term girl left), which wasn't much anyway.

Every year the St Vincent de Paul ladies brought in a present for all the girls in the section. Long-term prisoners would have a specially chosen gift that cost a little more than the average present under the tree. They, of course, did most of the Christmas sewing and this was our yearly thank you. St Vincent's obviously went to a lot of trouble to pick out things that specially suited the long-term girls. Smiley was given some craft work one year, Hypo received a book on tapestry, Froggie a book on gardening, and I received a book on knitting. The last year I was in prison I was given a beautiful little book called *101 Embroidery Stitches*, along with some nice soap and talc. Those who were in over Christmas on shorter terms would receive soaps, powder or hand cream, just little gifts from Coles supermarket that cost about $3 to $6 each perhaps, but they were nice and the girls appreciated them. One or two spare presents were left also in case girls came in the night before. The officers put them under the tree and labelled those for any newcomers.

Once we were given our presents, that was it for the day. We could do what we wanted. Well, what we wanted to do was be with our families. Nobody wanted to be alone, but everyone usually headed glumly back to their cells. We could go to a Christmas service run by the Catholics, but that was about all. Television only had Christmas services and carols, and the officers were reluctant to turn on the television in the morning anyway, even though we could watch it if we wished.

I used to go across to Mass, simply because it was something to do and Del was a Catholic and wanted company as the service was in the male section. It was often the only church service of any sort that we had a chance to attend, and that in itself was a change. We sang Christmas carols and they had a little leaflet with various readings and order of service. Usually only twenty or thirty prisoners were there. The others all seemed to prefer to sleep, play pool or simply brood on what their families might be doing at home.

They made a big deal about Christmas dinner and I was interested to see it. Those still in from the year before told me, 'You get free lollies and drinks and they bring cake across. You get turkey, Christmas pudding and a good meal.' Well, they might have done that one year, but they sure didn't do it while I was there. When Christmas dinner came across, the girls couldn't believe their eyes. Yes, we got Christmas pudding—tinned pudding with custard, and lumpy custard at that. Lunch was an ordinary cooked meal except that it had some very dried-up turkey for the meat. My vegetarian meal came across as normal except instead of the usual whole, hard-boiled eggs, they had actually cut them in half, whipped up the middles with mayonnaise and *piped* it back in. Wow! At least the guy had tried though. We got a can of Coke and a packet of lollies each. I wished it was Fanta as I didn't drink Coke. It wasn't, however, so that was that.

Three-quarters of the lollies were the standard jail issue this year, and the other quarter were a different variety. That only led to fights; some of the new girls went to grab the packets they wanted, and the girls who had been in longer and were more assertive informed them that this wasn't the way we did things. In the end, the officers distributed them.

The unwritten rule was that the girl who had been in longest had the first selection, and went down the list according to time inside, so Smiley had first pick as there was a packet allotted to her, even though she was diabetic. She could then decide to trade or hand them out generally. She wanted to swap her chocolate-filled caramels for my unwanted Coke. Great! That meant I got some different lollies, as the rest were mostly barley sugar with a few packets of Willow Mints. As I got four packets of barley sugar a week (instead of the tobacco and papers the smokers got), I soon decided I never wanted to see one again in my life; I used to leave mine in the fridge for everybody to eat. They mounted up so much that unless a girl with a real sweet tooth came in, we would have spare lollies everywhere.

If I didn't accept lollies regularly, the nasty screws often cancelled the whole ration. In order to keep the lines open until somebody came in and wanted lollies, I would accept at least half my rations every time and tip the oldest surplus out in the rubbish and hope not to be caught.

By Christmas afternoon, tempers were quite short. Everybody was doing her best either to provoke the others or avoid being provoked, yet still appear cheerful on the surface, even though we all felt pretty depressed.

Often the girls wrote long family letters on Christmas Day. By late afternoon, after an extra sleep, there really was nothing left to do but head towards the television. Something bright and cheery would have taken our minds off where we were, but no, there was always a film—usually an old replay—about family Christmases at home and how everything turned out right in the end. That was usually turned off, as it made the girls more miserable than ever.

Sometimes we had videos instead, picked for our section by the screws. The first officer in got the best selection for his or her block. A good officer would request the officer choosing them to get certain videos. If an order hadn't been put in, a good afternoon shift officer would select the best available. Sometimes we'd have replays, but only because they were better than the alternatives. It seemed they usually picked the videos with the most action, crime or bloodshed—not, to my way of thinking, the types of movies to calm people in criminal institutions. All they did was fester a desire for violence and give an added lust for revenge. I wasn't the only one who had that opinion; other girls and a number of the screws did too. Christmas was the only day we had extra videos, which were normally only on Saturday mornings. Later in my prison term we got them on Sundays as well, so I got to see them, as I didn't watch those on my Sabbath.

Eventually Christmas Day ended with regular lockup and the thought of work tomorrow as usual. There was no doubt that by the end of the day everybody was glad to see it over and go back to the normal routine again.

I had noticed a growing tendency, when requests came in, for me to be booked further and further ahead for outside jobs. Some of these were voluntary, but some I knew the prison was paid for. Whereas they would accept only one or two jobs to begin with, now they were so frequent that I was spending most of my working time on the sewing machine.

It astounded the screws that unorthodox requests I deliberately put through often managed to get passed. (Privately I thought it was because of my sewing, so I pushed the limits.) On one occasion, the ads for CCs (corn chips) were on, and the slogan was, 'You can't say no'. Every time somebody offers you a corn chip, you must nod your head and say yes. So, near Christmas, I decided for a lark to put them on one of my special buy sheets. I put in brackets next to the request for corn chips, 'You can't say no'. Believe it or not, whoever was on that day did not say no and I actually got them much to everyone's amazement!

Some evenings I sat in my cell reading my letters and trying to study. If I turned my cell light off (so that only the security lights were on) I could look straight south and see in the moonlight a little bit of water and mile after mile of desert landscape. It was not true desert, but from a southern point of view, desert enough. I had flown over that land many times and I knew just how far away home was, south straight out of my window. I could look at the stars and know that they were the same stars they saw at home, and 'wish upon a star' to say good-night to my darlings at home.

Foster mum Jan Hughes later wrote and told me that Kahlia regularly blew a kiss out of her window each night to the stars so they would transport it to Mummy too. She also discovered that violet leaves were the shape of a heart (which she could not yet draw herself) and used them to trace around to make me picture 'letters', as hearts represented love.

Often I would wish for dark. Sleeping with the light on was something I always hated. I love the peace and tranquillity, the calmness, the eternal feeling that night brings.

The prison is situated on an ironstone ridge and the girls' section ran right along the centre of that, so when we got a storm, any lightning was attracted to us. When it ran round the razor wire on our verandah roof or hit the grate in the middle of our courtyard it didn't attract us nearly so much!

When the wet *finally* arrived we got hot, wet days with hot, sticky nights. The air stayed at saturation point most of the time, so there were frequent thunderstorms. There was momentary relief while it was raining, but as soon as the rain stopped and the sun came out again it started steaming. Then you'd wish it hadn't rained after all. We had so much water we didn't know what to do with it. Everything was waterlogged.

Storms in Darwin are wild and wonderful things; there is always something primitive, basic and totally majestic about them. Often in the wet season I sat on my bench with my feet up, the top metal louvre open a crack, watching the wind whipping the trees wildly and the water coming down in torrents, flash flooding over the road.

Sitting in the day room because it was too wet to go outside, we often saw the lightning hit the perimeter fence and the rolls of razor wire along the top of the cyclone fencing would illuminate like a Christmas tree as the lightning sparkled and spat right around from one section to another. Lightning often blew the bell on the gate. For some months it appeared the wet season storms would time themselves nicely for the afternoon shift change, so the officers would get soaking wet leaving or arriving. If we knew there was a nasty officer on, we often hoped that just once they might manage to touch the bell as the lightning hit.

Sometimes water would fill the drain through the backyard, up to nearly 60 centimetres (24 inches) deep and two metres (2 yards) wide. It would soon run a banker, and pour in 10 to 15 centimetre (4 to 6 inch) deep streams off the roadways, banks and lawns, to be taken very quickly to the larger storm water drain outside and away. Within a quarter of an hour of the rain stopping, there would be very little water left. Within half an hour, there was just a trickle in the bottom and the violent runoff marks in the sand to remind you that a little while before there had been a storm.

A Six-Foot Tantrum

One day Zee, a very tall girl, was brought in. Although she didn't appear to be very old, she was about 185 centimetres (6 feet) tall. After she had gone through registration, we discovered that she was only fourteen. She had been sent to prison because she was causing problems with other children and the staff in Northern Territory juvenile care. For her own protection, as well as others', she was sent to us while they decided her fate.

The first couple of days were all right, although she was a bit sulky. We soon realised she was also very lazy. We got sick and tired of cleaning up after her. She smoked but wasn't used to roll-your-own cigarettes, which was all the prison supplied, so she grumbled and conned various girls into rolling them for her. (The girls had even taught me, for fun. They thought it was a real hoot to teach a non-smoking minister's wife how to do it and even how to roll a joint!) After a while everyone got tired of rolling her cigarettes and told her to roll her own. She made a tremendous mess (on purpose I'm sure because we wouldn't do it any more) all over her lap, then brushed it onto the floor, wasting a lot of tobacco. Because she also used three or four matches to light a cigarette, she frequently ran out and wanted to use everyone else's. The girls, who also had to exist on rations, soon refused to give her any extra matches. At the end of the day's work, when everyone had to quickly clean the day room, emptying the ashtrays and sweeping up the sewing cottons, she would get up and leave her mess for everybody else to deal with.

Finally, after many complaints to the screws, one of them actually saw her rolling cigarettes and brushing the tobacco off onto the floor as usual. The screw said, 'You can't make a mess like that and expect the others to clean it. You will have to clean it up please, Zee.'

Zee said, 'No, I won't.' That is one thing you don't say to an officer, particularly a decent one who is *asking you* something instead of *telling you*. She replied, 'I beg your pardon, young lady. I want you to clean up your mess.'

Zee looked at her again and said, 'No. I am not cleaning that up.'

The officer turned to her and said, 'Go and get a dustpan and brush and sweep it up *this instant*, or you are going on lockup.'

Very grudgingly, Zee got the brush and dustpan and started cleaning up. She did a very haphazard job, so she was told to do it again. That was it; she threw a tantrum, swearing at the officer and throwing the brush and dustpan down. Before she could blink she was grabbed and manhandled out. The other screw appeared pronto, and as Zee was struggling, yelling and screaming, they simply locked her in her cell and left her there. As we were full and she was new and a known problem, she was already in the security cell, but had all her gear in with her as we did in the ordinary cells.

That was by no means the end of the story. We started to hear ripping noises, and after a while, we were sure she was tearing up her gear. We told the screws who went to look but she apparently heard them and hid what she was doing. As they couldn't see anything, they left. As soon as they went, the ripping noises started again, and continued for the next half hour. The next shift came on and did their routine change over inspection.

She was obviously hiding something she was sitting on, so they told her to get up. Eventually she did and they discovered she had shredded all her sheets and her spare uniform and was starting to tear up the uniform she had on, and her bedspread. Zee had covered everything with the bedspread, so the real damage hadn't shown until the last minute. All her gear was taken, she was given a nightie to wear and stripped of everything except her mattress and pillow, then left alone again. This made her even madder, and she started on the mattress, screaming all the time. She shredded her toilet paper over the floor and squirted water everywhere as well.

I could see her hand jammed under the tap, squirting water directly at the intercom system in the corner (the screws monitored her activities through it). If she hit it in the right place she would not only have electrocuted herself but short-circuited the intercom system. She might have been a naughty child but a tantrum suicide we could do without. She was secured under guard in another cell for a while so the maintenance guys could remove her taps, which meant she no longer had a way of washing or getting a drink.

It also meant the guys could report to the others what was happening. They usually had a chance to give us some news, too, at times like this, as the screws were busy with the disruption, so the prison grapevine thrived. The cell was cleaned out as much as possible with a broom, and Zee was locked up again, this time with the restraining belt and handcuffs so she couldn't get into any more mischief.

Night fell. The floor was still wet and Zee was now soaking too. Nobody felt sorry for her, even though it was going to be a cold night. Every time she was asked if she would behave so she could have some new gear and a mattress, she would scream abuse so, of course, the officers left her there. That night she wore her food. For a week she slept on the concrete floor and had nothing to do, not even a magazine to read because every time they went near her, she would start fresh abuse.

Then Zee was dressed and taken to the interview room to see her probation officer and within minutes she screamed like a wildcat, yelling that if she was let out she would behave herself, and if they still locked her up, she wouldn't. He calmly and reasonably told her she would have to prove that she could behave herself first. We heard great banging sounds and later discovered that she had thrown a chair at him. It was no wonder they had sent her to prison despite the fact that she was under age. She was taken back to the cell. On the way, she tried to pull the office screen door off the hinges, as well as kicking the potted plants.

It was nearly a fortnight before they could give her a bamboo mat to sleep on. By that time I think she had had enough of the concrete, so she didn't attack the mat. After almost three weeks, they were able to put bedding back in for her and give her something other than a nightgown to wear.

Eventually, she calmed down because she realised she was getting nowhere, and was finally let out with the other girls again. All she did then was complain she had been mistreated! Nobody wanted to know. In fact, by that time, two or three of us older prisoners decided that we'd had enough, too, and told her sternly that we didn't want to know about her problems, and until she grew up and showed some maturity she could not expect to be treated as an adult, but like the spoilt brat she was. She was rather stunned at that. As the oldest, and having a son only a little under eighteen months younger than Zee, I was voted spokesperson and told her if she wanted to be treated responsibly, she had to act that way. Just because she was tall and strong and could throw her weight around did not mean she was going to get respect from anyone.

We knew that Zee's father had died and as a result, not long after, her mother had died in tragic circumstances. Zee had not been fond of her mother and was initially glad she had died, but had later felt guilty about this and been confused. She had been able to dress up, get into bars and act like an adult because she looked mature and was so tall, but she didn't have the emotional maturity to go with it, and that was her undoing.

We spoke to her about pulling her weight along with everyone else, how she could help around the place, and what would make people like her. She was obviously terrified of going back to juvenile care because a number of the other kids had agreed to band together and 'do' her when she returned, and she knew they would. We told her if she wanted to earn herself a different reputation, she had to stop throwing tantrums and show a bit of cooperation. She actually listened. From then on, we noticed a big improvement. She started volunteering to sew on buttons and help with the mending during the day, she cleaned up her own messes and generally wandered around asking people if she could help here and there, even though as a remand prisoner she was not officially required to work. (They only had to do hygiene jobs like rubbish removal.)

That was one time I felt prison was actually beneficial—but again it was the prisoners that helped, not the system. The laws can't always deal equally and justly with everyone, and must have some discretion for dealing with the unusual—like Zee.

Putting the Media to Good Use

In Darwin there aren't four seasons, only two: the wet season (around Christmas) and the dry (around mid-year). In the dry season, this means mostly a hot, dry day and a crisp, cold night with a nasty wind-chill factor although you could get dull days. Out of the wind you could sunbake, but the wind could make you turn blue and shiver.

The dry season lived up to its name. The air was so dry clothes picked up static electricity and clung. The ground became parched and cracked. In order to keep the lawns around our section from turning into dustbowls, we would water them every day with several long hoses, taking it in turns to change them around, according to a roster. They were thick industrial- quality hoses, and joined together, so some were nearly 30 metres (100 feet) long. Having been used, they were wet and dirty. We were expected to wind them up around our shoulders, and do it quickly so we could get back inside, as the nights were cold and daylight short. It was a wet, dirty struggle. Often there were puddles of water through which you had to wade in your leather sandals to turn the hoses off or pick them up. By the time you had finished, your shoes were soaking and your feet freezing.

We had no slippers; gardening sand-shoes (if owned) were not to be worn in the cell block, and as you often had to put the hoses away on the way back from the office you couldn't put gardening shoes on beforehand. We were not allowed to go with bare feet, so we'd wash our feet with our sandals on to get rid of the dirt (washing didn't make them any wetter). They very quickly became cold and clammy and would often stay partly wet for days if we had no opportunity to sit in the sun and dry them. Our feet were often blue with cold at that time of year.

One of the nice officers got thick men's socks for us, which we wore quite happily at night and often during the day in winter when we were inside the section; they were very unglamorous black, brown, or army green, but at least they kept our feet warm. We would do our best to get the better-looking pairs if we were long-term and those who came in just for a week or two got the leftovers or none at all. We weren't supposed to wear them outside the section, so we would wear them till the last minute if we were on cleaning duty over the other side.

One of the new girls decided she was far too cold to do that, didn't realise the implications, and wore them cleaning. The screws with her, barely over rookie training and not knowing any better, said nothing the first day, so she wore them again. This time the superintendent saw her and tore strips off the screws for allowing her to wear socks in the first place. They weren't part of the prison uniform and therefore everyone's socks were to be confiscated. After that, we were only allowed to wear socks during sport. Most of the regulars then took up sport spasmodically in order to keep their socks, so they could still wear them to bed, in their rooms, or when decent screws were on.

One of the good officer then spoke to the superintendent direct and we were once again given permission to wear socks night and morning, except when visitors came across out of hours. We were thankful for the concession.

I have always felt the cold, and when winter came to Darwin, I almost froze. The temperature was between 33°C and 35°C (91°F and 95°F) during the middle of the day, but dropped down as low as 12°C (54°F) overnight with the wind chill lower at all times. The difference between the day and night temperatures meant I felt the cold more than ever as my body didn't acclimatise to the rapid change. We tried to shower before the sun went down or very shortly afterwards, so that the water was a little warmer (the last girl often got cold water as it was mainly solar heated). The decidedly nasty wind-chill factor didn't help in the draughty cells.

In order to keep warm, we would pull a blanket off our beds, double it over, wrap it around us like a sarong, and wander around in that. Sometimes the screws even wore parkas, with jeans on under their dresses, big socks, Ugg boots, and still had blankets wrapped around them when they were on midnight shift and thought no one was around. In the morning, of course, they wore the normal uniform, all longing to go home to warm up (and their office was centrally heated—trousers as part of the female officers' uniform were only introduced shortly before I left).

We were only supplied with two blankets, two sheets and a bedspread. For most of the time I was there, the bedspreads were thin terry-towelling, and completely ineffective for giving warmth. Mine was so threadbare, I could see through it. Occasionally, when there weren't many girls in the section, we had permission to get another blanket from one of the spare cells, but if extra girls came in, we had to give it back and then felt the cold worse than ever. Some screws used to take them from us for spite, saying, 'You've been stealing blankets. Two's the issue, that's it, now don't go stealing any more.' (They knew perfectly well you had been given the blanket though, otherwise they would have charged you for stealing, and they never did.)

There was always the problem of keeping the cell warm. I shut the bottom half of my outer window louvres, which helped keep out some of the draught. Most of the girls shut their top outer louvres as well, but it didn't make much difference as the wind whistled through the louvre cracks. I opened mine a *little* though, both for extra light and to prevent myself feeling so horribly claustrophobic (they were solid metal louvres), but I was still very cold, and had a lot of sleepless nights. Our inside louvres of course had to stay wide open at all times (except when you were actually on the toilet) for security. Shut or open, the wind just seemed to whistle around and come straight through my blankets.

One night, I was watching part of an old movie (we got lockup before it ended, as usual). A scene showed an old tramp stuffing newspaper up the legs of his pants, down his back and into his sleeves, before curling up on the park bench with a few more layers over him. I wondered if that really worked, and decided to try it. The next chance I had, I grabbed a newspaper before it went in the rubbish and took it down to my room (against the rules of course as I already had over the limit of books and mail in my room) and spread a layer two sheets deep between my blankets, with three sheets at the bottom where the wind came in worst. I tucked it all in, with my bedspread on top. It wasn't obvious and I had a warm night for the first time in ages. Thank God for old movies!

There was only one problem—it crackled shockingly. That initially kept me awake, but the warmth and my tiredness soon overcame that, and I fell into a dead sleep. I got up much refreshed the next morning, with lots of energy. For a couple of weeks I really enjoyed life, then Duckie said to me, 'Lindy, when we go past your cell, if you move, you rattle. Why does your bed rattle?'

I said hoping to put her off, 'What do you mean it rattles? Maybe it's got a screw loose!'

She said, in a puzzled tone, 'No, it's a funny noise, as if you were sleeping on paper.' Of course, I burst out laughing.

She said, 'Well, what's funny?'

I knew she was OK and wouldn't blast me so I said, 'Fair cop!' and told her it was newspaper.

She asked, 'Why? Do you have a hole in your bed?'

I didn't follow that reasoning, but merely said, 'No. It's warmer. Go and have a look.'

She thought I was having her on so went to look. When she came back, she said, 'That really works? Are you *that* cold?'

I said, 'I'm really *that* cold. I was freezing, and now I'm getting a good sleep.'

She said, 'Oh well, good on you, go for it.' I asked whether I would get into trouble and she said, 'If they don't inspect the beds in the morning, you'll be fine. If somebody does hassle you now, you can tell them I have given you permission.' (She was the second senior officer.) For the rest of that winter and the next, I kept newspaper down my bed and stayed warm.

I had an old innerspring mattress. When I went into prison it was fairly bad, but I learned to sleep between the springs. Because it was so old and I was overweight when I first went in, the bed continued to deteriorate quite quickly. Fortunately I lost weight in a hurry, because I had to sleep with my hip between two springs, my shoulder between another two springs, and if I lifted my knee up on one side I was able to put both legs down without springs sticking into them as well.

The security cell had a good mattress in it, until it was ripped and torn up by a temporary resident on a rampage. That was rather a waste because it was a much better mattress than many of us had. One of the girls decided to throw tantrums until she got a better mattress. As soon as she did, I grabbed her old one and almost had it in my cell when a new girl came in, and it had to be used for her.

I had my old mattress for another eighteen months, at the end of which time I was getting desperate. I had managed to get an extra blanket or two and had folded them up under my mattress to help fill some of the vacuum in the middle where the stuffing had disintegrated and left the springs digging up. I couldn't put the blankets on the top because they would have been visible and I would have had them confiscated, that would still have had the same effect and stopped the springs digging in so badly. Even then the bed was extremely uncomfortable. I had asked several times for a replacement but always had to wait. So had Smiley, whose mattress was almost as bad. By then I had been in prison over two years and knew the ropes much better. I was aware that when the chief went on holidays and we had an acting chief on duty, they would order things not normally ordered seeing they were only in that position temporarily and didn't have to answer for it later. They could always plead ignorance. It worked extra well when there was a relief supply officer on as well. Things our section had been told hadn't come in would then turn up.

Del, hearing that the supply officer had gone on holidays, complained about her mattress to Duckie the acting chief. When told it wasn't that bad, she threw a tantrum, so her mattress was inspected. They realised it wasn't very good, and a replacement was ordered. When I heard about her mattress, which was one of the best in the place, I decided it was time that I said something again too. I told Duckie I thought some of the other mattresses should be inspected, too, and suggested she go around the various rooms and check out *all* the beds.

One of the other girls, hearing the conversation, promptly told her Del had one of the *best* mattresses in the section so Duckie agreed to my suggestion, and asked me to show her what we considered the worst mattresses to be. I took her down and showed her a couple of them, which she didn't like at all, then when we got down to Smiley's bed and she leaned over to feel it I playfully pushed her onto it. She got the full effect of the springs, as Smiley did. She jumped up in a hurry, pronounced it *awful* and agreed it should be thrown out.

She said, 'OK, I can get four mattresses. You pick out the four worst ones, and we'll replace them. No, I'll do it, because I hear you have one of them.'

She did the full rounds then, inspecting everything. When she came to my room she took a look at my mattress, and said, 'I'm not going to even sit on yours. I can see how bad it is from here.' When I pulled the blankets out from underneath, she said, 'Don't. I don't want to see it. How ever could you sleep on that?'

I just looked at her.

She said, 'Yes, well, we won't discuss that.'

By that afternoon I had a new mattress and the following morning Smiley and two other girls did too. Del missed out and threw an absolute mickey. She stormed into the office, and had a yelling match with Duckie; Duckie won. Del then came out to have a go at me. Duckie, seeing Del's direction, forestalled her and told her to keep away from me or she would be put on lockup. If she had any complaints she could sleep on my old mattress for a night and then maybe she would keep her mouth shut, because she (Del) was a spoilt little brat and Duckie was getting sick of her tantrums. Del then had to wait several more weeks before any more new mattresses arrived.

Sleeping on my brand new foam mattress that night was absolute bliss. I could hardly believe that anything could be so soft. I had always hated foam mattresses before because of the way they heat up underneath you, but even that was preferable to having springs digging into me. In winter the extra heat would help compensate for lack of blankets. The mattress was so strange and new that I kept waking up all through the night. For weeks when I went into my room and sat down, its luxurious softness continued to surprise me. I remember one night I got up to go to the toilet and had been sleeping so well on that mattress that I was still half asleep. When I sank into bed again, with nothing poking into my bones, it was like being given a thousand- dollar bonus. That mattress was better than any birthday present I have ever been given.

Once Duckie had started investigating, she decided a lot of our bedding could go for rags. She ordered new bedspreads for the whole section to replace the very thin, mended ones most had. I had been guarding mine very carefully, hand-washing it in case it went into holes as most of the others had done. One girl even had a blue one mended with orange patches! If we wanted anything extra that was nice in our rooms, we had to make it (after gaining the usual limited permission of course). A number of the girls made patchwork floor mats for themselves out of the Christmas sewing scraps. I never desired to feel that permanent, but as girls left they handed their mats on to their friends. I was offered a number and had gradually collected some that went well together.

When the bedspreads came across Duckie offered me first choice as I was the oldest and had helped her with the ordering. There was one brown one among the blue and pink ones. Even though blue was one of my favourite colours, to be different would be great and the brown would go with the cream cell walls and olive green shelving and doors. The brown plastic stool I had been allotted was almost the same colour and my mats toned as well. What a change to have something remotely pleasing to the eye instead of a conglomerate hotchpotch.

The other two girls who had been there long term were allowed to choose their bedspreads also, then I was given the rest to dole out, and there were enough to put matching bedspreads on the top and bottom bunks of each cell except one so that the whole section then looked reasonably decent. We also acquired new sets of sheets, pillowcases and towels, all of which went into the storeroom (but we had other plans for them).

Wonder of wonders, we also received summer brunchcoats! A new rule was made: when we showered after dinner, we could put on our nightwear and housecoats and wear them when we came up to the day room. Before that (we had to shower quite some time before lockup) we had to put our uniforms on over our nighties unless we stayed in our cells. This meant we either put the smelly uniform we had worn all day back on or we put on our clean uniform for the next day. In the latter case it would be wrinkled for parade in the morning and that was also frowned upon.

We hung our towels and uniforms in our cell wardrobe. Each wardrobe had a hanging bar across it, but no coat hangers (they were considered a dangerous weapon). Some of the girls made makeshift hangers by rolling up a magazine, then tying it around the middle with wool and attaching it to the bar. Some even covered their 'hangers' with material, making them look reasonably fancy. The other alternative, which I chose, was to throw the uniform straight across the bar so it would sit nice and flat, placing my towel next to it.

In the wet the humidity prevented the towels drying quickly, and they were often still on the clothes line when we came in to shower for lunch after gardening, so temporary 'gardening' towels were issued and our own towels dried in time for the evening shower. Many of us used our towel in the evening, hung it up overnight to dry, used it for our morning shower and then wiped the shower down with it afterwards before sending it to the daily washing. That saved scrubbing the shower out again later, and it always looked clean and tidy. The towels did wear out quicker, though.

As soon as a good screw came on, we would tell them our towel was getting a bit thin and ask if we could swap it for one of the new ones. One by one we got the new towels and the thinner ones went back in the storeroom, to be issued to new girls or as gardening towels.

One weekend, Lena hurt her upper back slightly. She went to the office and asked for some liniment to rub into her shoulder, which she wanted Duckie to rub in for her. Duckie refused, telling her she had to administer her own medicine or go across to sister. With bad grace, Lena took the liniment and Froggie offered to rub it in for her. Lena was standing fully clothed at the *door* of her cell with her uniform neck slightly dropped. Froggie (a nursing aid) was standing outside, rubbing the ointment on Lena's shoulder, when Duckie came down and 'caught' them. She really ripped strips off them, saying there was a rule against 'this sort of thing'. She didn't mean rubbing ointment into someone's back; she was referring to lesbian activities. How she could interpret what Froggie was doing as lesbian, I don't know, but Lena knew the inference and snapped back at Duckie, 'How the fuck do you think I'm going to fucking well rub the fucking stuff into my own fucking back when I can't even fucking well get round there and fucking reach it, seeing I have fucking hurt the fucking bastard?'

Then they were both yelling at each other. Duckie walked off, telling Lena she was going to be charged for swearing. Lena answered back and Duckie promptly locked Lena in, then walked off. Lena called out after her, 'Oh, go fuck a duck! I'd get more sense out of a brick wall.'

Duckie turned around and, much to the amusement of all the girls who were now listening and watching, said, 'Oh, go fuck a duck yourself!' Officers were not supposed to use bad language, and could be charged for it too. Lena was duly charged for swearing and insolence, as well as having someone doing the wrong thing in her cell with the ointment. She spent a couple of days on lockup.

Froggie was called in. She was given a warning about such activities and told very nicely that, although she'd had nurse's training, she was not to practise it. That was what sister was for (despite the fact that it happened at the weekend, sister was off duty, and there was no way she would come in for that. She even changed the doctor's instructions at times if she felt like it, and you had no recourse for complaint about it because you couldn't see the doctor without her permission. If she said no, even over the phone without seeing you, you couldn't get near the doctor.) So Froggie said very demurely, 'Yes, sir.' She came out laughing. It showed how stupid and out of proportion some things could become in prison.

Detect(ive)able Brutality, An' All God's Chillun

One day a new girl was brought in; it was quite obvious she had been injured. Her head was bruised and her arm obviously sore. We supposed that she had been picked up for street fighting. The nursing sister was brought across to check her out and, from the conversation we could hear, the girl had been bashed, had concussion, bruises and a bad arm. The prison, of course, had to make an immediate report on her condition in case they were later accused of inflicting the injuries themselves. The girl later told us that the cops had kicked and bashed her at the cop shop when she was picked up for questioning. This was not uncommon for those who were picked up continually.

When Shelion's Darwin term ended and she was to be extradited to Queensland, she was terrified of being bashed on the way as she was still recovering from a recent operation, and was very tender in the stomach. Because of this she was very careful to have a medical examination before she left, and I understand she made arrangements for her lawyer to travel with her on the plane, at her own expense. The medical report was to go separately, and a doctor meet and accompany her into custody at the other end, to ensure no possibility of 'accidental' bashing. Parts of the body like limbs and faces are usually not touched as they are too visible. Bodies, therefore, are fair game—and she'd been there before.

After breakfast on her departure day she said her goodbyes apart from the final wave, then went to pack while we all went about our normal work. Everyone was miserable to see her go because she was a lot of fun. We were all friends now, and it wasn't as if she was going home and we could be glad for her. Extradition to where she was going meant more charges (her *one* charge turned into *ninety* odd when she arrived there!), so we weren't rejoicing. We knew she'd really set the law and cops alight down there in the past. They wouldn't forget her in a hurry.

I was cleaning my toilet and hand basin when a shadow fell across the wall. Shelion was standing directly behind me. As we were forbidden to be in each other's cells, I knew she had something she wanted to say to me alone. She was obviously finding it very difficult to speak, and finally said,

'I just want to wish you well and thank you for everything you've done. I would've liked very much to have got to know you before. I'm just ashamed that I listened to what others said about you and let myself be influenced instead of making my own mind up, like I normally do. I'd like to be able to stand up for you, but in the circles I'm in, they wouldn't understand. I can't. I hope you understand. I realise you shouldn't be here, and I want to wish you all the best. I wish I had your guts.' Near to tears, she bolted for the door. I was so taken aback I hadn't said a word and I didn't have a chance to speak to her later. I was impressed, as I knew what courage it had taken for her to say that, but I also felt sad for her. She was an obvious leader in her group, and yet she was so afraid of the opinions and the pressure of her peer group that she was fearful to say what she believed when it was not popular.

Some months later I had an inter-prison letter from her. She reiterated what she'd said before. She also said she had never thought much about Christianity, but she wished that she had some of what I had and, although she did not believe in God at all, she admired my faith and wished she had something like that to hold on to. She stated further that, much to her surprise, when she got back to Brisbane, her family had come to meet her, and her brother, who ruled the family with a fairly iron hand (despite their very individual lifestyles), had said how he fought for me and how much he thought I'd been wronged. Once she got over the shock of hearing that, she told him with delight that she agreed. Only then did she feel free to say openly what she felt.

Shelion was one of the tougher girls in the Brisbane prison (she had spent some years in there before, and her reputation was well known, with a multi-state history of drugs, robbery, violence, prostitution and forgery in the past), but she gradually discovered that every girl she met this time with whom she felt some empathy was a Christian. She started to investigate what made these girls different from the others. Gradually her way of thinking and lifestyle started to change. One day, I received another letter from her telling me she had become a Christian and thanking me for starting her thinking along those lines.

We kept in contact occasionally. Shelion moves around and I have no idea what her lifestyle is now, as we have unfortunately lost touch. Often ex-prisoners find great difficulty in changing the way they live when released because of the pressure society puts on them. But I know that, although she may not share the same background as the average orthodox Christian, and even if she resumed her former lifestyle, she has a private understanding with God.

Shelion, Lena, Del, Smiley and a number of others I met inside whose paths may not cross mine again have touched my life in various ways and will be remembered with affection. Our lives were similar for a time, and the bonding created then will remain. Although I may not agree with their lifestyles or activities, it helped me understand we are *all* God's children and I have no right to distinguish because of position, lifestyle, birth or trade, and that we should accept each other simply on the merits of what we *are*, not what others *think* we ought to be. Acceptance is something we all need. Often the lack of it drives people into desperate situations, causing them to do things they wouldn't normally do, if only somebody bothered to show them a little bit of love and human kindness.

Cuffs For A Dangerous Prisoner

My scalp had developed what initially looked like dandruff, but it later became itchy and looked like ringworm. It didn't matter how often I washed my hair, it was so itchy I felt like scratching till it bled. I was sent to the doctor who gave me something to put on it, to no avail. After a succession of products, none of which worked, he decided to send me to the skin specialist. That meant a trip to the hospital, which was a welcome change.

I had always thought a ride in one of those dog-boxes would be embarrassing; I'd seen prisoners in them and wasn't sure whether to wave or ignore them. I'd wave now as, having been in them myself, I know a ride in one is the only form of contact with the outside world you get, and is as good as going on a holiday or a picnic. We really enjoyed our trips, unless of course we were being brought to the prison in the first place! A visit to the dentist in town or to the hospital was quite something.

There was a new rule (due to the recent Gun Point prison farm escape and bashing) that handcuffs should be worn at all times during an escort from the section to wherever you were going. They would be removed ('at the officer's discretion') at the destination and replaced for the return trip. This seemed a bit odd; if you were going to escape, you would usually find it easiest at your destination among other people. But it was novel and most of the girls thought it a real hoot.

The handcuffs were put on and I climbed into the back of the van. Travelling along I discovered I could take them off without any trouble. If I was seen with the cuffs off, I could be charged for trying to escape. On the other hand, if they were just on my wrists but not fastened, the officer would be unlikely to notice. I hadn't seen that male screw before, so I left them draped over my wrists. As I climbed out at the hospital I said to Sunshine, 'Do you want some handcuffs?'

She said, 'Oh yes, just hang on and I'll get the key.'

I said, 'I don't think you need the key, you forgot to lock them.' Startled, she glanced at the male screw who wasn't attending, then grinned, 'Oh well, you didn't need them on in the first place. Here, give me them quick before he sees,' nodding to the male screw. She grabbed them, put them into her pocket, and off we went. On the way home we were still giggling about it, but she made sure she locked them properly this time as he *wasn't* a good screw.

The prescription I was given on that trip to the specialist didn't help my scalp condition and I had to go back again. This time, I had a rookie who had just finished her probation and was now allowed to do escorts on her own. She was very nervous, not quite sure of all the rules, and hadn't done an escort to the hospital before. When we got there, she asked me what to do with the handcuffs. I asked her what she meant, and she said, 'Well, do you walk into the hospital with them on; that's embarrassing! Do I take them off, or do I have to leave them on?' I thought that leaving them on would be interesting, but decided to leave the decision entirely up to her.

Mr Schubert was on escort with her. I had got to know him a bit, because he had been the male officer on hospital day shift when Kahlia was born. He was watching this little exchange from a distance with some amusement, his eyes twinkling because *he* knew that I knew perfectly well what happened to the handcuffs. The rookie asked him, 'What do I do?' He looked at me and then at her and (with a very straight face) said, 'Well, it's up to you. She's your prisoner, you're in charge, do whatever you think.' One word from either of us and the cuffs would have been smartly removed. Usually the cuffs were only left on when that prisoner was considered a 'runner', violent or dangerous. Mr Schubert obviously decided not to point this out to the rookie so the three of us walked solemnly into the hospital with me handcuffed. The locals were used to escorted prisoners, but handcuffed ones were uncommon and a signal to beware. I knew my physical appearance was now so different I was unrecognisable, so this could be amusing.

We went in the back way, and initially saw very few people. Once we got inside, however, and started going through the outpatients department, the number of people in the corridors and waiting rooms dramatically increased. They were craning their necks or surreptitiously trying to step out of the direct path of the 'dangerous' criminal being brought through. The rookie was aware of this, too, and, feeling very embarrassed, she said, 'Look, umm, I've got your file here. Would you like to hold it over the handcuffs? Or I'll . . . I'll take my jacket off, and you can carry that.' Mr Schubert was still playing deaf, but judging by the quirk of his mouth and the twinkle in his eye when the rookie wasn't looking, he was hugely enjoying the joke, as I was. I said to her, 'Why? Are you ashamed of your job?'

'No! No.'

'Well, what's the problem? It's me wearing the cuffs, not you and I don't care.' She blushed and said if I wasn't embarrassed it was OK. To watch the reactions of people I managed to scratch my head and nose as much as possible to make the handcuffs clank and jangle. No doubt about it; everyone was trying to keep out of our way, eyes lowered as we passed, but openly staring once we'd gone by. When we entered the waiting room, people took one furtive look and then continued what they were doing, studiously ignoring us. My looks were obviously no longer notorious.

I find it odd that if you are a criminal or regarded as one, you suddenly become socially 'unclean'. Juries with guilty verdicts are the same. You suddenly become an object of awe and *persona non grata*. I found it hilarious to think that a 155 centimetre, 44 kilogram (5 foot 1 inch, 98 pound) woman could be considered enough of a threat to make anyone wary.

I saw the specialist while still wearing my handcuffs. When I attempted to comb my hair after he had studied my scalp again (it was decided my scalp problem was stress-related having tried umpteen remedies to no avail), the rookie decided I couldn't possibly do my hair in handcuffs. She removed them and replaced them (incorrectly) after I had combed my hair. While giving me instructions, the nurse leaned over and whispered, 'What's with her and the handcuffs?' I answered softly with a big grin, 'She's a rookie; doesn't know any different.' The answering grin said it all.

We went back to the vehicle and I hopped in. As Mr Schubert was locking me in the back, he said, 'You little devil!' I quietly showed him the loose handcuffs. She had forgotten to tighten them. He raised his eyes heavenward and walked off whistling. As I was let out of the vehicle back at the section, I said to her, 'Oh, by the way.

Next time you handcuff somebody and leave the handcuffs on, you'll have to learn how to do it.' Whereupon I handed them to her, swinging. The look on her face was extremely comical. Mr Schubert burst out laughing then, and she realised he was all right. If he hadn't been safe, I wouldn't have done it, but seeing the expression on his face and on hers was worth it.

That night my mail contained a letter from Michael saying Kahlia was running out of clothes. I found that difficult to believe because she'd had such a large wardrobe when I left, however, I started to sew. I made two dresses an evening for several days, then had an evening doing the finishing touches. I put in a request form to send a parcel out and when it was OK'd I rushed around doing a few extras—shirts for the boys' birthdays, some Hobbytex mats for relatives and a stuffed grandma doll based on our Christmas sewing patterns for Kahlia's birthday. I was even allowed to hand the latter over in person.

I had several pieces of material with me and a number of others sent in from various people to make dresses for Kahlia. One piece was a stiff- looking, plain black, but little of it. I wasn't sure what to do with it, until I was sent some beautiful white guipure lace. Immediately I decided—it should be a roaring twenties style, with lace around the bottom of double- tiered frills, dropped waist with a tie, plain top, and round neck edged with lace. I set to work and cut it out. I had some black silk, which I used for the wide drop waist tie with bow front. It looked lovely—simple yet stunning.

When I showed the black dress to Michael among the others I had made, he nearly had a fit. Not another black dress!

I said, 'She's bigger, she's not a baby any longer. Little kids wear black, it's fine.' The next day Kahlia visited, with Michael carrying the offending dress in a plastic bag for her to change into so I could see it. She wanted to keep it on, but Michael refused point blank. Her other dresses were worn, but the black dress hung in the cupboard.

The family came up three times a year (in each holiday period) and Michael occasionally had an extra legal visit of an hour or two. All in all I saw the children twelve to sixteen hours per year. I also rang when I could as we were allowed to request a half-hour reverse-charge phone call once a month if we behaved. The calls were monitored, so you could not talk freely. I found this artificial and frustrating.

Later I wrote of Kahlia's reception of her doll:

> She has also acquired her birthday present at last from me—a rag grandma doll—plaited bun, glasses, cap, apron, and long-sleeved frock and knickers. It's almost as tall as she is. Her eyes opened wide when she saw it. She has changed quite a bit since last time. When she walked in the door it was like seeing my old baby snaps go colour and come to life, only she was a little fatter. It was quite an incredible feeling. I guess it's like seeing your own child the way a stranger does. Quite the oddest sensation.

On the first set of visits Kahlia would only watch me from a distance. She would not talk to or approach me. On the second occasion, she was a little older. Jenny had been telling her for weeks that they were going to have a special visit with her *very own* mummy who loved her *very* much. This time we managed to break the ice on the first visit.

Later in my letter I wrote:

> Dear 'Mummy Jenny' told my little Princess that "'Mummy Lindy' has sore lips—better kiss them better." Kahlia [during the visit] eyed me very seriously, then said, 'Yas' and very gently kissed me better. She promptly decided 'Kahlia has sore lips too', and I had better reciprocate! [I found it extremely hard to wait patiently for her to make the first move and not rush her. She later crawled onto my lap of her own free will and stayed there.] Jen told me she got quite excited each time they turned the corner and she would announce, 'Go see Mummy'. Aidan managed to get the measles while he was here, so missed a couple of visits. Reagan's eye doesn't give him so many headaches now, although bright light is still painful. Legally he is blind in his right eye now, but it appears he has a small percentage [under ten per cent] of peripheral vision.

When Jenny and Wayne had moved north for Wayne's master's degree, Dr Owen and Jan Hughes became Kahlia's second set of foster parents. They had two girls and four boys of their own. As they were also locals (Owen was head of the education department at Avondale College), Kahlia was still able to be near her father and brothers. The change once again was traumatic for all of us. Both foster mums had cork boards with my letters and photograph on it, so she knew she was loved and owned by a 'real' mum as well.

On a much later visit, when Kahlia was about two, she came in with her hands behind her back. I sensed something was afoot. Before she said hello, she whipped a small hairbrush from behind her back and said, 'Whose is dis?'

Ah! So I was to be tested. I explained how I'd bought it for Aidan. 'See the "A" on the back?'

Reagan had then inherited it, and now it was hers.

'Yas,' she nodded delightedly and went back to her brothers who were waiting at a distance. I saw them go into a huddle and heard one of them say, 'See, I told you mummy would know.' Kahlia's head nodded with excitement.

'What was that all about?' Michael asked me. I told him I figured I'd just passed the test.

He replied blankly, 'Oh, they didn't say anything to me about that.' Later Aidan told me my suspicions were correct. It didn't take long after that for Kahlia to regularly call me mummy of her own volition. Jan was really pleased as she had managed to get her to say 'Aunty Jan' now she was a little older too. But Mummy Jenny was always her special mum and it took Jenny several more years to get her to say 'Aunty Jenny'. Kahlia knows she has a ready welcome at either home whenever she wants it from her two special mums, two special dads, five special sisters and five special brothers. They all loved and cared for her as their own and couldn't have treated her better. She happily boasts now that not many kids have *three mums* and *three dads* (1988) and no less than twelve brothers and sisters. She has even been flower-girl for one of her foster brothers since, and is twice an important 'aunty' now!

Storming Around Tropical Style

It always made me nervous when the family visited during cyclone weather. I didn't want them caught in a cyclone. We had been waiting for days to see whether one would come. Nothing happened, the family left, and I breathed a sigh of relief. Then we were told to batten everything down, move the pot plants and chairs and put them away inside because the wind was coming again after all. We moved everything in a hurry and when lockup time came we went to bed. Nothing happened; the cyclone had gone elsewhere.

Then one night I was jogging a little later than usual at sunset. It somehow looked different. We'd had no warnings, but I instinctively knew a cyclone was coming. The sky stayed a peculiar midnight azure blue—the colour, I imagined, of a polar night. I said to Smiley, 'We will get a cyclone tonight.' She agreed. She mentioned it to one of the screws, who said, 'Oh Smiley, you and your things. No, it's fine.'

The wind started to get a little stronger but still no one worried and the peculiar colour of the night remained. It was lockup time, and the section settled quickly. Smiley had smiled conspiratorially on the way to her room and said, 'Cyclone come, you watch 'im.' As usual I was studying late, and as I watched, the trees started to bend violently while the wind increased. The bending gum trees formed a long row of dramatic arches. I thought they would snap. The thunder rolled in, with sheet and fork lightning. It was frightening yet magnificent, like time-lapse photography: dark, then a great light in the sky and everything was green; dark again, then another flash and everything was pink, orange and yellow—colours of the sunset. You could smell the sulphur, it was so close.

They should have listened to Smiley. The Aboriginal girls always knew. Now the midnight screw had to move all the loose items herself. She locked all the windows inside, and came around to check on the girls. Most of them were still asleep. She told me a cyclone was coming through, but it wouldn't hit us for several hours; we were presently getting the side winds. It was a strange feeling of excitement, fear, and elation. There was nothing more to see outside. There was a limit to the amount of water I could watch hit the grass and go down the drain on the inside of the section, so I decided to try to sleep. Presumably if it got worse, we would be taken over to the cyclone section on the other side. I got a little sleep, but decided I was more interested in watching the storm. When it grew worse, the screw ventured out again to check on the girls. Checks were less frequent in that violent weather, as nobody in their right mind would escape; more likely they would be frightened to death.

Sure enough, many of the girls were too frightened to stay in their cells alone, and were allowed to pair up for company during what was left of the night. By this time it was nearly 3 a.m.; we didn't have watches, but we could guess the time fairly accurately by the number of times the screw came around usually.

A lot of the girls had water running down the walls of their cells. We soon discovered the cells that leaked and those with uneven floors. As long as I stayed near my bed, my cell was dry. I figured I wouldn't be electrocuted even though I had to wade through a pool in one part of my room. The cell next door to me was nearly 5 centimetres (2 inches) underwater, and water was flowing out under the door. I decided that, if it got really bad, I would grab my mattress, jam it into the small space between the toilet and the wall and crawl in there. It was the most secure place and furthest away from the wind, and if the walls fell down, I would have the mattress and toilet to protect me. I had put my Bible, photograph album, some crocheting and a couple of letters in a plastic bag, and I intended to grab them if necessary.

The wind got wilder. I thought the cyclone must shortly reach its peak. Then it settled down and got really quiet for a while. When the screw came around again I asked her when the cyclone was due to hit us. She said, 'I think we are in the middle of it. It's not much of a cyclone.' Sure enough, that was it. There was more wind but the cyclone had moved on. The tail- end wind after the eye wasn't so strong. By morning there was very little to see except wet, sodden grass, and tired girls. But the cyclone gave us something different to talk about. That in itself was a change.

I discovered that on 15 February 1985 my mother wrote to Marshall Perron, the Northern Territory Attorney-General requesting that I be allowed day release for church privileges. It was for three meetings, which meant nearly all day! I was amused. Of course, they said no, but at least she tried. I was even more amused when I found out the quote she wrote on the top of that letter (something she always does on the top of her letters), but I don't know what Marshall Perron thought when he read:

> Watch your step—I have not appointed you—God has; and He will stand beside you and help you give justice in each case that comes before you. Be very much afraid to give any other decision than what God tells you to. For there must be no injustice among God's judges, no partiality, no taking of bribes . . . You are always to act in the fear of God with honest hearts.

I hope it made him pause and at least think of the responsibility his office had. Well, there was no harm in trying, but they weren't going to give an inch.

Finally, after trying to make *me* say I *wouldn't* see anyone, I managed to force the authorities into letting me do two interviews in an attempt to 'stir the pot' a bit more. It was finally agreed I could do an interview with Ita Buttrose without photos. She had the metal detector put over her before she was allowed in! The authorities were paranoid that somebody might be able to record *them* without their knowledge (mind you, it was all right if they did it to somebody else). Ita said that in all her years as a journalist she had never had that treatment before, and was quite amazed by it. The authorities monitored the interview closely.

One day a normally fairly reserved male chief was doing relief duty in the female section. When I was called into the office for something it came as a surprise when he suddenly said, 'I understand you are doing an interview with Frank Alcorta.' (A local Northern Territory reporter.)

I said, 'Yes.'

He expressed his concern. I thanked him, then said, 'I decided, because of his standing here and his position with the local paper, it's time I got some information across.' He looked at me with a little bit of a twinkle in his eye and said, 'Fair enough.' It was obvious that he was no longer worried.

When I did the interview a number of weeks later none of Ita's treatment was repeated. In fact, for part of the time he was there, they didn't even monitor the visit. It showed the great difference between the way they treated their cronies and anyone else. The published report turned out to be accurate and friendly.

At each stage we seemed to get an inkling of where the media interest was leading. During the first inquest a number of people commented they wouldn't be surprised if our story was turned into a movie. It had all the elements: religion, a small baby, a mother, hostile public rumours, Aborigines, the Outback, and the courts. It was obvious the basis was there if somebody was interested, but it really seemed to have an unreal element about it. Things settled down but occasionally we were still asked if anyone was going to make a movie. We just shrugged our shoulders. It seemed irrelevant. Then the case was reopened with the second inquest, and people, particularly reporters, started to talk freely about it having all the elements of a drama once more. Throughout the trial reporters and others were seriously saying, 'They will have to make a movie out of this—somebody will grab it.'

Hard Labour Made Easy

At all times Helena had the ability to look as if butter wouldn't melt in her mouth. She thought and acted quickly, and she had the ability to come out with an answer that sounded totally plausible, given a second's notice. She could lie with a straight face (you had to know her extremely well before you could tell whether she was lying or whether she was telling you the truth). Fortunately, most of the time she chose to tell the truth, but because it was usually outrageous, nobody believed her anyway. She had one major saving grace; if she was caught red-handed, she would not bother to deny it. She'd say: 'Right, I did it. Fair cop. That's it.' She was never upset by a fair cop, but if she had been set up or dealt with unfairly, whoever had done it would be well advised to look out.

While Helena was in prison, it seemed she spent more time in solitary and on lockup than the rest of the girls combined. She regularly answered back, was insubordinate, or mocked the officers. Punishing her was a problem. She would do whatever she liked, and there was no way to curb her activities. The screws discovered that, if they put her on lockup, she loved it, spending her time sleeping and writing poems.

They would take her pencil and paper away and she'd still write poetry, producing it after she got out; and they had no idea where her paper and pencil had come from. She never ran out of cigarettes, and they could not figure that out either as she was only allowed two a day, but she seemed to be chain-smoking. They could smell the cigarettes but could never catch her smoking. (One time when they body-searched her, she had cigarettes in the hem of her dress, but they were not found. Often cigarettes sat in full view along the grooves in her steel louvres, but still the screws missed them in the daily cell search. She loved seeing them miss the obvious.)

Shelion and I had been asked to dig out the storm water drain at the back of the section and make a crazy rock wall, using rocks gathered by the guys, which we cemented together. (There's a good bit of the gold off my wedding ring in that, too.

At that stage it was jammed on so tightly it wouldn't come off, and you try cementing with bare hands, without a trowel or gloves. Cement is a *great* hand lotion!) We had finished one of the two sides. Every time it rained, the hoses were running or it was windy, the soft dirt and sand we had dug out and threw up over the top would pour down into the drain again. The drain itself badly needed attention; weeds grew on the bottom. Although there was concrete under part of it, every time there was rain, up to 15 centimetres (6 inches) of sand and dirt would be left on the bottom. We spent a lot of time cleaning out the drains.

It was decided to make Helena build the rest of the drain on her own as punishment. She was to spend most of the day out there. It got very hot and the work was hard, but she loved it, in fact, she revelled in it. The officer who was supposed to watch her work got frazzled in the sun as Lena grew browner and fitter as the days went by. Soon she not only requested to go out earlier (rushing through her morning job to get out there, and coming in at the very last minute in the afternoon), but when she was called on report again at the end of her punishment to see how she'd gone, she requested she be given another week in the drain, because she wanted to finish it! That was the end. The screws could not believe she wanted to do such a terrible job. They gave up and let her.

When she played up after that, they'd say, 'I'm not putting you on report. I know you like lockup; I refuse to do it.' So if she felt like playing up—she did. The screws weren't game to leave her out or lock her in. She wanted to do the drain, and if they put her on that for punishment, they were giving her the very thing that she liked. How do you punish a girl like that? They took her things away and she seemed to get them anyway. 'No problem!' was her favourite saying. Let's face it, if you've got nothing in the first place, you can have nothing taken from you. She'd been on report so often that she went for months with nothing in her cell, it didn't seem to worry her—she enjoyed those times, and got to finish the drain!

Lena decided to do her part for my cause. Having decided long ago not to murder me after all, she got Medic, one of the older prisoners in at the time, to help her write an open letter to the press on her observations of me as a prisoner. She said she had 'grown to love and respect this woman', and said 'her stronger character attracts all the female prisoners who have failed in society and have weaker characters themselves'. Moreover, she added that I had become 'a guiding influence and my adviser to help me step into maturity'. She also wrote the Queen a copy of her original letter. She was refused permission to send the letters. They went to Correctional Services head office, then to the Government Minister, and all along the line they said *no*. She was officially told it was considered too dangerous, but was privately advised that if she felt so strongly she should smuggle the letters out. She did, adding a separate note stating her objection to being refused permission to write freely to her Queen! Friends duplicated the letter and sent it on to all the Parliamentarians. It also appeared in the newspapers later on.

Naturally, the Correctional Services Department in Darwin said that Helena's conduct in smuggling the letters out would be investigated and she would be disciplined. Tapioca himself *censored* the replies from the various *Parliamentarians.*

It seemed that Helena's conclusion in her first letter was correct: 'I don't think they want people to know the truth and want all to stay ignorant on this matter.'

On 13 November, in response to the growing public storm, Senators Gareth Evans and Peter Durack, who were both former Attorneys-General, publicly called for my release. Immediately, Stuart Tipple applied to the Northern Territory again for me to be released on licence.

I received a couple of phone calls from home, one during Kahlia's third birthday party, another one just before Christmas. Everyone was as high as a kite. The adults were too excited about the possibility of my coming home, I could tell. Although they were saying they were calm for my sake, they had thrown caution to the wind and had no intention of being calm. I found myself trying to calm them down, trying to tell them not to get too disappointed if it didn't work out. I was afraid for the children; I knew another disappointment would hit them very hard, and local rumours were again saying the answer was *no*.

Sending Evil Angels Flying

Then the press, which had been diligently covering everything (of course), really got into the act. When John Bryson's book, *Evil Angels*, was published by Penguin at the end of 1985, it gave a more intelligent analysis of the evidence at the trial than the public had had so far, plus the few things that had been made public since. By then we had been approached once or twice by Australian filmmakers about the possibility of doing a movie, and always we had replied, 'When this is over, come back and ask again. Right now we don't think it is the right time.'

Now we were approached again and this time we thought seriously about it because we thought it might help towards clearing our names and getting a commission started. Stuart said an English producer, Verity Lambert, had contacted him, but I still didn't want to have any contact personally.

I said, 'Look, tell her to put it on paper—and put it away for future reference.' But she was persistent, and then we heard she was buying the rights to John Bryson's book. That made us think seriously about it. She could make a movie with or without our permission like anybody else who had already written books—they simply did it. According to the public, that *is* your life story then, whether you like it or not, and we would have to live with it. I knew if she did that book, the court scenes were so comprehensive everybody would think that was all there was to know; and that was all the public would ever hear about what had really happened. Although a lot of his book was good, if they used no other source material for the movie, that would be it. Nobody would ever have a second bite at the cherry and once again, *our* entire story would be left out of it.

Bryson, a Melbourne-based barrister and author, had been covering my case for years. I remembered seeing him at the trial, head bent over his scribbling pencil.

Michael had spent half a day with John Bryson and I had only talked to him for one hour's visit in jail and knew that all I had managed to do was correct facts that I knew he would have wrong, because he had collected them from incorrect file footage. I pointed out problem areas and behind- the-scene implications and mentioned half a dozen things that were a burden on my heart because of the way they had been misrepresented continually. At the end of the hour he said that it had been very useful and that now he could go away and do the necessary research. He would actually have to rewrite a substantial amount and put it in the correct context.

When the book came out I was amazed at what he had written about the start of the Seventh-day Adventist church. I had understood that he had actually gone to Washington DC in the middle of winter and our church headquarters were shut because of snowdrifts, so he had to wait and return later to do his research. Whatever he managed to do, he finally wrote about William Miller and his 'Millerite' followers in 1844. They were First Day Adventists. Seventh-day Adventists actually weren't around at that stage. Their beginning was from three distinct groups from different areas, which eventually merged. In time the Seventh-day Adventist church was formed from the basis of those three amalgamated groups. Some of the former members of the Millerite movement later joined the new group. When I read what Mr Bryson said about the Millerites, equating them to Seventh- day Adventists, I thought, 'Goodness me, if this guy has got this much wrong, what in the hell is he going to say about our case?'

But on the case it was a different matter. Here it was accurate. He had done his research fairly well, although there were a few things that were wrong. I never could figure out, having actually been in a light, airy, cream painted room with fluorescent lighting that I had told him was similar to my cell, why he described my cell as being a dingy little room with a single electric light bulb hanging from the ceiling. What's more, he said I had scrawny fingers. Scrawny fingers! Mr Bryson, you watch out. I didn't think I was a bit scrawny. How would he have felt if I had described his bald pate?

Nevertheless, Bryson wrote a moving book, soon becoming a bestseller. *Evil Angels* was the focus for further public demands, led by the press, that my case must be reopened. It got so much publicity that Marshall Perron was stung into saying, 'I don't care what Mr Bryson or anybody else says.'

Well, obviously thousands—even millions according to Sir Reginald Sholl—did.

But it didn't have the ultimate effect this time. The Territory refused the application for my release on 25 November. Aidan was devastated and heartbroken, Reagan, as usual, noncommittal to others, and I spent my third Christmas in prison.

Individual local churches of my faith were tremendously supportive. I got cards signed by church groups and Pathfinder clubs; cards from children's Sabbath schools (like Sunday schools); letters and special projects from classes of Adventist schoolchildren; and dozens of letters from individual church members—people who were proud to say 'Lindy Chamberlain is one of us'. Occasionally I got a letter from our Division, assuring me that they were thinking of me. But the Division Headquarters was still different.

Our church officially and steadfastly refused to become involved in the public campaign, feeling that the case should be handled through the 'proper legal channels' without any extra pressure from them. Certainly they were still underwriting most of our legal expenses, but they refused to be more directly involved. The trouble, of course, was that they couldn't really stay apart because many people in the Australian community tended to be hostile to us because of our religion.

Where other churches and some Adventist churches had days of prayer, there was always the question: Why doesn't your church organise an Australia-wide day of prayer for your release? The only answer we ever got was that the church shouldn't take part in politics. This was political, and the church should be seen to take a back seat. Time and time again I wondered how, if that was so, they continued to guarantor us the money to fight. I couldn't help but wonder if they hadn't been bulldozed into it by Dr Magnusson that day in his office or later. Regardless of how it was done, we were grateful.

In fact, as the New South Wales Anti-Discrimination Board noted, our case 'had deleterious effects on [the church's] image in the eyes of the general public'.

It was not the church's case, of course, but the Seventh-day Adventist church was coming under a lot of pressure. I know that a number of our churches had had anti-Chamberlain graffiti written all over them and had had quite a problem getting it off. Some had garbage emptied all around their yards. Many had threatening phone calls. Early one morning, the caretaker of one of the Adventist institutions found beheaded animals on the front doormat. The south Queensland church convention ground had signs hung on the surrounding cyclone mesh fencing overnight. People arriving for church one Saturday morning were met with signs reading 'Dingo Fence'.

I wonder what would have happened if the church had taken our part more strongly, knowing us as they did, and also knowing that Seventh-day Adventists literally follow the Commandment that states: 'Thou shalt not kill'. This is why we usually choose to work as non-combatants in time of war, particularly as medical personnel. Adventists also do not believe in lying and cheating. It is a strong stand, but head office seemed determined to keep our beliefs off the record.

A number of times, our church members wanted to share in helping pay our legal costs. They felt that a lot of the rumours circulating around us arose simply because our church wasn't well known, so people considered that we were slightly weird. Over and over again we were confused with Jehovah's Witnesses, who don't believe in blood transfusions. We do; in fact, the Seventh-day Adventist church runs the largest private hospital system of any Protestant church in the world, second only to the Roman Catholic system.

Then there have been the rumours that we sacrifice our children. On the contrary, they are very important to us. The church runs modern private schools ranging from preschool education to doctorates. Once again this is second only to the Roman Catholic system worldwide. Our children come to our main church services, and to a person used to the quietness of a Catholic or Church of England service, it must seem very strange to walk into an Adventist church for the first time and hear the babble of young children, who sit and listen, play at their parents' feet, draw or whisper, as part of the family unit. Most of our churches even have a special story for the children as a regular part of the church service.

But the church steadfastly refused to oppose government authorities. Our church paper, the *Record*, said after the failure of the High Court appeal that 'the church must be seen as a body that supports and has confidence in the judicial system and in the authority invested in a democratically elected government and its officials and agencies. The church cannot, must not, dare not be seen as a body that challenges or defies judicial procedures or civil authority, or engages in any activity that appears to discredit that authority.'

Dr Norman Young, senior lecturer in the Avondale College theological department, said:

> Like most millennial groups, the Adventist church gives itself a central though unenviable role in the consummation of all things; it believes that it will finally become the unique focus of a united religio-political persecution. In the meantime the church is determined to do nothing either to deserve or precipitate this last- day holocaust, hence the church's conservative approach to the Chamberlain case.

A 'Lie' is Found

Part of my way of coping was to try and work my frustration off. I now did 5,000 pepper skips in under fifteen minutes, ending with double skips, and ran a minimum of 8 kilometres (5 miles) a night before doing at least half an hour of pushups, leg and stomach exercises (pity I'm not that fit just now).

I had just finished my jogging and exercise program, showered and settled in the day room with my tapestry, ready for the Monday evening news. We were all talking when I heard the headline words 'matinee jacket' and 'Ayers Rock' mentioned. We all pricked up our ears and everybody's attention focused on the news item. They were saying that what was thought to be Azaria's matinee jacket had been discovered at Ayers Rock. A young Englishman, David Brett, had been found at the base of the Rock several days after a fall, which had taken his life. The badly decomposed body had been severely damaged by animals—apparently the right arm had been chewed off by dingoes and goannas. The policeman in charge, Sergeant Van Heythuysen, roped off the area and called for volunteers to search for the missing parts of the body.

One of the volunteers on the Sunday was John Beasy who had been the mechanic in the garage at Ayers Rock in August 1980.

One hundred and fifty-three metres (170 yards) from the position where the rest of Azaria's clothes had originally been found, he discovered a piece of clothing protruding from the dirt. As he grabbed it and pulled it from the ground, he immediately recognised a dirty and bedraggled baby's matinee jacket. At the trial I had described Azaria's white Marquise matinee jacket, size 000, with a pale lemon edging. Remembering my description of the missing matinee jacket, he told the sergeant in charge (working next to him in the search line) that he thought he had found the Chamberlain jacket. John Beasy was apparently the only one in that whole lineup who had been involved in our case. Any other person finding the jacket would probably have assigned it to the growing heap of discarded clothing collected during the search. I think God was directing that particular man's search pattern.

The Crown had so instilled in people's minds that the jacket was only a lie, the sergeant had not realised that there was such an item missing. It was immediately isolated and later sent in to Alice Springs on 2 February 1986.

Having heard the internal talk about the jacket, a supportive person leaked the information of its finding to Mike Lester, whom the person had learned during the first inquest was a genuine and accurate reporter who would keep his word. Rather than just let us hear from the TV once more, Mike rang Michael to let him know but, failing to get through, contacted Stuart Tipple and informed him instead. We were then able to tell the Northern Territory we were aware of the find and wished to have the jacket identified (before it became mysteriously lost). Mike still got his exclusive as Channel 9 broke the story on the news that night.

Stuart had tried in vain to let me know about the finding before the public news but, as usual, had been unable to get through the red tape. It was not until Tuesday that Stuart was finally able to get through. He let me know the report was accurate, but we could not confirm that it was Azaria's jacket until I could view it for identification and he was busy arranging for this.

On Wednesday, I was asked to go to the Northern Territory police headquarters to see whether I could identify the jacket. Stuart and our own photographer, Les Smith, also came. Les was also the scientist who would be working on that material.

Even my escort this time interested me. I wasn't taken in the paddy wagon with the screws as usual. Mr Barrier from head office supplied his own car, and our chief Mrs Barham escorted me in the car. They would even have liked me to wear normal clothing, apparently, but hadn't thought quickly enough. Anybody else would have had to go in prison uniform. I didn't see why there should be any special privilege status. After all, I was only going to the Berrimah police station. There were elaborate security arrangements to enter the back gate, because the press had gathered at the front. As they were watching for a paddy van and not one of the normal, light-coloured cars, we drove unmolested to the back, the walkie-talkies notifying our progress. (We later returned to the prison in the same manner, despite the vigilance of the press.)

Inside I met Stuart who told me, out of the room, exactly what photographs Les needed for the rest of our scientists to start working. Les remained professionally aloof and didn't make any sign of recognition apart from saying, 'Good morning, Mrs Chamberlain'. Where the Northern Territory took a video of the whole event and also some still photography, Les went to some pains to get specific photographs with special lenses. When we went into the forensic examination room, Stuart said little. We were aware of the camera running, and we were keen not to give them the slightest indication of whether or not it was the jacket until we had elicited as much information as possible and seen what other damage there might be. They were being particularly fussy and were using white paper on the cadaver table and gloves for their hands. Only Sergeant Sandry was permitted to handle it. I wasn't allowed to touch the jacket because I might add damage to it. As they had maintained I damaged it in the first place, I really couldn't figure out why they would be worried about any more damage from me, especially in front of them, and on video! I was certainly not going to damage anything because I didn't want to disturb whatever dingo damage we could find.

I realised when I first looked at the jacket that it was indeed Azaria's jacket. If I had told the Northern Territory at that point they would have said immediately, 'Thank you very much' and whisked it away. We would not have seen it again for many months. We would have been unable to ascertain whether any further damage had been done later, or any material removed from it. We already knew it had been picked up by hand and pulled straight out of the ground, which would have disturbed evidence. It was obvious it hadn't been handled much more than that because it was very stiff, and no one was quite sure what was going to happen when it *was* handled.

After a good look at the front allowing Les to get plenty of pictures, I asked for it to be turned over. They went to a great deal more fuss, putting pieces of paper out to catch every little bit of dirt and filming all this, before turning the jacket over. As the outside of the jacket was much-weathered and faded, I needed to examine the cleaner inside area to look for any of the lemon edging for complete confirmation. The back was photographed, then it was turned inside out. I asked for it to be held up (so Les could get some long shots of it like that as well), then shots of it laid down. I could definitely see the yellow, and there was absolutely no doubt that it was the jacket Azaria had worn, but the top button was missing. We knew from the television that they had it, but it appeared that we weren't going to be shown the button. Stuart had told me before, 'Don't forget the button.' I approached Stuart and tried to whisper to him that it was definitely the jacket. I was still worried, however, that if I told them now, we may not get to see the button.

Superintendent Neil Plumb came across interrupted and said abruptly, 'Well, is it the jacket, or isn't it?'

I said, 'Look, I'm just trying to speak to my lawyer.'

'That's fine. I just want to know whether it's the jacket.'

I said, 'I want to speak to my lawyer first.' I turned away again to speak to Stuart, and Plumb tried to elbow in between us. I obviously wasn't going to say what I wanted to say with him standing there.

'Look, Mrs Chamberlain, we're wasting time. Will you please tell me whether it's the jacket or not, and we can get on with it.'

Stuart, realising I was not going to mention a word before I spoke to him, turned to Plumb and told him that he would like to speak to his client in private. We would then let him know.

Plumb snorted and said, 'Oh well, you can use my office.'

We said, 'Thank you very much,' walked out the door, looked at one another and said, 'Bet it's bugged—he was too keen. Let's go up the corridor.' No way would we go anywhere near his office! We said as little as possible, carrying on most of our conversation in the corridor on the move. He raised his eyebrows and I gave an almost imperceptible nod. Stu shrugged, indicating how I knew and I fingered my cuff, 'I can still see the elastic, and the colour.' There was no doubt to me. He nodded. The moment I'd put my fingers to the cuff we noticed them looking, and immediately, they went across to have a look at the cuffs of the jacket while we were out of the room. Then I asked him how to see the button.

He said, 'OK. Don't identify the jacket. Tell them the button is the last positive identification. We will get photographs of that as well. Then you can tell them.'

We went back again and Stuart said, 'Mrs Chamberlain would like to see the button.' Plumb ordered one of his subordinates, who took some minutes hunting for the button. Plumb, just before the button came in, suddenly announced that he wanted to point out to us a change in colour on the edging of a pale yellowish-lemon.

We replied that we'd noticed already.

He mumbled 'Oh' and looked at me. The button arrived. We got photographs and there was no doubt it was Azaria's jacket button, although it had been found a couple of feet from the rest of the jacket. The real button could have gone missing anywhere and some other button been found near it, so it was important to know it was the correct one.

After we'd got the photographs we needed, I told them it was my daughter's jacket. Plumb asked how sure I was of that. I told him I was as sure as I could be considering time. It had an identical pattern and colour. It had what was left of the elastic around the sleeves, and it had the same button. So I was as positive as I possibly could be that it was her jacket.

Without actually sitting guard over the jacket for over five years, there was always a chance that somebody had replaced the original jacket with a counterfeit. Even in your own home, if you put a plate on a bench, somebody could remove it in your absence and replace it with an identical plate in the same place. Without remaining continually by it, you cannot swear that it is your plate. You can only say it's the same type of plate in the same place. Hence legally I could not say, 'This is Azaria's jacket.' All I could say was, 'This is an identical jacket in all respects to the one I put on my daughter that night, and I am confident that this jacket is hers.'

As far as I'm concerned, the possibility of somebody planting an identical jacket out there was nil. We had been trying for some years in vain to get one of those jackets from Marquise, but it wasn't until the actual jacket was produced that they were able to identify it and supply one.

I gave Stuart a nod. He would be in contact with me as soon as possible. He and Les were on their way to Ayers Rock to check out 'the dig for further evidence'. I was then whisked away as quickly as possible.

I was grimly amused to learn much later from Les that, despite the 'care' taken folding the paper and to catch the dirt shakings and replace them in the box with the jacket, Sergeant Sandry dropped the box on the floor. Loose dirt and debris flew out of the cracks in the box. Embarrassed, he quickly picked up the box and made off with it, *leaving the spillage* on the floor (that bit wasn't filmed!). Evidently the box still wasn't lined and sealed for protection. Despite the floor show for our benefit, they *still* hadn't changed.

As Mrs Barham had been watching for me in the corridor, I gathered she and Mr Barrier would have known I had identified the jacket, so what more was there to say? There were only four girls left in. When I walked in I gave Helena a nod so she knew it was definitely the jacket, then went back to work, after which I did my own thing for the rest of the evening. I was fairly restless because my mind was obviously on other things. I'd gone for my jog and then did things outside the day room. I was interested to see how the news would report it that night.

When it came on, the girls, not realising I was listening outside, called out to me, 'Quick! Lindy! Come here, they're saying it's her jacket! Is it really her jacket?'

I said, 'Yes.' So they sat avidly watching the news which said I had inspected the jacket in Mr McCauley's office and more or less said I had identified it. They even quoted me telling Mr McCauley—I hadn't even known he was in the building. Who got it wrong? The press? Or was information deliberately passed on incorrectly?

Del, Smiley and Helena had been inside with me for about two years and the other girl had been in and out several times, so we knew each other reasonably well. They were all pleased and excited for me that the jacket had been found. The screws on duty weren't very pleasant but were endeavouring to get in my good books realising there was a strong possibility that things were swinging my way at last. They also knew I had every intention of writing a book. It is amazing how they think you will forget the bad times if they are nice for a couple of hours or days!

The news reported that the discovery of the jacket was very important because the Crown had denied its existence, claiming it was a fabrication by Mrs Chamberlain to get herself out of a hole. Five years later it had turned up, and the scientists were stating that it had been in that location all that time, despite the fact that the police had supposedly made an intense search in the area where the jacket was found. Later evidence revealed only six rangers had spread out and walked along that area of 200 metres (220 yards) four times. The area is so long and large that unless people were shoulder to shoulder, they would be unlikely to find anything in that sort of search. The jacket was underneath a bush and would have been fairly visible at the time, if the Aboriginal trackers had been allowed in, or an intensive line search had been made at the time, the rest of the clothes would have been found.

Already rumours that we had planted the clothes were known to the police and the obvious thing was to look for our footprints there. Nipper was familiar with our shoe prints as he had identified them at the tent site, so he would have been able to spot dingo, ours, or other human tracks in the area and dispel any doubts immediately, but the Aboriginals had been told not to search there initially. A week later, when the other clothes were found by Wally Goodwin, the Aborigines came down to observe too, (as they had been told not to search in this area), but were still not asked their opinions, or for tracking advice, and were not allowed close to the clothing. Despite their long-range view, the Aborigines later testified in court that they *had* seen dingo footprints and disturbance around the clothes despite being a short distance away. Derek Roff, the senior ranger, agreed.

When Labor was Actually Right

About the time Brian Martin, Northern Territory Attorney-General, was rejecting our submission and *Blue Book* material in what is now termed the Martin Report (saying the material damage and sound deadener under- dash were not considered anything new and the case could not therefore be reopened), a report from Behringwerke of Germany (manufacturers of the testing reagent Kuhl used) also arrived, claiming their reagent was bi- specific and therefore reacted to adult blood as well as foetal blood, when it wasn't used carefully with a set of very specific controls. In this case it certainly hadn't been. Bob Collins (who had been the Leader of the Opposition at the time Azaria died) got hold of the Report and was quite irate about its contents.

He sent the reports to Dr Scott, the Crown's own scientist in Adelaide. Scott was amazed as he read both the submission we had compiled and the Martin Report disclaimer, then he wrote his own report and sent it back. It was damning, attacking the Northern Territory for being irresponsible in the evaluation of important and painstaking scientific evidence.

That coincided with the finding of the matinee jacket. Frank Alcorta had initially been the speech writer for Paul Everingham in 1980, but was now the local reporter I had recently given an interview to and quite influential. He was called into Bob Collins's office and Bob threatened that if he didn't call Behringwerke himself in Germany to check the information that he was putting in the paper, he would report Alcorta to the journalists' Board of Ethics, because he hadn't checked his information. With that threat Bob dialled Germany on the spot and put a reluctant Alcorta on the phone. After talking to Behringwerke direct Alcorta came off the phone ready to write the truth.

He had really been double-crossed by those he had worked for and used so that if anything backfired he would be blamed for the misinformation. This was enough for him to hit where it hurt most and write a piece for his paper using Scott's report and ours, and the information from the phone call to Behringwerke, telling exactly what had happened.

Frank Alcorta then went to Ian Tuxworth and the government and showed them his piece. He also told them it would be run in the paper that day unless they *did something* about the Chamberlains' situation (let me out, announce a Commission. Something!). The presses would start to print at midday. Nothing happened.

Then Chief Minister Tuxworth, was hastily called back mid-morning from his monthly school inspection. Information started to flow to and fro between his office and that of the Northern Territory Administrator. At lunchtime he personally called the Northern Territory newspaper and asked them to hold the press, as he had the headline of the decade—Lindy was to be released. It was an unusual thing to do. He could have asked one of his secretaries to pass the information on, or indeed let the press secretary release the information, but Tuxworth called the press himself. In my opinion, if it hadn't been for Bob Collins twisting Alcorta's arm up his back, I would never have got out.

Thank you, Bob Collins!

Marshall Perron, the Northern Territory Attorney General, called Michael direct to let him know that I was being released. For an Attorney- General to ring a prisoner's husband personally is, I am sure, another 'first'. Perhaps it was a way for them to show what 'good guys' they were. Normally, at the very *most*, a secretary would let the current lawyers know (especially when they were as well known as ours), and let *them* tell us.

Michael received such a shock when he was told Perron was calling him, that he rang Stuart to see whether he should take the call. It could have been a trick for all he knew. Stuart said to go ahead. Michael, still suspicious, prepared to tape the conversation so we'd have a record for our lawyers if necessary. When the call came through Perron gave his reason for calling and Michael was so stunned he didn't press the record button. He missed his chance of taping history in the making.

Soon after, on that lunchtime of 7 February, Michael Perron held a press conference and made this announcement:

> I am here to advise that the Territory government has decided to institute an Inquiry into the Chamberlain case. The decision follows advice received from the Solicitor-General and Police Commissioner on what they regard as significant new evidence. They have advised me that the discovery of a baby's matinee jacket near the base of Ayers Rock and its subsequent identification by Mrs Chamberlain may have bearing on the case. The government proposes to take whatever steps are necessary, including the possible introduction of legislation at the forthcoming sittings of the Legislative Assembly, to set up the inquiry.

Perron added:

> I can also advise that a short time ago His Honour the Administrator accepted the advice of the Executive Council that the balance of Mrs Chamberlain's life sentence be remitted and that she be released from Darwin Prison. I expect that will take place this afternoon. The decision to so recommend to His Honour is made in the light of Mrs Chamberlain's need for unrestricted access to legal advisers to prepare for the inquiry.
>
> Although Mrs Chamberlain's remission is subject to the usual conditions of good behaviour, it is not my intention that she be taken back into custody regardless of the outcome of the inquiry.

But I did not find out about this until the next day. When I did, I must admit I asked if that meant I could now rob a bank to pay my legal bills!

What a coincidence that Perron's announcement to the general press came only minutes before the threatened newspaper release, when people would have found out that the Northern Territory government was withholding vital information.

Such was the saga behind my release, rather than the matinee jacket as the Northern Territory claimed. The jacket allowed them an excuse to release me, even though it had been found five days before Perron's announcement. If the jacket had seriously been the reason, I would have been released immediately I had identified it. The Northern Territory knew then that an inquiry should be called, but they did nothing at all until they were forced to.

I AM HERE TO TELL YOU . . .

It was my turn to clean the observation tower, with its flight of steps, past the control room and armoury. Most of the work was tedious and dusty, but once up in the tower you had a breathtaking view. This week it had been postponed till Friday instead of the usual Wednesday, so we didn't have to rush through for Sister Mary Louise's usual visit. Today it was quiet, a chance for a break in the usual boring routine, so we had a good look at the view, and took our time. We had finished cleaning and were on our way out when we were asked to wait in the administration offices. Neither Smiley nor I knew why, but there wasn't anything else to do apart from mending, so with a bit of luck the other girls would finish that before we got back.

The place seemed to be crawling with strangers and men from head office. Mercer was rushing about and looking distracted. Our accompanying screw was to take us back to the section in one of the prison vehicles. She went off to arrange this, then returned to wait. Finally, after what seemed ages, it dawned on Mercer that we were still there.

'Haven't you taken them back yet?' he exclaimed in surprised irritation to our screw. She explained that we were waiting for the vehicle.

'We can't wait for that. Just get them out of here. Here. Use my car, it's just outside, and you drive them back. You do have a licence, don't you?' Smiley and I decided that he must have had more trouble with the screws, head office or something and went off giggling. Fancy getting a ride in Mercer's car! That was a new one; we thought he really must be desperate! We began to wonder if Mercer had been given the sack or something.

When descending the stairs to the sallyport, we passed Mr Barrier and a couple of other chiefs on their way up. Mr Barrier looked pleased with himself and they all smiled and said hello. We had to wait until our screw brought Mercer's car inside so we could get in. When the gate went up we could see media—obviously the southern press were there too—and photographers with still and television cameras covering the gate. So that was it. Mercer was scared they would get a picture of me on the way back to the section while he dealt with whatever had happened to cause all the commotion. At least the mystery of the car trip was explained, as our screw didn't know what had happened and she was too new to ask the other officers. The guy on the gate didn't know what was happening either and hoped we would have been able to tell him.

'Well if it's anything to do with you, go for it,' he exclaimed. I assured him I didn't know of anything that would cause all that fuss.

The car drove in and off we went. When we got to the female section, the screw had to get out and open the gate and drive us right up to the block doors. Smiley was delighted; all the other girls would now see her arrive in style too. They obviously hadn't looked out the window for a while, so they hadn't seen the press, and were wondering what was taking us so long when they saw the car pull up. I walked in and went straight back to my machine. I had hardly sat down and started telling Lena about it, when Mercer and Barrier walked past the window on their way in. Lena immediately thought of her smuggled letters and that the crunch had finally come. She was just issuing me with hurried instructions for an indefinite time on lockup when I was called. Now she was sure they were going to try and put me through the mill about whether I knew who her contact had been.

Helena's letters supporting me had caused such a stir that they were still trying to find out who had helped her smuggle them out. They had come to the conclusion that a male screw (married of course, and in love with her) had carried the letter, but they hadn't been able to decide which one. We had a good laugh about that. If they knew how it had gone out, Mercer would probably have had a stroke!

I was busy assuring Lena I could cope with any of Mercer's questions when Mrs Barham came to hurry me up.

'Don't look so worried,' she said.

'I'm not,' I said, still thinking over what Helena had said and mentally discarding it because of the press. Maybe something had come up over the jacket again; the press were on the gates the minute there seemed to be any more news on it these days. I was still wondering about it as I walked into the office. Mr Barrier was at the desk and Mercer was left standing. He'd hate that, I thought. It seemed a bit unusual as Mr Barrier usually came over on his own, and he usually used the interview room instead of the office.

Mr Barrier didn't beat around the bush.

'Good afternoon, Mrs Chamberlain. I am here to tell you that you are to be given immediate release.'

'I see,' I said. Barrier looked at me blankly, slightly embarrassed. Well they could do the talking. What was I supposed to say? They knew the routine; I didn't.

Mr Barrier shifted his papers and then said he had in front of him a paper stating that I was to be released. He could read it to me, he said, or perhaps I would rather read it myself. I chose to read it myself so Mr Barrier handed it over and I stood silently reading it. It was fairly basic, but I was interested to note that I was released on licence 'until or if revoked'. I quietly questioned (sceptically) how long it would last until revoked, and was told that phrase really meant 'permanently'.

I handed it back and asked whether I could have a copy. They looked uncertain, then said they could get me a photocopy if that was all right as this was their only copy and it had to go into the files. I said thank you and stood there. (It finally arrived over four years later.) I am not sure whether they thought I should jump up and down and shout or what, but it was their move. I was wondering what trick the Northern Territory government was up to now, or what they wanted to cover up. (It wasn't until I saw Bob Collins the next day that I learned the real reason behind my release.)

Mr Barrier said he could drop me off somewhere, get a taxi for me, or whatever I wanted. I was now totally free as of that moment, and he admitted his instructions from town were to remove me from the prison as quickly as possible. I grinned—so did he.

I said, 'Thank you very much, but if you will allow me a phone call, I'll make my own arrangements.' He looked doubtful. I continued, 'Look, all due respects to you, if I go out with you, it will be in an open car in front of the press and I have no intention of being seen by them. I am going out of here unseen.'

Mercer snorted openly. They both voiced their opinion that there was no way I'd manage that. Mercer's scepticism stood out plainly but they'd been ordered to give me immediate release—get her out of the door as quickly as possible, get rid of her, let her go. I'd soon find out I wasn't smart enough to get out unseen, so why not humour me, Mercer's face said.

I was permitted the phone call. I kept my fingers crossed that Liz Parry would be home. She was there. I said to Mrs Barham, 'You'd better tell her to sit down first.' It was very unusual to get a local phone call. You could get long-distance ones, but local ones only in an emergency and Liz knew that. Mrs Barham said to her, 'I've got somebody to talk to you here, and you'd better go and get a chair because there's some news for you.' So I was handed the phone and there was silence.

I said, 'Are you there?' She said, 'Yes.'

'Well, I'm coming home.' There was dead silence. I said, 'You haven't fainted or anything have you? Did you hear what I said?' Then the kitchen sounded like a whirlpool. She squeaked incoherently over the phone and was obviously so excited she didn't know what to do. I said, 'This is quick, Liz. The plan goes into action. Can you get hold of John? And how soon do you think you can get them here?'

She said, 'Ooh, ah, er, I know where he is—both I think. I'll . . . I'll do it. Can I ring you back? And it won't be long. It should be within half an hour.'

I said, 'Thank you. See you later,' and hung up.

Sue Priory had come in unscheduled with Liz on my regular weekly visit that morning because someone else had dropped out. That had been a pleasant surprise and we'd had a great time. We joked about when she would turn into me, and how she would be ready any time, the sooner the better. Now, the same afternoon, Liz was able to ring her and tell her to drop everything and get back to the prison post haste. Sue didn't need a second invitation.

Mr Barrier asked me how long it would take me to pack. Would ten minutes be enough? Mrs Barham grinned and we both said it would take a bit longer than that to sign me out, as I had quite a bit of stuff. It was agreed that she would do all the normal paperwork and get my stamps and money in order, while I packed and signed out with one of the other officers there.

I was beginning to get excited, but there was no way I wanted Mercer or any of the others from the jail system up there to see just how I felt, so I maintained a calm exterior.

I wasn't allowed near the other girls now, so I couldn't tell them what was happening. The authorities didn't want them to know, so although they knew something had happened, they still didn't know what. Lena is very quick-witted; you don't have to tell her anything twice. As I came out of the office to go to my cell, she was watching. I pointed to myself, pointed outside and waved goodbye. She looked at me stunned, repeated my actions and mouthed the word 'home'. I nodded and she gave me the thumbs up. The next thing all the girls had their heads together and she was telling them what was happening. There was no way the prison could stop it; we usually found some way of communicating.

I guess I had learned to cover so well that nobody really knew what I thought except perhaps Mrs Barham—I had been around her a lot more and she was more observant than the others.

I went across to my cell to start packing. Everything I had taken with me had to be signed out, item by item.

Apart from the things I'd taken in I had acquired quite a lot in three years, I had made a number of things and had gifts that people had sent me. I also had a tremendous amount of mail and study material, and I didn't want to simply throw it into a box somewhere. I knew when I got home sorting articles I had in jail with me would not be top priority. I had to organise my things so I knew where to lay hands on them without unpacking everything. Space at home was also a priority (I'd no idea just how much until I walked in the door and saw how much had accumulated since I'd left).

I packed swiftly and sorted at the same time. They had hoped to get me out of the door in ten or fifteen minutes, half an hour at the most. Well, with several officers and myself working flat out, it took two hours to pack and check everything off the list in the property book. Even then, in the end, instead of searching through the property book for my listed items, Mrs Yardley said, 'Right, Lindy, you and I know what you've got. You're not coming back here looking for a shoelace. I'll call out items on the list and you tell me whether you remember you've got them.' As she read the list, I kept packing flat out.

I had some of Lena's stuff in my cell and tried my hardest to take it up to the day room where she was working because I wanted to give her a few messages before I walked out. No way! I was told to give it to one of the officers, who would hand it over. So, from being one of the girls who had been summoned across to the office, I suddenly became an untouchable visitor and intruder, not allowed to talk to inmates without permission. I was a private person who had to get out of there as fast as possible. Really, it was quite funny, although frustrating.

When I went to get some more property out of the property room, Pastor Bob Donaldson was being let in the gate. My immediate thought was, 'Oh, he knows, so he's come in.'

He said, 'Hello, how are you?'

I said, 'Fine, thanks,' very chirpily. He seemed to be just hanging around and I couldn't figure out why the prison was letting him. I had thought that, because I'd been at the cop shop identifying the jacket on Wednesday, his visit had been cancelled. The jail knew he was coming on Friday instead, so he presumed I knew too, but I didn't.

Finally as I rushed past Bob he said, 'You look like you're pretty busy. Is something going on?' Of course, he wasn't supposed to be speaking to me either.

I stopped dead and said in surprise, 'Haven't they told you?' He said, 'No, what?'

I said, 'Bob, I'm going home!'

He said conversationally, 'Oh, that's nice. When?'

And I said, '*Now*, Bob! I'm going home *now*! They've given me immediate release.'

Bob looked stunned, amazed, then pleased, and as it sank in, he blushed vividly as he always did when he was really pleased or excited. This time it was great to see. He looked as if he really wanted to pass the news on to somebody, but, of course, everybody there was an officer and they already knew. I rushed on and as I left I heard him ask whether he could help! That was the last thing they wanted; he was a visitor, but they really couldn't kick him out either. Bob found it particularly amusing because Mercer had hauled him over the coals about his visits, asking him what he was going to talk to me about and telling him what he was and wasn't allowed to do. Mercer had often talked to him. Much to Bob's delight, Mercer never really knew whether Bob understood him or whether he was a bit thick. We smiled to ourselves over that.

For once, Mercer lost control of the situation. It was even funnier within twenty minutes when Sue Priory arrived. Now Bob had someone to talk to and they both sat there, very excitedly talking about it, and talking to me and to anybody that went past them. Mercer was trying to keep everything very prison-like and officious but he was also trying to be pleasant as well. He made a real hash of it, but it entertained those looking on.

As I continued packing, more and more people arrived as it was shift changeover. Then the phone rang. Mrs Barham, who was buzzing in and out, trying unsuccessfully to hide how excited she was, told me that Michael was on the phone. Because of the noise I could take the call in the storeroom. She unlocked the door and said not to talk too long because the phone was ringing hot, then walked out.

I spoke on the phone, un-monitored for the first time in three years, and Michael answered, too excited to wait for me to get out; he simply had had to talk to me. He said, 'Don't you *dare* tell me you're cool, calm and collected this time and not excited.' Well, I was getting that way but I was still feeling pretty cool about it all, so I just said, 'Yes, darling,' and continued to talk. He sounded as high as a kite and I said to him, 'You sound like you're in heaven down there.'

He said, 'OK, I will.'

'What?' I said, thinking I had misheard. I was being told to finish the call then and I thought, 'I will *what*?' I said, 'Look, I'll ring you from Liz's.'

I finished my packing. By that time John Parry and Footsie were there, as well as Bob and Sue. I asked one of the screws if she would ask Lena to iron my dress for me. It was my plan to use the same dress home that I had worn to jail, to lead the press astray as much as possible. I got that dress for Sue and I wore another one that

I'd made for myself while in prison. Sue changed into my clothes, and I grabbed hers and put them with my luggage. We were nearly set to go.

Then I put on street clothes, high heels, and makeup—proper makeup, for the first time in years—and emerged to say goodbye.

The screws had lined the girls up to say goodbye. I could tell by the look on the girls' faces that they were having trouble getting used to seeing me in makeup and street clothes, looking much like I would in public! You could see it registering on some of the screws' faces also.

I noticed Lena had stationed herself at the end farthest away from the screws, so I started saying goodbye on the opposite end of the line, saying goodbye, giving the long-termers a hug, one by one. When I came to Helena, I gave her a longer hug so I could whisper I'd left gear behind for her and tell her where I'd put it. Smiley and Del talked to the screws, automatically decoying for us. Lena said quietly, 'Right, mate,' then loudly, 'I'll see you when I get out.' I knew she had it all. This solved several problems, not the least of which was that we weren't allowed to give things to each other; we could only leave things in the section and they would be at the mercy of the screws, who could decide whether to issue them, throw them away, use them themselves or simply let them disappear. She would have no trouble finding the stuff now she knew where to look.

There was a problem with cameras around the back of the section. We had seen press drive past a couple of times, and there was no shielding from that direction. So, as a shield, I asked Mr Mercer if he and his officers would mind milling about at the back of the van as if they were all saying goodbye to me. The luggage was loaded in Bob's four-wheel-drive in a hurry, and I was to hop in under cover of all the activity and lie flat in the back of John's station wagon.

One look and I said, 'Listen, guys, this is a dumb idea—I'll be nearly at window level. I might as well sit up in the front seat! Put the seats back up and I will curl up on the floor under the towel' (the only thing in there). That was the last place I wanted to get caught so it had to work! So I curled up on the floor, so that even if the press looked in the window, they could only see a towel on the floor—just as well I'm tiny; curled up in a ball, I am pretty small! So there I was.

Everyone spread out as Sue came out with one of the officers and they all dutifully said goodbye to her. She hopped in the car with Footsie and went. The van followed, the last car to leave carried John Parry in his overalls and me.

Sue waved out the car window to the girls, who had been watching our progress out the windows, fully aware it was a setup. They thought it was a great joke. Footsie slowed down initially then took off through the gate. The tinted window was up, so they didn't get a very good look at 'me'.

It was enough. The cameras trained on Sue and Footsie, with Bob and the luggage following. Bob couldn't have been there at a better time if it had been planned. John and I went through the gate without the press giving us much of a look. It just looked like a workman in an empty station wagon, who had gone in for some reason or other and was coming out again. John Parry was not known very much and really didn't seem to be part of what was happening. You see, two vehicles had come in together.

Bob was separate, and somewhere along the line they got their wires crossed and thought the two vehicles that were leaving together were the same two that had come in together. They didn't stop to think that the one they were ignoring was one of the original two!

When I thought everything was clear, I stuck my nose out to see what was happening. Suddenly I saw that we had managed to pass one of the reporter's vans. They were in a high vehicle, and were able to look straight down onto the floor of our vehicle. I ducked under the towel again in a hurry. Although they looked in our direction, they had not noticed me. They gave us a honk, passed, and took off after Footsie. We pulled up beside Footsie and Sue at the lights. The press stopped behind Footsie, who was going left; we were turning right. Sure enough, they followed Footsie, and just around the corner I was able to get up and climb into the front seat with John. As we were driving along, one of them must have got lost and came tearing up beside us. I ducked, but need not have worried; they were so intent on looking for Footsie's car that they didn't give us another glance. I sat up the rest of the way back to Parry's.

As we pulled up in the Parrys' driveway, Liz raced out to meet us, gave me a big bear hug and rushed me inside. We went upstairs and sat around grinning like Cheshire cats at what we'd pulled off. While everyone else was on a wild goose chase through the countryside, we were undetected far from the action. There was no one else to celebrate with; we were all excited and had nothing to do. (It always seemed that way—I was hidden somewhere, while everyone else raged and celebrated, the press invaded, or whatever.)

There was one thing I could not resist doing. I said to Liz, 'They took the bait, they're chasing Sue! I really want to ring up the press.'

John said, 'You can't.'

Liz said, 'Go on, do it. If you want to do it, do it!'

John just shrugged and gave up; so she looked up the number of the local Darwin television station, who also had their crew out chasing 'me'. I rang up. When the switchboard answered, I said, 'This is Lindy Chamberlain speaking. I just wanted to let you know that the crew you have out supposedly following me are chasing a decoy. I have already reached my destination. I have gone to ground and you may as well tell them all to go home, because they're chasing the wrong person.'

She said, 'Oh, just a minute and I'll put you through to the newsroom.' I hung up. They probably still think she had a crank call. It didn't come over the news that they were all hoodwinked, so they obviously thought that *she* had been had. Well, guys, I've got news for you. *You* were wrong!

I tried and *tried* to phone Michael. He was always engaged. I dialled so often I broke two fingernails and finally used a pencil.

While I was still trying to get Michael on the silent line, the other phone rang. It was Sunshine. Sunshine had been off duty when she heard the news and was so excited she wanted to ring somebody, and who better than her friend of many years, Liz. Liz put her hand over the phone and told me who it was, asking if I wanted to talk. I nodded, so she said to Sunshine, 'I've got someone here who would like to say hello to you', then handed the phone over and I spoke. Sunshine nearly leapt through the phone; she'd had absolutely no idea where I was. She had just wanted to share her excitement with someone and she'd hit the jackpot. I thought it was quite fitting that my first congratulations should come from one of the best officers in the prison.

Before too much longer the inevitable happened—the first press car arrived. John had said to me, 'What do you want to do about the press?' I said, 'I'm not giving interviews to them, John. I'm not talking to *anyone*. Just fob them off with whatever you like.' Nevertheless, if specific reporters called and said it was off the record, I would be inclined *to* talk to them because their reporting had always been accurate. Those guys *could* lie straight in bed at night! And I mentioned four names to John—Malcolm Brown (*Sydney Morning Herald*), Kevin Hitchcock (Channel 10 news), Mike Lester (Channel 9 news) and Kim Tilbrook (Adelaide *Advertiser*).

That was the end of the matter for a time.

I dialled Michael's number, my parents' number, and my brother Alex's number, in that order one after the other, continuously for nearly an hour and a half before I finally got through to my brother. After talking I said in exasperation, 'Will you go round to Michael and tell him, for goodness sake, to get off the phone? I've been trying to ring him for hours. Alternatively get him to ring me here at Liz's and I will stay off the phone.' Shortly Michael rang and said, 'Boy, you're early!'

I said, 'What do you mean? I've been trying to call you for an hour and a half; you've been on the phone.'

'But you said to ring at seven,' he said.

'What do you mean I said to ring at seven?' I exclaimed. 'I never said anything about what time. I said I'd ring you when I got here.'

He said, 'No, you said to ring at seven.' Suddenly I realised that when I had said to him, 'You must be in heaven' he thought I said, 'Ring at seven,' and he had been waiting thinking what a long time it was to wait.

After I had finally talked to Michael, other phone calls started coming in and Liz and I were busy talking in between. Nobody had visited yet because word hadn't got around where I was, but some reporters had started to gather outside to watch the house. I guess they figured that as Liz was my friend and visited me every week, if they watched her she would lead them to me.

After a bit John, who was lookout while Liz and I talked, said, 'Someone's coming in.' Liz and I stayed out of sight, and John answered the door. We heard voices, then John said, 'Sorry, I can't give you any information.' When he came back I said to him, 'Who was it?' He said, 'I think that might have been one of the ones on your list—It's a Mike Lester.' Mike had written to us both occasionally and once or twice to me while I was in prison. He'd also been the one who told us the matinee jacket had been found. I said to John, 'I'd love to see Mike again. Go and get him. Come up with some idea to get him back in again, then ask him if he will give you his word that he won't talk. If he does, he won't break it.'

John went back outside and called after Mike, 'Excuse me, can I see you again for a moment?' Mike came back with John. He'd had time to report that, if I was there, nobody was talking and he hadn't found out anything from Mr Parry. But, if you're a reporter and you're called back, you may find out something extra, so the curiosity of the other reporters was up.

What was Mike about to be told that they weren't? And why him?

John invited him in to the TV room downstairs. The back door was shut in case anyone else arrived, and John started talking to him generally, asking various questions. Then he said, 'I know you are reporting on the case. If there was somebody you particularly wanted to see, could you give your word that you would not report on it?' I was sitting round the corner at the top of the stairs, not that far away, if Mike had only known it, but Mike didn't know and I heard him groan and say, 'Oh, do you realise what you're asking me to do?'

John said, 'Yes, you'd have a scoop and wouldn't be able to say a word.' Mike thought for a moment, then agreed, 'If Lindy will see me, I'll give my word it won't go any further. You realise that if they find out, I could lose my job over this?'

John said, 'Yes. We won't mention it either, if you won't. [Mike has left that job now and I have his permission to tell this story.] It just depends. You know, you can leave a message and say hi, or . . .'

He said, 'No, I give you my word.'

Meanwhile I had crept far enough down the stairs to a point where I could see John and hear properly. Mike was sitting with his back to me, but John was facing me. They were just talking small talk. I was tired of waiting for him to tell me when I could come into the room. I looked at John, asking with signs if I could come in yet, but John was enjoying himself. He looked at Mike and said, 'Of course, you realise that you'll have to go out in front of your fellow reporters and pretend that absolutely nothing's happened.'

'Yes, I realise this,' Mike replied, 'I . . .' He suddenly realised that John was smiling at someone over his shoulder and what his words meant. His face lit up and he said, 'Do you mean she's . . .' Then John, with a big grin, nodded and said to me, 'It's OK, you can come in.'

I was out of the line of vision moving downstairs when I heard a thump on the floor. Mike had obviously bounded up in one stride. It had really thrown him because he hadn't realised just how close I was. I think he had virtually decided that I wasn't there, but he was about to be told my whereabouts. As I walked in the door, Mike's face was an absolute study. He was obviously lost for words, *really* thrown off his cool.

Normally immaculate when on the job, he had been running around in the sun in Darwin trying to get a tipoff with the other reporters and he was in off-duty T-shirt, shorts and thongs. It was very hot outside and he had been perspiring quite freely. I smiled and he extended his hands slightly, not knowing what to say or do.

I said, 'Well, am I going to get a hug?' That was all he needed to find his tongue again.

'You bet!' he said. He gave me the biggest hug of my life, I am sure. If I had been fragile, every bone in my body would have broken into about sixty thousand pieces on the spot. Then he pushed me roughly away from him and said, 'Let me look at you. Oh, my God, what have they done to you?' He hugged me again and sobbed on my shoulder.

That was probably the nicest response that anyone could get. To know that someone, almost a stranger, cared enough about you to show their feelings despite the presence of strangers in the room. His actions could be misconstrued but he didn't care. (He had already been teased simply because he took himself off the case; he believed in our innocence and felt he could no longer report in an unbiased way, so people said he must have become emotionally involved). He had—but not the way they meant.

After a while, he regained his composure and apologised, saying he was hot and sweaty, and if he'd known I was there, he'd have gone to change. (Goodness, I couldn't have cared less! I would much rather have had a genuine welcome than something contrived later on.) Then he looked at me again and he said, 'I was so scared you would come out of prison hard, but you haven't. You're the same person who went in. I know there are changes but not in that way, and I'm just so relieved.'

We sat down and talked for what seemed like ages. It had to come to an end, however, because we couldn't afford to run the risk of the other reporters noticing he was gone too long. Mike stayed there long enough to calm down and get his face in order and then, promising to contact me again, he and John walked outside. He paused around the corner of the house and took a big, deep breath, then John let him out the gate and said, 'Thank you very much, Mr Lester. I'll contact you again about that.' And walked off. Mike had to walk into the midst of his colleagues, take another deep breath, and pretend the world hadn't changed. It was interesting; we watched him from the window and he carried off the whole situation very well, characteristically shrugging his shoulders and obviously telling them there wasn't going to be anything for a while. He and his crew hung around for a bit longer and then left.

A lot of my friends had either guessed or been told where I was by then, and in a fairly short space of time after that, people started to arrive.

It was obvious there was definitely something going on at the Parrys', so it had to be something to do with Lindy. The reporters realised that somehow or other, I'd entered and hidden in that house, fooling them all. The news soon spread and the rest of the media arrived. They couldn't get in, however, nor could they get an interview with anyone coming and going. They were not talking, but were obviously excited and celebrating.

Much to the chagrin of the media, a celebratory party was clearly in full swing upstairs at the Parrys', Lindy obviously being the guest of honour. They even climbed trees and hired the neighbour's balcony to try and catch a glimpse of me, but in vain. What intrigued them was the fact that we were having an absolute ball without a champagne bottle in sight; we are all teetotallers. This fascinated the media so much it was commented on in the news. I couldn't see why it caused comment, but then I can never understand why some people have to be roaring drunk to have a good time (a post-party headache is often all they have to remind them of their 'good times').

Meanwhile we were desperately trying to contact Stuart. We knew he was somewhere at Ayers Rock with the matinee jacket dig, but not sure exactly where. We finally discovered he was in the air, coming back to Alice Springs. We wanted to notify him that I had been released. Stuart was prearranged to collect me from jail and take me home.

Michael wasn't terribly happy about this, but he saw the sense in avoiding reporters swarming all over us on a long plane trip while they took pictures of the Chamberlains together again after nearly three years. I wouldn't do that, and so Michael had reluctantly agreed to stay home with the kids instead of doing what he wanted to do—catch the first plane to Darwin.

Finally Stuart rang us; he had been paged mid-air between Ayers Rock and Alice Springs, he was pleased and still recovering. The forensic material he was taking back to Sydney and his luggage were already checked through and on the next plane. The plane was about to depart and he couldn't get the luggage off again. He had no one else to take the material through for him and it was at the end of several days at the Rock so he was also out of clothes.

He told me, 'I'll have to take this flight, then I'll take the turnaround flight from Sydney and pick you up. I'll ring you again from Sydney.' And that's what happened.

He reached Sydney, only to tell his wife Cherie that he had to leave again. Stuart and Cherie lived in Gosford, a several-hour return trip from Sydney, so they stayed with Cherie's parents in Sydney overnight. Stuart borrowed some clean shirts from Cherie's father (fortunately they were the same size), then he took off again for Darwin early the next morning.

When I finally went to bed on my first night out, I couldn't sleep. The very feel of it—I could actually hear the springs in it squeaking every time I breathed. I was so tired and yet so excited and the noise put me off. I ended up pulling the covers and pillow onto the floor, and slept there for the night. I hadn't had the new foam mattress in prison long, so it felt so much more like the hard, lumpy prison bed I was used to.

I got up very early in the morning and put all the blankets back on the bed so Liz and John wouldn't know. I wondered how long it would take me to get used to a normal bed. It was Sabbath but we hadn't made any attempt to go to church—why compromise security now? Liz and I stayed home. The church folk were told if anyone wanted to see me, they could feel free to come round to visit me at Liz and John's that afternoon, but they must not pass on any news to the press.

Liz had a visit booked with Helena that Saturday morning (she used to go to visit her sometimes as well as me).

She asked, 'What will I do now? Will I keep the appointment or not?'

I urged her, 'This is the chance to find out what happened there after I left, and to let her know what's going on. She'll be wondering. So have your visit.'

I had lots of visitors, so Liz went and returned with the name and address of one of Lena's friends who wanted to see me. Lena had vouched for his security, so I contacted him and said he could come and meet me if he wished. He soon turned up with a young woman in tow, which was unexpected, but as he had been told the visit must be confidential, we presumed she had been well vetted.

As soon as they left the girl contacted the press. It wasn't until the local paper came out that we realised she had been a plant and actually worked for the press. The girl didn't get much, though. She had wanted me to have a photo taken with them, but because we were being careful regarding security, we took the photo on our camera to send later instead of the little Polaroid they wanted to use. That would have ended up in the paper. You live and learn, and we were still learning—fast! I left Lena to deal with that matter, which she did in due time.

I was particularly delighted to have Mary Ehn and Sister Mary Louise come with another friend of theirs. As Sister was leaving I noticed she was holding something in her hand. She put her hand over mine and said, 'I want you to have this. It is rather special to me. It is the one I took with me to Rome when my father was so ill and the Pope blessed it.' It was her rosary ring. I was thrilled, and I treasure it very much. I may not be a Roman Catholic, but I know what the gesture meant to her.

The press wasn't expecting Stuart to come, so John was able to pick him up and bring him back to the house with little fuss. When he arrived there was more excitement and hugs all 'round. The flow of visitors suddenly increased again. I was still getting used to being a private person.

Because I only had two dresses with me (one was a winter dress), there didn't seem any point in getting them dirty, I wore one of Liz's long T-shirts and wandered around with bare feet, blessedly cool. It was bliss no longer wearing the prison uniform and sandals.

It was really odd to look into a full-length mirror, not having done so for three years. In fact, I'd barely looked into a mirror at all. In prison there were small mirrors in the administration staff rooms, which we cleaned at night, but they were too high to see more than your face and shoulders, and there was a slight distortion of the image too. For the first time since leaving home I could look at myself in the full-length mirror and see myself as others did. It was like meeting an old friend after a long absence. Similarities but so many changes.

I was so excited about going home that, between the Friday and the following Tuesday when I finally arrived, I lost 3 1/2 kilos (eight pounds). I was 42 kilograms (94 pounds) when I arrived home on my own doorstep. My desire to eat totally left me. To my chagrin I discovered that, although the food was good, my stomach couldn't tolerate the richness and variety I was now free to eat. The one thing I had really looked forward to was a drink of real milk, which John bought specially for me. It promptly gave me pains in the stomach and made me feel ill.

People continually came and went during the afternoon. The room was full of people when Bob Collins's head appeared as he came up the stairs. There were excited exclamations of, 'Bob! Here's Bob!' Someone called,

'Three cheers for Bob!' A concerted roar rose from the crowd (which I later learned frustrated the waiting media even more, as they did not know the part Bob had played in my release and couldn't figure out why he was so popular).

Bob gave me a big hug; he was excited too. His own party had eventually disowned him because he had maintained my innocence all along, and now at last he was being vindicated publicly. That was when he told us the saga of my release. If somebody in the government hadn't made the error of leaving the times on one set of memo copies (the rest had had the times deleted), no one would have been the wiser about how quickly the whole episode had taken place, or the reason for all the haste.

It was late before the last excited caller left. Liz, John, Stuart and I remained talking for a while before preparing for bed. At about 11.45 p.m., as we finally bade each other goodnight, the phone rang. It was Mike Lester.

Mike's visit on Friday had been brief, and I still had three years of catching up to do. I was also able to find out the stories that were going around, too. The press suspected I was in the house and guessed which plane I was catching (we were able to avoid the plans they had discovered and make alternative arrangements) but were still unsure whether the church people had fooled them with an elaborate decoy plan. Mike filled me in on the finding of Azaria's jacket and the various rumours about it. He also reported on the many things that had been happening in the outside world during the last four days concerning me.

Time flew by. As I was talking, idly looking out the window, I saw a man run out the back drive past the kitchen window, vault the gate and run off. I knew no one had come in that way because I'd been sitting facing it, so he had come in the other direction. What was he doing? There had been bomb threats, as some people were incensed that I was out of prison. Having had them in the past, we were very aware of this. I mentioned it in passing to Mike and he became very concerned, saying my description didn't fit any of the reporters (they were staking out the house and were rostered on in shifts) there that night. He thought I ought to wake John and get him to look around the outside. Mike said he would drive over to check the newsmen and see if he could find out anything. He would call back later.

I was inclined to treat it as a joke. As I was still elated at being out of jail; nothing was worrying me much at that stage. It struck me, however, that I should act. John and Liz's three boys were asleep in the other room, and there was no point in taking any risk just in case. I tiptoed in to try and wake John, but succeeded in waking Liz instead. She was immediately worried and woke John to do the rounds of the house.

At any sign of activity, the press crew was likely to turn their lights on and start filming. They were obviously sleepy, though, because they did not see John, armed with a torch, solemnly protecting his property in nothing but a pair of white jocks! It would have made hilarious footage. John saw Mike drive around and stop to talk to the pressmen but couldn't see anything abnormal in his yard. We talked for a while in whispers, trying not to let the press know what we were up to (noise carries at night; we could hear *them* talking outside).

It was only about three-quarters of an hour until we were due to make our escape. As we were all awake and I was packed, John thought we might as well leave.

A Great Scam

Liz and John had to get dressed and Liz was to ring the house we were going to. John had to get the truck ready. I was to finish shutting my cases, then wake Stuart up. (We'd let him sleep as long as possible, knowing he was tired.) John gave us strict instructions not to turn on any lights as this would let the press know what was happening.

I knew Stuart was in young Joshua Parry's room and the location of the bed, but not what other furniture was in the room, or where he'd put his suitcases. It was pitch black in there. I had visions of Stuart hitting me over the head, mistaking me for an intruder when I tried to wake him, but when I spoke his name he woke immediately, fully alert. I quickly told him our plans—he had ten minutes to get ready—then left to help load my gear in the truck. Liz and I were so excited we had started to get the giggles. The quieter we tried to be, the more things we walked into or dropped in the dark. John reprimanding us made us giggle even more.

Sure enough Stuart came down, hair combed, dressed and ready to go in the allotted ten minutes. Still in the dark, we crept outside. There was a streetlight close by, so we kept in the shadow of a huge banyan tree. John often had carpet cleaning or pest control jobs in office blocks at that hour of the morning, so it was not unusual for the truck to be moving at that time. Stuart was just as clumsy as Liz and I, and on the way to the truck we both nearly fell over a board lying in the middle of the path. Trying to tell one another to be quiet and say, 'Ouch' softly made us nearly fall over again laughing. We felt like a band of conspirators. We finally jumped into the cab of the big pest control truck, donned pest control hats, and sat there trying to stifle our laughter while waiting for John—not feeling half obvious! John's slogan was 'All our patients die'; we hoped we were going to be among the lucky ones that day.

John waited until Liz had driven out of the gate in the other direction and watched while the reporters took the bait and followed her. As if on cue, Footsie arrived as Liz was pulling out the driveway, and followed also. He had thought he would drive past early and check everything was OK for the escape just in case he was needed as an extra decoy. It couldn't have been better timed. With the two cars going together the press was sure I was aboard. They gave chase.

Liz had strict instructions from John not to drive beyond her capabilities. She was to lure the press as far away as possible so we could get clear. Then she was to return home. We had a quiet trip across town to a mystery destination, finally pulling up and unloading our gear into a guest flat under a high block house.

Upstairs we were introduced to Greg and Jill Dawkins, who were kindly giving us shelter. We learnt that the flat had been specially built so that Michael and the children would have a new place to hide on visits (as the press knew their regular accommodation), or in case we needed a place to escape to, like now. The flat had only just been finished and we were its first occupants. I was most grateful.

Greg and Jill gave us a warm welcome. While we were talking, Footsie and Liz arrived. They had led the press a merry dance! Liz had parked her car at home and then arrived with Footsie to see if we were OK. As neither the press nor John had returned to the Parrys' by this stage, Liz had presumed John knew Footsie's new plans.

Meanwhile, John arrived home and found no Liz. He waited, unaware of Liz's movements, and began to fear that she'd been kidnapped or something. Liz rang later to see he was OK, and he berated her for not following the plan as instructed. Liz was determined, however, to spend her last few hours with me—it was the only time we'd had together alone after nearly three years of weekly half-hour visits and Liz deserved that.

We had a lovely breakfast with our hosts, then Liz and I went downstairs to the flat to get some sleep. Stuart had a room upstairs, and talked for a while longer, then went back to bed too. It was shortly after dawn. Liz and I were too excited to sleep for more than half an hour and finally realised we were both lying there trying not to wake each other. We started chatting again, despite the fact that that was all the sleep I'd had that night. We talked and talked. When Stuart woke and came down to rouse us, he found us excited and ready to go. He had his camera, so we took photos and clowned around while waiting. The three of us were in top form.

Back at the Parrys', the press scouts had returned. John got the boys breakfast and organised them for the day. He was relieved to note that the rest of the usual press contingent turned up. That meant our plan had worked. If the media had suspected anything they would have left by now for the new location. Plan two could go into action.

To make the media continue to believe I was still there, people had to keep visiting. The cricket was on and Bob Donaldson was going to watch it with his boys. That was perfect, because he was the only other person in Darwin I knew as well as Liz. If he arrived with his family to watch the cricket at John and Liz's house, with a bit of luck the media would decide I was still there just having a quiet time with my closest friends before I left on the plane for home. It also meant there was someone to care for the three Parry boys until Liz and John got back. Seven boys watching cricket provided all the noise that was needed to convince the media they hadn't followed a hoax and that I hadn't left. So they waited, and waited, and waited . . .

Mike Lester, knowing we were giving the press the slip, hung around to see what would happen. As the time arrived for us to leave for the airport and nothing happened, the crews grew more and more anxious. John left on his own and no one bothered with him. Pleased with the way things were going, he turned up to see what we were all doing. (He still hadn't quite forgiven Liz, though!)

Just before I left I was handed two large sheaves of gladioli and mixed flowers that had just been delivered. What on earth was I going to do with them? They obviously weren't going to last much more than the trip, and yet I wanted to take them with me. Stuart laughed and said he was sure I would think of something to do with them, so they went with me.

We said goodbye to Liz and our hosts when Footsie returned, and piled into the vehicle to make our way to the airport. Paul Brann, now moved from the Alice to manage Ansett Industries in Western Australia, had said once before that if we needed any help he would be available. He can look quite fierce, and his karate experience and build are also off-putting. We thought it was wise to have some security plus the arrangements for the trip dealt with as one.

One phone call was enough for Paul. He hopped a plane to Darwin and was there for the trip to Sydney with us. He had arranged everything with the airport managers at each airport, and they were there waiting for us at each place. The trip went without a hitch.

The reporters had decided to stake out the airport also; there was one lone car under a tree near the entrance. As we passed we saw feet up in the driver's window. The car's occupant was obviously either reading or sleeping in the midday heat, and not watching the cargo bay or the trucks coming and going. We were able to go across there without hindrance.

Paul had arranged for our luggage to be checked straight in, including a big picture they were worried might get damaged.

I said to them, 'Look, it's unfinished. I don't mind. Just send it through as it is, anyway.' Finally, they said they would. We got the luggage checks and gave them to Stuart for collection at the other end, so I could be whisked away immediately.

We then hopped back in the vehicle to drive to the plane. Once again we passed the reporter on guard. This time, however, he followed us, but could not get past the barrier. Mike told us later that his news team had had an emergency radio call (I assume from him) telling them we had done it again and were already at the airport. This sent them into a flat spin and a high-speed trip to get to the airport before the plane left.

We drove up to the plane steps to board early; Paul was in charge, and obviously quite at home. Suddenly Stuart's words about the flowers were prophetic. Other press were now swarming inside the terminal barriers and I still had to get up the plane steps. The flowers were the perfect cover, so the press were unable to take photographs of me. (We had bills to pay; they weren't going to get useful photographs for nothing.) I put both arms around the flowers and hid my face behind them. The media had no idea how slim I was because the dress I was wearing was the fairly flowing a- line postnatal dress Jenny Miller had bought me for Michael's graduation. With Paul standing between me and the press, plus the flowers, all they could see was a blue dress and legs.

High Flying

Stuart and I sat in the seats right at the front near the door. We couldn't have been in a worse place for initial boarding. We pulled the blind down so no one could see in the window. Paul was seated directly behind us so that he could keep an eye on things and stop anyone who came too close. The rest of the passengers boarded, including the press. Paul gave me a newspaper and said, 'Here, they might try with their cameras as they walk past, so put that in front of you.'

I hurriedly put up the newspaper just in time. I forgot I still had a lap full of things though. My legs were too short to reach the floor (why are plane seats so high?) and the things started to slide off when I let them go to grab the newspaper. Reaction took over and I used the old prison sit—one leg across my knee at right angles to hold them there—forgetting that I now had to sit in a ladylike fashion.

One of the photographers snapped a shot; the result was a view of Lindy's dress, leg up, petticoat showing, and a newspaper over her head. When the girls in prison saw that they were highly amused, saying, 'That's the prison sit. She's forgotten she's out now.' I realised fairly quickly what I had done and was able to get Stuart to grab the stuff on my lap, so I could put my head behind the newspaper better and my leg down without anything else sliding. The stewardess informed us when the press was settled and strapped in, so I could drop the newspaper. Now the seating position was ideal and secure. Two press photographers were in the front seat across the aisle (opposite Paul and one seat behind us). They leaned across to Stuart and said: 'Sorry to bother you but we have been sent here because we have a job to do; we have been asked to get a photo. Can we take one, please?'

'Sorry,' said Stuart, 'no.' They said in that case they were warning us they would try all the way home. 'If she leans so much as an inch forward past you, she is fair game,' they told Stuart. They would take a photograph but they wouldn't try any tricks; they would play by the rules. For the rest of the trip down to Brisbane, if I wanted to lean forward to scratch my foot, stretch, or wriggle, Stuart had to lean forward too as a shield. The least movement and the cameras would go click, click. I couldn't even go to the toilet.

When we got to Brisbane airport, we discovered that there were two planes leaving at almost identical times. Our plane's new intake of passengers were almost exclusively pressmen, according to the airport manager. During a discussion between Paul and the manager it was decided to transfer us to the other flight in order to avoid as many press as possible.

We transferred and discovered that this flight had also now filled with media. We would have been better off staying on the original plane, as the seating arrangement there was slightly better. Many of the press photographers on this plane were pushy. Part of the way to Sydney one of the photographers walked up the aisle to our seat and tried to take photographs of me. Stuart, who was reading, used his magazine as a lens cover to stop the photographer. After almost a minute of trying with the camera on motor-drive, the man gave up. As soon as the photographer left Stuart remarked, 'Phew. That was worse than playing at the net.' (He is an A-grade tennis player.)

A little later another photographer started to get up with his camera, obviously intent on trying the same thing, and hoping to catch Stuart off guard. Paul, in the seat behind us, saw him coming and 'accidentally' jumped up at the crucial moment, knocking the photographer backwards into his seat again. Paul apologised profusely, as only he can, then wandered up to us and simply stood there talking to us. The photographer got the message and stayed in his seat.

The flight attendants had told the TV cameramen they were not to keep cameras out during the flight. They were also endeavouring to use the 'fasten seatbelts' sign as much as possible to keep them all in their seats during the flight for us, which was a great help.

When we landed at Sydney we could see banks of cameramen lining the viewing windows where we should eventually exit from the plane; the rest of the passengers were held up while we left first. It had been arranged, in conjunction with the airport officials and police, that I was to be transported in a staff mini-bus with other airline employees to act as decoys, to put the media off the scent.

Stuart, Paul and I walked across the tarmac from the plane to the door of the corridor that connected with the departure lounge.

Instead of entering that door, we slipped around the corner to the waiting mini-bus. By now other passengers were disembarking also. I stopped at the door of the bus to say goodbye to Stuart and Paul. I had given Paul a hug, and was just hugging Stuart too, when an enterprising cameraman came up behind us. We saw him just as he raised his camera. I went to jump backwards, Stuart threw me, Paul jumped between us and the pressman, and the flash gun went off all at the same time. I landed in a sprawled heap on the floor of the bus at the feet of about a dozen strange airport employees who were already seated in the bus. (I could just imagine the headlines if he had managed to get a photograph of me in Stuart's arms!) The security guys shouted, 'Go!' and the bus took off in a hurry, which made me lose my balance again. I had no idea where we were going, as the photographer had interrupted us before they had time to tell me the rest of the plans for my trip home, except that Stuart would collect my luggage and send it through the next day.

I felt a fool sitting on the floor of the bus still, so I simply said 'Hi,' while meekly collecting myself, then moved to a seat as the bus sped away over what looked like darkened runway.

I was just beginning to wonder if I had actually been abducted when the bus halted, and a cop opened the door. He mumbled something about getting out. I sat there blankly, thinking there was no way in the world that I was going to get out of that bus in the middle of nowhere with a cop. We were in the centre of what looked like a paddock. I could see lights far away in the distance. It looked pretty lonely to me. He moved off and spoke, then the internal light of a car parked a short distance away came on.

I was still sitting there dazed when he impatiently said, 'Well, come on. Get out.' I started to ask where we were when the car's back door opened and the policeman said, 'Hurry up. Your husband's waiting.' Only then did I realise it was Michael. I was rushed across by the policeman and he almost pushed me into the back seat of the car, and Michael's waiting arms. Michael had brought me a bunch of red roses, which were crushed between us as we embraced. The thorns that dug into me helped remind me not only to move, but that I was really on my way home and it wasn't just a dream.

The policeman spoke briefly to our driver, and we took off. As we went Michael introduced me to the driver, whom he said was a friend called John. I was not too sure about that; he seemed to be on very friendly terms with the police. Anyway, Michael was there and we were travelling fast following the cop car. It seemed awfully dark. It was—we had no lights. John pulled up to find the switch for the lights, and the police came back to see what was wrong. When they found out we had no lights, they wanted to know why we couldn't continue to drive without them! The lights found, we were off again, away over the back of the runway, behind the police vehicle. Finally we halted at a locked gate which led to a main road. The police had appeared extremely nervous to get us out and away as quickly as possible, and I thought they were rather rude about it, but Michael assured me they had been most helpful to him.

Now I was so tired I felt as if my head was swimming. I had only had two hours' sleep in the last sixty-one hours, and there was at least a two- hour drive home ahead of us. The lack of sleep, the excitement and the plane trip had caught up with me. Because of the press photographers hounding me on the plane and my hasty removal across the tarmac, I still hadn't been able to get to a toilet, and I had been drinking juice all the way home, too. I felt so uncomfortable I was beginning to feel sick. Michael holding me tightly wasn't improving matters either. We stopped at a service station where I could go to the toilet and walk about and stretch my legs a bit. The guys were really nervous about that and wanted to go with me! I knew I wouldn't be recognised, so it didn't worry me a bit. As soon as Michael (who *was* recognisable) and John realised I really *wasn't* recognised, they settled down.

I felt a lot better after that stop, but wished I could crawl into a hole and sleep for an hour before I had to meet the friends I knew were waiting to welcome me at home. Everything now seemed to be going by in a haze. The funny thing was, now I was away from the Northern Territory, it almost seemed as if I had only been away for a few weeks. Nothing seemed to have changed much. We wound our way through good old familiar Sydney, and out onto the tollway. Now changes showed. There was a new freeway system under construction with large stretches already opened. I thought it an improvement; at least the trip home would be faster than it used to be.

Just after the Gosford turnoff we detoured into a cemetery, of all places! I said I could do with a peaceful sleep, and both men just looked at me as if I was weird. It looked as if no one's sense of humour had changed at all, so I had to get used to some of the old regime again, I supposed. It turned out we were making radio contact with John's wife to find out the position of the press.

Mike Lester told us that we had been going to fly home by private plane. The plan had been discovered so that had to be aborted at the last minute, which was why a car had been used instead. The press was still covering the college airstrip and the main gates of Avondale College. A work van had been sent down to meet us, the driver and his mate were wearing overalls. We were supposed to lie down in the back of the van. Blow that for a joke! I'd had enough that day without that. It was finally decided we could get away with staying in the car as long as the van was there for emergency or decoy use, and off we went again. I found out later I was travelling in the latest model silver BMW that had been lent by a car dealer (which explained why John couldn't find the lights, as it was an unfamiliar vehicle).

Off we went again. We were only half an hour from home now and fortunately the time flew. We pulled up just down the road from the college gates and were given the latest on the two-way radio, then followed the work van in through the gates. Yellow ribbons were around the gates, and I saw a big 'Welcome home Lindy' sign as we flashed by. People stood around the gate waiting, even though it was midnight. They waved and clapped as we passed.

A number of the camera crews had left only about ten minutes before we arrived, obviously deciding we had stopped somewhere on the way home for the night, having given them the slip again. The last crews still lingering were rewarded for their patience and eagerly filmed the van as it went through the gates. At last they had done the right thing and got a scoop. The papers the next day reported our entry also—followed by a silver BMW. If only that crew hadn't been so suspicious of a decoy they would have looked at that silver car and seen Michael and me sitting up in the back seat with only a bunch of flowers for protection.

The driveway flashed past, we passed our old house (*that* was home, to me) and topped the crest of the hill. All the college and factory lights came into view. Nearly there at last. We swept down the hill to the gatehouse. The guy checked us with a big grin and a 'welcome home' on the way through. I could see children running, but didn't take much notice. My eyes were glued on the house less than one hundred metres away. Suddenly I realised one of those neighbourhood kids was yelling something, desperately trying to get our attention.

I looked again. There tearing along the footpath beside the car, just visible in the street lighting, was a little blond twelve-year-old boy, shouting, 'Mum! *Mum!*' Aidan! As the car was still pulling up in the driveway I opened the door and scrambled out and the excited little blond whirlwind cut the corner, jumped the fence and propelled itself into my arms. 'Welcome home, Mum, you're *home*!' I knew at last that I really was.

PART FIVE

Evidence of a Bloody Mess

HOME AT LAST

I knew I had close friends and family waiting for me, and that they were thoughtfully staying inside to let Aidan be the first to meet me. Michael informed me that Kahlia and Reagan were staying at Hughes's place overnight, seeing everyone knew I would be arriving so late; and that the Hughes would bring them around first thing in the morning. I had expected they would be asleep in their own beds and I would have at least been able to look at them. I was disappointed, but I knew it was a sensible decision.

When I walked through the open front door, there was a group of my closest friends and family, all standing not quite knowing what to do—or so I thought. I later learned they were all simply stunned. Although he didn't tell me (my mother told me years later) even my own brother didn't know me until I smiled. Later he went home and cried at the condition I was in. I *felt* quite healthy but I had lost 3 1/2 kilograms (8 pounds) through excitement and the shock of rich foods. I was so tired I felt sick, and when I looked in the mirror my skin colouring was almost a pale grey. My appearance shocked them so much, they didn't know what to say at first. This was something I encountered many times over in the next few weeks.

The initial pause was quickly covered and we were soon hugging, chatting and laughing. No one stayed long, it was nearly 1 a.m. and everyone realised the morning would bring a fairly heavy day and lots of visitors, so they wanted Michael and Aidan to have as much time alone with me as possible.

As soon as they had left, Aidan impatiently enquired, 'Have you shown her yet, Dad?'

'Shown me what?' I enquired.

Michael said, 'Well, go ahead. I guess you can.' Aidan grabbed my hand,

'Come and see, Mum, we've got you a present.' He promptly led me out the back door and towards the garage. Michael followed.

There inside the garage was a silver-grey car. Michael informed me It was from the government auctions, fairly new, and in very good condition. He had been buying it through a friend for some months, hoping that I would be coming home and be able to use it. Later, the car dealer told me on several occasions Michael almost had to give it up because he was unable to find the payments, but had eventually just managed. The whole family was thrilled about it. Aidan made me sit in the driver's seat and try all the electric buttons and gears. He was all set for me to take us for a drive and try it out right then, but I managed to convince him I was too tired and it was much more fun in the daytime. It was nicknamed GG short for Grey Ghost, because you couldn't see in the car windows (they were tinted very dark so stickybeaks could not see me).

Next Aidan took me on a tour of every room in the house, and started recommending which cupboards I might like to tidy out! Michael kept suggesting to Aidan that he was tired and might like to go to bed, and Aidan kept saying, 'No, I'm not, Dad.' Eventually I pointed out it would be a big day tomorrow and it would be a good idea if we all went to bed. I only got three hours' sleep before the phone started ringing in the morning.

I walked into my bedroom that first night and couldn't believe how much it had shrunk. My side of the bed was piled high with *more* material from the case. There were filing cabinets in the corner so before I could find some night clothes (or get dressed in the morning) Michael had to move a couple of cupboards so that I could actually open my drawers.

My own bed seemed very strange. It was nearly a month before I could sleep comfortably on it. A number of times I went to the living room when Michael was asleep and lay on the floor for a while until I was tired enough for the strangeness of the bed not to keep me awake.

Next morning I was still in bed and talking on the phone when a whirlwind blew down the hall. The bedroom door burst open and an excited little boy exclaiming, 'Mum!' propelled himself into the room and dived straight onto the bed—plonk on top of me. He made it in one leap but the smaller whirlwind behind him, also squeaking, 'Mummy!' had to break her leap, because the bed was too high and she had to struggle to get up, but she wasn't far behind. The phone went flying to the floor and was forgotten for a couple of minutes until I realised I should tell my caller to ring back later! Then Michael realised the kids were there and he came down to join us. It was a vastly different scene from the one written for the film *Evil Angels (A Cry in the Dark)*.

There was no hesitation on the part of any of the children in accepting me at home again, but life was not all roses. They had to get used to Mum telling them what to do again, and several times one or other of the boys exclaimed, 'But I always do that!', or 'But I always go there on my own!'. The additional parental influence was obviously going to mean some big changes. With Mum around they could no longer get away with doing things as they had with Dad. Even with their food, the boys were independent and quite capable of getting their own.

We had planned that Kahlia would come and go as she wished, gradually transferring her from the Hughes' household to ours, so it would not be so much of a shock. We had reckoned without madam's own determination. She had barely walked in the door when she simply announced, 'Good, I can stay in my own bed now you're home, and you can have a loan of my pillow if you like.' I thanked her and told her it was very nice but I did have one of my own, so maybe she could keep hers.

I learned that when she stayed for weekends she was used to sleeping with Michael in my side of the bed, so I hid a smile and didn't remind her that the pillow she was offering me was actually mine. We made her a bed at the foot of ours until we could set up something permanent for her, and that was fine.

Being able to do housework—like washing my own dishes, for instance—was not really too exciting because we had done our own in jail, yet picking up a vacuum cleaner and vacuuming the floor was almost a pleasure. A broom or a mop was no novelty, but a vacuum cleaner was. The few times I had used the old prison cleaner on Mr Sutton's office had seemed like exquisite pleasure, it was so *normal*. So was a telephone; many times I simply let it ring and realised too late I should answer it.

Getting out of prison was the oddest experience. In many ways it was as if the last three years did not exist, and I had simply come home after a short visit away. I noticed the change most at the supermarket when I went to grab my normal brand of something only to discover it wasn't made any more, or the wrapping had changed so it was unrecognisable.

Prices had skyrocketed beyond belief, so for quite some time I couldn't recognise whether something was a bargain or not. People expected me to be always looking over my shoulder to see whether the cops were about to arrest me as an escapee; I didn't, but I did feel weird whenever I saw police approaching. Fortunately most of the local guys were fairly nice so that helped me get over it a bit.

I found all sorts of unexpected things were different. Streets had more houses and taller trees. Some friends had moved away, others had new babies. Often I found that my place had been filled in people's lives. They were now used to *talking* about me—not having me *there*. They made room for me again, telling me it was great to have me home and everything was as it used to be, and with some it was, but mostly it was not.

In many subtle little ways I found I was no longer needed. I would move towards a familiar chair and find it taken, or walk into a room in my own home where family and friends were and, although they knew I was with them, they had obviously settled in their usual places. They got up, quite flustered to see me there, not quite sure what they should do or who should move. Although they *thought* they were doing a good job of hiding what had happened while I was away, combined with all the seemingly innocent information I had received from a lot of different people whilst I was in prison, it just didn't work. It was like screaming headlines. It is not surprising that when a husband or wife gets out of prison after a long term, the marriage often breaks up.

For nearly a month after I was released, most different foods would give me very bad stomach cramps or diarrhoea, and generally made me miserable. I had to limit myself to very small amounts of new foods, which could be as simple as a piece of pineapple, a peach, grapes, a savoury or spread. About the only things I didn't have a problem with were breads and sweet foods because they were amongst the few things we got fairly regularly in prison; often we filled up on them because the course before had been unpalatable.

Having salt used in cooking again made food taste completely different too. The food in prison had been relentlessly bland (except for chilli, which was sometimes applied with quite a heavy hand). Becoming re-acquainted with condiments and spices was a whole new taste sensation also. I'd had problems for the first month inside, now I was having the same trouble in reverse.

What to Do with the Media

Michael and I had to decide what to do about television appearances. We knew Mike Lester would like us to be interviewed exclusively by his employers, Channel 9, but as they wanted far too much from us, we had opted for a rival channel. It was not the amount of money offered that interested us, but the honesty and integrity of the company, the conditions, and which interviewer they wanted to use. We told Mike we would have liked to go with his channel but were afraid they wanted the wrong things. Mike asked exactly what we wanted, and whether we'd give him half an hour to negotiate. I notified Stuart to hold the contract for a while and sure enough, Mike rang back within half an hour and said he had the deal we wanted. So Channel 9 it was.

We were babes in the wood about what was expected of us, and we had to have a minder who would keep the rest of the press away from us. We asked for Mike instead of a stranger and they agreed. Mike was able to help us with the various interviewers, ferry us around and help keep our children happy while they were waiting for their interview and photo sessions.

We were new at making contracts with the media, but it was the only way we could have some control over their actions and prevent them taking advantage of us. Too many had done that too often before, and it wasn't going to happen again.

Mike suggested we get ourselves an agent and, as Stuart had voiced the same opinion, we were beginning to think seriously about it. Dealing on our own wasn't very satisfactory, as neither Stuart nor we knew the rules by which they played, and they were certainly different to normal business deals. It didn't sound like a bad idea to me, so we accepted Mike's offer to ask around and find out who the best agents might be.

The final factor in our decision to go with Channel 9 was the fact that I wanted to go to church on my first Sabbath home. The other channels wanted me to stay out of sight. That would have been like house arrest—exchanging one prison for another, and I'd already had to stay inside in Darwin. Channel 9 understood and offered to arrange security, so I was able to go to my thanksgiving service.

Being present for the first service in the brand new church at Avondale College was a goal I had always aimed at, but the opening date had been announced while I was still in prison. A couple of weeks later I heard it had been postponed but once again the opening day came and went while I was still inside, and again I was disappointed. Then I heard it had been postponed yet again. Finally, here I was home just before the first service. Wow! I was absolutely thrilled.

On the Friday I was called for a meeting of all the security men, so they could see who they were protecting. The college grounds looked as if they were under a state of siege from the media. Anyone they thought resembled me, even slightly, was followed around the district until the press discovered they were mistaken. My friend Julie O' Neal (nee Gillet) was followed on several occasions. Because of this, and the threats the college had received on my behalf, they were being cautious and coordinating with Channel 9.

The carpet wasn't down on the floor in the church, and the acoustics were not properly fixed, but it *was* the first service—and it was to be a thanksgiving service for my release! Ray Martin was present. He had been called back at our request specially to do the *60 Minutes* interview and we were to meet him after the service. There he was, right down the front among the children, thoroughly enjoying himself. Journalists from other Packer-related media outlets were also there that day, and we met some of them after the church service, but all rival organizations were kept out by the college and TNT Security. Packer had supplied the additional security to safeguard his own interests, but the college was glad of the boost. I later learned from one of the security men, their real fear was a threatened sniper during the church service itself.

The church was overflowing with friends, students, well-wishers and regular church members. Ian Goad, an ex-Federal police officer, had been asked by Jeff Rout of college security (he was great to work with) to help with the security. When my release was announced Ian had bought out the local shop's supply of yellow ribbons and put them around the college gateposts. Others had added more ribbons later. (I had to smile when I realised an ex-cop's ribbons were the first to greet me when I came home late from the plane!)

Sabbath dawned bright and sunny, and for once all of us were ready to go early. The children went across to Sabbath school, but it had already been agreed, for security reasons, that I was not to go until the main church service. The *60 Minutes* crew had already set up their cameras to record the whole service. We had chosen to sit at the back of the balcony, where we had a good view but would not be the centre of curiosity or a distraction to the service. The Avondale College church minister, a classmate from Michael's college days and a special friend of ours, Pastor Lyell Heise, had arranged a thanksgiving and praise service with lots of music. Towards the end of Lyell's talk he would call us up to the platform, so that the church members could see me and welcome me home.

Michael and I walked around to the back entrance and through the side door, where we were to wait until signalled. Lyell spoke about us while we were waiting, and the waiting made me nervous. Then he signalled us. As I stepped out in full view, somebody gasped—there was dead silence for a second or two, then one person started to clap and slowly the whole church joined in, ending in a standing ovation. I was so nervous already I immediately burst into tears. Lyell held his arms out to us. When we reached the pulpit he gave us both a hug. Michael spoke briefly first, then it was my turn. My voice didn't want to co-operate and Michael had his arm around me so tightly it hurt and I could hardly breathe so I had to move it lower.

I said,

> 'Words are totally inadequate to say what we feel and to express our gratitude for your love, and your care, and your prayers. It just reaches out like a blanket and surrounds us. It is totally tangible, you can feel it wafting across the miles.
>
> 'The real fight for justice is only just beginning. You might think it is finished, but believe me, it is only just beginning. This is not just for our

> freedom and our name to be cleared. It's for every Australian. We don't ever want to see this happen in Australia again.
>
> 'May God bless you.'

When I stopped speaking the whole congregation was silent.

After the service I stood at the main door with Lyell so people could greet me personally if they wished. I wanted Michael to stand with me but he would not. Each person was brief and to the point, but there could be no mistaking that I was loved and had been missed. When I finally left, I was exhausted but happy. Security escorted me back to the house where Ray Martin and some others were waiting with Michael and the children.

It was at this time I learned that woman in charge of TNT Security was Pat Stanley, an ex-screw (and later deputy superintendent) from Mulawa! She said she used to take Kahlia from Michael at the gate, and carry her across to the office to be handed over for me to feed! When I met her, I realised she had been the female officer who had escorted me that very early morning when I had been left alone in the office to shower and wait. I discussed this with her, remembering the surprised, questioning look on her face when she was told to leave me alone there. She said it had been highly unusual for a prisoner to be left alone like that, and the incident illustrated how much I was trusted—perhaps because they realised I should not have been there in the first place.

Sabbath afternoon passed quickly with friends and visitors calling. That night my close friends threw me a coming-home party on Jan and Owen Hughes's front lawn. Some of them had travelled from as far as Melbourne and Brisbane. My uncle, aunt and one cousin from America were passing through Australia that weekend, so were able to be there too. Once again everyone was happy and excited and it seemed as if my feet barely had time to touch the ground.

The next day it was time to get ready for the first interview with Ray Martin. We were all dressed up and on our way out to the car for the trip to the Hughes's, 10 kilometres (6 miles) away, where the interview was to be held. For Kahlia, the thought of sharing most things was fine, but this was the first time we had all gone out in the car together, and now it was a different matter.

Kahlia hopped into the front passenger seat, as she was accustomed, and when I went to get in as well, she wouldn't move.

'My seat!' she exclaimed. Michael told her he understood, then tried to cajole her into moving, but she was not at all pleased. I offered to let her sit on my lap but she wouldn't hear of it. Eventually, she opted to sit on the floor by my feet. Halfway there, Kahlia started pinching at my stockings with her fingernails.

The stockings were stretching, fortunately, so I pretended to ignore it. Suddenly, I got a rude shock—she bit me! Michael was extremely surprised. She continued to pout and give me baleful looks, which did not bode well for the interview. Nevertheless, when we got to the Hughes's, Jan managed to talk her out of it, and her sunny disposition soon returned.

In all, Ray Martin spent five days at Cooranbong interviewing Michael and me. The interview was screened on *60 Minutes* early in March 1986.

Ray pointed out that some people had formed bad impressions of me, and asked whether I could offer any explanation. I replied:

> If I cried, I was said to be putting on an act; if I smiled I was heartless. I knew there were people ready to jump on everything I did and said. I cried in private, behind closed doors. I didn't see any reason why they should see the effect on me. I wouldn't give them that pleasure. [I still feel like this.]
>
> I am definitely not going to lie down and die for something I didn't do. I have to clear my name and that of my family . . . I've been called a liar. I don't like it, because I know I am not.

Later I added,

> Would you lie and say you had done something that you have never done when you could tell the truth? It's made me very angry to think that I have been told over and over again that 'if you'd lied and said you'd done it you'd be out of jail, but if you tell the truth you stay in prison'. You shouldn't have to lie to get justice.

A very nice cartoon by Nicholson of the *Melbourne Age* emphasises that point. Two Aussie ockers are having a conversation over a barbecue and one says to the other: 'Release Lindy? Not as long as she continues to maintain her innocence!' That was published in December 1985, just before I was released.

When Ray asked me about the attitude of the Northern Territory I said,

> 'It was quite obvious by the time we got to the second inquest. It didn't really matter much what we said, the Northern Territory was not prepared to listen. They said to me outright: "If we don't get you this time, we'll get you next time. We'll have this inquest and another one until you get charged because we are going to get you. "'

Ray Martin had arranged for one of the jurors, Yvonne Cain, to come to Cooranbong to meet me. On the appointed interview day I went for a walk down the road and when she arrived they kept her talking. It had been previously arranged that at a given signal I would walk up behind her and the cameras would be rolling to catch our reactions. I had no idea what I would do or say when I came face to face with her.

Yvonne was not given any indication of what was happening. She was extremely nervous about being interviewed and meeting me, and did not realise the cameras were already rolling. When I was within 2 metres (6 feet) of her Yvonne realised that Ray was looking at someone over her shoulder. She glanced round but her expression did not change until Ray indicated who it was, and I said, 'Hello'. Then her face changed. She looked amazed, shattered, shocked and horrified. She put her hands to her face and said, 'Oh my God, what have they done to you!' We walked towards each other and she flung her arms around me, and we cried in each other's arms.

Yvonne kept repeating over and over that it was not right and that she was sorry. She had been unconvinced of my guilt but had allowed herself to be persuaded, along with a number of the others. Every time they came up with a reason for innocence, one of the more vocal and outspoken members of the jury countered it with what seemed to be a logical, scientific explanation for murder, which they found difficult to comprehend in its complexity. As they ran out of objections while the others still had not, they finally conceded guilt.

Several years later we met again, and when Yvonne showed me her notebook I learned some very interesting things about the way the jury thought about my case. She was the only juror to keep a diary and the other jurors all referred to her notes when it came to making a decision. She was amazed to learn that we had known the jury was split three ways (guilty, not guilty and uncertain) during the afternoon while they were still out. As she remembered, no one had entered the room, so we decided that the information we had received via the press from the police had come either from the rubbish bin which had been put out to be emptied, or from a bugging device in the room somewhere. Either way it should not have happened.

The notes Yvonne took were interesting. She noted for instance, that Joy Kuhl had a very easy to listen to manner, so they listened with avid attention, 'like a bunch of schoolchildren'. She was impressed that Joy Kuhl 'was able to give an answer and explanation to all questions fired at her by Mr Phillips, there seems to be no doubt to her that the blood in the car is foetal blood.' Yvonne said that, on the other hand, they had found Barry Boettcher difficult to understand as his evidence was too technical for them, and they did not like his presentation.

Some of her lay observations were interesting, and convinced me even more of the need for panels of specialist scientists to evaluate forensic evidence and to only place their agreed summary before the jury. For instance, of Professor Nairn, one of Australia's top pathologists and a consultant, Yvonne Cain had written, 'Professor Nairn only does blood tests maybe once a week, Mrs Kuhl does it every day and it is her only job.' Of Dr Baxter, Mrs Kuhl's boss, it had impressed them that he had agreed with all Mrs Kuhl's tests and could not be put off by Mr Phillips's cross- examination, so they concluded that there was no doubt that the blood found in the car could be foetal blood. Mr Cullerford, an expert from England, had somehow given them to understand that he 'invented the particular type of blood testing that had been used for detecting foetal blood.' With that impression, the fact that he had agreed with Joy Kuhl would weigh heavily, and the errors in methodology and interpretation went unnoticed. Specialists in these fields weren't swayed by presentation, but evaluated the facts and rejected Joy Kuhl's evidence.

Yvonne had written that the jury was very impressed with Professor Chaikin's evidence where he used the magnified photographs of cut fibre ends. I guess that was easier to understand. What a pity they were unable to view the photographs from the point of view of experts who realised that other types of cuts also looked like that.

Of Dr Harding's evidence, Mrs Cain noted, 'Cat's hairs were imbedded in the material probably for months, the other hairs were human. Dingo hairs were compared with cat hairs and there was no comparison.' How different it all was from what we knew to be true.

From Mr Kuchel, the botanist, they decided it was 'unlikely the jumpsuit had been dragged over the sand at the back of their tent. All the seeds and bits of plant that were found on the jumpsuit were all growing in the area that the clothes were found in.' That was another misconception, as we well knew.

Detective Sergeant Brown, the policeman who claimed to have found the space blanket, convinced them 'there was great doubt about the marks being paw prints. The blanket also had numerous cuts and pulls through normal wear and tear.' The fact that it had only been used once before that night and could not possibly be worn entirely slipped their notice. They were not impressed with either Miss Fogarty's or Constable Morris's handling of the evidence either, and also concluded Michael could not remember very much, but did believe it was a dingo that took his child.

Yvonne Cain found Murray Haby credible when he spoke of his tracking on the sandhill, and believed that I had come 'to his Kombi Van and asked for a torch saying the dingo had taken her baby.' Well it sounded like that to me too, although I knew I hadn't. I hoped to ask him about it one day. Of my evidence she wrote, 'very sad, had a low voice and cried a couple of times, still keeps to the original story. It is hard to think that she may be lying.'

From Yvonne Cain's notes I couldn't believe they had got things so wrong. Barker's oratory and clever cross-examination had obviously confused them. John Phillip's summary notes dwelt on Sally Lowe hearing Azaria cry, but his oratory did not carry the impression that Barker's did. Under that she had written 'Sounds so convincing.' Under the judge's summary she wrote 'Whew!' The fact that he had summed up for acquittal had gone unnoticed, and she told me she had understood him to mean we were guilty but had found him hard to understand. Obviously the others had also found him hard to understand.

The jury wondered why I had not given the alarm until I had gone in and out of the tent, but decided that the evidence could point to my having called out before after all, and that:

> They did not search, while three hundred people were out searching, Lindy and Michael went to the Uluru Motel at midnight and spent the night there. Next morning he did not ring the police to see if there was any news, he rang his mother and said a dingo had taken Azaria and they did not expect to find the body. After that they went out taking photos for newspapers, they were at the local Aboriginal camp taking snaps of the camp dogs when they bumped into the police and told them they were leaving the next day to Mt Isa. Lindy had suggested they take a trip out to the Olgas! How could they contemplate leaving so soon?

All the evidence from the eyewitnesses of us searching, and being told to move to the motel, then told to leave and go home by the police had been forgotten, and I'm not sure where the bit about photographing camp dogs came from—maybe that was meant to be identifying them for Derek Roff! With that misconception of the evidence, it was a wonder any of them thought we might have been innocent!

Yvonne questioned, 'Why didn't the defence test the blood in the car??? Was it because they didn't dare take the chance? Or did they, and obviously couldn't tell us the results!' The fact that Joy Kuhl had used all the material and there was none left, and that she had destroyed all her evidence so that we could not look at that either, seemed to have completely passed them by.

She queried:

> Did Mr Chamberlain carry the clothes in the camera bag on the night of the incident over to where the clothes were found. O' tol test showed up the baby could have been in the bag he could have thrown the baby in a dingo lair.

I don't know how they thought a baby would fit in the bag.

At seven o'clock that night they:

> ...all went down for another look at the car—tent. By this time it was dark and we noticed that the light from the passageway led to where the tent was. We placed the baby's basket with the doll in it and stood by the tent. There was no way that we could have seen that the baby was not in the basket, could barely make out the basket. When we got back we had a vote again, ten to two for guilty. At eight-twenty all guilty.

This is what Yvonne Cain wrote in her diary of that verdict: 29.10.82 8.30 p.m.

> GUILTY
>
> Awful feeling in the pit of my stomach. Shaking from head to toe, feel almost dizzy.
>
> LIFE HARD LABOUR, HORRIBLE IT SOUNDS LIKE SHE WILL HAVE TO SMASH ROCKS UP FOR THE REST OF HER LIFE (Sorry) what else could we do.

So much was explained by those notes—it was no wonder several members of the jury cried when the verdict was given. Yvonne told me it was a shock to her when I was sentenced to life with hard labour. It had not really sunk in that that was the only punishment possible for murder. Years later, when I spoke to Yvonne again, she told me she will remember the look on my face that day for the rest of her life—and I will remember her crying when the verdict was handed down. She said she felt like standing up and saying, Look we're only joking. We didn't really mean it.' But it was too late. If only she had!

Ray Martin was also hoping to interview the boys, promising to do it as painlessly as possible. In the end it was agreed that after some filming of them riding their motorbikes, Ray would stop them while they were relaxed and try asking questions. If they got upset, the interview would be aborted.

Ray began by asking Aidan how he was handling things and what he thought of people who said his Mum was guilty. Aidan immediately burst into tears. Ray tried asking about the night, telling Aidan he had been the only one with me that night, and maybe he could help clear up a few misunderstandings. 'Mum never wanted to do . . . She would never want to do that,' Aidan started to say and that was the end of that, he could go no further. I knew he meant that I would never want anything to happen to any of them, and that I would never kill any of them, but many members of the doubting public (thinking no doubt that he meant I had killed her by accident) took his words as just one more indication of my guilt.

Ray spent the next ten minutes gently calming Aidan down and explaining he had not meant to hurt or embarrass him. Ray's attitude at all times was very compassionate and straightforward. At no stage did he use any of the bulldozer tactics frequently used by the press we had mainly dealt with in the past. He lived up to his reputation of being a gentleman, and we realised that we could add one more genuine honest journalist to our list.

After we had done the interview for *60 Minutes*, and a companion piece for the *Australian Women's Weekly*, it was arranged with Kerry Packer for us to go somewhere unknown to avoid rival press finding and photographing me, so we went to a beach house belonging to a friend of ours. Mike Lester and Pat Stanley, who were still assigned to 'babysit' us, had rooms in a local motel. We drove around a bit, walked through the national parks and generally had a nice quiet time.

Michael was occasionally recognised, but I wasn't, as nobody knew what I looked like. Everybody was still expecting to see me very fat. Once while I was standing with my arm through Michael's, leaning on him and calling him, 'darling' the checkout woman in the local fruit shop—who saw him regularly—stopped him and said how pleased she was that his *wife* was back and would he please convey her congratulations. It was clear she didn't have any idea who I was and it was obvious what she thought. She later asked my brother who the young lady his brother-in-law had with him was. At the time I had teased Michael about people thinking he was with a girlfriend! I had thought it a joke but she sure didn't. Nor did he.

Some of the press found where we were and drove up and down local streets looking for us, so the beach house became unsafe. We were then taken to Kerry Packer's property near Scone in the foothills of the Barrington Tops, central New South Wales. We stayed on one of his farms; where there was a distance of 7 kilometres (4 miles) between the front gate and the house. Mike and Pat stayed in the house with us and we enjoyed our week driving around the farm and walking over the hills. We even had Kerry Packer's personal four-wheel-drive shooting wagon.

Except for the manager, no one knew we were there until the last morning, when the gentleman who lived in the house returned home to be told by his boss that he was to stay with them for a day or two because there was somebody living in his house! We met him before we left. Till then he hadn't known who it was, so he was quite intrigued to know he had had the Chamberlains as guests.

Michael's birthday was during that week so we all went in to town to celebrate. We couldn't find anywhere considered safe, so in the end we settled for take-away pizzas and ate them in the park. Quite a gale was blowing, and here we were around a table in the dark eating and laughing. We had a lot of fun. We thought the press would *never* believe what we were doing. I found it incredible that, three years after going to prison, I was celebrating Michael's birthday with one of the screws from Mulawa—

not to mention a reporter. While we were sitting there, a young man walked over and said, 'Hello, Michael, Lindy.' Surely we hadn't been caught, we thought—not now! But it was only a young man on his way to Avondale College who had recognised Michael and come across to say hello and lend his support.

The *Women's Weekly* article was due out that week too, so we went into the depot to see if we could get a copy of the magazine in advance. We couldn't; the carrier was virtually under pain of death not to give them away. This was where Mike came in handy as Kerry Packer's personal agent; he told them that Mr Packer wanted one. He pointed to Kerry Packer's wagon, which was fairly well known around the area, and said, 'If you have got any problems you can ring Mr Packer,' giving the correct home number. We were given three copies. We all sat in the cars reading the story for the first time. It was some of the first favourable press we had had for many a year.

With the *Women's Weekly* out on the streets, I didn't have to avoid the photographers any more so Mike asked me whether Michael was going to take me out to celebrate my release and my birthday. I had been really cooped up and had hardly seen anything since I had been released.

'Well, I don't know, I wouldn't mind celebrating, go somewhere nice, but it costs a fair bit and we haven't got that sort of cash,' I answered.

He said he couldn't see why Kerry Packer couldn't foot the bill and would work on it.

During a stay at a house near Woy Woy on the central coast of New South Wales, we went to a local supermarket for groceries. A number of people were in the queue behind us, but as nobody gave us curious glances, we thought we were unrecognised.

We had come out, put our groceries in the car, and were sitting in the front seats ready to drive back when I noticed one of the women who had been in the queue coming around the corner. She was tall and blonde, with rather Scandinavian or German features, and she was smiling and waggling her head from side to side in a most unusual manner. I thought at first she was a bit simple, but as she approached us it was obvious she was extremely angry.

She came right up to the car, and spat with all her might on the windscreen, giving us a peculiar look, somewhere between a grin and a leer, as she did so.

I chose to ignore the incident, choosing not to give her the pleasure of reacting. But it was different for Michael; his mouth dropped open and he stared at her retreating back. 'Did you see what she did?' he asked, incredulous. 'Yes,' I said, and went to carry on our conversation. But Michael wasn't listening. He looked aghast, and so utterly taken aback (his mouth open like a dead fish) that I burst out laughing, having a sense of the ridiculous that is often far too strong.

The woman saw me laugh and was more furious than ever, but Michael was seriously upset, and my reaction didn't help. He couldn't understand how I could laugh when something like that happened, but it was the sort of thing I had determined long ago would not affect me, so it had no power to hurt. (People who have seen *Evil Angels (A Cry In The Dark)* may remember an inaccurate re-enactment of this scene; a passer-by spits on the glass of a phone booth in which Meryl Streep is making a call, and she laughs hysterically.)

Now my face had been published on the newsboards, I found I couldn't go anywhere without creating a stir.

One day, shortly afterwards I was having my hair done in Nowra on the south coast of New South Wales. Tanya, the owner, was doing mine and one of her girls was doing another customer. After a while Tanya realised that the *Women's Weekly* with our family pictures on the front cover was right in front of the other customer and she couldn't put it away without looking conspicuous.

We wondered how long it would take the other customer to realise that the woman she was looking at on that magazine cover was actually in the shop with her. Shortly we noticed that she was looking at the magazine and then very carefully at me. Soon she commented, 'That's Lindy Chamberlain over there, isn't it? I recognise her. You know, I always thought she was guilty, but now I've seen her I know she couldn't possibly have done it. I can't wait to go home and tell my friends.'

The girl was so astounded that she made an excuse to come over and talk to Tanya and repeated in a low voice what the woman had said.

I said, 'Well, now you understand why I say some people will never believe because their reasoning is not rational.'

Even if I knocked on all the doors in Australia I still wouldn't convince some people. One has to learn to live with the percentage that decide where there's smoke, there's fire, and you *must* be guilty because it has been in the paper. There must have been *some* funny business even if it wasn't *actually* murder.

If I had thought I was well known before I had been mistaken. Now I found people who were complete strangers addressing me quite confidently either as 'Mrs Chamberlain' or 'Lindy', whatever happened to appeal to them. They talked to me as a friend, telling me about their families and the things that happened to them as if I knew them well. It was a very friendly feeling. If one has to learn to be in the public eye, albeit unwillingly, then it is nice to have that kind of public reaction.

At home there was a massive task awaiting me, and it couldn't wait if we were all going to live in that house. There were now three extra people moved in, and the same amount of space. Besides that, Michael had had to move all his study furniture up to the loungeroom in order to accommodate Lesley. Lesley was the mother of a friend of ours, and had been engaged as a permanent live-in nanny only a week before I had suddenly been released. We knew a lot of people would be calling when I first arrived home and it would take me a while to get things back to normal. So, she did the normal daily washing and ironing, kept the kitchen clean, prepared the meals, and got the children off to school.

Lesley would have to stay with us for at least a few months until the Commission dates were set, and we found out how much time would be involved in that as we would need her to look after the children while we were away.

I sat in the loungeroom, rearranging the furniture in my mind's eye. Just then a friend dropped in and I said, 'Good. Just in time to assist me. I want to move some filing cabinets and they're too heavy.'

He looked horrified and said, 'Where are you going to put more in here?' I said, 'Just wait and see. Can you help me?'

He said, 'Sure, we're on flexitime I can get one of the other guys as well and a trolley if you like. Give me half an hour.'

Michael was away on business so I shut the loungeroom doors and when he arrived home took him straight down to the bedroom. There was not one filing cabinet in sight.

He was amazed and said, 'It looks great. But what have you done with them?' Then I took him to the loungeroom, and he couldn't believe it. The floor space had doubled, but so had the number of filing cabinets. I had managed to get twice as much in, simply by the way I had arranged everything. He just stood there—stunned.

Finally he said, 'It's great, but don't move too much stuff *too* quickly or I'll get culture shock! I've lived with it like it was for so long.'

There were newspaper articles and sorting from our case in every available corner because no storage space was left. I didn't realise just how stacked the house was until the day after I got home when I started to look around and open various cupboards.

Reagan had twenty-two cartons of assorted toys, junk and clothes (clean *and* dirty) under and around both sides of his double bed. His room was so full that to get into his bed he actually had to climb in over the bed end! It was obvious that for some time, instead of sorting the mess, the housekeepers had thought, 'What's a quick way to deal with this? Here's a box, put everything in and stack it away.' Even the linen cupboard, which was in frequent use, had the oddest things crammed in it, and the other cupboards and drawers were worse. I slowly began to sort out every cupboard in the house.

For weeks this made more of a mess, because I had to pull things out of one cupboard that didn't belong there and leave them somewhere while I collected what should go in and straighten it out. Then I would tackle the next cupboard, so there was a growing pile of things I couldn't place yet. Between visitors and the regular daily schedule, Reagan's bedroom took me a full three weeks to sort out.

Moving into houses with small cupboards, I had soon learned to pack things very neatly and tidily, getting in a great deal. This talent came in handy. I put less-used things in suitcases and stacked them under the beds or down in the back shed (it had taken a fortnight to clean that up so I could stack more there).

Aidan's bedroom was much easier than Reagan's. He and I got in there together and three days straightened it out. He was quite proud of his room then. He was very excited that he had new curtains.

I said to him, 'Honey, they aren't new curtains. They're your old ones. Why didn't you hang them up before? Your bedspread has faded from the sun in the last three years and been ruined.'

He exclaimed, 'I didn't know I had any curtains.' In the trauma of my return to jail they had all forgotten I had just washed and ironed his curtains ready to hang back up. They had stayed where I left them for three years!

The kids grumbled about keeping their rooms tidy. Reagan maintained that he knew where everything had been before, and now he couldn't find a thing. I sat him down and explained where all his things were, and he was quite happy after that. Items that he had long been looking for had turned up. As the days went by and he found more and more precious 'treasures', it helped compensate for the fact that he had a mother at home telling him he must make his bed, and put his toys away every day because I would not tolerate another scrambled toy session. (Now he is the tidiest child in the house.)

We were all relaxing before bedtime one night. Reagan had had a shower after some considerable grumbling and was now happier and certainly looking better scrubbed and clean.

He had what looked like a boil forming on his leg and I asked to have a look at it. He told me it was really sore and to be careful. I looked—and couldn't believe it. It was not a boil, but a huge festering blackhead! I then inspected the rest of his legs and a number of other places were fast reaching the same state. He had huge deep blackheads covering the whole of his legs, and also some on his arms. Then we *really* had a serious talk about showers.

I said, 'Right, Sonshine, you are going to get very ill. Whether you like it or not, Mummy is going to get all those blackheads out and then you are going to go and have a good scrub in the bath again.' He was fascinated by the big ugly blackheads popping out of his legs, but did not appreciate the pain that accompanied it. At the end of a solid half hour he maintained he couldn't possibly stand any more.

I agreed now the worst were out and sent him off to the bath again, and said, 'Tomorrow night we'll do it again until they are all gone and you learn you must wash yourself *every* night. No good telling Daddy you have had baths when I know you haven't. I have been watching you for the three weeks I've been home (after three years' absence I had to take over gently) and little boys who go to bed in their school clothes and get up and wear them to school again the next morning with dirty food all down the front, and pretend they are clean knowing Daddy doesn't see them, are not doing the right thing. You do not get away with that any more now.'

He did a grumble and Aidan laughed and said, 'See, I told you you wouldn't get away with it when Mum got home.' Then I started on Aidan. Aidan had been more careful in his washing and didn't have any blackheads, but he also had been guilty of lying in his clothes on top of the bed and just throwing them under the bed and around the room and hoping he didn't get caught, or changing the top layer and not the underneath one. So I warned them I was going to keep a close eye on them for the next fortnight.

The fact that Michael had told them when they went swimming at night they didn't have to have a bath did not mean they could go without baths totally as long as they went for a swim occasionally. Even then, they should at least wash the chlorine off. We argued over whether or not we had a bath every night for several weeks, but Reagan's episode several nights in a row with the blackheads and the benefit that he felt afterwards soon convinced him that at least five nights a week a bath was a good thing and much more comfortable—particularly when he was covered in mud, sand and mulberry juice!

My bedroom was tidy, more or less, and the lounge was getting there so I could relax a little.

Kahlia was still sleeping on the floor at the bottom of our bed because there was nowhere else to put her at that stage. She had to have her own bed. Reagan's antique double bed from his nanna was packed up and we went searching for two singles. We couldn't get what we wanted and ended up with an unpainted set. We rearranged the room so we were able to put Reagan and Kahlia in together. We couldn't use a double decker as Reagan still fell out of bed (he sleepwalked) and Kahlia was too little for the top level, so they had twin singles.

Meanwhile they slept on the floor while Michael and I started to sand down and paint the beds. (We got three-quarters of the way through and the Commission started, and that was the end of that. We didn't finish their beds off until after the end of the Commission when we had shifted. Then they each had their own bedroom. Reagan, much to his delight, got the antique double bed back again.)

I found bags of brand-new clothes that had been given to Kahlia as presents, as well as some she had obviously worn on a day's outing, still with wet nappies and remnants of a picnic lunch all tidily wrapped up in a plastic bag and stuffed down the back of a wardrobe, under a bed, or in some cupboard. Michael didn't remember that they had been put there. Obviously someone thought they were putting things away but they had done it without having a look. Wet clothes were mouldy, even some new clothes had damage. Some clothes had been grown out of before I found them. Some first birthday cards to Kahlia and other mail, including a number of my letters to the children, had never even been opened and had been stuck in the most curious places.

Michael had told everybody, including the kids, that nobody was to touch my cupboards, no matter what. The kids told me he strictly enforced that with them, even when I had given them permission to look there.

But even those cupboards hadn't escaped; there were old wet nappies and food in mine as well. In fact quite a bit of the unopened mail had been stashed in those cupboards of mine or his.

Slowly but surely I sorted everything out. I threw out boxloads of rubbish that had been put away. I gave away clothes that had been grown out of. I removed every curtain in the house and washed or dry-cleaned them, and I cleaned the Venetian blinds. Then there was the problem of getting stains out of clothes.

Lesley must have washed and ironed all day for almost ten weeks before that job was finished. Eventually we managed to find the floors, the hallway having been the worst obstacle course as the dumping ground for anything still waiting to find a home.

One day the boys came home and could actually see the hallway. They were so excited; the house was becoming normal again. Aidan in particular was pleased. He said, 'It really feels like you're home, Mum. Things are looking like they used to look.' Although we had our differences over baths and keeping rooms tidy, the boys were really pleased to see me.

Food was another problem. They had been used to coming in and grabbing what they felt like and often feeding themselves before Michael got home at night. Aidan loved vegetables and would eat just about anything in sight. Reagan, we discovered, had been existing almost solely, when he could get away with it—which was most of the time—on Weet-Bix, toast and jam. No wonder he was looking pale and sickly. He had to have quite a stern talking to about his lack of vegetables, then all I had to do was remind him of his recent blackheads and the boils he had got while I was away at the first inquest. That assisted the food to go down the hatch very quickly! Even now he looks at some food and says, 'Ugh, yuk,' and I look at him and say, 'I beg your pardon.'

'Well, I'm eating it, I'm eating it. I just said "yuk",' he says. Occasionally it takes a little more persuasion than that, but basically he is a lot better with his food.

Aidan has developed hollow legs and eats almost anything within reach, and Kahlia is learning to eat some of everything.

Having only been home one week, I could not believe my eyes when out at Miller's place I saw one of our sons climb up on to the table and crawl more than a metre (a yard) along the middle of it, fetch what he wanted, and crawl back. I had almost convinced myself that I was hallucinating and really hadn't seen that at all when Jen caught my eye.

She looked at me, smiled and said, 'It's all right, Mum, there are some little things we overlook. Things will change. They will get better, don't worry. Dads do great jobs but there are some things that need a mother's touch and get sadly missed.'

Meals for the kids were riots at times. The table would only fit in a place where it could not be used by everybody at once, so they had forgotten how to have communal meals. Most meals were eaten on a tray in front of the television. By the time we had scrubbed the carpet clean in that room and got to the table, the boys looked at me aghast, and said that they didn't like sitting at a table.

I informed them that at least once a week we were going to have a family meal and they were going to learn some manners again! They would learn to eat properly with a knife and fork. They would learn to use serviettes, to sit still and not to bob up and down, to say 'pass' and 'please' and 'thank you' instead of reaching and grabbing for things. It is working—*slowly*—although we still have discussions about manners. Sometimes now they can be taken out to restaurants, although at one stage I wondered whether I would ever be able to do that!

One of the first items on my list of things to do was to get my art subjects sorted out and my correct marks credited. As soon as I could manage a break from my visitors, I went down to the art department to see the lecturer, Mr Painter. I wanted him to re-mark my fourth-year work now I was home. I knew I deserved an upgrade as a result of the mixup that had occurred between my first- and fourth-year work, while I was in jail. Then he informed me it really didn't matter! Somebody should have told me that Avondale College didn't have correspondence students; he had just marked my work to be nice, but I really couldn't count any of my grades towards my degree in Applied Arts. Besides, I hadn't done my second-year theory exam and as marks are organised pyramid fashion, nothing could be credited without that.

I was dumbfounded!

'What do you mean I haven't done the exam?' I said. 'Of course I did it.' He said, 'Not my exam.'

I said, 'Yes it was!'

I could even produce the letter saying he had sent me the exam. He informed me that in that case it had got lost on the way back, because he had never received it and the letters weren't in his file. But not only had I done the exam, I had received marks for it and been sent the next semester's work. He denied this and, as he was going on a year's leave, I was not able to get my letters and college studies (which were still packed after my release from Darwin) unpacked before he left the following day.

He would not take my word nor was he prepared to do anything about any of my subjects just then, but said if I repeated my art history class with his relief teacher, he would consider what to do about the rest when he returned! Meanwhile, I still possessed an official printout containing my art marks. I also had a letter stating I had received eighty per cent for that exam, which should have given me an upgrade in the subject. To top it off, the class he wanted me to join eventually had an assignment and a class participation assessment instead of an exam! (I had started it but was unable to attend, as I was away at the Commission.) Of course, I had done all my assignments and classes with him already anyway.

Feeling upset after that encounter, I went to see my other art lecturer, Curley. (My 'lost' assignment had been carefully handed back to me—untyped still in its original envelope, with the instructions written in full view on the outside—the first night I had arrived home.) Curley had forgotten by then that I had even been in his class. When I insisted he look it up, he checked with the other students and his record book and discovered I had indeed been in his class, and that he even had some of my marks recorded. As he had been the one to take the phone call telling me the Federal Court was on, he was probably distracted by the news and had obviously forgotten to mark the tutorial I had only just finished. He had also forgotten his agreement about my absence from lectures. I really should have been told Avondale doesn't have correspondence students and I would need to repeat the subject. Oh, and he was sorry about my photography assignment being lost. I would need to do that again too.

I said, 'Do you mean to tell me that you are not even going to look at this assignment?'

He said, 'No, I'm not. There's no point.'

This being the second such experience in a row, I was totally disgusted. I was so upset and so wild that no one had told me (that assignment had cost me hours of blood, sweat and tears, trying to study in a hostile environment) that I'd had enough. For the first time in my life I destroyed something that I had put a lot of work into. I ripped the assignment in half in front of him and walked out.

I then went across to the academic dean to see what I could do. I was in for another shock. I discovered that I had been given automatic withdrawals from some subjects which I was halfway through completing. Neither my lecturers in those subjects nor I had been informed of this, and it was not supposed to be done without consultation between the student and the college.

Most of the people I needed to see about it were away on vacation, so I asked for a letter from the academic office stating that a number of my subjects were under discussion. I needed this to hand to the coming Commission, because they had asked for full statements of our academic records to be included with our initial submissions. No one wanted to take responsibility and after visiting three different people, I could take the matter no further and had to give up.

The letter was important. There was one set of academic records held at the prison and another completely different set held at the college. This made it look as if I had lied to the prison in order to get extra study privileges. No one wanted to know about it.

I'd had complete cooperation with all the subjects I had completed for the Food and Family Management side of my course. The teachers were helpful, even finding required articles in the college library themselves, which they had photocopied and sent through for me when I had endeavoured to find the material in Darwin and been unable to. My marks had also been officially credited. It was interesting how two faculties could work so differently within the one college. One day I will finish my art course but where is another matter.

Just recently I saw Curley again and he asked me when I would be returning to the art department, as they missed seeing me around. I just grinned.

He said, 'You are not still having trouble with those subjects, are you?' I grinned again and kept looking at him. He said, 'I thought you had sorted that out.' I still grinned and looked at him. He looked puzzled and then said, 'It wasn't *my* subject, was it?' It was obvious he had forgotten once again. Incidentally, both he and Painter are still friends of mine.

Things were starting to settle into routine at last, when Stuart approached us again about the film producer Verity Lambert. She was very persistent and was coming over from England to meet John Bryson, the author of the book *Evil Angels*, for which she had bought the film rights and she would still like to talk to us too. I eventually agreed. Michael admitted then that he had actually spoken to her before on the phone or in person, and thought my meeting her would be worthwhile. Then Stuart said to us, 'I think you really ought to get yourself some sort of an agent first. It's getting too much for me, keeping the press off your backs. It would be good if you had someone who could just exclusively manage that side for you.'

As Mike Lester had once said the same thing, we rang him and he said that Harry M Miller was the name that kept coming up. He could put us in touch with some of his clients if we wished to check him out. That was the name of a guy who had written to me in jail or so I thought. Although it was apparently protocol to wait for him to contact us again, we did check him out with a number of his clients, and found they were all very happy with his representation of them, so we decided to give him a go. We arranged a meeting with him through Mike (via Graham Kennedy, I think).

On the appointed day we met Harry at his home, liked what we saw and decided he was OK. Harry must have done the same because he agreed to take us on. Later he asked me how we had initially heard of him. 'Well you wrote to me when I was in jail and offered to represent me,' I said. Harry looked blank. 'No I didn't,' he said. Then it was my turn to look blank. We eventually worked out that it was a practical joker meaning to be nasty, but whoever it was had done us both a good turn, as Harry is a top agent. (I later learned Harry usually chooses you—you don't choose him!) From then on Harry dealt with the press, and we thankfully ceased to be annoyed by them—most of the time anyway. Harry was able to take over any arrangements with Verity Lambert, and Stuart Tipple was gratefully able to concentrate on the preparations for the coming Commission.

Having lost all my horrible excess postnatal weight in prison, when I was released and came south it was summer and none of my clothes fitted me. A lot of the clothes I had had when we lived up north were suitable only for house wear, and I had no good Sabbath clothes as long frocks had been fashionable before I went to prison and now, of course, they were not. As for winter clothes, I had none whatsoever.

I had worn out all my underclothes in jail too; as one set wore out I would write to Michael and get him to send me some more from my drawer (then I had to go through the rigmarole of signing them into my property, waiting a while, asking to exchange the ones I had because I'd got 'sick of these for a while', then waiting again until I could throw the ones I was 'sick of' out!). Eventually I came home to a drawer totally empty of *my* underclothes, so I really needed a shopping spree. People, excited I was out, and realising the situation I was in, gave me money for clothes as a release present, so I had the fun of going out and buying clothes. I didn't have time to make them and I could enjoy the shopping I had been unable to do for years. Even then I hunted for bargains, and I found out where the second-hand shop was and got extra good value for my money.

I did a lot of my shopping in the Queen Victoria markets in Melbourne or the Vic Boutique, as it is often known. I was able to bargain like anyone else, until publicity on the film started. (Why is it that everyone automatically thought *we* were instant millionaires just because John Bryson sold his book rights?) When I went again during that time, one of the ladies at the 'Vic' looked at me and said, 'How about this for you?' I said, 'No, far too expensive.'

She just laughed and said, 'You can afford that, you are rich now.' Slowly the idea continued to be perpetrated that because a film was being made about us, we were rich and could afford anything we liked. My bargaining power in any given situation was virtually nil after that, and we read all sorts of stories about what we had done, or were supposed to be doing.

Everyone seemed to overlook the fact that it was John Bryson's book that the film was based on. We only helped with extra research on the personal side. For some reason people think that if a book or something is about you, you get the profit. The author gets the profits (it isn't a lot) and they *don't even have to ask your permission* to write about you—or to make a film. If they want to they can take the chance of being sued for libel, and just do it. If you have been convicted of a crime anyone can write libel or outright lies about you whenever they like, as some did to us, and you cannot touch them. There is no recourse, even though we have been cleared.

Robert Caswell had been chosen to write the movie, and the first time we met him was at a dinner to discuss research for the film. Poor Robert got off a direct flight from the USA and came almost straight to the hotel for dinner with Verity Lambert the producer, Greg Coote the assistant director, Harry Miller, Michael and me. I spent most of the evening talking to Greg Coote because I knew we wouldn't get to know him much and we would see a lot of Robert in the future, so I simply wanted to watch Robert without him being aware of it, and get to know, a little, what he was like. Michael spent most of the time talking to Verity Lambert, so Robert had to talk to Harry Miller.

Halfway through the meal, Robert joined in the conversation with Greg and me. Clothes sense was mentioned. I forgot I hadn't known Robert before, opened my big mouth and said, 'Well, you can't talk about style. Look at that horrid tie you are wearing.' Robert was dead silent for a minute, then punched me in the arm and said, 'Well, it's not mine.'

I said, 'Well, what are you wearing it for?' He glanced across to Verity, lowered his voice and said, 'Because all my luggage has gone astray and Verity said I had to! It is out of Roadshow's wardrobe and it was the best of some absolutely horrible ones.' (He liked bowties.)

That also explained why he was wearing jeans. We both laughed and the ice was broken. We all enjoyed the rest of the evening and it was decided that we would act as advisers in the movie so we could be sure of its accuracy.

We met Robert Caswell on our own the next day so we could get to know one another better. He summed Michael up in about the first five minutes, and to my surprise gave me a rundown on Michael's character that I couldn't have bettered myself. Robert told me later that it took him about four months to work me out. One thing he always did was to shake my hand and then hold it a moment longer than was polite, to see my reaction.

He said, 'I could tell by your eyes that you didn't like it, you got mad, but were too polite to tell me to get lost.' He said knowing that, he did it consistently as he wanted to test my self-control and endurance. Apparently I won, as I lasted longer than he did. Later he said, 'I got about ten words out of you for the first six weeks [it was actually a bit more] and that's all.' We laughed about that later as he said, 'Can't shut you up now!'

Shortly after that Fred Schepisi, the director, and his crew came to Avondale. We had arranged to pick them up and transport them all around, and arrange for access to various locations of significance to the film. These would later be duplicated in movie sets. This was well before any filming was to take place. About seven people arrived, including the heads of the wardrobe, art and photography departments.

Fred Schepisi interviewed as many of the real people involved in our case as he could, so he could study them and give the right interpretation to the actors when he was directing.

I found it disconcerting to have all these film people in my own home. I knew they had to be accurate, but I was ashamed of the state the place was in. There were still piles of letters, boxes, mending and things that literally had no place to be put, so the house looked very untidy, unlike the way I normally lived. I was afraid the impression these people gained would be transferred to the sets. I was always a very tidy person, so this was really disconcerting.

Robert Caswell did his research for the script by interviewing everyone he could, from Crown lawyers to Northern Territory police and forensic people, then on to Melbourne forensic experts, the Commission and Chamberlain lawyers. He went to Darwin officials, Northern Territory politicians and the media before he wrote the story. The final script was truth as he saw it, having gathered extensive information from all those involved, as well as the Chamberlains. (Schepisi changed it in places—especially the ending.)

Numbers of people have asked me what it felt like to be portrayed in a movie, and it isn't easy to describe. The whole idea slowly grew, and was accepted as inevitable, just another unreal thing that has happened to us in the past ten years. Although I helped with the research and saw some of the filming in progress, it still seemed unreal. Even now, when I look at Meryl Streep on the screen playing me, that whole part of my life still seems unreal: it seems to have so little to do with *me* as an ordinary person. I *still* can't figure out why there has been so much media hype and publicity about our case. To me, it is something that has happened to two ordinary people, albeit it shouldn't have.

To play Michael, the producers were looking at Michael York, who could have been made to look quite a lot like Michael. His accent was a bit English and he would have done a good job, but nowhere near as good as Sam Neill. We also thought of the Australian John Hanlon from *Play School*, who looks very like Michael and who had played him in the documentary drama by Frank Moorhouse. Then of course there was Richard Chamberlain, who also looks a bit like Michael and probably would have done a brilliant job too, except he was considered a little old for the part—I don't know why though. (Funnily enough, they've both got the distinct Chamberlain eyes, but Michael's come from his mother's side, I think. People often ask if they are related and one lady consistently calls Michael Richard because she is convinced that he is Richard and won't admit it!) Richard Chamberlain would have been my initial choice.

Then, out of the blue, they told us Sam Neill had the part so I borrowed the videos of *Robbery Under Arms* and *My Brilliant Career*. I vaguely knew who he was but Michael didn't. It was really interesting to say to Michael, 'Come and look at this. This is the guy who is going to play you,' and watch his mouth fall open. I was aware that Sam and Michael were somewhat similar to look at, but Michael hadn't been aware of Sam's existence.

I was asked at one stage who I would pick to play myself. Not considering an international actress, I had thought of Helen Morse, an Australian actress. Had they told me to make an international choice, I probably would have chosen Cissy Spacek.

Then they said, 'What do you think about Meryl Streep?'

I said, 'I don't know much about her. I've heard she comes across as being fairly cold. I think she is different from the parts she's played, probably. . . in fact, come to think of it, I don't think *I've* ever seen her in a whole movie at all. I have only seen bits and pieces.' Once I knew she was being considered, however, I got several of her videos out. I saw a couple I didn't like very much, but *Sophie's Choice* and *Out of Africa* I thought were good. I could see she was definitely a top actress, even if she didn't look like me.

Robert told me later that the first time he met Meryl Streep nobody knew whether she was going to take my part or not, and they all really wanted her. She was to meet Verity Lambert and Robert to make her decision. By this time, Robert was so involved with the story and realised what an injustice had been done that he wanted the best, as he knew how important the choice of actress was in making or breaking so many opinions. Meryl, it seemed, was everybody's first choice.

The first time they met was in New York with Fred Schepisi. Meryl had been sent Bryson's book, *Evil Angels*. She'd recently given birth to her second daughter and couldn't help identifying with me—in fact it upset her so much she threw it across the room and refused to read any further.

She made a rule of never reading screenplays sent to her home but when sent the *Evil Angels* script she sat straight down and read the first draft screenplay from cover to cover and immediately agreed to play me in the movie.

Fred Schepisi wasn't involved in the movie at that stage. He'd rejected the offer to write and direct it because he was daunted by the size of the story and the responsibility of getting it right when so many lies and distortions had been invented by sections of the media and police for so many years.

Meryl wouldn't accept that. She wanted to do the movie with an Australian director. She'd worked with Fred on another movie called *Plenty*, so they knew each other well and, fears or no fears on his part, *he* was directing this movie.

So Fred finally said yes and flew to New York with Robert for the first script conference. Robert wanted to make a good impression naturally, but he was so involved with the story and the injustice of it all that the first impression he made, after a year of research and writing, was not exactly the one he had in mind.

'Guess what?' he said when he phoned from America. 'I made a fool of myself. I got so worked up telling her about you and the way you'd been so thoroughly fucked by the Northern Territory government, police and judiciary, that I broke down and howled like a baby.'

Well, it didn't hurt, Meryl couldn't help but see that he really believed in what he was working on.

The only time I saw Robert cry like that was in a meeting with Harry Miller and someone else. By this time, Robert had worked on the movie for nearly twelve months and we knew him well. He was a really good mate, and we felt very comfortable with him. He got so worked up because Kahlia had been taken from me twice after I had already lost Azaria and how nobody must let that happen to anyone ever again, that he started to cry. He was trying to talk in the middle of it and got even more upset.

Michael immediately identified with him, but, sensing how embarrassed Robert would be at crying in front of Harry, I just laughed and said, 'Come on, it's not that bad. You'll get over it,' and tried to lighten the situation. Michael immediately told me off quietly, saying I was hard and unfeeling and it was inappropriate, and yet I knew that Robert would sense what I was trying to do.

Later when we talked about the incident and I told Robert what Michael had said, he said he *had* known what I was doing. We had a laugh about it, but it helped to illustrate my different reactions to things. My instinct had been to get up and give

Robert a hug and say, 'Listen, it's OK now.' And yet with a room full of men that was the last thing I was going to do because they would get the wrong impression. (One of Robert's friends had already asked him whether we were having an affair because we related so easily as friends!) Anyway, in the end Michael got up and put his arms around Robert and I think they both cried. Robert was embarrassed and apologised later when he calmed down, but it showed his deep humanity—and why he is such a great writer.

Robert's series, *Scales of Justice* is absolutely brilliant. Because of my experience with lawyers, police and courts, I could really identify with its accuracy. I had watched it in prison and later, when I was told he had been asked to write the screenplay for the book *Evil Angels* and I was wondering who he was, I was informed that he had done that series, so I felt at ease. He also wrote much of the Australian award-winning series, *The Sullivans*. I once said to him. 'How come it absolutely went to pieces after Grace died, and what happened?' He laughed, embarrassed, and said, 'that was the last episode that I wrote for the series, and I don't know what happened then.' Well, that explained it.

Sam—Ace of Actors

Robert Caswell rang and said Sam Neill had asked if he could meet us and would really appreciate it. Michael didn't think it was a good idea at first but eventually agreed so it was arranged Sam would come up and he would sleep in Aidan's bedroom, as it was the only decent room in the house. Michael went to the station to pick up Sam, who was arriving on the night train. He had asked how to come and Michael suggested he travel just as we did, and turn up like any other person.

Michael had been quite a while so I presumed the train was late as usual. I was on the phone when I heard the car arrive. I was facing the door as it opened and there stood Sam framed in the doorway, a smile on his face and a large pot of perfectly white azaleas in full flower in his arms.

I smiled, gave Sam a little wave and continued talking on the phone while Michael brought him into the loungeroom. When I had finished talking on the phone, I went in and was introduced. Sam's potted azaleas were all done up in cellophane with a huge white ribbon, and looked beautiful. Sam handed them over and said, 'Here you are, I have bought these specially for you.' (Michael was later to comment, 'How come you got the present when it is *me* he is playing?' I told him *he* could buy Meryl a present.)

Michael showed Sam over the college and they were away quite a long time, arriving back about 11 p.m. We all had a hot drink and sat talking for a while and then retired for the night. The next morning Sam met all the children and once again Michael spent the morning with him.

In the afternoon we went up the Watagan Mountains. Driving along some of the bush tracks we noted there were still fires in the area. Michael was checking to see that those burning a couple of days before had gone out but as we were driving along we saw a couple of patches that were obviously starting up again.

We stopped and Michael and Sam got out to investigate while I stayed up by the car watching. After some consultation, they apparently decided they were going to put the fires out. They grabbed big branches and were beating away at the fire for five or ten minutes.

Sam got his fire out first and came back to the car a little ahead of Michael. He had his shirt off and black soot on his face where he had been rubbing the sweat off his brow. His body was glistening with sweat and his hair falling in his eyes. I couldn't help smiling to myself. No one knew he was staying with us and they would have found it hard to believe we had him fighting bushfires, but Sam had obviously enjoyed himself.

Sam was initially very shy, but after I got to know him I realised he was simply quiet. Once he was used to a situation he was not shy but had quite an impish sense of humour. We chatted away as if we had been friends for years while we waited for Michael to come back.

We looked further along to see whether the fire was coming up the gully. As we could still only see smoke, not flames, we decided to go through another farmer's property to check where the fire was going and whether it was out of control.

We knocked on the farmhouse door and couldn't find anyone at home, so continued down to their back paddocks. They had orange groves through there and as we walked closer to the head of the valley we came across a section of very old trees with thick gnarled wood that had been left to grow wild. Fruit lay all over the ground; some oranges from the year before had gone dormant over the winter and ripened again in the spring, while others had fresh new oranges.

Michael and Sam were absolutely delighted. They picked some of the oranges and were wandering around like two schoolboys with the juice dripping off their elbows. I felt envious, as I am allergic to oranges. We had to walk over a stream on a little bridge with almost rotten timber and the area was quiet and picturesque. The fire was obviously more smoke than anything else and in no danger of hurting anyone, so we eventually climbed into the four-wheel-drive and headed for home.

We had just had lunch when somebody knocked on the door. To give Sam some privacy we had not told anyone that he was coming. Our caller was a very sharp-witted gentleman so we thought it more prudent for Sam to disappear.

Michael went to the door while I took Sam out the back and told him to wait around the corner until it was safe again. We would be as quick as possible. About ten minutes later I went to find Sam and couldn't immediately see him. Then I saw long legs sticking out from behind the rubbish bin. There was Sam, reading, sitting between the rubbish bin and another bin full of manure and potting mix!

When I told him it was safe to come inside he grinned and said, 'Would you believe I like it here? I'll be in shortly.' It was another quarter of an hour or so before he roused himself to get up and come inside. It was interesting to see somebody normally seen only on the screen comfortably perched on our path amongst our rubbish bins.

We discovered Michael and Sam had attended schools only a couple of kilometres apart in New Zealand; Sam probably even watched Michael play in inter-school sports teams.

Sam did a magnificent job in the movie. Only those who knew Michael well realised just how brilliant he was. It was more impersonation than mere acting. He had Michael's mannerisms and characteristics perfectly and not one of Sam's own mannerisms came across. It was only a pity that he wasn't nominated for an Academy Award for his acting, as Meryl Streep was.

After Sam had come to stay, Meryl decided that she would also like to meet us. The thought of Meryl coming to stay in that dumpy little house was rather horrifying. The house was so far removed from the way I liked to keep it, and the way it should look, I felt the impression she would get in that situation would not help her play me accurately so I said no. I still do not think she would have gained anything for her portrayal of me from that house.

Unlocking the Lock Lady

When Helena came out of prison she stayed with us for a while, sleeping on the loungeroom floor until she was established in her own flat. Leslie was having personal problems, and finding the boys hard to cope with on top of it all, so decided to leave. As we were due to leave for the Commission some time shortly, we needed someone else to look after the children while we were away. Lena figured if Leslie could look after things, so could she. After a trial period while we were busy with our legal preparation, and the boys being keen (the fishing, beach, and driving lessons didn't enter into their enthusiasm, of course), we finally agreed.

For many months after that, every time we had to go away Lena moved in, and Kahlia moved back to Jan and Owen Hughes. We had no idea what we were taking on, but then neither did she, and some interesting times were experienced by all after that, let me assure you! (Lena stayed until we didn't need her any more. She still drops in periodically to say hello, or for the kids' birthdays, or to introduce some of her friends. Occasionally she turned up drunk or in a wild mood, mostly I managed to settle her down, have a laugh, and send her away feeling a little happier.) And she still calls me mum.

Life with Lena around is certainly a lesson for the staid. It probably gave Michael a few extra grey hairs too!

Although things now seemed to be running smoothly in the legal arena, the trouble with the support groups was not over, though most were happy to see me free. The pressure to use their lawyers was on once again. The position had not altered. Although we all agreed to a round table conference, the individuals concerned were unable to arrange a convenient date when they could all be present, and so the conference was finally aborted.

The information circulating amongst a lot of the support groups had become so garbled that shortly after my release I decided it was time to make a personal statement. I had discovered that a considerable amount of money was being poured into the counter-support groups by genuine supporters. Many did not realise the money was being used to fund lawyers for work on my behalf that the groups then refused to hand over to me, to Michael or to our appointed lawyers. They also wouldn't give us any of the information they were supposedly working on. Even the offer of a totally new lawyer as a go-between was rejected.

Such was the confusion that I had to very specifically point out in a public statement approved groups and organizations and the non-cooperation of other groups, letting people know that I would not be held responsible for any donations given to other groups or for the way they used their donations.

I was once again assured that the information held by those lawyers was definitely new and cogent but no one would ever give any indication of what it was. As before, when asked, the support group leader said he had never seen the information because he had been told it was too complicated for him to understand, and he had just taken the word of the lawyers about it. The lawyers themselves told me that it was no different from what I had originally seen, which I knew to be merely a bad rehash of prior material of ours and a personal attack on the lawyers we had used so far. In the end, none of the work which had supposedly been done especially for me was ever handed over.

An Inquiry of What Sort?

I well knew my release hadn't stilled the storm of protest, argument and inquiry. Far from it. Certainly we had been assured that the Northern Territory would hold an inquiry, but as a *Sydney Morning Herald* editorial put it: 'What sort of judicial review?'

Firstly the Territory proposed a panel of three judges (one to come from overseas) to sit in Darwin. Lionel Bowen, the Federal Attorney-General, suggested that the Northern Territory should invite him to provide a Federal Court judge with Royal Commission powers. In Parliament he added:

> I think that it is worth commenting now—the *Sydney Morning Herald* alluded to it—that there appears to be very strong evidence that the forensic tests that were carried out were not in accordance with established procedures, and that was known to the prosecution. There is other evidence from forensic experts in Australia that the evidence given was not in accordance with what one would call scientific capacity or understanding of what should have happened in terms of undertaking those tests . . .
>
> The allegation is that there has been an attempt to cover up the actions of the administrators of justice in the Northern Territory in endeavouring to obtain a conviction, rather than looking at the fairness of the evidence that should have been presented to the jury. It is a matter of record that there is some comment from one member of the jury that the jury now feels that it might have had at least an opportunity to acquit the accused rather than otherwise. These are not new accusations; they are known to the government of the Northern Territory . . .
>
> The obligation now is to guarantee that the Inquiry be far- reaching, wide-ranging, and impartial. The only way to achieve that would be by having an independent inquiry with somebody appointed from outside the Northern Territory with the capacity to examine all the evidence that is now available.

Things had certainly changed since the Federal Government's constant statements that any reopening of our case was a matter for the Northern Territory alone.

Naturally, Bowen's words did not please Marshall Perron—nor indeed Paul Everingham. It would be fair to say that what Bowen said acted as a red rag to a couple of bulls. Perron challenged Bowen to repeat his remarks outside the protection of Parliamentary privilege, adding that they had attacked 'the integrity of eight judges, three Northern Territory Attorneys- General, the Territorial police force, the Territory Department of Law and Crown witnesses in the Chamberlain case'. Goodness me!

Nevertheless, in mid-March, six weeks after Perron's reply, the Northern Territory Parliament passed a bill providing for a Federal Court judge to be appointed to inquire into 'doubts that had arisen into the convictions of Michael and Lindy Chamberlain'. The Territory didn't have legislation that would allow them to set up a Commission of Inquiry, and a special statute had to be passed.

We had to find a new QC, after all. Michael McHugh was a judge of the NSW Court of Appeal (later to become a High Court judge), John Phillips was Director of Public Prosecutions, then Supreme Court judge (now the chairman of the National Crime Prevention Committee), Andy Kirkham our junior, who had become a QC, wanted to excuse himself so that we had free rein to criticise his work if we wished (he felt it was not ethical for him to accept a position where it could be claimed he was simply covering his own tracks—pity some others I could name hadn't felt the same), and Phil Rice had become a Northern Territory judge.

We contacted all our former QCs and asked them to make a short list of those they would recommend. Then we started going through the list. One had just returned from a long stint overseas and promised his wife he would only take local cases for the next twelve months; another one, Chester Porter, had just been chosen the night before to represent the Commission; another one would be otherwise engaged as the commissioner in charge of an inquiry in South Australia; and Fitzgerald had just been announced as the commissioner for the Queensland inquiry into corruption; the other two were already involved in cases. It seemed everyone we asked recommended the same men and we were experiencing problems.

Time was getting extremely short, and on one of Stuart's frequent reports he exclaimed he felt as if he was sitting at his desk with a huge hangman's noose getting lower and lower over his head as the time shortened. In desperation Stuart rang John Phillips's clerk again to see whether he couldn't possibly think of anyone else. The man exclaimed he couldn't think why, but he had forgotten the best man of the lot.

His name was John Winneke and the clerk would make enquiries for us as to whether he was available. That afternoon we received a phone call saying not only was Mr Winneke available but he would take the case. Stuart rang and formally engaged him immediately.

The word in the ranks was that Winneke should be a judge but kept refusing. He had been a commissioner himself on occasion. We learned later this was quite true and he didn't want to be a judge because he thought it was too boring; he preferred the more active bar table.

We soon heard, that after consulting with Lionel Bowen, Perron had accepted the Commonwealth's offer of a Federal Court judge with Royal Commission powers, and Justice Trevor Morling was appointed Commissioner. Mr Justice Morling, a committed Baptist, was to be assisted by Chester Porter QC, a Sydney silk, with William Caldwell as his junior and solicitors John Davis, Mark Buchanan, and Fiona Crosby. Representing the Northern Territory (after saying in the press that he wouldn't do it) was Ian Barker QC—again—with Michael Adams and Elizabeth Fullerton as juniors. Michael (Mick) O'Loughlin was the solicitor again. Mick was the only lawyer on the case from beginning to end.

A short while after I was released the boys noticed pressure at school again—Aidan in particular. As I observed, I realised there was a running war between Aidan, a number of his friends, and the Hump brothers with their mates. It got so bad that it wasn't only at school, but outside as well; in the Pathfinder Club, and even in church. One of the church junior leaders, who was also a high school teacher, caught them all having such an argument that he threw a bucket of water over them to stop it. When he told me later, I asked him what it was about. From what he had seen, he thought Aidan had been getting quite a lot of provocation and that Aidan's mates were sticking up for him but he didn't know the cause.

While I was still talking to the teacher, Aidan and his mates came along. They were talking happily to us when the Hump boys deliberately walked through the middle of our group instead of around us, making sure one elbowed Aidan in the stomach on the way. They pushed past the teacher who grabbed the kid by the back of the neck, told him to apologise and not to do it again, and sent him on his way. The teacher observed that the same sort of thing was happening at school.

When I talked to the people in Pathfinders, they said similar things. Something kept distracting Aidan from what he was doing and he would flare up and go for the other guy. As this was visible, although what had provoked him was not, he was the one who got the blame. My own research revealed the two Hump boys and their mates would mercilessly tease Aidan about me, and then burst into tears and run for their lives to an adult when chased. The fact that they were scared stiff (with good reason) and crying made it look as if Aidan and his mates had already had a go at them. Again Aidan would be in trouble.

I sat Aidan down with his mates and talked to them. If people wanted to be like that, the best thing was not to give them the satisfaction of knowing they were upsetting you, and they would get sick of doing it. They agreed to try.

There was a special night with all sorts of different games, competitions, booths and displays in the college auditorium. I had observed the Hump boys hassling others a couple of times during the evening, but Aidan was staying well away from them.

Kahlia wanted to go to the toilet, and on the way back I glanced across and saw Aidan pinned into a corner by a large man. I had no idea who the man was but as Aidan went to move out from under his arm, he was grabbed and shoved back against the wall again. It seemed the man must have arrived almost as soon as I had left with Kahlia, as I'd only been gone a couple of minutes.

Young Luke, Kahlia's foster brother, obviously quite upset, was saying something to this man about letting Aidan go. The guy finally turned and walked off, snapping at Luke on his way.

Luke, seeing me coming and wishing the man to know that I was not blind to what had happened, called out quite loudly, 'Hello, Mrs Chamberlain,' at which the big guy turned. Then I realised he was now with the Hump boys. Luke hotly told me the man was their father and he had pushed Aidan around because he reckoned that Aidan was fighting with his sons. Then he added, 'But, Auntie Lindy, the Humps came up here and were messing our game up and kicking it around and Aidan didn't do *anything*.' Mr Hump had turned around and was coming back.

Five foot one to what looked like six foot of anger is not a good match, but as he got near I said, 'What seems to be your problem, mate?' He was obviously thrown off guard, and cooled down, then said that my son was causing the problem. I asked him if he knew the reason and he told me a lot of rubbish about Aidan always picking on his sons.

I asked, 'Have you ever watched this fighting?'

'No.'

'Well, I *have*,' I said. 'Your boys are giving as good as they get.'

His mouth opened, but I continued, 'I think it is extremely cowardly of one child to attack another one because of his mother's reputation.' His mouth shut in a hurry and he mumbled that he didn't know that *that* was the case. I said, 'Well, I do. And usually children learn things from their parents. So you control your sons, and *then* I will tell my son to stop protecting himself and his mother.' I called Aidan and walked away, as his son swore after us.

After some further fuss at school, the Hump parents were called in and the headmaster, discovering there was a bad attitude towards us, gently informed the Humps it was not the sort of thing that the school appreciated. It was quite understandable Aidan had stood up for his mother under the circumstances, and would continue to do so. This was a problem their family had better deal with. Aidan had no further trouble.

The relationship between our boys, however, was developing from being competitive into a fully fledged war. While I was in prison, Aidan had been very conscious of the fact that he was the elder and in his father's absence he was in charge, and he expected his younger brother to obey him. Reagan, on the other hand, being only two and a half years younger, felt he was old enough to take responsibility for himself. Particularly with Mum home, he would take no more notice of Aidan. Aidan, of course, did not like this and was finding it very difficult to relinquish his 'father' role. There are still traces of him lapsing into the role of father and then realising that he does not have to any more. Neither Reagan nor Kahlia will accept being told what to do by Aidan any more. Mum is home. Dad is around. 'They are boss, not you!' The war has abated, but things still have not returned to normal. Somehow I wonder whether they ever quite will.

When we went to Melbourne to meet Jack Winneke, we were told he was in court and we should see him in action. We had been told the Derryn Hinch defamation case was on but it didn't register that Winneke was actually representing the TV personality. It didn't take long after our arrival for Hinch to be told that we were there, and he turned around to have a look at us, obviously ill at ease. His press reports had been very hostile to us, so he was certainly no friend of ours. We were told later he was uncomfortable because he thought we were there to listen to his defamation case and later have a go at him ourselves. (Well, that's a thought!)

Because of Hinch's high media profile, his case was being covered by other journalists, and word soon got around that we were in court. Although we were sitting at the back, a couple of the press slid in and asked whether we would like to make a comment. We said we wouldn't and they left. We decided to go early, so we could avoid the media waiting for Hinch. We intended to cross the road and wait for Mr Winneke, but when we opened the courtroom door, a whole group of journalists was waiting for us. Cameras were all around the door, and one woman in particular was very persistent and quite obnoxious.

The press followed us quite a distance down the street until we could go across to Mr Winneke's chambers and disappear. That night we heard on the headline news that I had upstaged Hinch at his own trial. The pictures showed us emerging from court with the press all around and following as if we were Pied Pipers. Hinch and his wife emerged not long after to depleted press ranks. It looked as if he had been bypassed at his own court case; certainly not what we had intended (or Hinch either, presumably!).

I was caught wearing casual clothes and it hit the newspapers and for the first time ever I got good press about what I was wearing. There were big headlines: 'New Style Lindy', etc. It really wasn't a new style, it was just me, but I had never been caught in casual clothes before. The press was in a mood to be wooed and pleased, and pleased they were. But some of the stricter church members were not, and they complained about me making a figure of myself in the newspaper and how I should not go to the press looking like that.

What does one do? How do you explain to people that you do not control the press? They find you where they will, you can't get away from them, you can't control what they put in the news or the way they do it. Until you have been in the situation I have, you find it very difficult. It is one thing to be used to dealing with the press for advertising or in a situation where they are on your side, but they will turn on you like a pack of wolves, and there is nothing you can do about it. Then you find out just how good and friendly the press are! You find you have absolutely no control at all, even if you are a media boss like Alan Bond or Christopher Skase, owning news networks has not stopped the press making mincemeat of them.

Whatever I had done hadn't been right so I decided to do my own thing, and at last the public saw me as I was, not as they thought I ought to be. I have grown to realise that it doesn't matter what people think of you, as long as you can be true to yourself. If you tried to please everybody, you end up pleasing no one. You can please some of the people some of the time, but all of the people never.

So, much to some people's horror at times, I do what I want when I want. I dress, talk and go how and with whom I want. I know my motives are pure, clear and honest. Whatever I do, I can stand before God with a clear conscience and if somebody else wants to misconstrue my actions, where I am, what I'm doing or who I'm with, that is their problem, not mine.

Still there was criticism, particularly from my own church members I was even given a book on what I was supposed to wear in court for the forthcoming Commission, and it said I was supposed to wear light woollen suits of a classical style, and shirts. I would like to see anybody do that in Darwin! They would have to be crazy. It may be air-conditioned inside court, but nobody, *nobody*, would be stupid enough to wear clothes like that.

By this time I had an agent and an adviser so I sat down and talked with them. They said, 'No, find your own style. Be neat and certainly don't wear anything outrageous, but wear what you want to. We have already looked at your dressing styles and there is nothing that we would recommend you change.' Thank goodness for that; I hated a lot of those dowdy matronly clothes people wanted me to wear.

We walked into Winneke's reception, where we found another man already waiting and presumed he was the junior counsel whom Stuart Tipple had engaged. We chatted for some time, and waited to be introduced to the stranger. When Jack Winneke came in, he was over 180 centimetres (6 feet) tall with huge, muscular shoulders and legs. No wonder he had been a good footballer in his day. We learned later he still worked with weights in the gym and jogged. Winneke introduced himself all round, but still no one introduced the stranger to us. Stuart arrived a little later and he and Winneke introduced themselves. Winneke said to him, 'You two know each other, don't you?' indicating the other gentleman in the room.

Stuart said, 'No, I don't.'

Jack, surprised, said 'Stuart Tipple, Ken Crispin.'

Stuart then said hello, and as we were looking blankly, Jack said to Ken,

'Well, you have met the Chamberlains, haven't you?'

He said, 'No,' and so did we. Stuart looked at us, we looked at him; we wondered how he got there. Jack laughed and introduced us.

As soon as we got out of the room, I said to Stuart, 'If you've never met him, where did he come from? How come you engaged him without interviewing him first?'

He replied, 'I didn't interview him, Michael did.' But I knew Michael didn't know anything about it either, and said so.

Stuart said, 'Well, he's the guy from Canberra that Michael said to give a go.'

I said, 'That meant to interview him and see if he was any good, because Betty Hocking recommended him. Michael thought you were going to interview him.'

Stuart said, 'I thought he meant to engage him, so I did. I don't know what he's like, but if it turns out we don't like him or he's no good he can go.'

Ken Crispin spent all his time outside talking to Michael. I thought he must have been trying to persuade him that he was needed on the team. We hadn't met Brind Zichy-Woinarski, the junior counsel Mr Winneke had engaged as 'a good one' yet either, and I hadn't decided whether we would need another barrister or not. It appeared Michael and I were entitled to be represented separately, so if we needed a bigger team we would take advantage of that.

As we were all going down in the lift after the meeting, Ken started to discuss the case. This would have been fine if we had been alone, but other people were there, presumably lawyers. We were anxious for the Northern Territory not to get any *prior* information, so we were very careful not to discuss anything in public where we could be overheard. Michael and I said nothing and Stuart gave abbreviated non-committal answers to Ken's comments and questions. When we got out of the lift, I grabbed Stuart and said, 'You tell that guy to keep his mouth shut, or he is out. We can't have that sort of thing.'

Unknown to Stuart or me, Michael had actually engaged Ken to work on his behalf though there had been some discussion about whether he would be briefed by Stuart or an independent solicitor. Ken had already sent back a number of briefs to clear his diary for the case and arranged facilities to computerise the evidence. But the inquiry was due to start in eight days and he still had no documents. He knew the transcripts alone ran to several thousand pages and he was becoming frantic about the lack of time to digest it. When the call for the Melbourne conference came through from Stuart, Ken took it as the full steam ahead signal, and couldn't understand why everyone looked at him as an interloper—of course he didn't know that Michael had said nothing to us. When he heard from Stuart, he presumed that Stuart was his promised solicitor, but the conference came to an end and he was still in the dark so he had tried to help Michael realise the urgency of the situation and the necessity of receiving his brief shortly. When we went to the lift he realised we were all going our separate ways and he was still no further ahead, so he made one last desperate attempt to find out where, when and from whom his brief was to appear. No wonder he talked in the lift! It wasn't until doing the legal work for this book that he finally discovered what had happened. We had a good laugh over that.

While we were in Melbourne we were called in to work on the research for the film, and I told the production team what all the real people who were to be acted in the film wore. Whether they usually wore un-patterned clothes, or checks, brown, blues, florals etc.; whatever I had observed in court or out so those in charge of the film wardrobe could dress them as accurately as possible. Of course, they had black and white press photographs of our clothes too, so I sat for ages with the wardrobe master describing colours and the styles of the backs. At least this time it wouldn't be like the sets in that awful Moorhouse documentary drama.

In *Evil Angels (A Cry in the Dark)* the Mt Isa set was very close to our real house, though the other one, at college, was really nothing like ours. They had to pick whatever they could get, because they couldn't get up to the college. It would have cost them a few million extra to do the filming there, although the setting was wonderful and they would have loved to use the college church. They had to use the Lilydale Academy (an Adventist secondary boarding school near Melbourne) campus and tiny church—some old Avondale students said it was wonderful to see the campus and recognise the place! We had to write and tell them the truth. But the grounds in some of the outdoor scenes weren't too dissimilar all the same.

Back on the legal scene, Ken turned out to be a real asset to the team. We had decided to take advantage of the two junior counsels after all, but each was to represent us both so it could not be misconstrued as indicating a rift between Michael and me.

Ken was quick-witted, good in cross- examination and approachable, with a keen sense of humour. With his 170 centimetre (5 feet 7 inches) frame and wavy pitch-black hair, he looked Greek or Italian, but is pure Aussie. Brind Zichy-Woinarski, on the other hand, was blond, as tall as Jack—over 180 centimetres (6 feet)—but a combination of muscle and sinew, making him slim and athletic. He usually swam 100 Olympic laps daily as well as working out on weights and some other sports. Based in Melbourne, Brind was in the same building as Jack, so they were able to work together quite easily. Ken, on the other hand, was in Canberra, and Stuart in Gosford, so the team had to travel quite a distance for liaison purposes.

We still needed a junior solicitor to assist Stuart, and advertised for one. Some applicants were very young people with no experience, some were just anxious to be appointed for the sake of the publicity, and some were genuine, but we thought they couldn't really handle the work. We eventually found a woman called Pam, and were quite pleased with her. Stuart had been looking for a female influence on the team to give another perspective, and also to join his office staff on a permanent basis later on. In Pam he hoped he had found the right person. We enjoyed her company and got on well with her.

The house was looking more like home, it had been cleaned and scrubbed from top to bottom now and all the cupboards were tidy. The constant flow of well-wishers had died down now and it was the first longer gap of relative inactivity I'd had so far. Kahlia was happy to be in her own home, and the boys were enjoying the novelty of a normal family life again. Each of the boys made the most of it in their own way.

Aidan enjoyed walking along with his arm around my shoulders or holding my hand, not caring that thirteen-year-old boys aren't supposed to do that. We did a lot of things together and he was very proud to let people know this was *his* Mum and she was home.

Reagan was happy too, but much slower to react outwardly—almost as if he was frightened I would be taken away again. On the night before we had to go to Darwin for the beginning of the Commission, I wondered why he hadn't come to say good-night. It suddenly dawned on me what the problem might be.

I sat down on his bed and said, 'Honey, are you worried that Mummy mightn't come back?'

He burst into tears and said, 'Yes.' Then I explained that we were only going away for a little while. I thought I had already done that quite thoroughly, but I could see that his own fears were predominant. He couldn't bear to get close and secure, then lose me again; he had been hurt too often before. After our talk he was much happier but still looked a little uncertain.

The next morning when we left, he gave me a big hug and, as nobody else was upset seemed quite reassured. I was haunted by his big, troubled eyes. It wasn't until we returned from Darwin and he could actually *see* me and hug me that he was totally reassured, however. As time wore on, he had the same reaction as Aidan and clung to me like a limpet, crawling onto my lap whenever and wherever he could; sometimes he would even nearly spill my dinner, but he somehow managed to find a space for himself and my plate. It took some time, though, for him to accept as normal that his mother came and went to the Commission on a regular basis.

Firstly we went to an official 'mention' to set dates and parameters for the case and to admit the lawyers. Chester Porter said that the procedure in the inquiry would be as follows: he would call all the witnesses, leaving counsel for the other parties to cross-examine as they wished. He also suggested that the matinee jacket should be examined by the Victorian Forensic Science Laboratory, pointing out that the scientists hadn't been involved in the case up till then. This meant, presumably, that they would be more likely to be impartial than some others we had known.

The Crown said the testing should be carried out by scientists they nominated, although they said experts on our side could be present. Jack Winneke asked for Porter's original proposal to be adopted, saying to Justice Morling, 'Rightly or wrongly, Your Honour, perceptions have arisen about the independence of various persons, including those whom Mr Barker now asserts are best qualified to carry out these tests.'

Justice Morling adopted Porter's suggestion. The inquiry was set to open for evidence on 5 June 1986 and we went home to finish preparing and wait. We had done most of what we could now, so the rest was up to the lawyers and scientists, and we knew they were all doing their best in every way possible.

When it was nearly time for us to leave for the first session we still had no funds. We had a meeting with our lawyers and were not sure who was paying for what—whether the Commission or Legal Aid was paying all our expenses, some or none. We didn't know whether we should try and get a private loan from somewhere or whether our church head office (the Division) would once again act as guarantor for the money needed.

There seemed to be no communication with them. Finally, we had a meeting with our new liaison person, Pastor Ron Craig, and asked him what was happening. The answer came back that the church was waiting to see what the Northern Territory was going to do and then they would make a decision. But the Northern Territory said they had no intention of making a decision for up to a month after the start of the Commission.

Time was getting short so we had a round table conference with the president, Pastor Walter Scragg, and several of the key treasurers and secretaries. We stated our position clearly and asked for some indication of their intentions. They said they would discuss it and let us know. Before they went I asked specifically whether they could let us know one way or the other at least a fortnight ahead as I would have to get private backing and have time to make travel arrangements if they declined.

I rang a couple of times and was told they were out. I left messages to ring, but nothing came through. Finally, time was getting so short that I asked Ron once again to actually go in and see them. He assured me they were working on it, that he had been in touch with them and he was sure he would have some information for me shortly. I presumed the answer was going to be yes, as they surely would not merely leave us in the air without backing at this late date, so I waited again. Three days before the Commission was due to start, I rang again. There was still no more information, but I was assured everything was in hand. Stuart was also unable to get any information.

Finally it was lunchtime on the day we were due to leave and there had been no message at all from the Division. Reagan was to go to Melbourne, Aidan to Byron Bay, Kahlia was once again staying with Jan and Owen Hughes (her foster parents) at Cooranbong, and we had to go to the Northern Territory. It was the only way we could place the children as Helena had to be away just then. We knew we were going to be away for an indefinite time and had done our best as it was during the school holidays, which meant a lot of the locals (with whom we could normally leave the children) were not around.

I got on to Ron Craig again. He said yes, he was aware of the problem—now when was the deadline? I was desperate; we were totally broke and I still had no idea of what was happening.

I said, 'Ron, you *know* it's today. I have got one child going tonight and one in the morning. We haven't got the money to pay for the tickets, let alone anything else. We will have to leave for Sydney in two hours. You have got one hour to get some sort of message back to me.' In the meantime I prayed.

In an hour's time I got a message back all right. Ron was working on it. He had seen Scragg, the president, who was busy and said he would talk to Ron later. I said, 'Why don't they just admit they haven't got the guts to say yes or no? They don't want to say either. They don't want to give us the money, but they don't want to hurt us, and they are leaving us in the lurch—nowhere! That's worse than saying no.'

Ron said, 'Oh, I don't think that's the case. I am going across now to where he is and I will wait for him there.'

When I didn't hear, I rang again and this time I asked for Pastor Scragg direct. I was told he was unavailable, so I asked for Ron Craig and finally got him. Well, it had been Division prayer time and he couldn't go in and get him out of there. But Ron once more assured me that they were praying for me.

Ron told me Scragg had been contacted that morning, he knew we had to know by a certain time, but he had to talk to his secretary first. His secretary had to talk to him, the treasurer had to talk to them both and they all had to talk to each other. I was getting the run-around, and so was Ron. It really wasn't fair that I let my feelings out on him, but let him have it I did. To have people consider that kneeling and praying was more holy than being of practical use, avoiding making a decision that would have taken them thirty seconds I thought was disgusting, and I went away totally disillusioned.

I was sobbing fit to break my heart and I said, 'God, what will I do?' Suddenly I remembered the name of a man who had offered any help that was in his power to give at any time. I rang the exchange, got his number and was put through to his office. He was in. I spoke to him and within two minutes I had the money for the air tickets, and had arranged to pick it up partly in cheque form and partly in cash, exactly as I had asked for it. He got his secretary to organise Reagan's tickets, escort and his seat for the bus that night also. I couldn't help contrasting that man who knew his own mind and wasn't afraid to say yes or no with those I had just been dealing with.

When we got to Brisbane, there was an urgent message for us to contact Pastor Ron Craig. He knew we had left, and I was in no mood to humour the Division. We were changing planes. The phone call would have made me miss the plane, so I ignored the message. Ron was coming to Darwin the following day and any information he had for us could wait until then. When we saw him in Darwin, the first thing he said was, 'I just wanted to tell you the Division is working on the problem.' I looked at him and said, 'Is that what the phone call was about yesterday?'

He said, 'Yes. I wanted you to know it was in hand.'

I said, 'Ron, I don't *want* to know. It is too late. I needed that money to catch the plane yesterday. I had to get a private loan. Thank God some private people don't think they are too holy to help others.' He looked hurt and started to explain, and I said, 'Look, Ron, I know it's not your fault, but quite frankly I am sick of the way we are being treated.'

Several weeks later the answer finally came. They would be happy to continue as our guarantors. They were very sorry for what had happened to us, and felt it was just as much the church's responsibility as ours. After all, Michael had been one of their ministers at the time, even though he'd been asked to resign in April 1984. At first he became assistant to the Avondale College Principal, and later moved into the library and archives. When Michael was unhappy over his work, they continued to offer him other jobs, ranging from academic to the Sanitarium factory, and groundsman at the College. Eventually they ran out of ideas, and didn't know what to offer, so suggested as soon as our court business was over we'd have a meeting with them to decide what other type of job they could place him in, meantime he was still to be paid at the church pension rate, with benefits.

Wherever we went we always had to stay near our lawyers so we were on hand for conferences and advice, so it was nice to have a break away and someone's home to treat as our own in Darwin. As well as the Parry's, the Noonan's residence became like a second home, although it too was a fair way from the courthouse. We could wander in any time, help Liz cook a meal, play with the kids, swim in the pool, or simply lounge on the floor, and it wouldn't bother either Liz. We'd simply turn up. It was nice to have that relaxation.

Although we didn't speak much to most of the reporters during the Commission, there were one or two besides Malcolm Brown and Kevin Hitchcock to whom we could talk without fear of being reported. We could briefly discuss general subjects without being reported by most of the rest of the reporters now, too. This made it much easier because we were mostly all using the same hotel dining rooms, gym, and swimming pool, and you couldn't avoid everyone; so there was a tacit agreement to leave us alone, as long as we didn't try to avoid the press at the *front* of the court.

One pressman did break the rule one day, though. I had been swimming laps when Brind and Melinda Woinarski came down to the pool. After initially teaching myself to swim during this time, Brind had assisted my technique by describing appropriate body movements during court breaks. This was the first time since I'd learnt to swim that Brind and I had managed to coincide near a pool, and I wanted him to show me how to swim butterfly stroke. A demonstration in the water was too fast and the pool too small for Brind's height, so he demonstrated on the edge of the pool. Not only did his actions forcibly remind me of a windmill, but trying to imitate him felt so funny I nearly fell in the pool laughing and Michael grabbed his ever-present camera. I jumped into the pool and Brind sat down before Michael had that shot in his archives, too.

As the camera was now out, Michael decided to take some photos anyway, which he stood chest deep in the pool to take. He was seen in the pool with his camera by a photographer from an upper storey window. At first he couldn't believe anyone would be in the pool with a camera, then realised it was Michael photographing me. After hearing all the evidence about Michael and his unusual camera habits, he just couldn't resist trying to get a shot that admirably proved the point. When he returned with his gear, Michael had finished and gone, so he took a shot of me finishing my laps instead. He later apologised for breaking the rules!

THE BEGINNING OF THE END

The first day in court Chester Porter reminded me of a cheeky, bright-eyed sparrow with eyes and ears everywhere. He was about Michael's height with silvery-white curls, and despite his age I could somehow picture him as an inquisitive seven-year-old and knew he wouldn't have changed all that much over the years. He had a habit of tilting his head to one side as he listened.

His opening address took nearly two days, and he went through all the main issues. He pointed out that the evidence fell into three categories: the primary evidence (i.e., that given by eyewitnesses on the night of Azaria's death); Michael's and my accounts; and the scientific evidence.

No possible motive, Porter said, had been found for me to kill Azaria. He added.

'The evidence of the witnesses who saw Mrs Chamberlain that day with her baby certainly is inconsistent with any intention then in her mind of killing the child. Rather they give the impression of an affectionate mother and father.' If the evidence of Sally Lowe, Greg Lowe, or Aidan was accepted, I was clearly innocent. Furthermore, Michael had left me alone with Aidan and Reagan on the day after Azaria's disappearance; Justice Morling commented that 'it might be thought unlikely that Mr Chamberlain would leave his wife with the surviving children if he had been told that she had murdered the youngest'.

Chester Porter moved on to the forensic evidence, saying that the two army giggle hats and the underdash spray in the car were being tested by the Victorian Forensic Laboratory. Other assertions to be raised in evidence and contested by new forensic experts were the nature of the hairs on the clothing and in the tent, the presence and type of blood in our car and the nature of the cuts to Azaria's jumpsuit, as well as my alleged handprint on the back of it. He hoped that these matters could be cleared up without the expense of involving overseas experts (so did we).

Porter said that Joy Kuhl's evidence was extremely important and very much in dispute, and noted that he intended to ask expert witnesses outright whether she was right or wrong; each expert would be asked to submit a simple statement of his or her position. He hoped, he said, that 'any surprises or playing of ambushes' could be avoided.

When he got to Cameron's evidence, which Justice Morling said had been very important at the trial, Porter pointed out that it was opposed by at least three experts.

Porter also referred to the Crown's statement that there were inconsistencies in my various statements, which indicated I had been lying. There were, he said, 'two extreme positions and there is no intermediate ground. Either this lady when she gave all these statements was a murderess, or she was a mother who had suffered frightfully and was being accused of murder.' Jack Winneke also made some important points when he addressed the court:

> We venture to suggest to Your Honour that their trial was unique in this regard in the history of Australian criminal law and that it fuelled rumour, speculation and innuendo. Very little of that was favourable to the Chamberlains . . . many rumours had circulated about the Chamberlains at the time when they came to trial in Darwin.
>
> Your Honour, our law prides itself on being able to bring people to trial in circumstances of fairness and before a jury free from preconceptions, but we will be submitting that the equipment the law has to ensure a fair trial did not operate in the case of the Chamberlains and that it was impossible, no matter how much care had been taken, to be satisfied that this trial took place in a climate free from preconception.

Mr Justice Muirhead was right when he said he had underestimated the influence of the press. We now know that Yvonne Cain, the only juror who kept notes, used the daily newspaper reports as notes on forensic and other matters which she had found too difficult to understand herself. It was a good argument for impounding the jury in very public cases.

Kulpunya Territory

The evidence began and among the first witnesses called—most of them for the first time—were some of the Pitjantjatjara people who had done the tracking when Azaria disappeared. Their skills were phenomenal, as we knew and as Kevin Hitchcock had found out when making his documentary.

While in prison with a number of Aboriginal women I was privileged to gradually learn a number of their customs. It fascinated me to observe them actually talking to one another within their heads in some form of mental telepathy.

One day I asked Smiley why she was not talking to the new girls from home and catching up on news. We had nothing to do, so it seemed a perfect opportunity to me and I thought they might have been holding back because they thought they would get into trouble during work hours. Smiley looked at me surprised and said, 'I do already.' When I asked her how, she pointed to her head, giggled and said, 'In here.' When I queried if she meant talking in their heads and was that why they sometimes laughed, she said yes. Then she proceeded to tell me all the updated news, which I knew could only have come from that silent conversation as I had been sitting next to her the whole time.

When new girls came in I witnessed them on a number of occasions catching up on news from home, sitting silently with the occasional giggle as some delightful piece of information was passed on.

On a number of occasions after that she told me things which sounded like superstitious nonsense—until early one morning she told me she would receive some bad news shortly and how she knew it. Later that afternoon, she was taken across to the superintendent's office and was told exactly what she had predicted to me. I had checked the time when Smiley had initially told me, and when I asked the screws later if there had been a time given, the time stated was exactly the time when she had told me. Although I still did not understand it, I learned to accept that some Aborigines have a unique way of communicating totally beyond the understanding of the whites. It was this method of mental communication that had been used by our friends in the car at the store on our trip home from the Rock all those years ago.

The girls told me that tribal Aborigines only count to four or five, and those numbers are only used proportionally to the whole amount. I also discovered that they speak in relation to the rising and setting of the sun and do not use directions of the compass This often means when asked to make references using compass directions as the white man wishes, they may say whatever sounds like a good direction.

The most important thing I learned was that a tribal Aborigine does *not* lie. They have no use for the white man's subterfuge and multiplication of words, so their answers are correct, direct and concise. This factor was to cause great discomfort to some who questioned their accuracy and integrity.

Having told the truth and been disbelieved, the Aboriginal people became offended. Because Nipper's evidence on the surface had appeared confused and he wore thick glasses with lenses akin to milk bottles, the Crown did not wish to call him at either the second inquest or the trial and were prepared to call evidence on his eyesight to discount his testimony. In order to save him from being ridiculed in an adversary situation we agreed not to call him either, but as soon as we knew there was a Commission it was a different matter.

I was able via my lawyers to convey to those in charge of the Commission, some of the knowledge I had gained from my friendship with the Aboriginal girls in jail. I was able to tell of the importance in which these matters were held by the Aboriginal women. Finally the Commission did the right thing and went direct to the Aboriginal Council to gain permission so the women could speak on their own behalf away from their tribal grounds. They were also to choose their own interpreters approved by their council, so they knew their evidence was translated accurately and in accordance with tribal protocol. The Commission went to a lot of trouble to make sure the Aboriginal people could give evidence in their own words, free from any pressure to give an answer other people seemed to want to hear.

There were four trackers; Nipper Winmatti (called to give evidence at the first inquest) Barbara Tjikadu (Nipper's wife), Daisy Walkabout, and Nui Minyintiri. The other male tracker had since died, and one of the women was not called.

Nipper's evidence was that the dingo came from the north and went around the tent to the western front entrance and from there backtracked, going east to the sandhill, travelled southeast a little, then once again turning westward to the Rock and Maggie Springs way.

When he was asked by the Crown, 'How far from that canvas floor outside the tent did you see the tracks that were in front of it?' he said, 'Tracks walk in,' and added, 'I seen the tracks with my own eyes. They had gone in and come out.' Nipper spoke English quite well, as well as his own native language, and chose to answer a lot of his questions in English, although Marlene Cousens was there as the chosen interpreter for the tribe.

When Porter asked Nipper, 'Are you able to say what it was the dingo was carrying?' Nipper said, 'It was the baby the dingo was carrying and he was trying to climb up the rise of the sandhill. It was really hard for 'im to climb up.' At the top of the hill, Nipper saw marks where the dingo had put Azaria down. 'The marks look like there was a hip bones like gone deeper into the ground and the heel of the foot.' Tracks began at the tent and could be tracked up the sandhill.

Throughout the case there was a lot of publicity from some of the support groups over the alleged involvement of a semi-tame dingo which it was said had adopted the ranger, Ian Cawood and his family. It was alleged that this dingo, generally known as 'Ding', was the dingo that had taken Azaria.

The evidence seemed clear that this animal had been shot after an attack on another child a number of weeks prior to Azaria's disappearance. But Nipper had been interviewed by various people on a number of different occasions and had been quoted as saying Ding was the culprit.

During the Commission it became obvious that Nipper was actually the only one who could really identify 'Cawood's Ding' out of a selection of photographs of various dingoes (and without his milk bottle glasses too, which meant his eyesight wasn't as bad as some would have liked us to believe). Despite the fact that Nipper agreed Ding had done it, he seemed to be saying when questioned closely that it wasn't the same Ding. This appeared really confusing until he volunteered the information that he called it Ding because white men seemed to want to call it that. He called it Kulpunya or dingo. (His wife Barbara was to give similar evidence later.) Suddenly I understood—and saw the same reaction on Chester Porter's face as I realised Nipper thought all dingoes, according to the white man, were called Ding. With that confusion straightened out, it became apparent that Nipper said he had seen the dingo that took Azaria before because he had seen it standing in the middle of the road outside his house on that very Sunday morning. He knew it was a strange dingo not normally resident at Ayers Rock. He had looked at its tracks then and had later recognised them as belonging to the culprit dingo.

Then we saw the video that Kevin Hitchcock had done with Nipper. On it Kevin asked, 'If you saw the dingo carrying the baby here do you think what has happened to Mrs Chamberlain is the right thing?'

Nipper answered, 'Yes, Mrs Chamberlain is right—not guilty.'

'She is not guilty?' he was asked.

'Yes,' Nipper stated.

'You think the dingo took the baby?' asked Mr Hitchcock.

Nipper said, 'The dingo is guilty.'

'So what did he [Frank Morris] say when you told him what you found?' Kevin asked later.

Nipper answered, 'He believed me right.'

'He believed you?' queried Kevin.

'Yeah,' said Nipper.

Kevin Hitchcock then asked, 'Nipper, when you were in the courtroom and they asked you a lot of questions, why didn't you tell them the information about the dingo carrying the baby here?'

'No—they never asking me at all,' Nipper said.

'They didn't ask you questions?' Kevin said surprised.

'No,' agreed Nipper.

Kevin said, 'If they had asked you in the court, you would have told them what you've told us now?'

Well, that was common sense. Nipper said, 'He should ask me and I would have been tell him.'

Kevin wanted to be sure, 'But they didn't ask?' he asked again.

'No,' said Nipper flatly.

Everything Nipper said was corroborated by the other trackers as well as Derek Roff, Murray Haby, the headmaster who initially found the tracks and imprints in the sand, Inspector Michael Gilroy and Sergeant John Lincoln of the Northern Territory police.

Nipper might have been the head spokesman and tribal elder, but Barbara was recognised as being the best tracker in the tribe.

Mr Porter was conducting Barbara's examination. 'Was Nipper with you all the time when you were doing this tracking you've told us about?' he asked.

'Yes, both of us,' was the reply. All Barbara's evidence was given through an interpreter.

'Did Nipper do any tracking when you were not there so far as you know?' asked Porter.

'No, we was always together,' she replied.

Chester Porter asked, 'This dingo that you've told us about whose tracks were outside the tent and whose tracks were near where the baby's clothes were found, did you know which particular dingo that was?'

Barbara's answer was, 'The same dingo that we seen at the tent.'

'I beg your pardon?' asked Mr Porter.

'The same dingo tracks that we seen at the tent,' the interpreter repeated.

'What was the answer?' asked the Commissioner.

Mr Porter supplied, 'The same dingo tracks as were in at the tent.' Mr Adams interjected, '"As we seen at the tent".'

Porter repeated, '"As we seen at the tent"—yes, I think you are right. Did that dingo have a name? Did the dingo have a name?'

The interpreter, Miss Cousens, interjected, 'I don't follow that, because how can they—if they only saw the dingo tracks, how do they know his name?'

Mr Porter answered, 'That has been something that has been puzzling me for a long time, Miss Interpreter, but unfortunately . . .'

He addressed Barbara. 'Have you ever seen that dingo's tracks before the time you saw it at the tent? Have you ever seen that dingo's tracks before the day you saw them around the tent?'

Barbara's reply was, 'Yes, we used to see them tracks before.'

Mr Porter then asked, 'Did you know which dog that was? Did you know which was the dog that had those tracks? I will put it another way. Have you ever seen the dog that made those tracks?'

The interpreter then said, 'I will just explain that question. "I know I've seen it with my own eyes, the big tracks that a dingo's made", but she wasn't referring to your question.'

'I see,' said Porter. 'Have you ever heard of a dog called Ding?'

Barbara's reply was, 'Ding—that's another word for that same thing which is called Kulpunya, which means . . .'

'Kulpunya?' questioned Chester Porter.

'Kulpunya,' she repeated.

'Which is the devil dog of Ayers Rock?' asked Porter.

'Yes,' was the reply.

'Tell her I will not be asking her any more questions about that and she need not worry—except this: You told me at Ayers Rock that women are not allowed to talk about Kulpunya. Is that right?'

The answer was, 'Yes, that's true because it's very sacred.'

'It is very sacred, yes,' said Mr Porter. 'Thank you, Barbara.'

Then it was the Crown's turn and the Commissioner questioned, 'Mr Adams?'

Adams jumped to his feet. 'Thank you, Your Honour. Who came and asked you to track?' was his first question.

'Derek. Derek. The ranger, Derek, or whatever his name was,' the interpreter replied.

Adams asked, 'Did you know him well?' The reply was, 'I know him very well.'

'Did he speak to you in English?' Adams wanted to know.

'He used to talk English,' she answered.

'What did he say to you?' questioned Adam.

Barbara's reply was, 'He told us to get up because there was big trouble at Ayers Rock.'

Adams wanted to know, 'Did he tell you what the trouble was?'

'Yes, he told us about the disappearance of the baby,' she answered through the interpreter.

'What did he tell you about the disappearance of the baby?' questioned Adams.

'That a dingo took the baby,' she stated.

'Did he ask you to go and look for the tracks of that dingo?' Adams asked.

Barbara's reply was, 'Yes, he did.'

Adams asked, 'When you went looking for those tracks, was he with you?'

'Yes,' was the reply.

'And Nipper was with you?' Adams continued.

'Yes.'

'Nipper's English is pretty good?' questioned Adams.

The interpreter stated, 'He could talk pretty well and they could understand what he was trying to say.'

Mr Porter asked, 'Did you talk to Derek yourself?'

'Yes.'

'Did you talk to him about the tracks that you saw?' asked Adams.

'Yes,' Barbara answered.

‘Now, you’ve told us that the tracks that you saw were those of a big male dingo?’ questioned Adams.

‘Told to Derek?’ she questioned.

‘You’ve told us that the tracks you saw were those of a big male dingo?’ Adams reiterated.

Barbara’s reply was, ‘Yes, I’ve seen male dingoes have big tracks.’

‘Yes,’ said Adams. ‘The track that you saw on the sandhill, was that a male or a female?’ he asked.

‘A big male,’ she stated.

‘Why did you think it was male?’ he wanted to know.

She answered through the interpreter, ‘I’ve seen—I have seen male dogs have big tracks—whatever they are—tracks.’

‘And you thought that that dingo was carrying something, did you?’ queried Adams.

‘Yes, I thought it was carrying the baby,’ was Barbara’s prompt reply. Adams changed the subject in a hurry. ‘I want to ask you something about dingoes generally, now, and not about this particular dingo?’

‘I know that . . . ? . . . big one, but I don’t know little . . . ?’ the translator said Barbara’s reply.

Adams asked, ‘I wonder if you would mind translating that, please.’

The interpreter explained, ‘I know the difference between a female’s—female dingoes have small tracks, and male dogs have big tracks.’

Adams said, ‘Yes, I understand that. Now, what kind of tucker or game do dingoes get around the Rock?’

The interpreter replied on behalf of Barbara, ‘When a dingo is hungry, they go after kangaroos.’

‘Yes. Do they eat goannas, as well?’ asked Adams.

‘If it’s hungry, it will kill a kangaroo or whatever—lizard, goannas. A dingo is a dingo, and if he wants a feed, he’ll kill to eat,’ was the reply.

‘Does it also kill rabbits, and eat them?’ he then wanted to know.

‘Yes.’

‘Now, this dingo track that you saw, that dingo could have been carrying a lot of different things. Is that right?’ Adams asked. He knew Barbara had been very specific, but it was worth a try. ‘. . . I know that . . . ?’ queried Adams of the partial reply.

The interpreter answered, ‘I know it was the child.’

‘I see,’ said Adams. ‘How do you know it was the child?’

‘Because I know if it kills a joey, it will take off with it, carry it,’ was the answer Barbara gave.

‘So could this dingo have had a joey?’ asked Adams, hopefully.

The interpreter queried, ‘Do you want me to explain that question to you?’

‘Yes,’ exclaimed Adams. ‘Could you give us her answer, please? It won’t embarrass me if you think it was a stupid question.’

The interpreter looked at her hands for a moment, thought seriously, then looked straight at Adams and said, '"You are talking your way with your ideas and you are talking about lies." Are you satisfied?'

Everyone except Adams immediately broke into laughter.

The Commissioner tried to intervene as it was obvious Barbara resented having her word questioned.

'Would you ask Barbara whether the dingo could have been carrying a joey?'

The interpreter asked, 'Come again? Could you say that again?'

The Commissioner repeated his question, 'Could the dingo have been carrying a joey?'

Quick as a flash, the answer came, 'Was a kangaroo living in the tent?' The Commissioner blushed slightly as the whole court roared with laughter.

Both Barbara and Miss Cousens looked slightly offended. I think, perhaps, they may have thought everyone was laughing at them, rather than at the discomfort of the Commissioner. To anyone slightly acquainted with Aboriginal thought processes, the stupidity of his question, to their way of thinking, was obvious and deserved a smart-alec answer. It wasn't meant to be funny.

Adams continued, 'Because you saw the dingo track at the tent is that why you believe it was carrying a baby?'

'Yes,' she replied.

Now for a dumb question. 'Have you often tracked dingoes before?' queried Adams.

'We track dingoes so we can kill it and get the hide to sell.' She lessened his ignorance of Aboriginal culture.

He changed his tack, 'What was there about the tracks that told you the dingo was carrying something?'

'I know when a dingo is hungry it will kill to eat and then it takes it,' she stated.

'In telling this story to us are you relying on something about the tracks themselves or something you know about dingoes,' Adams wanted to know.

That was too hard to translate. 'Could you put that another way, please?' He tried again, 'Was there anything special about the marks of this dingo that you saw?'

The interpreter answered, 'That answer was just they were big tracks.' Adams then wanted to know: 'The tracks that you saw near the clothes, I would like to ask you some questions about those now. You've told us that those were also the tracks of a big male dingo?'

'Yes.'

'Was that the only big male dingo around Ayers Rock or were there others as well?' he queried.

'There used to be a lot of dingoes there,' was the reply.

Now that was interesting. The reports we had been hearing for years might well have been true. What a pity he didn't go on to ask how many had been shot as a result of the attack on Azaria.

He continued, 'Were there a lot of big male dingoes there?'

'I used to see—there used to be, or there were a lot of male dogs there,' was her answer. Obviously something had changed the population.

Now Adams asked a crucial question: 'The tracks that you saw at the clothes—were they the same dingo or a different dingo to the one that you saw at the tent?'

'The same dingo tracks that were at the tent,' came the reply.

'How can you tell that they were—I am sorry,' Adams started and then realised what he had nearly got himself into. 'Could they have been the tracks of another big male dingo? The tracks at the clothes—could they have been the tracks of another male dingo, not the same one that was by the tent?' he asked (he sounded hopeful to me). Barbara explained through the interpreter: 'If I come to a spot where there's three or four different dingo tracks there, they might be all big. I know which is the mother, which is young and so on, and which is old and which is so and so.'

'I see,' said Adams. 'The tracks of the big male dingo that you saw by the clothes—that was the track of the same dingo that you saw at the sandhill, or could it have been the track of another big male dingo?' He sounded hopeful again.

'The same one,' she said.

'Can you remember whether there was anything special or different about that dingo track that enabled you to tell the difference between it and any other dingo track?' Adams asked.

This line of questioning was getting the better of the interpreter: 'I would like to tell you something first before you ask questions like that. When Aboriginal people see tracks, they know who it belongs to, what person went there, because they know the tracks, whereas if all these people got out of the courtroom now and walked barefooted, you can't tell, can you?'

'No,' exclaimed Adams.

The interpreter said, 'Aboriginal people can.'

Adams then asked tentatively, 'Is it a meaningful question to ask how it is, what it is, about the track that tells her?'

The interpreter translated for Barbara, 'When I saw the tracks, I knew which dog it belonged to. If another dog cut across, I knew it wasn't that one. I knew the one, the same one.'

The evidence continued about tracks of what appeared to be another dingo altogether.

The interpreter stated: 'They followed the tracks for a long way then they come back. Long way. I don't know how long.'

Adams asked Barbara, 'Why did you follow those tracks?'

'It's the wrong tracks,' was her reply.

'How did you know they were the wrong tracks?' Adams persisted. Barbara's explanation was patient instruction for novice trackers: 'We followed it. When we followed the tracks then we found out—if we kept following that track we might have run into the dingo that was at the tent. We might have cut across his tracks as we was following that other dingo tracks.'

Adams wanted to know, 'When you started off following that dingo's track did you think it was the right track or the wrong track?'

Barbara's answer was definite, 'Yes, we knew it was the wrong track.' Barbara's evidence then came to an end and it was quite obvious that she knew what she was doing and was not about to be swayed by clever court questioning.

Adams sat down again and leaned back in his chair. He was a big man and the chairs usually groaned audibly as he moved around. The court had been fairly quiet for some time when an audible crack was heard. Adams had broken another chair. By the time he had broken several of the nice padded office chairs at the bar table (and swapped each one for a new one belonging to one of our men) everyone had had enough and declared he should sit in the same chair each time to save on Commission expenses. Adams didn't think that very funny, and continued to pick new chairs. One day Ken Crispin, who was seated nearest to Adams, waited until Adams was cross-examining, then got up and exchanged the broken chair that Adams had given him for the unbroken one now vacated, that Adams had taken.

We continued to hear from rangers and police who had been at Ayers Rock at the time. They went into great detail about what they had seen, the particular areas and their own involvement with the searching and subsequent evidence. Too much of a similar thing could be pretty boring, and we had heard all this three times before.

Although we knew generally what was coming the next day, there were often surprises, although the day had gone smoothly so far. I had lost Michael again after court but he often went to get the papers immediately so I wasn't worried. I stepped out of the lift and saw Stuart waiting for me. I knew immediately something had happened again. I had seen that look on Stuart's face before and knew I wasn't going to like what he was about to tell me any more than he wanted to tell it. We had always had a 'straight from the shoulder' policy between us, and Stuart told me the Crown had had Michael followed (they had a whole file of evidence with names, dates, times, places and even photographs) and they were intending to use it the next day in court. I thought I was going to be sick. If there is a discrepancy between the publicly stated and privately acted behaviour of a person it goes toward establishing the character of a witness, and therefore whether they are to be believed or not.

Our lawyers countered this problem by saying we would then be forced to reveal skeletons in the Crown's own cupboard. We had to be prepared for anything so there had been a quick scramble to find Michael and talk to him so we could best handle whatever was thrown up in court the next day. They were having difficulties talking to Michael and wanted me to discuss it with him. When Michael returned to the room after talking with them he never mentioned the matter so I had to. Bringing the subject up to was one of the hardest things I have ever had to do in my life. Despite our problems I had hoped that the shock of being 'de-credentialed' by the church would resolve many issues, and our marriage might make it after all.

That night turned out to be the most devastating one of our whole married life for me. Everything I held dear and believed in had been challenged and people I had thought I could trust I now knew I could not, nor could I figure why it was my fault when I wasn't even there. I had already told Michael I would wait until he could straighten his priorities out, but that it could not be an open-ended wait. I had always felt that open acknowledgment of mistakes, together with honesty, repentance and getting on with your life whilst trying not to repeat the same mistakes twice was the standard to live by. It was this 'out of the shadows into the sunshine' policy that I tried to teach my children to live by also. If you have nothing to hide you cannot be threatened. That way your life is an open book and you never have to live in fear because no one can accuse you or threaten you secretly. It would have just as little power over me as it did when I was threatened with blackmail in prison. I told them to go ahead as I was not ashamed to have my life examined, so the attempt failed and they gave up.

After all the heartache, nothing was raised in the commission the next day and eventually we learned they had chosen not to bring the subject up. Towards the end of the commission our friend Pr George Rollo was called in by Chester Porter QC for the Commissioner, to discuss the same topic. Fortunately I had been having counselling sessions with George, (we had some joint ones also later) and he immediately knew what Porter was referring to, although I had not told George details or the extent of my knowledge, so George was able to answer in the balanced, intelligent way he was renowned for. During their discussion it was concluded it would not alter the outcome of the case given the overwhelming facts before the court now and that apart from the media enjoying it, it did not add anything, so it remained unmentioned.

Five or ten minutes before we were due to arrive at court up to the time we went inside, we were fair game as the media got a daily shot of us, unless there was a fresh crew who didn't know the routine. One day, they had been saying, 'Come on, give us a smile. I know you're bored with this but there's only a few more days to go.' Then, because his soundman was watching us instead of guiding the cameraman where he was going, the cameraman backed straight into a light post. The other guys laughed at him. Later the newsmen were talking about it and Kevin Hitchcock was there, so I asked how the cameraman was, since it had looked as if he had hit the post fairly hard.

Kev laughed and said, 'You know, we didn't think you had seen that. You never looked as if you noticed it at all.' At last I must have graduated in not letting my feelings show when I tried.

On another occasion, a new camera crew started to walk in front of us down the street, the cameraman moving backwards as usual.

I said to Michael, 'Tell them there is a brick wall. Put them off.' He did, and put the cameraman off enough to stop filming before he realised it was a joke. At times like that you would hear them mumble, 'Touché', and then they would leave us alone.

There was a recess from 19 June until 6 August, which meant we could all go home for a few weeks and prepare for the next round—police evidence, plus the primary witnesses such as Greg and Sally Lowe.

When I came out of prison I needed a good holiday, and a number of friends had suggested we holiday in the snow with them and learn to ski. When we discovered at the last minute that we had the break in the Commission, we planned to go skiing. That was something I had always wanted to do; it looked so *free*, and right then I wanted to feel nothing more than freedom. We rushed around, borrowed and bought some snow gear, hired the rest, and off we went. Having gone with friends before, our boys could already ski. They simply hopped on their skis and took off. Half the luck of kids! The rest of the family were novices. I must have fallen over more than thirty times that first afternoon. Just as well it was only a half day. It wasn't the skiing that made me so stiff, it was getting up again!

I eventually started going *down* the hill instead of *into* it and sure enough, when I finally mastered some skill, it did have that wild, free as a bird, exhilarating feeling. There is anonymity in skiing under goggles, hats and gloves; and it is a great equaliser. Rich and poor, famous and infamous, can end up splat on the snow! Skiing would have to be *the* favourite family sport.

It was time to go to Melbourne and Pastor Peter Stojanovic, our Yugoslavian friend, invited us to stay with them. Then I got to know Mary, whose name I learned was Marijana—which is much prettier. (Why are Australians too lazy to try and pronounce foreign spelt names?) She was a bubbly, fun-loving person and often very like myself.

Sometime later I said to her, 'I can't understand why you were so quiet the day I first met you. It's just not like you. You are never quiet.'

She looked a little shamefaced and said, 'Well, I have got to be honest, kiddo. You see, I thought you were guilty. I sort of hadn't purposely made up my mind and yet it was there in the back of my mind, but when I saw you there with Kahlia and I saw how you treated her, I realised you weren't the type of mother who would do something to your child, even accidentally. I had always thought what happened to Azaria must have been an accident and you were covering up.' She added, 'I realised that everything I had read about you, and how hard I thought you were didn't make sense when I met you. I was studying you and feeling ashamed of myself, and I simply didn't know what to say. I actually didn't want to go.' Peter came in at the end of this and said, 'Go where?' She said to him,

'We were just talking about the first time I met Lindy.' So he said, 'Ah, yes. You tell her about the cake.'

She said, 'No!' That was enough to get my curiosity going, so I asked her about the cake. She said, 'It's nothing!'

Peter said, 'She didn't want to make you a cake.'

Marijana whacked him across the ears and he ducked, laughing, 'But I fixed her because Marijana makes the good cakes and I told her that if she wouldn't make it I would get my sister-in-law to make it and that was enough to make her maka da cake. She made it at night after work.'

I wondered when she could have made it except after work, but still didn't realise until sometime later just how *long* those cakes took to make, and that Marijana was holding down three jobs to help pay off their house, having very little sleep and very little time with her family in between. Marijana had sacrificed quite a lot of that precious time in order to make a cake for a person whom she thought was guilty of murder. When they finished telling me the story, she laughed, gave me a big hug and said, 'Just as well I learned different, eh, kiddo?'

I guess that was really the start of our lovely relationship; it felt as if at last I had found the younger brother and sister I had always wanted. Peter, Marijana and I almost suffered withdrawal symptoms when we left one another in Melbourne that time. The three of us became so close that when we stayed with them Michael almost felt left out, even though they related to him in the same way.

As time went on Kahlia was very happy to be with me, and she remained happy and enjoyed my company so long as I did not try any disciplinary action when she misbehaved. As Michael was usually there at those times, she would brook no interference from anyone else and I was finding it frustrating. The final countdown came when we were in Melbourne for the movie preparation.

We were staying at Pete and Mary's place and the children were all going to go out with Pete, so she had to get dressed. It was winter and we only had a small suitcase each. Most of her clothes were already in the drier, so we didn't have a choice. When I went to dress her, she suddenly took a vehement dislike to her previously favourite dress. I insisted she put it on because it was the only thing dry, and she slapped me hard across the face and screamed. When Michael rushed in to find out what was the matter, he wanted to know what I was doing to her to upset her so. I explained and he left. He couldn't believe that Kahlia would slap anyone as he never had any problems, but then I didn't have chewing gum with me to assist in her co-operation.

I tried again with the dress and we had a repeat performance. This time I smacked her on the leg hard and told her not to do it again, 'Nice little girls don't hit people, especially on the face, and especially not mummies—and mummies would be very bad mummies if they let their little girls do it,' I explained. She raised her hand again and I said to her,

'Go on. You smack me, and I will smack you again, only it will be a lot harder this time.' She looked at me defiantly and I looked steadily back.

The other children in the room were extremely interested. They all told her smacking wasn't nice either. Finally, with the combined encouragement, the hand wavered and dropped but she continued to cry and scream. Michael returned. Then the crunch came. We had heated words about me trying to establish some relationship with Kahlia on my own without him rushing to her aid every time she opened her mouth. Kahlia stood by, an interested observer. Even though Michael recognised my right to look after her, the mental conditioning that she was 'his' was hard for him to overcome. Eventually he agreed to let me try and establish my relationship with Kahlia with no interference from him whatsoever for two weeks, after which he would see how Kahlia went. Kahlia had been well cared for by her foster parents, but the damage had been done by over-zealous well-wishers and baby-sitters who felt sorry for a motherless child and gave in to her every whim—and she had learned how to play it early so all her 'mums' had a job ahead of them.

Within about twenty minutes of that massive fight, out of the blue Kahlia walked up to me, tugged my dress and said, 'I love you, Mummy.' It was the first time she had ever done so with no interference. From then onwards, we were great mates. She had realised I really did care, even though I disciplined her, and that her mother had a right to do some things for her own good. I discovered that taking things from a woman's point of view and what 'we girls do' worked wonders. After that it took very few sessions to have a reasonably normal family life (that is, when we weren't away at court).

Meeting Meryl the Magician

When we went to meet Meryl Streep for the first time, we were going through the script with Fred Schepisi and had been told we would have lunch with Meryl and Sam. We had seen Sam, said hello and then gone into Fred's office.

Several times Fred had taken phone calls, although he had asked for none to be put through and I began to suspect the caller was Meryl. Lunchtime had come and gone and there had been no more mention of our meeting for lunch. We were still going through the script so Fred had decided to have some food sent in. Another phone call came through and he kept answering in monosyllables. This time I sat and watched him and in a gap in the conversation, I said, 'That's Meryl, isn't it?'

He grinned and said, 'Yeah.'

I said, 'How come she is not here? I thought she was supposed to be here.'

He said, 'Well, I thought it might put you off, don't you mind?' I said, 'No. I don't mind. It's fine by me.'

He said, 'OK, one of her kids has done something. She's gone off for a minute.'

When she came back on the phone he said, 'Look, get your gear on and get yourself down here,' and hung up. I said, 'Is she coming?' and he said, 'Hmm.' A short while later, I saw her walk to the door. She did exactly what I had done. Those stupid doors went the opposite direction to what you expected and you could stand there like a fool, trying to push them when they needed to be pulled and vice versa. Michael had obviously missed the conversation, which we thought he had heard, because he seemed totally unaware she was there. I knew what a fool I had felt with those doors, so I just grinned and waved at Meryl then kept reading through the script with Fred. Fred, on the other hand, was sitting there with a big grin on his face, a typical mannerism of his when he was watching people. Michael realising Fred was looking at something and that I kept glancing back, looked up, and there, unmistakably, was Meryl. Flustered from her battle with the doors, she burst into the room. Michael jumped up and his mouth dropped open. I thought there was enough electricity in the air without adding to it and, sensing that Meryl was slightly embarrassed from her struggle with the doors anyway, I decided to just sit back and watch.

Meryl walked towards Michael and Michael took a step towards her, and they stood there looking at one another and it passed through my mind: *Goodness, are they going to embrace or both burst into tears?* Then Meryl sort of laughed, which broke the tension, and they shook hands and said hello. Then she came and plopped herself down on the big couch next to me.

Much to my amusement, Meryl was as far removed as possible from the lady on the screen. Her bubbly, effervescent personality is totally opposite to the cool, calm, controlled exterior often shown in her acting. She laughs a lot, she bounces around a lot, she uses a lot of hand movements. She is a fun person to talk to and to be with. As he watched the three of us, Fred's grin, if anything, grew wider and wider. He made me think of an overgrown elf who had just watched his magic work and was totally enjoying the situation.

Fred told Meryl she had to sit down now and be quiet because we hadn't finished work and she could talk later. She pulled a bit of a face at him and asked what we were doing. When he said we were going through the script, she replied, 'Good, I've got mine here, I'll stay.' It was interesting to watch the by-play between Fred and Meryl. Although Fred was the director, it was obvious Meryl very subtly had the upper hand. If there was anything she really wanted to do, she probably would win in the end, although in the nicest way. It didn't look as if she would need to throw any primadonna tantrums to get what she wanted. She was so much the master of her acting ability, she knew just how far she could push her own talent, and knew her own limitations. Meryl quickly turned to the right page and as we went through the script, she asked occasional questions about the reason behind such a thing, what sort of expression I would use here or there, or what I would do with my hands (what a pity the mini-series didn't do this also).

After some time, Sam also wandered in and the five of us continued going through the script. We had a very profitable time, and it was something I know they were quite grateful for later.

Meryl asked whether we had our family with us, but we only had Kahlia that time. Meryl had her three children and husband in Australia with her as well. Her eldest daughter was similar in age to Kahlia, she said, so could Kahlia come and play? I said, 'Sure.' I rang up Pete Stojanovic and asked whether he could pick up Kahlia from the school where she was with his children for the day so she could play with Meryl's little girl. 'Just drop her off at Meryl's,' I said, 'and we can pick her up after work, or you can meet us there at a certain time.' Peter said he would and I left it up to him. Meanwhile, Meryl alerted the security guards to expect them.

Later that afternoon, when we had finished our discussions, Michael went somewhere with Sam and I left with Meryl to see her dresser, Roy. She was having a fitting for her wigs and a consultation about makeup, so Roy would be really pleased to see me. It was odd being chauffeur-driven by a man packing a gun and being accompanied by two big burly security men, but obviously very necessary because Meryl and I were going somewhere public together. We would have liked to do a lot more together, but it was too dangerous. As it was, Meryl had had threats because she had agreed to play my part in the film, and we would be at the most risk when we were together. So we tried to go most places separately.

We walked through the hotel and had a nice time with Roy, discussing Meryl's wigs. He also had a good look at my face shape and the type of makeup I wore and what shape I did my eyebrows.

Walking out of the hotel was a different experience. By then, even if they hadn't initially recognised Meryl, the staff had recognised me. They put two and two together, guessed who they would have walking through the foyer, and all managed to be standing round the desk in the foyer when we emerged. Meryl seemed to have the same attitude as I did; she carried on with her business as per normal and didn't let on she saw anything out of the ordinary, so people remained unaware that she had noticed their presence at all.

When we went back to Meryl's home and walked inside there was no sign anywhere of Kahlia and Meryl's little girl, though her son was there. He had just finished his first day at an Australian school and Meryl was anxious to know how it had been. She let out a squeal and ran to him. By that time I had got to the room and realised that Peter Stojanovic had made himself at home there and was stretched full length on the couch reading a magazine, while another gentleman sat in a chair reading another magazine over the other side of the room. This turned out to be

Don Gummer, a quiet, nice guy who didn't seem the least bit threatened that he had a famous wife and who obviously knew his standing within his own household and with his wife and children.

Meryl introduced her beloved family and picked up the baby who came out to her. She had been eating toast or something because she had it all around her mouth. Without the least worry, Meryl picked her up and kissed her and didn't mind sticky little fingers being wiped all over her face and jacket. She went waltzing out to the kitchen, and there was Marijana happily swapping recipes with Meryl's cook.

That was the sort of person Meryl was. Marijana said afterwards she had been very nervous about meeting a big star, someone who had long been one of her favourites, with so many awards. Pete later commented that Meryl was just like she should have been and if she had been any other way they would have been disappointed. It was obvious that whatever situation she was in, Meryl was at home with people and able to make them feel at home with her.

While in Melbourne Meryl decided we would all have a meal together. Fred and his wife Mary, Sam, Michael and I, all had dinner with Meryl and Don at their home. That was a test for the security men—there were about nine outside at one stage.

Halfway through the meal Meryl said to Fred, 'You watch.' Fred replied, 'You wouldn't.'

She said, 'Watch me.' She looked down towards Sam who was at the other end of the table carrying on a conversation with Michael, Mary and Don. Fred and I sat back and watched. Without doing anything that was different at all, Meryl carried on her conversation with Fred and me. We watched in amusement as Sam began to squirm.

After a while he looked up and said, 'Cut it out!' Meryl just looked at him and said, 'What?' very innocently. He went back to his conversation, trying to tell some sort of story, and a few moments later he looked straight at Meryl and said, 'Will you quit that? You are putting me right off, and I'm telling a story.' That was the end. Fred, Meryl and I dissolved into laughter and she simply said to Fred, 'Told you so.' Meryl had managed to get the same type of reaction from Sam as Michael had when I was having a conversation in another part of the room. It really was quite funny. No wonder they call her Meryl the Magician.

When we were called down to work on the film, we would occasionally go early or late and stay over the weekends with Marijana and Pete. On one particular occasion we were in a real party mood; Meryl and Sam came over for dinner with their families and we had an enjoyable time. Later none of us wanted to go to bed—except Michael.

We went and got some videos, and he went to bed when the children did after watching the first one. The rest of us sat up to watch the second one then Marijana went to sleep on the floor. When the video finished, Pete and I were still wide awake, so we decided to have a go at the kids' new video game. We managed easily at first, then it grew harder and at about two in the morning we decided if we stayed up any longer and laughed any more we'd wake Marijana, and Michael would stagger back downstairs and tell us all to go to bed, like naughty children, which would send us into more gales of laughter, so we went to bed.

Pete's boxing name, Peter Crystal, came from the fact that he wore glasses, not to any allusion that he was fragile, because fist and jaw were both made of iron. It was good whenever I needed to go somewhere to know that I had a good bodyguard as well as a friend with me.

Pete drove us out to see the *Evil Angels (A Cry in the Dark)* movie set the day before the first filming started, as the set dresser wanted me to set the tent up the right way for them. The whole campsite was reconstructed in a huge tin shed studio. Even the buses looked like dwarfs. We looked around and I fixed the tent, then the dingo trainer came in.

We were introduced to Evanné Chesson, and then she took us out to see her dingoes. She had only just taken over; the head animal trainer had quit the day before because he was afraid of the male dingo and couldn't control it. He decided it was too dangerous to work with so Evanné, who had been his assistant, took over. Her assistant, Dick Skinner, had been bitten by the same animal that morning. His hand was heavily bandaged. Evanné let us have an old fashioned biscuit tin that one of the dingoes had bitten through while having a little pre-dinner gnaw. The holes looked as if they had been made by small-bore rifle bullets.

I was carrying the tin around in a bag with me when I met Sam wandering around the set and showed it to him. Sam was quite concerned and asked whether Meryl had seen it yet. When I said no, he asked whether he could show it to her. Later he reported that when Meryl saw the tin, she went white. She was to work with those dingoes later that day and was not looking forward to going anywhere near them.

Evanné told us that the female dingo she trained for the tent scene had just had mouth surgery but was still easily tossing a 5 kilogram (12 pound) weight up in the air. She had thought a heavy weight might hurt her animal, but when told she needed only 4 kilograms (10 pounds), she wondered why all the fuss had been made in court!

Dr Tony Raymond from the Melbourne Forensic Laboratory had been appointed by the Commission to do all the blood tests, and was often to give the final word as arbitrator between the Crown and the defence as well. He had been asked to do the work on the matinee jacket, with scientists from both parties attending as observers. Dr Raymond was to be called several times to give evidence in various fields.

He said without proper controls in blood testing one could be mistaken in the reaction they were reading, and the so-called arterial spray was indeed sound deadener as Les Smith had claimed. He thought some elements of the original protein should be able to be picked up even in severely denatured stains. During the break, my father came up to me and said, 'You know, I can't believe it but Tony Raymond is so much like my father as a young man, I keep looking at him and expecting to go back in time to being a little boy.'

Tony Raymond was also one of those rare species, like Dr Andrew Scott from Adelaide, who often did police forensic work but was quite capable of keeping his mind on the job in front of him and not straying with his own opinions. He gave scientific fact only and did not stray into the realm of what might or might not be *thought* to perhaps be the case.

Some people could not be so objective about their own opinions. Although we received hundreds of letters when I got out of prison from people telling me how happy they were, I never received any from the key members of the particular support groups who had been badgering me to use their chosen lawyers. They had claimed I would never get any sort of an inquiry if I kept Stuart Tipple on, and now here we were in the middle of one. Nevertheless, when I came face to face with one of the key leaders in the ladies' toilet during that week in Melbourne, she did not introduce herself; when I finally asked their names, someone else introduced her. I asked, surprised, why *she* hadn't told me who she was and she said she didn't want to intrude! Even then she didn't tell me she was pleased that I was out of jail, let alone that she hoped everything would go well during the Commission. We had been fighting particularly hard for that Commission and so had all the support groups, so that seemed very strange to me. I never saw or heard from her again.

Back inside the courtroom a document was tendered by the Crown which had Ian Barker's name written on it. Barker said, 'I don't know why my name appears so prominently on that document, but I'd prefer it blotted out.'

Morling told him it didn't matter.

Chester Porter said to Barker in an audible aside, 'You don't know what a temptation it is to blot *you* out, Mr Barker!'

Barker just glowered while Porter grinned wickedly. I bet his teachers used to wonder what mischief he'd been up to each time they saw that expression cross his face as a child.

Evidence of a Bloody Mess

The Melbourne session was to be mostly the forensic side of the case, and the centrepiece of the Crown's case: the evidence of blood in our car. The Crown had said at the trial that I had sat in the front passenger seat, held Azaria out in front of me and cut her throat with a pair of scissors or a knife. As the throat was cut, an artery spurted blood at a trajectory of about forty-five degrees, producing the spray pattern found on the under-dash plate. More blood dripped downwards, producing the marks that Mrs Hansell, the drycleaner, had found on my tracksuit pants, and other blood dripped onto the carpet.

Blood had also run down the side of the seat hinge (this could only have happened if the passenger seat had been occupied), and there was more blood on the crossbar beneath the seat (underneath the carpet and underfelt but there was no blood on them of course). They said there was also blood on a towel, which might have come from a knife wiped clean, and blood on a pair of scissors, which might have been the murder weapon—or perhaps had been used to cut the jumpsuit later that evening. Barker had used the under-dash spray to prove that Azaria was dead, where she died and how. Kuhl had said that her tests established that two of the droplets cut from the spray pattern, the stains on and under the seat, the marks on the towel and stains in the camera bag that Michael used all came from an infant under three months old. And there were 'strong indications' that the blood on the scissors also came from an infant. If this piece of evidence was right, then the Crown case was proven.

Well, that was what the Crown had said—and enough people had agreed with them to imprison me for almost three years, but was it right? Alas, the Crown 'stuffed up' its science factually speaking, thereby drawing the wrong conclusion.

With the assistance of numbers of eminently qualified scientists, it was discovered that any baby killed in our car would have had blood made of a sand/bitumen mixture.

The fact remains that the most damning piece of evidence used to convict me, when understood, was the key to understanding what was wrong; and how and why I was convicted.

By the time the Commission got under way, Les Smith's research had proved that the under-dash spray consisted of sound-deadening material, for a start. And then a Sergeant Henry Huggins from the Victorian police force had examined the stains on the crossbar under the seat and on a 10 cent coin on the metal floor under the carpet. Barker used this evidence to make the car sound as if it was awash with blood, but when Sergeant Huggins looked at this he found a few problems with that proposition. The coin was *under* the carpet, and there wasn't any sign of blood *on* the carpet. And the carpet was original—the police knew this because the car seats had to be removed to replace the carpet, and when Metcalfe pulled them out he found the packing putty General Motors Holden use still in place. What a pity that the police weren't as careful in all their observations as Metcalfe had been that time! How much trouble they might have saved themselves! Huggins said the stains on the floor couldn't possibly have got there from blood flowing down the side of the seat without going on the carpet.

During the taking of Henry Huggins's evidence in Melbourne, we went with the court to view the car. Our friend Pete Stojanovic, who was driving us around was with us. He pointed out some runs down the rear left mudguard to me, and we were joking how like the Crown's famous 'blood' they were. I pointed these run marks out to Ken Crispin who, noticing Michael Adams quite close, remarked quite loudly for his benefit, 'This is bad. The Crown has been careless. They have spilt some.'

Adams couldn't resist rising magnificently to the Crown defence. He couldn't have realised Ken was having a crack at the blood planted by the mystery syringe theory (the car cage had been broken into and a syringe had been found in the car—it appeared to be a vet's syringe, but more than that tests and inquiries failed to reveal) and so he replied pompously, 'The Crown is *never* careless. Not in this case.'

It was just too good an opportunity to miss. I had been standing with my back to Adams, and continued my conversation with Ken as if we hadn't heard Adams. Loud enough for him to hear once again I said, 'Oh no, they are never careless. They are deliberate!' Ken choked back a chuckle, as we both heard Adams's snort of quickly intaken breath. As he was not being addressed, he could do nothing.

Joy Kuhl had used a chemical called orthotolidine to test for the presence of blood—and quite a number of forensic scientists gave evidence about that. They agreed generally that a positive result wasn't conclusive at all, and further tests should have been done. Leo Freney, of the Department of Health in Queensland, went so far as to say that 'If at the end of the day you've only got screening test positives, the scientific answer is no blood found', and it was 'quite wrong' to treat a positive reaction as even prima facie evidence of the presence of blood.

In his investigations Les Smith had to use an infrared spectrophotometer. He asked permission to use one from the Australasian Food Laboratories in Cooranbong. Bob Hoskin, the scientist in charge of it, became familiar with the case Les was working on and observed that he had read copper dust had an almost identical reaction to blood, so did some research for his own information. The results were as he had read and he passed the information on to our men.

Barry Boettcher went to Mt Isa himself and collected copper dust samples, which tested positive. He said, 'Since the Chamberlains lived at Mt Isa when Azaria disappeared, it would be expected that a number of their items would have collected Mt Isa dust capable of producing the peacock blue colour expected in a positive orthotolidine test with blood.' Joy Kuhl's description of the strongly positive reactions to tests on substances in the camera bag was, he said, 'a good description of the sorts of results that I obtained in literally dozens of tests at Mt Isa.' Chester Porter wryly observed that, as far as he knew, the Mt Isa district wasn't awash with foetal blood.

Years later, positive results were still being obtained from Michael's camera bag, but no confirmatory tests would show any expected reactions to blood at all—just copper.

We informed Dr Andrew Scott, the Adelaide Crown forensic biologist who then carried out some tests to check the information we had given him about copper dust giving a similar reaction. He found that it did. (Of course, Mt Isa is one of the biggest copper-producing areas in the world.) Copper dust fooled all but the most experienced operators, who indicated how difficult it was to tell, except from the time of the reaction. There were enough clues, but not enough for someone who lacked the experience.

Meanwhile, Mike Lester had been working, as he had promised, on arrangements to take us out to dinner while we were in Melbourne. Finally he had rung up and said, 'Guess what? You can go to dinner at Maxim's. I am taking you out and you can have some other friends as well if you like. Who would you like?' Mac and Lynley Potts, Guy and Phyllis Boyd, Peter and Marijana Stojanovic were all living in Melbourne at the time, and they all said yes with great pleasure.

We had a marvellous time. Part way through, Guy and Phyllis Boyd's daughter Lenore Stevenson (who had started the first petition and got her dad interested initially) and her husband Stuart called in on the way home from an evening engagement, so we were able to meet them as well. We were given a private room upstairs and had a ball. As the evening progressed, we realised ever-increasing numbers were going to the bathrooms, making sure they had a good look in on the way. Obviously the word had passed around. Fortunately we were now used to this so it didn't bother us.

When it came to dessert, as nobody had been able to make up their mind just exactly which of the delicious desserts they really wanted to have, most of us ordered different ones and then proceeded to swap our plates around the table trying everybody else's. The waiter took one horrified look at what we were doing and then with great aplomb, turned his back and busied himself in polishing the silver and wiping the drink bottles down.

We had to supply a lot of the drinks ourselves, because most of us were teetotallers, and for once in his life, the poor man wasn't quite sure which of the bottles we had went with which course. Much to my amusement, halfway through the meal those who had been drinking the non-alcoholic red wine had their glasses refilled (when they weren't watching) with my favourite de-alcoholised ginger wine that Mac and I had been drinking. A number of the others weren't so keen on it, and the look on Lynley's face when she discovered she had a mixture of red and ginger was worth seeing.

Having not been out to a place like that before, Lynley was trying to empty her glass, not realising that every time she emptied it, the waiter would fill it up again. Like most good Adventist girls, she had been taught not to be wasteful by leaving anything. So I enlightened her, and when he walked past her the next time, she got her hand out so fast and slammed it down so quick on the top of the glass he managed, with the greatest effort, to hide his surprise, and say, 'No more? Very well, ma'am.' At which she exclaimed 'It worked!' and heaved a delighted sigh of relief.

Marijana was having a great time and not worrying about what others thought. While the waiter was out of the room, Pete jumped up, grabbed the bottle and began filling everybody's glasses. The waiter came back, Peter continued, and the waiter gave up and went away laughing. Pete later said, 'He probably thinks we are the biggest hicks from the country, but I couldn't care less, I've had a great time.'

To top it all off, on the way out a Rolls-Royce stalled in front of us and Pete took great glee in offering the man a push!

Often it was easier for final consultations to take place just before the start of the next court hearing, so we would all meet a few days early in the city where it was about to take place. During the long spell of Commission in Darwin, Jack Winneke took his secretary, Joan Simmonds, along also. Joan was a cheerful, efficient lady whom we all liked. She managed to keep her finger right on the pulse of things, yet was quiet and unobtrusive about it. We enjoyed working with her and the rest of the team.

Pam, our junior solicitor, on the other hand, was experiencing difficulties. As time went on she had problems working with the men so eventually we decided, by mutual agreement, to part company.

Stuart started looking for another solicitor and again there were a number of applicants. While waiting for Stuart at his office one day, I noticed a young guy also waiting and presumed he was a client of one of the other solicitors. We went in to see Stuart. Kahlia was with us and she got bored, so she went outside to draw pictures for the secretaries in the office. Through the crack of the door she had left open I saw the young chap talking to her. Kahlia was carrying on quite a conversation and he was reciprocating in an animated and lively way, playing, drawing and joking with her, generally keeping her well entertained. (I later discovered he had a child of similar age himself.) When we were nearly ready to leave Stuart said he had interviews booked with some of the applicants that day.

I said to Stuart, 'That's one of them out there, is it?' and he said, 'Yes.'

I said to him, 'Well, I like the look of him, he seems to have a few brains about him and be fairly bright. If his legal credentials are OK, let's have him.' We returned home and later in the afternoon Stuart rang us to report on his interviews with the various solicitors. He said, 'Well, I've got one. He is just a young bloke, but he seems to be pretty capable and have a good attitude and I like his credentials.'

I said to him, 'He wouldn't happen to be the one who was sitting outside when we were there, would he?' And he said, 'Actually, yes. I had forgotten you had seen him. Yes, he is the one.'

David Re was twenty-five, about 178 centimetres (5 foot 10 inches) tall, slim, brown-haired, and a real beach bum given the chance (which wasn't often). He always had a sleepy little-boy look and a cheeky grin. He often reminded me very much of Aidan when he'd just woken up. Although he gave the impression of wandering around, not doing very much, that was only a cover for a quick brain.

His car looked as if a bomb had gone off inside it, particularly in the boot, and we frequently joked to him about the forensic nightmare he would have to suffer if ever it was searched as ours had been. Despite the look of his car, David's work in the office was very meticulous, tidy and detailed. We found his filing and referencing to be excellent. He quickly caught up on all the back work, and was a great asset to the team.

Dave was very much the radical. Although he was expected to dress soberly for courts, he would appear wearing bright red socks, or ties with 'things' on them. As soon as court was over he would change into lurid shirts and shorts, with startling colours. One of his favourite shirts was green, with huge red beetles all over it! Another had spiders, and he also went in for tropical sunsets and palm trees. When the Commission was over he went to work in Germany for a while and occasionally dropped us postcards. It was lovely—but he always forgot a return address, so he never got a reply. That was our David. (In 2001, he was working at the Nuremberg Trials.)

Because the eyewitnesses' evidence was so important and things became very complicated during the second inquest and the trial, they had been unable to see us after the house raid. They often longed to talk to us or send us a message of encouragement, but realised that their evidence was crucial and if they kept up continual contact with us, the Crown would simply say they were biased and were entering into collusion with us. The most help they could offer was to stay away and let their evidence speak out. The eyewitnesses wanted to say a great deal to the jury, but were told their extra evidence was irrelevant, so they were unable to give what they considered to be a complete picture.

Yvonne Cain from the jury told me they often noticed one of the witnesses trying to say something extra and being unable to—then they wondered what it was that was being kept from them.

Because of the way the Crown set up the evidence against us, all the eyewitnesses were effectively called liars by inference, so their reputations were also at stake. Because of their involvement in my case some of the eyewitnesses were given an extremely hard time and even had to change jobs because of it. Although people tend to think we were the only ones affected, some of the others involved lost thousands of dollars in wages or business because of our case. Although fares and accommodation were paid for court appearances, expenses such as childcare in their absence were not. Nor were witness fees and loss of wages often forthcoming with any degree of promptness. Some lost contracts and many lost friends as a direct result of their involvement with us.

After my conviction the eyewitnesses had lobbied and given public addresses, but none of them had ever felt totally satisfied about their court evidence.

When we returned to Darwin again just before the Commission resumed on 6 August 1986, they were getting so used to us in the hotels now they usually even gave us the same room, but preferred us to stay under a pseudonym because of security.

This time the first significant witnesses were Sally and Greg Lowe. Although the Crown tried to make them sound biased, they stood their ground and were able to speak fully for the first time. Sally initially gave substantially the same evidence as before. Yes, she had heard Azaria cry, no, it hadn't been a tape recording. She saw a few drops of blood at the front of the tent and a large pool about a third of the way in, and concluded that the baby was dead. Yes, it was definitely blood. No, Azaria had definitely not been dead at the barbecue. The difference in her evidence was that this time she was able to tell of the pressure brought to bear on her at the second inquest and the trial when the Crown had done its best to break her story (they had actually got legal advice about it when she returned home). She also said how she was told by the interviewers that they weren't interested in the dingo theory, and appeared to have their minds made up regardless. (All the eyewitnesses were to complain of the same thing as they took their turn in the witness box.)

Then came Greg, who produced at least one surprise for the court. For the first time he said he had seen me come out of the tent, put my arm around Aidan's shoulder, go towards the car and open the back hatch. I hadn't been carrying Azaria. So, if he was correct, I could not have taken Azaria from the tent to the car and cut her throat. There was no time when I was unobserved and could have carried out the murder.

Barker really went for him. Why hadn't Greg said anything about this before?

'You kept it from the police?' he said. 'You didn't remember it before the coroner? You kept it from Mr Phillips? You kept it from Mr Kirkham? You kept it from the jury? But now you are quite certain that it happened?'

Greg said, 'Yes' to all those questions. He said he hadn't mentioned it before because he hadn't realised until the second inquest how significant it was, and he hadn't been called as a witness then. When he and Sally had been grilled during Operation Ochre, the questions concerned whether Azaria was alive at the barbecue—not whether I had gone to the car. That hadn't come up until the possibility of my murdering Azaria was mentioned. He didn't want to say anything that could be used to prejudice the credibility of Sally's evidence (that she'd heard Azaria cry in the tent), or they could say he was lying to back her up. He'd taken legal advice and been told that he'd better not mention it at that late stage. Sally's evidence was crucial, so he didn't want that to happen. So he had kept quiet. Now, of course, he was accused, as predicted, of fabricating evidence.

Ken Crispin, who was cross-examining, commented, 'Well, in the light of what's happened this morning, you now think that advice was pretty good.'

'Objection!' called Ian Barker.

Greg said now he could speak freely he was prepared to swear I had left the tent without Azaria, accepted that he'd been charged with lying under oath, and said that 'anybody . . . whose evidence tends to support one way or another has been called [a liar] over many years'.

The primary witnesses—the Wests, the Whittakers, Bobbie Downs (now Mrs Elston) and others—all testified that, contrary to rumour, Michael and I had been extremely upset during the evening. Michael was clearly distraught but had been trying to put on a brave face, and I was in shock. No fewer than six people gave evidence that there was no sign of blood on my face, hands or clothes. The reaction was always the same on the part of anyone listening for the first time—amazement that there was such overwhelming evidence in our favour and shock that it could possibly have been disbelieved.

While in Darwin I continued to run daily, both for sanity and for fitness. Usually I ran alone, though occasionally I talked Kevin Hitchcock into running with me for company. Michael had pulled a muscle and was unable to do more than run around the small hotel block and had to settle for a workout in the gym instead. Eventually his leg improved and he started running properly again.

Knowing we were both running regularly again, Malcolm Brown asked to go jogging with us one day. He promised not to report it—he'd fallen from grace by reporting a jog he'd once had in the Alice with Michael after promising not to, so Michael was still wary. Finally Michael agreed, and we were to meet in the Botanical Gardens one morning. Malcolm turned up with his notebook in the back pocket. He did have a T-shirt on, but there were the familiar shoes, business walk shorts and the splay-footed running style, though there was no doubt he could move along at quite a nice pace and had nothing to be ashamed of as a runner. Certainly he was a lot fitter than most of his fellow journalists. We had a good run, and although we had eyed the notebook warily, it wasn't used. Malcolm had redeemed himself.

Knowing I usually jogged alone very early in the morning or at dusk, people would often ask whether I was afraid of drunk Aborigines or nasty whites, but I never felt in physical danger in Darwin. On my early morning runs along the foreshore, I would often come across groups of Aborigines just waking up in the park ready for a new day and they would call out,

'G'day, Lindy!' I would call back and they would wave and talk. They knew they were under no threat from me and I knew I was safe with them. They would have protected me themselves, if necessary.

As for the whites, the prison guys had already sent me a message that I'd been OK'd on the streets. I have always found if you treat the so-called criminals right, most are no different from anyone else; indeed, they can be a lot more loyal. But treat them wrongly, and they will give as good as they get and more. Their social conscience is less insistent than other people's, so others come off worse. Crims stick together and I was still a friend. I'd been inside with a lot of them, and word is passed around. When dealing with hostile press, I still find if any prison friends (or friends of theirs) are around, they immediately spring into action and some photographers have been at a distinct disadvantage.

Being well known by the Darwin crims was one thing, but getting cooperation from the prison to visit Smiley was difficult, as the fact that I was well known still freaked them out. Anything I did had to go through head office. I'd gone to the prison before and been sent to ask in town, so this time I went direct, and on 16 August 1986, I finally got in to visit with Smiley again and wrote the saga of the visit down. These are the words:

I talked with Barry Barrier yesterday and asked for a one hour visit between 8. 30 and 9. 30 with Smiley. He said he had to ask the secretary as my first visit had caused a backlash. 'You know what certain people say about ex-prisoners visiting prisoners.'

'The screws!' I said disgusted. 'Yes, but they do it all the time.' We both knew it wasn't ex-prisoners they were worried about. It was just me they were paranoid about.

'I know, but that's how it is,' agreed Barrier.

If I rang later in the afternoon he'd let me know if I could go. After court I rang and he said there was no problem; if I was there a bit before, they'd get a rattle on and I'd get my full time. I arrived on time, filled out the visitor's slips and was sent straight over. Surprisingly the visit was inside at a table and chairs under the breeze way. Their usual paranoia! Smiley was pleased. She hadn't been told I was coming so it was a nice surprise. She was talkative and we had a great visit. Lulu, Mim, Smiley's young sister, Del and the others were in. The lady who had helped Helena write her forbidden letter was back on lockup and waiting for sentencing. They had new rules now, with a screw permanently sitting at the table for meal surveillance, so they could no longer trade food. They also had to all sit until everyone was finished, then wash their own dishes in formation like little penguins. Smiley said they hated it. They also had a new screw with a nasty, bossy voice, who was not liked much. She didn't know how to smile and reminded me of the Chameleon. I was informed it was time to go—my half hour was up. I told them I had a one-hour visit approved by Barrier, so they went to check. Playing the usual trick there were no instructions for an hour visit so I must leave. I said goodbye to Smiley, and as Mr Stiff was now the chief, I went over to the office and asked 'Who mucked that up?'

Mr Stiff replied, 'You know we didn't.'

'Tapioca up to his old tricks?' I questioned. Mr Stiff looked embarrassed.

'We can't do anything—we were only instructed it's a half hour.' I grinned and left. It was a typical practice. I told the young screw at the gate, 'I will be taking this further,' and I did. I rang Mr Barrier again. Yes, he had told the prison. It was the same old story. The blockage in the communication pipeline was always too late to fix—and they were always very sorry when it was too late to remedy. I knew he meant it. He really had done his best, but I also knew who 'blocked the pipeline'! Typical!

Then it was back to the daily grind of court. During one of the recess periods, we heard that a dingo had attacked and badly gashed a tourist on the arm at Standley

Chasm. This had not been made public as the person was anti-Chamberlain and did not want to give the Commission any information that would help them. The ranger apparently thought the incident would affect tourism and wouldn't cooperate either. The press were told by a friend of the tourist (a witness of the resultant damage but not the attack) who wanted to help. So they tried to follow up the story but the tourist concerned told them in no uncertain terms to stay out of it.

We were unable to use the information, despite the fact that there had been a number of eyewitnesses to the attack, because we could not get cooperation from the tourist, the ranger involved or the eyewitnesses to the actual attack. We were informed that the tourist had been bitten through clothing which had not been damaged although the resulting gash had required stitches.

A Study in Collusion

We were now dealing with police evidence and Detective Sergeant Brown was in the box. Brown claimed he had made notes shortly after collecting the space blanket 'in my official notebook at the police station'. He 'compiled the statement for that [our] trial from the notebook'. During his evidence on 17 September 1982 Ken Crispin put the following to him:

'You were asked this: "When did you first make a statement about the events you described?" and you said, "Only several weeks ago." "Was that on 1 September this year?" You've answered, "Yes". "You then made a statement about events that had occurred two years earlier?—Yes." Do you recall that evidence?'

'That's correct, yes,' Brown said.

Later Crispin stated 'There was no suggestion by you in answer to that question, "No, that's not right. I made a statement the same day and I've refreshed my memory with that", was there?'

'No,' Brown said. 'I made notes of the conversation.'

'You didn't say that in your evidence, did you?' said Crispin.

'No,' said Brown.

Brown claimed 'the statement was compiled from the notes and notebook'.

'And can we take it then that the notebook would have contained terms substantially similar to these: "Chamberlain then said, 'there are paw prints in one of the corners; you can see it if you hold it up to the light.' Chamberlain then unfolded the mat and held it up in the living room. Chamberlain indicated two marks on the mat." Is that right?' asked Mr Crispin.

'Yes,' said Brown.

Brown said he hadn't seen anything that looked to him like paw prints, and couldn't 'speculate what anyone would think, reading my notes'. As the notebook was now lost he was asked by Porter if he would have entered the events in his police diary and he answered 'I would have, yes,' and that the diary was 'in Mt Isa', and he hadn't brought it with him.

The notebooks were not in the police files but in Brown's own possession. Chester Porter asked him, 'Sergeant, are you seriously suggesting that your past diaries and past notebooks are just kept in your locker, never returned to police custody?'

‘Yes,’ Brown replied.

The Commission had subpoenaed Brown’s notebooks, diaries and any contemporary relevant notes from the time and the crucial notebook was missing.

Porter asked, ‘Aren’t you supposed to return them to the—under police regulations or directions?’

‘Yes,’ said Brown.

Porter later asked, ‘But wasn’t the subpoena wide enough to cover the diary?’

‘It would have been, I suppose,’ said Brown.

‘Well, why didn’t you bring the diary along?’ asked Porter.

‘I didn’t think it would be relevant. It’s only an entry—it would be an entry that I merely went to the house,’ Brown replied.

‘I see,’ said Porter. ‘Well, the next matter that would have occurred would have been that Charlwood—Detective Sergeant Charlwood, I think he was then—would have collected the space blanket from you?’

‘Yes,’ said Brown.

Later Chester Porter asked, ‘Sergeant, what I want to put to you is this: the allegation has been made to you that you are a ring-in; that you were never there at all. I’m giving you an opportunity to draw attention to any contemporary document that would refute that allegation?’

‘I have none here with me,’ Brown replied.

‘And you were asked to produce them?’ asked Porter.

‘Yes.’

The Commissioner interrupted, ‘Sergeant, are you confident that your diary as distinct from your notebook would record your visit to the Chamberlain’s house?’

‘It is six years ago, but my recollection would be that I would have entered it in the diary,’ Brown stated.

‘Would it have been in accordance with police practice and your own practice to record such a visit?’ the Commissioner continued.

‘Yes.’

‘Now, Mr Porter, you’d better listen to this,’ said Commissioner Morling.

‘Would you have any objection to Mr Davis, who instructs Mr Porter, leaving the court to ring the Mount Isa police station for two purposes—three purposes: one, to locate your diary; two, to send it to Darwin, and three, to read out over the telephone to him the contents of it for 27 August 1980?’

‘Unfortunately the diary is probably in the locker also. I’d have to locate the diary. I couldn’t give any instructions. It may be in the locker; it may be elsewhere,’ said Brown.

Later in the evidence Porter said, ‘You’ve sworn this morning that you made an entry in your diary and that the diary is at Mount Isa police station?’

Adams for the Crown interjected. ‘He’s sworn that he believed he made an entry in his diary.’

Porter said, ‘Well, he qualified it later. There was no qualification when he first gave it to me.’

‘I can’t be 100 per cent sure that I made an entry in the diary six years ago,’ said Brown.

'But you didn't give me that qualification when I first suggested to you that you kept a diary and you ought to have made a note, did you? There was no qualification when you first answered me, was there?' said Porter.

Later still in the evidence, Porter asked, 'Can you tell us why you did not bring your diary?'

'At that stage, I didn't think it had any relevance,' said Brown.

'But didn't you yourself tell me yesterday that you thought the diary may well contain an entry about you going to the Chamberlain's house to collect the space blanket?' queried Porter.

'Yes,' said Brown.

'Before I ask you what inquiries you may have made in this matter—you were stopped at the airport yesterday, weren't you?' stated Porter.

'I was requested to return,' said Brown.

When the Mt Isa running sheets were later placed in front of Brown, the Commissioner said, 'Sergeant, can I suggest to you that it would have been better to answer that question "There is no entry", but you may be assured you will be given an opportunity to explain why in your opinion there is no entry, you see. But if you can just keep in mind to answer the questions you may be quite confident that anything you want to say will in due course come out.'

Later Porter asked 'You see I am putting to you that you know full well as a result of your conversations with Constable Boag yesterday, that the running sheets do not thereafter say who picked up the space blanket. There is no mention of you having picked up the space blanket and there is no mention of no dingo paw prints on a space blanket that didn't have any paw prints.' *[sic]*

Brown had made another statement the day before; it was now being tendered for identification and Brown was reading it.

Porter said, 'Sergeant, why is it necessary for you to read that? I simply asked you was that the statement you made yesterday. Well, is there any real need for you to read it right through again, just to make sure?'

'No doubt you're going to ask me some further questions about it. I'd like the opportunity to refresh my memory of everything that's in it,' Brown said.

'What, in case you say something now different to the statement which you made only yesterday?'

'No,' said Brown.

The next day Porter's questioning finally got back to the diaries.

'Would you agree with me there is not a word in it about your alleged visit to the Chamberlains on 27 August 1980?'

'I had just left it "general inquiries in relation to Azaria Chamberlain," and left the rest of it,' Brown said.

'Whereas it contains considerable information about every other visit you made that day in the Chamberlain case?' Porter said.

Adams objected and finally the Commissioner said, 'Mr Adams, I do think this is pretty, for this witness, pretty critical evidence. I don't think cross examination should be interrupted.'

Porter returned to the witness 'What do you say to my question Sergeant?'

'What is your question again?' asked Brown.

'That you have made no mention whatsoever in your diary entry that day of the visit to the Chamberlains' house whereas you have detailed in your diary every other attendance or visit in connection with the Chamberlains that you made that day?'

'In recording—a police diary is for my reference. All right?' Brown replied. 'It is compiled in association with the notebook. The note—I documented fully in the notebook the visit to the Chamberlain household. I have left it in general terms "Inquiries in relation to the Chamberlains" in my diary. I have listed the other inquiries made that day because they were not listed in the notebook.'

'You have now explained to me why it would not be in the diary, haven't you—you have now explained to me why this entry about going to the Chamberlains' house should not be in your diary, you have explained that, haven't you?' asked Porter.

'Yes,' said Brown

'If that is so, why did you suggest to me yesterday that it was in your diary and put us to the trouble of getting your diary all the way from Mount Isa?'

'Well, yesterday you questioned me on my memory of what I wrote in the diary on a particular day six years ago. I suggest to you, can you remember what you wrote in a diary about what you did six years ago? I never at any stage said I was 100% sure of what was written in the diary.'

Later, when Brown was in the box again, the Commissioner said, 'Sergeant you knew, in effect, that you were being accused by Mr Crispin of perjury when you left the witness box, did you not?'

'Yes,' agreed Brown.

'And you knew in effect, that he was accusing you of having committed perjury in 1982 at the Chamberlains' trial?'

'Yes.'

'They were, from your point of view, very grave allegations?'

'From my point of view they were totally ridiculous,' said Brown. Morling continued: 'And ones which you would want to clear yourself of as soon as possible?'

'Yes,' said Brown.

'As an experienced police officer didn't you think it was inevitable that if you had drinks, dinner and breakfast with the witness who was going to corroborate you that the suggestions which are now being made would be made?' asked the Commissioner.

'As a police officer I know that you don't discuss a case that you are involved in,' Brown said.

'Did you think it was inevitable that if you had dinner and breakfast with the witness who would corroborate you, that the comments which are now being made would be made?'

'No, I didn't think that.'

When Ken Crispin was completing his evidence, he said, 'I suggest to you that in your evidence here in the last few days you've told a litany of lies in an endeavour to lend credence to this story about your conversation with Mr and Mrs Chamberlain?'

'That is not correct. I told the truth,' said Brown.

Later, Ken Crispin said, 'Well, apart from your diary, any records at Mount Isa would be insufficient to enable somebody to identify who picked up the blanket?'

'I was able to say that I picked up the blanket because I had a recollection of it,' Brown said.

The Commissioner interjected 'Sergeant, we'll get to the end of your evidence much more quickly if you answer the question. That was not an answer in any shape or form to that question. Would you put the question again, Mr Crispin.'

Mr Crispin continued 'There are no records at the Mount Isa police station which would enable anybody to identify who picked up the blanket?'

'Yes.'

Ken Crispin said, 'Do you say that there are records that would enable one to identify who picked up the blanket?'

'I'm saying there aren't any records,' said Brown.

'And I'm asking you was it for that reason that you felt compelled to give evidence that you picked it up? asked Ken Crispin.

'No. I was the person that picked up the blanket,' stated Brown.

'Well was there some young constable that you wanted to keep away from the inquiry because he had a distressing streak of honesty?' asked Mr Crispin.

'That's total rubbish,' Brown said. Adams objected at this point.

Brown's superior, Gray, was called to the box. Porter questioned him: 'Were criminal investigation staff issued with an official diary in addition to an official notebook?'

'That is so,' replied Gray.

Porter continued, 'Was it the expected duty that each officer enter into his or her notebook and diary information as to the investigations carried out by them, and the diary to include the movements and activities of each police officer?'

'Yes,' agreed Gray.

Porter then asked, 'Was there a commissioner's instruction in existence that completed notebooks be held by the officer-in-charge of each police establishment concerned?'

'Yes,' Gray said.

Porter later continued, 'I've been through this already with you this morning, inspector. I want you to tell the commission now. As you know it's alleged that Sergeant Brown never went there at all?'

'I've read that in an eastern states newspaper,' Gray replied.

'Can you solve the problem for us? Can you tell us where there is a contemporary police record of Queensland which would clear this matter up?' asked Porter.

'Not that I am aware' answered Gray.

'To your knowledge has his visit ever been recorded in any police document?' Porter asked.

'I don't know,' Gray replied.

'Was it recorded in his notebook?'

'I don't know. I've never seen his notebook,' said Gray.

Later Ken Crispin asked Gray of his associations with Brown while in Darwin and the Commissioner interjected, 'Sergeant didn't you think it would be highly likely if you had dinner with him last night somebody like Mr Crispin would suggest to you that you had discussed the evidence?'

'That he should suggest?' asked Gray.

The Commissioner said, 'Didn't you think, as an experienced police officer, that if you associated with Sergeant Brown before you got in the witness box it would be unkindly suggested by somebody like Mrs Chamberlain's counsel that you had discussed the evidence you were going to give?'

'It is not an unusual allegation, Your Honour,'replied Gray. Commissioner Morling continued 'Didn't you think it would have been more prudent, under those circumstances, to have no association with him?'

'Well, we are both here on our own, both staying in the same hotel, and that wasn't my doing. We just went out and had drinks and had dinner,' Gray said.

'I am not suggesting you did or didn't have any discussions with him, but on reflection do you not think it would have been more prudent to have had no association with him?'

'Your honour, it is a matter for interpretation of a person's actions and there was nothing untoward,' said Gray.

Ken Crispin asked 'You were alive to the possibility that somebody might suggest some collusion between the two of you as a result of being together last night?'

'The mere fact of being in the same hotel together would possibly raise that,' said Gray.

Gray had said either Charlwood or Inspector Michael Gilroy had rung and asked him to pick up a mat or blanket with marks on it we had indicated we had. The NT police running sheets indicated differently, and Ken Crispin continued with his questioning.

'I'd suggest to you that in fact that on 27 August 1980 you didn't receive a phone call from Mr Gilroy at all, did you.'

'To my recollection, I did,' said Gray.

Ken followed up as the running sheets indicated 'I'd suggest to you that Mr Gilroy rang Inspector McNamara?'

'No, not that I know of,' Gray said.

'Whilst it may be that Inspector McNamara subsequently mentioned the telephone call to you, there was no call directly to you, was there?' Ken Crispin said.

'As far as I recall, Inspector McNamara left the station that day with a team of investigating detectives and in fact was at Cloncurry,' said Gray.

'I'd suggest to you sir, that you really don't have any clear memory of this conversation with Detective Brown about the blanket at all, do you?'

'I do; I do have an independent recollection,' said Gray.

Ken continued further on 'I suggest to you, sir, that in fact your recollection of that has been significantly been coloured by feelings of loyalty towards a brother officer?' *[sic]*

'I don't get carried away that way,' said Gray.

'You've certainly, on—you certainly don't suggest that you have any recollection whatever of seeing Mr Brown actually leave the police station to fulfil that errand?' Crispin asked.

'No, I didn't see him leave,' answered Gray.

'And it's quite within the realms of possibility, is it not, that he may have asked a more junior officer to fulfil that errand for him, given that all available officers of the Criminal Investigation Bureau were involved in a murder investigation?' Crispin wanted to know.

'There's that possibility, but it's most improbable,' Gray answered.

Malcolm Brown reported it this way in the *Sydney Morning Herald* of 1 September 1986:

> Irvine Gregory Brown, a Queensland police sergeant subpoenaed to give evidence and to bring all relevant documents, arrived in Darwin without his official diary. He said in evidence he did not think it relevant.
>
> A former Mount Isa inspector, Robert Crawford Gray, flew to Darwin to corroborate Sergeant Brown's evidence when Sergeant Brown was accused of perjury. Sergeant Brown and Mr Gray denied in evidence that they had been involved in collusion but agreed that they had met at Darwin airport and had had drinks and two meals together before Mr Gray gave evidence.
>
> Brought back to the inquiry and asked why he had done that, Sergeant Brown said the other policeman was a personal friend and had nothing to do with the case.'

In the same news article Malcolm Brown also said:

> The greatest difficulty the Morling inquiry into the Chamberlain conviction has had among the seventy-nine witnesses which it has heard has been with key policemen involved in the case down the years.
>
> Some officers, such as Inspector Graeme Charlwood and Senior Constable James Metcalfe, have told the inquiry they have done nothing to prejudice what they or other witnesses have had to tell the Commissioner, Justice Morling.
>
> But both have been seen during the recent sittings of the inquiry lunching with people whom—at least for the sake of appearances—they might have avoided.
>
> A former NT policeman, Peter John Buzzard, who flew from New Zealand to give evidence, was taken by Constable Metcalfe to NT police headquarters and met an assistant commissioner.
>
> Ian Barker, QC, who prosecuted the Chamberlains in 1982 and who represents the NT Crown and Police at this inquiry, feels exasperated at the line of questioning and Bar table comments by the counsel assisting, Mr Chester Porter, QC.
>
> When Mr Porter questioned whether the NT police were deliberately delaying or withholding documents or tape-recordings from the inquiry, Mr Barker lashed out, saying that all efforts were being made by police to cooperate.

The *Newcastle Herald* also reported on Metcalfe's activities:

> A police statement taken from a witness in the Chamberlain case was doctored when it was typed up and presented at the 1982 trial, it was alleged at the Chamberlain inquiry in Darwin yesterday.
>
> Constable James Raymond Metcalfe, of the Northern Territory police, was questioned about a statement taken from Rowan Christopher Tew, a radio mechanic, at Mt Isa in September 1982.
>
> Mr Tew said last week that he had seen blood in the Chamberlains' car when installing a cassette player in November, 1980, but could not be certain it was his own.
>
> He suffered from an arm injury which meant he sometimes bled without realising it, though he had checked his arm and found no cuts.
>
> Counsel assisting the Commission, Mr Chester Porter, QC, said the typewritten report given to the Chamberlains' defence team did not mention Floyd Wallace Hart, who also worked on the car but did not see any blood.
>
> Constable Metcalfe said the omission probably was a typing error.
>
> Counsel for the Chamberlains, Mr John Winneke, QC, said another omission in the typed statement was a reference to Mr Tew's inability to recognise police photographs of alleged bloodstains found in the car after he had worked on it.
>
> 'I am suggesting that what was given to the trial defence was a doctored version of Mr Tew's statement,' he said.
>
> The Commissioner, Mr Justice Morling, said he was astounded to learn that Constable Metcalfe had the duty of reading the inquiry transcript each day.
>
> Constable Metcalfe said he had been given the job by the NT Police Assistant Commissioner, Mr Neil Plum.
>
> 'I am astounded by that; I am absolutely astounded,' Mr Justice Morling said.

When Metcalfe was waiting to give some of his evidence, he wandered away to the police station next door. While he was away John Davis, the senior Commission solicitor, came looking for him. Apparently Metcalfe had been told to stay there and hadn't. Later he came back and sat down, two or three seats away from where my brother Alex was waiting to give his evidence about the space blanket (when he did he called Barker 'mate' several times without realising, which really cracked us all up!).

Several other people were also in the room waiting when John Davis once again returned looking for Metcalfe. This time Davis spied his quarry, and confronted him. John Davis is a tall, stern looking man. He leaned over Metcalfe, tapped him with one finger in the chest and, in a very stern but not nasty voice, much in the manner of a schoolmaster to a naughty teenager, told Metcalfe that when he was told to stay put, he was expected to *stay put!* After that Metcalfe, rather uncomfortable, did stay put—for a while at least.

We knew the police had checked the car, so did they, so we did not think mentioning it was of any significance. A lot of information that was available, and for us, was not called during the second inquest and trial because part of the transcript of the first inquest could simply be tendered and included. This way, of course, the judge read it—and the jury was supposed to, but Yvonne Cain, the juror, told me they never looked at any of it. She said she had thought they weren't supposed to. (I wonder how many other juries neglect to read and digest all those extra printed pages of information?)

This means, of course, that vital information (like that of Nipper) can be totally overlooked by the jury simply by careful legal planning and the accused is powerless to do anything about it.

When you are looking at a thing very closely for a long period of time, there are things that you know others know as well. You do not realise the significance of pointing them out again until it just about hits you in the face, or somebody else asks why you didn't mention it before. And so, the fact that the car had been looked at before did not seem to loom very large, while the huge quantities of blood that appeared to be around seemed to take on massive significance and proportions.

The inspection of the car that had taken place at Mt Isa before the first inquest turned into quite a saga. Once more, it became a very embarrassing point. Detective Sergeant Graham had looked at the car and said there was no evidence of any blood in it. Then Jim Metcalfe, another policeman, nearly a year later found something he thought was sticky, looked significant, and asked for tests. The tests were negative but, not satisfied, they scraped below the surface and got a positive reading.

This area had become known as the 'under-dash spray' and was supposed to be an arterial spurt from Azaria having her head severed from her shoulders with a pair of small, curving nail scissors. The police were sticking to their story, not admitting they made a mistake, so what could they do? Put the car in the dark during the first inspection of course—make it by inefficient torch light, and claim Sergeant Graham couldn't see properly. How very convenient!

Sergeant Graham being present at Aidan's record of interview from just before sunset onwards meant it was not possible for him to have inspected the car after dark. He must have done it in full daylight, with or without the assistance of a torch, and the car was in an area well lit by fluorescent light anyway. It was clear to see that the Commissioner was unconvinced by the claim that the direct beam of a Big Jim torch was not good enough on its own anyway.

Considering the part that big Jim Metcalfe played in the discovery of the under-dash spray, the torch brand being Big Jim caused its own ripple of amusement. Either Sergeant Graham hadn't touched the car and did the inspection by torch in the few minutes that he walked out of Aidan's interview to check whether the car was ready for me to leave immediately, and wouldn't admit he hadn't done it thoroughly—or he had done it thoroughly in broad daylight at the time he originally claimed to Scott on 1 October 1980. Either way, we'll never know because I wasn't there and he isn't telling.

Malcolm Brown said in his *Sydney Morning Herald* article:

> Barry William Graham, a former NT policeman, made a voluntary statutory declaration on July 9 that he had made a detailed inspection of the Chamberlains' car on October 1, 1980, and had found no signs of bloodstaining.
>
> Mr Graham was met at Darwin Airport by a NT police inspector and lunched in Darwin with Inspector Charlwood, who had asked him to examine the car.
>
> When Mr Graham gave evidence, he said he had searched the car for between two and two-and-a-half hours.
>
> Mr Porter pointed out that in his statutory declaration he had said 'three hours'. Mr Graham said that he had searched his memory more deeply and denied that he had been influenced in any way by policemen since arriving in Darwin.
>
> Cross-examined by Mr Barker, Mr Graham said he had been dissatisfied with the examination in 1980, since it had been night time and he had had to use a torch. Mr Porter pointed out that not a word of those qualifying statements had appeared in the statutory declaration.
>
> Inspector Charlwood was asked in evidence why he had lunched with Mr Graham.
>
> He replied: 'As an experienced police officer, I am aware witnesses should not talk about their evidence before giving it.'

It was just one more of those things. When Sergeant Scott came into the witness box at a later stage to talk about Aidan's interview, he also said Sergeant Graham had been there *during* the interview (i.e., after dark). By this time the issue was mostly forgotten and the significance of his information dropped into a large well of facts, so unless you were totally engrossed in the case, as we were, you missed.

The lighting on a variety of things (e.g. the tent, dingoes, blankets, car etc.) was continually used by the Crown as a reason for doubt, and the lighting at the tent site once again came up in Constable Francis (Frank) Morris's evidence. Once again he said it was bad, and once again we reminded him that he had come from a lit house (and car headlights). All the eyewitnesses except the Whittakers (who had been using a bright gas light on a stand) also said the lighting was good, as I had done, but that was long before the police were so interested in the whole issue. Now once again the lighting was used as a reason to doubt my word. The lighting test during the night view of the first inquest had been long forgotten.

The Crown was trying to push a theory of murder in the car and all the blood there, therefore there was no dingo and no blood in the tent. Sally Lowe said quite positively that she had seen a pool of blood in the tent and as they *didn't* want any blood there, to disprove her statement it *had* to be too dark to see.

Finally, after being reminded once again of the night view, the Commission made some enquiries and agreed that it did appear that there had been a view where it was agreed that the lighting was sufficient to read by.

Graeme Charlwood, now an inspector of police, always gives me the impression of having a big scar across his cheek, but he hasn't. He has such a smooth manner that he comes across as the nice boy next door.

I thought he was open and above board at the first inquest. He said he never talked to the press, but later I thought to myself, some things he said in court seemed contradictory, so later I had a question mark. Then when we talked in the car after the Operation Ochre raid, I realised I had initially underestimated him and I knew we were playing an intellectual game from then on. As he also realised that he was not going to put it over me any more, he was cagey. When he told me not to sell myself short because I had the brains to commit the perfect murder, I thought: Right. If you have all that evidence and you still reckon that you don't know, you are one of those men who make up their mind, and then seem to have an open mind. So I handled him like a slippery eel.

During his evidence we discovered that the Northern Territory police had a warrant for our arrest when they came to Mt Isa initially for our record of interview! That was surprising news for me. Despite the fact that this was an interstate warrant and reasons for requesting it and for extradition had to be given, the police had conveniently forgotten what those reasons were, did not have them written down anywhere and could not find the original warrant. One more amazing coincidence, I thought.

I also learned Inspector Gilroy had been taken across in 1980 in case I was hard to handle. They thought that perhaps I might co-operate better with Gilroy, seeing I had been dealing with him until then. I was not to know he was there unless it became absolutely necessary. (Except I happened to walk into the police station at a time when I wasn't expected and passed him on the stairs. That was the only glimpse of him I got the whole time that he was in Mt Isa.)

Once again Inspector Gilroy acted like a gentleman in the witness box. Frank Gibson was also one of the straight, decent breed of cops. Before the trial he had rung and offered to give a character reference for us. That takes a lot of guts for a cop. He knew he would be out on his neck, but was prepared to do it anyway. He had wrestled with his conscience for some time, and decided he couldn't live with being a coward and going against what he knew to be right. We didn't accept his offer because we didn't want to put him in a position where his livelihood was on the line, but they made it so hard for him he ended up resigning, so they pushed him out anyway. It interested me to note that although he had been our bodyguard and associated with us intimately during the first inquest, he was never called to give any evidence during the Commission.

We saw Frank, Bill Barnes and some others from the first inquest several times during our transit through Alice Springs and always enjoyed our times together. The last time I saw Frank I cajoled him (it wasn't hard) into giving me his head of security badge, and it is a treasured souvenir. That was the last time I saw Frank, some months later he died of a massive heart attack at work. I miss him.

Dr Irene Milne said that she had had no problems with me or my children; some of my ways might have been a little different from those of other mothers, but they were not wrong, all the same. Yes, she had heard that I had the baby at the surgery after a fall from a supermarket trolley. No, she hadn't seen the baby in the black dress, although yes, she had heard about it. When asked about the rumour that Azaria had been bashed, she said, to the contrary she had been well cared for. When asked which Mt Isa doctor had rung the police and told them that the name Azaria meant 'sacrifice in the wilderness', she said she had no idea.

It wasn't until Dr Irene Milne went home from the Commission that her brother, discovering when listening to the news about her cross- examination and that she had been asked about this, told her that *he* was the doctor involved who had rung the Alice Springs police and told them what he considered to be the meaning of Azaria's name. She was very upset to be misrepresented in this way, as it appeared the information in the first place had come from her about me being an unfit mother, and it had not. She rang the Commission, and told them. She was later recalled to tell the court the mystery doctor was her brother, and none of his information had come from her.

I was initially puzzled because, although he was in the same medical centre, he had never been my doctor. Nor to my knowledge had we even nodded hello, though I had seen him walk past once or twice. I couldn't tell whether he even knew who I was. But I discovered his friend and secretary was also the receptionist at the centre. The same woman who had been so hostile to us over Reagan's chicken pox.

When Dr Irene Milne was asked if there was 'considerable ill feeling', as Mr Porter put it, between her brother and Mrs Chamberlain, she denied it. If she had known what we did maybe she would have begun to wonder whether bitterness and resentment caused by reports of the chicken pox incident had precipitated that phone call.

Some Fishy Stories

After doing a bit of window shopping at lunchtime to relax before the next onslaught, I realised I was a bit late and was hastily eating my sandwiches as I raced back to court. There was nothing worse than rounding the corner and discovering I was being filmed. I was never quite sure whether I had food all around my mouth and whether or not they were using telephoto lenses for close-ups. The press told me they never print shots like that, but knowing a number of the things they did, I could never be quite sure. I do know they all have cork boards on which they keep their favourite, funny and worst pictures of people. Having seen some of the shots they have, I was not at all anxious to go on any of their cork boards.

In Darwin we had to walk along the corridor past the media room in order to get to the courtroom, it was interesting to see what the press were doing. It was not unusual to find them sprawled with legs on the tables, lounging back in their chairs, reading newspapers, doing crosswords, playing cards, drinking, sleeping, or simply sitting around talking with their backs to the monitors while court was in session.

One morning Malcolm Brown was looking very crestfallen. The press room was buzzing and there was some hilarity at Malcolm's expense. Voices carried from the newsroom along the corridor on the way to and from the courtroom, and we gathered part of the story. Later we were told somebody had knocked on Malcolm's hotel room door very late one night and woken him up, telling him the television set in the room of a new arrival was broken. Would he mind if his set were taken, temporarily as a replacement, and they would bring it back to him in the morning? Of course he agreed. He helped them take it from his room, shut the door and promptly went back to sleep.

In the morning it was discovered he'd actually assisted someone in stealing his own television set, and was highly embarrassed when he had to explain to the owners. He was never really sure the other reporters hadn't set him up either! But he could take it. Only Malcolm could fall for a story like that, though! He was a curious mixture of travelled-man-about-the-world who'd been there, done that, seen everything, and a naive little boy from the backwoods. A combination I'm sure made him more accurate and careful in his reporting than many other journalists who prided themselves on being hard-nosed.

Certain journalists always came into the courtroom and took full notes. Malcolm Brown was one and actually took verbatim shorthand in order to get his quotes correct. We soon knew those who were conscientious—their reporting was very accurate. Others had no intention of being accurate, they just looked for the key word or sensation for the day and then turned that into headlines. They mainly took the day off, and would go around asking the others, 'Anything happened? What are we writing today?' 'Can you give me a few lines? Couldn't be there that time.' 'I wasn't listening, what was said?' Then they would write up whatever they felt like.

The press got so much mileage out of our case and managed to keep it running for so long that, during the Commission, one of the newsmen told me there were a number of words that immediately caused a doubling of circulation. In fact, they were all calamities. The words, 'cyclone', 'tidal wave', or 'war' would immediately at least double a paper's sale. So would a headline with 'Lindy' in it. Initially the words 'Ayers Rock', 'Inquest', 'Dingo Baby' (or Mum), or 'Azaria' were better known, but eventually it was just my name—'Lindy'.

Most of our lawyers, except Phil, Greg and Pam, shared some of our interests: Peter jogged; John had a good solo voice; Andrew and Stuart were into tennis and jogging; Jack and Brind liked weightlifting and jogging; Ken (an asthmatic) liked public speaking; and David liked sunbaking. Sharing common interests helped the team work well together—and most had a good sense of humour, which I liked.

Because we had such long stays in Darwin, the legal team could choose to go home every few weekends to visit their families, or use their ticket to bring their wives up to visit them. Melinda Woinarski was an air hostess, so she was able at times to schedule her trips and have her off-duty days in Darwin with Brind, to his great delight as they hadn't been married long. Jack's wife, Sue, was a lawyer also—a junior counsellor with a good reputation. She was able to come to Darwin between her own briefs and stay. She enjoyed watching Jack work. Cherie Tipple also came with their preschool son James whenever she could.

Pam Crispin looked after their home acres and a preschool child, so she was sometimes able to come with Ken for the whole duration of a stay in Darwin and bring Timmy with her (their other two children were older). Timmy was quite a character, and in a stentorian voice that carried right throughout the foyer of the Sheraton in Darwin and up to the upper levels of its balcony, he would inform anyone who came within his line of vision, and was willing to listen, that his dad was a lawyer, and 'he's working on the Chamberlain case, you know.' He was very proud of that.

Everybody knew when Timmy was in residence. He was shy when you first met him, but as soon as he got to know you, he was outspoken and quite a trick. Sometimes Sue Winneke would look after him for Pam, so Pam could go into court (without having to worry about Timmy wriggling and talking) and hear Ken cross-examining. On one particular day Melinda Woinarski and I arrived in the foyer at the same time, and met Timmy and Sue coming in from an outing. We decided to sit down and have a hot drink together. Timmy thought sitting at a table was time for food and maintained he would like 'just some salmon sandwiches, thank you, waiter.' So the waiter left and brought back some beautifully served salmon sandwiches, with very attractive garnishes.

Timmy took one look at the sandwiches and said, 'No, I said salmon sandwiches, and that's not salmon sandwiches. What's all this stuff you've got on it? I didn't order that.' The waiter was doing his best to hide indignation plus a smile and Sue waved him off over Timmy's head and said, 'Never mind, Timmy, we'll fix that up.' She quickly whipped off the lettuce that was with it and the garnish and put it back together again. Timmy eyed it somewhat scornfully and announced loudly, 'In a place like this where the food is more expensive, you'd think they'd know how to make a decent salmon sandwich, wouldn't you?'

One afternoon after court we decided we would go and see the fish feeding. The others were going and I thought it was probably safe if I went as well, knowing of course that it was the wife of Marshall Perron, the former Northern Territory Attorney-General and Chief Minister, who ran the tourist centre which was in the Perrons' backyard. I didn't want to cause any embarrassment. I knew Michael and the children had been there once before without realising just exactly where they were and had accidentally run into Marshall Perron, so I was sensitive that a similar mistake was not made again because they may think this time it happened on purpose. We took young James Tipple with us, who was of a similar age to Timmy (both boys were actually a few months off Kahlia's age). Melinda, Sue, Michael and I and one of the local girls went. The boys had a great time, James being very well mannered and cautious, Timmy being rambunctious and loud, frightening the fish and throwing bread *at* them, instead of feeding them, and generally having a wonderful time. Mrs Perron recognised Michael and went to talk to him, and several of our lawyers' wives, who were with him, were introduced and started talking as well. I decided in the end that I would wander up too and was also introduced to her. The conversation was pleasant but I was aware of her being slightly uncomfortable. I couldn't help wondering what she would say to her husband that night, now she had met the lady who had caused him so many problems (and vice versa!).

The men in our Adventist church at Darwin arranged to take the lawyers to Shady Lagoon on a fishing expedition for barramundi. They were all set but at the last minute only the solicitors could go, as the others were called in for a legal conference, so off we went in three boats. The numerous crocodiles along the banks were huge and we were thankful to be in a boat. While we were trolling up and down for barramundi, we came across a huge old croc lying on the bank—about 6 metres (20 feet) long and over a metre (3 feet) across its back.

Steve Plahn, a local who was quite a clown, decided to see if he could make the croc move and cast a lure without the hook at it. The first cast went across its back and made no impression. He kept trying, and the next cast went straight through the croc's mouth across its teeth, but the croc stayed motionless.

By this time Michael had decided this would make a good photograph, so we backed in close with our boats facing out ready for a quick getaway, and cameras at the ready. Our local friend once again cast his lure at the crocodile in a bet to see whether he could get it through the croc's mouth again. He did, and as he reeled in this time the croc stayed still until the lure was about halfway through its mouth, then got up on its hind legs and its mouth sprang shut like a trap. The boats moved away in a hurry and the croc, amidst a great swirl of muddy water, disappeared beneath. We took off down the lagoon and waited quite some distance away to see where the croc would surface next, because if they surface underneath your boat and tip you out, that's often the end of you. Thinking about it later, I realised it was a particularly stupid thing to do, and yet one becomes almost blasé about the familiarity of the crocodiles up there, because there are so many. The same applies to dingoes—I couldn't help thinking later that just such lack of understanding that they are dangerous wild animals had helped cause the disbelief and storm over our tragedy.

Michael was lucky and managed to score a couple of nice barramundi. We decided to invite all the lawyers to dinner, and arranged a table big enough to seat the whole team and their families. Everyone accepted enthusiastically and waited with anticipation for their first taste of fresh Territory barramundi.

Cherie Tipple was normally a total vegetarian, as I am, but decided on this occasion she could handle a little bit of fish, as long as she didn't have to look at it too much. Michael knew the fish was being cooked whole, but had given strict instructions to the hotel chef that it was to have its head cut off before cooking, and had even made a special sauce for the chef to cook it in. The chef looked sceptical, but cook it he did.

The chef apparently decided he couldn't possibly spoil this beautiful big fish by cutting off its head and when it arrived at the table, there it was with its glazed eyes and big open mouth. Everybody knew Cherie couldn't stand a dead fish gaping at her so we all watched her as much as the fish. Her face was a real study. The chef placed the fish on the table right in front of her, with its glassy eyes staring. That was the end of Cherie. She said, 'Ugh!' and announced that she would not be eating fish that night, she would stay vegetarian after all. The chef was unimpressed at the lack of appreciation over his culinary masterpiece.

As soon as he had gone we moved that fish away from Cherie, who then had a beautiful vegetarian meal with me while everybody else enjoyed their fish.

Not all the Commission evidence was given in Darwin. From 6 October, it moved to Sydney.

During the recess, the Northern Territory sent Ian Barker, Michael Adams, Mick O' Loughlan, and two others in search of forensic material. In Mick O'Loughlan's own words, quoted in the *Northern Daily Leader* on 6 January 1990, 'When the Royal Commission was on we had to find experts in blood and so on. So two QCs, two barristers and me went around the world. We went to Germany, London, Canada and the US—it was a good trip.'

They refused to fund a similar trip for Stuart Tipple and Barry Boettcher to visit a number of forensic witnesses in Germany, Sweden and England. Fortunately the church came up with the money and they were able to go after all.

Meanwhile, Michael and I went home.

Studio Workshop

We hadn't been home long when we were told by Verity Lambert that the studio filming was almost finished and we could go to Melbourne to see some of it in progress. Michael took his cameras and we had a good look around the new sets, and had lunch with Sam and Meryl between shoots. Fred Schepisi and Verity also joined us.

Later during the filming, we dropped around to Meryl's place to say goodbye before we left and leave a little Christmas present for her children, knowing that we would not see them again. Meryl pulled up with her chauffeur just after we arrived.

We had been window shopping and, to my great delight, I had found a small Turkish rug on sale. As Meryl is a very warm person, she spied the rug and immediately asked to have a look. I unrolled it on the grass beside the footpath and she exclaimed delightedly over it with me.

The next thing we read headlines in the newspapers: 'Meryl and Lindy go shopping for Persian carpets'. That was as accurate as their statements that Meryl used to push her little fourteen-month-old boy around in the pram. 'He' was a girl; they couldn't even get *that* right.

Over Christmas we went on holiday with Pete and Marijana Stojanovic to Peter's parents' place at Melany in Queensland. While we paid for our trip up, they gave us free accommodation.

Peter's brother-in-law, Frank, owned an estate agency up there, and on his books was some land with a beautiful view over the Glasshouse Mountains. It would be ideal for a multi-million dollar exclusive resort and, as Michael had his video camera with him, Frank asked him to video the area for a short sales promotion documentary of the place.

Hearing the glowing reports, the rest of us decided we would go and see this wonderful piece of real estate. So, along with mums and dads, cousins, uncles, aunties and kids, we all piled into Pete's bus and off we went. We wandered around the farm and agreed it was a beautiful view, then some walked home while we went on to view

Frank's own farm and proposed home site. We left to go south again the following day, travelling as far as Brisbane with Pete and Marijana before going our own ways.

The next day Pete rang. He was very upset because there was a large item in the newspaper saying that the Chamberlains had bought, in conjunction with Ms Streep, a property worth several million to build a big hotel and resort complex. Frank, too, was upset. As far as we could ascertain, the story came from a rival estate agent. Somebody had seen us looking over the property, known Michael had been there filming and put two and two together making eight—a normal occurrence in our lives these days.

Meryl couldn't believe the tactics of the Australian press, declaring she had never met press like it anywhere in the world. We had told her about cameramen and reporters standing on our doorsteps with cameras rolling as we opened the door. She had found such stories hard to credit until one press crew got past her security guards and it happened to her. She was extremely annoyed about it. She found her experiences with them quite devastating and later declared her own experiences had certainly given her insight into what the press had put us through.

The press pestered her so much she couldn't move around freely and her security man told me she used to sneak out late at night when she'd finished the day's filming and go riding around Toorak in Melbourne on her son's bicycle. Her security men, whom presumably she thought she had avoided, would follow her a good distance away in their car with the lights out to make sure she was all right.

Meryl also received a lot of hate mail, including *duplicates* of nasty letters that had been sent to me. Many letters of support arrived also, and all this gave her a feeling for the part she could never have gained otherwise.

The mother of the little child who played six-year-old Aidan in the movie, told me later he had been told nothing about the movie he was working on, and thought Meryl was really Lindy Chamberlain. He worked out that everyone thought she had killed her baby, instead of the dingo from the scenes he appeared in, and he had got quite upset about it.

The exteriors of the church and house in Mt Isa were taken on location, as were the scenes inside the church, with a lot of the local Seventh-day Adventist congregation. The crew built the interior of our Mt Isa house in exact replica in the Melbourne studios. Every wall needed to be able to move. Two to five minutes was the maximum time taken in most cases to remove and/or replace a wall for the camera to get the right view, the carpentry crew told me proudly. Without this, rooms on screen apparently look smaller than they really are.

I did have discussions with Verity and the set dresser about the amount of junk they had around the place; it wasn't my habit to leave clothes on the top of dressing tables or have boxes of toys around. They would have been away in the cupboard or in use. At that stage, I didn't have a lot of things on kitchen benches either.

When they came to see us during the research for the movie, they took all sorts of measurements and pictures of the ornaments. They were trying to be as accurate as they could in the movie, and I suppose they weren't to know that that messy house was not the way we normally lived.

When I visited the set in Melbourne they asked me to rearrange the ornaments and things so they were as I'd had them in Mt Isa. When I did, Verity said, 'If we put around only what you say you had, they will think it's a film set and people don't really live here, because movies tend to make a house look emptier than they are.' So they added extra gear. To me the finished version still looked overcrowded and messy.

What they needed to realise is that some people do prefer tidy houses.

During the time I was working with Robert on the film research, I mentioned my Bible and the help it had been to me while I was in prison. I also mentioned the notes I had in the margins and how the binding had broken away through use. When he realised I had it with me at the Commission in Sydney he asked if he could see it, and after looking at it for some time asked if he might borrow it for a while. He had it for quite some months, even taking it to America with him and back.

When Meryl learned of my Bible's existence through Robert, she asked him if she could borrow it. Robert rang me and asked if I minded. I agreed, so he handed it over, instructing her it must be guarded with her life. She took great care of it, even carrying it in her hand luggage on the plane just in case any of the luggage went astray, I understand, and she also had it for a number of months.

Each scene played by Meryl or Sam was set up for camera focusing and angles before they arrived. This process often took some time and involved the removal and re-positioning of various parts of the set. In order not to tire the major stars, seconds were used for this process. One day, while watching the set up for the Mt Isa bedroom scene, I noticed the 'stand-in' Meryl was avidly reading, and was oblivious to all that was going on around her. Finally I asked Fred what had her so engrossed, as I was too far away to see other than that it was a book.

He grinned and said, 'You ought to know what that is. It's your Bible.' I was told later that Meryl always carried my Bible to the set with her.

Doggone It!

Helena was still looking after the kids, but she loved animals of any sort too. She was a real Pied Piper and visited the RSPCA and the pound regularly. Firstly she acquired dogs, the number varying from one to several depending on how many homes she had found for those she had rescued. Despite the fact that we had told Lena her dogs were barred from the house, there was a doggy smell and hairs in odd places. I would look at her and say, 'You've had the dogs in here again.'

'Oh, ssh, don't tell Michael.'

'Don't you realise you can smell them?' I asked.

'Oh, they *only* just come into the lounge and sleep with me. I sprayed the air freshener around and they are outside when you come home at weekends. The boys don't mind.' *I* did though.

I eventually gave up saying anything more, but a number of times Michael and Helena argued over the dogs. He threatened the dogs with expulsion (back to her place). He wasn't going to have dogs in his yard while he was away. She said if they went, she went. Then the boys joined in. We needed a babysitter/housekeeper, and the boys wanted Helena. With a shrug Michael gave in.

But the college was complaining. We continued to come home to face letters from Grumpy at the college about the dogs in our yard and how we should keep them contained. The fact that the college had managed to pull the fence down was not relevant. Helena said many rude words about it, and Grumpy promised to have the fence fixed, but it remained unmended. Eventually we paid Lena's wages to fix up a temporary fence.

Finally I gave one of Grumpy's letters to Helena and said, 'Look, girl, you'll have to deal with this yourself. We're sick of coming home to complaints about you and your dogs. We've told you what to do with them and we really wish you would, because it gives us a bad name if you don't do it. Read that.' She did. The next thing I knew she had dialled 'old Grumpy' on the phone and told him what to do with his bloody fence. She was really very polite—for Helena—but when he objected to her language, she let him have a dose of jail language, told him what she thought of him and hung up before he could answer. Well, I doubt whether he would have managed to find any words after that anyway—he would still have had his mouth open!

Well we didn't have time to attend to a lot of domestic quarrels, so Grumpy and Lena would have to work that one out themselves. The neighbours were used to Lena's menagerie by now—cats, rabbits, a tortoise and Reagan's blue tongue lizard and cicadas were only some of them—so if they could handle the noise, Grumpy could.

Meanwhile, it was time for us to go to Sydney for the session there. In Sydney George Rollo was a tremendous source of support. He had travelled to Melbourne and stayed with his daughter for the session there, but had not come to Darwin. Now it was in Sydney where he lived, he could meet us daily and go to the Commission. He often spent lunchtime with us walking or talking, whether we needed legal work done or whether I simply felt like shopping and Michael thought I should have a bodyguard. (I didn't think so, but George came with me to humour him.) Many are the dress and shoe shops that George and I explored, with him patiently waiting while I browsed. He was a tall, imposing man and, despite his age, not the type that many would be willing to annoy. We got to know one another well during that time and he treated me like one of his daughters, giving me counsel, encouragement and advice, as he also counselled with Michael.

During one of the court breaks I was invited to go to America as guest speaker at a women's convention but the consul at the last moment refused to give me a visa for the United States (because of my criminal convictions—they later gave me an open visa), so I asked George to go and give the speech in my place. He had about four days to get ready. He took some videos with him, and answered questions that normally would have been put to me. He probably knew more about our case than anyone else apart from myself and our lawyers. He had interviewed dozens of people, studied the case thoroughly, and then written his booklet *A Reason to Kill*, so he was quite capable of deputising for me.

Meanwhile, more and more forensic and scientific evidence was coming out. There was the matter of the stains on my tracksuit pants, which had never reacted scientifically to blood. The solvent used to remove them could have taken off any one of half a dozen other stains—fruit juice or milk shake, for instance. Besides, Mrs Hansell, the drycleaner, had noticed that the stains were stubborn; she'd had to repeat the treatment. Blood—especially fresh blood, as this was reputed to have been at the time—normally came out fairly easily.

My sleeping bag, cleaned at the same time, did react positively to foetal haemoglobin tests but the same cleaner with the same method had apparently effectively stopped the slacks from reacting. How inconvenient for the Crown—but then we *knew* it wasn't blood at all, but juice, milk, and travel stains.

Finally Tony Raymond was re-called to give evidence about them and he said that apart from testing negatively, if the Crown theory was correct he found it difficult to believe there had been nothing showing on the light green inserts on the sides of the pants.

Then we came to the immunological tests—which Joy Kuhl still insisted established the presence of infant blood in the car. But a whole barrage of local and overseas experts, including Professor Ouchterlony, who had developed the method she was using and other experts such as Professors Nairn, Boettcher and Leach, said that her tests had been inadequate and did not establish the presence of foetal haemoglobin in the car. Once again, we had to sit through diagrams, slides, and learned comments about tests with names like 'crossover electrophoresis', 'radial immunodiffusion', 'Ouchterlony', 'mono' and 'bispecific'. This was all *before* the Commission experts had the final say.

Professor Siegried Baudner from Behringwerke, the German manufacturing company of the antiserum, said that it was impossible to use the antiserum (used by Joy Kuhl for her testing) by itself to differentiate between adult and babies' blood. The antiserum had to be very strictly tested and controlled before being used in any testing. This had not been done. The antiserum was primarily designed for use in experimental laboratories.

We learned during evidence the interior of a car in Mt Isa can reach a temperature of 80°C (176°F). It seemed that if any blood was heated to that temperature for only half an hour, it lost all immuno-chemical reactivity. All one was likely to get from blood that had been subject to this degree of heat was non-specific reactions (i.e., you can only tell that it was blood of some sort, as Dr Scott had found with our tent, but not what type of blood). Now, our car had been exposed to outback heat, both at Ayers Rock and at Mt Isa and to the hot, humid conditions in Darwin in the suicide season. Not only that, but our car had a black interior and no air- conditioning. (Black gives higher temperatures again.) It had been examined—by Joy Kuhl—more than thirteen months after Azaria disappeared, and more than two years after we had picked up Keyth Lenehan, the bleeding hitchhiker, on the road.

The end result of all this, and many hours of scientific exposition and argument, was that even *if* all the tests Joy Kuhl had done *had* been carried out competently the Commission could not be satisfied that there had been *any* blood in the car *at all*. A number of experts agreed that if there had been 'significant quantities' of the blood found in 1981, they would have been able to pick up traces five years later. They hadn't.

After the Commission was well over, Joy Kuhl was quoted on 28 July 1989, by Christie McGee in the *Australian*. She reported that Kuhl admitted erring in the Azaria tests evidence, saying, 'In retrospect I would have reported the matter differently in that I would never have said that the substances tested revealed foetal blood.' What a pity she hadn't admitted that years earlier.

Eventually, Commission scientists testified that the only blood that was *ever* picked up in the car was some that they thought was from nasal secretion on the back of the driver's seat.

During the trial, Barker had argued it was impossible that the material tested on the under-dash spray could only be part of the spray pattern. It was blood, he said. This was part of his argument to the jury: 'It's baby's blood. It came, the Crown says, from the child when she was killed . . .' He ridiculed the real explanation of how the spray got where it was and what it really was. '[Mr Phillips our trial QC would] have said, Ha! He'd say that's high gloss. Quite obviously the anti-foetal haemoglobin antisera used in the forensic science laboratory of the Health Commission of New South Wales is sensitive to British Paints. Therefore he would have said the car was full of paint.'

The difficulties in explaining some of Joy Kuhl's evidence kept piling up. I wasn't unhappy about that in view of her attitude at the trial. The final crunch came with the evidence—ironically enough—of forensic pathologist Professor Ferris, a Crown witness. He said that, if Azaria had been killed in the car the way the Crown suggested, there would have been 'visible and readily detectable amounts of blood present in the car almost in spite of whatever means was used to conceal it'.

Yet none of the witnesses on the night had seen any blood at all and two of them were nurses, one of whom had sat in the very spot where I had supposedly done the dastardly deed. Not only had she got no residue (of what must have been a very hasty cleaning of blood) on her clothes, she had not smelt the unmistakable smell of fresh blood either; nor had either of the dogs who had put their heads in the car door to smell the clothes that night. None had been found when the car was searched six weeks later either. In fact no residual traces of blood had been found by anyone at *any* time. And so the Crown case, dependent on the 'evidence' of the blood, just collapsed.

We'd sat through this, day after day, to prove something I had always known.

The thought of someone getting up in the name of science and making the statements that some of the Crown scientists did amazed the true scientists. This has continued all the way through, whether the people be from outside sources or indeed from Melbourne Forensic Laboratories. They have been horrified at the state of information and the biased way in which it was actually put in front of the jury. Genuine scientists are extremely careful of their good name and careful to be objective and impartial in all their material. This is not a field for guesswork; science, when carried out properly in tests like this, is accurate. What may change is the interpretation of those facts, but this is where you turn to the top expert in the field, and we were able to have our information checked by people who *were* top experts in their field.

When material about the Crown Ouchterlony tests were sent to Professor Ouchterlony himself, he was scathing and indignant that his tests could be so misconstrued.

A Cutting Business

Ken Brown was the dentist who had been so incensed by the result of the first inquest that he requested the clothes for further examination. He took them out of the country, at his own expense, across to Professor James Cameron and Mr Bernard Sims in London. He gave the Londoners his own version of events, not telling them that there had already been an inquest and the method of death given. They gave opinions based on his information, which ended up starting the second inquest.

There was so much evidence relying on the size of Azaria's clothes on her body which should have been perfectly clear but seemed to continually be overlooked, so eventually John Winneke asked that I be returned to the box to give evidence on the sizing of her singlet.

The Commissioner asked me, 'You say that singlet which was in fact on her is size 1?'

'Yes.' I answered.

Michael Adams for the Crown then asked me, 'You recall—you've been cross-examined on it—you recall that description that you gave on television of the way dingoes can peel back the skin on a calf or cow. Do you remember that?'

'I can remember but I can't remember any details on it,' I told him.

'Well, you did not there refer to the size of the singlet?' he stated.

'It is not necessary, is it?' I asked.

'That was your view; it wasn't necessary?' he asked pompously.

'Well, why would it be necessary?' I queried again.

'Well now . . .' Adams was ponderous.

'I mean, the average person—It's common sense you wear clothes—any mother of a child, knowing the weight of the child, would know a certain size was too big or not. I mean, I basically felt that that was something that's common sense, but it doesn't appear to be.'

'Double 0 size or triple 0 size was the appropriate size for Azaria?' he asked.

'Yes.' I said.

Well, I had thought anyone would know if the jumpsuit and matinee jacket were that small then the singlet should be a similar size, not three or four sizes bigger! The discolouration was quite obvious where the singlet had been folded up by nearly a third and that should have told them *something*, surely. It had told Tony Raymond for the Commission forensic. Why were the Crown so persistently blind?

Now it was the turn of the dingo experts to have their say about the damage to Azaria's clothing. Chester Porter asked them a set series of questions.

'In or about August 1980, was it within the bounds of reasonable possibility that a dingo might attack a human baby?' he asked.

Rangers Ian Cawood and Derek Roff, Les Harris of the Dingo Foundation, and CSIRO dingo expert Dr Alan Newsome all said 'Yes'. Dr Lawrence Corbett of the CSIRO said he thought it was possible but unlikely.

‘Was it within the bounds of reasonable possibility that a dingo might carry the baby away for consumption as food?’

They all said ‘Yes’ again, and Les Harris added: ‘Well, at the risk of sounding silly, it would not have taken the baby for any other reason whatsoever but food. Given what I said a few minutes ago about the camping area being regarded as a common foraging ground, I would not expect a dingo to stay in that area once it had acquired food or prey which was beyond its capacity to eat on the spot. It would have removed it to a place where it was unlikely to be challenged for possession.’

All agreed that a dingo would have been able to carry the weight of a 4.3 kilogram (9 pound 7 ounce) baby with ease, and Ian Cawood said the dingo could take the baby to the den near where the clothes were found. Les Harris added, ‘I can only draw on my general observations of dingoes over more than a decade in the field and in captivity, and my opinion is that a distance of 4 to 5 kilometres and the weight of about ten pounds [4.5 kilograms] would present absolutely no problem to a dingo.’ The clothes had been found only metres away from a dingo lair that apparently had pups in it at the time; this was the lair Michael and I had filmed with Erwin Chlanda. It was the firm belief of the rangers and the dingo experts that it was highly possible Azaria’s body had been transferred back to the lair by the dingoes for their pups.

‘Does the dingo normally or occasionally bury its prey?’ asked Chester Porter. From time to time, came the answer. And, bearing in mind the extensive staining around the collar of Azaria’s jumpsuit, Porter then inquired: ‘Does the dingo have a habit, like the fox, of eating its prey head first?’

Les Harris said, ‘Again, this depends on the size of the animal. With the larger animals they tend to eat the contents of the abdominal cavity first and then move on to the solid meat, but with smaller animals they usually tend to eat the prey head first.’

The experts added that the dingoes at Ayers Rock frequently came into tents, and wouldn’t hesitate to enter them for food. Furthermore, Derek Roff and Ian Cawood said the dingo would have just kept on going with its prey, even if disturbed. (We found out that one in the camping area made off with a 5 kilogram (11 pound) leg of pork, which it took from an Esky with the lid *closed*, and didn’t stop even when it was hotly pursued by the owner.)

Unpredictable animals, dingoes. We heard evidence that they can pick up dolls by their clothing without causing visible damage; the one that night could have taken Azaria to the area where the clothes were found without ripping or tearing the jumpsuit significantly at all. Furthermore, dingoes can remove clothing from prey; Derek Roff said he had seen a dingo open a bar of chocolate without ‘ripping and tearing’ the paper. They are very fastidious creatures. A dingo could easily open the press studs of a jumpsuit with its nose or teeth, and could have taken a body from the clothing altogether without much damage to the fabric, as the Adelaide Zoo dingo tests showed.

Ken Chapman, one of our dingo damage experts, told me the Adelaide Zoo test nappy and Azaria’s nappy damage were almost identical. Once when he was working on them, a Crown scientist went to get it and brought the wrong nappy back, thinking it was Azaria's, as the nappy damage was so alike. Ken had had to tell them it was the *zoo* nappy!

So much for all those assertions—by so many people over the past six years—that 'dingoes don't do such things'.

Then there was the damage to Azaria's clothing. The wrangle about whether this had been produced by a pair of scissors, a sharp implement, or a set of dingo teeth, continued.

It wasn't until after a lot of their work had been done that Les Smith and Ken Chapman were able to get hold of Azaria's jumpsuit and have a look at the actual damage. Before that they had only been able to work with some photographs and the transcript. When they actually got access to photograph the jumpsuit, they had much more accurate information to go on.

Finally, just before the Royal Commission, they were able to get full access to the jumpsuit itself as they had had only limited access before that. Now they were able to research it, they became extremely excited. There on that jumpsuit was damage comparable to a lot of the material that they had been finding on Suzie's (Les's pet dog), the test dingo's, and on the initial Adelaide Zoo test jumpsuit which the Crown had done.

Much was made of the fact that they were not 'forensic' scientists, they were just 'ordinary' scientists. It was pointed out over and over again that all scientists are 'ordinary scientists' until they specialise in a field. Forensic scientists have academic scientists from universities teach them in the first place, and academic scientists usually develop the new methods.

The Crown complained that not knowing the ropes and pressure of forensic work, and being able to sit back in their 'ivory towers' meant these men did not understand the work of the practising forensic scientist. It seemed difficult to believe the Crown could be so stupid because, let's face it, if a man has time to specialise on a case and think about it and work it out, he will no doubt have more chance of doing difficult work than someone who is absolutely overloaded with cases and told to have results in a hurry.

It was no secret that when Dr Andrew Scott was asked to test for saliva he knew there was no test so he actually had to devise one. This was the first of many times untried 'new' scientific methods were used in our case. There were no forerunners on which to gauge the evidence or how to prepare and test it. Certainly there are forerunners in those areas now. Forensic labs linked with universities are able to go to their university and say, 'We have a problem. This needs further investigation. We don't have the time, will you take over and let us know what you develop?' Those labs are likely to come up with far more accurate work because they are dealing with as wide a range of experts as it is possible to get. Maintaining that someone who normally works in a general field is expert in all fields is ridiculous.

True scientists and specialists are willing to give expert evidence but will not go out of their fields. If they do not know the exact answer, even though they may suspect it, they will not speculate. Over and over again, we found those qualified by the experience of working in a laboratory, some without even degrees, were claiming to be expert at things which they obviously did not have a great deal of knowledge about at all.

Dentist Ken Brown's evidence backed by Mr Bernard Sims did not go unnoticed either. The Crown had named two men as authorities when dealing with this evidence, and defence material from Smith and Chapman was forwarded to them. One, Professor Ron Fearnhead, had been Sim's teacher, and the other, Professor Gosta Gustafson, was widely known as the father of modern forensic odontology. Both (top men in their world field) agreed that the damage to the jumpsuit was consistent with a dingo dog severance rather than known scissor cutting—and Professor Gustafson had the rare qualification of having actually studied dog bites. That effectively caused the Crown's dental experts to retire.

One day walking back from court to our offices which were a block away, we stopped at the lights to cross. We were all walking in a group and I was standing on one side talking to Ken Crispin. Suddenly arms went round me from behind and I looked around and up into the face of a complete stranger. He grinned at me and said, 'Just wanted to tell you I love you, I think you're terrific and you're doing a great job. Hang in there, lady.' The lights turned green and he disappeared across the road ahead of us and out of sight. It happened so quickly I was left speechless, but not Ken. He wanted to know if a good-looking man did that to me, how come a good- looking woman never walked up to him and did the same thing? We laughed and continued on our way. Having had a rather awful day in court, things were much brighter. It was little things like that from total strangers that have helped us survive the last twenty-four years.

As the Commission went on, people often grabbed my hand in the street as I walked by or crept up behind me to whisper in my ear that they were thinking of us or praying for us. Usually it was more subtle than the man at the lights, but meant just as much.

Back at court, when the jumpsuit, nappy and singlet were produced once again, we couldn't help noticing that the Crown lawyers tended to handle the clothes quite roughly. Michael Adams, the Crown junior, was seen on several occasions pulling and stretching at the edges of the cut fabric on Azaria's jumpsuit. Once he actually jabbed it with his pen. There are photographs showing that cut before he did so, and ones later on which show where his blue pen mark is visible. With this sort of thing done openly in court, one cannot help wondering what other mishandling of the evidence was done by lawyers, scientists, police or others before our men were originally allowed to look at it.

The Crown's array of experts had initially seemed very impressive until I reminded myself that 'x' equals an unknown quantity and a 'spurt' is a drip under pressure. Therefore an expert equals an unknown number of drips under pressure. After contemplating that equation, I could cope.

Much of the cut evidence was based on Professor Chaikin's evidence at the trial. He had claimed expertise in dingo cut material. John Phillips, when cross-examining

Professor Chaikin at the trial, had asked, 'Can we just return to the question I asked you? Apart from the zoo jumpsuit, you have not examined any clothing that's been bitten by a dingo?'

Chaikin answered, 'Correct.'

'Have you examined the body of any person that has been bitten by a dingo?'

No.'

'Have you seen a live dingo bite anything?'

'No.'

'Have you seen a live dingo?'

'Yes.'

'Where?'

'Ayers Rock.'

'Right,' agreed John Phillips. 'That didn't bite anything in your presence?'

'No,' said Chaikin stiffly.

'Well, in uttering the opinion that you have, you do it without having seen any of the matters we have just discussed, don't you?'

'Well, I claim that I have some expertise in the interaction between various objects with various properties and fabrics, and fibre assemblies, and I base my opinion and conclusions on that.'

'I will repeat the question. In stating the opinion that you have, that it was not a dingo's tooth that produced the damage, you do that without ever seeing a live dingo bite anything, don't you?'

'That's correct.'

'Yes or no, please?'

'Yes.'

Once again John said, 'You state it without ever having examined the clothing of a person who has been bitten by a dingo, don't you?

'I have, as I said, carried out experiments with dingo teeth on this particular fabric,' Chaikin hedged.

'Will you please answer my question? You state that opinion without ever having examined the clothing of a person who has been bitten by a dingo?'

'That's correct.'

'And you state that opinion without ever having examined the body of a person bitten by a dingo?'

'That's correct.'

It was hard to believe that all that knowledgeable evidence could be given on what damage could *not* be done by a dingo when he had *never* actually seen anything to base his opinion on.

Professor Chaikin said that cuts to the jumpsuit were caused by a sharp implement. He then went into a learned explanation of what he called 'planar array', which, he said, was an alignment of the severed ends of the fibres within a number of consecutive yarns. Now 'planar array' was a fancy phrase nobody had heard before, and we suspected that it had been invented solely for the benefit of the Commission. It was a word not used in any scientific publications elsewhere, and was a new name given to mean 'all in a line'. Now they stated that it was planar array *alone* that had given them the means of distinguishing a scissor cut from a dingo cut. When it was pointed out that this was not necessarily so, then it was the *length* of the planar array that became important.

So far we'd had demonstrations of cuts and tufts, loops and pile—all interesting for general knowledge tests, but of little actual relevance to my case, I thought.

There was a lot of evidence with electron microscopes, showing types of cuts produced by various instruments (including dingo teeth). Well, the evidence could have done with being plainer, but they preferred to keep it complicated it seemed.

When the Crown experts discovered dingoes made tufts as well, that went by the board. Test after test was done and even while our men were in the witness box the other side was again testing. The Crown tested up to the last moment, and some of the fabric cut experts were in and out of the box many times as the days went on.

During one of the Crown witness's examination I remember Ken Crispin sitting in front of me in court drawing, and my curiosity got the better of me. I knew he was feeling furious about the garbage we were all being subjected to. He would be doing some of the cross-examination in the same field later and had been reading for hours on end about the subject. Eventually I kicked the back of his chair and put my hand out. He grinned and said, 'Hang on,' then later turned and passed me a caricature of a certain gentleman, the one we were presently listening to, an expert it was said on cutting, who had told us that only scissors could cause little tufts to fall away. We knew of course that almost anything could cut and cause tufts, and we'd had a man in the box hit the jumpsuit material with a hammer on a hard surface. The blow actually cut through the material, leaving tufts. We were now watching the expert trying to worm his way out of that one.

Ken had drawn a cartoon showing 'planar array'. An 'array' of three wooden carpenter's planes, wooden because of the thick wooden heads some people had. Another picture showed an expert holding a book called *Ripping Yarns* (the experts' textbook) and pulling along a little toy wagon filled with knives, scissors and cutting implements—knitting needles, nail files, cane knives, kitchen knives, and for good measure, he had put in a chainsaw; all implements we had that the Crown might have alleged were murder weapons. That really cracked me up.

After all, the Crown did seem pretty confused about whether the damage had been caused by scissors, a knife, or something else. Ken Crispin pointed out, 'Professor Chaikin and that doyen of South Australian forensic evidence, Mr Cocks [a policeman with no scientific degree at all] are applauded when they give evidence of scissor cuts, but ignored when Dr Griffiths' brand-new Wiltshire Staysharp knife hypothesis is propounded [a new theory suddenly introduced one day at the Commission]. Dr Sanson, on the other hand, is applauded for his comments about the V cut in the collar, but ignored when he concedes that the remainder of the damage to the jumpsuit may be consistent with damage by a dingo.'

It remained for Dr William Pelton, another textile expert, to really cast doubts on the Crown's conclusions. He said he had carried out a study of the samples of cloth damaged by dingoes, and found twenty-eight points of similarity between dingo-damaged fabric and the damage to Azaria's jumpsuit. Twelve, he said, would have been difficult to reproduce with scissors, even if anyone *had* known what kind of damage to cause; four points of similarity would have been very difficult, if not impossible, to reproduce with scissors. The damage was a mixture of cutting and tearing and the yarns had been pulled in such a way that tweezers would also have had to be used if the damage had been caused by a human being.

It wasn't surprising, of course, that he concluded that it was 'highly unlikely' the damage had been caused by a human, and 'highly likely' it had been caused by a dingo.

The Commissioner finally declared they could not keep coming back and back again on their evidence. If they hadn't given it to begin with, they had better forget it, because nothing new was being told, they were just trying to pick at the credibility of the defence and Commission. There had to be an end. At the end of it all, a dispute over 280 millimetres (11 inches) was reduced to a 15 millimetre (half inch) section, and Dr Barry Hoschke, CSIRO textile expert called by the Commission, testified that in order to get a classic scissor cut the scissors had to be sharpened under a microscope and the fibres cut one by one! *I* must have sat up in the middle of the night doing that too, I suppose!

Dr Hans Brunner heard of the police investigation into Azaria's disappearance and volunteered to do the hair identification for them. He has been acclaimed as being a world 'authority on the identification of mammals by hair' and has written the standard textbook *The Identification of Mammalian Hair*—but his offer was rejected. When we contacted him, he had no problem identifying the hairs as belonging to a dingo, not a cat (which are as different as red and green to an expert). Eventually Harding agreed with Brunner's diagnosis, and when asked by Porter, QC to produce the rest of the vacuumed hairs, he had to explain they had been *lost* sometime after the trial. It had happened *again!*

One reporter found it so boring he regularly used to sleep. When Verity Lambert, the producer of *Evil Angels (A Cry in the Dark)*, came to the Commission to see it in action, she asked us which lawyer was which because she wanted to observe Ian Barker and his Crown assistants. During a break she said, 'You know, if I was doing a murder film, there is a man in there that would be absolutely perfect cast as a mass murderer. I'll show you which man later.' We all laughed and chorused, 'We know which one.' He was one of the better-known reporters on the case from one of the supposedly authoritative Australian newspapers.

Verity was quite aghast to realise that the reports considered authoritative by the Australian public were given by a man who was so untidily dressed, and who had actually sat with his back to the Commissioner, feet up on another chair, head thrown back, mouth open, asleep and *snoring* in the courtroom itself. (I observed him do this on at least one other occasion as well and was surprised the court orderly didn't have him removed.) She had read his material and it always seemed to have a strong Crown bias to her rather than being impartial. As she watched him go straight to the Crown afterwards and ask what the news of the day was and what he should write up, it was *so* obvious she became extremely upset and angry.

When endeavouring to get his research for the script from all sources, Robert Caswell had lunch with the chief of news in Rupert Murdoch's organisation. He came away absolutely astounded because the man had told him if the Chamberlains were found guilty it was far better for newspaper sales—a comment that stuck forcibly in his mind for years afterwards.

Another day Robert wanted to meet us for lunch because he had some research he wanted us to check, so we agreed. Michael decided to skip court at the last moment and return to Cooranbong and therefore avoid the research, which he disliked, without telling Robert. Robert timed his arrival at court well, because we were all just walking out for the luncheon recess. For once he was dressed up, jacket, slacks, shirt, bow tie, the lot—as a surprise. He normally wore jeans and a jumper. He looked great. Despite his having sat in court for a number of days to get the feel of things, the regular court attenders didn't recognise him. Knowing Michael wasn't back yet, they were very suspicious of this young man, all dressed up, coming to meet me.

As we waltzed off, he offered me his arm, and down the corridor we went, stifling grins, because we could see everybody staring. I said, 'You know, we will have eloped by the end of the day at this rate.' I wasn't wrong—people walked up to my parents, casually wondering who the young man with Lindy was. Mum, reading their minds as well as I had, said, 'Oh, don't you recognise him? He's the film writer who's been sitting in court. You know, the one who's been sitting near you.'

'Oh, of course,' they said. 'Didn't recognise him dressed up like that. She'll be all right then.' Mum hid a smile and said she was sure I would be.

We had decided to go to the Sydney Pancake House as they served vegetarian meals as well as meat so we could both have what we wanted. Normally, there was a good lunch at a reasonable price, with quick friendly service too; but on this day they were absolutely packed out. I said to Robert, 'I was wrong this time about it being empty, let's go somewhere else.' He said, 'No, no, you picked this place, we'll eat here. Let's go in. I'll try a little L. A. B. S. (Los Angeles Bull Shit), and see what happens.'

'What name?' asked the waitress at the door. Robert, quickly reading the booking list upside down, said, 'Uh, that one there.'

She said, 'What's the name?'

'Jenkin, yes, Jenkin, that's me,' said Robert. She laughed, 'You're not, you know.'

'Of course I'm not,' said Robert, 'but they *are* late, and if they were coming, you must admit they would have arrived, or at least rung you by now.' She admitted that was true.

He asked if the Jenkins had booked a good table and she pointed out a prime place beside the window. The waitress said, 'OK, you can have it.' As we made our way to it, I asked her, 'What will you do if they come?'

She said, 'Somebody will have left by then, but I doubt that they will turn up now.'

Well, we got great service. We had our papers spread out on a nice comfortable table set for two with plenty of extra room. Halfway through the meal, the waitress came by and we asked her whether the Jenkins had eventually arrived. When she said, 'yes' I asked, 'What did you do with them?'

She laughed and said, 'Well, actually they are seated down there.' I said, 'Oh well, that's not bad they still have a window table.'

'You're kidding,' she said, 'It's right opposite the kitchen entrance *and* the toilets. They have done nothing but complain the whole time since they got here, but as it is a window table they don't know this table was supposed to be theirs.'

Robert was all for getting up, putting on his best manner, waltzing up to them and saying, 'Oh, Mr Jenkins. Nice to see you. LA wasn't it?' It was with difficulty I stopped him, although I couldn't help appreciating the mental picture of a poor confused stranger confronted with that!

During lunch that day Robert said he had worked out why Barker was so successful in cross-examining Michael at the trial. As Michael in his role as a minister was conditioned to respond to pleas of help, every time Barker said, 'Can you help me?' Michael tried to respond, even when he had no knowledge of the subject, so he floundered badly and guessed. *We* knew that but the jury didn't. Barker got what he wanted.

As Michael and I were due in the box again shortly it was a useful observation. Robert asked if Michael would be upset if he explained this to him. I thought Michael would be most grateful. (Robert again arranged to take Michael to lunch on his own another day—while I went window shopping—and explain this to him. Michael saw the light and prepared himself not to 'help' Barker, so he didn't fall for Barker's line any more in the Commission.)

By the time we had finished talking we were late for court and the Jenkins had left. I bet they never knew how they lost that lovely table by the window. Obviously if you are dressed well and put on a confident manner, you can get away with an awful lot.

My turn in the witness box had finally arrived. Another dose of Barker didn't bring any sense of pleasure, in fact it didn't make any sense to me at all. It would just be more hours spent going over and over everything I had ever said to him before, and anyone else he could think of that I had spoken to as well.

My initial examination was taken by Mr Winneke as my counsel, instead of Mr Porter for the Commission as was usual. I understand this was so I could be cross-examined if necessary by Mr Porter, and because Jack knew our case better.

Jack Winneke took me quickly but thoroughly through all my evidence again for the Commission records, then it was Barker's turn. This time I didn't have a migraine like I had been unlucky enough to have all the other times he cross-examined me, and I was ready for him. Whether he was ready for me was another thing, though, because my guys at the bar table said his legs were visibly shaking when he got up to cross-examine, and stayed shaking. He seemed to jump around all over the place with my evidence and continually returned to the same points in some type of circular argument, as if he hoped to get me to contradict myself.

I had already been in the box for days, and most of that time I was being questioned by Barker over and over on the same things. I mean, how much can one say about an incident that took only a few seconds? If you think the next paragraphs are boring and tediously repetitive, imagine how I felt after so many hours of it. We were discussing, if you could call it that, the dingo in the door of the tent, where I thought it had run, and if the dingo behind the car was the same one.

Barker continued 'How far were you away?'

I answered 'Probably about the same distance as from me to you now; maybe a . . .'

Barker interrupted. 'And the light, you've told us, was from the barbecue?'

'Yes,' I said.

'And the animal had . . . the animal was shaking its head?' questioned Barker.

'That's right, from side to side,' I agreed.

'Of course, a split second wouldn't have given you much time to see it move its head from side to side, would it?' Barker asked sarcastically.

'It depends how fast it's moving,' I answered.

Barker continued on, and now we were into previous evidence I had given, rehashing it again. He read: '"When I had previously yelled at the dingo it had run out of the tent across to the front of the car and into the shadow. As I was calling to Michael I was running in the direction the dingo had gone around the front of the car. Michael said, 'What?'—as I reached the front corner of the car, left-hand corner, at the time Michael answered—I noticed the dingo standing motionless and slightly behind the rear of the car in its shadow." Now, you were in no doubt, were you, when you said that—firstly, that the animal had run in front of the car and secondly, that the animal you saw behind the car was the one which had come out of the tent?'

'Either of those I was in some doubt about,' I stated.

'Why didn't you tell Charlwood you were in some doubt about it,' he wanted to know.

'He didn't ask me.'

'Because he didn't ask you, you didn't express any doubt?' he asked again.

'I had no idea when I gave this ROI the nit-picking ability that some lawyers possess. If I had known that I would have been very specific. Instead of a thirteen-hour interview you'd probably had a twenty-six hour interview and I would have been very, very exact. I wasn't,' I was bored with this rehashing, and disgusted.

'You were talking about a dingo that had taken your child, weren't you?' he asked.

'That's right. And that was what was taking my attention, not at the exact footsteps and the number of them and how many seconds they took,' I answered back.

'Are you saying that when you said that to Charlwood you were in fact in some doubt that the dingo behind the car was the dingo that had taken your child,' he asked.

'I was in some doubt that that was it, the same as I was in some doubt on the night; that I had seen the dingo in the tent; there was a dingo behind the car and reason told me it had to be the same, although there was some doubt in my mind that it was the same. In those situations you don't stop and weigh it up and ask logic—whether it's exactly true that such and such has happened or not; you take action and you move and you follow what is there.' It seemed some people needed very simple answers to understand some things.

'You saw it for about two seconds, didn't you, behind the car in constant view?' he continued on the same theme.

'I doubt that it would have been that long. It was a lot less time than the one I saw in the tent,' I answered.

'Looking at question ninety-five of the record of interview. Would you have a look at that. "When you saw this dingo standing behind the car did you have it in constant view until it disappeared into the scrub?"

'"Yes, it was a matter of about two seconds?"' he read.

'Yes, that wasn't standing for two seconds behind the car. I was chasing it at some distance that we're talking about there—back on into the dark,' I explained.

'You were so sure of its appearance that you in fact told Charlwood that if you were a better drawer you could draw it. Do you remember that?' he asked.

'The one that I saw in the doorway of the tent, yes, and that's head and shoulders [only showing].' He'd confused the two dingoes on purpose I'll bet.

'You're asserting as a sworn fact, aren't you, in the same way that you asserted the fact to Mr Charlwood; you didn't speak about impressions, you spoke about facts, did you not?' Barker queried.

'What I'm doing here is giving my version of the way I saw things that night. I was not stopped in this interview and nit-picked like you're doing now. We spent nearly two hours over this at the trial with you trying to get me to say that I actually watched it and you know very well I did not watch it in front of the car. It was only my impression,' I answered bored and impatient with the same questions over and over.

'Did you say this to the coroner?' Barker continued.

'It's quite obvious I said it to the coroner,' I answered impatiently.

'"When I yelled at it initially it had run across in front of the car"?' he questioned again.

'It was my impression that it had run across in the car, in front of the car, yes,' I explained again.

'"And the shadow of the fence and I headed in that direction"?' Barker asked again.

'That's quite right. I did head in that direction,' I agreed.

'"It had run and when I came round the corner of the car it was standing behind the car which would be probably in about the centre of the road." Do you remember saying that?' he continued.

'That's right. There was a dingo around there and I chased it,' I agreed again.

'"It"—you were talking about the one that come out of the tent. There's no question about that, is there?' He asked for what seemed the nth time. We had gone full circle again and were back to the question of the two dingoes again.

'There was a question in my mind. There is not a question in the way I have said here,' I explained patiently again. I really felt like telling him to concentrate and not ask the same thing. If he had listened the first time he'd know the answers off by heart now—we'd been through this so many times before, but he could always get lucky and bore me so much my concentration would slip and I might say something he would be happy with!

'You further said, "It would be about the centre of the road, well the centre between the railings, not actually the centre of the road. It was back in a shadow behind the car where it was fairly dark" and so on?' he reiterated.

'It was,' I agreed again.

'There was no question then that it was other than the dingo that left the tent, was there?' The man was a tiger for punishment.

'If you go over a little bit further you'll find where I'm telling the coroner that there was a question as—' I started.

He cut me off, 'Well, let's go to—'

'As to whether it was the same dingo or not.' I continued with my sentence. Two could play that little game. He didn't want me to point that out, it was too pointed.

He ignored me. 'Let's go to page eighty-six, where I think the coroner raised the matter. He said, "Why do you say that the animal you saw coming out of the tent was the same as the one you saw alongside your car shortly after?" You said, "Well, there's a possibility that it could've been a different dingo, for that matter. It was just the direction that it ran in and I just presumed (there were *many* later references to my presumption which the Crown found a major nuisance) that it was waiting for me to go over the road, to go in a different direction, and I had disturbed its pattern. I just headed in that direction and the dingo was standing there. It may have been another one. The coincidence of having two dingoes just a few seconds apart in the same area is rather high on the level of coincidences, that's all." Did you anywhere tell the coroner that you thought that the dog behind the car might have looked different to the dog that came out of the tent?' Barker plodded on.

'I don't think so. I don't think I was asked that question,' I answered.

Later on we were still going on the same subject. 'You see that you said, "He took fright and ran in front of our car which was parked right next to the next [tent]"?'

Well I followed what he meant and answered, 'Well, that's where I thought it had run.'

'Well, were you stating it as a fact or an impression?' he continued on.

'I'm telling him here what I thought had happened through my reconstruction of where I'd gone and where I thought it had gone,' I answered again.

'That was a reconstruction the next day, was it?' he ground on.

'It was a reconstruction that night in a split second. I couldn't run between the tent and the car, so how did I think that it would've?'

Barker continued, 'Did you express any doubt to Gilroy that it may have gone somewhere else?'

'No, I didn't,' I said.

'Did you suggest to him for example that it might have gone between the tent and the car?'

'No, I didn't. If he questioned me on it as to how I knew and was I exactly sure and had I watched it go, I probably would've answered all those questions to him then. Like I said to you before, I didn't before, I didn't realise how exactly specific and nit-picking you had to be in court.' I'd had enough of this nonsense.

'You say there's nit-picking to—' he started.

‘The way you act is nit-picking. Not all lawyers do that,’ I snapped.

‘Do you say that had Gilroy said to you,“Well, look, might this animal have gone between the tent and the car?”, you would have said, “Yes, it might”?’

‘That’s right,’ I answered, bored again.

‘Is that what you say?’ he asked. You’d think he’d get as sick of saying the same thing as I was of hearing it.

I reiterated the same thing again for him in a different way. ‘If he had’ve asked me had I watched it go exactly, the answer would have been, “No”. For starters, I had turned round after I saw it to tell the rest of the people at the barbecue that it was there. And after that I wasn’t interested in watching its progress because I’d seen what was in the tent.’

‘Were you trying to help Gilroy come to an understanding of what happened?’

‘Yes, and he was quite satisfied that I had helped him, but then he’s not you,’ I snapped at him again.

‘Did you try to assist Charlwood to come to an understanding of what happened?’

‘Yes.’

‘Could the witness please have the transcript of this Commission, 3598, 3599? This is a transcript of one of these television interviews. Do you understand—apparently made in late August or early September?’

‘Yes,’ I replied, ‘All done before the first inquest and before I realised how stupid some courts and lawyers are.’

‘Thank you,’ answered Barker. ‘Notwithstanding your view of certain lawyers, did you say to the public of Australia—I’m looking at page 3599—“I yelled at the dog. I thought the baby cry [cried]—he had disturbed her at that stage and went across in front of the car and ran, I thought, off into the distance.” Do you remember saying that?’

‘Yes, that’s right.’

‘Did you again suggest there anywhere that maybe it hasn’t run in front of the car?’ he wanted to know.

Mr Winneke asked, ‘I’m sorry, that it had . . . ?’ Barker corrected himself,

‘Had not run in front of the car?’

By this time I knew I was sounding extremely rude and antagonistic. If I didn’t let the court know it was purely personal, it could be misconstrued as being uncooperative to the Commission itself.

I started, ‘This description is sufficient for any intelligent public that is not nit-picking in court. I don’t like you, Mr Barker. I never have liked you. If you expect me to be polite to you, don’t. I don’t like your form of law and I don’t adhere to it and it’s—reason for your type of law that the reasons for these courts in Australia are in such a mess . . .’

The members of the public in the body of the court burst into applause and drowned out the rest of what I wanted to say. That frustrated me. I had wanted to state that if lawyers let witnesses tell the truth and did not try to twist it and spin it out so much, their pockets might have been thinner, but the backlog of cases might just have been caught up and a lot of taxpayers’ money saved into the bargain. And maybe, just maybe, we’d see justice come back to Australia.

The Commissioner couldn't overlook what I had done of course, and had to bring the court to order. 'Mrs Chamberlain, I can understand that you are under stress. I will not have that sort of conduct in this Commission.'

He then turned his attention to the rest of the court. 'I will not have that sort of conduct in this Commission. It will not do Mrs Chamberlain any good. I am sure she would resent it as I do, let alone counsel. And if it continues we will have to take steps to have it ceased.'

He turned to me again. 'Mrs Chamberlain, I can understand that you are under stress. You have very competent counsel representing you. You may be assured that if Mr Winneke thinks that Mr Barker is acting unfairly, or indeed if I do, if Mr Winneke thinks that he is asking you a question which you should not be asked, he would certainly object. There is no need for you to do anything else than to answer any questions which I rule you should answer.

'And those sort of asides will only delay the proceedings and also I can understand you may, as I say, be under stress, you ought to refrain from similar remarks. Yes, Mr Barker?' Barker said, 'Yes.'

Blow that. I knew very well that Barker was being legally correct, but that was not the point I was making at all. 'Your Honour, I also realise that Mr Winneke can only object on points of law because of the way the court is set up,' I said.

The Commissioner answered, 'Mrs Chamberlain, that is not the case. Mr Winneke can object to any question which he thinks you should not be asked and you may be assured that you will get a fair hearing in this Commission. You may also be assured—and let me tell you, so far and I am sure it will continue—there has been absolutely no reason for any complaint about the way Mr Barker is cross-examining you. It may be unpleasant but he is doing no more than his duty and he is doing it quite properly. Yes, Mr Barker?'

Well, that answer just proved my point. It wasn't wrong to be so carping the way our courts work today, and it should be, because it wastes time and gets no one anywhere. If that was a lawyer's duty done properly then they should all be sacked and the system reviewed in my opinion!

Barker finally ran out of steam after endless questions on the same topic, and Chester Porter had his turn. Mr Porter's questions were searching but he listened to the answers and got to the point without wasting the court's time, or mine.

'Can you come back to the next day. One can understand why—that's the day after the baby disappeared—one can understand perhaps why you would stay around and wait for them to bring word to you, and look after your other two children, but the next day you knew, did you not, that people were looking for your child?' Mr Porter asked.

Intelligent questions like that I was happy to answer. 'We had been told that morning that there was a smaller search, but they were trying to get the tourists out of it because it was confusing the trackers; they wanted to scale it down just to the Aboriginals and the trackers; and that they were having a little bit of trouble because they had too many volunteers that they really didn't want at that stage,' I explained.

Chester Porter continued later, 'The next morning you've heard the evidence that Michael was deliberately driving around to try and get a correct film for the Adelaide newspaper?'

'Yes,' I answered.

'You were with him at the time?'

I replied, 'I went in the bus, yes—just sat in the bus.'

'Didn't that strike you as a bit strange—that he should be concerned with getting films and taking pictures?' Mr Porter asked.

Well that was easy to answer. 'Not with Michael. Photography has always been something that can take his mind off something else and to me that was partly therapeutic and partly an escape mechanism that he uses from time to time, and that's just Michael,' I replied.

I knew this was something that had puzzled a lot of people, but no one who knew Michael was in the least surprised. (Besides, he had been asked to do it as a way of warning others, so of course he agreed.)

After three days of evidence, my time in the witness box came to an end, and Michael took the stand. This time he was much better with Barker after Robert Caswell's useful observations, and he didn't get nearly so uptight about it all. The whole way the Commission was run was much more low key than having a jury listening, so that also helped.

Meanwhile, during court, Felicity Moffit, one of the reporters, wore a beeper, and she would occasionally forget to turn it down when she walked into the court. Silence would reign, then you would hear a loud 'beep, beep, beep', and she would go crimson. It happened to her not once but a number of times. A similar thing also applied to Julia Shepherd, a reporter from the *Sun*, who used a tape recorder for her notes, as the press were allowed to do. When she pushed the wrong button, as Pastor Cozens had during the first inquest, we would get court played back, then hastily silenced in embarrassment.

One day at lunchtime Ken Crispin and I were waiting together at the lift to return to street level. It was a miserable day, with rainy cold weather outside. When we boarded the lift it was crowded. A woman casually said,

'It's not raining now.' Graeme Charlwood, who had also been at court that day, and was at the back of the packed lift, quipped, 'Not in here, anyway.'

'An astute observation,' said Ken.

Without thinking, I answered, 'Typical of a dumb cop.'

Ken grinned widely. For the rest of the way to the bottom floor the lift was very quiet, a number of the people were trying to hide large smirks, and I didn't even feel repentant.

As the Commission continued in Sydney, we stayed there during the week and went home on weekends. That was a great change from being away in Darwin for weeks on end. As the weeks wore on, all I ever seemed to do was go shopping on the way home from Sydney on a Friday afternoon, come home, pack it away, do the washing, the ironing, some cleaning, then repack and go back to Sydney on the Sunday evening.

The next week I never had any idea of what they had run out of, and often I guessed wrong. I would find some food gone off and other things I had expected to last for ages totally used.

Meanwhile Helena was doing her best to work locally during the day (she was making security screen doors—not bad for a reformed burglar!) and looking after the boys after school. Under the circumstances she did an excellent job. The number of times they bought chips for tea instead of cooking vegetables was more than I care to think about, though. When I tackled her about it she giggled, shrugged and said, 'I can't do everything. Besides, you know they hate eating veggies and I can't be *too* cruel. You can sit over them and make them eat them, but I am not going to. Well, not *most* of the time anyway. Why make myself tired by having a fight?' And so we had to be happy with that. She did see that they ate *some* vegetables and didn't get sick.

At least the kids were happy, and at this stage that was the main thing because we had to be away from them for so long. They were so pleased to have me back, seeing me at weekends was better than not seeing me at all. They were still fairly much used to looking after and fending for themselves (though not very efficiently!) and they adjusted much more easily than they would now they are older and used to me being home again.

Kahlia was staying at Auntie Jan and Uncle Owen Hughes' while we were away, so it was easier for her, but even she expressed the wish that she'd like to stay 'in my own home bed now please. Don't go any more now.' After so many months I was inclined to agree!

Near the end I got so tired of commuting between Sydney and Cooranbong, packing and unpacking, not to mention the late hours after court working on film research, that on a number of occasions I stayed down on the weekends in order to get some extra sleep and work done. The house was impossible to keep tidy just on weekends, so I finally left it alone. The kids were fed, happy and getting their homework done, so I settled for that. What did it really matter if the house was getting messy again as long as the kids were OK? There would be time to clean up again when all this was over.

Rather than walk in and feel depressed with what was happening around me as it got worse over the weeks, I simply went bush on the weekends, getting wood with Michael. The time spent in the open air was much more productive to a sound mind and a healthy body than what we had been doing the rest of the week, and helped keep me sane.

Pioneer reports of dingo deaths in early newspapers, diaries or books were not considered evidence when not on the actual coroner's report (our case still fits in this category also), even though inquests usually weren't held in cases when everyone was on the search to see what had happened firsthand anyway. If inquests *were* held, 'death by misadventure' was the usual listing, it not being considered relevant to put on the death certificate that the cause of death was actually a dingo, as everyone knew that. We knew that Aboriginal babies had been killed by dingoes, too. But because Aboriginal deaths did not have to be reported at that stage, there were no court records and the Aborigines themselves considered it a forbidden subject and would not discuss it.

Because of these factors, information regarding previous dingo attacks could not be considered as legal precedents—only irrelevant or misleading information.

During the trial we were aware, though the Crown was obviously not, that the child of a juror had once been attacked by a dingo. Only during the writing of this book was I informed the child was the son of Yvonne Cain (the juror who finally spoke forth) who had then lived in Alice Springs.

Not until years later did we finally manage to also contact the Cranwells, whose daughter Amanda had been attacked shortly before Azaria was taken. They came forward, apologising for not being in touch sooner—but they thought we had known about them all the time.

When we were preparing for the Commission, we wanted to check the second inquest death certificate to see what cause of death was now listed. Normally, you can apply for a death certificate and it is handed straight over. The Northern Territory did not want to release Azaria's, finally demanding to know what we intended to do with it before they would release it. We explained it might be for court action, and finally it arrived. We then discovered it was simply a copy of the first inquest death certificate, which had handwritten changes and was not a new official document at all. I often wonder what was the problem with asking for a death certificate for our own daughter, and why they were so paranoid.

Because there is currently no official court finding that lists Azaria as having been taken by a dingo, one wonders whether, when the same thing happens in the future, they will maintain once again that such a thing has never happened in Australian history. There are only newspaper reports and no official precedents; therefore it did not legally happen. Instead there is a current open murder verdict on the still standing second inquest.

There are things I would like to put in this book, but I cannot. I know certain facts but because the people who told them to me are in fear of their lives or jobs, and they have been unwilling to give evidence in court, I have not been able to prove certain things. This often happens. It frustrates the police who know about intimidated witnesses, and it also frustrates me. Both the defence and Crown at times are put in a position where they know something but cannot use it. There is just no way of getting over this fact while men threaten other men and carry out those threats. When one lives by fear, there is no remedy.

I certainly found truth in the old quote, 'What the world needs most is men, men who will not be bought or sold; men who will be as true to duty as the needle to the pole.' My father used to quote these words to me as I was growing up, and they made a profound impression on me. I can't remember who wrote them, but many a time in the last ten years I have been thankful for men who stood 'as true to duty as the needle to the pole'. Many other times, when I have desperately *needed* people with the guts to stand up and be true to duty, although they wanted to help, and although they knew we were innocent, they did not have a backbone any stronger than a jellyfish. They would help a little bit, but not enough to make themselves unpopular, not enough to take the hard line that was needed, not enough to turn around and say, 'I know the Chamberlains were set up; I know a dingo was responsible; I know that the Chamberlains were verballed.' There was too much at stake.

We knew of deals being done and could do nothing about it. Some scientists rang up our lawyers saying, they could do with the publicity the case engendered. 'Just tell us what you want us to say and we're quite happy to say it, whatever you want.' They didn't care whether the evidence was there or not! They couldn't understand when we said, 'No, thank you, we want a true, honest scientist with a backbone, who will say the information, whether it is for *or* against us. We want the *truth*.'

One day a strange man approached one of our lawyers and me just as we were walking in the door ready for court. I went on ahead and court started. My lawyer was only away a few minutes then came and went straight across to the Commission bar table. They listened intently then got straight up and went out, while our lawyer came and sat down. When I asked who it was I was told it was a Mr Perron, who was offering some vital information regarding dingo attacks on children.

Rather than have this information come from the defence it was better to come through the neutral Commission lawyers. Mr Perron was called to the box that day and gave evidence that while surveying in the top of north-western Australia, some Aborigines had asked him to help them shoot a dingo they had been tracking and chasing with spears. It had killed an Aboriginal baby. He was shown what remained of the baby's body, then had done as they requested. The dingo still had blood and tissue from the baby around its mouth when he shot it.

When asked why this had not been reported anywhere, he gave the stock answer that Aboriginal deaths did not have to be reported at that stage. He said his family all knew the story. This interested me. He was the father of Marshall Perron, the Northern Territory politician who was Attorney-General when I was released and later Chief Minister. Hard to forget that.

Nearly six and a half years after Azaria was taken I heard from my hospital acquaintance again (the one whose daughter was born sixteen minutes after Azaria). In her letter she stated that not only was her husband a policeman, but she had been a policewoman on maternity leave when we met. She had vigorously gone to my aid against the tide of opinion and the many rumours then running publicly and in the police station. In the end, the situation had got the better of her and, although she didn't believe them and *wanted* to see me, she was glad to use our transfer as an excuse to come and talk to me, and to study me silently with her little girl there. (On a visit just before we left Mt Isa.)

She apologised for studying me with the analytical impressions gained from her police training, but went away believing more firmly than ever that the rumours that said I had rejected Azaria and not treated her well in hospital because I was very unhappy to have a baby daughter were merely trumped up. My acquaintance offered letters in the form of statements from a qualified person as to my state of mind at the time which could be tendered at the Royal Commission. She was totally convinced I was innocent, and offered to give evidence to the Royal Commission also if we wanted her to, but the Commission was happy to accept her tendered letter. Her mother, who had also met me in hospital at the time, wrote a backing letter, and this was tendered also.

Childhood Memories

It was decided by Chester Porter that both Aidan and Reagan must be interviewed for the Commission. The lawyers weren't sure how much they would remember because they had been nearly seven and only four and a half at the time. Now they were thirteen and eleven and a half. We, of course, knew that if Aidan *would* talk, there was quite a bit he could remember.

In order to make the experience as painless as possible for the boys, it was arranged to go to the house of John Davis, the Commission solicitor, and meet Chester Porter there. Stuart picked the boys and me up and transported us to the address he had. When we got there, Chester Porter was already there and John's wife ushered us in to the family room to wait. The lawyers came out, said hello, and decided Reagan should go first. I was to wait with Aidan.

Reagan went in. As he waited, Aidan grew more and more uptight. He didn't want to go at all; then thought he should have gone first; then if they didn't come very shortly, he would go home. *He* wasn't there to be kept hanging around by *them*. It was no time to tell him to sit down and be quiet; he couldn't, he was too nervous. He walked round and round the dining-room table where we were waiting. About 45 minutes later Reagan came out, quite happily, and then Aidan was called in. He suddenly became very quiet when the door opened, then got up and went in. Reagan and I could relax, and very shortly Reagan saw the children of the household go past the door and wandered out to follow them. Soon the kids were involved in games, while I spent some time talking to John's wife, who brought us all a drink.

It seemed ages before Aidan came out. When he did, he had obviously been crying. Porter came out as well, thanked us and said he had appreciated being able to talk to the boys, then we left. This was one of the very few times when I actually spoke to Mr Porter direct. Although this was a Commission, not a trial, the accused do not mix readily with witnesses or with legal teams of the opposing or arbitrating party, even socially. It is not considered correct to say any more than 'good morning' or 'good afternoon' in passing and basically only if you are being looked at or spoken to directly. The rest of the time you pretend they don't exist and they do the same to you.

As we left, Aidan said to me, 'I thought you said he was going to be nice, he was awful,' and stomped off ahead. I raised my eyebrows at Stuart, who said, 'Porter was pretty tough on him. He made the unfortunate mistake of asking him whether he saw any blood straight off and he just cracked up and that was the end of that. He cried almost all of the way through, which I think exasperated Chester a bit, but he did answer the questions. Now Chester knows what Aidan can cope with. He answered all his questions directly and Chester will put him in the box, he knows what he can take. Reagan was a little brick, I was very proud of him. He told his story very succinctly and well, but unfortunately there is not a lot he can add, seeing he was sleeping most of the time. It is very difficult to ascertain whether the dingo walking over him was in his memory at the time or whether people have suggested it to him since.'

We tried to find the corroborative adult witness who he had told about being walked on. (It was one of his babysitters, but which one?) We found her in America after the close of the Commission, unaware that we did not know it was her.

Stuart also said Chester Porter had been impressed with the way both children gave their evidence. It had been patently obvious to anyone that neither of the boys had been coached or schooled in what they were to say, as the Crown had tried to imply.

For a long while afterwards Aidan maintained his refusal to give evidence at the Commission. He didn't care what *anyone* said.

I said to him, 'Sweetheart, it would really help Mummy and Daddy if you would, because you were there with me that night and they know you were there. If you refuse to give evidence it looks as if you are trying to hide something or that Mummy and Daddy are hiding something, and we are scared that you will say something that will tell them Mummy is guilty.'

'Huh!' he snorted, 'I'm not going. I tell you, I'm *not* going!'

Finally, when it came to it, right at the last minute, I said, 'Honey, you have got to go and that's it. I'm sorry if I've got to drag you there, but the Commission has said you have to go. Just make up your mind to it.' He became quieter. The weekend before he was to go he again said, 'I am not going, I tell you, I'm not going!'

'Honey, we've been over this. I don't want to do it again.'

'What's the point of me going in the box? They won't take any notice of you. Why would they listen to a kid? They will just say I'm lying, too. They won't take notice of any of the witnesses, and I'm only a kid.'

'Honey, that might be true, but you have got a good judge here . . .'

'Yeah, you said that about Porter. That he would be nice.'

'He had to know how much you could take in the box if Barker was nasty to you. He didn't want to put you through something you couldn't take, and he is the only man who can say you are OK because he has seen you.'

'Huh!'

Aidan was uptight all weekend, and finally when the time came for him to go in the box he got dressed without complaint in clothes of his choice. Reagan told him he looked good and that seemed to buoy him up a bit. True, he grumped at his brother, 'What would you know!' but when Reagan had gone out of the room he said, 'Suppose it's all right.' High praise for him.

It had been decided that Helena would be there so she could grab the boys and take them away as soon as possible afterwards. Despite the fact that she was a wild child herself, she could be calm and controlled when she had to. The boys liked her a lot because she had enough authority to pull them into line when necessary, but was enough of a kid to indulge in pranks and games and be lots of fun. Having laid huge guys out cold at times, she was also a reasonable bodyguard, even though she didn't look it. She sat in the gallery with Reagan and even managed to hold her tongue while Aidan was in the witness box.

Something seemed to be bothering Aidan, but I couldn't figure out what. He went with Stuart and eventually was called as a witness. He came in, very quiet and subdued after all his threats about what he was going to say and do in the box. He sat very quietly with his head down, and spoke softly while the judge and Porter quietly led him through their questions. He gave very brief answers and was obviously very upset. At the end of the time, the judge asked him one or two more questions and then, when Barker said, 'No questions', excused him. Our men didn't ask him anything either; they let him go in order not to compound the agony for him any more.

Despite the fact that he was upset, Aidan never quite broke down in court. Michael and I were very proud of him. We weren't sure how he was going to handle it and obviously a parent is nervous when a child is about to be put through a trauma.

Aidan went out, and when the break came he said, 'Well, when am I coming back in?'

I said, 'What do you mean?'

He said, 'When do I get a chance to have a go at Barker?' I said, 'Honey, you've had your chance. That's it.'

'No, I haven't! He never asked me any questions.'

'No, he's not going to ask you any questions.'

'Well, I want to tell him something, then.' I said, 'Honey, you can't. You've finished.'

'I can. I'm going back in.'

I said, 'Sweetheart, that's it. It's finished.'

'No, I'm going back in. I wanna tell him something.' Stuart came out then and said to me, 'What's the matter?'

I said, 'He wants to go back in and tell Barker something. He obviously wants to tell him what he thinks of him.'

Stuart said, 'Aidan, the judge asked you, was there any more you had to say, and you said no. It's finished.'

At that Aidan exclaimed, 'Aagh!' and went off mumbling to himself, absolutely furious.

I said to Helena, 'You had better chase him and see if you can take him up the Centrepoint Tower or something—anything to take his mind off it—and get him some lunch.'

Aidan came back that evening to where we were staying and stayed one more night with us before he, Reagan and Helena went back home. Helena said it had taken a while to get his mind off the court. I suspect that she might have taken them down to an arcade somewhere and let them have a go at the video machines to vent his wrath.

He never did tell me what he was going to say to Barker but it would have been interesting, as it looked as if he was going to tell him what he thought of him at long last! It would probably have helped if he had got rid of some of his pent-up anger, which instead, has had to simmer and very slowly die. I doubt Aidan's anger will ever quite go; certainly, our receiving compensation will help. For a couple of years after the Commission, all he ever said was, 'Well, when are they going to pay us compensation? They did it, they ought to pay!' And so they should.

Now, in longer stretches, I recognise 'my' children, but at times when I first came home I felt I was looking at total strangers, partly because of circumstances, partly because I hadn't been there in crucial stages of development. They were in one way the same children, and in another way they did things I found completely unacceptable. This has, fortunately for us all, improved greatly in the last four years. But it seems inevitable that while this rolling trauma continues, there will never be complete recovery for the Chamberlain family.

ADDRESSING THE MATTER

By the time the Commission had finished hearing evidence, the whole Crown case had vanished like thistledown in a breath of wind. The spray of 'arterial blood' turned out to be sound deadener, the 'blood' down the seat hinge and console (which was made to sound like buckets, but was simply 5 millilitres or one teaspoonful) was protein—probably caramel or chocolate milk shake, not blood at all. The camera bag had not been 'washed', but was simply worn and had copper dust in it, not foetal haemoglobin at all. The bloodstained handprints on Azaria's jumpsuit weren't even handprints and the 'blood' was only desert dust. There were dog hairs on the jumpsuit; paw prints on the space blanket; Azaria's blood on the mattress, the boys' jackets, our sleeping bags and Azaria's blankets (many times the amount of supposed 'blood' in the car, and correctly identified as Azaria's); and a great deal of evidence about dingo behaviour; as well as tracks in and out of the tent, on the sandhill with Azaria, *and* around the clothes.

Jack Winneke's address attacked the Crown case pretty thoroughly. The opinion evidence, he said, had been fundamentally wrong:

> The Chamberlains were the victims of it and have suffered a gross miscarriage of justice on account of it. Not only have they suffered the injury occasioned by the tragic loss of their daughter in circumstances entirely beyond their control, but they have suffered the insult of the convictions, the direct consequences which followed, and the ignominy thrust upon them by a lusting and disbelieving community.
>
> It is not, we submit, a murder case. It is rather a chameleon and a nightmare for the people charged.

He stressed that the significance of witnesses' evidence had always been obvious to the police and the Crown in the Northern Territory.

> And that is why, no doubt, they tried so very hard to break Mrs Lowe down, to use their own words, to such an extent that she and her husband went to a solicitor to see what rights she had as a witness. But having failed to break her down, it is now asserted that she is an unreliable witness. Another explanation might just be that the Northern Territory authorities, and particularly the police, are so obsessed with their belief of the Chamberlains' guilt that they have become quite unprepared to accept with an open mind any material that suggests to the contrary.

When he turned to the scientific evidence, he was very definite indeed:

> We submit to Your Honour that in the long run you should not hesitate to find that Professor Cameron's highly prejudiced opinion as to the

existence on this jumpsuit of handprints in blood is not only incorrect as a question of fact, but was uttered with carelessness and with the knowledge that it was likely to cause mischief back in Australia, and it did. This Commission should find, we submit, that Professor Cameron's opinion as to the cause of death is little more than speculation based on very tenuous support and expertise . . .

We submit that you should find that Mrs Kuhl was demonstrably wrong about the existence of foetal blood under the dashboard, and on the scissors, and on the camera bag, and on the chamois, and on the towel, and further, that the whole of her approach to her task was infected by lack of understanding of the task which she had at hand. Accordingly, we submit that you should find that the very damaging and prejudicial allegations made against the Chamberlains on the basis of her evidence really had no evidential foundation at all . . .

Insofar as Mrs Kuhl's evidence was used as a basis for suggesting that the Chamberlain car was awash with blood, and foetal blood at that, we submit that it was just plain wrong. The evidence before this Commission strongly supports the view, we contend, that whatever it was that Mrs Kuhl was dealing with in this car, it was not Azaria's blood, and indeed there is a very strong reason for suggesting that she was not dealing with blood at all, and that if she did find any blood in that car it was in minimal quantities and far more recent than it would have to have been if it was Azaria's blood . . .

The Commission now knows that the opinion, expressed at the trial, of the hairs found on Azaria's clothing as probably cat hairs was quite wrong; they were dog hairs. It also knows that there was no evidential basis for making the very damaging allegations that fibres found in the car and the camera bag came from the baby's jumpsuit after it had been cut, or that the hairs found in the camera bag may have come from Azaria. This Commission now knows, we submit, that the evidence given by Professor Chaikin to the effect that the jumpsuit had been cut by sharp scissors and not by a dog, and referred to by the Crown as unassailed and unassailable, is now very much assailed and, on his own concession, very much assailable . . .

In short, we submit that this Commission has a very graphic demonstration of the shortcomings of the expert opinion evidence relied upon so heavily by the Crown to convict the Chamberlains, and the net result of the evidence before this Commission is that the Crown, we submit, can no longer prove a cause of death, a scene of death, or an interference with the clothing by the Chamberlains.

. . . As this Commission now knows, dogs and dingoes can cut fabric, and very effectively cut it, with the carnassial teeth, and in doing so will produce tufts, will cut without disturbing the base fabric by way of distortion, and will produce fibre ends coming together in a plane. It is a

> regrettable fact, we submit, that none of this was realised by the experts who gave evidence for the Crown at the trial . . .
>
> One gets the impression that so many excuses or possible explanations or hypotheses have been put forward by the Crown that it has almost become an act of desperation to try and find some excuse for Mrs Kuhl, when in truth the real answer is that inexperience, incompetence, unreliability and prejudice have combined to produce results that were never there to be found in the first place.

When he had finished dealing with the scientific evidence, Jack Winneke summed up:

> We submit to Your Honour that in the circumstances of this case, once the opinion evidence has been swept away, you are left with the full glare of what we submit is reliable and independent eyewitness testimony that leads the reasonable mind to the conclusion that the Chamberlains could have had nothing whatever to do with the disappearance of their daughter, Azaria, whom they both loved and adored very much indeed, and that having regard to the totality of the material before Your Honour, Your Honour ought to come to the conclusion that they should be entirely exonerated.

It was an honest speech and Jack delivered it brilliantly. Ian Barker, when he rose to reply, of course, claimed that none of it was true.

> It is a waste of words to challenge the Crown to face up to what the Chamberlains' advisers see as impediments in the way of a finding adverse to their clients. They were, Your Honour, faced up to at the trial. No body, no motive, the cry, Aidan, the time element, the difficulty in washing the blood off her clothes, the problem of the disposal of the body, her demeanour, the disposal of the clothes—all these problems had to be confronted and set aside by the jury. They were no less real than they are now, and if they presented as immovable objects in the way of the Crown case, however irresistible, then the jury would have acquitted. But they did not.
>
> There is evidence before this Commission which, it is suggested, proves murder. In a separate submission, we contend that there is proof before Your Honour that the child bled in the car. If that be accepted, it is likely that she died in the car. Beyond that, we cannot make a submission which would enable the Commission to make a positive finding as to just how and when and where the child was killed. We cannot do so because the evidence is inadequate for the purpose and, with respect, we should not be challenged to do so.
>
> The Crown's position is that all the facts are not known and never will be known because the whole repository of all the facts is Mrs Chamberlain and she will not disclose what happened. We can, however, make submissions as to the likely cause of death . . .

Barker then attacked our credibility:

> Wherever you go in this case looking for things Mrs Chamberlain said about the events, it is very hard to find a consistent pattern. It is not the case, as Mr Winneke asserted, that there is a significant consistency in it all. Sure, the basic fact is consistent, that a dingo took the baby. But when you look for the details of how and why it happened, and what she really saw, it is like trying to put your finger on quicksilver; and when you examine it all, in the end it is impossible to know whether she is really saying she saw the dingo coming out of the tent from some distance back and yelled, 'The dingo's got the baby,' in other words she knew at that stage; or when she got to the door of the tent; or when she got into the tent and looked in the basket; or when she was leaving the tent. And what it is she thought she saw or thought was happening is submerged in this mass of conflicting stories which are not simply inconsistencies, but amount to irreconcilable accounts of what happened.
>
> The Chamberlains we submit were peculiarly and, indeed, startlingly inactive on the night she disappeared and thereafter. Their inactivity is explained by their sure knowledge the child was dead and would not be found. It is for this reason that so much was subsequently said about how quickly the baby would have been dead. In this regard, it is convenient to consider the evidence of both Mr and Mrs Chamberlain. At the very least, much of what was said publicly was wild exaggeration, and it is difficult to conceive of a grieving parent in the circumstances being moved to wildly exaggerate matters surrounding the child's death unless prompted to do so by self-interest and the consciousness of guilt.

Justice Morling interrupted to ask Barker how significant was the Crown's inability to establish any motive for my killing Azaria. Barker even skated over that, saying that he couldn't assign a reason, and the Crown had never tried to do so. If the Commission considered the improbability of a dingo being involved, and realised that I was the last person to see Azaria alive;

> then Your Honour may well come to the view that the question of motive is not of such importance, but is a matter of balancing one proved fact against another.

What facts? I thought.

Ian Barker said Jack Winneke's attack on the Northern Territory police was:

> carping and querulous and part of a rummage amongst the minutiae of the investigation to see what might be found which could possibly discredit the police. It serves only to confuse the issues arising from evidence obtained in the course of proper investigation.

He then came to the main thrust of the Crown case:

> Then, Your Honour, we come to the submission which is at the heart of the case, and that is what is the evidence as to the probability or improbability

of Azaria being taken from the tent by a dingo and Azaria's clothes being removed from her body by a dingo?

He said that the whole hypothesis was intrinsically improbable. Here we were again—his comments were a variation on the old statement we'd heard so often that 'dingoes don't do that sort of thing'.

Then Michael Adams took over the summary to defend Joy Kuhl's reputation:

> My submission is that she was competent. Dr Baxter, who had no love for her [they had argued and blamed each other in the witness box], believed that she was a competent forensic biologist. She had some years of experience; she knew what a result was . . . the techniques that she used were said by Mr Martin to be precisely the techniques he would have used. Dr Scott said it was not unreasonable for her to act in that way, although he would have liked to have seen adult controls on every plate. It is true that when she appeared in court her evidence was in some respect confused but in relation to the fundamental matter which is: did she see what she said she saw . . . they are reliable results . . .

Barker then came back into the fray, outlining the main features of the Crown case:

> Why there was no blood in the carry-basket; why there was no more blood in the tent; why there was no sign of active bleeding in the tent; why there was not massive spurting or splatters when the child was shaken as she must have been if Mrs Chamberlain is telling the truth, at the entrance to the tent; why there was no blood immediately outside the tent; why there was no blood in the tracks which are said to be the tracks of the animal; why there was no blood in the area of the depression, so called, where it is said the child might have been put down.
>
> It is really, with respect, impossible to imagine that all that could have taken place with the only blood being the small quantity we have been told about in the tent which stopped at the entrance to the tent and that fact, I respectfully submit, stands squarely in the way of the proposition that all this happened as the Chamberlains would have Your Honour believe. In our submission, the story is nonsense and it is a powerful reason for Your Honour finding that on this evidence there was a murder, and if there was a murder it could only have been at the hands of the child's mother.

Jack Winneke had very quietly sabotaged all that, simply by stating what Michael and I were supposed to have done on the night of 17 August:

> The case predicates that the Chamberlains were in some way able to separate the clothes from the body of the child and thereafter dispose of that body. It predicates that they, or one or other of them, sat down in the early hours of the morning with an armoury of equipment, be it scissors, tweezers, knives, sharp, pointed instruments or any other variety of weapon, for the purposes of inflicting a variety of damage to the jumpsuit,

> singlet and nappy . . . they were able to inflict damage which parallels . . . known dog damage.
>
> It postulates that they then jogged three kilometres in the dark, found a dingo den that even Roff and Cawood did not know existed, that they flattened the vegetation in a manner consistent with the way it would look if a dog had lain there and managed to do it in a way as to ensure that it was still seen a week later [without leaving our own footprints], and on the way in they dropped off the matinee jacket . . . in the course of doing this or at some other time, they rubbed the clothes so heavily in soil so as to thoroughly impregnate the garment and collect a teaspoon of soil inside it, but making sure that they got that soil from different locations.
>
> Having completed this rather remarkable exercise, they then stood back, as if in some form of benediction, and sprinkled the torn shreds of the nappy over the remainder of the crumpled heap and, as if to put icing on the cake, threw in a few dog hairs for good measure.

It was with considerable understatement that Jack said that all of this 'would not hold water'!

When we knew we were leaving Darwin and would not be seeing much more of the team, we decided to buy our guys goodbye presents. We went to Casey's Corner, a shop with the best selection of shirts in Darwin, and raided their stock. We managed to find a particularly lurid one for David, which he was absolutely rapt in. Brind was fairly easy, he had a good build and he liked trendy clothes, so we picked a great style in bright turquoise. It was a colour he had never worn before, but it suited him. Ken was a cinch, he loved red. Jack was a little harder but having heard him say he needed another casual white short-sleeved shirt, we finally found a nice style in his size.

Stuart was a problem. He was fussy and it took as long to find his shirt as all the others put together. We really didn't have a style that stood out as being 'him'. Finally we settled on one and gave it to him, though as a drop shoulder, loose style, we knew it was not what he was used to. They all put them on for a photo, but Stuart said very little, and I later said to him, 'I'm sure you hate that shirt.' He demurred, but when I insisted he admitted that he thought it was too big. I took him back to the shop to show him a number of others. Jennifer, a friend of ours, was the shop assistant, and we did our best to encourage Stuart into something slightly trendy but he was bent on picking conservative shirts.

I showed him one shirt I loved—it had a striped shoulder decoration—but he rejected it because he said it was 'too modern'. He finally picked one he liked, bought some other clothes and a new pair of jeans. Then we started searching for a shirt to go with the jeans. When Jennifer and I looked at the jeans he had picked, we looked at each other and she put her finger to her lips and went and picked up the shirt with the decorated shoulders again. I nodded. She took it back to Stuart and said, 'How about this? It would go very nicely.' By this time he had gone through all the shirts in the shop and not found what he wanted, so we persuaded him to try the striped shirt on. He said he'd take that one and asked, 'Why didn't you show me that one before?'

We both burst out laughing and explained it was the one he'd rejected. Stuart looked sheepish, laughed and said, 'Well, it does look good after all.'

A couple of weeks later, Cherie said, 'I love the shirt you talked Stuart into, nice and modern. I think it's good for men to occasionally have someone else tell them the same things their wives do.'

On 19 March 1987, the Commission adjourned. The barristers went back to Sydney, Melbourne and Canberra while Chester Porter and Bill Caldwell helped Mr Justice Morling to write his report.

We went around to say goodbye to the Noonans seeing it was our last time in Darwin and Tony *was* looking tired. I remarked to him that he was looking a bit off colour and he agreed he was a bit tired. Liz said he needed a break, but no more than that. I also mentioned to Michael that Tony didn't look too good and I hoped he wasn't sickening for something. Then I promptly dismissed the thought from my mind.

We went around saying goodbye to the rest of our Darwin friends, expecting it to be a long time before we visited them again, if ever, as the finding would be in Sydney.

Then Michael and I returned to Cooranbong to wait.

During filming, Stuart and his family were invited to go and see some of the movie being made, and when they were in Melbourne, where a lot of the filming took place, they accepted the offer. They went the day they were doing outdoor scenes at Lilydale Academy—for the outdoor Avondale College scenes. As they were watching, Fred said to Stuart, 'Do you want to be in the movie? How about you and your family being the walk- through extras in this scene?' Much to Cherie's delight, they walked past in the background and waved to 'us' just after the scene where Michael is striding ahead of the family (which *he* said was for 'security' reasons) across the college campus. It was one of the pieces that did *not* end up on the cutting room floor.

Michael, Reagan and I flew to Melbourne when Meryl was to do her last shoot and had been told we could go out to the set with Pete and Marijana. It was also being filmed at Lilydale Academy. In the end, Michael got upset, and flew straight home again.

The rest of us were enjoying watching the people who had been called back to do some refilming of one of the scenes. There was no dialogue in it, so neither Meryl nor Sam were nervous about having us there.

Sam wandered in the back door of the church where we were waiting for the cameras to finish setting up. He said hello, grinned, and said, 'Do you know what scene we are doing today?' When I said no he informed me it was a close-up take of me moving Michael's hand lower when I was giving my speech in the church during my homecoming thanksgiving service 'I know why you moved Michael's hand.'

'Yes, because he was squashing me,' I answered. 'I couldn't breathe properly.'

'Oh yes,' he said, with a grin on his face.

'Well, what do you think the reason was?' I asked.

'You just watch Meryl and see,' he said.

He left then because Fred was calling him. Meryl was already waiting down the front. They took their instructions from Fred and the signal was given: 'Lights. Camera. Action.' Sam, when he put his arm around her, moved his hand to Meryl's breast and she whacked him. Because we were on the opposite side of the church we had been able to see what he had done but the view of the church 'audience' was blocked by the rostrum podium. Pete, Marijana, Reagan and I, watching to see what it was he was going to do, immediately burst out laughing, as did Sam. Fred and Meryl, who had both immediately turned to remonstrate with him, realised he was looking down the back of the church, glanced in that direction also and realised it was a set-up, then they laughed too. After that, Sam behaved and the scene was over very quickly.

They were to walk out of the church afterwards for the final scene of the film. Reagan and I were able to sit behind the big camera and watch from the camera's point of view as Meryl, Sam, the boys and Kahlia, followed by the Millers, Irene Heron, the Hughes family and all the rest of the congregation filed out of the church to meet the media. (It was a fictitious scene Fred had written for the movie.) Reagan was particularly interested because it was the first time he had seen actual filming in progress.

As Reagan was running around afterwards in a break in the filming, a little girl came up to him very excitedly and said, 'Can I have your autograph please, Trent? You're playing Reagan, aren't you?' Reagan, with a big grin on his face, said. 'No, I'm not playing Reagan, I *am* Reagan.' The little girl didn't know what to do and went away. Reagan came in chuckling away to himself, thinking it was all great fun.

I said, 'Would you like to meet the boy who is playing you?' He said yes, so I said, 'We'll see if Fred can arrange it, but it might make him nervous, and if it does, don't be disappointed if Fred says no.' But Fred agreed and told us where to find 'Aidan' (Jason Reason) and 'Reagan' (Trent Roberts). There they were, all dressed up, looking reasonably like my boys. I said hello and told them who I was; their eyes brightened and we started talking. I said to Trent Roberts, 'Did you know that Reagan is here today?'

He said, 'No!'

I said, 'Would you like to meet him seeing you are playing him?'

'Oh yes, please,' he said.

Reagan was around the corner listening, but not where he could be seen, so I beckoned him. He came around the corner and there they were, face to face. They were actually quite alike (which none of the other five boys playing Aidan and Reagan at different ages were).

They eyed one another up and down with big grins and said hello rather shyly. Then Reagan said, 'I'm glad it's you sitting there in a shirt and tie in the summer and not me. I don't like wearing those clothes to church.' The boys grinned and said that it wasn't too bad; besides, they were getting *paid* for it!

The producers had had a terrible job getting children for the film. They had to get three sets of boys to play Aidan and Reagan at various ages and had to be particularly careful of the young ones. The young Aidan had quite a bit of acting to do, and if it wasn't any good it would spoil a lot of the movie, so they had to audition boys who could act well at the age of six.

The casting director, Rhonda Schepisi, told me if I had had ugly children she would have had a much easier job, as 'very good looking boys like yours, especially being *brown*-eyed blonds as well, are impossible to find.' They found plenty of blue-eyed blonds. They even investigated eye dyes and contact lenses and all sorts of things and decided in the end they would just have to settle for blond hair with blue eyes—as long as all six pairs of eyes matched, makeup could do the rest. Our boys thought that was a joke on the filmmakers; they couldn't play themselves in the final scene because they couldn't be matched with younger children.

I was there on the day they picked the children to play our boys at four and six years old; there seemed to be hundreds of kids running around the offices. In actual fact there were only about a hundred, but they were so lively and noisy it seemed like thousands.

It interested me to find out that they had actually gone to schoolyards to look for children. They also interviewed children who, not knowing the address but having heard there was to be a film and wanting a part in it, had simply written to the 'Azaria Chamberlain film'. The letters got to the film producers in the end. The little boy who played Aidan at six years in the film got his part simply by doing that.

The scenes Reagan and I watched that day were actually Meryl's last, so we stayed and all had lunch together. Sam still had a couple of solo scenes to do, then he also had finished, so we made the most of our time together. Meryl returned my Bible just before we parted, as she was due to leave for America the following day. She'd had the Bible re-bound as a surprise and she thanked me for the encouragement and inspiration it had given her.

Not long after we got home, out of the blue we had an urgent phone call from Liz Noonan, who was quite distraught. Tony had had pains in his stomach, and during the night he had told her she'd better get a doctor, as he didn't feel too well. The doctor rushed him to hospital and they did an exploratory operation. They discovered he had cancer which had already spread, and there was nothing they could do except stitch him up again, and break the devastating news that he only had three months to live.

Tony immediately stopped work; they sold up and moved to Adelaide, where Liz's family was, so Tony could see Liz and the children settled with family support around them.

Before Tony died we travelled over there to say goodbye to him. Michael got some fish for Liz and cooked dinner for them. Tony even managed a forkful. I wanted Tony to see his flowers, not have them wither on the grave where he would have no enjoyment of them, so I raided the local florist and persuaded her to let me choose and arrange my own, then took them with us to Tony. He enjoyed that.

Tony knew exactly what cancer meant. He had patients himself with the same thing. He knew every stage of his illness. Quite calmly Tony said, 'I know what's going to happen to me, I'll choke to death. That's what happens in the end because you can't move and the lungs fill with fluid. I'm not worried, it's just a momentary thing, because just after that happens I'll be with God, and there'll be nothing wrong with me, there'll be no more pain. It's really just a little thing and I can cope with that because I know God's with me.'

Tony's Catholic faith was very strong. He taught me that there is very little difference in confirmed Christians, regardless of their so-called religious tenets, and regardless of their colour or race. Tony's beliefs, except in a few small points, were very similar to mine, and yet if you studied the churches' beliefs there were wide gulfs. But God knows the heart, and we can rest assured that if we are sincere in what we believe, as long as we do not bypass what we know to be truth, God accepts our hearts for what they are. He does not count the brand name on our back.

Tony died a few weeks later, almost three months to the day of his diagnosis, and he left an ache in all our hearts. We'd already said our goodbyes so didn't go back for the funeral.

Liz felt someone special might turn up for the funeral though, and had purposely not named all the casket bearers. On the morning of the funeral she got a call from the priest. He said he had an unshaven man there who was either very upset or drunk, but was insisting on having Liz's address. His name was Greg Lowe. Liz was overjoyed. Greg was tired, upset, unshaven and belligerently determined to get to Liz. Sally and Greg had stayed with Liz and Tony in Darwin during the Commission. They had first got to know one another when the Lowes were touring (at the invitation of the support groups) giving a series of public meetings where the eyewitnesses gave their own evidence direct to the public to try and raise public support for an inquiry. The Noonans and Lowes had become firm friends. It was like that everywhere now with this case. Losing Tony was like losing a family member. Greg had got a loan to buy his ticket, left work, and travelled all night by boat, train and plane to be at the funeral. Liz asked him to be a casket bearer, so Greg said 'goodbye' to Tony.

THE END OF AN ERA?

At the end of May, Channel 9 in Sydney reported that Mr Justice Morling had quashed our convictions. This was a 'leak' that might have stemmed from information given in the Territory. The Report was delivered to the Governor-General and the Administrator of the Northern Territory under covering letters dated 22 May. In any case, the Report was not entirely accurate.

The Report was released (and tabled in the Northern Territory Parliament) on 2 June. It ran to 380 pages. (The *Sydney Morning Herald* published an edited version of the summary and conclusions on the following day.)

Mr Justice Morling had run through the evidence in detail. He said that since I was away from the barbecue area for only five to ten minutes, there would have been very little time for me to have cleaned up the car thoroughly.

> She was under observation by others, particularly Mrs Whittaker and Mrs West, for most of the time between the raising of the alarm and her departure for the motel later in the evening . . . It therefore appears that she had little or no opportunity to clean up any blood in the car after the alarm was raised and before leaving for the motel.

He pointed out that surprisingly few people had seen any blood in the car; in fact, none. He had a bit to say about Joy Kuhl, saying that there were 'fundamental objections to the acceptance of [her] findings of baby's blood in the area of the off-side rear hinge of the passenger seat and the floor beneath . . .' Her testing methods for detecting foetal haemoglobin had acknowledged drawbacks.

> At the trial Mrs Kuhl said that she used adult and foetal controls for all these tube precipitin tests. However, they are not recorded in her work notes, there is no laboratory result book record of the tests at all, and before the Commission she said that her evidence at the trial was incorrect and there were no adult controls in these tests.

He concluded that she:

> . . . lacked the considerable experience required to enable her to plan and to carry out these complex and difficult testing procedures, at least without careful guidance from a more experienced biologist. Indeed, there appears to be doubt whether any practising forensic biologist would have been sufficiently qualified to perform these tasks without extensive consultation with leaders in immunological research.

When all things were considered, Mr Justice Morling said, 'I conclude that none of Mrs Kuhl's tests established that any such blood was Azaria's.'

He said that he would have found the evidence that Azaria had been removed from her clothing difficult to accept, if it wasn't for the conflict of expert opinion on this question.

> However, Mr Roff's evidence cannot be lightly dismissed. He is a practical man with much knowledge and experience of dingoes. He is a disinterested witness. As senior ranger at Uluru National Park, it was not in his interests to support an allegation that a dingo had taken a child from a camping area within the park for which he had general responsibility . . .

Because Derek Roff's evidence had been supported and deferred to by others he said:

> . . . in the circumstances I conclude that, although a dingo would have had difficulty in removing Azaria's body from her clothing without causing more damage to it, it was possible for it to have done so.

Justice Morling quoted Michael's statement:

> 'On or about 8. 15 or 8. 20 we all saw what we considered a rather mangy forlorn specimen of a dingo, lurking just outside the barbecue enclosure. It appeared to be looking for food. It went into the shadows and then without any warning came back into the light of the barbecue area next to the gas bottles and pounced with frightening agility on a small, I guess you'd call it a field mouse, which we had sighted a few minutes earlier. This had been seen by the Tasmanian people as well as ourselves. My wife who had been nursing bubby then took her to the tent to lay her down to rest. I prepared some food for her while she was putting bubby down as she had not eaten much prior to this. She returned to have something to eat and as she was eating I think I thought I heard a faint cry from the tent. I think my words were, "Is that Azaria crying?" My wife said she would check it out and as she was proceeding back and into the tent her voice startled me when she cried out in horror, "The dingos *[sic]* got my baby." I was stunned and raced with the other man [Greg Lowe] madly towards and into the tent to see if this was so. That is, if the baby was missing. The sequence of events following this for some minutes is a little unclear. I was in a severe state of trauma. I felt useless. I raced for my torch, I think, and it would not go. I think that I ran into the bush madly hoping that in the darkness I might see either the dog or Azaria. I remember feeling very angry and frustrated because normally I pride myself with having very effective lighting and also, because my keys were not in my pocket, I could not switch the ignition of my car on in order to use the 100 watt searchlight that was in my glove box. My Tasmanian friend who had somewhere got hold of a torch had raced out into the bush in front of me and searched feverishly. I cannot remember much at the time for a few moments except that I came back to the tent in the hope that our eyes were playing tricks

on us. In other words that the dog might have left Azaria somewhere in an unlit corner under a rug, or bag, perhaps. But not so. The moment of truth that she really was gone hit me and realising now that I could do nothing alone cried out, I'm not sure if it was in my conscience or out aloud, "Oh God help me" (it was probably a silent cry) and raced along the southerly section of the road to elert *[sic]* any other campers that I could to see if they had a torch and could get out and start searching.'

Justice Morling went on to say:

> There is much in the evidence to justify a conclusion that Mr Chamberlain has a tendency to *describe events in theatrical language.* I think he also enjoys having an audience. These characteristics (which are exemplified in some of the language used in his statement I have quoted above) may account for some of the embellishments and exaggerations in his evidence. It is these exaggerations and embellishments which give some of his evidence a ring of unreality. In one of his interviews with the media he said that the great quantity of blood discovered in the tent led him to conclude that Azaria's death must have been swift. This statement was patently ridiculous and could not have deceived any person who saw inside the tent. The Crown relies upon it as showing that Mr Chamberlain is a liar but I think the statement does no more than reflect *his proclivity for hyperbole.*

In Michael's defence, Justice Morling had probably overlooked the fact that, by the time he gave that interview, I had already found more blood on articles than was at first apparent on the night.

Morling accepted us as truthful witnesses, and of me he said:

> The Crown claimed that some statements made for the first time by Mrs Chamberlain in her evidence before the Commission demonstrate a willingness on her part to make untrue statements in support of her claim of innocence. For instance, she told the Commission that Azaria's singlet was one size too big for her, whereas she had not previously claimed this to be the case. Again, before the Commission she said that she thought that Azaria had been asleep for only about ten minutes before she took her back to the tent to bed her down for the night. At all times previously she had stated that the child had been asleep for one-half or three- quarters of an hour. Yet again, before the Commission she stated for the first time that Aidan accompanied her from the tent towards the car when she went to obtain extra food for him. She had previously said that he stayed in the tent. I do not think any of these matters are of great importance. If any of her more recent statements are incorrect, and they may well be, their inaccuracy could be due to frailty or confusion of memory or a desire to obtain redress for an unjust conviction.

He continued:

> With the benefit of hindsight it can be seen that some of the experts who gave evidence at the trial were over-confident of their ability to form reliable opinions on matters that lay on the outer margins of their fields of expertise. Some of their opinions were based on unreliable or inadequate data. It was not until more research work had been done after the trial that some of these opinions were found to be of doubtful validity or wrong.
>
> If Mrs Chamberlain told her husband that she had killed Azaria, it was extraordinary conduct on his part to leave his two sons, the younger of whom was aged only three years in her sole custody on 18 August.
>
> Mr and Mrs Chamberlain's conduct at Ayers Rock on 18 August was strange whether or not Azaria had been murdered. Their conduct upon their return to Mount Isa is inexplicable if she had murdered Azaria. For instance, it is almost incredible that she should have told people there was blood on her shoes if she had murdered her daughter. Further, it was bravado of a high order for Mr Chamberlain to tell the police at Cooranbong that they had taken possession of the wrong camera bag if Azaria's body had been secreted in the one which he then produced.
>
> The Crown has no direct evidence of the Chamberlains' guilt to overcome the cumulative effect of all these formidable obstacles. Even so, their guilt would be established if, in spite of so many considerations pointing to their innocence, the conclusion was reached that it had been proved beyond reasonable doubt that a dingo did *not* take the baby. In the light of all the evidence before the Commission, I am of the opinion that *such a conclusion cannot be reached.*
>
> I shall state in summary form the effect of the evidence that leads me to hold this opinion. In doing so, it will be necessary to recapitulate some of the matters to which I have already referred in order to give a complete picture of the material (save for the Chamberlains' own testimony) which is directly relevant to this part of that Crown's case. It is also necessary to keep in mind that, under ordinary circumstance, it would be highly unlikely that a dingo would enter a tent, take a baby from it, carry it several kilometres to a den and there consume the body leaving the clothing in a position similar to that in which Azaria's clothing was found. But the question of Mrs Chamberlain's guilt or innocence is to be determined on the evidence and against the background of the circumstances as they existed at Ayers Rock in August 1980. It is not to be determined on the basis of preconceptions as to the likelihood of unusual animal behaviour.
>
> Before August 1980 dingoes in the Ayers Rock area frequented the camping area. At that time there were many dingoes in the area, some eighteen to twenty-five of which were known to visit the camping area. A number of attacks were made by dingoes on children in the months preceding Azaria's disappearance. In none of these did any child suffer serious injury.

About twenty minutes before Azaria disappeared Mr Haby saw and photographed a dingo which walked towards the Chamberlains' tent. A few minutes before the alarm was raised the Wests heard a dog growl.

On the night of 17 August dog tracks were observed on the southern side of and very close to the Chamberlains' tent. The same night Mr Roff and Mr Minyintiri, both experienced trackers and familiar with dingo behaviour, saw tracks of a dog carrying a load which they believed to be Azaria. It was within the bounds of reasonable possibility that a dingo might have attacked a baby and carried it away for consumption as food. A dingo would have been capable of carrying Azaria's body to the place where the clothing was found. If a dingo had taken Azaria it is likely that, on occasions, it would have put the load down and dragged it.

Hairs, which were either dog or dingo hairs, were found in the tent and on Azaria's jumpsuit. The Chamberlains had not owned a dog for some years prior to August 1980.

The quantity and distribution of the sand found on Azaria's clothing might have been the result of it being dragged through sand. The sand could have come from many places in the Ayers Rock region. The sand and plant fragments on the clothing are consistent with Azaria's body being carried and dragged by a dingo from the tent to the place where it was found. It is unlikely that, if the clothing had been taken from the Chamberlains' car, buried, disinterred, and later placed where it was found it would have collected the quantity and variety of plant material found upon it.

It would have been very difficult for a dingo to have removed Azaria from her clothing without causing more damage than was observed on it. However, it would have been possible for it to have done so. Mr Roff, the chief ranger at Ayers Rock and a man of great experience, thought that the arrangement of the clothing when discovered was consistent with dingo activity. Other dingo experts disagreed. I think it is likely that a dingo would have left the clothing more scattered, but it might not have done so.

The blood found in the tent was at least as consistent with dingo involvement in Azaria's disappearance as it was with her murder in the car. The pattern of blood staining on the clothing does not establish that the child's throat was cut with a blade.

The absence of saliva on Azaria's jumpsuit which was not conclusively proved at the trial is made more explicable by the finding of the matinee jacket which would have partially covered it. The fact that no debris from the baby's body was found on the jumpsuit is also made more explicable by the finding of the jacket. There is a great conflict of expert opinion as to whether the damage to the clothing could have been caused by a dingo. It has *not* been shown beyond reasonable doubt that it could not have been. There were marks on plastic fragments of the nappy similar to marks made by a dingo on another nappy used for testing purposes.

However, there was no blood on the nappy.

There was a dingo's den about 30 metres (32 yards) from the place where the clothing was found. There is no evidence that the existence of the den was known to the Chamberlains or, for that matter, to anybody else and in fact it was unknown to the chief ranger and his deputy.

It is impossible in the above summary to capture the whole effect of the voluminous evidence given on the matters which bear upon the dingo hypothesis but, taken in its entirety, it *falls far short of proving that Azaria was not taken by a dingo. Indeed, the evidence affords considerable support for the view that a dingo may have taken her.* To examine the evidence to see whether it had been proved that a dingo took Azaria would be to make the fundamental error of reverting the onus of proof and requiring Mrs Chamberlain to prove her innocence.

I am far from being persuaded that Mrs Chamberlain's account of having seen a dingo near the tent was false or that Mr Chamberlain falsely denied that he knew his wife had murdered his daughter. That is not to say that I accept that all their evidence is accurate. Some of it is plainly not, since parts of it are inconsistent with other parts. But if a dingo took her child, the events of the night of 17 August must have been emotionally devastating to Mrs Chamberlain. Her ability to give a reliable account of the tragedy may have been badly affected by her distress. The inconsistencies in her evidence may have been caused by her confusion of mind. Where her evidence conflicts with the Lowes' account of what she said and did in the few seconds after she commenced to run back to the tent, it may be the Lowes' recollection, not hers, that is at fault. The belief that people might unjustly accuse her of making up the dingo story might have led her, even subconsciously, to embellish her account of what happened, and this may explain some of its improbabilities. Her failure to see Azaria in the dingo's mouth is explicable if, as is quite possible, there were two dingoes, not one. These considerations afford at least as convincing an explanation for the apparently unsatisfactory parts of her evidence as does the Crown's claim that she was lying to conceal her part in the alleged murder. Having seen Mr and Mrs Chamberlain in the witness box, I am not convinced that either of them was lying.

In reaching the conclusion that there is a reasonable doubt as to the Chamberlains' guilt I have found it unnecessary to consider the possibility of human intervention (other than by the Chamberlains) in the time between Azaria's disappearance and the finding of her clothes. It is difficult, but not impossible, to imagine circumstances in which such intervention could have occurred. It is not inconceivable that an owner of a domestic dog intervened to cover- up its involvement in the tragedy or that some tourist, acting irrationally, interfered with the clothes before they were later discovered by others. There is not the slightest evidence to support either of these hypotheses but the possibility of human intervention is

> another factor which must be taken into account in considering whether the evidence establishes the Chamberlains' guilt beyond reasonable doubt. It was so recognised in some of the judgments given on the appeal to the High Court.

Finally, Mr Justice Morling said:

> It follows from what I have written that there are serious doubts and questions as to the Chamberlains' guilt and as to the evidence in the trial leading to their convictions. In my opinion, if the evidence before the Commission had been given at the trial, the trial judge would have been obliged to direct the jury to acquit the Chamberlains on the ground that the evidence could not justify their convictions. (Italics mine)

When the Morling Report was tabled in the Northern Territory Legislative Assembly, it was also tabled by the Federal government in the House of Representatives. (Lionel Bowen went back to his original view, saying that, in principle, the matter was one for the Northern Territory government to decide; this despite the fact that a Federal judge had presided over the Commission.)

Darryl Manzie, the Northern Territory Attorney-General (they seem to change them around fairly rapidly up there), said when tabling the Report:

> Mr Speaker, the Commission's Report will not satisfy everyone . . . it makes no declaration of innocence, but points rather to doubts and problems in the way of proving guilt. The Report stops a long way from saying that a dingo took Azaria . . . [it simply] says that the contrary has not been proved.

Well, it seemed they thought that to be some sort of vindication for the Northern Territory. As long as a dingo wasn't accused, that seemed OK with them.

Shortly afterwards, Manzie issued a press release. This is what he said: The Attorney-General, Mr Darryl Manzie, today announced that the Northern Territory Government had pardoned Lindy and Michael Chamberlain. Mr Manzie made the announcement in the Legislative Assembly this morning when tabling the [Morling] Report . . . He said the Northern Territory Government had accordingly moved to have the Chamberlains pardoned as soon as possible.

Meanwhile we could have gone to court, but we saw no point in laying ourselves open to the press watching our every reaction. We knew the press were allowed to have the finding beforehand so that they could sit and read it at their leisure in a locked room. As soon as it had been delivered, they would be let out to give their version to the public. We didn't have it; we still didn't get court material relevant to our case first-hand. We didn't want to hear the result via the radio or through some reporter. Nor did we want to be in the public eye. So we stayed in the nearby Sydney Boulevard Hotel; we were not actually at court but close enough.

We had agreed to do one interview and therefore save ourselves the humbug of the press calling. As soon as they knew we were contracted to one interview, the others would leave us alone; that particular television channel would keep the others at bay as well. A hotel room had been hired for the interview. There we were to await news of the finding from Stuart. Michael's cousin, Neroli Zaska, came over to keep us company, answer the door and the telephone.

We ordered tomato juice, soft eggs and toast for breakfast while we waited. After a long time we got Bloody Marys, hard fried eggs, bacon and toast. We returned it and the management apologised profusely. After another long wait we finally got tomato juice, raw eggs and burnt toast! By that time we had lost our appetites completely! It was time for the finding to be handed down anyway.

We heard a knock on the door and were told it was Terry Willesee and his crew. That meant the news was out already. At the same time Harry Miller entered the bedroom of the suite where we were to do the interview, and the phone rang. Harry answered it, and said Stuart was on the line. He had rung immediately from the court to let us know what had happened. We listened on the phone's loudspeaker as Stuart told us we had won at last and Morling had exonerated us. We were overjoyed. Then came the bombshell: 'The Northern Territory has announced they have given you a pardon.' It hit me like a bucket of ice water in the face. Michael was so excited—we were exonerated! At last, our names were cleared. We were exonerated! The meaning of the Territory's decision hadn't sunk in.

I said, 'Michael, don't you understand?'

All he said was, 'Aren't you listening girl? We are exonerated!' Nothing was going to calm him down at that moment, and why should I spoil it for him? It would sink in soon enough.

Harry looked at me and then at Michael.

I said, 'I suppose we have got to do this interview.'

I was not feeling the least bit elated. I excused myself, saying that I was going to freshen my makeup before I went in to face Terry Willesee and his crew. I really went to get myself together. Harry looked at me but said nothing and as I stood in the bathroom, fighting tears in an agony of spirit, he came to the door. I grabbed my hairbrush to pretend I was about to do my hair and Harry put out his hand and grabbed me round the wrist and held it in a vice-like grip.

Harry said, 'I know, young lady, I know what you are thinking. But you can do it. You can hold your head up high and go out there. You and I know the difference of what that means. You have got the guts, little lady, go out there and tell them what you think. You have something to say. Now's the time to do it while everyone will listen. Let them know what you think of them. You can do it.'

As I looked into his eyes, I knew Harry did understand. He was the only one in the room that day who knew just how much my sentence had hurt and how much clearing our names meant to me. Only the innocent who have been there can know just how much I hurt.

The Northern Territory slapped us in the face straight after the Commission had not pardoned, but *totally cleared us*. Now they took it away. Giving us a pardon was *not* in any sense an attempt to make amends. It is just a way of saying, 'Well, you've been a good little girl, so we will forgive you and will ignore the rest of your sentence, and this is a reward for being good.' I wasn't going to accept that. I had done *nothing* and I would not accept a pardon for something I was *not* guilty of. I knew Harry understood the difference.

I took courage. In the interview, I made it clear what an insult I thought the pardon was. It was really little different to being out on licence as I already was. Michael had *finished* his sentence and bond and they gave him a pardon after that! What for? Once again we announced that we would be seeking our names to be cleared. The difference between exoneration and pardon was pointed out to the Northern Territory, but they wouldn't change their minds. They would simply change their rule—and pass another law through Parliament; another precedent to allow us to go back to court again to clear our names—officially and legally.

The Shout of Innocence

Once again we were in no man's land, waiting for another court case. Meanwhile life had to go on. The boys settled into routine again and I was able to catch up on back filing and housework. Then Fred Schepisi rang to ask us if we could come to Sydney for a preview of the film. Robert Caswell and his friend, Liz, would be there and we asked if Stuart and Cherie Tipple could be there as well.

We travelled to Sydney with Stuart and Cherie, meeting Fred and the others at the Sydney studio for the viewing. Fred was obviously a bit nervous about what our reaction would be (after all, we could sue them if there was anything contrary to the evidence or that misrepresented it).

The six of us sat down in a row while Fred stayed at the back with the projectionist. When the movie started to roll I was really disappointed in the music. For much of it the characters could have been sunbaking on a tropical beach for all the relevance it had. Fred had said they didn't want the music to be too dramatic in case it took away from the drama of the story. Having lived through it I don't think anything could, so I don't know why he was worried. There is still no doubt in my mind that the 'Lindy' song I was sent in prison would have been better. Most of the movie lived up to my expectations and did not bring any surprises, although a lot of it was so realistic it was rather hard to take.

When the scene of the incident about Michael's evidence with Andy telling him he was 'a bloody bad witness' during the second inquest came on, Stuart had obviously forgotten it and I had forgotten it was in the movie. That scene was so accurate and brought back so many memories, Stuart and I immediately burst out laughing. Michael was very quiet. Afterwards he commented, 'I didn't know you two had set it up like that until then', which made us feel quite guilty as we realised he hadn't known anything about it.

The production staff had been most meticulous, even measuring the width of my wedding ring so they could make a proportional duplicate one for Meryl. One of the chief things about Meryl's performance was her ability as an American to try and adopt my Australian-New Zealand accent. Meryl told me later the way she learnt it was like learning a musical score. As she is a singer as well as an actress, she listened to tapes of my voice and then learned it in the way a singer learns a song. For an overseas audience, she did an excellent job, although most of my friends did not agree that it sounded like me, and were disappointed that she had not been better in her portrayal of me.

I personally thought that no other actress would have been able to do it better. I was very pleased with what she had done with the role, although both Meryl and I agree that there was not the scope in the script to portray a full-faceted personality, or anything much of the lighter side, so it did make me look harder than in reality.

One scene in the movie I have always disliked was the bedroom scene in the motel on the night of Azaria's disappearance. Although it was good acting, it did not strictly follow reality and to cap it all, when Meryl spread the sleeping bag on top of the bed, I wanted to jump up and tell her it would fall off! Sleeping bags are things you get *inside* if you are cold, with the blankets over the top.

I also disliked the ending. Fred and I had discussed this but he maintained the American public wouldn't understand if he put in Kahlia's real acceptance of me, without quite a bit of additional time (which they didn't have) spent in the previous part of the film explaining how Jenny and Jan had helped her accept the fact that her real mother had to be somewhere else and yet still loved her.

Much later, I told Fred over the phone I thought it looked funny. It was not a point of acceptance at all when Michael and the boys had to cajole Kahlia into coming to Michael and me, as written. If they *had* to do that scene, it would have been better to have had Kahlia voluntarily run after me, calling 'Mummy' and have the boys called to follow. Fred said, 'Hmm. You know, I reckon you might just be right.' But then we're all right in hindsight, and if that was the worst point of the movie, they did OK.

The movie had actually completed filming before the end of the Morling Royal Commission and they had written a coda to go after the ending. They were thrilled when the Commission turned out the way they had predicted, so held the ending until the next court case when they were able to change it slightly, and add the date and result of that finding before the final release of the movie.

Court's on Again

Life got back to normal again and soon we were due to fly to Darwin to set the parameters of the case and a date for the exoneration hearing.

When we arrived in Darwin for the meeting, we were told it would probably only take five minutes, but Michael Adams, representing the Attorney-General now instead of the Crown, disagreed. After the Commission and many months of evidence and a detailed finding, Adams stated to the three Northern Territory judges that the Commission finding was only *one of several* that could have been given, and he would like a number of weeks set aside in which to address them on the matter. He felt he was well qualified to represent both the Crown *and* the Chamberlains in this, but at *the end* of the time, if the Chamberlains were not satisfied, (which of course they would not be), they could then apply to have their own legal counsel address the court.

Jack Winneke mumbled mightily at that, and the rest of our guys' backs straightened perceptibly. After a few minutes' experience with Adams's verbosity, Judge Nader turned his back, chair and all, and gazed out of the window. Obviously Adams had not read anything about body language or he would have sat down there and then. The judges asked what was wrong with the perfectly good legal counsel the Chamberlains already had who were already familiar with the case. Adams, to me, did not seem to have an adequate explanation for that. The judges finally decided, after hearing a submission from Jack Winneke, that they would grant us leave to appear on our own behalf (this is not something that is automatic), and that, rather than spend the time in court (I'm sure from Nader's body language he would have heaved a sigh of relief over that), Adams was to prepare written submissions and we would be given time to reply in a written form also. He was given a length of time in which to write and then he stated that his program was full for a couple of months; he wouldn't be able to start until after that! Anyway, a date was set for each party to send their submission back to the judges (it would then be sent on to the opposing party). Eventually, after having already been given half the time for our submissions that the Attorney-General's Department was allowed, their submissions arrived barely on time (as we had learned to expect), and we had even less time than before for our reply. Nevertheless, ours was ready ahead of time (as usual) and handed across.

We returned to Darwin for, we hoped, the end of our legal battles. Jack Winneke had warned the judges before that he was afraid of several attempts at replies being made with no visible end in sight. Sure enough, minutes before we were to walk in the door for the finding, the Crown handed us a further submission, which was a reply to ours. We arrived just as Jack burst through the office door. He was steaming—they had done it again, as he had predicted.

We now had the choice of asking for a leave of right to reply, and therefore put off the date of the finding, or leave it unanswered and have them come back on us later (for reasons best known to themselves) saying that because we had not answered their submission, therefore we must have agreed with them, or had no answer.

Jack chose to merely stand and voice his objection, stating it was as he had feared, but because he did not want to hold the proceedings up it should go on the record that just because we had not replied, it did not mean we agreed. Jack sat down and Chief Justice Austin Asche began the finding. Justices Asche and Kearney both adopted the report of Justice Nader, but added some points of their own. Justice Nader proceeded with his finding, part of which read:

> In my opinion, upon a consideration of the adopted findings, there is a real possibility that Mrs Chamberlain did not murder Azaria and, therefore, the convictions of the Chamberlains ought to be quashed and verdicts and judgments of acquittal entered. Not to do so would be unsafe and would allow an unacceptable risk of perpetuating a miscarriage of justice.
>
> Having said so much, I would like to touch on a matter peripheral to this Reference. It may be thought that the mere acknowledgment of a doubt about the guilt of Alice Lynne Chamberlain is a half-hearted way for the matter to end. I would like to examine that sentiment for a

> moment. *It is rarely that a criminal trial positively establishes the innocence of an accused person.* If it does so, it does so by accident. The task of a criminal court is to ask and answer the question whether it is satisfied beyond reasonable doubt that the accused is *guilty* of the crime charged. If it is not so satisfied, the verdict should be one of 'not guilty': i.e., a verdict of acquittal. From the point of view of a criminal court, a verdict of 'not guilty' signifies that the jury is not satisfied beyond reasonable doubt of the guilt of the accused; it does not formally signify a positive jury finding upon the evidence that the accused is innocent. Such a positive finding is not the role of a criminal court, nor of this court. That is because under the criminal law a person is *presumed innocent* until the contrary is proved. It is not the court's function to establish innocence because, in the absence of a conviction, innocence is presumed: no finding is required. If the accused is not found guilty the presumption of innocence continues. So it is here. I have expressed the opinion that doubt exists as to the guilt of Mrs Chamberlain. I would categorise that doubt as a *grave* doubt. The doubt has arisen as a result of considering fresh evidence, in particular, the findings of the Commission. It is the existence of that doubt that demands the quashing of the convictions and the verdicts and judgments I propose. *The convictions having been wiped away, the law of the land holds the Chamberlains to be innocent.* (Italics mine)

Psalm 37: 6 in the *Living Bible* said, 'Your innocence will be clear to everyone. He will vindicate you with the blazing lights of justice shining down from the noonday sun.' And He had. God had seen us through and right had triumphed at last.

I really didn't want to let on how I felt and that was hard to describe, anyway. I guess it really hadn't sunk in yet that our names were cleared at last. The court was quiet with quite a few large smiles, but there wasn't the uproar there had been on other occasions. This time there was just the final relief that it was over for us at last (at least we thought it was).

Well, what the heck, I was going to give my guys a hug for all they'd done, regardless. People could say what they liked. I hugged Jack Winneke first. Why did they all have to be so *tall*! That set the mood and everyone started to move and talk or approach us.

I met Hannie Jones, a Dutch lady who owned a local art gallery in Darwin, one day when I walked into her shop browsing. We became friends and when our exoneration was to be announced, Hannie got someone to mind the shop and sat in court breathlessly awaiting the decision. She was really excited for us and came down to the front to congratulate us as soon as she could. After giving us a hug and telling us how thrilled she was, she returned to her business.

She had hardly been back in the gallery ten minutes when a policeman who was a regular customer came in. He exclaimed that he had not known she was a Lindy Chamberlain supporter and when she told him that she had been a friend and supporter for a number of years, he told her not to expect him to buy from her again, and he would see that word was passed around about her. Hannie was really upset at the threat!

We went back to the hotel as quickly as possible to avoid the press. Now everyone outside was celebrating and once again we were on our own with nothing to do and nowhere to go. But not for long. Within a few moments Suzie Priory (my prison 'escape' double) arrived bubbling and excited. A little later Liz Parry rang. Soon the phone and door were running hot with calls and knocks from our special friends in Darwin.

Stuart came by later, absolutely rapt at the finding. He told us it had once again created legal history because the judges had been so careful, not only to exonerate us, but to actually take care in spelling out specifically the fact that we were not only exonerated, but innocent. We had missed the implications of that when listening in the courtroom.

Soon it was time to fly home for the last time. To avoid being inundated with a rabble of press, Harry Miller organised transport and a limited number of interviews for us when we returned from Darwin. When we stepped into the arrival lounge at Sydney airport it was crawling with press and for once we were grateful for the protection of the Federal police; they took us through the initial crowds and out into a small anteroom. As we had seen our friends Lynne and Charles Lowe and their girls in the crowd, I grabbed Lynne's arm and swept her with me. When we were safely in the room we discovered Charles and one of the girls had been shut outside, so we were able to describe them and have them let in also.

We enjoyed a short and excited visit with them all, then had to be whisked away to get to the 2UE radio station for a live interview with Alan Jones.

On the way down in the escalator a cameraman jumped on in front of me at the last minute. He stood facing me with the lens of his camera less than 20 centimetres (8 inches) from my nose. I stifled the wild desire to poke my tongue out, and stood looking as indifferent as I could with *that* breathing down my neck.

When we emerged to where the car was waiting Michael discovered Harry had hired a white limo for us, and wasn't very pleased as he thought it would give people the idea that not only had we had our names cleared finally, but that we had also been granted compensation and were suddenly rich, which was far from the truth. Harry had a job explaining that it was the only vehicle that was big enough to pick everyone up at once, apart from a bus which he had no intention of hiring.

As the cameras were surrounding us, and it was the only vehicle there, Michael didn't have much choice. We climbed in. I enjoyed the ride and finally got to see television in a car. As we mainly got static and it was difficult to view, I figured it wasn't all it was cracked up to be after all.

We whirled into 2UE barely on time, and had instructions given to us hastily on the way as we walked through. Alan Jones was already on the air, and waved a greeting through the glassed partition as he spoke. In a break during the program we were ushered in. Our voice levels had already been tested and we were on before we had barely had time to say a decent hello. It was a fast and furious off-the-cuff interview, which seemed over almost before it began.

On our way home we used taxis and Harry's four-wheel-drive. I couldn't help smiling at the sudden change in status. Life was like that a lot these days. It just depended on who was organising and/or paying for it, what the latest news was, and whether we were flavour of the month for the press.

It's Party Time!

Whenever exoneration was mentioned, our friends had always declared that when it *finally* came through they were going to throw us a party. That sounded good to me. When we were finally exonerated and arrived home from Darwin, they said again, 'It's party time!' So we all joined together at a friend's place to plan a party.

Everybody was full of enthusiasm and some eager to assist. But when it boiled down to it *I* was mainly left to organise the party. It took me all my time for two weeks. Two of the *men* also helped me ring around, which I greatly appreciated. We didn't quite get through the guest list and it was cheaper in the long run to ring everybody to find out whether they were coming, because of the catering. I arranged for some locals to do the catering for the food. It was delicious and plentiful.

We only had a fortnight to get everyone together, because there was only one date when all our legal team was available.

When it came to the day before the party, the same men who had helped with the phoning appeared to help set up the tables. My brother's stepson also came around to lend a hand. He stayed working for a number of hours until I went home that night, confident that the place was completely prepared for the following evening.

My old friend Rosalie, her husband Breece and daughters came across the following day to help me organise the plates and cutlery. Apart from one other lass who arranged the flowers, that was the sum total of the local pre-party assistance I received for these preparations. By the time the six of us had decorated the tables, counted plates and cutlery and set out the chairs, the day was gone. Those preparing the appetisers began to arrive, so I left in a hurry to dress.

By the time of the party I was so exhausted I could have quite happily said, 'Right, now I will stay home and have a sleep and you can go to the party.' My eyes were just about falling out of my head.

We had asked the president, the secretary and only two or three select key members who had been particularly supportive of the major support groups. The Avondale College cafeteria held a minimum number, so by having a smorgasbord meal, we had been able to pack it with almost twice as many people as it was supposed to have.

People turned up for the victory party from Queensland, Western Australia, Tasmania, Victoria and South Australia; even as far afield as New Zealand. The only state that didn't have a representative was the Northern Territory, and that not by design. Liz Noonan, the ex-support group leader from there was present, but now she lived in South Australia.

Unfortunately, at the last minute there was a plane strike, so some of those for whom we had carefully arranged the date were unable to get there after all. Bob Collins was grounded in Canberra by the Parliamentary whip, as were all other politicians, for that weekend. Brind Woinarski had to stay behind because his wife,

Melinda, was shop steward for the airline union and had been receiving some pretty nasty threats. So, without her being able to come too, he felt he should care for and protect her rather than leave her home on her own. They had both been planning to come.

Jack and Sue Winneke had double-booked themselves, much to their disgust. Sue Priory, Footsie and others in Darwin were also stymied.

Liz and John Parry would dearly have loved to come but John was away for the weekend and Liz, believe it or not, was participating in the Centralian Masters' games. As her event was early on the day after the victory party, we figured that staying up late in the night and then flying back to Alice Springs wouldn't help. As it was, she did us proud. In her first ever competition at that level, and only her second competition in road walking, she got a bronze medal for the 10,000 metres road walk.

Sunshine had intended to travel from the other end of Australia as well, but she rang that afternoon to say she was unable to get there also. She was very disappointed. Nevertheless, we were able to put the party on video and one day we'll show it to those who couldn't come.

Sally Lowe and Michael's parents were staying with us. My parents were staying with my brother for the weekend, and a number of other party guests were staying in the boys' and girls' dorm guest rooms at college. We had arranged billets around the neighbourhood for those who wanted to stay and everything was set. Sally had come early so we could be alone together for the first time in years. She dealt with phone calls for me; and I don't know what I would have done without her.

Some of us had got together and helped pay for Sally's fare, but we didn't have enough to bring Greg across too (they had decided between them which one would come). After Sally had left, we discovered that Greg could also come up by car with some of the Melbourne support group. The only thing stopping him coming had been the cost of the trip. Like so many involved in the court case, Greg and Sally Lowe had been peripheral casualties. Greg had lost his job because of the hostility of his workmates, who knew he was involved in the Chamberlain case, and he had to transfer to another job. Then they were required to travel to different places to give evidence; they received their fares but not enough to cover their daily expenses and certainly not the babysitting fees. Sally and Greg had had to care for two babies during this time.

One tends to forget the things that witnesses have to go through simply because they have been subpoenaed to attend a court case. There is no way that witness fees cover the loss of a day's wages, plus meals. Their finances were stretched to the limit.

If anybody deserved to be at an exoneration party, the Wests, the Lowes, the Goodwins, Murray Haby, the Cranwells, certain key scientists and legal people did. Our friends and support group members wanted to meet them. We had told Greg we wouldn't give up on his coming until the last moment and he should be ready just in case. Eventually we gave him only a couple of hours' notice to catch the plane but he made it, even organising the children in that time. What we did forget was to tell him the party was formal, so he came in his jeans and nothing would persuade him to borrow some good trousers. He initially thought he would be out of place at a teetotal, vegetarian party, but he discovered a few mates and mingled happily with tinny in hand.

Some of the press who had been involved from start to finish and who had been accurate in their reporting were invited also. The evening was interspersed with speeches by a variety of guests and musical numbers.

The place was crowded. Although a good majority of the guests did not know one another, we had prepared name tags and people had a great time introducing themselves to people they had only talked to on the phone, written to, or heard and read about for a number of years.

The same applied to me. People to whom I had written for years but had no idea what they looked like, introduced themselves. There were also some people on our list whom we were unable to contact, whose addresses had been lost, or who for some reason or other, had been contacted too late and were unable to come. Nevertheless, there were some we had only been able to contact that afternoon who had managed to come. They just hopped into their cars in Sydney and drove. It was wonderful to see such a large, warm gathering of friends.

The highlight of the evening was Stuart's speech. To those who don't know him well, Stuart seems a quiet, polite and serious person. But underneath is a great sense of fun. His speech was a masterpiece. In a hilarious way he strung together the events of a nightmare. Some nightmare it had been! His speech had everyone laughing, even though a number of the guests had become involved as friends in the last couple of years and were unaware of many of the events that had taken place, and therefore the inferences made. One of the things that amused me in his 'nightmare' was when he had gone to jail, his sentence was to be 'the Chamberlains' lawyer forever, with no release!'

Although the gathering started between 7 and 7.30 p.m., the last speech was not given until 2 a.m. Many of the guests were reluctant to leave. By the time I had finished clearing the tables of food that needed to be refrigerated immediately, and the band had packed up, it was close to 4. 30 a.m. I left with the last carload and we went back to our house. Mike Lester drove me home in Graham Kennedy's Mercedes, which he had borrowed for the night. Greg and Sally, Mike, Michael and I decided we would have a hot drink. Greg and Sally then left for their bed in the girls' dorm now Greg was here too. Mike talked to us a little longer before he left to return to Sydney.

By the time I had washed and got ready to crawl into bed, Michael was snoring and the sun was coming up over the horizon. I wondered if it was worth going to bed at all, but I was so tired it didn't take long to be dead to the world. By nine Nanna and Pa were up and preparing breakfast; the kids, as usual, were wide awake and rearing to go.

With the party over and everybody tired but satisfied from the night before, we finally got word we had been able to arrange a private preview of the movie, which was almost ready for release. A number of our relatives and the witnesses were allowed to see it ahead of time. We had specially asked for this because we thought it only fair that they should be able to see it in privacy without having the local press pestering them for their initial reactions.

We counted heads and plane bookings were put off for another night so everybody (except the Wests) was able to stay until Monday. We had thought we would see more of the Wests. I had only waved to them across the room on the night. There were so many people, I had only been able to get around about fifty per cent of them, and then the Wests were gone.

I was told they were on their way back to Western Australia and was really disappointed until Sally Lowe, my trusty voluntary secretary said, 'No, they're not. I know exactly where they are. They're staying with their daughter in Sydney, and I think I can contact them. I've got one of their children's numbers in Perth, and if I ring her up she'll certainly know where they're staying.' Sally discovered that the Wests had not yet left, but were leaving later that afternoon or the next morning.

She left them a message saying if they could possibly stay, they could see the film and we would have a gathering in Sydney. Please ring. They rang back to say they could stay.

Filling in Some Final Gaps at Last

In the meantime we all decided to have a look at Michael's slides. He had intended to show them the night before, but decided the party was going too long. He had pictures of various events that had been talked about the night before and of the various people who had been involved in the case.

The Lowes, Goodwins, Habys, Hughes, Liz Noonan, Michael's parents, my parents, my brother and his new wife and family all turned out to watch the slides. That was an interesting experience because while some of us were very familiar with the people and the places, some were not except by name. So we sat together and discussed past memories. One of the photographs that Michael had was an aerial shot of the campsite, which particularly interested Sally. She had been trying for years to get a look at a similar photograph from the Crown, but they would not supply one.

The Whittakers had wanted to see a map of the area and some photographs of houses belonging to the rangers. They had followed dingo tracks to the back of one house, only to be told to leave as it had already been searched. They had told the police they had gone to a high-block house, but the police maintained it didn't exist. We also investigated this and, as the police said, there was definitely no high-block house in the area. The Whittakers, however, still insisted they had been at the back of a high- block house where there had been discussion on tracks; the search had been suddenly broken off in that area. They had always felt there was an unanswered question.

We were discussing the type of housing in Queensland and Max

Whittaker mentioned to me about this high-block house.

I said to him, 'There really aren't any high-block houses in that area at Ayers Rock. The rangers' houses are at the most a couple of feet off the ground. They are low-block and then they have bricks around the bottom and things like that.'

He said, 'Hang on. That *is* high-block.' I denied this, but he said, 'In Victoria that is known as a high-block house. A low-block is where you lay the cement straight on the ground, and anything off the ground is high- block.' We looked at one another and light dawned.

I said to Max, 'Oh, if only somebody had realised that you were a southerner. A high-block house in the north is a house that is two-storey level and actually has a garage, a laundry, or simply space underneath it! It is up high on stilts for coolness or because of flooding.'

This presented a totally different picture of the house he had gone to, and it was possible it *did* exist after all. When he looked at the maps he pointed out the general area. No one has a picture of those houses now, so it will never be possible to pick out the one he was talking about because the whole area is now an Aboriginal reserve. Max was told he would have had to cross a road to get to the one he thought it was, but when he looked at Michael's aerial photograph and pointed the direction he came in, there was *no* road to cross. There *was* a house where he thought the house was, however, but none of us knew to whom it belonged. Nor did Max know what the discussion that night at the house was about. I guess that is one question that will always disturb the Whittakers.

I was finally able to ask Murray Haby a question that had worried me for years. I knew I had met a gentleman running with a torch from down the Whittakers' end of the campsite and as he came *towards* me with that torch he had asked me for directions. I met him in the middle of the road on the run and pointed the way—we had no more than a few seconds' passing conversation. I later learned that man was Murray Haby, who had found the dingo's tracks and the impressions where the baby had been laid down that night. Those were the tracks that the Aborigines later identified as the culprit dingo's.

The Crown had asked Murray, 'Did Mrs Chamberlain come across to your van?' and he had said yes. I had always been told I went to the door of his van but I knew I hadn't. Some things might have been a little confused that night as the time went on, but that was not one of them. I couldn't understand why some strange man would say I had gone to his van, tell him the baby had been taken and ask him for a torch when I was yelling for the whole campsite to hear. Now finally, I was able to ask.

He looked startled and said, 'I never said that.' I responded, 'Well, my memory is that you must have been the man I met in the middle of the road.'

He said, 'Yeah, that's right.'

'Why didn't you say so?'

He replied, 'I did, I said you came across to my van.' Again we looked at one another and realised he was talking about coming towards the van and being met. I said I had come towards him, but the inference taken was that I had come right up to the van instead of going towards it. Such a *little* thing, and yet such a big misunderstanding, and one that was always claimed as proof that I was a liar. When I said I didn't go to Murray's van, the Crown took it as a point against his evidence, and a fact that there was something I wanted to cover-up.

Various witnesses questioned one another about why they did certain things that night, and we cleared up many points. With a round table discussion it was obvious that we were all on the same wavelength, regardless of the fact that in court it often appeared we had differing opinions. (Sometimes I think in a situation like that it would be far better for the judge to sit and listen to the people discuss the event together, then ask questions as a group, rather than the way it is done. Things would be much clearer if witnesses were able to throw all their evidence and ideas into the melting pot together. But even that would, of course, have its disadvantages if someone was corrupt and bought the witnesses.)

The day we went to see *Evil Angels (A Cry in the Dark)* a select group gathered—the Lowes, Wests, Liz Noonan, Michael's parents and mine, our three children, and my brother and his wife.

We went down to Sydney to watch it. We watched their reactions, saw Greg and Bill share a laugh as the film showed Greg spit a sausage on the ground at the barbecue and swear; it was so characteristic of Greg although an invented scene. That actor did a terrific job of being Greg Lowe. He was nearly as good as Sam Neill impersonating Michael.

As Liz Noonan had lived in Darwin and run the support group there in the most inhospitable environment, it was a bonus for her to see all these people together. A number of them had been guests in the Noonan home as they travelled. Quite often the witnesses were separate, but here she saw the lot together.

It was a bitter sweet experience for Liz because Tony had not long died; he had been very much her supporter and helpmeet in this. You could see she was thinking how much Tony would have liked being there.

Phyllis Boyd was in the same position. When Guy died unexpectedly it was as if part of us all had died. He was a very special man. On the party night we'd had a special toast to Tony Noonan, Guy Boyd and Sir Reginald Sholl, all of whom had died in the past few months, and were sadly missed by us and our support groups as well as by their friends and families.

The party had been appreciated and enjoyed by all. Mervyn Whittaker, one of the support group leaders, had been invited to the victory party. He travelled with other Victorian guests, Dr Jackson, a psychologist, and his wife, who had been regular correspondents and supporters while I was in prison.

Having been under stress from various reasons, Mervyn was finding it difficult to relax and sleep, so discussed what he might do to relieve the stress with Dr Jackson. He later informed me that the night had been such a tonic and emotional release of pent-up energy, stress and emotion that he had gone home on a high and from then on had not had any trouble. A number of other guests expressed similar feelings of release.

Let's Go to the Movies

During the time we had helped with the research for the movie, Robert Caswell laughed with us, cried with us, and shared every other emotion. His research was meticulous and every scene he wrote accurately depicted what happened. The inaccuracies usually occurred when the director, Fred Schepisi had a hand in altering the script. From my observations less than five per cent of it was touched by him, and that was mostly scenes taken from court transcripts. I must admit I often wondered why he received a co-credit for the writing.

Fred Schepisi's direction, though, was perfect and accurate, and although a writer does a good job, no film will be a success unless the director has also done his character research and is on the ball.

We got to know Robert and Liz (his lady, now wife) really well and enjoyed their company, as we still do. We meet them whenever they are back in Australia. They were actually in Australia when the movie was due to premiere. Robert had been asked to give an interview at the close of the first session.

This was primarily for all the press, and took place at eleven in the morning. Robert asked us whether we wanted to go. We would have liked to see it on a big screen but didn't want to get caught at the opening because of the press. Robert said, 'I can get you into the back of the theatre, I am sure I can. If you want to go, I'll try.' We said yes. The theatre manager agreed to let us in the back door and was told *not* to mention that the Chamberlains were arriving. So he helpfully announced, *to the press*, that we were coming and would be giving an interview afterwards. When we discovered what had happened, Robert said to him: 'Look, they can't come under those conditions. You have to get them in and out without being seen. It's *me* who's doing the interview, not them.'

With walkie-talkies and a great deal of difficulty, the theatre manager was able to take us through the bowels of the theatre, after taking us up the wrong stairs and having to edge his way across a narrow ledge he finally was able to get into the theatre and open the right door to let us into the back of the theatre balcony. The moment the final scene was over, as the credits were about to roll, we left the way we had arrived.

Michael and I were to go straight back to the hotel, while Robert went out the front to wait for his interview, Liz, as no one knew her, would go down to the toilets to catch any casual discussion on the movie and gauge how it went. She hung around for quite a while. Eventually she turned up at the hotel and said, 'Well, nobody said anything. It was extremely quiet, which means either it has affected them so much they can't talk, or they didn't go to that movie.' We later discovered most people were very quiet afterwards.

We waited and waited for Robert to arrive as arranged, then decided to order lunch anyway. We thought he must have misunderstood about where to meet, but he eventually turned up. His interview with Geraldine Doogue had been delayed for half an hour before she appeared. She had been extremely upset by the movie and, terrified that her fellow journalists would take photographs which would reveal her reaction, she had stayed inside the theatre until she felt she could control herself.

Nevertheless, she still can't have realised how bad she was because Robert said when she finally appeared she had two of her assistants holding her (one on each side) and her legs were buckling beneath her. She was still crying, and he sat there for nearly a quarter of an hour actually calming *her* down before they could do *his* interview.

It seemed she had been so strongly affected because initially she had laughed at dingo jokes on one of her programs. At the time Michael wrote to her, saying that this wasn't very good reporting, as she must remember the people involved in her stories *could* be sitting watching, just as he had been that night. She should consider she was laughing about real people. That forcibly struck home to her and she was careful in her presentations from then on. Later she actually met and interviewed Michael.

Now, having seen the movie, she was facing a lot of exactly what we had been through, and realising how callous her attitude had been. She found it much too close for comfort.

Many people wrote us letters of apology after that movie. They were people who realised how much they had been gulled by the bad press and helped contribute to our pain themselves, helping spread the rumours like a bushfire out of control pushed by the gale force winds of prejudice.

One young man wrote and apologised profusely for believing I was guilty, and said he had fought with his mother-in-law over it. I thought that was lovely, only it amused me that he didn't say he'd yet asked his mother-in-law to forgive him as well! I hope he saw the humour in the note I sent him. I thought letters like that took a lot of guts because one can say all sorts of things about an absent person who may never know you held that opinion of them. To admit a mistake and apologise for something that could have remained hidden takes a very strong person.

The reaction of overseas audiences was quite different from those in Australia. A friend of Robert's was recently on a flight from the Bahamas to the Los Angeles (lax) airport, the inflight movie was *A Cry in the Dark*. Although the flight had taken eight hours, for some reason the movie had been put on late and still had a quarter of an hour to run on arrival at Los Angeles. Most of the passengers refused to disembark until they had seen the ending. Eventually, the airline agreed that those passengers who wanted to, could stay on the plane while the rest of the movie was screened. Seventy-five per cent of the passengers stayed aboard to watch the end, after which they happily disembarked. The departure time of the return flight was delayed as a result.

The president of our church's Euro-Asian Division said, 'Thank you so much for making this movie. It is one of the best Christian movies we have seen this decade. It is very good for our church and explains things that we believe and is a very good Christian outreach.' In Germany they printed leaflets saying what Seventh-day Adventists believed, and giving people an invitation to attend a church service in an Adventist church. The church members stood out the front of the theatres and handed out these brochures when the movie, *A Cry in the Dark* opened, and all during the time it was in the theatres in Germany. But our local Australian Division advised us that a low profile would be best. They kept the same view they had had all along—the church couldn't be seen to be involved in things that were really a little political and they would prefer us not to give media interviews if we could help it.

Our church's overseas counterparts did not hold the same opinion about our public image as our local Division did. They were happy to have us over there to talk to them and give lectures, talks or church services. In fact some areas even asked us to permanently transfer across. I love Australia and wanted to stay here. My forebears helped explore and settle this island continent. They were free settlers—I added the convict stock later.

How much damage is done because those in authority are scared to stand up and make firm decisions? Are we responsible because we give these men the power to do things like this? Because we vote them in without knowing what they are really like? Because we are taken in by flowery speeches and nice smiles and handshakes and pats on the babies' heads? How responsible are we as a public for the people we put in ruling positions over us? It is all very well to blame Parliament and church officials for wrong decisions but, unthinking, we vote these people in.

Those in command are often a far cry from the warm-hearted reaction of Christians from other churches; the man on the street who raced after me, and gave me a huge bunch of flowers because he had seen me walking past and wanted to cheer me up; or the vivacious red-headed lady who grabbed me from behind and hugged me so excitedly in the ladies' room of David Jones and said, 'Just wanted to tell you I am proud of you. Keep fighting. I'm not a Christian but I have been praying every night for you.' Then she giggled and said, 'Well, maybe I'll get to be a Christian yet because I must pray to somebody, and I guess I would sure like to have the faith you have if anything like that ever happened to me.' Are you like the man at the door of our college Adventist church at my homecoming thanksgiving and praise service who got caught in the queue of people filing through to welcome me home and shake my hand? He was with his friends and family, who were obviously happy to see me, but *he* didn't want to know. I could see him coming and it was obvious he was extremely uncomfortable and didn't want to be anywhere near me; I could tell he thought I was guilty but he did not have the guts to turn around and say he didn't want to shake my hand.

I could respect someone who has the courage to disagree to my face, but not a coward who bends to peer pressure. As he came past me and went to slip out the door, I made sure I waylaid him and spoke to him. He answered, but he couldn't look me in the eye. My handshake must have felt as if it stung him because he got out that door faster than any other person in the queue.

But then life is full of surprises. Just recently I answered the phone and a young woman asked for Lindy. I have become fairly cagey about answering the phone because quite often the press have got hold of my phone number, or somebody really doesn't need to talk to me and is just being a nuisance, so I asked her what she wanted to talk about. Then I sensed that she was fairly upset, so I told her to whom she was talking. She told me that she had really just rung up to say how much she admired my strength. She was fairly new in the area and just wanted to ring up and say that, nothing more. She had written once a long time ago, but never posted the letter and suddenly had wanted to ring, had the presence of mind to find the phone number and out of the blue just rang up. Little things like that surprise you in life and give a sense of belonging and encouragement to keep on trying and fighting and struggling to get there in the end.

A PRICE TO PAY

Now years later, cosmetically you can't notice much that Reagan even had an accident; people usually don't notice until they have known him for while. You can see only a slight scar on one side of his face, and his eyes are a dark brown and the misshapen iris doesn't show much. It is when I see him playing sport, I realise most how much he misses that eye and how well he copes. He has wide peripheral vision, but he still suffers from occasional headaches. He plays with his computer and he reads, but every now and then he will come up and say, 'Mummy, I've got a headache. My eye hurts,' and he will go to bed early. Out in the sunshine, his eye hurts because as the scilia muscles have been cut; there is nothing to block off the bright light so he often squints.

When skiing he sometimes cuts in front of me and sends me flying because it is his blind side and he doesn't see me. Being not nearly as good a skier as Reagan, I can't stop as quickly and we both go splat. He apologises, but I know it isn't his fault. Others occasionally yell at him for the same reason thinking he is careless. I also know there are some sports he shouldn't participate in because of danger to his other eye; all restrictions that should never have been placed on him because of an accident that should never have happened.

For years I hoped he would be able to have a corneal transplant and see again through that eye, as there was nothing wrong with the retina. Then his eye became bloodshot with a lump on it, and he was told it was one of the stitches coming out. Only then was I also told the lens had been completely taken out of his eye all those years ago, and there is no hope of the sight in that eye changing. I had to break the news and saw the pain on his face as hope died. Those are the times when I feel the Northern Territory has much to answer for.

Tinder wrote that 'Yesterday's hurt is today's understanding rewoven into tomorrow's love.' Somebody sent me that little text in prison, and I sat it up against Reagan's picture, the picture of him with perfect eyes before his accident. Every time I looked at it, I knew that I understood a little more.

Finally the church held a meeting about Michael. He was really a little bit too well known to employ, other than the half-dozen jobs they had already offered him, they said, but they really needed our house. Perhaps we could find somewhere else to live and something else to do, but they would get back to us and have another meeting after we had been exonerated. Even with our wood business, people wanted to know all there is about us. Some were absolutely horrified that Michael cut and sold wood from the bush. Others thought it was marvellous. He also was increasingly booked as a wedding photographer and made a reasonable combined wage for himself. The church also continued to pay him his wage.

Though others may say, look at the Chamberlains, they are rich, it is not true. If it was, we would have earned every penny in such a way that nobody would wish to change places with us.

I've often heard people say, 'I envy you. You travel around the world. You are speaking here, you are speaking there, people want to see you, you are famous—or infamous, depending on their point of view. You can afford it, you've got nice clothes, and nice kids, it's all happening for you.'

When I have gone overseas on lectures people like to overlook the fact that many times I got no fee although my air fares, food, accommodation and babysitting was paid for by those I give my lectures to, and many a time I wouldn't have eaten if it wasn't. It has helped me exist at times.

Sure, I have nice clothes. I made or earned every one of them. On occasions I have borrowed my interview clothes from my designer friends Jean Bas, or Vivian Chan Shaw. I like nice things and I would love to be able to walk into the shops and buy what I want. Who wouldn't? Occasionally I have done an interview and done just that, and it has felt wonderful. Because we now charge money (and if you'd been misquoted and used by the press as often as I have, so would you!), so the media has paid, but I have always made sure of the reason for my buying and not spent willy-nilly.

When I came out of prison, we did a couple of big-money interviews, and gave half the money to the church and used the rest for legal expenses. The church had supported us right through and guarantored so many of our legal bills. We didn't realise that, because it was given in payment of a legal debt, our interview was considered work and was taxable—something we found out a number of years later. We didn't have the money then, we had no income, and there we were with a big back tax bill. I had tried to get a loan to tide me over until the Northern Territory gave us compensation, and had been only partially successful, so I wrote this book.

The advance I was given to pay a secretary and my expenses became the answer to my prayers. The contract was signed and the advance paid on the exact day the final payment of my tax was due. God answered my prayer, but He tested me right up until that day.

There is no doubt about it, when you look back at your life you can see the places where God has carried you through, where your stumbling footprints have grown so weary He has had to pick you up in His arms and carry you. You can see where you were strong and ran freely by His side. But there is no doubt that the times you are closest to Him are the times when He carried you in His arms.

If we can only stretch out our hand and leave it stretched out, even if we have no strength in our fingers to hold on to Jesus, He will hold on to us. When we say, 'No, let me go,' He won't force us, but is there, waiting with His hand outstretched. He will ride over those rough paths with us and will keep us safe and give us courage. But I learned, oh so many times, never to tell Him He could have my life if I was not willing to *give* it. Never to tell Him that my children were His to look after unless I was prepared to accept the way He thought best for them. Never to leave something in His hands if I wasn't prepared to accept the way He chose.

Many was the time I could not see which way He was directing, but I could look back later and see the reason for it. Often I wondered why I was going through a particular rough patch, and then a letter would arrive from a stranger; somebody who wanted to tell me that, because of *my* example, because of what had happened to *me*, because I came through that, then *they* could cope with *their* problems too. I knew once more that God had used me without my knowledge to help somebody else and, I guess, looking back over the last ten years, I know without a doubt that if I had to go through it all again because God wished me to, then I would, despite how hard it has been and despite the sacrifices I have had to make. I know God has given me the strength and richness I have needed for those times and I know God doesn't allow *anyone* to bear any greater burden than they can cope with *unless* He supplies the added strength needed to go through that experience, even though they may not realise it at the time.

If as many Australians went to church as those who are willing to worship at the shrine of forensic science, Australia's churches would be full and overflowing. We allow ourselves to be victims of the pride of science and technology in what has become very much a secular age.

What Happens Next?

Pre-exam nerves have nothing on being inside the courtroom, let me assure you. As you are weighed up from top to toe—and the gallery whispers none too softly—the jurors can see and hear it all. When lawyers make asides to their assistants or the police, often the stage whisper is loud enough for the jury to hear and 'relax with a bit of a joke'. In some cases comments just bordering on contempt of court are made, even during the examination of a witness in the witness box. When it is too open or disruptive the other counsel can 'object', and then the judge may direct the jury to disregard that remark and have it struck from the record, or even apologised for.

How ridiculous! Anyone who has ever said a word in haste in an argument knows even an immediate apology and acceptance does not erase the memory. People are not blackboards to be wiped clean—but it is the deliberate hurts, and the 'jokes' that make the most impression. It is the use, or rather misuse, of court psychology on the jury. The facts are of no consequence.

An unscrupulous lawyer will use every trick in the book to get the jury on his side. Hats off to the decent lawyers who won't stoop to that sort of manipulation.

Defence lawyers have only the information their client can supply, plus anyone who volunteers information, or that they can track down as possible witnesses from vague descriptions, but only as far as finances will allow. The Crown has much greater resources to draw from. Witnesses go to the police giving statements, and often request copies for themselves and to be given to the defence also. It was only by listening to news reports interstate that a number of our witnesses realised we had not been given their statements and didn't know of their existence, so they rang us and volunteered information—some of which was too late to use. *Then* we were able to elicit copies of *some* of these when the Crown was faced with it in court. I wonder how many others there still are that we know nothing of?

Piece by piece information came to light. The police, Crown and government in the Territory did everything to delay us finding out things, viewing court exhibits—giving us answers only after months of waiting. Then they have had the cheek to tell the public via the media they couldn't do anything until the Chamberlains' lawyers submitted some material—not admitting, of course, that they were the stumbling block. And how do you draw attention away from yourself while you do this? Why, leak another rumour about the Chamberlains, of course.

Time and time again people have threatened me, trying to make me admit something that wasn't true. They have tried saying that, because I took the trouble in jail to talk to girls from all walks of life, with all types of moral or immoral beliefs and backgrounds, that I was one of them, either engaged in criminal activity or, because of the impression people have of prisons, and because I freely talked to girls who were lesbians, some have tried to tar me with the same brush. They knew, of course, this was absolute rubbish. It is very easy to shrug your shoulders and try to ignore the taunts, but when it actually happens and it's a comment you're powerless to do anything about, it can still hurt.

Before I came out of prison, I had told the long-term girls if any of them were passing through they were welcome to come and see me. Often they said, 'When you get out, you won't want to know *us* because you come from a different life outside. You know all those posh people, you won't want to know us poor old jailbirds any more.' I assured them it would not make any difference to me, nor has it. When I've had the opportunity to visit or call any of them, or when the girls have telephoned or called in on me, I have always enjoyed seeing them, but those threats still remain each time one calls me. It really isn't accepted to have jail friends in polite society. That is something one is supposed to hush over. Well, I'm convict stock myself now so what have I to gloat over? The record books might have cleared my name but that will never take away the reality of my experience.

Why do people say I will forget? How can I? They have no idea. Oh, some things you forget, other things you will never forget, and they grow plainer or dearer with the time. You learn to cope better, sure, but the hurt and the memories still stay. Only some things fade with time. Only someone who has gone through it can understand the agony of having to sit there hour after hour while ghouls laugh and poke and make jokes and talk about your own flesh and blood as if it was an inanimate object with absolutely no relevance at all. And you learn to suppress your emotions and you learn to outwardly look as if it doesn't matter. You learn to cope with the regurgitating over and over and over of scientific facts and it becomes easier with time and it doesn't *seem* to hurt. But it hurts all the more when you see callous lawyers joking and saying, 'One up for me, boy, I got that one this time!' If only they stopped to think of the inside story and the personal cost.

This is your Australia. This time, all this happened to me—the next time it may be you, and if your case doesn't capture the national imagination, you won't have any hope of doing a thing. No one will want to know, and only a few close friends will care. You'll rot in obscurity like others I could name. It's time our legal system treated everybody equally and was allowed to determine truth and justice. We should not have to depend on political intervention when the appeal process is exhausted. Something needs to be done to tighten up methods and practices used in our courts today before it is too late—for all our sakes.

My own conviction was totally against the evidence of the eyewitnesses and—now—the available scientific evidence as well. The setups and cover- ups and concoctions used are obvious. The millions—yes, I mean millions—spent by the Northern Territory to put me in prison and keep me there would have gone a long way towards that railway and airport they wanted.

For over ten years now I have lived with rumour, innuendo and accusation over the death of my baby daughter, Azaria. I have tried to cooperate, but still this farce continues.

The Northern Territory may think they can hide, but unless something is done and soon, this tragedy could be repeated, another life will be lost, and the serenity of another Australian family shattered.

In a letter Lenore Stevenson wrote to me in November 1988, she aptly summed up the whole situation.

> People lost their jobs fighting for the principle of justice . . . not all Australians behaved like morons in those eight years . . . Although it is your private story (the loss of Azaria and the hell through which you struggled so admirably) there was a public side, the wider implications of which had ramifications for us all.
>
> What happens next time a horrible injustice occurs? Will people say, let the media take care of it, they did in the Chamberlain case, or let the government take care of it, they dealt with the Chamberlains justly in the end, or let the law courts take care of it?
>
> If people believe the small man's voice makes no difference, what happens next time?

What about you, reader of this book? Did you share with the police, with the crooked legal system, and with the crooked reporters? Did you share, sopping up every bit of fantastic news that they thought up, and feed their greed for money by buying it? Or did you buy the decent newspapers, those that didn't sensationalise the story, those whose circulations didn't go as high as the tabloids because they didn't falsify or dramatise the news that way?

Why blame the media? It is the public who demand the goods—so if there is no news today—well, spice it up to what the public wants or 'produce' some, and they do, and up go the reaction of demand and money and supply and greed. None can be blamed alone. All must share—producer, reporter, and consumer public. How much are we aware of what the person in the news really feels? How their family and friends feel? How it affects their lives? We all have preconceived opinions and jump to conclusions at some time or other in our lives.

Don't judge me just because my reactions weren't what you think yours would have been. How do you know I am not the one with the normal reactions, and you are the one who actually has the abnormal reaction. Just because someone's reaction is different from what you consider normal, it does not necessarily follow that they must be guilty simply because they reacted differently.

Did you read the truth, did you sign the petitions asking that the case be inquired into so all the truth could come out? Or did you say, 'No way, she's guilty, I don't want to know any more? I'm sick of hearing about them'?

Every defendant, guilty or innocent, deserves the right to have experts examine forensic material for their own trial as a second opinion, if for no other reason than to keep the exclusive 'forensic' scientists honest and on their toes, and stop any question of selective results by a biased scientist. Both sides are thus safeguarded.

Well, what do you think? Did you go to *Evil Angels (A Cry in the Dark)* and were you quiet afterwards because at last you began to understand? Or did you walk out thinking that what you saw was just 'the Chamberlain version', despite the fact that it had been well researched from both sides by Robert Caswell and the movie research department over a number of years?

What did you want? A story of my guilt—a story that told you about the sand that was claimed by Cameron to be a bloody handprint on the clothes, but was just desert dust? About the spilt milk shake in the car that was supposed to be foetal blood? About under-dash sound deadener that was supposed to be blood from my baby Azaria's throat? About the camera bag that was supposed to have the body stashed, that was simply copper dust from Mt. Isa, and had no blood at all?

And now we wait, we wait for the Northern Territory to pay us what they owe. I know they've done well out of us; they've had tourists, pressmen, lawyers, visitors, all of whom have gone to the Northern Territory because of this case. They've paid for accommodation, for food, for liquor, for souvenirs and tours; all money that's benefited the Territory and its tourist industry. But now we want what is *our* due from them. We are claiming an *ex gratia* payment for the wrong that has been done to us. I am innocent. They know that. And they have done an immense wrong to innocent people.

I know that God will see us through day by day until the Northern Territory pays for their mistreatment, if not because they *want* to pay us, because it is a precedent that *needs* setting, a lesson that Australians *need* to be taught. They cannot run roughshod over innocent people and not pay compensation for the injustice done.

What a person owns or does not own is irrelevant to compensation. It is something that is given to right a wrong. It wouldn't matter whether it was the Queen of England or a drunk in the gutter, both would be entitled to the same amount for the same wrong done. That is why I continued to fight for my right not to reveal personal details to the Northern Territory (until a newspaper did it for us, incorrectly of course) and for our right to compensation. It is the principle that strikes at the very roots of our freedom. Yes, they are entitled to every legal bill and expense we claim because we are asking for the payment of those expenses but for the *ex gratia* payment for wrongs to be righted, they need no information except the fact that we were innocent and they have done great wrong to innocent people.

I continued to fight, not only for compensation for me and my family, but also for correction of the findings in the second inquest, which still stood. My name still had to be deleted, as nominee, and now there was an open murder verdict for my daughter, and I *know* her cause of death was *not murder*. I know that there should now once again be a verdict that my daughter Azaria was taken and killed by a dingo. The Northern Territory know this too, but as long as they leave that verdict it relieves them of culpability and continues to hammer home the fact that they maintain the dingo was a lie.

Since the Morling Commission, they know positively that I did not kill my darling little girl, and all the way through the Northern Territory Crown claimed it was either Lindy Chamberlain or a dingo. Because the Commission was not asked specifically to decide whether or not a dingo killed Azaria, the Northern Territory has allowed the findings of the second inquest to stand and hope everyone will conveniently forget what they said before. They don't need to waste more public money on a new inquest, and they know it.

The second inquest should be annulled and a new verdict of death caused by a dingo entered—simply using the information available from their own Commission at no extra cost. There is no other possible decision. They know that. The Northern Territory must learn they have to pay for their mistreatment; they cannot evade their responsibility to me and my family.

No one ever again should go through what my family and I have. Governments, legal systems, the police, the press and the public must learn that they cannot ride roughshod over people—no matter how insignificant they may think them to be. There are still those who will stand up for truth and justice, thank God, like those in our support groups.

This is the principle I am fighting for, and will continue to fight for—we will all fight—until we win and injustice is acknowledged. Then, once and for all, justice will not only have *been* done, but will have been *seen* to be done, as the Northern Territory so aptly said.

My dad was right. What the world needs most is men who will not be bought or sold, but who are willing to stand up and be counted.

So, here we are ten years after Azaria's death, and still the rumours hurt—and the unfinished business continues.

PART SIX

Fourteen Years of Tears and Triumphs

A Book, Tears and Decisions

When I started writing this book, I was still living on hope and promises, trying to kid myself that one day we could once again get back on an even keel both publicly and privately. You can still love a person without loving the choices they make. What they choose to do is not who they are. Perhaps one of the hardest things in life is to see the difference between the person themselves and the choices they make. Behind the scenes I could no longer ignore the full facts of what continued to occur even after Michael no longer had his ministerial credentials. Barely out of prison, I realised nothing had changed. I was not blind, and soon had to face some of the hardest decisions of my life. Those decisions were to challenge everything I had ever held dear.

I had told Michael I would support him publicly when the Crown had come to us in the Royal Commission, as long as he did not try to blame me for his mistakes. I had also told Michael I was prepared to wait for him to sort himself out, but that this wait could not be open-ended. Many thought my marriage breakup was due to the case and the additional pressures of prison and press, but it was not. Michael and I had had many discussions on our relationship since I discovered he had been making choices not suitable to family life. Whether the public consider this right or wrong, I still believe in the Biblical definition of marriage and that marriage is for life, for better or for worse as the wedding vows state. Although I still loved the man beneath the public persona, he was not only still making choices that I could not continue to live with, but his personality was changing also. As the problems worsened I found I could no longer pretend everything was all right, and in situations that I found untenable because of the underlying currents, such as walking in and out of court with people jeering, my face and demeanour would go stiff and cold. Even my best friends (I had not confided in them) began to comment on it and it only added fuel to the rumours now circulating that I was a cold, unforgiving, frigid woman. I was still hoping for changes, but daily life was like walking barefoot on glass.

The negative effects on the whole family were so severe that something *had* to change, and drastically. I finally had to tell Michael I was no longer prepared to live as we were, and that I was divorcing him. Once again I had hoped this might be the catalyst needed. Contrary to other times when we had had this discussion I was not going to back down and change my mind. If you don't agree with something, you have to have the guts to stand up and say so even if it is unpopular; it usually will save you a lot of heartache later. I asked him to move out of my home, but he refused, so I moved down the hall. We had found an unfinished house at a bargain price and as I had saved some money for the deposit from the fee for an interview and could get a bank loan, I bought it as an investment, intending to finish it off slowly, then sell and rebuild on our dream block. Meanwhile we had built a large office for Michael behind a house which was divided into two apartments nearby. That was now in his name so I knew he had a choice of where to live.

While all this was going on I was also flat out writing this book, working 20 hour days six days a week and running behind schedule. Apart from my Sabbath I was only able to take off one hour per day, over supper, for the final six months. This was family time. I told Michael if he was serious about our marriage, he could court me all over again, and would have to prove to me that some of his lifestyle choices of the past were definitely over. I also promised to keep my mouth closed while he sorted himself out as long as he never tried to blame me for things that were not my choice. If that occurred then or in the future I would consider myself immediately released from that promise.

Future generations will not have to guess at the truth. They will be able to read the facts clearly. Although I have forgiven Michael, forgiveness is really for our own sake. By forgiving, we no longer need to carry the burden of resentment and in my case the only way I could do that was to pray for Michael to find peace within his own life. But, forgiveness does not mean that we will allow the injustice again.

Michael spent time with Kahlia during my one hour per day off, while I was writing, but the boys and I usually ate and did things alone. Kahlia told me later that she thought I had taken no time off, and hadn't known she was missing out on spending time with her Mum. My double study doors were open, and with my crew of two who were typing and collating we worked all hours of the day and night. Friends and visitors dropped in and most of our kids and their friends visited, even begging the computers to play games on if there was a gap in typing or editing. Ian Goad (an ex-Federal Cop) and Linda Driscoll (secretary extraordinaire) and I ate while we worked together, laughed together, and even cried together in turns over personal problems during that time. We learned to love each other, warts and all. Working as we did was highly stressful as they realised and shared my need to get everything super accurate, yet above all it was fun together. Although none of us would want to do it again, we really wouldn't have missed the experience either. At the end of it we thought we were all now expert enough to write a good book!

Meantime, on the marriage front, things were going from bad to worse. With my book being printed I headed north with the boys for my niece's wedding and decided to stay a few extra days with friends while there. Mum and Dad were heading straight home and I gave them my keys to stay the night in my home on their way south. They pulled up at my door only to see things being removed in my absence and decided to stay till I returned. On my return, after some discussion they went home to unpack, repacked for a long stay, locked up their home, and came back to help and support me, as Michael had not yet fully moved out. Thank God for wonderful parents.

Eventually Michael moved out totally just before the divorce became final. Fortunately the press missed that as I had to be present in court for the decree. We had told all the children they could choose where they lived. I refused to make them feel like meat on a bone. If they decided to change their decision at any time, they could. With that finalised I could breathe a little more at last and plan for my own future, although my heart bled at the loss of Kahlia who had decided to go with her father. She would come to me on weekends.

Compensations of All Sorts

Helena, my 'adopted' daughter from prison days, lent us a refrigerator, television, lounge suite, table and chairs, and a mattress for Reagan. Aidan wanted me to have his bed, but in the end he lent me his spare trundle bed and Grandma and Grandad his couch which made a double bed. Kahlia slept on the floor in my sleeping bag when she came home for weekends. She kept half her toys at each house. Mum and Dad bought me a set of saucepans and a dinner set. Reagan had his lawnmower, and I still had my bicycle, the camping cutlery, my office furniture, the dining room sideboard and chairs, the washing machine and dryer, all of which I had already purchased myself. Mum and Dad had brought their own blankets and pillows and I bought new down comforters for myself and Reagan. Aidan still had his own. We had wheels (our bicycles), furniture and we were happy again. Mum and Dad also had their car until I found an old station wagon for $2,500 a few months later.

I still had no regular income apart from the occasional interview. We had all been living off the advance on royalties for my book during most of the two years while I wrote and what with paying for the house, secretarial help, food, and school expenses it well and truly disappeared. Now we were being supported by Dad and Mum from their retirement pension, and when five and a half people are living on the old age pension you become very inventive. Threats of property settlement still hung over my head. Even though Michael and I both owned our own residences we still had the one joint piece of property where we had planned to build and settle, and the courts allow a further twelve months for either party to sue for anything further they wish for. I was hoping for an amicable settlement and access to family photos, videos, and the rest of my clothes.

Even though I did not have any regular employment, things now were very different without the constant tension in the household. I had a number of speaking tours in the USA and Canada booked, and, the fee helped with a few of the extra expenses like the car and a new mattress for Reagan, as well as some house payments. For nearly three years, Mum and Dad had paid the household bills and bought the food. Any extra money I earned from interviews went straight into house payments to a very tolerant bank—thanks, Westpac—and into school fees for our three children.

Eventually the Seventh-day Adventist church learned of my predicament when I fell well behind on the school fees and came to the rescue once again. They would now pay the kids' school fees directly to the school. They also arranged for me and the children to be covered by their medical policy through my parents' cover. I handled the phone call fine, then burst into tears of joy as soon as I hung up and went to tell Mum and Dad. I may have had my problems with certain individuals, but overall the church tried to be very supportive. They continued to pay Michael wages and to assist me with medical and school payments until we received compensation from the Northern Territory.

During one particularly bad period Aidan sold his precious motorbike and gave me the money for a house payment I couldn't meet. No wonder Mums cry! I promised him the minute I got compensation he would get a brand new bike of his choice. He eventually did but while it was parked at Michael's one night it was stolen. As he had not yet insured it and it was never recovered it was very disappointing for us all.

Most people think that, if they see someone on television, or if that person is well known for any reason, he or she must be rich. This made life extra tough for me. No one wants to hire someone with a public face for a normal job, and for me things went from bad to worse work-wise. I couldn't get a job anywhere. People were sympathetic, but explained feelings ran so high that, either their business would be boycotted because I was hated, or swamped with well-wishers trying to talk to me. Either was disastrous for business. I knew this was unfortunately true; I only had to venture out my door to go shopping. I couldn't blame prospective employers, but it didn't help me. During this time someone offered me a manual job. We discussed the day I would start and I was to ring for the location. Immensely relieved, and thinking the offer was genuine, I rang as requested, only to find out it was a joke. This hurt all the more because the person who made the offer was supposed to be a friend.

Smiling on the outside I felt devastated inside and had to fight depression continually. I still had a family to feed and a home to pay for. I tried direct sales and multi-level marketing, but although I was very successful in joining people up, I quickly realised they were for the most part more interested in having an association with me as an upline than they were in doing anything else, or even buying the product, so it proved to be a waste of time and money for me. It did give me confidence in myself and I made a lot of new friends, so I still count it a very positive experience.

Personal friendships had changed, though. A lot of longtime friends see divorced women as a threat and drop them socially until they remarry. I have never been able to figure that out, unless there are cracks in their own marriages they are trying to cover. As I had learned by experience it is a pretty tough blight on society when you cannot trust your own intimate friends.

It seemed that I had barely got my life into some sort of routine when Stuart Tipple rang and told me he needed me to get him submissions for compensation. Our lawyers had to put in legal papers stating why we deserved to be compensated. Along with the lawyer's papers we needed to supply as many letters, affidavits, and supporting documents, giving as many specific examples of witnessed trauma as we could. This had to be done for each member of the family individually, Michael and I as a couple, the children as unit, and the family as a whole, making eight different categories altogether. I could have given his office the names of the people I thought of and let them work on it, but as I would eventually have to foot the bill, I may as well do what I could myself—after all I was cheaper and just as efficient as a secretary in this case.

This meant hours on the phone. I'm sure the kids began to believe it was permanently glued to my ear. Soon papers started to come in from all directions and the job of collating began before I had even finished all the phone calls. Mum and Dad helped where they could and at least gave the kids a routine. Submissions had to be done for myself, Michael, the family as a whole, the children as a whole and each of the children individually. We had no way of knowing just how compensation would be looked at. I think that the children, as part of the whole debacle, should have been compensated in their own right, but eventually they were ignored in the overall scheme of things. The children and Grandparents are often ignored in the backwash but in this case they lived through the trauma almost as closely as we did. On top of that they had to endure the scorn of the public and the slur on their own names, as well as that of their loved ones.

With that out of the road and another indeterminate wait for the decision of the Northern Territory to be announced at their leisure, I settled back to wait again, but something was going wrong with my weight, and health in general.

My book was now out on the market in Australia, and also the UK and New Zealand. Some copies of the English versions were released in France also. When I had to do the publicity for the UK edition I swapped the first- class ticket the publisher provided for three economy tickets and took Reagan and Kahlia with me. Aidan was unable to come because he would miss the first six weeks of his senior year (Year 12) and he did not feel able to cope with that. After the London publicity was over we stayed in a friend's empty apartment and catered for ourselves. Then we took the underground all over London visiting all sorts of museums, galleries, churches, and other places of interest. We had a ball. We were there during the 1991 Gulf War, and three British soldiers held hostage at the time helped the children understand the effects of war far more clearly than the news could, as those concerned were from suburbs our bus passed through and we often overheard their neighbours talking about them and their families on the bus. Someone also bombed the prime minister's residence two minutes after we had been there, plus we had to evacuate a train station and take a detour by bus another time because of bomb threats on the tube. Between experiences like that and a weekend stopover during Chinese New Year in Singapore where I had been asked to speak, the experience was good for us all. The lifestyle in Singapore was so foreign to the kids that they came home with a new appreciation of their life in Australia, no matter how restrictive our finances were. It was a break we all needed.

Sometime later Commissioner Trevor Morling, who had been directed to recommend the amount of compensation for the NT to pay, asked me to meet him in Darwin and accompany him to the prison and show him over the various areas where I had lived and worked there, as it had changed somewhat since I had left. He also asked to view the accommodation where we had had to stay during the trial, and other related areas. Prisoners were now allowed to have a lot of things in their cells which were not even dreamt of in my day. The dining room and day room in the female section had been totally reconfigured.

The Northern Territory had decided the children were not to be given compensation and Mr Morling had heard I had requested the compensation to be half each for Michael and myself (due to various events later that year I was forced to change my mind). Morling asked my reasons because he said he found that surprising. When I told him, (Michael and I were still negotiating on final property settlement out of court), he asked me questions relating to my marriage. When I hesitated, he said 'Perhaps if I tell you what I know first, you will feel more comfortable.' He did and after that there was no further reason to hesitate, as he knew things even I didn't, so I explained my reasons.

Into the Light, a Chequebook and Compensation of All Sorts

Shortly afterwards, in January 1992, I had another speaking tour to do in the United States. The children were also invited as it was still in the Christmas holidays. This would give me a chance to have Reagan's eye reviewed by an internationally renowned Canadian eye specialist who had offered to help. Kahlia was all packed, but the day before we left she was forbidden to go, so the boys and I had to leave on our own.

Even though I had learned to mask it fairly well, I was always shy underneath, I hated going anywhere on my own and it took me a while to finally become comfortable with being single again. Although divorced and free to remarry according to Biblical beliefs, I was 'sick of men' as the saying goes. I never wanted anyone close enough to hurt me so badly again and intended never to have another permanent man in my life. During this trip I told God that if He thought it was not what He wanted for me, then He would literally have to make me trip over someone.

Barely a week later we were on our way back from Canada after having Reagan's eye checked. When met at the SeaTac airport near Seattle my host, Pastor Karl Haffner, said, 'Oh, by the way I hope you don't mind but I've asked my cousin Rick to help with the driving of the hire car and with the boys. That OK with you?' As it was the second time I had been there and I was quite comfortable with the arrangements made, I assured my host it was fine, although I was surprised to learn he had a local cousin. I was introduced to the cousin. When introduced I found the cousin quite forgettable, and couldn't even remember what he looked like or what his name was by the next day when he was to pick the boys and me up for an engagement. As the hire van had a flat tyre, and he had to tell us we were going to miss our first appointment, that did nothing to endear him to me.

God had other ideas. About a week later, during which time I had seen very little of Rick that made any conscious impression at all, he walked around a corner after Reagan and they were both looking at each other and laughing. It was many years since I had seen Reagan so relaxed, and I asked my host who the man was. He looked at me strangely, laughed, and replied that I knew who it was: his cousin Rick Creighton. Now I felt like a fool, especially as Reagan told me later that we had stayed in the same house all weekend and I had sat next to Rick at lunch! I knew I had missed something and noticed the influence he was having on Reagan. When we were out with Rick, shop clerks told Reagan to give the receipts to his 'father' or automatically gave us family passes; obviously we all looked comfortable together.

Four days later the truth hit me like a brick. I had fallen in love with Rick and I didn't seem to have had any say in it. After that we talked a lot when he had to drive me to engagements, but neither of us said a thing about feelings. After all, he was younger than me and he lived on the other side of the world. From his point of view I was a celebrity passing through who would see him as just Rick the bachelor cousin.

Aidan had returned to work by now (he is an electrician), and only Reagan and I were left. I had another appointment to have Reagan's eye checked, and Rick made me promise to call and tell him the prognosis as he and Reagan had become pretty close (and he had eye problems also). Both Reagan and I were shocked when we finally heard what the specialists had to say and not a little angry. With proper follow-up he need not have lost the use of his eye. Now it was too late to do anything more about it. Before leaving the States I called Rick as promised, and from then on he spent over a thousand dollars US per month on phone calls to Australia.

Rick was to arrive for his first visit to Australia on Friday 15 May 1992. He had already told me he loved me and now he was to meet the rest of my family and friends. Aidan had managed to write my 'new' car off a few months before and I was back to borrowing my parents' car or riding my bike again. I wanted independent wheels while Rick was in Australia, so Aidan lent me his 'new' vehicle which he had purchased from Michael. It was the duplicate of our original car which I had purchased from the film set of *Evil Angels* and called SAM after Sam Neill—so I enjoyed driving it again and now I had the wheels to meet Rick at the airport.

We took a ferry ride on Sydney Harbour on the way home. At one stage as we were leaving the ferry I said, 'Everyone is staring.' Rick missed my comment, put his arm around my shoulder and leaned closer to ask me to repeat it. I did, then said, 'So now you may as well just turn around and take a bow!' He looked puzzled, then caught on and turned unexpectedly to look behind us. Everyone was watching, and all eyes suddenly got interested elsewhere in a hurry. That was a shock to Rick. He knew I was well known, he just didn't realise how well known I was in Australia. He handled it well, though, and so I knew he would cope with the extra pressure that would bring to our relationship. That was the beginning of his crash course in handling the public and the media in Australia.

He also had a crash course in getting to know my friends. I had arranged a potluck lunch after church in order to introduce everyone to Rick at once. I knew if I hadn't done this they would all find excuses to call or drop in during the week. We all arrived home to find ourselves locked out. The house was deadbolted from the inside. My tough little prison friend Helena had just had a major run in with a man with a gun. He had also threatened her, "You're going back to jail, little girl", and as he had just come out of the bush near her caravan, and drugs had been mentioned, she knew she would have no hope if he had planted drugs somewhere on the large acreage. She was so frightened that she had crashed her car in an effort to get away from him, and so she had broken in to the only place where she felt safe (since her own mother had died she had long ago 'adopted' me as her mother, and my parents and her Grandparents, so she had come home). So much for all the security I had only just added to the house. When I finally managed to get the facts straight, I discovered that the police were on their way. They arrived before my guests and I had to spend the next couple of hours closeted away with Helena and two policemen while they took statements. As Helena was well known to them, the police took it very seriously knowing this was no act and she was not a person to scare easily.

Meanwhile my guests started arriving, and Mum insisted Rick answer the door and be the host. Thrown in at the deep end, Rick earned his place amongst my friends. He was questioned and scrutinised from every angle, including questions on how much money he had and what made him think he could bring up children or even had the right to! After such a grilling, he decided that if I had friends of that calibre looking out for me he didn't have any more worries that I might not be what I seemed. A few days later he proposed marriage and, knowing I had all the children's blessings, I accepted. Now came the awkward part. As soon as anyone knew we were engaged, the media would know and we would be mobbed. We told Harry Miller (my agent and, as I had called him at my book launch, my friendly human Alsatian guard dog) immediately, and he arranged an interview with *Woman's Day* to announce our engagement.

Like it or not, the only way you can guarantee that the truth alone is told is by a legally binding contract, and for a legally binding contract money has to change hands, even if it is only one dollar. It is as simple as that. There is nothing mercenary about it. If you do one interview you are able to control it and it also stops an uncontrolled 'feeding frenzy' of all the other media. Sure, there is always at least one news source that gets mad at missing out and so they print nasty or negative stuff, usually made up with just enough fact to look legitimate, with of course the perennial stuff about how they don't use 'cheque-book journalism.' Often the worst report is from one of the outlets you just turned down! The news media are running a business and they never offer money without expecting to make a profit, often a very handsome one. I have often been told that if I was about to be featured in a magazine or newspaper they automatically increased circulation, so no one loses. Sometimes people have said to me, 'Why don't you just stop pushing your story on the media? It would have died a natural death long ago'. I have never pushed my story on anyone. It is precisely because of the widespread public interest that the media continues to publish or broadcast tantalising snippets, bringing them the readers or viewers, who boost their rating. This leads to a demand for a full story, which they then purchase. Now everyone wants to read it and they have a ready-made market which in turn allows them a higher profit for the owners, and shareholders.

Some people just go for the highest dollar amount. I don't. I have chosen less money and opted for integrity instead. Someone who is willing to tell the truth without sensation, someone you can privately tell why it is not always helpful to open your mouth about something, even though you have right and the facts on your side, is worth more than money. Even in this book there are facts I would like to tell which I cannot because a person can still be sued even though they are telling the truth. Often, what is *not* said, or the questions that are deliberately omitted, hold the key to the truth about a situation. If it is about myself, have I not held back.

I now know quite a few media personnel in all forms (from daily print to electronic) whose word is their bond and whose integrity is high. Others can be dealt with because it is 'better the devil you know . . .' Still others I wouldn't talk to if they were the last person on earth no matter what they offered. Since 1990 you can guarantee that if the interview does not have a new, current photograph, I didn't do the interview and it is made up. From another point of view, when the media decides to make you its focus, when it is finished with you (if it ever is), then, because of the notoriety, you are often forced to make your living out of the situation they have created for you. The media always claim the public has a right to know, but it is usually their profits and ratings that hold the priority.

Well, like it or not, we wanted to announce our engagement on our terms, so we signed a contract. All contracts have an exclusivity clause, and as soon as the interview was done we had to disappear from home till the danger of being found by rival press was over, and our engagement announced to all. We decided on a trip north to let Rick see more of Australia and meet many more of my friends. This would be the ideal way to avoid the media while we waited for the magazine article to come out. We enjoyed the drive and time staying with Peter and Marijana Stojanovic in Brisbane, then were about to fly to friends in Cairns and Innisfail.

At the Brisbane airport we were unloading our bags from Pete's car, when he reached back in for the keys. Stunned he stood up and said 'Hey guys you didn't tell us compensation was through!' Now it was our turn to look stunned. He had just heard the headlines for the radio news bulletin. We all piled back into the car, bags on the footpath still, to wait for the radio news. Sure enough we had compensation. And sure enough the media was the first to tell us.

When Rick and I checked in separately for our flight (like strangers because we were under contract), Harry M Miller who had our itinerary (and through whom the newsmen were already trying to find me as I wasn't home) had already rung the airport to arrange for us to be whisked away out of sight as soon as we appeared. We went in a hurry through the non-public areas and into a secure room. There we were able to call Stuart Tipple and find out everything we had missed. It seems I am always somewhere else at all the right times for me, the wrong times for the media.

When talking to Stuart Tipple I found out Morling had chosen not to award compensation 50/50 despite my request. Although forbidden by court ruling to say how much compensation my portion was and being obliged to sign a statement saying I would never sue for more, I can say that, despite all the rumours, it was under a million dollars, and that was before I paid outstanding legal and other associated bills that the government did not cover. (They still left the church with about $750,000 outstanding in interest on the money they had borrowed to finance us. The church very kindly told me to simply forget about a lot of it, knowing I had no way of paying any more back to them.) There were also a lot of other bills I had 'inherited' which had to be paid also.

Taken out the back way to the plane we were able to stay out of sight the whole time and avoided detection for the two weeks until we returned to Brisbane.

Back at Pete and Marijana Stojanovic's again, Harry Miller rang and said that *60 Minutes* wanted to do a pre-taped interview with Michael and me together on the subject of compensation and that he thought I should do it. I agreed. I would have to leave immediately and they would pay my return flight. As Rick and I had driven up to Queensland it would mean he had to travel back on his own, and I would have to take a train home from Sydney, otherwise we would miss Kahlia who stayed with me on weekends. Alternatively, I could bring Kahlia back with me, so she could see her friends in Brisbane too, and we could all drive back together on Sunday. After negotiation it was arranged with Michael that a mutual friend would pick her up from his place and I would meet them at the Channel 9 studio. I left on the plane and arrived just in time to walk straight on stage as the cameras were rolling with the program introduction. As I was walking in, I asked my agent where Kahlia was and was informed she had not been able to come. As I knew Michael had left home after her escort had called to collect her, I knew there was no reason why he could not have at least brought her himself. I was disappointed and upset and had to face the camera immediately. Not only that, but I was still under contract from our engagement which was yet to be announced in *Woman's Day*.

My agreement with *60 Minutes* had stipulated that discussion was to be on compensation only, with no personal questions to be asked. I had to field three-quarters of the questions asked, as they dealt with whether I had a new romance in my life. I had my suspicions about who tipped them off. The atmosphere was hostile. The interview was to be edited immediately and shown for that week's program. When the cameras stopped rolling, I commented to Mike Munro that he had breached the contract in his questioning and that it was not ethical. After his shrugged shoulders and reply, as far as I was concerned he had just had his one chance and blown it. Never again. I was still fuming when I got back to Brisbane. It was no better when I saw the program on TV. Questions were out of context and you could see I was defensive, but it was not obvious why. I knew there would be a public backlash, and there was. It was one interview I should have refused to do or else walked off the set. I still have to live with the repercussions.

After a divorce becomes final, the courts allow a year for either party to contest the property settlement. Michael and I had already split everything except one last jointly held parcel of land, for which we were still negotiating a price. I was barely home from Brisbane and it was just before the twelve month period was up after the divorce, when a knock came on the front door and I opened it to receive a summons, signed on the same day as that awful interview. Michael was suing me after all. When he said in the interview that I deserved all my compensation but he was not happy with his, he knew that he already had court action in progress which would, in effect, reverse the amounts of Morling's decree.

With his "holiday" over, Rick left for work in the USA again. He had decided he wanted to tell his American friends about our engagement himself. As most of them had just about given up on his ever getting married he wanted to see their faces. He didn't bargain on the media though. When he got home he found all his friends already knew except one. Brad Jacobson, who Rick wanted to be the best man, had been camping and had not heard the half hourly announcements that ran all day in the Seattle media. After all Rick was a Seattle businessman so it was big news. The media were also staking out his work place. It had all been a baptism of fire for Rick but he handled it well.

Of Rumours and Promises Made and Broken

Life still wasn't smooth sailing. New rumours started that I had just walked out on my loving, supportive husband and children for Rick. As Michael was publicly saying he had no idea why I had divorced him, it added fuel to the rumours. Rick and his parents were put under a lot of pressure because of this. When one of Rick's favourite relatives found out, she was in tears over it. How could he have changed so much that he could break up a family? By the time his cousin found out that I was divorced before I even met Rick she had spent many agonising nights worrying over it.

We both had to spend a lot of time privately putting out fires started through rumour mongering, and unscrupulous 'leaks' to the press intended to misrepresent. Even now, rumours of this kind still persist in surfacing, and many can be directly traced. Primarily because of the persistent rumours Stuart Tipple advised me to approach the Seventh-day Adventist Church Divorce and Remarriage Issues committee for permission to Biblically remarry. Most of the time this procedure is ignored, in fact even though I was the daughter of a minister and had married one, I did not know it existed. Because I was such a high profile Seventh-day Adventist Stuart thought it would be wise for me to follow this procedure. The permission was granted, but it was not until 23 June 1993 that the official letter arrived. It stated that "after consultation with senior church administrators……. in their view, and taking into consideration all aspects of your situation, it was felt that there is no impediment to your marriage to Rick."

My weight was now climbing alarmingly despite no diet changes and the fact that I tripled the amount of exercise I did. Medical opinions varied. Now Kahlia, who was nine, told a counsellor that she was dissatisfied with her 'quality of life' and wanted to live with me now. Not only did Michael object, but her decision meant she would be going overseas, as Rick and I had decided to live in the USA. That meant a custody battle after all.

It also meant we had to have a fixed address in the States, and school enrolment for Kahlia, along with a dozen other details to prove that she would be looked after properly. That meant a change of plans and I had to fly to the States immediately and house hunt while Rick worked. After days of unsuccessful hunting all over the northern Seattle area, I finally found our home. It had 'ours' all over it, yet it looked way above our finances. When we went in I wandered one way and the agent went to find the builder. She came back really excited. The house had been on the market for over ten months because Americans were wary of the Wedgwood blue carpet (they prefer bone), and I loved it. It had been reduced to just over our price range and I knew I was home. When Rick saw it that night he did too. We bargained, got it for the right price, and signed the following day.

Then the 'fun' started. The owner of the flooring business Rick managed was having a traumatic time personally, and he just couldn't handle the media staking out the business and always trying to find Rick. He figured that Rick would find all the media attention and going from a bachelor life to being the head of a high profile family would be too great a challenge. He said Rick should have a long leave of absence without pay, or find another job. No amount of reassurance helped and

Rick lost his salary just when we needed it to guarantee a loan. This left us with a major problem.

We were in a financial bind now and as custody was now in legal hands Michael insisted on a $40,000 cash bond before he would let Kahlia attend our wedding. Michael finally agreed that it be held by Stuart Tipple as a mediator, but where could we come up with the cash? Once again the church came to the rescue and lent it to me, as the banks wouldn't—after all I was leaving the country, albeit temporarily.

We knew we would have to return to Australia immediately after our honeymoon as the custody and property court dates were set in February b1993. As we didn't know how long it would take, we had decided the whole family should not be split up, but would stay together for however long it took—and so far it had not been fast.

Although we had found the perfect wedding rings, we could not find an engagement ring we liked, so bought a loose diamond and I designed my own. With the ring, given during the support group meeting, still in my drawer I knew the perfect thing to use it for. I would have that special ring incorporated into my rings. The white gold went into a plain eternity ring with six of the diamonds channel set. One of the diamonds went missing, and the other two were set dead centre in each of two leaves on my engagement ring. In character with the leaves and vines on our wedding rings I had designed a wild briar rose in yellow gold, with a white gold leaf each side of it. White gold stamens held the heart shaped diamond at the centre of the rose in place. As a permanent reminder and thank you to all the support groups and the individuals in Australia who refused to believe lies, they were the perfect keepsake. The rings were ready to collect before our wedding.

We publicly took our vows at *La Vallauris* in Palm Springs California on 20 December 1992. This was as near to the halfway mark we could get for both families. It was also a nice private area where the media could not see in. We each wrote our own vows and kept them secret from each other before hand. Rick's vows came first:

> 'My Dear Lindy, Remember the morning we watched the sun come up over the Cascade Mountain range? From deep darkness the sky grew lighter and lighter. We couldn't see the sun, but the increasingly beautiful colours gave a foretaste of what was to come. And then a single shaft of pure, bright light broke through a cleft in the rocks, and flooded us with its warmth and beauty.
>
> Just so has been the beginning of the love that I have found in you! God has given to me a trust which cannot be valued, for He has gifted me with you, and your children. And with that trust He makes a covenant; a covenant by which He promises His leadership in our relationship if we choose to allow Him.
>
> Today we make this covenant publicly, with each other and with God. Together we dedicate our lives as one, to growing under His leadership into the full joy of what He desires for us.
>
> I thank God He has brought us together, for this love is Heaven sent. The deep darkness is past and warmth and beauty flood over us. Side by side we enter the future, remaining unfailingly true to each other and God above all.

My love, the intertwined vines on this ring symbolises the pure and irrevocable joining of our lives in love. And the white gold edging is a symbol of the protection of God surrounding our lives full circle, without beginning or end. This ring will declare to the world that I love you exclusively; that we belong—and are committed—to each other.

I love you Lindy! Thank you for you.'

And then it was my turn. I responded:

'As God sends a shaft of pure sunlight through the stormclouds, so too was the joy and unexpectedness of your love for me. I thank God He made you, and kept you, and sent you to me alone. You are my best friend. You have accepted me as I am and love my children as your own. You have shared so much of yourself with me and given me the ultimate compliment: You asked if I would let you could take care of me for the rest of my life and marry you.

Today I am letting you do just that because I love and trust you. You stole my heart before I was even aware that you were the key that would let my heart run free.

In return you gave me the most priceless gift of all—your own carefully guarded heart—openly and without reserve. I will guard that gift with my life. The love we have found together is rare and Heaven sent. I want to stand by your side, work with you, support you, relax with you, and laugh with you and our family as God intended marriage should be, through all that life will bring. Together we face a new beginning for all of us.

John Hampton Creighton IV: my darling, this ring will tell the world I love you, you are mine, and we are one. I love you so much. Thank you for being you.'

Aidan, Reagan, Kahlia, and I lit a candle each, then Rick lit one too. Simultaneously we all lit a large family candle, the symbol of one family, with one purpose—equality and a new united beginning. The kids were all excited that Rick had 'married us too' to quote Reagan (and they still remind him of that in friendly banter when they cause him work). To avoid the Australian press who were camped outside, when I changed into my going away clothes my cousin donned my wedding dress and left with one of the groomsmen. Aidan drove them in our car and in the ensuing car chase with the press, forgetting he was in America, he drove on the wrong side of the road, then turned left, only to find himself going up a one-way street the wrong way. Just as well it was at night. It was the accidental move that lost the chasing press. They probably decided the driver was crazy and they would all get booked if they followed. While the press followed them, we left quietly for the honeymoon suite on our own. Of course all our gear was in the car Aidan had and we had to wait for someone to collect it and bring it to us when the car returned. Everything arrived except my shoes and the camera, so we have no photographic memories from our first night hotel.

When we checked out in the morning we were to meet with everyone else, then go in convoy back to Los Angeles to drop our gear and take everyone to Universal Studios, and Disneyland before we all split up. We checked out of the Ritz dressed in our casual gear ready for the first day in a fun park but I felt ridiculous wearing beaded high heeled evening shoes! From then on the fun began.

During the wedding, a young friend of ours who was permanently confined to a wheelchair, 'nicked' a blank film from the official photographer and took himself out to the gathered paparazzi, and offered to sell it to them. They took the bait. Later that week we ran into him and his sister at Disneyland, having a ball on the $100 courtesy of the press (the magazine they sold the story to said it was $1,000, but then, the magazine also said I had black icing with red trim on my cake, and that the blond designer of the men's suits was my groom!). Being in a wheelchair Mike and his carer could avoid all the lines and could take one other person with them. They had already been on all the rides and so he offered to take Kahlia and her foster 'sister' Tiana with him to all the kids' rides that had huge long queues while we waited in yet another long queue. They were back and finished before we got our turn, so everyone was delighted. Universal Studios was just as much fun.

The big group of Australian guests then dispersed, and we went skiing for five days with the kids and two other families before Aidan had to leave for work back in Australia. Parting with him was very difficult, as it was the final split of our family, and he was finally on his own as an adult. Meanwhile Rick and I left for Hawaii while Pete and Marijana with their daughter Sharon, Kahlia and Reagan drove back home in our car to our house in Snohomish (northern Seattle), Washington state where they looked after them while Rick and I finally had two weeks' honeymoon.

We arrived in Kauai on the first tourist plane in after the hurricane 'Iniki' and that was as experience in itself. Nothing was as we had been informed and there was no food around. All the restaurants turned out to have nothing left but floorboards and stumps, even though the locals seemed to think they were still open! Most of the houses hadn't fared much better. Our villa had no window or floor coverings, nor did it have internal doors and the neighbour's front porch looked straight through into the bedroom. Seeing there were locals billeted there permanently and it was their habit to gather and sit on the porch, that presented rather a problem, so we checked out. We were lucky to find other places to stay both in the Waimea Canyon and further up the coast. The coastal cabana was divided into two and the other residents were local, rather colourful and fought a lot. One night there was such a fight that we thought one of them might end up in bed with us. They were throwing each other so hard against the wall at the head of our bed it kept bulging alarmingly.

Later we went on to the big island of Hawaii and stayed at Volcano. That was one of the highlights in my life as we got to see Kilauea volcano in full flow with the lava pouring into the sea and creating new land mass as it went. After talking to the rangers about the lava and discovering you could throw rocks into it safely, Rick and I had a great deal of fun throwing big rocks into the hot lava and watching them bubble and melt. We were safely able to get within half a metre (19 inches) of the front of the lava flow as it flowed uphill past a cave which sheltered us from the heat. Having done the traditional thing and had my luggage mislaid on the first inter-island flight, it finally caught up to me just before we left to go home.

Back in Seattle in early January we saw God's hand once again as we were trying to get our green cards in order to come back to Australia for the custody and property cases. When I entered America I had told the Immigration authorities we had to leave again shortly for the court case in Australia. The passport control people had told me we would have difficulty and to hang in there and not be put off when the local authorities told us it was impossible to do quickly. It could be done if only we persevered and refused to be put off. With that in mind when the local officials told me it was impossible I dug my toes in. (Prison had taught me that.) They wanted me to leave the window and I refused and kept arguing and asking to talk to the supervisor. With each successive supervisor we went through the same process, while the line behind us grew longer and longer and I stayed put. Finally the big boss came out and said if we waited we could have an immediate appointment. Just as they were locking all the doors and we thought we had been tricked after all, we were called in for our interview. The interviewer made a smart remark about Rick to Reagan, at which both the kids went to Rick's chair as if to protect him and told the guy what they thought. The interviewer went on to full names and birth dates et cetera then said, 'Sign here.' I was surprised and asked if he wasn't going to ask us any questions. He just grinned and said that with that reaction on the part of the kids to his teasing there was no doubt in his mind we had a real marriage and were a real family, not one invented for the sake of getting a green card. We walked out a few moments later with our temporary green cards. We later learned getting a card on the spot like this was unheard of. We also learned that if we had gone earlier, it would have put us into the previous financial year and as an American resident I would have had to pay fifty per cent of my compensation in taxes to the American government. God certainly helped us in the timing of all of that; the money had already been used for divorce bills, legal expenses, charity, and our house, since we couldn't get the bank loan we wanted. We were back to what we could earn ourselves.

Now new challenges faced us. We came back to Australia for an unknown period of time and Michael announced his own engagement. With another court case over our heads, we had no income. Rick had not received his Australian residency yet, so he was only on a visitor's visa and could not work officially. We were able to take over the management of a property for someone else and renovate it in lieu of rent, thus increasing the property value for them and saving us money at the same time. That kept Rick, Dad and the kids busy, while Mum helped me prepare material for the archives of the National Library of Australia. We were picking out key words and I was doing a mini précis of all the letters and papers, as well as collating and cross-referencing relationships and jobs. The National Library had offered to purchase them and it worked out that our "wages" thus earned were about two dollars per hour between Mum and me! This year, when unpacking some of my parents' things, we discovered several more unsorted boxes so I guess the job isn't finished yet.

Kahlia had told her father that she was back from America but refused to return to his house until he 'signed to say' she could go to live with her mother. She took her first foster Dad Wayne with her to pick up her clothes and make sure that her Dad understood that was what she really wanted. It still took time, and as the court case dealt with custody as well as property settlement, it was only finally settled one business day before we were to be in court. Kahlia waited anxiously outside in the car with Rick, as she said she wanted to know the result immediately, and if her father had not signed she wanted to be present in case she could talk to the counsellors herself. When I finally returned to the car several hours after I had left it, I nodded my head yes, and she burst into tears and turned to Rick to reassure herself that it was really true. I had to tell her several times before she really believed it was finally actually over.

Now we could prepare to leave. Rick and Reagan needed to leave almost immediately. School starts in late August, at the end of summer in America, and Reagan would be just in time to start his senior year. Kahlia and I would finalise the last of her paperwork, the remaining packing, and her American residency, then follow as quickly as we could. We made it in time for Kahlia to start her school on time also.

Being Cabbages, Not Kings

Finally all back in our own new home and country, life settled down into a peaceful routine we would never have been allowed to find in Australia. It was great to be part of the ordinary unknown masses again without being a curiosity and everyone watching the melding of a new family. This is hard enough without being in the spotlight.

Kahlia took to school like a duck to water, whilst Reagan, who is more reserved by nature, took it slowly. We enjoyed doing things as a family, and majority vote chose the activity of the day. We had a large activity room and it soon filled with local youth coming and going over the weekends. Life was good, and we started our own niche market publishing company which we sold when we came back to Australia.

For the first two years in America I ignored the telephone totally and only spoke on it when I simply couldn't avoid it. I spent hours in the garden, creating our own Garden of Eden, and later working for a landscape company, which I thoroughly enjoyed. I had never done much gardening before this, but for the first time we owned our own home and were free of the stress of the previous years and fully intended to stay put. I could 'nest' as Rick calls it because I had someone to share the burdens with. Rick, on the other hand, took me on and maintains—that itself—is nearly a full time job.

Rick ran our business and also acted as my personal secretary, and plunged headfirst into teenage parenting. He has always maintained this was the equivalent to a dock start whilst learning to barefoot water-ski! At first the kids tried to pit us against one another. The usual stuff- if Mum says no ask Dad etc—but they soon learned things didn't work that way. Rick always asked whether they had asked me yet and what I had said and I did the same. We were a team and if we did not agree with each other we discussed it in private and if the opinion was to be changed, the one who had given the original answer went to say that on more information the decision was altered. We upheld each other at all times. When asked once in an interview who wore the pants in the family, the interviewer was surprised to be told it was Rick. On further questioning, both Kahlia and Reagan agreed that Mum might sound like she was the boss but that Rick had the last word, and if he said yes or no that was it! He doesn't use his veto with the family very often as we usually do everything with majority rule, but when he does, it is always well thought out and with good reason.

It was wonderful to be in a partnership where each member of the family knew they were loved and wanted and of equal value to the others. It amused us to know people often asked our local church pastor Karl—who was Rick's cousin—what our family was really like at home because it looked too good to be true! The thing is, it really was like that. We all considered Rick a special gift from God. When parents agree and keep open communication between each other and their children, and have love, God and mutual respect as a basis for their marriage, there are no limits on that family.

We all worked as a team, playing, working, and praying together. We all shared the cooking, and had some interesting meals while Kahlia was learning, especially when teaspoons and tablespoons were interchangeable. I have always believed it was important to teach the boys as much as the girls so at the very least they were not helpless bachelors. Aidan in particular still hates ironing but he is an extremely good cook and no one likes ironing if it can be avoided. Kahlia can also use hammers, saws, drills, and lawnmowers but thinks weeding is the punishment from hell. Reagan took it all in his stride but would rather use a computer than anything else. Both the boys can hand or machine sew or wash, vacuum or cook as well. Rick too can cook a soufflé or do the mending as easily as he can fix the car, speak other languages, build a room, or race a snowmobile. It is no surprise they think he is wonderful. I think he is incomparable. To have a supportive man who is both gentle and strong behind you who loves you for who you are without a desire to change you is the most empowering thing I know. To know you are loved and supported even when you make mistakes and are no longer young or glamorous lets you become a whole person. I felt I could heal and grow with Rick in America and during our first two years, apart from avoiding phones, I emerged only for speaking appointments and tours, then hibernated at home again just enjoying my husband, home and family as an ordinary person again. In America we were not celebrities, we were just ordinary nobodies and we loved it. Eventually I was ready to face life and the world again.

It had been discovered that my weight gain was due to a very low thyroid and I was put on permanent medication. That halted my spiralling weight gain at last, but unfortunately didn't decrease it any, so now I'm related to Humpty Dumpty. I now learned how another large part of the population feels. I had to learn how to like myself all over again. My body was no longer totally exhausted but my muscles were screaming. All my stress had gone to my back and neck. During the first inquest I turned over in bed and both ends of my collarbone flew out of their sockets. I missed being matron of honour for one of my best friends because of it. Now my muscles were still in a mess and couldn't turn my neck more than a few inches either way. No one seemed able to help me. Finally I was put touch with 'Bear', a man who was head of a small advanced teaching foundation. He was reputed to be the best 'head' man in the US but he no longer took patients. Eventually he got tired of no hands on experience, and started consulting again one day per week. I got lucky and managed to get a referral. Finally I found relief. It has been a long slow extraordinarily expensive process, but I am finally almost back to what the rest of the population considers normal.

They Said … She Said … He Said …

In April of 1994 Reagan and Kahlia flew back to Australia to take part in Michael's wedding. They could not stay long as they had to take time off school, but it gave them a chance to catch up with friends and family, which they enjoyed.

With the children's return to the States, things quickly settled into a normal smooth routine, interspersed with the occasional media flurry over something. At one stage it was cheaper to get a round the world ticket than to just buy one direct home to see my parents and Aidan, so we took advantage of that. Rick and I both have friends scattered over England and Europe so it was a great chance to catch up to them, and the cost of food and a vehicle was little different to being at home. While on one of these trips we had a friend's daughter accompanying us and received an emergency call from Harry M Miller. The rumour was that Rick and I had fought all over Europe and had split up on our return home. Well first of all it was news to all of us as we were having a grand time despite the fact that I was on crutches or in a wheelchair with an ankle I had managed to break just before we left, and secondly we weren't even home yet. The interesting thing was that an interview seemed to often surface right when we needed an influx of cash for some reason or another. God certainly was watching over us. Down the track we often managed to discover where the rumours originated from, and the greater majority of those type of rumours had only one source. I guess some people have nothing better to do but I always wonder why they can't just enjoy their own lives and forget about others and make a life for themselves.

Next, rumours that I was a lesbian, or at least bisexual, surfaced, as they had done before. Supposedly, the worst part of this activity happened whilst I was in prison. Even if one had that proclivity, homosexuality is illegal in prison, and on the few occasions when some of the men were caught it caused a huge scandal and not just within the prison system. It also usually ended up in the paper and if I had ever been involved in such activity I'm sure it would have made national headlines! Even a breath of scandal would have ended up there. There are thousands of prison inmates over any given country who never involve themselves in any type of heterosexual or homosexual sex while in prison, just as there are thousands out of prison who choose to take a moral stand, whether for religious or other personal reasons, and remain celibate until married or in a long term relationship. This physical act of sex is the ultimate act of commitment between two people, and many choose to see monogamy as a sacred bond not to be broken by inconvenient circumstances. You may not like to deny yourself physically, but nevertheless it is a conscious choice that can be made and adhered to by choice of will. Failure to make a positive choice, is in fact making a negative choice by default, and you are still just as accountable for that choice. Many find it hard to turn off the mental switch of temptation, but it is not impossible with God's help. In my view, when you make any sort of commitment, whether in business, public, or private life, you stick to it even if you decide you wish you had not chosen to make the original commitment.

I could never understand why I was labelled a lesbian just because Helena and some of my friends were. Of course my hairdresser at the time was gay – now there goes proof that most women must be gay, as I'm sure we have all gone to a gay hairdresser at some time in our lives! I refuse to make a distinction between friends and acquaintances just because they see life differently to me. I personally do not agree with the gay and lesbian lifestyle, but I do approve of the individual people themselves. Once again, what they do is not who they are, and as long as they are not blatant in my own home or in front of me, then it has nothing to do with me. I may wish they would choose a different private life that I believe is in line with God's moral precepts, but that is for them and God to work out.

Rick and I remain friends with all types of people who are different from us and don't hesitate to make new friends. I believe that each individual is uniquely created by God and that a person's value is inherent, and therefore we have no right to set them apart or discriminate on basis of religion, nationality, or ethnicity. God loves us all freely and equally and gave his Son to die for us, so who am I to set myself above God and judge differently? Dividing our neighbourhoods and the world into 'us and them' has been the primary cause of tremendous heartache throughout the centuries. This does not mean that when our behaviour denies the inherent value of another human being that consequences should not be faced.

We wanted a copy of Azaria's death certificate that was correctly filled out and in the ensuing correspondence between Stuart Tipple and the Northern Territory, it was ascertained that the second inquest was not really complete. The murder verdict in the second inquest citing me had been proven wrong, and now the finding was wrong. Coroner Lowndes said a new finding could all be done in submissions. The Crown had agreed that they would not contest this time, but that they were happy for the Coroner to rely only on matters that we put in our submissions, plus the findings of the Morling Royal Commission and of the NT Supreme Court that had quashed our convictions. I could not have been happier and Michael also agreed, so Stuart set to work once again. When the date in December 1995 for a third inquest was finally set Rick and I travelled across from the States for the one-day finding. This time, being a civil rather than a criminal court, the finding is based on the opinion of one man and he only has to be swayed 51% to 49%. When we walked in just prior to court, we discovered the Crown had put in a last-minute submission after all.

Initially when listening to Coroner Lowndes I thought he was going to fly in the face of all the evidence of the Morling Inquiry and the Northern Territory Supreme Court and say I was guilty again, but he did not. Once again he cleared me, but then he went on to cause of death, and then we got a rude awakening. He threw in a puzzling comment about Sir Lancelot's shoe size and said it was far too long ago to know accurately what happened. Well, in this case at least, the living witnesses were still alive and it was no myth, so what Sir Lancelot's shoe size had to do with anything I failed to see. In the end Coroner Lowndes left the cause of death open. It was rather a blow as this time I was sure the finding would be definitive. Inside information as to why that particular verdict was reached abounded and criticism from the legal profession was high. One way or another my family still had to live with it. Once again we had an open finding which meant that the case could be reopened at someone's whim.

Healing or Hiding, Burglars and Citizens

Time passed and we were evaluating our future life plans. For several years we had been worried about my parents. They lived away from the rest of the family in Nowra, on the New South Wales south coast, and their home had been broken into several times, once when they were home in bed. My Dad took his hearing aids off to sleep and if Mum had raised her voice to tell him, the burglars would have known they were elderly folk. Mum prayed, then, as one of the burglars came across the adjoining room towards their door, she yelled at them to get out of there. Mum said the voice coming out of her gave her a fright and certainly gave the two burglars a fright, so much so that they literally left skid marks on the floor. No one could convince my mother otherwise than that God magnified her voice for her, and I for one believe her.

With things like this in mind, and my parents' health and age concerning us, we knew we had to make some hard life choices. Kahlia and I felt so much at home in America that it was as if we were Americans who had, as Kahlia put it, "just been born in the wrong country, that's all." Reagan was also at peace over there, but Aidan was in Australia and missing us, and we him. We were about to sell our lovely home and business and relocate. Once we did it would be another about seven years before we would be ready to do that again. Rick's parents were still young so we didn't need to worry about them, so what to do? After much prayer and heart searching Rick suggested we wrote lists, then both rated them in order of importance.

When we compared lists we both had family at the top. Rick looked at me and said, 'Honey I'm not going to push you into this, but it is time you stopped using this house as a security blanket and got on with your life and stopped hiding. You cannot have it both ways. Mum and Dad don't want to move and Aidan can't. If family is our priority we are really saying there is no decision left to make, we just need to accept that.' He was right of course (he nearly always is) and the rest of the list then became irrelevant, if family was important, then back to Australia it was. Rick always did have a way of making sense out of a jumble. No wonder the kids bring their friends home for counsel when they have problems to work out. (Once Reagan even rang from the dorm with a friend on the line who needed counsel.) With the house already sold and the furniture van arriving in a few days, we had only just made the decision in time. Kahlia hated the decision, and Reagan was away at college in America and old enough to decide for himself (within eighteen months he transferred back to Australia as well to be with family).

My American citizenship was almost through, six weeks away at most according to current rates. We decided that Rick and Kahlia would go ahead so Kahlia could start school on time for half year. She had just finished year ten with honours, and would jump straight in to mid year eleven. She did her year eleven easily in the six weeks before exams finding it so easy after the honours programs. Meanwhile I stayed with friends in the USA awaiting my call to interview and swearing in. Then a letter arrived saying there would be a national hold on all citizenships until further notice due to a backlog of cases. During this time I was not supposed to leave the country! I had several speaking engagements booked during this time in Australia, and was able to get a release from immigration to do these and still not jeopardise my citizenship, but I had to return immediately. If I arranged things properly I could manage to see my family at the same time. It was never enough of course and the phones ran overtime. Meanwhile Rick discovered what it was like to be a single father and deal with a teenage daughter. The fact that Kahlia didn't want to be in Australia didn't help and there were boys to deal with as well. Eighteen months later I finally got to return home permanently, and Reagan came with me. We drove from Seattle to Boston in mid-winter and dropped our car off with Rick's mother for her use. It took us a week, travelling through snow most of the way, or on ice, with sub-zero temperatures. We stopped at Niagara Falls on the way, and we missed Christmas, but were able to spend New Year with Rick's family.

Although we all needed to be here, Rick was the only one who took to it like a duck to water. He loves Australia. Facing the public attention again affected us all. In fact Rick complained it was like having a different family over here. The differences might have been subtle but they were there. Reagan started overeating, and got very depressed dealing with things that he had buried or not had to deal with whilst in America. Only now is he slowly climbing out of that and once again starting to show the son we know is buried underneath. In Australia, Kahlia was slowly settling in, and I went back to unpacking and gardening. I missed the green and the snow on the towering mountains that I loved. Still I had my family close, and now we had purchased property instead of renting, it was ours. We swapped house size for land size and although we loved our views the house that came with the land had to be made habitable for daily living rather than just as a weekender. The roof wasn't insulated and there were gaps everywhere. When there was a local mouse plague we found many more holes. The traps didn't seem to work and the best solution in the end was Rick chasing them with his shoe. He became an expert at catching them. It is only now, five years later, that I can finally say I fully accept being here.

Mum and Dad sold their home in Nowra and wanted to stay on the property too, so they moved in with us until we could get plans through council. In the end they never did move into their own house. My Dad loves keeping himself active and was happy as a pig in mud to have space around him and always something to do. If he wasn't helping me with the landscaping and couldn't find somewhere to dig or mow on the current project, he would come asking for a list of future projects. If we had to go away we always had to leave Dad a list so he could keep occupied.

We have an old quarry that lends itself perfectly to being an outdoor chapel so I had decided to make a wedding garden around it. The paddock around it was rocky and needed more soil. When taking a load to the dump one day we discovered they had free mulch there, so back we went with the trailer. After the first trip we devised a method with high sidewalls so we could get more per trip. Pitchforks worked best, and at the end of the load I worked inside the trailer tossing to the back and stamping it down while Dad threw it up to me. Mum got to collect the string and trash that we threw out of it. At eighty-four Dad could still swing a pick six hours a day. We got over 40 tons in less than two months. Of course we had to pitch it all off again at home also, but often I could have that done by the time Dad had his nap after lunch. Getting it off was a breeze compared to getting it on. On a good day towards the end we sometimes got two loads in a day.

The garden finally started to look like one, and the following winter we went rock collecting. Anywhere we travelled and saw a loose stone we brought it home. Many of them came from around our property, and lots from in the quarry. Now we were able to do the rock edges and finish some of the gardens. Cementing and placing the rocks and finishing the cement between them really kills your back and a lot of our rocks were huge!

A Midnight Epiphany

Rick normally only likes to garden if there is a machine attached, but he did the first edge while I was overseas so it was ready in time for our first function. During the middle of the night I finally knew what I wanted for Azaria. Part of one of the gardens would be a memorial garden with a fountain dedicated to my special daughter. The spot was perfect and reminded me of the Rock as it had a lot of exposed rock surface. A large boulder placed in the centre of that with a baby in a bath would remind me of the times I bathed her on the way to Ayers Rock, now known by its Aboriginal name of Uluru. They were happy times and it would be a beautiful addition to the Gardens. A memorial to a short but beautiful life that all could enjoy. I could hardly wait to tell Rick, but I managed to wait till morning. Later that day he came inside with a grin and said, 'Come with me. I think I have found your big rock and if I can do what I think I can, I can get it out with our own tractor.' That was interesting and nearly tipped the tractor up but he managed it and was able to place it in the centre of the garden for me. It had a flat section broken away just the size for the bath to sit. Absolutely perfect.

I commissioned John McNaughton, 'Jomac', a friend to do it, with a description of what I wanted. It was to be just a generic baby in the pose I wanted. John had never seen Azaria and decided not to look at photographs of her in case he was influenced. When he called us in to see the semi finished piece, I was pleased. He suggested I have wording around the edge of the basin instead of my original idea, but what, I wondered? Rick who was standing quietly in the background, immediately said,

'Celebrating Life'. I loved it. Just those words and her name 'Azaria Chantal Loren' was perfect. I made a few other minor suggestions to John on generic baby shapes and girls' hair versus boys' hair, we left. A couple of days later he called for us to meet him on the way to the foundry and said he would have his tools with him just in case. Mum went with us. When we saw the finished product, on the side of the road mind you, I couldn't believe my eyes. The finished piece was almost identical to Azaria. The only differences seemed to be that this baby had an 'outie' instead of an 'innie,' and one toe was longer! John fixed it on the spot and we stood in awe looking at it. He thought I was joking when I told him what he had unwittingly accomplished. Amazed he told us that he had been nervous about this commission (he knows how fussy I am) and had prayed about it. After that it had come together more easily than any other he had ever done. God works in mysterious ways when we ask.

Mum hadn't heard the conversation, and as soon as we arrived home she made a beeline for the hallway. I knew where she was going. She didn't know it was the first thing I had done as well just to make sure I wasn't simply wishing it to be that way. She came back and asked me if I had looked at that photo of Azaria lately. I grinned and said 'Yes. It's like her, isn't it? He didn't even have a picture either.' Mum could hardly believe it.

With the fountain sculpture finished it was a rush to get it mounted in time for the dedication. I chose March, my birthday, for the date in Azaria's twenty-first year and had invited all the eyewitnesses, lawyers, and many of those who were closest to me and the case. It was difficult to decide where to stop the guest list as I have so many friends. In the end it was closeness to me and Azaria that counted, after all it *was* my birthday! I asked Brian Warren to unveil the fountain as he used to babysit Azaria in Mt Isa for me and was one of the few who had actually known her. In the end he insisted I help him. It was an emotional and reflective time for all of us. The water dribbling from the sponge in the baby's hands made wandering tracks on the tummy and made it seem so real.

Amongst my many friends we had all sorts of photos of each other and all enjoyed a display of photographs Barry O' Brien had taken whilst covering the case over the years. I was also able to locate 'Sunshine' the female warder from my prison days and was delighted that she was able to come as well. She died not long after this event, as did George Rollo, and my heart misses them both. There were others I would have liked to invite from all the different sagas of my life over the last twenty years, but unfortunately I couldn't locate all of them. It is a pity when people move and leave no forwarding address. I figure I'm always easy to find care of Harry M Miller, Australia. Mail and messages are always forwarded. The rest of the day we ate and talked, and I was able to introduce my friends to each other and tell everyone what each one meant to me in the scheme of life. It was a happy time, and a lot of the eyewitnesses camped together and we had extra time together as well. Some of the folks had brought plants to add to the memorial garden or the friendship garden.

Stuart Tipple capped the day off with a speech during which he said:

> In considering what I was going to say today, I reviewed the invitation, 'A Celebration of Life'. As I read those words, 'A Celebration of Life' I thought, "Is it a celebration of life? Should it be a celebration of life? What are we here to celebrate?".
>
> Life is a journey … one common, unifying thing that we all have, is the fact that we have no control over our itinerary. We don't know where our next stop is going to be. We don't know what our triumphs and our

tragedies are going to be. We are all Cosmos Mariners. We are all on an individual and unique journey . . . Twenty-one years ago, our journeys intersected . . .

I became involved at the second inquest. It was obvious to me that the battle lines were drawn. This was going to be a trial. A trial of compelling eyewitness account versus scientific interpretations. A battle of rational, logical interpretation against bigotry and prejudice. I remember, at the end of that inquest, the prosecutor called the defence lawyers in and he said, "I'll tell you this," he said, "If she admits she killed her baby, she could get a bond, but if she keeps telling her lies, she is going to go to jail, and she is going there for life."

I remember my head spinning as I walked out of there, I kept thinking of '*The truth shall set you free*' John 8: 32. The truth shall set you free.

So the choice was given to Lindy: Lie, and be set free or tell the truth, and lose your freedom. Lindy told the truth, the eyewitnesses told the truth, the defence did their very best, but Lindy lost her freedom. However, she never, ever, was not free. She's never not been free to look each of you in the eye. She has never, ever, not been free to preserve the memory of a little girl that she loved, and who loved her in return.

In our journeys of life, we have many decisions that we have to make. When I received this Celebration invitation, I was so pleased to see that it was indeed a celebration because it could so easily have been something else. It could have been a memorial. It could have been a memorial of bitterness, of revenge, garnished with hate. I am so glad it is not, because I would not have been part of it.

One thing that my journey has taught me is that if you have that sort of baggage, you must discard it, because it hinders life's journey. When you think of the epitaph you would like, when you think about the highest office, the most accomplished sporting feat you aspire to; is that the epitaph you would want? Or would you, like me, want to have a different epitaph. Because I think the greatest honour, the greatest challenge, the greatest epitaph that you can have is to have a child, who loves you and remembers you as a loving parent. What greater epitaph could you have?

In this case Lindy suffered not just every parent's nightmare—the nightmare of losing a child—she suffered something beyond compare. Not only losing her child, but she was wrongly accused, and convicted, of her baby's death.

We are obsessed with how we are to be remembered . . .

Today is a Celebration. It's a celebration of Azaria's life journey. Be it short, it was significant. Be it short, it intersected all of us. It taught us more about ourselves, about others, and the world we live in.

Hundreds, thousands of words have been written about the life of Azaria. These words have been recorded in books, media, and transcripts. They can all be summed up in three lines: 'This is a story of a little girl who lived and breathed, and loved, and was loved. She was part of me. She grew within my body and when she died, part of me died, and nothing will ever alter that fact.'

Now *that*, that's an epitaph. That's an epitaph because the lady who felt the pain was able to write those words, and yet call today a Celebration. I know you have realised the significance of what is happening here today. The fact that you are here today means that you realise this is an important stop in your journey . . . Today we stop, we think, and we focus on a Celebration. A celebration of your life, a celebration of your journey. Let me suggest that we focus on that question I asked, "What is the most important? Your journey, or your destination?" Let me suggest to you it is your destination. The destination of choice should be, to find the truth. Without the truth, without Lindy having found the truth, without your support, and without the higher form of Truth touching her life, *today* would never have been a Celebration.

I thank you all for being here.

Casting about Stage and Screen

A lady named Moya Henderson had called me one day before I met Rick and asked if I would mind if she wrote an opera on the case. It was not the first request I had had about music over the years inspired by the case. Mostly they were very amateur pieces written with the hope that I would like it and help put the composer or artist on the way to stardom or a recording contract. Why anyone thought I had those contacts I don't know, but pieces continued to be sent to me with that in mind. Sometimes they were actually good, some even from known groups who were simply doing me the courtesy of letting me hear something they had already produced. My answer was always the same. I had no right to stop them legally, but I would ask them to remember that what they saw in the media was related to real people and a real loved child who had been lost. If the piece was defamatory they could be sued. I gave the same answer to Ms Henderson who assured me she wanted to be supportive, and that this was a great chance for Australian music. I never gave it another thought, until some time later I got an update telling me the librettist was to be Judith Rodriguez and that Opera Australia had given her a grant to write the opera. That made me realise the lady was a serious contender.

Years later I was informed a piece was to be included in the works in progress section of the Canberra Music Festival. The National Museum of Australia was to mount a small display to coincide with it. I was still living in America at the time and my friend Neville rang and told me he was interested in hearing it, as he was doing his PhD in Fine Art at the time, and as a consequence wanted to collect as much relevant data as possible.

The distorted tape we eventually received of the item from Neville reminded me of a cat with its tail on fire being pulled through a sieve backwards. Later we heard rumours the opera was refusing to put it on. We heaved a huge sigh of relief, and promptly forgot it.

The media always told us that the public would remain interested in our family and the legal case and never to expect the interest to go away. Well, after hearing nothing more about the opera for a number of years, we now lived in Australia. In a catch-up phone call from artist and friend Neville Dawson, he mentioned he was thinking of trying to get an exhibition in the Opera House foyer 'during the opera'. That was the first I knew that the opera *Lindy* had actually got off the ground and was to be performed, and my heart plummeted. Thanks to Neville I was able to get in touch with the director Stuart Maunder and get a copy of it. He was under the impression that I knew all about the opera being performed. From there I was able to get in touch with the composer Moya Henderson again and get a full copy of the opera. I was pleasantly surprised to find it wasn't what I had thought it would be like at all.

One is always nervous when their life is on display under someone else's interpretation but you are the one who has to live with the consequences. The full unchanged script had some misconceptions from the media and attributed some spiritual beliefs to me that are more generally held by the public at large. Other people are entitled to their own perceptions of life after death and that is fine by me, as long as they don't claim them as my beliefs. We had to have several chats over the differences the placing of a word could make in the meaning of some things. Between us were able to reach middle ground for the final version used in its inaugural performance in Sydney 2002. Although there were some skirmishes along the way it was able to be done amicably enough. The director Stuart Maunder, his crew, and the cast were all great to work with, and get to know.

Although the opera was modern, it received much better accolades than the opera officials had dared to dream, and received great reviews for the opera itself and its stars David Hobson as Michael, and Joanna Cole as myself, and for once I agreed with the media. The music score for Joanna's part as Lindy was so difficult that some stars had declared it impossible to sing, but Joanna did a great job. The cast put on a special performance for us and seventy close family and friends involved in the case before the media saw it, and they gave the cast, director Stuart Maunder, and composer Moya Henderson a standing ovation.

Unfortunately Michael was unable to attend the daytime performance and chose to go to the opening night. I had been asked to go to the opening of the opera, but the one thing the opera company never thought of when they chose the Friday night opening date, was that it was on my Sabbath and so I was unable to attend. Part of me was disappointed, yet I didn't really want to watch the opera while people watched me, so I wasn't too upset. I was glad to have seen it before the media did though, and was delighted how great it was on stage. Even though Stuart Maunder had said it was coming together better than they had hoped, I realised he had just been modest because it surpassed all our hopes. Over the four nights it was performed publicly it continued to receive standing ovations, even stamping and wolf whistles. The public response and ticket sales outper- formed opera company predictions so everyone involved were delighted. Apparently it is the first time an opera had been written about a real person and performed while the composer, librettist and the subject person are all still alive, and in this case, were all women.

Some years before the opera *Lindy* debut, I had agreed to sell the rights to my book for a mini-series on the case. This was to cover a totally different aspect that had never been covered in the media before. I understood it was to be the story of the forgotten people in the case – the children. The story was to be told through the eyes of Reagan, who was there at Azaria's birth, and was walked over by the dingo when it attacked and killed Azaria. Still today he suffers in coping with some of those memories and in my opinion he has been one of the most overlooked people in the case. Unable to find the corroborative adult at the time needed, he was forced to remain silent when he had something to say, and as Chester Porter, counsel for the Royal Commission said, would have made a 'great little witness'. The effects on the wider family are always overlooked in the concentration on facts, and Rick and I thought that a lot of good could come to a lot of people through this angle.

Eventually, after all the thousands of hours of research and hundreds of personal interviews that Simone North and Tony Cavanaugh, the writers and producers of the Liberty and Beyond mini-series did, they chose to go an entirely different direction. Enough time had now passed that people from both prosecution and defence felt they could talk freely. For Aidan it was a cathartic experience and we all noticed the difference in him afterwards. A number of others felt the same way. With a new government in power in the Northern Territory things were different there also. I was amazed to learn of the existence of a 1,200 page document written by the police on how best to combat the dingo, and also a Crown file of known dingo attacks. The Crown were aware of court precedents before my trial. What happened to presenting the whole truth and acting as an arbiter for justice?

What is the mini-series like? I don't know yet. Nor do I know at time of writing what it will eventually be called. I helped with research, contacts, old files, and consulted with the writers and heads of sets and costumes. Some was used, a good amount was not. I have seen a few clips that will be eventually edited and may be incorporated into the finished product. Craig McLachlan and Miranda Otto, the stars of the series, looked so real in the few partially edited pieces I saw that I had to look twice to tell the difference between the originals and the copies! The interior of the Mt Isa house was nothing like mine however and I haven't seen the other house set yet. Some of the clothes were copies of ones I had, but others definitely were not, nor were some of the colours, but that is just movie business. Locations were difficult to find, and TV usually does not have the budget movies do, so the producers make do as best they can.

Di Drew did a great job with the cast, getting the best out of them, and it was a pleasure to watch her in action on three different occasions. Getting to know the cast and crew a little bit in the small amount of time we spent on the set was a real pleasure. The general public impression of actors and their associated business and crews is wild, fast living, and rough. My impressions of the crews of both this mini series and the movie were that they were genuine, open, honest, friendly ordinary, people earning their living in a difficult and demanding job. The mini-series crew in particular were a really nice group of people, and I feel richer for meeting them.

Having met most of the cast, it is still hard to imagine some of them playing the parts they have been selected for, but then again meeting Miranda on the street you would not be able to pick the fabulous job she would do either, so one never knows. Will I like everything about the finished mini series? Of course not, because you cannot fit twelve years into four hours and feel a sense of completion. Some of the scenes are out of necessity often compilations of incidences that occurred to one or several people rolled into one scene. Not true in itself, but things in it are true for one person or another. There are some things that I may prefer not to have revealed about myself or some of the rest of the family but that doesn't mean they are not right. I am what I am, but like Meryl Streep before them, both of the lead actors told me they felt they did not have the scope to play their characters as they saw or knew them to be. Once again, you cannot condense into a few hours everything that happened over the twelve year period covered. Although I was unable to be on the set when they were working as it would be rather off putting for them to be acting the part of the person who is standing watching them, the time I spent with Craig, Miranda, and her husband Peter off the set was really enjoyable. They were all lovely people. Some of the bonds formed during this time will continue, I have no doubt.

Would I have done the mini-series differently if I had the choice? Undoubtedly, but it is not my choice to make and I can only sit back and watch. So why help in a project like this? As I have mentioned before, when you are in the public eye, anyone can do anything they like without your permission, so if given a chance to try and make something accurate, why would you not instead of complaining after the fact? At least you have a chance of explaining your point of view, even if you do not have control over the final outcome. I chose to take the consultant opportunity offered, as most of those people involved did, with or without a contract, though Michael did not.

My Hero

By Christmas 2002 my Dad had something go wrong with his varicose veins and much to his disgust couldn't work outside for a while, but it passed and we started on the last stage of one of the gardens. The extra cold –7°C (20°F) of the previous winter, followed by the drought had killed a lot of plants. Our dams ran dry and plants weren't established enough to withstand the drought. We even lost some full-grown gum trees. That set us back in opening the garden for weddings, but it is gradually recovering. Dad and I were about to start putting in the next water and rock feature, when he became ill. He was now eighty-seven and still looking twenty years younger. Over the next few months he was diagnosed with bowel cancer and it was well on its way.

Dad was "in good courage" as he would say and ready to meet his maker if necessary. He underwent what appeared to be a successful operation. The doctor had thought he had removed most of the cancer, but at Dad's age, eighty-seven, what remained usually grew very slowly. Dad recovered well but he still felt nauseous, then the bowel twisted and he had to go back for another operation. It looked like the cancer was growing again and growing fast, and the doctor gave him three months to live. I waited for Rick to come home so we could both tell Mum and Dad together.

They had just finished their supper when we went down to tell them. Mum cried quietly, and Dad sat quietly, asking a few questions. When we finished he thanked us, gracious as he always was, saying he would rather know than not know. We decided to make any preparations Dad wanted while he was still well enough to deal with it. The future looked bleak and filled with pain, but Dad's faith was as strong as ever. That was on Thursday. On Monday he had another appointment with the doctor and the decision was reached that it was probably only swelling after all, because the lump had suddenly disappeared.

As Dad still felt nauseous we decided to continue on with our plans just in case. Rick wanted to take the funeral service himself if Dad agreed and Dad was thrilled. Tuesday afternoon Dad and Rick spent three hours together arranging everything. They could not have been closer than if they had been related by blood. In the last few weeks everyone, including the great-grandchildren, had had occasion to visit. Wednesday morning the last of Dad's close contemporaries had either rung him or called him, and my brother and I had been visiting. Kahlia's twenty-first birthday was only three weeks away and she had been dithering over which version of the Bible she wanted her Grandparents to give her. I popped in to see Dad before I left for town to do some errands and pick up the Bible so Dad could be sure to sign it as Mum was getting anxious about it. I kissed Dad goodbye and told him not to get into any mischief I wouldn't get into. He laughed and told me I was a scamp. On his way for a walk with Mum later that afternoon he said he felt a bit dizzy and should perhaps sit first. He died in seconds of a heart attack. He died as he lived, with his boots on, facing life with courage. The only thing he had left undone was signing Kahlia's Bible. I hope my life will be just as complete.

We grieved for ourselves but not for Dad. He was in great pain and ready to go. The only adult I have ever met who I did not ever wonder if they were really ready to meet their maker. My Dad was my hero. He moulded my life with love and patience. I obeyed him as a child because I loved him and I knew he accepted me utterly. I wanted to always make him proud of me. To be morally strong, truthful at all times, and have the courage to stand up for your convictions even in the face of opposition and to personally know and love God is what my father taught me by example as well as word. He also taught me to stand up for and help those weaker or less fortunate than yourself, and to face life with humour and a smile. I miss him more than I can say.

While calling around to notify people of Dad's passing, Rick called the church office in Victoria and discovered there was a man trying to contact us. He claimed to have information on the disposal of Azaria's body. It was November 2003. They had been trying to get the message to us but it had not reached us. The next day Rick rang the man who would only identify himself as Frank. Rick again rang Frank in January and after talking to him for half an hour, with me listening to a lot of the conversation without Frank realising it, Rick suggested that he might like to talk to the Liberty & Beyond Production's investigators. They had some good investigators working with them and Stuart Tipple thought that would be a good idea if the man was agreeable. Frank wouldn't do it without my direct permission, so I picked up the phone. Frank apologised profusely, and gave me a mini précis of the story he told Rick. He told me his absolute proof that what he said was true was that he had kept in his possession the ribbons from the matinee jacket. The call ended soon after. Frank sounded sincere and I knew he believed what he had just said, but there was one big problem. The jacket had no ribbons in the first place, but the Crown had said it did and the newspapers carried the story that it had. What if there was some element of truth to it though? We called Liberty & Beyond and passed the information on and they took it from there, but were unable to verify the story, so we dropped it like so many others before it.

Right at the end of the mini series filming we bought a -new to us- vehicle, and on the way home stayed at our friends Pete and Marijana's. Next morning, wouldn't you know it, Pete, who rises with the chickens, knocked on the door and walked in with the newspaper in his hands. Frank Cole was headlines in all the papers even though he said he did not want publicity. Now we knew his full name. His story of shooting the dingo and finding Azaria and his mates burying Azaria's body and placing the clothes was in the media at last. Once again everyone else had been contacted and knew it was going to be in the paper but us. The story had changed a bit and there was no mention of his ultimate proof of the ribbons any more.

TV host Ray Martin contacted us and we discovered he and Michael had known about this man four years ago, but Michael had also dismissed it so Ray hadn't taken it any further. Now Ray said he sounded credible and soon had him on the television, and doing lie detector tests to prove his story. Lie detector tests carry no weight as evidence in court and they are inadmissible as concrete evidence. Maybe there is truth here somewhere and maybe not (at time of writing this I understand a police investigation is under way) but each story of this type is worth investigating because there is always the wild card chance there is a grain of truth hidden somewhere in it.

Dad wanted no cut flowers at his funeral, only donations to missions or white flowers and trees to plant in the wedding garden, and people honoured his wishes. In the memorial part of the garden are the two white Iceberg standard roses that stood one each side of my Dad's casket in the chapel. Dad would have enjoyed the way it looks now. We have had several functions in the gardens although we are still having water problems, but I look forward to the first wedding there. Birth, death, and marriage are all part of the cycle of life. I look at my unfinished water garden and don't have the heart to work on it yet. It holds too many reminders. One day I'll start again, and think of the richness my life has held as I wander in the garden and revisit the wonders God has allowed me to live through and the lives I have been a part of. I don't know what the future holds for me, but with God beside me I know I have nothing to fear. With Rick supporting me I hope I can be the example and encouragement to my children that my father was to me.

The echoes of the case continue to haunt Australia, and unfortunately another child has died since I gave my warning in the first part of this book. This time Clinton Gage, a 10 year old lad, was savaged and killed by a dingo whilst walking with his younger brother on Fraser Island, Queensland on the 30 April, 2001. Some said, 'Oh, but that was different, that was Fraser Island, and those dingoes are different.'

Try telling that to Clinton's parents. A dingo is a dingo regardless of where it lives, and some are more tame than others. They are still wild animals, and no matter how beautiful they are, precautions should be taken because they are a wild animal with wild instincts and you never know just when those instincts are going to surface. Some lions have made good pets too, but somehow we still don't want them roaming our streets or back yards as pets. What will it take to make Australians listen to the inherent dangers of our native country and take appropriate precautions? We may not be able to control nature, but we can at least educate ourselves in the best methods of protection from nature.

My life continues to be different to that of most people and still continues to make history. Even amongst tragedy, much good has come. The legal precedents alone have made Australia a fairer country, and the case has changed the way we see ourselves as a nation and hopefully, the way we read and hear our news services. I guess Di Drew, the director of the mini-series based on my book and other research, has best summed it up this way:

> 'The maturity of a nation is often stimulated by landmark events that change its direction and mould its thinking. Such was the case in Australia in the 1980s when baby Azaria Chamberlain disappeared at Ayres Rock. Never before had our nation been so captivated and so divided about a single issue.
>
> Over two generations we allowed ourselves to become obsessed by the mystery and seduced by the freedom to pass judgement. In our adolescence we presented a mob mentality; the stuff of witch hunts, of slur and innuendo. The paramour of immaturity.
>
> In 2004, I found myself at the helm of the mini series *Through My Eyes* traversing the remarkable lies, deceit, injustice, corruption, tragedy and ineptitude that came about because a woman stood firm in her truth and held fast to her faith. But even with the benefit of hindsight and the recognition of maturity the fact remains that a little girl lost her life and a mother still grieves.
>
> It is my deepest hope that we, as a nation, have matured to the point that we will never again see such a shameful episode repeated in our history.'

That is my deepest hope also. May it be a warning to other countries as well. You cannot ride roughshod over innocence and escape justice forever.

PART SEVEN

Will it Ever End?

WILL IT EVER END?

It is now thirty-four years since Azaria was born, and the saga surrounding the end of her life changed once more in 2012, so it's necessary to continue this book now, to make it complete.

To do anything other than write the facts of history in this book would be to attempt to re-write history the way I wish it to be. History is not always to our liking or even to our favour. Nevertheless we are stuck with it, good or bad, and that is what we have to live with. It became so obvious that others were trying to rewrite history in a multitude of ways so, in writing my book, I determined that it should be left as a historical record not only of my feelings and thoughts on what has happened in my life, but as a way to curate an overall narrative of the actual events that took place in 1980 with Azaria's death and the court cases that were to follow.

I originally named my book "Through My Eyes" because the book was written, as far as possible, through my eyes, through Sally Lowe's (now Shaw) eyes, through Greg Lowe's eyes, through Judy and Bill West's eyes, through Max and Amy Whittaker's eyes, through Aidan's eyes, and through Reagan's eyes.

As it is impossible to write without mentioning Michael, his part is taken from court transcript and quotes either from himself or others who were there at the time,. Otherwise it is left for him to tell his own story, at his request.

All the forensic evidence and discussion in the book was carefully perused by case scientist, Les Smith, who was involved in both the blood evidence and dingo damage "cuts" in order to make sure I had properly and accurately got all the scientific terms and interpretation spot on.

Two of my lawyers took a fine comb to the legal sections and discussions of themselves and the court. Other friends were chased down to check the sections on themselves.

In many places it is evident that I have used the personal writings of those involved, while others are concentrated and blended in or taken from interviews. This all meant that I was comfortable with the title, as it was a reflection of how everyone shown the manuscript felt they had been portrayed. It was through the eyes of all.

In Australia, England and New Zealand, most were familiar with my face and name, but once the book went international, it was the story and the phrase "The Dingo's Got My Baby" that was known so, to avoid confusion, I have changed my book title. My book is now known as "A Dingo's Got My Baby", but the book is identical, and still in Australian English and spelling.

It remains the aggregate experience of many people who suffered throughout my journey, in my personal hell, because they were not afraid to get involved with the evidence and get the truth out there. It was not only our family who were affected; the personal lives of the eyewitnesses were turned upside down because they told the truth about what happened that night, as they had witnessed it, regardless of pressure to change their evidence. Key lawyers and scientists also came under this intense pressure. The public hate many felt was almost tangible.

It would be easy to change and dramatise my story for public sympathy and fame, but this is the real story of real people, how and when it happened, and I feel to embellish it in any way would be dishonest both to history and to the memory of my beloved first baby daughter, Azaria.

I Want To Do Something Now

After the disappointment of the open finding of the third inquest (1995), Michael wanted me to sign papers giving permission for a whole new set of lawyers to take over the case and, further, he wanted me to agree that he would be the only one to instruct them. Why he thought I would do that I don't know, as I had never let others tell me what to do blindly. Michael had missed a good many of the legal conferences over the years and I was not at all sure he was up to speed on necessary details. And just why he would now choose not to use Stuart Tipple, but start from the ground up again, was beyond my comprehension. Stuart's grasp of our case was all-encompassing and his memory phenomenal, so why on earth would you want to throw that away? In the end I agreed to hear what Michael and his mysterious new lawyer had to say and planned to do, provided we met at Stuart's office and included him.

Rick and I arrived at the same time as Michael and two lawyers and proceeded into Stuart Tipple's conference room. The lawyers turned out to be Professor Ray Watterson from the Newcastle University and a colleague, a practising lawyer who worked on some of the cases the final year students undertook. He had come more as an observer and advisor, I think.

When the introductions were over and we got down to discussion, it was blatantly obvious within the opening thirty seconds that they were not in possession of the facts. Professor Watterson was proposing DNA tests and others which he was clearly under the impression had not been available at the time of the trial, or at least not done. I stopped him and suggested that to cut things shorter, perhaps Stuart could give them a brief version of the tests done and experts used. When Stuart did, their consultant looked thoughtful and the others stunned. Now realising all the ground they had been proposing to cover, and had been so excited about, was done and already in evidence, they wondered where they could help or how.

To quote Mr Tipple's notes "It was agreed that it would be fruitless making any application unless there was a change in the political climate of the Northern Territory and additional evidence could be collected and submitted to show that Mr Lowndes' finding that a dingo attack was 'an inherent unlikelihood and that one would not expect human beings and in particular young babies, to be taken and killed by a dingo' to be unsustainable."

We wanted to fix the inquest but how could that be done when all of our antagonists were still alive, and some even still in positions of power, and still maintaining we were guilty?

We had to have a plan and work around that, while we bided our time and awaited our chance. We felt we had one more chance and that was it. It felt a bit like the Chinese philosophy of planning for a thousand years, not just for a moment's gratification.

The Newcastle University team wanted to help but where could they go? It had all been exhaustively done before, except the dingo angle, and although we all had many cases of dingo attacks in our files, they would have to be collated for the time when they could go in with Mr Tipple's formal application and other submissions. This was something the Newcastle University team could do, as Stuart's were mostly in storage and mine were mainly in Canberra in the National Library. This would mean a trip down for me and Rick and a couple of days' work for both of us, plus a good few hours for Stuart and his staff.

Michael kept reiterating that he had files of dingo attacks, so it was obvious that if his team wanted to do something and were already working with Michael, that would be the way to go.

As Normal As It Gets - Mostly

Life settled back into what was, for us, a normal routine. Both Aidan and Kahlia found partners and decided to marry, with weddings three months apart either side of Christmas 2007. Both had the weddings the girls had dreamt of, and we had a very busy few months.

We get on well with both spouses, which is lovely for all involved and leads to much fun, love and involvement, despite the huge physical distance between us all. Just as well we all love travelling, but FaceTime is a brilliant advantage to all of us.

Over the years, in media interviews and personal talks and lectures, both Michael and I continued to state that we would not rest until there was no longer an open finding on the death certificate. On the thirtieth anniversary of Azaria's death I posted this letter on my website:

> **"A letter to Open Minded Australians.**
>
> "It is hard to believe it is thirty years since my darling baby was taken. For some odd reason everyone says you will soon forget. Why is it that people expect me to forget a part of myself? Why would you? Loss of a loved one, particularly a child is not something you forget any more than you can get out of your mind that you once attended school. That does not mean you dwell on it all the time. It is simply there in the fabric of your life and history. In some ways it seems forever and in others it is like yesterday still. Yesterday are the happy memories, and the years are the pain.
>
> "I choose to dwell on the happy memories and not on the pain.

Dwelling on the pain is only something that those who wish you harm hope that you will do. They want you miserable. I don't wish to be miserable. That is why I learned what forgiveness really is and put it in to practice. You always hear people say to forgive, but they don't tell you how to do it and that is key. Once you learn that, you wonder why you didn't do it before. Forgiveness is for yourself, it puts the responsibility on those who hurt you, and lets you get on with your life. It does not say it is OK to hurt me, then hurt me again. It simply says yes you hurt me, you had no right to do that to me but you did. I acknowledge that you did that and that I am not responsible for your actions. I will not take over the continuation of your actions towards me by allowing you or them to dwell in my mind and continue to fester and ruin my life. I have taken back control of my own life and head space and move forward. I am moving forward, not looking backward.

"So, have I forgiven everyone involved in creating the fiasco of the last thirty years and the public so willing to believe the worst and spread nasty rumours? Of course I have. I have handed the hurt back to those who caused it and it is up to them as individuals to ask God to forgive them for what they did, because I forgave long ago and moved on. Oh, and despite what some headlines have said in the last twelve months, that does include the police, politicians and lawyers of the NT. It would be nice to get a voluntary apology, but I am no longer holding my breath.

"Did you know that the truth is not a defence for libel in Australia? Ridiculous as that sounds that is the law as it currently stands. So if you tell the truth about someone you can be charged with libel if you say something a person has done wrong but which they want to remain hidden. They can have you charged in court because you told the truth and revealed their dirty dealings. Of course once you are in court (or under parliamentary privilege) you can say whatever truth or lies you like and no one can touch you for it. I believe one should be able to tell the truth openly without having to be dragged into court by corrupt people covering their trails. Unfortunately the way the law stands now I cannot tell you of any internal deals, deliberate lies, affairs or favours that I may know of that may make what happened in my case a lot clearer. If I did I would be charged with libel and the truth doesn't count in Australia yet.

"Now it seems like in the centuries to come there will still be arguments over who said what, where and how. It seems to me that it is ridiculous that people will believe all that stuff. Can they not even try to think for themselves but believe everything they are told to think by someone else? In the last couple of weeks I discovered I apparently did twice the amount of time in prison that I actually did, in Berrimah Prison no less, despite it being quite obvious that I was in Darwin Prison and Berrimah was only the suburb. Berrimah Gaol is in NSW. Only very subtle changes you say and nit picking. Yes, you are right that the difference is small in one way; it is only one wrong word. Now look at it another way. One prison does not exist at all and the other is thousands of kilometres away. Now it becomes not such a small thing but totally misleading. This is where lies and rumours start. When the truth is dealt with this way, subtly leaving a word out here and changing one there, then it goes into the archives unchallenged because someone else thinks it is too small to matter and another mistake is let slide or a deliberate omission or addition let go and you soon can bury the truth so deep that only the most vigilant will ever find it again.

"Of courses you can start rumours like the one where I was supposed to hit on the policemen who raided us! They wish! Of course they didn't bring that up in court. It is much easier to besmirch a person's reputation by starting a rumour or making a statement with no basis in fact that will surface accidentally or on purpose some time. Bury the fact that until the police told us we had to stay near the tent we had both searched. By belittling and burying it on the one hand and on the other use it as the excuse to say we sneaked away to bury Azaria's body, in the end was so successful that even the jury came to believe we didn't search, despite testimony to the contrary.

"It is no wonder that the eyewitnesses resent being disbelieved again and again when they hear and see the stupid lies and innuendoes resurface again and again. You see it is the questions not asked in court that are often the most important. For example, Murray Haby's evidence that he had found what the Aboriginals later confirmed were the tracks of the dingo that took Azaria and the marks where it had put her down. When we met him after he had given his evidence he told us he was not supposed to mention this, and only an odd question allowed him to say what he wished about what he had found. With selective or very technical evidence it is no wonder that modern day juries are no longer equipped to make an informed decision. We need an updated system for the modern age we live in so that there is less likelihood of the guilty going free because they take advantage of the current inadequacies and the innocent being charged because they expect the truth and fairness that a court was once based on. Now it is just a lethal game.

"Come on Australia. Surely you cannot be proud of the fact that you can let yourself be duped again and again and come back for more of the same. We used to be a proud nation who saw through corruption and were willing to give a fair go. How many times do you have to be hoodwinked and led along by the nose before you demand something better from our courts, police force, politicians and media? There are good, honest, truthful people in all these fields. We need to support them in their struggle to clean up their profession and stand for truth and justice. Hitler got as far as he did because good people didn't wake up to the importance of the small details that did not look threatening on their own, until the avalanche engulfed all and it was too late to fix.

"Painful as it may be at times we need to stand up and be counted. Change starts with the individual, the family, the local community, the town, the state, the country. It is not easy to decide not to let the small things slip, or give in to the bully because of the pain or embarrassment it may cause us, but if you don't do it you may as well die now. Grow a backbone before the world turns on you. Give up the desire for gossip and sensationalism. Use your brains for something useful. You may surprise yourself what you can achieve.

"I thank God that the Crown eyewitnesses in my case did have backbones as did quite a few ordinary Australians who were willing to stand up and say "hey I don't know what happened but something is not right here and we need all the facts" which paved the way for new legislation allowing for Royal Commissions in Australia now. This allows for all of the evidence, rumours, tip-offs and questions to be exhaustibly investigated. The Commissioner in our case was asked to find our guilt or innocence. Although we argued otherwise, he did not feel he had been given the power to rule on whether cause of death was a dingo or not so did not rule on that. Despite that (the Crown/prosecution always claimed that it was either me or a dingo), Morling in his finding said we would be guilty 'if, in spite of so many considerations pointing to their innocence, the conclusion was reached that it had been proved beyond reasonable doubt that a dingo did *not* take the baby. In the light of all the evidence before the Commission, I am of the opinion that such a conclusion cannot be reached.'

"Today our family will always remember it as the day truth was dragged in the dirt and trampled upon, but more than that it is the day our family was torn apart forever because we lost our beautiful little Azaria. She will ever be what this ongoing fight for justice has been all about. She deserves justice. In light of all the evidence before the Commission, this should be reflected on her death certificate and not the open finding that is there now. It is not like the eyewitnesses are dead or that there was not a recommendation from the Royal Commission. It would not take more taxpayers money to do it. The Commission was exhaustive, why not adopt the recommendation and stop wasting everyone's time, money and intelligence. Lindy or a dingo was the NT claim. Their own commission proved it was not me as I had told them all along, so why don't they accept their own claim? It makes one wonder are they too proud or too stubborn? Who knows the reason, but most of all please do not forget that a beautiful little girl died tragically on this date thirty years ago.

Regards, Lindy."

This was a familiar plea in my talks, speeches and interviews over the years.

Wow

I had been asked to speak in May 2010 for the annual Buddhist "Happiness and its Causes" conference. I was on a panel moderated by Margaret Throsby of the ABC on the subject of forgiveness. Of all the people over the years who listened to me talk, unbeknown to me, in this audience there was a woman who would make a difference in my life. Impressed by something I had said about forgiveness she went home and looked up my website and found the above letter. She then recommended to her friend, Delia Lawrie, who happened to be the Northern Territory Attorney-General, that she should also read my letter.

Next thing I knew an official letter came through my website on the 17th of August, 2010. It was from the NT Minister for Justice and Attorney-General, Delia Lawrie. I was at Rick's parents' place in Boston at the time, Rick printed it out and brought it to me with a big grin on his face, saying "I think this is a letter you will want to read," but he wouldn't give me any extra clues.

Curiosity high, I took the letter. It began:

> "I refer to the open letter posted on your website concerning the cause of death of your daughter Azaria.
>
> "In response to your letter, I have requested that the Registrar of Births, Deaths and Marriages conduct an inquiry . . ." and the letter continued with details of the process.
>
> Wow, was that a big hit out of the blue! I was simultaneously excited and dubious, as it wasn't an inquest and I was not sure if it had any teeth or could only check if it was one of the required official reasons allowed, and I already knew it was one of those. Despite that, I was thrilled with the progress.
>
> I mulled over it and decided to ask Stuart Tipple if he had also been notified, as that was the usual way we heard, and neither could we find anything in the news. I had to wait until office hours in Australia, then I called Stuart and he hadn't heard anything either, so I filled him in and sent him a copy of the letter. I asked him to makes a few enquiries and a few private phone calls while he was at it to find out the latest in the NT, and to see if anyone had dropped dead or changed their attitude yet.

Stuart's official notes read:

> "5. On 18 August 2010, Lindy asked me to advise as to: What Section 39 entails? Is it worth making submissions or better to do nothing?
>
> 6. On 18 August 2010, I forwarded Lindy a copy of Section 39 and advised: "It is unlikely the Registrar could or would enter a finding inconsistent with the Coroner. We have taken the executive decision to write to the Justice Adviser to clarify this matter and will keep you

informed."

Meanwhile I had also notified Harry Miller's the same day I had rung Stuart that, unless an announcement came from the NT themselves and was picked up by the news, I didn't want any to give any comment. Even then there was really nothing to say at that stage of events unless it was simply to say I was pleased with some movement. Too many times I had seen promising movements either stall or simply drop out of sight when the media became involved in NT business.

Stuart thought I should tell Michael but as we hadn't seen the NT announcement in the news yet, I did not wish any press leaks to come from me. Stuart kept pushing so after thinking over it for a while, I told Stuart he had permission to read the letter over the phone to Michael. He was flat out but would do it first thing on the next work day. He had hardly settled in to work and Michael beat him to it, calling to say he had got a letter.

It turned out that the Attorney General *had* released a statement on the 17th, however we had just not seen it. It read:

"Northern Territory Government

Media release

Delia Lawrie, Attorney-General

17 August 2010

Inquiry into Azaria Chamberlain's Registered Cause of Death

Attorney-General, Delia Lawrie, has asked the Northern Territory Registrar of Births, Deaths and Marriages to look into the cause of death stated on Azaria Chamberlain's death certificate.

'Lindy Chamberlain-Creighton has used the 30th anniversary of the death of Azaria Chamberlain to raise issues concerning the cause of death stated on her daughter's certificate,' Ms Lawrie said.

'I have written to the Registrar of Births, Deaths and Marriages and asked him to undertake an inquiry to determine if the registered cause of death on Azaria Chamberlain's death certificate is accurate.

'I have asked the Registrar to investigate under section 39 of the Birth, Deaths and Marriages Registration Act NT whether the particulars concerning the death of Azaria Chamberlain contained on the Register are accurate, taking into account the most reliable information that is currently available.

'I have also written to Mrs Chamberlain-Creighton, informing her of the inquiry into the registered cause of death on Azaria Chamberlain's death certificate.

'The cause of death currently listed on Azaria Chamberlain's death certificate is unknown.'"

Soon the press started in Australia and there was a typical media frenzy. Claims that the NT had finally been forced to re-open the case and that there was to be a fourth inquest were now made. There wasn't, of course, but you can't tell some people. I was so glad I had not given any statements. Checking the validity of the information would have been easy, but it seemed those doing interviews didn't bother to, and then it all went quiet again.

Everything seemed to happen at once, then. Mr Tipple's pithy notes read:

"For the assistance of all, we have reviewed our file and produced the following timeline:

7. On 19 August 2010, Northern Territory Registrar of Births Deaths & Marriages wrote to Lindy and Michael advising that he will be conducting an enquiry under Section 39 and Section 40 and invited submissions. In his letter the Registrar made the following observations: 'In the circumstance where a Coroner has conducted an exhaustive enquiry into the cause and circumstance of the death, having regard to all previous findings and the evidence disclosed through the exhaustive processes of the Commission, it would be at least in the absence of further evidence, be exceptional for the Registrar to reach some different conclusion.'

8. On 19 August 2010, wrote to the Attorney-General confirming that we will assist the Registrar but asked the Registrar to liaise with this office and advise the precise details that have been recorded and what will appear in any issued Death Certificate.

9. On 24 August 2010, received a response from the Registrar of Births Deaths & Marriages with a copy of the latest Death Certificate.

10. On 25 August 2010, 1 wrote to Michael confirming the correspondence invitation received and asking whether he would like us to represent him and if so, to provide details of any materials he would like us to consider.

11. On 31 August 2010, Michael rang and requested us to work with him and Ray Watterson, but that he would require at least 8 weeks."

Michael had always told me that he had his dingo files ready to go at a moment's notice, so I wasn't sure what the hold-up was, but as we were full steam ahead it didn't seem to matter to me, as long as whatever he was doing was the dingo files.

"12. On 1 September 2010, [Stuart] had a telephone attendance with Michael and advised he would be happy to receive any submissions from Ray Watterson and that any submissions should include the submissions made to a critique of John Lowndes' findings and incorporate new evidence of the CAC, and that there should be a joint approach, and that it would be best to try for a new Inquest.

So Stuart got busy.

13. On 7 September 2010, wrote to the Registrar of Births Deaths & Marriages advising that the inquiry should consider fresh dingo attacks and obtaining an extension of time."

Meanwhile, Stuart and I had been discussing options and we decided that Stuart should make a few personal calls behind the scenes again. Many of our support group members still resided in Darwin.

Finally we got answers. Stuart was so excited when he called back with answers to my questions, despite giving me the bad news first, as always.

Yippee!

In the process of ascertaining just what effect there could be from any actions of the Registrar, we discovered it was now a moot point anyway as the backlash over the media claims had made it a political hot potato and it was now basically dead in the water.

So why was he excited?

What Stuart was able to find out through all this, was that there was a new attitude now in at least some of the power sections of government, and that there were new personnel in the coronial system in the Territory. All systems were now go for a new application to be made to re-open Azaria's Inquest. Not only that, we knew *exactly* how we would go about it.

Excitedly he told me he was going to start writing initial submissions immediately he was "off the phone, with your permission of course." I was as quick to say go for it, as he knew I would be. There was a little more logistics talk, about how to keep both doors open without offending anyone, then we hung up; he to go to work immediately, and I to do a big "yippee" and fill Rick in as fast as I could. USA time was late when the phone call came through and we had been tired, but we were so excited it took us hours to calm down again!

The writing of submissions must be accurate, including all salient points you want to use, yet not give everything away before you have the go ahead to proceed fully. It is an exacting job and not something to be rushed, but still done as fast as possible, without neglecting the work of current clients at the same time.

I have rarely seen a lawyer work with the memory for detail, speed and accuracy with which Stuart Tipple is able to work. [Justice] Andrew Kirkham QC, AM, RFD, my then trial junior, is similar. Andrew has been asked to be a Judge, twice actually, and even agreed once then changed his mind and refused. It made me laugh when he said he realised he wanted a life rather than writing up judgements every weekend! Stuart likes the research, and has successfully refused all attempts to recommend or push him further up the legal ladder. It is a source of constant delight to me to know that all my other lawyers (and they are well into the double figures) have become Judges and Royal Commissioners, except for one that I know of. This is not a trend followed by those used by the Crown.

Stuart's notes state it very matter of factly then continue on:

"14. On 28 September 2010, advised Michael and Lindy that we do not believe the Registrar will be able to change anything without having a proper legal basis to do it and that the better approach would be to make an application under the new Coroner's Act under Section 44A to re-open the Inquest and consider the new evidence.

15. On 11 October 2010, wrote to the Attorney-General and advised: 'We confirm we have formed the view that the proposed inquiry into Section 39 of the Births Deaths & Marriages Registration Act will be too limited and unable to achieve the result and justice sought by our clients. We have formed the view the better course is for the Coroner to re-open the Inquest pursuant to Section 44A of the Coroners Act. Recent media reports have indicated your Department may well have formed the same view and would ask that you please advise in this regard. We look forward to hearing from you. '

16. On the same day, we made the following press release:
'Mrs Lindy Chamberlain-Creighton and Dr Michael Chamberlain applaud the Northern Territory Government's initiative in re-examining the recording of their daughter Azaria's death. Today, their lawyer Stuart Tipple has written to the Northern Territory Attorney General requesting that, rather than having an enquiry under Section 39 of the Births Deaths & Marriages Registration Act, it is more appropriate that the Coroner re-open the Inquest under his statutory powers.'

I then drafted submissions and in those submissions included the 15 reported dingo attacks which Michael had provided evidence of.

17. On 20 October 2010, the Northern Territory Attorney General replied confirming she does not have the power to require the Coroner to re-open the Inquest and requested any application should be directed to the Coroner's Office.

18. On 3 November 2010, the application was forwarded to the Coroner's Office.

19. On 3 November 2010, the Registrar, Births Deaths & Marriages wrote requesting submissions regarding his enquiry.

20. On 5 November 2010, wrote to the Registrar, Births Deaths & Marriages advising that in our view his enquiry into Section 39 is too limited and that we would be making an application for a new Inquest to the Coroner.

21. On 5 November 2010, press release confirming an application had been made to the Northern Territory Coroner requesting the Inquest be re-opened.

22. On 8 November 2010, Greg Cavanagh (now chief Coroner of the NT) responded acknowledging the application and because of his conflict (as our former Legal Aid junior trial lawyer, appointed by the Crown) has referred the matter to Coroner Elizabeth Morris.

23. On 16 November 2010, wrote to the Coroner (Morris) asking for an update on our application.

24. On 22 December 2010, Coroner responded advising the application is being considered.

25. On 26 August 2011, wrote to the Coroner requesting an update on the application and expressing disappointment that nothing had been heard.

26. On 16 November 2011, wrote to Greg Cavanagh advising that we have heard nothing from the Deputy Coroner and asking whether we could receive a report, otherwise we would be referring the matter to the Attorney-General.

27. On 21 November 2011, Coroner's office telephoned advising that our application was being investigated by an independent investigator and was being reviewed.

28. On 16 December 2011, Elizabeth Morris confirmed that she is determined to re-open the Inquest and advised: 'The parameters of the Inquest are that I am seeking and considering evidence as to the cause and circumstances of death of Azaria. I do not intend to receive evidence or submissions in relation to the police investigation nor the subsequent criminal proceedings and process.'

29. In January 2012, received and perused the Coroner's Brief of Inquest.

30. In January 2012, discussed with Rex Wild, Counsel Assisting, and he agreed that he will prepare his submissions and send them to us.

31. On 24 January 2012, Michael advised that he will be preparing some submissions himself. Advised that I would be delaying my submissions until I had read Mr Wild's submissions."

Stuart called to let me know what was happening, stating he had told Michael he would not be a party to it unless he could read it and I gave my permission too, as he worked on behalf of both of us. I sincerely hoped it would not annoy anyone by including things Ms Morris had already asked not to be included and I saw no reason to second guess Stuart's thorough work, but as Michael seemed determined do it, I gave my OK. I reiterated to Stuart that he make sure anything was not coming through him did not appear to be coming from me or on my behalf in any way, and on that basis Michael could be free to do what he felt he needed to.

Just as well I did, as when I finally saw the submission, it was also supposedly on my behalf and Stuart was able to advise Michael to amend that and a few other things immediately, which he did.

The frantic preparations continued. There are periods of intense work, then periods of nervous waiting while you await a response. Traditionally in the NT that had always been months, even years. Just how quick this would move we weren't sure, but wonder of wonders, this time, when it moved, it moved fast. Stuart's notes continue:

> "32. On 7 February 2012, read Mr Wild's submissions and began to prepare my own submissions.
>
> 33. On 20 February 2012, forwarded draft submissions to Rex Wild and requested him to amend some passages in his submissions.
>
> 34. Received Michael's submissions and requested him to make amendments.
>
> 35. Received Ray Watterson's submissions.
>
> 36. On 21 February 2012, Rex Wild agreed to make the amendments to his Submissions as suggested."

The Crown looking at things from an unbiased viewpoint was a novelty for me and I kept thinking I was just dreaming, or being lulled into a false sense of security. However, you have to give people the benefit of the doubt if you want to live in the world unafraid of paranoia or your own shadow, so I kept telling myself to believe and left it in God's hands. Meanwhile the simple words in Stuart's notes are a momentous understatement!

> "37. On 21 February 2012, forwarded my Submissions together with Ray Watterson's Submissions and Michael's Submissions to Mr Wild."

Professor Ray Watterson had prepared a submission on the range and power of a coroner, which was a subject he was considerably interested in. It was a good submission and the Coroner subsequently thanked him for it.

Mr Tipple's timeline continues:

"38. Prepared further evidence and Statutory Declaration of dingo attack from Josephine Arnold."

Here We Go Again

The date was set for the new inquest in Darwin, and we were now back home from helping out Rick's parents. Being away had its benefits as we weren't around for all the media disturbance and therefore were able to concentrate on what needed to be done instead of dealing with media. We were being pushed to sign contracts for exclusives, yet no one really knew if this was going to be all on one day, over two days, or two separate days. Nothing seemed right, so I resisted the urge to be pushed into anything. Of course you are always told it is your only chance to have your say and, as I have learnt, you have to say something or be hounded forever, so you have to make a choice about how you say it, and to whom.

In the end it didn't feel right and so I resisted and kept my options open. If it did go two separate days there would be nothing I wanted to say until I heard the final decision. I was sure I did not want to pre-empt anything. In the end we found out definitely the night before that the next day was for the entering of submissions only and we could have stayed home, but there is always the chance of hiccups in court that you may need to be on the spot for, and I have never hidden away, so I wasn't going to start now.

The trip went smoothly until we exited the plane and a gaggle of media surrounded the gate awaiting our arrival. They swarmed immediately, and as I had no intention of being forced to "stand and deliver" I kept pushing forward, saying "Excuse me, excuse me please" but there is just one thing wrong with that. Being short I could not see over all the heads to where I was going and, yep, I ended up at a glass window and had to turn around! Bummer! Stuart behind me wondered where I was heading and suddenly twigged when I came to a halt at the window. He quickly grabbed my elbow and said, "Escalator this way," then jumped on in front of me at the last moment to stymie a faster TV cameraman who had jumped on first. When they get lucky and do this, they turn around and video close up and the camera is nearly up your nostrils when they are tall and you are short like me! Not a nice experience at all. Even when standing a couple of steps higher than Stuart I'm still well protected. It's those broad shoulders again!

Rick had disappeared in the melee, and when I whispered his name as a question to Stuart, he just said "Car." As usual, Rick was on to the important details. As Stuart had a checked suitcase of legal submissions and papers we had to wait a while, but still had a fairly quick exit.

It is difficult to think that it is now thirty-two years ago that this all started. The old anxious, nervous feelings are still there despite the numerous times I've been to court over the intervening years.

Michael had also arrived, along with his lawyer, Ray Watterson and a bodyguard.

At the last inquest he had refused to give any statement generally as he had signed an exclusive contract, and as a result he was handled roughly in the scrum, and got thrown up against the wall in the scramble. Intentional or not it wasn't very nice, so this time he was prepared.

Stuart wanted to see Michael to brief him about the procedure the next day, so he tried calling but Michael wasn't answering his telephone, so he walked over to the other hotel. He got Michael's room number and went up, but it turned out to be the bodyguard's. They had swapped rooms, but only thing was, the bodyguard had the wrong room number and had no idea where Michael was! Stuart eventually found him in another room altogether! Conference over, Stuart arranged to pick Michael up so we could all arrive at court together the next day.

At Court it was very different this time. Harry Miller's office had got on to the Media Liaison lady, a position we hadn't heard of before, to see if things could be a little easier than last time. The lady was lovely and arranged to have police to control the crowd, leave us a place to pull up, and keep the media in a nice orderly row, provided we walked past them all reasonably slowly so they could all get their "shot" for the day. I had no trouble agreeing, so it was all set up. She also arranged a pre-court room so we didn't have to wait in the foyer along with everyone else, which was lovely of her.

We met in the morning at the appointed time, hopped in the booked taxi and were right on time to meet Michael, only he was not there and once again the bodyguard couldn't find him. Stuart tried ringing and we waited as long as we could while Stuart walked all over trying to find him. But he was nowhere to be found, so we had to leave without him or be late ourselves.

Our entry to the courthouse ran smoothly and was a welcome change from past court appearances. Michael just beat the Judge's entry.

Submissions on behalf of the Crown were entered into evidence, first by Council Assisting the Coroner Rex Wild QC, then an investigator on behalf of the Coroner gave her evidence of dingo behaviour and attacks in the intervening years This was based on investigation into our further dingo attack submissions which Stuart had made utilising Michael's dingo lists. Her notes and material was then entered in to evidence.

Stuart Tipple then handed our submissions in formally on behalf of the defence, along with Michael's submission. Although these are sent in earlier, they are always entered in formally to the court as well. This now makes them official and a matter of court record, open to all.

At the last minute Michael had announced he wanted to address the Coroner himself as well. I had agreed to let him do what he felt he needed to, but this now meant that I had to make a statement also. I had felt that everything and more was well covered by Stuart, but now I had to add a statement myself, so I chose to have Stuart read it on my behalf, as was the usual practice. Michael got up and spoke, saying in part, "Tragically, dingoes have killed children since Azaria.

"Since the loss of Azaria, I have had an abiding fear and paranoia about safety around dingoes. They send shivers up my spine. It is a hell I have to endure."

Stuart then read this personal letter for me:

"Coroner Elizabeth Morris

Dear Ms Morris

I thank you for the reopening of the inquest into the death of my daughter Azaria. I am often asked why I wanted the inquest reopened and why it mattered. 'Let it go' was most often the comment I heard.

Apart from the fact that that an open finding is just that - open, and therefore unsatisfactory to myself and family, I know it also leaves Coronial business unfinished. This is not just a matter of Lindy or Michael getting their own way. It is the only way I know to let Australians know once and for all that dingoes are dangerous. It is not a matter of 'provoke them and they attack' because they are otherwise shy, peaceable animals. Although I believe them to be beautiful creatures, they are sly not shy, cunning and strong. They are a wild animal doing what comes natural to a wild animal - hunting and opportunistically preying on the weaker object. Our Australian children and babies, and even injured adults alone in the bush, need to be protected from, and educated about, these animals.

Although we find many historical accounts in pioneer diaries, early news sheets and newspapers of dingo attacks and deaths, there is nothing before the attack on Azaria which established a legal precedence.

When Marshal Perron's father, Lionel, turned up at the Royal Commission and asked to present evidence, he told of the case of an approximately 12-month-old Aboriginal child that had been killed by a dingo. He saw the child's body and personally shot the culprit dingo which still carried evidence upon it. (Royal Commission transcript, pg. 4322/3) Despite this eyewitness evidence, it happened before Aboriginal deaths had to be recorded and therefore was still not counted as a legal precedence despite the reliability of the witness.

When pioneers discovered a death by dingo, they were experienced in the ways of the bush and knew what had happened. Today we are mainly a nation of city dwellers unused to the ways of the bush and suspicious of each other. We look to the law to tell us what to think and do, more than we use the now uncommon commodity of common sense.

Because the eye witnesses were pushed to the background, and rumour, speculation, and forensic science were originally deemed to be of more import, it has resulted in the sad fact that Australians have been misled and tricked into thinking the eyewitnesses to be 'liars or at best, fools', and that dingoes were poor maligned creatures that only attacked when provoked.

Because of these widely held misleading opinions I feel that it is my public duty to ask, as strongly as possible, for you to, once and for all, make a definitive statement on the inherent danger of these beautiful native creatures, so all can protect themselves and their children. Ignorance in this matter is not bliss, but the arbiter of unbelievable heartache. Please use your unique position to be the last Coroner, and the one who not only sets the record straight for my daughter's memory, but who strongly tells Australians and tourists alike, to beware and take precautions around these dangerous animals, no matter how friendly they look.

I know your job is difficult and not a popular one. My prayers are with you that the alarm may officially be sounded and recorded in the hope that other mothers may be informed and therefore protected from the heartache that I have endured.

Yours sincerely,

Lindy Chamberlain-Creighton."

This was now handed into evidence. A few details more on our behalf, then Stuart concluded and sat.

No one else had any more to add, so the hearing was held over until a date to be determined. Judge Morris needed to write her findings without hurry, around her current workload. She did not wish to be rushed. After a short conference over legalities in our allotted room, Michael did not want to leave together, so we waited awhile then left. There was nothing we could add to being glad that it was happening and there were no further comments at that time or reason to stay longer in Darwin, so we were able to get the plane home.

We had agreed to meet in the foyer of the hotel to wait for the taxi to the airport. Stuart arrived just as I came back from the bathroom, and decided a quick trip to the bathroom wouldn't be amiss for himself before the airport either, and left me with the bags. Rick arrived from checking out just as Stuart came back chuckling to himself. As soon as he got close enough to talk he asked me if I had seen what was in the toilets. Well duh! He was in the men's! Between chuckles he told me that it was rather off-putting as my face was over all the urinals! Turned out that the front page of the local paper was above each urinal, and I was on the front page that day. It really tickled Stuart's funny bone and made his day. Rick went in for a look, then they stood guard while I snuck in to see it also. Only in Darwin.

We had said goodbye to Michael and his crew so we didn't expect to see them again, but as we arrived at the airport there was Michael hiding behind the cars over the road with his camera, waiting to photograph us. The funniest thing about that was that the local press photographer caught him on film doing it, and it was in the paper the next day! I have no idea why he felt he had to hide, or that he wouldn't be seen.

Stuart's notes for the whole trip merely read:

"39. On 23 February 2012, attended the Coroner Court in Darwin."

Life went back to what is normal for us now, with real estate renovations and speaking engagements keeping us more than busy, as usual, until the finding date was announced. We told the family as a matter of course and all decided they didn't need to add to the media for the day but we would call them with the results the minute it was over. It was a long way for a few hours at best. Kahlia and Adam now lived on St Thomas in the US Virgin Islands, Reagan in Sydney, New South Wales, and Aidan and Amber in Port Hedland, Western Australia.

Rick made all the travel arrangements for ourselves and Tipples, and the finding date duly arrived.

As we packed our bags to leave we got a quick call from Aidan saying he would see us in Darwin tomorrow! After vacillating over it for two weeks he had finally made up his mind an hour earlier. Amber had managed to get tickets and they now had an hour to make the Perth plane so they could catch the only flight to Darwin the next day. He didn't want to look back and say "I could have gone, should have gone, why didn't I?" Then he would live with regret. Now he had to pay last minute fares and it cost them $7,000! At least they would be there and could sneak in without the pressure of anyone knowing they were coming. They hadn't even had time to book accommodation! I told him where we were booked just in case, and where Michael and his daughter, Zahra, had chosen to stay also. At least we had friends in Darwin that knew him and would find them a bed if necessary.

I quickly rang Reagan to see if he wanted to change his mind now, but he didn't feel he needed to be there and his absence would not cause him regret. Kahlia and Adam were living in the Virgin Islands and were unable to make it, but were primed to watch for news.

It was an uneventful trip up, and nice that Stuart had his wife, Cherie, with him this time. She hadn't been to Darwin since the trial and there were a lot of changes and a lot of memories. Michael was also on the plane, but minus his bodyguard this time as no-one had purchased him a ticket before he had arrived at the airport to leave, and by then the plane was full!

This time on arrival Stuart walked ahead of me so I could just follow his back and know the way to go. Even then he continually had to push through the media. It was those broad shoulders again! Rick had gone straight for the hire car and Cherie for their bags in order to make the process quicker, but we still had to wait for a while but not long before Rick pulled up with the car.

When we jumped into the car, the media had followed us all the way. A crusty older local trying to push past the scrum on the footpath commented, "Geez Lindy, ya can still pull a crowd!" Stuart thought that was a great shot as we pulled away from the curb. On the way to the hotel Cherie told me Stuart had a surprise for me, and when I started to ask, Stuart laughed and told me that I would see it in court the next day, so I had to be satisfied.

We did a drive through some main areas to give Cherie an update, then checked into our hotel and looked for food. Aidan and Amber had managed to get a room in our hotel as well so we were all able to get on the same floor, which was convenient and fun. We rang Aidan and found they were less than a block away, sitting at a sidewalk cafe having just finished lunch, so we walked down and joined them, all catching up as we ate. Then we made our leisurely way back to the hotel together. A number of locals wished me well, but mostly left us be.

That night Stuart wanted us all together for dinner as the next night could be hectic, and it was a relaxed way to have a heads up on the next day. Michael had his daughter, Zahra, with him and we all had a pleasant evening. We would all meet at our hotel the next morning at nine forty-five sharp to convoy together to court. This time there should be no mistakes as Michael and Zahra were to go with Aidan and Amber, and the court liaison had made the same arrangements as last time for us with the press and police so we wouldn't have any trouble.

As soon as Stuart walked into the hotel foyer the next morning for court I knew I had seen his surprise for me. He was wearing a new tie with little foxes all over it. What a great tie, and just like Cherie to source that! I was quite tickled with it, as they knew I would be. Very fitting, and as close as we could get, and let's face it, the canines need their representation in court too!

We all hung around and waited as long as we could but Michael didn't arrive so once again we had to leave or be late for court. Aidan was already really nervous and this didn't help.

I felt calm within myself and for myself, but anxious on Aidan's behalf as he had never been to court before this except his short time in and out of the witness box for the Royal Commission and that was years ago. Amber had never been near court or media before. I was proud of her as she handled it well and was a good support to Aidan throughout.

That was vastly different to having to walk into court in front of *all* the media. The reality of that is so different to the glimpses you see looking at it on television and imagining yourself in the scene.

Even if you are there as a Hollywood star it is not a fun thing to do. You are grabbed at, tripped with mic cables, banged on the head or in the face with cameras, and everyone is trying at once to get an exclusive despite you saying you have no comment to make. Having spoken to a number of stars over the years, I know they feel similar to how I did. Meryl Streep once commented that she thought Australian media were the rudest in the world. You are always aware there is only a split second between public and media love and hate, and no matter what you do, at some stage you will be damned if you do and damned if you don't. It is easier to deal straight, be yourself, and if your yes means yes and your no means no, and you are fair with everyone, your reputation will allow you a measure of respect from the media themselves, which makes it a little easier.

I had got used to the feeling over the years, but once again still felt nervous as we had to get out of the car. As I looked back at the second car to make sure they weren't having any trouble and had a straight walk in too, I was in time to see Aidan really struggling to keep it all together. That was almost the end of me too. With the court small and full, we had arranged extra seats the moment we knew they were coming and I didn't want someone who didn't know who Aidan was to stop them from entering the court room if they weren't with us. Someone else, probably media, had been excluded just that morning as it was, but family gets priority at a time like that.

The preliminaries were short and sweet, but already Aidan was upset, and barely holding it together. I always tell him it is my dad's fault, as the whole Murchison family cries easily when empathising, when angry or tired. I didn't dare look at him or I would start too, in sympathy. I was hidden behind lawyers, but every time the Coroner looked up she had a straight view of Aidan who was visibly upset throughout her finding. No wonder she became emotional herself near the end. Here was the effect on the little boy she had been reading about, now a man, right in front of her. This was not academic, but had human faces and feelings right in front of her.

Ms Elizabeth Morris SM began this way:

"1) This inquest has been reopened to receive information not available to previous inquests. My task is to consider and determine whether the whole of the evidence is sufficient to determine a cause of death of Azaria Chamberlain.

2) In the coronial jurisdiction, the test applied is a balance of probabilities test. Briginshaw v Briginshaw (1938) 60 CLR 336 supports the convention that reasonable satisfaction 'increases with the seriousness of the allegation'. A further factor referred to in Briginshaw as affecting the answer to the question whether the facts sought to be proved have been established to the reasonable satisfaction of the fact-finder is "... the inherent unlikelihood of an occurrence of a given description" having taken place.

3) Having considered all of the evidence, including evidence gathered of deaths and attacks by dingoes since the death of Azaria, I am satisfied, to beyond the required standard, of the following matters:"

She then proceeded to give a pithy summation of the campsite, Azaria's being taken, the alarm raised, the search, and the evidence of the eye witnesses, trackers, police and rangers from that night and the next few days.

"4) Mr and Mrs Chamberlain and their three children, Aidan, Reagan and Azaria, arrived at Uluru, generally known then as Ayers Rock on Saturday 16 August 1980, setting up their tent in the top camping area on the east side of the rock.

5) They were not alone, with six families in the camping area on the night of 17 August; the Wests, the Dawsons, the Habys, the Lowes and the Whittakers.

6) A common barbecue area was about 20-25 metres from the Chamberlain's tent. Mr and Mrs Chamberlain were in this area shortly prior to 8.00pm, preparing their evening meal. Aidan and Azaria were with them, but

Reagan was already in the tent asleep in his sleeping bag. Mrs Chamberlain was nursing Azaria, speaking to Mr and Mrs Lowe. Mrs Chamberlain then took Azaria and Aidan back to their tent area. She placed a sleeping Azaria in a bassinet in the rear of the tent and then went to get a tin of baked beans from their car for Aidan. Mrs Chamberlain then went back to the tent, and then returned to the barbecue area with Aidan.

7) Shortly after Mrs Chamberlain returned to the barbecue, Mrs Lowe heard a baby cry from the tent. Mrs Chamberlain went immediately to check on Azaria, and moments later cried out either "That dog's got my baby" or "My God, My God, a dingo has got my baby".

8) Both Mr and Mrs West heard the growl of a dingo or dog from the direction of the Chamberlain's tent fairly soon before they heard Mrs Chamberlain cry out.

9) Mrs Chamberlain initially ran in the direction she thought the dingo had gone, but then went back to check the tent. Others, including Mr Chamberlain and Mr Lowe then began an immediate search of the area and the surrounding sand dunes.

10) At around 8.25pm Mr Derek Roff, the ranger in charge of the area, arrived. He, along with Constable Morris, who arrived shortly thereafter, organised a search party consisting of some 250-300 people, who search the areas east, north and south of the tent until about 3.00am.

11) Mr Haby found tracks on the sand dunes east of the camp, along with a mark or imprint on the sand as though an object had been put down. Mr Roff also saw this imprint or drag mark, which he likened to a crepe bandage or resembling a knitted garment. Constable Morris also saw drag marks in that area, as well as tracks close to the rear of the tent.

12) Mr Roff and Mr Nui Minyintiri tracked a drag mark on the crest of a sand dune to the east of the tent. In Mr Minyintiri's expert opinion the tracks of a dingo that he saw showed that 'it walked as though it had some load on it . . . when I was tracking the dingo I knew, or I thought that it was carrying the baby for sure.' Mrs Barbara Winmati also assisted in attempting the next day to follow the tracks leading south from the tent, but after a considerable distance, lost the animal's trail."

There it all was again. Everything we had told them and all the activities we had known from the first of our nightmare and its immediate aftermath.

The Coroner went on to note in part of point 12 that "Mr Roff and Mr Nui

Minyintiri tracked a drag mark on the crest of a sand dune to the east of the tent. In Mr Minyintiri's expert opinion the tracks of a dingo that he saw showed that 'it walked as though it had some load on it . . . when I was tracking the dingo I knew, or I thought that it was carrying the baby for sure.' Mrs Barbara Winmati also assisted ..." This of course was the chief Ranger and two of the main Aboriginal trackers.

Her findings continued:

"13) Blood was found inside the tent on various articles. This blood was Azaria's."

Now Judge Morris turned to the forensic side of things and the Royal Commission:

"14) A Royal Commission of Inquiry into the conviction of Mr and Mrs Chamberlain was held between 8 May 1986 and 19 March 1987. His Honour, Justice Morling, delivered his findings on 22 May 1987. His Honour heard and received evidence, including evidence that had been heard at the criminal trial, as well as new evidence, including expert evidence, independent of that which was presented at the criminal trial proceedings. Given the thorough nature of the investigation of forensic and scientific evidence, there is little point or weight in further analysis. Many aspects of the scientific evidence in this case have been either misreported or misrepresented. Despite their thorough examination at the Commission myths still remain in the public domain in relation to clothing, blood, handprints, dingo hair and other aspects of the evidence. I have attached to these findings as an appendix, the report of the Commission, which formed part of the evidence before me, and which thoroughly and painstakingly addresses each of the forensic and scientific issues, and draws its conclusions from the best evidence available to it at the time.

15) In relation to that evidence, it is appropriate to adopt the findings of primary fact of the Commission ..."

Then she proceeded with her legal reasons for doing so, and continued on saying:

"In this case, there are several considerations that are relevant. The Commissioner is a Judge of a court. He has the experience and skills of a judge in evaluating evidence. The Commission conducted its inquiry in public over a long time, accompanied by much publicity. It heard many witnesses, including experts. One can be confident, bearing in mind all that had happened before the Commission was instituted, that no significant evidence was not given to and considered by the Commission. Everyone who had a legitimate interest in the outcome of the Commission was heard. The Commissioner was assisted by experienced counsel. He had the inestimable benefit of observing the witnesses. The report itself is cogent and internally consistent. There is nothing about the report that would cause concern that adopting its main findings may lead to error. For these reasons, I consider that the chief findings of the Chamberlain Commission should be adopted."

16) The Court of Appeal, like the Commission, had a focus on the criminal jurisdiction and the sufficiency of evidence … The Coronial jurisdiction has a different focus, that is, the identity of the deceased, the time, place and cause of death and relevant circumstances concerning the death. In findings, a Coroner may comment on a matter … and may also make recommendations on these issues connected with a death."

Justice Morris then continued on with:

"Evidence in relation to dingo related injuries and deaths

17) The evidence before the Commission in relation to dingoes, led the Commissioner to conclude:

Before August 1980 dingoes in the Ayers Rock area frequented the camping area. At that time there were many dingoes in the area, some 18-25 of which were known to visit the camping area. A number of attacks were made by dingoes on children in the months preceding Azaria's disappearance. In none of these did any child suffer serious injury.

About twenty minutes before Azaria disappeared Mr Haby saw and photographed a dingo which walked towards the Chamberlains' tent. A few minutes before the alarm was raised the West's heard a dog growl.

On the night of 17 August dog tracks were observed on the southern side of and very close to the Chamberlains' tent. The same night Mr Roff and Mr Minyintiri, both experienced trackers and familiar with dingo behaviour, saw tracks of a dog carrying a load which they believed to be Azaria. It was within the bounds of reasonable possibility that a dingo might have attacked a baby and carried it away for consumption as food. A dingo would have been capable of carrying Azaria's body to the place where the clothing was found. If a dingo had taken Azaria it is likely that, on occasions, it would have put the load down and dragged it."

There were more legal references, then she continued:

"Hairs, which were either dog or dingo hairs, were found in the tent and on Azaria's jumpsuit. The Chamberlains had not owned a dog for some years prior to August 1980.

The quantity and distribution of the sand found on Azaria's clothing might have been the result of it being dragged through sand. The sand would have come from many places in the Ayers Rock region. The sand and plant fragments on the clothing are consistent with Azaria's body being carried and dragged by a dingo from the tent to the place where it was found. It is unlikely that, if the clothing had been taken from the Chamberlains' car, buried, disinterred, and later placed where it was found it would have collected the quantity and variety of plant material found upon it.

It would have been very difficult for a dingo to have removed Azaria from her clothing without causing more damage than was observed on it. However, it would have been possible for it to have done so. Mr Roff, the chief Ranger at Ayers Rock and a man of great experience, thought that the arrangement of the clothing when discovered was consistent with dingo activity."

Justice Morris then noted, "Other dingo experts disagreed." Adding her own opinion, she stated "I think it is likely that a dingo would have left the clothing more scattered, but it might not have done so.

The blood found in the tent was at least as consistent with dingo involvement in Azaria's disappearance as it was with her murder in the car. The pattern of blood staining on the clothing does not establish that the child's throat was cut with a blade.

The absence of saliva on Azaria's jumpsuit which was conclusively proved at the trial is made more explicable by the finding of the matinee jacket which would have partially covered it. The fact that no debris from the baby's body was found on the jumpsuit is also made more explicable by the finding of the jacket.

There is great conflict of expert opinion was to whether the damage to the clothing could have been caused by a dingo. It has not been shown beyond reasonable doubt that it could not have been. There were marks on plastic fragments of the nappy similar to marks made by a dingo on another nappy used for testing purposes. However, there was no blood on the nappy.

There was a dingo's den about thirty metres from the place where the clothing was found. There is no evidence that the existence of the den was known to the Chamberlains, or for that matter, to anybody else and in fact it was unknown to the chief ranger and his deputy."

18) Available to this inquest was further evidence in relation to attacks on people by dingoes.

. . . A re-opening of an inquest is not an appeal against its findings. However, it appears that Coroner Lowndes (relying in 1995 on pre-1987 evidence and material) accepted the view stated by Commissioner Morling that the taking of Azaria was a novel case, for which there was no known precedent, and as such there was an inherent unlikelihood of an occurrence of such a nature.

21) Evidence tendered at this Inquest includes reports of attacks by dingoes

and dogs assumed to be part dingo or cross breeds. Reports from 1986 through to June 2010 include cases of both children and adults being attacked. In Queensland a 9-year-old boy died as a result of an attack by dingoes on Fraser Island in April 2001. In New South Wales a 2-year-old girl died in December 2005 from blood loss and shock from cranio-cervical injury from dog attack, being a part dingo crossbreed. In Victoria in February 2006 a 22-month-old girl died of chronic respiratory failure with contributing factors of blood loss from dog bites (the dog being described as a dingo/Labrador cross). Apart from these deaths, there were reports of various attacks and injuries, including records obtained from the Department of Environment and Resource Management in Queensland, regarding reported dingo incidents on Fraser Island.

22) The further investigation of this Inquest has not found any disappearance exactly like that of Azaria. However it is clear that there is evidence that in particular circumstances a dingo is capable of attacking, taking and causing the death of young children. Some of these attacks occurred prior to the disappearance of Azaria in Central Australia and were considered by the Commission. Others have occurred since and form part of the evidence before me.

23) In considering now all of the evidence, I am satisfied that the evidence is sufficiently adequate, clear, cogent and exact, and that the evidence excludes all other reasonable possibilities, to find that what occurred on 17 August 1980 was that shortly after Mrs Chamberlain placed Azaria in the tent, a dingo or dingoes entered the tent, took Azaria and carried and dragged her from the immediate area. Mrs Chamberlain, upon being alerted to Azaria's cry, returned to the tent area to see a dingo near the tent. Raising a cry which alerted others, Mrs Chamberlain then ran for a short distance after the dingo and then back to the tent, confirming that Azaria was missing.

24) Azaria was not seen again, despite the large search by many at the campsite and the more organised search once Constable Morris and Mr Roff were involved."

Cause of Death

"25) A Coronial Inquiry shall if possible find the 'cause of death'. As Azaria was never found, it is not possible to find the terminal cause or mode of her passing. However in Ex parte Minister of Justice; Re Malcolm; Re Inglis McClemens J said:

"I think that where the Coroners Act speaks of the cause of death it means the real cause of death namely the disease, injury or complication not the mode of dying as e.g. heart failure, asphyxia, asthenia etc."

The following passage from Jervis on Coroners was also adopted:

> "In order to distinguish between one sort of death and another it is necessary to consider not the terminal cause of death but the cause which was the real cause of death ... It is suggested that insofar as the terminal cause of death directly and consequently follows from a definable event, the death should be regarded as caused by the definable event."

Although some of the following information becomes more complicated than the social reader may wish, I have chosen to include it in my book so those with an enquiring mind or studying law can follow Judge Morris's full reasoning, but have left out the references and notations of the same throughout.

She continues:

"26) Traditionally, following English coronial law and practice, a finite range of verdicts or findings were available to a coroner when describing the manner of death. These include unlawful homicide, lawful homicide, suicide, misadventure, accident, natural causes and an open finding. However, in the Australian context this list is evolving, for reasons involving the different circumstances of death in this country as compared to England, as well as advances in medical and forensic science and the development of the National Coroners Information system, a database of coronial findings and recommendations.

27) Death by misadventure has been described as applying to those circumstances when the death has occurred as the result of a lawful or unlawful intentional human act unforeseeable leading to death. Accident has also been described as an unforeseen misfortune or mishap resulting in some physical injury or harm which has a causal connection with the death.

28) Whilst other definitions have sometimes been applied, neither of these two findings truly reflects the circumstances where a person has been taken or attacked by an animal. Sadly, these circumstances, in the Australian context, are not uncommon, and include shark, crocodile and other reptiles, dog and dingo. The National Coroners Information System report on animal related deaths identifies 254 deaths between 1 July 2000 and November 2010. The Northern Territory accounted for 24 of these deaths, clearly over represented on a per-capita basis.

29) Whilst some of these deaths could be classified as misadventure or accident (a fall from a horse, for example), others, such as bee, snake, shark, crocodile, dog and jellyfish are the result of the actions of the animal's own intention and/or inherent dangerousness.

30) It is evident that the traditional forms of finding should be expanded to include being taken or attacked by an animal."

Wow, this was history in the making again, a new landmark decision. I'm sure I was holding my breath, certain of what the ruling was going to be, yet I had to hear it spelled out in words. So often the Findings seemed obvious and yet at the last minute had fallen short. I hardly dared to believe. I was listening intently while she went over, yet again, Azaria's name, birth and parentage details, and where she died, then Judge Morris finally said,

"The cause of her death was as the result of being attacked and taken by a dingo."

Then she made some further recommendations:

"32) It is obvious, not just from these findings, but from other injuries and deaths since, dingoes can and do cause harm to humans …

33) … I do not intend to make any recommendations in relation to public safety and the control or management of dingoes in areas frequented by members of the public … Various wildlife and park management authorities around Australia are responsible for accommodating and balancing the needs of visitors and animals, including native wildlife. It is appropriate that they take measures to manage the now identified risks.

Dated this 12th day of June 2012
Elizabeth Morris
CORONER

"Mrs Chamberlain-Creighton, Mr Chamberlain, Aidan, and your extended families: Please accept my sincere sympathy on the death of your special and loved daughter and sister, Azaria. I'm so sorry for your loss. Time does not remove the pain and sadness of the death of a child."

Wow. The courage it took to do all that, knowing there were national and international media hanging on her every word and every emotion, I found incredible. The compassion in her voice and demeanour was obvious, and it seemed to me that she may have suffered a loss somewhere in her own life to show that depth of understanding. There was no showmanship or "I'm the Coroner, look at me" attitude. She was businesslike and efficient, yet compassionate. I wish our judicial system had more people of her calibre in it. If there were we wouldn't have so many miscarriages of justice to deal with in our world.

Stuart's notes simply conclude:

"40. On 12 June 2012, attended when the Coroner's findings handed down."

At Long Last

I can't describe my feelings.

Apart from listening intently to the finding, I was always aware that Aidan was visibly upset through it all, and I just wanted to hold him like when he was a tiny boy and kiss him better. He is a man who runs his own business now, though, and well aware that a hug and a kiss alone don't make the pain go away. It is something we all have to work through alone, despite the support of friends and family. It was lovely to find out later that some kind stranger had sent a beautiful arrangement of native flowers to his office, and that their secretary had put them on their kitchen bench to surprise them when they arrived home.

When I was asked later by the media what I was thinking and feeling at that moment, I answered that I wasn't sure, apart from being concerned about Aidan. Later Rick told me he could tell me what I was feeling. He said he felt my body "tense more and more and you got very still as it became apparent that she came close to uttering the words we were all waiting for. When she finally did say it, all that tension just drained out of you and you relaxed." Yeah, well I'll go with that.

If I had been home on my own I don't know if I would have smiled and relaxed or shouted "Yes!" and danced a jig! Anyway I was in court and just wanted to hold Aidan, at the end of a long journey that began when we walked happily together to the tent that night to put Azaria to bed and then raced carefree back to the BBQ. People tend to forget he went through all this with me, including following me back to the tent when I went to check on Azaria and made the horrible discovery that she was gone. He suffered all the following shock, blame and rumours that abounded from then on.

Reagan, too, deals with the ordeal he had that night when the dingo walked over him to get to his sister, and the fear that it had come back to get him when I rushed into the tent. Even as his mother I cannot conceive of the trauma of that, and yes, at the age of four, he was interviewed by police, and again for the Royal Commission, although they didn't call him because at the time we couldn't find a non-family adult witness who could corroborate his nightmares and evidence. Yep, well I still think it funny that he annoyed the police after he truthfully told them his sleeping bag was red and they basically called him a liar. Even though I intervened and told them he was being truthful, it was evident they were skeptical, so he fixed them by answering red to everything from then on 'til they gave up! Recently I asked him if he remembered why he'd done that, and he immediately told me it was because they treated him like a fool, and they were the fools so he stopped humouring them! Way to go, Reagan! I wouldn't have been able to get away with that. More's the pity, though. I would have loved to. All I do know is that the psychological results have been huge, and he is still struggling. Still, I am grateful that God kept his promise years ago to be with my kids, and to those on the outside looking in they are average, healthy human beings who have dealt with their family history remarkably well and turned out pretty normal considering!

Despite all their involvement, the Northern Territory maintained that the kids weren't affected, and didn't deserve compensation when we applied for it with ours.

So much for Justice. I think she cried that day too, if she had any tears left.

Kahlia too has her own scars to deal with from having her mother in prison during her most formative years. Being people's darling and being spoilt and fussed over, to suddenly being just an ordinary child, but still in the spotlight, brings its own problems that have to be dealt with. Through it all, problems or not, that's life, and how we choose to deal with it all is up to us. That is part of growing up, no matter what age we are, and I am proud of my kids regardless of their private battles.

Rick naturally got the first hug after court rose, then I honed in on Aidan and Stuart. To know it was over was a great feeling. Who got hugged next or in what order I can't remember, except when I looked up and saw Suzy Priori as she came running into the courtroom as others were leaving. She was my double when leaving prison. To share this moment together too was really special. We had already known that the small courtroom was full and you had to apply ages before to be allowed a seat, as the media knew, so she had missed out on being inside, but as she knew those guarding the door she was allowed in as soon as the court started to clear.

We were still talking and as Rex Wild QC was also still there packing up, I got Stuart to ask him if he minded signing the copy of my book for the National Library, which he did. It was not until after this that I noticed the cameras were still rolling even though the courtroom was now basically empty, and I couldn't resist asking if they had seen the "dingoes" on Stuart's tie. This apparently was aired and started a few rants on Twitter, about how tacky it was, or not.

Meanwhile, in the legal room outside the court we regrouped, ready to face the press. Rick called Adam and Kahlia to tell them immediately and discovered they had watched it live on the net already, as had Jack and Charlotte, Rick's parents in the US. Reagan was going to, but got involved in something and forgot. He went online to investigate when we told him, but maintained he knew they would have it right this time!

We all left together this time, stopping at the court doors to give a statement each. Michael went first this time.

My talk was short, thanking the Coroner for a long-time wrong righted, then Stuart Tipple for all his consistently hard work, and not forgetting his wife, Cherie, for continuing to patiently back him, despite all the pressures and horrid rumours she had had to put up with over the years as he worked solidly on our behalf. The eyewitnesses were not forgotten either. Stuart told the press we were going to walk around the courthouse to pick up a copy of the new death certificate, which was thoughtfully being prepared immediately, then would come outside again and stop to give them photo access. This made everyone happy; one more hit and then they would all leave us alone.

The process of picking up the certificate was quick and the photo session fairly painless. As long as they all got the shots they wanted and a close-up of the certificate they were happy. After Stuart held the certificate for the close up shots of it, I took my turn with it. After the initial rush I waited a little longer for one of the younger local reporters who was valiantly trying to use a tele camera he was obviously not that familiar with, while some reporter chick kept putting her iPhone in front of his lens. There was no real rush, but those waiting for Michael's turn had to wait a few seconds longer.

That done, it was straight across for my *A Current Affair* interview with Tracy Grimshaw. I had met her before when I did a thirtieth anniversary interview, so I knew they would deal fairly with me and I wouldn't have to worry about the rush editing job they were going to have to do to air it that night.

The interview was fast and short, then off to change for a photo shoot in the park where reporter, Peter FitzSimons, dropped in unannounced to see what I really thought about the dingo tie. I laughed and told him I knew they were foxes, but I chose to call them dingoes today for fun, and so dingoes they would be today. Tomorrow they would be foxes again. He was happy with that and nodded, saying he just wondered if I had known, then wandered off again. Apparently he got in touch with Stuart about it also:

> Stuart
>
> I think it was Oscar Wildean – right on the edge!
>
> Whatever else, it was an interesting choice. But I certainly would not present it as tacky. Just intereste (sic) in your perspective.
>
> Peter.
>
> Here is Stuart's reply:
>
> Peter,
>
> Very clever reply.
>
> Deferring to my wife's sartorial sense of style I asked her to find a suitable tie.
>
> Cherie produced the tie and asked what I thought.
>
> I recognised at once it was perfect for the occasion.
>
> It has proved to be a wonderful litmus test. Those that support Lindy without hesitation love it and those that have reservations are somewhere between your answer and claiming it to be downright tacky.
>
> Why is that?
>
> It's not the colour or the style. It's because it features a DINGO. They know that because they have been told, or read about it in the paper or perhaps had the energy to google it for themselves. Right? Well NO, actually, now look at the tie again. Do you still see a dingo or do you see what is really there?
>
> Of course a country boy like you would never mistake a fox for a dingo would you?
>
> Well not for long anyway.
>
> I hope the lesson we all learn from this tragic case and don't always believe what you are told or read in the papers. We can all make the mistake of seeing what we want to.
>
> Sadly I fear we haven't learned too much in the last 32 years."
>
> Regards Stuart Tipple.

Really! With all the important things that happened historically that day, and people get sidetracked by a throwaway tie comment! Yes, people don't learn not to jump to conclusions, but at least now they *have* been warned officially that dingoes are dangerous and maybe some lives can be saved as a result. Either way the new coronial laws will benefit many bereaved Australian families in the years to come.

The rest of the day was filled with viewing my *A Current Affair* interview, then dinner again with Stuart and Cherie, Aidan and Amber, and Michael. Zahra had opted not to come. When Michael did arrive, he did not appear overly relaxed and wanted to immediately question me if I meant what I said in my interview. I replied that of course "I meant it or I wouldn't have said it." He let it go at that with just an "Umm," and the talk turned general again. We left early as I had numerous short overseas TV link ups to do, then back to the hotel room to try to relax and get some sleep.

Next morning it was breakfast, packing, more interviews and off to the airport. One of the local reporters got us into the club lounge so it would be quieter for us but, of course, we had all forgotten that half the lounge would be media who were travelling first or business class! Oh well, they had what they needed and were happy to leave us alone or just to be social if we connected, so it was fine. During an uneventful trip home to Sydney Ray Watterson passed me a congratulatory note, and I noticed him sitting alone a bit behind me. I sent him a note back to say thank you and also for his contribution of a good submission to the Coroner on the range of her powers. As we were making our way to the luggage carousels and exits, he came alongside me and told me that he had almost not come as he didn't know if he could handle the inquest, but felt he would regret it if he didn't, so he purchased his ticket and came for the finale. Why? Because he had just had his own family tragedy. In the end he said it had helped him to come and I was glad he had. When Stuart stopped talking I told him and he went to speak to Ray also, then they went off talking together, while Cherie and I walked together. With only hand luggage I parted company with her at the bottom of the escalator, leaving her to say goodbye to Stuart for me (he was in the middle of lots of media collecting their TV cameras etc), and headed to where Rick was bringing our car, so I was able to disappear quickly.

A few days later Michael stopped me in Cooranbong and told me he had a proposition for me and that we needed to talk, which he wanted to do in person. Late for an appointment and booked solid for a week, I told him Rick was in the house next door and to tell him or arrange a time with him. It turned out he wanted to sue the NT, and those he was talking to had told him I needed to be involved for him to be successful. Thankfully Rick told him I meant what I said in my interviews and it was over for me. He was not happy but that was the end of the matter for us.

People ask me why I don't want to get even and get a decent compensation out of it. I have always been a firm believer that "If you are not a winner without a medal, you will never be one, with one." If you rely on other people to make things right for you so you can be happy, you will fail miserably. They created the pain in the first place, so why would you think you can force them to make you feel better?

You have a choice about what occupies your mind, whether you live in the past or the future, with sad memories or happy ones, with revenge or peace. I have forgiven myself for being caught up in others' nastiness, however fleeting or long-lasting, to not dwell on it, but to give the responsibility for the hurt and pain others have caused me back to the perpetrators, and move on.

It is now theirs to live with, forget, or choose to ask forgiveness for and rectify. It would be nice to think that those who have done wrong publicly would acknowledge that publicly, but I do not need that in order to be a whole person. They are the ones who ultimately have to answer to the God of the Universe for all of their actions. If asked for forgiveness I can happily give it, because I have already reclaimed my headspace and moved on.

Whenever I give my talk on "Who's the Tenant in Your Head" I am invariably approached later by someone who has finally grasped the concept of true forgiveness for the first time. Many have become hung up severely on the traditional version of forgiveness, where it is only for the perpetrator. It is not. That is pure arrogance. You are not God. You can only acknowledge and thank them for recognising their actions, and let them know that you took responsibility for your own mind, and moved on, and they are now released to move forward also.

Too often we become our own slaves to past regret and hurt. We need to learn to let go and give ourselves permission to take back control of our mind and move on to the future, which is bright with happiness and fulfilment. Don't throw it away for the sake of a past you cannot change anyway.

The Next Chapter In Life

Shortly after his fortieth birthday Aidan and Amber presented us with our first grandchild, a beautiful little girl they called Amelia Loren, Milly for short.

It is fun being a Grammy, and yes, I did spell that right, it's American. FaceTime and Skype are great to keep in touch, and video is awesome. As I write this she has just turned one.

Between our building projects and renovations, and my public speaking engagements, life is full and hectic. It is great to be able to help others with what I have learned throughout this experience and it is one way I can give back to the world for the support of the millions who prayed and worked on my behalf. We still need to work hard to earn our own living and our own retirement fund, but we enjoy our time off and travel as well.

Both my parents are now gone, and Rick's grow older and need yearly help with the "honey do" list. Life is all choices and balances. I love the US and would be happy being there permanently, but we need to be in Australia economically and family wise, so we split our time a little.

As all this is behind us now and the future is clear ahead, what does it hold in store? Life is to be lived with joy and without fear, and a new generation has joined the family ranks. Who knows what the future will bring, but with God by our side it will be awesome whatever happens.

REFERENCE MAPS

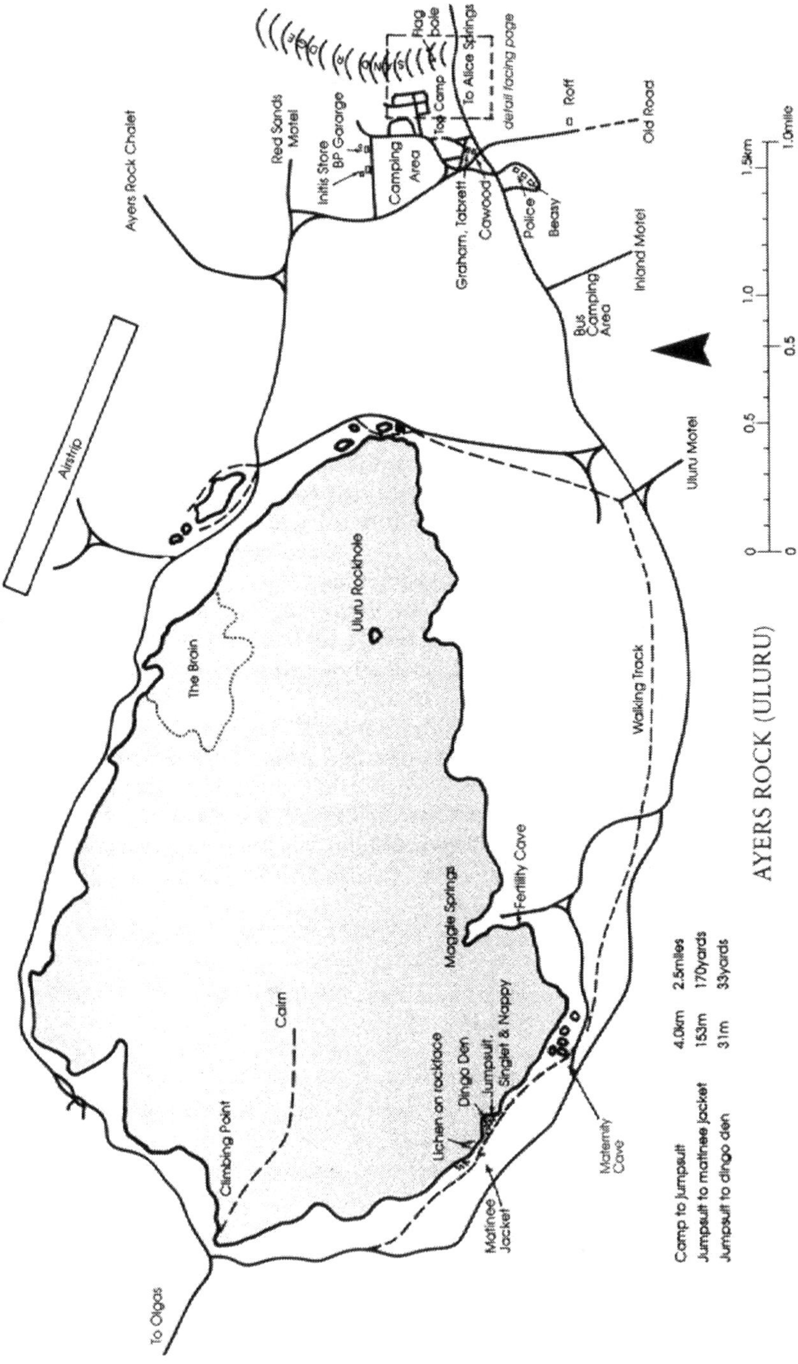

AYERS ROCK (ULURU)

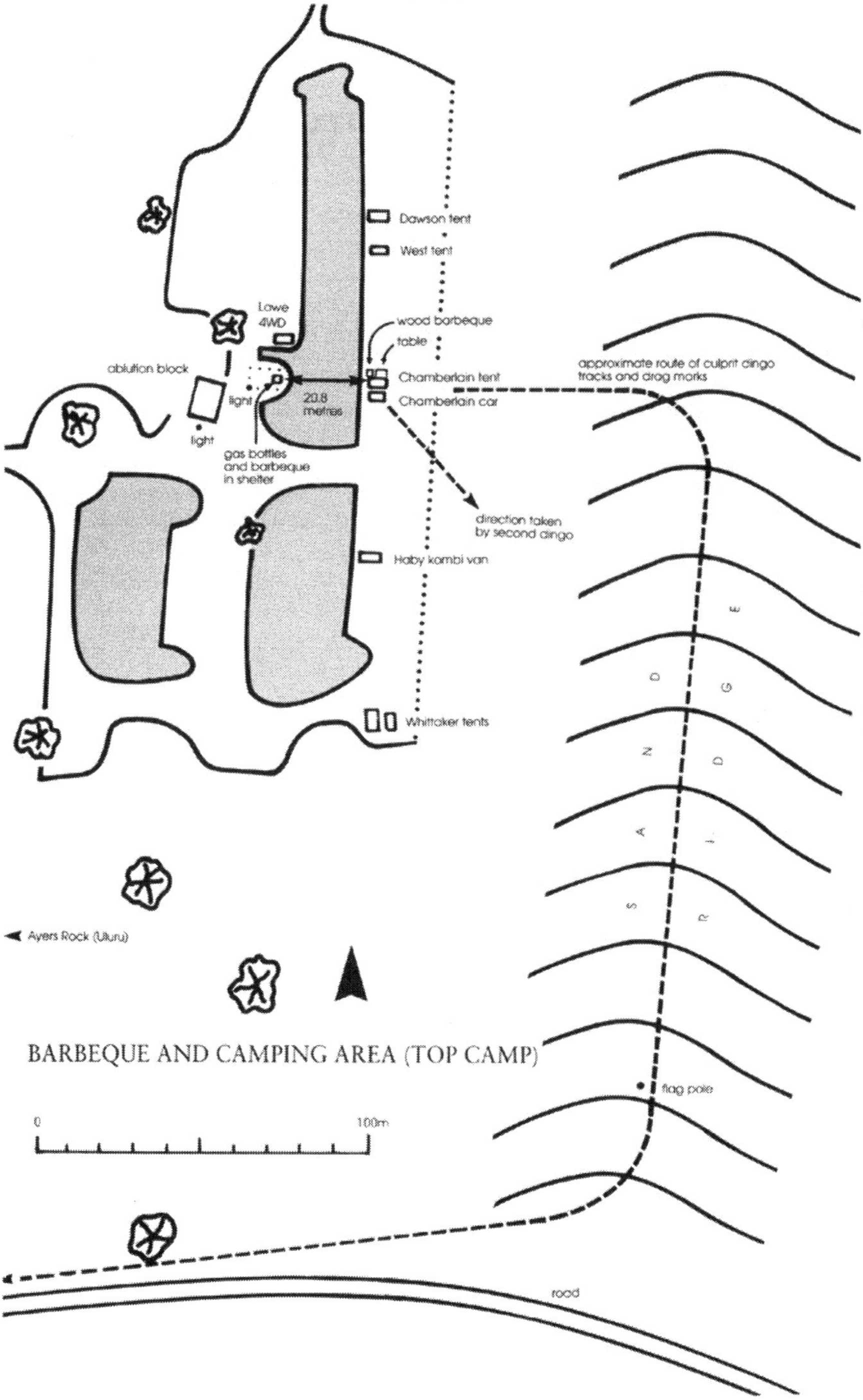

BARBEQUE AND CAMPING AREA (TOP CAMP)

ACKNOWLEDGEMENTS

If it wasn't for the encouragement of Robert Caswell, Stuart Tipple and George Rollo giving me the confidence to write this book, it may never have got off the ground. When the going got tough my Mum and Dad, my brother Alex, Marie Alford and Darryl Kent gave me the encouragement to keep at it. Marie and Darryl also spent many hours proofreading for me, along with Joy Cook and George Rollo. Linda Driscoll typed like the wind for hours on end, the computer groaning at her speed. Olive Landa and Ian Goad also typed for hours; there were many late nights and all night sessions with humour keeping us awake. My editor Jacquie Kent was lots of fun (and long-suffering when I edited her with frequent monotony). Les Smith and Barry Boettcher helped me edit the forensic, while Bill Barnes, Bill and Judy West, Greg and Sally Lowe, Lenore Stevenson, Yvonne Cain and Mum and Dad shared their letters, memoirs and diary notes with me. Liz Noonan, Liz Parry, Mike Lester and Helena Mantz also shared their memories of support groups, press and prison. Kevin Hitchcock helped me with the media point of view. Brian and Olive Hammond let me use their hide-away so I could work in peace. Harry Miller and Linda McClelland were great handling my agent business.

For the use of their photographs, my thanks go to: Barbara Brann, Michael Chamberlain, Ken Chapman, Margo Goodwin, Fairfax, David Hahn, Betty Hocking, Darryl Kent, Greg Lowe, Russell McPhedran, Melbourne Forensic Laboratories, Barry O' Brien and the Adelaide *Advertiser*, Bernie Ollevou, Lynley Potts, Tony Raymond, Les Smith, Stuart Tipple, Liz Ward (Noonan) and *Woman's Day*. Thanks also to Norm Young, Ken Chapman and Federation Press for the use of the reference maps. Maryann Ballantyne, Louise Lavarack, Mary Clark and Paul Judd from William Heinemann Australia also worked wonders meeting deadlines and putting up with me. Ken Crispin took most of the book with him on holiday to do a free legal check; Robert Blowes assisted him. Brind Zichy- Woinarski helped me with last minute research, and Stuart Tipple patiently produced earlier material. Michael and Norm Young helped locate transcript volumes and references.

My special thanks to the kids for being conscripted to pitch in with meals and dishes (without too much grumbling) and understanding while Mum had her head in a book; particularly to Reagan who went without his computer games for over a year while Mum used the computer!

For the reprint of my book my thanks go to East Street Publications, to Michaela Andreyev and Jane Macduff. My thanks to a wonderful editor Jacquie Kent who once again edited and to Justice Crispin for his sage legal advice again also. My thanks also go to Stuart Tipple, Miranda Otto, Di Drew, and Craig McLachlan for letting me quote them.

And lastly my thanks to my wonderful husband Rick for putting his life on hold while I went through the agony of writing about the last fourteen years and for helping me to edit and collate it.

APPENDIX 1

List of Names

A list of some key participants listed alphabetically by name:

Adams, Michael
Junior Counsel for Crown at the Morling Inquiry

Barham, Nancy
Head of female section, Darwin Prison

Barker, Ian QC
Senior Prosecuting Counsel

Barritt, Dennis
First Inquest Coroner

Baxter, Dr Simon
Senior forensic biologist, NSW.
In charge of NSW Forensic Lab and Joy Kuhl's boss

Boettcher, Prof Barry
Professor of Biological Science, University of Newcastle, NSW

Boyd, Guy & Phyllis, daughter Lenore
Sculptor (member of well-known Australian Boyd family of artists), started Australian Support Group movements

Bradley, Prof Keith
Professor of Anatomy, University of Melbourne

Baudner, Dr Siegried
Director of Behringwerke, West Germany

Brechwoldt, Roland
Dingo expert, NSW

Bresee, Prof Randolph
Textile expert, Kansas, USA

Brown, Kenneth
Dentist, University of Adelaide

Brown, Sgt Irvine Gregory
Police, Mount Isa QLD

Caldwell, William (now QC)
Junior Counsel assisting at the Morling Inquiry

Cameron, Prof James
Forensic pathologist, London

Cavanaugh, Greg
Junior Solicitor at trial

Cawood, Ian
Deputy Chief Ranger, Uluru National Park

Chaikin, Prof Malcolm
Textile expert, University of New South Wales

Chapman, Ken
Scientist. Cooranbong, NSW

Chamberlain, Amelia Loren (Milly)
Our first grandchild (to Aidan and Amber)

Chamberlain, Amber
Aidan's wife, née Martin

Chamberlain, Zahra
Michael Chamberlain's daughter from second marriage.

Charlwood, Det Sgt Graeme
(later Det Inspector) Northern Territory Police

Cocks, Sgt Frank
South Australian Police, Alice Springs

Corbett, Dr Lawrence
Dingo expert, CSIRO

Cornell, Dr Findlay
Biologist, NSW

Cozens, Pastor Bert
Seventh-day Adventist minister from Alice Springs

Cranwell, Amanda
Girl attacked by dingo at Ayer's Rock

Cranwell, Max & Phyllis
Parents of daughter attacked by dingo at Ayer's Rock

Crispin, Ken QC (now a Judge)
Queen's Counsel for Chamberlains at the Morling Inquiry

Culliford, Dr Brian
Forensic biologist, Metropolitan Police Laboratory, London

Dean, Peter
Solicitor for the Chamberlains at the inquests

Downs, Roberta (Bobbie) (now Mrs Peter Elston)
Nurse at Ayers Rock

Everingham, Paul (now in private law practice)
Chief Minister and Attorney-General of the Northern Territory
portfolio included Conservation Commission

Fernhead, Prof Ron
Odontologist, Japan

Ferris, Prof
Forensic pathologist, Canada

Fowler, Dr Craig
Forensic biologist, SA

Fullerton, Elizabeth
Counsel for the Crown at the Morling Inquiry

Galvin, Jerry
Coroner at the second inquest

Gilroy, Inspector Michael
Northern Territory Police
Goodwin, Wally
Tourist who found Azaria's jumpsuit

Griffiths, Dr Ross
Textile expert, University of New South Wales

Gufstafson, Prof Gosta
Odontologist, Sweden

Haby, Edwin Murray
Tourist who found imprint in the sand, Queen's Scout, school headmaster

Hansell, Mrs Joan
Drycleaner at Mount Isa

Harris, Les
President of the Dingo Foundation

Hart, Floyd
Person who installed radio-cassette unit in Michael Chamberlain's car

Heron, Irene
Family friend, carer at second inquest and trial

Hocking, Betty
Canberra MP, Leader of 'Plea for Justice' committee

Hughes, Dr Owen and Jan
Kahlia's second foster parents

Jones, Dr Anthony
Forensic pathologist, Northern Territory

Kirkham, Andrew (now QC)
Junior Defence counsel at second inquest and trial

Kuchel, Rex
Botanist, SA

Kuhl, Mrs Joy
Forensic biologist, NSW (now forensic biologist, NT)

Leach, Prof Simon
Professor of Immunology, Victoria

Lees, Colin
Family friend, camera bag witness

Lenehan, Keyth
The bleeding accident victim driven to hospital by the Chamberlains

Lincoln, Dr Patrick
Forensic biologist, London

Lincoln, Sgt John
Northern Territory Police, Alice Springs

Lowe, Greg
Tasmania tourist at BBQ area whilst Lindy took Azaria to the tent

Lowe, Sally
Tasmania tourist at BBQ area who heard Azaria cry

Mantz, Helena
Fellow prisoner in Darwin-now 'adopted' daughter

Martin, Brian
Solicitor General, NT

Martin, Dr Peter
Forensic biologist, London

McAulay, Peter
Commissioner, Northern Territory Police

McCombe, James
Tourist involved in search

McNay, Ashley
Counsel assisting the coroner at the first inquest

Metcalfe, Sen Constable James
Northern Territory Police

Adam Mills
Kahlia's husband

Miller, Wayne & Jenny
Kahlia's first foster parents

Milne, Dr Irene
Mount Isa medical practitioner who delivered Azaria

Morling, Mr Justice Trevor
Judge at the Morling Inquiry

Morris, Ms Elizabeth SM
Coroner for the Fourth Inquest

Morris, Sen Constable Frank
Northern Territory policeman at Ayers Rock

Muirhead, Mr Justice James
Judge at trial

Murchison, Avis Mrs
Lindy's mother

Murchison, Pastor Cliff
Lindy's father

Nairn, Prof Richard
Pathologist, Victoria

Newsome, Dr Alan
Dingo expert, CSIRO

Noble, Constable James
Northern Territory policeman at Ayers Rock

Noonan, Dr Tony & Liz
Heads of NT Support Group

O'Loughlan, Michael (Mick)
Crown Solicitor—First Inquest through to Royal Commission

Ouchterlony, Dr Orfan
Biologist, inventor of radial immunodiffusion or 'Ouchterlony' technique, Sweden

Parry, Liz & John
Lindy's friends, regular prison visitor, stayed with upon release

Pauling, Thomas (now QC)
Junior Prosecuting counsel at trial

Pelton, Dr William
Textile expert, NSW

Phillips, John QC (now a Judge)
Senior defence counsel at trial

Pleuckhahn, Prof Vernon
Forensic pathologist, Victoria

Porter, Chester QC
Senior counsel assisting Morling Inquiry

Ransom, Jenny (nee Richards)
Lindy's friend at Mt Isa

Re, David
Junior Defence Solicitor, Royal Commission

Rice, Phillip QC
Senior counsel for the Chamberlains at the first and second inquests

Robinson, Dr Vivian
Microscopist, NSW

Roff, Derek
Chief Ranger, Uluru National Park, NT

Rollo, Pr George
Seventh-day Adventist pastor, family friend

Sanson, Dr Graham
Zoologist, Melbourne

Scott, Dr Andrew
Senior forensic biologist, SA

Scott, Constable Maxwell
Police biologist, NT

Sims, Bernard
Odontologist, London

Smith, Les
Scientist, Cooranbong, NSW

Sturgess, Desmond QC
Counsel assisting coroner at second inquest and prosecuting counsel at trial

Tew, Rohan
Person who assisted Hart in installing radio-cassette unit in Michael Chamberlain's car

Tjikadu, Barbara
Best Aboriginal tracker, wife of Nipper

Tipple, Stewart
Senior Solicitor for the Chamberlains throughout all proceedings (except first inquest)

Torlach, Mr DM
Soil expert, NT

Vernon and Rosalie
Victoria family in camping area at time of Azaria's disappearance

Watterson, Prof Ray
University of Newcastle Law dept., Michael's lawyer friend.

Ward, Phil
Businessman, wrote book *What the Jury Were Not Told*, stood for NT Parliament

West, Judith, William and Catherine
Western Australia family in nearby tent at time of Azaria's disappearance

Wild, Rex QC
Assistant to the Coroner, Fourth Inquest

Whittaker, Amy
Nurse and social worker

Winmatti, Nipper
Aboriginal tracker. Headman of the tribe and traditional owner of Ayers Rock/Uluru

Winneke, John QC (now a Judge)
Senior Counsel for the Chamberlains at the Morling Inquiry

Young, Norm
Avondale College Theology lecturer, wrote book *Innocence Regained*

Zichy-Woinarski, Brind (now QC)
Junior Counsel for the Chamberlains at the Morling Inquiry

Judges and counsel involved in the appeals, Members of Parliament, journalists and others who made public statements are identified in the relevant chapters.

APPENDIX 2

Timeline of Events

June 11, 1980	Azaria Chantel Loren Chamberlain born.
August 17, 1980	9 weeks, 4 days, approx. 10lb. (4.5kg) Azaria was taken from the tent at Ayers Rock by a dingo
August 24, 1980	Wally Goodwin finds jumpsuit, booties, nappy & singlet, matinee jacket still missing.
October 1&2, 1980	Police statements (ROIs) given by all four Chamberlains at Mt. Isa, and car searched
February 20, 1981	Alice Springs Coroner Denis Barritt finds that a wild dog or dingo took Azaria; that no member of the Chamberlain family was responsible for her death, but there was unknown interference with the clothes. Ken Brown requests to do further tests.
September 20, 1981	Operation Ochre - Chamberlain's home raided simultaneously with the homes of all other key and some eye-witnesses.
November 20, 1981	NT Supreme Court (Darwin) quashes first inquest and orders a new one.
February 2, 1982	Second Inquest Coroner Gerry Galvin commits Lindy Chamberlain to trial on the charge of murdering Azaria. Michael Chamberlain is charged as an accessory after the fact. ("Inquest by Ambush") $5,000 bail and $5,000 surety.
September 13, 1982	Trial begins in Darwin, NT Judge Justice James Muirhead of the Supreme Court presiding. Called the "Trial of the Century".

October 29, 1982	Lindy, heavily pregnant, is found guilty of 1st Degree Murder and sentenced to life imprisonment. Michael, as accessory after the fact, receives an eighteen month suspended sentence.
November 17, 1982	Kahlia born in custody.
November 18, 1982	Federal Court bail application upheld pending 1982 appeal. Decision held overnight. $300 bail.
April 29, 1983	Federal Court unanimously rejects appeal. Lindy is held at Mulawa Women's Prison, then transferred to Darwin after application for bail pending High Court appeal fails. Kahlia goes to live with foster parents Wayne & Jenny Miller.
July 19 & 27, 1983	Solicitor Stuart Tipple applies for Lindy's temporary release due to Reagan's eye accident. Request not granted.
February 22, 1984	High Court Appeal fails in a split judgement of 2 to 3.
May 3, 1984	A Petition of 131,000 signatures (later 150,000) presented to Sir Ninian Stevens, the Governor- General.
November 17, 1984	Applied for release on licence because of transfer of Kahlia's foster parents. Application denied. Kahlia goes to new foster parents, Dr Owen and Jan Hughes.
June 4, 1985	Recently formed "Innocence Committee" submits new evidence to the NT government, and makes an application for an inquiry.
February 3, 1986	Stuart Tipple is tipped off that the missing matinee jacket of Azaria has been found during a search for missing body parts belonging to a fallen climber at Ayers Rock. The matinee jacket had been held at the Alice Springs Court House since January 31.
February 5, 1986	Lindy finally sees the matinee jacket and positively identifies it.
February 7, 1986	Senator Bob Collins forces local reporter Frank Alcorta to check his sources. He does, and is so infuriated he

	writes an article for the local paper and shows it to the NT Government, threatening to print it if Lindy is not released from jail by 12 noon, or an Inquiry is called. They do both.
June 2, 1987	After a fourteen month Royal Commission Justice Trevor Morling hands down his finding and clears the Chamberlain's of all guilt or responsibility. If he had been asked he finds support for the view that Azaria was taken by a dingo. In response the NT offers them a Pardon. (This still indicates guilt in Australia.)
October 21, 1987	A new act of Parliament is forced through to allow the Chamberlain's to return to court to clear their convictions.
November 4, 1988	Release of the film *Evil Angels* (*A Cry in the Dark*). It polarises the nation.
September 15, 1988	The Supreme Court of Darwin quashes all convictions and declares the Chamberlain's totally innocent. The court also adopts Morling's view that Azaria was taken by a dingo if they had been asked.
Jan/Feb 1990	Lindy tells Michael she wants a divorce.
June 27, 1991	The Chamberlain's divorce becomes final. Kahlia chooses to live with Michael and visit Lindy, Reagan stays with Lindy and visits Michael. Aidan divides his time between the two homes.
February 1992	Lindy meets Rick Creighton during a speaking tour of the USA.
May 19, 1992	Rick proposes marriage; Lindy accepts.
May 25, 1992	Compensation paid to the Chamberlains by the Northern Territory government.
May 28, 1992	Michael starts divorce property settlement proceedings which includes a cash settlement.
June 8, 1992	Lindy's engagement, to American Rick Creighton, is announced.

July 1992	Kahlia asks to return to live with Lindy and custody proceedings are started.
December 20, 1992	Rick and Lindy are married, and choose to live in Washington State, USA.
March 10, 1993	Michael announces his engagement to Ingrid Bergner (Goldsmith).
April 28, 1993	Lindy is awarded custody of Kahlia and Reagan (at the request of both children), and the divorce joint property settlement is finally agreed before the court date.
December 24, 1993	Michael pays Lindy for her half of jointly owned property.
April 10, 1994	Michael marries Ingrid Bergner.
December 13, 1995	Findings of the Third Inquest are announced. NT Coroner John Lowndes reiterates that neither Lindy nor Michael were in any way involved with the disappearance of their daughter. He leaves the cause of death 'open' however.
August 1998	Lindy & Rick, wishing to be closer to Lindy's ageing parents, and to Aidan, return with Reagan and Kahlia to live in Australia.
October 2002	Debut of the opera *Lindy* with Opera Australia.
November 2004	Mini series *Through My Eyes* is broadcast on Australia's Channel 7 network.
5 November 2007	Kahlia's wedding
7 February 2008	Aidan's wedding
February 2010	Reunion of eyewitnesses and Chamberlains
5-6 May 2010	Lindy speaks on Forgiveness panel at *Happiness and Its Causes* conference
17 August 2010	NT Attorney General writes to Lindy, saying that she is going to have the Registrar look into the 'open' finding on Azaria's death certificate.

24 February 2012	Attend court in Darwin for Fourth Inquest Submissions before Coroner Elizabeth Morris SM
12 June 2012	Coroner Elizabeth Morris SM hands down her finding into Azaria's cause of death. She finds that "The cause of her death was as the result of being attacked and taken by a dingo."

APPENDIX 3

An Outline of the Judicial Procedure Pertaining to the Chamberlain Case

An Outline of the Judicial Procedure Pertaining to the Chamberlain Case

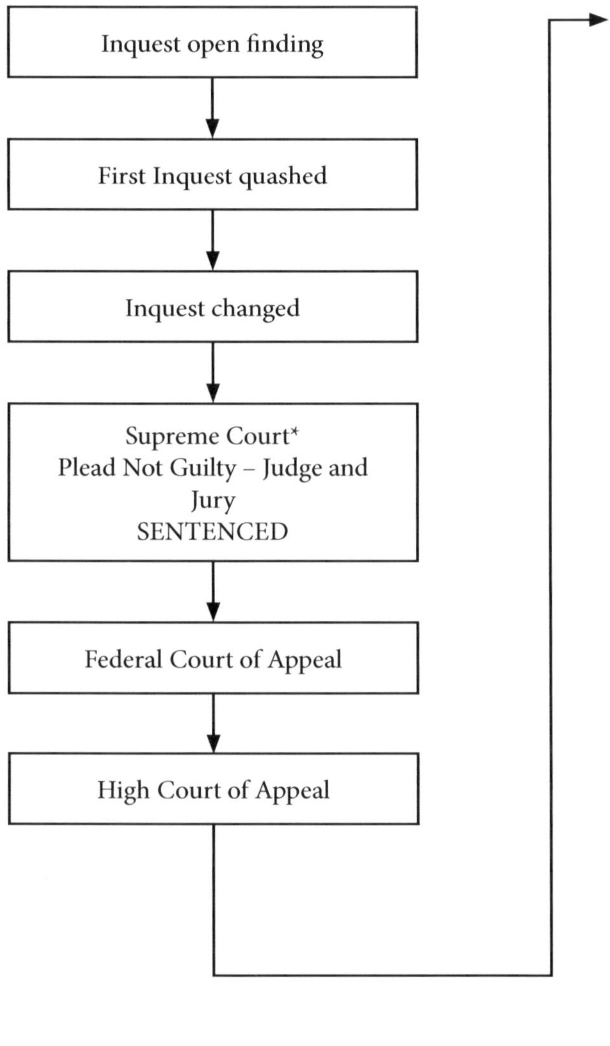

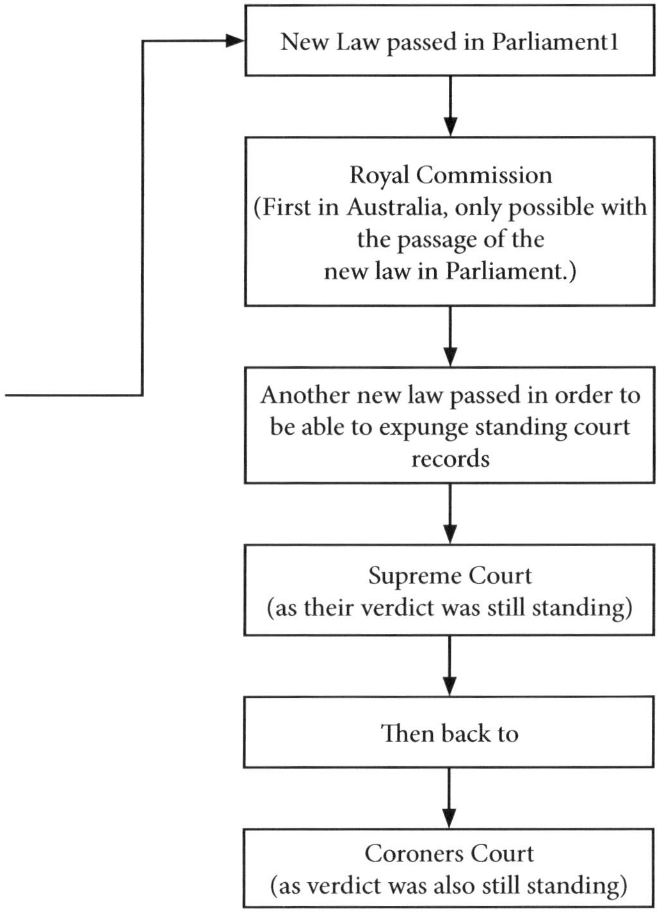

* These courts are also courts of appeal. An appeal can only be based on evidence already presented in the Supreme Court or on lawyers' mistakes or the misreading of legal rules. In our case there were several appeals to each ofthese courts between each court case.

[1] Due to public pressure, a new law is passed in Australia to allow a new legal process of inquiry to be held into any matters where it is suspected that the whole truth has been unable to be revealed or has been withheld for any reason. Previous to this, the High Court had been the final legal step in Australia although other countries had provision for a further step. This allows an exhaustive inquiry of all evidence, no matter how insignificant and is extremelywide ranging and thorough.

Photo by Jen Larson

Lindy Chamberlain-Creighton's autobiography details the life of an extraordinary Australian. Lindy is quite literally our own piece of "living history". Happily married to American Rick Creighton, they reside in Australia's Hunter Valley.

There is still enormous media interest in Lindy and her life. She is an entertaining, articulate person who does seminars, lectures and keynote addresses on a variety of topics including how to deal with stress; grief; forgiveness; privacy and the media's responsibilities in news reporting; lawyers' responsibilities to seek the truth and be impartial; and prison life – what it is really like inside and how it differs from the public's perception.

You may contact Lindy's website at www. lindychamberlain. com